European Politics in Transition

European Politics in Transition

FOURTH EDITION

Mark Kesselman
Columbia University

Joel Krieger
Wellesley College

Christopher S. Allen
University of Georgia

Stephen Hellman
York University

David Ost
Hobart & William Smith Colleges

George Ross
Brandeis University

Houghton Mifflin Company   Boston   New York

Editor in Chief: Jean J. Woy
Sponsoring Editor: Mary V. Dougherty
Senior Development Editor: Frances Gay
Editorial Assistant: Tonya Lobato
Senior Project Editor: Tracy Patruno
Senior Cover Design Coordinator: Deborah Azerrad Savona
Senior Manufacturing Coordinator: Marie Barnes

Cover Photo: Netherlands, Amsterdam, Leidsestraat, busy street scene.
Ed Pritchard. © Tony Stone Images

Printed in the U.S.A.

Library of Congress Control Number: 2001131515

ISBN: 0-618-05450-2

3 4 5 6 7 8 9-DOC-05 04 03 02

Brief Contents

Contents

Part III: Britain   151

JOEL KRIEGER

Part IV: France   231

MARK KESSELMAN

Part V: Germany 315

CHRISTOPHER S. ALLEN

Part VI: Italy   411

STEPHEN HELLMAN

Part VII: East-Central Europe in Transition 513

DAVID OST

Maps

Preface

When we first published *European Politics in Transition,* a colleague offered a friendly caveat about our choice of title. After all, aren't transitions supposed to be relatively brief and demarcated? The theoretical issue is worthy of extended analysis. Indeed, much discussion in the literature on regime change focuses on the thorny question of when democratic transitions begin and end. Whatever one's position on this debate, we are confident that the period since the third edition of *European Politics in Transition* was published in 1997 indisputably deserves to be considered a transition—and an unfinished one at that.

Who would have wagered then that the timetable for launching the euro would be respected, that the European Central Bank would succeed in acting as central banker for the bulk of the member states of the European Union (EU), and that the EU would be steadily moving toward integrating a significant number of new member states in East-Central Europe (as well as considering Turkey)? Given the increasing centrality of the European Union in the politics of member states (and the candidate members treated in the chapters on East-Central Europe), we have opened *European Politics in Transition* (following the Introduction, which provides a general framework) with an expanded section on the EU. We have planned *European Politics in Transition* so that instructors can assign sections in the order they prefer. But by placing the EU front and center, we wish to highlight its

centrality to the comparative politics of Europe. The section on the EU is now expanded and organized to parallel the chapter outline of the country sections, an indirect tribute to the quasi-polity-like character of the EU.

We have also expanded our coverage of the EU in the country sections to permit running analysis of the interplay between the EU and national politics. Four of the five chapters of the country treatments now include a subsection on the EU. Thus, we identify the EU as the last historical juncture in the first chapter of each country section; in the second chapter, we provide a subsection on European integration; the third chapter of each section emphasizes the European dimensions of governance and policy-making; and the fifth chapter in each section includes the challenges of European integration.

The fact that we stress that European politics is in transition is not intended to deny important continuities in the politics of the countries studied in this book. As in the third edition of *European Politics in Transition,* we organize our treatment within the same framework for measuring continuity and change that is used in *Introduction to Comparative Politics* (Houghton Mifflin, revised edition, 2000), a general introductory text that we co-edit with William Joseph. The four themes that frame the book, and that are introduced and analyzed in the Introduction, provide a useful way to organize the detailed descriptions of political institutions, processes, and forces analyzed in the country sections. The four themes include (1) the state in a world of states, (2) governing the economy, (3) the democratic idea, and (4) the politics of collective identity. We believe that these themes are a useful grid to chart the statics and dynamics of politics in the countries selected for study in this book. They also provide instructors rich possibilities for organizing comparative analysis.

We continue to believe in the centrality of political economy in understanding European (and, indeed, any country's) politics. For this reason, we devote one of the five chapters in each country section to governing the economy. Indeed, the increasing importance of the EU—as well as the intense debates around EU policies and decision making—underline that the problems of an industrial (and postindustrial) society are far from solved, and that an adequate understanding of *European Politics in Transition* requires close attention to political economy. With that said, the character of Europe's political economy, as well as economic policy, is a moving target. In the first two editions of this book, we focused on the postwar settlement, based on cross-class growth coalitions in the economic and political sphere, propelling interventionist states to pursue policies directed toward Keynesian counter-cyclical demand management and ample provision of social services. We continue to describe the postwar settlement, but it is now past history, a historical juncture that has been succeeded by a mix of market-friendly EU regulation and national state deregulation.

At the same time, there is no consensus within and among the states analyzed in *European Politics in Transition* about the proper mix of state and market forces. If European integration and the demise of communism have discredited a doctrinaire form of nationally based state-directed socialism, the center or center-left remains a major—indeed, at the time we write, *the* major—political force in Europe. Moreover, on the center-right of the spectrum, a more moderate approach that combines a commitment to neo-liberalism with a greater concern

to cushion citizens from the dislocating effects of global market forces has replaced the more doctrinaire form of neo-liberalism popular in the 1980s and 1990s. There is a lively debate within European politics about the appropriate extent and character of state intervention in the mixed economy. At the same time, adherents of the Third Way try to press their claims for a new orientation that transcends left and right.

As three of our four themes suggest, we also highlight the importance of dimensions other than political economy in the shaping of European politics. The first of these themes involves the dynamics of state formation. Notwithstanding the great power of the EU, European states continue to occupy center stage. The 2000 EU summit at Nice illustrated that the moment has not yet arrived when important EU decisions will routinely be made by majorities that do not include the representatives of most member states or reflect the interests of the most powerful. In order to understand European politics, it is essential to accord critical attention to how states are organized and to their executive, representative, and judicial institutions.

A second theme also not directly related to political economy (although with important indirect connections to it) is the democratic idea. Such diverse issues prominent in the recent past as the democratic deficit exacerbated by the growing weight of the EU, political scandals, and political reforms like the gender parity law passed in France in 2000 and a set of constitutional reforms underway in Britain illustrate that the meaning and practice of the democratic idea continue to generate extensive public attention.

The third theme highlights that political identities are wide-ranging and variegated. Although class and economic cleavages continue to divide the body politic, we also emphasize the importance of collective identities based on ethnicity, gender, and age. Which of these cleavages becomes salient in given countries and at given times, how they interact and are connected to partisan cleavages, and differences in their intensity and impact across countries are puzzles that instructors will doubtless wish to explore.

We have made several other significant changes in the organization of the country sections to improve coverage. The first chapter in each country section includes a subsection discussing the geographic setting (size, population, resource base, etc.) and the political implications of the geographic setting, and a subsection linking themes and implications. The second chapter includes a subsection on the generation gap, and the subsection on each country in the international political economy takes on issues of globalization. The fourth chapter has a new subsection on political parties and the party system, and the treatment of collective identity explicitly treats social class, citizenship, and nationality, as well as ethnicity and gender, while our treatment of representation and participation includes coverage of protest and social movements. As a result, instructors who have previously used *European Politics in Transition* will find that this edition both reflects the approach we have developed in earlier editions and involves a top-to-bottom updating and refinement of our coverage to reflect epochal developments and scholarship of the past few years.

We have been fortunate to receive excellent advice from many colleagues, including Margaret C. Gonzalez, Southeastern Louisiana University; Kerstin Hamann, University of Central Florida; Jonah D. Levy, University of California, Berkeley; Neil Mitchell, University of New Mexico; John D. Nagle, Syracuse University; Susan E. Penksa, Westmont College. We are grateful to the superb staff at Houghton Mifflin Company, including Mary Dougherty, Fran Gay, and Tracy Patruno, and at Books By Design, Nancy Benjamin.

M. K.
J. K.

European Politics in Transition

P A R T

I

Introduction

Mark Kesselman/Joel Krieger

"It was the best of times; it was the worst of times." We borrow the famous opening from Charles Dickens's *A Tale of Two Cities*, set in London and Paris during the French Revolution in the late eighteenth century, to describe the tumultuous character of the current transition in European politics. In a manner reminiscent of the period of violent revolutions in Dickens's time, the European continent may be, as it was when Dickens wrote, at the close of one era and the beginning of another.

Does Europe comprise, as it has for centuries, discrete sovereign states, animated by national identities and interests? Or have processes of European integration inaugurated more than a half-century ago produced a European Union (EU) that is a genuinely transnational polity?[1] More than ever before, students of European politics must weigh and evaluate both propositions, for each captures important truths about contemporary Europe. Considered side by side, they identify the current transition in European politics marked by the challenges of overlapping jurisdictions, multilevel governance, and negotiated sovereignties.

Of course, there is far more at play in Europe than tensions between nation-states and the EU. The revolutions of 1989 in Eastern and Central Europe marked the disintegration of much of the communist world. When the Berlin Wall, which divided East and West in both physical and symbolic terms, was dismantled brick by

brick in November 1989, the architecture of Europe was forever altered. Within a year, Germany was unified after nearly a half-century of cold war division, and by the end of 1991, the Soviet Union had splintered into fifteen troubled republics. The destruction of the wall, resulting from the pent-up pressures for change originating in the East, opened the floodgates between East and West Berlin, East and West Germany, and Eastern and Western Europe. The result was a massive movement of ideas, commodities, capital, technology, and people. Immediately, the people of East-Central Europe faced rapid and often disorienting dual transitions to market economies and democratic polities. These transitions, as well as the increasingly close ties between Eastern and Western Europe, are fundamentally redefining the political geography and the identity of Europe.

In a sense, the wall has come down in intellectual terms, and the patterns of development and questions we ask about East and West are not as dissimilar as they were before. Without neglecting the distinctive historical and institutional legacies of the nations of East-Central Europe, we can now—perhaps for the first time since the early twentieth century—consider some critical common themes. We can study the political causes and consequences of changes in economic performance and investigate in each country the growing demands for political participation by those who do not consider themselves

1

Europe

0 ⊢——————⊣ 300 Miles

0 ⊢——————⊣ 300 Kilometers

Reykjavik ★ ICELAND

NORWAY
Oslo ★ SWEDEN
★Sto

NORTH
SEA

DENMARK
★Copenhagen

BALTIC S

ATLANTIC
OCEAN

IRELAND
Dublin ★

BRITAIN
London ★
Chunnel

NETHERLANDS
★Amsterdam
Rhine
Elbe
★Berlin
Vistula
GERMANY
★Bonn
POLAN

Brussels ★
BELGIUM
Luxembourg
Paris ● LUX.
Loire
Seine
Danube
Prague ★
CZECH REP.
SLOV

FRANCE
Vienna ★
Bratisla
Bu
HUNGAR

Bern ★
SWITZERLAND
AUSTRIA

Rhone
Po
Ljubljana ★
SLOVENIA
Zagreb ★
CROATIA

PORTUGAL
Lisbon ★
Tajo
Madrid
★
Ebro
BOSNIA-
HERZEGOVINA
S
★Saraj
ADRIATIC SEA

SPAIN
ITALY
Corsica
★Rome
MONTENEGRO
Tirane ★
ALBAN

Balearic Is.
Sardinia

MEDITERRANEAN SEA

★Rabat
Algiers ★
Tunis
★

MOROCCO
ALGERIA
TUNISIA

adequately represented through the formal channels of government. We can consider the ebb and flow of xenophobic and hypernationalistic movements. And we can study the complex interplay of international and domestic politics within a context of increasing global interdependence and European integration. Indeed, we have just sketched out the four key themes that frame our discussion of European politics in transition, at the level of each country we analyze and at the level of the EU: the interaction of states within the international order; the role of states in economic management; the challenges resulting from demands for more participation, transparency, and accountability facing the transitional democracies of East-Central Europe, the durable democracies of Western Europe, and the EU itself; and the political impact of diverse sources of social identity and group attachments.

What Makes Europe . . . Europe?

This book is about the politics of Europe, a politics shaped by specific country-by-country as well as regional histories, cultures, political systems, and institutional genealogies. The countries of EU Europe share important similarities in levels of development and longstanding democratic traditions with the United States and other capitalist democracies, such as Canada, Japan, and Australia. Yet there is a quite distinctive European model of political governance and social policy, and there are significant country-by-country variations. Similarly, the countries of East-Central Europe share some common experiences and challenges with transitional democracies in other parts of the world, such as Argentina or Nigeria, but the challenges they face are compounded by their need to develop democracy and the market economy at the same time; few other transitional democracies in regions outside East-Central Europe must confront a nearly half-century legacy of command economies. Moreover, the postsocialist pathways that these countries follow are highly

influenced by specific national trajectories.[2] Finally, countries in the region are straining to join the EU, a situation that presents economic and political opportunities and challenges.

European Politics in Transition investigates both the whole and the parts: European politics at a critical juncture in the geographical and political-institutional integration of the region and the different ways specific countries have addressed common challenges such as competitiveness, integration, democratization, and social diversity. Before undertaking the systematic study of European politics, we need to clarify some important issues concerning the meaning and practice of democracy, the organization of the economy, and the cultural context for vibrant market-based democracies.

What Is the Meaning—or, Rather, Meanings— of Democracy?

As with many other important concepts, debate over the meaning of democracy is contentious. The wide popularity of the term conceals some important ambiguities, and we can identify contending positions on many key issues regarding the very definition. Should democracy be defined solely on the basis of the procedures used to select top governmental officeholders? That is, for a political system to qualify as democratic, is it sufficient that occupants of the highest offices of the state be selected on the basis of free, fair elections in which opposing parties are allowed to organize to present candidates and all citizens are entitled to cast a vote for a contending party? Or must there be respect for citizens' civil liberties (including rights of free expression, dissent, and privacy), regardless of what a democratically elected government might desire? What is the relationship between religious practice and the exercise of political power? To what extent must all citizens be guaranteed certain minimum economic and social rights in a democratic regime, as distinct from political and civil rights (such as the right to vote and criticize the government)? Otherwise put, what is the relationship between democracy defined in purely procedural terms and democracy defined as a system that promotes substantive equalities among citizens?

Despite the many debates about the meaning(s) of democracy, a rough consensus has emerged among practitioners and students of comparative politics or "comparativists." It is generally agreed that for a political system to qualify as democratic, the following conditions must obtain:

- Selection to the highest public offices is on the basis of free and fair elections. For an election to qualify as fair, votes must be counted accurately, with the winning candidate(s) selected according to preexisting rules that determine the kind of plurality or majority required to gain electoral victory.

- All citizens possess civil and political rights—the right to participate and vote in elections periodically held to select key state officeholders—and civil liberties—the rights of free assembly, conscience, privacy, and expression, including the right to criticize the government.

- Political parties are free to organize, present candidates for public office, and compete in elections.

- The opposition party or parties—those not represented in government—enjoy adequate rights of contestation, that is, the right to organize and to criticize the incumbent government.

- The elected government develops policy according to specified procedures that provide for due process and the accountability of elected executives (at the next election, through judicial action, and, in parliamentary systems to parliament).

- The political system contains a judiciary with powers independent of the executive and legislature, charged with protecting citizens' civil rights and liberties from violation by government and other citizens, as well as with ensuring that governmental officials respect constitutionally specified procedures.

Although these six points make a useful checklist of the essential elements of a democracy, several qualifications should be added. First, this definition does not claim that electoral out-comes are always (or possibly even often) rational, equitable, or wise. Democracy specifies a set of procedures for making decisions, but it does not guarantee the wisdom of the outcome. Indeed, as we discuss below, in the fourth qualification to the checklist, we believe that political outcomes in all democracies, both elections to office and the decisions of officeholders, are systematically and importantly influenced by economic inequalities that limit the ideal of "one person, one vote."

Second, no government has ever fully lived up to democratic standards. All democratic governments at various points in their histories have violated them to a greater or lesser extent. For example, Britain retained a system of plural votes for certain citizens until after World War II, and French women did not gain the right to vote until 1945.

Third, the way that the constituent elements of democracy on the checklist are interpreted and implemented is often debatable and sometimes becomes a very contentious political issue. For example, in the 1990s, there was intense controversy in France about whether Muslim girls should be permitted to wear a head scarf, which signifies adherence to Islam, to public school. On the one hand, some school principals prohibited girls from wearing the scarf on the grounds that France is a secular state with a legal ban against proselytizing in public schools. On the other hand, defenders of the practice argued that Muslim girls were exercising the fundamental right of self-expression.

Fourth, economic inequalities load the political deck. Wealthy citizens, powerful interest groups, and business firms can use their substantial resources to increase their chances of winning an election or influencing public policy. This creates a tension in all democracies, to a greater or lesser degree, between the formal political procedures (such as voting), in which all are equal, and the actual situation, in which the affluent are, in novelist George Orwell's famous phrase from the satirical novel *Animal Farm*, "more equal" than others because of their ability to have greater political influence.

The tension between citizens' economic inequalities and their equal right to participate in the choice of elected officials and governmental policies—that is, the tension between "one person, one vote" and "one euro, one vote"—is found in all European democracies and is typically a source of intense political division. Opposing political coalitions advocate very different governmental policies that reflect the interests of their distinctive socioeconomic constituencies. Three key areas of policy difference involve the following issues:

- The distribution of tax burdens. Although all governments levy taxes on citizens and businesses to support government activities, who pays how much is often a source of intense political debate.

- Governmental economic priorities. Should economic policy be directed above all toward restraining inflation (a particular concern for the affluent or elderly, since inflation threatens to reduce the value of their assets and savings) or toward reducing unemployment (which traditionally has harmed working people the most)?

- The extent of governmental spending for social programs. How much can and should be spent on the public provision of job training, unemployment compensation, old-age pensions, assistance to the needy, and other programs that are part of what is commonly called the welfare state?

Finally, although all democracies share the six key elements outlined above, democracies vary widely in their political institutions. A common classification of democracies is based on differing relationships between the executive and the legislature. In presidential systems, such as in the United States, the chief executive (the president) and the national legislature are chosen in separate elections, and there is a sharp separation of powers between the executive branch and the legislature. This system is actually an unusual form of democracy. Most of the world's democracies (including Britain, Germany, and Italy) have parliamentary governments in which executive and legislative powers are fused

rather than separated: the chief executive (whether called prime minister, chancellor, or president) and the cabinet are chosen from the legislature and generally are the leaders of the dominant party in parliament.

The formal and informal rules of the game for reaching and exercising power are very different in presidential and parliamentary systems. In presidential systems, members of the legislature jealously preserve their autonomy. Because the legislature is elected separately from the president, it is constitutionally authorized to set its own agenda, initiate policy proposals, and defy presidential directives. Presidents have resources that they can deploy more or less effectively to persuade the legislature to go along, but even when the same party controls both the presidency and the legislature, the key word is *persuade.*

In parliamentary systems, the legislature may serve as a forum for dramatic policy debate, but it represents neither an independent source of policy initiatives nor a decisive obstacle preventing the government from legislating its own proposals. On rare occasions, a rebellion within the ranks of the majority party (or coalition) in parliament brings down the cabinet, that is, forces the chief executive to resign. One can count such examples on one hand in post–World War II Britain and Germany. The fact that this happens all the time in Italy suggests the value of studying particular systems, as we do in this book, rather than engaging in generalizations about political systems.

"So what?" you may ask in response to this discussion of political institutions. Good question![3] Ponder what difference the type of system makes as you study parliamentary and presidential systems in this book. And note how rare presidential systems are—a point that may be surprising for those who think that the U.S. presidential system is typical.

The distinction between presidential and parliamentary systems does not exhaust the range of institutional variation within industrial democracies. You will discover that France's hybrid semipresidential system is quite different from both. France has a dual executive, with both a directly elected president and an appointed prime minister. As you will learn, these differences raise the kinds of questions that are at the heart of comparative politics: How do different political institutions and procedures give concrete expression to the same democratic values? What consequences do these differences have for the effectiveness of government and the distribution of resources?

Debates about political institutions involve central questions about relations among social groups, for the way that power is organized affects the structure of political conflicts and coalitions and the outcome of governmental decisions and policies. Nor are debates regarding the choice of the appropriate manner of organizing state institutions ever fully settled. Britain, the nation with the longest parliamentary democratic tradition (it is centuries old), has recently experienced renewed controversy regarding the distribution of powers between levels of government, as well as the extent of autonomy appropriate for the constituent units of the United Kingdom (which comprises Scotland, Wales, and Northern Ireland, as well as England). In France, an important reform in the 1980s provided for the decentralization of political power to regional and local governments. As a result, France's centuries-old pattern of state dominance and centralization is being altered. In East-Central Europe, citizens and political elites evaluate presidential and parliamentary models as they craft new democratic regimes.

What Economic System for Democracy?
Capitalism, Socialism, and Democracy

For a political system to be democratic, does the economy have to be organized in a particular fashion? A longstanding debate pits advocates of very different positions on this issue against one another. To sketch the context broadly, one can identify two ways to organize modern economic life. In a capitalist system, production is organized within the framework of voluntary (market) exchanges between private participants. The bulk of economic decisions—notably, what goods will be produced, by what methods, and by whom—are private and are made by private individuals who own and control productive assets. Their decisions are based on the goal of reaping the highest possible profits from selling goods in the market. In a socialist system of production, key decisions concerning the organization of the economy are considered public, not private. They are made by public officials, who may include elected representatives, state planners, and administrators, as well as workers who produce goods (in the case of the self-managed firm).

Many scholars contend that democratic political institutions cannot flourish unless the economy is organized within a capitalist framework. They believe that democracy requires leaving substantial power in the hands of individual citizens, and citizens cannot have this requisite power if government makes the key decisions involving the organization of production, exchange, and consumption. In this view, public control of the economy is both inefficient and tyrannical. On the other side, some assert that for a system to be democratic, there must be a significant measure of democratic decision making in both the formal sphere of politics and within the economy. The distinguished democratic theorist Robert Dahl explains why. Private "ownership and control [of business firms] contribute to the creation of great differences among citizens in wealth, income, status, skills, information, control over information and propaganda, [and] access to political leaders. . . . Differences like these help in turn to generate significant inequalities among citizens in their capacities for participating as political equals in *governing the state.*"[4] In this view, democracy is crippled when some of the most important decisions affecting the character of the entire society are made by affluent citizens and private business firms that are not democratically cho-

sen or accountable. The relationship among capitalism, socialism, and democracy is an issue of
vital importance.[5] When reading about individual countries in this book, consider how political
movements and governments have addressed
the question of whether capitalism is a necessary condition for democracy, an impediment—
or both.

Although the political and scholarly debate
on the relationship of capitalism, socialism, and
democracy has not been fully settled, all the
countries covered in *European Politics in Transition*, as well as other democracies throughout
the world, have capitalist economies. Moreover,
you will discover when reading about the countries in this book that there is a broad similarity
among democratic capitalist countries in the relationship between democratic political institutions and capitalist economic institutions. The
political economies of stable democracies generally involve quite extensive state intervention
in the economy alongside extensive market
competition by privately owned and controlled
firms. The characteristic situation has often
been called a mixed economy and was described
by political scientist Adam Przeworski as a
system "that relies on [state] regulated markets to allocate resources and on the state to assure a minimum of material welfare for everyone."[6]

Within the broadly similar context of a mixed
economy, however, we find extensive variation
from one democratic country to the next regarding the precise balance between state regulation and free markets. Some of the major political conflicts in democratic regimes—both the
longstanding durable regimes of EU Europe and
the transitional democracies of East-Central Europe—concern the extent and priorities of state
economic intervention, in particular, the opti-
mum policies to achieve trade-offs among a variety of desirable goals: high employment, low
inflation, economic growth, provision of welfare, international competitiveness, and so forth.
For each country, we discuss the form that these
conflicts have taken. Look for the range of policy
differences in this arena, consider what differ-

ence they make for citizens in these countries,
and develop your own position on the most desirable form of political economy.

The Cultural Context

Are there particular historical and cultural req-
uisites of democracy? Comparativists have long
debated whether democracy requires specific
cultural orientations. In an important contribution on this question, *Making Democracy
Work*, Robert Putnam looks at the energetic and
effective way that Italians in the north used
newly created regional governments to improve
their situation; he compares their success with
the relative failure of Italians in the south to exploit the possibilities created by the regional
form.[7] What made democracy work better in
the north? Putnam suggests the greater extent
in the north of what he calls *social capital*, that
is, the ability of northerners to coordinate their
efforts to work for the common good. In the
south, in contrast, citizens were less likely to
combine their energies to make the new regional governments an instrument for economic and social advancement; in other words,
social capital was lacking. Putnam claims that a
key difference between the two regions, which
explains why social capital was more prevalent
in the north, is that northerners are more likely
than southerners to trust their fellow citizens to
engage in common public pursuits.

Can we extend Putnam's argument to the
global scale? Are some cultures more hospitable
to the kind of trust and pragmatic compromises
that are essential for democracy to work? Or, as
Sidney Tarrow, a sympathetic critic, charged,
does Putnam mistake effect for cause? Tarrow
suggests that the greater extent of trust and social capital in the north was nurtured by Italian
state policies favoring the region.[8] The debate
between Putnam and Tarrow in part hinges on
the question of which is more important in explaining effective political and economic performance: state policies or political cultural attitudes. Consider this question as you read about

the relatively successful cases of democracy that comprise *European Politics in Transition* and assess the range of experiences among the democratic transitions in East-Central Europe.

A somewhat different question about the cultural base of democracy is whether, for democracy to flourish, there must be broad agreement or consensus on the democratic rules of the game, notably democratic procedures and the acceptance of the electoral verdict even for those on the losing side. The 2000 U.S. presidential election underlined the relevance of this issue in even the most established democracies. In *The Civic Culture*, a contemporary classic in comparative politics, Gabriel Almond and Sidney Verba claimed, by comparing the distribution of political attitudes in five nations, that citizens in democratic regimes are more likely than citizens in authoritarian regimes to trust government and accept the values of both participating in government and accepting directives from their government.[9] In a rejoinder to this approach, Dankwart Rustow countered, "The basis of democracy is not maximum consensus. It is the tenuous middle ground between imposed uniformity (such as would lead to some sort of tyranny) and implacable hostility (of a kind that would disrupt the community in civil war or secession). There must be a conscious adoption of democratic rules, but they must not be so much believed in as applied, first perhaps from necessity and gradually from habit. The very operation of these rules will enlarge the area of consensus step-by-step as democracy moves down its crowded agenda."[10] Consider the applicability of these two quite distinct claims to each country study and particularly to the case studies of East-Central Europe, where the development of democratic civic cultures remains an abiding challenge.

The Approach: Four Themes

This book seeks to go beyond "textbook" understandings. Politics in the narrow sense of governmental institutions and formal political pro-

cesses (that is, politics as "how a bill becomes a law") is only part of a far more complex story, which encompasses not only political parties, voting behavior, and the institutions of government, but also the emergence of powerful forces in society outside the government, as well as the interaction of international and domestic factors. Within European nations, politics has always involved social movements—from the English Chartists and popular movements on the Continent in the 1830s and 1840s, who demanded rights of political participation and democracy (some of which still have not been achieved), to Green parties in many contemporary Western European nations that struggle for women's rights, nuclear disarmament, and ecological concerns and that reject big government and big business. European politics also involves class conflicts between working people and the financial and business elites, conflicts that force the state to intervene in the economy by regulating market forces, managing industrial disputes through political negotiations, and determining how the wealth of society is divided among competing social groups. European politics today involves regional, ethnic, racial, and gender divisions, as well as the politics of the EU and relations between Eastern and Western Europe, within a context of intensified global interdependence.

To make sense of the large volume of information presented in *European Politics in Transition*, we structure our study of European politics around four core themes that we believe are central for understanding the transition that European politics is experiencing now:

1. The interaction of states within the international order
2. The role of states in economic management
3. The particular challenges facing European democracies and the pressures for more democracy
4. The political impact of diverse sources of social identity, including class, gender, ethnicity, and religion

These four themes provide a framework for organizing the extensive information on political institutions, processes, conflicts, policy, and changes that we present in the country chapters. The themes help explain continuities and contrasts among countries. We will also suggest a way that each theme highlights some puzzle in comparative politics that helps illuminate our understanding of European politics.

Before we introduce the themes, we offer several warnings. First, our four themes cannot possibly capture all of the infinitely varied experience of politics throughout the world. Our framework in *European Politics in Transition* provides a guide to understanding many features of contemporary comparative politics. But we urge students (and rely on instructors!), who through study and experience know the politics of the United States and many other countries, to challenge and augment our interpretations. Second, we want to note that a textbook builds from existing theory but does not construct or test new hypotheses, which is the goal of original scholarly studies. The themes are intended to crystallize some of the most significant findings in the field of contemporary European politics. Although these themes can usefully be applied to politics anywhere in the world, they serve here as an analytical tool to reveal both the specificity of national experiences and the distinctiveness of a European model of politics.

Theme One: A World of States

The theme that we call *a world of states* highlights that since the beginning of the modern era several centuries ago, states have been the primary actors on the world stage. For better or worse, since the seventeenth century, it has been state officials who send armies to conquer other states and territories, states whose legal codes make it possible for business firms to operate within their borders and beyond, and states that regulate, through immigration law, the movement of people across borders. Courses in international relations focus primarily on interaction

among states or other cross-border transactions. In *European Politics in Transition*, we emphasize a key feature of the international arena: the impact on a state's domestic political institutions and processes of its relative success or failure in competing economically and politically with other states.

No state, even the most powerful, such as the United States, is unaffected by influences originating outside its borders. Today a host of processes associated with *globalization* underscore the heightened importance of intensified cross-national influences. A wide array of general and specialized international organizations and treaties, including the United Nations and regional organizations or trade blocs like the EU, challenge the sovereign control of national governments within their borders. Transnational corporations, international banks, and currency traders in New York, London, and Tokyo affect countries and people throughout the world. A country's political borders do not protect its citizens from environmental pollution or the spread of infectious diseases. More broadly, developments linked to technology transfer, the growth of an international information society, immigration, and cultural diffusion have a varying but important impact on the domestic politics of all European countries.

Today, in the early years of the twenty-first century, nations are experiencing intense pressures from an expanding and increasingly complex mix of external influences. In every country, politics and policymaking are shaped in important ways by influences that come from outside its borders. But international political and economic influences do not have the same impact in all countries, and some states help shape the institutional form and policy of international organizations in which they participate. It is likely that the more advantaged a state is—as measured by such factors as level of economic development, military power, and resource base—the more it will shape global influences. Conversely, the policies of less advantaged countries are more extensively shaped by other states, international organizations, and broader international constraints.

Furthermore, when states pool their political and economic resources, they can leverage their influence in the international setting. Perhaps the foremost example in the world today is the EU, to which most of the countries analyzed in this book belong. As Part II, devoted to the EU, describes, it has been no easy matter for former rivals like France, Britain, and Germany to form an integrated economic region in which many key decisions are made in Brussels, the headquarters of the EU. The EU fits uneasily in a world of states, but international organizations like the EU (along with the North American Free Trade Association, the World Trade Organization, and others) are increasingly important.

The theme we identify as *a world of states* includes a second important focus: similarities and contrasts among countries in how they formed as states. We study the ways that states developed historically, diverse patterns in the organization of political institutions, the processes—and limits—of democratization, the ability of the state to control social groups in society and sustain power, and the state's economic management strategies and capacities. We observe how state formation and the position in the international order of states are linked. For example, compared to other states, the British state had (and continues to have) a less developed capacity to steer British industry. The state was less concerned with the competitiveness of the British domestic manufacturing industry because of the commanding position within international finance enjoyed by the private financial institutions comprising the City of London (London's financial district, equivalent to Wall Street in New York). Moreover, the vast scope of Britain's colonial empire meant that trade with the colonies could sustain the British economy. Consequently, the British state intervened less extensively and private firms were allowed to develop in a freer fashion than was the case for France and Germany.

A Puzzle: To What Extent Do States Still Remain the Basic Building Blocks of Political Life? Increasingly, the politics and policies of states are shaped by external actors as well as by the more impersonal forces of globalization. At the same time, many states face increasingly restive constituencies who challenge the power and legitimacy of central states. In reading the analysis of the EU, the four country case studies, and the in-depth treatment of East-Central Europe, try to assess what impact pressures from both above and below have had on the role of the state in carrying out its basic functions and in its relationship to its citizens. Has the EU developed to the point that it is a *transnational polity* as important—or perhaps more important—to Europe as the countries we study? What is the relation between member states and the EU?

Theme Two: Governing the Economy

The success of states in maintaining their authority is greatly affected by their ability to ensure that an adequate volume of goods and services is produced to satisfy the needs of their populations. Certainly the inability of the Soviet economic system to meet this challenge was an important reason for the rejection of communism and the disintegration of the Soviet Union. Conversely, the relatively great political stability of the wealthy industrialized nations described in this book is closely linked to their superior economic performance. How a country organizes production and exchange—that is, *governs the economy*—is one of the key elements in its overall pattern of development. Countries differ widely in the relative importance of agriculture versus basic industry versus high-tech and service-based production in their economies, how successful they are in competing with other countries that offer similar products in international markets, and the relative importance of market forces versus government control of the economy.

An important goal in the contemporary world is to achieve durable economic development. Effective economic performance is near the top of every country's political agenda. The term *political economy* refers to how governments affect economic performance—and how economic performance affects a country's political processes. We accord great importance to political economy in *European Politics in Transition* because we believe that politics in all countries is deeply influenced by the relationship between government and the economy.

A Puzzle: What Factors Foster Successful Economic Performance? This is a question that students of political economy have long pondered—and to which there are no easy answers. Consider the apparently straightforward question of whether states that intervene more vigorously to manage the economy outperform states with less developed capacities for economic management. France developed an extensive array of financial and industrial management tools in the postwar period. This directive approach was often praised as a means to promote vigorous economic modernization and growth. British policymakers tried (quite unsuccessfully) to copy French planning institutions. Through unification, Germany's social market economy—a complex interplay of laissez-faire and extremely sophisticated state-centered policies (which formed a very different policy from France's state-centered approach)—created an economy that was the envy of the world. Yet in recent years, Britain's less-is-more approach to governing the economy has been quite successful, French planners have been criticized for some notable failures, and observers of Germany wonder whether its model of economic governance can survive.[11] Indeed, as some of the more distinctive features of French and German economic governance have been eliminated in recent years, a frequent topic of discussion among European specialists is whether a convergence is occurring in the economic policies of European countries.[12] In reading the country studies as well as the analysis of East-Central Europe, try to decide what stance of the state is most likely to produce economic success, whether there are distinctive contrasts across countries, and whether countries are becoming more similar in their approach to governing the economy.

Theme Three: The Democratic Idea

Our comparative studies indicate a surprising level of complexity in the apparently simple theme of the *democratic idea*. We focus first on the near universality of the claim that citizens should exercise substantial control over the decisions that their states and governments make. Especially since the collapse of Soviet communism, democracy has no viable contender as a legitimate basis for organizing political power in the contemporary world. (Perhaps nationalism, especially when fused with religion, might be considered an alternative, but even many forms of religious nationalism claim to be based in democracy.)

In discussing the democratic idea, we focus second on the diverse sources of support for democracy. Democracy has proved appealing for many reasons. In some historical settings, it may represent a standoff or equilibrium among political contenders for power, in which no one group can gain sufficient strength to control outcomes alone.[13] Democracy may appeal to many people in authoritarian settings because states having democratic regimes often rank among the world's most stable, affluent, and cohesive countries. Another important pressure for democracy is the widespread popular desire for dignity and equality. Even when dictatorial regimes provide some of the benefits often associated with democratic regimes—for example, sponsoring development or using ideological appeals to garner popular support—intense pressures for democracy remain. Although authoritarian governments can suppress demands for democratic participation for a long period, our discussion of East-Central Europe in this book provides abundant evidence that the domestic and, in recent years, international costs of doing so are high.

Third, we emphasize the potential fragility of transitions from authoritarian to democratic rule. That popular movements and leaders of moderate factions within authoritarian regimes often overthrow undemocratic regimes and force the holding of elections does not mean that democratic institutions will endure. As our case studies of Poland, Hungary, and the Czech and Slovak Republics demonstrate, a wide gulf exists between a *transition* to democracy and the *consolidation* of democracy. Historically, powerful groups have often opposed democratic institutions because they fear that democracy will threaten their privilege, whereas disadvantaged groups may oppose the democratic process because they see it as unresponsive to their deeply felt grievances. As a result, reversals of democratic regimes have occurred in the past and will doubtless occur in the future. The country studies in *European Politics in Transition* do not support a philosophy of history or theory of political development that sees a single (democratic) end point toward which all countries will eventually converge. One important analytical work, published in the early phase of the most recent democratic wave, captured the fragility of the process of democratization in its title: *Transitions from Authoritarian Rule: Tentative Conclusions About Uncertain Democracies.*[14] The difficulty in maintaining democracy once established is captured in the observation that it is easier for a country to hold its first democratic election than to have its second. Hence, the fact that the democratic idea is so powerful does not mean that all countries will adopt or preserve democratic institutions.

Moreover, even when democracy has become relatively secure, we do not believe that it can be achieved in any country once and for all. Indeed, our *democratic idea* theme suggests the incompleteness of democratic agendas even in countries (several of which are included in this book) with the longest and most developed experiences of representative democracy. In virtually every democracy in recent years, many citizens have turned against the state when their living standards were threatened by high unemployment and economic stagnation. Social movements have targeted the state because of its actions or inactions in such varied spheres as environmental regulation, reproductive rights, and race or ethnic relations. Comparative studies confirm that the democratic idea fuels political conflicts even in long-established democracies because there is invariably a gap, even in the most egalitarian and longest-lived democracies, between democratic ideals and the actual functioning of democratic political institutions. Witness, for example, the extensive degree of economic and political inequality in Britain, France, and Germany, countries classified as among the most democratic in the world. Nor do challenges to democracy originate only with contestatory movements: public officials in even the most stable democracies have violated democratic procedures by abusing their power, from police on the streets to cabinet ministers. Examples include acceptance of bribes, other instances of corruption, and the use of illegal force against citizens.

In order to analyze more deeply the underpinnings of democratic stability, *European Politics in Transition* confines its attention to countries with extensive democratic traditions. With the exception of states in East-Central Europe, which adopted democratic institutions after the collapse of communism in 1989, all the countries surveyed in this book have been democratic for longer than a half-century.

A Puzzle: Democracy and Stability. Comparativists often debate whether democratic institutions contribute to political stability or, on the contrary, to political disorder. On the one hand, democracy by its very nature permits political opposition. One of its defining characteristics is that competition is legitimate among those who aspire to gain high political office, as well as among groups and parties defending different programs. Political life in democracies is turbulent and unpredictable. On the other hand, that political opposition and competition are legitimate in democracies paradoxically has the effect of promoting acceptance of the state even among opponents of a given government. Because opposition movements are free to express their opposition in democratic regimes, the result is greater political stability. Evidence for this claim has recently been provided by an important study involving a large number of cases, which finds that economic disruptions are much less destabilizing for democratic regimes than authoritarian regimes.[15] In reading the country studies in this book, look for stabilizing and destabilizing consequences of democratic institutions and the particular challenges that long-standing democracies face.

Theme Four: The Politics of Collective Identity

How do individuals understand who they are in political terms, and on what basis do groups of people come together to advance common political aims? In other words, what are the sources of group attachments, or *collective political identity?* At one point, social scientists thought they knew. It was generally held that age-old loyalties of ethnicity, religious affiliation, race, gender, and locality were being dissolved by economic, political, and cultural modernization. Comparativists thought that class solidarities based on the shared experience of work or economic position more broadly had become the most important source of collective identity. And it was believed that as countries became politically modern or mature, groups would pragmatically pursue their economic interests in ways that were not politically destabilizing.[16] We now know that the formation and interplay of politically relevant collective identities are far more complex and uncertain.

In the industrial democracies, the importance of identities based on class membership has de-

clined, although class and material sources of collective political identity remain significant in political competition and economic organization. In contrast, contrary to earlier predictions in social science, in many countries nonclass identities—affiliations that develop from a sense of belonging to particular groups based on language, religion, ethnicity, race, nationality, or gender—have assumed growing significance.

The politics of collective political identity involves struggles to define which groups will be full participants in the political community and which ones will be marginalized. It also involves a constant tug of war over the relative power and influence—both symbolic and material—among groups. Issues of inclusion and priority remain pivotal in many countries, and they may never be resolved. One reason that conflict around this issue can be so intense is that political leaders in the state and in opposition movements often seek to mobilize support by sharpening ethnic, religious, racial, or regional rivalries.

A Puzzle: Collective Identity and Distributional Politics. Once identity demands are placed on the political agenda, can governments resolve them by distributing resources in a way that redresses the grievances of the minority or politically weaker identity groups? Collective identities operate at the level of symbols, attitudes, values, and beliefs and at the level of material resources. However, the contrast between material- and nonmaterial-based identities and demands should not be exaggerated. In practice, most groups are animated by both feelings of loyalty and solidarity *and* the desire to obtain material benefits for their members. But the analytical distinction between material and nonmaterial demands remains useful, and it is worth considering whether the nonmaterial aspects of the politics of collective identities make political disputes over ethnicity, religion, language, or nationality especially divisive and difficult to resolve.

In a situation of extreme scarcity, it may

prove well-nigh impossible to find any compromise among groups, even when their conflicts revolve only around clashing material interests. But if at least a moderate level of resources is available, such conflicts may be easier to resolve because groups can "split the difference" and get a share of resources that they find at least minimally adequate. This process, which refers to who gets what, or how resources are distributed, is called *distributional politics*. However, the demands of ethnic, religious, and nationalist movements may be difficult to satisfy by a distributional style of politics precisely because the group demands more than merely a larger share of the economic pie. The distributional style may be quite ineffectual when, for example, a religious group demands that its religious values be imposed on the whole society—or, for that matter, that it be allowed to engage in practices prohibited by law. Similarly, how can the difference be split when a dominant linguistic group insists that a single language be used in education and government throughout the country? In such cases, political conflict tends to assume an all-or-nothing quality. The country studies in this book examine a wide range of conflicts involving collective identities. It will be interesting (and possibly troubling) to ponder whether and under what conditions such conflicts are subject to the normal give-and-take of political bargaining.

These four themes provide our analytic scaffold. With the four themes in mind, we can now discuss some of the common features and issues studied in the country studies that comprise *European Transitions in Politics,* as well as how the text is organized.

European Politics in Transition: Critical Junctures

European political systems are dynamic, not frozen, models. They respond to complex challenges and are shaped by preexisting institutional and cultural legacies, by battles lost and won, and by the exigencies of everyday life as it is experienced—and understood—by ordinary citizens, who make a host of messy demands on their governments. In this section we look at some of the major stages and turning points in European political development.

Industrialization, State Formation, and the Great Divide

For several decades following World War II, it was common for students, scholars, and policymakers to think of two Europes: East and West. The meanings we attach to the political arrangements for any part of the globe emerge historically, and the words we use have important political and ideological implications. For example, an expression like *First World,* which refers to Western Europe, Japan, and the United States, and *Third World,* which refers to the less economically developed states of Latin America, Africa, and Asia, may reflect a Eurocentrism in which the economically dominant West is given pride of place. And terms like *Western Europe* and *Eastern Europe* are as much political and ideological as they are geographical. In this case, the terms were linked to the cold war divide that pitted the United States against the Soviet Union, each allied with European states.

When we look at the evolution of modern European societies, we see two fundamentally transformative processes at work: the emergence of the modern state and the advent of developed capitalism linked to the Industrial Revolution. Absolutist states emerged in Europe during the sixteenth century. Monarchies with firm, centralized authority replaced the more localized and personal administration of power that characterized the large number of small principalities, city-states, leagues, and so on scattered throughout medieval Europe. The introduction of permanent bureaucracies, codified laws, national taxes, and standing armies represented the arrival of the first modern European states. In the competition among the widely varied political units of the time, victory went to monarchs who devised more efficient methods of governing—bureaucracies—and more productive economies.[17]

By the eighteenth century, new economic developments associated with capitalist industrialization began to push the state beyond its increasingly archaic monarchical forms. Although bitter feuds between landowners and monarchs were not uncommon, absolutist regimes were generally linked by economic, military, and political ties to the traditional landholding aristocracy. With the Industrial Revolution, the owners of manufacturing enterprises, the bourgeoisie, increasingly gained economic prominence and political influence. A growing incompatibility between old state forms and new economic demands fostered revolutionary upheavals that ushered in more modern constitutional forms of the state. Industrialization and state formation were closely linked historical phenomena: the European states that we recognize today follow from earlier eruptions associated with the growth of capitalist market forces and the struggle for power between the old, landowning classes and the modern, urban bourgeoisie.

There is another point, however, that is crucial to an understanding of both the history of European societies and the organization of this book. Until the Russian Revolution in 1917 and the subsequent post–World War II division of Europe, there was no natural division in Europe between east and west. In earlier centuries, absolutist states in Central or Eastern Europe—Austria, Prussia and Russia—existed alongside similarly centralized bureaucracies in France, Spain, or England. (The situation in Eastern Europe was complicated by the breakup of the great multinational empires, notably the Ottoman and Austro-Hungarian empires, and the creation of a host of small new nation-states after World War I.)

With the Russian Revolution and the emergence of socialist states in Eastern and Central Europe in the aftermath of World War II, a great divide split Europe into East and West. This distinction was reinforced by the United States and the Soviet Union as part of a global campaign to win allies and secure geopolitical and ideological dominance. For over a half-century, profound differences in political and economic processes separated the capitalist democracies of Western Europe from the socialist societies of Eastern Europe.

The passing of communism in East-Central Europe in the 1990s has created not only new geopolitical territories but new intellectual terrain. For the first time, we can ponder both the deep historical roots of divisions within Europe and the possibility (at this stage, nothing more than that) of a new pan-European polity fostered by the EU. The process of strengthening European-wide ties would be fostered if the existing members of the EU agree to accept as "candidate countries" for membership the thirteen states that have applied to join from East-Central Europe (as well as Turkey). Yet the risk of new and bitter divisions within Europe also derives from this very same process of widening the EU because of the likelihood that some states will be admitted and others excluded.

To understand the current transition in Europe, a useful historical baseline is the period following World War II. This was when the framework was established that at first regulated political conflict for a generation and then itself proved the source of new challenges beginning in the late 1960s that pressed forward the agenda of European integration.

Our account centers on Western Europe, the major focus of *European Politics in Transition*. We will also consider briefly the evolution of East-Central Europe. In the West, the key domestic political tension involved the relationship between relying on private market forces to promote economic growth as opposed to extending state control over the economy, as well as strengthening democratic rights, political participation, and social equity. The solution fashioned after World War II, which set the stage for an unprecedented period of prosperity and political stability, was linked to the widespread adoption of a new approach to economic management (known as Keynesianism, which we discuss below) and the extension of the welfare state. The new political formula involved cooperation among the state, organized labor, and organized capital around the quest for economic growth as a way to resolve the problem of class conflict. During a moment that some thought would last forever, it appeared that economic growth organized within a capitalist framework was not only compatible with but depended on steadily expanding democratic participation and welfare state social reforms.

Postwar stability declined when the social and economic bases of the postwar settlement crumbled. Gradually cooperation among classes gave way to conflict, new non-class-based social actors appeared, and the possibility and desirability of linking economic growth, welfare state expansion, and democratic participation were challenged. This is the story that we now recount in fuller detail.

World War II and the Emergence of the European Model

The years following World War II represented a period of rapid economic growth in Western Europe, sustained by secure and widely popular regimes. In Germany and Italy, the Christian Democrats ruled throughout the period, and in Britain, Labour and Conservative governments shared a mainstream consensus. In contrast to the economic depression and social instability of the interwar period, the years following World War II reflected an unusual degree of social harmony. (These observations must be qualified in the case of southern Europe, as we discuss later in this section.)

During this period, many scholars and political elites believed that sustained social, economic, and political conflicts were a thing of the past. Sociologist Daniel Bell described "the end of ideology" and the waning of ideological passions; political sociologist Seymour Martin Lipset proclaimed that the fundamental problems of industrial society had been solved. In brief, economic growth seemed to provide the solvent for reducing class antagonisms. The more radical social movements that sought fundamental change in the organization of society and the control of economic resources appeared outmoded. "The performance of capitalism since the end of the Second World War has been so unexpectedly dazzling," wrote an observer in 1965, that "it is hard for us to believe that the bleak and squalid system which we knew could, in so short a time, have adapted itself without some covert process of total destruction and regeneration to achieve so many desired objectives."[18]

The political regulation of the market economy temporarily succeeded in the postwar period in appearing to reconcile economic efficiency and social equality, capitalism, and democracy. In the new situation, a cross-class consensus on the value of economic growth—expanding the pie—largely displaced traditional class conflicts regarding how that pie should be produced and distributed.

Although class conflicts persisted in Europe, especially in southern Europe (Italy and France among our studies), the general trend was toward a consensus on the value of state regulation of market forces. The most common approach, often described as *neocorporatism*, involved direct negotiations between representatives of labor unions and organizations composed of business firms over prices or incomes, with the coordination and guidance of the state. A key shift was that the state persuaded organized labor to moderate its demands for substantial wage gains, autonomy, and control of the workplace in exchange for extensive benefits, including full employment, stable prices, welfare programs, and automatic wage increases. And it persuaded employers to recognize the legitimacy of labor unions, in both representing workers in the workplace and participating in decisions about the entire economy. These understandings and arrangements—what came to be called the *postwar settlement*—helped to end the era of strife associated with the transition to an industrial capitalist order.

The postwar settlement was linked to changes within technology and the organization of production and consumption—what some scholars have termed a shift to a *Fordist system* of mass production and consumption. The American industrialist Henry Ford has lent his name to the two key elements of Fordism because he was among the first to introduce the new techniques. First, in the realm of production, Ford pioneered the quintessential consumer durable—the automobile—relatively cheaply. The secret was to simplify production by introducing fewer parts (often interchangeable from one model to another) that were brought together to produce the finished automobile through assembly-line methods that divide the work into repetitive, simple operations. By standardizing the production process and the skills that workers needed, Ford was able to lower the cost of automobiles dramatically.

Second, Fordist production techniques made it possible not only to engage in mass production but also to affect patterns of consumption fundamentally. Because assembly-line work was so repellent, Ford was forced to pay workers more than the prevailing wage. The indirect result was that, thanks to the greater purchasing power enjoyed by workers at Ford and other large firms, the potential market for goods—automobiles and other mass-produced consumer durables—dramatically expanded. The social consequence of Fordism was to produce an extensive body of semiskilled manual industry workers, which became one of the largest groups in the societies of Western Europe. These workers were able to enjoy some of the material benefits of industrial production, especially when the postwar settlement integrated the newly expanded industrialized working class into political arrangements.

With the benefit of hindsight, particularly in the light of renewed political conflict since the late 1960s, it is now evident that the new harmony of the postwar settlement derived from an unusual set of circumstances. The absence of severe conflict resulted from the dislocations of war, which exhausted political passions, dictated that priority be placed on rebuilding war-torn economies, and placed a premium on cooperation within and among the states of Europe. At the same time, the division of global influence between the United States and the Soviet Union reduced the possibility of pan-European unity and placed the states of Western Europe in a situation of economic and military dependence on the United States. *Pax Americana* meant that Western European nations lacked the material means to challenge the United States's leadership, even as the perceived threat of a Soviet military invasion quelled potential political conflicts.

U.S. military, political, and economic intervention promoted European recovery and helped prevent the emergence of radical regimes in Western Europe. Nevertheless, despite the aims of some policymakers in the United States, convergence between U.S. and European political systems was limited because historical differences between the two regions were too strong to be overridden. Two factors are particularly important: the difference in the configuration of class forces in Western Europe and the role of the state. European workers were more conscious of their class affiliations and often defined their lives in terms of their participation in political parties and in party- and class-linked subcultures that provided strong bonds of friendship and community. European workers were likely to organize along class lines in the political sphere and support a range of parties—labor, social democratic, socialist, communist—that sought to extend state control over the private market system as well as expanded social provision.

Moreover, large numbers of working people in southern Europe were fundamentally, and quite openly, opposed to the entire capitalist system. Thus, contrary to the U.S. experience, political party cleavages within European politics reflected to a considerable extent the class divisions that remained from the emergence of industrial capitalism in the nineteenth century. The pattern of political opposition in Western Europe was complex. Long-standing differences in religious identity, conflicts over secularization, and regional loyalties motivated political choice in Italy, West Germany, and France. In contrast to the United States, however, a fundamental axiom of political life involved the continued conflict between the working people (organized through trade unions and socialist parties of one variety or another) and the propertied classes (manufacturing elites and those linked to the world of finance, organized through business associations and bourgeois parties). If the gulf between classes diminished, it remained the central source of partisan conflict.

Class conflict was often reinforced by a religious cleavage. The split was not so much between those of different religious affiliations. The large majority of Europeans were Christian. Rather, churches (often preeminently the Catholic Church) supported Christian Democratic and other conservative political parties, while there was mutual hostility between organized religion and parties of the Left.

The role of the state—the bureaucracy, parliament, and the entire range of national governmental institutions—was far greater in Western Europe than in the United States. In Europe, state action within the economic realm was extensive, including substantial provision of welfare benefits, direction of fiscal and monetary policy, regulation of industrial relations, and vigorous efforts to sponsor industrial growth and restructure failing industries. In the postwar period, states throughout Western Europe extended their activities in both the economic and social welfare spheres. For example, in many countries, a wave of nationalization of industry after the war resulted in state-owned enterprises controlling basic industries like steel, energy, and air and rail transport.

Therefore, the social harmony of the 1950s and 1960s did not lead to an Americanization of Western European politics. Rather, the two factors that most clearly distinguished Europe from the United States—party mobilization along class lines and activist state institutions—produced a special (Western) European model of politics that was more statist than what occurred in the United States but was unmistakably capitalist. A new class compromise ushered in an era of unprecedented growth and political stability from the end of World War II to the late 1960s and early 1970s. (We review below how this period of class and ideological reconciliation was shattered by renewed class conflict and the 1973 oil crisis.)

The process of constructing political harmony involved negotiating a set of nationally specific arrangements in each of the Western European countries, in which a wide array of state, business, trade union, and political party elites participated. It was at this time that the welfare state was consolidated, high levels of employment were achieved, anticapitalist forces were marginalized, and an unusual degree of social, industrial, and political consent for mainstream and reformist policies was secured.

Both the nature of political participation and the character of the economic system underwent significant changes as the European model emerged in the postwar period and as it has developed in the intervening half-century or more. Although contemporary European politics can no longer be charted against the benchmark of agreements that were negotiated in the 1940s and 1950s, the postwar settlement remains a critical juncture of great importance. Indeed, the agenda for European integration advanced by the EU to an important degree has transferred the logic of the postwar settlement—negotiations over distributive politics sustained by a normative appeal to common fates—from the national to the European level. Two major challenges involve whether the

growth of EU institutions and policies throughout Western Europe can achieve the same result
as occurred in the postwar settlement and (even
more daunting) whether the same process can
be extended by the eastward expansion of the
EU.

The Transformation of Political Parties. Political
parties played a key role in organizing a motif
for political participation and consent within the
emergent European model. However, as parties
were transformed in the process of organizing
and sustaining the postwar consensus, they also
eventually destabilized its social basis, thereby
weakening its underlying foundations.

The structure and behavior of political parties
were transformed, as parties with explicit organizational and ideological links to the working
classes and parties linked historically to the interests of economic elites competed by appealing to broader constituencies. As an alternative
to more adversarial ideological appeals, parties
of both the Left and the Right often sought to
generate broad-based electoral support. They
did so by representing themselves to the electorate not as the party of the working class or
the economic elite, but as the best modernizing
party—the one that could master technological
change and guide the national economy in a
complex system of international interdependence. (One scholar termed this a shift from
class-based, ideological, mass parties to "catch-
all" parties that sought to "catch" the support
from voters of diverse social classes.)[19]

As parties began seeking interclass support
on election day and were less concerned with
mobilizing stable subcultures around contested
class-based issues, class identities began to erode
relative to nonclass forms of self-identification,
including region, age, and religion. In a later period, social movements based on these and other
non-class-based factors further supplanted citizens' class identities.

A New Political Framework. The new political
framework that developed in Western European

nations after World War II involved a tacit alliance between the organized working class and
large-scale business, an arrangement that had
not existed in the past and would crumble by
the 1970s. Under the guidance of the state, the
two groups cooperated in a manner that stimulated economic growth, political moderation,
and social harmony. While states intervened extensively to regulate the economies and ensure
nearly full employment, higher wages, and expanded social welfare provision, the working
class was asked to accept as its part of the bargain severe limits on both its industrial and political demands.

Adam Przeworski has elaborated a theoretical
model that helps illuminate the conditions for
the emergence and functioning of the postwar
settlement. The political arrangements organizing this model are known as social democracy, in
which a center-Left party closely allied with the
labor movement controls the government to
orient state policy along the lines described
here. According to the social democratic model
that Przeworski elaborates (and which is a formalized model of what existed in considerable
measure in practice in the postwar period), the
working class must be sufficiently organized,
cohesive, and centralized that it can act in a
unified manner, and workers must gain a reasonable assurance from business and the state
that they will receive a steady stream of benefits, including high employment levels, regular
wage increases, and welfare state provisions. In
return, the organized working class, through its
accepted leaders within the trade union and socialist party spheres, finds it worthwhile to
moderate demands in ways that enable business
to carry on profitable activities.[20]

Working-class moderation had several elements. In contrast to a more class-divided past,
workers came to accept the prerogatives of capitalist control, in the overall organization of the
economy and within the production process. In
effect, demands for annual wage increases and
welfare state programs became a substitute for
the satisfaction of demands that were more

threatening to capitalist production (for example, workers' control over the pace, content, and conditions of work or over investment decisions, industrial policy, and technological innovations).

The model indicates that business must also accept constraints in order for the new agreement to work. Business firms must renounce the arbitrary exercise of their power in the workplace and political sphere and agree to provide workers with high levels of wages and employment. Finally, for the agreement to succeed, the state must do its part—for example, by regulating interest rates and engaging in countercyclical demand management (taxing and spending in ways that reduce economic instability), sponsoring political institutions that promote active class collaboration, and expanding welfare state programs. More generally, the state must appear to be a neutral arbiter serving the general interest, rather than siding unduly with either employers or workers. If the state were seen as favoring business interests, workers would protest rather than cooperate; if the state were seen as favoring workers' interests, capitalists would register their dissatisfaction by refusing to invest (what has been dubbed a capital strike), and economic stagnation would result.

In Przeworski's model, the postwar settlement pattern of class relations appears to have replaced traditional zero-sum conflict, in which the gains of one class are achieved at the expense of the other. Class compromise seems to represent a situation of positive-sum cooperation, in which citizens from both major classes, as well as other groups, gain from mutual cooperation and restraint. In fact, however, the appearance of universal benefit was misleading. Not all classes and social forces gained from the creation of the new, rationalized capitalist order. Although industrial workers (whether in blue-collar or office positions) began to enjoy the benefits of the consumer society, they continued to be subjected to the harsh conditions of industrial labor. Given a shortage of labor, owing to

rapid economic expansion, millions of immigrant workers were recruited to northern Europe from southern Europe (Portugal, Spain, Italy, Greece, and Turkey) and Eastern Europe (especially Poland and Yugoslavia), as well as from Africa and Asia. Immigrant workers were assigned the most menial positions and received low wages and meager welfare benefits. They were denied citizenship rights and were subjected to discrimination in housing and educational opportunities. Women also received fewer benefits from the new order, as a result of their unequal position in employment and in the domestic sphere, and their decidedly unequal treatment in welfare state provisions.

Labor Movements, Social Democracy, and Western European Politics. These reforms were first set in place in the 1950s. However, important political and economic differences generally divided the capitalist democracies in Europe by a north-south dimension: the nations of northern Europe (represented in this book by Britain and Germany) and those of southern Europe (represented by France, a mixed case, and Italy).

Workers in northern Europe were more likely to gain citizenship rights early and to be included within the dominant system. In West Germany (but not in Britain), labor unions were more unified, and workers gained greater benefits from the system. As a result, they were more likely to be moderate in their political stance. In contrast to southern Europe, working-class elements were not excluded from the decision-making process nor did they remain hostile to the existing economic and political order in significant numbers. Indeed, social democratic governments in northern Europe initially sponsored most of the major policy innovations that composed the postwar settlement. Then, by a process that French political scientist Maurice Duverger called "contagion from the left," moderate conservative governments emulated these reforms.[21] In northern Europe (including Britain), trade union leaders conducted national negotiations with top-level associations of business or with government. In West Germany, and to a lesser extent in Britain, they restrained rank-and-file rebelliousness against the deals that were struck.

Labor movements in southern Europe were divided internally by ideological and religious differences, and this found expression in rival national confederations, engaging in bidding wars for members at the workplace, firm, and industry levels. National union leaders had neither the authority nor the mandate to negotiate with business representatives and the state, and rank-and-file workers often refused to abide by any agreements that were struck. Business was likely to be opposed to unions on ideological grounds and, in any event, unions could not, and were not inclined to, offer management the kinds of benefits that unions routinely provided in northern Europe. Thus, the working class was relatively excluded from the ongoing economic order, which strengthened its tendency toward oppositional values and protest activity.

This comparison of labor movement dynamics in northern and southern Europe finds an important parallel in workers' political activity. For example, in the two northern European nations covered in this book, two-thirds or more of all workers were unified in a single socialist party, and these parties were either the first or second most powerful in their respective party system. The British Labour Party and the West German Social Democratic Party alternated as the governing party with center-Right parties and played crucial roles in promoting progressive reforms. These social democratic parties made a vital contribution to forging the class compromise that prevailed in northern Europe, and this participation had significant consequences. Within social democracy, the compromise was tilted moderately in favor of working-class interests: the state provided more expansive welfare benefits, tax laws were more progressive so that income inequalities were somewhat narrowed, and state policies placed a higher priority on full employment.

In southern Europe, workers divided their

support about equally among communist, socialist, and more conservative Christian democratic parties. Within the Left, the communist and socialist parties were highly antagonistic in France throughout the period and in Italy in the 1960s. As a result, the Right governed in these countries, although sometimes in complex and unstable coalitions. This circumstance reinforced workers' exclusion from the political community and also fostered more conservative state policies.

France is a mixed case in our analysis of the north-south split regarding the postwar settlement. Although it industrialized rapidly after World War II, and thus in this respect converged with northern Europe, its political and cultural patterns—notably a high degree of ideological conflict, labor militancy, and political fragmentation—were reminiscent of southern Europe.

Despite important differences in the way that political conflict was structured in the various Western European nations and the north-south split that we have identified, there was a broad convergence in the policies sponsored by the major Western European governments. One reason was that rapid industrialization and urbanization required the expansion of housing, education, old-age pensions, and unemployment insurance. Another was that given the preexisting tradition of activist states in Western Europe, it is not surprising to find that states were deeply involved in meeting the new social and economic needs. Far more than in the United States, Western European governments shared major responsibility for providing all citizens with basic services, including housing, medical care, and old-age pensions. The means varied through time and from country to country. For example, in the immediate postwar period, when the Left was often dominant and the Right discredited in many countries by the fascist era, popular pressure led governments to extend substantially the nationalized public sphere. When governments did not directly organize facilities and services—and pressures for nationalization quickly subsided in the 1950s—they provided public assistance programs and subsidies so that most citizens were entitled to a minimum of what was defined as necessary for a decent existence. A third reason for a trend toward convergence was the creation in the late 1950s of the European Economic Community (EEC), which provided for lower tariffs and a harmonization of economic policies among member states. As a result, national governments increasingly came to emulate each other's policy innovations.

Nonetheless, national differences persisted as a result of variations in historical evolution, political culture and institutions, and the specific balance among social forces and political parties. In the country sections of this book, we review the particular policy orientation adopted by each state. Nevertheless, there were some common elements on the postwar policy agenda of all the Western European states covered in the book.

Planning: Economic Regulation and the Keynesian Welfare State. Within the economic realm, the state engaged in ambitious efforts to achieve the goals of full employment, growth, economic modernization, and assistance to export-based industries. In the first years of the postwar period, priority was given to economic reconstruction, especially in basic industries such as coal and steel, mining, and transport. At this time, governments were under pressure from labor and often took over direct control (nationalization) of key industries. The state's economic steering capacity was strengthened by the development of planning techniques within newly created planning agencies or in finance and economic ministries. Although what passed for planning was often a mixture of hopes, estimates, guesses, and policies, planning did serve to moderate conflict among social actors, reduce bottlenecks in production, set sectoral goals, and build support for streamlining industry through technological innovation. Planning also aimed at reducing class tensions through the

creation of tripartite commissions of representatives from organized labor, capital, and the state.

In more general terms, there was a broad convergence in the economic and social policy orientation of European states for a few decades after World War II. The *European model* of economic regulation, as it informally came to be known, involved vigorous state intervention with the twin aims of maximizing economic growth *and* ensuring that the fruits of economic growth would be diffused throughout the population. Two key terms can be suggested to summarize the policy mix: *Keynesian economics* and *the welfare state.* Taken together, the policy package is sometimes referred to as the *Keynesian welfare state.*

Keynesian economics was inspired by the distinguished English economist John Maynard Keynes. His work centered around understanding the causes of the Great Depression of the 1930s, when the industrialized economies of Europe and North America stagnated, living standards plummeted, and unemployment soared to unprecedented levels, reaching as high as 20 percent. Keynes sought to devise policies to end the depression and prevent the recurrence of future depressions. He argued that the orthodox economic policy orientation that Western European and North American governments were following in the 1930s made economic problems worse. Rather than accepting fiscal orthodoxy, which stipulated that governments should cut spending when times were hard, Keynes advocated precisely opposite policies. He reasoned that the Great Depression was caused by declining demand for goods and services, which deterred new investment (since investors calculated that low demand meant that markets did not exist for new production). According to Keynes, when governments cut spending, which orthodox economics claimed was necessary for governments to live within their reduced means, this *further* reduced demand, thereby contributing to the downward spiral of dwindling demand and investment. On the contrary,

Keynes claimed, governments should boost spending during hard times—thereby countering the "natural" movement of the business cycle—in order to bolster demand and stimulate new investment. (This is why Keynes's economic recommendation is often called *countercyclical* demand management.) In brief, he posited that a more vigorous, activist government stance would reverse the trend toward stagnation and provoke upward growth. Keynesian economics thus came to be understood as involving vigorous government intervention through high levels of spending, to ensure overall (aggregate) demand, which would stimulate economic growth.

Keynes's name is also associated with the welfare state, the second leg of the new policy orientation that developed during the Great Depression and following World War II. He argued that the provision of welfare service, that is, an expanded welfare state, provided an ideal outlet for the additional government spending. Prior to the 1930s, government spending for the most part was devoted to defense, the maintenance of internal order (police), and education. Keynes argued that a desirable way to increase government spending during economic downturns was to redistribute resources to those most in need—the unemployed, sick, and economically dependent members of society. The term *welfare state* refers to the series of programs that transfer funds to citizens to meet social needs (transfer payments, such as unemployment insurance, pensions, and family allowances) or involve direct government provision of goods or social services (housing, medical care, job training, and the like). The origins of such programs lie earlier than the Great Depression. However, it was during the 1930s, and especially after World War II, that the welfare state expanded to alter the political economies of European countries fundamentally.

Rapid urbanization and industrialization produced pressure for state measures to prepare workers for the labor market and to cushion workers, pensioners, the infirm, and the unemployed from economic dislocations. These programs attempted to undercut opposition to capitalist expansion and to promote expansion by training workers to acquire the skills that business firms wanted. Among the welfare measures that the state sponsored were public construction and ownership of housing, provision of medical services, and funds for unemployment insurance and pensions. Although Western European welfare state programs were far more successful than those in the United States in reducing the human costs of rapid industrial expansion, the welfare state involved relatively little redistribution of power and resources among classes. Instead, it helped to encourage broader acceptance of the new order by redistributing resources across age groups (from adult workers to young children and elderly citizens) and preventing extreme inequalities.

Modernization of Political Institutions. After World War II, power shifted from parliamentary to executive institutions within the state. This shift involved two elements. First, the balance of power within the state shifted from parliament to the bureaucracy. The decline of legislative bodies was justified by the presumed need for speed and cohesion in policymaking. Parliamentary institutions are designed to represent diverse interests and promote debate among options, but they move quite slowly and are fragmented. The executive, on the other hand, is organized to act decisively in order to implement decisions effectively. Second, there was a shift of decision-making power within the executive. On the one hand, with the state involved in more far-flung activities, power gravitated upward, with prime ministers and their staffs exercising greater power of oversight and control over their cabinet associates and line agencies. On the other hand, because of the state's increased involvement in macroeconomic and policy activities, economic ministries gained greatly increased influence in the day-to-day administration of governmental policy.

The desire for increased political efficiency

was linked to the decline of class conflict and the perceived reduction in ideological passions: Why engage in protracted debate if everyone agrees on the desirability of economic growth within the prevailing capitalist economy? An unusual degree of consensus did not preclude differences among European political parties. Leftist parties were more inclined than rightist parties to favor redistributive measures; moreover, the entire political balance within Western Europe was substantially more to the left than in the United States.

Western European nations also differed quite substantially in their political-institutional mix. Southern European countries preserved a central role for parliament in making and toppling governments, possibly as a reflection of the greater political tensions in these states. (The situation changed drastically in France with the advent of the Fifth Republic in 1958, when Charles de Gaulle redesigned political institutions to limit parliament's role.) In northern Europe, government formation reflected electoral party choice, as opposed to party maneuvering in parliament (the situation in southern Europe). Moreover, stronger executives managed more enduring governments. For example, in West Germany, the Center-Right was in power without interruption from 1949 to 1966 (and shared its government with the Social Democrats in a Grand Coalition for three years thereafter). In contrast, governments changed every six months on average in France (until the founding of the executive-dominated Fifth Republic in 1958), and the fragmented, multiparty system prevented stable and cohesive leadership throughout the postwar period in Italy.

The European Model: Crises, Variations, and Challenges

Through the late 1960s, the European model we have described prevailed (with variations from nation to nation) throughout Western Europe, as governments successfully managed economic and welfare policies and the major social classes maintained their modernizing alliance with the state. For the most part, the central trade-off of the national postwar settlements held: Governmental steering mechanisms fostered full employment and economic growth, while increased social and welfare expenditures helped purchase relative social harmony and labor peace. The tension between democracy (now meaning participation through interest associations and cross-class political parties) and capitalism (now meaning politically regulated "modern capitalism" with extensive public holdings) was reduced—some thought forever.

Suddenly, and virtually without warning, this social harmony shattered, and a new era of political uncertainties began. This critical juncture unfolded in two stages. It was succeeded in the 1990s by what might be considered the beginning of a whole new era in European politics.

Stage One—From the Late 1960s Through the Mid-1970s: The Price of Success. In a way, the renewal of political conflict was rooted in the process of economic growth itself, which generated a host of political tensions that had been obscured by the strong grip of organized labor, capital, and the state. With state regulation aimed at forcing the pace of economic growth rather than reducing its damaging social consequences, the balance of costs and benefits shifted. Urban sprawl, traffic jams, and congestion became common. Forests were destroyed and rivers poisoned by industrial pollution. Migrants from rural areas and "guest workers," the euphemism for immigrant workers, jammed into hastily constructed blocks of high-rise flats that began to ring older central cities.

Women were drawn into the paid labor force in high numbers as a result of a tight labor market and an increase in clerical and governmental service positions, but they were recruited to poorly paid, subordinate positions. Economic growth was achieved in part through the introduction of new technology, which displaced skilled workers and posed threats to workers' health and safety. Labor unions ignored the damaging effects of economic growth on workers and on the social and physical environments. Furthermore, they generally failed to represent the interests of groups outside their traditional constituency of skilled, male, industrial workers.

The rapid expansion of the educated, urban middle class helped spark the early phase of militant protest. Many university students were radicalized by opposition to the U.S. military action in Vietnam as well as to the rigid authority patterns they encountered closer to home in their universities, political parties, and families. Many sought nontraditional goals: They wanted production to be democratically organized, resisted the traditional demands of marriage and career paths, and were the first to warn of environmental dangers from corporate abuses.

Political scientist Ronald Inglehart has coined the term *postmaterialism* to describe the values espoused by many educated youths in the postwar generation.[22] He discerns an intense generational cleavage created by the very different conditions under which prewar and postwar generations reached political maturity. Those born before World War II craved material and physical security because this was what they most lacked as a result of the Great Depression and military cataclysm. In contrast, Europeans born after the war were raised in a period of relative material security linked to the postwar settlement. With the rapid expansion of higher education throughout Western Europe in the 1960s, linked to brisk economic growth, they were more likely to be highly educated and to have the confidence born of expecting to gain stable and well-paid jobs.

Rather than expressing satisfaction and political quiescence, the postwar generations took their material advantages for granted and developed higher expectations. They resented, more than their parents did, being forced to submit to hierarchy, whether, for working-class youth, the tedium and mindlessness that characterized as-sembly-line production jobs, or, for middle-class youth, the tedium of the rigid hierarchies they encountered in corporations, universities, and government. Postwar youths were more likely than their elders to be affronted by the human and physical costs of military confrontation and economic growth. They sought to pursue nonmaterial goals, including self-expression, a sense of community, and autonomy. Because they were less integrated within established institutions, they were inclined to express their frustration through unruly protest. For example, Inglehart finds (comparing materialists and postmaterialists in a later period) that those committed to postmaterialist values are four times more likely than those committed to materialist values to engage in protest activity. Postmaterialists are also more likely to support single-issue grass-roots protest movements. "Though the pure Postmaterialist type constitutes only one eighth of the public," he writes, "they consistently furnish an absolute majority of the movements' activists."[23]

But we should beware of assuming that the rebellion of the late 1960s was rooted only in the new middle class. A key element contributing to the outbreak of protest in the late 1960s, which scholars often overlook in their fascination with new sources of opposition, was the rebellion of the industrial core of the working class. As the pace of economic change increased, workers were forced to endure intensified work tempos, increased occupational hazards, and tedious work. Blue-collar workers, particularly those in unionized sectors linked to social democratic parties, challenged the centrist slide of socialist and social democratic parties.

In order to understand the 1960s rebellion, we need to appreciate how it represented a confluence of diverse sources, somewhat in the manner of "the perfect storm" described in Sebastian Junger's book (and later film) of that name. That is, although there were some common grievances linking the diverse groups that protested in the 1960s, the sources were also quite diverse. "The movement" was a sprawling coalition of industrial workers, newly militant white-collar working classes, urban, educated middle-class youth, and women and nonwhites neglected by traditional unions and leftist parties. The groups might not have had such a tumultuous effect, but for the fact that they came together at one moment to create a surging political movement.

Finally, the growing incapacity of states to provide economic rewards in accordance with the postwar settlement combined with leftist critiques—focusing on disregard for ecology, nuclear power, and youth and women's movement issues—to spawn a resurgence of ideological divisions and forces on both the Left and Right. Although these responses to the decline of the postwar settlement combined in somewhat different ways in each of the Western European states, we can discern a general pattern in the political crisis and transition that succeeded the postwar settlement.

In the late 1960s and 1970s, there was a massive and unexpected eruption of what one study termed the "resurgence of class conflict in Western Europe." The most dramatic instance occurred in France in May 1968, when nearly half of all French workers, students, professionals, and civil servants staged the largest general strike in history. In Italy, during the "hot autumn" of 1969, workers and allied groups waged widespread grass-roots struggles, outside established political party or legislative channels, for workplace control, political influence, and provision of social necessities like health care and housing. In Sweden, industrial relations became far more conflictual in the 1970s than previously and culminated in a general strike/lockout in May 1980.

In the 1970s, as the crisis deepened, antistate protest began to break with the nineteenth-century heritage of class-dominated politics. What one observer called "the increased transparence of political power and the state" combined with the state's growing inability to ensure economic prosperity, which a restive and fragmented set of constituencies had long taken for granted. Political scientist Suzanne Berger notes:

In the seventies, the dominant political response to the new transparence of the state [was] to try to dismantle it, not to take it over. While this response is not without precedent in European history (the conservative Right often proposed this in the nineteenth century) never before has this conception of politics shaped new political ideas on both the Left and the Right. What has to be explained is why virtually all new political groups and thought in Western Europe have come to focus, in one way or another, on the issue of the breakup of the state; why virtually all new political organization has taken place outside the orbit of the political parties.[24]

Thus, a "crisis of governability" accompanied the new electoral volatility and the weakening of traditional patterns of party opposition. At the same time, increasingly influential political ideas and campaigns emerged outside and against conventional parties from the New Left and New Right: the women's movement, both neofascist and antiracist responses to immigration; nuclear disarmament agitation; environmental protest; and taxpayers' revolt.

If economic growth had continued unabated in the 1970s, social harmony might have been restored. However, the slowdown of Western Europe's economies reinforced the crisis of the postwar settlement. Many causes have contributed to the continued erosion and replacement of the postwar settlement, and each represents a new item on an emerging policy agenda that has made it increasingly difficult for any government to maintain popular support.

Traditionally in the vanguard of industrial production and technological innovation, Europe began falling behind in the contest for global competitiveness in key industries in the 1970s. First, Japan and the United States gained dominance in high-tech industries, causing a trade imbalance in this sphere. Equally serious, newly industrializing countries in the developing world—including South Korea, Taiwan, and Brazil—displaced Western Europe in basic industry, including steelmaking, textile production, and shipbuilding. Furthermore, as opposed to the continued expansion of the wage-earning ranks in the postwar years, tendencies developed toward structural unemployment. Ironically, a major reason was the development of high-tech innovations that saved on both capital and labor, with the result that fewer workers were needed to maintain a constant or even expanding level of output.

Changes within the organization of production contributed to the erosion of the postwar settlement. Fordism began to be an inefficient way to produce in the new era of the microelectronic revolution. As production shifted from mass-produced goods to diverse and often smaller-scale production strategies and to service-based industries, the semiskilled (often male) industrial working class began to shrink as a proportion of the employed population. On the one hand, this fragmented the working population, complicating neocorporatist bargaining based on unified social actors. On the other hand, technological change brought about new collective identities, based on new skills and social groups newly involved in production; for example, the number of female workers expanded rapidly. These changes were difficult to accommodate within the framework of privileged institutionalized bargaining with the state by the representatives of labor and business (neocorporatism) associated with the European model.

Western Europe was affected by the wider recession that began with the sharp increase in oil prices in 1973–1974. The cost of petroleum exports by the oil-producing developing countries grew at the expense of the industrialized nations of the West. The extremely high levels of popular support for the welfare state in Western Europe meant that most governments were unable to reduce welfare state benefits significantly Meanwhile, trade union power limited labor market adjustments, and the increasingly global scale of production encouraged an outflow of investment from flagging Western European economies.

More generally, increasing economic integration meant that national governments were less able to regulate their domestic economies.

Whereas some governments, often in the smaller European nations, flourished by developing the means to adapt rapidly to international economic imperatives, flexibility in most nations was impeded by rigidities that had developed through the years of the postwar settlement. In general, though with notable exceptions (among the larger European nations, West Germany was especially dynamic), Western Europe suffered a decline in international competitiveness. The result was higher rates of unemployment and inflation, slower productivity growth, and meager increases in living standards. The golden years of the postwar settlement were over.

Stage Two—From the Mid-1970s to the Mid-1980s: Experimentation and a Rightward Turn. Provoked by the political protest and poor economic performance that began in the late 1960s, a relatively brief phase of political experimentation occurred from the 1970s to the mid-1980s, when governments of the Left and Right promising new departures were elected in many Western European nations. Initially, political momentum took a leftward turn. For example, northern European regimes devised mechanisms enabling workers to participate in decisions regarding technology change and occupational health and safety. In France, the Socialist government of François Mitterrand, elected in 1981, substantially expanded the nationalized industrial and financial sectors.

Political momentum soon shifted toward the right as constraints deriving from the international economy and the opposition of domestic forces rendered unworkable the extension of direct state economic management or welfare benefits. Although no Western European government was highly successful in either mobilizing political support or promoting successful economic performance, the Left failed utterly to develop a new beginning.

If the postwar settlement was intimately associated with social democracy, the 1980s were an opportunity for a conservative counterattack.

For example, in Britain the Conservative government of Margaret Thatcher mounted a massive and quite successful assault on the power of labor unions and privatized both public housing facilities and nationalized industrial firms. Equally significant, it fostered important changes in British political culture, enhancing support for initiative and entrepreneurship at the expense of collectivity. Rightist coalitions promising tax reductions were elected in Denmark, Norway, and elsewhere, often replacing social democratic incumbents.

The Left also failed to shape state policy in the streets, through grass-roots movements. The most important failure involved the extraordinary outpouring of indignation in the early 1980s opposing the decision of the North Atlantic Treaty Organization to modernize intermediate-range nuclear missiles stationed in Western Europe. Although millions mobilized throughout Western Europe (and peace movements developed in East-Central Europe as well), the effort failed and the United States succeeded in stationing intermediate range missiles in Germany.

The uncertainty, loss of confidence, instability, and general decline that prevailed in Western Europe in the early 1980s was captured by the pungent term *Eurosclerosis,* which began to be heard at the time. Europe had lost its bearings following the long period of postwar reconstruction and growth, and where the drifting was destined to stop, nobody knew. Yet since the late 1980s and 1990s, there has been a revitalization of Europe, amid new issues, problems, and challenges.

From the 1990s to the Twenty-First Century: A New European Model?

Sometime in the 1980s, the vitality disappeared from the European model inspired by the postwar settlement of social democratic mixed economies, left versus right political contestation, and national policy models. Although sig-

nificant elements of the European model remain—Europe's welfare state sector remains far more extensive than its counterpart in the United States—Europe has witnessed the emergence of a new model of politics since the 1990s, the product of both a renewal of the process of European integration and a distinctive new domestic policy mix pursued by governments that reject Keynesian economic policies. We are now living through a critical juncture in European political development of historic proportions, whose ultimate significance is yet to be determined.

From State to Market to the Third Way. Across the political spectrum, there has been a significant shift in expectations about the role of the state in economic management. Unions have lost power, and middle-class politics is ascendant. The state continues to play an important role in the new political economy, but the role consists of activity to bolster rather than curtail the operation of markets. The dominant tendency in Western European politics currently seems to be a powerful backlash against the principles of compromise and the balance of public and private power that were presupposed by the postwar settlement and the welfare state. There is general agreement on lowering taxes, reducing state economic intervention, and relying more on market forces to shape socioeconomic outcomes (an orientation widely referred to as *neoliberalism*). Although many of the state steering mechanisms and welfare programs put in place during the postwar settlement have survived, the momentum for expanding political regulation of the marketplace is gone; instead, the dominant tendency is for welfare state retrenchment and the reinvigoration of private market forces wherever politically feasible. As Gøsta Esping-Andersen has observed, "Many believe that the welfare state has become incompatible with other cherished goals, such as economic development, full employment, and even personal liberties—that it is at odds with the fabric of advanced postindustrial capitalism."[25] In a similar vein, many have argued that global competition advantages countries that allow private market forces free rein, such as Britain, which has emerged as the EU champion for attracting foreign direct investment, and disadvantages countries such as France and Germany, which retain powerful regulatory mechanisms.

This shift toward neoliberalism does not sweep other political concerns off the board. Many of the concerns that began to undermine the postwar settlement in the late 1960s, including environmental and other quality-of-life matters, the demand for autonomy and community, and opposition to intrusive public and private bureaucracies, continue to fuel social and political movements. And conservative parties are often less suited than left-of-center ones to respond effectively to these new issues on the policy agenda. In fact, at the dawn of the new century, the appeal of neoliberalism was so pervasive that politics had become very muddy. It was increasingly difficult to define Left and Right in traditional pro-market or pro-state terms, and that frame of reference for defining political loyalties seemed increasingly outdated.

Into the breach, a new policy orientation has emerged in Europe as center-left politicians and parties, led by Britain's Tony Blair, with Germany's Gerhard Schröder a powerful ally, try to go "beyond left and right." This *third way*[26] attempts to transcend distributional politics, which it considers unsuited to an era of intensified global competition, and combine the best of traditional appeals of Left and Right: the social justice concerns of classic social democracy with reliance on the economic dynamism of the Right. By the turn of the twenty-first century, EU Europe was dominated by left-of-center governments, but few (Lionel Jospin's Socialists in France were an exception) considered themselves traditional European social democrats. While in some countries such as Italy, third-way politics was not a defining orientation, the approach was gaining a great deal of attention. As distinguished observer of Europe Ralf Dahrendorf commented, "In fact, the

Third Way debate has become the only game in town—the only hint at new directions for Europe's politics in a confused multitude of trends and ideas."[27]

To be sure, the arrival of a new political orientation that challenges and significantly recasts the European model does not mean the eradication of the old model. Class and occupational boundaries remain politically important, albeit sometimes in unusual ways. For example, as jobs become scarce, an important cleavage pits those occupying stable jobs against those with precarious employment or none at all. As private sector jobs become unstable, an important cleavage pits private and public sector workers against one another. At the same time, the waning of long-standing debates between socialists and conservatives means neither the end of political ideologies nor the consecration of a centrist consensus. Witness the rise of new forces, groups, and parties that challenge the established order. Without wishing to equate them, we observe other orientations that have gained increased importance: the environmental movements and their political expression (the Greens are now solidly represented in the European Parliament), plus anti-immigrant xenophobic forces in virtually every country. Thus, although the third way may not be the only game in town, it casts a long shadow over Europe and captures, for the time being, the most important new dynamic.

Old States and the New Europe. When the Treaty of Rome created the European Economic Community in 1957, many scholars confidently predicted the steady growth of European economic and political integration. Despite steps in this direction, the path was far more tortuous than many expected. Indeed, the economic turbulence beginning in the mid-1970s brought the process to a crashing halt, as European states became more concerned with protecting their domestic economies than with cooperating on a European-wide level. By the early 1980s, this produced the Eurosclerosis alluded to earlier.

The same forces that drove domestic political change in the 1980s also impelled political leaders and prominent business executives to cast their lot with a strengthened EU. When French president François Mitterrand reluctantly concluded in 1984 that France could not achieve domestic reflation on its own, he cast about for a new policy direction. He decided to join forces with German chancellor Helmut Kohl in a joint effort to revive France and Germany's ailing economies through increased European economic cooperation. In so doing, the leaders of Western Europe's two major states, along with prominent business leaders and officials in the EU, rescued the EU from decline. When the Maastricht Treaty on European Union was ratified in 1992, a new era began in Western European politics. Maastricht deepened economic integration, incorporated some aspects of foreign relations, defense policy, and policing and addressed the endemic demands for greater internal democracy. The regulatory and institutional changes in the framework of the EU since the early 1990s range from specific provisions expanding the organization's scope—which mandate the free movement of commodities, capital, technology, and labor—to infrastructural concerns of standardizing technical production norms and redrafting labor and other codes, as well as unresolved issues, including the Social Charter to enhance workplace and social rights and a common currency, the euro, launched in January 1999 by eleven of the fifteen member countries (Greece joined in January 2001 to make it twelve of fifteen).

Henceforth, the story of the domestic politics of Western European countries cannot be told without paying close attention to the increased importance of the EU. Other transnational influences associated with globalization have also become more powerful, for example, volatile capital flows in an era of international financial deregulation. But after a close look at the evolution of the EU in Part II, we highlight in the rest of the book the many ways that EU institutions have shaped the domestic political economies of member states.

The EU is not only a source of economic progress and political optimism. It has become a target for popular discontent by streamlining European economies, standardizing production norms, and ending state subsidies for domestic producers, as well as imposing harsh convergence criteria that require pursuing austerity policies in order to create a common currency. The situation since the deepening of the EU has been described as the New Europe. It is very much a mixed blessing: on the one hand, a revival of Europe's economic fortunes; on the other hand, widening divisions between European citizens who are winners and losers depending on education, training, and occupation. The shift in power toward the EU has also limited the capacity of the member states to regulate their own economies and societies, increased tensions over the definition of citizenship and national identity, and produced a "democratic deficit"—concerns over citizen control and institutional transparency and accountability—at the level of EU institutions. It is not yet clear what the outcome of this important transition in European politics will be. Moreover, beyond the future of the EU loom even larger issues: the declining specificity of national political and economic processes, the future of the nation-states of Europe, the relationship between Western and Eastern Europe, the identity of Europeans, and the integration of Europe in the global economy and political order.

Whatever the future of the EU and the larger issues it inspires, it is quite clear that the current transition in European politics is intertwined with the emergence of the EU as a transnational polity to rival the central importance of the countries whose political systems we study.

Conclusion

Western European politics is in transition from a stable postwar past to an uncertain future; from a set of conflicts dominated by class-based politics to a more complex political dynamic defined by both centrist and more radical versions of a politics beyond Left and Right; and from a situation of national autonomy to a web of European integration. With citizen trust in parties and governments eroded and economies under considerable stress, it is understandable that European political leaders sought new answers in new institutions. The EU may succeed in maintaining Europe's traditional favored place in the world, but that is by no means clear.

Paradoxically, despite the extraordinary upheavals of the past fifteen years, the persistent social and economic stresses, and the myriad future uncertainties, one again hears echoes of the "end of ideology" in Western Europe as in the United States. (An influential book published in the 1990s was entitled *The End of History*.)[28] Yet as with the liberal pragmatism of the 1950s, it is doubtful that the new third-way pragmatism of the early twenty-first century will escape challenge. There are simply too many stresses and unanswered questions, including how to reconcile regional and ethnic diversity with national unity, national cultural differences with the evolving EU, a strengthened Western European Union with the attempt to preserve national governmental autonomy, and persistent (and often disappointed) demands for economic growth with concerns about inequality and unemployment as well as environmental and social costs.

The future of East-Central European nations and their relations with Western Europe are especially thorny issues. With the demise of the Soviet Union, the nations of East-Central Europe have become freer to develop in more pluralist and more diverse ways. Although this may produce greater individual freedom and economic modernization, in some cases it has also fostered some of the worst features of unbridled capitalism (inflation, unemployment, increased inequality), as well as xenophobic tendencies. In the 1990s, many Eastern European nations suffered wrenching economic dislocations, involving soaring prices, massive layoffs, and regional inequalities, after market forces were unleashed in formerly protected and tightly regulated economies. As for relations between East-Central and Western Europe, will the election of democratic governments committed to strengthening market forces in Eastern Europe encourage the emergence of a continental movement toward unification? Or will it precipitate new tensions within and among the nations of Europe?

European Politics in Transition seeks to understand the historical, economic, social, and institutional forces that have shaped the transition to the New Europe. Directly following this Introduction, we provide a comprehensive analysis of developments in the EU. We then closely examine the major Western European nations: Britain, France, Germany, and Italy. We analyze more briefly Poland, Hungary, and the Czech and Slovak Republics (and consider Yugoslavia), the most important nations in East-Central Europe.

In each country study, we begin with a description of the historical legacy of state formation, which continues to have a significant impact on political forces and policies, and a broad overview of contemporary political institutions and challenges. In the second chapter in each part, we analyze the historically specific features of both the postwar settlement and the shift since the 1970s toward the more market-oriented political economy. The third chapter in each part analyzes institutions of policy formation and implementation: the government and executive generally, public and semi-public agencies, local government, and the judiciary. The fourth chapter analyzes institutions of political representation, notably legislatures, political parties and elections, modes of organizing interests, and contestatory movements. The last chapter in each country part focuses on the current transition: new political forces, cleavages, and policies; the impact of the EU; and likely directions of change. The influences of the EU on domestic politics and policy are thoroughly integrated into each country study.

It is quite a challenge to understand the political systems and changing dynamics of contemporary Europe. We hope that the timely information and thematic focus of European politics in transition will both prepare and inspire you to explore further the endlessly fascinating terrain of European politics.

Notes

1. The organization was called the European Economic Community (EEC) until the 1980s, when it became the European Community (EC). Since 1993 and the ratification of the Maastricht Treaty, it has been called the European Union (EU). In the remainder of this book, we usually use the current designation, European Union or EU, unless historical context calls for an earlier version.

2. For a superb study of this issue, see David Stark and Laszlo Bruszt, *Postsocialist Pathways: Transforming Politics and Property in East Central Europe* (Cambridge: Cambridge University Press, 1998).

3. For attempts to answer the question, see Alfred Stepan and Cindy Skach, "Constitutional Frameworks and Democratic Consolidation: Parliamentarism Versus Presidentialism," *World Politics* 46, no. 1 (October 1993): 1–22, and Juan J. Linz and Arturo Valenzuela, eds., *The Failure of Presidential Democracy* (Baltimore: Johns Hopkins University Press, 1994).

4. Robert A. Dahl, *A Preface to Economic Democracy* (Berkeley: University of California Press, 1985), pp. 54–55 (emphasis in the original).

5. For a classic discussion of this issue, see Charles Lindblom, *Politics and Markets: The World's Political Economic Systems* (New York: Basic Books, 1977).

6. Adam Przeworski, *Democracy and the Market: Political and Economic Reforms in Eastern Europe and Latin America* (Cambridge: Cambridge University Press, 1991), p. xi.

7. Robert Putnam, with Robert Leonardi and Raffaella Y. Nanetti, *Making Democracy Work: Civic Traditions in Modern Italy* (Princeton, N.J.: Princeton University Press, 1992).

8. Tarrow, Sidney, "Making Social Science Work Across Space and Time: A Critical Reflection on Robert Putnam's *Making Democracy Work*," *The American Political Science Review* 90, no. 2 (1996): 389–399.

9. Gabriel Almond and Sidney Verba, *The Civic Culture: Political Attitudes and Democracy in Five Nations* (Boston: Little, Brown, 1963). See also Gabriel Almond and Sidney Verba, eds., *The Civic Culture Revisited* (Boston: Little, Brown, 1980).

10. Dankwart A. Rustow, "Transitions to Democracy: Toward a Dynamic Model," *Comparative Politics* 2, no. 3 (April 1970): 363.

11. See Wolfgang Streeck, "German Capitalism: Does It Exist? Can It Survive?" *New Political Economy* 2, no. 3 (1997): 237–256.

12. Herbert Kitschelt, Peter Lange, Gary Marks, and John D. Stephens, "Convergence and Divergence in Advanced Capitalist Democracies," in Kitschelt, Lange, Marks, and Stephens, eds., *Continuity and Change in Contemporary Capitalism* (Cambridge: Cambridge University Press, 1999), chap. 15

13. This view was first put forward in Rustow's classic article, "Transitions in Democracy." More recently, it has been developed by Dietrich Rueschemeyer, Evelyne Huber Stephens, and John D. Stephens, *Capitalist Development and Democracy* (Chicago: University of Chicago Press, 1992).

14. Guillermo O'Donnell and Philippe C. Schmitter, *Transitions from Authoritarian Rule: Tentative Conclusions About Uncertain Democracies* (Baltimore: Johns Hopkins University Press, 1986).

15. Adam Przeworski et al., *Democracy and Development: Political Institutions and Well-Being in the World, 1950–1990* (Cambridge: Cambridge University Press, 2000), chap. 4. For a classic statement of the opposing view, see Samuel Huntington, *Political Order in Changing Societies* (New Haven, Conn.: Yale University Press, 1968).

16. For a survey of political science literature on this question, see Mark Kesselman, "The Conflictual Evolution of American Political Science: From Apologetic Pluralism to Trilateralism and Marxism," in J. David Greenstone, ed., *Public Values and Private Power in American Democracy* (Chicago: University of Chicago Press, 1982), pp. 34–67.

17. Perry Anderson, *Lineages of the Absolutist State* (London: New Left Books, 1974), Douglass North, *Structure and Change in Economic History* (New York: Norton, 1981), Hendrick Spruyt, *The Sovereign State and Its Competitors: An Analysis of Systems Change* (Princeton, N.J.: Princeton University Press, 1994), and Charles Tilly, *Coercion, Capital and European States, A.D. 990–1992* (Cambridge, Mass.: Blackwell, 1993).

18. Andrew Shonfield, *Modern Capitalism: The Changing Balance of Public and Private Power* (Oxford: Oxford University Press, 1980), p. 3.

19. Otto Kirchheimer, "The Transformation of the Western European Party Systems," in Joseph LaPalombara and Myron Weiner, eds., *Political Parties and Political Development* (Princeton, N.J.: Princeton University Press, 1966), chap. 6.

20. Adam Przeworski, *Capitalism and Social Democracy* (New York: Cambridge University Press, 1985).

21. Maurice Duverger, *Political Parties* (London: Methuen, 1954).

22. See Ronald Inglehart, *The Silent Revolution: Changing Values and Political Styles Among Western Publics* (Princeton, N.J.: Princeton University Press, 1977), *Culture Shift in Advanced Industrial Society* (Princeton, N.J.: Princeton University Press, 1990), and *Modernization and Postmodernization: Cultural, Economic, and Political Change in 43 Societies* (Princeton, N.J.: Princeton University Press, 1997).

23. Inglehart, *Culture Shift*, p. 380.

24. Suzanne Berger, "Politics and Antipolitics in Western Europe in the Seventies," *Daedalus* 108 (Winter 1979): 33.

25. Gøsta Esping-Andersen, "After the Golden Age? Welfare State Dilemmas in a Global Economy," in Gøsta Esping-Andersen, ed., *Welfare States in Transition: National Adaptations in Global Economies* (London: Sage, 1996), p. 1.

26. For the classic statement of this approach, see Anthony Giddens, *The Third Way: The Renewal of Social Democracy* (Cambridge: Polity Press, 1998).

27. Ralf Dahrendorf, "The Third Way and Liberty: An Authoritarian Streak in Europe's New Center," *Foreign Affairs* 78, no. 5 (September–October 1999): 13.

28. Francis Fukuyama, *The End of History and the Last Man* (New York: Free Press, 1992).

Bibliography

Anderson, Perry. *Lineages of the Absolutist State.* London: New Left Books, 1974.

Benjamin, Roger; Neu, C. Richard; and Quigley, Denise, eds. *Balancing State Intervention: The Limits of Transatlantic Markets.* New York: St. Martin's Press, 1995.

Berger, Suzanne, ed. *Organizing Interests in Western Europe: Pluralism, Corporatism, and the Transformation of Politics.* Cambridge: Cambridge University Press, 1981.

Dalton, Russell J., and Kuechler, Manfred, eds. *Challenging the Political Order. New Social and Political Movements in Western Democracies.* New York: Oxford University Press, 1990.

Downing, Brian M. *The Military Revolution and Political Change: Origins of Democracy and Autocracy in Early Modern Europe.* Princeton, N.J.: Princeton University Press, 1992.

Esping-Andersen, Gøsta. *Social Foundations of Post-Industrial Economies.* New York: Oxford University Press, 1999.

Golden, Miriam, and Pontusson, Jonas, eds. *Bargaining for Change: Union Politics in North America and Europe.* Ithaca, N.Y.: Cornell University Press, 1992.

Goldthorpe, John H., ed. *Order and Conflict in Contemporary Capitalism.* Oxford: Oxford University Press, Clarendon Press, 1984.

Hall, Peter A., ed. *The Political Power of Economic Ideas.* Princeton, N.J.: Princeton University Press, 1989.

Hobsbawm, Eric. *The Age of Extremes: The Short Twentieth Century, 1914–1991.* New York: Vintage Books, 1994

Hollifield, James F. *Immigrants, Markets, and States.*

Cambridge, Mass.: Harvard University Press, 1991.

Hollingsworth, J. Rogers, and Boyer, Robert, eds. *Contemporary Capitalism: The Embeddedness of Institutions.* New York: Cambridge University Press, 1997.

Hollingsworth, J. R.; Schmitter, Philippe C.; and Streeck, Wolfgang, eds. *Governing Capitalist Economies: Performance and Control of Economic Sectors.* New York: Oxford University Press, 1994.

Inglehart, Ronald. *Culture Shift in Advanced Industrial Society.* Princeton, N.J.: Princeton University Press, 1990.

Katzenstein, Peter J. *Small States in World Markets.* Ithaca, N.Y.: Cornell University Press, 1985.

Kitschelt, Herbert. *The Transformation of European Social Democracy.* Cambridge: Cambridge University Press, 1994.

Kitschelt, Herbert; Lange, Peter; Marks, Gary; and Stephens, John D., eds. *Continuity and Change in Contemporary Capitalism.* Cambridge: Cambridge University Press, 1999.

Laver, Michael, and Schofield, Norman. *Multiparty Government: The Politics of Coalition in Europe.* Oxford: Oxford University Press, 1990.

Lichbach, Mark Irving, and Zuckerman, Alan S., eds. *Comparative Politics: Rationality, Culture, and Structure.* New York: Cambridge University Press, 1997.

Marglin, Stephen A., and Schor, Juliet R. *The Golden Age of Capitalism: Reinterpreting the Postwar Experience.* New York: Oxford University Press, 1990.

Martin, Andrew, et al. *The Brave New World of European Unions: European Trade Unions at the Millennium.* New York: Berghahn, 1999.

Moore, Barrington, Jr. *The Social Origins of Dictatorship and Democracy.* Boston: Beacon Press, 1966.

Offe, Claus. *Contradictions of the Welfare State.* Cambridge, Mass.: MIT Press, 1984.

Rueschemeyer, Dietrich; Stephens, Evelyne Huber; and Stephens, John D. *Capitalist Development and Democracy.* Chicago: University of Chicago Press, 1992.

Shonfield, Andrew. *Modern Capitalism: The Changing Balance of Private and Public Power.* Oxford: Oxford University Press, 1980.

Stark, David, and Bruszt, Laszlo. *Postsocialist Pathways: Transforming Politics and Property in East Central Europe.* Cambridge: Cambridge University Press, 1998.

Tarrow, Sidney. *Power in Movement: Social Movements and Contentious Politics.* New York: Cambridge University Press, 1998.

Tilly, Charles. *Coercion, Capital and European States, A.D. 990–1992.* Cambridge, Mass.: Blackwell, 1993.

P A R T

II

The European Union and the Future of European Politics

George Ross

C H A P T E R

1

The Making of
the European Union

The European Union (EU) stands out as one of the great political success stories of the twentieth century. In 1950 six continental nations, only recently the most mortal of enemies, agreed to create the European Coal and Steel Community (ECSC). In 1958, in the Treaty of Rome, the same six agreed to create the European Economic Community (EEC), through which they would construct a "common market." By the millennium, over four decades later, the EEC had become the EU, in the process expanding from six to fifteen member states (and eventually toward thirty). European integration has led its members to cede autonomy to a new system of transnational and sometimes supranational institutions. The result is a new Euro-level system of politics.

With its roots in limited economic integration, the EU has moved toward a unified economy that rivals that of the United States. Governed by common rules from a common center, it has been instrumental in creating European prosperity and is an unquestionable asset to regional and world peace. It also has helped consecrate and consolidate democratic politics in Western Europe, a laboratory for experiments in new forms of governance and a model for other regions. Yet the EU is simultaneously a miracle and a mystery: a miracle because the politics of European modernity seemed to rule it out, and a mystery because it confounds conventional notions of political science.

Modern Europe invented the idea of sovereignty, which posited ultimate political power within territorial boundaries and vested authority in the hands of the sovereign, however defined institutionally. Another European invention, the nation-state augmented sovereignty by tying it to a nation unified by national identity. Citizenship, in this light, involved common outlooks, common loyalties, and a common language. Sovereign European territories also founded the contemporary world of states, often dated to the 1648 Treaty of Westphalia that ended the Thirty Years' War. Practitioners in this new world of states developed maxims of statecraft, eventually elaborated and codified in scholarly theories of international relations. Sovereignty established national boundaries around the use of power and force. International society became a system composed of sovereign states, by definition autonomous and in control of the uses to which their national resources might be put. In theory, no state was to interfere in the internal business of another, but because no higher political authority existed beyond national states, the international system was "anarchic." Thus, every state had to prepare for the worst, mindful that the superior power of some other states might leave it open to invasion and conquest. In this system of self-interest and self-protection, nation-states with superior power could threaten weaker ones to secure compliance on political issues, including those governing domestic matters. Building the means to prevent this coercion, maintain national security, and establish international bargaining power thus became essential. The miracle of the EU is that transnational integration has developed in precisely this region of the globe where the pathologies of sovereignty, the nation-state, and the international system have been most often demonstrated.

The EU is today an organization of states whose powers are consecrated in and limited by international treaties. Scholars have traditionally called such arrangements "international organizations"; the United Nations and the World Health Organization are classic examples. International organizations are, in theory, limited to administering policies that sovereign nations delegate them. The mystery of the EU is that it is a genuine transnational polity whose decisions significantly limit the sovereignty of its members. Just as important is that its members have developed a predilection for solving problems through the EU rather than nationally. Jacques Delors, for a decade (1985–1995) the president of the European Commission, often called the EU "an unidentified flying political object." For example, the EU is both federal and confederal. The rules governing its decisions are baffling; in some policy areas, decisions are taken by majorities, while in others, decisions must be unanimous. Legislation can be proposed only by the European Commission, whose members are not elected but appointed by member states. The EU Council of Ministers is composed of ministers from national government, the products of democratic national elections, yet the Council's workings have always been shrouded in secrecy. The EU has had a directly elected European Parliament since 1979, yet this body has had serious power for only a very few years, and because there is no European government elected on the basis of a program, it has no majority and no opposition. Absent as well is any European-level "we the people." Instead, the EU encompasses multiple peoples in many societies with different national identities and languages.

Critical Junctures

European integration has been a cumulative process of small steps, with each step a response to issues that European nation-states felt unable to handle on their own. Over time, this process has transformed the EU from a problem-solving arena of last resort to a place where European nation-states brainstorm, anticipate, and act in what they have increasingly understood to be their common interests.

"Nevermore War Amongst Us . . ."

For centuries the European continent was the site of bloody wars whose terrifying costs reached their peak in the first half of the twentieth century. By then, given new technologies and new ways of mobilizing populations, the pursuit of national interests in the international state system had turned suicidal. World War I (1914–1918), the result of long-standing European tensions nourished by careful alliance building, saw millions of young men killed and maimed in trench warfare over minuscule plots of land polluted by poison gas and artillery shells. This "war to end all wars," as U.S. President Woodrow Wilson called it, precipitated the end of the Russian Empire in 1917, brought communism to power, broke apart the Austrian Empire, left Central and Southern Europe divided among unstable small nations and territorial grievances, and caused the collapse of the German Empire. In Germany the new Weimar Republic was doomed by internal disagreements and by the punitive Treaty of Versailles (1919). Italian democracy, even more vulnerable, ominously succumbed to a fascist coup in 1922.

The interwar period (1918–1939) was a time of frightening instability, despite efforts to create transnational organizations like the League of Nations. Conflicting territorial claims and virulent nationalisms proliferated. Wild economic cycles, some nourished by the Treaty of Versailles, culminated in the collapse of the international financial system and the Great Depression. Economic disruption stimulated barbaric political extremism. In these years, Hitler and the German National Socialists conceived their own plans for uniting Europe, while Stalin and the Soviet Communists liquidated internal opponents in wholesale fashion. A civil war in Spain cost hundreds of thousands of lives and left the Spanish people under an illiberal regime. Fascism under Mussolini led Italy from disaster to disaster. Everywhere, intense class conflict nourished political unrest, even in areas where democracy continued to function. In the 1930s, the future of democracy in Europe and the world looked perilous indeed.

Europe's disorders then culminated once more in brutal war. In World War II millions upon millions of soldiers and civilians died, well more than 20 million in the Soviet Union alone (many of starvation). Pushing the technique of mass murder to new depths, the Nazis killed 6 million Jews in the Holocaust plus untold others they deemed undesirable. Atrocities of all kinds were magnified by new machinery that belligerents had come to possess. Populations were moved around Europe's map against their wills. Innocent civilians were routinely bombarded from the sky, sometimes instantly incinerated, as in the terrible firebombing of German cities by the Allies. Nuclear weapons, developed first by Europeans and Americans, were not used in Europe, but only because their development came too late in the war.

This gigantic human catastrophe ultimately brought down the fascist regimes of Germany and Italy (those in Spain and Portugal persisted into the 1970s). The war also diminished the appeal of illiberal political regimes, with the important exception of Stalinist communism to the East. In many countries, wartime Resistance forces bearing democratic ideals and social reform came to power in the postwar period. The United States, Great Britain, France, and the Soviet Union jointly occupied conquered Germany, tried Nazi war criminals (most notably at Nuremberg), and reflected on how to prevent anything like nazism ever recurring.

Europe in 1945 was at a historic turning point. Economically, it was prostrate. Cities, factories, and transportation networks lay in ruins, and because European treasuries were empty, money to reconstruct them was unavailable. Politically, Europe existed in the shadows of two superpowers, the Soviet Union and the United States—allies in the war but adversaries soon thereafter in a cold war that would last more than four decades. In this climate, Western Europeans had to cast about for new ways to solve their problems. One response was greater integration. For six Western European countries—Italy, France, West Germany, Belgium, the Netherlands, and tiny Luxembourg—the search for a new system began in the ECSC in 1950 and culminated in the 1958 Treaty of Rome that established the European Economic Community (since 1994, the European Union, or EU).

Fine-Tuning the Golden Age?

Europeans of the 1950s were pleasantly surprised when their economies began a virtuous cycle of growth and change. This Golden Age tied an Americanized system of mass production and consumption to Keynesian macroeconomic policy in which states acquired large new roles. Full employment, formerly a dream, briefly became a reasonable goal, and states redistributed part of the system's profitability in new or expanded social programs, backed by broad political coalitions that included the collective representation of groups long excluded. These postwar settlements underpinned the first great triumph of representative democracy in continental Europe's history. Ultimately they embodied shared aspirations for a general European model of democratic exchange, one that institutionalized class conflict through the representation of producer groups—both capital and labor.

These postwar settlements, however, were *national* systems, and they varied from country to country. National politics decided the most important matters of policy and distribution. In this context, the EEC, or Common Market, the first stage of European integration, was a supplement to Western Europe's thriving national economies.* The EEC's central role was to fine-tune the Golden Age, subject to the guidance of its member states. The Common Market came to provide useful services in support of the different national developmental models of its members. For example, its customs-free area created a larger trading space, so that the burgeoning industrial national champions in many of its member states could export more. Its Common Agricultural Policy (CAP) stimulated the modernization of agriculture, promoting rapid gains in efficiency together with a decline in rural populations, which in turn caused migration into expanding areas of urban employment. Finally, the EEC's common external tariff established a useful buffer against the harsh winds of the international market and the economic power of the United States.

Eurosclerosis, Europessimism, and the Collapse of National Postwar Settlements

EEC members   (nine after 1973 when the United Kingdom, Portugal, and Ireland joined) responded to the oil shocks and "stagflation" of the 1970s in different ways. Some continued to apply older Keynesian techniques, others turned to monetarism, and still others, like Britain after 1979, attacked labor organizations to lower wages. In a common market, however, such policy divergence could be dangerous, particularly in the broader context of currency fluctuations stimulated by the end of the U.S.-sponsored in-

*The European Union (EU) came into being when the Maastricht Treaty was ratified in November 1993. The politics and institutions of European integration were called the EEC (European Economic Community) or, colloquially, the Common Market until the 1970s, when it became the EC (European Community).

ternational financial system. When EEC member states lost their way in the 1970s, the Common Market very nearly died with the postwar settlement.

Only in 1985, after a decade of "Eurosclerosis," did energy return to European integration. By then the situation had changed dramatically. The buoyant growth of the Golden Age was gone. Europe had lost economic vitality and position relative to its competitors. Full employment had given way to high unemployment. The challenges were many, and so was the possible range of responses. Each member state might have chosen its own ways, almost certainly at the cost of European integration. But Europe's experiment did not founder. Instead member states agreed to several hundred measures to "complete the single market" by the end of 1992. This program was designed to dismantle protected national economic arrangements and create a more competitive Europewide "single economic space." Rather than act as handmaiden to national economic development projects, the EC would henceforth seek to transform national economies by promoting new economic liberalization. The culmination was the 1991 Maastricht Treaty on European Union (ratified in 1994, when the label "EU," for "European Union," became official). At Maastricht, member states agreed to establish the Economic and Monetary Union (EMU) to create a unified European monetary policy, the European Central Bank to run it, and a single European currency, the euro. Also meant to be a turning point to political integration, Maastricht proposed a new common foreign and security policy and new collaboration in justice and home affairs.

The Millennium: Puzzles Within Puzzles

International turbulence from the collapse of the Soviet empire and the end of the cold war brought new issues and problems in the 1990s. The 1992 single market program, despite much hype, failed to bring promised economic growth. Instead a deep recession began in 1992 and lasted for nearly five years. Unemployment rose above 10 percent (more than 20 million people were unemployed), and the figure would have been higher had the never-yet-employed young and the never-again-to-be-employed middle aged been fully counted. The semiskilled manufacturing jobs that Europe had expanded with postwar prosperity disappeared by the hundreds of thousands without being replaced.

All of these developments fed identity crises in European societies. As economic changes introduced in 1992 helped undermine national models, people lost confidence that national governments could respond to their needs. As national politicians tended to scapegoat Europe for their inability to produce for their constituents, new public awareness of the EU's significance collided with growing recognition that the public had not been fully consulted. From the beginning, European integration had been worked out by diplomats and leaders behind closed doors. Despite discussion of "democratic deficit," these stealth methods of decision making had not been burning issues during the Common Market period, when successful national models had created strong national identities and a sense of effective participation in national democratic systems. In the 1980s, however, renewal of European integration had undercut parts of these national models, and by the 1990s, feeling was widespread that Europe was seriously eroding the sovereign capacities of European nation-states to confront their own destinies, hence short-circuiting national democratic processes. At the same time, conviction grew that important decisions made at the European level were beyond democratic control. One consequence was a series of national populist movements, xenophobia, and anti-immigrant hysteria, which appeared like ghosts from a repressed past. In particular, the belief spread that political elites were unreliable and often corrupt.

As Maastricht became unpopular in the mid-1990s, the prospects for EMU became doubtful. The policy convergence that EMU demanded was much more of a strain than anyone had anticipated and would clearly cost a large number of jobs. Yet any thwarting of it would have been an incalculable defeat. As the EU moved toward the January 1999 deadline for setting up EMU, analysts worried, wavered, and criticized, but the German government stood solidly behind the process, reassuring those who had feared that a unified Germany might move away from the EU.

EMU success meant that the process of integration went forward. Puzzles within puzzles remained, however. For example, what was the EU to do with the ex-Communist countries of Central and Eastern Europe (CEECs)? Immediately after 1989 the EU, involved in "deepening" its internal processes, had lacked the resources to confront the issue. It did set up new programs to channel aid to the CEECs and negotiated agreements with most of them for freer trade. It also encouraged CEEC aspirations for eventual EU membership. The large differences in economic and political development between Western and Eastern Europe seemed to require such a piecemeal approach. By the second half of the 1990s, however, the EU clearly had to move toward full incorporation of the CEECs.

At issue were the conditions for bringing these new recruits into the EU. Plans for accession were drawn up in the late 1990s, and negotiations began. By agreeing to admit new CEEC members, the EU was taking the lead in organizing new trans-European economic interdependencies and helping the CEECs to modernize and share Western European prosperity. By enlarging to its east, the EU would also be exporting and underwriting the consolidation of democracy in countries where democracy had but fragile indigenous roots. It would have been hard to imagine a more important frontier for the EU. Perhaps because of the magnitude of these responsibilities, many in the EU were wary and ambivalent.

Issues raised by EU enlargement challenged

the EU's existing institutional arrangements. EU institutions had been designed in the 1950s to work for six members. With thirty members, they required serious change, or they might stop working altogether. Reconsidering institutional structures opened a host of complicated questions, however. Was the EU meant primarily for market building, as some important member states maintained? Or was market building meant as a launching pad for the broader unification of Europe? Moreover, a great debate on institutions—really a long-overdue constitutional discussion—could not avoid issues of democratic legitimacy.

The end of the Soviet threat also upset the comfortable predictability of Europe's cold war security. Maastricht proposed, in vague and general terms, the creation of a common EU foreign and security policy and spoke of the eventuality of a European-level defense capability. Yet because some EU member states were patently uninterested in pursuing these matters, policymakers proceeded mainly to seek better coordination among EMU members and more effective EU representation to outside parties. Still the questions remained. How would Europe confront potential new security problems in its own backyard? What would be the division of labor between the North Atlantic Treaty Organization and Europe in any such confrontations?

Lurking in these nested puzzles were questions about the EU's position in the world in general and, in particular, its relationship with the United States. The United States had facilitated the founding of the EU, and the frozen international structures of the cold war had provided certainties as it matured. The end of the cold war, however, occurred as Europe was becoming an economic region as large and potentially as productive and innovative as the United States, suggesting a rebalancing of economic power and the possibility of growing rivalry, particularly in trade conflicts. The implications of EMU success were similar. Greater European–U.S. coordination on vital issues would be

needed, but for decades the United States had grown accustomed to primacy. Finally, the cold war division of labor between the United States and Europe in foreign affairs in which the responsibilities of the EU were regional and those of the United States global became subject to change.

Europolitics and European Politics in Transition

Europolitics, the politics of European integration, is one of the fundamental reasons that national politics in Europe are at a moment of important transition. Fifty years of economic integration have had huge effects on national political autonomy. As the EU goes beyond economic integration, shrinking national sovereignty will become even more tangible. Europolitics has thus become more significant, in part at the expense of European national politics. Open EU-wide market structures have transferred decision making from national governments to markets. The site of market regulation has largely shifted substantially from individual nations to the EU. The EU has also assumed responsibility for monetary policy, perhaps the most important dimension of economic policymaking. Finally, since Maastricht, parts of foreign relations and defense policy, along with issues of immigration and policing, have begun to move toward the EU. For member states, therefore, whatever the gains from European integration, a great deal has—willingly—been lost. For the citizens of EU member states, these losses may be even greater as national polities lose discretion in macroeconomic, fiscal, industrial, social, and other policies. The programs that politicians present at election time may still presume these margins of discretion, but as the EU encroaches, politicians can do less (however much they claim to be able to do), and citizens lose the means to make changes through national political systems.

In all this, European politics has become a

multilevel system of governance. As European politics in transition, it happens locally and nationally within nation-states. At neither level, however, can actors do what they used to do. Europolitics is itself multileveled. Localities, regions, and interest groups of all kinds may "do" European-level politics. National governments themselves spend more and more time thinking about and doing Europolitics. As a result, the flow of information to citizens has become harder to organize and less transparent. These changes are particularly difficult to address because they are badly understood and the interests arrayed to profit from them are strong.

Europolitics has given political actors a much wider choice among levels of government to seek what they want. In general, however, political actors vary greatly in their capacities to use these new opportunities. Multinational companies, for example, can work at all levels and play them against one another. Those who work in these same multinationals are individual citizens who face greater constraints. The European arena presents national political elites with a place to set medium-range goals more easily than they can in the more congested politics of their own countries. When they are successful, as they have been in recent years, the consequences of their Euro-level decisions, targeted on large problems and medium-range remedies, constrain national democratic choices. De facto, the European political arena structures a priori the options available in national politics before citizens have had a full chance to deliberate and decide. Europolitics provides an ideal location to make decisions that would have been difficult nationally. Yet when the consequences of such constraints are felt nationally, the same elites who made the decisions can then scapegoat a mythical Europe for limiting national choices. Europolitics still takes place in a construction site. Therefore, can Europe handle the challenges that it faces?

CHAPTER

2

Politics
and Economics

The idea of European integration has a past. Immanuel Kant wrote about it in 1789. Saint-Simon speculated about it in France slightly later. In 1849, Victor Hugo presided over a Congress of the Friends of Peace calling for a United States of Europe. Would-be conquerors—Napoleon, Hitler, and Stalin—and those desirous of frustrating their conquests had their own notions of European unity. More practical conceptions emerged after World War I. In the 1920s Count Koudenhove-Kalergi, a Central European aristocrat, mobilized a substantial pan-Europe movement. Other such movements, on smaller and more workable scales, even led to serious negotiations. A customs union between Belgium, Luxembourg, and the Netherlands, for example, very nearly came into being in the 1920s. A high point came in 1929 when Prime Minister Aristide Briand of France made an eloquent plea for European federalization to the League of Nations. The integrationist current between the wars was, however, chronically divided about how to proceed. The rise of fascism closed the debate, and massive geopolitical changes after victory over the Nazis in 1945 was required to open it again.[1] The emergence of the United States as a superpower was the first key change. The cold war, structured around United States–Soviet confrontation, which then reconfigured Western European politics, was the second. These two changes in the balance of international power created the new constraints and opportunities that led Europeans to begin the process of integration.

"Europe" Is Born

As victory approached in World War II, the United States was more concerned with establishing a viable postwar international trading regime than with regional integration. U.S. leadership reconstructed the capitalist world's financial underpinnings in the Bretton Woods system (named after the New Hampshire hotel where final deals were struck in 1944). Bretton Woods involved a commitment by the United States to make the dollar a global reserve currency backed by a conversion value fixed in gold. The United States was also decisive in founding the World Bank and the International Monetary Fund (IMF). The IMF and World Bank in turn established institutional means to allow individual trading nations to run occasional deficits in international payments and to police the system of trade. The General Agreement on Tariffs and Trade (GATT), a multilateral organization to promote free trade, dates from this period as well.[2] In all this, the United States demonstrated its desire to be the trustee of the international trading system, a very important gesture in reconstructing market economies after the Great Depression and World War II.

The Europeans were flat broke. European states faced huge rebuilding tasks with little to trade and no money to pay for what they bought. The United States thus became a creditor, not only bailing out the British in 1946 but also, in an ad hoc way, helping almost everyone else. The Marshall Plan (1947) established the United States as the financier of European recovery. It made billions of dollars available to reconstruct European economies, with the principal provision only that the Europeans talk to one another about putting the money to good use. Even the Soviet Union and its Central and Eastern European satellite countries were initially invited. They refused to participate.

In Western Europe, the Marshall Plan promoted greater economic coordination, in particular through the Organization for European Economic Cooperation (OEEC, today the OECD, the Organisation for Economic Cooperation and Development, a leading think-tank about economic issues). The Western Europeans used Marshall Plan aid in ways suited to national goals that they themselves defined. Well invested, the funds provided a foundation for Western European modernization along the consumerist lines that the United States had already pioneered. It also allowed Western European nations enough financial space to consolidate the social reforms instituted in the wake of the war. Finally, it solidified their attachment to the United States.[3]

Postwar Alliances, Postwar Stalemates

Soviet intentions for Europe soon became clear in the aftermath of the war. By 1947, in its Central and Eastern sphere of influence, the Soviet Union had set about establishing "popular democracies"; in fact, they were neither democratic nor popular but dominated by local Communists mimicking Soviet ways and backed by Soviet military power. The Soviets could consolidate their bloc because of their massive military presence. Furthermore, European geography (Paris was only a few hundred miles from Soviet territories), together with the power of Communists in West European domestic politics, nourished American fear that a Soviet offensive westward would be difficult to stop. The outbreak of the cold war, the four-decade-long standoff between the United States and the Soviet Union, thus coincided with the Marshall Plan.[4]

Cold war rearmament formed the immediate geopolitical background for European integration. The United States took the biggest and first step by committing resources to the most massive peacetime military buildup in its history. It then promoted and largely financed Western European nations to follow its lead. The chosen instrument was the North Atlantic Alliance, founded in 1949, which stationed large numbers of U.S. troops and materiel strategically throughout Europe as a backbone force to block any offensive from the East. Europeans and other allies were expected to do their part as well, integrated under a unified North Atlantic Treaty Organization (NATO) command structure.

With the construction of an anti-Soviet alliance, U.S. military power became hegemonic over Western Europe, and Western European defense efforts in the European theater thus had to focus on NATO tasks, subordinating long-standing European rivalries. As long as the cold war continued, armed conflict among Western Europeans, the scourge of the first half of the twentieth century, was off the agenda. This change in European relations did not occur smoothly, and the rough patches played forcefully in developing European integration. For example, the United States insisted early on that the Germans be included in the new alliance, a decision that meant rehabilitating rather than punishing Germany. Rehabilitation involved the creation of a new German polity in 1949— the Federal Republic of Germany—carved out of the three zones occupied by the United States, the United Kingdom, and France. The Soviet zone became the German Democratic Republic, consolidating a division of Germany that would last four decades. Even more crucial to the United States was the need to rearm the new West Germany, now the front line of anti-Soviet defense.

These rapid geopolitical changes occurred simultaneously with widespread, initially inconclusive, talk about European integration. All parties agreed that Europe needed to shake its habit of staging a horrific bloodbath every second generation. Practically, however, much militated against success. Penury meant that European economies had to be nationally coordinated through price controls, rationing, and wage limitations, measures that made transnational economic integration difficult, at least for the immediate postwar years. Each Western European country faced a different set of social and economic concerns, and national strategies differed greatly. Notions of European integration also varied, and approaches were hard to conciliate. Open advocates of integration, always a small vanguard, were themselves divided. Federalists wanted supranational institutions (international institutions with power over nations) and even talked of a United States of Europe. Intergovernmentalists sought cooperative arrangements to preserve a maximum of national sovereignty. Beyond these differing visions were disagreements about what should be integrated and where the process should start.

"Europe" did have some early successes.[5] For example, the customs union of Belgium, the Netherlands, and Luxembourg (Benelux) opened in 1948 was an important precedent. But more common were failures and dead-ends. France and Italy negotiated a customs union in 1947, but the French parliament refused to ratify it. France, Italy, Belgium, the Netherlands, and Luxembourg then tried to negotiate a customs union and also failed. In 1949–1950, the British and Scandinavian countries failed to agree on a free trade zone. The most spectacular setback occurred at the Congress of Europe in The Hague in May 1948. There, apostles of integration from sixteen European countries debated almost everything, to an impasse. There were some significant results, like the Council of Europe, created in 1949 and located in Strasbourg, which created a Court of Justice that would subsequently play an important role in the advocacy of human rights in Europe.

Integrating Coal and Steel

The first great breakthrough occurred with the creation of the European Coal and Steel Community (ECSC) in 1950. The ECSC emerged out of one of Europe's most dangerous chronic problems: French–German relationships. The French, overrun by the Germans three times in seventy-five years, were understandably averse to this happening again. Their initial strategy was to fragment Germany and neutralize its heavy industrial areas, but the French steel industry in Lorraine, rich in iron ore but poor in coal, needed a steady supply of imported coking coal. The closest source was the Ruhr, so negotiations to create an International Ruhr Authority began in 1947. Cold war geopolitics encouraging rapprochement and U.S. goals for rehabilitating Germany rendered the French strategy unrealistic, however.

Working on the Ruhr problem was the man whose contributions to early European integration stands above all others, Jean Monnet, then head of French economic planning.[6] Facing strong U.S. pressure for a new French policy on Germany, Monnet proposed the ECSC to integrate the French and German coal and steel industries together with those of any other European democracies caring to join. This broad proposal meant a transnational pooling of the most important economic sectors of the time, central to both economic success and war making.

Monnet and Robert Schuman, the French foreign minister, were creative in proposing what became the Schuman Plan. In the spring of 1950, Schuman, persuaded by a memorandum from Monnet, circulated the plan only to those ministers he thought would be favorable to it. Then, with a majority, he rushed it rapidly through the government and announced it with great pomp to a press conference on May 9, 1950, only hours after the government's approval. The first few sentences of Schuman's declaration speak to the high stakes in question:

World peace cannot be safeguarded without creative efforts at the level of the dangers that menace it. . . . The contribution that a Europe that is
organized and vital can bring to civilization is indispensable to the maintenance of peaceful relations. By championing the idea of a United Europe
over the last twenty years France has always
sought to serve the cause of peace. Europe was not
built and we had war. . . . Europe will not be made
all at once, nor will it be made in a single holistic
construction: It will be built by concrete achievements that will create solidarity in facts. Assem-
bling European nations demands first that the secular opposition between France and Germany be
eliminated. The actions that are undertaken ought
therefore first to involve France and Germany.[7]

German chancellor Konrad Adenauer quickly
accepted the Schuman Plan. ECSC was thus a
fait accompli before governmental, public, and
partisan debate had occurred in either France or
Germany. The French and Germans immediately asked other European countries to join the
negotiations on ECSC, and on May 25 Luxembourg, the Netherlands, Belgium, and Italy
signed. Together with these four, France and
Germany signed the ECSC treaty in 1951, and
the new community was officially created in
July 1952, presided over by Monnet himself.
The British refused to join or even to negotiate.
The government claimed that things like ECSC
were not compatible with the United Kingdom's
Commonwealth ties and global positions.

Behind Monnet's clever idea and cleverer political operating lay a functionalist vision that
persisted in the "grand theory" of European integration.[8] He reasoned that integration would
be doomed were it to depend on resolving a
huge range of matters in one giant constitutional transaction. It would be much more feasible and success more likely were integration to
be founded on transnational approaches to
important but limited and specific problems.
Monnet hypothesized further that if sectoral integration began in an important economic area,
integration would spill over into new areas,
given the interdependencies of modern economies. Coal and steel were a good place to begin.

Because the United States was seeking to nor-
malize French and German relations, coal and
steel could become central to this normalization.

Monnet and Schuman knew that the United
States would not accept waffling for long before
imposing its own solutions, which would almost
certainly involve restoring full German control
over the Ruhr and the Saar. Both the French and
Germans thus had an interest in negotiating
their own agreement. The French could argue
plausibly with the Germans that French public
opinion would accept normalization only if arrangements neutralized threats from Germany's heavy industries. Among the Germans,
industrial interests wanted a new economic deal
that would open markets. Both sides also faced
immediate concern about potential overproduc-
tion in coal and steel. Chancellor Konrad
Adenauer—a grizzled veteran of German politics, former mayor of Cologne, Buchenwald
prisoner, and a Christian Democratic party
leader like Robert Schuman (who, moreover,
was from Lorraine)—saw in the Schuman Plan
prospects for a new departure with the French.
Most important, it would introduce the new
Federal Republic into the high diplomacy of
Western democracies.

The ECSC would be a customs union in coal
and steel that would end national subsidies and
barriers to trade. As its institutional architecture
became a model, Monnet's concern with institutional structures turned out to be of vital importance to European integration. His most controversial proposal for institutional innovation was
the ECSC High Authority, a supranational
agency that could work above, beyond, and
sometimes despite ECSC member states. The
appointed High Authority was granted independent power over a range of matters, including taxation, planning, competition policy (antitrust measures), and extreme shortages in
demand and supply. In certain circumstances, it
could decree a situation of "manifest crisis" and
then take dramatic measures. Monnet's original
plan proposed that the authority would be un-
constrained, but in the negotiations, a watchdog

Committee of Ministers was added, empowered to take broad policy decisions by majority vote on proposals from the High Authority. Finally, ECSC had an advisory assembly, appointed by the parliaments of ECSC members, in addition to a supranational court with jurisdiction over ECSC matters.

Integrating the Europe of Postwar Settlements

In the wake of the ECSC treaty, advocates of integration tried to adapt the "Monnet method" of sectoral integration to other areas. Usually, however, they failed. Separate French and Dutch proposals for Europeanizing agriculture went nowhere in 1950.[9] A French proposal for a European transport authority never got off the ground. A multilateral proposal to establish a European political community was drafted in the early 1950s, but the parties never agreed to it. The 1952 French proposal for a new European Defense Community (EDC) was another of Monnet's schemes to advance integration by seizing on a pressing problem in one sector—the need to find acceptable ways for the Germans to rearm—a prospect that frightened most non-German Europeans. In the enveloping cold war, which became a hot war for two years in Korea after June 1950, some form of German rearmament became inevitable. Two options were available: a carefully controlled German integration into NATO (the U.S. choice) or Monnet's EDC, which would have created a transnational European army containing German troops. EDC collapsed, however, when the French, who had first proposed it, refused in 1954 to ratify it (a combination of anti-NATO Communists and nationalist Gaullists did it in). The U.S. option thus prevailed, and in October 1954 the Paris Agreements were signed, creating the Western European Union (WEU, a European organization for defense coordination in NATO) admitting the Germans to NATO, and resolving the Franco-German dispute over the

Saar. The result was a four-power treaty (France, the United States, the United Kingdom, and Germany), granting the new German Federal Republic full sovereignty.

The notion of European integration remained very much alive, however, supported by leaders in the ECSC "six." Significant ideas and experiences were accumulating with agreements like the Benelux customs union. The institutional models of the ECSC also made strong impressions on Europe's elites. Critical leadership came from the Benelux. The Belgian Paul-Henri Spaak seized on the idea of a Common Market, which had been proposed by Dutch foreign minister Johan Beyen, and worked his way around Europe to persuade other leaders of its merits. The Beyen-Spaak approach was more ambitious than the minimalist "free trade area" favored by the British. Advocates of a Common Market proposed significant common policies and supranational institutions.[10]

A conference in Messina, Italy, in June 1955 was the turning point. Led by Spaak and other Benelux politicians, the ECSC six announced their commitment to create a European Common Market and Euratom (a European atomic energy agency), and work toward the harmonization of European social policies. Spaak was asked to prepare further proposals, and his report of May 1956 suggested "a European Common Market . . . [leading to] a vast zone with a common economic policy" plus Euratom. The two Treaties of Rome in 1957 were the result, officially founding EEC and Euratom.[11] Underlying the agreements were deals between France and Germany. The French wanted Euratom but were much less enthusiastic about the Common Market; nevertheless, because of their rejection of the EDC, they felt obligated to accept an EEC with safeguards rather than blocking it. Chancellor Adenauer believed that the Common Market would help the German economy and grant the Federal Republic more sovereignty and legitimacy. The Germans wanted trade liberalization in industrial products. The French were willing to agree only in exchange for a common agricultural policy that gave them preferential access to other EEC markets plus access to tropical products from their colonies and former colonies. The French feared building a Common Market prior to a harmonization of wages and social protection programs and imposed conditions. On the emerging institutions, the Germans were more supranationalist than the French, a difference that remains to this day. The British stayed away, disagreeing with the EEC's supranational dimensions and skeptical that the proposals would actually be implemented. This time, however, they mounted a counteroffensive, promoting in 1959 the European Free Trade Association (EFTA), which encompassed the Scandinavian countries, Iceland, Portugal, Switzerland, and Austria. EFTA involved free internal trade but no common external trade barriers or policies.[12]

The Preamble to the Rome EEC Treaty promised "to lay the foundations of an ever-closer union among the peoples of Europe." Article 2 stated:

> The Community shall have as its task, by establishing a Common Market and economic community and by progressively approximating the economic policies of Member States, to promote throughout the Community a harmonious and balanced development of economic activities, a continuous and balanced expansion, an increase in stability, an accelerated raising of the standard of living and closer relations between the States belonging to it.[13]

Establishing the EEC

The Common Market was the core of the new EEC. It proposed a staged removal of direct and indirect barriers to trade (tariffs, customs duties, quotas, barriers flowing from national standards) and rules for common trading relationships among member states to abolish "obstacles to freedom of movement for persons, services and capital." It would grow behind a common external tariff and commercial policy toward third countries. The EEC Treaty's other objectives included common policies in agriculture, transport, a "system ensuring that competition in the Common Market is not distorted," and procedures for coordinating economic policy and controlling balance-of-payments disequilibria. Member states would be obligated to harmonize their legal systems on Common Market matters. There were also provisions for a European Social Fund, a European Investment Bank to promote the development of less-developed regions, and association arrangements for overseas former colonies and territories.[14] With the exception of internal tariff liberalization, where steps were set out in detail, the EEC Treaty was a "framework agreement"; it announced general purposes but left concrete programs to be worked out through implementation in the EEC's first period. The treaty did set out a schedule for filling in these very large details. The entire process of putting into place the Common Market, referred to as the *transitional period*, was to last twelve years, divided into four-year segments. The practical substance of the EEC, however—its common policies and its institutions—remained to be worked out after Rome.

The signatories' underlying hope was that the Common Market would eventually lead to a unified European economy. The logics of market liberation and positive rule making to build a Common Market might ultimately spill over toward political unity—an assumption that foresaw contagion from the common "lower" politics of trade and markets into the "high politics" of federalism and foreign policy.[15] Where sovereignty was not explicitly delegated to Europe by treaty, policymaking remained national. The EEC was thus empowered to do only what these treaties allowed; conversely, what the treaties did not allow was forbidden territory. Although this explicit limitation may have been comforting at the time, the boundaries between national and EEC prerogatives soon became less rigid and clear, largely because of the treaty's framework nature.

The Rome EEC Treaty modeled the EEC's institutions on those of the ECSC. The European Commission, the EEC's executive in Brussels, was granted exclusive power to propose policy (as well as duties to implement and safeguard the treaty). The EEC "legislature," which voted Commission proposals up or down, was a Council of Ministers representing each national government, coordinated by a presidency that rotated among member states every six months. In terms of political philosophy, legitimacy for EEC decisions derived from the democratically elected national parliaments that appointed members to the Council of Ministers. A European Court of Justice, located in Luxembourg, would entertain litigation in those areas (mainly trade related) where the Rome Treaty granted EEC laws precedence over national statutes and precedents. A European Parliament, located in Strasbourg, was derived from the ECSC Assembly and composed of members appointed by national parliaments.

The glue of the new EEC was to be the European Commission, acting as strategic planner and activist for the integration process. Implementation of programs was almost always left to national governments and administrations, exhaustively consulted before any proposals were advanced. In theory, Commission activities would be constrained not only by the treaty but also by the preferences of member states, which determined what the Council of Ministers would entertain. In general, however, as long as it could find a suitable treaty base (treaty provisions allowing action) and plausible political support from member states, the Commission had the power to propose far-reaching changes. Many founders shared Monnet's view that the Commission should act as a motor whose most important job would be to expand the EEC's mandate over time. This "Monnet method"— the French term often used is *engrenage* (literally "getting caught in the gears")—was a way of being federalist without frightening too many people.

The Council of Ministers, the EEC legislature, made its decisions according to rules spelled out in the treaty. Most important decisions in the EEC's initial years were to be taken unanimously because they bore large implications for the eventual division of prerogatives between member states and the EEC. But once the Common Market had been established, there was to be a change to qualified majority voting (QMV), a way of weighting member state votes by size to reach a numerical majority. Larger member states would get more votes than smaller ones, and majorities had to reach a certain threshold to allow blocking minorities. This mechanism meant that as time went on, member states could be outvoted on significant matters.

The European Parliament, for two decades an assembly whose members were appointed from national parliaments (from 1979 its members were directly elected), had very little power, such that few people cared what it did. It was consulted on certain matters. It could debate an annual report that the Commission was required to submit. Although it never did so, it could also dismiss the Commission on a vote of censure (two-thirds vote among at least half of the total number of sitting members of the European Parliament—MEPs) and it could bring action against other EEC institutions before the European Court of Justice (ECJ) for "failure to act." Finally, it could pose questions to which the Commission was obliged to respond, a process that eventually became a regular "question time." Its role in EEC legislating, however, was minimal. It could give opinions and submit amendments, but neither Commission nor Council was obliged to do more than consider them.

The new EEC was an open-ended experiment. The Rome EEC Treaty defined in very general terms what it could and could not do, but its scope of action was left to trial, error, and struggle. Its institutions were similarly defined. A general division of labor was set out, with precise balances and roles left to define in practice. Because the Commission would have to carve a role from member states' prerogatives, the plan was a recipe for struggle between it and the

Council of Ministers. The Council's opacity made it simultaneously vulnerable to challenge over democratic legitimacy and open to member states' politicians seeking to circumvent and constrain their own national political lives through Euro-level decisions. The initial impotence of the Parliament created a dynamic of parliamentary agitation for increased power. The ECJ, the final major institution set up by the Rome Treaty, was charged with ensuring that "in the interpretation and application of this Treaty the law is observed."[16] In practice, this provision allowed it to make European law through interpretation and the accumulation of jurisprudence, creating another open-ended scenario. Finally, in a Europe of nations without any "we the people," the EEC was bound to have problems of democratic legitimacy and accountability.

First Years

The new EEC flourished in buoyant economic conditions. In a new spirit of optimism, the population of EEC countries began to grow rapidly, rebuilding their economies on the U.S. model of consumerism and mass production. New houses, roads, schools, and infrastructure proliferated. Europeans began to taste the joys of cars, household appliances, seaside holidays, and television. By the 1960s, the peak decade of the postwar boom, average growth in EEC member states was more than 5 percent every year, and trade among EEC members was growing even faster.[17] European societies were also integrating nationally more deeply than ever before, given solidification of democratic institutions, new commitments to social justice and redistribution of wealth, and, above all, economic change.[18] With a larger economic pie to distribute, nations had a wider range of stakeholders: groups with strong interests. Capitalists, politicians, civil servants, and interest groups of all kinds—labor, conservatives, socialists, young and old—all perceived the new order as a setting in which their purposes might be attained.

Was this coincidence of reasserted national models of political economy and the coming of European integration paradoxical? Not really. European integration began successfully *because* the reconfiguring of national social and economic models was the order of the day. As economies soared, each European society depended more on trade with the others. European integration opened the way to both such trade and complex political interdependence. The Germans needed Europe to rebuild their self-respect after the Nazi era. Others needed Europe to keep the Germans in their place. The French thought that they could use Europe to implement their grandiose foreign policy goals. The Italians saw the EEC as a source of regional development money and an external stimulus for modernization. The Benelux countries wanted the EEC because they needed broader markets, as did the Germans. Smaller countries hoped that supranationality in EEC institutions would protect them against larger states. All actors needed the United States' military strength during the cold war, and the United States preferred that Europeans should coordinate their actions.

That European integration and national change coincided did not mean that their coexistence was easy. The EEC's designers hoped that integrationist activists in Brussels, particularly at the Commission, would rapidly Europeanize more and more activities. Tension was thus deliberately built into EEC structures between a relatively narrow treaty mandate and the new institutions set up to implement it. On the other side of the ledger were national development models and leaders with little desire to see the EEC's mandate enlarged or its supranationality expanded. The problems crystallized as the new EEC carried out the schedule of activities prescribed by the Rome EEC Treaty. The first years brought the building of new institutions and common policies, with each process requiring tough bargaining among member states. Creating the customs union went easily, and the goal of ending internal tariffs was reached early. The EEC also established itself quickly as an interlocutor in important international trade negotiations like those of the GATT, one of the key institutions set up in the Bretton Woods period to pursue freer and fairer international trade. In both cases, the Rome EEC Treaty specified what needed to be done.

The framework parts of the treaty, where matters were not spelled out, were the hardest to work out. A Common Agricultural Policy (CAP) had to be built despite serious differences among member states and so became the major arena where the power balance between Commission and Council was struck. The Commission, backed by the Dutch and the Italians, proposed a strong, economically liberal program. Its plan was discarded en route because it threatened French and German systems that cosseted farmers and distorted markets. The outcome was a scheme of price supports for agricultural goods that protected EEC farmers from market pressures, governed by logrolling between farmers' organizations and national agricultural ministers at the expense of EEC taxpayers and consumers. In other policy areas, dealing was not easy either. Commission attempts to promote common transport and regional and industrial policies were blocked, for example, despite the explicit intentions of the Rome Treaty.

The early years of the EEC demonstrated the limits of national commitment to pooling sovereignty in favor of a strong European Commission. President Charles de Gaulle of France became the symbol of member states' insistence on the last word. The belated British candidacy for membership in 1961 was a first turning point. Negotiations for including the United Kingdom were difficult. The British sought significant exceptions to the Common Market, and de Gaulle disliked their too intimate "special relationship" with the United States on foreign policy and defense. Still, all but the French had reached agreement when, in January 1963,

de Gaulle broke off the talks and denounced the United Kingdom for seeking to make the EEC into a "free trade area" and an appendage of Anglo-American purposes.[19]

The French president was not finished. His next confrontation, this time with other EEC members, was about the very definition of European integration. De Gaulle was a firm French nationalist who, when in opposition before 1958, had opposed European integration. In power, however, he had changed his mind, deciding that France needed Europe economically and that the right kind of EEC might allow the French to exercise strong international power. He thus advocated a "Europe of nations" where important decisions would be taken through negotiations among governments and opposed supranational institutions, in particular the Commission. The Rome EEC Treaty did contain supranationalist hopes, yet because of its framework nature, it left openings for frustrating these hopes. De Gaulle announced his colors in 1961 in the French Fouchet Plan for European political cooperation in foreign policy; the plan was eventually rejected. The French president was determined to make his point nonetheless. Whether Europe should be confederal (intergovernmental) or federal (with supranational decision making) was the fundamental rift.

The European Commission became the French president's major target. The Commission's first president, Walter Hallstein, was determined to use the possibilities of the Rome EEC Treaty in the budgetary area to finance the CAP. When negotiations stalled, the French chose not to participate in the final logrolling process that had been characteristic of such situations earlier, and in September 1965, they withdrew from the Council of Ministers (the "empty chair" episode). The treaties proposed that after January 1966, the Council could decide certain matters by qualified majority, so that a nation might be outvoted. De Gaulle reasoned that with qualified majority "France . . . would be exposed to having its hands forced in almost any economic matter, hence social and often even political." The crisis led to victory for de Gaulle in the Luxembourg Compromise of January 1966. Unanimity in the Council of Ministers became the EEC decision-making norm for nearly two decades, with any member state retaining a veto. Hopes for the Commission as activist for ever-broader integration were thus dashed; the Commission became thereafter a timid actor and the Common Market an intergovernmental operation.[20] From this point, no matter what measure the Commission proposed, the Council could stop it unless all governments agreed.[21]

De Gaulle was speaking for France, but he was also pronouncing the realities of the EEC's first period. The Common Market happened at the high point of Europe's postwar boom. With Keynesian economic policy outlooks, extensive welfare states, highly institutionalized industrial relations systems, regional development policies, and deepening domestic markets for consumer goods, most governments enjoyed positions at the epicenter of economic and social regulatory mechanisms. These profoundly national models of development posed clear limits on Europeanization. As long as national trajectories in macroeconomic, industrial, and social policy were successful, there would be no demand for major transfer of activities to a supranational level.

European integration was still important, however. Predictable international trading arrangements, articulated around national states, were essential for each country's success. The EEC, which negotiated external trade arrangements and saw to the fairness of internal European trade, provided its member states with important trading tools that they could largely shape and control. The administration of a common external tariff provided some protection from the harsh winds of open international trade. Simultaneously, the EEC provided a buffer against and a subsystem within the United States—coordinated Bretton Woods system of trade and payments. The EEC customs-free zone facilitated a substantial increase in in-

ter-EEC trade in goods; in the decade before 1970, EEC internal trade rose from less than 40 percent of total member state trade to nearly 60 percent.[22] This trade increase brought more new economic growth. Finally, making agriculture the EEC's major common policy—at French insistence— occurred at a moment when farming had to be modernized and most farmers removed from their farms. If EEC efforts could cushion these changes and, whenever possible, be assigned political blame for them, so much the better for national policymakers.

EEC institutional and policy development thus stalled at the level that its member states needed. The Common Market became a handmaiden to continental Europe's postwar boom, a useful tool for certain purposes but unwelcome in other areas. The further Europeanization of economic processes that the Rome Treaty had originally proposed—the movement of capital, for example—was not in the cards, since it would have undercut key components of different national models. Moreover, frequent lamentations about the absence of greater economic policy convergence went unmatched by action, since national control over macroeconomic policy (taxation, credit, and monetary policies, in particular) was critical to the developmental models most member states were pursuing. The Commission learned to administer ably, particularly in agriculture, refining its skills at setting soybean prices and subsidizing tobacco fields. When it dared to propose more, it was all too frequently ignored.

Dark Clouds of Crisis

With the first twelve-year phase of implementing the Rome Treaty completed successfully and on time, the early 1970s brought new reflection about the EEC's future. Although the Luxembourg Compromise meant that such reflections had to start with member states, leaders expressed new energy for the European project. The 1969 Hague Summit concluded that progress beyond the Common Market might be possible toward a single European economic space, as the Rome Treaty had foreseen. The Hague Summit, the first after de Gaulle's 1969 resignation, also set out plans to widen the EEC to include the British, Danish, Irish, and Norwegians and deepen it by giving the Community larger budgetary powers, foreign policy coordination (European Political Cooperation), and movement toward Economic and Monetary Union (EMU).

Action followed. The EEC expanded from six to nine members in 1973. The British, Irish, and Danes joined, signaling the effective end of EFTA competition with the EEC. Norway also negotiated entrance, but the Norwegian people voted against it in a referendum. The EEC further gained new financial autonomy, acquiring its "own resources" (that is, direct revenue streams) from levies on agricultural products, import duties, and a small percentage of national value-added taxes (VAT). EEC institutions had depended on direct funding by member states' budgets, leaving them vulnerable to constant quibbling and second-guessing. Direct sources of revenues gave them greater breathing space and autonomy. There was also new ambition in regional development through the creation of the European Regional Development Fund (ERDF) and social policy.

The world, however, was changing, and in troubling ways. Policy divergences among key member states were broadening. The French, determined to minimize EEC supranationality, disagreed with the Germans about plans for EMU set out by Pierre Werner, the Luxembourg prime minister, and had strong misgivings about Germany's new *Ostpolitik* (a systematic opening to the socialist countries of Central and Eastern Europe). *Ostpolitik*, in turn, reflected deeper changes in the cold war environment, including détente and U.S. recognition of China, which reopened debate about foreign policy issues. The first effort at enlarging the EEC did not go smoothly either, since the deal with the United Kingdom was troublesome. British prime minister Edward Heath had been so eager to get in that he paid too high a price. As a re-

sult, in EEC jargon, the British became a "net contributor" to the EEC budget, paying in much more than they got back to finance a CAP from which British agriculture received few returns. This arrangement caused political difficulties in the United Kingdom, leading Harold Wilson, Heath's Labour successor, to demand renegotiation and hold a national referendum. British membership survived this challenge, but the problem of British net contributions was not resolved.

Meanwhile a sea-change was turning monetary policy into a nightmare. The United States, threatened by international market changes, vulnerability to imports, and chronic trade deficits, decided to end the Bretton Woods dollar/gold standard. The dollar and other currencies would then float in value against each other. The consequence was fluctuating, often volatile, exchange rates fed by speculation in currency markets, which made all countries more vulnerable. The new system was particularly treacherous for the EEC, with its multiplicity of currencies. Volatile exchange rates, unchecked, made it difficult to sustain the Common Market. Just the prospect made European markets difficult to forecast, dampening enthusiasm and slowing trade growth. Floating exchange rates also tempted member state governments to use monetary revaluation as a trading weapon and made running the CAP more difficult. The CAP was based on a price-support system to provide adequate incomes to farmers. With prices capriciously changing in different countries because of monetary floating, CAP administrators constantly had to adjust price supports, a difficult task and a new source of tension.

EEC leaders were aware of the new dangers and sought new policies to cushion their effects. In 1972, the EEC agreed to establish a currency snake—an arrangement to keep EEC currency values within 2.5 percent of one another—within a broader tunnel of floating exchange rates. At the same time member states, by accepting the recommendations of the Werner Report of 1970, pledged to reach full EMU by 1980. The Werner Report proposed establishing a single European currency and central banking system, but the good intentions of those member states committed to EMU were swept away in the fallout from the 1973 oil shock, which fueled Europe's already inflationary economic environment. [23] Europe was completely dependent on imported oil, and prices in Europe jumped rapidly. Unions pushed for higher wages, companies for higher prices, and governments for more revenues to sustain programs. Inflation spiraled. Efforts to fine-tune policies to cope with these new problems revealed a perplexing economic situation characterized by *stagflation* —simultaneous inflation and sluggish growth. The "snake in the tunnel" did not survive the consequent confusion.

Europe's Golden Age was ending. Growth levels declined, as Table 2.1 shows, while unemployment, which many had decided was a thing of the past, grew (see Table 2.2). Maintaining state expenditures for social programs became more difficult while public finances became more precarious. EEC member states, assuming the changes to be temporary, improvised, mak-

Table 2.2 Average EEC Unemployment Rates, 1960–1984 (in percent)

	1960–1967	1968–1973	1974–1979	1980–1984
Belgium	2.1	2.3	5.7	12.1
France	1.5	2.6	4.7	8.5
Germany	0.8	0.8	2.8	5.5
Italy	4.8	5.8	6.7	9.5
Luxembourg	0.0	0.0	0.4	1.4
Netherlands	0.7	1.2	3.1	9.4
Denmark	1.6	1.4	5.5	9.9
Ireland	4.9	5.6	7.6	12.7
United Kingdom	1.5	2.5	4.2	10.5

Source: Tsoukalis, *New European Economy*, Table 2.2, p. 23.

ing matters worse. Productivity, profit margins, and investment levels declined, and European industry began to lose competitive advantage.

Europe's failures in the 1970s were constructed of the same materials as its earlier successes. The 1960s had deepened tendencies toward inflexible labor markets, inflationary price tensions, and statist forms of economic management. These tendencies, in turn, shaped responses in the 1970s when economic circumstances began to change. Organized labor had a clear interest in protecting jobs, postwar reforms in industrial relations, and social policy. The political Left, whose strength was based largely on labor, had its own large stake in postwar strategies. Capital had depended on the national state for favors, protection, and subsidies. Finally, state managers had their own interests in the status quo. Political structures and coalitions therefore led national governments virtually everywhere to accentuate the national developmental strategies that earlier had worked so successfully in ways that made matters worse.

EEC member states needed "more Europe" in the form of greater international coordination

Table 2.1 EEC Annual Economic Growth Rates, 1960–1984 (in percent)

	1960–1967	1968–1973	1974–1979	1980–1984
Belgium	4.7	5.2	2.3	1.5
France	5.7	5.6	2.8	2.7
Germany	4.5	5.0	2.4	1.0
Italy	5.7	4.9	3.5	1.9
Luxembourg	2.8	6.1	1.3	2.1
Netherlands	5.2	5.5	2.6	0.7
Denmark	4.8	4.0	2.0	1.7
Ireland	3.9	5.4	5.0	2.6
United Kingdom	3.2	3.4	1.6	0.8

Source: Loukas Tsoukalis, *The New European Economy*, 2d ed. (London: Oxford University Press, 1993), Table 2.1, p. 22.

of monetary, macroeconomic, industrial, and trade policies. Most were convinced, however, that the national strategies that had worked so well during the postwar boom could be revitalized. The consequence was growing divergence in national policies. In macroeconomic policy, the French and the British tried renewed Keynesianism and exacerbated precarious situations. The Italians, who had confronted major social rebellion in the early 1970s, forged social reforms, which created major new economic rigidities, leading to political turbulence in the 1980s. Only the Germans did better. After a rare experiment with Keynesianism, they turned to anti-inflationary monetarism engineered by the Bundesbank (the German National Bank) and restructured in ways that made the German model an object of international admiration in the 1980s. One tendency across all the EEC, however, was renewed protectionism. Because tariffs could not be raised, nontariff barriers spread rapidly, often through state aids to industry, to save jobs. Such techniques threatened the effectiveness of the Common Market as a trade area.

The Common Market had risen in the 1960s as an instrument of a successful "Europe of States." In the volatile context of the later 1970s, the EEC, still an instrument of the national development strategies of its member states, began a downward spiral. The brief optimism of the early 1970s evaporated, and EMU plans were abandoned. "European political cooperation" arrangements struck for promoting foreign policy collaboration among EEC members stabilized in minimalist forms.[24] An ambitious new social policy program, proclaimed in 1974, had few results. The CAP fell on hard times, with bureaucrats obliged to run a cumbersome system of transfers to compensate farmers for currency fluctuations across member states. At the same time, CAP policies were becoming a system of perverse incentives, encouraging farmers to produce more whether or not there was market demand for their products. Mountains of butter, lakes of milk, and oceans of wine

dotted the EEC landscape. The British resented paying more than their share to finance the CAP, and the British contribution became a ticking bomb in EEC deliberations. Europe was not dead, but it had been reduced to a forum for deals in which member states sought narrow ways out of crisis.

Creative responses to these challenges were not lacking. Given the balance of institutional power struck in the 1960s, however, they were primarily intergovernmental. Informal summits of heads of state and government, convened at least once in each Council presidency, became a new institution, the European Council (fully integrated into EC treaties in the 1980s), which combined high-level strategic guidance with a regular forum to decide important issues that other European institutions had been unable to resolve.[25] In 1974 this new European Council decided to introduce direct elections to the European Parliament, held for the first time in 1979. This was an important step toward strengthening the role of Parliament and deepening EEC legitimacy. The European Parliament also gained some new budgetary power, partly because of the creation of "own resources" for European institutions. Thus, in 1975 Parliament was given decision-making authority, within limits, over noncompulsory expenditure (i.e., EEC spending that was not dictated by long-term commitments like the CAP, which remained within the power of the Council), plus the right to reject the budget as a whole.

The most significant intergovernmental innovation in the 1970s was the European Monetary System (EMS). Thinking about an EMS began after the failure of the "snake in the tunnel," indicating that member states were not going to carry out commitments to create EMU. EMS was proposed publicly by Commission president Roy Jenkins in 1977, but it really came about through negotiating efforts by French president Valéry Giscard d'Estaing and German chancellor Helmut Schmidt in 1978–1979.[26] EMS was a "two-speed" system: All EEC members belonged to EMS, and the EEC Monetary Committee (central bankers from each country) played a key administrative role. Membership in the EMS exchange rate mechanism (ERM) was voluntary, however, and included only countries willing to accept the ERM's monetary constraints (the British, for example, did not join until 1990). ERM participants had to keep the value of their currency within a narrow band of reference (plus or minus 2.5 percent) tied to a weighted basket of all member currencies. Mechanisms for market intervention to help threatened currencies stay within the narrow band were negotiated along with ways to realign the relative ERM currencies against one another, should the need arise.[27] EMS would prove to be a significant link between the EC's 1970s crisis and the renewal of integration in the later 1980s.

Monetary integration of some kind was almost inevitable if European integration was to survive. The issue was its precise nature. In this context, EMS was very important. The negotiations between the French and the Germans that structured the system turned out less favorable to the French (and other potential EMS members with currencies weaker than the deutsche mark) than they originally hoped. The French wanted an EMS that would work in mildly deflationary ways, together with mechanisms that would share the costs of fluctuation and revaluation among both strong and weak currencies. They got instead a system that was much more deflationary than they desired, dominated by the Bundesbank, which left weaker currency members most responsible for adjustment. EMS thus turned out asymmetrical, giving more power to the Germans (and particularly to the Bundesbank) than to others.[28]

EMS notwithstanding, the underlying dynamic of European integration in the early 1980s was centrifugal force. Germany, the one success story, restructured its economy in a context of stable prices. It coexisted in the early 1980s, however, with the first years of a new Socialist administration in France determined to pursue statist and inflationary policies. At the

same time, Thatcherism in Britain went its own way, and Reagan and the U.S. Federal Reserve induced the deepest international recession since the 1930s. Finally, the EEC itself was paralyzed by annual budget disputes in which British governments petulantly demanded their money back, following a doctrine of just return, according to which the financial contributions of member states should be roughly equal to funds coming back from the EEC. The issue was real enough. The CAP was the bulk of the EEC budget; British agriculture was small and very efficient. Thus, British contributions to the EEC budget went overwhelmingly to French and Italian farmers. When others resisted British demands for change, the British prevented them from doing anything else.[29]

The EEC's supranational potential had receded. Vital signs had not disappeared, but the body was not stirring. The European Parliament, fresh from its 1979 popular election and seeking new ways to make its mark, drew up a draft treaty on European Union (EU) in 1983–1984, which would eventually contribute to the newly energized environment that began in 1985.[30] There were other ambitious plans, but they were quickly deposited in libraries. The ECJ made judgments that would later be very significant, none more important than the *Cassis de Dijon* case of 1979 (Revue-Zentrale AG v Bundesmonopolverwaltung für Branntwein, ECC 120/78), which announced a new method for product standardization through mutual recognition of one another's rules, rather than negotiation to create common rules.[31] The ruling was central in revealing the protectionism hiding behind standard setting and provided an important legal basis for Commission strategy after 1985. But with certain prophetic exceptions, largely in industrial policy, the Commission itself proposed little and implemented less. Brussels accumulated a parts bin of good ideas for European change that would be significant later, but they languished in filing cabinets for the moment. The clouds of Europessimism had set in.

Globalization and the Liberal Renewal of Europe

By the mid-1980s an extraordinary turnaround had begun, with EEC institutions changed in ways that increased the willingness of member states to accept European solutions to their problems. The European Commission came alive as a proposition force for EU development, and its rebirth coincided with a realization by European elites that postwar settlements were no longer sustainable. The return of Europe became part of a new strategy to diminish the role of national states in economic and social life, reinvigorate market relationships, and create a solid new regional economic bloc structured around a liberated European market setting. All of this was designed to confront the newly threatening market environment that we now call globalization.*

Nowhere to Go But Up?

A key to EU renewal lies in the failure of the French Left. Socialist François Mitterrand, elected president of France in May 1981, brought a program to reinvigorate and deepen the French postwar settlement. It involved new nationalization, statist industrial policy and planning, industrial relations reforms giving more power to unions and workers, devolution of powers from the center to the regions, redistributive shifts in social protection programs, and Keynesian stimulation of the economy, including extensive public sector job creation. Yet the external context did not bode well. The Federal Reserve–Reagan recession in the United States touched Europe deeply, and the fate of the new EMS was uncertain.

The Mitterrand experiment ran quickly into difficulties. The Left government failed to devalue the franc immediately and preemptively,

although France's inflation level was already much higher than Germany's (13.4 percent versus 6.3 percent). The new Keynesianism fueled this disparity in inflation levels while other Europeans, led by the Germans, pursued price stabilization. Pressure on the franc led to three devaluations through March 1983, negotiated through EMS. The first, in October 1991, was unproblematic. The second, in June 1982, saw the Germans insisting on changes in French domestic policies, in particular a wage freeze. The French had to comply, and the Mitterrand government began to change its approach, turning toward austerity. Still, relative French inflation continued.

By winter 1982–1983, the French faced tough choices: leave EMS or stay and find an entirely different domestic strategy. Leaving EMS might allow programmatic continuity in relative autarky, but the risks of failure were high. Staying in EMS at the cost of major policy changes also had its risks. The debate in elite circles was heated, with Mitterrand listening carefully to both sides. Behind this disagreement were longer-term policy problems. Since the Gaullist 1960s, the French had believed that domestic *dirigisme* (statist economic steering) was compatible with European integration, as long as the French economy thrived and French diplomacy prevented Europe from imposing undue constraints. The Gaullist position was that French *dirigisme* provided the tool box that could give France the edge to be the key European player. March 1983 brought divorce between the two basic elements of this earlier French policy on Europe. Postwar settlement and Gaullist *dirigisme* were no longer compatible with European integration. France did not have to abandon the goal of being the EU's leader, but it would have to find new ways of achieving this position.

The French wanted a large and, if possible, unilateral German revaluation within EMS. The Germans refused, and the French threatened to leave. Eventually a joint revaluation of the deutsche mark and franc was negotiated. The

---

*Technically the European Union did not exist until the Maastricht Treaty was ratified in 1994. Because the EU was the product of processes analyzed in this section, however, the name EU will be used.

Germans again insisted on new French austerity measures, including new constraints on the budget and a monetary policy to wring out inflation. The process was a striking—perhaps even humiliating—confirmation of German hegemony in EMS. Mitterrand decided to stay in the EMS, but French elites began to believe that this option required strengthening French positions relative to Germany in financial and monetary affairs.[32]

This decision signaled the end of European hopes that postwar settlement strategies could continue. By 1984 the French had a new strategy focused on European integration. Mitterrand's hope was to conquer new political power at the European level using France's position between the Germans, who were economically powerful but whose past still left them politically weak, and the British, whose anti-European stance left them unable to seize initiatives on a European level. In this he sought to compensate for the loss of national control that the French economic policy turnabout of 1983 implied.[33] The most important immediate result was that the economic policies of major EU members converged to a point where new common action was plausible.

The French presidency of the EU in the first half of 1984 began the renewal of European integration, quickly resolving the issues underlying Europessimism. At the Fontainebleau European Council in June, for example, a French and German "good cop—bad cop" tactic settled the "British check" problem (Margaret Thatcher's insistence on a reduction in British budgetary contributions). The French and Germans proposed a partial rebate of British contributions to the EU budget and threatened Mrs. Thatcher that refusal could have dire consequences.[34] Spanish and Portuguese accession to the EU, which had been held up by the Greeks (who, having joined the EU in 1982, were using the new enlargement to seek "side payments" from EU members) was also reopened. Finally, Jacques Delors, the former French minister of finance and one of the designers of the French

policy shift, was appointed president of the European Commission. Delors was a good fit for the job, a front-ranking European political figure of proven strategic capacities and a convinced, very knowledgeable activist for European integration.

Toward a "Single Market"

Jacques Delors announced his new approach barely one week after his new Commission took office in 1985. "Is it presumptuous to announce . . . a decision to remove all the borders inside Europe from here to 1992?" A White Paper entitled *Completing the Internal Market,* quickly labeled the "1992" program, composed in record time by the Commission, was the first big step.[35] The White Paper elaborated nearly 300 measures to unify the EU's still largely separate national markets into an "area without internal boundaries in which the free movement of goods, persons, services and capital is ensured." Internal border posts would come down, and cross-border formalities for goods would be simplified. The creation of common product norms and standards across markets would occur rapidly, through either mutual recognition or, where needed, framework legislation. Different methods and rates of value-added taxation, which had become obstacles in cross-border trade, would be harmonized. The White Paper also included a detailed timetable of legislation, proposal by proposal, over two consecutive Commission terms (eight years) leading to 1992.

The White Paper launched the renewal of European integration. The "1992" slogan simplified a complex of measures in ways that generated public interest and enthusiasm: "1992" would "get Europe moving again." The White Paper played carefully to broader political realities with its liberalizing, deregulatory, and supply-side vocabulary. Member states had their own reasons to buy in. The Germans, facing rising unemployment, hoped to profit from new trade. The French saw it as a way of enhancing their diplomatic power. The British, reluctant Europeans adamantly opposed to new cessions of sovereignty to the Community, wanted liberalization and deregulation in principle.

After the White Paper was first discussed, the Milan European Council of June 1985 agreed to call an "intergovernmental conference [IGC]" to modify the Rome Treaties. Treaty revisions, particularly on institutional questions, had been suggested for years. The European Parliament had been seeking ways to create new EU momentum, and the Council of Ministers had appointed the Dooge Committee to reflect on ways of bringing EU institutions closer to the public. Enlargement to Spain and Portugal, scheduled for January 1986, would increase the number of EU members in need of development assistance, so treaty revisions about transferring resources from EU North to South seemed prudent. Finally, carrying out the 1992 program necessitated changes in EU decision-making practices.

The IGC was the first major reconsideration of the EU treaties since 1957. The result was the Single European Act (SEA, ratified in 1987).[36] Its most important contribution linked completing the single market to changes in EU decision making. The unanimity of the Luxembourg Compromise now had to give way to decisions by qualified majority vote (QMV) in most White Paper areas. Only the most sensitive single-market matters (fiscal policy, border controls, issues concerning the movement of people, and workers' rights) still required unanimity. Member states could henceforth be outvoted on important issues. In addition, because these new Council decision-making processes clearly changed the context for evaluating the EU's democratic legitimacy, the SEA linked new QMV to an extension in Parliament's amending power, codified in a new "cooperation procedure." In QMV matters, the Parliament could henceforth propose amendments that the Commission had to approve or reject. If the Commission approved, the Council could change the legislation only by unanimity. The SEA also proposed expanding areas in which the EU could act legally to include regional development policy ("economic and social cohesion"), research and technological development, and environmental policy. Finally, the SEA formally consecrated the European Council and European political cooperation (foreign policy coordination) in the treaty and pronounced in vague but premonitory ways about the need for further monetary integration.

Shrewd work won public support for the 1992 program. Business enthusiasm supported the White Paper and SEA because they appeared serious. Economic policy elites were sensitive to the Commission's efforts to argue for 1992 through the Cecchini Report, a panoply of economic studies about the "costs of non-Europe" that outlined what EU members would lose economically if they did not go through with the 1992 program. Generating labor enthusiasm was more problematic, as the single market was likely to threaten jobs in a context of rising unemployment.[37] Breaking down barriers between national markets also opened prospects for social dumping, in which corporations could relocate in areas of the Community with lower social overhead costs. The Commission thus focused much effort on labor, in particular by promising the opening of social dialogue at the European level: "confidence-building" discussions between Euro-level "social partners" (invoking another clause in the new SEA). The European Parliament was also a useful source of support. The increased power that the SEA gave the Parliament—the cooperation procedure—intensified communications between Brussels and Strasbourg and moved Parliament further into the Commission's camp. Also, paradoxically, skepticism about the Community contributed to the Commission's success. The EU had had so many problems by the mid-1980s that there was a tendency to discount any new initiatives. Thus many, including some important leaders, believed that even if completing the single market was announced, it would probably not amount to much, an attitude that helped minimize opposition to Commission plans.[38]

The most important source of support for the new policies was good economic luck. Awareness that something new was happening in Brussels coincided with an upturn in European economies, more coincidence than cause and effect. It helped the 1992 program and the SEA nonetheless. That Europe's new activism could be associated with a renewal of growth, prosperity, and job creation made it much easier to move forward.

The Commission, backed by France and Germany, immediately sought to build on its new prestige and credibility to promote even further change as rapidly as possible.[39] The first, and perhaps most significant, novelty was the Delors budgetary package of 1987. The EU then faced a number of separate problems. First, it had a real budgetary crisis. Next, regional development policies had to be redesigned in the light of the SEA's new commitment to economic and social cohesion. Finally chronic financial bleeding from the CAP had gotten worse. The genius of the Delors package was to join solutions to these three problems into a single program. Its quest for a five-year commitment to a greatly enlarged Community budget (which would include a fourth "own resource" based on a member state's gross domestic product) would give the Commission more budgetary latitude and avoid annual money fights. It also proposed changes in the CAP, including new cost stabilization mechanisms and a five-year program of guidelines for capping CAP spending, which might also keep chronic budgetary squabbles over agriculture off the table until 1993. The reform of the structural funds was in large part a response to new Spanish and Portuguese EU members, who wanted new regional development help because the completion of the single market would initially hurt poorer regions more than the better off. The reform brought the first really substantial European-level commitment to redistribution between richer and poorer member states. New cohesion policies would coordinate EU resources on a set of objectives.[40]

The budget for regional aid was doubled from 1988 to 1992, when it amounted to 25 percent of Community spending. Most important, spending the funds thus made available was done in a planned way. Multiyear programs were shaped and overseen by the Commission in accordance with a new principle of subsidiarity (policy worked by the most efficient level of government closest to the constituencies touched by it). Regions and localities generated ideas, and final community support frameworks (CSFs) were determined after contractual negotiations between the Commission and member states. The sums involved, if modest in absolute terms, were large in relation to the investment needs of poorer EU countries.

EMU proposals came next, barely after the ink had dried on the budget deal. At Hanover in June 1988, Delors persuaded the European Council to make him chair of a top-level committee of central bankers to bring forth new proposals for EMU.[41] Edouard Balladur, French finance minister, first called for new discussions to create a European central bank and a single currency in 1987. There were good arguments for EMU. It would reduce transaction costs, prod restructuring of European financial industries, and make intra-European factor costs more transparent. Wages would then reflect national productivity, and national budgetary and fiscal policies would have to reflect real economic fundamentals better, a good way for member state governments to externalize reforms. In international terms, EMU's single currency could become a reserve currency to rival the dollar, useful to Europe since the United States had used its currency many times to shore up its domestic economy at others' expense. EMU could be a giant step in promoting new European integration.

The bottom line, however, lay elsewhere. The French wanted more control over monetary policy because of their repeated problems in EMS. EMS had become an asymmetrical system in which the German Bundesbank consistently pushed others around, often threatening not to cooperate unless others accepted a hard line on price stability and monetary matters.[42] Others, the Italians in particular, were interested in helping the French. The French concern was not only about power, although this was certainly important. It mattered in addition to construct a new institutional basis for European monetary policymaking that would be less constrained toward price stability and more growth friendly than German domination of EMS had turned out to be. The problem with the French–Commission strategy was that the Germans had a clear bargaining advantage. If they did not like what they saw happening, they could refuse to move forward, and there would be no EMU at all. The French counted divisions among the Germans. The Bundesbank could be counted on to defend its positions in monetary matters. The Kohl government, on the other hand, had priorities beyond monetary policy in the realm of European integration.

Delors had a long-standing interest in monetary matters, having begun his career at the Banque de France, chaired the European Parliament's monetary committee, and been Mitterrand's first finance minister. He had also carefully kept the Commission's monetary affairs portfolio to himself when assigning tasks to his new Commission and thereafter had assiduously attended the monthly meetings of European central bankers in Basel. This familiarity was important, since work on the Delors committee was intense. The British delegate, Robin Leigh-Pemberton, chairman of the Bank of England, was sent by Margaret Thatcher to say no, and Karl-Otto Pöhl, the head of the German Bundesbank, was hostile. Neither stopped progress, however, and the Delors report set out the basic outlines for EMU that would eventually prevail: an independent European Central Bank committed to price stability, a gradual three-stage approach, and careful policies about convergence. The report spelled out the monetary side more than the economic policy side, however, implying a "bankers'" EMU.[43] The Delors report came to the European Council at Madrid in June 1989, when all EU members but the United Kingdom approved a new Intergov-

ernmental Conference to inscribe EMU into the treaties.

With EMU well under way, the Commission began moving in even more controversial directions. Awareness of the redistributive consequences of the single market made new social policy initiatives conceivable. The May 1989 Community Charter of Fundamental Social Rights, or Social Charter, was the product. It involved "solemn commitment" on the part of member states (only eleven, given furious British opposition) to a set of wage earner rights and was meant to make good on unfulfilled social promises the EU treaties base already contained. The Commission next produced an "Action Program" of nearly fifty proposals to implement the Social Charter. Unanimity decision rules on most matters meant, however, that little beyond workplace health and safety proposals, decided by qualified majority under SEA, would get through immediately, although the Maastricht Treaty later opened the way to many of the others. The SEA had also included a new article stating that "the Commission shall endeavor to develop the dialogue between management and labor at European level which could, if the two sides consider it desirable, lead to relations based on agreement." The social dialogue that followed was initially about confidence building, engaging employers and unions in habits of European-level discussion, which in time might create mutual respect and trust. It would take well into the 1990s before genuine contractual dealings would happen.[44]

By 1989 unforeseen and far-reaching changes in Europe's broader environment were on the horizon, however. The EU emerged from, and had been sustained by, the cold war. In "Western" Europe, as of 1989, there were twelve EU members and a limited number of other small nations, mostly remaining members of the EFTA, with the credentials to be EU members (which they would become in 1995). To the East lay "existing socialism," appallingly inefficient and oppressive, but cordoned off by Soviet power. Western Europe and the EU were protected by NATO and U.S. power. These arrangements had persisted for so long that they were assumed to be eternal. But in November 1989, the Berlin Wall came down, bringing the collapse of existing socialism and the end of cold war predictability. Europe's map and agenda changed almost immediately. To 1989 the EU's major regional concern was North-South integration on the western side of the iron curtain. Beginning in 1989, East-West matters came onto the table.

The year 1989 was a moment of joy for Europe and the EU, deeply inscribed in collective memory by the spontaneous dismantling of the Berlin Wall on November 9. But it also created a difficult new political puzzle. EU Europe had turned an important corner toward deepening the meaning of integration and was moving decisively toward genuine economic union, a single economy, and a single currency, with initiatives for greater political union on the horizon. The end of the cold war presented the EU with new issues that might potentially attenuate this deepening. First, Germany would be reunified, implying an increase in Germany's European weight and change in its outlooks. Next, the former socialist societies of Central and Eastern Europe would need assistance to modernize and democratize. "Deepening" had precedence over "widening." What had been initiated in 1985 had to be completed.

Of all the consequences of 1989, German unification was the most urgent, since it was not a question of "Eastern Europe" but of the place of Germany in the Community. The Commission took the lead in welcoming German unification, although Prime Minister Thatcher and President Mitterrand both were much more cautious. Jacques Delors thus announced in January 1990 that East Germany was "a special case. . . . There is a place for East Germany in the Community should it so wish." The next step was to prepare the immediate integration of the "five new länder" into the EU, which occurred after the March 1990 GDR elections in the German Democratic Republic.[45] Commission staff

had by then worked out a package of EU policies to help out. The wisdom of this course seemed self-evident. A Germany anchored at the center of the EU was the sine qua non of the Community's future. And it was essential for the development of the EU to enhance the commitment of the Federal Republic, rapidly becoming the EU's dominant member, to the Community's future.

As the implications of 1989 became clearer, the EU's leaders perceived opportunities for Europe to occupy new international political space. The EU conducted "foreign policy" for its members in trade and commercial matters, and its members retained virtually complete responsibility for the high politics of foreign policy. At the cold war's end, however, might it not be possible to enhance the Community's foreign policy capabilities? Thus, the French and Germans prodded the Dublin European Council in June 1990 to call a second IGC on political union, to be held simultaneously with the EMU conference. "Political union" included issues of foreign policy capacity and democratization, the first desired by the French, the second by the Germans.

The climax came in 1991 in the Maastricht Treaty on European Union.[46] Maastricht was Europe's initial response to economic globalization and the end of the cold war. The negotiations went on for a year. EMU was relatively easy to deal with. The 1989 Delors report had set out a program that the talks could follow, and the unequal balance of power between the Germans and French pointed to the ways in which final differences would be resolved. Germans, asked to give up their most important national symbol, the deutsche mark, wanted EMU to provide ironclad guarantees about price stability and financial responsibility, which the French wanted to relax. The British opposed EMU altogether, and it thus was necessary to prevent them from sabotaging the IGC. British opposition was neutralized by a formula allowing the United Kingdom to opt out of EMU, which also forbade it preventing anyone else from joining (with the Danish also opting out). The Spanish were intent on getting more North-South redistribution out of the EMU tasks, and ways had to be found to provide them with side payments without disrupting things. They were given a "Cohesion Fund"—more redistribution to compensate for the costs of EMU.

German–French differences posed larger problems. The first involved convergence criteria that would oblige potential EMU members to align their policies prior to final passage to EMU. The French supported the idea in principle, but the final harsh convergence terms were included because the German Bundesbank wanted to make sure that profligate EU member states—Italy in the first instance—could be kept out of EMU. Convergence targets were thus set for budget deficits (3 percent of GDP), longer-term debt (60 percent of GDP), inflation, interest rates, and currency stability tied to an average of the best results across the EU.

The next large differences were about timing. The Delors committee's three-stage progression had officially begun with the elimination of capital controls in the single market in 1990 (and involving ECOFIN—the Council of Finance Ministers—"mutual surveillance" of member state economic policies to coordinate convergence). Stage 2, which the Delors report proposed for 1994, would create the European Central Bank (ECB) and system of central banks to "apprentice" for roles in final EMU. The date of full EMU was then tentatively set for 1997, depending on how many member states were eligible because they met the convergence criteria targets. The Germans rejected this timetable, largely because of the costs of unification. Stage 2 was thus watered down to become a "European Monetary Institute" to prepare the final stage and "monitor" convergence. The French also wanted an "economic government" to set the Community economic policy, but the Germans refused, making EMU rather more monetary than economic. The Germans also

won complete independence for the proposed ECB dedicated to price stability.

The timing of stage 3, when the new ECB would prepare the single currency, was vague until the very last minute, to the chagrin of the French, who insisted that movement to EMU had to be made irreversible. Penultimate proposals on the table could have made things contingent on a minimum number of eligible member states, perhaps postponing EMU forever. The final compromise, French in origin and backed by the Italians, set a first possible date for January 1997, when a majority of states would have to be eligible to go forward. More important, it also fixed a date, January 1999, when EMU would happen no matter how many were eligible. This, the lone French victory on critical EMU matters at Maastricht, ultimately ensured that EMU actually happened.

The "political union" IGC was another story. The idea of talking about political union—a common foreign and security policy, greater democratization of the Community, more efficient institutions, and coherence among monetary, economic, and political action—had emerged only in spring 1990. This had given very little time for careful preparation, although the negotiations brought out fundamental disagreements about the desirable nature of European integration between "federalists" and "intergovernmentalists" and between member states that wanted European integration in the political area and those that preferred minimalism. Ambitions for coordinating EU foreign and defense policies, again largely French, ran up against member state disunity after the end of the cold war. The proposed common foreign and security policy divided "Atlanticists" insisting on the preeminence of NATO from those that desired more independent European positions. This particular disagreement was exacerbated by the Gulf War, which raged during the critical first months of the negotiations. Thus, the language finally hammered out about a European Common Foreign and Security Policy (CFSP) was tentative. Member states might decide on general areas of concern and on joint actions within these areas, but the rules for decision making made it difficult for Europe to act, let alone in time to have an effect. On "justice and home affairs," directions were set to extend the Schengen arrangements (named after the town where first agreements had been struck) for opening borders that had been struck earlier among some EU states. A "Europol" for coordinating police information and action would be created to offset the security problems of the abolition of internal borders, minimal standards for EU citizenship were set out, and common approaches to immigration policy and political asylum were envisaged. These proposals, like those for CFSP, were really declarations of intent. Finally, two new institutions, a Committee of the Regions and an Ombudsman, were established, and the power of the Court of Auditors was enhanced.

The most tangible products of political union were new powers for the European Parliament. Up to Maastricht, the Council of Ministers was the EU's "legislator," voting Commission proposals up or down. The SEA had allowed the Parliament to propose amendments but withheld final decision power. Maastricht allowed the Parliament to "codecide" with the Council on all QMV issues. This change was a real step toward remedying the democratic deficit and enhancing the EU's public credibility. Unfortunately, it came encased in cumbersome procedures. The Parliament also acquired the right to vote proposed Commission presidents up or down.

The final Maastricht document (135 pages long) was difficult even for insiders to read. It was also complicated in a constitutional sense. The "architecture" of Europe was one of the negotiators' central arguments. There were heated disagreements between those who wanted a federalist "tree" with everything connected to a common trunk (the Community) and a "Greek temple" with three separate "pillars" topped by

a connecting pediment/preamble. The temple won out. Maastricht innovated in moving the EU into those policy areas closest to the heart of remaining member state sovereignty, the CFSP (the second pillar) and justice and home affairs (the third). But no consensus existed to make these areas into community matters. Instead they were hived off to become separate, intergovernmental, entities. The "Community," focusing primarily on economic integration, was the first pillar.

Title I of the Treaty on European Union thus set out "common dispositions" and general goals. Then came the pillars. The first was a modified Community, while the second and third were consecrating intergovernmental arrangements for a Common Foreign and Security Policy and justice and internal affairs. The "European Union" (EU) encompassed all of the temple, becoming an entity much greater than the Community. The whole is illustrated in Figure 2.1.

The temple's pediment made the European Council the major strategist of European integration. The intergovernmental nature of the two non-Community pillars placed important policy matters beyond the Commission's effective reach (even if the CFSP pillar did grant the Commission a small role). EMU, although formally within the Community pillar, somewhat sidelined the Commission as well. The treaty's new subsidiarity clause, if vague, was also directed at limiting the Commission's actions, perhaps through litigation, only to those matters that demonstrably could not be undertaken at national or subnational levels. Finally, the increased powers to the European Parliament, in what Maastricht called the codecision procedure, could also reduce the Commission's proposing role. All told, Maastricht implied a shift away from supranationality toward intergovernmentalism at the institutional cost of the Commission. The reasons were easy to understand. As European integration moved into fundamental dimensions of national sovereignty in

	Common Pediment Common Principles and Objectives Articles A through F of the Maastricht Treaty Key Actor for Strategy and Coordination: European Council		
	Community Pillar 1	**Pillar 2**	**Pillar 3**
Content	• European Community • European Coal and Steel Community • Euratom (Titles II, III, and IV of the Maastricht Treaty)	Common Foreign and Security Policy (CFSP)	Cooperation in matters of justice and internal affairs (policing transnational crime, migration)
Principle of Governance	Community method Commission importance ECJ jurisprudence	Intergovernmental Council importance National jurisprudence	Intergovernmental Council importance National jurisprudence

Figure 2.1   Maastricht's Greek Temple

economic, monetary, foreign, and defense policy, member states wanted to retain as much control as they could.

Maastricht's solemnity masked uncertainty about implementation. What Maastricht said and what it led to were certain to be different since much of the treaty was vague and open-ended. The actual configuration of important new areas (EMU, CFSP, and others) would be contingent on attitudes and circumstances after Maastricht. EMU, the most detailed part of the new treaty, itself faced an unpredictable future. The ultimate meanings of other Maastricht provisions, the clauses on European citizenship, for example, or the third pillar on justice and internal affairs, were impossible to foresee.

After Maastricht: Years of New Dangers?

European leaders saw Maastricht as a conclusion. Ratification would be unproblematic, they felt, since governments would not have signed without knowing that they could produce approval. EU life would then go forward because there was a complicated and interconnected package of diplomatic and financial problems to be resolved. As it happened, however, doing important business as usual was difficult. Conditions around the European political system changed rapidly after Maastricht. The process of ratifying Maastricht in member states uncovered substantial public opposition to the EU's forward movement. European economies then turned sour. In all this there occurred significant backlash against the Commission, and the balance of institutions in the Europolitical system began to shift.

Business Not as Usual

The GATT Uruguay Round negotiations came to a head in the immediate post-Maastricht period. They had stagnated in the later 1980s in large part because agriculture was being discussed for the first time and the EU wanted to keep changing the CAP off the table until Maastricht had been completed. Without CAP reform, the Uruguay Round could not be successfully concluded, however, and European business interests wanted a successful conclusion for more trade liberalization and, if possible, the extension of multilateral trade agreements to services, intellectual property, and foreign direct investment.[47] This put farmers and their powerful interest groups in a difficult position to resist CAP reform, something that they might well have done otherwise. CAP reform was, in turn, tied to the development of a second "Delors package" of medium-term budgetary changes. "Delors I" was coming to its end, and, given the size of the CAP budget in overall EU expenditures, "Delors II" needed clarity on how much agriculture would cost.[48]

The outlines of a CAP reform came from the Commission in early 1991. The CAP would begin shifting away from price supports to maintain farmers' income toward a system of set-asides (deficiency payments) in which farmers would be paid not to produce. This was roughly the way the United States subsidized its farmers. Deficiency payments had the advantage of distorting prices less and bringing them closer to world market prices. Eventually this would limit European surplus dumping on the international market, one major goal of those pressuring the EU for change. In order to keep the farmers from rebelling, however, the new CAP would be as expensive to taxpayers as the old one.

CAP reform moved haltingly until May 1992 when a deal was struck (after a fifty-hour-long meeting) whose seriousness was underlined by the protests that it provoked. The stage then was set for clearer dealings on the Uruguay Round. The end game was tougher than expected, however. The Americans were obdurate. On the EU side, the French minister of agriculture threatened that France would not cooperate. Each side eventually made concessions on agriculture and split their differences on other matters (with the French insisting on protection for European cultural products like films). But the tension around the end game publicly divided the EU negotiators and tarnished the image of the Commission.

CAP reform did clarify the atmosphere around the second Delors budgetary package, which proposed growth in the EU budget somewhat less than that of Delors I. Council discussions of the Delors II package were difficult, however. The British argued against it, the Belgians and the Italians, ordinarily staunch Europeans, agreed with them, while the Germans, several constrained by the exorbitant costs of unification, pronounced it inconceivable for the Community budget to grow twice as fast as member state budgets. Only the South really liked Delors II because of the proposed increase in structural funds. The debate showed the growing reluctance of more prosperous parts of the Community to underwrite solidarity and cohesion and, more generally, to finance the EU. This was an ominous sign that the member states that counted were no longer willing to invest in the growth of the EU.

The first signs of public unhappiness with the EU appeared in the spring of 1992. Denmark and Ireland had both called referenda to ratify the Maastricht Treaty. The Danes were traditionally unpredictable about European integration. The Danish Parliament and major parties favored the treaty, but Danish voters had very nearly voted down the SEA in a referendum in 1986. On June 2 the Danes voted Maastricht down by 50.7 percent to 49.3 percent, a margin of 46,000 votes. The "no" voters were a curious mixture of "under-Denmark" (the poorer, the less skilled, public sector white-collar workers), the majority of women, and Left and Right political extremes. The Danes, who owed much of their prosperity to the EU, disliked the political side of Maastricht, seeing in it an undesirable change in the contract they had signed in joining the EU, which was, they thought, only for economic purposes.[49] Success in the Irish referendum (69 percent to 31 percent) was minor solace.

The day after the Danish "no," President Mitterrand announced a similar referendum for September 1992. Mitterrand, who believed European integration after 1985 to be his own work, reasoned that a successful referendum might restore its momentum. His calculation was bad. By August polls were at fifty-fifty, with "no" forces leading in momentum. France's *petit oui* (a "tiny yes," with 51 percent voting "yes" and 49 percent "no") saved, but hardly endorsed, Maastricht. Like Denmark, the French "tiny yes" was rich, urban, and well educated.[50] The "noes" were farmers (connected with the CAP), workers, lower-level white-collar workers, and the less well educated.

Euro-euphoria was over. The old issue of democratic deficit in the form of public suspicion that decisions were being made by elites in mysterious ways rose again. Just behind this was one of the most problematic dimensions of European integration. National democratic processes were very short term and had become even more so with innovations in the media and campaigning. In this context, European institutions presented an opening to take decisions with medium and long-term effects. These decisions would later feed back into national democracies as constraints coming from "outside." Europe thus provided a welcome instrument for elites who wanted to reconfigure domestic political arenas without paying the domestic costs. The 1992 program had initially been accepted— tacitly—by public opinion because it involved few short-run costs. For several years, when intention was being translated into legislation, "1992" was but a slogan. But when the liberalizing effects of the 1992 program began to have real consequences, European peoples reacted.

The Edinburgh European Council in December 1992 cobbled together a solution to the Danish problem, allowing the Danes to opt out of significant parts of the Maastricht deal that Danish leaders had earlier signed.[51] When the Danes were asked in spring 1993 to reconsider ratifying a treaty from which they had managed largely to extract themselves, they voted yes.

Face was saved. Edinburgh also passed the Delors II package in slightly watered-down form. A set of programs would be sustained until the end of the century, the Commission's budgetary autonomy would be guaranteed, and the all-important commitment to regional redistribution would be sustained.

There were other logics at work to diminish enthusiasm for European integration, however. The beginning of a precipitous economic downturn in early 1992 played an enormous role in darkening the skies. Growth stagnated again, as it had prior to 1985. Unemployment, the single most salient issue in member state politics, began to shoot up again, as Table 2.3 shows. Cyclical downturn was coming on top of the employment, reducing the effects of the 1992 program itself, and companies were shedding labor as they restructured for the single market. Observers also remarked that the Maastricht EMU proposals, with their stringent convergence criteria, would make it very difficult for member state governments to stimulate economic activity. Even within such constraints, however, budget deficits shot up and cast new doubt on whether the EMU convergence criteria were feasible at all.

The worst had yet to come, however. Beginning in summer 1992, fluctuations of the German deutsche mark and the U.S. dollar led financial flows toward Germany, weakening other EMS exchange rate mechanism currencies.[52] This was largely because the German Bundesbank, upset about the monetary terms of unification and worried about rising inflation, had tightened German monetary policy more than needed. Every member state that wanted to stay within the fluctuation limits of the ERM was thus obliged to keep interest rates higher than it would have liked, making countercyclical stimulation of their economies nearly impossible. German policies made recession deeper and more intractable than it should have been, but this was only part of the story. The post-Maastricht political environment itself fueled turbulence in currency markets. A major ERM

Table 2.3   EU Unemployment Rates, 1975—1998

	Excluding East Germany					Including Eastern Germany					
	1975	1985	1990	1991	1992	1993	1994	1995	1996	1997	1998
Total Unemployed (millions)	5.0	14.8	12.0	12.7	13.6	17.76	18.47	17.85	18.16	17.93	16.95
Unemployment Rate (percent)	3.7	9.9	7.7	8.1	8.2	10.7	11.1	10.8	10.8	10.6	10.0

Sources: European Commission, *Employment in Europe 1999* (Luxembourg: EC, 2000), excepting 1992 and 1995, which are from *Employment in Europe 1997* (Luxembourg: EC, 1997).

realignment might have stopped the problems quickly, but few wanted it because of the negative effects that it might have had on the French referendum campaign. Many policymakers, with their eyes on the EMU convergence criteria and the coming of EMU Stage 2 in 1994, had come to see the ERM as a proto-EMU with fixed exchange rates (the ERM had not been realigned since 1987).

The result was an explosion of currency speculation, leading first to Black Wednesday, September 16, 1992, when the British left the ERM.[53] The Italian lira left the same day, the Spanish peseta was devalued, and the Spanish, Portuguese, and Irish very quickly reintroduced exchange controls. Subsequently the currencies of Finland, Sweden, and Norway, three EFTA candidates for EU membership, cut loose from earlier pegging to the EMS. In January 1993, the Irish pound was devalued. The storm was not over, however.

In the wake of September 1992 and the French referendum, the franc came under speculative siege. It was saved initially by huge joint German–French intervention efforts. For years the French had pursued a "strong franc" policy to root out inflation and restructure the French economy at the cost of high unemployment and growing economic insecurity. The new Center-Right government after legislative elections in March 1993 was charged with preparing the scene for 1995 presidential elections, and it

made sense for it to stimulate the economy in a countercyclical way by lowering interest rates. But the new government could do so only in limited ways before the franc would fall below its ERM limit, unless the German Bundesbank (the "Buba") was willing to lower its own rates.

Whether the "Buba" would be willing to do so was doubtful, and this was all the money markets needed. Prime Minister Balladur would be pushed to lower French rates, the Bundesbank was unlikely to help out, and the franc's value would then slip. Speculation would cause the franc to fall further, and it was a solid bet that Balladur would be unable to raise French interest rates to counteract it, for reasons of domestic politics. Devaluation, or some equivalent change, was likely.[54] In mid-July 1993, when the Bundesbank refused anything more than a token reduction in rates, speculators shifted into high gear. With the Bank of France running out of reserves, harsh and complicated negotiations revalued the range of ERM fluctuation to allow more room for currency floating. This solved the speculation problem for the time being. EMU was at the heart of Maastricht. EMS stability was one of the rocks on which the EMU proposals had been built. The EMS crisis threatened the credibility and implementation of EMU.

Maastricht was in trouble in other areas. At the very moment in 1991 when Maastricht negotiators were creating words for a Common

Foreign and Security Policy, the first serious armed conflict in Europe since 1945 broke out in Yugoslavia. The Yugoslav Federation had been precarious for some time, but in the spring of 1991, it began to disintegrate with declarations of independence by Slovenia and Croatia. Slovenian circumstances were unusual because the province had few Serbs and Belgrade's attempts to respond with force fizzled within ten days. But the Serb core of Yugoslavia was prepared to go to war to occupy Serb-populated territory anywhere else in the federation, and it did so in Croatia in July 1991. The foreign policy unity of EU member states, stretched already by the Gulf War, was tenuous at best at this point. Their differences prevented effective response on Yugoslavia, in particular because the French were initially pro-Serb and the Germans pro-Croat. The EU did organize an international peace conference at the Hague in September 1991. This did not prevent the Germans from recognizing Croatia and Slovenia in January 1992, largely discrediting the EU's impartiality and undermining the peace conference. The EU did well to mediate a cease-fire.

When Bosnia-Herzegovina declared itself an independent republic and was recognized by the EU and others, the Serbs sent in troops to prevent success, encouraging systematic ethnic cleansing in predominantly Serbian areas. Further attempts at EU-UN mediation failed. Ultimately it took battle fatigue and the application of U.S. muscle to stabilize Bosnia through the 1995 Dayton Accords. Prior to Dayton, European leaders had denounced the United States for its unwillingness to accept serious involvement in Yugoslav peace brokering. After this, many of the same leaders began denouncing the United States for its unilateralism. In the background, new trouble was already brewing in Kosovo.[55]

The Yugoslav crisis deepened public doubt about EU. Watching Dubrovnik being bombed and Sarajevo dying nightly on television news was heart-wrenching. Millions of refugees fled, many to Germany. Intellectuals effectively expressed their anguish about European impotence, helping Europeans to understand the horror of the events. Alas, any instruments available to the EU, given its disunity, were easy for Yugoslav president Slobodan Milosovic to parry. Mediation did not work, and sanctions imposed had little influence. Unanimity decision rules made EU action with real clout, including militant intervention, out of the question. The United States initially waited for Europe to sort out the problems, but when the Americans arrived, they naturally invoked their superior power, and Europeans felt humiliated. If the Community was little use in dealing with situations like Yugoslavia, then what use was it more generally?

When the Going Gets Tough, Do the Tough Get Going?

The quiet way in which the 1992 period ended on January 1, 1993, spoke volumes. The single market had not quite been completed, and there were delays in VAT realignment, opening up public procurement (where the obduracy of various governments was impressive), liberalizing energy markets, and transposing important legislation. The failure to remove airport passport controls by the target date was visible evidence that free movement of people lagged behind the three other EU freedoms. Formal ratification of Maastricht in October 1993 did not do much for morale either, since it was overshadowed by the grim economic situation.

In late 1993, the Commission tried to retake the initiative with a White Paper, *Employment, Growth, and Competitiveness*, whose goal was to propose a new medium-term development strategy. Its economic analysis was hard-nosed. For the central problem, unemployment, "there is no miracle cure." None of the solutions offered—protectionism, a "dash for economic freedom" (through government spending), reducing job sharing at the national level, and/or a drastic cut in wages—would work. The European economy's growth rate had been shrinking over decades, unemployment rising over trade cycles, investment declining, and the EU's competitive position worsening across the board. The single market had been helpful but not enough. The rest of the world, confronted with the same challenges, had also been responding.

The White Paper proposed employment policy as the place to begin. Europe should set a target of creating 15 million new jobs by the year 2000. New competitiveness would flow from "creating as favorable an environment as possible for company competitiveness" in the advanced technology areas, where the future lay. Making the single market work and cooperating to make European regulation simple and consistent were important goals. Member states should also provide stimuli for flexible small and medium-sized industries and accelerate the establishment of the trans-European networks (TENs) in infrastructure (particularly telecommunications) mandated by Maastricht. These TENs could rapidly cut transaction costs and push Europe further toward the information society, where new comparative advantage might be found. They would also help integrate Eastern Europe.

The key phrase in the White Paper was that "the new model of European society calls for less passive and more active solidarity." There should be a negotiated, decentralized, and rapidly evolving "sort of European social pact" in which "new gains in productivity would essentially be applied to forward-looking investments and to the creation of jobs." Wage earners would be asked to accept raises set below productivity gains in the interests of job-creating investments. Solidarity across generations and regions, plus preventing poverty and social exclusion, were fundamental. Most important, however, was developing flexible national employment systems, beginning with commitment to lifelong education. Employment arrangements, both outside and inside firms, should be modified by active labor market policies to en-

courage mobility. The cost of unskilled and semiskilled labor should be reduced by lowering social insurance expenses. Unemployment policy also needed an overhaul to enhance incentives to reenter the labor market.

The White Paper was serious, elegant, and prescient. It could make a difference only with the goodwill of member states, however, and here changing times were evident. In 1985, consensus had been possible about completing the single market. The 1994 White Paper pointed toward deepening Europe's regional uniqueness, but many member states did not want this. Moreover, even those willing to contemplate new deepening disagreed about what it should involve. Finally, the EU had accepted three new former EFTA applicants that officially joined in 1995: Austria, Sweden, and Finland (the Norwegians rejected membership in a referendum for the second time). All of these small societies had their own ideas, and this made the EU equation even more complicated.

The political voices who had promoted the renewal of European integration in the 1980s were also leaving the stage. President Mitterrand lost virtually all political credibility before retiring in 1995. The British Conservatives had become stridently adamant in their Euroskepticism. The Italians, almost always pro-EU, were mired in the scandals that Italians came to call "the end of the First Republic." The Spanish prime minister, Felipe Gonzalez, leader of the EU South, was on the way to losing power. And Jacques Delors left the Commission presidency in January 1995. Only Helmut Kohl remained.

Keeping the Future Open

The great burst of integration that had begun in 1985 seemed to have ended a decade later. No better illustration of this was the conflict around naming a successor to Jacques Delors as Commission president. Advocates of finding a weak new president, unlikely to stir things up, and without the energy and intelligence that had been Delors's forte won out. The new president was Jacques Santer, former Luxembourg prime minister. Subsequently the Commission lost most of its proposition force energy. National leaders evidently wanted power to shift back to the member states, the Council of Ministers, and the European Council—in other words, to themselves.

The Maastricht negotiators provided a way to take the temperature of the Union by asking for another IGC to review the workings of their treaty after five years. The new conference was convened in 1996 and concluded at the Amsterdam European Council in June 1997. The Amsterdam Treaty provided an accurate portrait of a newly cautious and conflicted EU. According to one participant, "Many governments did not want to reform anything in depth."[56]

In the foreign policy area, decisions were deferred on extended Community trade competence to services and intellectual property. On defense, integrating the WEU into the EU was put off. CFSP structures were strengthened with creation of a planning staff, an early warning unit, and, most important, a High Representative for the CFSP, (roughly, a single spokesperson) who would also serve as secretary-general of the Council of Ministers.[57] CFSP decision rules were also clarified. The European Council could henceforth define common European strategies unanimously, and the Council could implement them with QMV. When neither common strategies nor Council decisions existed, however, CFSP decisions had to be unanimous. This was softened by a new provision that allowed member states to exercise "constructive abstention" on CFSP matters. Rather than simply blocking things, dissenters could opt out of a particular decision, provided only that the total of abstentions was not more than one-third. Another significant innovation was incorporation of the so-called Petersberg tasks—a set of regional crisis management and peacekeeping objectives set out by WEU in 1992 into the treaty.

In matters of freedom, security, and justice (the renamed third pillar), Amsterdam brought more changes. It enunciated conditions under which member states might be disciplined (even suspended) for infringing basic principles of democracy, human rights, and the rule of law. It also included new language against racial and gender discrimination and on data privacy. Commitment to a zone of freedom, security, and justice demonstrated clear new concern for incorporating human rights into the EU treaties. When defined legally, through either a specific EU Charter of Rights or ECJ jurisprudence, this would be very important. Finally, third pillar matters had been very slow getting off the ground after Maastricht, in particular because of the requirement of unanimity for decisions. Amsterdam thus proposed a gradual (five-year) shift of key policy matters about free circulation of persons, including immigration and asylum policies, from the third to the community pillar.[58] The third pillar remained intergovernmental on matters of criminal justice and policing, including Europol, a new agency for police cooperation foreseen by Maastricht, whose operationalization had been difficult.

Perhaps the most interesting breakthrough in the Amsterdam Treaty was in social policy, a matter that had not been on the IGC's agenda at all. The reasons were the EU's frighteningly high level of unemployment and the shift from Center-Right to Center-Left governance in member states that had begun in the second half of the 1990s.[59] One change was the promotion of the Maastricht Social Protocol to full treaty status because of New Labour's willingness to sign on. The Social Protocol had created an ingenious procedure for promoting Euro-level social dialogue between the social partners (i.e., unions and employers). Even without the British, these had led to negotiated legislation (agreements then given the force of law by Council decision) on parental leave and atypical employment (part-time and short-term work), important pieces of the Social Charter Action Program. Amsterdam's real innovation was to introduce a new clause into the treaty committing the EU to achieve a "high level of employment" to be implemented by the development of a "coordinated strategy."

Putting employment policy into the treaty provided some counterpart on the job creation side to EMU preparation that had obliged deflation and austerity.[60] Member states were enjoined to produce national action plans for employment development following a set of common guidelines from the Commission for the first employment policy exercise at Luxembourg in November 1997. The Commission could also provide new incentives to harmonize these national plans. The clear intent was to oblige member states to target their economic and social resources on employment matters, then to compare different national plans to make them more complementary and promote the emulation of best practices. In itself, this was an interesting innovation in method. The Commission here was not a legislator. Instead it was to be a facilitator, managing a process in which plans originating in the member states might be "Europeanized."

Amsterdam was least successful in the area of general institutional reform. From the beginning, key member states were not in the mood for constitutional debates despite evidence that EU institutions did not work well and fell short in democratic responsibility and accountability. The urgent issues were more prosaic than these, however, related to eventual EU enlargement to the CEECs. If institutions were not reformed, a large influx of new members could paralyze both Commission and Council. Amsterdam did not confront these issues. Instead it called for yet another IGC beginning in 1999 specifically targeted on them.

Jacques Delors, who knew his EU history, was fond of describing European integration as "a few years of success, more years of crisis and many more years of stagnation." European successes had invariably been followed by disagreement, then by long moments of relative paralysis. The renewal after 1985 had happened after European integration's worst crisis. The end of the post-1985 forward movement left European integration in another crisis. Maastricht and the end of the cold war had cooled enthusiasm for integration. But they had also left urgent matters on the table that virtually compelled Europe to continue moving forward almost despite itself. The programming of the Amsterdam follow-up to Maastricht was one good example, and there were others. EMU was programmed unless Europeans found dramatic reasons to stop it, and it was hard to imagine any reasons that would be good enough to camouflage the huge, perhaps terminal, defeat that reneging on EMU would be. Maastricht's vague provisions on foreign and defense policy pointed to post–cold war dilemmas that Europe would have to face, one way or the other. Europe's international security situation had changed profoundly. The issue of enlarging the EU to the ex-Socialist countries in Central and Eastern Europe was created by 1989, not by Maastricht. Even if some member states regarded new enlargement as too much trouble, there was no conceivable way that could cover EU abdication of its responsibilities to unify all of Europe in an interdependent order of prosperity and democracy.

The "Eurosclerosis" period of the 1970s and the EU crisis that finally ended in 1985 might well have been terminal. Had not certain basic choices been made by leaders to renew European integration, the "Common Market" might well have been the furthest point of advance, destined to disintegrate, slowly but surely, in time. The 1990s crisis of European integration was different. Commitments, mechanisms, and institutions had been built after 1985 that would inevitably drive European integration forward. Uncertainty remained, however, about which roads would be taken.

Notes

1. See W. O. Henderson, *The Origins of the Common Market* (London: Frank Cass, 1962).

2. Fred Block, *The Origins of International Economic Disorder* (Berkeley: University of California Press, 1977), is a good source.

3. On the general circumstances surrounding the Marshall Plan, see Alan Milward, *The Reconstruction of Western Europe, 1945–1951* (London: Methuen, 1984).

4. The best general study of U.S. influences on European integration is Peter Duignan and L. H. Gann, *The United States and the New Europe* (Oxford: Oxford University Press, 1994).

5. See Pierre Gerbet, "The Origins: Early Attempts and the Emergence of the Six (1945–1952)," in Roy Pryce, ed., *The Dynamics of European Union* (London: Croom Helm, 1987), pp. 40–44.

6. See François Duchêne, *Jean Monnet: The First Statesman of Independence* (New York: Norton, 1994).

7. First paragraph of the Schuman declaration of May 9, 1950, my translation, from Joe Boudant and Max Gounelle, *Les Grandes dates de l'Europe communautaire* (Paris: Larousse, 1989), pp. 14–15.

8. For a succinct selection from earlier writings on the theory of European integration, see Brent F. Nelson and Alexander C-G. Stubb, eds., *The European Union: Readings on the Theory and Practice of European Integration*, 2d ed. (Boulder, Colo.: Lynne Rienner, 1998), pt. 2.

9. John Gillingham, *Coal, Steel, and the Rebirth of Europe, 1945–1955* (Cambridge: Cambridge University Press, 1991).

10. Jean Monnet, whose intelligence and agility had been so important earlier, fell behind. He had lost none of his fervor but chose to focus it on a new proposal, which turned out to be a mistake, rather than on the customs-free area that would become the heart of the new EEC. Following his "functionalist" method, he sought another sectoral area to integrate, atomic energy, which he thought would become central to the civil economies of European societies, given Europe's penury in oil. Euratom, the European atomic energy agency that he advocated, would, he thought, use this future source of energy to bind European economics together even more. But alas, Monnet had not understood the role of cheap oil in Europe's future. See Andrew Moravcsik, *The Choice for Europe* (Ithaca, N.Y.: Cornell University Press, 1998), chap. 2. This is an invaluable source for the objectives of EU member states at critical choice points in EU history, as well as for accounts of the multilateral negotiations that occurred at these points.

11. For further information, Timothy Bainbridge, *The Penguin Companion to European Union*, 2d ed. (London: Penguin, 1988), is invaluable.

12. See chapter 7 in Alan Milward, *The European Rescue of the Nation State* (Berkeley: University of California Press, 1992).

13. The best way to begin understanding the EU is to read the treaties themselves. The EEC Treaty of Rome, along with the ECSC, Euratom, and the Single European Act (1987), are found in EC, *Treaties Establishing the European Communities* (Luxembourg: EC, 1987). For Article 2, see p. 125.

14. Ibid., Article 3.

15. Jean Monnet's *Memoirs* speak in explicitly functionalist terms. Ernest Haas reformulated these terms into academic integration theory. See Haas, *The Uniting of Europe*, 2d ed. (Stanford: Stanford University Press, 1968), and Leon Lindberg, *The Political Dynamics of European Integration* (Stanford: Stanford University Press, 1963).

16. Stephen Weatherill and Paul Beaumont provide an excellent and approachable review of the ECJ and EU law in *EC Law* (London: Penguin, 1993).

17. Loukas Tsoukalis, *The New European Economy*, 2d ed. (Oxford: Oxford University Press, 1993). Chapter 2 reviews these early years.

18. On this Golden Age, see Andrew Glyn and Alain Lipietz in Stephen Marglin and Juliet Schor, eds., *The Golden Age of Capitalism* (Oxford: Oxford University Press, 1990).

19. Consult Miriam Camps, *Britain and the European Community, 1955–1963* (Oxford: Oxford University Press, 1964), and Stephen George, *An Awkward Partner: Britain in the European Community* (Oxford: Clarendon Press, 1990).

20. Stanley Hoffmann has written perceptively of this in *The European Sisyphus: Essays on Europe,*

1964–1994 (Boulder, Colo.: Westview Press, 1994), esp. chap. 3.

21. One further, relatively small, change was the negotiation of a treaty in 1965 (entering into effect in 1967) that fused the executives of the three European Communities into one. The Brussels Commission thus became the Commission of the ECSC and Euratom, hence the "Commission of the European Communit(ies)."

22. See Andrea Boltho, ed., *The European Economy* (Oxford: Oxford University Press, 1982).

23. In the wake of new warfare in the Middle East, OPEC (the Organization of Petroleum Exporting Countries, dominated by the Middle Eastern oil-producing nations), which for years had seen its revenues decline in consequence of Western inflation, doubled members' oil prices. A second shock in 1979 had similar effects.

24. On EPC, see Simon Nuttall, *European Political Cooperation* (Oxford: Clarendon Press, 1992).

25. On the European Council, see Simon Bulmer and Wolfgang Wessels, *The European Council* (Basingstoke: Macmillan, 1987).

26. EMS was a "two-speed" affair, including only some EC members (not Britain, for example). See Peter Ludlow, *The Making of the European Monetary System* (London: Butterworths, 1982).

27. Such revaluation occurred twenty-six times between 1979 and 1999 (when EMU came into existence). Everyone agreed that it should have occurred even more often.

28. The story of how this happened is told succinctly in Dorothee Heisenberg, *The Mark of the Bundesbank* (Boulder, Colo.: Lynne Rienner, 1999), chap. 3, and with a different analytic choice in Morvacsik, *Choice*, chap. 3.

29. Margaret Thatcher's *The Downing Street Years* (New York: HarperCollins, 1993), contains several trenchant discussions of the "British check" issues. See Chapter 18 in particular.

30. On the "draft treaty," see Roland Bieber, Jean-Paul Jacque, and Joseph Weiler, eds., *An Ever Closer Union: A Critical Analysis of the Draft Treaty Establishing European Union* (Luxembourg: EC, 1985).

31. See the discussion in Weatherill and Beaumont, *EC Law*, pp. 430ff.

32. Heisenberg, *Mark of the Bundesbank*, notes at this point, "The EMS had been changed permanently into a system in which the German economic model was institutionalized and other economic policies would not be viable" (p. 84).

33. Mitterrand had been very careful to cultivate the German government even before the 1983 shift. His dramatic gesture of support for Chancellor Helmut Kohl (who had recently displaced the social democrat Helmut Schmidt in 1982 when the Free Democrats shifted allegiance) in his pro-Euromissile speech to the Bundestag in January 1983 created an important new friendship. His relationship with Kohl was pivotal for the rest of the story.

34. On budget problems, see Thatcher, *Downing Street Years*, pp. 537–541.

35. Delors describes the ways in which he decided on the single market approach in his preface to Paolo Cecchini, *The European Challenge* (Aldershot: Wildwood House, 1988).

36. The SEA was *single* because there is only one text to modify all of the EU treaties and to remind member states that it was to be ratified in all-or-nothing ways, and not because of the single market.

37. Michael Emerson, *What Model for Europe?* (Cambridge, Mass.: MIT Press, 1988), has a contemporary discussion of employment.

38. Altiero Spinelli, one of Europe's grand old federalist figures, commented, after the SEA, that the "mountain has given birth to a mouse." When the act was presented for ratification to the French parliament, for example, Prime Minister Chirac, at that time a Gaullist whose party bristled with anti-Europeanists, judged that so little was likely to follow that it was not worth spending political resources opposing it.

39. Delors and his team used the metaphor of "Russian dolls" when discussing their approach. See George Ross, *Jacques Delors and European Integration* (New York: Oxford University Press, 1995).

40. The largest, "Objective 1," was aid to less-developed regions (largely in the South). The objectives also included funding to reconvert de-industrialized areas (often in the North), programs to confront long-term employment, help to enter the labor market for unemployed young people (those below the age of twenty-five), and, finally, development and structural adjustment aid in rural areas.

41. Delors had earlier been instrumental (despite Prime Minister Thatcher) in inserting language fa-

vorable to new monetary initiatives into the Single European Act. Jean Quatremer and Thomas Klau, *les Hommes qui ont fait l'euro* (Paris: Plon, 1999), pp. 150–151.

42. In 1988 the Bundesbank had pronounced that EMU was quite unnecessary given the success of EMS.

43. Bundesbank president Karl-Otto Pöhl suggested his own EMU program in June 1990. Membership would be restricted to the strong currency countries of the deutsche mark zone and France.

44. On social dialogue, see Stephan Leibfried and Paul Pierson, *European Social Policy* (Washington, D.C.: Brookings, 1995). See also Andrew Martin et al., *The Brave New World of European Unions* (New York: Berghahn, 1999), chap. 8.

45. See European Commission, *The Impact of German Unification on the European Community* (Luxembourg: EC, 1990).

46. For a description of Maastricht from inside the Commission, see Ross, *Jacques Delors*, chaps. 3–6.

47. On the GATT Uruguay Round negotiations, which ended in 1993, see Hugo Paemen and Alexandra Bensk, *From the GATT to the Uruguay Round* (Leuven: Leuven University Press, 1995). Hugo Paemen was the EU's head negotiator.

48. A readable and detailed discussion of the CAP in its various guises is found in Wyn Grant, *The Common Agricultural Policy* (New York: St. Martin's, 1997).

49. The Danes had supported membership in 1972 by 63 to 37 percent and ratified the Single Act in 1986 by 56 to 44 percent. See Toivo Miljan, *The Reluctant Europeans* (London: Hurst, 1977).

50. Results and analysis can be found in *Le Monde*, September 22, 1992.

51. Richard Corbett's "Governance and Institutional Developments," in Journal of Common Market Studies, *The European Community 1992* (Oxford: Blackwell, 1993), p. 35, provides a dense summary of the European Council's "decision" on Denmark, a highly irregular ruling for which the EC treaties made no provision.

52. David Marsh, *The Bundesbank: The Bank That Rules Europe* (London: Heinemann, 1992), provides a shrewd overview of the bank's position. See also John Goodman, *Monetary Sovereignty: The Politics of Central Banking in Western Europe* (Ithaca, N.Y.: Cornell University Press, 1992).

53. The best recapitulation of these events is in *Financial Times*, December 11, 1992.

54. See *Economist*, July 17, 1993, for a review of the developing situation.

55. See Geoffrey Edwards, "The Potential and Limits of the CFSP: The Yugoslav Example," in Elfriede Regelberger, Philippe de Schoutheete, and Wolfgang Wessels, eds., *Foreign Policy of the European Union: From EPC to CFSP and Beyond* (Boulder, Colo.: Lynne Rienner, 1997).

56. Franklin Dehousse, *Amsterdam: The Making of a Treaty* (London: Kogan Page, 1999). On the Amsterdam preparations, see Geoffrey Edwards and Anton Pijpers, eds., *The Politics of European Treaty Reform: The 1996 Intergovernmental Conference and Beyond* (London: Pinter, 1997). For a good and accessible review of the finished product, see European Commission, *The Amsterdam Treaty: A Comprehensive Guide* (Luxembourg: EU, 1999).

57. Javier Solana, former Spanish foreign minister and secretary-general of NATO, was appointed the first High Representative in 1999.

58. There would be a five-year transition phase, however, during which the Council would set out new rules about external borders, asylum, and judicial cooperation by unanimity. The so-called Schengen Accord was also incorporated into the treaty, with the United Kingdom and Ireland given an opt-out. The Schengen agreements (named after the place where they began) concerned the free circulation of people inside the Schengen "area." This area had begun with agreements among a limited number of member states and steadily expanded to almost everyone in the 1990s. Since they did not involve everyone, however, they were not legally EU arrangements. Amsterdam made them so.

59. The new French Socialist government wanted a good deal more, however, in particular, the constitution of a Euro-level "economic government" to stand as a macroeconomic policy counterpart to EMU and the ECB. The economic government would have the power to outline large economic policy goals to which the ECB would have to listen. The French lost this at Amsterdam but continued to return to it in various forms thereafter.

C H A P T E R

3

European Institutions

The EU lives in a dense forest of Brussels office buildings, most of them grimy, utilitarian, and unattractive. The history of this European quarter reflects the evolution of the EU. In the 1960s, with the Common Market successfully launched, the European Commission moved into a gigantic, glass-faced, X-shaped office building. The offices of the commissioners were on the top floor of the Berlaymont (as the building was named), with grand views over Brussels. The Commission's administrative divisions, or directorates-general (DGs), lived mainly on the lower floors. The idea of this grand design was to make everyone accessible to everyone else. It was undercut, however, by an interior that was grim and difficult to understand. The Council of Ministers' headquarters next door on the unpleasant wind tunnel of Brussels' Rue de la Loi was smaller and nondescript, symbolizing that most of the Council's work was done in the member states. As the Commission gained power in the 1980s, it progressively colonized the entire area, decentralizing the DGs and lobbies into more dull new buildings. Decentralization made people walk from building to building and gave the area some daytime street life and a lively restaurant scene, where EU civil servants and lobbyists could congregate over lunch.

The year 1991, when Maastricht was negotiated, was important in both fact and symbol. In June, Commission leaders learned that the Berlaymont was filled with dangerous asbestos, and they decamped forthwith. Commissioners and their staffs went up the street to the more modest Breydel building, and the administrative services dispersed all over Brussels.[1] As the Commission's power and influence waned, the Berlaymont sat derelict, while the building czars debated whether to demolish or rebuild it and, most important, where to find the money to do either.

The mid-1990s brought the Santer Commission (1995–2000), and the neighborhood began to change again. Immediately across the street from the empty Berlaymont, a new Council headquarters was built, extremely large and pompous, in reddish-beige marble redolent of a mausoleum. This new building announced clearly that the Commission was in trouble and the Council ever more in charge. In the meantime, the Berlaymont had been covered by huge white plastic sheets, as if it had been loaned out to pop artists. In the distance, towering on the horizon, was something that looked like a gigantic metal beer barrel. This was the Brussels home of the European Parliament, whose star also rose in the 1990s. Nothing has ever been simple for the Parliament, however, for several hundred kilometers away in Strasbourg, another large and costly new home for it was also being built.[2]

The "Triangle" Plus One

Changes in the Brussels European Quarter have mirrored those among EU political institutions. The EU is a complex of organizations built among and around nation-states. Although it is not a sovereign entity, it does exercise some measure of sovereignty. It does not have a constitution, but substantial elements of one appear in the treaties that have created it. The EU is young and in constant evolution; thus, the balance of power among its institutions has varied over time, while new institutions have periodically appeared.

The Maastricht Treaty reconfigured pre-1991 European institutions by creating the "Greek temple" structure of three interconnected pillars (see Figure 2.1). The "Community" pillar encompassed what European integration had built prior to Maastricht. Institutionally dense and complex, it exists as a triangle of institutions: the European Commission, the Council of Ministers (behind which now stands the European Council), and the European Parliament. Because European integration is a community of law, this triangle operates within a body of jurisprudence from the European Court of Justice (ECJ).

European Commission

The Rome treaties gave the European Commission three major prerogatives:

1. It has exclusive right to propose EU legislation in the form of regulations, directives, and recommendations.
2. It oversees the implementation of EU policy, monitoring member state transposition of EU law into national statute and following up implementation.
3. It is the guardian of the treaties, ensuring that European law is observed and, if need be, bringing member states and private bodies before the ECJ.

The Commission also has a fourth, de facto, role, and it may be the most important:

4. It is an intellectual and political collective to reflect on and agitate for the future of European integration.

The Commission has specific policy competencies where its actions are like a partial federal government. It has the duty of administering EU competition (antitrust) policies, for example, to maintain a level playing field across the single market. In doing so, it polices state aid to industry, cartel-like activities, and mergers and acquisitions. It can act to prevent the emergence of monopoly market power. It can tell member state governments not to subsidize national industries and fine them if they do not obey. It must be notified of all large mergers, and it can disallow mergers that in its judgment will lead to abuses of market power, as it did at least thirteen times over the past decade. It administers the Common Agricultural Policy (CAP), regulating Europe's hugely expensive and complex agricultural operations, sometimes even exercising its vanguard responsibilities to reform agricultural policy. It has a large role in European environmental policy. It regulates workplace health and safety across the EU. It administers, and to some extent designs, the structural funds for developing the EU's poorer regions. It has a significant architectural role in European-level research and development strategies and programs. It draws up the EU budget. It represents the Community externally in trade matters. It also represents member states in a number of international organizations and has information offices throughout the world and diplomatic delegations in many countries. And these are only its larger duties.

Since the 1995 enlargement of the EU to fifteen member states, the Commission has had twenty members. Each large member state (Germany, France, Italy, the United Kingdom, and Spain) appoints two commissioners and smaller member states one each. Terms of service for commissioners were four years until Maastricht, when they changed to five years to coincide with the electoral life of the European Parliament. The Commission president is designated by the European Council. After Maastricht, the Parliament also gained the right to scrutinize the qualifications of newly nominated commissioners and the president.[3] The Parliament cannot block appointment of specific commissioners, but it may withhold approval of the entire Commission, although it has never done so. The Amsterdam Treaty gave Parliament the right to approve the nomination of the Commission president prior to, and separate from, its right to approve the entire Commission.

The Commission proper (the twenty commissioners) is a *college* of equals. Understanding the idea of college is essential to understanding how the Commission works. The Commission president has few of the powers of appointment, policy direction, arbitration, and ultimate authority over decisions of a prime minister. His basic sources of influence come from presiding over the Commission's business, coordination, agenda setting, and chairing (aided by the Commission's general secretariat and legal services, which report to the president).[4] There are two vice presidents of the Commission who stand in when the president is absent. Commissioners are all required to swear "to be completely independent in the performance of their duties . . . [and to] neither seek nor take instructions from any government or from any other body." The president assigns each commissioner a portfolio of precise tasks before entering office, involving directing and leading one or several of the Commission's services (the DGs).

The assignment of portfolios is a critical moment for each Commission and Commission president, as portfolios for the Prodi Commission illustrate (see Table 3.1). Some tasks are much more important and more coveted than others. The trade commissioner, for example, is at the very core of European trade policy, and the competition commissioner has great power over the shape of economic activity in Europe and beyond. Individual commissioner nominees and member states are thus greatly concerned about the appointments, so that the power of the president in assigning jobs is constrained. Commissioners themselves do not have ministerial powers over their administrative areas. They direct their services politically but in accordance with programmatic lines to which the entire Commission has agreed.

The Commission meets every Wednesday, three times a month in Brussels and once in Strasbourg, to be present at the monthly plenary sessions of Parliament. It usually takes off the month of August, when governments and governance tend to shut down across Europe. Decisions are taken after collective debate, to which each commissioner is expected to contribute. Broad participation in debate is the heart of the college method. Ministers in classic governments argue briefs related to their ministry and participate in other areas only as informed spectators. As members of a college, commissioners participate in all decisions, and their influence depends on their ability to do so effectively. Collegiality is designed to produce consensus. The Commission votes only when there is no consensus.

So that commissioners can keep on top of the very broad range of matters that come before the college, they are assisted by cabinets, or personal staffs. Cabinets, composed of a half-dozen ambitious operatives recruited from inside and outside the Commission's services, do the legwork necessitated by collegial organization. Because all commissioners must be prepared to discuss and decide anything and everything, each must be fully informed about all business. Each must also be represented in lower-level policy development on anything even remotely close to the commissioner's specific portfolio. Part of the cabinet serves as an intelligence gatherer on the entire range of issues on the Commission floor, while another part works more closely with services pertinent to the commissioner's portfolio and substitutes for the commissioner at multiple policy preparation meetings that occur before each Wednesday's full college meeting.[5]

The cabinet system, borrowed from French and Belgian practices, has always been controversial, although it is difficult to see how the Commission could function as a college without something equivalent. Cabinet members are envied. Most Commission civil servants work vertically, that is, in their specific administrative

Table 3.1   Prodi Commission, 2000–2005: Commissioners and Portfolios

Name (country)	Portfolio
Romano Prodi (Italy)	President
Neil Kinnock (United Kingdom)	Vice president of administrative reform
Loyola de Palacio (Spain)	Vice president of relations with the European Parliament, transport, and energy
Mario Monti (Italy)	Competition
Franz Fischler (Austria)	Agriculture, rural development, and fisheries
Erkki Liikanen (Finland)	Enterprise and information society
Frits Bolkestein (Netherlands)	Internal market
Philippe Busquin (Belgium)	Research
Pedro Solbes Mira (Spain)	Economic and monetary affairs
Poul Nielson (Denmark)	Development and humanitarian aid
Günter Verheugen (Germany)	Enlargement
Chris Patten (United Kingdom)	External relations
Pascal Lamy (France)	Trade
David Byrne (Ireland)	Health and consumer protection
Michel Barnier (France)	Regional policy
Viviane Reding (Luxembourg)	Education and culture
Michaele Schreyer (Germany)	Budget
Margot Wallström (Sweden)	Environment
Antonio Vitorino (Portugal)	Justice and home affairs
Anna Diamantopoulou (Greece)	Employment and social affairs

area, while Cabinet members work horizontally, across the services, putting them in much better positions to build the broad networks of contacts that make them more visible and lead to promotion more quickly. Cabinet work is demanding on time and personal life, and grateful commissioners more often than not try to find good new positions for their staffs before the ends of their terms. Cabinet service has thus become the best way for Commission civil servants to rise rapidly in the ranks.

Some veteran and skilled cabinet staffers often serve several different commissioners over the years and become invaluable central players in making the Commission work. The career of

Michel Petite, Romano Prodi's *chef de cabinet* in 2000, is a case in point. French, but bilingual in English. and gifted with a first-rate legal mind, Petite served from 1985 in the cabinet of Lord Cockfield, primary author of the "1992" White Paper, then shifted to providing advice on tax policy in the cabinet of Christiane Scrivener before finally joining the Delors cabinet in 1991, where he was a key operative during the Maastricht negotiations. In the mid-1990s he worked as head of the Commission's merger control unit in the competition policy directorate, then joined the Commission's three-person negotiating team for the Amsterdam Treaty negotiations. After a year as Commission Fellow in residence at Harvard University and a brief new appearance in the competition policy area, he was called by Prodi.

Despite a mythical reputation as the unstoppable "Brussels bureaucracy," the Commission administration is very small, with fewer than 20,000 people—roughly equivalent to the staff of a midsized European city. From this total there are 5,000 A-grade staff officers, the "real" European civil servants (or "Eurocrats," as the press calls them). The distribution of A-level posts among nationals of each EU member is carefully observed, with some jobs regularly allocated to particular nationalities. Each major administrative unit is headed by a general director (A-1 in rank), and the general directors hold the Commission's highest administrative posts. A-level jobs are coveted. They are interesting compared to most national civil service jobs, well paid, and exempt from national taxes (although the EU itself taxes them). A-levels are recruited primarily through an annual European-wide competition from thousands of applicants for each opening (the number of available jobs varies annually, depending on budgets and retirements).

The Commission also employs several thousand translators and interpreters, necessary because of its obligation to translate all official Commission documents into eleven languages and for simultaneous translation during meetings. The workaday languages of the Commission are English, French, and German. Native speakers of the most widely used languages gain considerable political advantage, for language confers some power in itself. For a long time, French was predominant, partly because the Commission was designed and built by the French and the Belgians. Since the end of the Delors commissions in 1995, however, English has made advances. German is rarely used. The remainder of the Commission's personnel provide clerical and other support services, including thousands of jobs for Belgian locals paid well above going rates in the local labor market.

At its best, the Commission sees itself as devoted to the noble cause of advancing European integration. This dimension of the Commission as an institution with a mission rather than simply an ordinary, routine-driven, civil service can have both positive and negative effects. At those relatively rare moments when it has relative power in the EU institutional triangle, the Commission can be a hotbed of commitment, hard work, and energy. During bad moments, when its role is limited, it can be full of demoralized grumbling, as hierarchical and inflexible as any national civil service in ways that demotivate second-level officials, whose jobs become dull and whose careers are blocked. Of course, like any other complex administration, the Commission is subdivided by functional divisions, which always have a tendency to become feudal and self-contained. Moreover, because it is multinational, the Commission has national cliques, clans, and rumors similar to other international organizations. Also because the Commission is a political as well as an administrative organ, the political affiliations of the people within it matter.

The Commission's most important job has been to conceive initiatives, justify them to the Council of Ministers in particular, and then persuade others that they should be enacted. This function, however is necessarily limited, because the Commission rarely proposes de novo. In most cases it is acting as a filter, translating the desires of others and the requirements of international agreements into specific proposals. One observer, a former member of Jacques Delors's personal staff, calculated that in the very busy year of 1991, only 6 percent of the Commission's proposals came from its own initiatives (a similar count in 1998 estimated 5 to 10 percent).[6] Twenty-eight percent were linked to international agreements; 21 percent followed requests from the Council or member states; 17 percent modified existing texts or were needed because of ECJ decisions; 12 percent resulted from general framework programs approved by the Council (research and development, for example); 8 percent were obligatory under the treaty (setting agricultural prices, among others); and 8 percent originated from requests from firms, particularly concerning trade practices (requests for antidumping actions, for example).

The Commission spends much time sounding out politicians, national ministries, lobbies, producer groups, and other Euro-level institutions, in particular, the Council and the Parliament. Commissions and their administrations are aided, usually in institutionalized ways in particular areas, by several thousand advisory, management, and regulatory committees, made up of member state civil servants. The interchanges between the Commission and these committees are governed by codified rules called *comitology*. Following these rules, the Commission faces different levels of consultation and differing obligations to respond to what it is told. The Commission is also the object of intense lobbying. Finally, the actual implementation of most Community measures is mainly left to member state administrations, monitored by the Commission.

In general, the Commission can initiate proposals only in the areas allowed and implied by the treaties. Its original prerogatives were largely sectoral, including the CAP, competition law, and common external trade policies (the administration of tariffs and negotiating bilateral and multilateral trade negotiations, including the General Agreement on Tariffs and Trade). The 1985 White Paper, *Completing the Internal Market*, extended the Commission's role as a proposition force by making it responsible for producing the measures in the 1992 program, plus a wide range of ancillary activity, particularly in the setting of standards and the regulation of workplace health and safety. The Single European Act (SEA) also gave the Community expanded competencies, in particular in economic and social cohesion (regional redistribution policy), environmental policy, and research and development. In more routine areas, the Commission prepares the annual Community budget for submission to the Parliament and Council of Ministers and, since the first "package," a pluriannual budgetary program.

Maastricht clarified Community and Commission prerogatives and made some important changes. Article 3 defined the twenty policy areas where the Community could act (meaning where the Commission had the power of proposal), either exclusively or concurrently with member states (see Table 3.2). Many of these were traditional, sometimes with the scope of Community action expanded, but there were several new areas, including public health, education and training, and consumer protection. Maastricht also included a new article (3B) that consecrated "subsidiarity" by decreeing that the Commission and Community should act, even where the treaty did allow, only where objectives could not be achieved by the member states themselves.[7]

Table 3.2   The Twenty Areas for Community Action—Maastricht List

1. Elimination of customs duties and quantitative restrictions on goods traded among member states, as well as other equivalent practices

2. Common external trade policy

3. An internal market with free circulation of goods, people, services, and capital

4. Measures to promote the entrance of and free circulation within the internal market, eventually to include visa policies

5. Common policies in agriculture and fishing

6. Common transport policies

7. Competition law

8. Rapprochements of national legislations for the functioning of the common market

9. Social policy involving the European Social Fund

10. Reinforcement of economic and social cohesion (regional policy)

11. Environmental policy

12. Enhancing the competitiveness of Community industry

13. Promotion of technological research and development

14. Encouragement for establishing and developing trans-European networks (in telecommunications, transport, and energy)

15. Contributing to a high level of public health

16. Contributing to quality education and training as the flowering of member state culture

17. Policies of development aid

18. Association with overseas territories (mainly colonies) to help trade and pursue efforts of economic and social development

19. Contributing to the enhancement of consumer protection

20. Measures in the areas of energy, civil defense, and tourism

---

Maastricht also reconfigured Community prerogatives in important areas of common policy areas. Economic and social cohesion became a fundamental mission, meaning, in legal terms, that all EU policy areas and Commission initiatives were to integrate commitment to regional development. The treaty also established a Cohesion Fund to compensate poorer countries for the costs of Community environmental policy and the trans-European networks (TENs), new Community-wide public works projects in transport, telecommunications, and energy infrastructure established by Maastricht. The treaty contained a new article that made it possible for the Community and Commission to be involved in industrial policy, but unanimity in Council decision making was required. Maastricht enlarged the scope of Community research and development policies beyond science and technology to areas such as health and the environment. Environmental policy, which the new treaty also promoted to a fundamental objective, was henceforth to be decided by qualified majority decision making in all but a few areas. Finally, Maastricht added a social protocol, originally signed only by eleven member states, with the British opting out (they opted in

at Amsterdam), which allowed new space for social policy.

The Amsterdam Treaty beefed up provisions enjoining equal treatment between men and women in the workplace and obliged such matters to be mainstreamed through all EU activities. In practice, this meant that all Community activities were supposed to consider environmental, regional, and equal opportunity concerns—a tall order! The Amsterdam Treaty also reinforced consumer protection powers. Finally, it programmed the five-year shift of significant tasks related to justice and home affairs (the third pillar—free movement of persons, immigration and external border control, asylum law) into the Community pillar and hence into the Commission's orbit. The grandiloquent rubric of this shift, "establishing an area of freedom, security and justice in five years," may turn out to be the treaty foundation for a Community charter of basic rights (above and beyond the commitment of individual EU member states to standards for human rights). For the five-year transition period (until 2003), the Council was charged with designing new rules in these areas (excepting asylum and immigration, where the five-year period does not apply), deciding by unanimity, and the Commission would then administer these rules. Thereafter, any new decisions would be made by qualified majority voting (QMV).

The Commission's power and position in the European political system have varied historically. When it first tried to assert itself as an agenda setter in the 1960s, it was stopped abruptly by the French. The Commission did not become irrelevant, however, because it retained large regulatory powers in the Common Market. It then rose to the height of its powers between 1985 and Maastricht, helping the EU to overcome "Eurosclerosis" and undoubtedly achieving its highest level of prestige and influence. During these years, it annually proposed more legislation than most national governments did, while moving omnivorously into new policy areas. After Maastricht, public opinion and the member states determined to halt growth in Commission power. The last years of Jacques Delors's presidency were difficult, and his successor, Jacques Santer, did not command the same influence.

Santer's first claim was that the Commission would henceforth "do less and better," but it achieved only the first of these goals. Conflict with the Parliament over Commission practices grew to the point where the Parliament threatened to refuse discharge (close the books) to the 1996 annual budget. The Commission's downward spiral then culminated after a scathing report on its stewardship from a blue-ribbon committee appointed by the Parliament, which documented a number of inadequate Commission administrative practices. The entire Santer Commission could do little but resign collectively in response. Romano Prodi, Santer's successor, was thus forced to preside at a historic low point in power and credibility. Time will tell whether the Commission will recover.[8]

Council of Ministers

In the official portrait of the EU, the European Commission was agenda setter and executive and the Council of Ministers the legislator. Originally the Council decided alone on proposals from the Commission, which for the most part had been discussed by Parliament. Since Maastricht, the Council codecides with Parliament on most Community pillar issues and is also the center of Pillars 2 and 3 on Common Foreign and Security Policy (CFSP) and justice and home affairs. The Council comprises ministers empowered by their governments to decide European issues, and it is where member states, the fundamental "citizens" of the EU, express their preferences.

There are in practice several different ministerial councils whose membership varies with the matters discussed. The largest issues come before the General Affairs Council, comprising foreign ministers (the label implies, correctly,

that the basic decision-making processes of the EU are diplomatic). The second most important council is ECOFIN, composed of economics and finance ministers, whose work has expanded tremendously. Close to twenty other policy areas have their separate councils of specialist ministers; agriculture ministers deal with the Common Agricultural Policy (CAP), for example, and the Internal Market Council (no official defense ministers council exists yet, but it is in the works). The multiplicity of different councils functioning in the name of the Council of Ministers creates problems of coordination that are not always well resolved. Coordination is even more difficult because of the sheer number of Council meetings: on average in the 1990s, there were ninety per year, so the Council is more or less permanently in session.

The Council's decision rules add complexity. The Rome EEC Treaty foresaw three different voting systems—unanimity, QMV, and simple majority—depending on the issue area. The Luxembourg Compromise narrowed things to unanimity on almost anything important. One consequence was that the Council rarely voted at all. The SEA, however, applied QMV across a wide range of matters, including almost everything involved in completing the single market. Maastricht and Amsterdam extended the scope of QMV further, but far from completely. QMV, or weighted majority voting, distributes voting power in accordance with the relative size of different member states.[9] After the most recent enlargement in 1995, sixty-two votes (70 percent) were needed to pass a measure under QMV. Agreement of two large and two smaller member states can therefore become a blocking majority of twenty-six.

Issues and voting rules in the Council are also correlated with different interinstitutional processes. Council–Parliament dealings may involve QMV plus codecision, cooperation (amending), and simple consultation, in addition to special QMV-Parliament rules on EMU matters. Council unanimity, restricted in scope over time, can still involve codecision, consultation, and simple assent by the Parliament. Sometimes the Council, deciding by itself, uses QMV (on trade policy and some international agreements, for example), and sometimes it requires unanimity. Only expert insiders master all of these rules, which themselves have been changing with the frequent intergovernmental conferences (IGCs) to change the treaty.

The Council does not deliberate and decide by itself any more than the Commission does. The most important of the Council's helpers is COREPER (a French acronym for Committee of Permanent Representatives), whose members the *Financial Times* once called "the men who run Europe."[10] The permanent representatives in COREPER are member state ambassadors to the EU, their deputies, and top staff. They are their countries' front line in Brussels and do much of the work to shape ultimate Council decisions, filtering and refining matters to come before the Council, much as the cabinets do for the Commission. In their processes, they hammer out as much consensus as possible among themselves (referred to as "point A" matters), leaving the ministers with only the 15 to 20 percent remaining areas of disagreement ("point B" matters). The residency of permanent representatives in Brussels is often long, and they tend to be experienced veterans with full mastery of EU lore, networks, and methods.[11]

COREPER itself does not work alone either. The initial sorting out of decisions to consider is done for it by 150 to 200 lower-level working committees, where thousands of national civil servants and experts participate.[12] COREPER also coordinates and largely staffs a number of high-level functional committees, including the Political Committee (involving member state and Commission foreign policy political directors from European Political Cooperation) that prepares the work of the General Affairs Council and, since Maastricht, CFSP. The K4 Committee coordinates a range of third pillar matters.[13]

Deliberations of the Council of Ministers have been mysterious. Outcomes are announced to the public, but internal processes are not. Minutes have never been circulated, even in summary form. Rising worries about Europe's legitimacy after Maastricht led to largely cosmetic efforts to reveal this mystery. Thus, a few television broadcasts have shown parts of Council proceedings, on certain matters the Council has allowed its votes to be known, and since 1995, the media, after complicated legal proceedings, can get more detail. The inside knowledge gleaned thus far, however, has been limited, in part because much of the Council's work is done in bilateral and multilateral discussions between member states before anything reaches the Council room.[14]

The presidency of the Council rotates among member states every six months in an agreed order, organizing and coordinating Council work. The presidency also oversees Council–Commission relationships. Because the prerogatives of the European Parliament have grown through cooperation and codecision, the presidency now also coordinates demanding Council–Parliament interactions, including submission of its own annual program to the Parliament. The presidency presides over and prepares the European Council summits. In all of these activities, it can play an important role as power broker and package builder among member states. Finally, the presidency has traditionally spoken for the EU externally on foreign policy matters (excepting trade). For foreign policy activity, the acting presidency has been aided by the previous and next presidency, the so-called *troika*.[15] The development of the CFSP and the third pillar (which is in part directed outward to other countries) has broadened the presidency's foreign policy role while establishing a place for "Mr. Common Foreign and Security Policy" to give a single voice in EU foreign dealings.

An effective presidency can exercise considerable power, and effective presidencies have been important. French and German presidencies in the 1980s were critical in regenerating the momentum for integration, for example. British presidencies, in contrast, have brought caution. EU lore that smaller members are not likely to be successful presidents is not always accurate. Little Luxembourg, for example, presided over the most difficult negotiations for the SEA and the Maastricht Treaty; Belgium, with its strong pro-integrationist sentiments, has similarly been important; and the Portuguese presidency in the first half of 2000 was particularly innovative. The rotating Council presidency is not always the most effective of EU institutions. Discontinuities in leadership can often disrupt the flow of business.

The Council of Ministers relies on a Council secretariat of some two thousand people (a scant 300 A-level administrators, plus legal linguists (experts in legal translation), translators, and secretaries, in the new Council building in Brussels. The organization of the secretariat is different from the Commission's, with a staff for the secretary-general, legal services, and only seven DGs. The Council secretary-general, who has his own large cabinet, has become a very important person recently.[16] The Commission has always regarded the Council secretariat, rightly and ruefully, as a rival whose goal is to keep the Commission from exercising too much influence. The secretariat provides services and continuity to the rotating Council presidency—one of the primary reasons that the presidencies of small countries can work. The secretariat organizes and takes minutes of all Council ministerial and subministerial meetings, an enormous job. It is responsible for accurate translation of all official EU actions into all official languages—hence, the importance of legal linguists. The Amsterdam Treaty increased the stature and power of the Council secretariat when it established the position of High Representative for Foreign Policy ("Mr. CFSP") who is also the official Council secretary-general, although an associate secretary-general actually runs the office. Javier Solana, former Spanish foreign minister and secretary-general of the North Atlantic Treaty Organization (NATO) was named first "Mr. CFSP" in 1999. It is too early to know precisely how significant this change will be, but the new arrangements clearly endow the secretariat with clout in the foreign policy and defense areas that may make the institution even more important in time.

The European Council—really a "super-council" of ministers—came into being in 1974 as an institutionalization of regular summit meetings of EU heads of state and government. The Maastricht Treaty consecrated it formally as the body that gives the EU the impulsion it needs and defines its general direction. One might say that the European Council is the EU's board of trustees, the highest representatives of Europe's "owners," the member states, acting through summit meetings at least once, but usually twice, during each six-month Council presidency. The European Council supplements the strategic capacities of the key triangle institutions, the Commission and Council of Ministers. It is prepared by the sitting Council presidency with the help of the Council secretariat. The European Council strategizes the EU's immediate future for all three pillars, including the Community one, and settles outstanding issues.

European Council meetings are very exclusive. Only presidents or prime ministers plus one other minister (usually the foreign minister), the Council secretary-general, and the Commission president and secretary-general sit in the room—only thirty-three people in today's EU of fifteen members. This small size is designed to facilitate frank and open discussion and produce clarification of what is possible. The summits are carefully prepared to narrow the agenda to the most important outstanding matters. During the actual European Council, which is always brief—usually two days—legions of civil servants and technicians deploy in meeting rooms, hotels, and other places within the reach of cellular phones. They provide proposals, wording, and discussion when needed. The negotiating begins with a visit from the president of the European Parliament, who makes a declaration on behalf of the Parliament and then leaves. Then issue after issue is discussed, the easy ones resolved quickly and harder ones saved until later. After the second session is a working lunch, when the leaders separate from their foreign ministers to begin confronting the most difficult problems, while the foreign ministers expedite the rest. If important matters remain, as they almost always do, the last few hours of any European Council are very intense. The product of each European Council—the so-called presidency conclusions—reflects the agenda for the meeting. It contains comments about international events, instructions about policy initiatives for the Commission and Council to take up, and pronouncements on larger issues of the EU's future.[17] The importance of the European Council is clear from a partial list of its most important recent conclusions (see Table 3.3).

The balance of EU power tipped toward intergovernmental bodies in the 1990s, primarily at the expense of the Commission. This shift occurred partly because of exhaustion at the end of the Delors period and the subsequent feck-lessness of the Santer Commission. It also occurred because the progress of integration has foregrounded matters that fall closer to the heart of member state sovereignty—issues like foreign policy, defense, immigration, policing, internal security, and EU enlargement. Many of these matters are currently outside the Community pillar and thus legally intergovernmental. Also the more complicated and weighty the agendas are of the EU's intergovernmental institutions—the Council of Ministers, in particular—the more difficult it has become to generate clear resolution to problems. This is yet another signal that new scrutiny of EU institutions, with an eye to serious reform, is urgent. In the meantime, however, many observers have noted the Council's tendency to pass decision-making tasks upward so that the European Council is now a default decision maker for the EU. The danger in this shift is that the European Council conducts a very brief meeting when many things must be done. The more the Council of Ministers dodges bullets, the more bullets

the European Council must bite. More important, it is much easier, and much more likely, that bilateral deals between member states bypass European institutions altogether.

European Parliament

The European Parliament (EP) began as the successor to the European Coal and Steel Community (ECSC) assembly, composed of unelected members with little power who were appointed by member state governments.[18] The Parliament has since evolved slowly into an influential institution. Since 1979 it has been directly elected.[19] Seats in the Parliament are currently allocated among member states as shown in Table 3.4.

Candidates to the EP run on national party tickets. Once elected and in Strasbourg, national party groups then form European-level family coalitions. The Socialists, who have created a transnational party of European Socialists, and the Christian Democrats (who now include the British Conservatives) grouped in the European Peoples' Party, are by far the two largest EP groups.[20] Until 1999 the Socialists were larger, but the balance shifted slightly in the 1999 elections, oddly enough at a moment when the Left was in power in most EU member states. The Socialist-Christian Democrat EP pivot reflects the center of gravity of continental European party politics and can be found at work in other EU institutions, underlining general European commitment to social market economies. Both the Social Democrats and Christian Democrats accept that there can be no substitute for market mechanisms. They both also reject hard-line neoliberalism that advocates markets' making *all* important decisions. They both thus believe in a European model of society, with extensive welfare state programs and negotiated decisions among capital, labor, and other organized groups.

Elections to the EP, held every five years, have always been second-order national elections.

Table 3.3   Major Conclusions of Recent European Councils

European Council	Product(s)
Fontainebleau, 1984	Solved "British check" issue; expansion to Spain and Portugal unlocked; appointment of Jacques Delors
Milan, 1985	Approved "1992" White Paper; decided intergovernmental conference to modify treaty
Brussels, 1987	Adopted first Delors budgetary package (reform of structural funds)
Madrid, 1989	Accepted Delors report on Economic and Monetary Union (EMU); discussed Social Charter
Dublin, 1990	Decided German reunification within the EU
Rome, 1990	Opened two IGCs—on EMU and political union
Maastricht, 1991	Maastricht Treaty
Edinburgh, 1992	Adopted second Delors budgetary package; negotiated ways to allow Denmark to hold second Maastricht referendum; decided to negotiate enlargement to four European Free Trade Association countries
Brussels, 1993	Discussed White Paper on *Growth, Competitiveness and Employment*
Brussels, 1994	Designated Jacques Santer as president of Commission
Essen, 1994	Discussed Commission paper on enlargement to Central and Eastern European countries
Madrid, 1995	Decided date to proceed to final EMU stage; named new European currency the euro
Turin, 1996	Opened IGC to review Maastricht
Dublin, 1996	Proposed EMU stability and growth pact
Amsterdam, 1997	Conducted final negotiations on Amsterdam Treaty
Luxembourg, 1997	Start of Amsterdam employment policy processes
Cologne, 1998	Wide-ranging discussions on European Strategic Defense Program
Helsinki, 1999	Adopted "Headline Goal" on creation of European rapid reaction force by 2003
Lisbon, 2000	Industrial policy summit on information economy
Nice, 2000	End of IGC to reform EU institutions for enlargement

Any election held in any European country is understood by national politicians to indicate the relative strength of national political forces. Thus, when European issues are discussed during Europarliamentary campaigns, they tend to be transparent proxies for national political conflicts and concerns.[21] This subordination of Europarliamentary electoral politics to the issues and rhythms of national political life may even have intensified in the 1990s, given the disaffection of national publics from Europe. In general, it has made the European Parliament a training ground for aspiring national politicians yet unable to break into national politics and a parking lot for national politicians who have been voted out of national office. These tendencies have not, however, prevented the occasional presence in Parliament of important politicians.[22]

The Parliament elects its own president and

Table 3.4 Distribution by Member State of Seats in the European Parliament, 1999

Country	Seats	Country	Seats
Austria	32	Italy	87
Belgium	25	Luxembourg	6
Denmark	16	Netherlands	31
Finland	16	Portugal	25
France	87	Spain	64
Greece	25	Sweden	22
Germany	99	United Kingdom	87
Ireland	15	**Total**	**626**

executive bureau for periods of two and one-half years. The president presides over parliamentary sessions, participates in periodic interinstitutional discussions with Commission and Council counterparts, and addresses member state heads at European Council summits. The bulk of the hard work is done by nineteen permanent committees, which produce detailed, thoughtful reports in their functional areas, often made even more interesting by the degree of political consensus that has tended to prevail about what Europe should be.[23] The centrality of committees has also made them the logical target for the enormous army of lobbyists whom the EU has acquired.

The importance of Committee business is part of the explanation for the strange spectacle that visitors to parliamentary sessions often witness. Ushered into the gallery of the EP's "hemicycle," visitors are likely to see a vast room nearly devoid of human presence. There will be a staff person here and there, someone up on the dais presiding, and several seemingly lost members of the European Parliament (MEPs) distributed around the room, either speaking because their turn has come (after which they tend to leave) or waiting for the president to recognize them. Fortunate visitors may see a momentary flood of MEPs to their seats for a scheduled vote. At these moments,

usually quite disconnected in time from relevant debate, votes on several different matters are taken electronically. After MEPs have pushed their buttons a requisite number of times, with the results immediately tallied on an electronic scoreboard, the crowd mills out. The room looks like a real parliamentary assembly only when it is being addressed by commissioners, particularly the Commission president, who report and answer questions regularly, prime ministers, heads of state, and other visiting dignitaries.

An astute visitor would also notice that speakers in Parliament are often more strident than those in national parliaments. With the European Parliament largely elected by proportional representation and the power it has acquired, the European political system still has no government and opposition. As a result, MEPs feel less restraint than MPs in national parliaments where free expression is limited by disciplined loyalty to a coalition or party. Thus, Greens in the EP are very green; populists are cuttingly populist; Leftists are really on the Left; and Right extremists can be truly extreme. Ian Paisley, the extreme Right Northern Ireland Unionist, and Jean-Marie LePen, the French populist xenophobe, were both outspoken MEPs. More often, however, the European Parliament reflects a do-good progressivism, as discussions and documents from its social affairs' and women's committees show.

The Parliament originally had only consultative power, with legislation proposed by the Commission that the Council decided after considering Parliament's opinion. This odd constitution of a legislative body without de facto legislative power created a parliamentary lobby for correcting the Community's "democratic deficit."[24] The episodic growth in Parliament's powers since its founding is partly a consequence. In the 1970s it acquired deliberative powers in the establishment of the Community's annual budget, making it an important object for lobbying and allowing it to intervene indirectly in important policy areas. The Parliament also discovered that it could delay decisions, because time limits for delivering its consultative opinions were vague.

The SEA created a cooperation procedure for most single market legislation (which, as reconfigured at Maastricht, also covered proposals made in transport policy, regional development, social policy, development cooperation, and specifically legal and economic matters). The cooperation procedure created a legislative process with two readings (see Figure 3.1). The Commission proposes simultaneously to the Council of Ministers and Parliament. The Parliament then gives a general opinion, and the Council produces a "common position" that Parliament can then accept, reject, or amend. Acceptance means that the legislation is adopted. Rejection allows the Council to overrule the Parliament, but only by unanimous decision. The Parliament then has three months to propose amendments by an absolute majority of its membership, leading to negotiations with the Commission. If the Commission supports the amendments, the Council had three months to accept them by QMV, reject them unanimously, or do nothing and see the legislation die. If the Commission did not support the amendments, the Council can unanimously approve the amended proposal or its earlier common position. The complexity of this process should not obscure its importance. The cooperation procedure endows Parliament with important amending powers, giving it new influence over the Commission and Council, both of which have been obliged to develop new approaches to the Parliament.

Creating the cooperation procedure did not make the EP into a "real" parliament, however. It still can neither propose nor reject legislation on its own. It has gained the power of rejecting some legislation with Maastricht's codecision procedure (effective after the treaty's ratification in 1993, only a few brief years after the SEA came into effect). Codecision should be understood literally, in the sense that Parliament and the Council actually codecide on Commission proposals as if they were two separate leg-

---

First Reading

1. Commission proposes initially.
2. Parliament gives its initial opinion.
3. Council prepares its Common Position.

Second Reading

4a. Parliament approves or fails to act within three months (one month extension possible). The measure passes.
4b. Parliament rejects (absolute majority of members). Text fails unless Council revotes Common Position unanimously.

Figure 3.1   Overview of the Cooperation Procedure

---

islative houses. After Maastricht, codecision applied to a wide swath of issues: the free movement of persons, the internal market, education, culture, public health, consumer protection, TENs, research and development, and environmental action. The codecision process set out at Maastricht was exceedingly complex, however. In a first legislative reading, it was the same as the cooperation procedure. But if Parliament did not pass or amend the proposal, a second reading ensued. Parliament then could indicate either that it would reject the Council's common position (by an absolute majority of members) or propose amendments. The Council could then adopt these amendments by QMV, and if the Commission accepted them, the proposal was adopted. If the Commission did not endorse the amendments, the Council had to accept them unanimously and then pass the proposal by QMV. If the Council could not generate unanimity for the amended act, it then could convene a conciliation committee composed of an equal number of Council members and parliamentarians. The conciliation committee then had to reach agreement on a joint text within six weeks. Council and Parliament then got six weeks more to adopt the new text. If one or the other refused, the text was rejected. If the conciliation committee could not agree on a joint text, the Council could return to its original common position and vote on it, possibly including some of Parliament's amendments, by QMV. Parliament then had six final weeks to review the proposal, which, if rejected by an absolute majority, finally died.

Parliament also has the formal prerogative of consent on a series of different basic decisions: applications from prospective new members, important international treaties, matters concerning European citizens' rights to reside and travel in the EU, and changes to the statutes of the EMU system of European central banks. It must also pass the Commission's multiyear programs on regional development aid and research and development. It must be consulted on basic choices in the CFSP and is informed about Pillar 3 on internal and judiciary policies. Maastricht also gave the Parliament power to constitute temporary committees of inquiry, receive petitions, and name an ombudsman (which it had an exceedingly difficult time doing). In addition, the Rome Treaty granted Parliament the right to bring the Commission and Council to the European Court of Justice (ECJ) if they did not act in areas where the treaty enjoined them to do so. At a later point, it also acquired the right to go to court over infringement of its own powers by Council actions. The Parliament has significant budgetary powers. Finally, Maastricht created new ways of enhancing Parliament's oversight of the Commission, in particular its prerogative of approving the appointment of a new Commission and being consulted about new Commission presidents. Extending the Commission's term from four to five years to coincide with the parliamentary term was yet another Maastricht effort to make the Commission more responsive to Parliament.

However much the Maastricht negotiators had hoped to confront the democratic deficit, the new powers they gave to Parliament, particularly in codecision, were structured in such complicated ways that they remained opaque to outsiders, in particular to ordinary citizens. The Parliament could scrutinize, report, investigate,

and evaluate. But the diverse paths that it had to follow were difficult even for an expert to follow. Depending on who was counting, there were as many as *twenty-two* different ways for the Parliament to decide. Parliament therefore became better equipped to scrutinize the actions of other EU institutions, but at the cost of its ability to communicate complicated matters to European citizens.

The Amsterdam Treaty worked to simplify the Parliament's roles. The largest post-Maastricht problem was the variation in Council decision making correlating with varying parliamentary procedures. Where Council required unanimity, the cooperation procedure continues. Amsterdam extended the scope of QMV and firmed up the correlation between QMV and codecision, which became, in the Commission's words, "the general rule."[25] The major remaining exception is agriculture, where the Council need only consult Parliament (presumably because the CAP cuts close to member governments' electoral concerns). The cooperation procedure persists only for specific matters concerning EMU. The Commission's "general rule" conclusion was overoptimistic, however, because Maastricht had made key issues of CFSP and "justice and home affairs" intergovernmental, hence largely outside the Parliament's scope. Finally, as Figure 3.2 indicates, Amsterdam also simplified the codecision procedure, removing the byzantine third reading that Maastricht had created. Thus, if Council and Parliament are unable to reach a compromise in a conciliation committee, the proposal in question is rejected. This procedural change represents a significant shift in influence, as the Council is now under much more pressure to strike deals with the Parliament.

The most striking aspect of the European Parliament's history is its steady acquisition of power, in large part because of the chronic problems of legitimacy that European integration has created. Applying rough-and-ready standards of democratic responsibility and participation, decisions of major import to the lives of EU

First Reading (same as cooperation)

1. Commission proposes initially.
2. Parliament gives its initial opinion.
3. Council prepares its common position.

Second Reading

4a. Parliament approves. The measure passes.

4b. Parliament proposes amendments to common position or makes statement of intent to reject (three months' time limit + one month extension).

4c. Conciliation committee (half from Council, half from Parliament) convened to seek agreed-on joint test (six weeks).

5a. The measure passes if joint text agreed.

or

5b. If Council reverts to common position and Parliament votes it down by absolute majority within six weeks, the measure fails.

or

5c. Passage if Parliament fails to vote or fails to vote it down within six weeks.

Figure 3.2   Overview of the Codecision Procedure

member state citizens could not legitimately be made through multilateral diplomatic negotiations and an unelected Commission. The transformation of an appointed European Assembly without real power into today's codecider was a logical way to confront this dilemma. European national democracies are parliamentary democracies, and it was logical to approach the democratic deficit issue by progressively endowing a European Parliament with real power. The process has been prodded forward energetically by the Parliament itself, which has been more effective as a lobbyist for its own position than as a parliamentary body. There is no reason to assume that this dynamic will not continue. Council QMV correlated with codecision has been extended considerably, but there are still significant matters to which these procedures do not apply. Because many of these matters were

placed outside the Community pillar at Maastricht, in pressuring for new powers the Parliament will be pressuring for bringing them into the Community.

So much is almost inevitable. In the medium term, however, growing parliamentary power and influence are bound to expose the other dimensions of the EU's democratic deficit. The absence of a substantial Euro-level political culture among European citizens (excepting, of course, Europeanized elite groups) is fundamental. The reasons that this absence persists are complex, and it is clear that it is bound to continue as an issue. Notwithstanding, there are some ways in which innovation at the European level could facilitate change. Parliaments traditionally become effective when their deliberations connect with the pursuit of specific platforms. This happens when they deliberate the proposals of governments that have sought specific mandates for their programs. Some form of Euro-level government and opposition structure would give Europarliamentary debate the clarity that it currently lacks. It would also help promote the development of the genuine Euro-level parties and coalitions that would be better armed to bring European issues to European citizens without being obscured by today's mediation through national politics. Such developments are not yet on the agenda, however.

The Parliament did have an epiphany in 1999, however, and presaged an even stronger future. During much of the Santer period, there was parliamentary restlessness about the Commission's sloppy work habits, cronyism, and even corruption. Matters began coming to a head in late December 1998 at a hard-nosed parliamentary plenary session about the discharge (book closing) of the 1996 budget. A successful censure vote might then have happened had the two major party groups agreed on what to do. Instead the Socialist group, afraid of provoking an institutional crisis, backed off. In a gesture of reconciliation, and perhaps relief at getting off the hook, the Commission agreed that an independent committee of experts should investigate the charges that had been made. The Committee's report, issued on March 15, 1999, was a crushing indictment of the Commission.[26] There had been fraud in contracts to outsiders, in part because Commission services were overburdened with new work and unable to keep up. Several commissioners had put family members on the payroll. One, Edith Cresson of France, was even keeping her dentist, a "longstanding friend," on expensive retainer as a "scientific expert."[27] The experts documented many instances of Commission work done with blithe disregard for propriety—often, as with nuclear cleanup projects in the countries of Central and Eastern Europe (CEECs) out of haste created by pressure rather than venality. In general, as the report noted, "It is becoming difficult to find anyone [in the Commission] who has even the slightest sense of responsibility."[28] With this report in hand and with Commission president Santer unable to remove Cresson from the Commission because the French would not allow it, the Parliament looked set to pass a censure vote. Instead, the Commission resigned as a bloc.[29]

Commentators made much of this series of events, seeing in them a real advance for democratic accountability in the European political system. The Parliament had every reason to feel further empowered by what happened. Indirectly the crisis pushed the Commission to undertake a number of major internal reforms that it had been postponing for years, not least because of internal resistance. DGs were reorganized and renamed, the national flagging of key jobs was attenuated, career paths were made more transparent, and a number of other important changes were made with the Romano Prodi presidency, under the leadership of Neal Kinnock, one of the British commissioners. How much the Parliament will be stimulated to strengthen its roles and whether the Commission will reform itself sufficiently remain to be seen.

European Court of Justice

Europeans are a people of the law, and European integration is ultimately a legal construct. Today, European law is superior to and supersedes member state law. Recognition of this hierarchy was not automatic. The European Court of Justice, born in the European Coal and Steel Community Treaty, had a mission to establish the primacy of European Community law and has been the major institutional actor in its recognition. If treaties and legislation have provided a skeleton for the EU's de facto constitution, the case rulings of the ECJ have provided its sinews and ligaments. The court's role in recent times has been of such importance that there has been hue and cry about "judge-made law" and excessive judicial activism.[30] (See Table 3.5.)

The ECJ sits in Luxembourg and is composed of fifteen justices and nine advocates-general. Each judge is named for a six-year term by member state governments, with half the Court renewed every three years. The justices elect their president for a three-year term. Advocates-general review cases to provide legal opinion to the judges but do not rule on fundamental legal matters. The court can sit in plenary sessions when it wishes, but must do so when dealing with matters brought by a Community institution or member state. Otherwise, it subdivides its work among six chambers (of three and five judges each), with the possibility of anyone sending matters to the full court. The decisions are binding on member states and their citizens. The huge workload of the court led to the establishment of a Tribunal of First Instance (comprising fifteen judges) by the SEA, primarily to decide complex matters of fact in litigation brought by individuals and companies. Decisions concerning questions of law (and not of fact) can be appealed from this court to the full ECJ. (See Figure 3.3.)

Recourse to the ECJ occurs in many ways. The most significant route has been via the preliminary ruling procedure. A national court pre-

Table 3.5   Some Significant Decisions of the ECJ

Decision	Importance
Costa v. ENE, 1964	Central in establishing the supremacy of EU law itself.
Van Duyn v. Home Office, 1974	Gave individuals the same right to take employment in another member state as nationals of that state, a landmark ruling about the free movement of people.
Defrenne v Sabena, 1976	Based on Article 119 of the Rome Treaty, which enjoined equal treatment between men and women in employment, the case opened up the EU to a wide range of social policy initiatives and further rulings with major consequences in attenuating gender discrimination in EU labor markets.
Vereniging Bond van Adverteerders v. Netherlands State, 1988	Obliged member states to open up national telecommunications services to competition, an important step in the liberalization of service provision.
Cassis de Dijon, 1979	Perhaps the most famous of the recent cases, it decreed that member states must base their acceptance of EU goods from other member states on the principle of "mutual recognition," thus assuming that all member states have reasonable product standards. This ruling, which allowed the EU to avoid unending negotiations to harmonize product standards, was of huge significance to the single market program.

sented with a case about the legality of European law forwards the case for preliminary ruling to the ECJ; with ECJ advice, the national court then settles the case in question. National courts may also ask the ECJ outright whether a specific national statute conforms to EU law.[31] Anyone, whether a European institution, government, or individual, can ask the court to rule on the legality of European legislation and other measures within a two-month time limit in so-called annulment proceedings. Next, the Commission or a member state can ask the ECJ to decide if a member state has failed to fulfill its EU legal obligations. Member states, other EU institutions, or individuals may also bring cases against a particular institution for failure to act when it ought to have under EU treaties. Cases for damages against Community institutions may be considered as well. Member states and EU institutions may also ask for rulings on the compatibility of international agreements with EU law. Recourse to the ECJ, which has handed down more than three thousand decisions since

the days of the ECSC, has increased with the growing salience of European integration for member states and individuals. The court's rulings have also become central in the evolution of European integration, often serving as policy and political switchpoints.

In another effort to give Europeans a sense that there was more to European integration than economics, Maastricht introduced "European citizenship" into Community law (Article 8).[32] All citizens of member states became citizens of the EU with the right to move about and live in any member state (subject to exceptions, mainly concerning work). EU citizens living outside their own country can vote and be elected in municipal elections in their country of residence and in elections to the European Parliament. Every EU citizen is entitled to full diplomatic protection from any member state embassy and consulate. EU citizens also acquired rights to petition the European Parliament and a new ombudsman/mediator. These clauses on European citizenship clearly bore the

**Governments of the member states appoint
fifteen judges and six advocates-general by common accord for six-year terms**

COURT OF JUSTICE
Full Court: Fifteen judges
Two chambers with five judges, four chambers with three

TYPES OF PROCEEDING

Actions for failure to fulfill obligations under treaties (Commission or member state v. member state)	Actions for annulment (against Council or Commission)	References from national courts for preliminary rulings to clarify the meaning and scope of Community law
	Actions on grounds of failure to act (against Council or Commission)	Opinions
	Claims for damages against the Community	

COURT OF FIRST INSTANCE
Twelve judges

Direct action by natural and
legal persons (except anti-
dumping cases), staff cases,
ECSC actions

Figure 3.3   European Court of Justice

potential for considerable elaboration and expansion as precedents for new legislation and future litigation.

New Institutions with Open Futures

By far the most important product of the Maastricht Treaty was Economic and Monetary Union (EMU), which, although officially part of the Maastricht community pillar, is independent of the "Community" method. The key EMU institution is the new European Central Bank (ECB), sitting atop a system of European central banks. Its central task is to manage the euro, the new single European currency. EMU has a strange status. The ECB has complete autonomy in the monetary sphere, as befits the desires of member states for an independent central banking system. The president of the Council and one Commission member participate, without a vote, on the bank's governing board. National finance ministers and the Council have limited prerogatives otherwise.

The new bank makes key decisions about monetary and, indirectly, economic policy. Here lies one of the key ironies of Maastricht. Behind initial French proposals for EMU, one goal was to gain more control over the Bundesbank and German economic policy, which had come to govern European monetary policy. The EMU set out at Maastricht, in contrast, looked like the German system writ large, devoted exclusively to the pursuit of price stability, as the severe convergence criteria to prepare membership in the 1990s demonstrated. More generally, monetary policy, central in the general economic policies of all EU countries, is made by unelected central bankers. Whether the EMU system proves effective or not, its independence provides significant issues for democratic accountability.

The institutional complexes of the second and third Maastricht pillars are both intergovernmental, involving state-to-state negotiations. They are thus built on different foundations from the Community pillar. Their very recent establishment means that they are in flux and consequently difficult to define. The second pillar, encompassing the CFSP, grew out of a notion, unequally shared among EU members, that the time was ripe to transform the existing system of European Political Cooperation (EPC) on foreign policy matters into a confederal foreign and defense policy. EPC was a long-standing system of information sharing and exchanging views (including a network for sending diplomatic ciphers, COREU) which aimed at foreign policy coordination without infringing on member states' national autonomy.[33] The products of EPC were usually solemn declarations about world problems. The idea of CFSP was to expand EPC into arrangements that would bind member states in foreign policy and, in the last analysis, the defense area as well. The Maastricht agreements (in Title V) were, however, vague and unwieldy. CFSP was EPC plus a new possibility of joint action.[34] The key change was the introduction of procedures to operationalize joint actions, the pooling of sovereignty for specified foreign policy purposes.

The procedures in the new treaty were so complicated that if obliged to follow them to the letter, the EU would have rarely been able to agree on principles, and then only on relatively harmless issues. Even with agreement about the desirability of joint action on something significant, these procedures were so daunting that the EU would be too late to do much. The CFSP was thus more of a declaration of intent that the EU would eventually enter into the foreign policy area than it was an immediately practical set of policies.*

The foreign policy record of the EU since Maastricht has been marked by failure to act effectively, with Yugoslavia the major, and most damaging, case (although there have been others—Rwanda, for example). Even before Maastricht, major EU members were divided about the dissolution of the Yugoslav Federation. The Germans wanted rapid recognition of new republics, the French wanted to keep the federation alive, and the British wanted to do nothing that might encourage common EU foreign policy, even though they were willing to collaborate bilaterally with others. As the crisis emerged, national preferences varied, and the EU, as an actor, was sidelined and powerless. The Germans eventually got their way in early 1992, leading everyone to recognize Croatia and Slovenia, a gesture that widened warfare to Bosnia. In the meantime, weak EU efforts to promote negotiations between the conflicting parties were quickly integrated into battle plans as tactics to gain momentary advantage. Europe was unable to mount the effort needed to intimidate and persuade the belligerents to talk seriously. Only when NATO could be mobilized, as the United States became more concerned, was some progress possible. Because Maastricht's CFSP agenda had been to establish a European foreign and defense policy independent of the United States, the story was a bitter defeat, although not as bitter as events were for the peoples of the former Yugoslavia.

Maastricht's vision of common European defense removed an important taboo, but until very recently the consequences have been small. The French had long wanted to make the Western European Union (WEU) into the arm of the EU, but faced strong disagreement about WEU relationships to NATO. Should it be a subordinate European pillar of NATO, coequal with the United States, or should it be quasi-independent? There were also issues about who might

---

*The EU has observed elections in Russia and South Africa, engaged in some regulation of goods that can be used both for civilian and military purposes plus antipersonnel mines, and sent out a few humanitarian and other aid packages to the former Yugoslavia and Palestine.

belong. Article 5 of the WEU Treaty was a mutual aid clause—an attack against one member would thus be considered an attack against all. This raised issues about the several neutral EU member states. Some of these matters were confronted, but very slowly. The practical and architectural problems in the way of any common EU defense loomed very large until the end of the 1990s.

The third pillar, on justice and home affairs, less declaratory than the CFSP, is still somewhat inchoate. It was premised on commitment to the free circulation of individuals within the single European market and the concomitant issue of external border controls. There were precedents prior to Maastricht in the 1985 Schengen declaration by France, Germany, and the Benelux countries governing free circulation of people (the removal of internal border controls). Schengen was a model adopted by the most committed countries that others would follow when they were ready. Most, excepting Denmark, the United Kingdom, and Ireland, ultimately signed the agreement, and Schengen was formalized as a legal convention in 1990 and brought into the Treaty at Amsterdam.[35] Some transnational cooperation among police forces also preceded Maastricht through the so-called Trevi group. Title VI of Maastricht sought to formalize these matters, opening new paths to much greater cooperation and specifying questions of common interest, including asylum policy, rules for external border controls, immigration, the fight against drugs, policies against international fraud, and judicial, police, and customs cooperation. The treaty pointed toward a considerable transnational centralization of information and action. Because matters such as internal security and crime control are fundamentally national, Pillar 3 is intergovernmental.

Progress on Pillar 3 was halting until the Amsterdam Treaty, however, when the Schengen Accord (the legal corpus accumulated since the Schengen agreement) was finally inserted into the treaties. Schengen's apparatus, including information-circulating techniques and agreements about transnational surveillance and police pursuit, has been difficult to put into place. Some EU members have doubted others' reliability in upholding deals, in particular because of the growing political salience of issues concerning immigration. By 1996 the free circulation of individuals inside the single market had begun in only seven of fifteen member states. Difficult discussions went on about immigration policy and on a common (more restrictive) asylum policy. The establishment of Europol, an organization to centralize police information and exchanges, proposed by the Germans, stalled in disagreements among member states.

EMU, CFSP, and European defense are all very contemporary matters. In some cases they are changing rapidly in form and content and are better considered works in progress than fixed institutions. Chapter 5 will focus on the key evolutionary processes for the EU in the first years of the new millennium and will return to these works in progress in their unfolding, and sometimes quite surprising, detail.*

---

*There are other European institutions of lesser importance. For example, a Court of Auditors scrutinizes financial operations, reviews EU accounts, and evaluates financial and budgetary management. There is also an Economic and Social Committee (ECOSOC), which must be consulted by the Commission and Council on economic and social issues (although the ECOSOC's opinions have no binding effect). ECOSOC, composed of appointed delegates from national labor movements, employers, professionals, and consumer organizations (which meets ten times a year in plenary and more often in specialized subgroups), is an essential sounding board for EU institutions concerning the likely reception of new policies by organized interests. Finally, Maastricht established a new Committee of Regions along the ECOSOC model. Its purposes are similar, directed toward regionalizing consciousness of the EU and creating more direct linkages between regional actors and EU institutions.

Notes

1. At one point the Commission thought that it would move into a building occupied by the Belgian secret service. At least for symbolic reasons, this plan was not a good idea, and the Commission was fortunate that it did not work out.

2. Each member of the European Parliament (MEP) thus had offices, faxes, and computers in two different places, between which he or she had to travel several times a month. Brussels was the place where committees and party groups met. Strasbourg was where the Parliament met in plenary session. A fleet of trucks transported parliamentary files and other materials from Brussels to Strasbourg and back each month. There were several flights a day on the same route, transporting the people concerned— MEPs, commissioners, lobbyists, journalists and others—chock-a-block full for the one week a month when the Parliament was in Strasbourg but largely empty the rest of the time.

3. It did this for the new Santer Commission in 1995. In these hearings, the Parliament made critical comments on the qualifications of several new commissioners to do the particular jobs for which they had been tentatively designated. The Commission's general composition was not changed, but some changes occurred in the attribution of tasks to specific commissioners

4. The Amsterdam Treaty introduced a new clause (Article 163 EEC) that "the Commission shall work under the political guidance of the President," but it is too soon to know what difference this has made.

5. Cabinet representatives of different commissioners meet as policy proposals take on form on their way to the Commission meeting. First a "sous-chef" group involving commissioners hammers out the largest possible degree of consensus. If a text passes muster at this level, it then goes to the weekly "chefs' cab" meeting, usually on Mondays, where cabinet heads discuss the text further, again to achieve as much consensus as possible. When full agreement is reached at "chefs' cab," the text goes into the Commission agenda as an item needing no further substantive discussion. The full Commission meetings thus discuss only the texts and points that remain in dispute. The organizational backbone of this process is the cabinet of the Commission president, which presides over all of these many meetings

6. The 1991 figures come from Fabrice Fries, *Les Grands débats européens* (Paris: Editions du Seuil, 1995). The 1998 estimate is from John Peterson and Elizabeth Bomberg, *Decision-Making in the European Union* (New York: St. Martin's Press, 1999), p. 38.

7. The new "subsidiarity" clause was vague and general. There were attempts to make the concept more precise in 1992–1993, particularly at the Edinburgh European Council in 1992. The Commission had to prepare a complicated paper to define subsidiarity, and numerous threats were uttered about the Commission's meddling in certain areas (particularly social and environmental policies), but very little concrete was done. The consequence, however, was significant intimidation of the Commission, which from that point was exceedingly careful when it acted.

8. Many observers of European integration have been arguing for some time that the Commission's future lies in embracing its substantial regulatory state roles rather than seeking to restore front-ranking agenda setting and political roles.

9. The numerous inequities in this system of weighting should be obvious. For example, each German citizen is undervalued compared to everyone else in the EU. Each citizen of Luxembourg, on the other hand, is worth considerably more than any other EU citizen. For these and other reasons, the need to reweigh relative voting power QMV is one of the thorniest institutional issues presented by the prospect of enlargement to the countries of Central and Eastern Europe. Fiona Hayes-Renshaw and Helen Wallace, *The Council of Ministers* (New York: St. Martin's Press, 1997) is the best source on everything pertaining to the Council.

10. *Financial Times*, March 11–12, 1995

11. There are two COREPERs. The second is where the ambassadors work on higher political matters, with the first where their deputies work out more technical issues.

12. Hayes-Renshew and Wallace, *Council of Ministers*, p. 98. I have drawn heavily on their Chapter 3.

13. There is also a Special Agriculture Committee, which, an exception proving the rule, is not in the COREPER orbit.

14. For example, there are biannual official Franco-German summits and many more informal meetings to coordinate strategy and action. The French and British and Germans and British have similar arrangements. How much of the EU's basic movement is designed in such ways is unknowable, but it is certainly large.

15. On the Council presidency, see Emil Kirchner, *Decision-Making in the European Community: The Council Presidency and European Integration* (New York: St. Martin's Press, 1992). Also See Guy de Bassompierre, *Changing the Guard in Brussels: An Insider's View of the EC Presidency* (New York: Praeger, 1988).

16. At present there are twelve official languages: Spanish, Danish, German, Greek, English, French, Irish Gaelic (which, although official, is not a working language), Italian, Dutch, Portuguese, Finnish, and Swedish.

17. The presidency conclusions for the most recent European Councils are available at http://www.Europa.eu.int.

18. The best book on the Parliament is Martin Westlake, *A Modern Guide to the European Parliament* (London: Pinter, 1994). See also Francis Jacobs, Richard Corbett, and Michael Shackelton, *The European Parliament*, 4th ed. (London: John Harper, 2000).

19. The treaty specified that the mode of election should be uniform across the Community, but uniformity has not quite been achieved. Everyone except the British, who stick with their traditional first-past-the-post single-member-constituency system, uses some form of proportional representation.

20. The other, much smaller, groups include, in order of strength, the Liberals, Greens, European Democratic Alliance, European Right, Left Unity (Communists), and Rainbow Group. There are also a few unaffiliated members.

21. This is the consensus of different studies of the 1994 polls. See Cees van der Eijk and Mark N. Franklin, eds., *Choosing Europe* (Ann Arbor: University of Michigan Press, 1996), and Juliet Lodge, ed., *The 1994 Elections to the European Parliament* (London: Pinter, 1996).

22. To take only the French, overrepresented in this category, former president Giscard d'Estaing has made an important new career in European affairs after his defeat for reelection in 1981, and former prime minister Rocard has more recently taken Europarliamentary affairs to heart. Before he became Commission president, Jacques Delors also learned a great deal about Europe and European monetary affairs as an MEP after 1989.

23. For a revealing ethnographic view of the Parliament, see Marc Abelès, "Political Anthropology of a Transnational Institution: The European Parliament," in *French Politics and Society* 111 (1995): 1.

24. See Shirley Williams, "Sovereignty and Accountability in the European Community," in Robert Keohane and Stanley Hoffmann, *The New European Community* (Boulder, Colo.: Westview, 1991).

25. European Commission, *The Amsterdam Treaty: A Comprehensive Guide* (Luxembourg: EU, 1999), p. 59.

26. For the report, see http:/www.europarl.eu.int/experts/en/2.htm.

27. Ibid., sec., 8, "Allegations of Favouritism," p. 1.

28. Cited in Desmond Dinan, "Governance and Institutions 1999: Resignation, Reform and Renewal," in Geoffrey Edwards and Georg Wiessala, eds., *The European Union: Annual Review of the EU 1999/2000* (Oxford: Blackwell, 2000), p. 7, sec. 9 of Experts Report.

29. The outgoing Commission then assumed caretaker status until a successor was appointed in the autumn of 1999. Jacques Santer, ironically, found a new job for himself after the June 1999 elections to the European Parliament when he was elected an MEP from Luxembourg.

30. Perhaps the most eloquent presentation of this position is Hjalte Rasmussen, *On Law and Policy in the European Community* (Dordrecht: Martinus Nijhoff, 1986).

31. Desmond Dinan, *Ever Closer Union* (Boulder, Colo.: Lynne Rienner, 1999). chap. 10.

32. It is interesting to note that the original treaties dealt mainly with Europeans as "workers," that is, marketized individuals. It was the ECJ that over the years has progressively expanded this notion to incorporate broader dimensions of citizenship, laying the groundwork for the insertion of citizenship into the treaty.

33. Political cooperation occurred at four different levels: European Council meetings, meetings of foreign ministers wearing their EPC hats (as opposed to their Council of Ministers caps—a venue that often caused the same people to change the name of the conversations they were carrying on), regular meetings of the political committee, which included the political directors of foreign ministers plus the Commission political director, plus various working group meetings. EPC is presided over by the Council presidency.

34. For a condensed summary, see European Commission, *European Union* (Luxembourg: EC, 1992).

35. The British absence from the Schengen list should not be taken as yet another example of British Euroskepticism. The United Kingdom has a different internal system of keeping track of people than continental Europe. In British law, individuals cannot be stopped randomly for identity checks, and the United Kingdom has no national identity cards. Control over presence in the United Kingdom must therefore be carried out at the borders.

C H A P T E R

4

The EU
and Its Policies

The making of policy in any political system is a complicated matter. Policy making in the EU is even more dense and difficult to understand than in national contexts. On any issue there are myriad linkages within, between, and external to European institutions. Inside these institutions are multiple and overlapping political, professional, national, and friendship networks, together with policy communities on any problem. Policymakers have to observe hierarchies, take short-cuts, follow routines, and be creative to make things happen. Furthermore, as the story of Europe shows, the relative power and resources of the different European institutions change as policy develops. In these ways Europolitics and Europolicymaking resemble those of any mature political system, but they are even more opaque because the EU is not a sovereign state.[1] In the policymaking realm in general, the EU involves interactions between an institutionally unique Commission, multilateral negotiations between national governments, and the activities of a parliament that does not act at all like national parliaments. The policymaking stories that follow illustrate the EU's policymaking uniqueness.

The Single Market

The program for completing the single market exemplifies the core of European policymaking. European integration first thrived around the common market, a customs-free zone surrounded by a common tariff toward the external world. Structuring a common market in agriculture involved particular problems—hence, the Common Agricultural Policy (CAP). There were also flanking policies to help the common market function. The common market was clearly meant as but the first stage of something much broader, but the success of national postwar settlements and the effects of economic change in the 1970s choked off prospects and ambitious plans of the early 1970s. Economic and Monetary Union (EMU), regional redistribution, and greater EU involvement in social policy were shelved. Worse still, economic problems and policy divergence quickly led member states to limit cross-border trade, despite the customs-free zone. The achievements of the 1960s were therefore threatened. It was the single market program that revived and may have saved, European integration.

The Commission's White Paper, *Completing the Internal Market*—the "1992" program—demonstrated Commission agenda setting at its most astute. Its 282 proposed measures (which had become nearly 1,406 by 2000) implied new economic objectives, extensive new economic integration, and ultimately greater political integration. The program was meant to create a completely open market around "four freedoms" of movement in goods, services, capital, and people. The general logic emphasized deregulation and market building. The 1992 program would give firms greater economic space to innovate, grow, prosper, develop the capacities to win on a global scale, and transform earlier national economic outlooks to a new European perspective. The single market involved relocating some sovereignty to the market itself, away from the member states accustomed to deciding many market regulations in political ways. The new policy also created openings for "re-regulation" on a European level, since the single market needed new flanking activities. The Commission therefore sought new competition and environmental, regional, commercial, research and development, and other policy competencies. The Commission also aimed to enhance its own powers within the Europolitical system. Table 4.1 describes the major axes of the 1992 program.

The Single European Act (SEA) established qualified majority voting (QMV) for single market matters and empowered the EU in new regulatory areas.[2] Market building implied state building, hence provisions in the SEA to promote economic integration in environmental, regional, and other policy areas. The Commission saw the 1992 program as endowing Europe with the space for economic renewal and opening up new prospects for European political integration. Success in implementing each set of proposals, the Commission hoped, would create a new context where member states would need to agree to further new proposals to confront the unforeseen implications of their initial agreements. If the process went well, a rolling movement of Europeanization would occur.

The most strenuous period of activity in the history of European integration followed. Each significant change necessitated legislation, and EU legislative output during the 1985–1992 period was vast, easily comparable to that of any member state, although it slowed considerably thereafter. All this legislation had to be drafted by the Commission, which could use some ideas from earlier years that were in its files and the all-important new approach to standard setting

facilitated by the ECJ's *Cassis de Dijon* ruling, which allowed mutual recognition and avoided endless multilateral bargaining. Still, to produce the single market proposals, the Commission strained its internal and political resources to the limit and so may have paid a large price. The leadership had a clear choice between using the Commission's existing creaking and groaning organization or reforming its operations, but it judged the tasks at hand too pressing to take time for reform, and thus laid the groundwork for difficulties that arose later in the 1990s.

Planning was itself immense. The program had to be scheduled over eight years with clear year-by-year priorities coordinated with the Council of Ministers and Parliament. Once scheduling was clear, commissioners and their administrations had to draft materials, involving political strategizing plus wide consultation with interests, committees, national-level administrations, along with COREPER (a French acronym for Committee of Permanent Representatives) and other Council bodies. Prepared texts then had to be submitted officially to the Council and Parliament (which might offer amendments), then negotiated through with both until a result was achieved. The work was not finished at this point either. Member states were obligated to transpose the new measures into their national law, and these processes had to be monitored and policed, through the European Court of Justice (ECJ) if necessary.

Inside the Commission, proposals involving many different Directorates-General (DGs) necessitated incessant meetings, task forces, and legal advice from the Commission's legal services (which examined everything to ensure that proposals were in line with treaty stipulations) coordinated by commissioners' personal staffs and commissioners themselves. In the first stages of drafting, tough and energetic oversight came from the cabinet of Commission president Jacques Delors. The resultant proposals then filtered upward through Commission processes until the Commission was satisfied with their quality, before official submission to

Table 4.1   Synopsis of 1992 White Paper Provisions

Measures to Regulate	Markets for			
	Products	*Services*	*Persons/ Labor*	*Capital*
Market access	Abolition of internal border controls Approximation of technical regulations, value-added tax, and excise taxes	Mutual recognition, end licensing restrictions in banking and insurance, transport deregulation (air and road)	End of border controls on persons Relaxation of residence requirements for EU citizens Right of establishment for professionals	Abolition of exchange controls Securities issued in one country admitted in another Facilitate industrial cooperation and migration of firms
Competition	Paper on state aids to industry Liberalize public procurement Merger control	New competition policy for air transport Approximation of fiscal and regulatory practices	European "vocational training" card	Proposals on takeovers and holdings Approximation of double taxation, security taxes, parent-subsidiary links
Market functioning	Proposals on research and development in telecoms and information technology, standards, trademarks, corporate law, and the like	Approximation of regulation in banking, consumer protection in insurance, EU permits for road haulage EU standard for bank cards	Approximation of income tax provisions for migrants, training provisions Mutual recognition of diplomas	European economic interest grouping European company statute Harmonization of property laws Common bankruptcy provisions
Sectoral policy	CAP changes Reduce subsidies in steel	Common crisis regime in road transport, air transport policies, rules on mass risks insurance	Silence on labor market	Strengthen European Monetary System

Source: Adapted from Table 4.2 in Helen Wallace and William Wallace, *Policymaking in the European Union*, 4th ed. (New York: Oxford University Press, 2000), pp. 95–96.

Council and Parliament. This filtering was a complicated process in which each commissioner's cabinet had to review every piece of each proposal and take a position. During the long period in which the Commission generated new measures, it also made extensive efforts to drum up support. Were it possible to total the number of meetings and translation and textual changes needed for all this, the figure would be huge.

One of the more daunting tasks was harmonizing technical standards and norms. For manufactured goods, the White Paper proposed mutual recognition and a new approach in which the only legislation involved minimal standards for workplace health and safety, moving Europe into the area of labor standards and social policy. This included writing framework directives, like the 1989 Machinery Directive, which specified security minima for all kinds of machinery.

Toys, boilers, machines using gas, elevators, pleasure boats, and construction products were among the products regulated. The White Paper also necessitated directives promoting compatibility of different utility and transport systems. Beyond minimum standards, it was also necessary to promote the voluntary creation of European norms and standards for products, a task contracted out to semipublic European standards organizations.

Deregulation and then reregulation for items as common as food and agricultural products was a huge job that involved harmonizing public health standards and specifying additives and materials in contact with food processing, labeling, food hygiene, and the like. This area proved particularly controversial, leading to constant rumors about the Brussels bureaucracy's desire to regulate ancient local tastes out of existence. The Danes were thus forbidden from using an additive that allowed them to color imitation Greek feta cheese. The French went into a mild uproar about regulations on natural camembert cheese. The British press had a field day when an administrative mistake about additives threatened to forbid the production of flavored potato chips. The Germans, who defined product standards for beer in ways that prohibited foreign beers that had not been brewed to German standards from being called beer, had to be taken to the ECJ. Controversies over the height of tractor seats and pollution standards for cars were fierce. Although member states had approved all these programs, the Commission repeatedly found itself with serious public relations problems.

The free movement of services presented its own difficulties, beginning with technical definitions of what services actually are (a problem that trade negotiators for the General Agreement on Tariffs and Trade were also beginning to face). Limits on market liberation protected against "races to the bottom" by providers seeking to lower costs by lowering levels of regulation. Public services and the provision of public goods of one sort or another (utilities,

certain transportation networks) were also allowed some sheltering from market mechanisms, although the extent of such sheltering became, and remains, a difficult issue. The 1992 program led to deregulation in financial services (e.g., harmonizing banking laws, mutual recognition of other standards), insurance, telecommunications, international transport, and audiovisual transmission. Creating free movement of capital was another central matter, leading to directives on stock and bond trading, commercial loans, and stock exchanges, which eventually led to lifting all limits on capital movement. The free movement of people has been the most difficult area, partly because of intergovernmental problems in working with police and the judiciary. Even so, the rights of EU citizens to work and live in member states other than their own were established, along with different procedures for recognizing the equivalencies of professional certifications.

The Commission's energetic production of legislation created backlash. The Commission was indeed sometimes heavy-handed, and member states took to accusing it of meddling and bureaucratic imperialism. This indignation, plus the desires of some countries to slow European integration, provided reasons to include the subsidiarity clause in the Maastricht Treaty.[3] The discussion also had its consequences for the Commission's behavior. The last two years of the Delors Commission presidency were marked by much greater Commission self-restraint. And when the time came to appoint Delors's successor, there was major conflict among member states. The French–German candidate was the Belgian prime minister, Jean-Luc Dehaene, but he was vetoed by the British, who wanted a much less activist president. Jacques Santer was the compromise result.

The program was not fully in place by the end of 1992, leaving a number of tasks for the remainder of the 1990s. Several of these remain. Forward movement on food, veterinary and phytosanitary standards, intellectual and industrial property, and corporate taxation was slow.

Creating single markets in utilities, which had been state monopolies, was even slower. Telecommunications deregulation took off only in the second half of the 1990s. Electricity deregulation is just now beginning. Open markets in many public procurement areas remain far away. The important proposal on European company law that would allow European-level incorporation remained in contention until the Nice Summit in 2000. Transposition of some matters already legislated is also incomplete. Enough was done, however, so that four years after 1992, the Commission could calculate that the single market had created hundreds of thousands of jobs, raised investment levels, and created an annual 1 percent increase in income across the EU.[4]

The EU Budget

One axiom that apprentice political analysts need to know is that, for any political system, budgets reveal matters of fundamental importance. The EU budgetary trends in Tables 4.2 and 4.3 demonstrate this principle.

The most significant insight that these numbers offer is that the EU budget, although it expanded rapidly from the 1980s into the 1990s, is still very small compared to those of its member states.[5] The EU is held to a total expenditure level of less than 1.27 percent of total members' GNP. Average budgets of EU member states are around 40 percent of their own gross domestic product (GDP). This comparison requires caution, to be sure, because EU policies may shape member state expenditure patterns without the EU's spending a great deal. Still, the EU's financial clout is much smaller than those of its member states. In this respect, as in others, the EU is not really a state but not quite a nonstate.

Combined, the CAP and structural fund expenditures compose about 80 percent of EU spending. Redistribution of resources is one, among many, defining characteristics of a state and both of these items are redistributive, although in different ways. The CAP takes revenues from taxpayers (and consumers) and redistributes them to farmers and rural areas, and to a degree across national boundaries. The structural funds promote development by transferring money from wealthier to poorer areas of the EU. Were one to remove these two big-ticket items, the EU budget would be very small indeed. Funding in other areas, including the EU's spending inside and outside its boundaries, is only 20 percent of the total budget.

The EU's budgetary allocations are extremely

Table 4.2   Financial Perspective Through 2000, Delors II Package, 1992 (m. ecu 1993)

	1993	1994	1995	1996	1997	1998	1999
Agriculture	35.23	35.1	35.72	36.36	37.02	37.7	38.4
Structural funds	21.28	21.88	23.48	24.99	26.53	28.24	30.00
Internal policies	3.94	4.08	4.32	4.52	4.71	4.91	5.10
External action	3.95	4.0	4.28	4.56	4.83	5.18	5.60
Administration	3.28	3.38	3.58	3.69	3.80	3.85	3.90
Reserves	1.50	1.50	1.10	1.10	1.10	1.10	1.00
Total	69.77	69.94	72.48	75.22	77.99	80.98	84.09
% gross domestic product	1.20	1.19	1.20	1.21	1.23	1.25	1.26

Source: *Official Journal of European Communities* (93/C 331/01).

Table 4.3   Financial Perspective Through 2006, EU 15: *Agenda 2000* (1999 euro)

	2000	2001	2002	2003	2004	2005	2006
Agriculture	40.9	42.8	43.9	43.8	42.8	41.9	41.7
Structural funds	32.0	31.5	30.9	30.3	29.6	29.6	29.2
Internal policies	5.9	6.0	6.1	6.3	6.4	6.5	6.6
External action	4.6	4.6	4.6	4.6	4.6	4.6	4.6
Administration	4.6	4.6	4.7	4.8	4.9	5.0	5.1
Reserves	0.9	0.9	0.6	0.4	0.4	0.4	0.4
Preaccession aid	3.1	3.1	3.1	3.1	3.1	3.1	3.1
Total	89.6	91.1	94.2	94.9	91.9	90.1	90.7
% gross domestic product	1.13	1.12	1.18	1.19	1.15	1.13	1.13

Source: David Galloway, "Agenda 2000—Packaging the Deal," in Geoffrey Edwards and Georg Wiessala, *The European Union, Annual Review 1998/1999* (Oxford: Blackwell, 1999), Table 1, p. 21.

important when EMU is taken into account. Economic theory suggests that single currencies work best when they exist in relatively homogeneous areas and when there is enough "fiscal federalism" to compensate for likely periodic regional and sectoral shocks. Such shocks are more easily cushioned when financial transfers are available, whether in the form of "automatic stabilizers," like the unemployment compensation that most member states use within their territories, or flexible systems of regional transfer payments. Labor mobility is another important way of cushioning shocks, as the U.S. example suggests. Workers in depressed sectors or regions thus bear some of the cost through migration to areas where employment opportunities are better. In the EU, however, labor is mobile mainly within member states and in specific small transnational regions (the French–Belgian border region, for example, and the French–Swiss–German area around Basel). Language and cultural barriers present nearly insuperable obstacles otherwise. EU member states are thus potentially vulnerable to such shocks, yet because resource transfers to shocked areas remain overwhelmingly national, member states will have to bear the adjustment costs, and most have few ways to allocate these costs. National

wage levels and welfare state programs provide the major remaining sources of economic flexibility in the absence of fiscal federal remedies and national capacities.

Tables 4.2 and 4.3 also show that EU budgetary growth as a percentage of member state GNP, which shot up in the 1980s, had stabilized by the late 1990s. For some time to come, the availability of new money for any purposes is therefore likely to be limited because the costs of carrying out CAP reform in the medium term—that is, shifting to deficiency payments from price supports to fit the international trade situation better—must involve steady-state expenditures to placate agricultural interests. And when new funding becomes available in agriculture, it will undoubtedly be needed to phase the countries of Central and Eastern Europe (CEECs) into EU agricultural policy norms. Similar constraints apply to the structural funds. To find preaccession funding for potential CEEC memberships, it has already been necessary to reconfigure regional development guidelines at considerable pain to some current EU members.

The act of transferring national revenues to other nations in the broader interests of Europe is one of the more interesting modifications of

Table 4.4 Transfers in EU Budgets as a Percentage of Member State GDP

	1980	1984	1988	1994
Belgium	−0.32	−0.41	−0.79	−0.16
Denmark	0.70	0.70	0.38	0.15
Germany	−0.28	−0.39	−0.60	−0.90
Greece	—	2.34	3.30	4.62
Spain	—	—	0.46	0.74
France	0.08	−0.07	−0.22	−0.25
Ireland	5.00	4.01	4.30	3.94
Italy	0.21	−0.29	0.02	−0.58
Luxembourg	−0.15	−0.93	−1.20	2.12
Netherlands	0.32	0.27	0.60	−0.64
Portugal	—	—	1.45	2.55
United Kingdom	−0.35	−0.24	−0.30	−0.18

Note: A negative transfer indicates a net contribution as a percentage of GDP.

Source: Tsoukalis, 2d ed., Table 9.1.

Table 4.5 Member States' Shares in EU Financing and EU-15 Gross National Product (1997 data)

	Share in EU Gross National Product	Share in Financing EU Budget
Austria	2.6	2.8
Belgium	3.1	3.9
Denmark	1.9	2.0
Finland	1.4	1.4
France	17.2	17.5
Germany	26.0	28.2
Greece	1.5	1.6
Ireland	0.8	0.9
Italy	14.2	11.5
Luxembourg	0.2	0.2
Netherlands	4.5	6.4
Portugal	1.2	1.4
Spain	6.6	7.1
Sweden	2.7	3.1
United Kingdom	16.1	11.9

Source: Wallace and Wallace, *Policymaking in the European Union*, Table 8.3, p. 234.

national sovereignty flowing from European integration. Table 4.4 provides a rough index of these transfers in recent years. Modification of sovereignty, however, has always been somewhat precarious. The British were too eager to get in when they negotiated the financial dimensions of their membership in the 1970s, and they ended up paying disproportionately. The issue of the "British check" later became prominent in high-level discussions. Prime Minister Thatcher's strident announcements that "I want my money back" and her willingness to block progress on other issues is a live memory.

Over time, the more prosperous EU member states have become net contributors to the budget, as Tables 4.4 and 4.5 show. One reason that the EU budget stabilized in the late 1990s is that members insisted on clear limits to their willingness to transfer taxpayers' incomes to other member states. Even if countries accept redistribution, the issue of proportionality remains. What is a "fair" contribution, measured against those of others, and what criteria should be used to decide? This matter is complicated, largely because the common policies that redistribute EU revenues affect member states in unexpected ways. The British, for example, have always felt unjustly treated, because the logic of the CAP favors countries with large agricultural establishments (France's, for example), while Britain's agricultural presence is small. Yet the shortfall in U.K. contributions shown in Table 4.5 explains growing impatience on the part of other EU members with the continuing British "rebate" that Mrs. Thatcher negotiated in 1984. The Italians benefit greatly, explaining part of their eager and persistent "Europeanism." The Spanish, despite their relative poverty, feel similarly to the British.

Since the mid-1980s, the budgetary process

has had two steps. The more important is largely intergovernmental, involving a "grand rendezvous" every five years or so to achieve agreement on medium-term programmatic and expenditure patterns. Three times thus far (1987, 1992, and 1998–1999), the Commission has drawn up extended budgetary projections involving significant changes in programmatic goals along with large budgetary increases, while also pledging budgetary discipline to keep within multiyear guidelines. These programs are extremely useful because they prompt middle-range planning for EU activities and, once negotiated, create relative freedom from financial squabbling for EU institutions, the Commission in particular, in the short term. But they have always been difficult moments of truth.

The Commission budget DG drafts the package with the assistance of the president's cabinet and other DGs. This political exercise is characterized by very delicate processes of investigation (really prenegotiations) to see what budgetary changes the member states will bear. Once it makes this determination, it must devise a strategy for funding the activities that it most wants to pursue. To create bargaining room for its preferred options, the Commission typically asks for more money than it can really expect to get. Tough, hard negotiations are thus inevitable. They usually begin with the publication by the Commission of a closely argued paper in favor of its maximum demands. These papers—for example, *Making a Success of the Single Act* (1987), *From the Single Act to Maastricht and Beyond: The Means to Match Our Ambitions* (1992), and *Agenda 2000* (1998)—are invaluable sources about the Commission's most profound goals.[6] Their titles also show the Commission's efforts to tie budgetary deals to changes in the EU treaties.

Leaders of the member states, meeting as the European Council, must then negotiate a final compromise. These moments have always been difficult. At Brussels in 1988, for example, after the Delors I package had failed at Copenhagen,

member states pledged to double regional development funds over five years. They also signed on to a controlled growth of CAP spending, the introduction of a new redistributive revenue stream (tied to GNP), and a new "own resource ceiling," so that by 1992, the EU budget would not exceed 1.2 percent of member states' combined GDPs.[7] The later 1980s were years of economic growth. Even so, the first package passed only because the Germans were willing to finance new expenditures. With the size of the structural funds on the table, struggle between richer and poorer members was particularly sharp. The final product was therefore a huge success for the Commission.[8] At Edinburgh in 1992, the deal on a seven-year financial perspective (covering 1993–1999) involved another near-doubling of regional policy funding, reflecting the power and resolution that the "cohesion" countries (Spain, Portugal, Greece, Ireland—the EU's poor members) had come to have in EU financial struggles. By Edinburgh economic circumstances had changed, however. The Germans faced a huge bill for unification and were unwilling to repeat the generous gesture they had made in 1988. This, combined with recession, the desire on the part of some member states to slow the forward movement of European integration, and public disenchantment with the EU, created a budgetary standstill that persisted throughout the 1990s and beyond. Thus, the Commission did not do as well as it had in 1988 when the final deal was struck. Having asked to raise the budget ceiling to 1.37 percent of GNP, it had to accept 1.27 percent. The British presidency's efforts to cut the Commission's requests back even further were defeated.[9] A similar situation existed at the end of the 1990s, when the *Agenda 2000* budgetary discussions occurred. Enlargement to the CEECs was on the horizon, and because of new transfers associated with this, almost all of the EU-15 would become net contributors, further dampening any remaining enthusiasm for raising the budget.

With revenue growth decided by these grand

rendez-vous debates among member states, the second level is an annual budgetary discussion on expenditures. The European Parliament is an important participant in this second level. It has no control over revenues, but it does have some power over expenditures. The exercise begins when the Commission drafts an annual budget, usually by late May, which goes to the Council and Parliament. The Council examines it (having had considerable input already), and the Parliament officially adopts it by the end of July. The draft budget is divided between compulsory and noncompulsory expenditures, with the Council of Ministers having the final word on compulsory expenditures (defined as those items needed for the EU to meet its internal and external obligations, such as treaty and legislative commitments). The Parliament has the last word on noncompulsory expenditures. The balance between these two expenditure types shifted from 80–20 in the early 1980s to 50–50 by the mid-1990s, making Parliament a prime target for lobbyists.

The Parliament's first reading on the final draft occurs in early autumn. At this point it can ask for modifications to compulsory expenditures and amend proposals for noncompulsory items up to a preestablished maximum rate of increase. The revised draft then goes to the Council of Ministers, which makes its final decisions on compulsory expenditures in November. Parliament's second reading, in December, focuses on noncompulsory expenditures. Once it has reached conclusions, it can accept the entire budget by a majority vote of its members and three-fifths of the votes actually cast. If it rejects the budget, a system of "provisional twelfths" comes on line, with monthly expenditures allowed only to the limit of one-twelfth of the previous year's total.

Parliament's involvement in budgetary matters does not end with a vote on expenditures. When the budgetary year is over, the Commission must submit a financial statement to Parliament, which is then obliged to approve or reject in the discharge procedure. In this, the Parliament's own work is supplemented by a statement from the Council and a very important, and often critical, annual report from the EU's Court of Auditors.* The timing of the discharge procedure is complicated. During the first year after the budgetary year in question, the Commission and the Court of Auditors prepare their reports. Not until the next year, however, or two years after the budgetary exercise to be discharged, do Council and Parliament actually review the auditors' report. The Council then must recommend to Parliament whether to vote discharge. Parliament then debates and votes resolutions. In November of this second year, the Commission usually prepares a new report responding to Parliament's resolutions. This timetable means that a Parliament, whose term is five years, spends its first two years considering the discharge of two budgets implemented before it was elected, and in its entire term it gets to consider only two budgets in which it has been directly involved. The discharge procedure, complicated and technical, is important. It was the discharge debate on the 1996 budget at the end of 1998, for example, that began the processes leading to the momentous resignation of the Santer Commission in 1999.

The Common Agricultural Policy and the Structural Funds

The CAP continues to be a source of legend and publicity (rarely good) about European integration. Put in the Rome Treaty to create a Common Market in agricultural products and modernize a then-backward European agricultural sector (Article 37), the CAP was one of the EU's first difficult projects. Financial administration was the job of the European Agricultural Guarantee and Guidance Fund (EAGGF), adminis-

---

*The Court of Auditors, in place since 1977 and based in Luxembourg, became a "European Institution" at Maastricht, giving it the power to bring cases to the ECJ.

tered by the Commission. The CAP's double price system involved price supports for agricultural products that kept Community prices above those on the world market. The Commission therefore set internal or indicative prices for each agricultural product market and established intervention prices to enable the EAGGF to buy up products for storage and export when prices fell below a certain point.

European agriculture modernized quickly, in part because of the CAP, and by 1968 had become an exporter. Perverse consequences from the double-price system appeared quickly. Farmers were encouraged to produce too much, leading to surpluses stored at additional expense and, when necessary, dumped on the international market. Other major agricultural producers, like the United States and Australia, were displeased. The CAP also created incentives for larger farmers to overuse chemical fertilizers to increase yields, causing pollution. By the later 1960s, these developments were worrisome enough to prompt serious reflection on change, but by then farmers in key member states had created powerful groups to protect their vested interests. The CAP thus persisted, along with its costly absurdities. Pressures to reform the CAP mounted as the policy produced repeated budgetary crises and diplomatic problems.

When monetary turbulence became a concern in the 1970s, the Commission acquired the new task of administering "green money," a hugely complicated operation of compensating farmers for fluctuations in exchange rates. As time went on and tasks multiplied, DG VI (the agricultural affairs DG) became the largest single administrative unit in Brussels. Inside its buildings, specialists counted carrots, standardized measures, administered milk quotas, and sold surplus goods on the world market. They also policed farmers to ensure that they were actually producing what they claimed, for fraud was constantly tempting in such highly regulated markets. They disbursed vast amounts of money, made valiant attempts to account for it, and tried to determine how much more would

be needed for years to come. And as these brave civil servants prepared to propose prices and regulations for specific areas to discuss with Parliament, they were incessantly lobbied by hard-nosed farmers' organizations and agriculture ministers. The whole system was overseen by a COREPER Committee on Agriculture, and each particular product area had its own management committee.

The CAP has been redistributive in many ways, not all felicitous. In simple terms, it shifts income from taxpayers to farmers through the EU budget, with some member states getting more than others. Several poorer countries (Greece, Ireland, and Spain), along with two much wealthier ones (Denmark and France), have been beneficiaries. Danish farmers have received the largest per capita payments. Germany has lost the most, followed by Italy and the United Kingdom. Parallel transfers from consumers to farmers have also occurred through the price-support system of income maintenance, which has kept European prices higher than world prices, although the reforms of the 1990s have lessened this disparity. The price support system, when it has led to the international dumping of agricultural goods, involves transfers from Europeans to others and storage costs, and subsidies to exports had become the CAP's single largest spending category by the 1990s.[10] Additional and obvious transfers occur between urban and rural areas, in two simultaneous directions: toward more inefficient agricultural regions and to very efficient producers, like French wheat farmers, who have hidden politically behind their laggard colleagues.

Negotiations about the CAP became acrimonious soon after its inception, with certain member states, Britain and the Netherlands in particular, rebelling against huge transfers to phantom Italian tobacco growers, Bavarian hop growers with large black Mercedes cars, gigantic French beet sugar conglomerates, and prosperous Danes. From time to time, small changes occurred, particularly beginning in the 1980s.

Quotas on milk production were established and, in 1986, the Delors I package introduced stabilizers to reduce subsidies automatically once dangerously high levels of production were reached. The Delors I package also introduced multiyear projections for the CAP budget. Still, the costs per EU citizen continued to rise into the 1990s.

The most important CAP reform to date began in the early 1990s. The Commission was then in the middle of negotiating the Uruguay Round of the General Agreement on Tariffs and Trade (GATT), and agricultural policy became the major issue in dispute between Europe and the United States. The CAP's price support system and surplus dumping on the world market were the big problems. Because member states had high stakes in freer trade, the protectors of the CAP were isolated. Refusal of major reform could have led to collapse of the most important round of multilateral trade negotiations in history, so the Commission could use threats from GATT partners to corner farmers and their political allies. The Commission proposed reducing guaranteed price levels—a 30 percent drop in grain prices and 15 percent in beef prices in three years—and shifting aid toward land setasides, that is, deficiency payments rather than price supports (more like the U.S. model of subsidies). The battle was noisy, and the French came close to blocking both CAP reform and the Uruguay Round, but in 1992 CAP reform was accepted. Movement since has been further away from price supports toward direct income subsidies for eligible farmers. But because paying farmers off was an important part of the politics of achieving reform, the new approach was not designed to save money. Nonetheless, the 1992 changes have begun undercutting some of the CAP's perverse incentives, helping in international trade and decoupling aid for farmers from agricultural prices.

A more recent concern is to find a way to adapt the CAP to Eastern European agriculture. CEEC applicant countries with large agricultural sectors will probably be granted transition periods before full participation in the CAP, but enlargement eventually raises the prospect of more reform. Moreover, the United States and other important agricultural exporters have not given up attacking the CAP for the problems it causes for international trade. The World Trade Organization's (WTO) new dispute mechanisms, for example, have been clogged with U.S. complaints about the EU's banana regime, creating a spectacle in which the EU has tried to protect special arrangements for "ACP countries" (colonies and former colonies of Africa, the Caribbean, and the Pacific), and overseas territories against accusations by the United States made on behalf of two very large companies (Chiquita and Dole), neither of which actually grows bananas in the United States. Disputes have also arisen about American exports of hormone-fed meat and genetically modified agricultural products, which the EU is reluctant to accept, raising very complicated questions about the management of health risks in agricultural trade. Here, more issues will be discussed before and during the next WTO round, and these discussions may prod further CAP reform and, simultaneously, more trade problems. In the meantime, the EU has been arguing that agricultural subsidies (presumably not trade distorting) are justifiable on environmental grounds. Defenders of the CAP thus now define it as a policy for maintaining rural landscapes and farmers, touted as guardians of ecological balance.

As reforms come and go, making the system even more complex, the number of farmers declines year after year, the average age of farmers rises, and the cost of the CAP never shrinks. Those farmers who remain are very well organized and quite capable of exercising severe political sanctions on their home governments for decisions they do not like. Therefore, reforms require that farmers be paid off to accept them. There are clouds over the CAP's future, however. Member states may be unwilling to pay indefinitely for the current level of CAP subsidies.

Since the later 1980s the structural funds

have been the EU's second largest budgetary item. Regional development policy, like the CAP, is an expression of solidarity between some Europeans and others, in this case between the better-off and less-developed regions. It was not always thus. There was a small bow to regional development in the Rome Treaty, a payoff to the Italians for their southern problems. The 1970s brought the founding of the European Regional Development Fund (ERDF) to complement the EAGGF Guidance section (responsible for structural operations in agriculture) in agriculture and the European Social Fund (charged with human capital spending). Excepting the EAGGF, the sums were small, the funds were not coordinated, and the funds were seen as supplements to member state national budgets rather than expressions of solidarity. It took enlargement to less-developed member states—Ireland in 1973, Greece in 1981, Spain and Portugal in 1986—to create pressure for more energetic efforts. The SEA in 1986 introduced new articles making economic and social cohesion a new common policy.

The reform of the structural funds of 1988 sought to target the combined effects of the three funds on regional development and double their funding over five years to 25 percent of the EU's total budget. The structural funds have since been reconsidered in every large budgetary negotiation, in each case connected with the results of an intergovernmental conference (IGC) and treaty changes. When the Delors I budgetary package ran out in 1992, just after Maastricht, the Delors II package programmed yet another doubling by 1999. A third reconsideration, tied to Amsterdam, led to a more complex package in 1999 that anticipated enlargement to some CEECs. The amounts have become quite large, upward of $40 billion, by 1997. The principles for the reformed funding up until 1999 have been as follows:

- *Concentration* around priority objectives
- *Partnership*, involving close cooperation between the Commission and the "appropriate authori-

ties" at "national, regional, and local level" in each member state and at every stage in the policy process
- *Additionality*—that EU funds should complement, rather than replace, national funding
- *Programming* multiannual, multitask, and multiregional programs rather than uncoordinated individual national projects.[11]

The Commission has assumed the central planning role in all this. The funds, in addition to supplementary loans from the European Investment Bank, are targeted to the following objectives:

- Objective 1: Assisting underdeveloped regions
- Objective 2: Aid to deindustrialized regions
- Objective 3: Combating long-term (over twelve months) unemployment and integration of young people (under age twenty-five) into the labor market
- Objective 4: Helping workers adapt to technological change
- Objective 5: (a) Structural reform of agriculture and (b) aid to rural areas

After the accession of Sweden and Finland in 1995, a sixth objective, for Arctic regions, was added.

The first objective, assisting the underdeveloped areas of the EU, receives by far the largest amount of funding, roughly two-thirds. For the period prior to *Agenda 2000*, all of Greece, Ireland, Portugal, Corsica, Sardinia, Sicily, southern Italy, all of Eastern Germany except Berlin, and most of Spain were Objective 1 areas. The Maastricht Treaty added a "cohesion fund" to subsidize the "cohesion countries'" participation in the EU's environmental and transport policies.

The amounts involved, if modest in absolute terms, have been significant in relation to the investment needs of poorer EC countries. Although disaggregating the effects of the structural funds from other variables is difficult, they have made an important contribution to growth in aggregate demand in these areas. The estimated average impact of EU grants is shown in Table 4.6.

The reform of the structural funds also enhanced the Commission's institutional prominence, placing another big-ticket item on the EU budget alongside the CAP. The Community and Commission acquired another common policy to justify their continued importance, and the Commission put itself at the center of regional policy design. The different DGs involved in the actual planning around the DG for regional development are strategically placed to encourage certain kinds of development in poorer and declining areas of the EU. Most often this encouragement focuses on modern infrastructures (transport, telecommunications, energy), new small and medium-sized enterprises, and occupational training schemes.

Member states have done their best to interfere in the Commission's workings in regional development, however, in ways that tended to renationalize the process in the 1990s. Eastern Germany and southern Italy, for example, received much more from the funds than did comparable regions in other parts of Europe. This, and the scatter-plotting of small projects funded from Brussels (probably indicating national patronage politics), point to the working of factors other than those strictly related to regional development.[12] Here yet again one can measure the consequences of the weakening of the Commission in the interplay with member states.

The cumulative effects of such programs and their multiplier effects to help poorer regions catch up cannot yet be known. In the meantime, however, the structural funds have provided incentives to member states to avoid "races to the bottom" through strategies of low wage and minimal welfare states. A bonus for the Commission is that regional levels of government in poorer areas increasingly have stakes in European integration. The structural funds are also good for the economies of the donor member states because they increase purchasing power in the cohesion countries to spend on goods and

Table 4.6   Estimated Annual Impact of Structural Funds, 1989–1993

	Average Annual Growth Rate, 1989–1993	Estimated Annual Impact of Structural Funds
Greece	1.6	0.5
Spain	1.5	0.2
Ireland	4.6	0.3
Italy	1.5	0.1
Portugal	2.6	0.7

Source: EC Commission, *Fourth Annual Report on Implementation of the Reform of the Structural Funds*, p. 85.

services from the rest of the EU. Structural fund programs have also been catalysts for much-needed administrative reforms and changes in recipient states. A case could also be made that EU regional development aid has helped consolidate democracy in Greece, Spain, and Portugal, the three southern countries that emerged from dictatorships in the 1970s. Yet the cohesion countries have had to submit to greater intervention from Brussels than other member states, lessening their "subsidiarity."

After the Amsterdam Treaty, the prospect of Eastern European EU memberships began changing the playing field. The *Agenda 2000* proposals had to take account of the political barriers to budgetary expansion that had appeared in the 1990s. Thus, the Commission programmed a steady state expenditure on the structural funds (0.46 percent of Community GDP) through 2006 that would include 20 percent of funding for pre- and postaccession help to new EU members. Accomplishing this objective meant taking money from existing structural fund recipients in Western Europe, so the Commission proposed to redefine structural fund objectives so that the percentage of the EU-15 population getting funding would drop from slightly over 50 percent to 35 to 40 percent. The Commission also sharpened targeting for unemployment problems in Objective 2 regions (declining areas within the more prosperous North) and cut the number of structural fund objectives from six to three. Objective 1, aiming at less developed regions, was retained but with tougher eligibility criteria; Objective 2 aimed at declining areas; and Objective 3 involved training and employment policies.

Struggle inevitably followed. Cohesion areas whose living standards had risen above the 75 percent of EU average cutoff point for funding found these changes hard to accept. Even after a continuation of Cohesion Fund money was held out as a peace offering, they tried to block the changes. Northern member states then insisted on their pet projects. The results, hammered out at Berlin in 1999, were not quite what the Commission had hoped. Funding for prospective new members was protected, but the general funding level was reduced. The number of programs and amount of funding for Community initiatives where the Commission had considerable power were reduced. The method employed by key member states to strike the Berlin compromise involved recognition of "particular situations" in member states that would be funded, structural fund principles and objectives notwithstanding.[13] The Commission was thus weakened, and further renationalization occurred. The future of the structural funds was more uncertain than it had been since 1987 as a result. The actual admission of new members later in the 2000–2006 budgetary period was bound to change existing arrangements even more.

Competition and Industrial Policy

Articles 85 to 94 of the Rome Treaty established a policy to ensure that "competition in the internal market is not distorted." The object was to provide an instrument to knock down artificial walls protecting special producer interests inside the EU. The Commission therefore does much of Europe's antitrust policy. Anticompetitive behavior by firms—unfair market power, trusts, and monopolies—is outlawed, and

the Commission reviews cases above a certain size threshold. It also reviews state aid to firms (e.g., subsidies, grants, special tax advantages) that could create unfair market advantages. Article 90 applies less stringent rules to publicly owned undertakings. Article 89 grants the European Commission responsibility for enforcing these rules. Its powers were enhanced after 1989 when, after seventeen years of hesitation by member states, it was given the right to oversee and control mergers.[14] If companies could use their market power to limit competition or governments could favor their home enterprises, there would be little point in creating a single market. The Commission is also given rights to investigate and impose penalties (with ECJ review possible). Beyond these provisions the Commission must submit an annual report to the European Parliament.

The Commission's power over competition law is important, particularly since the single market. The powers are both negative—prevention and repression of illegal behaviors—and positive—regulatory and authorizing. The Commission's competition policy DG is charged with the bulk of competition policy. Its 200-strong A-level staff of lawyers and economists monitors conditions, devouring the business press and observing market developments. Since 1989 it has had merger control units to oversee merger proposals. The competition policy DG can request information from firms and carry out investigations. Member state governments are required to inform the Commission of aids and subsidies. Each year the DG looks into hundreds of cases, submits the most important cases to the broader Commission for consideration, and informs member states when their state aid practices are under investigation. Commission proceedings are often heated, because competition matters are important to member state governments and firms. Because Commission credibility may be at stake, however, there is considerable give and take, and ultimately the ECJ sets legal limits to the Commission's operations by way of litigation from other European institutions (a specific Court of First Instance handles most competition cases).

Serious Commission investigations into potential violations are more often than not concluded informally, with firms and member states redefining their plans. When informal dealing fails, the Commission may levy quite substantial fines. French state-owned companies like Renault and Pechiney, the Belgian chemical giant Solvay, and the Swiss–Swedish packaging company Tetrapak were all fined in the early 1990s, for example. Major cartels have been ferreted out and dismantled in several areas. The play of national interests may have allowed other potential violations to escape sanctions, of course, but these instances are not documented.

The merger control regulation, effective in 1989, provided the Community and Commission with a powerful new tool, first used in 1991 when the Commission voted to forbid the takeover by Alenia-Aerospatiale, a producer of commuter airliners, of DeHavilland Canada, an important North American company. The procedure, which caused conflict within the Commission, involved legal judgments about the nature of markets and the likely restraint of trade were the merger to be allowed. Interests pressured the Commission from all sides.[15] Subsequent cases have been less spectacular, but all have contributed to the development of procedures and jurisprudence in the area. Altogether, the Commission struck down a dozen large merger deals in a decade from the nearly 1,000 it has handled, and it has obliged reformulation before approving numerous others.

The problem of state aids is difficult for governments trying to help out important national firms because jobs and votes may be at stake. Moreover, some member state governments—and the French are not alone—maintain traditions of *dirigisme* (state-centered industrial policy) notwithstanding the single market. Community competition law has nonetheless become more active and effective where government-controlled companies engage in commercial activities, where governments have been constrained to behave as private owners would have. In the airline industry, for example, heavily subsidized national carriers ran up against Commission efforts to deregulate the EU airline market. Thus, national airlines (Air France, Alitalia, and Iberia, among others) were granted one last bailout chance, provided that subsidies were accompanied by plans to make the carriers competitive. The treaty also grants the Commission certain powers to deregulate what once were called natural monopolies in telecommunications and energy (in Article 90), but results have been slow. Promoting things like third-party access to monopolized energy networks has raised political disputes, with the introduction of energy liberalization stalled until 1999. Telecommunications deregulation, which took a decade to produce, was in place by 1998 and then stimulated frenetic merger and acquisition action. The Commission and Community have also become much more active in regulating intellectual property. One of the haziest competition policy areas, however, is defense industry. The end of the cold war provided strong new incentives for European defense contractors, most of which remained national champions, to cooperate and merge. The Commission may allow new market power in these areas as part of the CFSP.

Complicated jurisprudence separates EU competition policy competencies from those of national governments and courts. Moreover, in some cases, the benefits of limiting competition can be deemed to outweigh its disadvantages. In smaller matters, the Commission observes a de minimis rule (a threshold below which the EU does not act). EU competition policy is in constant evolution as the European market changes. In matters involving public services such as telecommunications, energy supply, railways, and post offices, opening markets without undercutting the equitable provision of public goods remains a legal and political frontier. The private sector has been in persistent furor over exclusive distribution arrangements (car dealerships constrained contractually by manufacturers, for example) and franchises. There has also been persistent debate about establishing an EU antitrust agency independent of the Commission, but this has never reached a point of decision.

Paradoxically, the EU and Commission are charged to pursue competition policy and industrial, or "competitiveness," policy simultaneously. The first area is primarily concerned with creating free and open market conditions uncluttered by private and public market power, while the second involves the use of public power to promote industrial success. The paradox continues to strain EU consensus. Member states with strongly liberal positions are eager to see strong competition policy and dislike industrial policy, while those with more statist traditions typically seek greater public support for competitiveness.

EU industrial policy stretches back to the European Coal and Steel Community (ECSC), which had strong powers over producers and did not hesitate to use them. More than once, for example, the ECSC invoked a situation of "manifest crisis" to implement structural changes. The EU has also been involved in similar activities to reconfigure troubled industries. In recent times, for example, it has acted to restructure shipbuilding and textiles. Often it has provided packages of financial aid, subsidized training programs, and enacted trade protection to promote cooperation among firms. Most such actions have been of the "bailout" type. But by the 1990s, the problem of industrial policy had changed. Aid to rust belt areas and industries was partly taken over by Objective 2 of the structural funds. The new issue is the general vulnerability of European industry, including its most up-to-date sectors, to more intense global competition. The question today is less that of organizing and cushioning decline than of promoting innovation. Already in the early 1980s the EU, prodded by Commission activism, had started funding research and development. The pioneering Esprit program, which provides funding to transnational research cooperation among companies mainly in the electronics

area, is now but one example among many EU-sponsored research and development efforts organized in a long list of titles (Jessi, Eureka, which is more intergovernmental, and many others). The Esprit experience, however, illustrated the problems and paradoxes promoting the development of a European-level industrial backbone in electronics. The Information Society DG (formerly XIII), the Commission's high-technology agency that administers Esprit and other such programs, has been accused by liberals of French-style *dirigisme* and of being in the pockets of the big electronics companies, and both criticisms may be justifiable. Yet despite accusations, research and development programs have proliferated.

The SEA granted the EU broader responsibilities in research and development. The Commission now produces an overall multiyear program, which Parliament then reviews, that puts together and plans funding for multiple activities. Maastricht expanded the mandate to include research in environment and health. The Fourth Framework Program for research and development for the period 1994–1998 totaled a bit more than $13 billion.

The effort, however, has been hampered by difficulties and controversies. Should the EU help out Japanese and U.S. firms located in Europe, or European multinationals whose intention it may be to outsource production outside the Community? Should it help European firms deeply enmeshed in strategic alliances all over the world? Should the EU promote pure research, or should it help firms bring products closer to the market? Heavy-handed Commission efforts to use standard-setting prerogatives for high-definition television in the early 1990s, largely at the behest of large consumer electronics firms, were a political and technical fiasco, as were similar efforts to use EU money to entice big computer firms into greater collaboration.

In the first half of the 1990s the Commission devoted serious efforts to making better political and intellectual sense of the competitiveness versus competition policy paradox with a new doctrine of framework industrial policy. Industrial policy could be justified if it sought to remedy European disadvantages due to market imperfections (e.g., competitive advantages in the international market that flowed from earlier government help to industry or prior monopoly situations) and to provide new incentives to all European market actors, without distinction, to pursue new competitive strategies. At the heart of this outlook were incentives to retrain workers and promote industrial cooperation within the single market. This framework approach was applied when the time came to create a single market for automobiles, a moment when Europe also had to face the likelihood of increased foreign (particularly Japanese) market penetration in cars. Complicated negotiations with the Japanese led to a ten-year-long voluntary trade restriction deal slowing Japanese entrance, accompanied by a major package of Community aid to European car producers that provided incentives to modernize.

The paradox persists despite such sophisticated new arguments. Divergent member state perspectives about politically based efforts to intervene in market activities are not easily resolved. Those who believe that signals coming from the market should be the ultimate guide to producers' decisions, like the British, are skeptical about anything resembling industrial policy. Others, like the French, believe that there needs to be a consciously woven European industrial fabric to allow Europe to compete successfully. These differences were played out in the Maastricht Treaty, which included a new clause allowing industrial policy but restricted it by requiring unanimity and also included a clause declaring the need for trans-European networks (TENs) in transport, telecommunications, and energy. The Commission has tried desperately over the years since Maastricht to get the European Council to provide adequate funding to underwrite a list of priority TENs projects, including roads, railroads, and information highways. The reluctance of the European Council to cooperate has been patent, however. In the meantime, the Commission itself continues to squabble internally about such matters.

The most important recent steps occurred at the Lisbon European Council in spring 2000, where EU heads of state and government adopted a much stronger liberalizing program to promote the information society, more flexibility, and new social policy objectives promoting new labor market openness. It was Lisbon's approach to implementation that was particularly interesting. Following the approach of the Luxembourg employment policy, Lisbon proposed the method of open cooperation (MOC) in which general objectives would be set out by Commission and Council, member states would make national plans, best practices would be highlighted, and benchmarks would be established. EU legislation played little role in this MOC approach. Its purpose is to engender genuine coordination in a voluntary way, relying on the effectiveness of the exercise to build confidence and spread knowledge to get member states to change their industrial policies.

Social Policy

The EU has traditionally had few powers in social policies (the welfare state, labor standards, and industrial relations). The Treaty of Rome's social provisions were limited to labor market mobility, training, and equal opportunity between men and women (Article 119), but even here little indicated the ways that prescribed "harmonization and cooperation" should be achieved. The treaty also created a European Social Fund to make "the employment of workers easier, increasing their geographical and occupational mobility within the Community," again with vague indications about scope and implementation. The diplomatic setting more than the treaty constrained early EU social policy action. The early years of the EU coincided with the consolidation of modern national welfare states, and the EU's architects perceived social policy as the heart of national sovereignty. The

EU thus grew together with as wide a variety of social policy regimes as it had members. Attempts to transcend this diversity in the earlier 1970s largely failed. Progress in equal treatment was made only because of legislation after the ECJ's 1976 *Defrenne v Sabena* decision (which made equal treatment a matter of direct legal effect on individuals).[16] The 1985 White Paper made little mention of social policy either. Member states were not eager to give the Community new latitude in social policy.[17]

Workplace health and safety is the area where the EU had its greatest early effects in social policy. The snail's pace of harmonization in this area prompted searches in the 1980s for a new approach in which framework directives for products were limited to defining "essential safety requirements" or other "requirements of general interest" and no longer laid down detailed technical specifications. The new approach brought some speed-up in health and safety harmonization, but it took the SEA's qualified majority (in Article 118A) to accelerate the pace. Moreover, in the SEA's new Article 100A, where decisions are still governed by unanimity rules in social areas, the Commission was required to "take as a base a high level of protection" whenever those measures concern "health, safety, environmental protection and consumer protection." The SEA thus specifically enjoined that the Commission promote a "race to the top" in workplace health and safety. The Commission used Article 118A to formulate the Third Health and Safety Action Program for the period 1988–1993 containing directives that have now been enacted. Thus, by the mid-1990s, a solid body of European-level health and safety regulation was on the books.

The major social policy innovations came with the Delors Commission's Community Charter of Basic Social Rights for Workers in 1989. The charter was a "solemn commitment" to a set of "fundamental social rights" for employees. It made no legal addition to the Treaty of Rome or the SEA but instead sought to gather together and make good the unfulfilled social promises that the Community's treaty base already contained. The teeth of the Social Charter were contained in the Action Program that followed (November 24, 1989), involving forty-seven measures. Here, however, the Commission was on shaky political grounds with the Action Program because, with the exception of health and safety, unanimity was still required in the Council of Ministers. In areas beyond health and safety, therefore, legislating proved difficult, if for no other reason than British opposition.

The SEA also included a new Article 118B stating that "the Commission shall endeavor to develop the dialogue between management and labor at the European level which could, if the two sides consider it desirable, lead to relations based on agreement." Social dialogue became a high Commission priority, involving discussions among the Union of Industrial and Employers Confederations of Europe (UNICE), the employers' association, the European Trade Union Confederation (ETUC), and the public sector employers' association Confédération Européenne des Employeurs Publiques (CEEP). Neither the ETUC nor UNICE, both essentially Brussels lobbies, were initially empowered to negotiate, and for a long period social dialogue was an exercise in confidence building that revealed contradictory purposes. UNICE wanted to frustrate Commission legislative purposes. ETUC, in contrast, wanted as many concrete proposals as possible.

The Commission then tried to provide incentives for European-level social partners to bargain, which began to work in the early 1990s under the pressure of legislation from the Social Charter and the Maastricht negotiations. The Commission's proposals on treaty change ultimately found their way into a Maastricht Social Protocol. This suggested initially that when the Commission wanted to propose action in the social policy area, it would first announce its intention to the social partners, who might then decide to negotiate in the area. If negotiations succeeded, their results could become a substitute for EU legislation. If the social partners were unable to negotiate, then the Commission could go ahead with legislation. The employers, to that point opposed to European-level bargaining, decided that accepting such a "negotiate or we'll legislate" clause would be preferable to legislation, which would eventually become a constraint.

At Maastricht, British prime minister John Major refused to accept this new social policy proposal. Twelve member states then agreed to a protocol in which eleven would accept the new social clauses. After Maastricht's ratification in 1993, the Commission reproposed a directive, which had been blocked several times since 1970, for establishing European Works Councils (EWCs) in multinational companies. These committees of workers and management empowered to gather information and discuss corporate strategies would be established, on the basis of negotiations, in every "Community scale group of undertakings." EWCs would encompass all of an undertaking's operations within the EU, with their competence limited to transnational, as opposed to national, matters concerning the group in question. The Commission went through the various steps needed to allow the social partners to decide whether they preferred collective bargaining to legislation, which they ultimately did not. A directive was passed in the fall of 1994.

The next Commission proposal, on parental leave, actually worked under Social Protocol proceedings. A framework agreement on parental leave, to be translated into national settings by subsequent negotiation, was negotiated by the social partners in later 1995 and became law the next year. Negotiations to regulate different dimensions of atypical work (part-time and short-term contracts) were also successful in the later 1990s. The British finally signed up to the Social Chapter at Amsterdam in 1997. By that point, however, the EU had lost the little enthusiasm it might have had for legislating in core social policy areas. Employment and competitiveness had become much more important concerns. The EU's influence in social policy remains limited, however. What exists is a patchwork, including equal protection and health and safety legislation, together with Social Charter directives and the opening of EU-level bargaining life. The core welfare state is not part of any conceivable EU mandate, except in indirect, long-term ways. The conventional welfare state matters remain solidly ensconced behind borders of national sovereignty.

Future directions may be different if the Amsterdam–Luxembourg employment policy initiatives take root. At Amsterdam, an important employment clause was added to the treaties because of the coincidence between high European unemployment and the election of large numbers of Social Democrats in member states. The employment cause spawned the so-called Luxembourg Process (the first large meeting was held there in fall 1997). The idea was to set specific goals for a European employment strategy, charging member states each to produce national action programs (NAPs). The Commission then would consider these programs, all seen together, to promote new convergence and emulation of best practices. The exercise was then to be repeated every year. This was the first effort to employ the MOC.

The four large goals were employability (equipping people with the proper skills), entrepreneurship (facilitating the founding of new business and new employment opportunities), adaptability (promoting flexibility in work), and equal treatment (nondiscrimination). The Commission's leaders in social policy also expressed hope that the employment strategy could be tied to a similar process of harmonization being developed for macroeconomic policy to constitute a "European employment pact." The employment strategy aimed to promote new job creation policies with active labor market policies (in particular, enhanced skills training and life-long education) and to prod reforms of pertinent welfare state programs to minimize the poverty traps that developed when programs like unemployment benefits kept people out of the labor market for so long that they had minimal chances of returning.[18]

Whether this new approach will bear fruit cannot yet be known. It is most likely to make a difference if the return to higher economic growth that appeared in the later 1990s continues. Most interesting is the change in perspective that it embodies. EU institutions are not here engaged in legislating and decreeing things that all member states must then do. The employment strategy instead aims to create synergies between European institutions and member state governments around principles and guidelines about which all can agree. Success will follow if member states involve pertinent groups in their populations, take the guidelines seriously, and emulate the good ideas of others.

European social policy has always been constructed around a logic of subsidiarity recognized by the EU treaties. EU member states were the appropriate venues for democratically confronting the social problems that their citizens faced, and the EU was better placed to harmonize and coordinate those matters from the wide range of different member states' policies that might create barriers to a European market. The employment strategy embodies new recognition of these realities. This new approach, if it proves effective, could well be replicated in social protection programs (pensions, health care), education, and tax policy.

Environment, Transportation, and External Trade

The range of EU common policies is now vast. Community environmental policy began tentatively in the late 1960s with a directive on classifying, labeling, and packaging dangerous substances. Activity grew with Action Programs and participation in international environmental accords in the 1970s, and a dedicated Commission Environmental DG was set up in 1981. Activity thus grew until environmental policy became part of the treaty in the SEA (Article 130r–t). Maastricht then listed environmental policy among the fundamental areas so that environmental considerations should henceforth be part of all EU action. Maastricht also ex-

panded the use of QMV voting in the environmental area.

Environmental policy was an obvious choice for EU regulation, because environmental problems are, or may become, externalities for any member state and are thus better addressed from a transnational center. Moreover, with the completion of the single market after 1985, different national standards of environmental protection might easily have become the source of nontariff barriers to trade. The EU, and the Commission's DG, have worked primarily on the basis of multiyear action programs, which the Council and Parliament approve. The treaty sets out a set of general principles of policy formation: primacy on preventive action, "the polluter should pay," and correction at the source of problems. In recent years much Euro-level intervention has been couched as sustainable development. Environmental programs have promoted the codes of conduct, particularly through "green labels" on products. The treaty also advocates firms use of a new "eco-audit." A wide range of legislation has been passed about water and air pollution, noise, waste disposal, and transport of dangerous substances. Environmental impact assessments are now compulsory for all projects above a certain size. EU-level environmental policy has been consistently a favorite of public opinion, and for some time the Commission tried very hard to make its mark through new projects. The annual rating of the quality of bathing beach water was one way it devised to fly the EU flag.

By the 1990s, however, certain member states, including the United Kingdom, had begun vocally to resent EU "meddling" in environmental matters. Others, like Spain, which received the new cohesion fund at Maastricht partly in compensation, objected to the high costs of compliance. The Commission's most daring proposal, a tax on carbon dioxide emissions, has been bogged down in the Council amid lobbying for years, however, and environmental policy has become a favorite target for arguments about the need for subsidiarity.[19] Nonetheless, EU environmental policy is in many respects a genuinely federal approach to environmental problems. It has been effective in deciding ways to share the diminution of greenhouse gas emissions, for example. The EU also is an important international agent in multilateral environmental negotiations. Here, as in social policy, one sees today a mix of approaches, reflecting a more mature recognition of the meaning of subsidiarity, with multiple policy focuses ranging across global programs, EU-wide programs, and efforts to coordinate national and local policies.[20]

The Treaty of Rome specified that the new EEC could also have a "common transport policy" (Articles 3 and 74), originally limited to rail, road, and inland waterways but extended in the SEA to air and sea transport. Until well into the 1980s, however, little was actually done. In fact, in 1982 the European Parliament brought suit against the Council for "failure to act," and it took an ECJ decision in 1985 to spur some action. The problem was engineering the difficult trade-offs between transport costs, which made the European market a more difficult place to circulate people and goods, and the national transport systems of railroads, roads, internal waterways, and airlines that were run as subsidized public enterprises. Until the single market, these trade-offs were settled in favor of member states' interests.

In the late 1980s the Commission was granted a number of new powers, first to free up air transport by beginning to deregulate fare and route structures, a process still underway. The Commission produced a first package of new rules here in 1987 and two more in the 1990s. The result of the process will undoubtedly be the end of subsidized "national champion" airlines and the emergence of genuine trans-European companies with fuller rights of cabotage (picking up new passengers in countries other than their own). Developing a more effective and economically sound air transport system is now contingent on creating a new trans-European air traffic control system, however, and this may be some time off. Similar changes are slowly happening in sea transporta-

tion, in which the Commission seeks internal market deregulation in exchange for help in making EU maritime companies more globally competitive. Roads and railroads are a more difficult problem. In both of these areas, plus telecommunications, Maastricht sanctioned the development of TENs. Getting member states to agree to finance the TENs has proven difficult, however, and the programs have moved forward slowly. Nonetheless, the (limited) ability of the EU to provide financial underwriting has given it considerably increased power over national planning in these areas. Connectability and standards will be important in the future. For high-speed trains, for example, having to change locomotives at national borders because of different electricity currents leads to a considerable loss in the improvements that new rail technology can bring. Moreover, networks that connect formerly peripheral parts of the EU, particularly in the South, and Europe's post-1989 openings to the East are economically vital for everyone concerned.

Forging a consistent trade policy toward the outside world had been from the beginning one of the central pillars of creating a common, then a single, market. By the 1990s, the policy had become tremendously important in international trade, because the EU was by far the largest and most open trading zone in the global system (comprising 38 percent of total world trade). Administering the common trade policy is one of the Commission's major responsibilities, carried out by the international trade DG, and the international trade commissioner has become a figure comparable to the U.S. trade representative on the world scene. The work has rarely been easy. The Commission has to bargain internationally on the basis of mandates granted by member states and reviewed constantly in give-and-take with Council and Parliament. As in many other areas, EU member states have tended to have different approaches to trade policy. Northern industrial countries are free traders, loath to interfere in trade flows, while the South, including France, has leaned toward managed trade relationships as tools for shaping domestic economies. This complexity has led to a situation in which some matters are EU–Commission responsibilities, some are mixed, and some remain in member state hands. In particular, member states have persistently denied the Commission competence in areas of trade in services and intellectual property.

The EU occupies different places in the complex layering of the international trade system, each of which has to be treated differently. Its treaties, for example, give privileged trade positions to the ACP countries, whose trading relationships with Europe are regulated separately (the ACP countries are exempt from EU customs). The EU has also contracted association agreements with the CEECs that involve gradually freeing trade in most areas. The Commission also negotiates for the EU in important multilateral trade dealings like GATT and WTO and deals with specific countries as well, largely through the EU's trade and diplomatic delegations in most world capitals. The Uruguay Round, which lasted several years, saw huge conflicts between the EU and the United States over agriculture, ending in a major change in European trade policy in the area (the level of European trade subsidies of key products was lowered substantially). Ensuing international trade discussions over services and intellectual property ended with European–U.S. agreement to disagree over trade in audiovisual materials, with Europe insisting on the cultural importance of protecting film and television. The Uruguay Round was a moment of serious internal conflict in the Commission, charged with the negotiations, between the Commission president, seeking to bring the refractory French into a final deal, and the commissioners for external

trade and agriculture. The WTO, which emerged from the Uruguay Round, has since consistently been an arena of disputes between the United States and Europe about bananas, beef hormones, mufflers for airplanes, genetically modified organisms, American tax havens for exporters, and other matters. Managing these endemic conflicts diplomatically has been a constant challenge for the EU.

The most frequently used short-term trade tool in the EU's tool box, under GATT and WTO rules, is the procedure to respond to dumping (the practice of selling goods below market prices to penetrate markets). Anti-dumping measures, taken by the Commission after appeal from industries in the Community, have been used recently at a rate of twenty per year, a figure that some observers claim is too high. Article 19 of the GATT Treaty also allowed invocation of "safeguard clauses" allowing temporary protection in urgent situations.

Given the controversies around globalization, the EU's position in international trade and its complex internal arrangements for making and executing policy in this area are bound to be central in years to come. Matters that used to lie outside multilateral trade gatherings such as environmental and labor standards are now on the table. Private diplomacy by large economic interests and the development of a lively international civil society, largely composed of protest groups and nongovernmental organizations, are new facts of life. The Seattle ministerial meetings of the WTO in 1999, with its street protests and ultimate breakdown, may have been harbingers of future conflicts. Here the EU will have new openings to act creatively.

Notes

1. For readers who desire to focus more deeply on policy, Helen Wallace and William Wallace, *Policymaking in the European Union,* 4th ed. (Oxford: Oxford University Press, 2000), is an ideal source.

2. See Andrew Moravscik, "Negotiating the Single European Act," in Robert Keohane and Stanley Hoffmann, eds., *The New European Community* (Boulder, Colo.: Westview, 1991).

3. Later, when Maastricht was about to go into ef-

fect, efforts were made to make the idea of subsidiarity clear. The Edinburgh European Council of 1992 featured a formal discussion of the matter on the basis of a paper prepared by the Commission.

4. European Commission, *The Impact and Effectiveness of the Single Market*, Brussels COM (96) 520 final, 1996) October 30. The Commission puts out regular information, including a biannual *Single Market Scorecard*. See http://www.europa.eu.int/comm/dgs/internalU.S.market. See Alasdair R. Young and Helen Wallace, "The Single Market: A New Approach to Policy," in Wallace and Wallace, *Policymaking in the European Union*.

5. The best recent work on EU finances is Brigid Laffan, *The Finances of the European Union* (London: Macmillan, 1997).

6. *Making a Success of the Single Act* (Luxembourg: EC, 1987); *From the Single Act to Maastricht and Beyond: The Means to Match Our Ambitions* (Luxembourg: EC, 1992); *Agenda 2000: Financing the European Union* (Luxembourg: EC, 1998).

7. Over time agricultural levies and sugar duties, never large, have steadily declined; the valued-added tax resource, which had reached 68 percent in 1988, has also declined, with the "fourth resource" climbing from 10.6 percent in 1988 to its current level.

8. See Brigid Laffan and Michael Shackleton, "The Budget, Who Gets What, When and How," in Wallace and Wallace, *Policymaking in the European Union*.

9. Michael Shackleton, "The Delors II Budget Package," in Neill Nugent, ed., *The European Community 1992: Annual Review of Activities* (Oxford: Journal of Common Market Studies/Blackwell, 1993), covers this ground well.

10. Elmar Rieger, "The Common Agricultural Policy: Politics Against Markets," in Wallace and Wallace, *Policymaking in the European Union*, p. 192.

11. Taken from Box 9.2 in David Allen, "Cohesion and the Structural Funds, Transfers and Trade Offs," in Wallace and Wallace, *Policymaking in the European Union*.

12. See Loukas Tsoukalis, *The New European Economy Revisited* (New York: Oxford, 1997), chap. 9, for an excellent review of these issues.

13. Allen, "Cohesion and the Structural Funds," p. 258, provides a list.

14. For general discussions, see European Commission, *EEC Competition Policy in the Single Market* (Luxembourg: EC, 1989); Stephen Weatherill and Paul Beaumont, *EC Law* (London: Penguin, 1993), chaps. 22–27.

15. See George Ross, *Jacques Delors and European Integration* (New York: Oxford University Press, 1995), chaps. 4–5.

16. A set of directives then led to a progressive widening of the meaning of equal treatment to include most elements of the labor contract, including hiring and firing, access to training, working conditions, social security programs, and discrimination against women around certain family issues (e.g., pregnancy and employment security). By the mid-1980s the Commission had set up an "equal protection unit" in its Employment and Social Affairs DG and begun to produce "medium term action plans" establishing priorities. Since then, steady action has raised member states' standards.

17. In the SEA, the application of qualified majority decision making in the general area of harmonization (Article 100A) was excluded for two single market areas central in the EU's very thin social policy legacy: provisions "relating to the free movement of persons" and those "relating to the rights and interests of employed persons."

18. See European Commission, *European Employment and Social Policy: A Policy for People* (Luxembourg: EC, 2000).

19. For a detailed listing of EU environmental actions, see EC Committee of the American Chamber of Commerce in Belgium, *EU Environment Guide* (Brussels: EC, 1995), chap. 1.

20. See Alberta Sbriagia, "Environmental Policy: Economic Constraints and External Pressures," in Wallace and Wallace, *Policymaking in the European Union*, chap. 11.

C H A P T E R

5

Europolitics in Transition:
Four Challenges

European integration has succeeded beyond its founders' dreams. The EU is more and more the place where European nations seek to solve their problems and is clearly irreversible in any conceivable future. It would now be hard to find areas in the lives of EU member states and citizens where European matters have not penetrated. We can no longer understand the politics of Europe only by comparing national systems.

European integration may have succeeded, but it is far from concluded. The EU has taken on much greater importance in recent times, often because EU member states have sought to solve crises through deepening the EU. Deepening the EU, in turn, has repeatedly created new situations in which the EU must continue to grow and change. With a new century, European integration has now spilled over so much that Europeans cannot avoid addressing the really hard questions about what they have done. "Where is the EU going?" "What is it for?" "Who is it for?" This final chapter examines four of the largest challenges confronting Europe EMU, enlargement, security policy, and reforming EU institutions to demonstrate why these questions need to be answered.

Economic and Monetary Union as a Beginning Rather Than an End?

EMU was the heart of the Maastricht Treaty, the great leap forward for European integration in

the 1990s. Nothing was guaranteed by the deal that member states concluded in 1991, and the EMU that actually began on January 1, 1999, might well not have happened. EMU now exists, and Europeans will have real euros in their pockets by 2002 to buy wine in France, beer in Germany, grappa in Italy, and schnapps in Austria, wherever they come from in the EU. This has opened up a host of new challenges however.

Recall the years from Maastricht to the mid-1990s. The French and others wanted EMU to gain greater voice in economic and monetary policy than they had in the European Monetary System (EMS) dominated by the Bundesbank and its single-minded pursuit of price stability. The 1980s provided periodic demonstrations that EMS gave the German central bank the power to intervene in the domestic policies of other EMS members. Maastricht did produce EMU, but the Germans had greater bargaining strength, and the French did not get what they wanted, symbolized by the convergence criteria that enjoined a future of unremitting austerity with few margins for maneuver on all potential EMU members. The process begun at Maastricht thus was bound to be more complicated than appointing euro-bankers, renting a building in Frankfurt, letting them introduce the euro, and then decreeing another victory for European integration.

For some time there was doubt that EMU would ever see the light of day. Almost immediately after Maastricht, the EU went into crisis. Public opinion support abruptly collapsed, with EMU the main lightning rod. Currency speculators then found fertile ground for quick and profitable dealing in the inadequate preparation of different national currencies for EMU. The EMS, meant to be an island of stability, turned into a volcano. Simultaneously the Bundesbank, confronting the costs of German unification, jammed its monetary policy brakes to the floor just when other EU member states were facing the most serious recession since 1945. No one then had the space to pursue countercyclical policies, and unemployment went up to new postwar highs. This had another consequence, however: No member state was able to think seriously about taking the specific measures necessary to meet the Maastricht convergence criteria.

The years immediately before January 1, 1999, produced an EMU miracle, but it was far from aesthetically beautiful. The Germans worried about the capacities and wills of their eventual EMU partners, in particular, the Latins. The Germans had long desired to keep Italy and perhaps Spain out of EMU because both had propensities to financial laxity. Moreover, everyone, including the Germans, fell behind in preparing EMU because of the recession. The deadline for deciding who could join EMU was in 1998, based on the accounts for 1997. This left little time for potential members to prepare and greatly enhanced the danger that short-term, one-off approaches to the convergence criteria, including creative accounting, would prevail over deeper behavioral changes. And to the degree to which these dangers were realized, EMU could turn out to be precarious.

The German response was severe and predictable. The German finance minister began advocating new, and even stricter, convergence criteria that would remain in force long after the final stage of EMU began in 1999. This led in 1996 to discussion of strict limits on member state budgetary deficits under EMU (3 percent maximum, which implied deficits of 1 percent in normal times to create reserve capacities) to be enforced by automatic and very large financial penalties for miscreants. The "stability and growth pact" confirmed at Amsterdam in June 1997 could lead to automatic major penalties on those whose budget deficits went beyond 3 percent if their gross domestic products (GDPs) dropped less than .075 percent (those countries that could not point to crisis conditions to justify larger budget deficits). In situations where recessions were serious, however, the Council of Ministers might be more flexible.

Why the Germans might have been worried became clearer in the chaotic, brief period before the May 1998 meeting when final EMU membership was decided. The Italians, with a budget deficit of 7.7 percent (versus the target 3 percent) and a cumulated debt of 124 percent (versus the target of 60 percent) in 1995, looked hopeless. The bulk of Italian effort was a tough "Eurotax" to raise government revenues. There was also clever manipulation of interest rates on government bonds. Neither measure really touched fundamental budgetary behavior, however, although together they rapidly lowered the budget deficit. On the general debt issue, the Italians anticipated that things would be fudged, since the Belgians had the same problem and the Belgians were necessary for EMU. The Spanish deficit in 1995 was 6.6 percent, leading the Commission to threaten suspension of regional development payments if things did not improve. The 1996 Spanish budgetary exercise turned out much better, with the new Aznar government benefiting from a significant drop in interest rates. Subsequently, renewed Spanish growth and astute austerity measures brought Spain into line. The French, without whom there could not realistically have been an EMU, trod their own road. Faced with a deficit of more than 5 percent in 1995, President Jacques Chirac almost immediately reneged on his extravagant (and mildly anti-EMU) campaign promises. The French then shifted the pension fund assets of France Telecom, which was being privatized, to the revenue side of the national budget, gaining a precious half-point against the Maastricht convergence criteria with the stroke of a pen.

This particular tactic provoked soul searching in the Commission, which was supposed to prevent "book cooking," but it finally gave in for the greater good of EMU. Even the German government tried clever accounting, proposing at the last minute to revalue the Bundesbank's stock of gold. This maneuver was disallowed domestically, but the Germans were barely able to sneak under the 3 percent barrier anyway.

On May 3, 1998, the heads of state and government declared eleven member states (the "euro-11") eligible for EMU, and the leadership of the European Central Bank (ECB) was then appointed. Full EMU began on schedule on January 1, 1999. It was more the beginning than the end, however, since it was certain to be a crucible for further change. The relative absence of an "e" in EMU (i.e., an economic policy dimension) remained controversial, for example. Throughout the second half of the 1990s, the French had agitated for an "economic government" to coordinate the economic policies of EMU member states and generate macro- and microeconomic signals for the ECB. The logic behind this, beyond French desire to get a larger piece of EMU action, was that without some such arrangements, ECB policies would stand alone as EU economic policy guidelines, as the convergence criteria had from the mid-1990s, leaving separate EMU governments as policy "takers" from the ECB, with fragmented resources to respond. This, in turn, would make it very difficult to achieve an appropriate "policy mix" in what came to be called "Euroland." EMU instigated more spillover, therefore, not least because its original architecture challenged member states to find euro-level counter-institutions to the ECB. Skirmishing about the formation of a special "euro-X" group of EMU participants within the broader ECOFIN (where all fifteen ministers of finance sat) continued, with de facto consecration of a euro-11 group achieved by 2000 (euro-12 in 2001, when Greece joined EMU). The fact that non-EMU members were outside the euro-11 created one more fissure in the unity of EU policy discus-sions, however, and whether the euro-11 will be enough to facilitate greater economic policy coordination—the absent "e" in EMU—is a large question for the future.

In the meantime, EMU raises specific coordination issues that must eventually be confronted, many with their own spillover potentialities. Member states retain fiscal policy prerogatives under EMU, for example. Competition in fiscal policy to gain competitive advantage is already a problem. More aggressive tax dumping, which is at least conceivable, could threaten a taxation "race to the bottom," further hollowing member state capacities to pursue social and other policies that European voters clearly continue to want. On the other hand, new euroregulation to promote better tax harmonization would further infringe on central areas of member state sovereignty. How difficult this puzzle might turn out was illustrated by the long-lasting effort to create withholding taxes on income from savings to curb tax evasion. Little Luxembourg (which lives from banking) and larger Great Britain (for which banking is also central) fought others to a standoff without reaching the desired withholding tax. A compromise was achieved in 2001.

The transition to Stage 3 of EMU on January 1, 1999, was well prepared. Creating the new ECB and locking together of eleven currencies went seamlessly. The first year of EMU was full of surprises nonetheless. To great general relief, European economic growth resumed in 1998–1999. For the first time in what must have seemed like ages, unemployment began to decline, falling to below 10 percent by the end of 1999. Widespread anticipation that the new ECB might nip new growth in the bud from fear about future inflation proved unfounded when the new system produced a surprisingly accommodating monetary policy, with low nominal and real interest rates. The major criticisms of the new system were that the ECB had problems communicating, causing confusion in markets. Although harsh neoliberal arguments continued about the inadequacy of continental "structural reforms" (meaning welfare state reform and labor market flexibility), contributing to suboptimal use of available human capital, there was also evidence that things had actually changed considerably in these areas.[1]

The next surprise was less positive. Prior to 1999 many experts had predicted that the new single currency would start strong and perhaps even appreciate versus the dollar. The opposite occurred. Between January 1999, when the euro was valued at 1 euro to $1.18, and autumn 2000, the value of the euro fell over 25 percent, before climbing upward a bit at the beginning of 2001. Amid hand-wringing about credibility, the indignity of a "weak currency," and "undervaluing," the euro's weakness, although hard on EU tourists in North America, provided strong stimulus to new "Euroland" growth by pumping up exports (in particular to the United States) without stimulating new inflation. Some even began to talk about the coming of a "new economy" in Europe, following that of the United States, but without its undesirable social effects. Moreover, the euro proved successful as an alternative currency denomination for a wide range of corporate and governmental bond issues, a sign pointing toward midrange "legs" as a reserve currency.

These short-term considerations pointed to longer-run questions. The euro's slide raised the issue of international exchange range management, particularly with the dollar. How would coordination between Europe and the United States proceed in the exchange rate area? A stable international monetary environment is in everyone's interest. But to the degree that the euro becomes a serious rival to the dollar, older ways of managing exchange rate matters, where the United States called important shots, might have to be modified. How would the costs of economic adjustment within Euroland be distributed? Would EMU's "one size fits all" monetary policy enhance broader welfare, or would it privilege that of certain regions to the advantage of others? The ECB's initially accommodating policies, for example, worked well for

France and Germany, which needed new growth, but it also heated up the smaller economies of Ireland and Portugal, obliging their governments to adjust. What would happen when this kind of effect touched France and Germany?

Would EMU stimulate member states to undertake the structural reforms actually needed to complete transition to the new economy? Would it be able to steer a good course between monetary gentleness that allowed too much laxity on reform matters and harshness that might destroy the uniqueness of the humane European model of society? This was, of course, a fundamental matter of social policy. EMU could eventually enjoin great harmonization of member state social policies or, at the very least, much greater coordination. The Amsterdam employment policy initiatives, in which member states were asked to produce national action plans around a set of job creation objectives after which the Commission tried to promote the adoption of "best practice," were the model for such a "method of open coordination." Social policy is one of member states' most important remaining prerogatives, however, and one of the most important political currencies for national politicians to distribute in electoral competition. The issue of how much social policy coordination would be needed in EMU versus how much member states would be willing to allow will certainly be part of the EU's future agenda.

The structural reforms anticipated from the workings of EMU will also involve relations between banks, companies, and governments. One of the desired, and likely, goals of EMU is to promote a genuine European single market in capital worthy of the size and strength of the single market more generally. This has great implications for a plethora of long-standing sheltered national arrangements between banks and firms, as well as the currently nationalized nature of particular financial markets. In different ways, most large continental economies were built around financing by "patient capital" from banks and other financial organizations' making longer-term capital placements that al-lowed firms to plan in the longer term. Good ex-amples were to be found in relationships be-tween large German banks and huge companies like Daimler-Chrysler and Siemens. With an open euro-wide capital market, such relation-ships would have to give way to a shareholder-oriented culture, resembling that of the United States. Whatever the advantages and disadvan-tages of this, it is certain to upset older ways of doing things.

New financial market arrangements also im-ply change, and perhaps euro-regulation, of le-gal structures in banking and financial areas. Spillover in these directions, which market de-velopments will push, will be contentious. Finally, the more robust and "American" the euro-capital market became, the more it would become influential in national debates about so-cial and other policy reform. Demographic and economic conditions meant that most EU states were facing major issues of pension reform, for example. Traditional public and semipublic re-tirement programs were certain to fall under in-creasing siege from capital-hungry financial markets seeking to capitalize pension programs (e.g., by allowing part or full financing through mutual funds). Were this to occur, even in part, the nature of the European model of society could change in major ways.

A final open question should be asked. Where will the candidates for enlargement fit in EMU? Most will not be eligible for immediate EMU membership, although accession agreements will all contain timetables and programs for eventual membership, since EMU is part of the *acquis communautaire* (the accumulated legal structure of the EU). For some time this will make EMU much more of a two-speed club, with the countries of Central and Eastern Eu-rope (CEECs) joining Denmark, Sweden, and the United Kingdom as EMU outsiders. The im-plications of this for EMU are difficult to fore-see, but the implications for the EU more broadly are clearer. A solid core of member states will become "insiders," with ongoing rea-sons to meet and coordinate economic matters separately from the non-EMU "outsiders" (in an expanded euro-11, for example). The outsid-ers will then have to find ways to cope. This, as we will see, is in line with some recent sugges-tions about building stronger flexibility provi-sions into the EU Treaties to facilitate such "two-speed" arrangements. A multi-speed EU would be very different from the one that emerged after the Treaty of Rome, however.

Will "Western" Europe Become All of Europe? Enlarging the Union

European integration was launched by six Western European continental nations, but it was never meant to be restricted to them. In the 1970s, three new members from The European Free Trade Association (EFTA)—the United Kingdom, Ireland, and Denmark—joined. Then in the 1980s, when three countries that had lived under authoritarian regimes—Spain, Por-tugal, and Greece—proved willing to democra-tize and marketize, the Union accepted them. In the mid-1990s, three more EFTA countries— Austria, Finland, and Sweden—joined. Impor-tant precedents were set in this growth from six to fifteen. The EU was not only an exclusive club for rich countries but also had responsibili-ties to help nurture new members toward stable democracy and prosperity. Extending the EU to cover Western Europe (excepting Switzerland and Norway) has been a great success, and new members with different perspectives on integra-tion have enriched EU life.

As enlargement became a regularized prac-tice, the EU formalized the obligations of new applicants. The key stipulation was acceptance of the *acquis communautaire*. Applicants thus could not pick and choose the Europe they wanted to join but had to accept the Europe that earlier members had created.

Those applicants that joined early and whose social, political, and economic arrangements were similar to those of the EU's original members did not find these EU entry fees exorbitant. As the EU developed, however, and particularly since the mid-1980s, the *acquis* has broadened and deepened. Today's enlargement discussions involve a codified *acquis*, divided into thirty-one chapters, well over 70,000 pages long.

The Chapters of the Acquis Communautaire—2000

1. Free Movement of Goods
2. Free Movement of Persons
3. Free Movement of Services
4. Free Movement of Capital
5. Company Law
6. Competition Policy
7. Agriculture
8. Fisheries
9. Transport
10. Taxation
11. EMU
12. Statistics
13. Social and Employment Policy
14. Energy
15. Industrial Policy
16. Small and Medium-Sized Undertakings
17. Science and Research
18. Education and Vocational Training
19. Telecommunications and Information Technologies
20. Culture and Audiovisual Policy
21. Regional Policy
22. Environment
23. Consumers and Health Protection
24. Justice and Home Affairs
25. Customs Union
26. External Relations
27. Common Foreign and Security Policy
28. Financial Control
29. Financial and Budgetary Provisions
30. Institutions
31. Miscellaneous

Enlarging the EU to the formerly communist areas to the east means imposing Western European standards and ensuring that these standards are observed. Most newly democratizing CEECs have limited recent experience with Western-style democracy, state-of-the-art complex market economies in an open international economy, up-to-date administrative and judicial practices, and other accoutrements of life that existing EU members take for granted. The first enlargements will thus be complicated, daunting, and perilous exercises. Long transition periods are needed in some policy areas because some applicants will be unable to join otherwise. Ensuring the acceptance of the *acquis* will oblige diligent follow-up for years. If new members lack institutional or administrative capacities, or, quite as important, the will to make the new arrangements work, big problems could emerge. What, for example, would follow for the entire EU if substantial cheating on the rules were tolerated? What if certain new members were unable to ensure the rule of law fully? What if the internal political existences in new democracies develop political movements and decisions that are inimical to the principles of the EU?

It took the EU some years to accept the principle of enlarging to the CEECs. When the cold war ended in 1989, the EU was engaged in intense deepening among existing members. It was politically imperative, for example, to facilitate the rapid unification of Germany in 1990 because the position of Germany in the EU was central to the future, even though in the tense moments prior to unification, some EU leaders (including Thatcher and Mitterrand) vacillated. When the issue of the CEECs emerged, the EU's choice was to pursue deepening while reassuring the CEECs that if immediate enlargement was unrealistic, the EU would soon turn to them. The first gestures toward the CEECs were bilateral trade and cooperation agreements with particular countries.

At the 1989 G7 Summit (an annual meeting of leaders of the world's wealthiest countries), the EU then assumed the tasks of coordinating and delivering aid to Poland and Hungary (originally food and humanitarian aid, including that coming from outside the EU) through the new PHARE program (a French acronym for aid for rebuilding the Polish and Hungarian economies). PHARE was eventually extended widely to cover infrastructural investment; assistance to business; educational, training, and research aid; funding for environmental protection (including nuclear safety); and agricultural restructuring in thirteen CEECs.[2] The EU also helped found the European Bank for Reconstruction and Development to provide private investment in the CEECs.[3] Next, beginning in 1990, the Union negotiated "association agreements" (quickly renamed "Europe agreements") with ten CEECs, to prepare "a new pattern of relationships in Europe." Europe agreements included political cooperation on foreign policy matters, trade agreements aimed toward establishing a free trade area, economic, cultural, and financial help, plus the beginnings of the alignment of EU and CEEC "associates" legislation on key market matters (primarily competition rules and intellectual property). The European agreements did not point clearly toward eventual EU membership for the CEECs, however, and some EU members were unwilling to open up markets to CEEC trade in areas where the CEECs might be competitive.

The 1993 Copenhagen European Council was a turning point, declaring that the EU was willing "conditionally" to accept eventual membership provided the CEECs met four criteria:

- Stable institutions (guarantee of democracy, the rule of law, human rights, minority rights)
- A functioning market economy and capacity to cope with competitive pressures inside the EU
- The ability to adopt the *acquis communautaire*
- The proviso that the EU had the capacity to absorb new members without endangering ongoing integration

Despite Copenhagen's declarations, however, there were evident hesitations about enlarge-

ment among member states and inside the Commission.

The Essen European Council in 1994 set out a detailed "preaccession strategy," scheduled regular enlargement meetings, and began detailed preparations for integrating the CEECs into the single market. Essen also promised new policies for supporting the CEECs on infrastructure, environmental policy, Common Foreign and Security Policy (CFSP), Justice and Home Affairs, and other matters. The Madrid European Council the next year then asked the Commission to prepare "opinions" on possible candidates (the first strong step to enlargement) as a major study on the effects of enlargement on existing EU policies, particularly the Common Agricultural Policy (CAP) and the structural funds, and budgetary implications. Madrid also proposed that new accession negotiations begin six months after the Amsterdam Intergovernmental Conference (IGC) ended. Hesitations persisted, however. The Germans, in particular, wanted only three CEECs to join: Poland, Hungary, and the Czech Republic.

The Amsterdam Treaty was supposed to begin the institutional reform processes to allow EU institutions to work after CEECs joined. In this respect, as in others, Amsterdam was an inadequate compromise. It extended qualified majority voting (QMV), but not by much, backed away from talking about the number of commissioners and the weighting of Council votes in an enlarged EU, and allowed "flexibility" (by which several members might integrate faster than the others, with the others' consent) but only in extremis. It settled minor matters, like limiting the size of the Parliament. Amsterdam postponed things, therefore, and called yet another IGC on institutional reform for 1999. It was clear that EU members were skeptical about whether, when, and in what circumstances the EU would actually enlarge. More important, until enlargement was truly at hand, they were unwilling to engage in serious institutional reform.

The enlargement process was nonetheless

underway. The Commission, charged with preparing opinions on candidates and researching enlargement and its impacts, compiled a 1,300-page document, *Agenda 2000*.[4] The Commission judged that none of ten CEECs had fulfilled the Copenhagen criteria, but that the Czech Republic, Estonia, Hungary, Poland, and Slovenia were within reach, and it recommended that negotiations with them be opened.[5] The Luxembourg European Council in 1997 then decided that formal negotiations would open with all ten candidates plus Cyprus (henceforth referred to as the Luxembourg Group), with the first five and Cyprus beginning detailed screening discussions with the Commission (which would do the actual work, with the Council standing behind it). Dealings with the second five would proceed in a multilateral, and thus slower, way. Of these, Bulgaria, Latvia, Lithuania, and Romania were moving forward, but far slower than the Luxembourg Group, while Slovakia was further behind because of its authoritarian regime. Negotiations with the Luxembourg Group opened in 1998 amid new disagreements about the division of the candidates into two groups. The Helsinki European Council in 1999 then recommended that full accession negotiations be started with the left-behind five, henceforth called the Helsinki Group.

By late 2000 only the easiest *acquis* issues had been settled and then mainly for the Luxembourg Group (discussions with the Helsinki Group had barely opened). The June 14, 2000, Commission scorecard noted satisfactory talks with almost everyone on *acquis* chapters about statistics, small and medium-sized undertakings, science and research, education and vocational training, and CFSP. Beyond this, there had been successful dealings with the Luxembourg Group on Fisheries (excepting Poland), industrial policy, telecommunications and information technology, consumers and health protection, financial control (excepting the Czech Republic), and EMU (a framework deal involving transitional phases). This left the big items wide open, however, including the "four freedoms" (free movement of goods, persons, services, and capital), competition policy, agriculture, transport, taxation, energy, culture and audiovisual policy, regional policy, the environment, justice and home affairs, the customs union, and financial and budgetary matters.

Tough bargaining remained. The reformed CAP is too expensive to be applied directly in the candidate countries, Poland in particular. Negotiating long transition periods could be a dodge, however. On the one hand, the EU insisted that CEECs accept all of the *acquis*. On the other, existing EU members felt entitled to exempt themselves from extending part of this same *acquis* to new applicants when it would cost too much. Free movement of people, another bedrock of the *acquis*, provided another example. The Germans demanded that it be restricted with Poland (and potentially with others, with transition periods again hiding the restrictions) for fear of adverse domestic political and economic consequences.[6] The structural funds provided another burning question. The CEECs all need more investment funding to catch up economically. The Commission's *Agenda 2000* budgetary proposals and the 1999 Berlin European Council anticipated the accession of most, if not all, of the Luxembourg Group. The Commission foresaw that member states, particularly the net contributors, would be in no mood to increase spending to help the CEECs. It concluded that regional development commitments (including the cohesion fund) for the existing EU-15 would have to be cut back to provide pre- and postaccession aid for the CEECs, while in general, structural fund growth would have to slow (implying less help for the CEECs). This led to changed structural fund goals with prorated payoffs to the existing EU members that stood to lose. The candidate countries were ghosts at the table in this tough discussion.[7]

Whether EU enlargement from West to East will live up to announced noble intentions is an open question. It has been a long decade since the end of the cold war, and the processes underway are unlikely to bring the first new members before 2004. Member states are at cross purposes. Some, like the United Kingdom, advocate early enlargement because they see it weakening prospects for federal European integration. Others, which claim to favor enlargement, prefer not to be constrained in scheduling it. Cross-cutting disagreements exist about which of the many applicant countries should be welcomed first.

The enlargement story parallels that of EMU. Existing EU member states, for their own reasons, are hesitant. New enlargement is bound to be risky and costly. Despite this, in 2004–2005 there will be accession for the first of the Luxembourg Group—Poland, Hungary, and the Czech Republic—with Slovenia and Estonia, very small countries, not far behind. In the meantime, there is danger that as the costs of entrance become clearer, public enthusiasm in the CEECs about the EU may wane. Moreover, given differences of opinion and the EU's obduracy about concessions that might hurt the interests of existing member states, the process is unlikely to appear very noble. Much is at stake, however. The most likely scenario is slow enlargement to the CEECs that can most easily fit into the EU. This will leave the least developed CEECs waiting longer. While one could hope that this will not be significant, it could, however, leave those that fall behind more vulnerable to poverty, illiberal political movements, and instability, all churning away on the EU's borders. With bad luck, crises threatening European stability could develop.

Enlargement is certain to bring surprises. The Union will have to reform its institutions to make enlargement work. Enlargement will change the external borders of the EU, bringing new neighbors and new issues about security and immigration. To the degree to which some CEECs are different from Western European EU members, the internal balance of the EU will change. Bringing 100 million more people into the EU and raising their living standards to EU levels will take time, patience, and expense. Success will consolidate a prosperous and democratic European continent.

A Big Switzerland? The EU as Regional Power or Global Presence?

In the cold war world, there was no space for autonomous European foreign political and military power. International rivalries inside Western Europe were unthinkable because superpower balance had removed military confrontation from the Western European equation. The deepening successes of European integration from 1985 onward greatly enhanced the EU's power in the world, particularly in economic matters, as Table 5.1 shows.

The end of the cold war created a new situation. The EU was obliged to learn rapidly. Moving forward in economic realms was the EU's history. But what then? Commission president Jacques Delors repeatedly and rhetorically asked whether the EU would remain a "big Switzerland"—an economic giant but a foreign policy dwarf. With the United States continuing to guide the North Atlantic Treaty Organization (NATO) with a firm hand and with NATO's interests constraining the EU's definition of its own interests in foreign policy and security matters, being a "big Switzerland" had its advantages.[8] It would allow the EU to act on the economic matters that it did best while allowing Europeans to focus on what they wanted most: being prosperous. It could also be cheaper than any alternative, particularly as larger EU states faced dramatic post–cold war defense reviews. Finally, it would allow member states to maintain what remained of their sovereignty in the foreign political arena.

It took a while after 1989 for Europe to take the full measure of post–cold war geostrategic changes. The British and the Germans remained prepared to play their part in staving off a Soviet invasion long after the Soviet Union had ceased to exist. The French, who left the NATO command structure in the 1960s although re-

Table 5.1   The EU as "Economic Giant" by the Numbers

	EU-15	Eurozone (euro-11)	United States	Japan
Population, 1999 (millions)	375	291	271	126
Gross domestic product per capita, 1999	19,819	20,012	30,173	22,023
Share of world exports, 1998	19.7%	NA	16.3%	9.4%
Share of world imports, 1998	18.3%	NA	21.6%	6.5%

Source: EU Delegation, *The European Union and World Trade* (Washington, D.C.: EU Delegation, November 1999).

maining officially in the alliance, had invested vast sums in an independent nuclear deterrent to provide the backbone of a European anti-Soviet defense with autonomy from the United States. This never happened, and after 1989 the French were left with sophisticated nuclear weapons and not much else, given how much these weapons had cost, aimed at targets in newly friendly CEEC countries. The Italians, Spanish, and others with lesser international ambitions faced analogous situations. EU member states had to do something to update their security outlooks, if only to avoid looking foolish within NATO. When this became apparent, however, domestic economic problems stood in the way.

The EU's sad relations with the former Yugoslavia loomed large in the change that had occurred by the end of the 1990s. The Union's fecklessness in the face of extreme brutality in its own neighborhood was humiliating. A variety of posturing—solemn statements, high-powered delegations, economic sanctions, attempts at mediation, flattering diplomacy, and more—fell short first in Croatia, then in Bosnia, and ultimately in Kosovo. EU policy was incoherent and not backed by convincing power. It took tough U.S. diplomatic brokerage to impose a new status quo in Bosnia. The Dayton accords may have been followed by a lot of hard European work, because Europeans provided the peacekeeping forces on the ground, but the humiliation stung.[9] The United States had the as-

sets and could present the credible threats that made things happen, and this allowed it to call the shots. The Europeans did not have the assets and could not call the shots, although the events were happening in Europe.

Between Bosnia and Kosovo, the EU did move forward slowly, in particular in the Amsterdam Treaty. Wordings and decision rules on CSFP were changed, and flexibility became a theoretical possibility because of new clauses on "constructive abstention." The Western Economic Union (WEU) was also given new capacities and put on a course of merger with the EU, and a "Mr. CFSP" was created and appointed. Quite as important, the Petersberg tasks (set out originally in 1992 as possible new activities for the WEU) were included in the treaty, opening to humanitarian intervention, peacekeeping, and regional crisis management that the EU could legitimately regard as its own business without conflict with NATO. None of this was spectacular, however, and portended a long period before sufficient EU unity of purpose existed to overcome the "big Switzerland" option.

In 1993–1994 NATO, reviewing its positions, opened to the possibility of a new "European pillar" and recognized the need for "Combined Joint Task Forces" ("coalitions of the willing" for crisis management) and a "European Strategic Defense Initiative." In certain circumstances NATO also would make its assets available to Europeans.[10] During the same period, key EU member states began to review their defense positions. British reassessments concluded that new European security tasks would involve rapid crisis management intervention in and around Europe itself. Ambiguity about NATO positions then became very important. Crisis management in Europe implied the possibility of British (and European) interests in actions that might not engage the United States. Would the United States allow Europe to use NATO assets if it disapproved of European goals? The French, particularly vocal about this issue, moved in 1995 to end conscription and build a professional army, in the process rejoining parts of the NATO planning apparatus.[11] They agreed with the British that building the capabilities for rapid response conflict management tasks was the central strategic challenge. There already were embryonic efforts in the German–French Eurocorps and other experimental European transnational military arrangements.

If a European strategic defense identity (ESDI) was logical, the questions became, What kind? and Was the United States in favor of serious European autonomy? Amsterdam sketched out a European role around the Petersberg tasks that, if not separate from NATO, might be semiautonomous. The French were eager because this provided a way of redefining Gaullist outlooks for new circumstances. The Germans could be counted on to wait until the United States and NATO gave their permission, while the British, if they ran true to course, would hew to the U.S. position. It took an unexpected initiative on the part of the new British prime minister, Tony Blair, to change things. The Blair government did another defense review soon after taking office, and Blair was shocked how badly Europeans were prepared for new crisis management tasks.[12] He brought his shock to the Pörtschach European Council in fall 1998, announcing that the European foreign policy and defense situation was "unacceptable" and marked by "weakness and confusion." This announcement was

followed by a Joint Declaration on European Defense by Blair and Chirac at a bilateral meeting in St. Malo in early December.

The St. Malo declaration advocated rapid implementation of the Amsterdam CFSP provisions, particularly in defense policy, to give the "Union . . . the capacity for autonomous action, backed up by credible military forces, the means to decide to use them, and a readiness to do so."[13] The Vienna European Council endorsed St. Malo in December 1998. Kosovo reinforced the momentum. The United States called, and fired, most of NATO's shots in ways that did not please elite European opinion. Quite as important, the Europeans were unable to make major contributions to the bombing offensive. Where they participated, their equipment was not modern enough. Some planes could not fly at night, for example, and others could not fly at all. They had few of the high-technology tools—smart bombs, guidance systems, and the like—at the heart of the effort. And they were completely dependent on the United States for intelligence (satellites), command and communications tools, and airlift capacity. The Kosovo campaign was another humiliation for EU members, in other words; once again, after the United States had directed and starred in the military production. Europeans then paid for less spectacular jobs like reconstruction, humanitarian assistance, troops, and policing on the ground.

The Cologne European Council in June 1999 made a number of basic decisions. Defense policy structures would be built within the CFSP pillar, and "alternative options such as developing the autonomy of WEU, the exclusive focus on ESDI within NATO, or the establishment of a fourth pillar within the EU were dismissed."[14] The Helsinki European Council six months later committed to 50,000 to 60,000 troops "capable of the full range of Petersberg tasks," which could be deployed within sixty days and sustained for one year (implying double the number of troops in readiness) by 2003. The Council of Ministers would set up new structures for political and strategic control over these forces. Most important, the "European Council underlines its determination to develop an autonomous capacity to take decisions and, where NATO as a whole is not engaged, to launch and conduct EU-led military operations in response to international crises. This process will avoid unnecessary duplication and does not imply the creation of a European army."[15]

The EU thus appeared set on building a new defense identity in a few years that would give it a range of new tools to combine the military and nonmilitary dimensions of crisis management. Appearances, once again, could be misleading. Increasing levels of defense spending are called for, for example, if Europeans are to acquire what they now lack to achieve autonomy, including expensive satellites, intelligence systems, smart weapons, airlift capacity, independent planning capacities, and new command and control systems. In times of budgetary stringency, the money is not certain to be forthcoming. Increased coordination of the European defense industry is absolutely necessary, but carrying it out to a successful conclusion will be a complicated and uncertain process. It is also conceivable that the more tangible a new European security identity becomes, the tenser EU relationships with NATO and the United States will become. The United States has reason to salute a new "European pillar" in NATO, which a new European security program would institute. A relatively autonomous European defense operation may be less to U.S. tastes, however. As a French commentator has noted, Americans and Europeans "indulge in incompatible dreams. The US wants to be number one, while minimizing the cost to the lives of its soldiers or to its economy. Europeans want to keep the US as the ultimate insurance policy as they evolve towards a common identity."[16] In this situation there is space for serious disagreement. What happens when and if Europe moves to achieve its Helsinki goals will be well worth

watching. Both European commitment and American patience are likely to be tested. The new Europe could begin reflecting about whether it was merely a bloc with regional interests or something bigger, with global interests.[17]

European Institutions: Democracy and Legitimacy?

The Eurosystem was never designed as a system of governance, let alone a state, and it did not begin in a search for an ideal constitution. Many who participated in composing the initial treaties hoped that great political and institutional flowers would eventually bloom from limited beginnings. But they had little idea what varieties were likely to grow, if any. They also knew that since European peoples were not really prepared for any great changes, the garden would have to grow plot by plot. "Europe" would first have to prove its usefulness. The new European experiment was purposively begun in economic matters at the center of multiple interdependencies. In time, the founders hoped, "Europe" would grow through spillover.

The EU's institutional triangle of an appointed Commission, intergovernmental Council of Ministers, and weak Parliament, plus other institutions like the ECJ, were designed to allow the EU's six original members to work together for limited purposes. In the EU's brief history, the scope and prerogatives of all these institutions have expanded beyond anyone's anticipation. Accompanying the EU's expanding mandates and membership, European leaders have periodically updated the treaties on which the system is based. Since 1985 there have been precious few moments when the EU has not been either digesting the changes of a recent IGC or preparing for a new one

By the beginning of the twenty-first century, however, European leaders were aware that the EU faced major constitutional issues. In the words of Joschka Fischer, the German foreign minister,

> In the past, European integration was based on the "Monnet method" with its communitarization approach in European institutions and policy. This gradual process of integration, with no blueprint for the final state, was conceived in the 1950s for the economic integration of a small group of countries. Successful as it was . . . this approach has proved to be of only limited use for the political integration and democratization of Europe.[18]

Fischer was opening a rare great debate on Europe's future goals. Other leaders also recognized the unique nature of the situation and made their own careful contributions to this debate. British prime minister Tony Blair, for example, queried

> Europe, yes, but what sort of Europe?
> . . . The trouble with the debate about Europe's political future is that if we do not take care, we plunge into the thicket of institutional change without first asking the basic question of what direction Europe should take. . . . The need for institutional change does not derive either from a fear that Europe is immobile or that it is time to upset the delicate balance between Commission and governments: it derives from a more fundamental question.
> . . . The most important challenge for Europe is to wake up to the new reality: Europe is widening and deepening simultaneously. There will be more of us in the future, trying to do more. . . . The issue is: not whether we do this, but how we reform this new Europe so that it both delivers real benefits to the people of Europe, addressing the priorities they want addressed; and does so in a way that has their consent and support.[19]

Every proposal for reform raised further questions, however. Try as member states might to confine things to institutional "plumbing," the entire design of the EU's "house" was really the issue. EU institutions have worked to get the Union into the new century, but in convoluted, sometimes obscure ways. Institutions that are already creaking, groaning, opaque, and distant with fifteen members could seize up for good in an enlarged EU. The EU's growing responsibilities in a globalizing world put a new premium on institutional efficiency. Yet EU institutions, unprecedented experiments in transnational governance, are unmapped territory for democratic responsibility.

Institutional Plumbing and the 2000 Intergovernmental Conference

The contemporary problems of EU institutions are clear. The Commission has been vulnerable from the outset, handicapped because commissioners are appointed, because these appointments have not always been of the highest quality, and because the Commission's services are perceived as a high-flying, sometimes self-righteous crowd of technocrats unaccountable to anyone. This is not really the Commission's fault. The treaties gave it highly visible roles as energizer, animator, vanguard, and rule maker of European integration, and these roles exposed it as a target for opponents of integration and a scapegoat for member state leaderships to shift the blame for what they themselves have wrought. When the Commission has been weak, it has been easy to characterize as a band of parasitic meddlers. When it has been strong, it has faced counteroffensives from other institutions and member states.

Other EU institutions have had their own problems. The Council of Ministers has become highly complicated, fragmented into a proliferation of meetings and specialized committees. The General Affairs Council (of foreign ministers), which is supposed to be the Council's coordinating organ, has great trouble keeping up, in part because foreign ministers and their staffs have too much to do in addition to EU matters, but also because of the growing crush of EU business. The permutations and combinations of constant negotiation among numbers of mandated national delegates in multiple areas have created slow decision making and more than occasional deadlock. All too often matters get passed up to the European Council, where they take time from the priority tasks of longer-term reflection and goal setting. Beyond this, if the Parliament's power has grown rapidly in the last two decades, it does not know what its place and mission really are. The rotating presidency of the Commission does not work well and does not allow sufficient continuity. When, after enlargement to thirty, member states will exercise the presidency only every fifteen years, it is unlikely to work much better. The "economic government" issue about EMU is serious, and without resolution, Europe's economic policy mechanisms may be seriously hindered. There are important administrative services in the EU's new areas, particularly CFSP and justice and home affairs, that are fragmented between and inside the Council and Commission and sorely demand better ways of working.

One cannot overlook the larger problems of the changing balance of power among the triangle institutions. The Commission, in particular, has been weaker or stronger, depending on the moment. Intergovernmental, as opposed to "Community," ways of operating appear and reappear. The Parliament's increasing power has had an impact on the relative power of Constitution and Council. Innovation creating the cooperation procedure nourished an important alliance between Commission and Parliament. The codecision procedure then nourished new alliances between Parliament and the Council. And then there is the very real matter of democratic deficit—the Union's ongoing difficulty at building acceptable relationships of responsibility, accountability, and legitimacy with Europe's peoples. The negative results of the 2000 Danish referendum on EMU were only one reminder of this.

As Joschka Fischer underlined, the EU has grown, following the Monnet method, by adding functions for existing institutions rather than reflecting on and redesigning these institutions. The 2000 IGC was mandated to confront the most immediate issues that enlargement posed. In the words of three experts charged by

the Commission to think about institutions and enlargement:

> A significant increase in the number of participants automatically increases problems of decision making and management. Interests are more different, discussion is slower, decision more difficult, management more complex. Problems in the working of the European institutions are already apparent today. . . . They are bound to increase.[20]

Without considerably more QMV, national vetoes will increase geometrically in a variegated EU of thirty members, and prospects for paralysis will rise commensurately. Enlargement (and more QMV) also necessitated a reweighting of votes in the Council so that majorities would more accurately reflect the size and population of member states. Next, simply adding new commissioners to the existing twenty (already the limit of effectiveness) could destroy the Commission's capacity to function as a college.[21] The IGC also focused on finding broader procedures for greater "reinforced cooperation" to allow the more energetic and ambitious member states to forge ahead of others in particular dimensions of integration (as EU members already had done in EMU and the Schengen group). Finally, the IGC drew up the European Charter of Rights, which member states supported, that might eventually integrate into the treaties.[22]

These were urgent problems but also the easy ones. The Treaty of Nice in December 2000 did not bode well for the tougher problems that lay behind them, however.[23] There was tit-for-tat bargaining on extending QMV, which fell far short of the objective of removing unanimity in forty areas. On matters of lesser importance, QMV progressed, but on the five matters that counted, deadlock persisted. There was some progress on external trade matters (on services and intellectual property, with France insisting, however, on maintaining unanimity on culture, health, and education). Unanimity will continue on both fiscal and social policy, however, largely because the British insisted. Finally, where

QMV was extended, in areas like immigration and regional policy, long transition periods were set out. On immigration, QMV would not come until 2004, with the Germans also insisting on maintaining a veto beyond this date on the final definition of EU asylum policy. The solution for the structural funds on which the Spanish insisted to the end was, alas, typical. QMV would indeed be introduced, but not until 2007. What this meant was that Spain (and allies) would retain a veto through the beginnings of enlargement to the CEECs and through the negotiation of the EU's next new budgetary package, itself likely to be for six years, in effect a veto that would last until 2012!

Reweighting Council voting (which included establishing the number of Council votes that new members would receive) became a bitter struggle, particularly between larger and smaller members. The larger members won. If the four largest members of the EU-15 voted together, they would constitute a blocking minority, even if all smaller countries wanted something (this was done in part by raising the threshold for QMV). This result was possible, however, only after very difficult bargaining between the French and Germans, with the latter seeking more power because of their post-unification population growth. The relative weight of larger versus smaller members grew in general. The new QMV system will not come into effect until 2005, however, yet another index of existing member states' desires to protect their positions during a difficult moment of transition.

The smaller countries won on Commission size, however. In 2005 the large countries would lose their second commissioner, but all members would get one commissioner. When the EU reached twenty-seven members, the matter of having fewer commissioners than members could be reconsidered, but only unanimously, implying at least a decade before anything new would happen. The only real advance was that designating the Commission president could be by QMV rather than unanimity. Possibilities

for reinforced cooperation (less than a majority of EU members deciding to move forward on their own) were increased.

Reinforced cooperation, already sketched very restrictively at Amsterdam, was designed to facilitate an avant-garde of member states moving ahead of others (accepted out of fear that an enlarged EU might otherwise settle into deadlock). The Nice Treaty removed the possibility of member states' vetoing reinforced cooperation, but made it impossible for any vanguard to move forward in ways that would undercut either the single market or the *acquis communautaire*. Thus, at least eight members had to be involved, and reinforced cooperation had to be within areas that the treaty allowed; it could not restrict Schengen or involve significant defense and foreign policy issues, and it had to proceed within clear procedural guidelines.

Perhaps the most important result of Nice was official commitment to hold another IGC in 2004 that would confront larger constitutional matters.[24] This was a solid indicator about how much Nice involved reluctance to work on relatively simple changes. There was no mystery behind this. Even such simple changes produce relative winners and losers and shift balances of power and influence. More QMV would remove potentially paralytic veto points, but almost all member states had their favorite veto targets, and when they were put on the same negotiating list, the list got long. Reweighting QMV involved taking votes away from today's small countries and reassigning them to larger ones and could have reconfigured the relative powers of larger members, particularly France and Germany, which fought furiously about this. Keeping the number of commissioners small enough to allow the Commission to function meant that some countries would either not get commissioners or that their commissioners would get second-class jobs. In reinforced cooperation, the problem was less in finding new words to allow some members to go faster than in anticipating what this might lead to. In general, Nice was the longest European Council meeting in EU history, and member states waited until the very last conceivable moment to strike a very small deal.

Toward a Great Debate?

Institutional redesign will be the EU's order of the next decade, because the harder questions still need to be addressed. Getting the institutional architecture straight is only part of the problem. The treaties need to be rewritten, yet another job that was put off at Maastricht, Amsterdam, and Nice. Understanding the treaties is difficult even for legal scholars and inside operators, but it is possible to simplify them to be more understandable for broader publics. The most general of EU principles could be enunciated briefly and clearly, as they are in many national constitutions. Clarifying subsidiarity is also possible by specifying the juridical spaces in which the EU, member states, regions, and localities live. Then the particular competencies of each level could be set out.[25] These tasks will presumably be at the heart of the 2004 IGC. Joschka Fischer, a prime mover in issuing the call for the new IGC, underlined his reasoning in a May 12, 2000, speech in Berlin:

> These three reforms—the solution of the democracy problem and the need for a fundamental reordering of competences both horizontally, i.e. among the European institutions, and vertically, i.e. between Europe, the nation-state and the regions—will only be able to succeed if Europe is established anew with a constitution, in other words: through the realization of the project of a European constitution centered around basic, human and civil rights, an equal division of powers between the European institutions and a precise delineation between European and nation-state level.[26]

Europe indeed needs a constitution. Discussing this need leads inexorably to fundamental questions of Europe's real purposes and goals—in Eurospeak, the EU's "finalities." Fischer has perhaps summarized it best:

> Ten years after the end of the cold war and right at the start of the age of globalization one can literally almost feel that the problems and challenges facing Europe have wound themselves into a knot which will be very hard to undo within the existing framework: the introduction of the single currency, the EU's incipient eastern enlargement, the crisis of the last EU Commission, the poor acceptance of the European Parliament and low turn-outs for European elections, the wars in the Balkans and the development of a Common Foreign and Security Policy not only define what has been achieved but also determine the challenges still to be overcome.
>
> Quo vadis Europa? is the question posed once again by the history of our continent. And for many reasons the answer Europeans will have to give, if they want to do well by themselves and their children, can only be this: onwards to the completion of European integration. A step backwards, even just standstill or contentment with what has been achieved, would demand a fatal price of all EU member states and of all those who want to become members; it would demand above all a fatal price above all of our people.[27]

Fischer (echoing Jacques Delors and others) proposed a "very simple answer: the transition from a union of states to full parliamentarization of a European Federation."[28]

French president Jacques Chirac, speaking to the German Bundestag a month later, put a different inflection on things, advocating movement forward within existing structures and stressing that

> for the foreseeable future nations will remain the first references for our peoples . . . [and] . . . to envisage their disappearance would be as absurd as denying that they have already chosen to exercise parts of their sovereignty in common and that they will continue to do so. . . . So . . . let us give up our anathemas and simplifications and agree, finally, that the institutions of the Union are and will remain original and specific.

Chirac went on to propose reforming existing institutions by democratizing them, clarifying the division of tasks among the different levels of European governance by applying the principle of subsidiarity, and, above all, opening up the prospects of reinforced cooperation to allow a "pioneer group" of nations around France and Germany to forge "better coordination of economic policies, reinforce defense and security policy and be more effective in the struggle against crime." [29]

In the fall of 2000, the British weighed in. Predictably, Tony Blair was less grandiose and ambitious than his continental colleagues:

> Europe is a Europe of free, independent sovereign nations who choose to pool that sovereignty in pursuit of their own interests and the common good, achieving more together than we can achieve alone. The EU will remain a unique combination of the intergovernmental and the supranational. . . . Such a Europe can, in its economic and political strength, be a superpower . . . but not a superstate.
>
> We should not therefore begin with an abstract discussion of institutional change. We begin with the practical question, what should Europe do? What do the people of Europe want and expect it to do? Then we focus Europe and its institutions around the answer. . . . The problem Europe's citizens have with Europe arises when Europe's priorities aren't theirs. No amount of institutional change, most of which passes them by completely, will change that.[30]

Blair went on to suggest, among other things, enhancement of the European Council via an annual agenda submitted to the public, changes in the rotating presidency of the Council, a second chamber of the European Parliament composed of representatives of national parliaments that could "politically review" EU legislation, and "enhanced cooperation" but not as a "mechanism of exclusion." The EU's "constitution," he added, will, "like the British constitution . . . continue to be found in a number of different treaties, laws and precedents. It is perhaps easier for the British than for others to recognise that a constitutional debate must not necessarily end with a single, legally binding

document called a Constitution for an entity as dynamic as the EU."[31]

These speeches make clear that the issues are so large that European leaders hardly know where to start. The "Community" method has created a strange political animal that is rapidly moving beyond its original economic territories into the heart of member state sovereignty in foreign and military matters and justice and internal affairs. And even in its existing situation, the Union has a large number of genuinely federal functions: the CAP (which still desperately needs change), EMU, regional development, competition policy, single market regulation, environmental policy, and a federal judiciary. It also has a number of intergovernmental or "confederal" policy areas with non-Community institutional structures, particularly in the CFSP and justice and home affairs areas. Most European insiders agree that the dynamics in play portend more Euro-level politics, at the cost of national prerogatives, in both market and economic areas and in new political unity areas.

Divisions among "federalists" and intergovernmental "confederalists" who also want more Europolitics are profound, based on very real differences in interests. Some smaller countries, like the Netherlands and Belgium, want a federation and more supranational Europolitics as a shield against domination by collusion among the bigger countries like Germany and France. Differences between both these camps and others that want to restrain any growth in Europolitics, like the Danes, the British, and perhaps the Swedes, are also profound. Given vast disagreements, therefore, any full-blown constitutional conference could create more problems than it could solve. Serious institutional reform will probably occur piecemeal, if it occurs at all. But to the degree to which EU institutional cacophony and ineffectiveness continue, the EU will suffer, and those who would prefer that it not move forward will win. Something must happen in the next decade, one way or the other. The future of the EU is at stake.

The Democratic Dilemma

Behind debates about institutional change lie issues about the future of democracy in Europe. European integration has always presented delicate problems for democratic theory and practice. EU member states agreed to pool significant dimensions of sovereignty from the Rome Treaty onward, particularly in all-important economic areas. This pooling, through the Monnet method, was meant to enhance economic success and the general welfare across the Union, but it created a Euro-level political system that poses serious problems for citizen scrutiny, control, and exercise of preferences over decisions.

The Rome Treaty established a system with a distinct lack of transparency and direct political responsibility. The European Commission, with its formal monopoly of proposal, was appointed. The Council of Ministers, the EU's colegislature, and the European Council, the EU's strategic guide, are intergovernmental and have always functioned behind screens of diplomatic secrecy. From the viewpoint of member state polities, Europe is "foreign policy," and this has allowed national elites to shroud European activities behind executive prerogative. The European Parliament, despite its growing power, remains an odd body to which no government is responsible and which has no majority and opposition, making for very foggy debates and communications with European peoples. European law is juridically superior to national law, but the origin and nature of European law are poorly understood by citizens, and the workings of the ECJ are difficult to understand. Finally, all of these institutions work with a baffling multiplicity of decision-making processes that only specialists can truly follow.

Real democratic politics in Europe remains national politics. There exists as yet little European political culture. Despite this, national parliamentary discussions rarely foreground European issues, and elections to the European Parliament remain tightly linked to national political debates. With notable exceptions—Denmark, for example, which constitutionally obliges its national parliament to debate European issues and submit key Euro-level legal matters to national referenda—most national parties and interest groups have only begun to embrace European matters. One could fault member state leaders, analyze the reasons for their behaviors, and investigate the institutional and other incentives at the national level that encourage such practices. But whatever this might turn up, the gap between the thickness of national democratic deliberative practices and the thinness of analogous practices at European level is clear.

In the euphoria at the end of the cold war, it was common to assume that "democracy was democracy" in the sense that once a society had confirmed its choice of constitutional political institutions committed to the rule of law and regular, free electoral consultations, the story had been told. In the strange but widely accepted formula, the enormous post–cold war achievement of democratic ways was "the end of history." One issue overlooked in this euphoria was fundamental, however. Even where the basic definitional criteria for democracy are satisfied, democratic life is subject to change. Democracy is a historically dynamic process, not a fixed object. Economic shifts, citizen preferences, the shape of social structures and social problems, relationships between sovereign nations, the scope of markets, and a host of other factors create variety in the nature of democratic life over time and between different democratic societies. In effect, *there may be more, less, or different democracy* in different places and times.

In Europe, as elsewhere, change has been occurring rapidly, even in societies long certified as democratic. Patterns of social stratification have changed. "Workers" have declined, and those remaining are diversified in situation and outlook. The "middle classes" have become pivotal in their roles as consumers, producers, and voters. "Elites," earlier based primarily on the power of wealth, are more bureaucratized and technocratic. Populations have been aging in ways that challenge intergenerational patterns of distribution and place new strains on social protection systems. Over the past two decades, the rate of economic growth has dropped, rendering earlier expectations of government less realistic, with important consequences in terms of citizen confidence in politics and politicians. The downturn in growth has increased economic insecurity and brought high unemployment, greater inequality, new poverty, and social exclusion Labor unions, key to the "neocorporatist" postwar patterns of representation, have been weakened and lost political influence. Organized interests of all kinds have changed their strategic and tactical repertoires.

Patterns of political representation have changed significantly in consequence. The effects of television, for example, raise deep questions about the role of media in political representation. Televisual campaigning is very expensive and has obliged political parties to seek new sources of funds, often in technically illegal ways that made the 1990s a decade of scandals. Modern polling and political advertising, if they are useful to politicians to target particular constituencies and "median voters," help short-circuit older patterns of aggregating preferences and create new ones. The role and nature of political parties have changed. The mass membership parties pioneered by European social democracy are being replaced by elite-run electoral machines. Decentralized popular social movements, earlier obliged to seek effective political expression under the wings of these parties, now are heard in quite different ways.

Most important, the declining economic importance of national boundaries has altered policy agendas and diminished national state capacities. Europeanization and globalization have undercut earlier simplistic assumptions of relative national autarky, bringing a sea change in the theory and practice of economic policy. Economic boundaries are much more permeable. Financial markets are now in a position to constrain and sanction many national policy choices. Sovereignty has been lost, sometimes from choice, often unwillingly. Politicians now have considerable difficulty responding to the expressed needs and desires of citizens for levels of economic and social security that had earlier been assumed. In general, issue repertoires in democracies have shifted in consequence of social and economic change. Older statist approaches have been under siege for some time, and social democratic parties have shifted perspectives toward "third-way" perspectives, in which the state and the market coexist in less antagonistic, supply-side ways. In a period of what many perceive to be relative deprivation, immigration has once again become a central political issue, and new populist impulses have appeared, many bearing messages of intolerance.

If similar changes can be tracked in most democratic capitalist societies, in Europe, unlike elsewhere, they have been occurring in the context of European integration. The EU's democratic deficit has been less or more pressing to the degree to which decisions made at the European level have themselves been significant to EU citizens. Thus in the common market first period, roughly into the early 1980s, Europe was not perceived as weighing greatly on what really mattered. This has changed dramatically in recent years. European integration, for better or worse, has become decisive in shaping the day-to-day lives of all EU citizens. Since 1985, substantial national state capacities and control have been transferred away from EU member states. In some areas, capacities have been relocated from familiar national democratic places to less familiar and less democratic transnational ones, shining new spotlights on the insufficiencies of the Brussels institutions. In addition, important matters that had been debated publicly and decided democratically at national level have been shifted toward the market.

The story is even more complicated. Decisions producing this relocalization of state capacities have often been made by European-level methods whose relationships to democracy are murky. Europe has become a choice location for making decisions either by "foreign affairs" methods shielded from public scrutiny or by the "Monnet method" of engineered spillover (the Commission's preferred approach). The methodological problem is significantly multiplied because these decisions often are based on a different temporal logic from those in national democratic lives. Euro-level deliberations are privileged locations for medium- and longer-term choices whose ultimate consequences ordinary Europeans ignore when the choices are made, and ignorance is created structurally by the shorter-term time horizons that govern domestic political arenas where politicians must always have their eyes focused on impending elections. There has also often been explicit desire on the part of Euro-level decision makers not to stress their longer time horizons in public discourse. Europolitics has thus become a very useful way to circumvent the many blockages and veto points of national politics. The perverse dimensions of this are clear. When elites use Europe to reconfigure national arrangements to give them the kind of policy breathing space they think they need, they then often turn around and shift the blame for the disruption that follows onto Europe. The consequences of such Euro-level decisions targeted on large problems and proposing medium-range remedies are likely to constrain national democratic choices at a later point. The effect is that the European political arena, with its perceived democratic deficiencies, effectively structures many options in national polities before these polities have had a chance to deliberate and decide.

The ways in which democratic representation and accountability work in EU member states vary but are sufficiently well understood by citizens to allow the legitimization of national authority. The same cannot be said for the EU, which is a promiscuity of different types of representation. National political elites are represented in the workings of the Council of Ministers and the European Council, but given the intergovernmental ways of these institutions, they can skirt accountability in many ways, diluting the importance of their provenance in national elections. The Commission is not supposed to represent any particular Europeans but to serve "Europe." The Parliament does not yet engage the attention of those who elect it. Members of the European Parliament are elected, for the most part, because of the national positions of their parties, not because of voters' acquaintance with European matters. The muddied picture of political responsibility that these voters get of Europe undoubtedly helps this since they cannot really know, in Europolitical terms, what they are voting for. There is no clear choice between parties on Europolicy lines, largely because there is no choice between Europlatforms and governments. The European Parliament may do good work analyzing and scrutinizing proposals sent to it, but very few people know about this work, and even fewer understand where it fits politically.

If there can be *different* democracy and also *more or less* democracy, then we must be very attentive to the effects of Europolitics for democracy in Europe. The most obvious observation is that the ramshackle EU institutional complex makes democratic responsibility and accountability more difficult than it needs to be. But it is not at all obvious what to change and how to change it. Designing transnational democratic politics is a dramatically new problem that must take place against the background of changing democratic politics more generally. Moreover, given the wide range of difference across the EU, basic constitutional change is dangerous for European integration. Politicians and leaders are thus faced with a daunting choice between confronting the EU's democratic dilemma at the potential cost of disrupting integration or moving forward with integration and hoping for the best.

Those who have built Europe are democrats and people of the law, but European institutions as they currently exist do not facilitate the clarification of issues of democratic responsibility and accountability. Institutional muddiness, however innocently created over decades, is not likely to produce politically innocent behavior. Postwar settlements in Europe created extremely dense national systems of political exchange, often fenced by difficult-to-change rules and powerful organizations. European integration, particularly since the mid-1980s, has been designed to undercut the parts of these settlements deemed barriers to European economic success. Some actors, including business interests, have been able to adjust their strategies to influence these processes successfully. Other actors, particularly those with deeply rooted national resource bases, have been less flexible. In brief, European integration has helped some groups more than it has helped others. The changes wrought by European integration justify questioning whether Europe in the twenty-first century will have different democracy or less democracy.

Notes

1. For a review of the first year of EMU, see Organisation of Economic Cooperation and Development, *EMU One Year On* (Paris: OECD, 2000).

2. The Commission, which assumed major responsibility for PHARE, quickly found itself overwhelmed. It did not have enough qualified personnel and finances. In consequence, many things were done in a rough-and-ready way that would come back to haunt the Commission.

3. For a subtle and thorough review of enlargement matters, see Elrich Sedelmeier and Helen Wallace, "Eastern Enlargement: Strategy of Second Thoughts?" in Helen Wallace and William Wallace, *Policymaking in the European Union,* 4th ed. (Oxford: Oxford University Press, 2000).

4. European Commission, *Agenda 2000: For a Stronger and Wider European Union* (Luxembourg: EU, 1998).

5. This made a total of eleven candidacies, since the Commission had already given a positive opinion on civil-war-divided Cyprus in 1993.

6. On the current state of the CAP, see Elmar Rieger, "The Common Agricultural Policy: Politics Against Markets," in Wallace and Wallace, *Policymaking in the European Union.*

7. The expression is from Brigid Laffan and Michael Shackleton, "The Budget: Who Gets What, When and How," in Wallace and Wallace, *Policymaking in the European Union.*

8. At Maastricht, EU member states had clearly been loath to give up their remaining foreign and defense policy autonomy, because in most instances it remained a real source of international leverage. The Gulf War helped set the stage for this reluctance, simultaneously dividing the Europeans and pushing them into line behind U.S. goals. The EU's disarray after Maastricht then facilitated a relatively rapid U.S. strategic reevaluation, particularly with NATO. NATO thus moved to reconsider its missions and expand in ways that guaranteed it a strong position in European security matters for the new era, even while the United States withdrew most of its troops and cut back on defense spending. On NATO changes, see David S. Yost, *NATO Transformed* (Washington, D.C.: United States Institute of Peace, 1998).

9. See Fraser Cameron, *Foreign and Security Policy of the European Union* (Sheffield: Sheffield Academic Press, 1999) pp. 50–55; Anthony Forster and William Wallace, "Common Foreign and Security Policy," in Wallace and Wallace, *Policymaking in the European Union.* Chirac also demanded that NATO name a French officer for the Mediterranean region, which caused a stir and limited France's rapprochement.

10. Yost, *NATO Transformed,* chap. 4.

11. The Germans were behind and ended their review only in 1999. While ending conscription was politically impossible, they reflected on the new situa-

tion otherwise in similar ways to the French and British.

12. Forster and Wallace, "Common Foreign and Security Policy," p. 484.

13. Cited in Cameron, *Foreign and Security Policy*, p. 78.

14. Ibid., p. 79. NATO, at its fiftieth anniversary festival, had earlier given its blessing to a strengthened European security and defense policy.

15. Presidency Conclusions, Helsinki European Council, December 10–11, 1999, Title II.

16. Dominique Moisi, "What Transatlantic Future," in Werner Weidenfeld, ed., *Creating Partnership: The Future of Transatlantic Relations* (Gütersloh: Bertelsmann Foundation, 1997), p. 99.

17. In this light, another recent Bertelsmann Foundation publication, *Enhancing the European Union as an International Security Actor* (Gutersloh: Bertelsmann Foundation, 2000), makes very interesting reading.

18. Joschka Fischer, "From Confederacy to Federation—Thoughts on the Finality of European Integration" (translation of advance text of speech at Humboldt University, Berlin, May, 12, 2000), p. 6.

19. 10 Downing Street, "Prime Minister's Speech to the Polish Stock Exchange," October 6, 2000, www.number-10.gov.uk.

20. Richard von Weizsäcker, Jean-luc Dehaene, and David Simon, *Report to the Commission on "The Institutional Implications of Enlargement"* (Brussels: European Commission, October 18, 1999), p. 5.

21. For a succinct summary of the issues, see ibid.

22. For the draft Declaration on Fundamental Rights in the EU, see http://db.consilium.eu.int, the Council of Ministers' web site, and follow the links.

23. The only available version of the Nice Treaty available at time of writing was *Trait de Nice, Texte provisoire agréé par la Conférénce inter-gouvernementale sur la réforme institutionnelle* (SN 533/00, Brussels, December 12, 2000).

24. At Nice, the European Parliament was also slightly enlarged, and the Germans gained some seats relative to the French.

25. See the effort at such a rewrite by specialists at the European University Institute in Florence, *Basic Treaty of the European Union* (draft) (Florence: Robert Schuman Centre for Advanced Studies, 2000). For another such effort in a totally different vein, see "Our Constitution for Europe," *Economist*, October 28, 2000, pp. 17–22.

26. Fischer, "From Confederacy to Federation—Thoughts on the Finality of European Integration," p. 6.

27. Ibid., p. 1.

28. Ibid., p. 4.

29. Chirac made a major speech in response to Joschka Fischer in Berlin on June 27. The citations are from German Foreign Ministry, French text, June 27, 2000, my translation.

30. Blair, p. 8.

31. Ibid., p. 9.

Acknowledgments

Writing a textbook chapter on the EU is a daunting task that I have undertaken here because I am deeply troubled by the lack of understanding among North Americans (including social scientists) of the importance of European integration. I would like to express gratitude to the DAAD (Deutscher Akademischer Austausch-Dienst) for kindly including me in the Germany 2000 program, from which much new knowledge came about German European outlooks and enlargement. Debi Osnowitz has been a great editor and will be an even greater sociologist as soon as she ceases taking on ungratifying jobs like this. Brandeis University has helped with the editing task. The European Commission Delegation in Washington, D.C., has done a great job in keeping American scholars working on the EU encouraged and informed (particularly Hugo Paemen, Gunther Burghardt, Fraser Cameron, Jonathan Davidson, and Bill Burros). The Minda de Gunzburg Center for European Studies and the European Union Center at Harvard University (particular thanks to Reneé Haferkamp, Andy Moravcsik, and Joseph Weiler) have been a great help. Jane Jenson was tolerant and kind, as always. Almost certainly some of what I have written will annoy some of these wonderful people and great institutions. As perhaps the greatest "European" once commented on something I had written, "You intellectuals always have a perverse critical side to you." Sadly, from the point of view of my relationship with him, he was correct. On the other hand, that is what we are supposed to be. None of the above colleagues and friends are responsible for errors and tendentiousness.

Bibliography

Dinan, Desmond. *Ever Closer Union.* 2d ed. Boulder, Colo.: Lynne Rienner, 1999.

Duchêne, François. *Jean Monnet: The First Statesman of Interdependence.* New York: Norton, 1994.

Duignan, Peter, and Gann, L. H. *The United States and the New Europe.* Oxford: Oxford University Press, 1994.

Edwards, Geoffrey, and Pijpers, Anton, eds. *The Politics of European Treaty Reform: The 1996 Intergovernmental Conference and Beyond.* London: Pinter, 1997.

Edwards, Geoffrey, and Wiessala, Georg, eds. *The European Union: Annual Review of the EU 1999/2000.* Oxford: Blackwell, 2000.

George, Stephen. *An Awkward Partner: Britain in the European Community.* Oxford: Clarendon Press, 1990.

Gillingham, John. *Coal, Steel and the Rebirth of Europe, 1945–1955.* Cambridge: Cambridge University Press, 1991.

Grant, Wyn. *The Common Agricultural Policy.* New York: St. Martin's Press, 1997.

Hayes-Renshaw, Fiona, and Wallace, Helen. *The Council of Ministers.* New York: St. Martin's Press, 1997.

Heisenberg, Dorothee. *The Mark of the Bundesbank.* Boulder, Colo.: Lynne Rienner, 1999.

Hoffmann, Stanley. *The European Sisyphus, Essays on Europe, 1964–1994.* Boulder, Colo.: Westview Press, 1994.

Keohane, Robert, and Hoffmann, Stanley, eds. *The New European Community.* Boulder, Colo.: Lynne Rienner, 1991.

Kirchner, Emil. *Decision-Making in the European Community: The Council Presidency and European Integration.* New York: St. Martin's Press, 1992.

Laffan, Brigid. *The Finances of the European Union.* London: Macmillan, 1997.

Leibfried, Stephan, and Pierson, Paul. *European Social Policy.* Washington, D.C.: Brookings, 1995.

Ludlow, Peter. *The Making of the European Monetary System.* London: Butterworths, 1982.

Martin, Andrew, et al. *The Brave New World of European Unions.* New York: Berghahn, 1999.

Moravcsik, Andrew. *The Choice for Europe.* Ithaca, N.Y.: Cornell University Press, 1998.

Nelsen, Brent F., and Stubb, Alexander C-G., eds. *The European Union: Readings on the Theory and Practice of European Integration.* 2d ed. Boulder, Colo.: Lynne Rienner, 1998.

Paemen, Hugo, and Bensk, Alexandra. *From GATT to the Uruguay Round.* Leuven: Leuven University Press, 1995.

Peterson, John, and Bomberg, Elizabeth. *Decision-Making in the European Union.* New York: St. Martin's Press, 1999.

Pryce, Roy, ed. *The Dynamics of European Union.* London: Croom Helm, 1987.

Regelsberger, Elfriede; Schoutheete, Philippe de; and Wessels, Wolfgan, eds. *Foreign Policy of the European Union: From EPC to CFSP and Beyond.* Boulder, Colo.: Lynne Reinner, 1997.

Ross, George. *Jacques Delors and European Integration*. Cambridge: Polity Press/Oxford University Press, 1995.

Tsoukalis, Loukas. *The New European Economy Revisited*. Oxford: Oxford University Press, 1997.

van der Eijk, Cees, and Franklin, Mark N., eds. *Choosing Europe*. Ann Arbor: University of Michigan Press, 1996.

Wallace, Helen, and Wallace, William. *Policymaking in the European Union*. 4th ed. Oxford: Oxford University Press, 2000.

Westlake, Martin. *A Modern Guide to the European Parliament*. London: Pinter, 1994.

Weatherill, Stephen, and Beaumont, Paul. *EC Law*. London: Penguin, 1993.

Web Sites

General EU Web site, *http://www.europa.eu.int*.

Other official EU Web sites:

Council of Ministers, *http://www.ue.eu.int*.

Court of Justice, *http://www.curia.eu.int*.

European Central Bank, *http://www.ecb.int*.

European Commission, *http://www.europa.eu.int/comm*.

European Council, *http://www.ue.eu.int*.

Eurostat, *http://www.europa.eu.int/eurostat.html*.

European Parliament, *http://www.europarl.eu.int*.

European Union in the United States, *http://www.eurunion.org*.

Jean Monnet at Harvard Web site (useful for tracking down new scholarly work on the EU), *http://www.law.harvard.edu\programs\jeanmonnet\euatharvard*.

U.S. State Department, European Affairs, *http://www.state.gov/www/regions/eur*.

PART

III

Britain

Joel Krieger

CHAPTER

6

The Making of the
Modern British State

British Politics in Action

The familiar maxim, "A week can be a long time in politics," took on new meaning in Britain during September 2000 as a fuel crisis quickly erupted into a serious political challenge to Prime Minister Tony Blair. On Thursday, September 7, the story broke that angry farmers and truck drivers were mounting protests outside an oil refinery in northwest England. French truckers are famously contentious and had won concessions from their government in the form of a 15 percent reduction on fuel taxes the previous week, but few expected a similarly aggressive turn to direct action in Britain. But by the weekend, protests were threatening delivery at every refinery in Britain as discontent over high fuel prices spread across Europe.

The rising cost of gasoline in Europe has presented a huge headache to motorists. In Britain, as elsewhere, the high cost of petrol (gasoline) has become a serious threat to those whose livelihood puts them behind the wheel or requires that their products be transported by vehicle. As the ninth ranking oil producer in the world, the United Kingdom is in far better shape about oil than other European countries. Nevertheless, the prices in Britain are the highest of all, with premium unleaded gas at the time of the protest costing about $4.37 a gallon. Although the Blair government tried to turn the mounting anger against oil companies and the Organization of Petroleum Exporting Countries, it was clear as

the week wore on that Blair was on the hot seat. For a start, taxes account for a higher percentage of the cost—a whopping 76.2 percent—than anywhere else in the European Union (EU) countries (gasoline taxes in the United States count for 22.8 percent of the pump price, less than one-third the levy paid by Britons). Moreover, it is clear that the ferocity and effectiveness of the protests took the government by surprise and that Blair, who is often accused of aloofness and arrogance, misplayed his initial response.

On Monday, September 11, as panic buying mounted and fears grew that hospitals might soon be forced to cancel nonemergency procedures and schools might have to shut down, Blair refused to compromise on fuel taxes and seemed tone deaf to the protesters' laments. "We cannot and will not alter government policy on petrol through blockades and pickets," intoned a defiant prime minister. "That's not the way to make policy in Britain." By the following evening, 90 percent of the petrol stations in Britain had run out of unleaded gas. Overnight, Queen Elizabeth, on the advice of the prime minister and cabinet, declared a state of emergency. By Wednesday, September 13, hospitals, schools, and social services were being hard hit, small businesses were crippled by the protests, and food stocks were dwindling. Blair's promise to get things back to normal by evening only inflamed the situation, but by the end of the workweek, the protest's informal leaders called

off their action. They had proved their point, nearly bringing Britain to a halt, and focused the country's attention on their concerns. The protesters quit while they were ahead without promises of concessions, but amid strong hints that the next budget would include cuts in fuel taxes—and before they could be blamed for loss of life or the failure of critical services. As the blockades came down, opinion polls showed 80 percent of the country behind the protests.

It was a week that Britain would long remember. Although like any government, Labour—dubbed "New Labour" by Blair, who had taken over as party leader in 1994—was experiencing its share of midterm troubles, Blair was still riding high. He had been elected in a landslide in 1997 and had maintained his political momentum well past any honeymoon period. Through August, New Labour held an apparently unassailable lead, averaging 15 percent, and the party had held a continuous lead over the conservatives for a remarkable period of eight years, going back to the government of Conservative John Major. Understandably, Blair was viewed as invincible, and pundits had begun looking to the next general election, which was expected in May 2001 before the outbreak of foot-and-mouth disease caused a brief delay. But as the fuel protests wound down, opinion polls showed the unthinkable: The Conservatives had surged past Labour. For the first time, people were asking whether Tony Blair could lose the next election. In the end, the election held on June 7, which decisively returned Labour to office, provided an emphatic rejoinder.

As dramatic as these developments were, the importance of the week's events may go well beyond the snap polls and Blair's embarrassment, because the political orientation Blair represents has great significance for British politics, as well as for European politics more generally. With his election in 1997, Blair raised expectations throughout the country by asserting a new brand of politics beyond Left and Right. Blair committed government to an ambitious program of modernization defined by a set of chal-

lenges: to develop top-quality public services especially in education and health, take tough action on crime, forge a new partnership with business, introduce radical constitutional reforms, and reconfigure Britain's relationship with Europe. In addition, Tony Blair's bold leadership and enormous popularity, backed by a long streak of economic prosperity, have helped make London a chic European capital and Britain a much vaunted trend setter. French entrepreneurs and job seekers are looking for opportunities at the end of the Channel tunnel and German chancellor Gerhard Schröder is being hailed as "the German Blair."

"Blairism" has been widely discussed as a potential third-way model of government that would meld concerns for social justice with a commitment to market-based economies. As a result, the victory of Blair's New Labour created a rare opportunity for a government to look beyond opinion polls and electoral competition and attempt lasting political change. Were the protests over the cost of gasoline a momentary diversion and a "heads-up" for Blair—or a sign that the third way is more style than substance? The ultimate balance sheet on New Labour will offer some important lessons about prospects for political innovation within established democracies.

Geographic Setting

Britain is the largest of the British Isles, a group of islands off the northwest coast of Europe, and encompasses England, Scotland, and Wales. The second largest island comprises Northern Ireland and the independent Republic of Ireland. The term *Great* Britain encompasses England, Wales, and Scotland but not Northern Ireland. We use the term *Britain* as shorthand for the United Kingdom of Great Britain and Northern Ireland.

Covering an area of approximately 94,000 square miles, Britain is roughly two-thirds the size of Japan or approximately half the size of

France. In 1995, the population of the United Kingdom was 58.6 million people; the population is projected to peak at 61.2 million people in 2023.[1] To put the size of this once immensely powerful country in perspective, it is slightly smaller than Oregon.

Although forever altered by the Channel tunnel, Britain's location as an offshore island adjacent to Europe is significant. Historically, Britain's island destiny made it less subject to invasion and conquest than its continental counterparts, affording the country a sense of security. The geographic separation from mainland Europe has also created for many Britons a feeling that they are both apart from and a part of Europe, a factor that has complicated relations with Britain's EU partners to this day.

Critical Junctures

Our study begins with a look at the historic development of the modern British state. History shapes contemporary politics in very important ways. Once in place, institutions leave powerful legacies, and issues placed on the agenda in one period and left unresolved may present challenges for the future.

Formation of the United Kingdom

In many ways, Britain is the model of a unified and stable country with an enviable record of continuity and resiliency. Nevertheless, the history of state formation reveals how complex and open-ended the process can be. Some issues that plague other countries, such as religious divisions, were settled long ago in Great Britain proper (although not in Northern Ireland). Yet others, such as multiple national identities, remain on the agenda.

British state formation involved the unification of kingdoms or crowns (hence the term United *Kingdom*). After Duke William of Normandy defeated the English in the Battle of Hastings in 1066, the Norman monarchy ex-

tended its authority throughout the British Isles. Although Welsh national sentiments remained strong, the prospects for unity with England were improved in 1485 by the accession to the English throne of Henry VII of the Welsh House of Tudor. With the Acts of Union of 1536 and 1542, England and Wales were legally, politically, and administratively united. The unification of the Scottish and English crowns occurred when James VI of Scotland ascended to the English throne as James I. Thereafter, England, Scotland, and Wales were known as Great Britain. Scotland and England remained divided politically, however, until the Act of Union of 1707. Henceforth, a common Parliament of Great Britain replaced the two separate parliaments of Scotland and of England and Wales.

At the same time, the making of the British state included a historic expression of constraints on monarchical rule. At first, the period of Norman rule after 1066 strengthened royal control, but the conduct of King John (1199–1216) fueled opposition from feudal barons. In 1215, they forced the king to consent to a series of concessions that protected feudal landowners from abuses of royal power. These restrictions on royal prerogatives were embodied in the Magna Carta, a historic statement of the rights of a political community against the monarchical state. Soon after, in 1236, the term *Parliament* was first used officially to refer to the gathering of feudal barons summoned by the king whenever he required their consent to special taxes. By the fifteenth century, Parliament gained the right to make laws.

The Seventeenth-Century Settlement

The making of the British state in the sixteenth and seventeenth centuries involved a complex interplay of religious conflicts, national rivalries, and struggles between rulers and the fledgling Parliament (see "Critical Junctures in Britain's Political Development"). These conflicts erupted in the Civil War of the 1640s and the forced abdication of James II in 1688. The bloodless political revolution of 1688, subsequently known as the Glorious Revolution, marked the "last successful political coup d'état or revolution in British history."[2] It also confirmed the power of Parliament over the monarchy. Parliament required the new monarchs, William and Mary, to meet with it annually and to agree to regular parliamentary elections. This contrasted dramatically with the arrangement enjoyed in France by Louis XIV (1643–1715), who gained power at the expense of the French nobility and operated without any constraint from commoners.

By the end of the seventeenth century, the framework of a constitutional (or limited) monarchy, which would still exercise flashes of power into the nineteenth century, was established in Britain. For more than 300 years, Britain's monarchs have been answerable to Parliament, which has held the sole authority for taxation and the maintenance of a standing army.

The Glorious Revolution also resolved long-standing religious conflict. The replacement of the Roman Catholic James II by the Protestant William and Mary ensured the dominance of the Church of England (or Anglican church). To this day, the Church of England remains the established (official) religion, and approximately two dozen of its bishops and archbishops sit as members of the House of Lords, the upper house of Parliament.

Thus, by the end of the seventeenth century, a basic form of parliamentary democracy had emerged, and the problem of religious divisions, which continue to plague other countries throughout the world, was settled. Equally important, these seventeenth-century developments became a defining moment for how the British perceive their history to this day. However divisive and disruptive the process of state building may have been originally, its telling and retelling have contributed significantly to a British political culture that celebrates

democracy's continuity, gradualism, and tolerance.

As a result of settling its religious differences early, Britain has taken a more secular turn than most other countries in Western Europe. The majority of Britons do not consider religion a significant source of identity, and active church membership in Britain, at 15 percent, is very low in comparison with other West European countries. In Britain, religious identification has less political significance in voting behavior or party loyalty than in many other countries. By contrast to France, where devout Catholics tend to vote right of center, there is relatively little association between religion and voting behavior in Britain (although Anglicans are a little

Critical Junctures in Britain's Political Development

1688	Glorious Revolution establishes power of Parliament
c. 1750	Industrial Revolution begins in Britain
1832	Reform Act expands voting rights
1837–1901	Reign of Queen Victoria; height of British Empire
1914–1918	World War I
1929–1939	Great Depression
1939–1945	World War II
1945–1979	Establishment of British welfare state; dismantling of British Empire
1973	Britain joins the European Community
1979–1990	Prime Minister Margaret Thatcher promotes "enterprise culture"
1997	Tony Blair elected prime minister

more likely to vote Conservative). Unlike Germany or Italy, for example, politics in Britain is secular. No parties have religious affiliation, a factor that contributed to the success of the Conservative Party, one of the most successful right-of-center parties in Europe in the twentieth century.

As a consequence, except in Northern Ireland where religious divisions continue, the party system in the United Kingdom has traditionally reflected class distinctions and remains free of the pattern of multiple parties (particularly right-of-center parties) that occur in countries where party loyalties are divided by both class and religion.

The Industrial Revolution and the British Empire

Although the British state was consolidated by the seventeenth century, its form was radically shaped by the timing of its industrial development and the way that process transformed Britain's role in the world. The Industrial Revolution in the mid-eighteenth century involved rapid expansion of manufacturing production, and technological innovation. It also led to monumental social and economic transformations and resulted in pressures for democratization. Externally, Britain used its competitive edge to transform and dominate the international order. Internally, the Industrial Revolution helped shape the development of the British state and changed forever the British people's way of life.

The Industrial Revolution. The consequences of the Industrial Revolution for the generations of people who experienced its upheavals can scarcely be exaggerated. The typical worker was turned "by degrees . . . from small peasant or craftsman into wage-labourer," as historian Eric Hobsbawm observes. Cash and market-based transactions replaced older traditions of barter and production for local need.[3]

Despite a gradual improvement in the stan-

dard of living in the English population at large, the effects of industrialization were often profound for agricultural laborers and particular types of artisans. With the commercialization of agriculture, many field laborers lost their security of employment, and cottagers (small landholders) were squeezed off the land in large numbers. The mechanization of manufacturing, which spread furthest in the cotton industry, upset the traditional status of the preindustrial skilled craft workers and permanently marginalized them.

The British Empire. Britain had assumed a significant role as a world power during the seventeenth century, building an overseas empire and engaging actively in international commerce. But it was the Industrial Revolution of the eighteenth century that established global production and exchange on a new and expanded scale, with particular consequences for the making of the British state. Cotton manufacture, the driving force behind Britain's growing industrial dominance, not only pioneered the new techniques and changed labor organization of the Industrial Revolution but also represented the perfect imperial industry. It relied on imported raw materials and, by the turn of the nineteenth century, already depended on overseas markets for the vast majority of its sales of finished goods. Growth depended on foreign markets rather than domestic consumption. This export orientation fueled an expansion far more rapid than an exclusively domestic orientation would have allowed.

With its leading industrial sector dependent on overseas trade, Britain's leaders worked aggressively to secure markets and expand the empire. Toward these ends, Britain defeated European rivals in a series of military engagements, culminating in the Napoleonic Wars (1803–1815), which confirmed Britain's commercial, military, and geopolitical preeminence. The Napoleonic Wars also secured a balance of power on the European continent favorable for largely unrestricted international commerce (free trade). Propelled by the formidable and active presence of the British navy, international trade helped England take full advantage of its position as the first industrial power. Many scholars suggest that in the middle of the nineteenth century, Britain had the highest per capita income in the world (it was certainly among the two or three highest), and in 1870, at the height of its glory, its trade represented nearly one-quarter of the world total and its industrial mastery ensured highly competitive productivity in comparison to trading partners (see Table 6.1).

During the reign of Queen Victoria (1837–1901), the British Empire was immensely powerful and encompassed fully 25 percent of the world's population. Britain presided over a vast formal and informal empire, with extensive direct colonial rule over some four dozen countries, including India and Nigeria. At the same time Britain enjoyed the advantages of an extensive informal empire—a worldwide network of independent states, including China, Iran, and Brazil—whose economic fates were linked to it. Britain ruled as a hegemonic power, the state that could control the pattern of alliances and terms of the international economic order, and often could shape domestic political developments in countries throughout the world. Overall, the making of the British state observed a neat symmetry. Its global power helped underwrite industrial growth at home. At the same time, the reliance of domestic industry on world markets, beginning with cotton manufacture in the eighteenth century, prompted the government to project British interests overseas as forcefully as possible.

Industrial Change and the Struggle for Voting Rights. The Industrial Revolution shifted economic power from landowners to men of commerce and industry. As a result, the first critical juncture in the long process of democratization began in the late 1820s, when the "respectable opinion" of the propertied classes and increasing popular agitation pressed Parliament to expand

Table 6.1   World Trade and Relative Labor Productivity

	Proportion of World Trade (%)	Relative Labor Productivity[a] (%)
1870	24.0	1.63
1890	18.5	1.45
1913	14.1	1.15
1938	14.0	0.92

[a]As compared with the average rate of productivity in other members of the world economy.

Source: Robert O. Keohane, *After Hegemony: Cooperation and Discord in the World Political Economy* (Princeton, N.J.: Princeton University Press, 1984), p. 36. Copyright 1984 by Princeton University Press. Reprinted by permission of Princeton University Press.

the right to vote (franchise) beyond a thin band of men with substantial property, mainly landowners. With Parliament under considerable pressure, the Reform Act of 1832 extended the franchise to a section of the (male) middle class.

In a very limited way, the Reform Act confirmed the social and political transformations of the Industrial Revolution by granting new urban manufacturing centers, such as Manchester and Birmingham, more substantial representation. However, the massive urban working class created by the Industrial Revolution and populating the cities of Charles Dickens's England remained on the outside looking in. In fact, the reform was very narrow and defensive. Before 1832, less than 5 percent of the adult population was entitled to vote—and afterward, only about 7 percent.

In extending the franchise so narrowly, the reform underscored the strict property basis for political participation and inflamed class-based tensions in Britain. Following the Reform Act, a massive popular movement erupted in the late 1830s to secure the program of the People's Charter, which included demands for universal male suffrage and other radical reforms intended to make Britain a much more participatory democracy. The Chartist movement, as it was called, held huge and often tumultuous rallies, and organized a vast campaign to petition Parliament, but it failed to achieve any of its aims.

Expansion of the franchise proceeded very slowly. The Representation of the People Act of 1867 increased the electorate to just over 16 percent but left cities significantly underrepresented. The Franchise Act of 1884 nearly doubled the size of the electorate, but it was not until the Representation of the People Act of 1918 that suffrage included nearly all adult men and women over age thirty. How slow a process was it? The franchise for men with substantial incomes dated from the fifteenth century, but women between the ages of twenty-one and thirty were not enfranchised until 1928. The voting age for both women and men was lowered to eighteen in 1969. Except for some episodes during the days of the Chartist movement, the struggle for extension of the franchise took place without violence, but its time horizon must be measured in centuries. This is British gradualism—at its best and worst (see Figure 6.1).

World Wars, Industrial Strife, and the Depression (1914–1945)

With the matter of the franchise finally settled, in one sense the making of the British state as a democracy was settled. In another important sense, however, the development of the state was just beginning in the twentieth century with the expansion of the state's direct responsibility for management of the economy and the provision of social welfare for citizens. The making of what is sometimes called the *interventionist state* was spurred by the experiences of two world wars.

The state's involvement in the economy increased significantly during World War I. The state took control of a number of industries, including railways, mining, and shipping. It also

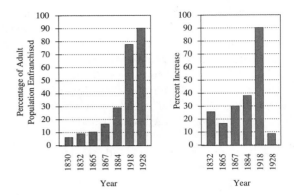

Figure 6.1   Expansion of Voting Rights

Expansion of the franchise in Britain was a gradual process. Despite reforms dating from the early nineteenth century, nearly universal adult suffrage was not achieved until 1928.

Source: Jorgen S. Rasmussen. *The British Political Process*, p. 151. Copyright © 1993. Reprinted with permission of Wadsworth, an imprint of the Wadsworth Group, a division of Thomson Learning. Fax 800-730-2215.

set prices and restricted the flow of capital abroad and channeled the country's resources into production geared to the war effort. After World War I, the state remained active in the management of industry in a rather different way. Amid a set of tremendous industrial disputes, the state wielded its power to fragment the trade union movement and resist demands for workers' control over production and to promote more extensive state ownership of industries. This considerable government manipulation of the economy openly contradicted the policy of laissez-faire (minimal government interference in the operation of economic markets). The tensions between free market principles and interventionist practices deepened with the Great Depression beginning in 1929 and the experiences of World War II. The fear of depression and the burst of pent-up yearnings for a better life after the war helped transform the role of the state and ushered in a period of unusual political harmony.

Collectivist Consensus (1945–1979)

In the postwar context of shared victory and common misery (almost everyone suffered terrible hardships immediately after the war), reconstruction and dreams of new prosperity and security took priority over ideological conflict. In Britain today, a debate rages among political scientists over whether there was a postwar consensus. Critics of the concept contend that disagreements over specific policies concerning the economy, education, employment, and health, along with an electorate divided on partisan lines largely according to social class, indicated politics as usual.[4] It seems fair to say, however, that a broad culture of reconciliation and a determination to rebuild and improve the conditions of life for all Britons helped forge a postwar settlement based broadly on a collectivist consensus that endured until the mid-1970s.

Collectivism is the term coined to describe the consensus that drove politics in the harmonious postwar period when a significant majority of Britons and all major political parties agreed that the state should take expanded responsibility for economic governance and provide for the social welfare in the broadest terms. They accepted as a matter of faith that governments should work to narrow the gap between rich and poor through public education, national health care, and other policies of the welfare state, and accepted state responsibility for economic growth and full employment. Collectivism brought class-based actors (representatives of labor and management) inside politics and forged a very broad consensus about the expanded role of government.

Throughout this period, there was a remarkable unity among electoral combatants, as the Labour and Conservative mainstream endorsed the principle of state responsibility for the collective good in both economic and social terms. Although modest in comparative European terms, the commitment to state management of the economy and provision of social services

marked a new era in British politics. In time, however, economic downturn and political stagnation caused the consensus to unravel.

Margaret Thatcher and the Enterprise Culture (1979–1990)

In the 1970s, economic stagnation and the declining competitiveness of key British industries in international markets fueled industrial strife and kept class-based tensions near the surface of politics. No government appeared equal to the tasks of economic management. Each party failed in turn. The Conservative government of Edward Heath (1970–1974) could not resolve the economic problems or the political tensions that resulted from the previously unheard-of combination of increased inflation and reduced growth (*stagflation*). The Labour government of Harold Wilson and James Callaghan (1974–1979) fared no better. As unions became increasingly disgruntled, the country was beset by a rash of strikes throughout the winter of 1978–1979, the "winter of discontent." Labour's inability to discipline its trade union allies hurt the party in the election just a few months later in May 1979. The traditional centrist Conservative and Labour alternatives within the collectivist mold seemed exhausted, and many Britons were ready for a new policy agenda.

Margaret Thatcher more than met the challenge. Winning the leadership of the Conservative Party in 1975, she wasted little time in launching a set of bold policy initiatives, which, with characteristic forthrightness, she began to implement after the Conservatives were returned to power in 1979. Reelected in 1983 and 1987, Thatcher served longer without interruption than any other British prime minister in the twentieth century and never lost a general election.

Thatcher transformed British political life by advancing an alternative vision of politics. She was convinced that collectivism had contributed to Britain's decline by sapping British industry and permitting powerful and self-serving unions to hold the country for ransom. To reverse Britain's relative economic slide, Thatcher sought to jump-start the economy by cutting taxes, reducing social services where possible, and using government policy to stimulate competitiveness and efficiency in the private sector.

The term *Thatcherism* embraces her distinctive leadership style, her economic and political strategies, as well as her traditional cultural values: individual responsibility, commitment to family, frugality, and an affirmation of the entrepreneurial spirit. These values combined nostalgia for the past and a rejection of permissiveness and disorder. Taken together and referred to as the *enterprise culture*, they stood as a reproach and an alternative to collectivism.

In many ways, the period of Margaret Thatcher's leadership as prime minister (1979–1990) marks a critical dividing line in postwar British politics. She set the tone and redefined the goals of British politics like few others before her. In November 1990, a leadership challenge within Thatcher's own Conservative Party, largely over her anti-EU stance and high-handed leadership style, caused her sudden resignation and replacement by John Major. Major served as prime minister from 1990 to 1997, leading the Conservative Party to a victory in the 1992 general election before succumbing to Tony Blair's New Labour in 1997.

New Labour's Third Way

Some twenty electoral records were toppled, as New Labour under the leadership of Tony Blair (see the box) won 419 of the 659 seats in Parliament, the largest majority it has ever held. Blair was propelled into office as prime minister with a 10 percent swing from Conservative to Labour, a postwar record. More women (120) and members of ethnic minorities (9) were elected than ever before. In addition, the political undertow of this electoral tsunami was fierce. The Conservative Party, which had been in power since Margaret Thatcher's 1979 victory and was

one of Europe's most successful parties in the twentieth century, was decimated. More cabinet ministers lost their seats than ever before. The Conservatives were nearly wiped off the map in London and other major cities and were shut out altogether in Scotland and Wales.

After Tony Blair's election in 1997, there was an unmistakable sense in Britain that something extremely interesting and potentially significant was happening. Blair's willingness to experiment with ideas and policy and his call to modernize almost anything in the grasp of government contributed to a sense of political renewal and intellectual ferment in Britain.

New Labour aspired to recast British politics, offering what it referred to as a "third-way" alternative to collectivism and Thatcherism. Everything was at issue, from the way politics is organized to the country's underlying values, institutions, and policies. In electoral terms, New Labour rejected the notion of interest-based politics, in which unions and working people naturally look to Labour and business-people and the more prosperous look to the Conservatives. Labour won in 1997 by drawing support from across the socioeconomic spectrum. It rejected the historic ties between Labour governments and the trade union movement, choosing instead to emphasize the virtues of a partnership with business.

In institutional and policy terms, New Labour's innovations were intended to reverse the tendency of previous Labour governments in Britain to provide centralized statist solutions to all economic and social problems. Blair promised new approaches to economic, welfare, and social policy; British leadership in Europe; and far-reaching constitutional changes to revitalize democratic participation and devolve (transfer) specified powers from the central government to Scotland, Wales, and Northern Ireland.

In the early months of his premiership, Blair displayed effective leadership in his stewardship of the nation during the period after Lady Diana's death and his aggressive efforts to achieve a potentially historic peace agreement for

Tony Blair

Born in 1953 to a mother from Donegal, Ireland (who moved to Glasgow after her father's death), and a father from the Clydeside shipyards, Tony Blair lacks the typical pedigree of Labour Party leaders. It is very common in the highest ranks of the Labour Party to find someone whose father or grandfather was a union official or a Labour member of Parliament (MP). The politics in the Blair family, by contrast, were most closely linked to Conservatism (as chairman of his local Conservative Party club, his father, Leo, had a good chance to become a Conservative MP). Often, like Tony Blair's two predecessors—Neil Kinnock from Wales and John Smith from the west of Scotland—leaders of the Labour Party also have distinctive regional ties. In contrast, Blair moved to Durham in the north of England when he was five years old, but spent much of his youth in boarding schools; moved south when he was old enough to set out on his own; studied law at Oxford; and specialized in employment and industrial law in London—and returned to the north only to enter the House of Commons from Sedgefield in 1983. Thus, Blair has neither the traditional political or regional ties of a Labour Party leader.*

Coming of political age in opposition, Blair joined the shadow cabinet (an opposition party's would-be cabinet) in 1988, serving in turn as shadow minister of energy, then employment, and finally as shadow home secretary. An MP with no government experience, he easily won the contest for party leadership after his close friend and fellow modernizer, John Smith, died of a sudden heart attack in the summer of 1994. From the start, he boosted Labour Party morale and raised expectations that the party would soon regain power. As one observer put it, "The new Leader rapidly made a favourable impression upon the electorate: his looks and affability of manner appealed to voters whilst his self-confidence, lucidity and clarity of mind rendered him a highly effective communicator and lent him an air of authority."† Blair has gone from strength to strength, combining winning style with firm leadership, eclectic beliefs, and bold political initiatives. A figure to reckon with (some have predicted he will become the dominant figure in British politics for the next quarter-century), his lack of familiar roots and ideological convictions make Blair, for many, an enigmatic figure.

*See Andy McSmith, *Faces of Labour: The Inside Story* (London: Verso, 1997), pp. 7–96.

†Eric Shaw, *The Labour Party Since 1945* (Oxford: Blackwell, 1996), p. 195.

Northern Ireland, with far-reaching constitutional implications. Blair's government registered higher popularity at the end of its first year than any other government at a comparable stage since opinion polling was introduced. Moreover, despite a round of scandals, resignations, and quarrels between ministers in the winter of 1998–1999, New Labour was riding high in the polls as it approached the halfway point of its first term in office. By the summer of 2000, however, a rash of embarrassing leaks

from Blair's inner sanctum, including a document written by the prime minister that revealed him stewing over "a sense that the government—and this even applies to me—are somehow out of touch with gut British instincts," contributed to a growing sense that New Labour was spinning its wheels. Many observers, Labour supporters among them, suggested that Blair and his team were better at innovative-sounding ideas than at delivering the goods. Factionalism in the party and among the leadership was reemerging and skepticism growing that key promises, for example, in health care and education (respectively, to reduce waiting lists for hospital services and class sizes) might not be met. And then Blair stumbled dramatically during the fuel crisis. To be sure, even after the fuel crisis, Blair remained a formidable leader, and Labour was the prohibitive favorite to remain the governing party after the next election, but the third way had lost more than a little of its luster.

Britain in the Euro Era

In May 1998, eleven EU countries, led by Germany, France, Italy, and Spain—but not including Britain—signed on to the single European currency, the euro. One month later, the European Central Bank was established, operating with considerable institutional and political independence, and charged primarily with maintaining price stability and advancing the economic policies of the EU. At the beginning of 1999, exchange rates were locked in, the euro became legal tender, and euro-based foreign exchange operations began. Already, without Britain's participation in the single currency, much of the action on trading floors in the City (London's financial center) is conducted in euros. The conversion timetable calls for the introduction of euro bills and coins for everyday use on New Year's Day 2002 and the withdrawal of the legal status of national currencies by the end of February.

The introduction of the euro reflects the larger vision of creating a more fully integrated EU, or what many have called (some approvingly and some derisively) a "United States of Europe." More concretely, financial analysts point to increased trade, reduced transaction costs, and substantial savings on cross-border commerce. With a population larger than that of the United States and with a bigger gross domestic product (even without further enlargement), an integrated Europe poses a formidable competitive challenge to the United States. In addition, many observers expect that monetary union will accelerate and make irreversible a tendency toward greater European political and foreign policy cooperation.

Britain's decision thus far not to join the Euro-club (since January 2001, with the accession of Greece, the United Kingdom is one of only three outsiders) remains a significant nondecision in both economic and broader political terms. Its implications and the challenges ahead are discussed further in Chapter 10.

Themes and Implications

The processes that came together in these historical junctures continue to influence present developments in powerful and complex ways. Our four core themes in this book, introduced in Part I, highlight some of the most important features of British politics.

Historical Junctures and Political Themes

The first theme suggests that a country's relative position in the *world of states* influences its ability to manage domestic and international challenges. A weaker international standing makes it difficult for a country to control international events, shape the policy of powerful international organizations, or insulate itself from external pressures. Britain's ability to control the terms of trade and master political alliances during the height of its imperial power in the nineteenth century confirms this maxim. In a quite different way, the theme of the world of states is also confirmed by Britain's reduced standing and influence today.

As the gradual process of decolonization defined Britain's changing relationship to the world of states, Britain fell to a second-tier status during the twentieth century. Its formal empire began to shrink in the interwar period (1919–1939) with the independence of the "white dominions" of Canada, Australia, and New Zealand. In Britain's Asian, Middle Eastern, and African colonies, the pressure for political reforms leading to independence deepened during World War II and in the immediate postwar period. Beginning with the formal independence of India and Pakistan in 1947, an enormous empire of dependent colonies more or less dissolved in less than twenty years (although the problem of white-dominated Rhodesia lingered until it achieved independence as Zimbabwe in 1980). Finally, in 1997, Britain returned the commercially vibrant crown colony of Hong Kong to China. The process of decolonization ended any realistic claim Britain could make to be a dominant player in world politics.

Is Britain a world power or just a middle-of-the-pack country in Western Europe? It appears to be both. On the one hand, as a legacy of its role in World War II, Britain sits as a permanent member of the United Nations Security Council, a position denied more powerful and populous countries such as Germany and Japan. On the other hand, Britain has remained an outsider in the EU, more often than not playing second fiddle in its "special relationship" to the United States—a bond of language and culture that creates an unusually close alliance—and declining in influence in the Commonwealth (an association of some fifty states that were once part of the British empire). In particular, British governments face persistent challenges in their dealings with the EU. As Margaret Thatcher learned too late to save her premiership, Europe is a highly divisive issue. Can Britain afford to remain aloof from the fast-paced changes of economic integration symbolized by the headlong rush toward a common currency (the euro), already embraced, despite growing qualms, by every leading member state except the United Kingdom? It is clear that Britain does not have the power to control EU policy outcomes. Will British governments, beginning with Tony Blair's, find the right formula for limiting the political fallout of EU politics and at

the same time find the best approach to economic competitiveness?

A second theme examines the strategies employed in *governing the economy* and the political implications of economic performance and the choices government makes in the distribution of economic goods and public services. Since the dawn of Britain's Industrial Revolution, prosperity at home relied on superior competitiveness abroad, and this is even more true in today's environment of intensified international competition and global production.

When Tony Blair took office in 1997, he inherited a streak of prosperity in Britain dating from 1992—an enviable circumstance. The Blair government could thus work to modernize the economy and determine its budgetary priorities from economic strength. Will Britain's "less-is-more" laissez-faire approach to economic governance, invigorated by New Labour's business partnership, continue to compete effectively against the more directive state-centered models of France and Germany? Can Britain achieve a durable economic model with—or without—fuller integration into Europe? How can we assess the spending priorities and distributive implications of the third-way politics of the Blair government? Britain will never again assume the privileged position of hegemonic power. It is positioned well to make the most of its role as a competitive middle-of-the-pack European power, but in these perilous times of intense global competition, success is not a given, and Britain faces a host of challenges.

A third theme is the potent political influence of the *democratic idea*, the universal appeal of core values associated with parliamentary democracy as practiced first in the United Kingdom. Even in Britain, issues about democratic governance, citizen participation, and constitutional reform have been renewed with considerable force.

As the traditionally sacrosanct royal family has been rocked by scandal and improprieties, questions about the undemocratic underpinning of the British state are asked with greater urgency. Few reject the monarchy outright but, especially after the perceived insensitivity of the royal family in the aftermath of Diana's death, the pressure to modernize the monarchy, scale it down, and reduce its drain on the budget gained new intensity. Perhaps most significant, questions about the role of the monarchy helped place on the agenda broader issues about citizen control over government and constitutional reform. As a result, in November 1999 a bill was enacted to remove hereditary peers from Britain's upper unelected chamber of Parliament, the House of Lords, although to facilitate passage, the government agreed to keep ninety-two hereditary peers as an interim measure in the modified second chamber.

Long-settled issues about the constitutional form and unity of the state have also reemerged with unexpected force in recent years. How can the interests of England, Wales, Scotland, and Northern Ireland be balanced within a single nation-state? Can the perpetual crisis in Northern Ireland be finally resolved? Tony Blair has placed squarely on the agenda a set of policies designed to reshape the institutions of government and reconfigure fundamental constitutional principles to address the "troubles" in Northern Ireland and modernize the architecture of the United Kingdom to recognize the realities of a multi-nation-state. Key policies include the formation of a Scottish Parliament and a Welsh Senedd (or Assembly), and the negotiation of a peace agreement for Northern Ireland that would contain a comprehensive set of new political institutions and power-sharing arrangements—some involving the Republic of Ireland—with far-reaching constitutional ramifications. Clearly, democracy is not a fixed result even in the United Kingdom, but a highly politicized and potentially disruptive process, as constitutional reform has taken a place front and center in Tony Blair's bold agenda.

Finally, we come to the fourth theme, *collective identities*, which considers how individuals define who they are politically in terms of group attachments, come together to pursue political goals, and face their status as political insiders or outsiders by virtue of these group attachments. In Britain, an important aspect of the politics of collective identities is connected to Britain's legacy of empire and its aftermath. Through the immigration of its former colonial subjects to the United Kingdom, decolonization helped create a multiracial society, to which Britain has adjusted poorly. As we shall see, issues of race, ethnicity, and cultural identity have challenged the long-standing British values of tolerance and consensus and now present important challenges for policy and the prospects of cohesion in Britain today. Indeed, the concept of "Britishness"—what the country stands for and who comprises the political community—has come under intense scrutiny. At the same time, gender politics remains a significant issue, from voting results that show clear differences in the party preferences of men and women (a gender gap) to questions of equality in the workplace and positions of political leadership. Moreover, the specific needs of women for equal employment opportunities and to balance the demands of work and family have assumed an important place in debates about social and employment policies.

Implications for Comparative Politics

Britain's privileged position in European and comparative politics textbooks—it almost always comes first among country studies in these books—seems to follow naturally from the important historical firsts it has enjoyed. Britain was the first nation to industrialize, and for much of the nineteenth century, the British Empire was the world's dominant economic, political, and military power, with a vast network of colonies throughout the world. Britain was also the first nation to develop an effective parliamentary democracy (a form of representative government in which the executive is drawn from and answerable to an elected national legislature). As a result of its vast empire, Britain had tremendous influence on the form of government introduced in countries around the globe. For these reasons, British politics is often studied as a model of representative government. Named after the building that houses the British legislature in London, the Westminster model of government emphasizes that democracy rests on the supreme authority of a legislature—in Britain's case, the Parliament—and the accountability of its elected representatives. Traditionally, the Westminster model and the values of consensus building and stability on which it rests have served as one standard (the U.S. political system has been another) for countries struggling to construct democratic political systems. Finally, Britain has served as a model of gradual and peaceful evolution of democratic government in a world where transitions to democracy are often turbulent, interrupted, and uncertain.

Today, more than a century after the height of its international power, Britain's significance in comparative terms must be measured in somewhat different ways. Modernization is the watchword of the Blair government, and the level of public support given Blair ever since his extraordinary 1997 victory, the advantages bestowed on prime ministers by the formidable levers of power they control, and the strength of the British economy provide a platform for success. Therefore, Blair's ability to succeed—or his failure—in forging a left-of-center business partnership, implementing constitutional reforms, and balancing national interest with supranational pressures for European integration will send important signals to governments throughout Europe and beyond. Is innovation possible in established democracies with powerful institutional and cultural legacies that tend to set limits on radical change? Can a politics beyond Left and Right develop coherent policies and maintain enduring support? Can constitutional reforms help bind together a multiethnic, multinational state? In fact, contemporary Britain may help define an innovative new model for middle-rank established democracies in a global age.

Notes

1. Jenny Church, ed., *Social Trends* 27 (London: The Stationery Office, 1977), p. 28.

2. Jeremy Black, *The Politics of Britain 1688–1800* (Manchester: Manchester University Press, 1993), p. 6.

3. E. J. Hobsbawm, *Industry and Empire* (Harmondsworth: Penguin/Pelican, 1983), pp. 29–31.

4. See Duncan Fraser, "The Postwar Consensus: A Debate Not Long Enough?" *Parliamentary Affairs* 53, no. 2 (April 2000): 347–362.

C H A P T E R

7

Political Economy
and Development

The timing of industrialization and of a country's insertion into the world economy are important variables in explaining both how and how successfully the state intervenes in economic governance. Both the specific policies chosen and the relative success of the economic strategy have significant political repercussions. Economic developments often determine political winners and losers, influence broad changes in the distribution of resources and opportunities among groups in society, and affect a country's international standing. In this chapter, we examine the politics of economic management in Britain and consider the implications of Britain's less-is-more, laissez-faire approach. We begin with a historical overview of Britain's economic development and its experience of the postwar settlement. We then consider, in turn, the principles of British economic management, the social consequences of economic developments, and the political repercussions of Britain's position in the international economic order.

The Postwar Settlement and Beyond

To understand the postwar settlement in Britain and come to terms with the contemporary debate about economic management, we must first step backward to analyze the historical trajectory of British economic performance. In addition to its claim as the first industrial nation,

Britain is also the country with the longest experience of economic decline. In a way, it was a victim of its own success and approach to economic development. From the eighteenth century onward, Britain combined its naval mastery and the dominant position created by the Industrial Revolution to fuel expansion based on the foreign supply of raw materials and foreign markets. With plenty of profits available from this traditional overseas orientation, British entrepreneurs became complacent about keeping up with the newest industrial techniques and investing in machinery at home. Secure in the advantages of empire and the priority of international trade over domestic demand, the government stuck to its belief in free trade (low tariffs and removal of other barriers to open markets) in the international realm and a hands-off approach at home. With low investment in the modernization of industrial plants and little effort to boost efficiency by grouping small-scale firms into cartels and trusts as the Americans and Germans were doing, Britain slipped behind its competitors in crucial areas: technological innovation, investment in domestic manufacturing, and scale of production facilities.

By the 1890s, Britain's key export, textiles, was slipping, and the international position of the machine-tool industry, which Britain also had dominated, was collapsing even more rapidly. Both Germany and the United States had overtaken Britain in steel production, the key

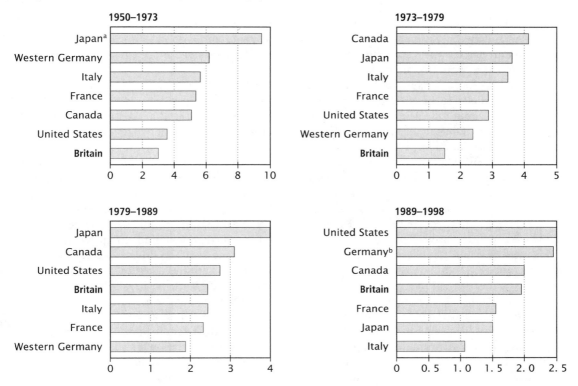

Figure 7.1 Britain's Relative Economic Performance: Annual Percentage Growth of Gross Domestic Product

Improved economic performance leaves room for improvement but inspires growing confidence in the United Kingdom, both at home and abroad.

[a] 1952–1973.
[b] Western Germany before 1991.
Source: *Economist*, March 25, 2000. Copyright © 2000 The Economist Group, Inc. Reprinted with permission. Further reproduction prohibited. www.economist.com.

indicator of competitiveness at the time, and the gap was widening. In 1901, the largest U.S. steel company alone was producing more steel than all of England![1] Thus, Britain has been concerned about relative economic decline for more than a century.

A quarter-century ago, there was not much to admire in the British economy. Growth and domestic investment were low and unemployment high, and in 1976 the government received a Third World–style bailout from the International Monetary Fund to help stabilize the economy. Britain was routinely called the "sick man

of Europe." However, throughout the 1980s and 1990s, Britain's growth rate was right in the middle of the pack of the seven richest countries, or G7 (see Figure 7.1). During the same period, which spans the Conservative governments of Margaret Thatcher and John Major, as well as that of Labour's Tony Blair, living standards (whether measured by gross domestic product per capita or purchasing power parity) also place Britain in the middle of the G7 and the group of twenty-nine Organisation for Economic Cooperation and Development (OECD) industrialized countries. Living standards are significantly below those of the United States and Japan, and roughly correspond to others in Western Europe. As the *Economist* observed, "Britain is neither an economic paradise nor a wasteland."[2] Perhaps because both praise and blame would have to be shared across party lines, debates about the health of the British economy are a mainstay of domestic politics. And, of course, a middling record leaves room for improvement. That said, the difference in the relative position of the British economy from a generation ago has not gone unnoticed. Moreover, despite continuing concern about a productivity gap between the United Kingdom and key competitors, as well as endemic concern about rates of domestic investment and spending on research and development, there are heady grounds for optimism. For one thing, Britain avoided the high unemployment and recession that plagued many of the member nations of the European Union (EU) in the mid-1990s. For another, according to spring 2000 EU statistics, the size of Britain's economy had overtaken that of arch-rival France to become the fourth largest in the world (after the United States, Japan, and Germany). The state of public finances looked healthier than in most of Europe, the unemployment rate (at 5.5 percent in September 2000) was substantially lower than in France (9.7 percent) and Germany (9.5 percent), and Britain was winning the competition for foreign direct investment (FDI). The United Kingdom was attracting more foreign investment than China and 30 percent of all the FDI in EU member nations. Investors and economists observed that the British economy was not performing with the eye-catching growth or productivity of the U.S. economy, but it displayed a very able European performance record, and that represented a startling turnaround from a quarter century ago. Moreover, Britain's strong performance outlasted that of the U.S., which began slowing late in 2000.

In analyzing our *governing the economy* theme, some scholars have suggested that states that have institutionalized effective relationships with organized economic interests (such as France and Germany in Europe and also Japan) have enjoyed more consistent growth and stronger economic competitiveness. It is true that Britain's annual growth rates were lower than those of Japan, Germany, and France from the end of World War II through the 1970s. Rather than institutionalizing a dense network of relationships among government agencies, business, and labor, Britain preserves arm's-length state relationships with key economic actors. With British political culture trumpeting the benefits of free-market individualism and with New Labour reinforcing Thatcherism's appeal to entrepreneurship, competition, and industriousness in the private sector, the British experience becomes a critical test case for analyzing the relative merits of alternative strategies for governing the economy.

In the first years of the new century, it appears that the trend toward greater and greater government regulation and management of the economy has reversed, breathing new life into the old economic doctrine of laissez-faire. In large part because of the success of the British and U.S. economies, as well as the missionary zeal of New Labour and New Democrat policymakers, laissez-faire economics—or neoliberalism, as it is called today—seems to have the upper hand. Neoliberalism is a touchstone premise of Tony Blair's New Labour. Government policies aim to promote free competition among firms, interfere with the prerogatives of entrepreneurs and managers as little as possible, and create a business-friendly environment to help attract foreign investment and spur innovation. At the same time, Britain's Labour government insists that its third way—as distinct from conservative or conventional Center-Right projects—can blend the dynamism of market forces with the traditional Center-Left concern for social justice and commitment to the reduction of inequalities. How "new" is New Labour's approach to economic management? Are Britons across the spectrum enjoying the fruits of relative prosperity? How has the growing importance of the EU and the economic processes of globalization changed the political equation? In this chapter, we analyze the politics of economic management, beginning with a historical overview of Britain's economic development. Then we consider in turn the principles of British economic management, the social consequences of economic developments and policy, Britain's relationship to the EU, and the political repercussions of Britain's position in the international economic order.

State and Economy

Whereas late industrializers, like Germany and Japan, relied on powerful government support during their industrial take-off period, England's Industrial Revolution was based more on laissez-faire, or free-market, principles. When the state intervened in powerful ways, it did so primarily to secure free markets at home and open markets for British goods (free trade) in the international sphere.

With control of crucial industries during World War I and the active management of industry by the state in the interwar years, the British state assumed a more interventionist role. After World War II, the sense of unity inspired by the shared suffering of war and the need to rebuild a war-ravaged country helped crystalize the collectivist consensus. In common with other Western European states, the British state both broadened and deepened its responsibilities for the overall performance of the economy and the well-being of its citizens. The leading political parties and policymaking elites agreed that the state should take an active role in governing the economy.

The state assumed direct ownership of some key industries (nationalization). The state also accepted the responsibility to secure low levels of unemployment (referred to as a policy of full employment), expand social services, maintain a steady rate of growth (increase the output or gross domestic product), keep prices stable, and

achieve desirable balance-of-payments and exchange rates. The approach was characterized by what has come to be called Keynesian demand management, or *Keynesianism* (after the British economist John Maynard Keynes). State budget deficits were used to expand demand in an effort to boost both consumption and investment when the economy was slowing. Cuts in government spending and a tightening of credit and finance were used to cool demand when high rates of growth brought fears of inflation or a deficit in balance of payments. Taken together, this new agenda of expanded economic management and welfare provision, sometimes referred to as the Keynesian welfare state, directed government policy throughout the era of the collectivist consensus.

During the first two decades of the postwar order, Britain shared with other European industrial democracies a very favorable set of economic conditions that helped underwrite the new and experimental approaches to economic governance and smooth over political disagreements. Increasing worker productivity encouraged a solid rate of domestic investment. At the same time, Britain enjoyed low inflation, virtually full employment, and a steady rate of growth. In comparison with the interwar period, Britain's postwar economic growth rate of 2.8 percent represented a record of solid achievement. However, this was far short of the much-vaunted "miracles" of economic growth that occurred elsewhere during the same twenty-year period: 6.7 percent in West Germany, 6.0 percent in Italy, and 4.5 percent in France.

It is likely that the scale of Britain's postwar boom was limited by the continuing pattern of weak investment in domestic industry, magnified by relatively low investment in the research and development of new production technologies. British competitiveness was weakened further by the higher proportion of out-of-date plants and equipment than in the cutting-edge economies of the day (owing to the longevity of British manufacturing and the fact that factories were left relatively undamaged by war, when compared to Germany or Japan). In addition, the country faced a relatively abrupt adjustment to the end of the empire, with all the loss of commercial advantages that entailed. With respectable but unspectacular growth rates, British policymakers faced less room for maneuver than their counterparts, a factor that reinforced their natural caution in developing welfare state policies or pursuing new agendas for economic governance.

Two central dimensions—economic management and welfare policy—capture the new role of the state. Analysis of these policy areas also reveals how limited this new state role was in comparative terms.

Economic Management

Like all other states, whatever their commitment to free markets, the British state intervenes in economic life, sometimes with considerable force. Some states, such as France, Germany, and Japan, exercise strategic control over the economy to guide it and enhance competitiveness. These countries coordinate macroeconomic policy (intended to shape the overall economic system at the national level by concentrating on policy targets such as unemployment, inflation, or growth) with industrial policy (aimed at enhancing competitiveness by promoting particular industrial sectors).

To this day the British have not developed the institutions for state-sponsored economic planning or industrial policy that some of their competitors have created. Instead, apart from its management of nationalized industries, the British state has limited its role mainly to broad policy instruments designed to influence the economy generally (macroeconomic policy) by adjusting state revenues and expenditures. The Treasury and the Bank of England dominate economic policy, which has often seemed reactive and sometimes skittish. As senior officials in these key finance institutions respond to fluctuations in the business cycle, the govern-

ment reacts with short-term political calculations that abruptly shift policy agendas. As a result, state involvement in economic management has traditionally been relatively ineffectual. An ongoing stop-go cycle of reversals has plagued policy, which has had relatively little effect on natural business cycles and was unable to prevent recessions during 1979–1981 and 1990–1992.

Despite other differences, this generally reactive and minimalist orientation of economic management strategies in Britain bridges the first two eras of postwar politics in Britain: the consensus era (1945–1979) and the period of Thatcherite policy orientation (1979–1997). How has the orientation of economic policy developed and changed during the postwar period? How new is New Labour when it comes to economic policy?

The Consensus Era. Before Thatcher became leader of the Conservative Party in 1975, Conservative leaders in Britain generally accepted the terms of the collectivist consensus. These Conservatives were also modernizers, prepared to manage the economy in a way consistent with the Keynesian approach and to maintain the welfare state and guarantee full employment.

Declining economic competitiveness made the situation for mainstream Conservatives and, indeed, for any other government, more complex and difficult. By the 1970s public officials no longer saw the world as one they understood and could master; it had become a world without economic growth and with growing political discontent. Edward Heath, the Conservative centrist who governed from 1970 to 1974, was the first prime minister to suffer the full burden of recession and the force of political opposition from both traditional business allies and resurgent trade union adversaries. Operating in an era marked by increased inflation and reduced growth (stagflation), Heath could never break out of the political constraints imposed on him by economic decline.

From 1974 to 1979, the Labour government of Harold Wilson and James Callaghan reinforced the impression that governments could no longer control the swirl of events. The beginning of the end came when trade unions became increasingly restive under the pinch of voluntary wage restraints pressed on them by the Labour government. Frustrated by wage increases well below inflation rates, the unions broke with the government in 1978. The number of unofficial work stoppages increased and official strikes followed, all fueled by a seemingly endless series of leapfrogging pay demands that erupted throughout the winter of 1978–1979 (the "winter of discontent"). There is little doubt that the industrial unrest that dramatized Labour's inability to manage its own allies, the trade unions, contributed mightily to Thatcher's election just a few months later in May 1979. If a Labour government could not manage its trade union allies, whom could it govern? More significant, the winter of discontent helped write the conclusion to Britain's collectivist consensus and discredit the Keynesian welfare state.

Thatcherite Policy Orientation. In policy terms, the economic orientations that Thatcher pioneered and that Major substantially maintained reflected a growing disillusionment with Keynesianism. In its place, monetarism emerged as the new economic doctrine. Keynesian demand management assumed that the level of unemployment could be set and the economy stabilized through decisions of government (monetary and fiscal or budgetary policy). By contrast, monetarism assumed that there is a "natural rate of unemployment" determined by the labor market itself. Monetary and fiscal policy should be passive and intervention limited (so far as this was possible) to a few steps that would help foster appropriate rates of growth in the money supply and keep inflation low.

By implication, the government ruled out spending to run up budgetary deficits as a useful instrument for stimulating the economy. On the contrary, governments could contribute to overall economic efficiency and growth by reducing social expenditure and downsizing the public sector, by reducing its workforce or privatizing nationalized industries. Monetarism reflected a radical change from the postwar consensus regarding economic management. Not only was active government intervention considered unnecessary; it was seen as undesirable and destabilizing.

New Labour's Economic Policy Approach. Time will tell whether New Labour thinking on macroeconomic policy, backed by new political will, can end the "short-termism" of economic policy and provide the cohesion previously lacking.

In British commentaries on New Labour, much has been made of the influence of revitalized Keynesian ideas and reform proposals.[3] In some ways, government policy seems to pursue conventional market-reinforcing and pro-business policies (this approach is often referred to as neoliberalism). In other ways, the New Labour program stands as an alternative to Thatcherite monetarism and traditional Keynesianism. Whether New Labour's approach to economic management constitutes a distinctive third way or a less coherent blend of disparate elements is a matter of political debate.

The first shot fired in the Blair revolution was the announcement within a week of the 1997 election by the chancellor of the exchequer (finance minister), Gordon Brown, that the Bank of England would be given "operational independence" in the setting of monetary policy. The decision transferred from the cabinet a critical, and highly political, prerogative of government. With Brown attuned to the pressures of international financial markets, and the control of inflation and stability the key goals of macroeconomic policy, the transfer of authority over monetary policy confirmed the neoliberal market orientation of economic policy. Moreover, the institutional change in monetary policy has received high marks from the OECD, which, in its most recent analysis of the United Kingdom (issued in June 2000), credited New Labour with making real progress in ending the boom-and-bust cycle. The Paris-based inter-governmental organization noted approvingly that the new monetary policy regime has "per-formed well thus far, not least in comparison to the previous regimes." With an observation that must have made Gordon Brown smile with de-light, the OECD concluded that the new credi-bility of monetary policy was also "a major rea-son why a wage-price inflation spiral need not flare up."[4]

As innovative and effective as monetary pol-icy may be in the context of Britain's historic weakness in this area (and this is no small ac-complishment), it locates New Labour econom-ics firmly in the familiar tradition of neo-liberalism. In other ways, however, New Labour's approach is refreshingly contemporary in analysis and may signal a third way. Above all, it emphasizes pragmatism in the face of global economic competition. Since capital is in-ternational, mobile, and not subject to control, industrial policy and planning that focus on the domestic economy alone are futile. Rather, gov-ernment can enhance the quality of labor through education and training, maintain the labor market flexibility inherited from the Thatcher regime, and help attract investment to Britain. Strict control of inflation, low taxes, and tough limits on public expenditure help pro-mote both employment and investment oppor-tunities. At the same time, economic policy is directed at enhancing the competitive strength of key sectors and developing a partnership with business through research and development, training, technology, and modernization poli-cies. New Labour is very focused on designing and implementing policies to create new jobs and get people—particularly young people—into the workforce; amid skepticism, there are some indications of success. Blair, his economic policy team, and his supporters hope that this approach will help build a stable and competi-tive economy, one in which all Britons have a stake (New Labour refers to its vision as "the stakeholder economy").[5]

Political Implications of Economic Policy. Dif-ferences in economic doctrine are not what matter most in policy terms. In fact, British governments in the past have never consis-tently followed any economic theory, whether Keynesianism or monetarism, in the making of economic policy. Today, the economic policy of New Labour is pragmatic and eclectic. The polit-ical consequences of economic orientations are more significant: Each economic doctrine helps to justify a broad moral and cultural vision of society, provide motives for state policy, and ad-vance alternative sets of values. Should the gov-ernment intervene, work to reduce inequalities through the mildly redistributive provisions of the welfare state, and sustain the ethos of a car-ing society (collectivism)? Should the govern-ment back off and allow the market to function competitively and thereby promote entrepre-neurship, competitiveness, and individual au-tonomy (Thatcherism)? Or should government help secure an inclusive stakeholder economy in which business has the flexibility, security, and mobility to compete and workers have the skills and training to participate effectively in the global labor market (New Labour)? As these questions make clear, economic management strategies are closely linked to social or welfare policy.

Social Policy

Observers have noted that the social and politi-cal role of the welfare state depends as much on policy goals and instruments as on spending levels. Does the state provide services itself or offer cash benefits that can be used to purchase services from private providers? Are benefits limited to those who fall below an income threshold (means-tested) or universal? Are they designed to meet the temporary needs of individuals or to help reduce the gap between rich and poor?

The expanded role of government during World War II and the increased role of the Labour Party during the wartime coalition government led by Winston Churchill prepared the way for the development of the welfare state in Britain. The 1943 Beveridge Report provided a blueprint for an extensive but, in comparative European terms, fairly shallow set of provisions. The principal means-tested program is social security, a system of contributory and noncontributory benefits to provide financial assistance (not services directly) for the elderly, sick, disabled, unemployed, and others similarly in need of assistance.

In general, welfare state provisions interfere relatively little in the workings of the market, and policymakers do not see the reduction of group inequalities as the proper goal of the welfare state. The National Health Service (NHS) provides comprehensive and universal medical care and has long been championed as the "jewel in the crown" of the welfare state in Britain, but it remains an exception to the rule. Compared to other Western European countries, the welfare state in Britain offers relatively few comprehensive services, and the policies are not very generous. For the most part, Britons must rely on means-tested "safety-net" programs that leave few of the recipients satisfied.

The Welfare State Under Thatcher and Major. The record on social expenditure by Conservative governments from 1979 to 1997 was mixed. Given Britons' strong support for public education, pensions, and health care, Conservative governments attempted more limited reform than many at first anticipated. The Thatcher and Major governments encouraged private alongside public provision in education, health care (insurance), and pensions. They worked to increase efficiency in social services, reduced the value of some benefits by changing the formulas or reducing cost-of-living adjustments, and

contracted out some services (purchased them from private contractors rather than providing them directly). In addition, in policy reforms reminiscent of U.S. "workfare" requirements, they tried to reduce dependency by denying benefits to youths who refuse to participate in training programs.

Despite these efforts, the commitment to reduced spending could not be sustained, partly because a recession triggered rises in income support and unemployment benefits (included under the "Social Security" heading in Figure 7.2). In addition, the cost of health care rose dramatically in Britain, as in all other industrial democracies, because costs were linked to such nonpolicy factors as the increasing age of the population. Looked at in comparative perspective, benefits per head have been below the EU average and considerably below those in Germany or the Scandinavian member states (they are higher, however, than in the United States or Japan).

To a degree, however, this general pattern masks specific and, in some cases, highly charged policy changes in both expenditure and the institutionalized pattern of provision. In housing, the changes in state policy and provision were the most extensive, with repercussions in electoral terms and in changing the way Britons think about the welfare state. Early on, Thatcher's housing policy became a major test case of her vision of society, as she emphasized private ownership and responsibility. Even before she was prime minister, Thatcher made housing a high-profile issue. During the 1979 campaign, she promised to give all tenants in council (public) housing the opportunity to buy their homes at up to 50 percent below market value.

She kept her promise. By 1990 more than 1.25 million council houses were sold, particularly the attractive single-family homes with gardens (quite unlike public housing in the United States). Two-thirds of the sales were to rental tenants. Thatcher's housing policy was extremely popular. As one observer noted,

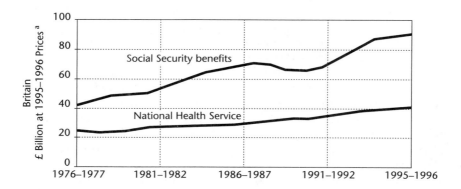

Figure 7.2   Real Growth in Social Security Benefits and National Health Service
Expenditure in Britain, 1976–1996

Despite efforts to reduce the cost of the welfare state, especially during the period of
Conservative governments from 1979 to 1997, Britain experienced real growth in both
social services and health care provisions.

---

[a]Adjusted to 1995–1996 prices using the GDP market prices deflator.
Note: In Britain "social security" refers to a variety of social benefits, including pensions,
unemployment benefits, sickness benefits, child benefits, and single-parent benefits.

Source: From *Social Trends* 27, 1997 Edition, ed. Jenny Church, p. 137. "Social Trends" Office for
National Statistics © Crown, copyright 1997.

housing "was electorally crucial in dividing a working-class movement, deeply disillusioned by the apparent inadequacies of the Welfare State and politically embittered by the economic policies pursued by the Labour government after 1976, by its populist appeal to the anti-bureaucratic, individualist and self-sufficient ideology of home ownership."[6] By one calculation, between 1979 and 1983 there was a swing (change in the percentage of vote received by the two major parties) to the Conservative Party of 17 percent among those who had bought their council houses.[7] By 1987, the swing by new buyers from Labour to Conservative was down to just 2 percent over the national trend, however. Because the rise in adjustable mortgage rates (some 6 percent in 1988–1989 alone) fueled a steep increase in monthly mortgage payments, the housing issue no longer worked to the advantage of the Conservative Party. Indeed it may have started cutting the other way.

Despite great Conservative success in the campaign to privatize housing, a strong majority of Britons remain stalwart supporters of the principle of collective provision for their basic needs. Thus, there were limits on the government's ability to reduce social spending or change institutional behavior. For example, in 1989 the Conservative government tried to introduce market practices into the NHS, with general practitioners managing funds and purchasing hospital care for their patients. The British Medical Association strongly objected, and many Britons were worried that the creation of an "internal market" would create incentives for doctors or hospitals to cut corners and reduce services to those with the fewest options. Many voiced fears that the reforms would create a two-tier system of medical care for rich and poor.

Major worked to distance himself from Thatcher's perceived disregard for the plight of the less fortunate. In fact, his government increased welfare spending, in part to persuade the electorate that Conservatives could be trusted on the "caring" issues. Characteristically, and with some quiet success, Major took a pragmatic nonideological turn in welfare policy, looking for cuts and improvements at the same time, within a general framework that preferred means-tested to universal benefits. Nevertheless, the political damage was done. Before the 1992 election, Labour gained a commanding lead over the Conservatives on the health issue: A majority of two-to-one judged it the best party to run the NHS.[8] Clearly, a lack of confidence in the Conservatives on the "caring" issues hurt Major substantially in 1992.

An overwhelming majority of Britons—87 percent—rely exclusively on the NHS for their health care, and nearly all receive most of their critical care in NHS hospitals. As the 1997 election approached, polls made clear that the health service had knocked unemployment out of first place as the most urgent issue on people's minds. Opinion surveys also confirmed that voters usually blamed the Conservatives for problems in these areas, and they even blamed Tory social policies for increases in crime. Indeed, a majority of the Conservatives' own supporters worried about what might happen to health and other social services with another Tory government. Nothing else propelled the Labour landslide in 1997 more than the concern for the "caring" issues, and despite the setback Labour suffered over Blair's handling of the fuel crisis and the foot-and-mouth disease epidemic, the traditional advantage Labour enjoys on these issues helped secure victory for Blair's New Labour in June 2001.

New Labour Social Policy. As with economic policy, social policy for New Labour presents an opportunity for government to balance pragmatism and innovation, while borrowing from traditional Labour as well as from Thatcherite options. Thus, the Blair government rejects both the attempted retrenchment of Conservative governments that seemed mean-spirited and the egalitarian traditions of Britain's collectivist era that emphasized entitlements. Instead, New Labour focuses its policy on training and broader social investment as a more positive "third-way" alternative. At the same time, New Labour draws political strength from the "Old Labour" legacy of commitment on the "caring" social policy issues.

For example, following Bill Clinton, his New Democratic counterpart in the United States, the prime minister promised a modernized, leaner welfare state, in which people are actively encouraged to seek work. The reform of the welfare state emphasizes efficiencies and attempts to break welfare dependency. Efforts to spur entry into the labor market combine carrots and sticks. Positive inducements include extensive training programs, especially targeted at youth, combined with incentives to private industry to hire new entrants to the labor market. The threats include eligibility restrictions and reductions in coverage. Referred to as the "New Deal" for the young unemployed, welfare reform in the United Kingdom has emphasized concerted efforts to create viable pathways out of dependence. Although beginning with a focus on moving youth from welfare to work, New Deal reform efforts expanded in several directions. The New Deal was quickly extended to single parents and the long-term unemployed. In 1999, the government launched a "Bridging the Gap" initiative to provide a more comprehensive approach for assisting sixteen- to eighteen-year-olds not in education, employment, or training to achieve clear goals by age nineteen through a variety of "pathways" (academic, vocational, or occupational). "Better Government for Older People" was launched in 1998 and followed quickly by *All Our Futures,* a government report issued in the summer of 2000 with twenty-eight recommendations to improve the quality of life and the delivery of public services for senior citizens. The gap between the lofty goals and the government's delivery on promises to the elderly was illustrated by the derisive response of many older Britons to the 1999 increase of 75 pence ($1.10) in their weekly state pensions. In a rare moment of post–fuel crisis humility, Blair granted the point in his speech to the Labour Party's annual convention in September 2000, calling the token increase a mistake and assuring his audience—and the nation's pensioners who compose nearly a quarter of the electorate—"we get the message." And, in return, the prime minister, as well as the chancellor of the exchequer, Gordon Brown, left the unmistakable message that the final preelection budget would include a more significant increase, especially for lower-income pensioners.

Although the jury is still out on the follow-through and effectiveness of New Labour social and welfare policy initiatives, the intent to create innovative policies and approach social policy in new and more comprehensive ways is clearly there. Late in 1997, the government inaugurated a Social Exclusion Unit staffed by civil servants and external policy specialists, located within the cabinet office, and reporting directly to the prime minister. It was charged broadly with addressing "what can happen when people or areas suffer from such problems as unemployment, poor skills, low incomes, poor housing, high crime environments, bad health, and family breakdown." The Social Exclusion Unit has been actively involved in developing the New Deal initiative as well as in writing reports and recommending policies to take on problems such as truancy and school exclusion, homelessness, neighborhood renewal, and teenage pregnancy. This collaborative effort to identify comprehensive solutions to society's ills and reduce the tendency for government to let marginalized individuals and groups fall by the wayside even during good economic times captures the third-way orientation of the Blair project.

Nevertheless, New Labour, like all other governments in Britain and many other countries, will be accountable above all for the failure or success of more traditional social policies, especially health care and education. Even the generally favorable OECD report already referred to gives the Blair government low marks on

health care, noting that the resources are "chronically overstretched" and that the ratio of doctors to population and level of spending are low for a developed country. It cautions that health care results in the United Kingdom are in some ways mediocre, with cancer survival rates, for example, more typical of Eastern than Western European norms, and raises doubts about the effectiveness of NHS reforms. Until class sizes and waiting lists for treatment are reduced, the electorate will not let New Labour off the hook on education and health care. For a great many Britons, these core policies, much more than the battle against social exclusion, will determine the measure of success of New Labour's social policy.

Society and Economy

What were the *distributional effects*—the consequences for group patterns of wealth and poverty—of the economic and social policies of Thatcher and Major? To what extent are the policies of Tony Blair's Labour government designed to continue—or to reverse—these trends? How has government policy influenced the condition of minorities and women? It is impossible to ascertain when government policy creates a given distribution of resources and when poverty increases or decreases because of a general downturn or upswing in the economy. The evidence is clear, however, that economic inequality grew in Britain during the 1980s before it stabilized or narrowed slightly in the mid-1990s, and that ethnic minorities and women continue to experience significant disadvantages.

As British journalist Peter Jenkins observed, a host of Thatcher-era policy outcomes—high unemployment, changes in tax policy that increased the tax burdens of the poor relative to the rich, the reduction in the real value of welfare benefits—led to increased inequality. In the 1980s there was much talk in Britain of "two nations," rich and poor, and a frequent (usually critical) characterization of Thatcher, accordingly, as a "two-nation Tory." Jenkins took the analysis a step further, suggesting that the upward pressure on the top end of the economic scale and the downward pressure on the bottom end had created a three-tiered society of "the haves, the have-nots, and the have-lots."[9]

Data confirm this pattern. Between 1980 and 1990, for those at the ninetieth percentile, incomes grew by 47 percent compared with only 6 percent at the tenth percentile. In the early 1990s the gap stabilized; by 1994 real incomes were growing at both ends of the spectrum, and the gap between incomes for the top and bottom 10 percent narrowed. Similarly, the proportion of people whose incomes fell below 40, 50, or 60 percent of the national average grew rapidly throughout the 1980s but declined by 1994.[10]

Policy initiated by the Conservative Party particularly during the Thatcher years tended to deepen inequalities. The economic upturn that began in 1992 combined with Major's moderating effects on the Thatcherite social policy agenda served to narrow inequality by the mid-1990s. Since 1997, as one observer noted, Labour has "pursued redistribution by stealth, raising various indirect levies on the better-off to finance tax breaks for poorer workers."[11] As a result, since 1997 Britain has witnessed a modest downward redistribution of income. A strong economy, concerted attention to social exclusion in its many forms, and a 1999 pledge by the prime minister to eradicate child poverty augur well for a further modest narrowing of the gap between rich and poor in Britain. But, as a 2000 report, *Poverty and Social Exclusion in Britain*, indicates, there is much more work to be done to improve the standards of living of many Britons. The report found almost a quarter of households in Britain living in poverty in 1999, compared to 14 percent in 1983.

Inequality and Ethnic Minorities

Poverty and diminished opportunity disproportionately characterize the situation of ethnic minorities (a term applied to peoples of non-European origin from the former British colonies in the Indian subcontinent, the Caribbean, and Africa). Official estimates place the ethnic minority population in Britain at around 3.3 million, or just under 6 percent. Indians compose the largest ethnic minority at 27 percent; Pakistanis and Bangladeshis represent about 23 percent; and Afro-Caribbeans, 23 percent. Due to past immigration and fertility patterns, the ethnic minority population in the United Kingdom is considerably younger than the white population. More than one-third of the ethnic minority population is younger than age sixteen, nearly half is under twenty-five, and more than four-fifths is under forty-five. (By contrast, only about one-fifth of whites are under age sixteen, fewer than one-third under twenty-five, and three-fifths under forty-five.) Thus, despite the often disparaging reference to ethnic minority individuals as "immigrants," the experience of members of ethnic minority groups is increasingly that of a native-born population. Among those under age twenty-five, 92 percent of people of Indian descent, 76 percent of Pakistani or Bangladeshi descent, and 80 percent of black people were born in the United Kingdom.[12]

Britain has adjusted slowly and, by most accounts, poorly to the realities of a multicultural society. The postwar period has witnessed the gradual erosion of racial, religious, and ethnic tolerance in Britain and a chipping away at the right of settlement of postcolonial subjects in the United Kingdom. During the Thatcher era, discussion of immigration and citizenship rights was used for partisan political purposes and assumed a distinctly racial tone. Ethnic minority individuals, particularly young men, are subject to unequal treatment by the police and considerable physical harassment by citizens. They have experienced cultural isolation as well as marginalization in the educational system, job training, housing, and labor markets. Recognizing these problems, in 2000 the government brought to Parliament a bill to amend the Race Relations Act by outlawing direct and indirect discrimination in all public bodies and place a "positive duty" on all public officials and authorities to promote racial equality.

There is also considerable concern about the apparent rise in racially motivated crime. Official figures released in spring 2000 for London show a dramatic increase in the number of "racial incidents" from 5,876 in 1997–1998 to 23,346 in 1999–2000. Worse still, of the nearly 25,000 racially motivated crimes in London, nearly 15,000 were violent. Although part of the increase may be attributable to changes in reporting procedures (traditionally police officers determined whether a crime would be treated as racial crime, but for 1999–2000 the characterization of a crime as racially motivated relied mainly on the testimony of the victim), there is widespread perception that hate crimes are on the rise in major metropolitan areas with significant ethnic diversity.

The sense of cultural isolation within the ethnic minority communities seems strong, and these perceptions have deepened ethnic identities or identities based on countries of origin or descent, as distinct from British identities. "In defining ourselves we sometimes say we are English or Welsh or Indian or Jamaican," observed the Afro-Caribbean social theorist and cultural critic Stuart Hall. "Of course this is to speak metaphorically. These identities are not imprinted in our genes. However, we do think of them as if they are part of our essential natures."[13] Few in the minority communities are likely to identify themselves simply as part of a national culture—as English—without reference to their subnational minority identity.

In general, poor rates of economic success reinforce the sense of isolation and distinct collective identities. Variations among ethnic minority communities are quite considerable, however, and there are some noteworthy success stories. For example, among men of African-Asian, Chinese, and Indian descent, the proportional representation in the managerial and professional ranks is actually higher than that for white men (although they are much less likely to be senior managers in large firms).

Also, Britons of South Asian, and, especially, Indian descent enjoy a high rate of entrepreneurship. In contrast to Britons of Indian descent, who have enjoyed the greatest mobility into business and professional careers, those of Bangladeshi descent are at the other end of the spectrum. As the latest arrivals and migrants from a predominantly peasant economy, they have faced a set of acute problems: they enter an industrial urban economy with few marketable skills; their proficiency in English is low; and they are the object of outright discrimination. Despite some variations, employment opportunities for women from all minority ethnic groups are limited. The largest employment concentrations are in the "other nonmanual" category (42 percent of Pakistani, 47 percent of Indian, and 54 percent of Afro- Caribbean women), followed by "semiskilled manual" (45 percent of Pakistani, 34 percent of Indian, and 25 percent of Afro-Caribbean women). There is only limited representation across all other job levels.[14]

A distinct gap remains between the job opportunities available to whites and those open to ethnic minorities in Britain (see Table 7.1). It is clear that ethnic minority groups are overrepresented among low-income households in the United Kingdom. Nearly two-thirds of Pakistani or Bangladeshi households are located within the bottom fifth, and fewer than one-fifth of whites may be found there. Blacks (persons of African or Caribbean descent) are also overrepresented in the bottom one-fifth, although not to the same degree.

Inequality and Women

Women's participation in the labor market when compared to that of men also indicates marked patterns of inequality. The Thatcher and Major governments made it clear that management flexibility in hiring part-time workers to lower labor costs would take priority over efforts to reduce gender inequality in the workforce. As a result, the proportion of work-

Table 7.1 Distribution of Disposable Income in Great Britain by Ethnic Group, 1994–1995

Ethnic Group	Bottom Fifth of Group	Top Four-Fifths of Group
White	19%	81%
Black	27	73
Indian	27	73
Pakistani/ Bangladeshi	64	36
Other ethnic minorities	36	64
All ethnic groups	20	80

Source: Jenny Church, ed., *Social Trends* 27 (London: Social Trends, The Stationary Office, Office for National Statistics, 1997). © Crown, copyright 1997.

ing women in part-time employment increased. Not only are part-time jobs less secure and lower paid, they also provide fewer pension rights, opportunities for advancement, and employment protections than full-time work. Thus, in the context of cutbacks in provision for home care, employment policy tended to "confirm the old ideas that women worked only for pin money [money to spend for nonessentials] or should stay at home and care for their husbands, children and sick or elderly relatives."[15] In addition, government policy tended to worsen the often precarious situation of female heads of household when the eligibility for income maintenance was tightened and the value of benefits reduced.

In fact, most women in Britain work part time, often in jobs with fewer than sixteen hours of work per week and often with fewer than eight hours (in contrast, fewer than one in every fifteen men is employed part time). More than three-quarters of women working part time report that they did not want a full-time job, yet more women than men (in raw numbers, not simply as a percentage) take on second jobs. In addition, women are far less likely to be

self-employed than men; in 1996, there were roughly three self-employed men for every woman.

A 1997 survey from Eurostat, the statistical arm of the EU, confirms that employment conditions for women in Britain trail those of their European counterparts. The survey reports that in several EU countries, women still get paid substantially less than men, measured in hourly earnings, even when they have comparable education and work in the same industry and occupation. However, the differential is greatest in Britain, where it is just below 25 percent. Moreover, when the overall mix of jobs and the effects of sex segregation in the labor market are taken into account, including both full- and part-time workers, the gap increases to 36 percent, and the gender pay inequality in the United Kingdom remains the worst in the EU. To complete the picture, when women move up the job ladder, patterns of inequality actually deepen. Women in management positions in the United Kingdom receive only two-thirds the pay of their male counterparts.[16]

The Blair government remains committed to gender equality in the workplace and affirmed its resolve to address women's concerns to balance work and family responsibilities. It has taken a number of steps to aid women at work and help reconcile the demands of family and employment. The government has implemented (or proposed) a set of "family-friendly" work-related policies, including unpaid parental leave of up to three months (the EU standard accepted by the United Kingdom under Blair as part of the Social Charter) to supplement the statutory leave package (six weeks at 90 percent pay plus twelve weeks at half-pay plus roughly $90 per week) and the right to refuse to work more than forty-eight hours per week. Other measures include a commitment in principle to filling half of all public appointments with women, a review of the pension system to ensure better coverage for women, draft legislation to provide for the sharing of pensions after divorce, tax credits for working families as well as for child care, and a National Childcare Strategy. Nevertheless, the United Kingdom is likely to remain an EU outlier in the provision of day care, with responsibilities remaining primarily in private hands and the gap between child care supply and demand far greater than elsewhere in Western Europe. Moreover, the government has continued the Conservative policy of promoting management flexibility, so it seems likely that the general pattern of female labor market participation and inequality in earnings will change relatively little in the years ahead. A spring 1999 report commissioned by the cabinet office's Women's Unit confirms a significant pattern of inequality in lifetime earnings of men and women with an equal complement of skills, defined by both a gender gap and a "mother gap."

The Generation Gap

There is another widely discussed and equally significant gap that helps shape British politics: the generation gap. In fact, its dimensions are most clear at the point where gender and generational differences come together, and they have done so acutely in elections. The issue of a gender gap in voting behavior has long been a mainstay of British electoral studies. From 1945 to 1992, women were more likely than men to vote Conservative. In addition, since 1964 a "gender-generation" gap has become well established and was very clear in the 1992 election. Among younger voters (under thirty years old), women preferred Labour, while men voted strongly for the Conservatives, producing a fourteen-point gender gap favoring Labour; among older voters (over sixty-five years old), women were far more inclined to vote Conservative than were their male counterparts, creating a gender gap of eighteen points favoring the Conservatives.

The modest all-generation gender gap that favored the Tories in 1992 (6 percent) was closed in 1997, as a greater percentage of women shifted away from the Conservatives (11 per-

cent) than did men (8 percent). As a result, women and men recorded an identical 44 percent tally for Labour. The gender-generation gap continued, however, with younger women more pro-Labour than younger men and the pattern reversing in the older generation. Moreover, one of the most striking features of the 1997 election was the generational dimension: the largest swing to Labour was among those in the age group eighteen to twenty-nine years (more than 18 percent), and among first-time voters; there was no swing to Labour among those over age sixty-five.[17]

After the 2001 election, analysis pointed to a generation gap in turnout. BBC exit polls revealed that young voters had the lowest turnout, most often saying the election "didn't matter." The new Home Secretary, David Blunkett, worried aloud that youth had "switched off politics."

What are the implications of this overlay of gender and generational voting patterns? For one thing, it seems that a party's ability to recognize and satisfy the political agendas of women in Britain may offer big political dividends. Studies suggest, first, that issues at the top of the list of women's concerns (e.g., child care, the rights and pay of part-time workers, equal pay, support for family caregivers, domestic violence) do not feature strongly in the existing policy agendas of the political parties. Second, to the extent that women and men care about the same broadly defined issues, women often understand the issues differently than men do and express different priorities. For example, while men (and the three major parties) consider unemployment the central employment issue, women emphasize equal pay and pensions, access to child care, and the rights of part-time workers. Third, research indicates that distinct sets of issues concern different groups of women. For example, older women are most concerned about pensions and transportation. Due to the overrepresentation of women in lower-paid part-time jobs, working women express particular concern about the minimum wage and the treatment of part-time workers.

Mothers find the level of child benefit more important than issues of tax cuts. Finally, younger women strongly support policies that would help them balance the responsibilities of work, family, and child care.[18] This last point may be the most critical. Like the focus on "working families" in the U.S. presidential campaign in 2000, political parties in Britain recognize that the successful political management of the gender-generation gap is becoming a critical electoral battleground. In particular, winning the support of working mothers or younger women who plan to become working mothers could pay huge political dividends.

On other aspects of the generation gap, there is far less clarity. The political apathy and self-interested materialism of the "youth of today" receive wide comment, but there is little evidence that can disentangle the attitudes of the millennium generation from the different stages and accompanying social and political attitudes each generation acquires during its life cycle. Nevertheless, there has been one surprising and potentially telling public opinion blip on the controversial issue of Britain membership in the single European currency. Despite the widespread belief that the "euro NO" group was dominated by crotchety old fogies, polls in September 2000 showed that the opposition to joining the euro was actually highest among those eighteen to twenty-four years old, at a whopping 80 percent. Trying to shed their unhip image, the "Noes" recruited singer Geri Halliwell, formerly of the Spice Girls, to their campaign, and worked hard to press the claim, as one "No" campaigner put it, "that you can be young, tolerant and still opposed to the euro." Calling the battle of the euro a "cultural war," he added, "Our message should be 'Yes to sex and drugs in Amsterdam, but No to the single currency.'"[19]

The Dilemmas of European Integration

Since the beginning of the Industrial Revolution in the eighteenth century, Britain has been more dependent than most other countries on international commerce for the creation of wealth. Because Britain's economy is more interdependent with the global economy than most other leading industrial powers, it faces considerable external pressures on its economic policy. The dilemmas of European integration most vividly illustrate the interplay between economics and politics in an era of global interdependence.

Britain was humbled when its applications for membership in the European Community (EC) were blocked in 1963 and again in 1967 by France. Worse, since its admission in 1973, Britain's participation in the EC (in November 1993, it became the EU) has tended to underscore its reduced international power and ability to control regional and global developments. Many Britons remain skeptical about the advantages of Britain's political and economic integration with Europe and are uneasy about the loss of sovereignty that resulted from EU membership.

Economic Integration and Political Disintegration

During the Thatcher and Major years, the issue of economic integration bedeviled the prime minister's office and divided the Conservative Party. The introduction of the European Monetary System (EMS) in 1979 set the stage for the political dramas that followed. The EMS fixed the exchange rates among member currencies (referred to as the exchange rate mechanism, or ERM), and permitted only limited fluctuation above or below. Intended to stabilize European economies and promote trade among members, its success depended on the willingness of member states to pursue compatible economic strategies—and on their ability to maintain similar growth rates and levels of inflation. In retrospect, this plan seems highly unrealistic. How likely were Spain, Portugal, Greece—or even Britain—to keep pace with Germany in the period of heady economic competitiveness before unification? But there was tremendous pressure to set up the ERM before political disagreements or recession could close the window of opportunity.

Thatcher opposed British participation in the ERM throughout the 1980s, insisting on British control of its economic policy. However, when her domestic economic policy failed to stem Britain's rampant inflation, Thatcher's anti-EC stance pitted her against senior ministers and leaders of Britain's EC partners, as well as against the bulk of the British business community. It seemed that everyone but Thatcher thought participation in European integration would ease inflation in Britain and enhance its competitiveness. In the end, Thatcher succumbed to the pressure to give up a measure of economic sovereignty, in effect, to Germany and its central bank (the Bundesbank), whose decisions would force Britain to follow in lock-step. She permitted Britain to join the ERM in October 1990. Ironically, just one month later, she was toppled from office by a coup led by those in her own party who most deeply resented her grudging attitude toward integration.

For the new government of Prime Minister Major, participation in the ERM held enormous symbolic and political significance. As chancellor of the exchequer, he had quietly pressed Thatcher to join, and as prime minister, he staked his reputation on its success. He hoped that participation would stabilize European trade, reduce inflation, and pull Britain out of a stubborn recession.

Implications of Maastricht and the Common Currency

The Treaty on European Union (usually called the Maastricht Treaty for the small Dutch town where it was negotiated in 1991) represented a bold agenda for economic and monetary union and for deeper cooperation on foreign policy and security matters. Maastricht also established a plan to phase in a single EC currency and control of national monetary policy by a European central bank. In addition, Maastricht gave treaty status to the Community Charter of the Fundamental Social Rights of Workers, more commonly known as the Social Charter.

Unlike Thatcher, Major positioned himself as pro-Europe and was solicitous of his allies. But he stood his ground at Maastricht. Negotiating well, Major secured a crucial opt-out clause for Britain. The United Kingdom would not be bound by the Social Charter or by any single currency plans. Unfortunately for Major and the Conservatives, almost before he could enjoy his Maastricht victories, Major's integration strategy faced a nearly fatal setback.

In September 1992, the EMS collapsed under the impact of downward pressures in the British economy and the strains of German unification. The prime minister's reputation was badly damaged, and the momentum for economic unity among EC countries was abruptly stalled. The Thatcherite anti-Maastricht hard core in the Conservative Party dug in against him on the key issues of economic and monetary union, thereby undermining his leadership and forcing him to squander his political capital on the lost cause of party unity on Europe. Major never recovered, and it took several years before plans for economic integration in the EU were put back on track. Remarkably, a single European policy (the ERM) led to Thatcher's downfall and politically haunted John Major throughout his premiership.

Developments in European integration present a formidable hurdle for Tony Blair or any successor government (this is discussed further in Chapter 10). Few in Britain find it easy to countenance a common currency in place of the pound sterling (the British currency), a symbol of empire and national autonomy. Britons are also extremely reluctant to lose direct control over monetary policy to the European Central Bank (ECB), particularly given the loss of nearly 30 percent of the value of the euro against the dollar in the period between its launch in January 1999 and the high-visibility rescue mission spearheaded by the ECB in September 2000. But since Tony Blair's Britain wants to assume leadership in Europe and position itself on the cutting edge of globalization, Britain faces a significant dilemma over the euro. The political repercussions of economic and monetary considerations will help shape the challenges that New Labour, future governments, and the country face in the years ahead.

Britain and the International Political Economy

The term *globalization* is often applied as a general catch-phrase to identify the growing depth, extent, and diversity of cross-border connections that are a signal characteristic of the contemporary world. Discussion of the concept often begins with accounts of the increasing globalization of economic activities, seen in the reorganization of production and the global redistribution of the workforce (the "global factory") and in the increased extent and intensity of international trade, finance, and foreign direct investment. Some have argued that the radical mobility of factors of production, especially the capital of the "electronic herd" of investors and financiers who can shift vast sums of money around the globe at the speed of a mouse-click has fatally weakened the capacities of nation-states. Students of comparative politics by and large argue, however, that claims of the demise of national policy controls and national economic models have been exaggerated. Each country study will illuminate the particular features of national economic models as they are shaped by the international political economy, all set against the critical backdrop of domestic policy legacies and political constituencies and programs.

Britain plays a particular role within the European and international economy, one that has been reinforced by international competitive pressures in this global age. For a start, FDI favors national systems like those of Britain (and the United States), which rely more on private contractual and market-driven arrangements and less on state capacity and political or institutional arrangements. Reasonably enough, foreign investment tends to steer clear of production systems like that of Germany or the Scandinavian countries, which rely more on citizenship status, institutionalized coordination, and state-sponsored arrangements. Due to such factors as low costs, political climate, government-sponsored financial incentives, reduced trade union power, and a large pool of potential non-unionized recruits, the United Kingdom is by far the favored location in Europe for FDI.

From the mid-1980s onward, the single market initiative of the EU has attracted foreign investment by according insider status to non-EU-based companies, so long as minimum local content requirements are met. Throughout this period, all British governments have, for both pragmatic and ideological reasons, promoted the United Kingdom as a magnet for foreign investment. For the Thatcher and Major governments, FDI was a congenial market-driven alternative to state intervention as a means to improve sectoral competitiveness, especially in the automobile industry. It had the added benefit of exposing U.K. producers to "lean production" techniques and management cultures and strategies that reinforced government designs to weaken unions and enforce flexibility. New Labour has continued this approach, which helps advance its key third-way strategy orientation to accept globalization as a given and seek ways to improve competitiveness through business-friendly partnerships.

FDI is only one part of a bigger picture. *Fairness at Work*, a White Paper published in May 1998, helped establish New Labour's framework for enhanced individual rights and benefits of workers in important domains such as unfair dismissal, maternity and parental leave, and minimum wage, bringing the United Kingdom closer to European norms. Nevertheless, as the prime minister confirmed in his foreword to the document, "Even after the changes we propose, Britain will have the most lightly regulated labour market of any leading economy in the world." In very important ways, New Labour accepted the legacy of eighteen years of Conservative assaults on trade union powers and privileges. It has chosen to modernize—but not reshape—the system of production that proliferates nonstandard and insecure jobs without traditional social protections, a growing sector in which women and ethnic minorities are significantly overrepresented. As a result, within EU Europe, Britain has assumed a specialized profile as a producer of low-technology, low-value-added products through the use of a comparatively low-paid, segmented, weakly organized, and easily dismissable workforce. Tony Blair's Britain preaches this model of "flexible labour markets" throughout EU Europe, and its success in boosting Britain's economic performance in comparison to the rest of Europe has won some reluctant admirers, even converts.

Thus, Britain has been shaped by the international political economy in important ways and hopes to take full advantage of the economic prospects of globalization, even as it also tries to reshape other European national models in its own image.

As our world-of-states theme suggests, a country's participation in today's global economic order diminishes national sovereign control, raising unsettling questions in even the most established democracies. Amid complicated pressures, both internal and external, can state institutions retain the capacity to administer policy effectively within distinctive national models? How much do the growth of powerful bureaucracies at home and complex dependencies on international organizations such as the EU limit the ability of citizens to control policy ends? We turn to these questions in Chapter 8.

Notes

1. See Paul M. Kennedy, *The Rise and Fall of British Naval Mastery* (Atlantic Highlands, N.J.: Ashfield Press, 1992), pp. 186–189.

2. "A British Miracle?" *Economist*, September 16–22, 2000, pp. 57–58.

3. Will Hutton, *The State We're In* (London: Jonathan Cape, 1995).

4. Organisation for Economic Cooperation and Development, *Economic Survey: United Kingdom* (June 2000), p. 11; http://www.oecd.org/eco/surv/pdf/unitedkingdom00.pdf.

5. See Stephen Driver and Luke Martell, *New Labour Politics After Thatcherism* (Cambridge: Polity Press, 1998), pp. 32–73.

6 Michael Jones, *Marxism Today* (May 1980): 10.

7. Ivor Crewe, "Labor Force Changes, Working Class Decline, and the Labour Vote: Social and Electoral Trends in Postwar Britain," in Frances Fox Piven, ed., *Labor Parties in Postindustrial Societies* (New York: Oxford University Press, 1992), p. 34. See also David Marsh and R. A. W. Rhodes, "Implementing Thatcherism: Policy Change in the 1980s," *Parliamentary Affairs* 45, no. 1 (January 1992): 34–37.

8. Kenneth Newton, "Caring and Competence: The Long, Long Campaign," in Anthony King, ed., *Britain at the Polls 1992* (Chatham, N.J.: Chatham House, 1993), p. 147.

9. Peter Jenkins, "Thatcher's Britain," *Geopolitique*, no. 31 (Autumn 1990): 14–15.

10. Jenny Church, ed., *Social Trends 27* (London: The Stationery Office, 1997), pp. 98–99.

11. Steven Fielding, "A New Politics?" in Patrick Dunleavy et al., eds., *Developments in British Politics 6* (New York: St. Martin's Press, 2000), p. 2.

12. Office of National Statistics Social Survey, *Living in Britain: Results from the 1995 General Household Survey* (London: The Stationery Office, 1997).

13. Stuart Hall, "The Question of Cultural Identity," in Stuart Hall, David Held, and Tony McGrew, eds., *Modernity and Its Futures* (Cambridge: Polity Press, 1992), p. 291.

14. Gail Lewis, "Black Women's Employment and the British Economy," in Winston James and Clive

Harris, eds., *Inside Babylon: The Caribbean Diaspora in Britain* (London: Verso, 1993), pp. 73–96.

15. Bob Jessop, Kevin Bonnett, Simon Bromley, and Tom Ling, *Thatcherism* (Cambridge: Polity Press, 1988), p. 48.

16. Melanie Bien, "A Woman's Place Is in the Workplace—But Pay Her More," *European*, December 11–17, 1997, p. 35.

17. Pippa Norris, *Electoral Change in Britain Since 1945* (Oxford: Blackwell, 1997), pp. 133–135; Pippa Norris, "A Gender-Generation Gap?" in Pippa Norris and Geoffrey Norris, eds., *Critical Elections: British Parties and Voters in Long-Term Perspective* (London: Sage, 1999).

18. Joni Lovenduski, "Gender Politics: A Breakthrough for Women?" *Parliamentary Affairs* 50, no. 4 (October 1997): 708–719.

19. "Culture Wars on Europe, " *Economist*, September 9–15, 2000, p. 68.

CHAPTER
8

Governance
and Policymaking

An understanding of British governance begins with consideration of Britain's constitution, which is notable for two significant features: its form and its antiquity. Britain lacks a formal written constitution in the usual sense; that is, there is no single unified and authoritative text that has special status above ordinary law and can be amended only by special procedures. Rather, the British constitution is a combination of statutory law (mainly acts of Parliament), common law, convention, and authoritative interpretations. Although it is often said that Britain has an unwritten constitution, this is not accurate. Authoritative legal treatises are written, of course, as are the much more significant acts of Parliament that define crucial elements of the British political system. These acts define the powers of Parliament and its relationship with the Crown, the rights governing the relationship between state and citizen, the relationship of constituent nations to the United Kingdom, the relationship of the United Kingdom to the European Union (EU), and many other rights and legal arrangements. Thus, it is probably best to say that "what distinguishes the British constitution from others is not that it is unwritten, but rather that it is part written and uncodified."[1]

More than its form, however, the British constitution's antiquity raises questions. It is hard to know where conventions and acts of Parliament with constitutional implications began, but they can certainly be found dating back to the seventeenth century, notably with the Bill of Rights of 1689, which helped define the relationship between the monarchy and Parliament. "Britain's constitution presents a paradox," a British scholar of constitutional history has observed. "We live in a modern world but inhabit a pre-modern, indeed, ancient, constitution."[2] For example, several industrial democracies, including Spain, Belgium, and the Netherlands, are constitutional monarchies, in which policymaking is left to the elected government and the monarch fulfills largely ceremonial duties. In fact, Western Europe contains the largest concentration of constitutional monarchies in the world. However, Britain alone among Western democracies has permitted *two* unelected hereditary institutions—the Crown and the House of Lords—to participate in governing the country (in the case of the Lords, a process of reform was begun in 1999).

More generally, the structure and principles of many areas of government have been accepted by constitutional authorities for so long that appeal to convention has enormous cultural force. Thus, widely agreed-on rules of conduct, rather than law or U.S.-style checks and balances, set the limits of governmental power. Most of the time, such conventions constrain state officials from overstepping generally agreed boundaries and prevent any state institution from achieving undue concentration of power.

For example, after a general election, the Crown (since 1952, Queen Elizabeth II), whatever her likes or dislikes for the individual or her very private political preferences, will certainly invite the leader of the victorious party to form a government. Similarly, that leader (now serving as prime minister) will surely ask the queen to dissolve Parliament within five years, thereby introducing a new general election. Neither activity is required by statute or specified in a written constitutional document, but no one in Britain harbors the least doubt that governments will be formed and Parliaments dissolved as required by the constitution, that is, by binding custom.

Nevertheless, the absence of a single document of binding authority means that rules of conduct may be less than clear when a situation lacks sufficient precedent. For example, if no party is quite victorious after a general election—if none has a clear-cut majority by itself in the House of Commons (a condition known as a *hung Parliament*)—the conventions that govern the formation of a new government are not terribly clear.

As a leading constitutional authority recently observed, if the expectation that a general election would deliver a majority government no longer held, "the Crown would presumably have to decide what the conventions were, and since party agreement is only one element in the make-up of conventions such an agreement might not be conclusive."[3] It may seem curious that such a *venerable* constitution is also *vulnerable* in such a basic matter as the formation of a government, but it is nonetheless.

This example underscores an important aspect of British government: absolute principles of government are few. At the same time, those that exist are fundamental to the organization of the state and central to governance, policymaking, and patterns of representation.

Organization of the State

What are the central organizing principles of the British state? First, the core constitutional principle of the British political system and cornerstone of the Westminster model is parlia-

mentary sovereignty. Parliament can make or overturn any law; the executive, the judiciary, and the throne do not have any authority to restrict or rescind parliamentary action. Only Parliament can nullify or overturn its own legislation. In a classic parliamentary democracy, the prime minister is answerable to the House of Commons (the elected element of Parliament) and may be dismissed by it. That said, by passing the European Communities Act in 1972 (Britain joined the European Economic Community in 1973), Parliament accepted significant limitations on its ability to act with power. It acknowledged that European law has force in the United Kingdom without requiring parliamentary assent and acquiesced to the authority of the European Court of Justice (ECJ) to resolve jurisdictional disputes. To complete the circle, the ECJ has confirmed its prerogative to suspend acts of Parliament.[4]

Second, Britain has long been a unitary state. By contrast to the United States, where powers not delegated to the national government are reserved for the states, no powers are reserved constitutionally for subcentral units of government in the United Kingdom. However, the Labour government of Tony Blair has introduced a far-reaching program of constitutional reform that promises to create, for the first time, a quasi-federal system in Britain. Specified powers have been delegated (the British prefer to say *devolved*) to legislative bodies in Scotland and Wales, and potentially in Northern Ireland. "Boldly put, at least in terms of its governance the UK is not united," noted a pair of political scientists writing about multiple levels of governance in the United Kingdom. "Scotland, Wales and Northern Ireland in key domestic areas of decision-making can go their own way whether it is over university fees, beef on the bone or policies in relation to local government."[5] In addition, some powers have been redistributed from the Westminster Parliament to an authority governing London with a directly elected mayor, and additional powers may be devolved to regional assemblies as well.

Third, Britain operates within a system of fusion of powers at the national level: Parliament is the supreme legislative, executive, and judicial authority and includes the monarch as well as the House of Commons and the House of Lords. The fusion of legislature and executive is also expressed in the function and personnel of the cabinet. Whereas U.S. presidents can direct or ignore their cabinets, which have no constitutionally mandated function, the British cabinet bears enormous constitutional responsibility. Through its collective decision making, the cabinet—and not an independent prime minister—shapes, directs, and takes responsibility for government. Cabinet government stands in stark contrast to presidential government and is perhaps the most important feature, certainly the center, of Britain's system of government.

Finally, sovereignty rests with the Queen-in-Parliament (the formal term for Parliament). Britain is a constitutional monarchy: The position of head of state passes by hereditary succession, but nearly all powers of the Crown must be exercised by the government or state officials. Taken together, parliamentary sovereignty, parliamentary democracy, and cabinet government form the core elements of the British or Westminster model of government, which many consider a model democracy and the first effective parliamentary democracy. The absence of legally enforceable limits to the exercise of power raises questions about the gap between democratic ideal and political reality in Britain. Can a willful prime minister overstep the generally agreed limits of the collective responsibility of the cabinet and achieve an undue concentration of power? How well has the British model of government stood the test of time and radically changed circumstances? What are the constitutional implications of Blair's reform agenda?

These questions underscore the problems that even the most stable democracies face. They also help identify important comparative themes, because the principles of the Westminster model were, with some modifications, adopted widely by former colonies ranging from Canada, Australia, and New Zealand to India, Jamaica, and Zimbabwe. So British success (or failure) in preserving citizens' control of their government has implications reaching well beyond the British Isles.

The Executive

The term *cabinet government* is useful in emphasizing the key functions that the cabinet exercises: responsibility for policymaking, supreme control of government, and coordination of all government departments. However, the term does not capture the full range of executive institutions or the scale and complexity of operations. The executive reaches well beyond the cabinet. It extends from ministries (departments) and ministers to the civil service in one direction, and to Parliament (as we shall see in Chapter 9) in the other direction.

Cabinet Government

After a general election, the Crown invites the leader of the party that emerges from the election with control of a majority of seats in the House of Commons to form a government and serve as prime minister. The prime minister usually selects approximately two dozen ministers to constitute the cabinet. Among the most significant assignments are the Foreign Office (equivalent to the U.S. secretary of state), the Home Office (ministry of justice), and the chancellor of the exchequer (a finance minister or a more powerful version of the U.S. treasury secretary).

The responsibilities of a cabinet minister are immense. "The Cabinet, as a collective body, is responsible for formulating the policy to be placed before Parliament and is also the supreme controlling and directing body of the entire executive branch," notes S. E. Finer. "Its decisions bind all Ministers and other officers in the conduct of their departmental business."[6] In contrast to the French Constitution, which prohibits a cabinet minister from serving in the legislature, British constitutional tradition *requires* overlapping membership between Parliament and cabinet. Unlike the informal status of the U.S. cabinet, its British counterpart enjoys considerable constitutional privilege and is a powerful institution with enormous responsibility for the political and administrative success of the government.

The cabinet system is a complex patchwork of conflicting obligations and potential divisions. Each cabinet member who is a departmental minister has responsibilities to the ministry that he or she must run; and unless the cabinet member is a member of the House of Lords, he or she is also linked to a constituency, or electoral district (as an elected member of Parliament, or MP), to the party (as a leader and, often, a member of its executive board), to the prime minister (as an appointee who shares in the duties of a plural executive), and to a political tendency within the party (as a leading proponent of a particular vision of government).

The cabinet room at 10 Downing Street (the prime minister's official residence) is a place of intrigue as well as deliberation. There is an old maxim about British politics: "Where there is death, there is hope." And short of death, there is always the chance that the prime minister will fail. Either way, almost inevitably the prime minister's successor as party leader and potential prime minister will emerge from the ranks of current or former cabinet members. From the perspective of the prime minister, the cabinet may appear as loyal followers or as ideological combatants, potential challengers for party leadership, and parochial advocates for pet programs that run counter to the overall objectives of the government.

Against this background of drama and high-stakes scheming, the convention of collective responsibility normally ensures the continuity of government by unifying the cabinet on matters of policy. The principle of collective responsibility binds all ministers to support any action taken by an agency in the name of the government, whether the action was discussed in the cabinet or known to the minister in advance. This requirement makes the probability of parliamentary support extremely high. In principle, the prime minister must gain the support of a majority of the cabinet for a range of significant decisions, notably those governing the budget and the legislative program. The only other constitutionally mandated mechanism for checking the prime minister is a defeat on a vote of no confidence in the House of Commons (discussed in Chapter 9). Since this action is rare and politically dangerous, the cabinet's role in constraining the chief executive remains the only routine check on his or her power. Collective responsibility is therefore a crucial aspect of the Westminster model of democracy. Prime ministers, however, reserve the option to develop policies in cabinet committees, whose membership can be manipulated to ensure support, and then to present policy to the full cabinet with little chance for other ministers to challenge the results. In addition, the principle of collective responsibility requires that all ministers support any action taken in the name of the government, whether or not it was brought to cabinet. Does collective responsibility effectively constrain the power of prime ministers, or does it enable the prime minister to paint "presidential" decisions with the veneer of collectivity? Collective responsibility is a fluid principle, combining constitutional, ethical, and practical managerial components.[7] Its meaning is contested and its operational application subject to the discretion of the prime minister. In fact, each prime minister's quite distinctive treatment of the cabinet is an interesting test case for the elasticity of a "part written and uncodified" constitution.

A politician with strong ideological convictions and a leadership style to match, Margaret Thatcher often attempted to galvanize loyalists in the cabinet and either marginalize or expel detractors. Therefore, controversial issues (such as the proposed reorganization of health provision in 1988–1989) were often decided by hand-picked cabinet committees or in combination with personal advisers and senior civil servants. In this way, Thatcher often avoided full cabinet scrutiny of critical policies.

In addition, she was increasingly accused of intimidating opponents within the cabinet by shuffling cabinet posts and threatening dismissal. By keeping cabinet members off guard and casting out those who challenged her leadership, Thatcher reduced the diversity of opinion represented in the cabinet and limited its classic functions as a powerful instrument of collective deliberation. Thatcher even went so far as to refer to cabinet members as her "political advisors," and they were "made to feel their major responsibility lay upwards to Downing Street rather than outwards to parliament and country."[8] The reliance on personal advisers outside the cabinet in order to circumvent the responsible cabinet minister came to a flash point in October 1989 when one of Thatcher's longest-serving and respected ministers, Chancellor of the Exchequer Nigel Lawson, resigned in a dispute over the role of the prime minister's personal economic adviser. In the end, Thatcher's treatment of the cabinet helped galvanize the movement to unseat her as party leader and stretched British constitutional conventions.

John Major returned to a more consultative approach, in keeping with the classic model of cabinet government. "When John Major became Prime Minister it was as though he had read textbooks on British constitutional theory, had observed very closely the circumstances of Margaret Thatcher's downfall, and had come to the conclusion that he was going to do things differently—very differently."[9] By instinct, he was inclined to hold back his own views and permit open discussion, regarding dialogue as an opportunity to consolidate the commitments of sometimes reluctant ministers to cabinet decisions. Especially in the early years, his management style in cabinet, partly owing to temperament and partly to the lack of fixed ideological positions on many issues, was very consultative. After Thatcher's tight control, ministers were delighted with their new free-

dom. At the same time, on several key issues, Major was able to exert his leadership style to good effect, forging agreement, despite some initial differences of view, on the use of British troops in Bosnia, policy developments in Northern Ireland, and some key (and quite divisive) policy decisions on Europe.[10] In time, after the 1992 election and especially after Britain's abrupt departure from the Exchange Rate Mechanism (ERM), the collegiality of Major's cabinet broke down, leaks came in torrential downpours, and dissension in the cabinet crippled the government. Major lacked the leadership capacities to purge cabinet or effectively demand loyalty. As one observer put it, he "was forced, therefore, to hope that the doctrine of collective responsibility would produce the teamness he could not engender."[11]

Tony Blair, like Thatcher, has narrowed the scope of collective responsibility. Cabinet meetings are dull and perfunctory, and debate is rare. Decisions are taken in smaller gatherings by the prime minister, a few key cabinet members, and a handful of advisers. In a striking example of this process early in the Blair premiership, right after the election when the full cabinet had not yet met, the government announced the decision to free the Bank of England to set interest rates. Blair has accentuated the tendency for shorter cabinet meetings (they are usually less than an hour) that are not intended to inform members systematically of critical issues and cannot seriously take up (much less resolve) policy differences. Observers note that Blair has tried to exert very tight control of the cabinet as well as the policy agenda and has done so in a manner that raises questions about the significance of collective deliberation.

Both Blair and his close aides seem skeptical about the effectiveness of committees (including cabinet as well as cabinet committees). The prime minister prefers to coordinate strategically important policy areas through highly politicized special units in the Cabinet Office such as the Social Exclusion Unit, the Women's Unit, and the UK Anti-Drugs Co-ordination Unit. Finally, to supplement (or perhaps replace) the power of collective decision making and responsibility in the cabinet as a vehicle for securing the commitment of ministers, Blair has vastly expanded the role of one-on-one meetings with ministers. Thus, in the first twenty-five months in office, Blair held 86 cabinet meetings, but 783 meetings with individual ministers (compared to the 272 held by Major over the same period).[12] In a lecture at the London School of Economics that caused quite a stir, a highly regarded historian and former writer for *The Economist*, Peter Hennessy, quoted a variety of Whitehall insiders (*Whitehall* is a street name referring to the London nerve center of the civil service) who lamented that Blair had killed off cabinet government grounded in collective responsibility. Comparing Blair with the other recent prime minister often blamed for eroding the principle and limiting the practice of cabinet government, one of the luminaries was quoted as saying that "Blair makes Margaret Thatcher look like a natural consulter; to be a minister outside the inner loop is hell."[13] As if to make clear that styles of leadership and their effects on cabinet authority have no party labels, Hennessy concluded that the cabinet has become even more marginal under Blair than it was during Thatcher's premiership.

Alongside collective responsibility, members of the cabinet assume individual responsibility for personal or private misconduct and, more important, administrative or political misjudgment. Responsibility is taken seriously: it means resignation. Since 1900, more than a hundred ministers have resigned, although far more often for personal misconduct or to avoid being fired than out of high political principle or to take responsibility for an error of judgment in their departments. One classic illustration of the latter (and its political use to insulate the prime minister) was the resignation of the foreign secretary, Lord Carrington, and two colleagues after the Argentine invasion of the disputed Falkland/Malvinas Islands in 1982 for failing to anticipate the attack.

On balance, cabinet government represents a durable and effective formula for governance. It is important to remember that the cabinet operates within a broader cabinet system or core executive as it is sometimes called (see Figure 8.1). Since the prime minister is the head of the cabinet, his or her office helps develop policy, coordinates operations, and functions as liaison with the media, the party, interest groups, and Parliament. Both cabinet committees (comprising ministers) and official committees (made up of civil servants) supplement the work of the cabinet. In addition, the treasury plays an important coordinating role through its budgetary control, while the cabinet office supports day-to-day operations. Leaders in both the Commons and the Lords, the *whips*, help smooth the passage of legislation sponsored by the government, which is more or less guaranteed by a working majority.

The cabinet system ensures that there is no Washington-style gridlock (the inability of legislature and executive to agree on policy) in London! On the contrary, if there is a problem at the pinnacle of power in the United Kingdom, it is the potential for excessive concentration of power by a prime minister who is prepared to manipulate cabinet and flout the conventions of collective responsibility.

Bureaucracy and Civil Service

Policymaking at 10 Downing Street may appear to be increasingly concentrated in the prime minister's hands. At the same time, when viewed from Whitehall, the executive may appear to be dominated by its vast administrative agencies. The range and complexity of state policymaking mean that in practice, the cabinet's authority must be shared with a vast set of unelected officials.

Cabinet members have the formal title *secretary of state for X*, where *X* designates the ministry, such as Defense or Employment. A few have a special title such as chancellor of the exchequer. To help bridge the closely linked functions of policymaking and implementation of policy, each secretary has a few political assis-

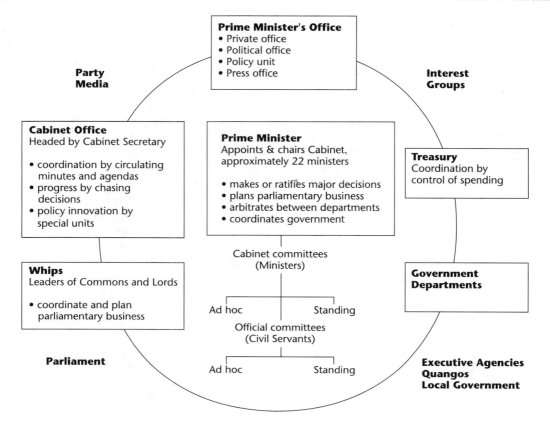

Figure 8.1   The Cabinet System

The cabinet is supported by a set of institutions that help formulate policy, coordinate operations, and facilitate the support for government policy. Acting within a context set by the fusion of legislature and executive, the prime minister enjoys a great opportunity for decisive leadership that is lacking in a system of checks and balances and separation of powers among the branches of government.

Source: *British Politics: Continuities and Change,* Third Edition, by Dennis Kavanagh, p. 251. Crown copyright material is reproduced under Class License with the permission of the Controller of HMSO and the Queen's Printer for Scotland.

tants (appointed by the prime minister in consultation with the secretary). These *ministers of state* may take responsibility for specific policy areas and often assume some discretionary authority over policy. *Junior ministers* act as intermediaries with the nonpolitical bureaucracy of the civil service and may also assume responsibility for particular departmental duties. (A junior minister may be referred to as a parliamentary undersecretary of state or, where the senior minister is not a secretary of state, simply a parliamentary secretary.)

Since ministers of state and junior ministers are nearly always MPs (or occasionally lords), the fusion of legislature and executive is expressed in the daily management of departments. These political appointments are highly sought as the inside track to subsequent cabinet membership, and they are paid positions. Ministers of state and junior ministers are considered to be part of the government and, together with the members of the cabinet, may number roughly one hundred. Since even ministers below the level of the cabinet are bound by the principles of collective responsibility and their career trajectory probably depends on loyalty to their superiors, the government begins every debate in the Commons with a large, absolutely solid voting bloc. "The crucial core of support," notes one scholar of British politics, "is referred to somewhat derisively as the payroll vote."[14]

How is the interaction between the civil service and the cabinet ministers (and their political assistants) coordinated? A very senior career civil servant, called a *permanent secretary*, has chief administrative responsibility for running a department. The permanent secretaries are assisted, in turn, by other senior civil servants, including deputy secretaries and undersecretaries. There are approximately 75,000 senior executives a few rungs down from the level of interaction with ministers and junior ministers. In addition, the minister reaches into his or her department to appoint a *principal private secretary*, an up-and-coming civil servant who assists the minister as gatekeeper and liaison with senior civil servants. In April 1999, there were 460,040 permanent civil servants (measured in full-time equivalents, FTEs) of whom 421,340 were working full time, down from a height of 735,400 FTEs in 1979, a decline of one-third.

Although "permanent secretaries are the main filter through which departmental business is purified, reduced and made palatable for ministerial consumption," the interface between politicians and administrative officials is somewhat more diffuse.[15] It is difficult to draw a hard-and-fast distinction between policymaking and policy implementation or administration, and successful policy requires that career civil servants at a variety of levels be able to translate a policy goal into concrete policy instruments, notably acts of Parliament (but also policy directives and other instruments). Since nearly all legislation is introduced on behalf of the government and presented as the policy directive of a ministry, much of the work of conceptualizing and refining legislation that is done by committee staffers in the U.S. Congress is done by civil servants in Britain. As a practical matter, ministers are not routinely involved in the day-to-day affairs of government departments. And even when they are, they often lack the expertise and insider's knowledge of the bureaucracy. In practice, civil servants, more than ministers, assume operational duties and, despite a certain natural level of mutual mistrust and incomprehension, the two must work closely together. To the impartial, permanent, and anonymous civil servants, ministers are too political, unpredictable, and temporary—and they are tireless self-promoters who may neglect or misunderstand the needs of the ministry. To a conscientious minister, the permanent secretary may be protecting "his" or "her" department too strenuously from constitutionally proper oversight and direction. Whatever they may think, no sharp line separates the responsibilities of ministers and civil servants, and they have no choice but to execute policy in tandem.

Civil servants are engaged in a wide range of activities. Approximately 18 percent provide services of one kind or another to the public, for example, sickness benefits or pensions, or they work in job centers at the heart of the welfare reform initiatives or issue driving licenses. Some 10 percent work for the Home Office, including those staffing the prisons. More than one-fifth work for the Ministry of Defence, and about 13 percent work for Inland Revenue (the equivalent of the Internal Revenue Service in the United States). The rest are involved in various duties relating to policy and administration—for example, generating statistics about social and economic trends, programming the "open government" web sites (numerous web sites with information about government policies and proposals), or advising ministers. The civil service also includes some 30,000 industrial staff, the majority of whom work for the Ministry of Defence—loading ships in naval dockyards, for example. Many of the activities traditionally undertaken by civil servants are now carried out in executive agencies established since a 1988 report on more effective government management. In addition, quite a range of administrative functions previously performed in-house within state entities are now provided through the contracting out of services to the private sector. In 1999, the civil service composed about 2 percent of the total workforce and the public sector (including local government, central government and public corporations) accounted for approximately 18 percent of the workforce.

Like ministers, civil servants are servants of the Crown, but they are not part of the government (taken in the more political sense, like the term "the administration" in common American usage). The ministers, not the civil servants, have constitutional responsibility for policy and are answerable to Parliament and the electorate for the conduct of their departments. A change of minister or government, whatever the cause, does not mean a change in departmental staffs. Civil servants are highly respected for their adherence to traditions of anonymity and political neutrality, and for the technical expertise and continuity they lend to policymaking. The German social theorist Max Weber (1864–1920), one of the founders of modern sociology, described the attributes of a modern bureaucracy: hierarchy, defined spheres of responsibility, routine procedures, professionalism, and, above all, rule-governed administration. Like the Westminster model of government, the structure and behavior of the British civil service is often considered a model of politically insulated, efficient administration, free of the partisanship, insider dealing, and corruption found in many bureaucracies, particularly in postcommunist, postauthoritarian, and postcolonial regimes. When we examine policymaking further at the end of this chapter, we will see that this characterization is only partly accurate.

The significant influence of civil servants (and the size of even a streamlined bureaucracy) raises important questions about the proper role of unelected officials in a democratic polity. Indeed, the civil service has been assaulted from many directions. Since the early 1980s, the pace of change at Whitehall has been very fast, with governments looking to cut the size of the civil service, streamline its operations, replace permanent with casual (temporary) staff to deal with peaks in workload, and enhance its accountability to citizens. Beyond these pressures, the frustration of civil servants was deepened by Thatcher's evident impatience with the customs of impartiality and drawn-out procedures that slowed her aggressive policy agenda.

In addition, the reinvigoration of parliamentary select committees has complicated the role of the civil service. Traditionally, ministers serving as the political heads of departments—and not civil servants—take responsibility for policy and face scrutiny in Parliament. Constitutionally, civil servants have no responsibility or role distinct from their minister. The system assumes that civil servants are not answerable for policy and will keep the operations of their department (embarrassing to a minister or otherwise) confidential. Although tradition requires senior civil servants to testify on behalf of their ministers, the more aggressive stance of select committees in recent years has for the first time pressed them to testify, in effect, *against* their ministers, if necessary to satisfy parliamentary concerns about misconduct or poor judgment. Some describe a situation of crisis and loss of morale. Many civil servants are worried about the uncertainty of their position. With day-to-day operational responsibility for the affairs of state resting with the civil service, they know that ministerial responsibility is often a fiction, and they are worried about the unpredictable scrutiny they now face.

As a result of this ongoing modernization of Whitehall (known as new public management, NPM), the civil service inherited by New Labour is very different from the civil service of thirty years ago. It has been downsized and given a new corporate structure (divided into over 120 separate executive agencies). Few at the top of these agencies (agency chief executives) are traditional career civil servants. More generally, a tradition of a career service, in which nearly all the most powerful posts were filled by those who entered the bureaucratic ranks in their twenties, is fading. Many top appointments are advertised and filled by "outsiders." The Blair government seems unlikely to reverse the NPM trends toward accountability, efficiency, and greater transparency in the operations of the executive bureaucracy, although many have expressed concern that New Labour has done—and will continue to do—whatever it can to subject the Whitehall machine to effective political and ministerial direction and control.[16] Constitutional changes such as devolution and the prospect of a Freedom of Information Act hold the possibility of directly and indirectly reforming the civil service further.

Public and Semipublic Institutions

Like other countries, Britain has institutionalized a set of administrative functions that expand the role of the state well beyond the traditional core executive functions and agencies. The ebb and flow of alternative visions of government in the postwar period, from collectivist consensus to Thatcherism to New Labour, have resulted in substantial changes in emphasis. We turn now to a brief discussion of "semipublic" agencies—entities sanctioned by the state but without direct democratic oversight.

Nationalized Industries

The nationalization of basic industries was a central objective of the Labour government's program in the immediate period after World War II. Nationalization symbolized Labour's core socialist aspiration affirmed in the famous Clause IV of its party constitution ("to secure for the workers by hand or brain the full fruits of their industry . . . upon the basis of common

ownership of the means of production, distribution and exchange"). Between 1946 and 1949, the Bank of England was nationalized, and coal, iron and steel, gas and electricity supply, and the bulk of the transport sector became public corporations. By 1960, nationalized industries accounted for about 18 percent of total fixed investment, produced about one-tenth of the national income, and employed some 8 percent of the U.K. workforce.[17]

Replacing private entrepreneurs and acting through government-appointed boards of directors for each industry, the state now hired, bargained with, and fired workers; paid the bills; set pricing policies; and invested, planned, and presided over a vast industrial empire. Nationalization created state monopolies backed by public financing that could operate more efficiently than the smaller undercapitalized firms they had replaced. The state takeover of industries was designed to ensure the cheap and reliable provision of essential fuel supplies and transport, facilitate a modicum of central coordination of personnel and investment planning, and improve productivity.

The nationalized industries have operated by principles that give all of the advantages and none of the risk to private capitalists—for example, "buy dear" (at a high price) from the private sector and "sell cheap." Private firms made a profit from selling materials and equipment and saw their costs of production drop with the steady and relatively cheap supply of basic fuel and energy, for example. During the 1970s and especially since Thatcher's rejection of the collectivist consensus in 1979, the boards of the nationalized industries have practiced increasingly hard-nosed strategies toward labor unions. The coal miners' strike of 1984–1985, the longest and most violent industrial dispute in postwar Britain, illustrates this approach. More generally, extensive privatization sharply reduced the scale and political significance of the public sector. During the eighteen years of Conservative government beginning in 1979, nearly a million workers transferred from public to private sector employment, and by 1995 the output of the nationalized sector was less than half the percentage of gross domestic product it had been in 1975.

Before assuming leadership of the Labour Party, Blair argued that a revision of Clause IV was necessary to make it clear that the Labour Party had broken with its past. He reiterated that goal in his first speech as leader to the party conference in October 1994, and within months, a new Clause IV was in place that speaks to middle-class aspirations and rejects the notion that the capitalist market economy is immoral or inherently exploitative. For New Labour, a return to the program of public ownership of industry is unthinkable. Instead, when thinking of expanding state functions, we can look to a growing set of semipublic administrative organizations.

Nondepartmental Public Bodies

Since the 1970s, an increasing number of administrative functions have been transferred to quasi-nongovernmental organizations, better known as *quangos*. In Britain, there are three traditional kinds of nondepartmental public bodies: executive bodies, tribunals, and advisory bodies or agencies. Quangos have increasing policy influence and enjoy considerable administrative and political advantages. They take responsibility for specific functions and can combine governmental and private sector expertise. At the same time, ministers can distance themselves from controversial areas of policy, such as arms sales or race relations.

Despite Thatcher's attempts to reduce their number and scale back their operations by the early 1990s, a new generation of powerful, broadly defined, and well-funded quangos had replaced the smaller-scale quangos of the past. In 1990–1991, quangos were spending three times as much as they had in 1978–1979. The growth was particularly significant in locally appointed agencies, including bodies with responsibility for education, job training, health, and housing. By the late 1990s, there were some 6,000 quangos, 90 percent operating at the local level. They were responsible for one-third of all public spending and staffed by approximately 50,000 people. Key areas of public policy previously under the authority of local governments are now controlled by quangos, which are nonelected bodies.

Some observers have expressed concern that the principle of democratic control is being compromised by the power of quangos, which are not accountable to the electorate. Some argue that the growth of local quangos has contributed to the centralization of power, as agencies appointed by ministers take over many functions of local government. Although critical of the "quango state" while in opposition, New Labour took a more measured approach once in government, emphasizing reforms and more democratic scrutiny. The elected authority in London, as well as the Welsh Assembly and Scottish Parliament, acquired extensive powers to review and reform many of the quangos under their responsibility. In addition, the Blair government issued a set of proposals on quangos through the cabinet office (in June 1998), including potential requirements for published reports and open meetings, increased scrutiny by House of Commons select committees, and increased representation of women and ethnic minorities on quangos.[18]

We will return later to consider local government in Britain, but we move now to a discussion of a set of formal institutions both within and outside the executive.

Other State Institutions

Although British public administration extends well beyond its traditional focus on finance or foreign affairs or law and order, these policy areas remain critical. In this chapter, we examine the military and police, the judiciary, and subnational government.

The Military and the Police

From the local bobby (a term for a local police officer derived from Sir Robert Peel, who set up London's metropolitan police force in 1829) to the most senior military officer, those involved in security and law enforcement have enjoyed a rare measure of popular support in Britain. Public opinion polls show that the army and the police rank first and second, respectively, among the institutions in which Britons have confidence. Constitutional tradition and professionalism distance the British police and military officers from politics. They harbor virtually no political ambitions and have traditionally steered clear of partisan involvement. Nevertheless, in recent decades both institutions have been placed in more politically controversial and exposed positions.

In the case of the military, British policy in the post–cold war period remains focused on a gradually redefined set of North Atlantic Treaty Organization (NATO) commitments. Still ranked among the top five military powers in the world, Britain retains a global presence, and the Thatcher and Major governments deployed forces in ways that strengthened their political positions and maximized Britain's global influence. In 1982, Britain soundly defeated Argentina in a war over the disputed Falkland/Malvinas Islands in the South Atlantic. In the Persian Gulf War of 1991, Britain deployed a full armored division in the United Nations–sanctioned force arrayed against Iraq's Saddam Hussein. Under Blair's leadership, Britain was the sole participant alongside the United States in the aerial bombardment of Iraq in December 1998 and again in February 2001, in the early days of the administration of George W. Bush. Since the mid-1990s, the British have supported diplomatic efforts to stabilize the territories of the former Yugoslavia; in 1999 the United Kingdom strongly backed NATO's Kosovo campaign and pressed for ground troops.

The broad-based popularity of these missions must be measured against the more controver-

sial role of the military in the dispute in Northern Ireland. After a civil rights movement calling for Catholic political and economic equality helped provoke Protestant riots in the autumn of 1969, the British government sent troops to Northern Ireland. During the height of the "troubles," in a context set by paramilitary violence on all sides, the reputation of the army was tarnished by its use of techniques that violated civil liberties. The powers that security forces used to detain suspects were found to violate the European Convention of Human Rights. In addition, a set of extremely embarrassing decisions by the European Court of Justice on Human Rights concerning Britain's interrogation procedures in Northern Ireland resulted in procedural changes in the British treatment of suspects. Subsequently, the court ruled that Britain unlawfully killed three Irish Republican Army members in a 1988 action by undercover soldiers in Gibraltar. The British army was also subject to accusations that it was used as a partisan political instrument to repress Irish nationalism.

As for the police, which traditionally operate as independent local forces throughout the country, the period since the 1980s has witnessed growth in government control, centralization, and level of political use. The coal miners' strike of 1984–1985 raised significant questions about the political roles forced on the police (and, as we shall see, the judiciary) by the Thatcher government. In practice, police operated to an unprecedented—and perhaps unlawful—degree as a national force coordinated through Scotland Yard (London police headquarters). Police menaced strikers and hindered miners from participating in strike support activities. This partisan use of the police in an industrial dispute flew in the face of constitutional traditions and offended some police officers and officials. During the 1990s, concerns about police conduct focused on police–community relations, including race relations, corruption, and the interrogation and treatment of people held in custody. In particular, widespread criticism of the police for mishandling their investigation into the brutal 1993 racist killing of Stephen Lawrence in South London resulted in a scathing report by a commission of inquiry in 1999. The case raised basic questions about police attitudes toward ethnic minorities, as well as their conduct in racially sensitive cases, and focused renewed attention on necessary reforms.

The entire criminal justice system, including the police and the judiciary, has received harsh scrutiny in recent years. In July 1993, the Royal Commission on Criminal Justice proposed 352 recommendations for overhauling criminal justice. The report left few satisfied and underscored growing concerns that problems abound.

New Labour has advocated expanding police–community partnerships and improving relations with ethnic minority groups. At the same time, it considers tough action on crime as part of its broader approach to community that places considerable emphasis on the responsibilities of individuals and citizens (communitarianism). In an interesting twist, in 1996 Blair dispatched to New York City the person tapped to be home secretary in the future Labour government to study that city's success in reducing street crime. New Labour then adopted the "zero-tolerance" approach trumpeted by New York's Republican mayor, Rudolph Giuliani.

The Judiciary

The function of the British judiciary has been far more limited than that of its French, German, or U.S. counterparts. In the United States, for instance, the Supreme Court used an 1803 decision known as *Marbury v. Madison* to secure the principle of *judicial review*: its right to decide the constitutionality of actions by the executive and legislative branches of government, thereby limiting their power. In Britain, the principle of parliamentary sovereignty has limited the role of the judiciary. Courts have no power to judge the constitutionality of legislative acts (judicial review); they can only deter-

mine whether policy directives or administrative acts violate common law or an act of Parliament.

Since it cannot rule on matters of constitutionality and is never called on to set policy on controversial issues (such as a woman's right to abortion or the limits of affirmative action), the British judiciary is generally less politicized and influential than its U.S. counterpart. In recent decades, however, governments have pulled the courts into political battles over the rights of local councils, the activities of police in urban riots, and the role of police and trade unions in industrial disputes. For example, in the 1984–1985 coal miners' strike, the courts interpreted the new Employment Act of 1982 very broadly and froze the entire assets of the miners' union. This decision helped tip the balance in the dispute toward the government. Also concerning the miners' strike, in a decision that confounded many, the Court of Appeal rejected an unusual application by the local police authority in Northumbria to compel the home secretary to withdraw instructions for the use of tear gas and plastic bullets to disperse the miners. At a stroke, the decision showed the new and controversial political role of the courts, advanced the centralized cabinet-level (hence, political) control over policing, and affirmed an ancient royal prerogative against the local police authorities.

Jurists have also participated in the wider political debate outside court, as when they have headed royal commissions on the conduct of industrial relations, the struggle in Northern Ireland, and riots in Britain's inner cities. Some observers of British politics are concerned that governments have used judges in these ways to secure partisan ends, deflect criticism, and weaken the tradition of parliamentary scrutiny of government policy. Nevertheless, Sir Richard Scott's harsh report on his investigation into Britain's sales of military equipment to Iraq in the 1980s, for example, indicates that inquiries led by judges with a streak of independence can prove highly embarrassing to the government and raise important issues for public debate.

Thus, it seems that the courts—newly activist and politicized (by British, if not U.S., standards)—are increasingly called into the breach when the normal interplay of party, interest organization, and institutional politics cannot resolve contemporary disputes. This development raises serious questions about British democracy. Should nonelected officials, as all senior judges are, be granted such a crucial role in resolving disputes among interests in society and, indirectly, in influencing the direction of social and economic policies? Constitutional reform may increase the set of highly politicized demands on the judiciary in the United Kingdom. It is too early to tell, but it seems likely that the devolution of powers within the United Kingdom, granting enumerated powers to the Welsh Assembly and a broader general competence to the Scottish Parliament, could produce jurisdictional disputes similar to those found in federal systems such as Germany and the United States.[19] Finally, another tier of involvement has been forced on British courts by the United Kingdom's extranational entanglements with the EU, discussed later in this chapter.

Subnational Government

Since the United Kingdom is a state comprising distinct nations (England, Scotland, Wales, and Northern Ireland), the distribution of powers involves two levels below the central government: national government and local (municipal) government. Because the British political framework has traditionally been unitary, not federal, no formal powers devolved either to the nation within the United Kingdom or to subnational units (states or regions) as in the United States or Germany. Initiatives undertaken by Blair's government promise far-reaching constitutional changes in the distribution of power between the U.K. government and subcentral national units.

Although no powers have been constitutionally reserved to local governments, they historically had considerable autonomy in financial terms and discretion in implementing a host of social service and related policies. Before 1975, elected local governments set their own spending and taxation levels through the setting of *rates*, or local property taxes. In the context of increased fiscal pressures that followed the 1973 oil crisis, the Labour government introduced the first check on the fiscal autonomy of local councils (elected local authorities) by introducing *cash limits* (ceilings on spending) beginning in fiscal year 1976–1977. In 1980, the newly elected Thatcher government introduced the Local Government, Planning and Land Act, further tightening the fiscal constraints on local government. Finally, in 1982, the central government set a ceiling on local rates (a *rate cap*).

In this era of constraint, local councils tried a variety of experimental approaches. Conservative councils began to contract out (and thereby privatize) services to private enterprise. Labour councils pursued a range of socialist or progressive initiatives, including the promotion of local job opportunities, the creation of nuclear-free zones, the reduction of fares for public transportation, and the funding of community groups. The struggle between left-wing Labour councils and the right-wing Conservative government bent on reducing welfare provision and limiting local control over budgets pushed the role of local councils to the forefront of British political debate. The outright abolition of London's progressive and multiculturally oriented city government (the Greater London Council, GLC) under the leadership of Ken Livingstone, and several other metropolitan councils in March 1986, completed the political onslaught on local autonomy.

Riots in several British cities in 1981 and 1985 and the much-vaunted Battle for London—the campaign of resistance to the GLC's abolition—provoked some of the most hard-edged debates about democracy in recent British history. Given the GLC's emphasis on ethnic minority cultural initiatives and its campaign for equal opportunity and political access, the struggle also highlighted the racial dimension of British politics.

In 1989, the Thatcher government introduced a poll tax, an equal per capita levy for local finance, to replace the age-old system of rates. This radical break with tradition, which shifted the burden of local taxes from property owners and businesses to individuals, and taxed rich and poor alike, was monumentally unpopular. The poll tax proved a tremendous political liability, maintained the local edge to national politics, and helped lead to Thatcher's departure. As in other areas of public policy, Major tried to depoliticize local government. He quickly replaced the poll tax with a new local tax linked to the value of properties, although he kept policies in place that centralized and controlled local finance.

Although much of New Labour's agenda concerning subcentral government is focused on the political role of nations within the United Kingdom, devolution within England is also part of the reform process. Regional Development Agencies (RDAs) were introduced throughout England in April 1999 as part of a decentralizing agenda, but perhaps even more to facilitate economic development at the regional level. Despite the fairly low-key profile of RDAs and their limited scope (they are unelected bodies with no statutory authority), they open the door to popular mobilization in the long term for elected regional assemblies. In addition, the Blair government placed changes in the governance of London on the fast track. New Labour introduced no plans to reconstitute the GLC or return to a city government the powers currently enjoyed by quangos and by London's boroughs. Nevertheless, the introduction of a directly elected mayor of London in May 2000 proved embarrassing to Blair, as the government's efforts to keep Ken Livingstone out of the contest backfired. The official Labour candidate finished third to Livingstone, who beat the Conservative candidate by more than 200,000 votes and, with characteristic panache, began his victory speech with an obvious allusion to the abolition of the GLC, by remarking: "As I was saying before I was so rudely interrupted 14 years ago . . . I want an all-embracing administration that will speak with one voice on behalf of London." Even before the debacle of the mayor's race in London, Blair and New Labour appeared genuinely ambivalent about decentralization with the loss of direction and control it entails. In the aftermath, it was even clearer that constitutional reform, once begun, can take on a life of its own.

The European Dimension

In addition to devolution and constitutional reform, British politics has been fundamentally restructured by the delegation of more and more authority to the EU. As one observer neatly summarized this watershed development, "The result is a new kind of multi-level political system in which political power is shared between the EU, national and subnational levels, and decisions taken at one level shape outcomes at others."[20]

The European dimension has significantly influenced law and the administration of justice. Parliament passed the European Communities Act in 1972 to seal Britain's entry into the European Community (EC), with the provision that existing EC law be binding on the United Kingdom. In any conflict between British law and EC (now EU) law, EU law prevails. The act specifies that British courts must adjudicate any disputes of interpretation that arise from EU law. In addition, the Treaty of Rome (the treaty that formed the EC, to which the United Kingdom is bound by the terms of its membership) specifies that cases that reach the highest domestic appeals court—the House of Lords—be sent to the European Court of Justice (ECJ) in Luxembourg for final ruling.

As a member of the EU, Britain is bound to abide by the ECJ, as it applies and develops law as an independent institution within the EU. For example, two decisions by the ECJ led to the enactment of the Sex Discrimination Act of 1986, since previous legislation did not provide the full guarantees of women's rights in employment mandated to all members by the EU's Equal Treatment Directive. The pace of supranational influences on Britain, in legal as in other policy areas, will doubtless increase as EU measures of economic and political integration proceed. Politically, the binding nature of EU laws and regulations is likely to fuel the fear that Britain is losing sovereign control, whether to jurists in Luxembourg or bureaucrats in Brussels. Moreover, the expanding scope of EU influences is likely to widen the role of the judiciary within British affairs. Since the EU's dispute resolution process relies to a much greater degree on legal instruments than has the domestic U.K. political system, the growing role of the ECJ as an agent of European integration promises to expand the role of the legal and judicial process in British political disputes.[21]

Moreover, as a signatory to the European Convention on Human Rights, Britain is required to comply with the rulings of the European Court of Justice on Human Rights (ECJHR) in Strasbourg, the judicial branch of the Council of Europe. The incorporation of the European Convention on Human Rights (ECHR) into U.K. law with the passage of the Human Rights Act in 1998 has far-reaching potential for advancing a "pluralistic human rights culture" in Britain and providing new ground rules in law for protecting privacy, freedom of religion, and a wider respect for human rights.[22] Perhaps an indication of its broad influence to come, the adoption of the ECHR forced the United Kingdom to curtail discrimination against gays in the military.

In administrative and political terms, the consequences of the European dimension are equally profound. Both ministers and senior civil servants spend a great deal of time in EU policy deliberations and are constrained both directly and indirectly by the EU agenda and directives. Although still effectively in charge of many areas of domestic policy, more than 80 percent of the rules governing economic life in Britain are determined by the EU. Even when the United Kingdom has opted out, as in the case of the common currency, European influences are significant. Decisions by the Council of Finance Ministers and the European Central Bank shape British macroeconomic, monetary, and fiscal policies in significant ways. Nor are foreign and security policy, the classic exercises of national sovereignty, immune from EU influences, since multilevel governance has been extended to these spheres by the EU's Common Foreign and Security Policy.[23] Little is certain about the processes of European integration, except that they will continue to shape and bedevil British politics for many years to come.

The Policymaking Process

Parliamentary sovereignty is the core constitutional principle of the British political system. However, when it comes to policymaking and policy implementation, the focus is not on Westminster but rather on Whitehall (the London street that once housed government ministries and whose name still connotes the world of ministers and civil servants). In many countries, such as Japan, India, and Nigeria, personal connections and informal networks play a large role in policymaking and implementation. How different is the British system?

The interaction between the cabinet secretary and his or her junior ministers and their counterparts among the career civil servants—notably the permanent secretary, deputy secretary, and undersecretary—reveals much about the policymaking process. Policymaking emerges primarily from within the executive—from the efforts of what is sometimes called the *partisan executive* (the ministers) and the *merit executive* (the career civil servants, who are duty-bound to turn policy goals into instruments, then implement the executive orders and acts of Parliament that result).

Unlike the U.S. system, in which policymaking is concentrated in congressional committees and subcommittees, Parliament has little direct participation in policymaking. Britain preserves decision making for the corridors of Whitehall. However, the policymaking process involves much more than just a collaboration between high-flying junior ministers and anonymous mandarins (a term originally referring to officials in Imperial China and used colloquially to describe traditional top career civil servants who are generalists steeped in the culture of Whitehall).

Decision making is strongly influenced by *policy communities*—informal networks with extensive knowledge, access, and personal connections to those responsible for policy. In this "private, specialized, and invariably 'closed' world," civil servants, ministers, and members of the policy communities (sometimes referred to as *subgovernments*) trade expertise and mutual recognition of authority. This is the make-or-break context in which policy is made.

A cooperative style, even a coziness, develops as the ministry becomes an advocate for key players in its policy community and as civil servants come perhaps to overidentify the public good with the advancement of policy within their area of responsibility. For example, some have accused the Ministry of Agriculture, Fisheries and Food of defending farmers and manufacturers in their effort to boost food prices and profits. In a similar vein, classic patron-client relations develop in which "sponsor departments" advance the interests of the sectors affected by their policies. This describes, for example, the relationship between the Department of Health and Social Security and the medical establishment for much of the postwar period. In the late 1980s, however, efforts by the Conservative government to introduce unpopular internal market reforms in health care broke the cooperative policy styles and sent doctors rushing into the Commons and the committee rooms to battle legislation they had been unable to rewrite or block through the normal functioning of their policy communities.

As we see in Chapter 9, the breakdown of the collectivist consensus transformed politics at many levels, from the policymaking process to the organization of interests and the broad dynamics of representation and political participation.

Notes

1. See Philip Norton, *The British Polity*, 3d ed. (New York: Longman, 1994), p. 59, for a useful discussion of the sources of the British constitution.

2. Stephen Haseler, "Britain's Ancien régime," *Parliamentary Affairs* 40, no. 4 (October 1990): 415.

3. Geoffrey Marshall, *Constitutional Conventions: The Rules and Forms of Political Accountability* (Oxford: Oxford University Press, Clarendon Press, 1986), pp. 220–222. The discussion of conventions associated with a hung Parliament follows closely from Marshall's account.

4. See Philip Norton, "Parliament in Transition," in Robert Pyper and Lynton Robins, eds., *United Kingdom Governance* (New York: St. Martin's Press, 2000), pp. 82–106.

5. Jon Pierre and Gerry Stoker, "Towards Multi-Level Governance," in Patrick Dunleavy et al., eds., *Developments in British Politics 6* (New York: St. Martin's Press, 2000), p. 31.

6. S. E. Finer, *Five Constitutions* (Atlantic Highlands, N.J.: Humanities Press, 1979), p. 52.

7. Chris Brady, "Collective Responsibility of the Cabinet: An Ethical, Constitutional or Managerial Tool?" *Parliamentary Affairs* 52, no. 2 (April 1999): 214–229.

8. Donald R. Shell, "The British Constitution in 1984," *Parliamentary Affairs* 38, no. 2 (Spring 1985): 131.

9. Anthony King, "Cabinet Co-ordination or Prime Ministerial Dominance? A Conflict of Three Principles of Cabinet Government," in Ian Budge and David McKay, eds., *The Developing British Political*

System: The 1990s, 3d ed. (London: Longman, 1993), p. 63.

10. Dennis Kavanagh and Anthony Seldon, *The Powers Behind the Prime Minister* (London: HarperCollins, 1999), pp. 206–239.

11. Brady, "Collective Responsibility of the Cabinet," p. 223.

12. Kavanagh and Seldon, *The Powers Behind the Prime Minister*, pp. 275, 281.

13. Brady, "Collective Responsibility of the Cabinet ," p. 214.

14. Jorgen S. Rasmussen, *The British Political Process* (Belmont, Calif.: Wadsworth, 1993), p. 84. Consult this work for a clear and useful explanation of the organization of the executive and the relationship between ministries and civil service.

15. Gavin Drewry and Tony Butcher, *The Civil Service Today* (Oxford: Basil Blackwell, 1988), p. 21.

16. Kevin Theakston, "Ministers and Civil Servants," in Pyper and Robins, eds., *United Kingdom Governance*, pp. 39–60.

17. Simon Mohun, "Continuity and Change in State Economic Intervention," in Allan Cochrane and James Anderson, eds., *Politics in Transition* (London: Sage, 1989), p. 73.

18. Tony Wright, ed., *The British Political Process* (London: Routledge, 2000), p. 280.

19. See Gillian Peele, "The Law and the Constitution," in Dunleavy et al., *Developments in British Politics 6*, pp. 76–78.

20. Simon Hix, "Britain, the EU and the Euro," in Dunleavy et al., *Developments in British Politics 6*, p. 48.

21. Gillian Peele, "The Law and the Constitution," in Dunleavy et al., *Developments in British Politics 6*, pp. 69–87.

22. See Bhiku Parekh et al., *The Future of Multi-Ethnic Britain: The Parekh Report* (London: Profile Books, 2000), pp. 90–102.

23. For a useful discussion of the repercussions of the EU on British governance, see Simon Hix, "Britain, the EU and the Euro," in Dunleavy et al., *Developments in British Politics 6*, pp. 47–68.

C H A P T E R

9

Representation and Participation

Parliamentary sovereignty is the core constitutional principle defining the role of the legislature and, in a sense, the whole system of British government. No act of Parliament can be set aside by the executive or judiciary, nor is any Parliament bound by the actions of any previous Parliament. Nevertheless, in practice, the control exerted by the House of Commons (or Commons) is not unlimited. In this chapter, we investigate the powers and role of Parliament, both Commons and Lords, as well as the party system, elections, and contemporary currents in British political culture and identity. We also assess the political significance of collective identities in Britain (social class, nationality, ethnicity, and gender) and discuss patterns of political participation and social protest.

The Legislature

Is Parliament still as sovereign in practice as it remains in constitutional tradition? Clearly, it is not so powerful as it once was. In the mid-nineteenth century, from roughly the 1830s to the 1880s—after monarchical control of government ended but before the formation of modern mass-membership parties—the House of Commons was vastly more powerful than it has ever been since. During this "Golden Age of Parliament," it collaborated in the formulation of policy, and members amended or rejected legislation on the floor of the House. Contemporaries even referred to Parliament's "elective function," owing to its frequent role in the seating and unseating of governments and ministers.[1] From the period of the Reform Act of 1867 onward, with the growth of mass-membership parties, functions that Parliament had exercised during the Golden Age were transferred elsewhere. The function of selecting the government moved downward to the electorate at large. At the same time, the legislative and policymaking function tended to move upward to the cabinet and government.[2] As a result, the Commons now does not so much legislate as assent to government legislation, since (with rare exceptions) the governing party has a majority of the seats and requires no cross-party voting to pass bills. Moreover, in the postwar period, the enormous range of economic and social welfare responsibilities and the sheer complexity of policies have meant that in Britain (as elsewhere), the balance of effective oversight of policy has shifted from the legislature to executive agencies.

In this section, we discuss, in turn, the legislative process, the House of Commons, the House of Lords, and reforms and pressures for change.

Legislative Process

To become law, bills must be introduced in the House of Commons and the House of Lords, although approval by the latter is not required.

The procedure for developing and adopting a public bill is quite complex. The ideas for prospective legislation may come from political parties, pressure groups, think tanks, the prime minister's policy unit, or government departments. Prospective legislation is then normally drafted by civil servants, circulated within Whitehall, approved by the cabinet, and then refined by one of some thirty lawyers in the Office of Parliamentary Counsel.

According to tradition, in the House of Commons the bill usually comes to the floor three times (referred to as *readings*). The bill is formally read upon introduction (the first reading), printed, distributed, debated in general terms, and after an interval (from a single day to several weeks), given a second reading, followed by a vote. The bill is then usually sent for detailed review to a standing committee of between sixteen and fifty members chosen to reflect the overall party balance in the House. It is then subjected to a report stage during which new amendments may be introduced. The third reading follows; normally, the bill is considered in final form (and voted on) without debate.

After the third reading, a bill passed in the House of Commons follows a parallel path in the House of Lords. There the bill is either accepted without change, amended, or rejected. According to custom, the House of Lords passes bills concerning taxation or budgetary matters without alteration and can add technical and editorial amendments to other bills (which must be approved by the House of Commons) to add clarity in wording and precision in administration. After a bill has passed through all these stages, it is sent to the Crown for royal assent (approval by the queen or king, which is only a formality), after which it becomes law and is referred to as an act of Parliament.

House of Commons

In constitutional terms, the House of Commons, the lower house of Parliament (with 659 members at the time of the 2001 election), exercises the main legislative power in Britain. Along with the two unelected elements of Parliament, the Crown and the House of Lords, the Commons has three main functions: (1) to pass laws, (2) to provide finance for the state by authorizing taxation, and (3) to review and scrutinize public administration and government policy.

In practical terms, the Commons has a limited legislative function; nevertheless it serves a very important democratic function. It provides a highly visible arena for policy debate and the partisan collision of political worldviews. The House comes alive when opposition members challenge the government, spark debates over legislation, and question the actions of cabinet members. During *question time*, a regular weekly feature of Commons debate, ministers give oral replies to questions submitted in advance by members of Parliament (MPs) and offer off-the-cuff responses to follow-up questions and sarcastic asides (often to the merriment of all in attendance). A half-hour session each week is allotted to the prime minister's question time, when the prime minister and the leader of the opposition engage in highly charged verbal combat. The exchanges create extraordinary theater and can make and unmake careers. The ability to handle parliamentary debate with style and panache is considered a prerequisite for party leadership.

The high stakes and the flash of rhetorical skills bring drama to the historic chambers, but one crucial element of drama is nearly always missing: The outcome is seldom in doubt. The likelihood that the Commons will invoke its ultimate authority, to defeat a government, is very small. MPs from the governing party who consider rebelling against their leader (the prime minister) are understandably reluctant in a close and critical vote to force a general election—which would place their jobs in grave jeopardy. Only once since the defeat of Ramsay MacDonald's government in 1924 has a government been brought down by a defeat in the Commons (in 1979). Contemporary constitutional conventions provide a good deal of wiggle room for the government. It was once taken for granted that defeat of any significant motion or bill would automatically result in cabinet resignation or a dissolution of Parliament. However, it is now likely that only defeat on a motion that explicitly refers to "confidence in Her Majesty's government" still mandates dissolution. For now, the balance of institutional power has shifted from Parliament to the governing party and the executive.

House of Lords

The upper chamber of Parliament, the House of Lords (or Lords), is an unelected body that comprises hereditary peers (nobility of the rank of duke, marquis, earl, viscount, or baron), life peers (appointed by the Crown on the recommendation of the prime minister), and law lords (appointed to assist the Lords in its judicial duties and who become life peers). The Lords also includes the archbishops of Canterbury and York and two dozen senior bishops of the Church of England. There are roughly 1,200 members of the House of Lords, but there is no fixed number, and membership changes with the appointment of peers. Not surprisingly, the Conservatives have a considerable edge in the upper house with just over one-half of peers; Labour runs a distant second at roughly one-sixth. About one-third are *crossbenchers*, or independents.

The House of Lords is the final court of appeal for civil cases throughout Britain and for criminal cases in England, Wales, and Northern Ireland. This judicial role, performed by the law lords, drew international attention in 1998 and 1999 when a Spanish court attempted to extradite General Augusto Pinochet of Chile on charges of genocide, torture, and terrorism. In modern times, however, the Lords has served mainly as a chamber of revision, providing expertise in redrafting legislation. Although the Lords does not act as a serious impediment to

the government, it can slow legislation and encourage modifications. Since the 1970s, government "defeats" (adverse votes) have generated considerable interest and sometimes encouraged compromises. During the Thatcher years, the House of Lords took on a highly visible and surprisingly adversarial role, voting against the government 155 times. In 1994, the Lords forced the Major government to modify the Police and Magistrates' Courts bill, especially with reference to the powers of the home secretary to appoint members to local police authorities. Most dramatically, Lady Thatcher used the Lords as a forum for challenging the more conciliatory stance of the Major government toward Europe. The government suffered 79 defeats during the calendar years 1997–1999 and an additional 20 defeats through September 2000.

The House of Lords attracts a variety of opinions. Some MPs on the Labour Left (and others) have persistently called for its abolition as an undemocratic body. Others view it, like the Crown, with a tolerant affection. In 1999, the Blair government appointed a Royal Commission on the Reform of the House of Lords (the Wakeham commission) and in the same year introduced legislation to remove the right of hereditary lords to speak and vote. In January 2000 the commission recommended a partly elected second chamber, enumerating three alternative models. One interesting possibility is that the second chamber might give representation to the devolved governments within the United Kingdom, as well as to regions, thus taking on a role somewhat similar to the Bundesrat in Germany.

Reforms in Behavior and Structure

It is a sign of the contemporary decline of the Commons that constitutional commentators through the mid-1990s stressed the independence of the Lords. But the more significant development is the shift in power toward the executive and especially the cabinet: "Supposedly, Parliament, Lords no less than Commons, checks and controls the executive. In practice it is the other way around."[3] How significant are contemporary changes in the House? How far will they go to stem the tide in Parliament's much-heralded decline?

Behavioral Changes: Backbench Dissent. Since the 1970s, backbenchers (MPs of the governing party who have no governmental office and rank-and-file opposition members) are markedly less deferential than in the past. A backbench rebellion against the Major government's European Union (EU) policy took a toll on the prestige of the prime minister and contributed to his historically low approval ratings. A resolute leader with a very large majority, Blair seems less likely to face significant rebellion from Labour MPs and, at the same time, is more able to tolerate it. Nevertheless, episodic divisions have occurred—for example, over social welfare policy and the treatment of trade unions and related industrial policy. It is extremely likely that any decision to join the euro would inspire more significant backbench rebellion. After Major's problems with backbench dissent, many commentators argued that weaker party discipline had become a permanent condition, but more evidence is necessary before we can be certain that the open challenges to Major were more than merely a passing reflection of the exceptional divisions over Europe in the Conservative Party.

Structural Changes: Parliamentary Committees. In addition to the standing committees that routinely review bills during legislative proceedings, in 1979 the Commons revived and extended the number and "remit" (i.e., responsibilities) of *select committees*. Select committees help Parliament exert control over the executive by examining specific policies or aspects of administration.

The most controversial select committees are watchdog committees that monitor the conduct of major departments and ministries. Select committees hold hearings, take written and oral testimony, and question senior civil servants and ministers. They then issue reports that often include strong policy recommendations at odds with government policy. As one side effect of the reform, the role of the civil service has been complicated. Traditionally, ministers take responsibility for policy and face scrutiny in Parliament. Historically, senior civil servants have testified on behalf of their ministers, but due to the more adversarial posture of select committees, for the first time they have been required to testify in a manner that might damage their ministers, revealing culpability or flawed judgments. As a result, the powerful norms of civil service secrecy have been compromised and the relationship with ministers disturbed.

On balance, the committees have been extremely energetic. Power is another issue, however, because the committees' direct influence on legislation and their ability to hold executive departments or the government accountable are limited. For the most part, when the committees have been effective, it is because they have served to publicize and critically evaluate government policy. They serve as magnets to attract otherwise scattered criticisms and give them the visibility and prestige of a parliamentary audience. Reform bodies have recommended that select committees be given greater resources and powers, perhaps including a role in confirming appointments and a capacity to compel the testimony of ministers. Radical changes in procedure, political culture, and tradition would be necessary to make select committees powerful watchdogs approximating the role of their counterparts in the U.S. Congress.

In 1997, a Modernisation Committee was established, providing an avenue for the Commons to assess procedures and conventions critically. The committee's reforms have been generally regarded as productive but limited. Perhaps the most significant modernizing reform was the 1998 changes in the system of scrutinizing EU affairs. These included the introduction of new committees and the strengthening of informal links with EU institutions.

The prospects of parliamentary reform are limited by its very character and function within the broader political system. One knowledgeable insider recently observed:

> The executive's control of Parliament, along with the dominance of party, will always mean that political considerations are likely to overrule the wish to subject the government to more vigorous scrutiny, especially when the issues involved are politically sensitive. There is also the fundamental fact that Parliament is a legislature in which the ambition of most of its members is to join the executive.[4]

As a consequence, demands for significantly greater scrutiny over government are not likely to be made and even less likely to be accepted.

Political Parties and the Party System

Like the term *parliamentary sovereignty,* which conceals the reduced role of Parliament in legislation and the unmaking of governments, the term *two-party system,* which is commonly used to describe the British party system, is somewhat deceiving. It is true that since 1945, only leaders of the Labour or Conservative parties have served as prime ministers. From 1945 through the 2001 election, the Conservative Party won eight general elections and the Labour Party an equal number. It is also true that throughout the postwar period, these two parties have routinely divided some 90 percent of the seats in the House of Commons. But a variety of other parties—centrist, environmental, nationalist, and even neofascist—have complicated the picture of party competition.

Labour Party

As one of the few European parties with origins outside electoral politics, the Labour Party was launched by trade union representatives and socialist societies in the last decade of the nineteenth century and formally took its name in 1906. From its inception in a Labour Representation Committee, supporters sought to advance working-class political representation and to further specific trade unionist demands. In the years preceding World War I, the party expanded its trade union affiliation but made only weak progress at the polls. Labour secured only 7.1 percent of the vote in 1910, but the radicalizing effects of the war and the expansion of the franchise in 1918 nearly tripled its base of support. In 1918, it received 22.2 percent, even with a shift of emphasis from the defense of trade union rights to explicitly socialist appeals. Its landslide 1945 victory promoted a party with deep working-class roots and a socialist ideology to major player status in British politics. At the same time, Labour began moderating its ideological appeal and broadening its electoral base.

Early in the postwar period, it was clear that Labour Party *fundamentalism,* which stressed state ownership of industry and workers' control of production, would take a back seat to a more moderate perspective that advocates the projects of the collectivist consensus (this shift was referred to by contemporaries as *revisionism* or *Labourism*). During the height of Labourism (roughly 1945 to the mid-1970s), party identification and electoral behavior displayed a strong correlation with occupation. In the 1950s and early 1960s, those not engaged in manual labor voted Conservative three times more commonly than they did Labour; more than two out of three manual workers, by contrast, voted Labour. During this period Britain conformed to one classic pattern of a Western European party system: a two-class/two-party system.

The period since the mid-1970s has been marked by significant changes in the party system and a growing disaffection with even the moderate social democracy associated with the Keynesian welfare state and Labourism. The party suffered from divisions between its trade unionist and parliamentary elements, constitutional wrangling over the power of trade unions to determine party policy at annual conferences, and disputes over how the leader (a potential prime minister) would be selected. In 1981, a centrist breakaway of leading Labour MPs further destabilized the party.

Divisions spilled over into foreign policy issues as well. Although Labour has been generally internationalist, persistent voices within the party challenged participation in the European Community (EC) on the grounds that EC policy would advance the interests of business over labor and damage the standard of living of working Britons. However, by the late 1980s, Labour began to look to the EC as a means of resisting attacks on the principles of the welfare state at home. In particular, the EC's adoption of the Social Charter to extend workers' rights and protections in 1989 helped turn Labour into a pro-EC party. On defense issues, there was a strong pacifist and an even stronger antinuclear sentiment within the party. Support for unilateral nuclear disarmament (the reduction and elimination of nuclear weapons systems with or without comparable developments on the Soviet side) was a decisive break with the national consensus on security policy and contributed to the party's losses in 1983 and 1987. Unilateralism was then scrapped.

The 1980s and 1990s witnessed a period of relative harmony within the party, with moderate trade union and parliamentary leadership agreeing on major policy issues. Tony Blair's immediate predecessors as party leaders—Neil Kinnock (who served from 1983 until Labour's defeat in the March 1992 election) and John Smith (who replaced Kinnock and served as leader until his death in May 1994)—helped pave the way for New Labour by abandoning socialism and taking the party in a new pragmatic direction. It seems clear that for the foreseeable future, there will be no return to Labour fundamentalism. Labour has become a moderate left-of-center party in which ideology takes a back seat to performance. (The challenges that New Labour faces are discussed further in Chapter 10.)

Conservative Party

The pragmatism, flexibility, and organizational capabilities of the Conservative Party, a party that dates back to the eighteenth century, have made it one of the most successful and, at times, innovative Center-Right parties in Europe. In contrast to some leading conservative parties in Italy and Germany, it has been a secular party wholly committed to democratic principles, free of the association with fascism during World War II that tainted the others. Although it has fallen on hard times in recent years, it would be unwise to underestimate its potential as both an opposition and a governing party.

Although the association of the Conservative Party with the economic and social elite is unmistakable, it is also true that it was the Conservative government of Prime Minister Benjamin Disraeli (1874–1880) that midwifed the birth of the modern welfare state in Britain. The creation of a "long-lasting alliance between an upper-class leadership and a lower-class following"[5] made the Conservative Party a formidable player in British politics. Throughout the postwar period, it has also routinely (with some exceptions) provided the Tories, as Conservatives are colloquially called, with electoral support from about one-third or more of the manual working class. Even in Labour's landslide victory of 1997, 29 percent of manual workers voted Conservative.[6]

Several ideologies of governance have developed within the Conservative Party, and there is no consensus about their relative significance. Some scholars see a cleft in the party between hierarchical and paternalistic attitudes on one side and individualistic free-enterprise traditions on the other. Others argue that the Conservative Party represents the interests of one class (the bourgeoisie or property-owning class) and not the nation as a whole; and ideological currents and factions within the party can be largely explained by the divisions of interest among different capitalist elements (for example, financial versus manufacturing interests or domestic versus internationalist interests). The analysis here, by contrast, tends to emphasize the shift, starting with Thatcher, away from the principles of the collectivist consensus that Labour and Conservative elites had shared for three decades.

Contemporary analysis of the Conservative Party must also emphasize the cost to the party of the internal divisions over Britain's role in the EU. The Tories have seldom, if ever, experienced divisions as serious as those over Europe in the 1990s. The bitter leadership contest that followed Major's resignation after the 1997 defeat only reinforced the impression of a party in turmoil. The new party leader, a centrist, William Hague, had his work cut out for him. The Conservatives were divided between the "Euroskeptics," who reject further European integration, and those who support integration balanced by a firm regard for British sovereignty. In addition, despite party support for a unitary—not a federal—arrangement, the Conservatives under Hague had no choice but to find credible positions on the constitutional reforms that were already in the pipeline and some, like devolution, that have every considerable support, especially in Scotland. Finally, although economic and social policy divisions were eclipsed by the clash over Europe, Conservatives faced inner disagreements on social policy, industrial policy, and the running of the economy.

The pro-business and pro-market orientation of Blair's Labour Party and its perceived centrism limit the options for Conservatives in advancing economic and social policy that would mark out a distinctive alternative to Blair. Interestingly, much as Blair's New Labour bears a kinship to New Democrats in the United States,

Hague's policy orientation, as well as some rhetoric, seemed to take a page from President George W. Bush's play book. Hague introduced a more inclusive social agenda and sprinkled his speeches with references to "compassion" and "caring." While opposing government initiatives such as adoption of the European Social Charter and the minimum wage, Hague nevertheless tried to improve the Conservatives' reputation on the "caring" issues by allowing that increased expenditures on education and health were necessary. In a clear effort to differentiate the Conservatives from Blair's third way, Hague launched a "British Way" initiative, appealing to "Middle England" and traditional values of entrepreneurship, individualism, and loyalty to local and national institutions.[7] In a related development, the party adopted hard-line positions on asylum seekers, gays, and ethnic minority rights that raised questions about tolerance and its much trumpeted compassion.

Buoyed by improvements in polling numbers and the sense of Labour adrift, Hague spoke confidently to the Conservative Party conference in October 2000, the last he anticipated before fighting an election. Insisting that New Labour was nothing more than a fashion and that "nothing is more unfashionable than a fashion that is out of fashion," the Conservative leader asserted that the party was ready for government. Having solidified the party on Europe around the broadly popular anti-euro posture, Hague faced a new division in the ranks between more libertarian and authoritarian traditions of conservatism, inspired by the juxtaposition of two convention speeches. One speech by the party's spokesperson on law enforcement that called for "zero-tolerance" policing—including automatic fines for people caught with small amounts of marijuana in their possession or even in their bloodstream—was derided as "zero common sense" by a leading conservative daily and called unworkable by a leading police organization. The other, by Michael Portillo, a former tough-minded defense secretary, was an uncharacteristically personal appeal to the party for more understanding and acceptance of diversity in sexual orientation and ethnicity. Whatever the divisions, the Conservatives faced the election with a confidence they had not experienced for several years, hoping for a good showing, although not expecting victory. But the election proved a stunning repudiation. A bid to lower taxes backfired with an electorate demanding better public services. Nor did the anti-euro stance gain support. Within hours of the result, Hague announced his resignation.

Liberal Democrats and Other Parties

Since the 1980s a changing roster of centrist parties has posed a potentially significant threat to the two-party dominance of Conservative and Labour. Through the 1970s, the Liberal Party, a governing party in the pre–World War I period and thereafter the traditional centrist third party in Britain, was the only centrist challenger to the Labour and Conservative parties. In 1981, the Social Democratic Party (SDP) formed out of a split within the Labour Party. In the 1983 election the Alliance (an electoral arrangement of the Liberals and the SDP) gained a quarter of the vote. The strength of centrist parties in the mid-1980s led to expectations of a possible Alliance-led government (which did not occur), and observers of British politics began to talk about a party system with "four major national parties" (Conservative, Labour, Liberal, and SDP).[8] After the Conservative victory in 1987, the Liberal Party and most of the SDP merged to form the Social and Liberal Democratic Party (now called the Liberal Democrats, or the LD).

Under the leadership of Paddy Ashdown, the Liberal Democrats fought the 1992 election from the awkward stance of "equidistance" from the two major parties. After a disappointing result—17.8 percent of the vote and only twenty seats in the Commons—the party changed its position in 1994 and began working more closely with Labour. Most important, the

two parties created a Joint Constitutional Committee that developed a degree of unity on proposals for constitutional reform. Many credit the Liberal Democrats with inspiring Blair's constitutional agenda. Nevertheless, under Ashdown's effective leadership, the Liberal Democrats preserved their independence in the 1997 election. They targeted the seats where they had the greatest chance of victory, with impressive results. Although their share of the vote actually slipped slightly between 1992 and 1997 (from 17.8 to 16.8 percent), they won more than twice as many seats (forty-six). Amid a growing debate about the relationship between Labour and the Liberal Democrats, early in 1999 Ashdown unexpectedly announced his intention to resign as leader and was succeeded by Charles Kennedy, an MP from the Scottish Highlands who had previously served the party as spokesperson for European affairs and for agriculture and rural affairs.

The appeal of smaller parties in Britain is constantly shifting. One party, the Greens (formed in 1973 by environmentalists and the oldest Green Party in Europe), surprised everyone (themselves included) by achieving a 15 percent third-place showing in the June 1989 elections to the European Parliament (but winning no seats). With public opinion surveys ranking "pollution and the environment" as the third-most common concern,[9] the major parties hustled to acquire a greenish hue. But the Green Party failed to capitalize on its 1989 showing. By the mid-1990s, party membership declined, and environmental activists focused on a wide range of grassroots initiatives. In 1997, it ran only ninety-five candidates (down from 253 in 1992), with very little impact (it averaged only 1.4 percent in the constituencies it contested).

The National Front (formed in 1967), a far-right, neofascist, anti-immigrant party, won seats on local councils and entered candidates (unsuccessfully) for Parliament. After the National Front faded in the late 1970s, the British National Party (BNP), formed in 1983, emerged as the most visible far Right party. Concentrating its electoral strategy on impoverished inner-city constituencies, in 1997 it ran fifty-seven candidates who registered a meager 1.3 percent average share of the votes cast. In addition to these Center, environmental, far Right, and single-issue parties, Britain has several national parties, which are described below as part of the discussion of trends in electoral behavior.

Elections

British elections are exclusively for legislative posts. The prime minister is not elected as prime minister but as an MP from a single constituency (electoral district) averaging about 65,000 registered voters. Parliament has a maximum life of five years, with no fixed term. General elections are held after Parliament has been dissolved by the Crown at the request of the prime minister. However, for strategic political reasons, the prime minister may ask the Crown to dissolve Parliament at any time. The ability to control the timing of elections is a tremendous political asset for the prime minister. This contrasts sharply with a presidential system, characteristic of the United States, with direct election of the chief executive and a fixed term of office.

Electoral System

Election for representatives in the Commons (who are called members of Parliament, or MPs) is by a "first-past-the-post" (or winner-take-all) principle in each constituency. In this single-member plurality system, the candidate who receives the most votes is elected. There is no requirement of a majority and no element of proportional representation (a system in which each party is given a percentage of seats in a representative assembly roughly comparable to its percentage of the popular vote). Table 9.1 shows the results of the general elections from 1945 to 2001.

This winner-take-all electoral system tends to exaggerate the size of the victory of the largest party and reduce the influence of regionally dispersed lesser parties. Thus, in 1997, with 45 percent of the popular vote, Labour won 419 seats. With 17 percent of the vote, the Liberal Democrats, despite targeting their most winnable constituencies, won only 46 seats. Thus, Labour received fewer than three times as many votes as the Liberal Democrats, but won more than nine times as many seats. Such are the benefits to the victor of the system.

With a fairly stable two-and-a-half party system (Conservative, Labour, and Center), the British electoral system tends toward stable single-party government. However, the electoral system raises questions about representation and fairness. The system reduces the competitiveness of smaller parties with diffuse pockets of support. In addition, the party and electoral systems have contributed to the creation of a Parliament that has been a bastion of white men. The number of women and ethnic minorities holding seats has grown in recent elections, however. In 1992, 60 women were elected as MPs out of 650 seats (9.2 percent), an increase from 42 members in 1987 (6.3 percent). Also in 1992, 6 ethnic minority candidates were elected, up from 4 in 1987, the first time since before World War II that Parliament included minority members. The 1997 election may represent a breakthrough for women: the number of women MPs nearly doubled to a record 120 (18.2 percent). In addition, the number of black and Asian MPs rose to 9 (1.4 percent). Despite the trend of increased representation of women and minorities, they remain substantially underrepresented in Parliament.

Trends in Electoral Behavior

Recent general elections have deepened geographic and regional fragmentation on the political map. British political scientist Ivor Crewe has referred to the emergence of *two* two-party systems: (1) Competition between the Conser-

Table 9.1 British General Elections, 1945–2001

	Percentage of Popular Vote						Seats in House of Commons					
	Turnout	Conservative	Labour	Liberal[a]	National Parties[b]	Other	Swing[c]	Conservative	Labour	Liberal[a]	National Parties[b]	Other	Government Majority
1945	72.7	39.8	48.3	9.1	0.2	2.5	−12.2	213	393	12	0	22	146
1950	84.0	43.5	46.1	9.1	0.1	1.2	+3.0	299	315	9	0	2	5
1951	82.5	48.0	48.8	2.5	0.1	0.6	+0.9	321	295	6	0	3	17
1955	76.7	49.7	46.4	2.7	0.2	0.9	+2.1	345	277	6	0	2	60
1959	78.8	49.4	43.8	5.9	0.4	0.6	+1.2	365	258	6	0	1	100
1964	77.1	43.4	44.1	11.2	0.5	0.8	−3.2	304	317	9	0	0	4
1966	75.8	41.9	47.9	8.5	0.7	0.9	−2.7	253	363	12	0	2	95
1970	72.0	46.4	43.0	7.5	1.3	1.8	+4.7	330	288	6	1	5	30
Feb. 1974	78.7	37.8	37.1	19.3	2.6	3.2	−1.4	297	301	14	9	14	−34[d]
Oct. 1974	72.8	35.8	39.2	18.3	3.5	3.2	−2.1	277	319	13	14	12	3
1979	76.0	43.9	37.0	13.8	2.0	3.3	+5.2	339	269	11	4	12	43
1983	72.7	42.4	27.6	25.4	1.5	3.1	+4.0	397	209	23	4	17	144
1987	75.3	42.3	30.8	22.6	1.7	2.6	−1.7	376	229	22	6	17	102
1992	77.7	41.9	34.4	17.8	2.3	3.5	−2.0	336	271	20	7	17	21
1997	71.4	30.7	43.2	16.8	2.6	6.7	−10.0	165	419	46	10	19	179
2001	59.4	31.7	40.7	18.3	2.5	6.8	+1.9	166	413	52	9	19	167

[a]Liberal Party, 1945–1979; Liberal/Social Democrat Alliance, 1983–1987; Liberal Democratic Party, 1992–2001.

[b]Combined vote of Scottish National Party (SNP) and Welsh National Party (Plaid Cymru).

[c]"Swing" compares the results of each election with the results of the previous election. It is calculated as the average of the winning major party's percentage point increase in its share of the vote and the losing major party's decrease in its percentage point share of the vote. In the table, a positive sign denotes a swing to the Conservatives, a negative sign a swing to Labour.

[d]Following the February 1974 election, the Labour Party was thirty-four seats short of having an overall majority. It formed a minority government until it obtained a majority in the October 1974 election.

Source: *New Labour Triumphs: Britain at the Polls*, ed. Anthony King (Chatham, N.J.: Chatham House, 1998), p. 249. Copyright © 1998 by Chatham House. Reprinted by permission. For 2001 results, http://news.bbc.co.uk/hi/english/static/vote2001/results_constituencies/uk_breakdown/uk_full.stm.

vative and Labour parties dominates contests in English urban and northern seats and (2) Conservative-Center party competition dominates England's rural and southern seats.[10] In addition, a third two-party competition may be observed in Scotland, where Labour–national party competition dominates.

The national parties have challenged two-party dominance since the 1970s. The Scottish National Party (SNP) was founded in 1934 and its Welsh counterpart, the Plaid Cymru, in 1925. Coming in a distant second to Labour in Scotland in 1997, the SNP won 21.6 percent of the vote and six seats. With its greatest strength in agenda setting on devolution, it is likely to play a vocal and potentially influential role in the ongoing processes of constitutional reform. The Plaid Cymru contested every seat in Wales in 1997 but won only four seats where Welsh is still spoken widely. Its experience is another illustration of the effects of the first-past-the-post system. With its support concentrated in districts where Welsh is spoken the most, the Plaid Cymru won four seats despite polling a modest 9.9 percent. By contrast, with support more evenly spread, the Conservatives polled 19.4 percent in Wales and won no seats. With the Tories shut out in both Wales and Scotland in 1997, the prospects of a common two-party pattern of electoral competition throughout Britain are more remote than ever before.

For now the winner-take-all electoral system has preserved two-party dominance in parliamentary representation. But the popular vote tells a different story: Between 1974 and 1997, the combined share of the popular vote for Conservative and Labour averaged under 75 percent. The British electoral system is more complicated than it seems at first glance.

In fact, one of the most significant features of the 2001 election was the further weakening of two-party dominance. With Charles Kennedy, the leader of the Liberal Democrats, running an effective, plain-spoken campaign—arguing, for example, that improvement in public services would require tax increases—the party in-

creased its vote tally by nearly one-fifth overall. They won fifty-two seats, the most since 1929, and knocked the Tories into fourth place in the popular vote in Scotland. As the Conservatives entered a period of introspection and battles for party leadership, the Liberal Democrats could credibly claim that they were, in effect, the leading opposition party.

Collective Identities

The sources and relative strength of diverse group attachments have shifted in Britain in recent decades under the combined pressures of decolonization, which created a multiethnic Britain, and a fragmentation of the experiences of work, which challenge a simple unitary model of class interest. National identity has become especially complicated in the United Kingdom. At the same time, gender politics has emerged as a hot-button issue.

Social Class

Given the two-party/two-class model that has traditionally dominated British politics, the most influential interests have been those linked to class and occupational interests. During the period of consensus that framed politics from the end of World War II until the 1970s, business interests and trade union organizations vied for influence over economic and social policy. Equally important, governments tried very hard, but often without success, to gain the cooperation of these interests in the formulation and implementation of policy.

During the 1970s, the long years of economic decline culminated in an actual decline in the standard of living for many Britons. Also for many, the historic bonds of occupational and social class grew weaker. Union membership fell as jobs continued to be lost in the traditional manufacturing sectors. More damaging, unions lost popular support as they appeared to bully society, act undemocratically, and neglect the needs of an increasingly female and minority workforce.

Throughout the postwar period until Thatcher's administration, British governments struggled to reduce the frequency and duration of strikes, constrain the political power of trade unions, and limit wage increases in both the public and private sectors. They tried two somewhat contradictory policy approaches. On the one hand, governments sought to restrict trade union rights by law (for example, by the 1972 Industrial Relations Act of the Heath government). On the other hand, they tried to expand the involvement of the national association of trade unions, the Trades Union Congress (TUC), in the design and implementation of policy. Why not "turn the poacher into the gamekeeper" and involve trade union leaders in the enforcement of voluntary wage restraints? For example, the 1974–1979 Labour government negotiated a series of highly visible social contracts to hold the line on rising wages in return for promises of expanded social provision, initially with the TUC and subsequently with individual trade unions. When these agreements fell apart, strikes erupted in the 1978–1979 winter of discontent, leading to Thatcher's victory the following May. Labour and Conservative governments alike tried both approaches, with only fleeting success.

Under the Conservative leadership of Thatcher and Major, governments held class-based interests at arm's length and worked to curb their political and industrial power. A formidable combination of legislated constraints, trade union defeats in industrial disputes, and massive unemployment (particularly in the traditionally unionized manufacturing sectors) helped crystallize a pattern of decline in union membership, militancy, and power. Although Blair's reasons are different—he emphasizes the realities of the new global economic competition—he has done little to reverse the decline in union influence. As many have noted, "tough on the unions" is a core premise of New Labour, and this has contributed to a fundamental ero-

sion of the collective strength of working people in the United Kingdom.

How has the arm's-length approach introduced by the Conservatives influenced the ability of business to advance its interests? Medium-scale manufacturing industries are organized politically through the Confederation of British Industry (CBI). In general, Thatcher remained aloof from interest pleading. As a result, organizations like the CBI that traditionally operated on the executive developed closer relations with Parliament. In general, the work of interest groups and lobbyists in the Commons has increased considerably in recent years. Ironically, Blair's business partnership opens new doors to both midsized industry and larger transnational corporate interests and financial interests. The influence of the City of London (the capital's financial district) over economic policy remains considerable.

Citizenship and National Identity

As political scientist Benedict Anderson observed, national identity involves the belief in an "imagined community" of belonging, shared fates, and affinities among millions of diverse and actually unconnected citizens.[11] Since the 1970s, the question of what constitutes "Britishness"—who is included and who excluded from the national political community—has become increasingly vexed. What constitutes "Britishness"? Of what may citizens be justifiably proud? How has the imagined nation stood the test of time? These questions are increasingly difficult to answer.

Questions about fragmented sovereignty within the context of the EU, the commingled histories of four nations (England, Scotland, Wales, and Ireland/Northern Ireland), and the interplay of race and nationality in postcolonial Britain have created doubts about British identity that run deep. As ethnicity, intra-U.K. territorial attachments, and the processes of Europeanization and globalization complicate national identity, it becomes increasingly difficult for U.K. residents automatically to imagine themselves Britons, constituting a resonant national community.

The 1970s also saw the emergence of a growing gap in the economic prospects of North (suffering industrial blight and high unemployment) and South (more prosperous and competitive). In addition, pressure for devolution and growing nationalist sentiment in Scotland and Wales fueled a center-versus-periphery division. Finally, working-class identity and politics were stigmatized as government sharply criticized the behavior of unions. The traditional values of "an honest day's work for an honest day's pay," resistance to cutbacks in wages or changes in work assignments, and solidarity among coworkers in industrial disputes were characterized as "rigidities" that reduced productivity and competitiveness.

Thus, the imagined community of Britain fragmented into smaller communities of class, nation, region, and ethnicity that existed side by side but not necessarily in amiable proximity. Can New Labour re-create a more cohesive political culture and foster a more inclusive sense of British identity? Unlike Thatcher, Blair is a conciliator, and he has worked hard to revitalize a sense of community in Britain and extend his agenda to the socially excluded. The efforts of the Blair government to forge unity and build community and the obstacles it faces are discussed in Chapter 10.

Ethnicity

Britain is a country of tremendous ethnic diversity. As of mid-2000, more than one-tenth of the population (5.75 million people) had community ties or personal histories outside Britain. Almost 6 percent (3.25 million people) were of African, African-Caribbean, or Asian descent. In Greater London, a little more than one-third of the population have community backgrounds outside Britain, and slightly more than one-fifth have backgrounds in Africa, Asia, or the Caribbean. The authors of a recent commission report on multiethnic Britain explained:

Many communities overlap; all affect and are affected by others. More and more people have multiple identities—they are Welsh Europeans, Pakistani Yorkshirewomen, Glaswegian Muslims, English Jews and black British. Many enjoy this complexity but also experience conflicting loyalties. [12]

In Chapter 7, we discussed the economic and social dimensions of ethnic inequality. In political terms, the last two decades have seen increased attention, both negative and positive, to the role of ethnic minorities in the United Kingdom. The politicization of immigration in the 1979 election marked an intensification of this process. It also underscored the resentment white Britons felt toward minority communities who maintained their own religious beliefs and cultures. Thatcher promised tougher nationality legislation to restrict immigration, expressed sympathy for those who harbored "fear that [England] might be swamped" by nonwhite Commonwealth immigrants, and associated minorities with lawlessness. In a similar vein, during the 1984–1985 miners' strike, she denounced the miners as the "enemy within," comparing them to the external Argentine enemy during the 1982 Falklands/Malvinas war. Thatcher symbolically expelled some groups— ethnic minority communities and the unrepentant miners—from the national community. In this way, Thatcherism involved an attempt to redefine national identity by implicit appeals to a more secure, provincial, and unified Britain. This approach also had the effect of making those in the ethnic minority communities feel marginalized or excluded.

Many have asserted that "black" and "British" is a contradiction. In defining themselves, ethnic minorities are prone to say they are Pakistani or Jamaican or Muslim, but some do not feel very British. (The challenges of multiethnic Britain are discussed further in Chapter 10.)

Gender

In Chapter 7, we discussed the social and economic inequality women face and the gender-generational gap in voting patterns. We noted that the issues women care about most—child care, the treatment of part-time workers, domestic violence, equal pay, and support for family caregivers—do not top the list of the policy agendas of any of Britain's political parties.

Has New Labour significantly changed the equation? In 1997, Labour made a concerted effort to attract female voters and was handsomely rewarded. Especially notable were the extensive efforts to improve women's prospects for selection as candidates, pursuant to the goal set at the 1992 annual conference that half the seats being vacated by retiring MPs and half of the most winnable seats should be contested by female candidates. In addition to specific policy statements, the appointment of a series of shadow ministers for women, who worked hard to mobilize support through women's networks and organizations, contributed to Labour's success in reversing the gender gap.[13] The unprecedented election of 120 women MPs and the appointment of a significant number of women onto the Labour front benches raised hopes that 1997 would mark a critical breakthrough for women's representation in the Commons and in positions of government leadership.

On the matter of women's political concerns, however, the results are far from clear. New Labour did not feature women's political agendas in the campaign and did not deliver on one of the explicit promises made: that New Labour's first cabinet would include a minister for women. More important, the early dispute over cuts in child benefits for single parents divided Labour MPs, Labour supporters, and, reportedly, even policymakers. It also raised some important questions about New Labour's approach to the family, which seemed to privilege marriage and, in the eyes of some, the traditional view that the wife should mother and the father provide the principal financial support for young children.

It is probably fair to say, on balance, that Labour did well among women voters less because of any specific pledge (such as a minister for women) and more because it made the effort to listen to concerns that women voiced. In adopting a universalist—rather than a "rainbow coalition"—approach, New Labour declined the opportunity to address women's concerns specifically in its key electoral pledges, but Labour stalwarts would insist that they addressed key concerns that women and men shared in talking about health care, crime, and education. They would point with pride to the policy directions spurred by the social exclusion and women's units.

Will the gender gap tilt toward Labour in 1997 driven by the interests and identities of young women become a case of "easy come, easy go"? In the absence of concrete policy achievements that respond to political agendas grounded in women's experiences of work and family life, it is hard to place women decisively in Labour's column. Such policy innovation would require a substantial reconsideration of the way society organizes domestic and work life and explicit policy attention to the necessary mediations between social needs and the demands of paid work. How much longer should public policy in Britain operate on the gendered assumption of a forty-hour workweek with a partner working part time and willing to take on the necessary domestic tasks? Many women in Britain are quick to suggest that tax credits for working families and efforts to encourage businesses to adopt more family-friendly policies, however laudable, have not changed the basic equation.

Protest and Social Movements

Since the 1970s, class-based interest bargaining has declined, while movements based on ethnic and gender attachments (sometimes referred to as new social movements, NSMs) have grown in significance. These movements have changed the landscape of politics in Britain. By contrast to the traditional interest-group-oriented social movements, the NSMs tend to be more fluidly organized and democratic, less oriented to immediate payoffs for their group, and more focused on fundamental questions about the values of society. For example, in the 1970s and 1980s, the women's peace movement protested Britain's participation in the North Atlantic Treaty Organization's nuclear defense and organized a string of mass demonstrations. In general, following the NSM approach, the women's movement in Britain has remained decentralized and activist. It has been less involved than the American women's movement, for example, in legislative lobbying or coalition politics. The British feminist movement has emphasized consciousness raising, self-help, and lifestyle transformations. The movement has spawned dozens of action groups, ranging from health clinics to battered women's and rape crisis shelters, to feminist collectives and black women's groups, to networks of women in media, law, and other professions. More recently, women have confronted government over inadequate child care provisions and the difficulties posed for women's daily struggle to juggle the demands of work and family.

Simultaneously, the subcultures and countercultures of black Britain have been a vital source of NSM activity, often expressed in antiracist initiatives. "Rock Against Racism" concerts in the 1970s brought reggae and skinhead bands together in public resistance to the National Front; today, lower-profile efforts are made to sensitize local councils to the cultural and material needs of ethnic minorities and to publicize their potential political clout. Efforts to secure improved housing have been a persistent focus of ethnic minority political mobilization. Like the women's movement, such movements are decentralized and culturally engaged. They are much less focused on legal challenges, legislation, or coalition building than comparable movements in the United States.

In recent years, partly in response to what are perceived as unsettling and undemocratic processes of globalization, political protest has been on the rise in Britain. A radical strain of anticapitalist anarchism has gained strength. As protesters demand more accountability and transparency in the operations of powerful international trade and development agencies, a "reclaim the Streets" march in London in June 1999 resulted in over eighty arrests and the equivalent of over $3 million damage to the City of London (the equivalent of Wall Street). In addition, London became the site of protests timed to correspond with the Seattle meeting of the World Trade Organization (WTO), which generated some 100,000 protesters in November 1999.

Above all, since the mid-1990s the level and intensity of environmental activism have been unprecedented. The combined membership of Greenpeace and Friends of the Earth swelled substantially above 600,000 by 1993, but the level of environmental activism really took off with the growing attention to genetically modified (GM) crops in the late 1990s. A newly radicalized movement, worried that long-term consumption of GM food might be harmful and that once let loose, GM crops—referred to derisively as "Frankenstein food"—might cross-pollinate with "normal" plants, captured the popular imagination. A host of direct-action protests erupted in the summer of 1999, some including the destruction of crops. Opinion polls indicated that nearly 75 percent of the population did not want GM crops in the United Kingdom, and in November 1999, the government announced a ban on commercially grown GM crops in Britain until at least 2003.

A quite different kind of activism spread to the countryside among a population not usually known for political protest. Farmers who had been badly hurt by the BSE ("mad-cow disease") and other rural populations concerned about the perceived urban bias of the Labour government launched massive protests, including as many as 250,000 people in 1998, to defend fox hunting! And as we know, massive demonstrations that cut across constituencies and enjoyed huge popular support erupted in September 2000 to protest high fuel prices.[14]

In their classic study of the ideals and values that shape political behavior, political scientists

Gabriel Almond and Sidney Verba wrote that the civic (or political) culture in Britain was characterized by trust, deference to authority and competence, pragmatism, and the balance between acceptance of the rules of the game and disagreement over specific issues.[15] These developments suggest that quite powerful political subcurrents persist in Britain, posing significant challenges for British government.

Notes

1. Philip Norton, *The Commons in Perspective* (Oxford: Basil Blackwell, 1985), pp. 11–26. For a discussion of the historic decline of Parliament, see also Norton, "Introduction: Parliament in Perspective," in Philip Norton, ed., *Parliament in the 1980s* (Oxford: Basil Blackwell, 1988), pp. 1–19; and Dennis Kavanagh, *British Politics: Continuities and Change* (New York: Oxford University Press, 1988), pp. 222–224.

2. Norton, "Parliament in Perspective," p. 4.

3. *The Economist*, November 5, 1983, p. 64.

4. Tony Wright et al., *The British Political Process* (London: Routledge, 2000), p. 232.

5. Samuel H. Beer, *The British Political System* (New York: Random House, 1973), p. 157.

6. See David Sanders, "Voting and the Electorate," in Patrick Dunleavy, Andrew Gamble, Ian Holiday, and Gillian Peele, eds., *Developments in British Politics 5* (New York: St. Martin's Press, 1997), pp. 45–74.

7. For an excellent treatment of Hague's strategy, see Steven Felding, "A New Politics?" in Patrick Dunleavy et al., eds., *Developments in British Politics 6* (New York: St. Martin's Press, 2000), pp. 10–28.

8. Henry Drucker and Andrew Gamble, "The Party System," in Henry Drucker et al., eds., *Developments in British Politics 2*, rev. ed. (London: Macmillan, 1988), p. 60.

9. Market and Opinion Research International, *British Public Opinion* 13, no. 6 (July 1990): 4.

10. Ivor Crewe, "Great Britain," in I. Crewe and D. Denver, eds., *Electoral Change in Western Democracies* (London: Croom Helm, 1985), p. 107.

11. Benedict Anderson, *Imagined Communities*, rev. ed. (London: Verso, 1991).

12. Bhiku Parekh, *The Future of Multi-Ethnic Britain: The Parekh Report* (London: Profile Books, 2000), p. 10.

13. For a detailed account of the efforts by Labour, as well as the Conservatives and Liberal Democrats, to attract women voters, see Joni Lovensduski, "Gender Politics: A Breakthrough for Women?" *Parliamentary Affairs* 50, no. 4 (1997): 708–719.

14. For an excellent discussion of social movements and protest from which this account of anticapitalist and environmental mobilization was drawn, see Helen Margetts, "Political Participation and Protest," in Dunleavy et al., *Developments in British Politics 6*, pp. 185–202.

15. Gabriel A. Almond and Sidney Verba, *The Civic Culture: Political Attitudes and Democracy in Five Nations* (Princeton, N.J.: Princeton University Press, 1963); Almond and Verba, eds., *The Civic Culture Revisited* (Boston: Little, Brown, 1980); and Samuel H. Beer, *Britain Against Itself: The Political Contradictions of Collectivism* (New York: Norton, 1982), pp. 110–114.

CHAPTER
10

British Politics
in Transition

In the fall of 1994, cease-fire declarations made by the Irish Republican Army (IRA) and the Protestant paramilitary organizations renewed hope for a peace settlement in Northern Ireland. Then, in a dramatic new development in early spring 1995, British prime minister John Major and Irish prime minister John Bruton jointly issued a framework agreement, inspiring mounting optimism about a political settlement. Although Major did what he could to secure public and parliamentary support, he lacked the necessary political capital to bring the historic initiative to fruition.

With his landslide victory, Tony Blair had political capital to spend, and he chose to invest a chunk of it on peace in Northern Ireland. Blair arranged to meet Gerry Adams, president of Sinn Fein, the party in Northern Ireland with close ties to the IRA—and shook his hand. He was the first prime minister to meet a head of Sinn Fein since 1921. Blair later spoke of the "hand of history" on his shoulder.

Under deadline pressure imposed by Blair and the new Irish prime minister, Bertie Ahern, and thirty-three hours of around-the-clock talks, an agreement was reached on Good Friday 1998. It specified elections for a Northern Ireland assembly, in which Protestants and Catholics would share power, and the creation of a North-South Council to facilitate "all-Ireland" cooperation on matters such as economic development, agriculture, transportation, and the en-

vironment. Much was left unclear, for example, the details of how and when the IRA would give up its weapons (called "decommissioning" in Northern Irish parlance) and questions about the release of prisoners affiliated with the paramilitary groups. It did not address the reform of the police force in Northern Ireland, which is overwhelmingly Protestant and partisan and does not enjoy the confidence of the Catholic community. Nevertheless, despite doubts about the fine print, both parts of Ireland voted yes in May 1998 in a referendum to approve the peace agreement. It appeared that a new era was dawning in Northern Ireland.

Like the spiral of political violence that can shake peace efforts in the Middle East at any time, handshake or not, devastating bombs have exploded in Northern Ireland since the agreement, and violent turf battles within and between each camp have created fear and repeated crises in the peace process. The Northern Ireland secretary, Peter Mandelson, felt compelled to suspend the devolved power-sharing government in February 2000, less than three months after it began, under Protestant Unionist pressure concerning the timetable for decommissioning of IRA weapons amid allegations of bad faith on both sides. In January 2001 Peter Mandelson, a close confidant of Tony Blair's, was forced to resign as Northern Ireland Secretary over allegations of financial improprieties. The downfall of a very powerful cabinet insider was a blow to the government but signaled no changes in Northern Ireland policy. Through the winter of 2001, recurring crises over weapons—deadlines, procedures governing inspections by an international commission, what sort of interim meetings could take place—strained relations between the parties to the dispute and threatened to disrupt the Good Friday Agreement. Insisting that Sinn Fein cabinet ministers be barred from discussion until the IRA disarmed, hard-liners in the Protestant camp created a rash of challenges to David Trimble, the Ulster Unionist leader who remained committed to the success of the process. Sinn Fein, in turn, accused Trimble of sabotage and warned that the IRA would not be able to control its own dissidents if the power-sharing arrangements were unilaterally dismantled

Although nothing is certain when it comes to Northern Ireland, the political resolve on all sides seems firm, if battered, and this time the violence has tended to bring the divided communities closer together in the cause of peace. Certainly Blair and his Irish counterparts have the will to see the process through, and they have shown considerable fortitude and political courage in the effort thus far.

There can be no greater political challenge for a British prime minister than peace in Northern Ireland. And, to be sure, Blair's initiative displays in full measure his willingness to find innovative solutions and provide decisive leadership. In that sense, it is a central part of his government's program. In addition, the "troubles" in Northern Ireland confirm the important proposition that unresolved tensions in state formation shape political agendas for generations. The "troubles" reflect enduring political tensions flowing from antagonistic collective identities, as differences in political power and economic privilege enflamed cultural (in this case, religious) divisions. Northern Ireland, however, is but one of a host of challenges facing Britain on Tony Blair's agenda. With the prospects of peace probably uncertain for years

to come, Blair is unlikely to risk too much political capital in one place.

Continuities, Transitions, and Changing Agendas

As our Democratic Idea theme suggests, no democracy, however secure it may be, is a finished project. Even in Britain, with its centuries old constitutional settlement and secure institutional framework, issues about democratic governance and citizens' participation remain unresolved.

Constitutional Reform

Questions about the role of the monarchy and the House of Lords have long been simmering on Britain's political agenda. Since the traditionally admired royal family was battered by scandal and misconduct in the 1990s, these concerns about the undemocratic foundations of the British state have gained credibility. "Why is the House of Commons not sovereign?" wondered one observer somewhat caustically. "Why does it have to share sovereignty with other, unelected institutions?"[1] Few reject the monarchy outright, but there is more grumbling than ever before about the role and deportment of the Crown. When a fire at Windsor Castle in 1991 brought the issue of royal finances to the fore, the cost to taxpayers of the expensive and bedraggled monarchy was openly debated, and the queen agreed to pay taxes "voluntarily" for the first time. In the mid-1990s, publicity surrounding the marital problems of Lady Diana and Prince Charles subjected the monarchy to intense criticism. In 1997, the initially cool and standoffish reaction of the royal family to Diana's death alienated many Britons and created an unprecedented level of popular antipathy toward the Crown. Although Charles's increased informality and evident devotion to his sons helped improve his standing after Diana's death, questions about the role of the monarchy helped place on the agenda broader issues about citizen control over government and constitutional reform.

The balance of power among constitutionally critical institutions remains a major issue of contemporary political debate. One well-respected observer of the British constitution recently noted, "The Commons is hobbled. It is constricted on one level by strong, oligopolistic political parties. On another, it is virtually neutered by a modern executive whose reach (vis-à-vis its own policy) far exceeds that of any other executive in the Western world."[2] Add to these concerns the role of the unelected House of Lords and the absence of an "entrenched" bill of rights (one that Parliament cannot override), and it seems appropriate to raise questions about the accountability of the British government to its citizens.

In fact, constitutional reform may become New Labour's most enduring legacy. The Blair government has begun to implement far-reaching reforms of Parliament, including the removal of the right of hereditary peers to speak and vote in the House of Lords and the redesign of the historic upper chamber. In addition, the European Convention on Human Rights has been incorporated into U.K. law. Moreover, new systems of proportional representation have been introduced for Welsh and Scottish elections, as well as for the European Parliament, and the possible use of proportional representation in U.K. general elections has been placed on the reform agenda. New Labour's inability to control the outcome of London's historic mayoral contest in May 2000 illustrates the difficulties that may accompany far-reaching measures to devolve and decentralize power.

Finally, the initiatives in Northern Ireland and power-sharing arrangements between Westminster and national assemblies in Scotland and Wales raise the prospect of further basic modifications of U.K. constitutional principles. Devolution implies both an element of federalism and some compromise in the historic parliamentary sovereignty at the heart of the Westminster model, with uncertain and potentially unsettling consequences. It is too early to be sure about the success of these reform initiatives, but it is certain that the constitutional reform agenda is highly significant. The May 1999 elections to the Scottish and Welsh parliaments, which produced national parties as the main rival to Labour in both places, already introduced major changes.

The range and depth of New Labour's constitutional reform agenda represent a breathtaking illustration of a core premise of our Democratic Idea theme, that even long-standing democracies face pressures to narrow the gap between government and citizens. If the British feel themselves removed from day-to-day control over the affairs of government, they are hardly alone. And despite the questions Britons raise about the rigidities of their ancient institutional architecture, others throughout the world see the Westminster model as an enduring exemplar of representative democracy, stability, tolerance, and the virtues of a constitutional tradition that balances a competitive party system with effective central government.

Identities in Flux

Although the relatively small scale of the ethnic minority community limits the political impact of the most divisive issues concerning *collective identities*, it is probably in this area that rigidities in the British political system challenge tenets of democracy and tolerance most severely. Given Britain's single-member, simple-plurality electoral system and no proportional representation, minority representation in Parliament is very low, and governments have been slow to respond to concerns about cultural isolation.

There are deep-seated social attitudes that no government can easily transform. Although immigration policy is no longer a hot-button issue, immigration still inspires fear among white

Britons of "multi-culturalism and cultural dilution" and conjures very negative and probably prejudiced reactions. According to a 1996 survey of social attitudes in Britain, about two-thirds of the respondents believed that the number of immigrants should be reduced, about one-half felt that immigrants take jobs away from those born in Britain, and approximately one-quarter said that immigrants increase crime rates.[3] In fall 2000 the report of the Commission on the Future of Multi-Ethnic Britain raised profound questions about tolerance, justice, and inclusion in contemporary U.K. society. In a powerful and controversial analysis, the report concluded that "the word 'British' will never do on its own. . . . Britishness as much as Englishness, has systematic, largely unspoken, racial connotations."[4]

How about other dimensions of collective identity? The situation is fluid. The electoral force of class identity has declined in Britain for the time being, as have the strike rates that signal working-class militancy. New Labour's efforts to develop a partnership with business and keep trade unions at arm's length have positioned a weakened labor movement as an "internal opposition," challenging the government on industrial relations and economic policy. On the positive side, the economic vitality of the 1990s and the early years of the new century has created some pockets of renewal in the north of England and taken some of the edge off North-South divisions. In addition, the increased prospects of a political settlement in Northern Ireland offer the hope that discord over national identity may be reduced in a profound way. More unsettling, the agreement in Northern Ireland, the constitutional reforms in Scotland and Wales, and the processes of Europeanization all involve some weakening of the central authority of Westminster and Whitehall. Thus, British identity, which is already weakly felt, will lose some of its institutional security at the same time that European identity is pulling from above and regional, ethnic, and national identities are pulling from below.

The Challenges of European Integration

From 1989 to 1997, the seemingly endless backbiting over the Social Charter and Maastricht in the Conservative Party sidetracked Thatcher and Major and cost them dearly in political terms. Britain's traumatic withdrawal from the Exchange Rate Mechanism in 1992 stands as a warning that deeper European integration can be economically disruptive and politically dangerous. In the years ahead, Britain's decision whether, when, and under what conditions to join the single currency will almost certainly prove a serious challenge to New Labour's managerial skills and unity.

Thus far, the government has opted to play down the political significance of the euro. At first, Blair and his followers began to make the case for the "yes" campaign, despite government assurances that the promised referendum on the euro would not be held until after the subsequent general election. Despite some strong hints early in 1999 that the government would ultimately support entry, Foreign Secretary Robin Cook claimed that "the high-water mark of European integration has already been reached"; Chancellor of the Exchequer Gordon Brown repeatedly assured listeners that the decision on entry into the single currency will be based on how high the euro scores on a series of economic tests.[5]

Most observers note, however, that the issues swirling around British participation in the single currency are profoundly political and that the tide of European integration is rising. In fact, the matter of Britain's participation in the euro seems likely to create significant political pressures for New Labour. Unofficially, key members of the government support British participation in the single currency, and the decision to free the Bank of England from direct government control was a powerful indication that Blair and Brown intended to create the proper conditions for British entry. However, the prospect of all but irreversible and comprehensive European integration has inspired significant resistance within New Labour and among the public. Polls in early 1999, after the launch of the euro, showed that the gap between supporters and opponents of the single currency had narrowed, but a solid majority of respondents were still against U.K. membership.

Early in 2000, the euro fell below parity with the dollar, and public opposition to the euro pushed opinion polls two to one against participation. The government began to back off its implicit support for the "yes" option and determination to hold a referendum soon after re-election. By the fall of 2000, despite concerted efforts mounted by the European Central Bank (ECB) to stabilize the euro, the common currency had lost nearly one-third of its value against the dollar since its launch in January 1999. In a significant tactical departure, an increasingly wary Blair refused to speculate on how the euro was doing with reference to the economic tests but observed that under the current circumstances, he would vote "no" in a referendum.

For countries that have joined (or will join) the euro club, the ECB has acquired critical economic policy powers that have reduced national sovereign control. Participation holds significant consequences for price stability and for the capacity of national governments to manipulate interest rates and exchange rates to cushion declines in demand and limit unemployment. In addition, the euro will create pressure for coordination of tax policies. Economic and monetary integration therefore has potentially quite significant repercussions for standards of living and distributional politics at home. Inevitably New Labour will have to face head-on these issues and the political divisions that will almost certainly follow. The euro will cast a long shadow over New Labour's strategies for *governing the economy*, and perceptions about Blair's handling of the U.K. position on the euro are likely to have tremendous political repercussions for years to come.

In addition, United Kingdom–European Union (EU) relations in general, and their acute focus on the single currency, underscore the importance of our *world of states* theme. In Chapter 6, we discussed the expectation that a middle-rank power, even in European terms, would encounter difficulty in managing the domestic impact of decisions by regional blocs, and here the British case is no exception. Britain is no longer a world power and cannot rival Germany or France in its influence on EU developments. "Euroskepticism" all but crippled the Conservative Party in the 1980s and through the 1997 election, and New Labour seems increasingly reticent about committing itself to first-tier participation, which would have required an early endorsement of the euro. The poorer countries in Europe, led by Spain, which worked very hard to be accepted as a charter member in the euro club, see integration as an engine of prosperity and greater political influences. By contrast, uncertain about participating in a game it cannot dominate, Britain continues to pay the price in terms of real and symbolic loss of influence for its ambivalence about Europe.

British Politics in Comparative Perspective

For many reasons, both historical and contemporary, the British case represents a critical one in comparative terms, even though Britain is no longer a leading power. How well have three centuries of constitutional government and a culture of laissez-faire capitalism prepared Britain for a political and economic world it has fewer resources to control? Does Britain still offer a distinctive and appealing model of democracy? What are the lessons that may be drawn in time from Blair's New Labour—a modernizing politics that aspires to go beyond Left and Right?

Until the Asian financial crisis that began in 1997, it was an axiom of comparative politics that economic success required a style of economic governance that Britain lacks. Many argued that innovation and competitiveness in the new global economy required the strategic coordination of the economy by an interventionist state. Interestingly, however, the United Kingdom escaped the recession that plagued the rest of Europe for much of the 1990s, with six solid years of uninterrupted growth between 1992 and 1998, and it outperformed Germany throughout much of the 1980s and 1990s.

The reasons for Britain's success and its economic prospects for the future continue to fuel debate inside the United Kingdom and attract considerable attention elsewhere. Perhaps Britain has already reaped the competitive benefits of ending restrictive labor practices and attracting massive foreign investment looking for a European base with few restrictions—and it is time to introduce a German-style high-skill, high-wage workforce and give it similar opportunities to participate in management. Or perhaps Britain's "less is more" approach to economic management, augmented by Tony Blair's business partnership and welfare reforms that encourage active participation in the labor force, provides an important and timely alternative to the more state-centered and interventionist strategies of Germany, France, and Japan. Time will tell, and partisan debate will probably never end, but the British approach has gained favor in recent years. In many countries throughout the world, politicians are looking for an economic model that can sustain economic competitiveness while preserving individual liberties and improving the plight of the socially excluded. Tony Blair's third way—a political orientation that hopes to transcend Left and Right in favor of practical and effective policies—will be carefully watched and, if it is successful, widely emulated.

Beyond the impressive size of Blair's victory, nothing about the May 1997 election was clearer than the unprecedented volatility of the electorate. In previous elections, commitment to party (partisan identification) and interests linked to occupation (class location) had largely determined the results. In 1997 attachments to party and class had far less influence.

Beginning with the historically low turnout, the 2001 election underscored, as one journalist put it, that "instinctive party support" based on class and partisan traditions has been replaced by "pick and choose" politics. The tendency of voters to behave as electoral shoppers lends a perpetual air of uncertainty to elections.

The most notable feature of today's electorate is its unpredictability. What are the consequences for government and for electoral politics if voters at each election feel totally free to choose whichever party they like? What variables, if any, have replaced the traditional influences on voting behavior?

It seems that Blair's success in transforming Labour into New Labour blunted the social basis of party identification. At the same time, the modernization agenda of New Labour resolutely emphasized fiscal responsibility over distributive politics. As a result, it seems that specific issues and the needs of voters mattered more than deep-seated attachments. People voted as consumers of policies: They asked themselves who would make it easier for them to find a good place to live or pay their mortgage, get the health care their family needs, best educate their children—and what role the government would play in underwriting or providing these goods.

In addition, the British political scientist David Sanders has suggested that class and party identification may have been replaced by "the growth of alternative sources of identity—apart from class—that have no obvious attachment to the established political parties,"[6] including ethnicity, gender, and other increasingly important ways in which people define themselves. As the discussions of gender and politics in Chapters 6 and 9 suggest, gender presents the most interesting case for the electoral influence of alternative collective identities, as women link their

"Fuel Tax Protesters Tie Up Chancellor." This cartoon shows Chancellor Gordon Brown trapped by protesters in September 2000 demanding reduced taxes on fuel. The government refused to give in to demands during the heat of the direct action campaign, but Brown's prebudget statement in November was calculated to relieve pressure on the government before the anticipated general election.

Source: *Spectator*, September 16, 2000, p. 12. Drawing by Jonathan Wateridge, courtesy of the *Spectator*.

voting decisions to a specific set of needs that vary by generation and material circumstances.

As our introductory vignette in Chapter 6 about the fuel crisis illustrates, without the traditional constraints of partisan and class identities, citizens (whether as voters or as political activists) can shift allegiances with lightning speed. "What have you done for me lately?" becomes the litmus test for leaders and politicians. Short-term crises in policy and perception send opinions flying all over the map, and citizens behave like consumers with little brand loyalty,

following short-term policy preferences or the most confidence-inspiring management team. In Blair's case, it appeared by November that September's crisis was old news. The prebudget statement by Chancellor Gordon Brown promised a package of freezes and cuts in fuel taxes plus large reductions in vehicle excise duties amounting to the equivalent of $3.2 billion—or some 24 cents a gallon for ordinary motorists and twice that for truck drivers. Perhaps not coincidentally, the government was back on top, with snapshot polls giving Labour 45 percent and the Conservatives 34 percent.

The election in June 2001 was, paradoxically, a landslide and a powerful reminder that much of the electorate was waiting to be convinced that New Labour could deliver on its core promises of improved schools, hospitals, transport, and protection against crime. In winning 40.7 percent of the popular vote and a very commanding majority of 167 in the Commons, Labour achieved an historic result. For the first time, the party won two emphatic electoral victories in a row and was poised to lead the country for two full successive terms. Nevertheless, despite the overwhelming mandate, at 59.4 percent, the lowest turnout for a general election in Britain since 1918 indicated widespread apathy and skepticism (although, of course, a low turnout also reflected a sense that the outcome was never in doubt). Many wondered aloud whether in its second term New Labour could dispel the notion that it was "more spin than substance." Even an exuberant Tony Blair noted that the mood in 2001 was more sober and less euphoric than it had been on election night four years earlier. Everyone seemed painfully aware of unfulfilled promises and the challenges that lay ahead.

In this era of uncertain democratic transitions, divided leadership, and intense global pressures on economic competitiveness, Britain's response to contemporary challenges will be closely watched. These are tough times for national governments to maintain popular support and achieve desirable goals. Can a popular and resolute leader who is riding a wave of economic prosperity in one of the most secure democracies govern effectively? If not, many will conclude that these tough times just got tougher.

Notes

1. Stephen Haseler, "Britain's Ancien Régime," *Parliamentary Affairs* 40, no. 4 (October 1990): 418.

2. Ibid., p. 420.

3. Lizanne Dowds and Ken Young, "National Identity," in Roger Jowell, John Curtice, Alison Park, Lindsay Brook, and Katarina Thompson, eds., *British Social Attitudes: The 13th Report* (Aldershot: Dartmouth Publishing Company, 1996), pp. 141–160.

4. Bhiku Parekh, *The Future of Multi-Ethnic Brit-ain: The Parekh Report* (London: Profile Books, 2000), p. 38.

5. "Goodbye to All That?" *European*, April 27–May 3, 1998, p. 5.

6. David Sanders, "The New Electoral Battlefield," in Anthony King et al., *New Labour Triumphs: Britain at the Polls* (Chatham, N.J.: Chatham House, 1998), p. 221.

Bibliography

Beer, Samuel H. *Britain Against Itself: The Political Contradictions of Collectivism.* New York: Norton, 1982.

Driver, Stephen, and Martel, Luke. *New Labour: Politics After Thatcherism.* Cambridge: Polity Press, 1998.

Dunleavy, Patrick, et al. *Developments in British Politics, 6.* New York: St. Martin's Press, 2000.

Giddens, Anthony. *The Third Way: The Renewal of Social Democracy.* Cambridge: Polity Press, 1998.

Gilroy, Paul. *"There Ain't No Black in the Union Jack": The Cultural Politics of Race and Nation.* Chicago: University of Chicago Press, 1991.

Hall, Peter A. *Governing the Economy: The Politics of State Intervention in Britain and France.* New York: Oxford University Press, 1986.

Hall, Stuart, and Jacques, Martin, eds. *The Politics of Thatcherism.* London: Lawrence and Wishart, 1983.

Hobsbawm, E. J. *Industry and Empire.* Harmondsworth: Penguin/Pelican, 1983.

King, Anthony, et al. *New Labour Triumphs: Britain at the Polls.* Chatham, N.J.: Chatham House, 1998.

Kavenagh, Dennis, and Seldon, Anthony. *The Powers Behind the Prime Minister: The Hidden Influence of Number Ten.* London: HarperCollins, 1999.

Krieger, Joel. *British Politics in the Global Age. Can Social Democracy Survive?* New York: Oxford University Press, 1999.

Landes, David S. *The Unbound Prometheus: Technological Change and Industrial Development in Western Europe from 1750 to the Present.* Cambridge: Cambridge University Press, 1969.

Marsh, David, et al. *Postwar British Politics in Perspective.* Cambridge: Polity Press, 1999.

Marshall, Geoffrey. *Ministerial Responsibility.* Oxford: Oxford University Press, 1989.

Middlemas, Keith. *Politics in Industrial Society: The Experience of the British System Since 1911.* London: André Deutsch, 1979.

Norris, Pippa. *Electoral Change in Britain Since 1945.* Oxford: Blackwell Publishers, 1997.

Parekh, Bhiku, et al., *The Future of Multi-Ethnic*

Britain: The Parekh Report. London: Profile Books, 2000.

Pierson, Paul. *Dismantling the Welfare State? Reagan, Thatcher, and the Politics of Retrenchment.* New York: Cambridge University Press, 1994.

Riddell, Peter. *The Thatcher Decade.* Oxford: Basil Blackwell, 1989.

Särlvik, Bo, and Crewe, Ivor. *Decade of Dealignment: The Conservative Victory of 1979 and Electoral Trends in the 1970s.* Cambridge: Cambridge University Press, 1983.

Shaw, Eric. *The Labour Party Since 1945.* Oxford: Blackwell Publishers, 1996.

Thompson, E. P. *The Making of the English Working Class.* New York: Vintage, 1966.

Wright, Tony, ed. *The British Political Process.* London: Routledge, 2000.

Web Sites

http://www. open.gov.uk/

http://www.official-documents.co.uk

http://www.parliament.uk

http://www.cabinet-office.gov.uk/

http://www.scottish.parliament.uk/

http://news.bbc.co.uk

http://www.mori.com/

P A R T

IV

France

Mark Kesselman

CHAPTER

11

The Making of the
Modern French State

French Politics in Action

The city of Nice, on the Côte d'Azur, France's famed Mediterranean coast, is best known for its elegant hotels, restaurants, and casino. Along with its neighbors Cannes, Saint Tropez, and other neighboring resort towns, Nice has attracted the rich and famous for generations. In December 2000, two other groups assembled in Nice. The first group was composed of heads of member states of the European Union (EU). They met at the invitation of French President Jacques Chirac, as France was nearing the end of its rotating six-month term as presiding country of the EU. EU summit meetings are usually dull affairs. Political leaders pose for photo ops, offer toasts at state dinners, ratify decisions negotiated in previous working sessions by EU technocrats and member state administrators, and return home. This time, the presence of a second group at Nice made for a very different summit conference.

The second group was large—in fact, it numbered over 80,000—and its members were neither rich, famous, nor powerful. It was primarily composed of trade unionists from twenty-six countries but also included activists from countless organizations challenging neo-liberal economic policy within the EU and internationally, as well as promoting environmental protection, immigrant rights, and human rights. About four-fifths of the participants were French, the rest were from Italy, Spain, and other European countries. The gathering was unprecedented in several important respects. For the first time on such a wide scale, trade unions from throughout Europe—which often disagree on priorities—agreed on a common set of demands. The focal point of protest was the Charter of Fundamental Rights adopted at the Nice summit. European trade unions sponsored what one observer termed "the largest European trade union demonstration in history" to protest that, in their view, the Charter does not provide adequate rights, has the legal status of a declaration by member states but not a treaty commitment integrated within EU law, and fails to provide enforcement mechanisms and penalties for noncompliance.[1] Trade union confederations throughout Europe also signed a common declaration in preparation for the Nice summit, calling for a five-year plan of EU-wide measures to promote social provisions and job creation.

The EU demonstrations at Nice brought together trade union militants and community activists, two groups that rarely cooperate. Participants traveled to Nice to protest that a small number of officials, many of whom were unelected and not directly accountable by democratic processes, made EU decisions behind closed doors that deeply affected all Europeans. The protests may be considered the first Euro-demonstrations ever. They had a somewhat familiar air, however, in that they resembled protests at Seattle, Washington, a year earlier, when a World Trade Organization ministerial meeting was disrupted by widespread demonstrations, bringing together trade unionists and nongovernmental organizations (NGOs) from throughout the world. Familiar, too, was the police response at Nice—baton charges, tear gas assaults, and numerous arrests. Nor were the Seattle and Nice demonstrations unique. Between the Seattle and Nice protests, demonstrations disrupted meetings of international political and economic leaders held in Davos, Switzerland; Prague, the Czech Republic; and Washington, D.C.

The EU demonstrations at Nice dramatically highlight the fact that France's fate is closely intertwined with that of Europe. They also highlight the strains between governing elites and large numbers of discontented citizens throughout Europe. Interestingly, the supranational EU indirectly promoted cooperation among traditionally rival forces in France in a way that had never happened before. It is noteworthy that French trade unions—typically rivals rather than allies—worked together to mobilize their members for the Nice demonstration. Significant, too, is that French unions joined with diverse groups from other sectors of French society, such as ATTAC (described in Chapter 15), an organization seeking to create a tax on international financial speculation. These developments suggest that the EU, and France's involvement in the global political economy more generally, are promoting a restructuring of traditional French identities, cleavages, and alliances. In brief, the Nice demonstrations invite us to reflect on what is enduring and what is changing in French politics.

Geographic Setting

France is among the world's favored countries, thanks to its temperate climate, large and fertile land area, relatively low population density, and high standard of living. However, the country is poorly endowed in natural energy and mineral resources. For example, France must import most of its petroleum, a reason that the government has sponsored an intensive nuclear power program since the 1950s. France must also import most minerals, a result of an initial scarcity of reserves and years of extensive exploitation. Thus, France must concentrate its efforts on producing high-value-added products to compete internationally.

With a population of 60.7 million, France is one of the most populous countries in Western Europe, but its large size—221,000 square miles—means that its population density is low. An unusual feature of French national territorial boundaries is that some overseas territories, such as the Caribbean islands of Guadeloupe and Martinique and the Pacific island of Réunion, are considered an integral part of the country. (They therefore have a fundamentally different status than colonies do.) Their inhabitants are French citizens who enjoy full civil rights and liberties; for example, like other French citizens, they elect representatives to the French legislature to represent their locality.

France's gross national product (GNP) of over $1 trillion and per capita income of $23,500 make the country among the most affluent in the world. Most families own a television, a VCR, a telephone, and an automobile. Half own their own home. France ranked second among the 174 countries of the world in the 2000 UNDP Human Development Index, a widely respected measure of the overall quality of life compiled by the United Nations.

France occupies a key position in Europe, bordering the Mediterranean Sea in the south and sharing borders with northern European countries (Belgium, Switzerland, and Germany) on the north and east, Spain in the southwest, and Italy in the southeast. France is Britain's closest continental neighbor; the two are separated by a mere twenty-five-mile stretch of the English Channel, which became even closer since 1994 with the opening of the "Chunnel," the railroad

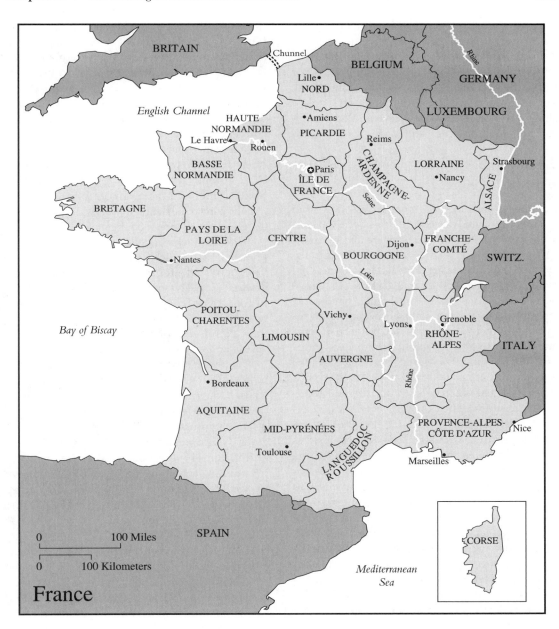

BRITAIN

Chunnel

BELGIUM

GERMANY

Rhine

Lille

NORD

English Channel

HAUTE
NORMANDIE

Amiens

PICARDIE

Reims

LUXEMBOURG

Le Havre

Rouen

LORRAINE

Strasbourg

BASSE
NORMANDIE

Paris
ÎLE DE
FRANCE

CHAMPAGNE-
ARDENNE

Nancy

ALSACE

BRETAGNE

Seine

PAYS DE LA
LOIRE

CENTRE

Dijon

FRANCHE-
COMTÉ

SWITZ.

Nantes

BOURGOGNE

Loire

POITOU-
CHARENTES

Bay of Biscay

Vichy

Lyons

Grenoble

RHÔNE-
ALPES

ITALY

LIMOUSIN

AUVERGNE

Rhône

Bordeaux

AQUITAINE

MID-PYRÉNÉES

LANGUEDOC-
ROUSSILLON

PROVENCE-ALPES-
CÔTE D'AZUR

Nice

Toulouse

Marseilles

CORSE

0   100 Miles

0   100 Kilometers

SPAIN

Mediterranean
Sea

France

tunnel under the English Channel that links the two countries. France has quite secure natural borders of mountains and seas on all sides, save for the open plains of the northeast. The flat, open terrain separating France from Germany enabled German forces to invade France

three times in the nineteenth and twentieth centuries.

France has a modern economy, and the bulk of the population work in the industrial and service sectors. However, agriculture continues to occupy a significant place in the economy, and because the country was predominantly rural until quite recently, an even stronger place in the country's collective memory. Moreover, the proportion of French who live in rural areas and small towns remains high. No other French city comes close to rivaling Paris, the capital, in size and influence, and Paris, Lyons, and Marseilles are the only large cities in France.

Critical Junctures

A central feature of French history—from premodern times to present—has been the centrality of the state. France was created by monarchs who for centuries laboriously knit together the diverse regions and provinces of what is present-day France—actions that provoked periodic protest. The French have often displayed toward the state both enormous respect for its achievements and intense resentment because of its frequently high-handed intrusion into local life. Moreover, the state played the key role in structuring French political life. The pattern of vigorous state activity and popular backlash persisted until recent times. However, the increasing political and economic importance of the EU, as well as decentralization reforms initiated in the 1980s, have jostled the French state's preeminence. Until the 1990s, for better or worse, political attention and energies were exclusively focused on Paris—the national capital and seat of the admired and feared ministries that governed French life. Nowadays, Paris must vie for preeminence with regional and local governments throughout France—as well as Brussels, headquarters of the EU, Frankfurt, where the European Central Bank is located, and Strasbourg, home of the European Parliament.

Creating Modern France

For five centuries at the beginning of the modern era, the area that is now France was part of the Roman Empire. It was called Gaul by the Romans (the source of the term *Gallic*, sometimes used to describe the French). It took its current name from the Franks, a Germanic tribe that conquered the area in the fifth century A.D., with the breakup of the Roman Empire. The Merovingian dynasty ruled France for several centuries, during which time most of the population became Christian. It was succeeded by the Carolingian dynasty, whose most noteworthy ruler, Charlemagne, briefly brought much of West Europe under his control during the Holy Roman Empire in the ninth century.

Following Charlemagne's death, the empire disintegrated. Norsemen from Scandinavia established a duchy in Normandy, in northwest France, from which their ruler, William the Conqueror, led a force that invaded England and defeated English troops at the Battle of Hastings in 1066. (The Bayeux tapestries, woven soon after the invasion and now displayed in the Bayeux museum in Normandy, describe the invasion and battle in rich detail.)

During the next two centuries, a succession of powerful French monarchs patiently and tenaciously sought to unify France against the fierce resistance of powerful provincial rulers and groups in Burgundy, Brittany, and other regions. France was nearly overrun by the English during the Hundred Years' War (1337–1453). Joan of Arc, a peasant, finally led French forces to victory over the invading English army. Along with Charlemagne and a handful of other historic figures, she remains a symbol of intense national pride.

France flourished during the next several centuries, especially after Henri IV (who ruled from 1589 to 1610) ended fierce religious wars between Catholics and Huguenots (Protestants) by issuing the Edict of Nantes in 1598. The edict granted Protestants limited religious toleration. In the sixteenth century, France and England competed in acquiring colonial domination over North America. The rivalry between the two eventually ended with France's defeat, symbolized by the signing of the Treaty of Paris in 1763, when France accepted British domination in North America and India. (At a later period, France engaged in further colonial conquests in Africa, Asia, and the Caribbean.)

The seventeenth and early eighteenth centuries were the high point of French economic, military, and cultural influence throughout the world. France was the most affluent and powerful country in Europe, as evidenced by exquisite chateaux throughout France, some still standing, built by monarchs and aristocrats. France was also the artistic and scientific capital of Europe, home of the Enlightenment in the eighteenth century, the philosophical movement that emphasized the importance of using scientific reason to understand and change the world.

The Ancien Régime

French political life was shaped for centuries by the attempt of French monarchs to undermine local loyalties and foster uniform rules throughout the country. From the seventeenth century, the powerful king Louis XIV (1643–1715) sponsored the creation of a relatively efficient state bureaucracy, separate from the Crown's personal domain and the feudal aristocracy. France began to be administered according to a legal-rational code in which standardized regulations were applied throughout the country. France was a pioneer in developing the absolutist state, which has shaped French development ever since.

But the modernizing, absolutist state created by Louis XIV and other monarchs coexisted with an intricate and burdensome system of feudal privileges that peasants and other common people increasingly resented. Another target of popular discontent was the Catholic Church, a large landowner, tax collector, and ally of the feudal authorities. This complex patchwork of institutions was later called the *ancien régime*, or old regime. (See Table 11.1.) Furthermore, the monarchy collected taxes not only to finance a modern legal and administrative system but also to support the extravagant and wasteful court at Versailles.

Table 11.1 Major French Constititutional Regimes

Ancien régime (Bourbon monarchy)	Until 1789
Revolutionary regimes	1789–1799
Constituent Assembly, 1789–1791	
(Declaration of Rights of Man, August 26, 1789)	
Legislative, 1791	
Convention, 1792–1795: Monarchy abolished and First Republic established, 1792	
Directory	1795–1799
Consulat and First Empire (Napoleon Bonaparte)	1800–1814
Restoration	1814–1830
July Monarchy	1830–1848
Second Republic	1848–1851
Second Empire (Louis Napoleon)	1852–1870
Paris Commune	1870
Third Republic	1870–1940
Vichy regime	1940–1944
Fourth Republic	1946–1958
Fifth Republic	1958–Present

Worse, Louis XIV and his successor, Louis XV, accumulated massive state debts as they pursued a series of military adventures in Europe and colonial conquests overseas. For most of the period from the mid-seventeenth to the mid-eighteenth century, France was at war with its neighbors. As historian Simon Schama notes, "No other European power attempted to support both a major continental army and a transcontinental navy at the same time."[2] France was the most powerful nation in Europe in the seventeenth century. But in the eighteenth century, Britain began to challenge France's preeminence, thanks to the economic advantages that Britain reaped from the Agricultural and Industrial Revolutions. France's stagnant economy could not generate the resources to compete with an increasingly productive England. As a result, the French monarchy had to borrow to compete. By 1788, French state debt was so large that interest on past loans consumed over one-half of current state expenditures.[3] When Louis XVI tried to raise taxes, the bulk of which fell on the common people, the reaction this provoked sealed the fate of the French monarchy.

The Two Faces of the French Revolution, 1789–1815

An angry crowd burst through the gates of Paris's Bastille prison on July 14, 1789, and freed the prisoners, launching the French Revolution. This was soon followed by the toppling of the French monarchy and the entire *ancien régime* of nobility and feudal privileges. The First Republic was proclaimed in 1792. These momentous events marked the beginning of a new era in French and world history. France was the first European nation in which a revolution abolished the monarchy and established a republic based on the belief that all citizens, regardless of social background, were equal before the law. It is difficult to overestimate the impact of the revolution on people's thinking. Historian Lynn Hunt observes, "The chief accomplishment of the French Revolution was the institution of a dramatically new political culture. . . . The French Revolution may be said to represent the transition to political and social modernity, the first occasion when the people entered upon the historical stage to remake the political community."[4]

The revolution was at the same time a *national* revolution, which affirmed the people's right to choose their own political regime; an *international* revolution, which inspired national uprisings elsewhere in Europe and sought to expand French revolutionary values internationally (often through military means); a *liberal* revolution, which championed the value of individual liberty in the political and economic spheres; and a *democratic* revolution, which proclaimed that a nation's identity and the legit-

imacy of its government depend on all citizens having the right to participate in making key political decisions. These provocative ideas have since been diffused on a global level.

The revolution was not without flaws. At the same time that the revolutionary regime was changing the course of world history by proclaiming the values of liberty, equality, and fraternity, it could be harsh and intolerant toward opponents. (At the extreme, during the Reign of Terror, the Revolution guillotined those found guilty by revolutionary tribunals.) Historian Joan Landes has analyzed how, despite some reforms responsive to women's demands (for example, short-lived divorce legislation), the revolutionary ferment was quite hostile to women: "The [First] Republic was constructed against women, not just without them, and nineteenth-century Republicans did not actively counteract this masculinist heritage of republicanism."[5]

In other ways, too, the revolution left a complex legacy. Alexis de Tocqueville, a French aristocrat and writer in the nineteenth century, brilliantly identified two quite opposite faces of the French Revolution: it both produced a rupture with the *ancien régime* and shared the goal pursued by French monarchs of strengthening state institutions. In particular, many of the centralizing institutions created by Napoleon Bonaparte, the popular general who seized power and proclaimed himself emperor in 1802, remain to this day. Napoleon established the system by which state-appointed officials called *prefects* administer localities and the Conseil d'État (State Council), which supervises the central administration. And he promulgated the Napoleonic Code of Law, an elaborate legal framework.

Since Napoleon's defeat and exile in 1815, French politics has often revolved around the question of how to reconcile state autonomy—the state's independence from pressure coming from groups within society—with democratic participation and decision making. Compared to some other successful democracies, notably Britain, France has been less able to combine the two within a stable political regime. The French state successfully developed the capacity to regulate important as well as quite trivial areas of social life. For example, the Ministry of Education tightly controls the curriculum in all public schools; and until quite recently, the Ministry of the Interior kept close watch on the names that local governments assigned to city streets and vetoed proposed changes it disliked. While citizens often sought state help, they also resented its heavy hand and periodically took to the streets in opposition. The result was extensive political instability.

Many Regimes, Slow Industrialization: 1815–1940

France spent much of the nineteenth and twentieth centuries digesting and debating the legacy of the Revolution. The succession of regimes and revolutions for more than a century after 1815 can be interpreted as varied attempts to combine state autonomy and direction with democratic participation and decision making. After Napoleon's final defeat in 1815, there were frequent uprisings, revolutions, and regime changes. The monarchy was restored to power in 1815 but was overthrown in a popular uprising in July 1830, which installed a distant royal cousin, Louis Philippe, as king. In 1848, another revolution produced yet another regime: the short-lived Second Republic. Louis Napoleon, the nephew of Napoleon Bonaparte, overthrew the republic after three years and proclaimed himself emperor. When France lost the Franco-Prussian War of 1870, the Second Empire was swept away by a revolutionary upheaval that produced the Paris Commune, a brief experiment in worker-governed democracy. The Commune was violently crushed after a few months, to be succeeded by the Third Republic, created in 1870 under the shadow of military defeat and civil war.

Despite its less-than-glorious origins and the fact that it never commanded widespread support, the Third Republic turned out to be France's most durable modern regime, lasting until 1940. (The second most durable regime is the current one, the Fifth Republic, which was created in 1958.) The Third Republic was described, in a famous phrase by nineteenth-century sociologist Ernest Renan, as that regime "which divides us [French] least." It was a parliamentary regime with two powerful legislative bodies, the Chamber of Deputies and Senate. Its institutions were designed to prevent decisive leadership, given the recent legacy of Napoleon's illegal seizure of power and the ideologically and fragmented state of French society. Yet the republic survived the terrible ordeal of World War I and held firm against extremist forces on the Right during the 1920s and 1930s, when republics were crumbling in Germany, Italy, and Spain. It was cast aside when France was defeated by Germany in World War II, in part a result of the Third Republic's inability to mount an effective military challenge to the Nazi forces.

The succession of regime changes in the nineteenth and twentieth centuries highlights the existence of sharp cleavages and the absence of political institutions capable of regulating conflict. However, in sharp contrast with the dizzying pace at which regimes came and went, the rate of economic change in France during this period was quite gradual. Compared to Germany, its dynamic neighbor to the northeast, France chose economic stability over modernization.

There have been endless attempts to explain why France did not become an industrial leader in the nineteenth century. Although it began the century as the world's second most important economic power, fairly close to Britain in terms of economic output, by 1900 France trailed the United States, Great Britain, and Germany in industrial development. A large peasantry acted as a brake on industrialization, as did the fact that France was poorly endowed with key natural resources, notably coal, iron, and petroleum. Historians have also pointed to the relatively underdeveloped entrepreneurial spirit in France. Within the ranks of the middle class, professionals, administrators, and shop-keepers outnumbered industrial entrepreneurs. In general, French manufacturers excelled in sectors that did not fuel industrial expansion, notably agricultural produce for local markets and custom-made luxury goods (silk weaving and porcelain), which did not lend themselves to mechanized production and for which mass markets did not exist.

Another factor inhibiting industrial development was the slow growth of the French population. In the middle of the nineteenth century, France was the second most populous nation in Europe (after Russia). However, although the British population more than tripled in the nineteenth century and the number of Germans more than doubled, France's population increased by less than one-half.[6] France had 15 percent of Europe's population in 1800 but only 8 percent in 1950.[7] Slow population growth meant smaller demand and less incentive for businesses to invest and increase productivity.

More important than technical or demographic factors was the role of the state. In Britain, the government removed restrictions on the free operation of market forces, and in Prussia (later Germany), Bismarck imposed industrialization from above. By contrast, the French state aimed to "maintain an equilibrium among industry, commerce, and agriculture and attempt[ed] to insulate France from the distress and upheaval that had struck other nations bent upon rapid economic advance."[8] France retained some of the highest tariff barriers in Western Europe in the nineteenth and early twentieth centuries. The purpose of this protectionist policy was to shield small producers—farmers, manufacturers, and artisans—from foreign competition. Economic historian Richard Kuisel observes that "rarely, if ever, did [the French state] act to promote economic expansion, plan development, or advance economic democracy."[9]

Yet the state did not confine its economic ac-

tivity to purely protectionist purposes. In a tradition that dates back to Colbert, the finance minister of Louis XIV who directed the creation of the French merchant marine, the state sponsored a number of large-scale economic projects. For example, in the 1860s under Louis Napoleon, the state consolidated several small railroad companies and organized an integrated national rail network; encouraged the formation of the Crédit Mobilier, an investment bank to finance railroad development; and guaranteed interest rates on the bonds sold to underwrite railroad construction.

Through much of the nineteenth century and well into the twentieth, however, the state sought to preserve political stability rather than promote economic modernization. Slow economic growth did not prevent political conflict. But it did contribute to France's humiliating defeat by Germany in 1940.

Vichy France (1940–1944) and the Fourth Republic (1946–1958)

World War II was one of the bleakest periods in French history. When France was overrun by Germany in 1940, the Third Republic collapsed, and Marshal Pétain, an aged military hero, signed an armistice that divided France in two. The north was under direct German occupation; the south was controlled by a puppet regime, whose capital was at Vichy, presided over by Pétain. The Vichy government collaborated with the Nazi occupation by providing workers and supplies for the German war machine. It had the dubious distinction of being the only political regime in Western Europe that delivered Jews to the Nazis from areas not directly under German occupation. About 76,000 Jews, including 12,000 children, were sent to Nazi death camps. Vichy not only failed to protect foreign Jews who had fled to French soil for asylum but organized its own program of imprisoning French Jews and sending them to Nazi concentration camps.

Although the vast majority of French quietly accepted France's defeat and meekly complied with the Vichy government's directives, a small resistance movement developed within France. Charles de Gaulle, a prominent general in the Third Republic, publicly broke with Vichy and advocated armed opposition to the regime. He assumed leadership over communist, socialist, and progressive Catholic opposition forces and consolidated them into what became known as the Resistance. Although France actually contributed little to the Allied victory—indeed, it provided labor and materiel to help the Nazi war effort—de Gaulle's skillful actions enabled France to gain acceptance as a member of the victorious coalition and obtain one of the five permanent seats on the United Nations Security Council following the war.

To salvage French honor after World War II, de Gaulle helped create the myth of a broad and powerful Resistance movement against Pétain. In fact, the Vichy regime had encountered little opposition, and the Resistance was quite limited. Most French citizens, including the vast majority of civil servants, had cooperated with the Vichy regime. It took fully half a century after the end of the war for a French president to apologize publicly, in the name of the state, for the crimes committed by the Vichy regime. In 1995, President Jacques Chirac declared in a public address, "Those dark hours will forever tarnish our history and are a disgrace to our past and to our tradition. We all know that the criminal madness of the occupying forces [the Nazis] was assisted by the French, that is, the French state." Until then, postwar presidents had criticized individuals who cooperated with the Nazi regime but had not acknowledged the French state's responsibility.

It has taken decades for the French to grasp the extent that public and private authorities, as well as ordinary citizens, collaborated with the Nazi regime—more so in France than in any other country in Western Europe. In 1998, an opportunity was provided when Maurice Papon, a former official of the Vichy regime—who later exercised high administrative and political positions in the Fourth and Fifth Republics—was tried for complicity in crimes against humanity. The Papon trial provided an intensive opportunity for millions of French to learn the shameful record of the Vichy period. Journalist Adam Gopnik observed, "The Papon trial was the central, binding event of the . . . year in France, a kind of O.J. trial without television or a glove. It was the longest, the most discouraging, the most moving, at times the most ridiculous, and certainly the most fraught trial in postwar French history."[10]

In 1945, following the Nazi defeat, de Gaulle sought to sponsor a regime that would avoid the errors that in his view had weakened France and contributed to its moral decline and defeat by Germany. He believed that the institutional design of the Third Republic, in which the executive was completely dependent on parliament, blurred the responsibility for governing and prevented forceful leadership. He proposed creating a regime in which the government was independent and powerful.

De Gaulle at first failed in this attempt. Having just overthrown the authoritarian Vichy regime, French citizens opposed creating a new republic with a strong executive. De Gaulle abruptly resigned as leader of the provisional regime drafting a new constitution and mounted an unsuccessful campaign against the new republic that resulted. The constitution of the newly created Fourth Republic was in fact very similar to that of the Third Republic.

The Fourth Republic, which survived for a dozen years (1946–1958), embodied an extreme form of parliamentary rule and weak executive. The constitution gave parliament a near-monopoly of power, which it exercised in a quite destructive fashion: governments were voted out of office an average of once every six months! This situation was in part due to the fact that many parties were represented in parliament because the National Assembly, the powerful lower house, was selected by proportional representation. As in the Third Republic, rapid shifts in party alliances, as well as a lack of discipline within parties, meant that governments lacked the cohesion and authority to make tough decisions and develop long-range policies. Although the Fourth Republic was often described as highly unstable, the situation might better be described as one of political stalemate.

Neither the Vichy regime nor the Fourth Republic satisfactorily combined state direction and democratic participation. By their opposite excesses, they underlined the need for devising a new constitutional framework that would promote stable, democratic rule.

Despite some important achievements, notably setting France on the road to economic expansion and modernization, the Fourth Republic was unable to take decisive action in many important spheres. The regime was severely handicapped by the fact that powerful political forces, notably the Communist Party and de Gaulle's political movement, were well represented in parliament and strongly opposed one government after another. The Fourth Republic's failure to crush the Algerian independence movement, which opposed French domination of the North African colony, provided de Gaulle with the opportunity to regain power. By threatening to lead a military rebellion against the republic, he pressured parliament to authorize him to scrap the constitution and propose a new constitutional framework more to his liking. The constitution of the Fifth Republic, drafted under his direction, provided for a vastly strengthened executive and weakened parliament.

The Fifth Republic (1958 to the Present)

The contrast between the Fourth and Fifth republics provides a textbook case of how institutions shape political life. The Fourth Republic could be described, unkindly but accurately, as an example of all talk and no action: While parliament endlessly debated, and voted to make and unmake governments, elected political leaders did little to address the nation's pressing problems. On the other hand, the Fifth Republic created institutions in which leaders could act decisively but, at least in the early years, were hardly accountable to parliament or public opinion.

The history of the Fifth Republic is closely linked to the growth of the European Union (first known as the European Economic Community), which was created one year before the birth of the Fifth Republic. The European Union (EU), as it later came to be known, helped to knit together historic rivals France and Germany, foster economic growth, and increase Europe's economic and political role internationally. The growing economic and political integration of Europe, thanks in significant measure to French leadership within the EU, represents a fundamental change after centuries of intense conflicts within Europe. The Fifth Republic has reaped handsome benefits from the growth of the EU.

Although de Gaulle became first president of the Fifth Republic in the unsavory circumstances of a possible military intervention, he was able to command wide popular support because of his historic position. Resistance hero, commanding presence, and one of the political giants of the twentieth century, de Gaulle was able to persuade the French to support a regime in which democratic participation was strictly limited. He defended the new constitution on the grounds that a parliamentary regime along the lines of the Fourth Republic or the British Westminster model was not appropriate for a country as divided as France. Although the new constitution was approved by a large majority in a popular referendum, de Gaulle's high-handed governing style and the centralized institutions of the Fifth Republic eventually provoked widespread opposition. The most dramatic example was in May 1968, when students and workers engaged in the largest general strike in West European history. At the height of the May uprising, half of France's workers and a larger proportion of students were on strike. For weeks, workers and students occupied factories, offices, and universities, and the regime's survival hung in the balance. Although de Gaulle temporarily regained control of the situation, he was discredited and resigned from office the following year.

The Fifth Republic was severely tested once again in 1981. Until then, the same broad political coalition, representing conservative forces, that took power in 1958 won every single national election. In 1981, the Socialist Party candidate, François Mitterrand, was elected president, and in the parliamentary elections that followed, his allies swamped the conservative coalition. Despite fears that the Fifth Republic would not be able to survive a socialist government, the institutions of the Fifth Republic proved highly successful at accommodating political alternation.

President Mitterrand's Socialist government

"What!?? The president's a Socialist and the Eiffel Tower is still standing!??" "Incredible!"

Source: Courtesy Plantu, Cartoonists & Writers Syndicate, from *Le Monde*.

sponsored one of the most ambitious reform agendas in modern French history, including changes that strengthened the autonomy of the judiciary, the media, and local governments. The centerpiece was a substantial increase in the number of industrial firms and financial institutions in the public sector. However, by seeking to extend the sphere of public control of the economy, France was swimming against the international economic and political tide. During the 1980s, the predominant tendency elsewhere in the industrialized world was to strengthen private market forces rather than extend public control. (Margaret Thatcher in Britain and Ronald Reagan in the United States were elected to leadership positions at nearly the same time that Mitterrand captured the French presidency.) When the Socialist experiment began to provoke an economic and financial crisis in 1983–1984, the government reluctantly decided to reverse course. Since then, French governments of Left and Right alike have generally pursued market-friendly policies. As a result, the ideological war of Left and Right in France, which raged for centuries, has declined. Since the 1980s, frequent changes in the governing coalition have occurred, but there has been extensive continuity in economic policy.

Does the convergence between the major political parties of Center-Left and Center-Right mean the end of major political conflict in France? Not at all. Several new issues have emerged to divide the French electorate and challenge French political institutions.

France in the Euro Era: Decline or Renewal?

Although no single event can be identified as a critical juncture in the first years of the new millennium, it may be appropriate to single out France's increasingly close involvement in the EU, highlighted by the adoption of the euro, for special mention. In the 1970s, political scientist Stanley Hoffmann described France's dilemma as "decline or renewal?" The same words can be used to identify the dilemma that the euro was designed to address.[11] The euro symbolizes the powerful way that France's fate is now so intensely intertwined with that of the EU. Few national symbols are as important as a country's currency. Since the creation in 1991 of the Economic and Monetary Union (EMU) as a key element of the Maastricht Treaty, which deepened the process of European integration, most member states of the EU have been moving toward introducing the euro, at first alongside and eventually in place of their own national currencies. At first merely a bookkeeping device, the euro assumed physical form in 2002 when actual bank notes and coins entered into circulation. Beyond the fact of the euro stands the fact that France is now deeply enmeshed in the institutions and policies of the EU. Although the process of European integration has been occurring ever since the creation of the European Coal and Steel Community in 1950, the adoption of the euro in the current period may well signify the tipping of the balance toward Europe in a way that qualifies as a critical juncture.

Along with Germany and several smaller European countries, France helped form the EU to promote economic growth and political stability. Indeed, France played a key role in the early 1980s in reviving momentum toward European integration. Has French membership achieved that aim? The answer is mixed. On the one hand, as Chapter 12 will analyze, although the French economy has been flourishing, it can hardly be qualified as a complete success. Our major focus in this book is on political developments. And on that score, the news seems even less promising. A cluster of recent developments produces the impression of political instability and even crisis within French politics. One ingredient is the rapid-fire series of electoral shifts that have occurred. From 1986 to 2001, there were six presidential and parliamentary elections in France. In every single one, control shifted from the ruling coalition to the opposition. For example, two years after electing conservative Jacques Chirac to the presidency in 1995, voters elected a socialist parliamentary

majority headed by Lionel Jospin. As a result, Jospin became prime minister and shared executive power with a considerably weakened President Chirac. Voters thus are quick to demonstrate their displeasure with the "ins"— although it does not take them long to register their displeasure with the new ruling coalition! A second ingredient is that an endless series of political scandals has tarnished the reputation of many leading politicians, including party leaders, cabinet ministers, and the two most recent presidents (Mitterrand, president from 1981 to 1995, and Chirac, elected in 1995). Third, a growing number of French citizens have turned against the major governing parties of both left and right, preferring to abstain or support fringe parties. Fourth, many scholars assert that underlying these changes is the fact that the French political system is unable to deal effectively with pressing social and economic challenges, declining but persistently high levels of unemployment, French participation in the EU, and the meaning of French national identity in an era of globalization.

Themes and Implications

Our analysis of the evolution of French development has identified some key turning points in French history. We can gain greater clarity on French politics by highlighting the distinctive ways that France has addressed the four key themes that provide a framework for analyzing European politics in transition.

Historical Junctures and Political Themes

Analyzing the four themes that frame *European Politics in Transition* suggests how important is the current transition in French politics. The situation in France has changed quite dramatically within the past decade with respect to every one of the four.

France in a World of States. France's relationship to the rest of Europe and other regions of the world, particularly Asia and Africa, has heavily shaped state formation. For over a century following Napoleon's defeat in 1815, the country displayed an inward-oriented, isolationist orientation. For example, France erected high tariff barriers throughout the nineteenth century and first half of the twentieth century to minimize international trade. Nevertheless, it participated aggressively in the new imperialism of the late nineteenth century, creating a new French empire in Southeast Asia, North and sub-Saharan Africa, and the Pacific. For close to a century, France exploited the mineral and other resources of its colonies with little regard for their own development. But the arrangement also spared France from competing in the global economy, which contributed to its relatively slow pace of technological and industrial development.

France's tortured relationship with Germany—the two fought three devastating wars in less than a century—has weighed heavily on state development. The fact that the two countries developed cordial relations after World War II, in part thanks to the mutually beneficial expansion of the European and world economy, has provided France with a vastly increased measure of security. The alliance between the two countries has been vital in promoting closer European economic and political integration within the EU. At the same time, France and Germany continue to compete, although now it takes the form of economic rivalry between business firms rather than military confrontation.

No longer in the first rank militarily, France remains an important player on the world stage. For example, it is a major nuclear power and among the world's leading arms exporters. France has been an important participant in the Western alliance led by the United States. But in contrast to Britain and Germany, for example, France has often been a gadfly to the United States. For example, under President de Gaulle's leadership, France withdrew from the military command structure of the North Atlantic Treaty Organization in the 1960s and ordered U.S. troops stationed in France to leave. Similarly, when in 1998 the United States launched air strikes against Iraq because of President Saddam Hussein's refusal to allow access to U.N. weapons inspectors, Britain participated alongside the United States, and Japan and Germany supported the action. France registered public opposition (although less intensely than did China and Russia).

The French state has been a powerful, capable instrument helping the country adapt to the challenges posed by global economic competition. In recent decades, the state skillfully promoted internationally acclaimed high-tech industrial projects, including high-speed rail travel (the TGV), leadership in the European consortium that developed an efficient wide-bodied airplane (the Airbus), an electronic telephone directory and data bank (the Minitel), and relatively safe and cheap nuclear power plants. The fact that the French state has played such a key role in nation building and in economic and cultural development is why, as one observer notes, "No other nation in the world has as dense and passionate a relationship with the State as does France."[12] Yet France's statist tradition is under siege as a result of increased international economic integration and competition, highlighted by French participation in the EU, as well as ideological shifts and citizens' demands for more autonomy.

Governing the Economy. Our discussion of France's statist tradition is useful in understanding the way that France organizes governance of the economy. In the period following World War II, the French pioneered in developing methods to steer and strengthen the economy. As a result of planning, state loans and subsidies to private business, and crash programs to develop key economic sectors (e.g., the steel industry), the French economy soared. However, state direction has created problems in the current era, when rapidly changing technology and economic globalization put a premium on flexibility. The French state can be compared to a stately ocean liner that can move powerfully once the direction has been set but has great difficulty changing course.

The Democratic Idea. France has had a complex relationship to the democratic idea. On the one hand, its deeply rooted statist tradition is quite hostile to democratic participation and decision making. On the other hand, France has been deeply attached to two divergent democratic currents. The first dates back to eighteenth-century philosopher Jean-Jacques Rousseau. The theory of direct democracy that Rousseau inspired claims that citizens should participate directly in political decisions rather than merely choose leaders who monopolize political power.

A second powerful democratic current in French political culture, fearful that direct democracy can culminate in demagogic leadership, stresses the value of representative democracy. Many opponents of de Gaulle criticized him for violating the representative democratic tradition and furthering *le pouvoir personnel* (personal power). The parliamentary tradition opposes anything that smacks of direct democracy. It advocates instead delegating power to the people's elected representatives in parliament.

Despite their great differences, the two democratic traditions share with each other and with the statist tradition an important common feature, one that could be considered a central pillar of French political culture until recently. All three have traditionally opposed the concept of a written constitution, interpreted by an independent judiciary, limiting state power. The French have rarely viewed a constitution with the reverence many Americans feel toward the U.S. Constitution. And they have even more vehemently opposed an independent judiciary limiting the executive and legislature. A key change in French political culture since the 1970s has been the development of widespread support for the Constitution of the Fifth Republic and the right of the Constitutional Council to strike down governmental decisions as contrary to the Constitution.

France's democratic theory and institutions face important challenges. One problem stems from French participation in the EU, which exhibits what has been dubbed a "democratic deficit," that is, too much administrative direction and too little democratic participation and representation. Another strain derives from the continuing difficulty of reconciling state autonomy and democratic participation within France. For example, as we shall analyze in Chapter 13, the French executive centralizes enormous powers and exhibits a relative lack of accountability. The kind of democratic deficit that many assert is a weakness of the EU may also be said to characterize France's own political system.

Politics of Collective Identity. French national identity has always been closely linked to state formation. The Revolution championed the idea that anyone who accepted republican values could become French. The French approach to citizenship and national identity encourages immigrants to become French citizens on condition that they accept dominant cultural and political values. Such an approach stresses that what binds people are shared political values rather than common racial or ethnic (i.e., inherited) characteristics.

At the same time, the French have been quite strongly divided by social, economic, and cultural cleavages. There has long been a working-class subculture, closely linked to the powerful French Communist Party (Parti communiste français—PCF), as well as a Catholic subculture, in which the Church played a key role. In recent decades, these subcultures have declined in importance. Occupational shifts, notably a drastic decline in blue-collar jobs and the rapid expansion of a white-collar service sector, have blurred class boundaries. During this period, the PCF went from being one of France's most powerful parties to a minor party. There has also been a dramatic decline in religious observance. As a result, the Catholic Church is no longer a powerful source of collective identity.

In the realm of collective identity, then, the legacy of the past weighs less heavily than in other areas. The whole issue of citizenship and collective identity has been complicated by economic difficulties and immigration. While class cleavages have declined, the relentless operation of market forces means that many French lead a precarious existence, for example, the long-term unemployed or those engaged in part-time or temporary work. In the past, major socioeconomic (class), ideological, and cultural (religious) cleavages were closely aligned with partisan (political party) cleavages. Nowadays, major issues, such as attitudes toward Europe and the globalized economy, often split partisan groupings. The result is that durable identities inherited from the past have declined in importance and have not been replaced by stable new collective identities.[13]

At the same time, the traditional pattern of French national identity has been challenged, with conflict fueled recently by ethnic differences and globalization. After World War II, French economic reconstruction and industrialization were fueled by a large wave of immigrants from North Africa. Although immigration was severely restricted following the economic slowdown in the 1970s, the issue of immigrants and their status in French society erupted into the political arena in the 1980s and 1990s. A new political party, the National Front, gained widespread support by blaming many of France's problems, especially unemployment, urban decay, and crime, on immigrants and their children. At the same time, many children whose parents were immigrants consider themselves fully French yet refuse to conform to dominant cultural norms. They have affirmed their pride in being Algerian and Muslim, demanding cultural autonomy and the right to be different in their dress, food, and religious practice.

French national identity is also jostled by French participation in the EU and, more broadly, an opening of France's geographic and cultural horizons as a result of globalization. (Recall the Nice summit demonstrations described at the beginning of this chapter.) Decisions affecting French citizens are increasingly made outside France—by officials in Brussels, Belgium, headquarters of the EU, and by corporate executives and bankers in Frankfurt, London, New York, and Tokyo. The French can no longer believe what was always to some extent a myth: that they lived in a self-contained world that they refer to (because of France's geographic boundaries) as the hexagon. At the same time, France participates vigorously in shaping decisions made outside its borders. Along with Britain and Germany, France is one of the "big three" of the EU and a world-class economic competitor. A key issue is how effectively France will confront the challenge of closer integration in the European and world political economy.

Implications for Comparative Politics

The study of French politics potentially offers rich lessons for the study of comparative politics. France has continually tried to reshape its destiny by conscious political direction, and it provides a natural laboratory in which to test the importance of variations in institutional design. To illustrate, comparativists debate the impact of diverse electoral procedures. Since French electoral procedures (along with many other features of political institutions) have often changed in a brief period, comparativists can make fine-grained comparison of the impact of institutional variation.

At a more general level, the French have often looked to the state to achieve important economic and political goals. In countries without a statist tradition (for example, the United States and Britain), private groups rely to a greater extent on their own efforts. What can we learn from comparing the two approaches? What are the strengths and weaknesses of statism?

France also provides a fascinating case of a country that seeks to combine a strong state and strong democracy. The French do not believe that a state that acts vigorously need be undemocratic. In practice, however, combining the two is no easy matter. How successful is the French attempt? What can it teach people about this issue?

As a leading participant in the EU, France provides students of comparative politics with an excellent case of a country seeking to forge close economic and political ties with its neighbors while retaining an important measure of autonomy. The EU is an extraordinary experiment in regional cooperation. But participation involves costs as well as benefits. What kinds of strains have been produced within France as a result of its membership in the EU? How effectively has France been able to shape EU institutions?

A place to begin our analysis of current French politics is with France's political economy, for the way that a country engages in economic management deeply influences the functioning of its political system.

Notes

1. This account of the Nice summit is based on participant observations and unpublished material kindly provided by Gérard Alezard and Jacques Capdevielle.

2. Simon Schama, *Citizens: A Chronicle of the French Revolution* (New York: Knopf, 1989), p. 62.

3. Perry Anderson, *Lineages of the Absolutist State* (London: New Left Books, 1974), p. 111. This section also draws on Theda Skocpol, *States and Social Revolutions: A Comparative Analysis of France, Russia, and China* (New York: Cambridge University Press, 1979).

4. Lynn Hunt, *Politics, Culture, and Class in the French Revolution* (Berkeley: University of California Press, 1984), pp. 15, 56.

5. Joan B. Landes, *Women and the Public Sphere in the Age of the French Revolution* (Ithaca, N.Y.: Cornell University Press, 1988), pp. 171–172.

6. William H. Sewell, Jr., *Work and Revolution in France: The Language of Labor from the Old Regime to 1848* (Cambridge: Cambridge University Press, 1980), p. 199.

7. Georges Dupeux, *La société française, 1789–1970* (Paris: Armand Colin, 1974), p. 10.

8. Richard F. Kuisel, *Capitalism and the State in Modern France* (Cambridge: Cambridge University Press, 1981), p. 15.

9. Ibid., p. 16.

10. Adam Gopnik, *Paris to the Moon* (New York: Random House, 2000), p. 107.

11. Stanley Hoffmann, *Decline or Renewal? France Since the 1930s* (New York: Viking, 1974).

12. Laurence Ménière, ed., *Bilan de la France, 1981–1993* (Paris: Hachette, 1993), p. 12.

13. Pierre Brechon, Annie Laurent, and Pascal Perrineau, eds., *Les Cultures politiques des Français* (Paris: Presses des Sciences Po, 2000), *passim*.

C H A P T E R

12

Political Economy and Development

France is one of the world's leading economic powers. It has the fourth highest gross national product, ranks fourth in terms of world trade, and is the second largest importer and exporter of capital. A key to understanding France's successful economic performance is the vigorous role that the state plays.

During the early period of industrialization in Western Europe, from the late eighteenth century through the nineteenth century, the French state pursued a quite distinctive goal compared to the British and German states. Along with the United States, these nations were the world's leading economic powers in the nineteenth century. In Britain, the world's first industrialized power, the state sought to remove restrictions on the free operation of market forces. In Prussia (which consolidated neighboring states to form Germany in 1871), the state fostered industrialization from above. The French state, by contrast, aimed to "maintain an equilibrium among industry, commerce, and agriculture and attempt[ed] to insulate France from the distress and upheaval that had struck other nations bent upon rapid economic advance."[1] This situation could last only so long as the state was able to protect France's economy and the nation from external threat. However, this became increasingly difficult and eventually proved impossible. The low point was reached when the Third Republic collapsed, and Marshal Henri Pétain signed an armistice with

the Nazi regime that signified France's virtually total defeat.

The Postwar Settlement and Beyond

When France was liberated and the Fourth Republic was created in 1946, influential groups concluded that the state had to seek economic modernization. At this time, a fundamental transformation occurred in the state's relationship to the economy. "After the war," economic historian Richard Kuisel observes, "what was distinctive about France was the compelling sense of relative economic backwardness. This impulse was the principal stimulus for economic renovation and set France apart from other countries."[2] Two scholars have described the postwar shift as "a new French Revolution. Although peaceful, this has been just as profound as that of 1789 because it has totally overhauled the moral foundations and social equilibrium of French society."[3]

State and Economy

The new French Revolution ushered in sweeping changes in the economy, society, and values. As a result of its long statist tradition, France was potentially well equipped to develop the institutional capacity to steer the economy. Kuisel describes the French state's approach as follows:

France resembled other capitalist countries in developing an arsenal of institutions for managing the economy. . . . Yet France found its own way to perform these tasks. It lodged responsibility in new public institutions and staffed them with modernizers. It relied heavily on state intervention and planning. . . . The result was a Gallic style of economic management that blended state direction, corporatist bodies, and market forces.[4]

From guardian of the established order, the state became the sponsor of social and economic progress. For example, it began to provide cradle-to-the-grave social services, including family subsidies, day care facilities, old-age pensions, public health care, unemployment insurance, and public housing. The French welfare state eventually became one of the most extensive in the world. The state exercised its new role in several ways.

Planning

Soon after World War II, the French developed what they called *indicative planning*. A national Planning Commission, comprising civil servants appointed by the government, set national economic and social priorities for the next four or five years. The Planning Commission was assisted by modernization commissions, comprising public and private officials, which established targets for specific economic and social sectors. Successive plans sought to establish the maximum feasible rates of economic growth, propose crash programs for the development of specific industries and regions, and identify high-priority social goals such as educational targets. The state then used the plan as a basis for setting legislative and budgetary priorities. Perhaps more important than the specific goals that were pursued was that planning helped change France's political culture. The process of planning fostered the belief that change was to be welcomed, a sharp contrast to the past conservative pattern.[5]

Planning developed broad support in part because it was not imposed in a heavy-handed fashion. In contrast to many of France's traditionally large, top-heavy bureaucracies, the planning agency was a small, flexible agency, staffed by dynamic, young problem solvers. Unlike Soviet-style planning, French plans were not legally binding but were the product of an informal consensus among public and private officials. The planning process provided a way to share information and streamline economic decision making.

The process did not represent interests equally. At its core, it encouraged the formation of a close alliance between the state and dynamic producer interests, especially large, technologically advanced firms seeking to compete in world markets. The interests of small businesses, trade unions, and consumers were largely ignored. Critics charged, quite correctly, that planning was undemocratic because important decisions affecting France's future were made behind closed doors and important voices were excluded from the planning process.

Dirigisme *Under de Gaulle*

Planning began in the Fourth Republic, but the first steps were halting and uncertain. Vigorous leadership to overcome conservative forces opposing change was provided after 1958, when Charles de Gaulle, the most influential politician in twentieth-century French history, regained power and created the Fifth Republic.

De Gaulle was a complex, controversial, and contradictory figure. On the one hand, he was a faithful representative of traditional France, deeply attached to the values of order and hierarchy, which earned him the enmity of the Left. On the other hand, his personal leadership and the republic that he created provided the force to undermine traditional forces and restructure the French political economy.

Economic Management

General de Gaulle's return to power in 1958 ushered in a period of state-led industrialization and growth based on a distinctive pattern of indicative planning. The state bureaucracy expanded the scope of its activity and developed specific instruments to promote economic modernization. The state steered cheap credit toward favored sectors and firms, and in key industrial sectors it encouraged the creation of large firms, which later came to be called "national champions." The French described the new relationship between the state and economy as *dirigiste* (directorial), which highlights the state's importance in steering the economy. Many key economic decisions were made in governmental ministries, especially the Ministries of Finance, Economy, and Industry, as well as the planning agency. The state thus stepped in to compensate for the relatively weak role played by private entrepreneurs.

Four key elements of the *dirigiste* approach can be identified. First, the French state engaged in intensive efforts to coordinate economic policymaking through the planning process, the government, the Ministry of Finance, and other agencies.

Second, the state used subsidies, loans, and tax write-offs to achieve its economic goals, such as industrial concentration, specialization in new fields, and technological innovation. For much of the postwar period, the state provided the bulk of capital for new investment, limited the outflow of French capital, created a host of parapublic banking institutions, and closely regulated private bank loans. The central aim was to provide "favored sectors with access to credit at subsidized rates."[6] The other side of the coin (given the lack of private sources of business credit) was that inefficient firms or firms located in sectors to which the state assigned low priority were unable to obtain state financial assistance.

Third, as we have seen, the state developed plans to restructure specific sectors, including steel, machine tools, and paper products. The Ministry of Industry pressured medium-sized industrial firms to merge in order to create "national champions" able to compete in world markets. These giant firms were privileged partners of the state and received ample resources to

ensure their success. Fourth, the state created and managed entire new industries in sectors where it decided that private enterprise was not up to the job. Some of these state-created and -managed firms were in the vanguard of technological progress throughout the world. In sum, in the French economic model, the state was a (indeed, *the*) chief economic player.[7]

France's Economic Miracle. During the period one French economist has called "the thirty glorious years" (1945–1975), the planners and their allies were remarkably successful. The rate of French economic growth was among the highest of any European nation and second only to that of Japan, a striking contrast with the 1930s, when the French economy declined at the rate of over 1 percent annually.[8] (See Table 12.1.) Economic growth made for higher living standards. The average French citizen's income nearly tripled between 1946 and 1962, producing a wholesale transformation of consumer patterns.[9] For example, between 1946 and 1962, the proportion of homes with running water more than doubled. The number of automobiles registered in France increased from under 5 million in 1959 to 14 million in 1973. The number

Table 12.1 Average Growth Rates in Gross National Product, 1958–1973

Japan	10.4%
France	5.5
Italy	5.3
West Germany	5.0
Belgium	4.9
Netherlands	4.2
Norway	4.2
Sweden	4.1
United States	4.1
United Kingdom	3.2

Source: Bela Belassa, "The French Economy under the Fifth Republic, 1958–1978," in *The Fifth Republic at Twenty,* ed. William G. Andrews and Stanley Hoffmann (Albany: State University of New York Press, 1981), p. 209.

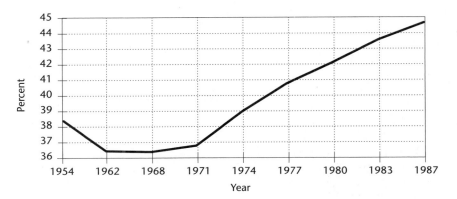

Figure 12.1   Women in the Labor Force

Source: INSEE, in Louis Dirn, *La Société française en tendances* (Paris: PUF, 1990), p. 108.

of housing units built annually increased from 290,000 to 500,000 during the same period. In sum, after a century of economic stagnation, France leapfrogged into the twentieth century.

May 1968 and Beyond: Economic Crisis and Political Conflict. Despite the dramatic economic growth of the 1950s and 1960s, many resented the way that economic restructuring had been carried out. Political scientist Peter A. Hall identified a central dilemma in the planning process: "The reorganization of production to attain great[er] efficiency tends to intensify the social conflict that planning is also supposed to prevent."[10] The most dramatic evidence of the regime's fragility occurred in a massive wave of unrest in May 1968. The opposition movement was triggered by a variety of causes: government-imposed wage restraint, the reduction of trade union representation on the governing boards of the social security (public health) system, and the rapid expansion of higher education. (Universities had been hastily constructed, and students received little guidance.)

May 1968 was a massive movement of diverse groups united in their opposition to the way that a distant state was deciding their fate with little grass-roots consultation or participa-

tion. The movement ushered in a period of intense labor mobilization. Strikes in the early 1970s were frequent and often involved highly militant tactics, such as seizing factories, sequestering managers, and even organizing production directly. Striking workers challenged harsh authority in the workplace, speedups in the pace of work, and technological innovations that increased workplace hazards. A rapid increase in female employment beginning in the early 1970s (see Figure 12.1) also produced some important strikes when women protested unequal treatment.

As a result of their militance, workers gained increased rights and benefits, and the state and employers' associations sought to achieve stability by organizing collective bargaining at industrywide and national levels. But a political challenge from the Left and widening economic crisis thwarted these efforts.

In 1972, the two largest left-wing opposition parties, the Communist Party (Parti Communiste français, PCF) and the Socialist Party (reformed and renamed the Parti socialiste—PS—in 1969), forged a coalition that seemed poised to gain power. The alliance, named the Union of the Left, advocated substantial economic and social changes, notably increasing the number of state-owned banks and industrial firms, labor law reform, and increased social welfare spending.

Economic Instability. The Left's fortunes were further improved because economic strains in the 1970s tarnished the reputation of the governing conservative coalition. First, when the substantial shift of workers out of agriculture and from rural to urban areas began to reach its limit, gains in productivity began to slow. Furthermore, France was badly damaged by international economic shocks in the 1970s. Heavily dependent on imported oil, France was squeezed when petroleum prices increased sharply in the 1970s. The restructuring of international capitalism in the 1970s damaged French industry in two ways. On the one hand, developing nations, such as Taiwan, South Korea, and Brazil, began to outcompete France in such basic industrial sectors as textiles, steel, and shipbuilding. French firms not only became less competitive internationally but also lost substantial shares of the domestic market to foreign competition. Hundreds of thousands of jobs were eliminated in these three industries alone; for example, more than one-third of all steelworkers were permanently laid off. Entire regions were devastated.

On the other hand, the French economy was battered by technological advances achieved by other industrialized nations. France was too small to be a world leader in microelectronics, bioengineering, and robotics, and U.S. and Japanese producers rapidly captured markets in these fields. Thus, at the very time that the country needed to generate increased exports in order to finance the increased costs of petroleum, French firms were losing export markets to the fastest-growing Third World nations, where wage costs were low, and importing high technology from advanced capitalist leaders.

These trends provoked a crisis in the French model of development. The postwar approach was highly successful in sponsoring crash programs for industrial reconstruction and mod-

ernization. But in the new, more competitive world, it was necessary to adapt rapidly, decentralize economic decision making, and outcompete foreign firms. Success today is achieved by creative breakthroughs, not emulation. The inadequacy of the postwar approach was driven home by the Socialist government in the early 1980s.

French Socialism in Practice—and Conservative Aftermath. After conservative governments failed to meet the economic challenges of the 1970s, the Left finally gained the chance to try. A new era began in 1981, when the Socialist and Communist parties gained power after twenty-three years in opposition. François Mitterrand soundly defeated incumbent president Valéry Giscard d'Estaing in the 1981 presidential election.

Immediately on gaining office, Mitterrand dissolved the conservative-dominated National Assembly. Capitalizing on Mitterrand's popu-

"It's touching to see all these graduates."
(ANPE is the state employment office.)

Source: Courtesy Plantu, Cartoonists & Writers Syndicate, from *Le Monde*.

larity, the Socialist Party obtained an absolute majority of seats, giving the government a free hand to enact its reform proposals. The Socialist government sponsored a range of economic measures to revive the ailing economy, create jobs, and recapture domestic markets. The major reforms were as follows:

- A hefty boost in social benefits, including increases in the minimum wage, family allowances, old-age pensions, rent subsidies, and state-mandated paid vacations (from four to five weeks each year)
- The creation of public sector employment
- A vigorous industrial policy, including state assistance to develop cutting-edge industrial technologies (including biotech, telecommunications, and aerospace)
- A hefty expansion of nationalization in the industrial and banking sectors

On two previous occasions French governments had extended public control over the economy: the Socialist government of Léon Blum during the Popular Front of 1936–1938 and in 1946 after the end of World War II. Between 1981 and 1983, the Socialist government went further. As a result of the nationalization measures, public sector firms accounted for 28 percent of gross domestic production (an increase of 7 percent), 23 percent of French exports (compared to the previous level of 11 percent), and 36 percent of investments (from 29 percent).[11] Thirteen of France's twenty largest industrial firms and virtually all banks were now in the public sector.

The Socialist approach was a radicalized version of the postwar *dirigiste* approach, supplemented by newly created mechanisms for increasing participation by rank-and-file workers and labor unions in economic decision making. For example, labor unions gained greater rights on the shop floor and at higher levels, and procedures were created for worker consultation on production processes, technology, and occupational health and safety.

Many French citizens reaped significant benefits from the Socialist program, and many of the newly nationalized firms, which were in financial difficulties when they were nationalized, were put on a firmer footing thanks to the infusion of government subsidies. But the program failed in one decisive respect: It did not revive economic growth, which was needed to create new jobs and generate the revenues for the added government spending. There were two reasons. First, French business executives and international investors were hostile to the government's policy orientation. Rather than investing in French industry, they exported capital to safe havens abroad. Second, an international economic recession in the early 1980s meant that French firms had difficulty exporting their products, whereas the benefits distributed by French government spending were often used to buy foreign imports. In brief, many of the benefits from the government reforms were reaped by foreign firms.

Many of the Socialist reforms helped to modernize the French economy, society, and state in the long run. However, in the short run, the cost of the reforms provoked a severe economic crisis that drove France to the brink of bankruptcy. Budget deficits soared, international investors avoided France like the plague, and France's international currency reserves were rapidly exhausted. Something had to give—and fast.

The crisis cruelly demonstrated how limited was the margin of maneuver for a medium-rank power like France. Mitterrand's government was soon forced to choose between reversing its reformist course or adopting strong protectionist measures to shield France from international pressures. The latter strategy involved high risks, because it would require France to pull out of European Union (EU) monetary arrangements, and it would doubtless provoke international isolation, especially since conservative-minded leaders held office in Washington, Bonn, and London at the time. After intense soul searching, Mitterrand ordered a complete about-face in economic policy in 1983. The decision to turn back from radical statism was one of the most important made within the Fifth Republic and set France on a conservative course from which it has not departed since.

France's failure to achieve autonomous development in the early 1980s has had profound ideological and policy consequences, both within France and elsewhere. First, it served to discredit both France's traditional statist pattern and the possibility of a nationally based radical or democratic socialist economic course. Although the state continued (and continues) to play an important role, that role changed from attempting to extend and democratize state control in the early 1980s to bolstering market-based production in which private actors—above all, business firms—gain substantial power.

Second, the indirect effect of the French failure was to propel European integration forward. French policymakers, from Mitterrand down, concluded that if France was to play an important role in the world, it could not go it alone. They turned to the EU as the next best alternative to domestic power and autonomy. As one scholar observes, "It was only in 1983, with the turn-around in the economic policy of the French government, that the French started . . . to become more pro-European, and started to see European integration as a way of compensating for the loss of policy autonomy."[12] Mitterrand made a virtue of a necessity, going from a lukewarm attitude toward European integration to becoming a leading sponsor of European economic, monetary, and political integration. For this process to occur, however, France needed to renounce the statist direction of the economy and accept an economic orientation that was congruent with the process of wider European market unification. The topic that we now describe is the domestic component of the EU's strategy of promoting a common (and privately controlled) market in goods, capital, and population movements.

France's Neoliberal Modernization Strategy. The new policy adopted in 1983 sought to promote free markets, so that the state would defer to private decision makers on a host of key economic matters. This does not mean that the French state has completely withdrawn from economic governance. Although it has relaxed control over the economy, it maintains significant direct and indirect influence over market forces. Among the elements in this "neoliberal modernization strategy" are privatization, deregulation and liberalization, and economic policies in conformity with EU directives.[13]

Privatization. In the early 1980s, the Socialists initiated an ambitious nationalization program. Part of their "right turn" in 1983 involved halting this process. Within a short time, the government began privatizing what had only recently been nationalized.

The trend toward privatization was pursued with greater vigor by conservative governments, which governed in 1986–1988 and in 1993–1997, and in more moderate fashion by the Socialist government elected in 1997. A large number of state-owned industrial firms, investment houses, and banks were sold to private investors. The sweeping change reflects an assumption—quite new to France—that the state should no longer own or direct firms that are in the competitive sector, that is, subject to market competition as opposed to firms in a monopoly position. The state retains ownership of most public transportation, power, and communications systems, but even these organizations, which previously enjoyed a privileged position, are slated for privatization in the future.

Although privatization apparently represents a total shift from public to private control, this appearance is misleading. First, the state granted a small number of large investors (with whom it has close relations) a controlling share in privatized firms in order to maintain informal state leverage and management stability. Second, the state often retained a considerable voice in the management of the privatized firms because state-owned firms and banks (notably, the giant savings bank network that operates through the postal system) were usually among the favored few investors (the "hard core," as they were called) who purchased controlling blocks of stock in the newly privatized firms.[14] Third, state influence continued in an indirect way as a result of continuity in managerial ranks. Many of France's largest firms, including privatized firms, are directed by executives who are graduates of state-run elite schools. They remain steeped in a statist tradition, are life-long members of state networks (the *grands corps*, described in Chapter 13), and move back and forth between positions in the public and private sectors. Thus, there remains a dense network of relations between the state and private business firms.

Most of the sales of newly created shares in the privatized firms were highly successful. Privatization also altered French social structure by substantially increasing the number of stockholders in France. The number of French citizens owning shares of stock increased from under 2 million to approximately 8 million, which helped promote what conservative governments called "people's capitalism" in France.

Opponents of privatization—primarily on the left of the political spectrum, and especially the Communist Party—charged that the process represented the sale of vital public assets at bargain-basement prices and that the most affluent citizens were reaping the lion's share of the benefits. In some cases, employees of firms slated for privatization waged strikes, on the grounds that their hard-won benefits—good wages and fringe benefits, job security, and rights to representation within the firm—would be in peril. In general, their fears were justified. Indeed, one of the forces driving privatization was the desire to cut costs by reducing employee benefits. Political leaders reasoned that it would be less damaging politically if cutbacks were carried out by executives of private firms. These strikes, often in key sectors like transportation, have caused considerable disruption and political damage for the government.

Privatization has occurred in other West European countries (not to speak of formerly communist countries in East and Central Europe). However, within Western Europe, the move is especially noteworthy in France because it marks such a departure from the traditionally preeminent role of the state.

Deregulation and Liberalization. Before the shift from *dirigisme* in 1983, the state exercised close supervision over the economy. State regulations defined technical standards; specified market share; set prices, interest rates, and terms of credit; and even determined where investments were permitted. Policymakers provided themselves and private firms with the space to pursue these policies by erecting stiff tariffs to shield French producers from the harsh discipline of competition. The state regulated labor markets to protect workers. It limited employers' freedom to schedule work-time and promote and fire workers. For example, employers required administrative authorization for layoffs, and to obtain such approval usually meant providing workers with significant benefits. For many matters, employers needed the approval of administrators in a host of bureaus and ministries. In brief, the French economy often seemed to be strangled by kilometers of red tape.

Some state regulations were beneficial. Consumers benefited when the administration set high standards and rigorously enforced them. For example, the French transportation network had an enviable safety record. Workers benefited when state labor inspectors prevented arbitrary employer actions.

However, since 1983 there has been a strong trend toward deregulation. For example, employers no longer need to obtain administrative authorization to lay off workers, and they have greater freedom to schedule work in a flexible manner. Price controls have been largely eliminated.

Deregulation has been especially sweeping in the financial sector, where the dense framework of state supervision, subsidized loans, differential interest rates, and credit rationing has been substantially eliminated. Today, market forces, not Ministry of Finance officials, determine who should receive loans, how much, and at what interest rates. Private firms are forced to fend for themselves, both for better—since they are forced to be more efficient—and for worse (since loans are given according to strictly economic criteria, which may ignore social needs).

Deregulation has meant that French firms can no longer rely on tariffs, technical standards, and government policies to prevent foreign competition. French businesses must now compete with foreign firms both at home and abroad. The result has been dramatic: France is now a world leader as both a destination for foreign investment and a source of investment abroad. In brief, the new policy stance relies heavily on market competition to achieve economic and technological modernization.

Impact of the European Union. France's participation in the EU has further reduced the state's role in economic management. It was no coincidence that when Mitterrand abandoned more traditional Socialist goals in 1983, he turned toward revitalizing European integration. Some scholars assert that he exchanged the project of socialism within France—which proved unrealistic in any event, in part because of the existence of conservative governments elsewhere—for a European project.

The adoption of the Single European Act in 1987, the Maastricht Treaty in 1991, and the Stabilization Pact in 1997 tied France ever more tightly to its European neighbors. The Maastricht Treaty required member states to adopt austerity measures, called *convergence criteria,* in order to qualify for participation in a common European currency, the euro. States had to cut annual budget deficits to under 3 percent of the gross domestic product (GDP) (in the mid-1990s the French government deficit was nearly twice this amount), limit total public debt to under 60 percent of the GDP, and grant their central banks independence so that

they could pursue anti-inflationary economic policies.

The policy changes mandated by Maastricht often conflicted with traditional patterns of the French political economy. For example, the Banque de France, France's central bank, was traditionally under government control; it regulated the banking industry and set interest rates in accordance with government policy. However, the government sponsored legislation in 1994 to enhance considerably the independence of the Banque de France. Directors of the bank now are appointed for fixed terms of six years and cannot ordinarily be dismissed.

The adoption of the Economic and Monetary Union (EMU) in 1991, and the launching of the euro in 1999, are crucially important. The European Central Bank (ECB), comprising mostly bankers, was created in 1998 to control the euro for the eleven member states whose currencies were due to be replaced by the euro in 2002. Most members of the EU participated in launching the euro; the major exception was Britain, as described in Chapter 7.

The ECB has the authority to regulate interest rates, the euro's exchange rates, and the size of the money supply of member states. Critics charge that the single-minded pursuit of price stability comes at the expense of other worthy goals, such as economic growth and job creation, and one of Prime Minister Jospin's aims was to persuade other governments in the EMU to give priority to economic expansion and job creation.

The goal of currency reform is to produce a vast, unified economy. The eleven states have an economy as large as that of the United States: each accounts for about one-fifth of the world's total annual production. Creating a common currency made it easier for firms in the EU to invest and trade across borders of the member states. Presumably this produces gains in efficiency, which should provide benefits to all concerned. But the adoption of the euro, as well as other measures promoting greater economic integration, also involves costs for states and citizens. When states like France delegate to EU officials power to regulate the currency, interest rates, and the exchange rate, state officials and citizens lose control over core elements of sovereignty. This restricts the arenas in which citizens and state officials can influence policy choices. The "democratic deficit" within the EU may signify reduced accountability by those who make key decisions affecting economic and social life.

Not surprisingly, the new policy initiatives encountered stiff popular resistance. French voters came within a hair of rejecting the 1991 referendum on the Maastricht Treaty. Even more dramatic was the reaction in 1995 when the government announced a program of austerity measures designed to qualify France for the launching of the euro. In 1995, conservative Prime Minister Alain Juppé, at President Chirac's direction, announced cutbacks in state social programs, including retirement benefits for railway workers, civil servants' salaries, and reimbursement for medical costs. As we describe in Chapter 15, the massive strikes by public sector workers (in varied sectors, including transportation, postal service, and schools) threatened the Juppé government's very existence. However, despite marginal differences among the economic policies of different governments since 1983, none has openly challenged the orientation chosen at that time.

The End of Dirigisme *or* Dirigiste *Disengagement?* If the French have turned toward neoliberalism, they have done so in a distinctively French manner. Political scientist Vivien Schmidt observes that France has not

> abandoned its statist model. . . . The state . . . remains embedded in French culture and embodied in its institutions, with change able to come only through the state, not against it. . . . Governments have not stopped seeking to guide business, albeit in more indirect ways . . . and they as always play a primary role in deciding the direction of economic growth and the shape and organization of economic activity, even as they engineer the retreat of the state.[15]

Schmidt calls the shift in France's political economy "*dirigiste* disengagement." In recent years, the state has supervised the retrenchment of industries like steel and shipbuilding, rather than supervising their expansion, as occurred in the earlier period.[16] It has steered the French economy toward integration within the EU and has shifted its efforts toward exerting influence on EU institutions. This is *dirigisme* of a different—and less overbearing—sort, but for better or worse, statism is still alive and well in France. Moreover, reduced state control does not necessarily signify increased freedom for French consumers, citizens, or workers since it has been accompanied by increased control by the EU and giant corporations headquartered in France or elsewhere.

Welfare State

In part because of working-class pressure, exercised in the streets and through political parties, the French have enacted among the most extensive package of welfare state programs of any other country in the world. State-provided and/or -financed social services (the social security system, as it is called in France) begin before birth, for pregnant women are entitled to free prenatal care, and extend through old age, with pensions, subsidies for home care, and nearly free health care. French families have access to excellent low-cost public day care facilities, staffed by teachers with advanced training who receive good salaries. Families with more than one child receive a monthly subsidy.

Public education is excellent in France, and all students who pass a stiff high school graduation exam are entitled to virtually free university education. An extensive system of public housing and rent subsidies makes housing affordable for most citizens. Workers enjoy a minimum wage far higher than the level prevailing in the United States, five weeks of paid vacation annually, and the right to job training throughout their working lives financed by a tax on employers. There is an extensive system of unemployment insurance and benefits for retraining in the event of layoffs. A program created in 1988 provides a minimum income for the long-term unemployed. The extensive system of social provision promotes solidarity and enables most French citizens to live in dignity. However, the price tag for the welfare state is high. Public expenditures (including spending by the state, local governments, and welfare state agencies) constitute about 55 percent of France's annual production (GDP). This represents an increase of 11.5 percent since 1970, most of which financed the soaring costs of social programs.[17]

The French are fiercely attached to their system of extensive social protection and regard it as an alternative to the American market model. In the American model, state services are meant only to provide the bare minimum for those who cannot afford to purchase services in the private market. In France, it is generally believed that the state should provide generous benefits on a universal basis—not only to the very poor. An American journalist described the French welfare state "as a global ideological rival" to the American social and economic pattern.[18]

At the same time, economic inequalities are severe in France and are increasing. In 1975, the wealthiest 10 percent of French households owned 40 percent of all assets; twenty years later, the wealthiest tenth owned 50 percent.[19] For much of the 1980s and 1990s, France's unemployment rate was among the highest in Western Europe, exceeding 12 percent in the mid-1990s. Governments of Left and Right loudly proclaimed their determination to address the problem but failed to bring down unemployment. In the past several years, international economic expansion has finally helped. But in 2001, unemployment remained above 9 percent, meaning that millions of French remained without jobs.

The Jospin government's signature reform to reduce unemployment was work sharing. In 1998, the government sponsored a reduction in the legal workweek to thirty-five hours, with the aim of encouraging job creation. The plan was bitterly opposed by business groups and conservative parties, which claimed the plan would be economically ruinous. In fact, the results were far less dramatic. Not only has the French economy continued to expand, but employers have obtained significant gains from the reform.

The law mandated that specific procedures for reducing the workweek would be established by collective bargaining between employers and labor unions, which gave employers considerable leverage. By 2000, over 4 million workers were covered by such agreements. Although about 400,000 jobs have been created in France each year since 1997, it is difficult to determine how many of these were created by reducing the workweek. One reason is that the reform authorized employers to schedule work more flexibly, both within given weeks and seasonally. Employers had long complained that they were hindered by rigid work rules—regulations that labor unions characterized as reasonable protection against employer coercion. By increasing flexibility to schedule work, firms were able to increase output from the existing workforce. Thus, contrary to many dire predictions, the reform has brought benefits to both business and labor.

Despite the state's provision of social services, free market competition generates winners and losers in France as elsewhere—and in an age of global competition and rapid technological change, there are losers aplenty. The French have coined the term *the social fracture* to describe the existence of a permanently excluded group of citizens—those without stable jobs, the long-term unemployed, the poor, and the homeless. The number of homeless in France has been estimated at between 200,000 and 500,000, and soup kitchens organized by nonprofit organizations serve 500,000 meals daily to the poor.[20] Nearly 2 million citizens receive grants under the minimum income program for the impoverished and long-term unemployed. Although the program was designed to help reintegrate this group into the French economy and society, few recipients of the grants have been able to find stable employment. Thus, despite France's prosperous economy and ample welfare state, many citizens are excluded from full participation in French society. One result is increased social unrest. In 1997, unemployed workers occupied many of France's unemployment offices, to the great embarrassment of the recently elected Socialist government of Lionel Jospin. The Jospin government proposed a package of measures to assist the unemployed and the excluded, but the problem has not been resolved.

A related dilemma in recent years involves the rising costs of the welfare state. On one hand, the "Sécu" (shorthand for the social security system of health and retirement benefits) is among the most popular public programs in France. Prior to 1995, not even conservative governments dared attack it frontally. However, social programs are increasingly costly, due to rising medical costs, high levels of unemployment, a slowdown in birthrates (which means fewer active workers are available to contribute to finance welfare benefits), and a growing ratio of retired to younger workers. The proportion of elderly will double by 2050. Currently, there are 3.0 French adults who work, for every retired worker; in 2050, the ratio will drop to 1.5 workers, for every retired worker. At the same time, the government faces severe pressure to contain costs, as a result of international economic competition, citizen opposition to tax increases, and France's participation in the EU.

These conflicting pressures have produced intense political controversy. Prime Minister Alain Juppé's proposal for reorganizing the public health system in 1995, involving benefits cutbacks, provoked extensive strikes that immobilized France at year's end and swept the conservative coalition from office in 1997. But the pressures to reduce state spending did not vanish.

One of the key reasons for rising welfare costs is that so many French citizens cannot find work. Thus, there are fewer workers who pay the taxes that support the welfare state and more citizens who are claimants for state benefits. Since the 1980s, France has experienced double-digit unemployment rates, among the highest of the industrialized nations. Youth, immigrants, and women are considerably more likely to be out of work, and the Socialist government sponsored a plan in 1997 to create 700,000 jobs in the nonprofit and public sector for unemployed youth. For years, voters have consistently ranked unemployment the most important problem in France, and successive governments' inability to reduce unemployment has contributed to the frequent electoral gyrations of the recent period. (Conversely, the fact that unemployment declined since the late 1990s considerably improved Prime Minister Jospin's poll standings!)

Society and Economy

One problem area in France that has traditionally hindered economic performance has been relations between management and labor. Typically French workers have gained benefits by protest at work and in the streets rather than by cooperating with their employers, the typical pattern in Germany. It took the May 1968 uprising for labor unions to gain the right to organize plant-level locals. Until the Socialist government sponsored labor reforms in the early 1980s, including the obligation for French employers to bargain collectively over wages and hours, French workers did not enjoy benefits that workers in northern European nations had gained decades earlier. Because the labor movement has traditionally been quite weak, it was especially vulnerable during the recent period of economic crisis and restructuring. The French labor movement has suffered severe declines in membership, and less than 10 percent of the wage-earning population currently belongs to a labor union.

Inequality and Ethnic Minorities

France long prided itself on its ability to integrate ethnic minorities. The contrast with Germany is quite striking in this respect. The French conception of citizenship was political rather than based on blood, that is, ethnic ties.

Yet France's vaunted openness was partially misleading, for there has also been a long tradition in France of suspicion (or worse) toward the foreign-born. In the French conception, immigrants could become members of the French community but on condition that they accepted the French language and culture—in brief, assimilated, rather than preserving their own traditions. Moreover, as we will see in Chapter 14, in recent years France has spawned a chauvinist, anti-immigrant, and quite racist party, and racist attitudes have become all too widespread.

Inequality and Women

The place of women in French society is fairly secure but far from equal. On the one hand, France has been at the forefront of providing social services, such as excellent public and nonprofit day care facilities, which enable women to work outside the home. France resembles the Scandinavian countries in not imposing a "marriage tax" on earnings, whose effect is to discourage female employment. As two specialists observe, whereas in Germany, "family policy confirms and strengthens the antagonism between maternity and employment, in France the model of the 'working mother' . . . is fully integrated into the family policy. . . . State policies in France are crucial in supporting high rates of participation in full-time employment by diverse groups of women."[21] Another specialist observes that the female-friendly and family-friendly policies place France "at the forefront of developments in employment policy designed to make child-bearing compatible with employment."[22] These policies, along with a veritable cultural revolution in attitudes about women's appropriate role, have contributed to an enormous increase in female employment rates in recent decades. The proportion of women aged twenty-five to forty-nine years old in the paid labor force soared from 49 percent in 1970 to 79 percent in 1998. The excellent state of child care facilities also helps explain why 72 percent of women with two children have jobs.[23]

However, women are far from achieving economic and social equality in France. For example, there continues to be a wage gap in France as in most other countries (in France, it is 20 percent).[24] Inequality persists in other spheres as well, for example political representation, although a landmark reform adopted in 2000 mandated equal gender political representation. (See Chapter 14 for the details.)

The Generation Gap

An ironic result of France's extensive welfare state arrangements is to create a quite sharp and inequitable generation gap. While welfare state programs provide generous treatment for the elderly, young people are treated much less well. One reason that young people face difficulty finding jobs is that the legal protections and economic benefits provided for stably employed workers limits job creation. Thus, young people disproportionately absorb the costs of a generous welfare state. One result is that unemployment rates are far higher among the young. Whereas in the United States the unemployment rate for young workers is double that for older workers; it is five times higher in France.[25]

Recent government measures to deregulate (introduce greater flexibility) into labor markets have proved a mixed blessing for the young. Although the result has been to reduce the level of unemployment, which especially benefits those seeking their first job, two-thirds of those who are newly hired receive fixed-term work contracts rather than permanent employment contracts, which were typical in the past. Furthermore, during the 1990s, the proportion of part-time workers in the labor force (many of whom are young, and usually women) increased from 12 to 17 percent—lower than in the United States and about average for Europe.[26]

The Dilemmas of European Integration

A government-commissioned study of France's long-term prospects observes, "[EU] legislation has assumed an increasingly important place in French economic and social life."[27] In such varied domains as the structure of business organizations, labor relations, the regulation of food and medicines, and even cultural life, the EU provides a regulatory framework. France's economic orientation has shifted in the postwar period from carrying on the bulk of its economic exchanges with its former colonies in Asia and Africa toward economic integration within the EU. For example, over 60 percent of French imports and exports are currently with other member states of the EU.

Yet one should not consider the EU as simply external to France. After all, along with Germany, France has been key in determining the shape and activity of the EU. And the two most influential leaders of the European Commission have been French; the first was Jean Monnet (known as the Father of Europe), the second, Jacques Delors, president of the European Commission in the 1980s and 1990s. (See Chapter 2.) Furthermore, European integration provides immense benefits and opportunities. If the EU had not been created after World War II, Western Europe might have succumbed to the agonizing conflicts that followed World War I. On the economic level, if it were not for the EU, Europe could not aspire to its status as a world-class economy, along with the United States and Japan. Moreover, European integration has provided cultural benefits. The French have become more open to the outside world thanks to the mobility promoted by membership in the EU.

Young French citizens are especially likely to identify their fate with Europe. In response to a public opinion poll that asked whether respondents considered themselves to be European as well as French, the proportion of those eighteen to twenty-four years old who answered yes was 38 percent, compared to 27 percent of those twenty-five to thirty-four years old, 33 percent of those thirty-five to forty-nine years old, 31 percent of those fifty to sixty-four years old, and 24 percent of those over age sixty-five.[28]

Yet the EU provides challenges and dilemmas as well as opportunities. At the most basic level, membership in the EU, especially following adoption of the Maastricht Treaty and the creation of the euro within the European Monetary Union, threatens the distinctively state-led pattern by which France achieved economic success and cultural distinctiveness. It therefore poses an especially great challenge in France. The style of economic governance in the EU is closer to that in Britain or Germany than France. EU regulations prohibit states from engaging in the kind of *dirigisme* that was the hallmark of the French state in the postwar period—for example, credit rationing, subsidies, and state ownership. As a result, France is forced to make greater adjustments in its style of economic management than is the case for other member countries of the EU.

An excellent illustration both of how EU policies constrain French domestic policy choices and how French officials retain a margin of maneuver occurred in 1997. Despite the EU's requirement to limit government budget deficits, the newly elected socialist government led by Prime Minister Lionel Jospin was able to pursue its domestic priorities of job creation and work sharing. Jospin financed the added costs not by budget deficits but by higher taxes on business firms and affluent taxpayers. At the same time, his government lobbied the EU to give higher priority to job creation.[29]

The weight of the EU is evident in virtually every policy area imaginable. For example, in 2000, the European Court of Justice (ECJ) overturned a French law dating from the nineteenth century that banned night work for women.

The legislation had been designed to protect women and promote family life. The ECJ held that the prohibition constituted gender discrimination. If parliament had not agreed to comply with the ECJ's ruling and abolish the law, France would have incurred a stiff fine.

Whether the new commitments are desirable is one thing. But quite apart from their wisdom is the fact that decisions on vitally important matters are now decided in Brussels, not Paris (although the French of course play a leading role in EU decisions). As a result, French policy autonomy is vastly diminished, and the fates of France and the EU are intertwined in ways that were inconceivable before the 1990s.

France and the International Political Economy

France benefited for centuries from its relatively large size, skilled workers, and a large internal market. By going it alone, the French economy performed quite well until the 1970s. France remains a major world economic power. But as global economic integration and competition have increased, France chose to pool its resources with other European countries within the framework of the EU.

The Socialist reformist experiment of the early 1980s described earlier may have been France's last attempt to pursue solitary state-directed economic expansion. When the attempt failed, President Mitterrand proposed revitalizing Europe as an alternative project. The decade that followed witnessed an enormous expansion in the scope and intensity of European economic integration.

The way that France participates in the international political economy will continue to have an important influence on domestic politics. But how international influences are refracted in internal politics depends heavily on the shape of political institutions and partisan coalitions. We analyze these issues in the next two chapters.

Notes

1. Richard F. Kuisel, *Capitalism and the State in Modern France* (Cambridge: Cambridge University, Press, 1981), p. 15.

2 Ibid., p. 277.

3. Henri Mendras with Alistair Cole, *Social Change in Modern France: Towards a Cultural Anthropology of the Fifth Republic* (Cambridge: Cambridge University Press, 1991), p. 1.

4. Kuisel, *Capitalism*, p. 248.

5. See Peter A. Hall, *Governing the Economy: The Politics of State Intervention in Britain and France* (New York: Oxford University Press, 1986).

6. John G. Goodman, "Monetary Policy and Financial Deregulation in France," *French Politics and Society* 10, no. 4 (Fall 1992): 32.

7. John Zysman, "The Interventionist Temptation: Financial Structure and Political Purpose," in William G. Andrews and Stanley Hoffmann, eds., *The Fifth Republic at Twenty* (Albany: State University of New York Press, 1981); John Zysman, *Political Strategies for Industrial Order: State, Market, and Industry in France* (Berkeley: University of California Press, 1977); and Hall, *Governing the Economy*.

8. Kuisel, *Capitalism*, p. 264.

9. Andrews, Introduction to Andrews and Hoffmann, eds., *The Fifth Republic*, p. 4.

10. Hall, *Governing the Economy*, p. 163.

11. Laurent Ménière, *Bilan de la France, 1981–1993* (Paris: Hachette, 1993), p. 18.

12. Amy Verdun, *European Responses to Globalization and Financial Market Integration: Perceptions of Economic and Monetary Union in Britain, France and Germany* (New York: St. Martin's Press, 2000), p. 177.

13. Peter A. Hall suggested the term "neo-liberal modernization strategy" to describe the economic

policy followed by successive French governments since the mid-1980s. See his "From One Modernization Strategy to Another: The Character and Consequences of Recent Economic Policy in France" (paper presented to the Tenth International Conference of Europeanists, Chicago, March 15, 1996).

14. The best study of the process in English is Vivien A. Schmidt, *From State to Market? The Transformation of French Business and Government* (Cambridge: Cambridge University Press, 1996), chaps. 5–6.

15. Ibid., p. 442.

16. For some fine case studies of the process, see Anthony Daley, *The State, Labor, and Adjustment in Steel* (Pittsburgh: University of Pittsburgh Press, 1996), and W. Rand Smith, *The Left's Dirty Job: The Politics of Industrial Restructuring in France and Spain* (Pittsburgh: University of Pittsburgh Press, 1998).

17. Commissariat général du plan, *Rapport sur les perspectives de la France* (Paris: La Documentation Française, 2000), pp. 41, 46.

18. Roger Cohen, "Paris and Washington Speak Softly," *International Herald Tribune*, October 20, 1997.

19. Commissariat général du plan, *Rapport sur les perspectives de la France*, p. 30.

20. See *Le Monde*, October 22–23, 1995; and Assayers-CGT, *Rapport sur la situation économique et sociale, 1994–95* (Montreuil: VO Editions, 1995), p. 9.

21. J. Monk and M. D. Garcia-Ramon, "Placing Women of the European Union," in M. D. Garcia-Ramon and J. Monk, eds., *Women of the European Union: The Politics of Work and Daily Life* (London: Routledge, 1996), pp. 16, 20.

22. J. Fagnani, "Family Policies and Working Mothers: A Comparison of France and West Germany," in Garcia-Ramon and Monk, eds., *Women of the European Union*, p. 133.

23. Commissariat général du plan, *Rapport sur les perspectives de la France*, p. 54.

24. Ibid., p. 17.

25. Fondation Saint-Simon, *Pour une nouvelle république sociale* (Paris: Calmann-Lévy, 1997), p. 44.

26. Commissariat général du plan, *Rapport sur les perspectives de la France*, p. 64.

27. Ibid., p. 45.

28. Philippe Méchet, "Français, êtes-vous Européens? Oui pourquoi pas . . . ," *Revue politique et parlementaire* 101 (March–April 1999): 15.

29. George Ross, "Europe Becomes French Domestic Politics," in Michael S. Lewis-Beck, ed., *How France Votes* (New York: Chatham House, 2000), chap. 4.

C H A P T E R

13

Governance and Policymaking

Despite the frequent changes of regimes in France in the past two centuries, three important underpinnings of the French state have remained nearly constant—at least until recently. First, for centuries, there was nearly universal agreement on the value of a unitary state. Since the French Revolution, subnational governments have been regarded as an administrative arm of the state based in Paris, their primary purpose to help implement national policy. Although most French remain committed to maintaining the unitary character of the state, an important change occurred in the 1980s when the Socialist government transferred substantial powers to local governments. A new spirit of local autonomy is evident.

Second, most French supported the long-established tradition of statism, reviewed in Chapters 11 and 12, which claims that the state should play an active role in directing the society and economy. As we saw in the previous chapter, this tradition has also been challenged within recent years.

The third change involves limits on state action from within the state itself. Until recently, the French accorded relatively little importance to the principle of constitutional supremacy. It may be surprising to learn that a nation that emphasizes the importance of formalized legal codes and that, along with the United States, boasts the modern world's first written constitution did not consider that the constitution should be scrupulously respected. French political practice reflected the view that representatives chosen by democratic elections should have a free hand to govern and not be hindered by constitutional or judicial restraint. Judges in France have traditionally enjoyed little autonomy and, indeed, have been considered part of the executive branch. This too has changed in the recent past. The Constitution of the Fifth Republic has generally come to be regarded as the authoritative source for allocating power among political institutions; the judiciary has gained the vital power to strike down legislation and executive decisions on the grounds that they violate the Constitution.

Organization of the State

The Fifth Republic is usually described as a semi-presidential system, combining elements of presidential and parliamentary systems. In a wholly presidential system, such as in the United States, the executive and the legislature are chosen separately, and neither is answerable to the other. The legislature and executive have independent powers, and neither controls the agenda of the other. Moreover, both institutions have fixed terms in office, and neither the government nor the legislature can force the other to resign and face new elections. There is one exception to this generalization. The legislature has the power to impeach and force the president to resign in the unusual case when it deems that the president has committed treason or other grave misdeeds that the Constitution specifies as grounds for impeachment. In France, the procedure (which has never been used in the Fifth Republic) works as follows: for a president to be impeached, a text must be voted in identical terms by an absolute majority of both houses of parliament. The president's case is then judged by a High Court of Justice comprising twelve deputies and twelve senators elected from and by the two houses.

In a parliamentary system, as in Britain, the executive and legislature are fused. The government is accountable to Parliament and must resign if Parliament passes a motion of no confidence. At the same time, the government has substantial control over the parliamentary agenda and can dissolve Parliament, thereby provoking new elections.

In the Fifth Republic, both the president and parliament are popularly elected. The government is appointed by the president but is answerable to parliament. As in parliamentary systems, the National Assembly (the more powerful house of parliament) can force the government to resign by voting a motion of no confidence—what the French call a *motion of censure.*

Why is the Fifth Republic a *semi*-presidential system? The "semi" refers to the fact that in several respects—notably, the existence of a government that is responsible to parliament—the legislature and executive are not wholly separate, as they are in a pure presidential system. The system is called semi-*presidential,* not semi-*parliamentary,* because the executive dominates parliament, not the other way around. Whenever the political system of the Fifth Republic deviates from the purely parliamentary or the purely presidential model, the result is to strengthen the executive—primarily the president. The executive largely controls the parliamentary agenda and can dissolve parliament and provoke new elections. There is thus a fusion of executive and legislative powers characteristic of parliamentary regimes in a manner

that strengthens the executive. But there is a separation of powers in that the National Assembly cannot pass a censure motion forcing the president to resign. The result is a particularly sharp imbalance between executive and legislature.

Despite criticism that the executive is unduly powerful, the Fifth Republic is one of the most stable regimes in French history. One poll found that 61 percent of the French judged that political institutions have functioned well in the Fifth Republic. An overwhelming majority of 89 percent supported popular election of the president, a controversial innovation when it was introduced in 1962, and 91 percent approved of the constitutional provision that provides for the holding of a popular referendum.[1] For the first time in modern French history, political conflicts are now played out within a widely accepted institutional framework. At the same time, there has been general agreement that an unduly powerful presidency imbalances the regime. A constitutional amendment adopted in 2000 that shortened the president's term from seven to five years has partially allayed this criticism. Nonetheless, debate continues about the desirability of further institutional reforms to democratize the regime.

Since the beginning of the 1980s, the Fifth Republic has survived two important political challenges: first, a shift in political control (alternation) from one political coalition to another; and second, *cohabitation,* as it is called by the French, or power sharing, the situation of divided control when opposing coalitions control the presidency and parliament.

The first alternation in the history of the Fifth Republic occurred in 1981, when the conservative coalition that ruled since the beginning of the Fifth Republic was defeated by the Socialists. Contrary to widespread predictions that the shock would destabilize the regime, the institutions of the Fifth Republic proved quite adequate to the challenge. Since then, alternation has become a normal feature of French political life.

For many years, the French judged that if opposing forces were to gain control of the executive and legislature—that is, cohabitation—political stalemate (or worse) would occur. The unthinkable finally did occur in 1986. Five years after François Mitterrand was elected president, parliamentary elections produced a conservative majority in the National Assembly, and Mitterrand appointed as prime minister Jacques Chirac, leader of conservative forces. The event proved to be the mouse that roared. The two found workable solutions to governing together, and despite a few tremors, the regime held firm. The first period of cohabitation ended in 1988, when Mitterrand was reelected president. He immediately dissolved the National Assembly and succeeded in sweeping a Socialist plurality into power. When a new period of cohabitation began in 1993, following a conservative victory in legislative elections that year, the rules of the game for such a situation were firmly in place. Even less uncertainty occurred when the third period of cohabitation began in 1997. This time, conservative Jacques Chirac, elected president in 1995, was forced to appoint Socialist leader Lionel Jospin prime minister. By now, all political actors were thoroughly familiar with their parts, and the play proceeded quite smoothly.

Three reasons might be advanced to explain why political institutions have been able to overcome the challenges of alternation and cohabitation. First, the ideological distance between Left and Right had declined *prior* to these challenges. The gap diminished even more after the Socialist government moderated its policies in 1983–1984. Second, the Constitutional Council (a court whose powers are described subsequently) has effectively maintained a balance (equilibrium) among institutions. Finally, public opinion polls suggested that most French citizens wanted political institutions to function normally. These developments signify a profound change in French political culture, involving a diminution of ideological intensity and the rise of a more moderate, pragmatic political style.

The Executive

Besides Russia, France is the only major country with a semi-presidential system. In parliamentary regimes, the head of state—either a president or a monarch—exercises purely ceremonial duties, while the bulk of executive power is wielded by the head of government, who is responsible to parliament. In France, the president is not only the head of state but also enjoys substantial policymaking and executive power.

The president is far from all-powerful, however, since he (there has not yet been a woman president of France) shares executive and policymaking powers with the prime minister and the cabinet. Particularly during periods of cohabitation, the prime minister's constitutional powers sharply limit presidential leadership. Although the president names the prime minister and other members of the government, the National Assembly (the lower house of parliament) can force the government to resign by voting a motion of no confidence. Thus, when the National Assembly is controlled by a majority hostile to the president—the situation during cohabitation—the president must bow to political realities and appoint a government representing opposing political forces. In this situation, the government, not the president, controls most major policy decisions. It thus makes a vital difference whether the president can count on the support of a parliamentary majority. As Mitterrand's and Chirac's presidency demonstrates, the same president can shift from commanding enormous power (when in control of a parliamentary majority and a loyal prime minister) to exercising a quite modest role (when forced to confront a prime minister and parliamentary majority leading an opposing coalition). When both president and prime minister possess independent power, the two have important reasons to seek to cooperate (despite their political differences) since voters might punish both leaders if gridlock occurred.

To describe France as having a dual executive, as many do, obscures the power of the bureaucracy, a third key element of the executive. The bureaucracy is a large and sprawling organization that reaches far and wide to regulate French society. The three pillars of the executive provide the motor force of the French state.

The President

As long as both the executive and the legislature are controlled by the same party coalition—what we will term *united control*—the powers of the French president are immense. (We analyze below the very different situation during cohabitation—what we will term *divided control* of the executive.) The president combines the independent powers of the U.S. president—notably, command of the executive establishment and independence from legislative control—with the powers that accrue to the government in a parliamentary regime—namely, control over parliament's agenda and the ability to dissolve parliament and force new elections. Indeed, the government, under the president's direction, controls parliament more tightly than is the case in other parliamentary democracies. The result is a greater degree of executive dominance than in virtually any other democratic nation.

The president occupies the office at the very top of this commanding edifice. The presidency has become so powerful for three reasons: (1) the towering personalities of Charles de Gaulle, the founder and first president of the Fifth Republic (who was president between 1958 and 1969), and François Mitterrand, the Socialist president who held office from 1981 to 1995; (2) the ample powers conferred on the office by the Constitution; and (3) the political practices of the Fifth Republic.

Presidential Personalities. Charles de Gaulle (1890–1970) was unquestionably the most influential politician in modern French history. He first achieved prominence in leading the Resistance forces in France during World War II in opposition to the Vichy regime, allied with the Nazi occupation. After de Gaulle succeeded in toppling the Fourth Republic in 1958, he designed the Fifth Republic to facilitate strong leadership in order to enable France to exercise maximum power on the world stage. As first president in the Fifth Republic, de Gaulle exercised towering leadership.

The two presidents after de Gaulle, Georges Pompidou and Valéry Giscard d'Estaing (both were de Gaulle's political allies), were pale shadows of the Fifth Republic's first president. The next president who used presidential powers to the full was François Mitterrand. Mitterrand was a youthful leader in the Resistance during World War II and an ally of de Gaulle, but personal ambition soon divided the two. When de Gaulle returned to power in 1958, Mitterrand charged that the Fifth Republic was undemocratic and that de Gaulle had created a presidential office that would allow him to exercise power in an arbitrary and authoritarian manner. In the 1960s and 1970s, Mitterrand helped direct the opposition leftist forces against de Gaulle, de Gaulle's policies, and the Constitution of the Fifth Republic. During this period, Mitterrand twice ran for president, losing both times. However, he succeeded in remaking the Socialist Party into a major alternative to the Gaullist coalition, and in 1981, on his third try, he defeated the incumbent president, Giscard d'Estaing. Thus began Mitterrand's fourteen-year reign, the longest presidential term in the history of the Fifth Republic.

The supreme irony is that, as president, Mitterrand ruled in a manner strikingly similar to that of his arch rival, de Gaulle. Many of the criticisms he had leveled at de Gaulle were applied to Mitterrand as well: He was solitary, capricious, and monarchical in his governing style. As he humorously remarked soon after taking office in 1981, "The institutions of the Fifth Republic weren't created with me in mind, but they suit me fine!" Under Mitterrand, the Left became fully integrated within the institutions of the Fifth Republic. Mitterrand was largely responsible for the Socialist government's initial attempt to pursue a radical reform agenda, as well as for its right turn in 1983. He worked closely with German chancellor Helmut Kohl to promote European economic integration and monetary union.[2] He promoted policies that left little latitude to Jacques Chirac, who succeeded Mitterrand as president in 1995. In part because Mitterrand had created a framework that was difficult to change, in part because Chirac was soon forced into a period of power sharing with the Socialist Party—winner of the 1997 parliamentary elections—Chirac did little to enhance presidential power.

The Constitutional Presidency. The president is the only political official directly chosen by the entire French electorate. The system of direct election provides the president with powerful personal support and probably bolsters the legitimacy of the entire regime. During the first forty years of the Fifth Republic, the president—the only official chosen in a nationwide election—was elected for a term of seven years. (The office of vice president does not exist in France; if a president dies in office, a new election is held after a brief campaign, and the newly elected president begins a fresh term.) The long term further bolstered presidential power but also provoked complaints. Given the enormous powers of the presidential office, there were periodic proposals to reduce the presidential term. Critics charged that it was undemocratic to elect someone to such a powerful office for seven years without adequate mechanisms of accountability. After many unsuccessful reform attempts dating back to the 1970s, President Chirac and Prime Minister Jospin agreed in 2000 to sponsor a referendum to reduce the president's term to five years. The reform was approved by voters and takes effect for the 2002 presidential elections.

The reform will doubtless do much to promote greater balance among France's political institutions. Furthermore, it will considerably reduce the likelihood of cohabitation in future years, since henceforth both the president and members of the National Assembly, the powerful lower house of parliament, will be elected for five years. The first presidential and parliamentary elections held under the new system will be in 2002. Thus, the same political coalition will probably win both elections.

Why should a reform so often proposed yet never implemented have passed this time? It was no surprise that Prime Minister Jospin supported it: most French political leaders did—that is, unless they were elected president, at which time they suddenly had second thoughts about the wisdom of such a reform! So why didn't President Chirac act the way his predecessors did? The reason is probably that when he proposed the reform, he was sixty-eight years old and doubtless planned to run for reelection in

Reducing the Presidential Term to Five Years.

Source: Plantu, Cartoonists & Writers Syndicate, from *Cassettes, Mensonges et Vidéo* (Paris: Le Seuil, 2000), p. 109.

2002 when his first term expired. Chirac hoped to forestall charges that he would be too elderly to serve a second seven-year term.

The Constitution of the Fifth Republic endows the president with the ceremonial powers of head of state, the role occupied by the president in previous regimes. He is the fortunate occupant of the resplendent Elysée Palace in a fashionable section of Paris, he is the symbolic embodiment of the majestic French state, and he enjoys preeminence over the prime minister at international diplomatic gatherings.

The Constitution also grants the president important political powers that had belonged to the prime minister in the past, as well as new powers not previously exercised in previous republics. Thus, the president both symbolizes the unity and majesty of the state and actively participates in political decision making. (Table 13.1 lists the Fifth Republic's presidents and their terms of office.)

In order to be nominated for president, a candidate must obtain the signatures of hundreds of local elected officials throughout France. (Unlike the U.S. Constitution, there is no minimum age requirement or necessity to be a citizen.) Potential candidates with solid local connections do not have much difficulty getting on the ballot. At every election there are typically five or more candidates. In reality, only candidates nominated by the major political parties (see Chapter 14) stand any chance of winning.

A two-ballot system of election is used for presidential elections. To win on the first ballot, a candidate must obtain an absolute majority, that is, over 50 percent of those voting. If no candidate receives a majority, there is a runoff election between the two front-runners. Given the fact that many candidates compete at the first ballot, it is unlikely that any candidate will gain an absolute majority. There have been runoffs in every presidential election held by universal suffrage in the Fifth Republic thus far.

Presidents are eligible for reelection without limit. President Giscard d'Estaing was seeking

Table 13.1   Presidents of the Fifth Republic

President	Term
Charles de Gaulle	1958–1969
Georges Pompidou	1969–1974
Valéry Giscard d'Estaing	1974–1981
François Mitterrand	1981–1995
Jacques Chirac	1995–Present

reelection in 1981 when he lost to François Mitterrand, and he toyed with the idea of running again in 1988 and 1995. Only Mitterrand served two full seven-year terms, and given the 2000 constitutional amendment limiting the president's term to five years, it is probable that this record will stand for many years.

The Constitution grants the president vital political powers, including the right to do the following:

• Name the prime minister and approve the prime minister's choice of other cabinet officials, as well as name other high-ranking civil, military, and judicial officials.

• Preside over meetings of the Council of Ministers (the government). Note that the president, not the prime minister, is charged with this responsibility.

• Conduct foreign affairs, through the power to negotiate and ratify treaties, as well as to name French ambassadors and accredit foreign ambassadors to France.

• Direct the armed forces, bolstered by a 1964 decree that grants the president exclusive control over France's nuclear forces.

• Dissolve the National Assembly and call for new elections. However, if the president has dissolved the National Assembly, he or she cannot do so again for a year.

• Appoint three of the nine members of the Constitutional Council, including its president, and refer bills passed by parliament to the council to determine if they conform to the Constitution.

Four other constitutional grants of power strengthen the president's position. Article 16 authorizes the president to assume emergency powers when, in his judgment, the institutions of the republic, the independence of the nation, the integrity of its territory, or the execution of France's international (treaty) commitments is threatened.

Article 89 authorizes the president, with the approval of the prime minister, to propose constitutional amendments. An amendment must be approved by a majority of both houses of parliament and ratified by either a national referendum or a three-fifths vote of a congress comprising both houses of parliament. The amendment procedure has been used with increasing frequency in recent years. Eleven of the fifteen amendments to the Constitution until 2001 were added since 1992. Recent amendments have regulated France's participation in the EU, use of the referendum procedure, the financing and supervision of the public health system, reducing the presidential term, and mandating gender equality for party nominations. The accelerated tempo of amendments suggests that recent developments have jostled hitherto stable political arrangements.

Article 11, amended in 1995, authorizes the president to sponsor a national referendum to approve policy initiatives or reorganize political institutions, provided that the proposed change is first approved by the government. The use of the referendum in the Fifth Republic creates a direct link between the president and citizens, and thus represents a sharp break with French parliamentary traditions and practice. Because of the fear that a popular leader would assume dictatorial powers (recall the example of the two Napoleons, who did just that), it was generally agreed until the Fifth Republic that the president should be a distant and ceremonial political figure. One of de Gaulle's most important legacies was to replace this tradition with one of a strong president with direct links to the people.

The referendum was used several times in the early years of the Fifth Republic to consolidate support for the republic. But use of the referendum is a high-risk strategy. When voters rejected a referendum that de Gaulle called in 1969 to approve his proposal to restructure the Senate and create regional governments, he resigned from office, on the grounds that he had lost popular confidence.

Because of the precedent that a president whose referendum is defeated should resign, later presidents have been reluctant to sponsor referenda. President Pompidou sponsored one referendum; President Giscard d'Estaing, none; President Mitterrand, two; and President Chirac, two. Although all five referenda were approved, they received such lukewarm support—turnout was embarrassingly low—that the "victories" probably caused the president as much harm as good.

Presidential power is greatly bolstered by Article 5, which directs the president "to ensure, by his arbitration, the regular functioning of the governmental authorities, as well as the continuance of the State. He shall be the guarantor of national independence, of the integrity of the territory, and of respect for . . . agreements and treaties." Because the president is the sole official charged with arbitrating and guaranteeing national independence, the Constitution confers on the office enormous legitimacy and power over the state machinery.

The Political President. The Constitution creates a powerful office on paper. To be effective, a president must translate formal powers into the actual exercise of influence. A president has important resources to pursue this goal, but success is far from certain.

The fact that the president is the only official to be elected by the entire nation sets the office apart. The democratic legitimacy conferred by electoral victory provides a powerful weapon that can be used in the president's combat with the opposition and can also be useful in keeping the president's own political associates in line.

Presidential leadership is given a powerful boost when the president commands a parliamentary majority, which in effect means the support of the dominant party coalition in the National Assembly. Two key developments occurred in this respect in the 1980s. First, prior to Mitterrand's election in 1981, the ties between the incumbent president and the dominant party were somewhat muted. De Gaulle professed to disdain parties, even the one formed to support him; although Pompidou helped consolidate the Center-Right party that was the primary organized source of his support, he ostensibly maintained distance from the party; and Valéry Giscard d'Estaing's power did not derive from his leadership of a party (the small party he led was far less important than the dominant party in the governing coalition, the Gaullist Party). Mitterrand, however, reached the presidency in 1981 thanks largely to his effective use of the Socialist Party (Parti socialiste—PS). "For the first time since 1958," notes a French political scientist, "[a president] did not derive his authority from recent governmental experience or personal charisma but from his leadership of the dominant party."[3] Moreover, unlike Presidents Pompidou and Giscard d'Estaing, who on election severed their links to the party organizations with which they had been associated, Mitterrand continued to maintain close ties with the PS.

Mitterrand's reliance on the PS did not mean that the party had much influence over government policy. As one observer points out, there is not "a single [major] instance when the Socialist Party leaders, or its parliamentary group, imposed a policy decision on the government."[4] Rather, as in the parliamentary regimes reviewed in this book, control of the dominant party was used to cement the executive's legislative leadership. Doing so might require occasional compromise. But the PS generally remained as docile during the Mitterrand presidency as did the Socialist-controlled parliament.

If President Mitterrand can be considered the first president in the Fifth Republic who was a genuine party leader, President Chirac is the second. Just as Mitterrand molded the PS to become the instrument of his personal and presidential ambitions, the same can be said about Chirac's leadership of the Rassemblement pour la République (RPR), the neo-Gaullist party that he directed from 1974 on. The two presidents both benefited from the resources provided by party leadership, although close identification with the party can also prove a liability, especially since political parties are generally unpopular in France.

A president who shares party sympathies with the parties allied within the majority party coalition in the National Assembly is able to name a loyal prime minister and government, and parliament generally supports the president's policies. This was the situation for the nearly three decades from the beginning of the Fifth Republic until 1986. However, the election in 1986 of a conservative parliamentary majority opposed to President Mitterrand represented a fundamental break in the previous pattern of presidential leadership. Since then, periods of cohabitation (1986–1988, 1993–1995, 1997–present) have alternated with periods of united control, although the reform reducing the president's term to five years adopted in 2000 will make divided control much less likely in the future.

De Gaulle and successive presidents have used their formal and informal powers to the hilt; the result has been to increase presidential power further. In addition to the constitutional power to designate prime ministers, presidents have successfully claimed the ability to dismiss them as well, thus making the government responsible not only to the National Assembly, as specified in the Constitution, but also to the president. Except during the periods of cohabitation, prime ministers have accepted the fact—nowhere specified in the Constitution—that they serve at the president's pleasure. Presidents have also assumed the power, formally delegated by the Constitution to the government, to develop policy and intervene in virtually any domain that they choose. (The situation is very different during cohabitation.)

The unusually extensive powers of the president have led two political analysts to suggest a dual circuit of political representation in France. On the one hand, there is the system of "classic representation, which stretches from the people to the government, connected by political parties and parliament. The other system, more difficult to specify, directly links the nation to the chief of state."[5] Although in some respects the United States might also be said to exemplify dual representation, there is no counterpart in Congress comparable to the French prime minister and government. During periods of cohabitation, conflict between the two heads of the executive potentially can pose the risk of destabilizing French institutions. The fact that this has not occurred is in part because both officials fear voters' reprisals if they did not seek mutual accommodation.

The Prime Minister and Government

Anyone who referred only to the Constitution would be surprised that presidents have made the key policy decisions during most of the Fifth Republic. The Constitution designates the government, not the president, as the preeminent policymaking institution. Article 20 states that the government "shall determine and direct the policy of the nation. It shall have at its disposal the administration and the armed forces." And Article 21 authorizes the prime minister to "direct the action of the government. He [the prime minister] is responsible for national defense. He assures the execution of the laws." Thus, when governments follow the president's lead, it is because of *political dynamics* rather than *constitutional directive*. In analyzing the policymaking process, it is essential to distinguish between periods of united party control of the presidency and National Assembly and periods of divided control.

The government (also known as the cabinet) is a collective body under the prime minister's direction. The Constitution directs the president to appoint the prime minister, who is usually leader of the major party in the dominant parliamentary coalition. The prime minister in turn nominates and the president appoints other cabinet ministers. Most cabinet ministers are powerful members of the coalition that controls parliament. (Given France's multiparty system, described in Chapter 14, it is highly unusual for one party to gain an absolute parliamentary majority. Therefore, the typical situation is that parties that are ideologically close ally in order to command a majority of parliamentary seats.) Cabinet ministers direct government departments and propose specific policy initiatives, which, after receiving the approval of the government and president, constitute the legislative and administrative agenda.

Although the president appoints the government, the Constitution specifies that it is responsible only to the National Assembly. This means that a government is not constitutionally obliged to resign at the president's request. Only the National Assembly can force a government to resign, by voting a censure motion (a procedure described in the next section). Here is one of the important differences between periods of united versus divided party control. Every prime minister, when there has been united party control, has publicly affirmed the president's right to replace the prime minister and government.

The reason that, prior to 1986, there was such uncertainty about how cohabitation would work in practice is that the Constitution of the Fifth Republic is hopelessly confused regarding the respective powers of the president and government. Put differently, there is both a presidential and a parliamentary "reading" of the Constitution. The fact that the Constitution assigns some of the same key powers to *both* the president and prime minister contains the seeds of potential conflict when there is divided control.

Article 21 states that the prime minister is "responsible for national defense," but Article 15 designates the president as "commander of the armed forces" and directs him to preside over key military policymaking committees. Similarly, Article 21 makes the prime minister responsible for directing the government and ensuring the execution of the laws, and it empowers the government to direct the bureaucracy; yet Article 5 mandates the president to ensure the regular functioning of governmental authorities and Article 9 directs him to prepare the agenda and preside over weekly meetings of the council of ministers (that is, the government)! Given the confusion generated by the Constitution, it is no wonder there was so much uncertainty about how cohabitation would function.

The prime minister and other government ministers have extensive staff assistance to help them develop policy proposals and direct the immense and far-flung bureaucracy. For example, the prime minister's office includes the general directorate of the public service, the general secretariat of the government, and the general secretariat of defense. These agencies coordinate policy and supervise its implementation by the departments that comprise the executive. The informal division of labor that makes the prime minister responsible for directing the daily workings of the bureaucracy and the president responsible for formulating the overall policy orientations is evident in the fact that the president's personal staff numbers around 50 and the entire staff of the presidential office is 600 to 700. Thus, presidents can at best intervene only selectively to enforce their preeminence. Nonetheless, when the president leads the dominant parliamentary coalition, to which the prime minister and other cabinet ministers belong, there is no confusion about who ranks number one within the executive. During periods of united control, there has never been a major instance when the prime minister and government have not accepted presidential leadership. However, when control is divided, during power sharing, the president must beat a dignified retreat from center stage and cultivate the image of a statesman presiding over France's longer-run destiny but not immersed in shaping the government's policy orientation.

The prime minister is the second most powerful position in the Fifth Republic. The Constitution specifies that the prime minister directs the bureaucracy (Article 20) and the government (Article 21), and has exclusive responsibility for issuing regulations, which have the force of law (Articles 21 and 37). Most prime ministers have been prominent politicians, and the office is regarded as a stepping stone to the presidency. Thus far, two prime ministers—Georges Pompidou and Jacques Chirac—subsequently became president; several others, including Socialists Michel Rocard and Lionel Jospin and Gaullist Edouard Balladur, have actively sought the presidency.

During periods of united government, the prime minister's most unpleasant function is to serve as a lightning rod to deflect criticism from the president. At these times, prime ministers are expected to take responsibility for unpopular decisions and give the president credit for popular actions. As a result, prime ministers generally become increasingly unpopular and are replaced after two or three years in office. Political scientist Robert Elgie describes the thankless position of prime minister: "When things go well, the President often receives the credit. When things go badly, the Prime Minister usually takes the blame. If things go very badly and the President starts to be criticized, then the Prime Minister is replaced. If things go very well and the Prime Minister starts to be praised, then the Prime Minister is also replaced."[6]

The prime minister is responsible for leading the cabinet and ensuring its cohesion, which requires him or her to arbitrate conflicts among cabinet ministers over policy and budget priorities. This is no easy matter, for the cabinet always comprises a coalition of parties with divergent programs and interests. Moreover, it includes France's most prominent and ambitious politicians, who possess an autonomous power base. Cabinet ministers, who are usually senior politicians from parties in the governing coalition, direct the various government ministries. Cabinet positions differ widely in power. The minister of finance informally ranks second to the prime minister, because, given the ministry's role in setting spending priorities, it exercises great power over other government ministries. The Ministries of Defense, External Affairs, and Interior also rank high in importance. Particular ministers may have influence disproportionate to their cabinet position because of their political clout, access to the president, or strategic position in the ruling party. Thus far in the Fifth Republic, there has been one woman prime minister, Edith Cresson, who directed a Socialist government in 1992–1993.

As we have seen, the prime minister's role is especially important during periods of cohabitation, when he or she assumes full responsibility for policy formulation and implementation. Of course, this is the situation of prime ministers in all parliamentary democracies—save that prime ministers in other systems do not have to contend with a popularly elected president from a different party coalition. The prime minister's difficult task during cohabitation is to convey the impression of being fully in control so as to gain credit for any positive developments, yet to avoid prolonged confrontation with the president, for this would prove highly unpopular.

As with cabinets in most other political systems, the French cabinet is not a forum for searching policy debate or collective decision making. Cabinet meetings are occasions for announcing decisions made elsewhere and for fulfilling formalities required by the Constitution, such as approving nominations to high administrative positions. The most important policy decisions are made at a higher level—at the Elysée Palace or Matignon (official residence of the prime minister)—or by interministerial committees, which bring together ministers from several departments for a specific policy area. Interministerial committee meetings are smaller and more informal than full cabinet meetings, and are presided over by the president, prime minister, or their representatives. They are a forum for fuller discussion and decision making.

Bureaucracy and Civil Service

The most prominent officials in the French state are found in the Elysée, the Matignon, and ornate government ministries scattered throughout Paris. The day-to-day work of the state, however, is performed by a veritable army of administrators who number 2.5 million—one for every twenty-four French citizens! Given France's long-standing *dirigiste* tradition, the bureaucracy has enormous influence over the country's social and economic life. The Fifth Republic further bolstered the influence of the bureaucracy by limiting parliament's legislative power and authorizing the bureaucracy, under the prime minister's direction, to issue legally binding regulations equivalent to laws.

Key positions at the top of the bureaucracy, the sector on which we focus here, command great power. The bureaucracy offers among the most prestigious and powerful career possibilities in France. Having proper educational credentials is essential, since the top posts are reserved for graduates of selective educational institutions, called *grandes écoles*. Competition for admission to these schools is intense; of the over 1 million students enrolled in higher education at any given time, only 52,000 are at a *grande école*. At the very top of the educational pyramid are the handful of the most select *grandes écoles*, which admit about 3,000 students annually.[7]

Students who graduate at the top of their class at a *grande école*, especially the two most prestigious ones, the École Nationale d'Administration and the École Polytechnique, are admitted into an even more select fraternity: one of the *grands corps*—small, specialized, cohesive networks of civil servants. Membership in a *grand corps* is for life and guarantees a fine salary, excellent position, and considerable power. Members of a *grand corps* leapfrog to the top of the bureaucracy at a remarkably young age. The *grands corps* have informally colonized key positions in leading ministries, meaning that positions in a given sector are reserved for members of a given *corps*. Recently members of the *grands corps* have also gained top executive positions in large industrial firms and banks. And they are well placed to launch political careers, often running for parliament after compiling some administrative experience. Many members of the *grands corps* have become cabinet ministers, several became prime minister, and two—Valéry Giscard d'Estaing and Jacques Chirac—were elected president.

Among the many influential bureaucratic positions, particular mention should be made of what the French term a ministerial *cabinet*, that is, the personal staff advising a government minister. (In order to distinguish the *cabinet*, or personal staff, from the cabinet that is composed of government ministers, we italicize *cabinet* when referring to the former agency.) Members of a *cabinet* are not strictly speaking part of the bureaucracy (during the period they are serving in a *cabinet*). Rather, their job is to advise the minister on policy and partisan matters and informally supervise the bureaucracy in the minister's name. French ministers have considerable power over the line bureaucracy thanks to the help provided by their *cabinets*.

Given the French state's retreat to a more modest role since the 1980s, one might have expected that the *grandes écoles* would decline in importance. But the schools have adapted well to the increased importance of the private sector. After several years of obligatory service in the state bureaucracy, many graduates now migrate to the private sector and obtain attractive positions in large banks and corporations. One study found that nearly half of all chief executives of France's 200 largest firms are graduates of the two top *grandes écoles*.[8]

But all is not well in the French administration. The retreat of the state has affected the morale and social position of civil servants. The increased power of the private sector, as well as the European Union's (EU's) increased role, signifies that the civil service is no longer larger than life. Moreover, the civil service was regarded in the past as an impartial and nonpartisan instrument. However, once the Gaullist regime blurred the previously sharp boundaries between the civil service and the policymaking/political apparatus, with civil servants moving into high political office, the civil service's reputation for impartiality suffered.

Public and Semipublic Institutions

Since World War II, France has had an important array of public sector enterprises in basic industry, transportation, energy, telecommunications, and services. Furthermore, the state controlled many investment decisions, both directly, through state-owned industrial firms, and indirectly, as a result of the credit policies of state-controlled banks and the Ministry of Finance. This sector has been sharply reduced by the sale of state-owned enterprises beginning in the mid-1980s. There are still large and powerful semipublic agencies that remain, for example, Electricity of France, the sprawling agency that enjoys a monopoly on the distribution of electricity throughout France. But like the civil service, semipublic agencies no longer enjoy the prestige and power of yesteryear.

Other State Institutions

Given the far-flung reach of the French state, many state institutions would warrant close attention. We focus here on those that have the greatest power or those (like the Economic and

Social Council) that may lack extensive power but are designated by the Constitution.

The Military and the Police

In all countries, the military and police are key executive agencies that provide the coercive force to enforce state decisions. In some countries, the armed forces play an important role in shaping policy and directing the state. In France, the army has traditionally played a minor role in politics. However, in some exceptional but important cases, the army has played a key role, most recently in 1958, when it helped topple the Fourth Republic and return de Gaulle to power.

The French armed forces have traditionally been regarded as a pillar of the republic, mainly because the army was recruited by conscription (all French male youth were subject to the draft). The army was seen as a device for socializing French youth from diverse social backgrounds. However, the French pattern seemed quite old-fashioned and costly in an age when mass armies involving draftees with relatively little training have been replaced elsewhere by professional armies. In 1996, President Chirac undertook a major break with the past when he ended conscription, cut back the army, and placed far greater emphasis on professional recruits.

For many years, France deployed its armed forces in its former colonies in Africa and the Pacific to protect repressive regimes. In the process, France made a mockery of its proclaimed commitments to democracy and universal human rights. For example, international human rights organizations charged France with bolstering a murderous regime in Rwanda that engaged in widespread genocide against the Tutsu population. Prime Minister Jospin announced a reversal of the French policy, and the downsizing of France's armed forces may contribute to the policy shift.

The police forces in France enjoy considerable freedom in carrying out their duties—far too much freedom, according to many. The "forces of order," as they are called in France, have a reputation for abusing power, including illegal surveillance, arbitrary actions, and even torture. Immigrants and French citizens from North Africa, black Africa, and the Caribbean are especially likely to be subject to identity checks, strip searches, and other indignities. The judiciary and high executive officials have rarely acted vigorously to restrain the police. At the same time, public opposition to arbitrary police activity has increased, so the situation may improve.

The Judiciary

Traditionally the French judiciary had little autonomy and was considered an arm of the executive. In the past two decades, however, this condition has changed dramatically. The shift has been nicely captured in the title of an influential study by a French constitutional scholar. *The Metamorphosis of French Democracy: From the Jacobin State to a State of Law* analyzes the fundamental shift in French political culture linked to the growth in the powers of the Constitutional Council, as well as the increased power of independent administrative regulatory authorities in such varied sectors as the audiovisual industry, trading on the stock market, and commercial competition.[9]

The Constitutional Council. Possibly no other political institution in the Fifth Republic has gained more power since the founding of the Fifth Republic than the Constitutional Council. As one study of the council observes, "Originally an obscure institution conceived to play a marginal role in the Fifth Republic, the Constitutional Council has gradually moved toward the center stage of French politics and acquired the status of a major actor in the policy-making system."[10]

Members of the council are named for staggered nine-year nonrenewable terms by the president of the republic and the presidents of the National Assembly and Senate, each of whom names three members. The president of the republic names the president of the council. Those named to the Constitutional Council are generally distinguished jurists or elder statesmen who are considered not to be highly partisan. The first woman ever named to the council was appointed in 1992, and the council is hardly representative of France's diverse socioeconomic groups.

Three changes have been most important in strengthening the powers of the Constitutional Council and the judiciary more generally:

- Broadening access to the Constitutional Council. At first, only the president of the republic and the presidents of the two houses of the legislature could bring cases to the council. A constitutional amendment passed in 1974 authorized sixty deputies or sixty senators to bring suit. As a result, the council is now asked to rule on most important legislation.

- Broadening the council's jurisdiction to include the power of judicial review, that is, the power to invalidate legislation that in its opinion violates the Constitution. This key change occurred as a result of the council's skillful strategy. Although this development is unprecedented in French history, the council now routinely exercises sweeping power in a bold and continuous fashion. If the primary innovation of the Fifth Republic in the first years of the republic was to consolidate the dominance of the executive over the legislature, the primary development since then has been to consolidate the primacy of the Constitution, as interpreted by the Constitutional Council, over both the legislature and executive. The change has involved a substantial expansion of the powers of the council and a greater equilibrium of powers within the regime.

- Transferring the power to appoint judges from the executive to magistrates elected from among the rank of judges. This change required a constitutional amendment in 1993. The same amendment created a new Court of Justice of the Republic to try cases against government ministers accused of criminal acts committed while in office. The court comprises six deputies and six senators, elected by the two chambers of the leg-

islature, and three senior judges. The change was designed to allay public criticism after former government ministers were accused of criminal responsibility for allowing contaminated blood stocks to be distributed for blood transfusions, causing numerous patients to contract the HIV virus.

The Constitutional Council has periodically been the object of intense criticism when it has issued judgments that antagonize influential political forces. The council's composition is one reason that it may become the focal point of criticism. Owing to their nine-year terms, and particularly with the increasing frequency of political alternation, the majority of council members may have been appointed by political opponents of an incumbent government. Although council members do not vote simply on the basis of partisan affiliation, political leaders seize on party differences to criticize council decisions they oppose, as occurred, for example, when the council struck down several laws sponsored by the government of Prime Minister Balladur between 1993 and 1995. In one case in 1993, the government angrily sponsored a constitutional amendment to overturn a council decision that limited the government's effort to restrict the legal rights of those seeking political asylum. And the government further sought to restrict the council's ability to overturn legislation by a constitutional amendment in 1995, which stipulates that a referendum can pass legislation that in effect may violate the Constitution. The effect is to bypass the council's review procedure in such cases.

These changes contributed to the judiciary's growing independence and to the belief that the government, including its highest officials, should be responsible to an independent judiciary. Ironically, the changes were a belated and inadequate response to the widespread and continuing perception that the executive has all too often acted above the law, in both the conduct of official business and ways that border on corruption. For example, press exposés in 1995 revealed that high government officials, including Jacques Chirac and Alain Juppé and their relatives, occupied government-owned luxury apartments at below-market rents. Earlier, in 1993, the revelation that Socialist prime minister Pierre Bérégovoy had received a large interest-free loan from someone accused of financial misdeeds led to Bérégovoy's suicide. In general, these reports have fueled the call for a judiciary independent of political influence and free to hold politicians legally accountable for their actions.

The French judicial system of Roman law, codified in the Napoleonic Code and other legal codes (for example, those governing industrial relations and local government), differs substantially from the pattern prevailing in Britain, the United States, and other nations inspired by the common law system. Courts accord little importance to judicial precedent; what counts is existing legislation and the codification of legislation in specific subfields. French judges also play an active role in questioning witnesses and recommending verdicts to juries. A judicial authority, the *juge d'instruction,* is delegated responsibility for preparing the case. Criminal defendants enjoy fewer rights against the prosecution than in the U.S. or British system of criminal justice.

State Council. Administrative courts in France are very important because of the great power of the bureaucracy and the wide scope of administrative regulations (recall that many areas regulated in other democratic systems by laws are the subject of administrative regulation in France). The French administrative system includes a hierarchy of about thirty administrative courts. At the apex is the Conseil d'État (State Council), which hears cases brought by individuals alleging that administrative regulations and actions violate their rights. The State Council advises the government in drafting new legislation concerning the constitutionality, legality, and coherence of proposed laws. It can also rule that there has been a false or erroneous application of the law, and that damaging consequences might result from implementing administrative regulations. Although the government can overrule the State Council, it rarely does so, because the council's opinions command enormous respect. (Members of the Conseil d'État belong to one of the most powerful and prestigious *grands corps.*) One State Council ruling that had an important impact on French political life declared that European Community treaty provisions and regulations take precedence over French legislation, ministerial directives, and regulations. (This principle was later enshrined in a constitutional amendment in 1992.) The council plays an important role as a watchdog on the executive, especially important in the French political system, where the executive has such great autonomy.

The Economic and Social Council

The Constitution designates the Economic and Social Council as a consultative body composed of representatives of various interests, including business, agriculture, labor unions, social welfare organizations, and consumer groups, as well as leading citizens from cultural and scientific fields. The council has issued some influential reports on matters pending in parliament. But it is little known to most French citizens, has no formal legislative or administrative role, and exercises meager political influence.

Subnational Government

Until the 1980s, responsibility for regulating local affairs was in the hands of field officers who represented national government departments—prefects, supervisors of civil engineering, financial officers, and so on. Locally elected municipal governments were quite weak, and the local governmental structure was extremely fragmented: There are over 36,000 village and city governments in France, more than all the local governments in other major Western European countries combined.

The Socialist government's first major reform in 1981 was a fundamental overhaul of local government. State supervision of local governments was reduced, regional governments were created, and localities were authorized to levy taxes and engage in a wide range of activities. The Socialist government sponsored legislation limiting the number of elected offices that a politician could hold concurrently. Until then, the system known as the *cumul des mandats* (accumulation of mandates) permitted politicians to hold multiple elected positions simultaneously. Prominent political leaders often cumulated the office of mayor, member, and possibly president of the departmental council, deputy or senator, and/or member of the European Parliament—all at the same time!

The decentralization reform is widely recognized as one of the Left's greatest achievements. As a result of the transfer of substantial taxing and spending authority, local governments became more autonomous and vibrant. For example, regional governments organized public transport facilities to reduce dependence on automobiles, and local governments sponsored cultural activities to revitalize their areas. The decentralization reform has taken firm root and is popular among most French citizens, political parties, national politicians, and local officials.

The European Dimension

Although we review political institutions of the French state in this section, political institutions in France, like those in other member states of the EU, no longer function in isolation from EU institutions. There is such tight integration between the two levels that domestic French public officials spend much of their time participating in EU decisions and implementing EU

decisions. The process begins at the top, since the president, prime minister, and cabinet are constantly involved in shaping EU decisions. The process is most apparent during the six-month period when, as a result of rotation within the EU, a given country occupies the EU presidency. When this occurs, as was the case for France in the second half of 2000, the French state takes a leading role in preparing the EU's agenda.

President Chirac hosted other EU member heads of state in the stormy meeting of the EU Council that met at Nice in December 2000. French cabinet ministers presided throughout the second half of 2000 at meetings of their ministerial counterparts. Thus, to cite one example, the French agriculture minister coordinated the attempt to reform the EU's Common Agricultural Policy, involving subsidies and price supports for farmers in the EU.

On the other side of the equation, French officials spend much of their time implementing policies that are shaped at the EU level. Jacques Delors, a French political leader who for years served as president of the Commission of the EU, claimed that about 80 percent of the legislation regulating French affairs now originates in Brussels (the seat of the EU). Whether the topic is the quantity of fish that French commercial trawlers are permitted to harvest or standards for pharmaceuticals marketed in France, French bureaucrats usually implement regulations that reflect EU as well as French administrative decisions. To take another domain, French law courts now routinely defer to decisions by the European Court of Justice when they decide cases brought within France. When analyzing the way that French political institutions function, it is sometime difficult to unravel where the "EU" begins and "France" leaves off.

At the very beginning of the process of European integration, the French government created an administrative agency within the prime minister's office to serve as a link between the French bureaucracy and EU policies and personnel. It is known as the Secrétariat Général du Comité Interministériel pour les Questions de Coopération Économique Européenne (General Secretariat of the Interministerial Committee for Questions of European Economic Cooperation—SGCI) and comprises administrative officials of different state agencies. Through negotiations among representatives of the various French executive departments affected by a particular EU decision, the SGCI seeks to develop a unified French position on pending EU decisions. It also seeks to coordinate the implementation of EU decisions by the French bureaucracy. In recent years, the French parliament succeeded in gaining the right to be consulted on those issues that the EU Council was considering that could be considered to fall within the legislative domain. More generally, EU matters have gradually become integrated into the French domestic process of decision making and bureaucratic implementation. As a leading expert on the question observes, "This evolution proves that Community policies are no longer assimilated with foreign policy within the French government. It also perfectly illustrates how a domestic political process can be gradually 'Europeanized.'"[11]

Integrating EU-level matters within the French state's administrative policymaking process is one thing. Finding ways to promote public awareness and debate about these issues is quite another. Part of the EU's democratic deficit results from the chasm between what forms the focus of public debate in the national arenas of EU member states, on the one hand, and decisions made by politicians and administrators in the EU and national states, on the other. France is no exception here. The Jospin government elected in 1997 was the first to highlight the linkage between EU policies and French domestic policy choices—decades after EU policies began to affect France's economy and society. As George Ross identifies the challenge: "What is at stake in the long term is whether European-level politics can be articulated more adequately

with the various dimensions of French political life."[12]

The Policymaking Process

Until 1986, the beginning of the first period of cohabitation, there was great unity of purpose and a nearly hierarchical chain of command linking the president, government, bureaucracy, and parliament. The president, often in consultation with the prime minister, formulated major policy initiatives. The government, assisted by the formidable bureaucracy, developed the detailed legislative proposals and administrative regulations for implementing policy. And the parliament generally approved the government's proposals (although as we will see in the next chapter, the government could not take parliamentary approval for granted).

During the periods of cohabitation (1986–1988, 1993–1995, and since the 1997 parliamentary elections), the policymaking process has been quite different. The prime minister has had the dominant voice in policymaking, and the president has retreated to the political wings.

Divided control affects policy implementation less than policy formulation because cabinet ministers and their *cabinets* direct the process of implementation regardless of relations between the president and government, and also because bureaucratic agencies possess considerable autonomy to manage their own affairs. Although often forced to bargain with interest groups for their support in order to implement policy, the bureaucracy usually has the upper hand. However, one cannot predict the details of policy *outcomes* merely by knowing the content of policy *decisions*. The bureaucracy is itself often divided by competition among different ministries and bureaucrats have expertise and power that can be used to protect their own and their agency's interests.

In France there are few opportunities for

those outside government to influence executive decisions. The Constitution enshrines executive dominance at the expense of the legislature and popular participation. In particular, the Fifth Republic accords parliament precious little autonomy—a striking contrast to the British, German, and other parliamentary regimes.

Nonetheless, the executive is not all-powerful. First, electoral swings produce party alternation in office, which often results in policy shifts. Second, strikes, demonstrations, and other forms of protest have periodically erupted and influenced the direction of policy. Third, the Constitutional Council has gained an important role in the policy process. Finally, the freedom of the executive and the French state more generally have been severely limited by France's participation in the global economy, especially French membership in the EU.

As France has become more integrated within the EU and the wider global arena, the gulf has widened between political decision makers and ordinary citizens. There is widespread criticism of decisions made behind closed doors in Paris, Brussels, and elsewhere. Many fear that deci-sions made in this manner provide handsome benefits for privileged interests at the expense of vulnerable groups. One result has been periodic strikes and protests, as we describe in Chapters 14 and 15. In order to address this democratic deficit, there are increasing calls for institutional reforms within France and at the level of the EU. One response was the reduction of the French president's term to five years. But the change has not allayed criticism of the imbalanced nature of the semi-presidential system. Among other constitutional reforms proposed to strengthen representative elements are authorizing parliament to participate in setting budgetary priorities and limiting the president's power to dissolve parliament.

The system of political representation has been under particular stress recently and political stability shaken because of conflicts involving political identity and inequality. As described in the next chapter, with the exception of a notable reform legislated in 2000 designed to assure gender parity, representative institutions have not adapted effectively to these challenges.

Notes

1. Jean Charlot, *La Politique en France* (Paris: Livre de Poche, 1994), p. 27.

2. Ronald Tiersky, *François Mitterrand: The Last French President* (New York: St. Martin's Press, 2000).

3. Hugues Portelli, *La Politique en France sous la Ve République* (Paris: Grasset, 1987), p. 229.

4. Olivier Duhamel, "The Fifth Republic Under François Mitterrand: Evolution and Perspectives," in Stanley Hoffmann, George Ross, and Sylvia Malzacher, eds., *The Mitterrand Experiment: Continuity and Change in Mitterrand's France* (New York: Oxford University Press, 1987), p. 152.

5. Jean-Marie Donegani and Marc Sadoun, "Vie et mort de la Ve République," *Le Débat*, no. 106 (September–October 1999): 152.

6. Robert Elgie, *The Role of the Prime Minister in France. 1981–91* (New York: St. Martin's Press, 1993), p. 1.

7. Ezra Suleiman, "Les élites de l'administration et de la politique dans la France de la Ve République: Homogénéité, puissance, permanence," in Ezra Suleiman and Henri Mendras, eds., *Le recrutement des élites en Europe* (Paris: La Découverte, 1995), p. 33.

8. Michel Bauer and Bénédicte Bertin-Mourot, "La tyrannie du diplôme initial et la circulation des élites: La stabilité du modèle français," in Suleiman and Mendras, eds., *Le recrutement des élites en Europe*, p. 51.

9. Laurent Cohen-Tanugi, *La métamorphose de la démocratie française, de l'État jacobin à l'État de droit*, rev. ed. (Paris: Gallimard, 1989).

10. John T. S. Keeler and Alec Stone, "Judicial-Political Confrontation in Mitterrand's France: The Emergence of the Constitutional Council as a Major Actor in the Policy-making Process," in Ross, Hoffmann, and Malzacher, eds., *The Mitterrand Experiment*, p. 176.

11. Christian Lequesne, "France," in Dietrich Rometsch and Wolfgang Wessels, eds., *The European Union and Member States: Towards Institutional Fusion?* (Manchester: Manchester University Press, 1996), p. 191.

12. George Ross, "Europe Becomes French Domestic Politics," in Michael S. Lewis-Beck, ed., *How France Votes* (New York: Chatham House, 2000), p. 112.

C H A P T E R

14

Representation
and Participation

The Constitution of the Fifth Republic grants the executive an astonishing array of powers and severely limits popular participation, representation, and legislative autonomy. These arrangements were inspired by Charles de Gaulle, principal architect and first president of the Fifth Republic. De Gaulle believed that political parties and parliament had overstepped their proper role in the Third and Fourth Republics. The Constitution of the Fifth Republic was designed to ensure the independence of the executive and limit the influence of political parties, organized interests, and parliament.

For better or worse, de Gaulle did succeed in limiting parliament's influence. But the framework failed to prevent the proliferation of well-organized, centralized parties that he opposed. The irony is that the growth of strong parties has helped achieve the goals for which de Gaulle designed political institutions in the first place: decisive leadership, extensive popular support, and political stability.

De Gaulle's decision to provide for popular election of the presidency has been the major factor in the development of strong parties. In order to maximize their chances of winning the all-important contest, parties had to become centralized, powerful organizations. Yet political parties have served better to facilitate strong executive leadership than to provide channels for expressing opposition to the executive. As a result, and especially given the absence of other effective means of representation, France's

centuries-old tradition of popular protest against state authority persists and political stability is constantly threatened by protest in streets, factories, and offices.

The Legislature

In the French political system, the operative assumption seems to be that parliament should be seen but not heard. In France's semi-presidential system, parliament lacks the autonomy and separation from the executive that legislatures enjoy in presidential systems, yet it cannot hold the executive accountable, as legislatures in parliamentary systems can. The French parliament provides a poor forum for important national debates, fails to represent conflicting interests adequately, and has proved a feeble mechanism for checking abuses of power. With that said, parliament does provide a means by which the government negotiates compromises within the majority coalition, and it has gradually gained power since the early years of the Fifth Republic.

The French parliament is bicameral. The two chambers are the National Assembly and the Senate. In the Third and Fourth Republics, parliament was regarded as the sole voice of the sovereign people. Under the Fifth Republic, parliament is no longer the seat of sovereignty and has been stripped of many powers. The Constitution limits the areas within which parliament is authorized to act. At the same time, the executive is granted extensive powers independent of parliament, as well as numerous weapons to control parliamentary activity.

The executive can choose to dissolve the National Assembly before its normal five-year term ends. The decision to dissolve is delegated to the president, but the prime minister and government are closely involved in the process. (The executive cannot dissolve the Senate, but the Senate's powers are limited in any event.) When the executive dissolves the National Assembly, it cannot do so again for a year.

Until 1997, whenever a president dissolved the National Assembly, the president's allies won the elections that followed. Examples include de Gaulle's dissolution of the National Assembly in 1962, following the censure of his prime minister and government, and Mitterrand's dissolutions of 1981 and 1988, both times following his election as president. This pattern was not repeated in 1997, when Chirac miscalculated that an early dissolution of the National Assembly (in which Chirac's conservative alliance had a lopsided majority) would produce a fresh mandate for his coalition. When parties opposed to Chirac, led by Socialist Party head Lionel Jospin, won the elections, some critics charged that Chirac should resign in order to maintain the dignity and honor of the presidential office. He did no such thing—and quietly prepared to take his revenge, by gaining reelection at the next presidential election in 2002.

Article 34 of the Constitution, which defines the scope of parliament's legislative jurisdiction, represented a minor revolution in French constitutional law. Rather than authorizing parliament to legislate in all areas except those it designates as off-limits, the Constitution enumerates areas in which parliament *is* authorized to legislate. Outside these constitutionally specified areas, the executive can issue legally binding regulations and decrees. Even within the areas of parliamentary competence, Article 38 authorizes the government to request parliament to delegate to the government the power

to issue ordinances with the force of law. This may happen, for example, if the government wishes to save time, avoid extensive parliamentary debate, or limit unwelcome amendments. The referendum procedure described in this chapter provides yet another means for the executive to bypass parliament.

Within the limited area of lawmaking, the Constitution grants the government extensive powers to control legislative activity. The government is mostly responsible for establishing the parliamentary agenda, and as in other parliamentary regimes, most legislation coming before parliament is initiated by the government, not backbenchers or the opposition. (In one typical year, 1989, eighty-four of ninety laws passed by parliament were government initiated.)[1]

The government's control over parliament's legislative and other activity is bolstered by some additional measures. Under Article 44, the government can call for a single vote—known as the *vote bloquée* ("blocked vote," informally known as the package vote)—on all or a portion of a bill. The government can select which amendments will be included with the text. Governments have used—or, according to the opposition, abused—the package vote procedure to restrict debate on many key legislative texts.

The government can curb parliament further by calling for a confidence vote on either its overall policies (Article 49, clause 1) or on a specific piece of legislation (Article 49, clause 3). This provision applies only to the National Assembly, since the Senate cannot vote censure, that is, bring down a government. When the government declares a confidence vote, its motion is considered to have been approved—in the absence of a vote supporting the government—unless the National Assembly passes a censure motion within twenty-four hours.

The Constitution imposes an especially severe restriction for a censure motion to pass. An absolute majority of the National Assembly must vote in favor of censure. Thus, deputies who are absent or abstain in effect count as supporting the government. (Members of the National Assembly are known as deputies; members of the Senate are known as senators. Together the two groups are known as members of parliament.) The government uses these formidable weapons not only to check opponents but to keep in line deputies from its own coalition who might otherwise be tempted to oppose the government on a particular policy. When opposing the government might cause it to fall, in which case it might dissolve the Assembly and provoke new elections, the government's supporters are much more inclined to silence!

Deputies can also submit motions to censure the government on their own initiative. Such a motion must be signed by one-tenth of all deputies in the National Assembly. The procedure for passing this kind of censure motion is the same as that called by the government.

Given that the government normally commands majority support in the National Assembly, it need not worry about being forced to resign by a vote of censure. In fact, only one censure motion has ever passed since the creation of the Fifth Republic. In 1962, the majority of parliament was enraged when President de Gaulle convened a referendum to approve his initiative to elect the president by popular vote. Unable to vote censure of de Gaulle (since the Constitution does not make the president accountable to parliament), the National Assembly vented its spleen by censuring de Gaulle's prime minister and close associate, Georges Pompidou. However, parliament emerged weaker from the combat, because following the censure vote, de Gaulle promptly dissolved parliament and called new elections. When the Gaullist coalition won a legislative majority, de Gaulle sealed his victory by again designating Pompidou to head the government.

Articles 38, 44, and 49 give the government powerful weapons with which to limit parliament, exceeding those possessed by the government in virtually any other democratic regime. When a government relies on these powers to overcome parliamentary resistance, which oc-

curs frequently and on important legislation, a loud outcry is heard from the opposition. However, it has been impossible to abolish these devices because governments of both the Left and Right have found them highly useful, especially when government has a slim parliamentary majority, is internally divided, or seeks to legislate an ambitious agenda quickly.

The government employed these devices handily during the period it was most vulnerable in the Fifth Republic, between 1988 and 1993, when the Socialist Party (PS) had a plurality but not a majority in the National Assembly. The prime ministers of the period were forced to rely on shifting coalitions and constitutional gimmickry to survive and pass legislation. They accurately calculated that disagreements among the diverse opposition parties—including the Communist Party, the Center-Right parties (the Union des Democrates pour la France, UDF, and the Rassemblement pour la République [RPR]), and the Front National (FN)—were so great that the parties would not want to ally against the Socialist government. When in 1990, the Communist Party did join with the Right in voting a censure motion in opposition to a proposed reform of the social security system, the maneuver constituted an unprecedented alliance of the heterogeneous opposition forces. (The government survived, thanks to support from unaffiliated deputies.) The prime ministers at this time—Michel Rocard, Edith Cresson, and Pierre Bérégovoy—used the device of the confidence vote to pass key features of their legislative agendas, including annual budgets and the creation of a minimum income program. Their examples suggest that when the government has a slim majority, constitutional engineering has in fact helped produce stable governments. On the other hand, the use of such devices (especially when they are not necessary to ensure a government's survival) reduces parliament to a rubber stamp, limits the opportunity for useful national debate of vital political issues, makes it difficult for opposition parties to challenge government policies, and forces discontented groups to take to the streets rather than channel their demands through parliament.

Political scientist John Huber has analyzed how the package vote and censure procedures serve an important and little-noticed purpose.[2] Whereas most observers have focused on how these measures are a weapon that the government can use to limit parliament's autonomy, Huber emphasizes their utility as a way for the government to promote binding agreements among the parties represented in the majority coalition. This approach takes its point of departure from the fact that the partners in a coalition are also rivals. In brief, the package vote and censure motion provide the prime minister with resources to negotiate and enforce agreements among his or her supporters.

Parliament has more limited control over the budgetary process than in other areas of legislative competence. Members of parliament are prohibited from introducing budget amendments that will raise expenditures or lower revenues. Furthermore, parliament must approve the budget within seventy days after it has been submitted by the government or the government can enact it by decree (although this has never occurred in the Fifth Republic). Parliament's minimal role in the budget process vastly reduces its ability to participate in establishing national priorities. For this reason, there have been recent calls to enlarge its competence in this area.

In some parliamentary systems, parliamentary committees—as the French term them, commissions—play a vital role. But not in the Fifth Republic. There are six permanent commissions: foreign policy; finances and economy; defense; constitutional changes, legislation, and general administration; cultural, family, and social affairs; and production and exchange. (Special commissions also may be appointed to examine especially important legislation, as occurred regarding the Socialist government's nationalization reform in 1981.) Commissions are responsible for reviewing proposed legisla-

tion. Although they may propose important changes, the government can employ constitutional powers to reject unwanted modifications. The Constitution also authorizes parliament to create commissions of inquiry to control the executive, but few have been created, and they have proved quite ineffective.

In recent years, parliament has modestly increased its standing. When some powerful party leaders occupied the position of president of the National Assembly or Senate (roughly equivalent to the British speaker of the house), they sponsored changes to provide members of parliament more opportunities to question cabinet ministers. Members of parliament have successfully exploited the right to amend government-sponsored bills. Parliament's informal power has further increased in two kinds of situations. First, rank-and-file deputies count for more when the government does not have a large majority in parliament, a frequent occurrence in recent years. Second, cohabitation has enlarged the possibility for parliamentary maneuvering. Although members of parliament often grumble at the restrictions under which they labor, there is little prospect that the situation will be drastically changed, since it would require governments to voluntarily relinquish their power.

The National Assembly is by far the more powerful chamber of parliament. Only it can censure the government, and it has the decisive role in passing legislation. The Senate has enormous power in one key area—the constitutional amendment process. Since its approval is required for amendments to pass, it has coequal power in this domain with the National Assembly and possesses a veto power over constitutional changes.

Most bills that receive serious parliamentary consideration are introduced by the government in either the National Assembly or Senate. After review and possible amendment by one of the six standing commissions, the bill is submitted to the full chamber for debate, further amendment, and vote. If a text is approved, the second chamber considers it.

If a bill is passed in identical form by the two chambers, it becomes law (unless struck down by the Constitutional Council). If the two houses vote different versions or the Senate rejects a text approved by the National Assembly, a joint commission from the two seeks to negotiate a compromise, which is again considered by both houses. The government can expedite this process and ask both houses to reconsider and approve an identical text. If all else fails, the government can ask the National Assembly to override the Senate, and if the bill is approved by the National Assembly, it becomes law despite the Senate's opposition.

After a bill is passed, the Constitution authorizes the president of the republic, president of either chamber of the legislature, or sixty deputies or senators to request a review by the Constitutional Council. The council can strike down those portions of a bill or the entire text that it judges to be in violation of the Constitution. If the council has not been asked to rule within one month after a bill is passed, it becomes law and can never be reviewed by the council.

Why would the National Assembly and Senate have different positions on a policy issue? One reason is that members of the two houses are elected by different procedures and represent different interests. Deputies—that is, members of the National Assembly—are chosen from single-member districts for five years (unless the government dissolves the chamber before the end of its normal term). There are currently 577 seats in the National Assembly; thus, there are 577 districts. A two-ballot procedure is used, similar to the one for presidential elections. A candidate must receive an absolute majority of the votes cast to be elected on the first ballot. (Elections are held on Sundays to encourage turnout.) If no candidate does—the usual situation—a runoff election is held the following week. Unlike the presidential election, in which only the two front-running candidates may compete at the runoff, any candidate receiving at least 12.5 percent of the votes can compete in the runoff. Typically, however, parties on the Left and those on the Right negotiate

alliances in which they agree to support the best-placed candidate from the alliance in each district. The result is that parties agree to withdraw less well-placed candidates in the coalition, even if they obtain over 12.5 percent of the vote. Parties entering into these agreements stand a much better chance of seeing their candidates elected. However, fringe parties, like the FN, can exercise an important influence if many of their candidates clear the 12.5 percent threshold and refuse to withdraw in the runoff.

Since party alliances typically reflect the Left-Right divide, the system used to elect the National Assembly contributes to polarization within French politics. But the major effect of the system is to maximize the chances of a stable majority emerging in parliament, and it thereby bolsters political stability in the entire political system. This is why political scientist Jean Charlot claims that the two-ballot single-district system "has proved ... one of the most solid underpinnings of the Fifth Republic. The electoral law ... weakens or even neutralizes the natural tendency of the French and their parties toward division."[3]

By design, the two-ballot system penalizes small, isolated parties that cannot form agreements with major parties. The most dramatic case in recent years is that of the FN. In the 1997 parliamentary elections, the FN obtained 15 percent of the popular vote, but because its supporters were spread throughout France and the FN could not ally with a large party, it failed to elect a single deputy.

The procedure used to select senators means that the chamber is responsive to different interests. The 322 senators are chosen for nine-year terms by mayors and town councillors from each *département* (the 100 administrative districts into which mainland and overseas France is divided). (Twelve senators are elected by nonresident French citizens.) Rural interests are substantially overrepresented; although one-quarter of the population lives in villages of under 1,500, 40 percent of the local officials electing senators represent these communes (localities). The Senate is thus particularly zealous in defending the interests of small towns and villages.

Political Parties and the Party System

We have described the irony that the emergence of powerful political parties—the very factor that de Gaulle feared would nurture division, instability, and paralysis—has promoted political stability in the Fifth Republic They have done so by making possible stable leadership and political alternation in office. Popular support and political stability increase when elections represent a choice between alternative political coalitions. In recent years, however, the decline in ideological distance between the Center-Left and Center-Right has reduced the importance of the electoral outcome; many French citizens feel unrepresented by *both* of the two major alternatives. The result is declining support for the major established parties.

Popular election of the president has produced polarization and "presidentialization" of the party system. *Polarization* describes the tendency for the electorate to divide into two camps as a result of the procedures used to elect the president. *Presidentialization* means that parties give priority, in terms of their program, internal organization, alliance strategy, and leadership, to winning the next presidential election. Parties are organized to be efficient electoral vehicles, and the process favors leaders who project an appealing image and perform well on television. The party shapes its program to capture the widest possible audience, which produces a tendency toward ideological moderation. As French parties have moved in this direction, some observers have described French politics as becoming "Americanized," for the emphasis on winning the presidential elections, the focus on candidates' personalities, and ideological centrism are major features of American politics.

Counterpressures, however, constantly challenge the trend toward polarization and presidentialization. In particular, because the major

parties neglect certain groups in their march toward the ideological center, opportunities have opened up for a variety of fringe parties. The result is a countertendency toward fragmentation within the party system. Splinter parties have performed especially well in elections to the European Parliament and to municipal and regional councils, where the stakes are lower and at which representatives are chosen by proportional representation (PR). Since seats are allotted in PR according to the proportion of votes each party receives, there is less incentive for parties to ally or for voters to cast their ballot for large parties. Consequently, small parties generally fare better in elections held by PR.

The Major Parties

In the past several decades, three major parties have vied for dominance, and each has held top offices within the Fifth Republic.

Rassemblement pour la République (RPR). Parties on the right of the French political spectrum have traditionally been numerous and fragmented. Under de Gaulle's leadership, a new party was created, which—largely because of his popularity—dominated the Fifth Republic in the early years. The RPR, as it is now known, never had a precise program. It was originally created to support de Gaulle's personal leadership and his somewhat vague program of championing France's national independence, providing strong political leadership within France, and modernizing French society and economy while retaining France's distinctive cultural heritage.

Beginning in the mid-1970s, the RPR slipped from first place. Jacques Chirac, who became leader in 1974, lost presidential bids in 1981 and 1988. The RPR temporarily regained its premier role in the Fifth Republic when Chirac won the 1995 presidential elections and named Alain Juppé, a close ally, as prime minister. By winning a swollen parliamentary majority in legislative elections in 1993, the conservative sweep was complete. However, the victory celebration soon ended. When in late 1995 Juppé proposed cutbacks in social benefits (which we analyze in Chapter 15), severe strikes shook the regime to its roots. Chirac tried to regain control by dissolving the National Assembly and calling new elections in 1997. But the attempt backfired, and the victory of the Socialist-led coalition led to another period of cohabitation for the remainder of Chirac's first term.

The social base of the RPR generally reflects its conservative orientation. Business executives, professionals, the highly educated, and the wealthy are more likely to favor either the RPR or the second conservative party. In the runoff ballot of the 1995 presidential election, 67 percent of respondents in a public opinion poll who identified themselves as well-off favored Chirac. (The bulk of voters who reported themselves as having low income voted for Chirac's Socialist opponent, Lionel Jospin.)

Union des Démocrates pour la France (UDF). Created in 1978, the UDF was an umbrella organization for several small Center-Right parties that opposed de Gaulle and the RPR. The party's major leader was Valéry Giscard d'Estaing, president from 1974 until his defeat for reelection in 1981.

There were good reasons at first to have two major Center-Right parties. The two differed sharply on many issues: The RPR strongly supported de Gaulle, the UDF opposed him; the UDF supported European integration, the RPR was divided on the issue; the RPR favored state direction of the economy, the UDF preferred free enterprise. But de Gaulle is long gone, and disagreements over other issues do not so much pit the two parties against each other as divide them internally. Moreover, because of the polarizing logic of the French electoral system, the RPR and UDF usually join forces during most campaigns, and they formed a coalition government after the 1986 and 1993 parliamentary elections.

For years, Jacques Chirac and Valéry Giscard d'Estaing remained political rivals, and the parties remained distinct and often opposed organizations. The situation changed in 1995 when Chirac outmaneuvered Giscard in the campaign leading up to the presidential elections. When Chirac won the election itself and began a seven-year term, the aging Giscard began to withdraw from active political life. The UDF began to disintegrate, with a prominent leader of the UDF bolting to form a separate party. At the same time, the dividing line between the RPR and UDF became increasingly blurred. In 1998 the parties formed a loose coalition, the Alliance for France; many speculate that they will eventually merge to form a single party.

Parti Socialiste (PS). The PS is one of the major success stories in contemporary France. From a party of aging local politicians and schoolteachers in the Fourth and early Fifth Republics, it became the vanguard of a new France in 1981, when it swept presidential and parliamentary elections. Since 1981, the PS has been France's dominant political force. It has profoundly shaped present-day France by accepting the institutions of the Fifth Republic, changing its policy orientation, and undertaking a series of sweeping reforms.

Three factors explain the Socialist success. First, the Gaullist coalition that ruled the Fifth Republic became increasingly rigid and conservative. Second, the May 1968 protests exposed the weakness of the Gaullist coalition and its potential for defeat, especially if the PS could meld a coalition of the industrial working class with the new white-collar groups whose ranks were being swelled by rapid economic growth. Third, François Mitterrand, who became leader of the PS in 1972, helped fashion it into a new breed of socialist party. Although it continued to advocate substantial reforms, it kept its distance from the working class and labor unions.

The PS reached power in 1981 by advocating substantial, even radical, changes, and it sponsored a whirlwind of reforms in its first years in office. However, when President Mitterrand re-luctantly decided on a dramatic about-face in 1983–1984 after the government encountered severe economic difficulties, French socialism lost its ideological bearings. By abandoning its reformist approach in 1983 and championing conservative policies long defended by its con-servative opponents, the Socialist movement seemed hopelessly confused.

As Mitterrand's long presidency drew to an end, his reputation was tarnished by a series of scandals involving his close personal associates and by revelations that, before becoming a Re-sistance leader during World War II, he was ac-tive in a far-right organization in the 1930s and was awarded a decoration by the Vichy regime. The PS was further discredited by the fact that many of its leaders were accused of crimes rang-ing from abuse of power for personal enrich-ment to running illegal money-laundering op-erations to finance the party. The low point was reached in 1993 when the PS was soundly de-feated in parliamentary elections. Historian Donald Sassoon observed, "At the end of the Mitterrand experiment, the French Left ap-peared more devoid of ideas, hopes and support than it had been in its entire history."[4]

But the PS has demonstrated remarkable re-silience. PS candidate Lionel Jospin performed creditably in the 1995 presidential elections, coming in a close second in the runoff to Jacques Chirac, and Jospin led the party to victory in the 1997 parliamentary elections, enabling him to form a Socialist-led government. Thus, the PS has controlled the presidency or the govern-ment, or both, since 1981, except for the brief period from 1995 to 1997. (During much of this time, however, it has had to share power with conservative parties.)

What explains the party's durable electoral success? For one thing, although its achieve-ments fell far short of its ambitious goals, its policies have proved quite effective. It presided over a thorough overhaul of the French econ-omy and played a leading role in strengthen-ing European integration. Another major PS

achievement was to broaden support for the Fifth Republic. Until 1981, conservative forces had exercised a monopoly of power. The PS demonstrated that the Left could gain high office and represent the interests of previously excluded groups. A final reason for PS success was the weakness of conservative forces, due to internal divisions between the two Center-Right parties, the fact that neither party had a leader able to rival François Mitterrand, and the de-fection of many conservative voters to the far-right FN.

Small Parties

The three political parties that dominate the French political system do not command uni-versal support. Especially as their programs be-came increasingly alike, many voters believe that none of the major parties is responsive to their concerns. As a result, there is significant support for several small parties, whose com-bined forces are quite substantial. The result is relatively great fragmentation within the French party system.

Parti Communiste Français (PCF). From 1945 until 1981, the PCF was one of the largest politi-cal parties in France. It presented itself as the heir to the French revolutionary tradition, proud of its close links to both the French work-ing class, whose electoral support was key to the party's strong position, and the Soviet Union. For much of this period, the PCF's stated goal was to replace France's capitalist system— which, it argued, was undemocratically orga-nized and exploitative—by public ownership and control of the economy. This put the party on a collision course with other political parties and forces (save for small ultra-left groups).

Since its creation at the time of the Bolshevik Revolution, the PCF's internal organization, like that of orthodox communist parties elsewhere, was based on the concept of democratic central-ism. In practice, this meant that the distribution of power within the party was long on centralism and short on democracy. The party's top leaders, especially its secretary general and his closest associates in the secretariat, chose party officials and decided the party's general orientation. Critics in the party's ranks were quickly isolated and expelled from the party.

PCF support began to dwindle because it adapted too little and too late to the political, social, and economic modernization that transformed France beginning in the 1960s. Wave after wave of dissidents failed to persuade party leaders to reject the Soviet model, promote internal party democracy, and modernize the party's ideology and program. From commanding over 20 percent of the vote in elections in the postwar period, PCF electoral support fell to under 10 percent by the 1980s. Although it joined the PS in the governing coalition elected in 1981, it was a very junior partner, and it left the government in 1984 in protest against the Socialists' right turn.

Two other factors contributed to weakening the PCF. The party had close ties to France's largest trade union, the Confédération Générale du Travail (CGT). But when workers began to desert the CGT in the 1970s, this weakened the PCF. Finally, the dismantling of the Soviet Union, a momentous change in world politics, left the PCF isolated and somewhat discredited. Many of the kinds of voters who would have supported the PCF in the past, especially workers, youth, and the less educated, have drifted to the FN, whose coarse opposition to established parties is appealing to those on the margin of French society. In brief, the party is a shadow of its once-mighty self, and its decline has moved the entire political spectrum toward the right.

The PCF survived the disintegration of the Soviet Union. Its leader, Robert Hue, won 9 percent of the vote in the 1995 presidential elections and the party's candidates won 10 percent of the vote in the 1997 legislative elections. The party retains an important base by running many local governments. The PCF allied with the PS and Green Party to win the 1997 parliamentary elections, and two PCF leaders were appointed to the Jospin government.

Front National (FN). The FN has existed for decades, but its rapid rise in the 1980s was fueled by high unemployment, fears about increased crime, and the choice of a handy scapegoat: immigrant workers and their families.

The FN is one of the first openly racist political parties in Western Europe in the contemporary period. Its slogan "France for the French" implies that immigrants, especially those who are not white, are not "truly" French. Although party leaders have engaged in anti-Semitic and anti-immigrant rhetoric across the board, their favorite target has been Arabs from Algeria, France's former North African colony. The FN advocates depriving immigrants of employment, social benefits, and education and, if possible, deporting them. In the 1990s, the party broadened its program and increased its support by proposing simplistic solutions to other problems that trouble the French. It advocates authoritarian measures to deal with France's rising crime rate and fiercely opposes European economic and political integration, which in its view fuels unemployment and dilutes French national identity.

FN leader Jean-Marie Le Pen, a dynamic, articulate orator, has powerfully contributed to the FN's success. In both the 1988 and 1995 presidential elections, Le Pen gained 15 percent of the first ballot vote, just behind the major candidates. In 1998, however, he was convicted of assaulting a political opponent and, under French law, was barred from holding public office for two years. The party was therefore deprived of its most popular leader for the 1999 elections to the European Parliament. One of Le Pen's close associates challenged him for the party leadership. In the conflict that followed, the party split, and its future prospects suddenly dimmed.

The FN's popularity has posed a dilemma for the Center-Right: Should it reject the FN outright or make concessions in a bid for its support? For example, in regional elections in 1998, three UDF leaders were expelled from the party when they accepted FN support to retain their seats as president of regional councils. When one of the three was later readmitted to the party, it caused a severe split within the UDF.

The FN was a vanguard party of sorts in Europe in recent times to insult ethnic minorities openly and advocate racist and authoritarian measures. (Parties in Austria, Denmark, and elsewhere later followed the FN's lead.) Moreover, FN propaganda has borne fruit. In a 1998 poll, 40 percent of French respondents—twice as many as Germans or British—reported holding racist beliefs. Despite the crisis within the FN in 1998, it has already had a substantial impact on French politics. This is why political scientist James Shields claims that "the rise of a powerful extreme-right party in France is arguably the most important political development of the past fourteen years."[5]

Les Verts (Greens). While the major political parties have traditionally been quite indifferent to environmental issues, by 1990 French citizens ranked ecology fourth in importance among their preoccupations.[6]

The state's relative indifference to environmental concerns provided the potential for a Green movement in France. For example, France has the largest nuclear power program in Western Europe. The state-controlled nuclear power and electric power agencies are often described as states within the state because of their isolation and overbearing approach, and the Greens first reached public notice by sponsoring antinuclear protests.

The Greens had been on the French political scene for years before achieving a major breakthrough in the 1989 European elections, gaining 10.6 percent of the vote. The success was linked to the "new look" that the party adopted in the late 1980s, which appealed to young, well-educated voters, who provide the bulk of support for the Greens. At this time, it abandoned a leftist orientation and claimed that it was "neither Right nor Left" but Green.

To an even greater extent than other parties, the Greens have been divided by the personal ambitions of their leaders. In the 1993 parliamentary elections, the Greens split into two parties in part because of rivalry between two Green leaders. Nonetheless, the larger grouping of the Greens allied with the PS in the 1997 parliamentary elections, and party leader Dominique Voynet was appointed minister of environment in the Jospin government.

The Greens continue to be intensely divided. At the party congress held in late 2000, the party was split into six factions. Although Voynet succeeded in cobbling together a majority of delegates' votes and retained her leadership of the party, the party's electoral support has stagnated. It has failed to persuade the Socialist-led government to change the system of electing deputies to the National Assembly from the single member district plurality system to PR, which would increase the party's representation in the National Assembly.

Elections

French voters go to the polls nearly every year, to vote in a referendum or in elections for municipal, departmental, or regional councillor, deputy to the European Parliament or National Assembly, and president. (See Tables 14.1 and 14.2.)

The decline of the Communist Party means that for the first time in two centuries, the far Left is not a major force in French politics. A key to its decline is the massive desertion of young voters, who traditionally were quite likely to vote for the Communist and other parties on the far Left. Whereas 30 percent of young voters supported the PCF in the late 1970s, this proportion plummeted to 10 percent in the 1980s and 1990s.[7]

Some scholars describe the shift as the normalization of French politics, in that French po-

Table 14.1   Electoral Results, Elections to National Assembly, 1958–1997 (percentage of those voting)

	1958	1962	1967	1968	1973	1978	1981	1986	1988	1993	1997
Far Left	2%	2%	2%	4%	3%	3%	1%	2%	0%	2%	2%
PCF	19	22	23	20	21	21	16	10	11	9	10
Socialist Party/Left Radicals	23	21	19	17	22	25	38	32	38	21	26
Ecology	—	—	—	—	—	2	1	1	1	12	8
Center parties	15	15	18	10	16	{21	{19		{19	{19	{15
Center-Right	14	14	0	4	7			{42			
UNR → RPR	18	32	38	44	24	23	21		19	20	17
Far Right	3	1	1	0	3	0	3	10	10	13	15
Abstentions	23	31	19	20	19	17	30	22	34	31	32

Note: Percentages of parties do not add to 100 because of minor party candidates and rounding errors.

Sources: Françoise Dreyfus and François D'Arcy, *Les Institutions Politiques et Administratives de la France* (Paris: Economica, 1985), 54; *Le Monde*, March 18, 1986; *Le Monde, Les élections législatives* (Paris: *Le Monde*, 1988). Ministry of the Interior, 1993, 1997.

Table 14.2   Presidential Elections in the Fifth Republic (percentage of those voting)

Candidates	December 1965		Candidates	June 1969		Candidates	May 1974	
	1st Ballot	2nd Ballot		1st Ballot	2nd Ballot		1st Ballot	2nd Ballot
Right Center-Right								
de Gaulle	43.7%	54.5%	Pompidou (UNR)	44.0%	57.6%			
Opposition-Center								
Lecanuet	15.8		Poher (Center)	23.4	42.4	Giscard (Center-Right)	32.9%	50.7%
Left								
Mitterrand (Socialist-Communist)	32.2	45.5	Defferre (PS)	5.1		Mitterrand (PS)	43.4	49.3
			Duclos (PCF)	21.5				
Abstentions	15.0	15.5		21.8	30.9		15.1	12.1

Note: Percentages of votes for candidates do not add to 100 because of minor party candidates and rounding errors.
Sources: John R. Frears and Jean-Luc Parodi, *War Will Not Take Place: The French Parliamentary Elections of March*

litical patterns increasingly resemble politics in northern Europe and the United States. Two related changes have contributed to normalization. First, the ideological distance between political parties has declined as a result of the PCF's waning support and the PS's greater moderation beginning in 1983. For example, 57 percent of the electorate report that they see little difference between the PS and the Center-Right parties.[8] Second, alternation between parties of the Center-Left and Center-Right has become common. An indication of increased volatility is that in every one of the five legislative elections held between 1981 and 1997, the governing majority changed. Such shifts were unthinkable in the first decades of the Fifth Republic. Alternation has become so routine partly because political conflict has become so moderate, at least among the major parties.

These changes represent a fundamental restructuring of the French party system and political life. Yet before concluding that the new

era signifies political health, we should note some disturbing trends. Indeed, scholars have identified a crisis of political representation and the party system.

To begin, support for those parties not part of the select "cartel" of governmental parties has climbed in the past few years: the combined vote total of peripheral candidates in the 1995 presidential election was 38 percent. Other voters who demonstrated opposition to the "cartel" include the 3 percent of voters who deliberately spoiled their ballots at the first round to manifest their discontent, as well as some portion of the 22 percent of nonvoters. Thus, over half the electorate chose not to support candidates from the major parties of Center-Left and Center-Right. As the major parties move closer together, citizens become skeptical that parties can make a difference, and fewer citizens bother casting a useful ballot.

In a related vein, voting patterns have been increasingly volatile, as evidenced by greater

Table 14.2   (cont.)

Candidates	April–May 1981		Candidates	April–May 1988		Candidates	April–May 1995	
	1st Ballot	2nd Ballot		1st Ballot	2nd Ballot		1st Ballot	2nd Ballot
			Le Pen	14.4%		Le Pen	15.0%	
Chirac (RPR)	18.0%		Chirac (RPR)	19.9	46.0%	Chirac Balladur	20.8 ⎱ 18.9 ⎰	52.6%
Giscard (Center-Right)	28.3	48.2%	Barre	16.5				
Mitterrand (PS)	25.8	51.8	Mitterrand	34.1	54.0	Jospin (PS)	23.3	47.4
Marchais (PCF)	15.3		Lajoinie	6.8		Hue (PCF)	8.6	
	18.9	14.1					20.6	

1978 (London: Hurst, 1979), p. 6; *Le Monde, L'Élection Présidentielle: 26 avril–10 mai 1981* (Paris: Le Monde, 1981), pp. 98, 138; *Le Monde*, April 28 and May 12, 1988; *Journal Officiel*, May 14, 1995.

vote switching among parties. Political scientist Pascal Perrineau notes, "A new type of voter is emerging, less docile to social and territorial allegiances, less faithful to a party or political camp, and less involved in the act of voting. . . . He or she is likely to change his or her mind from one election to another, or even from one ballot to another in the same election."[9]

When regional governments were created, it was said that they might absorb the discontent generated by popular disillusionment in national politicians and institutions. However, turnout in regional elections declined from 78 percent in 1986 to 68 percent in 1992 to 58 percent in 1998.[10] In an exhaustive study of political participation in France, the Perrineau research team found that political participation in France has not so much diminished—in fact, they claim, it has increased as a result of participation in voluntary associations.[11] The researchers found that citizens are more individualistic than in the past, that is, less attached to their former fixed allegiances of class, region, and so on and more volatile in their voting choices. The result is that the French are not so much depoliticized as disillusioned; for the political system—including established parties, the administration, and the government—cannot respond to their aspirations.

At the same time, virtually every major political party, and most of the minor ones as well, are wracked by internal dissension. The causes may differ: hostility to the leadership's rigidity within the PCF; a succession struggle within the PS; a stalemate among UDF leaders. But beyond particular factors, existing parties seem ill equipped to confront the social, economic, and cultural changes sweeping France. This failure helps explain the success of the FN and the Greens in restructuring the political agenda.

A final trend is the recent wave of scandals involving political leaders. In recent years, the procession of politicians prosecuted for financial shenanigans includes former cabinet ministers, the president of the Constitutional Court, and prominent mayors. A major cause is the increasing integration of the political and business worlds, provoked at the subnational level by the fact that local governments gained increased powers in the 1980s to regulate land use and other aspects of economic life. Another cause is the high cost of financing political campaigns. Thus, numerous politicians (including the mayors of Cannes, Lyons, and Paris and the leader of the PS) have been convicted of diverting funds for their personal use or to finance their party. In response to the public outcry, four party finance laws were passed between 1988 and 1995 to root out political corruption. The legislation authorizes public funds for parties and candidates, limits private political gifts for parties and candidates at all levels, and establishes ceilings for campaign expenditures in elections from municipal council to the presidency. An independent election commission was created in 1994 with the power to disqualify candidates who violate campaign finance laws.

However, fresh evidence that political corruption is not a thing of the past occurred when two scandals erupted within weeks of each other in late 2000. First, a reporter released a videotape made by a former close aide of President Chirac that described how the president presided over a vast corruption scheme while mayor of Paris. The aide channeled illegal kickbacks from housing contractors in Paris to bolster Chirac's and his party's power. President Chirac could not be indicted at the time, since French courts have held that an incumbent president cannot be prosecuted—a ruling prompted by an earlier suit in connection with allegations that President Chirac had used government funds while mayor of Paris to pay party workers. But the videotape is a time bomb that can explode after Chirac leaves office.

Within weeks after the release of the videotape, public indignation and disgust further increased following revelations of a kickback scheme among the three major parties, the RPR, UDF, and PS. During the early 1990s, just when reforms were supposedly cleaning up political finance by limiting private political contributions and providing public campaign subsidies, these ostensibly rival parties were conniving to share illegal payments of around $100 million from builders in the Paris region who landed high school construction contracts. (Other political parties may also have shared some of the proceeds.) A host of political leaders, once again possibly including President Chirac, were implicated and numerous prosecutions were sure to occur. Newspapers characterized the revelations as the greatest political scandal in the history of the Fifth Republic and called on those responsible to leave public life.

Collective Identities

Economic problems, urban problems, and France's changing relation to the international order pose challenges that ideologies, party organizations, and loyalties forged in the past are ill equipped to meet. The two most important examples are the decline of Marxism, along with the related decline of the PCF, as well as an erosion of working-class self-identification; and a dramatic decline in Catholic religious observance, along with the weakening of the Catholic Church and social networks that formerly promoted the Right's social cohesion. In addition, the issue of immigration has posed a challenge for French national identity.

Organized Interests

Most scholars agree that the overbearing French state has typically tended to limit possibilities for social movements as well as for private interests to organize and regulate their own affairs. The Fifth Republic reinforced this tendency by strengthening the executive. Organized interests are still able to play a significant role. In some sectors, interest groups compete with each other. In others, the state provides for extensive consultation with private interests by creating advisory bodies on which they are represented.

There is a great variety of possible relations between administrative agencies and interest groups. At one extreme, the National Federation of Farmers' Unions (FNSEA) exercises immense power. Its representatives serve on the administrative commissions that set levels of agricultural prices and subsidies. In some respects, it is difficult to distinguish where the bureaucracy ends and the FNSEA begins. Another powerful organization is the major business association, the Movement of French Business Firms (MEDEF). Trade associations and labor unions play an important part in administering the far-flung public health system, as well as state-financed vocational training programs. Representatives of interest groups also serve on a peak-level advisory body, the Economic and Social Council (described in Chapter 13). At the other extreme, French labor unions are exceedingly weak.

Social Class

For centuries, France was among the countries in which class cleavages periodically fueled intense political conflict. When Karl Marx looked for an example of advanced economic development in the nineteenth century, he studied Britain, which, he advised his German readers in the Preface to *Das Kapital*, provided a guide to their own economic future. However, when he looked for clues to how political and class conflict might develop, he chose France as his example. His historical writings on the revolutions of 1830 and 1848 and the Paris Commune of 1871 are powerful analyses of the conditions under which workers mount a challenge to the political and economic system.

Yet a watershed change in collective identities occurred during the 1970s and 1980s. Under the impact of economic change and ideological reorientation, large numbers of French citizens (especially manual workers) shed their self-identification as members of a social class (see Table 14.3).

Table 14.3   Proportion of French Citizens Identifying Themselves as Members of a Social Class

	December 1976	March 1983	April 1987
Total	68%	62%	56%
Occupation of respondents			
Higher executives, professionals	68	67	60
Middle executives, school teachers	57	66	63
Office workers	64	62	59
Manual workers	74	71	50

Source: *L'Expansion*, March 20 to April 27, 1987, in Louis Dirn, *La Société française en tendances* (Paris: PUF, 1990), p. 63.

This does not mean that the importance of class divisions has disappeared from France's collective memory. It is striking, for example, that large majorities of citizens express support in public opinion polls for the periodic strikes and demonstrations by transportation workers, farmers, and others, which cause widespread disruption and great personal inconvenience. But social class is no longer a major dimension of partisan cleavage. Political parties today do not seek support on the basis of class, and the major parties' class base has become increasingly similar.

The most extensive decline in class identification has occurred in the ranks of manual workers. There are many reasons for the declining importance of working class identity—a tendency found throughout Europe. One reason is the massive economic restructuring that has occurred since the 1970s, with a shrinking of basic industries (including steel, shipbuilding, automobiles, and textiles), which has produced the closing of some of the largest plants and a general downsizing of the industrial workforce.

Thus, the number of manual workers in France has shrunk by one quarter in the past several decades.

Another reason for declining working class identity is the changing character of the trade union movement, a traditionally important source of working class identity and activity. French labor unions are weak and highly divided. The overall rate of labor union membership in France has plummeted from over 20 percent to fewer than 10 percent of the labor force since the 1970s, among the lowest rates of all industrialized democracies. The bulk of union members are found among public sector workers, including administrators in state and local government, health care and postal workers, teachers, and employees of public and semipublic agencies.

The French trade union movement is highly fragmented. There are five umbrella trade union confederations claiming to represent workers throughout the economy, as well as independent unions in specific sectors (such as teachers). Some independent unions are highly militant and critical of what they regard as the moderation of the major confederations. Each confederation pursues its own course, often opposed to that of the others. Traditionally divisions were heightened because each confederation was allied with a competing political party. The largest confederation, the CGT, was closely linked to the Communist Party. The confederations' ties to political parties have weakened in recent years, but their mutual rivalry continues.

The low rate of unionization and divisions among unions are key factors in understanding unions' weak influence. Nonetheless, unions command far wider support among workers and the general public than their small size would suggest. For example, although one need not be a union member to stand for election to representative mechanisms like works councils, most of the candidates who are elected are nominated by trade unions. Moreover, unions repeatedly mobilize large numbers of nonmembers, along with their own militants, to participate in strikes and demonstrations.

Yet because of their meager size and internal divisions, trade unions have relatively little direct influence in shaping public policy. For years, the labor movement could not persuade the state to legislate even minimal protection for union officials in the face of arbitrary employer actions. Unions have had little voice in formulating and implementing policies of direct concern to workers and unions. Under these conditions, they have typically been forced to express their demands by direct protest—a more dramatic but often less effective means than behind-the-scenes meetings with administrative officials. Their main influence lies in blocking policies they oppose, such as the Juppé government's social reforms, rather than in persuading the government to adopt policies they favor.[12]

Citizenship and National Identity

The French have traditionally taken pride in the fact that citizenship rights have been granted in a highly inclusive fashion. As sociologist Rogers Brubaker describes in his classic comparison of the two major continental states of West Europe, *Citizenship and Nationhood in France and Germany,* the French conception of citizenship was traditionally based on the principle of territory, whereas the German conception was based on blood or ethnicity.[13] The Latin terms that social scientists use to describe the contrasting approach to defining criteria for citizenship are *jus soli* and *jus sanguinis.* In the first case, anyone born on French soil, including the offspring of parents who are not citizens, automatically possesses citizenship rights. Furthermore, France has traditionally imposed few residency or other requirements for immigrants to become French citizens. Thus, the French defined membership in the political community on the basis of political criteria. The French approach, dating from the Revolution of 1789, reflected the belief

that whoever accepted French political ideals and culture was granted legal rights of citizenship. This approach contrasts sharply with the German conception of citizenship, which reflects the belief that the German political community is defined by blood; that is, one could be a citizen only if one's ancestors were German. These different approaches had an important impact on political practice: French naturalization rates have been four or five times higher than those in Germany, and the disparity in inclusion within the political community is far greater yet for second- and third-generation immigrants. In brief, according to political sociologist Charles Tilly, France has "served as Europe's greatest melting pot."[14]

As in many other areas of French political and cultural life, there has been an important change in the domain of citizenship in the recent past. Although France has not fundamentally altered its conception of citizenship, there have been important conflicts on the question. The marginal changes that have occurred in the legal definitions and requirements for gaining citizenship rights speak volumes about the shift to a more exclusive conception of membership in the French political community. The shift in conceptions of citizenship is closely related to the issue of immigration.

Ethnicity

France has traditionally attracted large numbers of immigrants. Indeed, in 1930, there was a higher proportion of immigrants in France than in the United States, a country known as a major destination for emigrants.[15] Tilly observes, "A country whose fertility began to decline very early, France has depended on immigration for the bulk of its population increase since the nineteenth century."[16] So what? Historian Gérard Noiriel's pathbreaking studies provides an answer. Noiriel suggests that the successive waves of immigration "allowed the country to preserve its rank on the international scene, whereas many observers in the late nineteenth century had predicted its irremediable decline."[17] He points to the fact that immigrants were the bulk of iron miners in the 1920s, when France was among the world's major steel producers. And in the period of rapid economic growth after World War II, immigrants built most new French homes and highways—usually working for low wages under harsh working conditions. Thus, immigrants have made an invaluable and insufficiently recognized contribution to France's economic performance.

But it is not sufficient to stress their quantitative contributions. France's justly esteemed reputation as one of the world's scientific and cultural centers rests in considerable part on the contributions of immigrants. In the twentieth century, we can point to scientist Marie Curie, philosopher Henri Bergson, writers Paul Verlaine and Guillaume Apollinaire, painters Pablo Picasso and Marc Chagall, and composer Igor Stravinsky. Even the quintessentially French actor Yves Montand was of immigrant background.

Although the flow of immigrants to France has slowed, recently arrived immigrants continue to enrich France. An illustration from sports: members of the 1998 French World Cup soccer champions constituted a veritable rainbow coalition. The rules of World Cup stipulate that national teams can recruit only citizens of their own country. Among the French players were Zinedine Zidane, whose parents are Algerian immigrants, Lilian Thuram, whose parents are from Guadeloupe, and Marcel Desailly, who hails from Ghana. Other players were of Armenian and Polish descent. Nothing could have better symbolized the fact that France is a country of immigrants.

The fact that the history of France cannot be understood without highlighting the important role of immigrants does not mean that relations between immigrants and native-born French have been harmonious. For example, early in the twentieth century, tensions often ran high between immigrants arriving from Poland, Italy, and Portugal and native-born French. But conflicts around the issue of immigration have intensified in recent decades. Part of the explanation involves cultural conflict and anxiety about France's national identity in an era of globalization. Brubaker has emphasized the traditionally close link in France between nationhood, citizenship, and common cultural values:

> In the French tradition, the nation has been conceived in relation to the institutional and territorial frame of the state. . . . Yet while French nationhood is constituted by political unity, it is centrally expressed in the striving for cultural unity. Political inclusion has entailed cultural assimilation, for regional cultural minorities and immigrants alike.[18]

The not-so-hidden reverse side of the coin of French inclusiveness has been strong pressure for immigrants to renounce their cultural heritage and assimilate dominant French political, social, and cultural values.

There has been an important change recently centering on the right of immigrants and their children to obtain French nationality. The issue surfaced publicly for the first time in the 1980s when the FN challenged the notion that immigrants' children should automatically be granted citizenship rights.[19] The FN's slogan summed up the shift toward considering citizenship a right, not a privilege: "To be French, you must deserve it." The two major Center-Right parties, influenced by the FN's growing popularity, partially embraced its exclusionary stance in the 1986 legislative election campaign. They proposed changing citizenship regulations to deprive second-generation immigrants (that is, children born of immigrant parents) of the automatic right to citizenship. The Center-Right parties proposed that henceforth, second-generation immigrants be required to apply for citizenship. At the same time, administrative officials could decide to reject the application under certain circumstances. A major reason for the proposed change was the allegation that recent immigrants (who were Muslim) were not willing and able to accept dominant French values compared to earlier immigrants. The position reflected the view that there were bedrock conflicts between "French" and "Muslim" values. Although sometimes defended with rational arguments, the position often reflected a chauvinist rejection of all things Muslim. It also equated Muslim values with the most extreme fundamentalist tendency within Islam, which in fact few North African immigrants in France supported. In brief, the recent conflict over immigrants' status suggests a troublesome loss of collective self-confidence in France.

Brubaker notes that the proposed change in citizenship law "was unprecedented even in longer-term historical perspective."[20] Although the Center-Right government elected at the time retreated from its position because of both technical obstacles to sponsoring a change and a firestorm of protest from the Left, students, labor unions, and human rights groups, later conservative governments did narrow citizenship rights. The Jospin government partially reversed the change. The Socialists sponsored a new nationality code that granted children of foreign-born parents automatic citizenship—but only when reaching the age of eighteen, rather than at birth, the original situation that conservative governments had altered. In brief, the issue of citizenship rights has become politicized in a way that it never was before. That this is the case testifies above all to widespread anxiety about the meaning of French national identity, as well as a chasm between many nationalist white French citizens and second- and third-generation North African immigrants. Brubaker rightly stresses that the traditional inclusive approach remains strongly entrenched in France. Indeed, for the 2001 municipal elections, for the first time, citizens of other EU member states living in France were authorized to vote and even run for town councils. This reform, mandated by the EU, symbolized how the EU may enrich France's traditionally inclusive conception of citizenship. Thus, the French have

not abandoned their liberal approach to citizenship. However, this long-established orientation has become a target of criticism. Differently put, Noiriel suggests that, since the 1980s, "The view that immigrants represented a threat to 'national identity,' originally launched by the far right, was held by large sectors of the public."[21] Sad corroboration of this view is that, in public opinion polls, French citizens consistently display significantly higher levels of racist attitudes than are found in other EU member states.

France's ailing economy is another reason that the issues of immigration and cultural identity have assumed such importance in the recent past. Indeed, France's economic difficulties and conflicts over the meaning of French national identity are closely intertwined. Immigrants were tolerated when they were needed to perform necessary jobs like building roads, homes, and automobiles. Recently, however, the shift to a service-based economy, as well as lagging economic growth, has reduced the number of unskilled and semiskilled jobs, and there is a surplus, not a shortage, of workers. The result is that immigrants and their children are far more likely to be unemployed. In addition, recent immigrants prove a convenient target for those native-born French living a precarious existence—and for politicians eager to reap political gains from the difficult situation.

The major controversy over immigration centers on the status of the most recent wave of immigrants, who are mainly Muslims (and often Arabs) from North Africa (above all, Algeria, and also Morocco and Tunisia). There are about 4 million Muslims in France, 2 million of them French citizens. Many arrived in France during the 1960s, mostly from Algeria, when there was a large demand for foreign workers willing to work for low wages on public works projects, and the French government helped organize the recruitment of workers from North Africa. Since the mid-1970s, with the onset of economic stagnation, successive governments have often used brutal means to stop the flow of

new immigrants. (New immigration is now prohibited, save for families of already-established
immigrants and applicants for political asylum.)
As a result, the number of new immigrants arriving yearly has fallen from 250,000–300,000
to 100,000–120,000.[22] (Note that issues of immigration and identity came to the fore *after*
new immigration to France had flowed to a
trickle.) The conspicuous presence of police carrying out identity checks in Métro stations and
elsewhere symbolizes the government's determination to expel undocumented immigrants,
that is, those who migrate to France without
official authorization.

The Muslim community in France is quite diverse and divided—by country of origin, degree
of religious observance, and generationally.
Among the most politically active groups is the
Beurs, the roughly 1 million children of immigrant parents from North Africa. Although the
Beurs have made energetic efforts to achieve social mobility (with women far more likely to
succeed than men), Muslims in France are often
considered second-class citizens and the object
of widespread hostility. Every year they are the
object of racist attacks.

The explosive mix just described has stimulated the growth of new parties and movements.
In the early 1980s, FN leader Jean-Marie Le Pen
failed to gain the required number of signatures
from local politicians to run for president. Ten
years later, the FN was the fourth largest party
in France. The party's slogan, "France for the
French," does not answer the question, "Who
(and what) is French?" But its simplistic and
racist approach has reshaped the structure of
ideological conflict and public opinion. For example, many French citizens on the economic
and social margin have been persuaded by the
graffiti that the FN sprays in prominent places:
"3 million immigrants = 3 million unemployed," which falsely implies that immigrants
cause unemployment.

There has also been intense mobilization in
support of the undocumented immigrants and
against racism. On several occasions, undocumented immigrants have camped out in
churches to dramatize their plight. The Jospin
government was squeezed from both sides in
1998 when it sponsored legislation to review
and regularize the situation of qualified undocumented immigrants. On the one hand, conservatives lambasted the government for being
"soft" on immigrants. On the other hand, the
Left severely criticized the Interior Ministry for
rejecting the claims of half the 150,000 applicants for regularization and announcing that
they would be deported. Leading artists and intellectuals, led by four of France's most famous
filmmakers, launched a movement of solidarity
with the immigrants and opposing the government. The action was highly embarrassing to a
socialist government proudly proclaiming its
commitment to human rights and humanist
ideals.

Gender

Women, the largest "minority"—in reality a 51
percent majority—have traditionally been
highly underrepresented in the French political
system. There has never been a female president of the republic and only one prime minister: Edith Cresson, who served briefly under
President Mitterrand and was the object of considerable ridicule, in part because of her gender.
This situation is changing dramatically as a result of a constitutional amendment passed in
1999 and legislation adopted in 2000 designed to
ensure women equal political representation.

France may be said to be the home of mod-
ernist feminist thought. Philosopher and novelist Simone de Beauvoir's *The Second Sex* published after World War II is a landmark in this
regard, and in the 1960s and 1970s French feminist theorists contributed to reshaping literary
studies throughout the world. However, there is
considerable gender inequality in France, and
women's movements, like many other social
movements, have been relatively weak in the
face of a distant state. Moreover, state policy often has been unresponsive to women's concerns,

partly as a result of their meager political representation. Contraception, for example, was illegal in France until 1967. Abortion was banned until 1974. A law outlawing sexual harassment was passed in 1992. However, although the legislation prohibits sexual harassment by supervisors, it is silent on the issue of harassment by fellow-employees. Moreover, the concept of a hostile working environment does not exist in French law.[23] On the other hand, legislation outlaws publishing sexist material, and France's extensive welfare state benefits, including public preschool facilities and health programs, serve women's interests.

For many years, France was among the industrialized democracies in which women were most underrepresented. Feminists highlighted the injustice of the fact that although over half the electorate, women constituted no more than 10 percent of the National Assembly. When a law was passed in 1982 mandating that women constitute at least one-fourth of municipal councils, the Constitutional Council struck it down on the grounds that this violated a constitutional mandate of equal treatment of all citizens. In part as a result of a cross-party coalition of female legislators, pressure mounted to amend the Constitution in order to resolve the deadlock. In 1999, the Jospin government sponsored such an amendment in order to "encourage equal access for women and men to political life and elected positions." Landmark legislation passed in 2000 implementing the amendment goes beyond even the most advanced countries (in Scandinavia) to promote gender equality in political representation. The parity law, as it is called, requires all political parties to nominate an equal number of men and women. Public campaign subsidies are significantly reduced for any party that fails to comply.

The 2001 municipal elections were the first held since the reform was adopted. (The 2002 legislative elections will also be governed by the parity law, which means that the number of female deputies will soar.) The 2001 municipal elections produced a dramatic increase in

women's representation. Nearly without exception, election slates in towns throughout France had as many women as men. From one election to the next, the number of women on France's town councils increased from about 7,000 to 39,000, nearly half of the 83,000 municipal councilors in the villages and towns over 3,500 population to which the law applies. Within several years, women should achieve close to equal representation within all of France's representative institutions.

Two questions immediately posed by this development are: Will these gains also be translated into a comparable increase in women's representation at the highest executive positions, notably, the government and office of president and prime minister? And will women's increased political representation promote legislative and policy changes that produce social and economic equality between men and women? The parity law thus provides a laboratory test of whether increasing political representation produces legislation that addresses gender inequality in the wider society.

Protest and Social Movements

Although Fifth Republic institutions were designed to discourage citizens from acting autonomously, they have not always succeeded. France has a long tradition of direct protest. Throughout the nineteenth century, regimes were toppled by mass opposition in the streets. More recently, the May 1968 uprising was "the nearest thing to a full-blown revolution ever experienced in an advanced industrial society" and a vivid reminder of how fragile political stability can be in France.[24] A repeat performance occurred in December 1995, when transportation workers brought Paris and other large cities grinding to a halt. And in 1999, France was at the forefront of protests over the quickening pace of globalization. (We describe the 1995 and 1999 protests in Chapter 15.)

The overall number of strikes has declined as a result of high unemployment. However, the strikes that do occur are often highly militant and disruptive. Among the groups resorting to strikes and demonstrations in recent years were farmers, fishing interests, postal workers, teachers, high school students, truckers, railway workers, health care workers, and immigrants and their offspring—and that is only a partial list! At the same time, protest movements are neither unified—the diverse protests enumerated above are united only by the angry claim that political institutions serve their interests poorly—nor linked to political parties that can adequately represent their demands.[25]

The picture thus far is of a trend toward less frequent strikes and demonstrations while those that occur are likely to be militant, extensive, and disruptive. Another trend in recent decades is a dramatic increase in the number of civic associations that bring citizens together for sports, leisure, cultural, and generally nonconfrontational purposes. Whereas about 20,000 new

associations were created in 1975, the number increased to 60,000 new associations annually in the current period. Although these statistics reveal a sharp rise in civic membership, the French remain less likely to join such associations than citizens of neighboring countries. Whereas 39 percent of the French report belonging to one or more associations, the comparable figures are 53 percent in the United Kingdom, 58 percent in Belgium, 67 percent in Germany, and 84 percent in the Netherlands.[26]

The Fifth Republic erected sturdy institutions to strengthen the state. But an adequate balance has not yet been struck between state action, on the one hand, and citizen participation and representation, on the other. Thus, when specific challenges develop, as we review in the next chapter, established channels often fail to provide an effective forum to debate and address problems.

Notes

1. Olivier Duhamel, *Le Pouvoir politique en France* (Paris: Editions du Seuil, 1993), p. 256, n. 1.

2. John D. Huber, *Rationalizing Parliament: Legislative Institutions and Party Politics in France* (Cambridge: Cambridge University Press, 1996).

3. Jean Charlot, *La Politique en France* (Paris: Livre de Poche, 1994), p. 21.

4. Donald Sassoon, *One Hundred Years of Socialism: The West European Left in the Twentieth Century* (New York: New Press, 1996), p. 571.

5. James G. Shields, "Le Pen and the Progression of the Far-Right Vote in France," *French Politics and Society* 13, no. 2 (Spring 1995): 37.

6. Olivier Duhamel and Jérôme Jaffré, "Le malêtre de la gauche," in Olivier Duhamel and Jérôme Jaffré, eds., *L'État de l'opinion, 1990* (Paris: Le Seuil, 1990), pp. 9–20.

7. François Platone, "Le vote communiste: le verre à moitié plein," in Pascal Perrineau and Colette Ysmal, eds., *Le vote surprise: les élections législatives*

des 25 mai et 1er juin 1997 (Paris: Presses de Sciences Po, 1998), p. 187.

8. Charlot, *La Politique en France*, p. 159.

9. Pascal Perrineau, "Election Cycles and Changing Patterns of Political Behavior in France," *French Politics and Society* 13, no. 1 (Winter 1995): 53. For further analyses of this issue, see Daniel Boy and Nana Mayer, eds., *L'Électeur a ses Raisons* (Paris: Presses de la Fondation Nationale des Sciences Politiques, 1997), and Michael S. Lewis-Beck and Richard Nadeau, "French Electoral Institutions and the Economic Vote," *Electoral Studies* 19 (2000): 171–182.

10. Pascal Perrineau and Dominique Reynié, Introduction to Perrineau and Reynié, eds., *Le Vote incertain: Les élections régionales de 1998* (Paris: Presses de Sciences Po, 1999), p. 12.

11. Pascal Perrineau, ed., *L'Engagement politique: Déclin ou mutation?* (Paris: Presses de la Fondation Nationale des Sciences Politiques, 1994).

12. See Anthony Daley, "The Hollowing Out of French Unions: Politics and Industrial Relations After 1981," in Andrew Martin and George Ross, eds., *The Brave New World of European Labor: European Trade Unions at the Millennium* (New York: Berghahn Books, 1999), and Herrick Chapman, Mark Kesselman, and Martin A. Schain, eds., *A Century of Organized Labor in France: A Union Movement for the Twenty-First Century?* (New York: St. Martin's Press, 1998).

13. Rogers Brubaker, *Citizenship and Nationhood in France and Germany* (Cambridge, Mass.: Harvard University Press, 1992).

14. Charles Tilly, Foreword to Gérard Noiriel, *The French Melting Pot: Immigration, Citizenship, and National Identity* (Minneapolis: University of Minnesota Press, 1996), p. vii.

15. Patrick Weil, *La France et ses étrangers* (Paris: Gallimard, 1991), p. 28.

16. Tilly, in Noiriel, *The French Melting Pot*, p. vii.

17. Noiriel, *The French Melting Pot*, p. 240.

18. Brubaker, *Citizenship*, p. 1.

19. This account draws on ibid. and Noiriel, *The French Melting Pot*.

20. Brubaker, *Citizenship*, p. 143.

21. Tilly's paraphrase of Noiriel's position, in Noiriel, *The French Melting Pot*, p. xii.

22. Patrick Weil, "Immigration, nation et nationalité: Regards comparatives et croisés," *Revue française de science politique* 44, no 2 (April 1994): 308–326.

23. See Amy G. Mazur, *Gender Bias and the State: Symbolic Reform at Work in Fifth Republic France* (Pittsburgh: University of Pittsburgh Press, 1996).

24. Stephen Bornstein, "States and Unions: From Postwar Settlement to Contemporary Stalemate," in Stephen Bornstein, David Held, and Joel Krieger, eds., *The State in Capitalist Europe: A Casebook* (Winchester, Mass.: George Allen & Unwin, 1984), p. 64.

25. See Guy Groux, "Culture protestataire et opinion publique: Un lien ambigu," in Pierre Bréchon, Annie Laurent, and Pascal Perrineau, eds., *Les Cultures politiques des Français* (Paris: Presses de Sciences Po, 2000), chap. 11.

26. Commissariat général du plan, *Rapport sur les perspectives de la France* (Paris: La Documentation Française, 2000), p. 86.

C H A P T E R

15

French Politics
in Transition

The pace of change throughout the world is doubtless accelerating as space and time are compressed by the incredible technological advances of recent decades, and national borders become more porous as a result of increased transnational economic, political, social, and cultural flows. While the extent and character of the changes wrought by globalization are complex, controversial, and often obscure, the fact that the world is changing cannot be disputed. These observations apply to France no less than to other countries in the world. What kinds of changes—and continuities—in French politics emerge from our analysis?

Continuities, Transitions, and Changing Agendas

What a distance separates French politics in the early years of the new century from politics even a few years earlier. Political conflict in the 1970s and 1980s—as well as the major political parties—were arrayed quite neatly along a Left–Right ideological continuum linked to social class divisions. In the 1970s, attention was riveted on the opposition between an alliance linking the Communist and Socialist parties, based on a radical reformist program, and the conservative Center-Right parties. In the early 1980s, the reform initiatives of the Socialist government dominated the news. When the Center-Right coalition gained a parliamentary

majority in 1986, its first priority was to roll back many of the reforms.

By the mid-1990s, however, the Center-Left and Center-Right generally agreed on the major political priorities. All three major parties accepted France's mixed economy, consisting of the coexistence of a strong role for the state but also heavy reliance on private market forces. All three accepted that for the sake of further European integration (notably, the launching of the euro), it was worth making unpleasant economic policy choices, including cutbacks in state spending, especially social spending, in order to reduce government deficits and the public debt. This general policy orientation dated from the mid-1980s and had been pursued by Socialist and conservative governments for a decade. By the mid-1990s, then, it appeared that significant ideological controversy, at least among the major political parties, had ended.

Yet in retrospect, the calm that prevailed was the prelude to the storm. We review here political challenges in 1995 and 1999 that highlight continuities and changes in France's political agenda—and the inadequacy of the existing system to confront that agenda.

The Strikes of December 1995:
May 1968 Revisited?

In late 1995, France was rocked by a series of strikes and demonstrations whose extent and intensity recalled those of May 1968. An analysis of the strikes reveals the important elements of change that have recently occurred in France, important elements of continuity, and the importance of the transition and challenges that France is confronting.

Dashed Expectations: The 1995 Elections and Thereafter. The origins of the massive strikes in 1995 may be found in the conjunction of France's severe economic difficulties, the expectations raised by Jacques Chirac's 1995 presidential election campaign advocating a change, and the disillusionment that was created when Chirac renounced his electoral pledges.

In Chapter 12, we reviewed how France has been undergoing extensive economic restructuring, which has produced both modernization for many industries but also devastation for entire regions and sectors of the population. Since the Socialists' "turn" in 1983, governments of Left and Right had promoted the intensive modernization of French industry by a program involving deregulation, privatization, high interest rates, and social retrenchment.

In the 1995 presidential election, the Movement for the Republic (RPR) candidate Jacques Chirac attempted to differentiate himself from another conservative candidate, as well as from Socialist party candidate Lionel Jospin, by holding out the hope that things could be different. As a respected journalist commented in a book about Chirac's campaign, "He was forced to adopt the strategy of an outsider, gambling that victory would go not to a candidate proposing continuity, but to the candidate who advocated change."[1] For the first time since the Socialist party's U-turn of 1983, a candidate from one of the "big three" centrist parties challenged the consensus that there was no alternative but to pursue austerity policies. In a famous phrase during the campaign, Chirac declared, "The pay stub [i.e., a decent wage level] is not the enemy of employment." And when Chirac gained election, it was no surprise that in his victory

speech, he proclaimed, "Our battle has a name: the struggle against unemployment."

Chirac's strategy was electorally successful but later proved politically costly. Only months after he had escalated expectations that things could be different and that government policy would accord priority to reflation and social ends, he was forced to orchestrate an about-face. The need to comply with the strict fiscal requirements of the Treaty of Maastricht collided with Chirac's electoral promises, and the promises lost. In a television interview in October 1995, he announced that his initial optimism about the possibilities for reflation were mistaken. The situation was more difficult than he had foreseen, and there was no alternative to returning to fiscal orthodoxy. His words were quickly followed by actions.

The Cold Shower of Further Austerity. Immediately after Chirac's interview, Prime Minister Juppé announced a series of major reforms, which—in both form and substance—represented virtually a declaration of war on labor unions, especially those in the public sector. Without prior consultation with unions, Juppé proposed tightening requirements for civil servants' pensions and ending preferential retirement benefits for particular categories of public sector workers: railway workers, electrical and gas workers, and postal workers. Juppé called for revamping the state-run railway system, including partial privatization, closing unprofitable sectors, and laying off workers. And he proposed to overhaul the social security (health care) system, in particular the method of financing and delivering health care. His plan included tightening benefits and limiting future increase in expenditures; partially transferring control to parliament (that is, the government) from the previous system, in which unions had a major role; and modifying the system of financing health care by increasing the number of those taxed and creating a new tax that would apply to virtually all citizens receiving income and state transfer payments. Furthermore, he mandated financial austerity for universities, including cutbacks in hiring of new staff, as well as limiting new construction and maintenance. In addition, government ministers hinted that new reforms would soon follow, including the partial privatization of France Télécom, the sprawling state telecommunications agency, and increases in income taxes.

The Response. Reaction to the proposed reforms was swift. The railway workers were the first to announce a strike, thus continuing a tradition of militant action by rail workers in France. (Although railway workers represent only 1 percent of all French wage earners, they account for one-fifth of all the work time lost due to strikes.) Other transport workers quickly followed their lead: Paris Métro workers and bus drivers, public transport workers in other French cities, and air traffic controllers and Air France personnel. France was quickly brought to a halt, as gridlock and miles of traffic jams immobilized Paris and other large cities. Massive demonstrations brought out ever more participants, climaxing in a 2-million-strong demonstration on December 7. As other public sector workers stayed home, the postal system ground to a halt, garbage began to accumulate on city streets, schools closed, and power slowdowns occurred.

In the face of this overwhelming and sustained opposition to the proposed reforms, Juppé retreated on some key points. For example, in 1996 he obtained legislative authorization to carry out the promised reforms by administrative decree. In fact, the major reason that President Chirac dissolved parliament in 1997 and called for new elections was that he gambled that a fresh electoral mandate would enable the Juppé government to sponsor further cutbacks. Chirac's miscalculation produced a Socialist parliamentary majority in 1997 and a Socialist government.

Although the strikes were of major significance in signifying the depth of popular opposition to the dominant orientation of eco-

nomic policy, they failed to alter that orientation in fundamental respects. The strikes reveal the continuing vitality of the French tradition of popular protest, and they highlighted how important French participation in the European Union (EU) is, both for shaping French policy and provoking popular opposition.

Oui to Roquefort Cheese, Non to Genetically Engineered Products (GMOs)

Several years after the strikes that protested the threat of social cutbacks, another movement sprang up to protest constraints imposed by the process of globalization and Europeanization. The movement is quite diverse and includes environmentalists, reenergized ultra-leftists, intellectuals, and farmers. We focus here on France's most recent heroic protest figure, José Bové, a farmer from the sheep-raising region of southwestern France where famed Roquefort cheese is produced.[2] Bové helped create an organization of small farmers in 1987 that opposed the agribusiness orientation of the National Federation of Farmers' Unions. Small farmers like Bové protested the standardized methods of farming that agribusiness corporations sought to impose (including the use of genetically modified seed), low-priced competition from Italy, Spain, and other members of the EU, and farmers' loss of autonomy resulting from centralization of food distribution and processing by large corporations. Bové achieved worldwide prominence in early 1999 when he led a march of several hundred people that ransacked a McDonald's construction site in southwest France. For Bové and his supporters, who quickly grew into the millions, McDonald's symbolized much of what was wrong about the EU and globalization: fast, standardized food produced by a U.S. multinational corporation, and which had little in common with traditional French cuisine and might include genetically engineered products (genetically modified organisms—GMOs).

Bové was arrested and sentenced to an unusually stiff penalty for property damage of ten months in prison and a $15,000 fine. Under intense pressure, the prison sentence was reduced to three months. Bové's bail was paid by a public subscription, and statements of support poured in from groups across the political spectrum. President Chirac announced that he personally was inspired by Bové's project of seeking to preserve national ways of farming, eating, and living in the face of the homogenizing forces of globalization.

In 1999, when the World Trade Organization met in Seattle to strengthen regulations requiring governments to guarantee free trade and investment, the French agriculture minister invited Bové to attend the conference and praised his efforts. (Bové smuggled 100 pounds of Roquefort into the United States and distributed it at the Seattle protests.) Meanwhile, Bové's crusade against McDonald's gathered steam, and McDonald's throughout France and the rest of Europe came under attack. When the United States imposed punitive tariffs on food imports to the United States from the EU in retaliation for the EU's ban in American hormone-injected beef in 2000, Roquefort cheese figured prominently on the list.

Bové continues to play a leading role in a worldwide struggle against globalization. He participated in the World Social Forum, held at Porto Alegre, Brazil, in 2001, a meeting of social movement organizations. While at the forum, he joined an invasion of an agricultural research facility run by Monsanto, a U.S. biotech firm, and helped destroy genetically modified corn and soybean plants. In short order, Bové has become a French cultural hero, whose opposition to what he regards as U.S. economic and cultural imperialism strikes a responsive chord among the French.

France is a center of the worldwide protests against globalization and the EU. A coalition named ATTAC, created in 1998, swiftly grew by 2001 to include 25,000 members and nearly 200 local committees throughout France and in other countries.[3] ATTAC has sponsored forums and demonstrations to oppose free trade and capital movements and supports a plan origi-

Globalization. This appeared when José Bové traveled to the Seattle meeting of the World Trade Organization in 1999.

Source: Planti, Cartoonists & Writers Syndicate, from *Cassettes, Mensonges et Vidéo* (Paris: Le Seuil, 2000), p. 36.

nally proposed by Nobel Prize laureate James Tobin to impose a worldwide tax on financial speculation. Along with trade unions from France and other European countries, ATTAC played an important role in the protests at the Nice summit of the EU described in Chapter 15. In brief, popular contention persists in France and will doubtless increase in the face of new sources of challenge.

New Issues and Sources of Partisan Conflict: Economy and Identity

French politics has entered a new era. On the one hand, traditional ideological conflicts have waned, and established political parties have moved closer together. The Center-Left Socialist Party has drained much of the support that in the past made the Parti Communiste Français (PCF) one of France's largest parties. The two major Center-Right parties uneasily coexist. Furthermore, ideological struggles involving fundamental differences over how to organize the economy have been replaced by debates occurring within the framework of centrist, pragmatic managerialism. There is thus widespread acceptance of a mixed economy blending state regulation and market competition.

Political institutions overcame the challenges posed by alternation and cohabitation in the 1980s. Moreover, significant institutional reforms in the past two decades, including decentralization, the shortening of the presidential term, and the requirement for gender parity in political representation, have produced a more balanced and equitable regime. Yet there is lively debate about additional institutional reforms. Some proposals call for a quite fundamental restructuring of the regime, for example, installing a more clear-cut presidential system by abolishing the office of prime minister and prohibiting the president from dissolving parliament. Other proposals involve significant but less fundamental changes, for example, increasing parliament's role in preparing the budget, drastic reform of the quite unrepresentative Senate, and further restrictions in politicians simultaneously exercising several elected mandates (the *cumul des mandats*). Although no proposal has yet received sufficient support to be adopted, intense debates about institutional reform will doubtless persist.

In addition to issues of institutional reform one can identify a more general problem of political participation and representation. As we saw in Chapter 14, established parties command ever smaller levels of support. Citizens are voting with their feet—by supporting dissident political parties or not voting at all. In brief, the established French political parties have been relatively unable to resolve two major issues: the economic challenge of ensuring adequate standards of living for all French citizens and the cultural issue of French national identity. Each is a difficult issue; in tandem, the two produce the major political challenge confronting the French political system.

"It's the Economy, Stupid." William Clinton became president of the United States in 1992 when, with the nation in recession, he promised to focus "like a laser" on the economy. This is a useful reminder that governments generally flourish when the economy flourishes and are punished when the economy stagnates. The uneven performance of the French economy in the past several decades is a large part of the explanation for the political gyrations that have occurred. Although the French economy has been considerably modernized and strengthened in the recent period, many French have paid a heavy price, notably by high rates of unemployment and a large number of marginalized, excluded citizens. The improvement in the economy in the late 1990s helped produce Prime Minister Jospin's exceptionally high poll standings, as did the Jospin government's sponsorship of assistance targeting youth, the excluded, and the long-term unemployed. But France's economic difficulties and associated social problems are too deeply rooted to be solved by simple legislation.

French economic difficulties are compounded by the French style of economic governance. In the postwar period, the French excelled at state-directed promotion of large firms producing projects for captive markets at home and abroad (the latter negotiated with foreign states), as well as at crash programs of industrial development (such as rail and road transport, aerospace, and telecommunications). In the current economic race, victory goes not to the large but to the flexible, and state direction may prove a handicap, not an advantage. Moreover, the cost of innovation in many new spheres now exceeds the capacity of a medium-sized power such as France.

As in many other countries, economic restructuring has produced social marginalization. In France, however, this situation has generated nationwide protest movements that have disrupted politics as usual. Recall the massive strikes in late 1995 that shook France to its roots and contributed to the overthrow of Alain Juppé's conservative government in 1997. (During the 1997 legislative election campaign, four-fifths of voters replied, in public opinion polls, that unemployment was the most important problem influencing their vote.[4]) Prime Minister Jospin faced a somewhat similar, if less intense, challenge in late 1997 when jobless workers stormed unemployment insurance offices throughout France to demand increased benefits and greater government assistance in finding jobs. The conflict temporarily subsided when he offered a carrot and a stick. The carrot consisted of a package of measures specifically targeting the long-term unemployed, as well as a mandated reduction of the workweek to thirty-five hours. The stick was that Jospin ordered the police to storm and evacuate the occupied offices.

An important question on France's political agenda is how to preserve the quite extensive welfare state, which provides fairly generous contributions enabling citizens to obtain high-quality child care, medical care, education, and job training. The French pride themselves on resisting the American model in which one's access to these goods and services depends on the extent of one's income. The French regard access to these goods and services as a right of all citizens. But can this conception survive when unemployment is high, the proportion of the working population (which finances such programs) is declining, and EU treaty obligations impose severe fiscal constraints?

The Challenge of European Integration

How can the French adapt to the challenge posed by the EU to French national distinctiveness, identity, and political, economic, and cultural autonomy? It may be no coincidence that the rise of electoral support for fringe parties coincides with the deepening of European integration in the past two decades. For example, an analysis of electoral patterns and European integration in France and Britain finds that voters' calculation of the costs and benefits of European integration plays a significant role in their vot-

ing choice. Specifically, "contributing to the success of the far right (and other small parties) in France are voter perceptions of attractive policy alternatives over economic integration not offered by the mainstream parties."[5] Similarly, there has been a resurgence in France of demands for regional autonomy and even, in the case of the island of Corsica, for independence from France. In the case of Corsica, there has been bitter and often violent conflict. The French government sponsored a reform in 2000 to grant Corsica special status, with a Corsican legislature given wider powers than other regional legislatures in France enjoy. But it is too soon to say whether this measure will resolve the Corsican conflict or prove too timid for Corsican nationalists and too much for French nationalists. More generally, an important unresolved issue is whether French national identity can be refashioned within the EU when the French values of liberty, equality, and fraternity have become more widely shared—and at the same time that minorities within France have begun to challenge the dominant model of cultural assimilation and seek to preserve their own cultural identities.

An official commission appointed to reflect on "The State and French Society in the Year 2000" asserted that because of its traditional patterns, France has severe handicaps in confronting the future. It asked, "Will the road toward democratic maturity, within the context of the globalization of values and a reduced role for national states, be more arduous in France than in other nations?"[6] In the light of the previous discussion, the answer seems quite obvious.

French Politics in Comparative Perspective

France has long provided an interesting case for comparative analysis because of its many attempts at state and regime making. By comparing the Fourth and Fifth Republics, we can study the impact of institutions on political outcomes. The same country was governed in two dramatically different ways within a short time. The experiment teaches what to avoid as much as what to emulate. The Fourth Republic demonstrated the pitfalls of a fragmented multiparty system with undisciplined parties and a parliamentary regime with a weak executive. The Fifth Republic demonstrates the danger of an isolated and overly powerful executive. The Fifth Republic has taken halting steps toward developing more balanced institutions, including a larger role for the Constitutional Council, stronger local governments, a shorter term for the president, and independent media. France's semi-presidential system may prove attractive to countries seeking lessons in political-institutional design.

France also provides an exciting opportunity to analyze the efficacy of institutional changes to address inequalities in political representation. By adopting the gender parity reform in 2000, France became the first country in the world to mandate equal political representation for men and women. The results of this bold experiment are being widely scrutinized and hold rich lessons for comparativists.

In addition, France pioneered another institutional reform involving intergroup relations when legislation was passed in 1999 creating a civil union between couples of the same or opposite sex, the civil solidarity pact (*pacte civil de solidarité,* or Pacs). The Pacs provides couples who register their association some of the legal rights hitherto enjoyed only by married couples. The innovation (which was strongly contested by groups championing traditional val-

ues) symbolizes a liberalization of French cultural attitudes.

On the level of political culture more generally, France has prided itself on its universalist yet distinctive role in history, deriving from its revolutionary heritage of liberty, equality, and fraternity. But at the same time that they have become increasingly accepted, both within France and globally, these values are less able to promote cohesion among French citizens. Another challenge to French political culture and national pride is that the French language—revered by the French for its beauty and precision, and a favored medium for international diplomatic communication—is rapidly being eclipsed by English. It is instructive to study how France adjusts to the process of abandoning its claim to being preeminent among the countries of the world. More generally, France is not alone in seeking to reconcile the conflicting claims of maintaining national cohesion in the face of extensive internal diversity and increasing integration in the international economic and political system. Nor is it the only country that struggles with the issue of how to maintain a cohesive political community while affirming the right of diverse groups with different cultural heritages to membership in that community. The way that a proud country like France seeks to address these many dilemmas can provide rich lessons for comparative analysis. In brief, more than thirty years after youthful French protesters chanted in May 1968, "The struggle continues," the words have lost none of their relevance.

Notes

1. Patrick Jarreau, *La France de Chirac* (Paris: Flammarion, 1995), p. 9.

2. This account draws on Kate Goldstein-Breyer, "Unidentified Fringe Movements: The Secret of their Success," unpublished paper, Columbia University, 2000.

3. Data from ATTAC, *Tout sur Attac* (Paris: Editions mille et une nuits, 2000), and interviews with leaders of the organization.

4. Roland Cayrol, "L'Électeur face aux enjeux économiques, sociaux et européens," in Pascal Perrineau and Colette Ysmal, eds., *Le vote surprise:*

les élections législatives des 25 mai et 1er juin 1997 (Paris: Presses de Sciences Po, 1998), pp. 100–101.

5. Kenneth Scheve, "European Economic Integration and Electoral Politics in France and Great Brit-

ain," unpublished paper, Harvard University, 1999, p. 29.

6. Bernard Cazes, Fabrice Hatem, and Paul Thibaud, "L'État et la société française en l'an 2000," *Esprit*, no. 165 (October 1990): 95.

Bibliography

Boy, Daniel, and Nonna Mayer, eds. *The French Voter Decides.* Ann Arbor: University of Michigan Press, 1994.

Brubaker, Rogers. *Citizenship and Nationhood in France and Germany.* Cambridge, Mass.: Harvard University Press, 1992.

Chapman, Herrick, Mark Kesselman, and Martin A. Schain, eds. *A Century of Organized Labor in France: A Union Movement for the Twenty-First Century?* New York: St. Martin's Press, 1998.

Daley, Anthony, ed. *The Mitterrand Era: Policy Alternatives and Political Mobilization in France.* New York: New York University Press, 1996.

Daley, Anthony. *Steel, State, and Labor: Mobilization and Adjustment in France.* Pittsburgh: University of Pittsburgh Press, 1996.

Duyvendak, Jan Willem. *The Power of Politics: New Social Movements in France.* Boulder, Colo.: Westview, 1995.

Friend, Julius W. *The Long Presidency: France in the Mitterrand Years, 1981–1995.* Boulder, Colo.: Westview, 1998.

Gaffney, John, and Lorna Milne, eds. *French Presidentialism and the Election of 1995.* Brookfield, Vt.: Ashgate, 1997.

Gopnik, Adam. *Paris to the Moon.* New York: Random House, 2000.

Hall, Peter A. *Governing the Economy: The Politics of State Intervention in Britain and France.* New York: Oxford University Press, 1986.

Hall, Peter, Jack Hayward, and Howard Machin, eds. *Developments in French Politics 2.* New York: Macmillan, 1998.

Howell, Chris. *Regulating Labor: The State and Industrial Relations Reform in Postwar France.* Princeton, N.J.: Princeton University Press, 1992.

Huber, John D. *Rationalizing Parliament: Legislative Institutions and Party Politics in France.* Cambridge: Cambridge University Press, 1996.

Ireland, Patrick. *The Policy Challenge of Ethnic Diversity: Immigrant Politics in France and Switzerland.* Cambridge, Mass.: Harvard University Press, 1994.

Keeler, John T. S., and Martin A. Schain, eds. *Chirac's Challenge: Liberalization, Europeanization, and Malaise in France.* New York: St. Martin's Press, 1996.

Levy, Jonah. *Tocqueville's Revenge: Dilemmas of Institutional Reform in Post-Dirigiste France.* Cambridge, Mass.: Harvard University Press, 1998.

Lewis-Beck, Michael S., ed. *How France Votes.* New York: Chatham House, 2000.

Mazur, Amy G. *Gender Bias and the State: Symbolic Reform at Work in Fifth Republic France.* Pittsburgh: University of Pittsburgh Press, 1996.

Noiriel, Gérard. *The French Melting Pot: Immigration, Citizenship, and National Identity.* Minneapolis: University of Minnesota Press, 1996.

Pierce, Roy. *Choosing the Chief: Presidential Elections in France and the United States.* Ann Arbor: University of Michigan Press, 1995.

Schmidt, Vivien A. *From State to Market? The Transformation of French Business and Government.* Cambridge: Cambridge University Press, 1996.

Simmons, Harvey G. *The French National Front: The Extremist Challenge to Democracy.* Boulder, Colo.: Westview, 1996.

Smith, W. Rand. *The Left's Dirty Job: The Politics of Industrial Restructuring in France and Spain.* Pittsburgh: University of Pittsburgh Press, 1998.

Stone, Alec. *The Birth of Judicial Politics in France.* New York: Oxford University Press, 1992.

Tiersky, Ronald. *François Mitterrand: The Last French President.* New York: St. Martin's Press, 2000.

Tilly, Charles. *The Contentious French: Four Centuries of Popular Struggle.* Cambridge, Mass.: The Belknap Press of Harvard University Press, 1986.

Web Sites

The French Embassy site in Washington, in English, *http://www.ambafrance-us.org/fnews.htm*

The French president's site, in French, *http://www.elysee.fr*

The prime minister's site, in English, *http://www.premier-ministre.gouv.fr/en*

National Assembly site, in French, *http://www.assemblee-nationale.fr*

French foreign ministry, in French, *http://www.diplomatie.gouv.fr/actualite/actu.asp*

France's most respected newspaper, *Le Monde,* in French, *http://www.lemonde.fr*

A center-left newspaper, *Libération,* in French, *http://www.liberation.fr*

A conservative newspaper, *Le Figaro,* in French, *http://www.lefigaro.fr*

P A R T

V

Germany

Christopher S. Allen

16

The Making of the
Modern German State

German Politics in Action

Any journey to Berlin today produces a powerful first impression. Construction equipment is virtually everywhere, and the noise and bustle accompanying this frenetic activity seem almost overwhelming to both new visitors as well as those who have not been there for several years.

Two things are driving this structural overhaul of Germany's largest city. First, as a result of unification in 1990, the German capital has moved from its former site, Bonn, a picturesque university city on the banks of the Rhine in the extreme western part of the country. Not only did this move make geographical sense, it also signified the completion of the commitment made by the founders of the Federal Republic in 1949 that, once unified, Germany would retain Berlin as its capital.[1] The erection of new ministry offices is responsible for much of this construction boom as older buildings are rehabilitated and newer ones spring up seemingly overnight. Second, Berlin's location in the middle of the former East Germany has presented German governments during the past decade with both an opportunity and an obligation to rebuild that region after forty years of Communist underdevelopment. The structural rebuilding of the city has had a powerful effect in raising both commercial and residential properties. It also has reinvigorated cultural and political life as the former divided city once again becomes a world capital.

The merging of the two states in 1990 was the second unification in modern Germany's brief history. The principalities that joined in 1871 to form the first modern German state (called the *Second Reich*) produced a remarkable—and often catastrophic—variety of political outcomes: an authoritarian pseudodemocracy, World War I, the ill-fated Weimar Republic, the fascist Nazi regime (the *Third Reich*), World War II and the Holocaust, the postwar partition into two Germanies, and finally, a modern reunification. Unlike Britain, whose democracy developed gradually over many centuries, Germany was able to establish a stable democracy only after great fluctuations in regimes, two military defeats, and a foreign occupation, and then only in part of its former territory. East Germany, which remained within the Soviet Union's sphere of influence, was ruled by a highly repressive Communist government until unification in 1990.

The return of the capital to Berlin not surprisingly has generated some fears as well as enthusiasm among both Germans and other Europeans. In many ways, the change in Berlin's physical and political status is a metaphor for both the challenges and the opportunities that Germany faces in the new century. For one thing, German unification conjures up fears among some of its neighbors regarding whether it will once again become a menace to the European continent as it did twice during the first half of the twentieth century. The rebuilding of

the Reichstag, the parliament building constructed by Otto von Bismarck, who founded modern Germany in 1871 and used by Hitler, drives some of the foreign anxiety about Germany's role in the new century. Realistically, an aggressive Germany is highly unlikely, but the country's unique history does not induce skeptics to give it the benefit of the doubt. Second, the frenetic and often ostentatious building boom in the new capital contrasts sharply with the dilapidated condition of much of eastern Germany that surrounds Berlin. The primary complaint that eastern Germans have of their western German cousins is that they are using their disproportionately high wealth to behave as carpetbaggers in the former German Democratic Republic (GDR). The faster that Berlin grows, the more obvious it is to eastern Germans how far they lag economically behind the rest of the country. Third, Berlin's rapid growth has served as a magnet not only for eastern Germans who wish to leave their smaller towns for the big city but also for others from both Eastern Europe and the rest of the world who are taking advantage of Europe's post–cold war open borders. The rapid immigration of foreigners into a part of Germany that was both ethnically and culturally homogeneous during the Communist years has proved combustible. Not only were these eastern Germans economically disadvantaged compared to their western fellow citizens, some saw the influx of immigrants as both an economic and cultural threat. Finally, the growth of Berlin as Germany's new capital raises once again in some minds the question of whether we are witnessing the evolution of a German Europe or a European Germany.

The new Berlin—and Germany as a whole—stand at a turning point that could lead in one of two directions. The first might see a consolidation of postwar successes in which the former East Germans achieve the material prosperity and democratic political culture of their western counterparts. This could help Germany to become the anchor in the expanding European Union (EU) as a partner—not a conqueror—of

its neighbors. The second path would be much more dangerous. It could see a rising social conflict, unstable domestic institutions, uncertain international relations including a weakened EU, and difficulties in responding to international economic competition.

Geographic Setting

Germany is located in central Europe and has been as much a Western European nation as it has an Eastern European one. A federal state, Germany is divided into sixteen states (or *Bundesländer* in German), many of which correspond to historic German kingdoms and principalities (e.g., Bavaria, Saxony, Hesse) or medieval trading cities (e.g., Hamburg, Bremen). It has a total area of 137,803 square miles (slightly smaller than the state of Montana) and a population of 82 million. (Table 16.1 presents a brief profile of Germany.) Comprising about 90 percent whose roots stem from within the borders of modern Germany, all of whom speak German as the primary language, they are roughly evenly divided between Catholics and Protestants. Germany has been relatively ethnically homogeneous; however, the presence of several million Turks in Germany, first drawn to the Federal Republic as "guest workers" (*Gastarbeiter*)—foreign workers who had no citizenship rights—in the 1960s, suggests that ethnic diversity will continue to grow. The new century saw a familiar echo of the importing of foreign workers in the 1960s. A shortage of information age workers among the German population induced Chancellor Gerhard Schröder's government to permit the immigration of several thousand Indian computer professionals with Internet and programming skills. Furthermore, increased migration across borders by EU citizens has also decreased cultural homogeneity, since approximately 10 percent of the country's population traces its origins outside the Federal Republic.

For a densely populated country, Germany

Table 16.1 Profile

Land and Population

Capital	Berlin
Total area (square miles)	137,803 (slightly smaller than Montana)
Population	82 million

Economy

Gross national product (GNP) per capita (1998, U.S.$)	$28,260
Average annual gross domestic product (GDP) growth rate (1987–1997)	1.5%
Women as percentage of total labor force	42%
Income gap: GDP per capita (U.S.$) by percentage of population	
Richest 20%	$37,963
Poorest 20%	$6,594
Total foreign trade (exports plus imports) as percentage of GNP	45%

has a surprisingly high 54 percent of its land in agricultural production. It comprises large plains in northern Germany, a series of smaller mountain ranges in the center of the country, and the towering Alps to the south at the Austrian and Swiss borders. It has a temperate climate with considerable cloud cover and precipitation throughout the year, a climatological feature that contributes to the famous German *Wanderlust*, as many often seek out warm weather destinations for their annual six weeks of paid vacation. For Germany, the absence of natural borders in the west and east has been an important geographic feature. For example, on the north it borders both the North and Baltic seas and the country of Denmark, but to the west, south, and east, it has many neighbors: the Netherlands, Belgium, Luxembourg, France, Switzerland, Austria, the Czech Republic, and

Poland. Conflicts and wars with its neighbors were a constant feature in Germany until the end of World War II.

Germany's lack of resources, aside from iron ore and coal deposits in the Ruhr and the Saarland, has tempered much of the country's history. Since the Industrial Revolution in the nineteenth century, many of Germany's external relationships, both commercial and military, have revolved around gaining access to resources not present within the national borders. The resource scarcity has helped produce an efficient use of technology since the industrial age, but in the past, the lack of resources also caused German leaders to covet those of their neighbors aggressively. This era appears to have ended, especially with the arrival of the EU.

Critical Junctures

Unification in 1990 represented a great triumph for democratic Germany, but this milestone also forces us to examine the specifics of *why* Germany was divided in the first place. By examining critical historical junctures from the eighteenth through the twentieth centuries, we can better understand Germany's dynamic evolution, including the havoc that earlier German regimes caused both the country's neighbors and its own citizens. This short review of the key periods that shaped modern Germany will take us through a volatile history of the country's nineteenth-century unification, the creation of an empire, two world wars, a short-lived parliamentary democracy, twelve years of Nazi terror, military occupation, forty years as a divided nation, and the uncertainties of European integration (see Table 16.2).

Nationalism and German Unification (1806–1871)

There have been many attempts to unify a German nation in European history. The first was the Holy Roman Empire founded by Charle-

Table 16.2   Critical Junctures in Germany's Development

1806–1871	Nationalism and German unification
1871–1918	Second Reich
1919–1933	Weimar Republic
1933–1945	Third Reich
1945–1990	A divided Germany and the postwar settlement
1990–1998	The challenge of German unification
1998–present	Germany in the euro era

magne in 800 A.D. (sometimes referred to as the First Reich). But this wide-ranging, loose, and fragmented "empire" bore little resemblance to a modern nation-state. (In fact, someone once quipped that it was neither holy, Roman, nor an empire.) For more than one thousand years, the area now known as Germany was made up of sometimes as many as three hundred sovereign entities. Only in 1871, under the leadership of the Prussian military leader Otto von Bismarck, was Germany united as a nation-state. Bismarck called it the Second Reich because the name suggested a German state that was both powerful and able to draw on centuries-old traditions.[2]

There are three main points to make about state formation generally, and German state formation in particular.[3] First, state building requires an evolution of collective identity beyond the family, village, and local region to one encompassing a broader collection of peoples. Clear geographic boundaries may help define such an identity. Britain, an island, and France, a region surrounded by rivers and mountains, both developed as nation-states centuries ago. Germany, on the other hand, occupied central European plains with few natural lines of demarcation.

Moreover, religious, linguistic, or ethnic differences can hinder the development of a national identity. The Protestant Reformation, led by the German Martin Luther in 1517, not only split Christianity into two competing sects but

also divided many European societies in ways that profoundly affected the evolution of nation-states. Bitter religious wars broke out among advocates of each side in many parts of Europe. Britain and France resolved these contests decisively in favor of Protestantism or Catholicism within their own borders, thereby getting rid of this decisive cleavage early on. In Germany, neither Catholics nor Protestants won, and the wars' extensive casualties deepened hostilities that lasted for centuries. Each side viewed the conflict as both a military and a spiritual war that needed forceful leadership. This clearly retarded the development of any liberal or democratic impulses in Germany. Although religious animosity subsided by the twentieth century, the north of Germany remains mostly Protestant and the south mostly Catholic.

Ethnic and linguistic divisions, sometimes involving widely different forms of spoken German, also delayed unification. Nevertheless, the similarities among Germans were great enough to produce a common cultural identity before the nation-state emerged. In the absence of clear geographic boundaries or shared religious and political experiences, "racial" or ethnic and cultural traits came to define Germans' national identity to a much greater extent than for other European peoples.

A second point is that nation-states can promote economic growth more easily than fragmented political entities can. By the time Germany joined the global economy, it lagged behind Britain and France in industrializing and securing access to the natural resources of the developing world. Germany thus was forced to play catch-up with these other developed states.[4] Nineteenth-century leaders felt that Germany needed access to more raw materials than were contained within its own borders. Combined with the awakened German nationalism of the late nineteenth century, this pursuit of fast economic growth produced an aggressive, acquisitive state in which economic and political needs overlapped. Whereas Britain and France entered the nineteenth century as imperial powers, Germany's late unification and late industrialization prevented it from embarking on this quest for raw materials and empire until the late nineteenth century.

Third, military strength is a fundamental tool that many nation-states use in their formation and consolidation. Yet the rise of militarism and a corresponding authoritarian political culture were tendencies that were exaggerated in Germany for several reasons.[5] The map of Germany shows a country with many neighbors and few natural geographic barriers. This exposed position in the central plains of Europe encouraged an emphasis on military preparedness by nineteenth-century German state builders, since virtually any of Germany's neighbors could mount an attack with few constraints. And the lack of a solid democratic or liberal political culture in the various German-speaking lands before unification in 1871 allowed Prussian militarism an even greater influence over political and civic life.

German nationalism did not just appear out of the blue in the late nineteenth century. It had a long history and deeply rooted origins. Prussia had been a major military force in German-speaking lands since the seventeenth century, and it became Europe's greatest military power by the time of the Seven Years' War (1756–1763). Yet Prussia and most of the rest of Europe were overtaken by Napoleon in the early nineteenth century, as the French emperor swept eastward as far as Russia. During this conquest, Napoleon consolidated many of the smaller German-speaking principalities, particularly those from the northwest to the northeast of what is now Germany. But Napoleon's reach exceeded his grasp, and he suffered defeat in 1814. The Prussians, under the leadership of Friedrich Wilhelm III, conducted a "war of liberation" against French forces and further consolidated German-speaking states, but now under Prussian control.

The rise in Prussian influence in German-speaking areas continued through the first half of the nineteenth century as Prussian socioeco-nomic forces and political culture spread throughout what is now northern and central Germany. Prussian leaders were flush with military conquest and supremely confident that their authoritative—and authoritarian—leadership suited an awakening German-speaking population. Political and economic currents such as free-market capitalism and democracy did not find strong roots in the Prussian-dominated Germanic principalities. Rather, the dominant features of Prussian rule were a strong state deeply involved in economic affairs (an economic policy known as *mercantilism*), a reactionary group of feudal lords called *Junkers*, a patriotic military, and a political culture dominated by virtues such as honor, duty, and service to the state.

In 1848, German democrats and liberals (*liberal* in the original European sense of favoring free markets) tried to challenge Prussian dominance by attempting to emulate the democratic revolutionary movements in France and other European countries. The growth of free-market capitalism and the evolution of greater democracy in the United States and Britain served as catalysts in both France and Germany, and the center for this movement was in Frankfurt am Main, then as now an important trading city. However, German democratic forces were even weaker than in France because the Prussian state and authoritarian political culture were so strong. Thus, free-market and revolutionary democratic movements were violently suppressed. Yet Prussia—and eventually a united Germany—were to experience a different kind of revolution—a "revolution from above," political sociologist Barrington Moore has called it.[6]

After the democratic revolution failed in 1848, the most famous of the Prussian leaders, Otto von Bismarck, continued to forge unity among the remaining German-speaking independent principalities. Bismarck realized that the spread of German nationalism required firm economic foundations. Thus, Prussia, and a united Germany, would need to industrialize and modernize its economy to compete with Britain, France, and the United States. However, after the turmoil of the 1848 revolution, a democratic and free-market approach was not possible. Bismarck then put together the unlikely, and nondemocratic, coalition of the feudal *Junkers* in the northeast and the new industrial barons from the growing coal and iron ore industries in the northwestern Ruhr River valley. This alliance among grain-growing landowners and new-money industrialists under the guidance of a strong state was Bismarck's revolution from above. In other words, Bismarck's revolution relied on an alliance of elites rather than a mobilization of democratic or working-class support, a form common to the French and American revolutions.

Prior to 1871, the rise of nationalism and the formation of a united Germany out of the divided German states produced intense conflict. Militarism, not surprisingly, was a key component of Prussian nationalist political culture, and Bismarck used his armies to unite all German-speaking peoples under his influence. Such aggressive nationalism produced three bloody conflicts in the 1860s, as the Prussian armies defeated Denmark (1864), Austria-Hungary (1866), and France (1870) in short wars in which the modern German boundaries were established. The culmination of Bismarck's aggressive nationalism was the unification of Germany into a second "empire" or Reich.

Second Reich (1871–1918)

The Second Reich was an authoritarian regime that had some of the symbols of a democratic regime but very little of the substance. The failure of the democratic revolution in 1848 meant that nondemocratic forces (industrial and landed elites) in the newly united Germany mobilized and controlled both political and economic power. And these forces constructed political institutions to retain this power. Bismarck's regime was symbolically democratic in

that the Iron Chancellor (Bismarck's nickname owing to his military successes and attacks on democratic forces) allowed for universal suffrage, but he retained real decision-making authority in nonelected bodies that he could control. The political dominance by nondemocratic forces took the form of a bicameral legislature consisting of a lower house (Reichstag) and upper house (Landtag). The Reichstag was popularly elected, but real power lay in the hands of the Landtag, the members of which were either directly or indirectly appointed by Bismarck. The Reichstag could pass legislation, but with little, if any, hope that it would become law.

Led by Bismarck for the first twenty years of the regime, the Second Reich saw as its primary goal rapid industrialization augmented by state power and a powerful banking system geared to foster large-scale industrial investment. Thus, it did not rely on British and American "trial-and-error" free markets. As Germany became a leading industrial power by 1900, the Second Reich was economically quite successful, developing such industries as coal, steel, railroads, dyes, chemicals, industrial electronics, and machine tools. The emphasis on the development of such heavy industries meant that the production of consumer goods was a lower priority. This pattern created an imbalance in which the industrialists reaped large profits while the majority of Germans did not directly benefit from the economic growth led by heavy industry. The resultant lack of a strong domestic consumer goods economy meant that a substantial portion of what Germany produced was directed toward world markets.

The rapid transformation of a largely feudal society in the 1850s to an industrial one by the turn of the twentieth century created widespread social dislocation and produced numerous forms of opposition. One was a general pressure to democratize the authoritarian system by providing basic rights for liberal (that is, free-market) and middle-class forces. A second was the growth of the working class and the corresponding rise of the militant Social

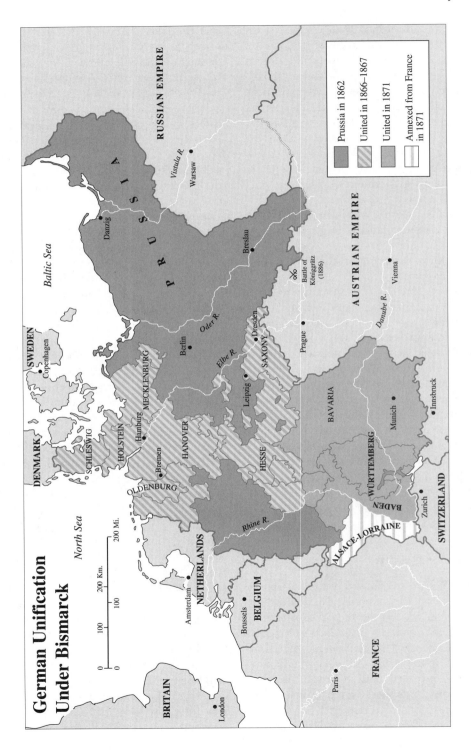

German Unification Under Bismarck

Legend:
- Prussia in 1862
- United in 1866–1867
- United in 1871
- Annexed from France in 1871

North Sea

200 Mi.

200 Km.

BRITAIN

London

NETHERLANDS
Amsterdam

BELGIUM
Brussels

FRANCE
Paris

SWEDEN

DENMARK

Copenhagen

Baltic Sea

RUSSIAN EMPIRE

Vistula R.
Warsaw

Danzig

P R U S S I A

SCHLESWIG

HOLSTEIN

MECKLENBURG

Hamburg

Bremen

OLDENBURG

HANOVER

Berlin

Oder R.

Breslau

Battle of Königgrätz (1886)

AUSTRIAN EMPIRE

Vienna

Danube R.

Prague

Dresden

Elbe R.

SAXONY

Leipzig

HESSE

Rhine R.

BAVARIA

Munich

Innsbruck

WÜRTTEMBERG

BADEN

Zurich

ALSACE-LORRAINE

SWITZERLAND

Democratic Party (Sozialdemokratische Partei Deutschlands, SPD). The SPD's primary goals were economic rights in the workplace and democratization of the political system. Greatly influenced by the writings and the active participation of Karl Marx and Friedrich Engels—who were, after all, Germans—the SPD grew as fast as the pace of German industrialization.

During much of his rule from 1871 to 1890, Bismarck alternately persecuted and grudgingly tolerated his democratic and socialist opposition. The combination of social and political pressures forced Bismarck, a conservative, to ban the SPD in 1878 but also caused him to create the world's first modern welfare state in the early 1880s to soften the rough edges of rapid economic growth. This combination of welfare and political repression (sometimes referred to as Bismarck's iron fist in a velvet glove) suggested that Bismarck was an astute politician who knew how far to push the opposition and when to give ground in the short term in order to maintain long-term political control.

Bismarck was also skillful in balancing the very different interests of the grain-growing feudal *Junkers* in East Prussia and the expanding industrialists in the north and west of Germany. In what has sometimes been called the marriage of iron and rye, these disparate social forces were united by mutual economic and political needs.[7] The *Junkers* needed a mechanism to get their agricultural output to market, and the industrialists needed a commodity (rye wheat) to ship on the expanding railroad system. Bismarck consummated the marriage with a tariff system that discriminated against foreign importers of steel and grain, giving German iron and rye greater breathing room. The marriage also helped the two reactionary forces remain united to stave off the clamoring democratic and socialist forces "below" them.

Bismarck used his skills to balance the divisive energy of nationalism with the need to maintain a coherent state policy. Invocation of nationalism enabled him to unite the diverse German-speaking peoples despite resentment by Bavarians and Rhinelanders (among others) toward the Prussian-dominated regime. But in time, nationalism proved difficult to contain. The spirit unleashed by a newly unified and rapidly industrializing Germany gave rise to a pan-Germanic feeling of nationalism among German-speaking Europeans in eastern Europe. This often took the form of militant anti-Semitism owing to the perception by some Germans that Jews had enjoyed a disproportionate share of wealth and influence in central Europe. In general, the pan-Germanic movement espoused themes that the Nazis later seized in justifying their claims of racial and cultural superiority.

Bismarck also powerfully influenced German political culture, with its state-centered emphasis that came to characterize the united Germany. The *Kulturkampf* (cultural struggle) was a prime example of Prussian, and Protestant, dominance. Led by Bismarck, it was essentially a movement against the Catholic Church, aimed at removing educational and cultural institutions from the Church and conferring them on the state. This action polarized the Church and many Catholic Germans and left a significant political legacy of both Catholic and Protestant influence in German politics to this day.

Clearly the unification of Germany in 1871 produced considerable economic strength in the late nineteenth and early twentieth centuries. However, as the tensions described suggest, it remained politically fragile, unstable, and undemocratic.

As the German economy grew during the latter part of the nineteenth century, German business and political leaders faced an immediate problem: How could rapid economic growth continue if they could not be certain of obtaining needed raw materials or having access to world markets to sell their finished goods? Although Germany possessed considerable iron and coal deposits, it had little else in the way of natural resources. It had neither the colonial possessions of Britain and France, nor the geographic advantages of the United States, with its largely self-sufficient domestic market and plentiful natural resources. Having little influence in either North America or Asia, Germany participated in what historian Geoffrey Barraclough has called "the scramble for Africa."[8] However, Germany was a latecomer in this region and was able to obtain colonies only in what are now the countries of Namibia and Togo, whereas the British, French, and Belgians obtained colonies in regions of the continent with more easily exploitable resources.

From 1871 until World War I, the foreign policy of the German state was primarily concerned with extending its colonial and economic influence, only to be repeatedly checked by other colonial powers. This situation inflamed German nationalists, causing German leaders to invest in the rapid development of the ship-building industry to equip a commercial shipping fleet and a powerful navy that could secure German economic and geopolitical interests.

The combination of numerous factors—an undemocratic domestic political system, the lack of profitable colonies, an exposed geopolitical position on the central European plains—joined with an increasingly aggressive nationalism to heighten Germany's aggression toward other nations. This volatile combination proved to be a blueprint for disaster and caused Germany to launch World War I.

Germany felt threatened by its inability to expand its economic and military resources and was allied with the Austro-Hungarian Empire. When the Austrian archduke Ferdinand was assassinated by a Serbian nationalist, the Austro-Hungarian Empire attacked Serbia (which was allied with Britain and France), and the war was on. Originally envisioned by German leaders as a brief war to solidify the country's geopolitical position and maintain socioeconomic power for dominant elites, it did neither. It turned out to be a protracted war that cost Germany both its colonial possessions and its imperial social order. The combination of weak leadership (Bismarck's successors were poor imitations of the original), lack of resources, and overconfidence in Germany's military prowess brought the Second Reich to an end at the conclusion of World War I. Germany's defeat and the collapse of the Second Reich left very weak foundations for the country's first attempt to establish a parliamentary democracy.

Weimar Republic (1918–1933)

Germany's military defeat in World War I had profound implications for questions of state formation and democracy. When the ceremonial head of state, Kaiser (King) Wilhelm II, abdicated the throne following the resignation of the last wartime government, Germany was without both a head of government (chancellor) and head of state (*Kaiser*). The political vacuum was filled by the large but politically inexperienced SPD, as all other leading parties of the Second Reich had been discredited by Germany's defeat. In 1918, this new leadership proclaimed Germany's first democratic government, one that some would later call accidental, owing to the SPD's unexpected assumption of power. The new government was born in defeat and lacked legitimacy in the eyes of many Germans. In other words it was a "republic without republicans."

This Weimar Republic, named after the city of Weimar where the constitution was drafted, was a procedural democracy in the sense of holding regular elections and having multiple parties. The German Reichstag appeared to function like many other democratic parliaments at the time, such as those of Britain and France. It contained a broad spectrum of political parties, from the far Left to the far Right. Yet its eventually fatal weakness was that too many of the right-wing political parties and social forces, as well as the Communists on the Left, did not accept the legitimacy of democratic government and actively tried to destabilize and undercut it.

The SPD leadership was on shaky ground from the beginning. The military leaders and industrialists who had so strongly encouraged

Germany's aggressive nationalism were never held accountable for their actions. They faced neither criminal nor political sanctions for leading Germany into a destructive war. In fact, the republic's first government turned to the army to help restore order during late 1918, when the newly formed Communist Party (Kommunistche Partei Deutschlands, KPD) and various leftist groups challenged the government's authority. By asking the undemocratic army to "defend democracy," the SPD undermined its ability to make major changes in German society.

The outcome of the war intensified the nationalist impulses of many conservative and reactionary Germans. Many in the military believed that "cowardly" democratic politicians had betrayed Germany at the signing of the Treaty of Versailles following the German surrender to the Allies on November 11, 1918. Stung by the reparations payments assessed on Germany by the Allies, along with the demilitarization of the Rhineland, a region bordering on France, German nationalists branded the Weimar leaders as "Jews, democrats, and socialists" who had sold out Germany's honor. By controlling various right-wing newspapers and magazines, the nondemocratic Right kept up a steady drumbeat of poisonous rhetoric that eventually crippled the regime.

A severe economic crisis in 1923, caused largely by Germany's attempts to deal with the reparations payments to the Allies, further played into the hands of the nationalists. Since the German economy was weakened by the mobilization during World War I, the added costs of the reparations payments made a bad economic situation much worse. The government's "solution" was to print more money. It used the shaky reasoning that a cheaper reichsmark (the name of the currency then) would reduce the real costs of the reparations. This was no solution at all, because the government kept printing so much money that by 1923, inflation reached astronomical proportions (e.g., one U.S. dollar was equal to approximately 12 million

reichsmark). Individual Germans were powerfully affected in numerous ways. At the height of the inflationary wave, people had to receive their paychecks twice per *day*, once in the morning and once in the evening after work. The cost of basic foodstuffs was literally rising hourly, and people who waited to buy goods after work (instead of shopping on their lunch break) would find the goods much more expensive. The simple act of depositing or withdrawing money at a bank also reached ludicrous proportions; some individuals used wheelbarrows brimming with nearly worthless reichsmark to go to and from the bank. To the nondemocratic right wing, the Weimar regime was a concrete example of a democratic government unable to create and supervise a stable economy.

In the early 1920s, Adolf Hitler, a little-known, Austrian-born, former corporal in the German army during World War I, founded the Nazi Party. *Nazi* is a German acronym for National Socialist German Workers Party. Although it sounds like the name of a left-wing party, the use of the word *national* is important here. Hitler used nationalism as a weapon to attack both parties of the Left, the SPD and KPD. He thereby undercut the socialist movements' German roots, which reached back to Marx and Engels. Taking advantage of a deepening economic crisis and a weakened democratic opposition, the Nazis mobilized large segments of the population by preaching hatred of the Left, of "internationalism" (the key philosophical underpinning shared by both the SPD and the KPD), and of "inferior, non-Aryan" races. Hitler unleashed powerful racist social forces antagonistic to democracy, which ultimately undermined it and caused its destruction.

After the Great Depression began in 1929, Germany became even more unstable, with none of the major parties of Weimar able to win a majority or even form durable governing coalitions. The Communists, Social Democrats, Catholic Center Party, Democrats, Liberals, Bavarian People's Party, Nationalists, Conservatives, and Nazis all had fundamentally different views on how Germany should be governed, and many of them were not committed to the idea of democracy. In the wake of this political instability, the early 1930s saw numerous inconclusive elections. The last several months of the Weimar Republic (1932–1933) witnessed no fewer than six elections, all resulting in minority governments. At no time did the Nazis ever receive a majority. Their high point in free and fair elections was 229 seats out of 609 in the vote during the fall of 1932. This election was considered the last one without violent Nazi intimidation of other political parties.

The Nazis relentlessly pressed for political power amid a population that continued to underestimate Hitler's real intentions and view his hate-filled speeches as merely political rhetoric. The Nazis were rewarded when Hitler induced Weimar's aging President Hindenburg, an eighty-four-year-old World War I general, to allow the Nazis to obtain cabinet positions in the last Weimar government in early 1933. Hitler immediately demanded the chancellorship from President Hindenburg, and received it on January 30, 1933. (Under the Weimar constitution, as in many other parliamentary systems, the head of state—the president—was assigned to choose the next head of government—the chancellor—if no one party or coalition received a majority of legislative seats.) Once in power, the Nazis began to ban political parties and arranged for a fire at the Reichstag that they tried to blame on the Communists. Hitler then demanded that President Hindenburg grant by emergency decree broad, sweeping powers to the Nazi-dominated cabinet. This act made the Reichstag irrelevant as a representative political body.

Thus, the parliamentary democracy of the Weimar Republic was short-lived. From its shaky beginnings in 1918, the very stability of the state was mortgaged to forces that wished its destruction. Ironically, the constitutional structure of the Weimar regime was relatively well designed. The two significant exceptions were the "emergency" provisions allowing for greater executive power in crises and the lack of a mechanism to form and maintain stable governing coalitions among the various political parties. The more elemental problem with Weimar, however, was that not enough political parties and social forces were committed to democracy. The Republic's critics included the military, many unemployed former soldiers, the Prussian aristocracy, elements of both the Catholic and Protestant churches, and large segments of big business. In addition, the KPD fundamentally criticized the Weimar Republic, but from the left. Unlike multiparty political systems in other countries, the Weimar Republic was plagued by a sharp and increasing polarization of political parties. Even parties expected to have at least some ideological affinities (the Communists and the Social Democrats, for example) were mortal enemies during Weimar. The KPD called the SPD social fascists, and the SPD saw the KPD as a puppet of Moscow. The Weimar constitution was an elegant document, but without broad-based popular support, the regime itself was continually under attack.

Third Reich (1933–1945)

Once the Nazis controlled the chancellorship and the government, their next priority was establishing total control of the political system and society. The initial step was the systematic banning of political parties. The first party to be banned were the Communists, next were the Social Democrats and their trade union allies, and after that almost all of the democratic political parties. Even the organs of civic society such as clubs, neighborhood organizations, and the churches were subject to Nazi control, influence, or restrictions on independent action.

Ultimately the Nazis used propaganda, demagoguery, and the absence of a democratic opposition, which had been relentlessly hounded and then banned, to mobilize large segments of the German population. Through mesmerizing speeches and the relentless propaganda ministry led by his aide Joseph Goebbels, Hitler used his total control of political power and the media to reshape German politics to his party's vision. This was a vision that did not allow opposition, even within the party. For example, after establishing power, the Nazis even turned on their own "foot soldiers," the brown-shirted storm troopers (Sturmabteilung, SA). The SA was a large but ragtag group of street fighters whom the party used in the 1920s and early 1930s to attack Communists, Socialists, and trade unionists. The SA also was used to seize and burn opposition newspapers, as well as to loot and destroy businesses owned by Jews, foreigners, and other opponents of the Nazis. However, once the Nazis had established control and political opposition had been neutralized, the storm troopers became a major liability. The SA and its leader, Ernst Röhm, believed that their valiant service should propel the SA to a stature equivalent or superior to that of the army. But to the ears of the Nazi leadership and the generals who had now embraced Hitler, this notion was mutiny. The Nazis dispensed with the SA in 1934 by ordering the grisly murder of Röhm and the entire SA leadership in a predawn raid by Hitler's elite guard (Schutzstaffeln, SS) on a storm trooper barracks in Berlin, an event now known as the Night of the Long Knives, since most of the SA leadership was stabbed while it slept.

Domestic policy during the first few years of Nazi rule focused on two major areas: consolidating and institutionalizing centralized political power, and rebuilding an economy that had suffered through the monetary chaos of the 1920s and the great depression of the early 1930s.

The Nazis' new centralized political authority was different from past German political patterns. Until the Nazis had come to power, German regional and local governments had enjoyed moderate political autonomy. Part of this autonomy was based on the independence that the German regions enjoyed while they were still sovereign states before the 1871 unification. Among the best-known semi-independent re-

gions were Bavaria, the Rhineland, including the industrial Ruhr valley, the Black Forest area in the southwest, and the city-states of Hamburg and Bremen. The Nazis chose to centralize all political authority in Berlin by making all regional and local authorities subject to tight, autocratic control. The main purpose of this top-down system was to ensure that Nazi policy on the repression of political opposition and of Jews and other racial minorities was carried out to the most minute detail. Such political centralization also enabled Goebbels's propaganda ministry to spread relentlessly the Nazi "virtues" of submission to authority, racial superiority, intolerance, and militarism. Nazi racist theories and practice were especially heinous, stressing Aryan racial purity and thus the persecution of Jews, Gypsies, and homosexuals as well as the sick and disabled.

The Nazis' economic program was also autocratic in design and execution. Since free trade unions had been banned, both private and state-run industries forced workers—and eventually slave laborers during World War II—to work long hours for little or no pay. The industries chosen for emphasis were primarily heavier industries (coal, steel, chemicals, machine tools, and industrial electronics), which required massive investment from the large cartels that formed in each industry, from the banking system, and from the state itself. Some segments of big business initially feared Hitler before he came to power. Yet with free trade unions suppressed, most of German industry endorsed Nazi economic policies. The Nazis also emphasized massive public works projects, such as creating the *Autobahn* highway system, upgrading the railroad system, and erecting grandiose public buildings that were supposed to represent Nazi greatness. These projects employed large numbers of workers and under extremely repressive conditions. The emphasis on heavy industry and transportation clearly favored military production and expansion. Almost all of the industries that the Nazis favored had direct military application, and the *Autobahn*, similar to the modern U.S. Interstate highway system, was built more to ease military transport than for pleasure driving.

During the Third Reich, Hitler fanned the flames of German nationalism by glorifying the warrior tradition in German folklore and exulting in imperial Germany's past smashing of rival armies in the mid-nineteenth century. In calling for a return to a mythically glorious and racially pure German past, he made scapegoats out of homosexuals, ethnic minorities such as Poles, Danes, and Alsatians, and especially Jews. In fact, the Germans' strident anti-Semitism helped give increased impetus to its growth in other European countries during the 1920s and 1930s. To nationalist leaders like Germany's Adolf Hitler, Italy's Benito Mussolini, Spain's Francisco Franco, and others elsewhere in Europe, anti-Semitism represented an important political force. It allowed these nationalist leaders to blame any political problems on this "external" international minority and target them as an enemy of nationalism who should be relentlessly persecuted and suppressed.

On international issues, the Nazis refused to abide by the provisions of the Treaty of Versailles signed by the Weimar government in 1918. One of these provisions called for severe restrictions on German military activity. After 1933, however, Nazi Germany began to produce armaments in large quantities using its heavy industry, remilitarized the Rhineland (the area of Germany closest to France), and sent aid to Franco's fascist army as it fought to overthrow the democratically elected Spanish republic from 1936 to 1939. The Nazis also rejected the territorial divisions of World War I, as Hitler claimed that a growing Germany needed increased space to live (*Lebensraum*) in Eastern Europe. He ordered the forced union (*Anschluss*) with Austria in March 1938 and the occupation of the German-speaking Sudetenland section of Czechoslovakia in September 1938. The Third Reich's attack on Poland on September 1, 1939, finally precipitated World War II.

"Enemies of the Third Reich"

Hitler's grandiose visions of German world domination were dramatically heightened by the conquests of first Poland and then the rest of Europe. By the summer of 1941, he began to turn his attention to the only other continental power that stood in the way of his goal of total European domination, the Soviet Union. Hitler assumed that defeating the Soviet Union would be as easy as his other conquests. Therefore, in the summer of 1941, he violated the Nazi-Soviet nonaggression pact by embarking on a direct attack on the Soviet Union. The attack was the end of German military success and the beginning of the Third Reich's defeat, a process that would culminate almost four years later, in May 1945. Yet even as defeat loomed in 1945, Hitler preferred to see Germany totally destroyed rather than have its national honor "besmirched" by total surrender.

Germany saw tremendous physical and human destruction. Approximately 55 million people died in Europe during World War II, with approximately 8 million of those being

German. In addition, Germany was occupied by the four victorious Allied powers (Britain, France, the United States, and the Soviet Union), and ceased to exist as a sovereign state from 1945 to 1949.

Clearly the most heinous aspect of the Nazi movement was the systematic execution of 6 million Jews and millions of other civilians in the concentration camps throughout Germany as well as occupied Central and Eastern Europe. Hitler explicitly stated in his book *Mein Kampf* (*My Struggle*) that the Germans were the "master race" and all other non-Aryan races, especially the Jews, were "inferior." But as with a lot of his other statements during his rise to power, many Germans chose to ignore the implications of this hatred or thought it was mere exaggeration. For example, a controversial book by political scientist Daniel Goldhagen makes a powerful case that many German citizens who were not directly connected to the Nazi extermination process nonetheless either ignored or turned away from clear evidence that systematic extermination of Jews took place.[9] Goldhagen argues that many Germans voluntarily participated in brutal violence against Jews not because they were forced to but because they were motivated by vicious anti-Semitism, the roots of which went back generations. The magnitude of Nazi plans for other races became apparent after Hitler came to power, but by then any chance of domestic opposition had passed. Persecution of Jews and other racial and ethnic minorities grew steadily more atrocious until Germany's defeat in 1945. First, the Nazis placed sharp restrictions on the freedoms of Jews and other persecuted minorities. Then property was confiscated and destroyed, culminating in the *Kristallnacht* (Night of Broken Glass) of 1938, in which Jewish stores, synagogues, and homes were systematically ransacked. Last, the concentration and extermination camps were systematically constructed and filled with Jews and other minorities. The Nazis placed most of the extermination camps in occupied countries like Poland, but one of the most

infamous was in Germany at Dachau, just northwest of Munich.

The Nazi period had a powerful impact on German state formation during the post–World War II years. It served as an "antimodel" of what any postwar democratic political system should avoid at all costs. Of course, the Nazi legacy has also served as a "model" for the various neo-Nazi groups that have sprung up in the Federal Republic of Germany (FRG), both in the mid-1960s and especially in the postunification years of the 1990s. Although there are constitutional prohibitions on neo-Nazi activities, numerous outlaw groups and their quasi-legal sympathizers still admire the horrors of the Third Reich. The number of active members of these groups is quite small, perhaps a few thousand at most, but some studies of public opinion show support for the goals, if not the tactics, of such groups at figures near 10 percent of the population. We examine these forces more closely in Chapter 18.

A Divided Germany (1945–1990)

From 1945 to 1949, a brief yet influential historical juncture, Germany was occupied by the four Allied powers. This was influential because the Western allies seemed to impose democracy "from above" in a way that was quite effective. Yet as we will see, postwar democratic German leaders shaped this new democracy in a fashion quite different from British or U.S. democracy. Germany, as evidenced by both World Wars I and II, had proved to be one of the most unstable and threatening members of the international political system during the late nineteenth and early twentieth centuries. Through both the Second and Third Reichs, Germany was viewed as an aggressive, acquisitive economic power and a political-military power that caused fear among its neighbors. This potent legacy of conquest and domination caused the victorious Allied powers (Britain, France, the United States, and the Soviet Union) to treat

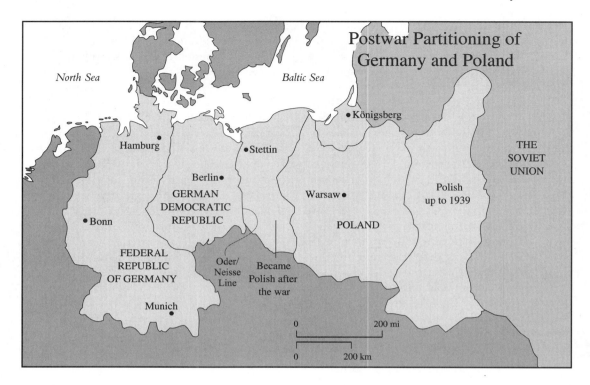

Germany differently from the other Axis powers, Japan and Italy. Unlike the latter two countries, Germany was occupied by the Allies, and its territory was divided into what soon became East and West Germany. At first, the reason for such a four-part physical dismemberment of the German state was that the country's history warranted such action. But the realities of the cold war soon offered a different and more powerful reason for Germany's division.

In the years of the postwar occupation, both German and Allied officials imposed several important constraints that continued in the FRG. The first was the reduction of the powers of the central state in domestic politics, replaced in part by strong regional governments. The second was the limitation of the FRG's role as an international political power. The Allied occupation authorities prevented the German military from having a legal independent status until the mid-1950s, and even then it was closely monitored and controlled by the Western Allies and eventually the North Atlantic Treaty Organization (NATO). Third, German politicians reformed the party system, helping to create parties that were broader and less driven by narrow ideological considerations alone. Perhaps the most significant reform was the merger of Catholic and Protestant interests into Christian Democracy, comprising the Christian Democratic Union (CDU) and the Christian Social Union (CSU), the Bavarian branch of this movement. During Weimar, the Catholics and Protestants had their own parties, which were often uncooperative with each other as well as with other parties. However, postwar Christian Democracy radically rethought German political conservatism by embracing democracy, social welfare, antinationalism, and antimilitarism. Yet it also retained its conservative core in its emphasis on religious, family, cultural, and homeland (*Heimat*) values. In short, for the first time in German history, it appears that political institutions were designed that apparently have produced stable democracy.

For the brief occupation period (1945–1949), Germany ceased to be a nation-state. It was only with the founding of the FRG in 1949 that a more stable, democratic form of government emerged and was known colloquially as West Germany. East Germany became a separate, Communist country at that time. While nation-statehood returned nominally to the two Germanies in 1949, the lack of German sovereignty during the 1945–1949 period created an important legacy that lasted for much longer than the occupation period. From 1949 until 1990, both Germanies, for different sets of historical reasons, did not take on the kind of political responsibilities that "normal" nation-states did. The Federal Republic deferred to the United States in matters of international relations, as did the GDR to the Soviet Union. Both the United States and the Soviet Union felt it important to constrain independent and international German political activity, a legacy that dated from the occupation period. This constraint produced for the Federal Republic a so-called economic giant—political dwarf syndrome that began to change only in the 1990s.

As the cold war intensified in the late 1940s and tensions grew between the Soviet Union and the other three powers, Germany became the dividing line between the two camps, and the two Germanies emerged. This division produced yet one more major historical juncture. Its most durable legacy was that it was a turning point in which an apparently stable democracy developed. How long the country would stay occupied and divided was not known during 1946 and 1947. The cold war, however, changed many of the immediate postwar expectations of what Germany's future was to be. The transformation of the Soviet zone of occupation into the GDR and its inclusion in the Soviet-led Warsaw bloc, as well as the creation of the FRG and its inclusion in NATO, seemed to preempt any discussion of reunification indefinitely.

The Federal Republic became a parliamentary democracy, characterized by constitutional provisions for free elections, civil liberties and individual rights, and an independent judiciary. However, it also banned both communist and neo-Nazi parties during the 1950s and 1960s, and it initiated state-sponsored purges of the civil service in the early 1970s to root out presumed radicals who were believed to have obtained positions in the bureaucracy.

Forces on the democratic Left such as the SPD, the Greens (the ecologically oriented, small-is-beautiful political party that first won Bundestag seats in 1983 and joined the SPD in a left-leaning coalition government in 1998), and the trade unions have strongly emphasized democratizing material resources. The clearest institutional examples are the legally mandated in-plant works councils (all firms with five or more employees are required to have independent organizations to represent worker interests) and firm-wide *codetermination* (that is, almost 50 percent of company boards of directors comprise trade union members). Beginning in the 1950s, this rank-and-file democratic participation, often called *democratic corporatism*, helped alleviate much of the social tension that had plagued Germany prior to 1945.[10] Under democratic corporatism, business, labor, and the government work together on economic and industrial relations issues and generally develop consensual policy solutions to national, regional, state, and local challenges. The Germans have spoken of their "social" (not "free") market economy because of the deeply entrenched belief that business must share in the responsibility to provide a stable order, for both the economy and, indirectly, society. The development of this set of institutional and political structures—a mixed economy, democratic corporatism, and a generous welfare state—in Germany, as elsewhere in Western Europe, has been called the *postwar settlement*. Although this settlement proved generally beneficial for the political economy of the FRG, it was not a panacea. For example, the treatment of immigrant workers within German industry has at times seemed more exclusionary than inclusionary. Also, the illiberal right-wing extremists who have stigmatized and attacked racial and ethnic minorities have often met with less than thorough prosecution of these crimes by the German state.

The Federal Republic's democratic traditions since 1949 have their origins in the successful creation of a durable and flexible set of political institutions. The parliamentary system is bicameral, with a lower house (Bundestag) and an upper house (Bundesrat). The lower house is directly elected, and the upper house is made up of delegates selected by the sixteen federal states. The chancellor (head of government) is similar in power to the British prime minister and attains office by virtue of being the leader of the majority party or coalition in the Bundestag. The largely ceremonial president (head of state) is similar to constitutional monarchs like Britain's Queen Elizabeth. The multiparty system of five major parties covers a wide political spectrum and provides representation for diverse, democratic political opinions, and the independent judiciary respects the rule of law. Finally, the comprehensive state provides generous benefits to German citizens and works closely with private-sector interests to maintain economic strength. However, the stresses placed on democratic institutions (both procedural and substantive) in the wake of German unification and European integration have caused many observers to reexamine German democracy in a more critical light.

The lack of democracy in the GDR—a "people's democracy," in Communist parlance—was a condition that remained throughout the GDR's history from 1949 to 1990. In fact, it was the East German regime that constructed the Berlin Wall in 1961. During the 1950s, many East Germans who wished to flee communism would travel to Berlin, which remained under the control of the four Allied powers. Once in the free Western sectors of the city, they could travel without restriction to the FRG and receive immediate citizenship. Hundreds of thousands of East Germans migrated west in this way, causing a labor shortage and a "brain drain" for the GDR. Finally, in August 1961, the GDR erected the wall, making travel to the West impossible. The GDR called the wall an antifascist barrier, supposedly meant to keep the West Germans from "invading" East Germany, but all Germans, East and West, realized that it solidified what many feared was a permanent division of Germany.

The GDR was a one-party state under the control of the Communist Party, which was known as the Socialist Unity Party (Sozialistiche Einheitspartei, SED). Although the GDR provided full employment, housing, and various social benefits to its citizens, it was a rigid, bureaucratic, Stalinist regime that tightly controlled economic and political life under the leadership of party chairmen Walter Ulbricht, Willi Stoph, and Erich Honecker. The GDR assumed a universal consensus about the "correctness" of communism; all public democratic dissent was suppressed as being deviationist and undermining the "true path of socialism." East Germans trying to flee to the West were subject to execution on the spot. Numerous memorials to escapees who were shot stand along the site of the former Berlin Wall. Many observers have argued that recent antiforeigner attacks, which have been strongest in the former East Germany, can be attributed partly to the lack of a genuine democratic tradition of dialogue, tolerance, and public discourse there.

For more than forty years, Germany's role in the international family of nations was a limited one. Not only did Allied and NATO restrictions prevent unilateral German political action, the *Grundgesetz* (Basic Law) prevented German troops from being used outside NATO (that is, largely Western European) areas. *Basic Law* is a term used instead of *Verfassung*, the literal translation of *constitution* since, in 1949, FRG founders believed that a constitution would be written only on German unification. (Ironically, after fifty years, the term *Basic Law* has become so ingrained that the name has stuck.) At the founding of the FRG and GDR, however, both West and East Germans believed that the country was likely to remain divided for the foreseeable future, which meant that the political role of the two German states was intentionally circumscribed by each of their alliance partners. Not only was the GDR restrained by the Soviet Union; so too was the Federal Republic limited by the Western Allies, NATO, and the presence of a seemingly permanent garrison of foreign military forces. Even as the West German economy grew strong during the economic miracle years of the 1950s and became the leading Western European economy by the 1960s, the FRG's political role remained much more limited. The GDR experienced a similar pattern. It apparently became the strongest of the Warsaw Bloc's economies. However, since unification, the massive rebuilding required in Eastern Germany has called into question the GDR's economic strength.

Germany's unification in 1990 took place rapidly and surprised West and East Germans alike. When the Berlin Wall was opened in November 1989, the two German states envisioned a slow process of increased contact and cooperation while they maintained separate sovereign states for the short term. But when the trickle of East Germans moving west turned into a deluge, the Kohl government was forced to take action to stem the influx of Eastern Germans into the West. One step was to provide a currency exchange whereby former East German currency could be exchanged for valuable West German deutsche marks. After hurried negotiations in late summer, the former GDR became part of the Federal Republic of Germany as five new FRG states.

Thus, through unification in 1990, the role of the German state in the international arena had remained muted. But the supposedly settled international political landscape that the cold war afforded, in which a divided Germany was taken for granted, was gone with the opening of the Berlin Wall and the coming apart of the Soviet Union. For better or for worse, Germany—as a single, powerful nation-state—had made a rapid reappearance on the international stage. This theme resonates throughout the chapters on Germany.

The Postwar Settlement

The postwar settlement in the FRG evolved in phases, or as Peter Katzenstein has called the first three of them, "republics."[11] These were not republics in the French sense, with separate constitutions; rather, Katzenstein associated them with the dominant political orientation of the respective FRG government in power at the time. In terms of governing coalitions, the period of the postwar settlement has swung from the moderate Center-Right (1949–1966), to the moderate Center-Left (1969–1982), to the moderate Center-Right (1982–1998), and now a democratic Left government (1998–). Together these governments produced a set of basic policy options—with minor variations depending on which of the two major parties led the coalition—that have maintained continuity throughout this long period.

Important characteristics distinguished the postwar settlement in the FRG from the settlements in other Western European nations. Among the most significant were the highly organized nature of the business community (greater than in other European countries), a weak central state and strong regional governments, an active tradition of worker participation within a strong labor movement (i.e., corporatism), influential quasi-public institutions shaping and implementing public policy at all levels of society, and a continued commitment to the welfare state by both major parties.

The development of welfare services in the Federal Republic springs from several points of origin. First, it was the conservative Bismarck who created the first welfare state in the 1880s to preempt the more radical demands of the Left. Second, it owes much to the European

"Find the money."
German policymakers worrying about the costs of
the welfare state.

Source: Atelier Rabenau/*Frankfurter
Allgemeine Zeitung.*

Christian Social tradition, a major ideological tenet in the CDU–CSU coalition, and also an important influence on the small, more free-enterprise-oriented Free Democratic Party (FDP). Both Catholic and Protestant churches have, for more than a century, espoused a belief in public spending for services as a responsibility of the strong for the welfare of the weak. Third, the unions' and the SPD's demands for increased public spending ensured that the Left was incorporated into the political order during the 1950s and early 1960s. Thus, the postwar settlement has produced a deeply rooted legacy of commitment to the public provision of welfare services.

We also want to elaborate a bit more on the concept of the German model, a theme used in much political science literature to describe how the FRG coheres in terms of its political and socioeconomic features.[12] German society is more "organized" than other countries in the sense that political institutions, social forces, and the patterns of life in civic society place more emphasis on collective action than does the individualism more characteristic of Anglo-Saxon

countries. Germans do have considerable individual freedoms; however, political expression, in both the state and civil society, revolves around group representation and articulation of a cooperative spirit in much of public action. Does it mean there is no conflict in Germany? Hardly! But it means that both private citizens and public authorities look to organized, collective responses rather than isolated individual action.

Helmut Kohl and the Challenge of German Unification (1990–1998)

Germany's unification in 1990 took place rapidly, surprising West and East Germans alike. When the Berlin Wall was opened in November 1989, the two German states envisioned a slow process of increased contacts and cooperation while maintaining separate sovereign states for the short term. But the initial slow flow of East Germans moving West turned into a stampede. When a currency reform provided East Germans with valuable West German deutsche marks, this move only fueled the migration westward in the summer of 1990. After a referendum on unification and intense negotiations in the late summer, the former East Germany was incorporated into the FRG as five new West German states (*Länder*).

Formal unification took place in the fall of 1990 as Chancellor Kohl, the "unification chancellor," won a strong reelection victory for his Center-Right Christian Democratic–Free Democratic coalition. The period of euphoria did not last, as the costs of unification placed increased stress on Germany's budget and democratic institutions. Unification has proved much more difficult than many observers first anticipated. Before unification, East Germany was considered the strongest of the Eastern European Communist economies. But the border opening and eventual unification soon showed that the East German economy was far more backward than most economists had thought. The Communist planned economy (sometimes called a *command economy*) was not sensitive to market signals since production of goods was determined more by rigid government dictates than by consumer needs. The East German level of technology was decades behind, especially when compared to the developed economies of the West. Simple telephone communication was usually an adventure, and the current unified German government has spent billions just to rebuild communication networks. Politically, East Germany was a state in which open political discourse and expression were discouraged, if not prohibited. Of course, people would meet and speak candidly among family or close friends, but a liberal democratic political culture did not exist.

Incorporating the disadvantaged Eastern Germany had an adverse impact on a wide range of public policies, including unemployment expenses, structural rebuilding funds, and the large tax increases necessary to pay for it all. The large number of unemployed in eastern Germany—approximately 20 percent, more than double the figure in the prosperous west—helped fuel scattered ultra-right-wing political movements. They sought out foreigners (often Turks) as scapegoats, and there were several vicious attacks on minority groups in the 1990s.

The difficulties of unification were complicated by raised expectations by the Kohl governments throughout the 1990s. In order to win the support of Eastern Germans, he sugarcoated the enormity of the unification process as well as its duration. In order to win the support of Western Germans, he had to convince them that the 7.5 percent "unification tax" imposed on them in the early 1990s would be money well spent. Unfortunately for Kohl, the longer the unification process remained incomplete, the less willing the German electorate was to give him continued support. He was able to convince voters to continue to support the Christian Democratic–Free Democratic government in the 1994 election, in which the coalition was returned to power, albeit with a significantly reduced majority.

As the 1998 election approached, Kohl felt confident that he would win reelection. He believed that German unification, despite its remaining challenges, and the EU in which Germany would play a leading role would ensure victory. The voters did not agree, handing the Christian Democratic–Free Democratic coalition a resounding defeat in the September 27 election. Successfully convincing Germans that a change was necessary, newly elected SPD chancellor Gerhard Schröder, a generation younger than Kohl, entered into a coalition government with the Greens for the first time in the nation's history. Significant too was the continued high support for the former communist party in Eastern Germany (over 20 percent), which enabled it to gain more than 5 percent of the total German vote. With almost 54 percent of the electorate voting for parties of the Left, clearly a new era had arrived in Germany.

The speed with which East Germany came apart after the fall of the Berlin Wall surprised everyone, not the least Helmut Kohl. Kohl can certainly be faulted for misjudging the economic and political costs of German unification. In fact, his overpromising of the pace of East German transformation in the early 1990s was a critical factor in his electoral loss in 1998. However, in acting quickly to integrate East Germany as five new *Länder*, when an independent, noncommunist East Germany proved unworkable in the spring and summer of 1990, Kohl helped alleviate what could have been a politically disastrous situation for both Germany and Europe.

Germany in the Euro Era

Germany's leaders from Konrad Adenauer, the first postwar chancellor, through Schröder all have been strongly enthusiastic toward European integration. In the late 1980s, Helmut Kohl realized the opportunity for Germany that a more formally united continent would present.

In its relations with other states after World War II, Germany has faced two different kinds of criticism. First was the fear of a too-powerful Germany, a country that had run roughshod over its European neighbors for most of the first half of the twentieth century. Second is the opposite problem, the so-called economic giant, political dwarf syndrome in which Germany was accused of benefiting from a strong world economy for much of the past fifty years, while taking on none of the political responsibility. The fact that these are mutually contradictory points of view did not spare Germany from criticism.

Yet an integrated Europe promised the possibility of solving both problems simultaneously. Germany will likely remain the economic anchor of the EU, and its membership in the EU will enable it to do things and take on needed political responsibilities that it would be unable to do on its own. Kohl realized this and was a firm advocate of all measures that would assist in a smooth, stable, and comprehensive EU. Germany, like all of the other European nations that supported integration, has tended to see the glass as half-full. From Germany's viewpoint, meeting both criticisms in the context of the EU was a positive-sum outcome.

However, the comprehensive integration process that began with the Maastricht Treaty of 1992 had an unusual mechanism of dealing with issues. European leaders, faced with fewer and more difficult tasks, made the choice to begin with the former and then address the latter. This meant that such relatively easy steps of easing intra-European trade and travel and allowing for workers to cross borders for employment as long as they had the requisite linguistic and job skills were taken first. The more complicated and difficult decisions, such as a single currency, monetary and fiscal policy, and democratic governance, were delayed. Optimistic European leaders, including the Germans, believed that a positive momentum, if not a "europhoria," would develop and thereby ease the transition toward continued integration.

In retrospect, the accelerating pace of European integration with its movement toward a common monetary policy, a European central bank, and a single (virtual) currency in 1999, followed by the physical elimination of all national currencies in favor of the euro in 2002 placed additional pressures on the Federal Republic. Many Germans wondered whether the anchor of stability represented by the redoubtable deutsche mark (DM) and the inflation-fighting Deutsche Bundesbank would begin to drift in the uncertain sea of the EU. At the turn of the century, many Germans began to realize the costs associated with European integration that might threaten the economic and political stability that they had so long prized during the first fifty years of the Federal Republic. The fall in value of the euro by some 25 percent in relation to the dollar in 1999 and 2000 was worrisome to Germans long accustomed to a stable and rock-hard DM. While the lower value of the euro meant it was easier for German industry to export goods, the higher prices for imported goods threatened to rekindle the age-old fear of German inflation.

With respect to open borders and seemingly free-flowing immigration, Germans also wondered whether Europeanization threatened to erode what it meant to be German. At the same time that immigration and political asylum increased in Germany during the 1990s, the birth rate, particularly in the former GDR, dropped precipitously. Far-Right and even some moderate right-wing politicians used these demographic changes to whip up nationalist support for decreasing the flow of migrants to the FRG. Ironically, these demographic changes also coincided with the inability of the highly regarded secondary educational system to produce enough skilled workers for the information age. Germany's vocational educational system and integrated apprenticeship system have worked exceptionally well for traditionally strong German industries, but they have been less effective in producing highly qualified information sector workers. This "tech shortage" reached such a critical mass in 2000 that the Schröder government began to recruit software specialists from

India who would be granted "green cards" (i.e., permanent residency status) upon their arrival! In other words, a new wave of *Gastarbeiter* was arriving precisely when some Germans were increasingly agitated about the immigration boom. In fact, some conservative politicians reacted to the arrival of the Indian software specialists with the phrase *Kinder statt Inder* (children instead of Indians), meaning that they would prefer that the government train German adolescents instead of inviting another wave of immigrants. The problem, however, was that the speed with which the German economy needed to embrace the information sector fully could not wait. The country needed both to increase Germany's presence in this complex sector and enable its traditionally strong industries to adapt to new forms of international competition. The economic pressures did not allow the luxury of waiting the several years for the German secondary educational system to get up to speed.

Finally, the issue of democratic governance was an additional European challenge. Like most other forms of increased integration among nation-states throughout history, economic integration generally precedes political integration. The EU has been no exception. However, in the rush toward integration, questions of political accountability have been less well emphasized. With fiscal and monetary policy essentially determined by either Brussels or the European Central Bank, where does democratic governance really lie?

Themes and Implications

We now step back and reexamine comparatively these historic junctures and political themes.

Historical Junctures and Political Themes

Germany's role in the world of states, the first theme, is contentious. For all states, military strength is a basic tool used to shape and consolidate. But in Germany, the rise of militarism and a corresponding authoritarian political culture were exaggerated for several reasons. Germany's exposed position in the central plains of Europe encouraged military preparedness because any of its many neighbors could mount an attack with few constraints. Since various German-speaking lands lacked a solid democratic or liberal political culture before unification in 1871, Prussian militarism exerted dominant influence over political and civic life. In other words, late unification accompanied by war created a state that caused tremendous fear among Germany's neighbors. The conduct of World War I and especially the Third Reich of the Nazis and World War II intensified this fear. Although more than fifty years have passed since the end of World War II and although Germany's independent political actions are constrained by the EU, many Europeans remain wary of Germany's international role.

The second theme, *governing the economy*, has been colored profoundly by Germany's late nineteenth-century state building. Clearly, nation-states can promote economic growth more easily than can fragmented political entities. Delayed unification and industrialization prevented Germany from embarking on the race for empire and raw materials until the late nineteenth century. By the time it joined the global economy, it lagged behind Britain and France in industrializing and securing access to the natural resources of the developing world and was forced to play catch-up. This pursuit of fast economic growth combined with the awakened sense of German nationalism in the late nineteenth century produced an aggressive, acquisitive state in which economic and political needs overlapped. This fusion of state and economic power enabled Hitler to build the Third Reich. Consequently, post–World War II policymakers and political leaders sought to remove the state from actively governing the economy. Thus, the postwar period saw the development of *Modell Deutschland* (the German model), a term often used to describe the FRG's distinctive political and socioeconomic features: coordinated banking and industrial relations, democratic participation by workers on the job, and extensive public sector benefits. This model looked unlike the free-market traditions of countries like the United States and Great Britain and the more state-centered democracies like France and Japan. Rather, postwar Germany developed an organized capitalist model that placed primacy on coordination among private sector actors to promote efficiency and competitiveness. As a counterweight to concentrated economic power, the Federal Republic also developed a strong labor movement that used democratic corporatism to participate in fundamental decisions that were often left to management in other countries. This model served Germany exceptionally well until the late 1990s, but its future is uncertain in the new era of the EU. Whether previously successful German economic institutions continue to function well in a unified Europe remains a question.

The *democratic idea*, our third theme, developed much later in Germany than in most other advanced industrialized countries. It was not until 1918 and the shaky Weimar Republic that Germany first attained democracy at all. And Germany's fragile democratic institutions were crushed by the Nazi takeover less than two decades later. Despite a formal democratic constitution, Weimar was a prisoner of forces bent on its destruction. Unlike stable multiparty political systems in other countries, the Weimar Republic was plagued by a sharp and increasing polarization of political parties. The constitution of the Federal Republic in 1949 was designed to overcome Weimar's shortcomings. A system of federalism, constitutional provisions to encourage the formation and maintenance of coalitions, and a streamlined political party system proved solid foundations for the new democracy. Electoral turnout of between 80 percent and 90 percent for almost all elections since 1949 suggests that Germans have embraced democracy, although skeptics argue that Germans were voting more out of duty than anything

else.[13] However, four peaceful, electoral regime changes in the past fifty years in which both government and opposition functioned more smoothly than most other democratic regimes may finally put to rest doubts about German democracy. The remaining uncertainty is how well and how quickly the democratic culture will penetrate former communist eastern Germany.

The fourth theme, the *politics of collective identities*, offers a unique look at the intersection of democracy and collectivity. More than in other democratic countries, German political institutions, social forces, and patterns of life emphasize collective action rather than the individualism characteristic of the United States. In other words, class is still important. Although it provides an important source of collective identity and is closely linked to party cleavages, it does not polarize and provoke stalemate. Religion too is an important collective identity, especially with the strong role that Christian Democracy plays in the political life of Germany. These collective identities should not imply that German citizens have less personal freedom compared to those in other developed democracies or that there is no conflict in Germany. It means that political expression, in both the state and civil society, revolves around group representation and cooperative spirit in public action. Certainly Germany's history from Prussian militarism through Nazism has led many observers to believe that collectivist impulses should be eradicated. However, to expect Germany to embrace a liberal, individualistic democracy as in the United States with no deep history of this is misguided. Germany's development of a collective identity since 1945 has relied on a redefinition of Germany in a European context. For example, one of the first provisions of the Social Democratic–Green coalition agreement was to alter Germany's restrictive immigration policies. The new law finally enabled long-established immigrants to gain German citizenship. Thus, German collective identity is changing.

Implications for Comparative Politics

Despite the surface similarities between Germany and the other Western European states covered in this book, there are substantial differences, and they give us a chance to develop and test more general theoretical claims in comparative politics. With respect to the organization of the state, the most significant difference between Germany, on the one hand, and England, France, and Italy, for example, on the other, is that Germany is a federal state, and the others are unitary. This German federalism has produced economic and political patterns quite different from those of its three major European neighbors.

Another important difference is that Germany's later industrialization produced a strong—though unbalanced—economic growth until after World War II. When this growth combined with nationalism and militarism in the late nineteenth and early twentieth centuries, Germany was feared by its neighbors, and with good reason. While late development can lead to catastrophic outcomes, it can also induce greater forms of cooperation and coordination among major actors, producing such institutions as corporatism.

A third difference arises from the delay in the development of democratic forms of representation until the Weimar Republic. Once it was destroyed by the Third Reich, parliamentary democracy did not return until the founding of the Federal Republic in 1949. Of course, the most significant difference between Germany and other Western European states is the Nazi period and the havoc the Third Reich caused. Many observers during the post–World War II period may have thought this difference had declined in significance. However, the racist attacks on foreigners by neo-Nazis force many to rethink whether the evils of the Nazi period are confined entirely to the past. Also, the unification with the former Communist East Germany is an obvious important difference between Germany and its neighbors. The economic, po-litical, cultural, and physical pressures of uniting two disparate societies have placed greater strains on the Federal Republic's politics and institutions than any other event since the state's founding in 1949. While postwar Germany has manifested most of the features of a stable capitalist democracy, these peculiarities and their legacies have created and maintained significant tensions within society.

Finally, Germany's role in the EU presents both opportunities and challenges to Germany and its neighbors. As the strongest European power, Germany has many economic and political advantages in an integrating Europe. However, it must deal with the suspicion that its twentieth-century historical legacy arouses in its neighbors, and it must also confront the question of whether its postwar political institutions, so well suited to it, will also suit Germany and other Europeans in the EU.

We suggest that the best way to answer these issues is to examine them historically, systematically, and rigorously through the prism of our four themes.

Comparative analysts seeking to understand Germany's history and future prospects have been guided by a number of assumptions that we explore more fully in the following four chapters. One is that relations among social groups—competing collective identities—have an important influence on a state's formation and development. In Germany's case, bitter religious, ideological, and regional social conflicts (among others) were partly responsible for delaying its unification and stable development. As a result, Germany lagged several centuries behind other Western powers in forming a modern nation-state.

Germany's late unification as a nation-state also gave it little time to develop strong civic and democratic institutions with which to address deep social divisions and fierce international competition. Democracies that evolve more gradually can usually meet such challenges more peacefully and effectively. In encouraging public discussion and compromise among competing social interests, such governments can diffuse potential conflicts and deliberate state options more fully. Germany's weak civic and governing institutions were unable to protect it and other nations from ruthless oppression by military elites who led the German people into two disastrous wars. These tragic experiences were to have a profound influence on the postwar development of West Germany's democracy. This suggests that the clever design of political institutions can promote democracy; witness the success of the Basic Law in reconciling the need for effective government and democratic participation.

Another assumption we consider is that a state's relationship with private interests is established early and shapes its ability to develop effective economic policies over time. Such relationships formed to govern the economy help determine a state's wealth and ability to manage changes effectively. In Germany's case, delayed industrialization may have proved beneficial once democratic institutions became stronger and better able to reconcile economic growth with political accountability. Like Japan, Germany's government has played an active role in

economic development from the start. In contrast, Britain and the United States industrialized early, with much less direct government intervention, and their economies rely much more on private market forces. Clearly, advanced industrialized democracies employ different economic policy models. In Chapter 17, we consider the implications of Germany's economic strategy for its postwar development.

A final assumption is that a state's position in the international system—measured in part by its resource base, level of economic development, and military power relative to other states—affects its ability to manage domestic and international pressures. By the time that Germany embraced industrialization in the late nineteenth century, it felt compelled to catch up with a world of more advanced industrial states such as Britain, France, and the United States, which had divided a large share of the world's primary resources and trade among themselves. Germany's intense effort to expand its industrial and military power through direct state involvement in the economy had important—and adverse—consequences for its development.

Notes

1. The FRG is also the name of the newly unified Germany, since the former East Germany officially reunified by joining the FRG as five separate, new federal states (*Länder*).

2. Prussia no longer exists as a state or province. It was an independent principality in what is now northeast and northwest Germany and part of Poland.

3. Charles Tilly, ed., *The Formation of National States in Western Europe* (Princeton, N.J.: Princeton University Press, 1975).

4. Tom Kemp, *Industrialization in Nineteenth Century Europe*, 2d ed. (London: Longman, 1985).

5. Gordon Craig, *The Politics of the Prussian Army* (Oxford: Oxford University Press, 1955).

6. Barrington Moore, *Social Origins of Dictatorship and Democracy* (Boston: Beacon Press, 1965).

7. Alexander Gerschenkron, *Bread and Democracy in Germany*, 2d ed. (Ithaca, N.Y.: Cornell University Press, 1989).

8. Geoffrey Barraclough, *An Introduction to Contemporary History* (Baltimore: Penguin, 1967).

9. Daniel Goldhagen, *Hitler's Willing Executioners: Ordinary Germans and the Holocaust* (New York: Knopf, 1996).

10. Philippe Schmitter and Gerhard Lembruch, *Trends Toward Corporatist Intermediation* (Beverly Hills, Calif.: Sage, 1979).

11. The concept of the "three republics" of postwar West Germany has been drawn from Peter A. Katzenstein, ed., *The Politics of Industry in West Germany: Toward the Third Republic* (Ithaca, N.Y.: Cornell University Press, 1989).

12. William E. Paterson and Gordon Smith, *The West German Model: Perspectives on a Stable State* (London: Cass, 1981).

13. Ralf Dahrendorf, *Society and Democracy in Germany* (Garden City, N.Y.: Anchor, 1969).

C H A P T E R

17

Political Economy
and Development

The Federal Republic of Germany (FRG) has clearly taken a development path that emphasizes cooperative interaction with a dense interest group network of key social and economic actors. Post–World War II Germany has avoided both of the imbalances that plague many other nation-states: in one, powerful private interests (typically the leaders of a sector of the economy) may "capture," or dominate, state policy; in the other, the state dominates or captures private interests. As we suggest in this chapter, by its unique forms of organized capitalism, combined with the social market economy, Germany has largely avoided the imbalance of state economic strategies that are subject to unpredictable changes and boom-and-bust cycles. This relative stability is all the more remarkable given the twin challenges beginning in the 1990s: German unification and European integration.

The Postwar Settlement and Beyond

The postwar settlement long seemed for many observers, both German and non-German, to be almost an immutable fact of nature. After emerging from its horrendous history during the first half of the twentieth century, the new FRG produced something quite different: a set of structures and institutions consisting of, first, an organized-capitalist, mixed-economy welfare state with a high degree of labor union

involvement and, second, a stable multiparty democracy. Yet like all other institutional arrangements, the FRG's were neither immutable nor without tensions. A number of challenges to the postwar settlement arose beginning in the 1970s, at the end of the economic boom years, and have continued through unification and the era of European integration. This chapter characterizes the consolidation and maturing of the postwar settlement and contrasts it with the new political economy from the mid-1980s to the present. Yet rather than representing solely a sharp conflict between two antagonistic policy options, the transition also witnessed important continuities.

The transcending of the postwar settlement—the emergence of a Third Republic, in Peter Katzenstein's formulation—took place during this transitional period in the early and mid-1980s. In this process, the political economy of the Federal Republic emerged from a period of economic uncertainty—what some called Eurosclerosis,[1] to achieve its position as the leading nation in the process of European integration and accomplish its unification with the former German Democratic Republic (GDR). This Third Republic was again led by the Christian Democrats, this time in the person of Chancellor Helmut Kohl, who was consistently underestimated by his critics. It was the Kohl Center-Right coalition of the Christian Democratic Union (CDU) and Christian Social Union (CSU) with the Free Democratic Party

(FDP) that enthusiastically embraced the concept of the single European market and pragmatically moved to consolidate the former GDR into the Federal Republic. The opposition (the Social Democratic Party, SPD, the Greens, and the former communist Party of Democratic Socialism, PDS, in the five eastern states) was much slower to embrace either of these two momentous developments, to their political detriment.

The following example provides concrete evidence of a challenge to labor market policy, an area that had directly benefited from one of the long-standing institutional relationships of the postwar settlement. It also suggests that the institutional capacity to address such problems, although sharply challenged, has not fundamentally eroded.

The thirteen-year SPD-FDP Center-Left coalition government (1969–1982) led by Chancellor Helmut Schmidt collapsed largely because of a dispute over economic policy. The SPD's left-wing rank and file (but not the chancellor) wanted increased stimulation of the economy, and the more moderate FDP did not. The FDP changed its coalition partnership and turned to the Christian Democrats. The new CDU/CSU-FDP coalition government, led by the new chancellor, Helmut Kohl, took office in October 1982 and faced the immediate problem of increased unemployment, owing largely to the residue of the twin oil shocks of the 1970s. One of the new government's immediate tasks was to shoulder the cost of sustaining the long-term unemployed through general welfare funds. However, a more serious structural problem lay beyond the immediate issue of cost: How could the Federal Republic's elaborate vocational education and apprenticeship system absorb all of the new entrants into the labor market? In a country that has prided itself on its skilled workforce, this issue represented a potential problem because it could have undermined one of the strong points of the German economy: the continued supply of skilled workers. This supply of highly skilled—and highly paid—workers has

been one of the linchpins of the postwar settlement generally, and the German model specifically.

Despite these threats in the early and mid-1980s, the unemployment compensation system and the vocational education and apprenticeship system both weathered this period during the first years of the Kohl government. In a concentrated effort, the national and state (*Länder*) governments, employer associations, trade unions, and works councils, using a variety of formal and informal institutional mechanisms, found ways to reinvigorate one of the core foundations of the Federal Republic's labor market. They did so by a combination of decentralized negotiations targeted to the specific needs of the labor markets of particular regions of the FRG. They used such existing institutions as codetermination (*Mitbestimmung*), the works councils (*Betriebsräte*) present in almost all German firms, and the country's elaborate vocational education system. This system allows employers, unions, and governments to participate in shaping the curriculum to the needs of particular regions. Although some regions lagged, principally northern German regions such as the heavy-industry Ruhr valley and the shipbuilding cities of Bremen and Bremerhaven, other regions prospered. Among the more successful regions were the southwestern region of Baden-Württemberg, where firms such as Daimler-Benz and Bosch have their headquarters outside the region's largest city, Stuttgart. The city of Munich and the *Land* of Bavaria (where the giant electronics firm Siemens is located) also prospered during the latter part of the 1980s to the mid-1990s.

The FRG has relied heavily on its skilled blue-collar workers throughout the postwar period. There has been much less decomposition of this segment of the working class because of its importance in the flexible-system production processes of such industries as machine tools, automobiles, chemicals, and industrial electronics. Although there has been some evidence of partial decomposition in weaker industries such as steel and shipbuilding, where there have been major job losses, blue-collar working-class decomposition was far less pronounced than in either Britain or the United States.

Because of this reliance on high-skill and high-wage manufacturing, the FRG has seen only a small growth of service-sector jobs. Unlike the United States, where a large proportion of the new jobs since the 1980s have been created in the service sector, Germany has resisted this option, largely due to the belief that low wages would result. Some individuals on the right wing of the FDP in the mid-1980s at first argued that the country should emulate the United States by creating new jobs in services. The SPD and the trade unions countered with the assertion that most service-sector jobs in the United States were low-paying jobs at fast food restaurants with few benefits. They argued that the strains placed on society by this plan for employment growth, in the form of insufficient economic demand (owing to low wages) and increased social spending (owing to lack of fringe benefits), would represent a net loss for German society. The plan for high-productivity, high-wage unionized employment had sustained the economy for many years, and most labor market actors preferred to retain their dependence on that policy path. The U.S. "solution," they believed, was the wrong choice. From the mid-1980s until the first years of unification, German industry had not listened to the siren song of service-sector jobs over manufacturing ones and had slowly reduced its unemployment in West Germany by relying on a traditional postwar pattern: manufacturing jobs in export-earning sectors.[2]

An additional institutional factor that prevented the decomposition of the working class was the residual strength of organized labor.[3] (The role of unions is treated explicitly in subsequent chapters.) Their purposeful response to the economic downturn of the late 1970s and early 1980s prevented the erosion of union strength that took place in other industrialized countries. For example, under the SPD-led governments, the unions were able to secure strong footholds in the political economy, which protected them during the more disadvantageous 1980s and 1990s. In 1976, under the SPD-FDP coalition government, the original codetermination law of 1952 was expanded to stop just short of the virtual full-parity codetermination that coal and steel workers had enjoyed since 1951. The 1952 law required firms with 2,000 or more employees to let 33 percent of the board members be chosen by the trade unions. In 1976 the figure increased to 50 percent. However, management retained the tiebreaking vote. In addition, in 1972, the SPD-FDP coalition government also extended the provision of the *Betriebsverfassungsgesetz* (Works Constitution Act) to provide more rights for trade unions inside the works councils and thereby solidified unions' positions in the workplace. Most significant, this continued maintenance of an institutionalized presence for unions enabled them to participate in shaping the direction of the Federal Republic's economy on their own terms rather than forcing them reflexively to oppose any overtures by either management or a conservative government.[4]

The strains on the social market economy beginning in 1990, exacerbated by the huge costs of unification, finally seemed to transcend the postwar settlement as it pressed on the upper limits of Germany's capacity to pay for these costs. Larger budget cuts than ever previously proposed in the FRG became imperative by the early 1990s. The completion of the European Union's (EU) single market, supposedly the grand culmination of a post–cold war spirit of German and European unity, proved more difficult to realize than its planners first thought. The immediate benefit in the early 1990s seemed only likely to strengthen the trends toward decentralization and deregulation already under way in Western Europe. More significant for the German regime, it threatened to disturb the organized capitalism of Germany's small and large businesses.

Organized capitalism in Germany consists

of an intricate, mutually reinforcing pattern of government and business self-regulation. Clearly, an Anglo-American push for deregulation would undermine these patterns. Plus, the rapid deregulation in European finance threatened Germany's distinctive finance-manufacturing links, which depend on long-term relationships between the two parties, not the short-term "deals" that quickly became fashionable in Europe. Thus, the trend toward Europeanization—in a way that challenged Germany's preeminent position—seemed to be incompatible with the highly consensus-oriented and coordinated nature of Germany's adjustment patterns.

In addition, tensions persist between former East and West Germans. The GDR economy was considered strong by Communist standards. It provided jobs for virtually all people, but many of these were not sustainable when Communist countries like the GDR collapsed. GDR industry, as in most of the other former Communist countries, was inefficient by Western standards, and most firms were not able to survive the transition to the West German capitalist system. Among the most serious problems were overstaffing and quality control. Consequently, many East Germans lost their jobs. For a time, they were generously supported by West German subsidies, but the recovery in the five new *Länder* lagged much more than the Kohl government originally thought it would. Easterners resented the slow pace of change and the high unemployment, and West Germans were bitter about losing jobs to easterners and paying increased taxes for the cleanup of the ecological and infrastructural disaster inherited from the former East German regime. This question of the durability of the West German model for a united Germany was raised anew with the large increase in the unemployment rate in the eastern *Länder* after unification in 1990.

On balance, the long years of the postwar settlement proved far more durable in Germany than in any of the other countries covered in this book. But the twin pressures embodied by German unification and European integration, combined with two new challenges to the political economy of the FRG toward century's end in the form of the information economy and Germany's high tax status, will be explored in the remainder of this chapter.

State and Economy

Other country studies in this book make a sharp distinction between economic management and the welfare state. We do not with respect to Germany for a very good reason. The relationship between economic management and the provision of public goods (i.e., welfare) is interpenetrated among private, public, and what Peter Katzenstein calls "para-public" institutions.[5] In other words, it is not easy to demarcate these two policy areas in Germany as it is elsewhere.

Germany has long been an organized-capitalist country in which two sets of groups, representing industry generally and employers specifically, are powerful and coordinated.[6] Rather than emphasizing individual entrepreneurship and small business as the defining characteristic of its economy, Germany has relied on an organized network of small and large businesses working together.[7] In addition, the banking system and financial community play a direct role in private investment and until recently have engaged in little of the financial speculation characteristic of Wall Street. Traditionally, they have seen their primary role as providing long-term investments for the health of the internationally competitive manufacturing industries, the foundation of the economy. This model generally holds for the regional and savings banks. However, a bifurcation has developed in the industry as the largest and best known of the German banks (Deutsche, Dresdner, and Commerzbank) have begun to move away from their traditional role and behave like large banks in New York, London, and Tokyo, unfettered by long-term relationships to domestic manufacturing firms.[8]

Government economic policy is indirect and supportive rather than heavy-handed and overly regulatory. It sets broad guidelines but often leaves the implementation of policies to coordinated negotiations among organized interests such as employers, banks, trade unions, and regional governments. This does not mean the government does not become involved in economic policymaking; it just does so more flexibly. The flexibility is produced in two ways. First, the German pattern of regulation addresses the general framework of competitiveness rather than the minute details more commonly addressed in other countries. In many cases, if the framework patterns are effectively drawn, microregulation is much less necessary. Second, among the major European economies such as Britain, France, and Italy, Germany has the smallest share of industry in government hands. This condition is accomplished by a cooperative federalism that delegates to the states the administrative powers of laws and regulations passed at the federal level. Both are integral parts of Germany's social market economy (*Sozialemarktwirtschaft*), discussed more fully later in this chapter.

Unlike Britain and the United States, Germany did not have the option of the kind of trial-and-error capitalism that characterized much of the early nineteenth century. By the time it unified in 1871, Germany was forced to compete with a number of countries that had already developed industrialized capitalist economies. German business and political elites realized that a gradual, small-firm-oriented industrialization process would face ruinous competition from Britain, France, and the United States. Thus, the German state in the late nineteenth century became a significant and powerful—if antidemocratic—force in the German economy. It did so by building on the foundations established by the formerly independent states—Prussia, Bavaria, and the others—that became part of a united Germany in 1871.

Regional governments developed their autonomy before unification, resulting in a tradition of strong public-sector involvement in economic growth and development. In the fragmented Germany of the late eighteenth and early nineteenth centuries, states had to develop governmental systems to provide for the material and social needs of their populations, and they had to do so without being able to rely on a centralized national state. These regional governmental actors worked both directly and indirectly with private economic interests, blurring distinctions between state and market.

The economic powers possessed by the modern states of the post–World War II Federal Republic are not products merely of the decentralized federalism that has characterized the political institutions of Germany. Rather, the *Land* governments have also built on a century-long pattern of regional-government involvement in both economic growth and industrial adaptation. The most common metaphor for analyzing industrial growth in Germany during the nineteenth century has been that of Alexander Gerschenkron's late-industrialization thesis.[9] This thesis maintains that Germany's transformation from a quasi-feudal society to a highly industrialized one during the latter two-thirds of the nineteenth century was characterized by a process of explicit coordination among government, big business, and a powerful universal banking system. German banks are universal because, then and now, they are capable of handling all financial transactions and are not segmented into savings and commercial branches, for example. This nineteenth-century pattern has often been called rapid German industrialization, although a more accurate account would call it rapid Prussian industrialization, since it was Bismarck's vision and mobilization of Prussian interest groups that proved the dominant force.

Although Germany was not unified as a nation-state until 1871, the foundations for economic growth and the most spectacular early leaps of industrial modernization took place before 1871. The creation in 1834 of the customs union (*Zollverein*) that removed tariffs among eighteen independent states with a population of 23 million people, was a crucial spur to industrial modernization as it greatly increased trade. This process was led by Prussia, and the dominant symbol for Prussia's hegemonic position was Bismarck's role in brokering the interests of grain-growing *Junkers* in the east with those of the coal and steel barons in the Ruhr. Bismarck used the development of the railroads as a catalyst for this marriage of iron and rye. He astutely realized that railroads were a primary consumer of coal and steel, yet they also provided an effective means of transportation to market for the *Junkers'* grain from the relatively isolated eastern part of Germany.[10] Although the Prussian-led image of rapid, state-enhanced industrial growth is important, the opening of trade among these independent principalities did not dislodge the distinct patterns of modernization that the less powerful states had developed on their own. Small-scale agricultural production remained in many parts of the southern states, particularly in Bavaria, and small-scale craft production continued in Württemberg, as well as in many other regions where feudal craft skills were adapted to the patterns of industrial modernization.

And because each of the states had different material needs and social circumstances, these regional governments perhaps did a more effective job of fulfilling needs than would a central state. Certainly Bismarck's welfare state measures brought economies of scale to those programs that needed to be implemented on a national basis. However, the strong role of the regional governments in the provision of certain specific needs continued, especially during the Second Reich of 1871–1918. Even as the Third Reich was overtaking the Weimar regime, the regional governments tried unsuccessfully to resist the Nazi state's goal of a massive centralization of policy.

Fundamental change was needed following the horrors of the Third Reich between 1933 and 1945, when the state worked hand-in-glove with German industry to suppress workers, employ slave labor, and produce military armaments. These events caused postwar policymakers to avoid such a strong state role in economic life under the Federal Republic. Unlike the French and Japanese states, which have been much more economically interventionist, the German state has evolved a rather unique relationship between the public and private sectors. Rather than seeing a relationship of state versus market, the German public and private sectors have evolved a densely interpenetrated association that avoids the kind of state planning characteristic of postwar Japan or France. It also has avoided the opposite pattern: the antigovernment free-market policies of Britain and the United States in the 1980s. Of course, the five *Länder* of the former GDR evolved no such balanced ground between state and market, as they were governed by a communist regime in which the state ruled and markets did not. This past contributes to eastern Germany's continuing delayed integration into the economic and institutional fabric of the unified FRG.

The key general concept in understanding the FRG's political economy is that the relationship between state and market is neither free market nor state dominant. Rather, the state sets clear general ground rules, which the private sector acknowledges, but then allows market forces to work relatively unimpeded within the general framework of government supervision. Since the time of the first postwar chancellor, Christian Democrat Konrad Adenauer, the Germans have referred to the relationship between state and market as the *social market economy*. Basically, the concept refers to a system of capitalism in which fundamental social benefits are essential—not antagonistic—to the workings of the market. Among the social components of the German economy are generously provided health care, workers' rights, public transportation, and support for the arts, among many others. In some respects, these benefits are similar to those provided by the Japanese and French states. However, the provision of some public benefits by means of organized private interests—the quasi-public Sickness Funds that provide for health insurance, for example—makes the German social market economy a blend of public and private action to support and implement public policies.

The major principle behind the social market economy is that of a market system embedded within a comprehensive framework that encourages the interpenetration of private and public institutions. State policy is a conscious choice to provide a general regulatory boundary, without involving itself in the minute details of policy implementation. The implementation of these framing policies produces a stable set of outcomes. It is organized and implemented by coordination among public- and private-sector actors that improves—rather than impedes—economic competitiveness. The politically independent Bundesbank (central bank) is just such an important actor (and is addressed in Chapter 18). Thus, the social market economy does not lie halfway between state and market but represents a qualitatively different approach. For example, German law in a particular area is often more general than specific, because it then expects that organized interests (business, labor, or other interest groups and social forces) will meet and negotiate the details within the law's general mandate. Moreover, strong, internally generated pressures from within each of these organized groups encourage their members to stay onboard and not depart from the negotiated collective outcomes. The combination of high wages, high social spending, and the necessity to keep German goods competitive globally provides concrete reasons that such group-oriented outcomes are beneficial for the major social forces in the FRG. Not surprisingly, the five *Länder* of the former GDR fit uneasily into the dominant West German model. Not only are eastern German firms generally less competitive than those in the west, the network of supporting institutions is either absent or is imposed by *Wessis*, a derogatory term akin to *carpetbagger* that is used to describe western Germans who try to exploit the less well-developed east.

The social component of the social market economy also differs from those of other countries. Although the Federal Republic has always been generous with the provision of welfare benefits, they serve more than just distributive income-transfer purposes. For example, two of the most important provisions, government savings subsidies to individuals and a comprehensive vocational education system, have direct and positive benefits for the competitiveness of the German economy. They create both a stable pool of investment capital and a deep pool of human capital that enables Germany to produce high-quality goods.

Such policies are based on the German system of framework regulation and can best be explained in the words of one of the shapers of post–World War II economic policy, economist Wilhelm Röpke:

> [Our program] consists of measures and institutions which impart to competition the framework, rules, and machinery of impartial supervision which a competitive system needs as much as any game or match if it is not to degenerate into a vulgar brawl. A genuine, equitable, and smoothly functioning competitive system can not in fact survive without a judicious moral and legal framework and without regular supervision of the conditions under which competition can take place pursuant to real efficiency principles. This presupposes mature economic discernment on the part of all responsible bodies and individuals and a strong impartial state.[11]

By this method, German economic policy during the post–World War II period has avoided the sharp lurches between laissez-faire-led and state-led economic policy that have characterized Britain.

Germany is a prime case of a high-wage, high-welfare country that has maintained its competitive world position far better than other advanced industrialized states for the almost thirty years since the oil crisis of 1973. Its success in combining strong competitiveness with high wages and social spending has surpassed even that of Japan. A high-skill emphasis in key export-oriented manufacturing industries is the specific path that German economic policy has taken to maintain its competitive position. The foundation stones of this system are the elaborate system of vocational education combined with apprenticeship training. It is implemented through the works councils, which are elected by all employees in all German firms with five or more employees. This system of advanced skill training has enabled Germany to resist the postindustrial, service-sector orientation that countries such as the United States and Britain have tried. Relying extensively on this elaborate apprenticeship training program, Germany has maintained competitive positions in such "old" manufacturing industries as automobiles, chemicals, machine tools, and industrial electronics. The Federal Republic's strategy for international competitiveness was not to develop new high-tech industries, thereby deemphasizing the fulcrum sectors, but to employ high-technology *processes* in these comparatively old-fashioned industries. Economist Michael Piore and political sociologist Charles Sabel have called such process innovation "flexible system manufacturing" because it emphasizes the high skill levels and flexibility of the German workforce, thereby enabling these industries to find crucial niches in world markets.[12] To Americans, Mercedes, Audi, and BMW automobiles are the most visible examples of the success of this strategy. By stressing the value that its highly skilled workforce adds to raw materials, Germany has defied predictions for almost thirty years that its industrial economy would erode, as have many other formerly manufacturing-oriented developed economies. Despite being poor in natural resources (like most of the rest of Europe), Germany maintains a surplus balance of trade and still has a large working-class population, which historically has *not* favored protectionism. With one in every three jobs devoted to exports (one in two in the sectors of automobiles, chemicals, machine tools, and industrial electronics), protectionism for German unions would be self-defeating. The skills of its workers help German industry overcome the costs of acquiring resources and paying high wages because German industry has emphasized high quality and high productivity as offsetting factors.

Enhancing this set of policies has been Germany's research and development strategy. It preferred not to push for specific new breakthroughs in exotic technologies or for inventing new products that might be years from market. Rather it chose to adapt existing technologies to its traditional, already competitive sectors. This has been the exact opposite of U.S. research and development strategy, for example. During the postwar years, this policy has enabled Germany to maintain a favorable balance of trade and a high degree of competitiveness. But how long would this model continue?

Early in the twenty-first century, however, the German political economy seemed less rosy than in previous decades. European integration and German unification have forced German industry and policymakers to examine whether this model remains appropriate or needs fundamental reexamination. Depending on others to make core discoveries and then quickly applying the technology to production is a delicate task that requires coordinated policies among all producer groups. Trying to institute the Western German policy among former GDR workers who come from a different industrial culture has begun to prove difficult. In fact, the speed with which the information age and the penetration of the Internet into all facets of economic and public life has caught the German model somewhat unprepared. Are Germany's prevailing economic practices and policy styles still relevant for the new information industries, as well as existing industries transformed by the process? Can the vocational and apprenticeship system produce the kind of workers needed in the new century? The answer is uncertain, because despite unemployment at between 6 percent and 7 percent, German industry had to recruit programmers, web designers, and network specialists from India to meet gaping shortages in these fields in Germany. However, the deregulation of Deutsche Telekom, the former state-run telephone service, has begun to spur a belated development in Internet and information infrastructure technology. The question for observers of German political economy is whether the traditional German industrial pattern of integrating and applying innovations first developed elsewhere will apply to the information age economy as well.

In general, however, Germany still seems well positioned among those developed countries to which the term *postwar settlement* applies in the sense of the embedding of a capitalist economic system within a parliamentary democratic polity. Given Germany's volatile history, these political and institutional arrangements were first imposed by the Allied powers as a way of preventing extreme economic and political outcomes. Once instituted, they were soon adapted and embraced by most of the major West German interest groups and political parties. The German state has played a guiding, though not imposing, role in developing and supporting the postwar settlement. Fearful of the excesses of centralized state control, manifested in extreme form by the Nazis of the Third Reich and the Communists of the GDR, German state policy has preferred to shape and frame outcomes rather than to control them directly. In general, social identities—the guest workers excepted—and political regulation remained relatively consistent from the founding of the Federal Republic until the 1990s. Here too, though, the postunification turmoil has created a much greater strain on the democratic political institutions of the Federal Republic.

With respect to state-society relations, we must stress the social market economy and its related concept of framework regulation, themes that will resonate throughout the three chapters that follow and are unique contributions to democratic practice in German society. These institutional patterns characterize the relationship between private and public sectors and among major interest groups in German society. Rather than the state-centered polity of France and Japan or the market-centered polity of Britain and the United States, Germany has adopted a fluid, interpenetrated set of policies that govern state and market relationships. Democratic corporatism and the role of interest groups in shaping public policies (and not just through state policies) are two examples. In effect, these processes of "negotiated adjustment" allow the state to delegate certain public functions to private actors in return for these private actors' taking responsibility for implementing public policy.[13] Also, Germany enjoys a kind of overlapping federalism (in the sense of national and regional governments explicitly coordinating policies), which has produced strong institutional continuity. For example, federal law is actually implemented by regional and local governments, thus avoiding some of the duplication that plagues different levels of government in the United States. This German framework regulation has been maintained for much of the postwar period, though the tensions produced by unification have clearly placed strains on this system.

Such strains are particularly evident in the newer states that composed the former GDR. The complex network of institutions that evolved in Western Germany for over forty years had to be created from scratch in the former GDR. Western German policymakers understandably attempted to transplant successful FRG models in a wide range of policy areas. Among these were labor market, educational, welfare, housing, and regulatory institutions, and virtually all of them were less successful in the five new *Länder* than in the other *Länder*. To scholars of institutional analysis, this lack of fit was no surprise. Wade Jacoby has written eloquently about just such "transplantation difficulty."[14] It is very difficult to impose institutional structures from outside. As Jacoby argues, successful adaptation of institutional change must be "pulled in" by indigenous actors in Eastern Germany. That takes time. Furthermore, one usually organized segment of German society, business, also suffered from organizational fragmentation. Competitive pressures, principally in the east but also in the west, saw a weakening of the solidarity that had long characterized organized capitalism and began to complicate the usually smooth-running industrial relations system.[15]

Clearly the organized-capitalist model is not an unadulterated success in the minds of all Germans. Both the Greens and the small, free-market-oriented sector feel that the organized, and perhaps closed, nature of producer groups privileges those who are inside the loop (such as industry organizations, employer groups, and the banking community) and excludes those outside. Moreover, the Greens are also critical of many business policies that they feel do not sufficiently guard against environmental consequences. The primary critique from the small-business sector is that the organized nature of large-firm dominance is not flexible enough in the creation of new products and industries. However, neither the Greens nor advocates of a more laissez-faire approach to economic policies have dislodged the dominant position of German organized capitalism in the shaping of economic policy. And the apparent limitations of the German model for Eastern Germany have been largely responsible for the continued presence of the former communist party, renamed the Party of Democratic Socialism (PDS). This party has served as an important tribune for Eastern Germans who would like greater resources from the federal government.

Beginning in the early 1990s, a sharp three-pronged challenge began to undermine the idea of a smoothly functioning German economic juggernaut. First, the Kohl government badly misjudged the costs of unification and the institutional resources necessary to integrate the five new *Länder*. By mid-1992, Kohl had finally acknowledged that the successful integration of the Eastern economy into the Western one would cost much more and require longer than originally predicted. Second, the structural challenges that the German political economy faced in the mid-1990s were far more extensive than any the Federal Republic had experienced since the 1950s. The amount budgeted in the early

1990s for reconstruction in Germany was approximately 20 percent of the entire FRG budget. In addition, funds from private firms and regional governments and other subsidies amounted to another 50 billion deutsche marks. Yet even these huge sums were not enough to make the assimilation process go more smoothly. There remains a large gap in productivity levels between the two regions. Third, the West German integrated institutions (even when working well) became difficult to transfer as a model to Eastern Germany.[16] For example, the Treuhand (the government reconstruction agency) privatized some 7,000 of the total of 11,000 firms that it had taken over in the former GDR as a result of the collapse of the old Communist economy. One of the most significant of the costs of this transition was the high unemployment in the eastern sector. Some 1.2 million persons were officially unemployed, and another 2 million were enrolled in a government-subsidized short-time program (part-time work with full-time pay) combined with job training. Yet the latter program had its funds cut as part of an austerity budget. In short, the magnitude of the problems in Eastern Germany has threatened to overwhelm the FRG's institutional capacity to handle them.

Some pessimistic observers finally began to suggest that these stresses placed the German political economy in a precarious position by the turn of the century. Germany's economic prowess has resided in certain manufacturing industries whose goods may be eminently exportable. But in these industries, many technologies must constantly be upgraded, and the cost of wages continues to rise. Throughout the 1990s, the combination of unification, European integration, the continued high-wage, high-tax, and high-welfare economy, followed by the pressures of the information economy on traditional "bricks-and-mortar industry led to the so-called *Wirtschaftsstandort* (literally, location for economic growth) debate. The essence of this turn-of-the-century criticism of the German economy was that the combination of domestic and international factors had made Germany a much less attractive place to invest for international capital to bring into Germany or for German capital to remain in the country. In direct response to this challenge, the Schröder government passed a tax reform package in July 2000 that seemed to address directly the major criticism of the *Wirtschaftsstandort* criticism by offering both personal and corporate tax cuts. Although this seemed to mollify the equities markets, it was not viewed with complete enthusiasm from the left-leaning rank and file of his Red-Green coalition (*red* is a colloquial term for all parties of the left, such as the SPD).

Thus, although the German model of economic growth has proved remarkably durable through almost all of the postwar period, the specific and demanding requirements of both unification and European integration have confronted this model with new pressures. The huge demands of unification are daunting enough. Complicating them is the need to align Germany's economic policies with those of its European neighbors.

Society and Economy

During the boom years of the mid-twentieth century, German economic growth provided a sound foundation for social development. The social market economy of the Christian Democrats was augmented by the SPD-led governments from 1969 to 1982, under which the supportive social programs of the 1950s and 1960s were extended and elaborated. Such growth and corresponding social policies helped avoid the occupational and regional conflict common to many other countries. To be sure, there were—and are—divisions in Germany's society and economy. However, the strong role of trade unions and the unwillingness of employers to attack their workers on wage and workplace issues (perhaps owing to trade union strength) minimized stratification of society and the workplace until the 1990s. Nevertheless, German unifica-

tion, European integration, and new competitive pressures on the German economy placed increasing strains on the social market economy by slightly increasing inequalities compared to the long preunification period of postwar prosperity.

Inequality and Ethnic Minorities

One indelible image of Germany in the postunification years was that of neo-Nazi skinheads setting fire to a hostel containing newly arrived immigrants while chanting *"Ausländer raus"* (foreigners out) as local German residents look on without intervening. Although such heinous acts have been relatively rare in Germany—and have also occurred in other European countries—Germany's history during the Third Reich continues to cause alarm bells to ring at the slightest hint of racial intolerance. Thus, among the concerns that affected the economy and society beginning in the 1980s was the role of ethnic minorities in Germany. The issue grew in prominence throughout the 1990s and has continued into the new century as unification and European integration intensify and immigration to Germany continues. The most contentious concepts are those of nationalism and ethnicity. Exacerbating the problem is the fact that the inhabitants of the former GDR were raised in a society that did not value toleration or dissent. Eastern Germans were also part of a society in which official unemployment did not exist. And the average GDR citizen rarely encountered, not to mention worked with, foreign nationals. West Germany, in contrast, has encouraged the migration of millions of guest workers from throughout southern Europe since the 1960s. At the same time, the FRG provided generous provisions for those seeking political asylum, in large part to try to overcome the legacy of Nazi persecution of non-Germans from 1933 to 1945. East Germany, on the other hand, was a much more closed society, as were most other Communist regimes. Thus, when unification arrived—and was overlaid on the migration of different ethnic minorities into both the east and west—few former GDR citizens responded positively to the contact with foreign nationals.

Former GDR citizens were expected, first, to adopt completely Western democratic habits of debate and toleration of diversity without missing a beat. Second, they were expected to deal with a labor *market,* which sometimes did not supply an adequate number of jobs. In other words, gone was a world of lifetime employment, and in its place was one where structural unemployment claimed as much as 25 percent of the workforce. Third, they were faced with a much more open and ethnically diverse society than they had ever known, and they often blamed the lack of employment on immigrants and asylum seekers. Consequently, many of those German citizens who were beginning to fall through the cracks of the German welfare state were also susceptible to racist pronouncements from demagogues who wished to blame ethnic minorities for all the major changes that had taken place in such a short time. The immigration of computer professionals from India in 2000 only added to the tensions.

Ethnic minorities—even long-term legal residents and new citizens of Germany—often face some on-the-job discrimination, particularly in occupations unprotected by a trade union or a works council. Not surprisingly, ethnic minorities—in Germany as in most other developed countries—have found themselves often employed in workplaces where they are required to perform menial and often thankless work.

Inequality and Women

Women's role in the German workplace is a growing issue. First, the increase in female participation in the labor force (see Table 17.1) has created a departure from traditional German experience. Although still at lower rates than in the United States, the participation of increasing numbers of female employees has created new tensions in an area where men had dominated virtually all positions of authority in both management and unions. The unions have made far greater strides than has management in providing expanded opportunities with responsibility and authority.

Perhaps the most significant obstacle that German women have to overcome is not so much the substance of the benefits that they receive but the premise on which women's role in German society is defined.[17] By any measure, Germany's universal welfare state benefits are generous to all citizens, including women, but it is helpful to understand the context within which rights are granted.

German welfare is a creation of conservatives and Christian Democrats and not that of the Left. It was Bismarck who created the first modern welfare state in the late nineteenth century—not out of the goodness of his heart but to stave off socialist revolution and preserve traditional German cultural values. Similarly, the postwar Christian Democratic creation of the social part of the social market economy was based on Christian values and envisioned a world of male breadwinners and women at home caring for—and having more—children. To be sure, the years of Social Democratic governance (1969–1982 and since 1998) have expanded benefits for women, but at its foundation women's benefits in German society have been tied more to their roles within the family than as individuals. This means that within the context of the labor market, individual German

Table 17.1   Labor Force Participation Rates, Ages Fifteen to Sixty-Five (in percentages)

	1993	1994	1995	1996	1997
Male	81.3	81.3	81.0	80.3	80.3
Female	62.3	62.7	62.6	62.3	62.8

Source: Federal Statistical Office, Germany, 1998.

women face discriminatory aspects and assumptions about their career patterns that American women have greatly overcome. As increasing numbers of women enter the German workforce, it is harder for them to achieve positions of power and responsibility as individuals than it is for their American counterparts. Perhaps this is one more manifestation of the differences between collectivist and individualist societies.

The Generation Gap

Modern generational issues first achieved political significance in the FRG with the emergence of the new social movements in the late 1960s. Several issues drove these movements, culminating in a wave of protests throughout West Germany in 1968, but here we concentrate on those that affect the economy.

These social movements grew increasingly influential in the early 1980s. Elements of the citizen action groups became core supporters of the Green Party formed in the late 1970s. In 1982, the presence of these groups—both the Greens and the young social movements outside the SPD—contributed to the final exhaustion of the SPD as a party of government. Willy Brandt, the first SPO chancellor, reflecting during the early 1980s on these developments, termed these movements "the SPD's lost children," meaning, in retrospect, that the SPD ought to have listened to and incorporated their concerns into party policy.

Although increasingly important in the Federal Republic, these youth-led social movements were not usually associated with what French sociologist Serge Mallet has called the "new working-class" phenomenon (i.e., a change in the composition of the working class from older, male, blue-collar workers to a more diverse mix, including younger, female, and service sector workers) that had been identified in other countries. Political scientist Ronald Inglehart has named these social movements "postmaterialist," in the sense that their concerns were not those of traditional Marxist materialism.[18] In fact, in Germany they have not relied on class as a primary category to define themselves, as many tend to be university-educated children of the middle class. They have thus not been able to create an identity strong enough to challenge the highly skilled working class's dominance in the structure of the Federal Republic. If there is a new working class, it has arisen within the trade unions as members have increased their skills to engage in the flexible system of manufacturing. The still-dominant working-class culture of the Federal Republic has acted as a barrier to the postmaterialist social movement's attaining further influence. However, they have attained an important vehicle for systematic political representation in the Green Party.

The next aspect of the generation gap comes at the other end of the demographic scale: pensioners and older workers. The German birth rate fell markedly in the last decade of the twentieth century, particularly in the former GDR. Demographically this has placed great pressure on the German welfare state because the combination of the low birth rate and the increasing age of the baby boom generation means that fewer younger workers will be contributing to the welfare and retirement benefits of an increasing elderly population. This time bomb has not yet fully hit German politics, largely because the Kohl government during the 1980s and 1990s essentially ignored it. In 2000 the Schröder government only began to address it in the context of the tax reform package. The Red-Green government has proposed augmenting the beleaguered public pension system with additional tax funds that will help Germans diversify their retirement options by developing tax-supported private pensions to accompany the public ones.

The Dilemmas of European Integration

The EU was embraced by most Germans and by the political and industrial establishment, especially in the first few years after unification. As

Europe's leading power, Germany stands to benefit greatly from successful European integration, since its position of strength will likely be enhanced by wider market opportunities. Many actions and policies that its neighbors might have met with cries of German domination become more internationally acceptable when seen as Germany's active participation as a member of the larger EU.

From its international position at the start of the new century, Germany has confronted a number of difficult issues. One open question regarding the EU for Germany has been whether successful German-specific institutional arrangements—such as its institutionalized system of worker (and union) participation in management, its tightly organized capitalism, and its elaborate apprenticeship training—will prove adaptable or durable in a wider European context. What may work well inside Germany may be dependent on German-specific institutional, political, or cultural patterns that will not travel well outside the Federal Republic.

The challenge for Germany in the EU is a difficult one. Germany's successful form of organized capitalism during the postwar period clearly made its economy more successful than that of any other European country. One might then think that in looking for a European-wide model on which to base EU economic policy, Germany might serve as an attractive template. This has not been the case, as EU economic policy seems modeled more on the British free-market policies of conservatives Margaret Thatcher and John Major. What explains this anomaly? The short answer is that institutions take longer to build and establish than do laissez-faire markets. Moreover, German-style organized capitalism has developed in a context specific to Germany and has been reinforced by thousands of overlapping and mutually reinforcing relationships built since the end of World War II. In short, German institutional practice is unlikely to extend beyond the borders of the FRG. The dilemma for the Germans is that to succeed in the EU economy will mean adopting the more free-market practices of the Anglo-U.S. model. The question for Germany is whether it will flourish in Europe using a model with which most of its economic actors are unfamiliar.

As for the question of the speed of European integration, countries that might see the value of emulating German institutions require not just strategies but also the means of implementing them. The lack of a cohesive European-wide institutional framework would severely hinder efforts to develop strategies appropriate to meeting the domestic and international challenges of European unification. Most other European nations know the goals to which they must aspire: a highly skilled workforce able to compete in international markets on some basis other than a combination of low labor costs and high-tech production strategies. But whether they can or want to emulate Germany's example remains to be seen, especially in the face of recent German economic difficulty. The preoccupation of Germans with their immediate domestic issues, plus the German-specific nature of the institutions of their political economy, has partially diminished the luster of German-style policies for the new Europe.

Germany and the International Political Economy

The postunification years have altered Germany's political role on the world stage. As a mature democracy and the leading European power, more is now expected from it. Germany's economic and political power continued through the postwar period and saw its high point during the years between 1960 and 1990. Yet after the momentous events of German unification and European integration, many observers in Europe, Japan, and North America assumed that Germany would take on greater political responsibility based on its position of economic strength and newfound political unity. However, the international indecision and inaction of the Kohl government in the 1990s suggested that Germany was not yet willing or able to do so.

Examples of this inaction were seen in the failure of leadership in areas such as the Gulf War, Somalia, and especially Bosnia. At that time, some still believed that Germany would remain a "political dwarf," at least in a geopolitical sense

Clearly Germany is being pressed to take greater political responsibility, both within the EU and as a sovereign nation-state, based on its economic resources and its political power as the leading European nation. Yet its first steps in the post–cold war arena of Eastern Europe demonstrated its lack of diplomatic skill. The country's initial inaction regarding Bosnia and the appropriate German and European policies toward the former Yugoslavia have literally paralyzed German (and European) foreign policy. Making a purposeful European response still more difficult was the Kohl government's impulsive recognition of Slovenia and Croatia, followed by its pronouncements legitimating Bosnia's separatist claims. This was a position opposed by other Western powers, and it partially precipitated much of the violence when the former Yugoslavia came apart.

Europe as a united entity might find developing a region-wide geopolitical policy easier to accomplish if more skillful leadership came from Germany. But leadership requires working with one's allies and not simply taking an independent position diametrically opposed to one's allies' interests. Obviously future military issues are very much bound up with this question of leadership in the EU. Whether the United Nations, the North Atlantic Treaty Organization (NATO), or the EU itself are to take military responsibility for Europe remains uncertain. This uncertainty has been prolonged by Germany's own ambivalence about its international political role. In their defense, the Germans have stressed the strains and huge costs of unification, as well as the difficulty of dealing with the political asylum issue. But Germany is experiencing nothing more than the obligations of political responsibility. Great nations have to find a way to do extremely difficult things at

times when it is not convenient, but Germany has not yet developed these kinds of skills.

However, the arrival of Gerhard Schröder as chancellor seems to have moved Germany's foreign policy in a more decisive direction. As the first chancellor with no direct memory of World War II (he was born in 1944), he is less willing to defer to the United States and NATO on all international issues. In fact, the combination of moving the capital to Berlin and Schröder's more independent foreign policy stance suggests that Germany's international political role might increase. German participation in the U.N. peacekeeping mission in Bosnia was one example, and agreeing to participate in opposition to Serbian aggression in Kosovo in 1998 was another. In opposition, the SPD and Greens had argued that because of the Third Reich's aggressive military expeditions to the east in World War II, it was impossible for the German military, under either U.N. or NATO auspices, to play a constructive role in Eastern Europe. Yet now in government, the SPD and Greens face increased international pressure that Germany play a leading role in European foreign policy and not shirk the responsibility. While some European neighbors might express anxiety about increased German political power in Europe, the alternative is a political vacuum by an indecisive EU, hardly a stronger option.

Other issues such as trade, economic competition with Japan, the type of monetary policy to be favored by the EU, and the general pace of economic integration remain areas of major concern, though less serious than the ones just mentioned. With the passage of the General Agreement on Tariffs and Trade in Uruguay in December 1993, as well as the contentious World Trade Organization conference in Seattle in 1999, some of the more difficult trade issues have ceased to be major areas of potential conflict. To its benefit, Germany, as a goods-exporting nation, has always favored an open trading system. Both its management and its unions have realized that exports represent both profits and jobs, and that to seek refuge in protectionism would be self-defeating. The threat from Japan seemed to recede somewhat in the late 1990s as the Japanese experienced the recession that had earlier beset both Europe and North America. Germany had developed a different strategy to deal with the Japanese economic challenge than had other Western nations. Instead of believing, as Britain and the United States did, that older manufacturing industries should be given up in the face of the Japanese competitive onslaught, the Germans felt that these industries could remain competitive with a high-skill, high-value-added approach. In large measure, this approach has succeeded and may give the German economy some breathing room as Japan struggles with its own recession.

Germany has enjoyed a greater degree of institutional stability since World War II than at any other time in its history. Even the momentous European and German changes in the late 1980s and to the present do not seem to have fundamentally undermined the political structure. Part of the reason for this stability has been the ability of dominant economic and political leaders to retain a balance between the private and public sectors. Nineteenth-century history showed Germans the important role that the state played in the unification of the country and the development of an industrial economy. Yet twentieth-century German history—both the Nazi years and the GDR experience—showed Germans the dangers in placing too heavy a reliance on centralized state authority. Even the Left has now realized that it must maintain a strong presence in both public and private sectors. The social welfare measures are important for their constituents, but so too are the institutions that workers have obtained within the workplace, and these institutions will be strongly tested as the five former GDR *Länder* struggle to attain the material benefits of the rest of Germany. Ultimately the lesson that the major actors in the Federal Republic's political economy seem to have learned from the confluence of Germany's pre–World War II undemocratic legacy, the GDR experience, and the FRG's post–World War II parliamentary practices is that a balance must be struck between the public and private sectors.

Notes

1. Mancur Olson, *The Rise and Decline of Nations: Economic Growth, Stagflation, and Social Rigidities* (New Haven, Conn.: Yale University Press, 1982).

2. Steven Cohen and John Zysman, *Manufacturing Matters* (New York: Basic Books, 1987).

3. Andrei S. Markovits, *The Politics of the West German Trade Unions* (Cambridge: Cambridge University Press, 1986).

4. For a comprehensive treatment of the West German trade unions during the postwar period, see Andrei S. Markovits and Christopher S. Allen, "West Germany," in Peter Gourevitch, Andrew Martin, George Ross, Stephen Bornstein, Andrei S. Markovits, and Christopher S. Allen, eds., *Unions and Economic Crisis: Britain, West Germany and Sweden* (London: Allen & Unwin, 1984).

5. Peter J. Katzenstein, ed., *The Politics of Industry in West Germany: Toward the Third Republic.* (Ithaca, N.Y.: Cornell University Press, 1989).

6. Rudolf Hilferding, *Finance Capital: A Study of the Latest Phase of Capitalist Development* (London: Routledge and Kegan Paul, 1981).

7. Gary Herrigel, *Industrial Constructions* (Cambridge: Cambridge University Press, 2000).

8. Richard Deeg, *Finance Capitalism Unveiled* (Ann Arbor: University of Michigan Press, 1999).

9. Alexander Gerschenkron, *Bread and Democracy in Germany,* 2d ed. (Ithaca, N.Y.: Cornell University Press, 1989).

10. Colleen A. Dunlavy, "Political Structure, State Policy and Industrial Change: Early Railroad Policy in the United States and Prussia," in Sten Steinmo, Kathleen Thelen, and Frank Longstreth, eds., *Structuring Politics: Historical Institutionalism in Historical Perspective* (Cambridge: Cambridge University Press, 1992), pp. 114–154.

11. Wilhelm Röpke, "The Guiding Principles of the Liberal Programme," in Horst Friedrich Wünche, ed., *Standard Texts on the Social Market Economy* (Stuttgart: Gustav Fischer Verlag, 1982), p. 188.

12. Michael Piore and Charles Sabel, *The Second Industrial Divide* (New York: Basic Books, 1984).

13. Kathleen Thelen, *A Union of Parts* (Ithaca, N.Y.: Cornell University Press, 1992).

14. Wade Jacoby, *Imitation and Politics: Redesigning Germany* (Ithaca, N.Y.: Cornell University Press, 2000).

15. Steven J. Silvia, "German Unification and Emerging Divisions within German Employers' Associations," *Comparative Politics* 29, no. 2 (January 1997): 194–199.

16. Jacoby, *Imitation and Politics.*

17. Joyce Mushaben, "Challenging the Maternalist Presumption: Gender and Welfare Reform in Germany and the United States," in Ulrike Liebert and Nancy Hirschman, eds., *Women and Welfare: Theory and Practice in the U.S. and Europe* (Rutgers, N.J.: Rutgers University Press, 2001).

18. See Ronald Inglehart, *The Silent Revolution: Changing Values and Political Styles Among Western Publics* (Princeton, N.J.: Princeton University Press, 1977); Serge Mallet, *The New Working Class* (New York: Monthly Review Press, 1968).

C H A P T E R

18

Governance
and Policymaking

The governing principles of the Federal Republic of Germany (FRG) are a reaction to the catastrophic experiences that beset previous regimes in Germany. When the Federal Republic was established in 1949, the primary goals of the founders were to work toward eventual unification of the two Germanies and, more important, avoid repeating the failure of Germany's only other experiment with democracy, the Weimar Republic.[1] Unable to accomplish immediate unification, the founders formulated the *Grundgesetz* (Basic Law) as their compromise. It symbolized the temporary nature of disunited Germany, since the founders preferred to wait until Germany could be reunited before using the term *constitution* (*Verfassung*).[2] However, their goal of ensuring a lasting democratic order was a more complicated problem. Two fundamental institutional weaknesses had undermined the Weimar government. First, provisions for emergency powers enabled leaders to centralize authority and suspend democratic rights arbitrarily. Second, the fragmentation of the political party system prevented stable majorities from forming in the Reichstag. This instability encouraged the use of emergency powers to break legislative deadlocks.

The founders of the postwar system, heavily influenced by the Allied occupation authorities, sought to remedy the abuse of centralized power by establishing a federal system in which the states (*Länder*) were given considerable powers, particularly administrative powers. It is paradoxical that a constitution owing so much to the influence of foreign powers has proved so durable. Under the Basic Law of the Federal Republic, many functions that had formerly been centralized during the imperial, Weimar, and Nazi periods—the educational system, the police, and the radio and television networks—now became the responsibility of the states. Although the federal Bundestag (the lower house) became the chief lawmaking body, the implementation of many of these laws fell to the *Länder* governments. Moreover, the *Länder* governments sent representatives to the Bundesrat (the upper house), which was required to approve bills passed in the Bundestag.

There was little opposition from major actors within the Federal Republic to this shift from a centralized to a federal system. The Third Reich's arbitrary abuse of power with respect to Jews, political parties, trade unions, and human rights in general had created strong sentiment for curbing the state's repressive capacities. In addition, political leaders, influenced by the presence in the Federal Republic of U.S. advisers, were inclined to support a federal system. Furthermore, the development of a federal system was not a departure but a return to form. Prior to the unification of Germany in 1871, the various regions of Germany had formed a decentralized political system. The regional states had developed such autonomous institutions as banks, universities, vocational schools, and state administrative systems.

By several methods, the new system overcame party fragmentation and the inability to form working majorities. The multiplicity of parties, characteristic of the Weimar Republic, was partially overcome by changes in electoral law. These procedures were designed to reduce the number of small parties and have resulted in a more manageable system. Only two large parties and four small ones have ever gained representation. The Bundestag is for several reasons more likely to achieve working majorities than the Weimar government did. Election laws require that the interval between elections be four years (except under unusual circumstances). This requirement gives an elected government the opportunity to implement its electoral goals and take responsibility for success or failure. The electoral system, explained in the section on the Bundestag in Chapter 19, was also changed from proportional representation under the Weimar system, which proved unstable, to a combination of proportional representation and single-member electoral districts. New constitutional provisions limited the possibility for the Bundestag to vote a government out of office. Under the Weimar constitution, negative majorities often garnered enough votes to unseat the chancellor but could not provide a mandate to install a replacement. In the Federal Republic this has been changed. The Federal Republic's head of government, as the leader of the dominant party or coalition of parties, now has control over the composition of the cabinet. The federal president is merely the ceremonial head of state. Under the Weimar constitution, the president could be called on to wield emergency powers. Hitler used this rule to manipulate the system under the aging President Paul Hindenburg in 1932–1933. In the Federal Republic, the president has been stripped of such broad power.

The principles of the Federal Republic's government contained in the Basic Law give the regime a solid foundation—one that in the short term has appeared capable of assimilating the five *Länder* that comprised the former German Democratic Republic (GDR) when unification occurred in 1990. And with the Federal Republic having survived for more than forty years, it is clear that the most important goals of the Federal Republic's founders have been fulfilled. Nevertheless, neo-Nazi movements and racist violence in the 1990s surprised many observers who thought these sentiments had long since been purged from German politics. Political scientist Ralf Dahrendorf had stated that until the arrival of the Federal Republic, Germany had been a premodern country, having never developed a liberal democracy.[3] From 1949 until unification, it had seemed much more like other Western industrialized countries. With the difficulty in integrating the two regimes after unification in 1990 and with increasing uncertainty regarding European integration, some of the more optimistic assumptions that Germany had purged its politics of antidemocratic elements came under greater scrutiny.

Organization of the State

Germany is a parliamentary democracy with a chancellor as head of government and a ceremonial president as head of state. From 1949 until unification, the capital was Bonn, but after a ten-year transition period, the Bundestag voted to move most of the parliamentary functions to the official capital, Berlin. In the early and mid-1990s, several ceremonial functions were held in the historic Reichstag in Berlin. But by 1999, after a massive renovation of the Reichstag and the building and rebuilding of numerous government ministries, almost all day-to-day activities were located in the new capital, with only a few ministries remaining in Bonn.

The Federal Republic's legislature is bicameral; the lower house—the Bundestag—has 669 members and the upper house—the Bundesrat—has 69 members. Unlike the U.S. Senate and the British House of Lords, the Bundesrat is made up of elected and appointed officials from the sixteen *Länder*. In this sense, Germany's constitutional system allows more governmental institutional overlap than in many other

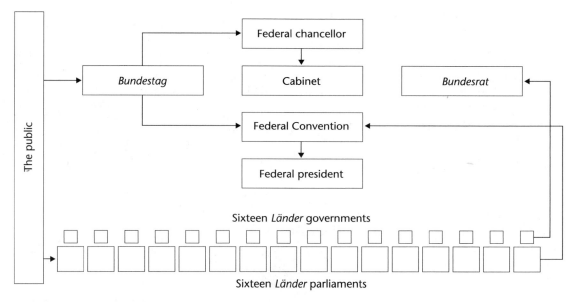

Figure 18.1   Constitutional Structure of Germany's Federal Government

countries that are either unitary (France, Italy, and Britain) or believe in sharp separation of powers within the federal government and a separation of powers between federal and state governments (the United States). The Bundestag members are elected in a basically proportional-representation system (explained in Chapter 19), in which the leader of the major party, who is usually the leader of the largest party in a two- or three-party coalition, is the chancellor. As in most other parliamentary systems, the chancellor must maintain a majority for his or her government to survive.

The German state is organized as a federal system, with the sixteen *Länder* having considerable authority independent of the federal government. Most important are those powers that authorize *Land* governments to raise revenue independently through the ability to own and operate firms, usually in partnership with private industry. Regional and local governments in Britain, Italy, and France have far fewer such powers. The functioning of the German federal government, however, is more like the parliamentary systems of its European neighbors.

There is a fusion of powers in that the chancellor (the executive) is also the leader of the leading party (or coalition) in the Bundestag. This contrasts with the U.S. separation of powers, in which neither the president nor his cabinet officials can simultaneously serve in the Congress. Generally in the Federal Republic, the executive dominates the legislature, but this authority comes from the chancellor's role as party leader coupled with a high level of party discipline. Most members of the governing parties support the chancellor at all times, as their own positions depend on a successful government. This circumstance has the significant result of avoiding the "lone ranger" syndrome, so common in the U.S. House and Senate, where individual members of Congress or the Senate act as independent political entrepreneurs.

The Executive

The division between the head of government (the chancellor) and the head of state (the president) was firmly established in the Federal Republic, with major political powers delegated to the chancellor. Responsibilities and obligations were clearly distinguished. For example, the chancellor could be criticized for the government's policies without the attack being perceived as a frontal assault against the state itself. In this sense, the division of the executive branch was crucial in gaining respect for the new West German state at a time when most of its neighbors remained suspicious of Germany's past. It was Chancellor Hitler, after all, who manipulated President Hindenburg in 1934 to increase the powers of the chancellor. When Hindenburg died shortly after, Hitler fused the offices of chancellor and president, producing the position of Führer (supreme leader).

The President

As head of state, the German president holds a much weaker position than that of the chancellor. Like constitutional monarchs in Britain, for example, German presidents stand above the political fray, which means that they take more of a ceremonial role than an active political one. The distinction between executive functions in the Federal Republic can be contrasted with the confluence of the roles of head of state and head of government in the United States. The president of the United States fills both of these roles, the implications of which have not always been positive for the country. Both Lyndon Johnson and Richard Nixon hid behind the head-of-state mantle by suggesting that criticism of their government's policies was unpatriotic. The German president has the following duties:

> As head of state, the president represents Germany in international affairs, concluding treaties with other countries and receiving the credentials of foreign ambassadors and envoys. He or she formally appoints and dismisses federal civil servants, federal judges, and officers of the Federal Armed Forces and may exercise the right of presidential clemency. He or she participates in the legislative process through the promulgation of laws,

the dissolution of the Bundestag, and the formal proposal, appointment and dismissal of the federal chancellor and the ministers. The political system of Germany assigns the president a non-partisan role, often of a ceremonial nature, with powers that rest largely on the moral authority of the office rather than on political power. An exception is the occurrence of a parliamentary crisis when no candidate can command the support of an absolute majority of Bundestag members. In this case, the president can decide whether the country is to be governed by a minority administration under a chancellor elected by a plurality of deputies or whether new elections are to be called (although the German President has never had to use the last provision).[4]

In May 1999, Johannes Rau was elected president by the Federal Convention (Bundesversammlung), an assembly of all Bundestag members and an equal number of delegates elected by the state legislatures (the equivalent of an electoral college) according to the principle of proportional representation. The presidential term is five years, and a president may serve only two terms. Rau replaced former President Roman Herzog. The important point about the German presidency is that in the case of a political crisis affecting the chancellor, the president would remain as an overseer of the political process, providing continuity in a time of national crisis.

The Chancellor

The Federal Republic's chancellor is elected by a majority of the members of the Bundestag. In practice, this means that the chancellor's ability to be a strong party leader (or leader of a coalition of parties) is essential for the success of the government. A government is formed after a national election or, if the chancellor leaves office between elections, after a majority of the Bundestag has nominated a new chancellor. The new leader consults with other party and coalition officials to make up the cabinet. These party leaders have considerable influence in determining which individuals receive ministries.

In the event of a coalition government, party leaders often earmark, even before the chancellor's election, members of their party who will receive certain ministries. Negotiations on which policies a coalition will pursue can often become heated, so the choice of ministers is made on policy as well as personal grounds.

Once the cabinet is formed, however, the chancellor has considerable authority to govern, owing to the power of the *federal chancellery* (*Bundeskanzleramt*). This office is, in effect, the first among equals of all of the cabinet ministries, enabling the chancellor to oversee his or her entire government efficiently, as well as to mediate conflicts among the other ministries. It is a kind of superministry that has wide-ranging powers in many areas. The chancellor uses this office and its professional staff to supervise and coordinate policy among the other cabinet departments, such as the ministries of economics, finance, interior, and labor and the foreign office, as well as less influential departments. The chancellor draws the professional staff largely from the high ranks of the majority party or coalition partner. Germany's party system and its parliamentary legislative body place a premium on long service, which is expected before advancement is possible. Consequently, party officials often develop specific areas of expertise that the majority party or the chancellor's office can draw on when positions need to be filled. Rather than relying on outsiders from other professions for cabinet positions (as the U.S. executive often does), the chancellors draw their cabinet officials from a pool of individuals with long experience in both government and the party in power.

The Federal Republic has had a history of generally strong chancellors. The first was Konrad Adenauer, who, as the leader of the Christian Democratic Union (CDU), served as the head of government from 1949 to 1963 and established the social market economy. A former mayor of Cologne in the Weimar years, he was known as *Der Alte* (the old man). His paternalism seemed reassuring to a majority of voters at a time when West Germany was rebuilding from the devastation caused by the war. His successor, Ludwig Erhard (CDU), had been economics minister under Adenauer and was widely credited with formulating the social market economy policies that produced the economic miracle during the 1950s and early 1960s. As chancellor from 1963 to 1966, Erhard was much less effective, however. Not only did he fail to respond to the slight recession that hit West Germany in 1965, he lacked Adenauer's decisiveness. Still weaker was Kurt Kiesinger (CDU), the chancellor of the 1966–1969 Grand Coalition of the CDU and Christian Social Union (CSU) with the Social Democratic Party (SPD). He was not a resolute leader, and his task was hindered by the increasing conflicts between the CDU-CSU and the SPD, and the strong foreign policy posture of Vice Chancellor Willy Brandt (SPD). It was also hindered by the growth of the Extraparliamentary Opposition (APO) on the Left and by the National Democrats (NPD), a reconstituted neo-Nazi party, on the Right. Although the Grand Coalition had fused the two major parties in government, it also meant that there was no authentic opposition party. This period of "consensus" government proved short-lived.

Following the 1969 election, the SPD became the dominant coalition partner from 1969 to 1982. Its thirteen-year tenure was largely due to the strong leadership of Chancellors Willy Brandt (1969–1974) and Helmut Schmidt (1974–1982). Brandt was mayor of West Berlin during the 1960s, and during his years as chancellor, he emphasized *Ostpolitik* (encouraging relations with East Germany and the Soviet bloc countries). This policy proved highly popular and was continued even under the Christian Democratic leadership of Helmut Kohl after 1982. Brandt was forced to resign in 1974 when one of his personal assistants was discovered to be a spy for East Germany. However, Brandt remained party chairman through the mid-1980s and was a unifying figure for the party following the coming to power of the Christian Democrats in 1982. Helmut Schmidt replaced Brandt in 1974 and during his term was highly regarded for his skill in managing the economy. Schmidt steered the West German economy through the first oil crisis and through troubled economic straits during the late 1970s and early 1980s. Under his chancellorship, the German economy performed better than those of other European countries. His primary weakness was his inability to retain a close relationship with the rank and file of the Social Democrats. When the Free Democratic Party (FDP), the SPD's junior partner in the governing coalition, broke with Schmidt in the early 1980s on economic policies, Schmidt lacked sufficient support among his own party to remain in power. As leaders of the SPD, both Brandt and Schmidt were adept at brokering conflicts between the left wing of the party and the centrist FDP coalition partner. Both also expanded and consolidated the welfare state.

Helmut Kohl took office in 1982. Many politicians and political observers underestimated his considerable political skills at their own peril. He expertly used the power of the chancellor's office: to hold the CDU/CSU-FDP coalition together; to fend off an attack from the right by the Republikaner (the Republican Party); and to keep the opposition SPD and Greens from making effective challenges to him in the elections of 1987, 1990, and 1994. Following the urbane and worldly Helmut Schmidt was a difficult task for the career politician from the city of Ludwigshafen in the state of Rhineland-Palatinate. Unlike Brandt and Schmidt, Kohl does not speak English in public and often seems ill at ease at ceremonial functions. He is a physically robust man who is said to typify to non-Germans avuncular and *gemütlich* (jovial) characteristics that seem more appropriate for German travel posters than as characteristics for a federal chancellor. Nevertheless, winning four consecutive national elections is no small accomplishment. Nor was shepherding Germany through the twin tasks of unification and European integration, his greatest accomplishments.

"The scalandal is . . . over?

Source: © Andreas Karl Gschwind.

Marring his post-chancellorship legacy, however, was a campaign finance scandal in 1999 in which he refused to reveal the names of donors who had made illegal campaign contributions to the CDU, a clear violation of German law. Kohl claimed, in defense, that he was only honoring his pledge to these individuals not to reveal their names. Kohl's transgressions severely damaged the electoral fortunes of the Christian Democrats in *Land* elections in 1999 and 2000, at a time when his successor as chancellor, Social Democrat Gerhard Schröder, was struggling. Kohl's political ignominy reached its apex when, at the tenth anniversary of German unification in October 2000, he was not invited to the celebrations in Berlin.

Gerhard Schröder, elected chancellor in 1998, is the first German political leader truly of the postwar generation. Unlike Kohl, who was a teenager during World War II, Schröder was born on the war's cusp, in 1944, in the small Lower Saxony town of Rosenburg. He was nevertheless profoundly affected by the war in one sense: his father, a German soldier, was killed on the eastern front in Romania. As a young man, Gerhard Schröder had to work while he completed his education, serving a stint in a hardware store before completing the first phase of his university studies.

In his twenties, he became active in Social Democratic party politics, belonging to the *Jungsozialisten* (Young Socialists), or *Jusos* as they are known colloquially. Schröder embraced Marxism, as did most other *Jusos* at the time; this fact is not surprising given the Marxist roots of virtually all social democratic, socialist, and labor parties throughout the world. By the time Schröder received his law degree from Göttingen University in 1976, he had already become an influential young politician in the SPD. He became a member of the Bundestag in 1980 and in 1990 was elected *Minister-Präsident* (governor) of Lower Saxony. Even in his early years in public life, Schröder had high ambitions. One evening in Bonn in the 1980s, Schröder, who had taken perhaps an extra glass of wine or two, was walking past the gate to the chancellor's office then occupied by Helmut Kohl, put his hands on the gate, and exclaimed: "I want to be in there!" Schröder's personal life is not without controversy; he has been married and divorced three times, and is now married to his fourth wife. During the 1998 campaign, the youth wing of Helmut Kohl's CDU used a gag slogan urging voters to reject Schröder and the SPD, stating, "Three women can't be wrong."

During the 1998 election campaign, Germany's incoming chancellor was compared with British prime minister Tony Blair and even with U.S. president Bill Clinton. Observers stressed one apparent thread that tied the three politically young (all are in their forties or fifties) political leaders together. As heads of "left" parties on their countries' respective political spectrums, they seemed to share an affinity for moving their parties toward more centrist positions. In fact, the SPD slogan for the 1998 campaign was *"die neue Mitte"* (the new middle), suggesting just such a moderate tendency on Schröder's and the SPD's part.

Some more leftist members of the SPD acted as a brake on some of Schröder's more centrist-leaning tendencies, especially Oskar Lafontaine, the former chairman of the SPD and Schröder's first finance minister. Schröder was interested in more supply-side measures, such as reinvigorating the economy with technological innovation and increased flexibility; Lafontaine relied on a more demand side approach, such as increasing the number of jobs, decreasing inequality, and targeting tax cuts and social benefits toward the working class and the trade unions, the SPD's largest constituency. Lafontaine drove such a hard bargain that he persuaded Schröder to give more authority to the Finance ministry, especially concerning European Union (EU) affairs, while reducing the role of the Economics Ministry. Yet Schröder retained the upper hand when he forced Lafontaine from his cabinet position in the spring of 1999 in a power play to bring the governing coalition back toward *die neue Mitte*. Schröder's intraparty triumph was so complete that Lafontaine also resigned his chairmanship of the SPD and gave up his Bundestag seat as well. The combination of Lafontaine's purging and Kohl's discrediting of the CDU gave Schröder needed breathing room as he consolidated his hold on the chancellorship in 1999 and 2000.

The office of chancellor has played a pivotal role in the Federal Republic. The clearly defined role of the chancellor within the federal framework has resulted in a far more effective office than was the case in the Weimar period. And by requiring that the chancellor be the head of the majority party or coalition, the Federal Republic has avoided the disastrous scenario by which Hitler terminated the Weimar regime in 1933. One feature of this change is that the chancellor's more limited role within the context of a federal system has constrained the ability of the central government to take sweeping action. Many Germans have seen this limitation of centralized executive power as a welcome improvement.

As in all other parliamentary systems, in Germany the head of government is the dominant member of a governing team. Chancellors select a cabinet of ministers who can best augment and support the executive branch. The most significant cabinet ministries are those of finance, economics, justice, interior, and foreign policy (the Foreign Ministry). Chancellors generally select cabinet members from leaders of their own party or of coalition partners. Decision making within the cabinet meetings is often quite formalized, with many of the important deliberations conducted prior to the official cabinet meetings. In many cases, chancellors rely on strong ministers in key posts, but some chancellors have often taken ministerial responsibility themselves in key areas such as economics and foreign policy. Helmut Schmidt and Willy Brandt, respectively, fit this pattern. The Economics and Finance ministries always work closely with the Bundesbank, the powerful independent central bank.

Perhaps the most significant source of the chancellor's powers is the constitutional *constructive vote of no confidence*. To overcome the weakness of the cabinet governments of Weimar, the Federal Republic's founders added a twist to the practice familiar in most other parliamentary systems, in which a prime minister is brought down on a vote of no confidence. In most systems, if prime ministers lose such a vote, they are obliged to step down or to call for new elections. In the Federal Republic, however, such a vote must be "constructive" in the sense that a chancellor cannot be removed unless the Bundestag *simultaneously* elects a new chancellor (usually from the opposition parties). This constitutional provision strengthens the chancellor's power in at least two ways. First, it means that chancellors can more easily reconcile disputes among cabinet officials without threatening the chancellor's position. Second, it forces the opposition to come up with concrete and specific alternatives to the existing government and prevents them from being oppositional just for opposition's sake.

Chancellors also face significant limits on their power. As we discuss in Chapter 19, the Bundesrat must ratify all legislation passed in the Bundestag, unless overridden by a two-thirds vote in the lower house. In addition, the Bundesrat generally implements most legislation passed in the Bundestag, so it is important

for chancellors to consider the position of the upper house on most issues.

Bureaucracy and Civil Service

Another crucial part of the executive is the national bureaucracy. The tradition of a strong civil service has deep roots that long predate the introduction of democracy. Particularly in a place like Germany, where the state long resisted the extension of democracy to all citizens, a position in the civil service was one in which service of the state, and not necessarily its citizens, was paramount. Even in the democratic parliamentary Federal Republic, the perception remains strong among officials that their responsibility is first to the state and only derivatively to its citizens. In Germany, positions in the bureaucracy are very powerful and are protected by long-standing civil service provisions. German civil servants (*Beamten*) had a reputation for being inflexible and rigid in the performance of their duties during the Second and Third Reichs. Even during the Federal Republic, when the bureaucracy has been under democratic supervision, there are certainly inefficiencies in the Federal Republic's public sector, as in all other public and private bureaucracies. Yet civil servants view the work that they perform as a profession—that is, more than just a job.

The most surprising fact about the German bureaucracy is that only approximately 10 percent of civil servants are employed by the federal government. The remainder are employed by the various state and local governments. In the years before the founding of the Federal Republic, most of the civil servants were recruited from the families of the reactionary nobility, but selection of bureaucrats in the Federal Republic takes a more modern form. Most come either from major German universities or from positions within the political parties. The federal bureaucrats are primarily policymakers and work closely with their ministries and the legislature. The bureaucrats at the state and local levels are the predominant agents of policy implementation, because the states bear most of the responsibility for carrying out policies determined at the national level. This overlapping of national, regional, and local bureaucracies is enhanced by the belief that certain crucial functions can be performed only by the public sector and that the civil servants' mandate is to perform these duties as well as possible. The ongoing institutionalized relationship among the various levels of the bureaucracy has produced more consistent and effective public policy than in some countries where federal and state governments are often at odds with one another.

Renowned for being officious, rigid, and unfriendly, the German bureaucracy has high—if grudging—political respect from the population. It is generally seen as efficient, although sometimes arcane. Selection of some bureaucrats is based on party affiliation. This derives from the traditional German pattern of "proportionality," in which all major political groups are represented in the bureaucracy. However, the 1970s witnessed attempts to purge the bureaucracy of suspected radicals, which tarnished the reputation of the bureaucracy for impartiality and fairness. Those who are chosen based on party politics—largely top federal officials—are in the minority. Selection to the status of civil servant is generally based on merit, with elaborate licensing and testing for those who advance to the highest professions. German bureaucrats are well known for a high degree of competence, especially when compared to the bureaucrats in most developed states. In the United States, for example, deep antagonism toward the public sector has demoralized most public-sector workers. In contrast, no such cycle of antagonism and demoralization has occurred in Germany.

Public and Semipublic Institutions

Public and semipublic institutions in Germany are powerful, efficient, and responsible for much national policymaking. In countries that had a feudal guild system of representation, such as

Germany, an inclusionary, often corporatist form of representation is common. Semipublic institutions combine aspects of both representation and implementation.[5] The corporatist interest groups are also very much intertwined with the Federal Republic's semipublic agencies, which we argue are institutions crucial for the functioning of the German political economy. Occupying a gray area encompassing both public and private responsibilities, the semipublic (or parastatal) institutions are an apparently seamless web that shapes, directs, implements, and diffuses German public policy.

In the late 1940s, the idea of a strong central state in Germany was discredited for two reasons: the excesses of Nazism and the American occupation authorities' strong affinity for the private sector. West German authorities faced a dilemma. How would they rebuild society if a strong public-sector role were ruled out? The answer was to create modern, democratic versions of those nineteenth-century institutions that blurred the differences between the public and private sectors. These institutions have played a crucial, and long unrecognized, role in the German political economy.

Political scientist Peter Katzenstein has written extensively about the parapublic agencies, calling them "detached institutions." He sees them as primarily mediating entities that reduce the influence of the central state as they generally operate from a principle of engaging all relevant actors in the policy community in continuous dialogue until appropriate policies are found.[6] Katzenstein finds that they have tended to work best in areas of social and economic policy, but less well in their interaction with the university system. Among the most important parapublic agencies are the Chambers of Industry, the Council of Economic Advisers (known colloquially as the Five Wise Men), the vocational education system, which encompasses the apprenticeship training system, and the institutions of worker participation (codetermination and the works councils). Even parts of the welfare system are parapublic, since the system of distribution for welfare benefits is often administered by organizations that are not officially part of the state bureaucracy. The most significant example is the *Krankenkassen* (sickness funds), which bring all major health interests together to allocate costs and benefits through an elaborate system of consultation and group participation.

The most important semipublic German institution for shaping economic policy, the politically independent Bundesbank, is not part of the government. This institution is both the bankers' bank (in that it sets interest rates) and the agency that determines the amount of money in circulation. This last point is the one that proved so contentious during the 1980s and 1990s. The Bundesbank's preference is for low inflation, both because this is a traditional demand of all central bankers and because of Germany's history of ruinous inflation during the Weimar Republic. The relevance for economic policy is that when the government wishes to expand the economy through increased spending or reduced taxes, the Bundesbank always prefers policies that favor monetary restrictions before fast economic growth. In other words, the government and the Bundesbank can be of opposite minds on economic policy, as has been the case in the years since unification. However, the introduction of the euro has also been accompanied by the creation of the European Central Bank (ECB). Modeled after the Bundesbank, the ECB would seem to be poised to favor Germany. But because it serves all of Europe, some Germans are concerned about not only future monetary stability but whether European and German monetary interests will continue to be harmonious.

One of the policy areas already mentioned merits more extensive discussion: the parastatal institutions involved in the implementation of policy concerned with industrial relations. This system of codetermination (*Mitbestimmung*) contrasts sharply with Anglo-American patterns. We cover this set of institutions here because the area of industrial relations in Germany is more than just a system of interest representation. It is also a shaper of public policy.

Providing for the institutionalized participation of workers—including, but not restricted to, union members—on the supervisory boards of directors of all medium and large firms, codetermination gives unions an inside look at the workings of the most powerful firms in the Federal Republic. Based on laws passed in the early 1950s and expanded in the 1970s, codetermination gives workers and unions up to one-half of the members of these company · boards. Unions can thus understand, if not control, how and why major corporate decisions are made on such issues as investment and application of technology. The problem for the unions in challenging management positions on contentious issues is that with the exception of the coal and steel industries, the laws always provide management with one more seat than workers have.

An additional institutional structure represents German workers and gives them access to the policy implementation process. In notable contrast to the trade unions' industry-wide role of representation, all shop-floor and plant-level affairs are the exclusive domain of the works councils (*Betriebsräte*), internal bodies of worker representation that exist in most German firms. The trade unions have historically addressed collective bargaining issues, whereas the works councils have concentrated on social and personnel matters. These lines of demarcation were much clearer than they became in the late 1980s and early 1990s with the development of more flexible workplaces, in the sense of team work groups and multiple tasks within specific job categories.

The unions' legitimation derives from a countrywide, multi-industry representation of a large number of diversified workers. The works councils, on the other hand, owe their primary allegiance to their local plants and firms. The two distinct and separate bodies definitely cause rivalries, periodic rifts, and different representations of interest. Despite the 85 percent overlap in personnel between unions and works councils and despite a structural entanglement between these two major pillars of labor representation in the Federal Republic, these divisions can produce tensions among organized labor. A period of general flux and plant-related, management-imposed flexibility in the mid- and late 1980s exacerbated these tensions. Specifically, the centrifugal nature of this dual system of representation lent itself to "minicorporatist" tendencies that partially undermined the large-scale, all-embracing solidarity claimed by the unions. The unions have by and large successfully avoided the proliferation of any serious plant-level divisions among workers, although there have been some significant exceptions.

Other State Institutions

The chancellor, the president, the bureaucracy, and semipublic institutions are not Germany's only important state agencies for governance and policymaking. Among other state institutions that deserve attention are the military, the judiciary, and subnational governments.

The Military and Police

The German military was historically powerful and aggressive from the eighteenth century (when it was the Prussian military) through World War II. In this two-century period, it was responsible for many wars and major acts of aggression. However, all changed after World War II, and the German military today is completely under civilian control and tightly circumscribed by law and treaty. Germany has a universal service option requiring all citizens over the age of eighteen to perform one year in military or civilian service. In 1990, Germany had approximately 600,000 men and women in the military, but in 1994 the Federal Government set a cap at approximately 340,000. Germany spends 1.5 percent of its gross domestic product on the military, far less than other major European

countries spend. Similar to the Japanese military, Germany's armed forces were legally proscribed from acting independently beyond the borders of the FRG since the end of World War II, first by the Allied occupation and later by the Basic Law. The end of the cold war produced two other important changes in German military policy: the reduction in U.S. armed forces stationed in Germany and the payments made to Russia for removal of soldiers and materiel from the former East Germany.

Under the provisions of the Basic Law, the German military is to be used only for defensive purposes within Europe and in coordination with North Atlantic Treaty Organization (NATO) authorities. Only very limited military activity under tightly reined approval (e.g., via NATO, the U.N., and perhaps eventually the EU) has altered the general prohibition. German participation in the U.N. peacekeeping mission in Bosnia in the mid-1990s was one example, and agreeing to participate in opposition to Serbian aggression in Kosovo in 1999 (a decision made by the Red-Green government) was another.

Since World War II, two generations of Germans have been educated to deemphasize the military and militarism as solutions to political problems. The irony is that it is difficult politically—and until recently, constitutionally—for Germany to commit troops to regional conflicts, even under U.N. auspices. Such issues are obviously related to Germany's aggressive historical role in the international political system. The dilemmas increase when the issue of Bosnia, Serbia, and the catastrophe of the former Yugoslavia is overlaid on this set of policy proscriptions. Part of the reason for German resistance to commit to military action other than strict defense of the Federal Republic's borders (the essence of NATO's cold war mission) is Germany's aggressive past actions in Eastern Europe. In fact, until their election in 1998, the SPD and Greens argued precisely that the Third Reich's aggressive military expeditions to the east in World War II make it impossible for the

German military, under either U.N. or NATO auspices, to play a constructive role in Eastern Europe. Yet after coming to power, the Red-Green government had to allow Germany to take on more geopolitical responsibility in the context of NATO and the EU. This has not been an easy issue, and it is made all the more difficult by the need for the Greens and left-leaning elements in the SPD to accommodate themselves to their power and responsibility.

Discussion of the German police needs to focus on two areas. The first is that of the postwar experience in the FRG, where police powers have been organized on a *Land* basis and—given the excesses of the Third Reich—have been constitutionally circumscribed to ensure that human and civil rights remain inviolate. To be sure, there have been episodes of exceptions, as the German police will never be as well regarded as the British "bobby." For example, during the dragnets for the Red Army Faktion terrorists in the late 1970s, many forces in the SPD and among the *Bürgerinititiven* (citizen action groups), the precursors to the Greens, argued that German police forces compromised civil liberties in their desire to capture the terrorists.

The second is that of the GDR's notorious secret police, the Stasi. The Ministry for State Security (Stasi's formal name) comprised some 91,000 official employees; moreover, in 1989, more than 180,000 East Germans and perhaps 4,000 West Germans worked as Stasi informants.[7] In proportion to the 16 million GDR citizens, the Stasi was more encompassing in the GDR than was the Gestapo during Nazi rule. Since unification, Stasi archives have been open to all, as the East Germans and later the FRG believed that full and open disclosure of Stasi excesses was essential in a democratic state.

The Judiciary

Autonomous and independent, the German judiciary generally makes its rulings consistent with accepted constitutional principles. It also

remains outside the political fray on most issues, although the ruling in 1993 limiting access to abortion for many women—in direct opposition to the law on abortion in the former GDR—was a clear exception to the general pattern. It also was criticized in the 1990s for showing far too much leniency toward perpetrators of racist violence.

The judiciary has always played an important role in Germany because of the deep involvement of the state in political and economic matters. Late to unify and industrialize, the central state was a much larger actor in Germany than in most other countries, necessitating an extensive set of rules to define such wide-ranging powers. Thus, the German state has historically been supported by a strong legal system. The relationship between the state administration and the judiciary during the 1871–1945 period was an extremely close one, yet it engendered many abuses. During the Second Reich, the court was used to safeguard the privileged position of those in power—for example, by failing to rule against the Reichstag voting system, which allowed the small number of Prussian estate owners to have a majority of power. During the Weimar period, the court frustrated the further implementation of democracy when it ruled against the workers councils' demands for increased power within the workplace. Hitler abused the court system extensively during the Nazi regime, inducing it to make a wide range of antidemocratic, repressive, and even criminal decisions. Among them were banning non-Nazi parties, allowing the seizure of Jewish property, and sanctioning the death of millions.

The Federal Republic's founders were most concerned that the new judicial system avoid those earlier abuses. One of the first requirements was that the judiciary explicitly safeguard the democratic rights of individuals, groups, and political parties, stressing some of the individual freedoms that had long been associated with the U.S., British, and French legal systems. In fact, the Basic Law contains a more elaborate and explicit statement of individual rights than exists in either the U.S. Constitution or British common law.

Yet the Federal Republic's legal system differs from the Anglo-Saxon legal tradition. The Anglo-Saxon legal system is characterized by adversarial relationships between contending parties, in which the judge (or the court itself) merely provides the arena for a legal struggle to take place. What emerges from these proceedings is an ad hoc system of laws. In countries with such a system, the courts are essentially only a neutral arbiter. In continental Europe, including Germany, legal systems are more codified, with roots in Roman law and the more modern Napoleonic code.

This means that the judiciary in the Federal Republic is an active administrator of the law rather than just an arbiter. Specifically, judges have a different relationship with the state and with the adjudication of cases than they do in Anglo-Saxon systems. This judicial system relies on a belief in the "capacity of the state" (as political sociologist Theda Skocpol terms it) to identify and implement certain important societal goals.[8] And if the task of the state is to create the laws to attain these goals, then the judiciary should safeguard their implementation. In both defining the meaning of very complex laws and implementing their administration, German courts go considerably beyond those in the United States and Britain, which at least in theory avoid political decisions. The German courts' role in shaping policy has been most evident in its ruling in 1976 on whether to allow the unions to obtain increased codetermination rights. The court allowed the unions to obtain near parity on the boards of directors but stated that full union parity with the employers would compromise the rights of private property.

The Federal Republic has a three-pronged court system. One branch consists of the criminal-civil system, with the Bundesgerichtshof (Federal High Court) at its apex. It is a unified rather than a federal system, making it not subject to the *Länder* governments' control. In fact, it tries to apply a consistent set of criteria for legal issues in the sixteen *Länder*. As a court of appeals, the Bundesgerichtshof is the judicial body that addresses cases that have been appealed from the lower courts. It handles the range of criminal and civil issues common to most industrialized states, passes judgment on disputes among the *Länder*, and makes decisions that would be viewed in some other countries as political.

The Bundesverfassungsgericht (Special Constitutional Court) deals with matters directly affecting the Basic Law. As a postwar creation, it was founded to safeguard the new democratic political order. Precisely because of the Nazis' abuses of the judiciary, the founders of the FRG added a layer to the judiciary, empowered for judicial review, to ensure that the basic democratic order would be maintained. The Federal Constitutional Court consists of federal judges and supporting staff.

Half of the court members are elected by the Bundestag and the other half by the Bundesrat. They may not be members of either house of parliament, the government, or of any of the corresponding bodies of a state. Furthermore, the constitution and procedure of the Federal Constitutional Court are regulated by federal statute, which specifies in what cases its decisions have the force of law. The statute may require that all other legal remedies must have been exhausted before a complaint of unconstitutionality can be entered and may make provision for a special procedure as to admissibility.[9]

The most notable decisions of the Bundesverfassungsgericht in the 1950s were the banning of both the ultra-Right Socialist Reich Party and the Communist Party as forces hostile to the Basic Law. During the early 1970s, when the Radicals Decree was promulgated, causing some leftists their jobs as teachers, bureaucrats, or other public servants, the Constitutional Court ruled on the cases of several individuals who lost their jobs as "enemies of the constitution." During the brief terrorist wave of the late 1970s, in which several prominent individuals were kidnapped or killed by the ultraradical Red Army Faction (RAF), this court was pressed into service to pass judgment on the undemocratic actions of the terrorists. But it also sanctioned wide, indiscriminate investigation of all those who might be supporters of the RAF. In a state that claimed to be an adherent of Western-style liberalism and was ruled by an SPD-led government, such far-reaching action disturbed many who were concerned about individual freedoms and due process.

The Bundesverwaltungsgericht (Administrative Court) is the third branch of the court system. Consisting of the Labor Court, the Social Security Court, and the Finance Court, the Administrative Court has a much narrower jurisdiction than the other two. Whereas the Bundesrat, with its regional divisions, concerns itself with the implementation of the law within geographical boundaries, the Administrative Court system concerns itself with the implementation of the law within functional boundaries. Through administrative decisions, the state and its bureaucracy occupy a prominent position in the lives of German citizens. Thus, this level of the court system acts as a corrective to the arbitrary power of the state bureaucracy. Compared to countries such as Britain and France, where much of public policy is determined by legislation, German public policy is much more often conducted by administrative action on the part of the bureaucracy. Through this court, citizens can challenge actions of the bureaucracy when, for example, they believe that authorities have improperly taken action with respect to labor, welfare, or tax policies.

Beginning in the 1990s, the courts have come under great pressure to deal with the intractable policy issues that unification and European integration have brought about. More and more, they are being drawn into the political thicket and coming under much more scrutiny regarding their decisions. The West German state also engaged in numerous clandestine searches for terrorists in the late 1970s, which many observers felt compromised the democratic rights of citizens who were unaffiliated with any terrorist organizations. Many critics wish that the courts would show the same diligence and zeal in addressing the crimes of neo-Nazis as they did in sanctioning those measures in the 1970s. However, the courts' response to the violence of the 1990s has not shown the same resolute action.

Subnational Government

Unlike the weakly developed regional governments of Britain and France, for example, the sixteen *Länder* of the Federal Republic enjoy both considerable autonomy and significant independent powers. Each state has a regional assembly (*Landtag*), which functions much like the Bundestag at the federal level. The governor (*Minister-Präsident*) of each *Land* is the leader of the largest party (or coalition of parties) in the *Landtag* and forms a government in the *Landtag* in much the same way as does the chancellor in the Bundestag. Each of the sixteen state elections is held on independent staggered four-year cycles, which generally do not coincide with federal elections and only occasionally coincide with elections in other *Länder*. Like the semipublic or parastatal institutions, subnational governments in Germany are powerful, significant, and responsible for much of national policy implementation.

Particularly significant is Germany's overlapping federalism, in which policies developed in the Bundestag are often explicitly implemented by *Land* governments. Recall that only about 10 percent of all public employees work at the federal level, meaning the remainder work for state or local governments. A good way to show how Germany's functional federalism works is with an example: industrial policy.

Regional governments are much more active than the national government in planning and targeting economic policy, providing them with greater autonomy in administering industrial policy. Precisely because the *Länder* were constituent states, they were able to develop their own regional versions of industrial policy (*Ordnungspolitik*). They could take action regionally in ways that the federal government could not do nationally, since the national government was discouraged from centralizing economic power. The *Land* governments undertook this intervention in the economy in the name of regional autonomy, not in the name of centralized economic planning. Furthermore, because different regions had different economic needs and industrial foundations, these powers were perceived as legitimate and appropriate by most voters. The *Land* governments encouraged banks to direct investment and loans to stimulate industrial development in the respective *Länder*. They encouraged cooperation among regional firms—many in the same industry—to spur international competition. In so doing, they avoided violation of the Cartel Law of 1957, because this coordination did not impede domestic competition. They also invested heavily in vocational education to provide the skills so necessary for high-quality manufacturing goods, the core of the German economy. Organized business and organized labor too had a direct role in shaping curricula to improve worker skills through the vocational education system. The *Land* governments have enhanced industrial adaptation by qualitatively shaping the framework for adaptation rather than adopting a heavy-handed regulatory posture.

The general pattern of regionally autonomous economic policy in the *Länder* has an important common denominator: the legitimacy of regional state intervention. However, not all states pursue the same economic policies; there have been various models of specific government involvement in economic policy and industrial adjustment in these regions. Specific long-standing patterns identified have included the organized flexible specialization of Baden-Württemberg, the twentieth-century late industrialization of Bavaria, and the managed decline and adjustment of North Rhine—Westphalia.[10]

German regional governments also differ from those in the United States in the nature of their politics. In the United States, state politics often revolves around personalities or issues of only narrow, parochial interest. This parochialism is partly due to the fragmentation of the U.S. political party system, in which national parties often have very little direct involvement with regional issues. The spirit of the "new federalism," begun under the Nixon presidency and continued with a vengeance under Presidents Ronald Reagan and George H. W. Bush, meant that fewer funds were available from the national government for state funding needs. In the Federal Republic, state politics are organized on the same political party basis as the national parties. This parallelism does not imply that national politics dominates local politics, but that voters are more often able to see the connection among local, regional, and national issues in ways that enhance both unity and diversity in the political system. Because the parties take positions and establish platforms for state and city elections, voters can discern the differences among parties and make choices based on issues as well as personalities.

This does not mean that personalities play no role in German regional politics. In fact, the nature of the party system in the Federal Republic places a premium on national political figures' paying their dues through service at the levels of local and regional party and government. Because regional and local party actors are tied closely to the parties at the national level, there is an affinity among actions taken at different political levels. Contrast this arrangement to that in the United States, where southern Democrats often choose to ignore the national Democratic Party on many issues. This connection in the Federal Republic among national, regional, and local politics may be one reason that voter turnout in German state elections far exceeds that in equivalent U.S. elections.

Just as overlapping responsibilities (*Politikverflechtung*) make separating the institutions of federalism difficult from the national to the regional level, this phenomenon is at work between the regional and local levels too. In fact, the cities of Bremen and Hamburg, which were members of the Hanseatic League specializing in foreign trade from the thirteenth to the fifteenth centuries, remain city-states. Even today, they have overlapping municipal and *Land* governments. The unified Berlin city government now also fits into this city-state category. Echoing the powers that the regional governments held in the years before German unification in 1871, FRG's local governments, growing out of such city-state traditions, have enjoyed far more power than their U.S. counterparts.

Local governments in the Federal Republic differ from those in Britain and France in their capacity to raise revenues by owning enterprises. For example, there is a wide degree of local government ownership of revenue-generating enterprises. This is due in part to the historical patterns of public-sector involvement in the economy, but has also sprung from the belief that these levels of government are the stewards of a collective public good. Supporting art museums, theater companies, television and radio networks, recreational facilities, and adequate housing complexes, and offering various direct and indirect subsidies for a city's inhabitants, are seen as crucial for maintaining the quality of life in modern society. Even during the recessions of the early 1980s and early 1990s, there were remarkably few cutbacks in ownership of public enterprises or these various types of social spending.

The European Dimension

The increased prominence of the EU offers both challenges and opportunities for FRG governance issues.[11] On the one hand, German policy formation at the European level is constrained because a much larger number of actors are involved in policies directly affecting the FRG. More significant, these actors generally operate in an environment quite different from the institutional continuity of German-style organized capitalism and democratic corporatism.

Because pragmatic pluralist relationships are much easier to establish at the EU level than the deeply entrenched institutional continuities of the FRG, the shared understanding among German actors with long years of interpenetrated relationships is much harder to establish at the EU level. Concretely, both the role of the Bundesbank and the cozy bank-firm relationships so long characteristic of the German model become decreasingly significant as the ECB usurps the role of the Bundesbank. In addition, the organized capitalist German mode—at least among the largest firms and banks—also gives way to a more Anglo-American deregulatory model. In that sense, what was unique about the German political economy in the postwar period becomes much less so the further European integration proceeds.

On the other hand, Germany possesses a significant institutional advantage over other European states as European integration continues. According to political scientist Vivien Schmidt, "To the extent that German institutional actors are now part of the larger, quasi-federal decisionmaking system that is the EU, this additional level of decisionmaking basically complements traditional German notions of democratic representation, by compounding their already compounded understanding of representation."[12] Unlike the unitary states of Britain, France, and Italy, for example, Germany has experienced fifty years of modern federalism. To the extent that the institutional structure of the EU is based on federalism, the organizational landscape for both German federal and regional actors is most definitely known territory. For example, one exceptionally important area within the EU is the complex of regional policies that enable Brussels sometimes to bypass national governments and implement directives within the regions of sovereign nation-states. While Britain and France have somewhat belatedly developed degrees of regional autonomy, the FRG has experienced regional political actors who can integrate themselves much more easily into the multilevel governance structures of the EU.

The Policymaking Process

The chancellor and the cabinet are the primary determinants of policymaking, but the executive does not wield arbitrary power in this area. Despite the strong executive role, the policy process in Germany is largely consensus based, with contentious issues usually heavily and extensively debated within various public, parapublic, and private institutions. While the legislature also has a general role in policymaking, the primary driving force is the respective cabinet departments and the experts on whom these institutions call.

If policymaking is shaped primarily through the executive, then policy implementation is more diffuse. Along with the role of the corporatist interest groups and various parastatal organizations, the Bundesrat plays a significant role in policy implementation throughout the Federal Republic. This policy implementation takes place in a wide range of areas. Among the most significant are vocational education, welfare, health care, and worker participation. We can illustrate implementation most clearly by using the example of a specific form of economic policy.

In such an organized capitalist, corporatist political system, much of the policymaking takes place on an informal basis between and among overlapping institutions. A system of framework regulation sets only outer boundaries, within which all actors must function, and leaves detailed implementation to ongoing discussions among the major actors. For example, supervision of the banking system consists of a few general forms of regulation but very few specific ones. This structure gives considerable power to a parastatal institution (the Federal Bank Supervisory Office) but also provides the private banks within the system both autonomy and responsibility (through self-regulation) for the implementation of policy affecting the important German banking industry.

There is considerable misunderstanding among many observers about exactly why and how institutions support the Federal Republic's

economic policymaking process. Many people misunderstand the role that these institutions have played in the process of flexible adaptation to competitive pressures that has enabled the German economy to outperform the economies of most other industrialized countries for much of the post–World War II period. At first glance, many observers of Germany see institutions such as regulatory agencies and parapublic interest groups that seem to inhibit economic freedoms. Yet closer examination reveals that German institutions regulate not the minute details but the general framework. Since all economic actors understand clearly the general parameters within which they must work, German regulatory policy is remarkably free of the nitpicking microregulations common to other countries. Moreover, many policies, particularly in the banking and manufacturing sectors, are reinforced by industry self-regulation that makes heavy-handed government intervention unnecessary.

What are the components of this economic policymaking process? First of all, it is a *system*, not just a collection of firms and discrete policies. It has followed a pattern in which business, labor, and the government work together from the outset of the process and develop consensual policy solutions to national, regional, state, and local problems. The Germans have spoken of their *social* (not *free*) market economy because of a deeply entrenched belief that business must share in the responsibility of providing a stable order, both for the economy and, indirectly, for society.

The foundation of this attitude lay in the fact that German business, labor, and government embraced a different conception of regulation from the one used elsewhere. Rather than seeing regulation as a stark choice between laissez-faire and heavy-handed regulation, Germany has used *Rahmenbedingungen* (framework regulation), which does not see a sharp market-state separation or a singly focused goal of regulating each government action toward the market. Rather, it contains the foundation of a looser, more encompassing framework for both the public and private sectors. This approach has produced a system that is often called externally rigid (in the sense of prohibiting easy entrance and exit with respect to firms and industry) but internally flexible (in the sense that large institutions and firms are often, to American observers, surprisingly flexible in adapting applied technologies to produce specialized goods). In short, this system regulates not the details but the encompassing rules of the game within which all actors must play.

Some would criticize such a system as being too cumbersome and inflexible. In fact, the relative slowness of the FRG in fully embracing the information economy would seem to confirm this stereotype. However, the Germans see a great advantage to this "all eggs in one basket" system in that it generally produces agreement on major policy direction without major social dislocation. Once agreement has been informally worked out among all the major parties, moving forward with specific legislation is easier. This process is generally less conflict oriented than in Britain, since the German parliamentary system takes more explicit steps to include wider support among major interest groups.

This consensual system has been greatly challenged recently by the extraordinary nature of unification issues, which have put this informal style of policymaking under tremendous pressure. Among the issues that have proved most intractable are the noneconomic issues of political asylum, racist violence, and various scandals that have tarnished the reputations of major public figures, both political leaders and leaders of major interest groups.

Notes

1. For two important accounts of the initial postwar uncertainty about the stability of German democracy, see Gerhard Ritter, *The German Problem* (Columbus: Ohio State University Press, 1965), and Ralf Dahrendorf, *Society and Democracy in Germany* (Garden City, N.Y.: Anchor, 1969).

2. Since unification in 1990, the term *Basic Law* has been retained because most Germans rightly associate the "temporary" term with the country's longest and most successful experience of democracy.

3. Dahrendorf, *Society and Democracy in Germany.*

4. http://eng.bundespraesident.de.

5. Parastatal institutions differ greatly from pluralist representation in countries such as the United States, where interest groups petition public authority for redress of grievances but themselves often stay at arm's length from the implementation process. See Robert Dahl, *Dilemmas of Pluralist Democracy: Autonomy vs. Control* (New Haven, Conn.: Yale University Press, 1982).

6. Peter Katzenstein, *Policy and Politics in West Germany: The Growth of a Semi-Sovereign State* (Philadelphia: Temple University Press, 1987).

7. John O. Koehler, *Stasi: The Untold Story of the East German Secret Police* (Boulder, Colo.: Westview Press, 1999).

8. Peter Evans, Dietrich Rueschemeyer, and Theda Skocpol, *Bringing the State Back In* (Cambridge: Cambridge University Press, 1985).

9. German Basic Law, Article 94, 1944.

10. Christopher S. Allen, "Regional Governments and Economic Policies in West Germany: The 'Meso' Politics of Industrial Adjustment," *Publius* 19, no. 4 (1989): 147–164.

11. Vivien A. Schmidt, "European 'Federalism' and Its Encroachment on National Institutions," *Publius* 29, no. 1 (Winter 1999): 19–44.

12. Ibid., p. 36.

C H A P T E R

19

Representation
and Participation

In the wake of unification and European integration, Germany has continued to search for a synthesis of democratic participation and extraparliamentary opposition that is neither exclusionary nor antidemocratic. In short, it still struggles with issues surrounding collective identities. The issue of resocializing disparate political cultures when respect for dissent and dialogue is not deeply ingrained is problematic for any society. However, the key issue for Germany in this regard is how to develop a system of democratic participation that encompasses both extrainstitutional groups and specific organized political institutions.

The Legislature

The legislature occupies a prominent place in the political system in Germany, with both the lower house (Bundestag) and the upper house (Bundesrat) having significant and wide-ranging powers. The Federal Republic of Germany (FRG) is similar to other parliamentary regimes having a fusion of power in which the executive comes directly from the legislative branch. In other words, there is no sharply demarcated separation of powers between cabinet and legislature.

The electoral procedures for choosing members of the two houses differ substantially, and their different orientations are a product of those different methods. For example, the

Bundestag elects its members directly by ballot; voters choose both individual district representatives and the political parties that represent their interests. The Bundesrat's members, on the other hand, are officials who are elected or appointed to the governments of the states (*Länder*). We elaborate on both legislative branches in this section. Both are broadly representative of major interests in German society, although some interests, such as business and labor, are somewhat overrepresented and ecological and noneconomic interests are somewhat underrepresented.

The executive takes up the specific legislative proposals, since such issues as the federal budget and taxation are required by the Basic Law to come from the executive. That most bills are initiated in the cabinet does not diminish the influence of Bundestag or Bundesrat members, however. Also, many different groups, both inside and outside the legislature, can propose different policies. However, the chancellor and the cabinet are prominent. In fact, since the chancellor is the leader of the major party or coalition of parties, it is somewhat incorrect to see a sharp division between the executive and legislative branches. Since parties are generally ideologically coherent, there is usually strong consensus within parties and within coalitions about both the input and output of the legislative process. Parties and coalitions depend on party discipline to sustain majorities, which places high priority on agreement about major legislation.

When the chancellor and his cabinet propose a bill, it is sent to a relevant Bundestag committee. Most of the committee deliberations are behind closed doors, so the individual committee members have considerable latitude to shape the details of legislation. The committees call on their own considerable expertise, but also solicit that of relevant government ministries as well as testimony from affected interest groups. This system appears to be a kind of insiders' club, and perhaps to some degree it is. However, the committees generally call on a wide range of groups, both pro and con, that are affected by the proposed legislation. This inclusive form of deliberation—specifically consulting the democratic corporatist interest groups—helps produce a more consensus-oriented outcome. In contrast, in countries with a more pluralist (that is, less inclusive) form of lobbying, such as Britain, legislation is likely to be more contentious and less likely to produce general agreement. Under pluralism, it is relatively easy for groups to articulate issues. However, unlike democratic corporatist systems, pluralist systems tend not to ensure access in a systemic way and also often produce comparatively haphazard policy.

After emerging from committee, the bill undergoes final readings in the Bundestag. Although the major parameters of the bill have already been defined, this debate in the Bundestag often produces considerable criticism from the opposition and sharp defense by the governing coalition parties. The primary purpose of such debate is to educate the public generally about the major issues being addressed. Following passage in the Bundestag, a bill must be approved by the upper house. Although usually accomplished easily, this approval also involves the Bundesrat's determining how a particular law will be implemented at the regional level.

The social composition of the legislature has been largely male and of professional or middle-class orientation, a statement true even of the supposedly working-class Social Democratic Party (SPD), which in the 1950s had a much greater proportion of blue-collar workers

elected to the Bundestag. From the 1950s to the 1970s, there were few women in the legislature, though this situation began to change in the 1980s and 1990s, particularly as the Greens—with their iconoclastic policies (and casual attire)—have seated a number of female Bundestag members (see Table 19.1).[1] The addition of newer parties, such as the worker-oriented ex-communist Party of Democratic Socialism (PDS, the party of former East German Communists) and the continued presence of the Greens, has increased variety in the backgrounds of party members. If these parties maintain their representation to the legislature, it will continue to erode the Bundestag's middle-class, professional profile.

The Bundestag

Until unification, the lower house of the legislature consisted of 496 seats: 248 elected in single-member districts and 248 elected by proportional representation from lists compiled by the political parties. After unification, owing to the representatives of the five new *Länder* of the former German Democratic Republic (GDR), the number of seats was expanded to 669. This figure exceeded the number of representatives in the British Parliament and caused a strain on the facilities in Bonn, as the Bundestag chamber

Table 19.1   Percentage of Women Members of the Bundestag

Year	Percentage	Year	Percentage
1949	6.8	1976	7.3
1953	8.8	1980	8.5
1957	9.2	1983	9.8
1961	8.3	1987	15.4
1965	6.9	1990	20.5
1969	6.6	1994	26.3
1972	5.8	1998	30.2

Source: Bundeszentrale für Politische Bildung, 1998.

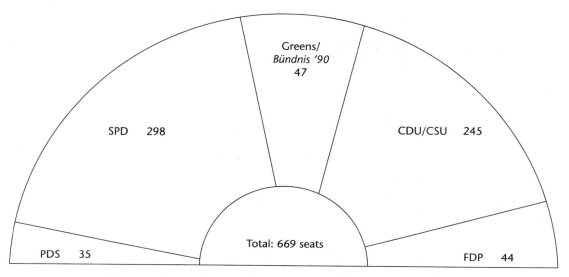

Figure 19.1   Distribution of Seats in the Fourteenth Bundestag (1998)

The Fourteenth German Bundestag was elected in September 1998. Currently, 669 deputies represent the Federal Republic of Germany's 61 million voters.

was not originally built to accommodate such a large number. The movement to the renovated Reichstag in Berlin in 1999 overcame that problem.

The German parliamentary system represents a synthesis between the British and U.S. tradition of a single legislator representing one district and the proportional-representation method more common in continental Europe, in which a group of party members represent a given region depending on the percentage of the party's vote in that region. This unusual combination of two systems resulted from a compromise between the British and U.S. preference for single-member districts and the prevailing German practice of multiparty representation. Single-member-district voting systems tend to produce a two-party system, and Germany wanted to ensure that all major parties, not just two, were represented. In practice, the German hybrid system, which is known as mixed-member (or personalized) proportional representation, requires citizens to cast two votes on each ballot:

the first one for an individual member of a political party, usually (but not always) from the district, and the second one for a list of national and regional candidates grouped by party affiliation. Thus, this system has the effect of personalizing list voting because voters have their "own" representative but also can choose among several parties. To ensure that only major parties are represented, only those winning 5 percent of the vote or having three candidates who win individual seats directly gain representation in the Bundestag (or in any *Land* or municipal government). This provision exists because in the late Weimar period, sharp conflict among parties opened the door for the Nazi rise to power; however, under the 5 percent rule, smaller parties tended to disappear, with most of their adherents gravitating toward the three major parties until the Green Party attained seats in the Bundestag in 1983. In the 1990 federal election, only the PDS and Bündnis '90 (an alternative, ecology-minded, former East German party, now merged with the West German

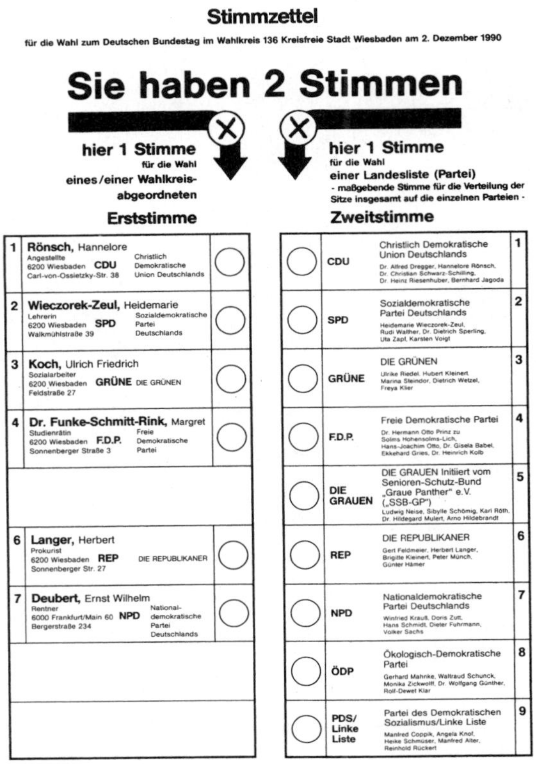

Figure 19.2   1990 Bundestag Election Ballot

With their "first vote," voters from the Bonn electoral district can choose a candidate by name from the lefthand column. The "second vote" in the righthand column is cast for a party list at the federal level.

Green Party) gained seats in the Bundestag as new parties. Both were successful in attaining representation in 1998 too, with the Greens joining the governing coalition for the first time. The extreme right-wing party, the Republikaner (Republicans), flirted with the 5 percent hurdle in several regional elections and threatened to exceed the threshold in the 1994 federal elections but ultimately received less than 2 percent of the popular vote.

Allocation of seats by party in the Bundestag, however, functions more like proportional rep-

resentation. Specifically, the percentage of total seats won by each party corresponds strongly with the party's percentage of the popular vote (providing the party receives the 5 percent minimum percentage to attain seats). For example, if a party's candidate wins a seat as an individual member, the candidate's party gains one fewer candidate from the list. In practice, most of the district seats are won by the two large parties, the Social Democrats and Christian Democrats (CDU), since the district vote is winner take all. The smaller parties' representatives, on the other hand, are almost always elected by the party lists. Thus, the list system creates stronger, more coherent parties. In countries with fragmented, individualistic parties, it is often harder to gain and hold effective majorities. In contrast, Willy Brandt's coalition governments from 1969 to 1974, joining the SPD and the Free Democratic Party (FDP), had extremely narrow margins, and only strong party discipline enabled Brandt to remain in power.

We discuss the political parties explicitly in the next section, but their general ideological coherence is essential to mention here, since each Bundestag member almost always votes with fellow party members. This party unity contributes to consistency in the parties' positions over the course of a four-year legislative period and enables the electorate to identify each party's stance on a range of issues. Consequently, all parties and their representatives in the Bundestag can be held accountable by voters based on their support for their party's positions on the issues. This party discipline, in turn, helps produce more stable governments.

One direct result of party discipline is that the Federal Republic has high electoral participation (80–90 percent at the federal level). Some observers have argued that German citizens vote in such high numbers out of habit or duty.[2] Given the remarkable stability in the voting patterns of the three main postwar parties, with little deviation in each party's electoral outcome from election to election, it is more likely that high electoral participation is due to clear party ideology. And the newer parties, with similar kinds of ideological coherence, would seem to confirm this. For the FRG's fifty years, voting participation rates have matched or exceeded those of all other Western European countries.

The tradition of strong, unified parties in the Bundestag has had some drawbacks, however. The hierarchy within parties relegates newer members to a comparatively long period of apprenticeship as backbenchers. (Senior party members sit in the front benches of the Bundestag, as in other European legislatures, leaving the rear seats for newly elected members.) In fact, some of the Federal Republic's most prominent postwar politicians at the national level built up their visibility and political skill through long service in *Land* or local government service before using it as a springboard for national political power. For example, former SPD chancellor Willy Brandt was mayor of Berlin at the time of the construction of the Berlin Wall in 1961, former SPD chancellor Helmut Schmidt was mayor of Hamburg, and Helmut Kohl was for many years the dominant CDU regional official in his home *Land* of Rhineland-Palatinate.

Although this system does educate younger members in party ideology, it also frustrates particularly ambitious young legislators. They can become even more frustrated when their party is in power, because the dominance of the party elders increases at that time. The federal chancellery, as an administrative unit comprising the chancellor's top appointed officials, often controls the Bundestag by setting legislative agendas and making key policy decisions. Most bills originate with the chancellery and the ministries rather than with the Bundestag or Bundesrat. Thus, party discipline tends to channel committee discussion well within the broad position the party itself has taken, and the structure of the Bundestag discourages individual action by legislators.

The chancellor and the party leadership can lose touch with the backbench members of their party. For example, in the early 1980s Helmut Schmidt took positions—against stimulating the economy and for allowing the stationing of additional U.S. missiles on German soil—to which the majority of his SPD were strongly opposed. Thus, when the FDP attacked Schmidt on economic issues, his own party's rank and file also criticized him. Ultimately, any leadership of a governing party that fails to respond to its parliamentary membership or its voters, or both, will be forced to resign or will lose in the next election.

The Bundesrat

As the upper house of the legislative branch, the Bundesrat occupies a position quite different from those of the U.S. Senate and the British House of Lords. The Bundesrat is the mechanism by which the federal system of the country actually works. It is responsible for the distribution of powers between national and state levels and grants to the states the rights to implement federal laws. It is literally the institutional intersection of the national and state governments. It consists of members of the sixteen *Länder* governments. The total number of seats is sixty-nine, an increase from forty-five prior to unification, with each *Land* sending at least three representatives, depending on its population. States with more than 2 million residents have four votes, and states with more than 6 million have five votes.

The political composition of the Bundesrat at any given time is determined by which parties are governing the *Länder*. Each of the sixteen *Länder* casts its votes in a bloc, depending on the views of the party or coalition in control of the state government at the time. Consequently, the party controlling the majority of *Länder* governments can have a significant effect on legislation passed in the Bundestag. And because *Länder* elections usually take place between Bundestag electoral periods, the Bundesrat majority can shift during the course of a Bundestag legislative period. For example, in the two years before the 1994 federal elections, the states governed by the SPD had a majority in the Bundesrat, which made it difficult for the Kohl government to implement all of its policies.

The Bundesrat must approve all amendments to the constitution, as well as all laws passed in the Bundestag that address the fundamental interests of the *Länder,* such as taxes, territorial integrity, and basic administrative functions. It also enjoys a *suspensive veto;* that is, if the Bundesrat should vote against a particular bill, the Bundestag needs only to pass the measure again by a simple majority to override the Bundesrat's veto. If a two-thirds majority of the Bundesrat votes against a bill, the Bundestag must pass it again by a two-thirds margin. In usual practice, however, the Bundesrat has not acted as a force of obstruction or gridlock. When the legislation is concurrent, that is, when the state and national governments jointly share administrative responsibilities in implementation of the particular policy, there is almost always easy agreement between the two houses. Also, if a party or coalition has a stable majority in the Bundestag, then any possible obstruction by the Bundesrat can be overcome. For example, during most of his term as chancellor, Social Democrat Willy Brandt faced a Bundesrat that had a one-vote majority of Christian Democrats. However, since his SPD-FDP coalition also had a slim but firm majority in the Bundestag, he was able to overcome their opposition on many issues and never lose a key vote.

The Bundesrat introduces comparatively little legislation. More bills are introduced in the Bundestag, though the majority of laws originate from the government itself through one of the ministries. However, the Bundesrat's administrative responsibilities are considerable. As *Länder* government officials, most of the members of the Bundesrat are considerably experienced in the implementation of particular laws. Their expertise is frequently called on in the committee hearings of the Bundestag, which are open to all Bundesrat members. This overlap

(*Politikverflechtung*) is a unique feature of the Federal Republic. Many Americans make the mistake of equating German and U.S. federalism. Yet *Politikverflechtung* provides a qualitatively different relationship between national and state governments. The Federal Republic avoids the problems of administrative jurisdiction that sometimes plague other decentralized, federal countries because many of the laws passed in the Bundestag are implemented at the *Land* level. This administrative arrangement enables the national government to use fewer employees than would be the case without *Politikverflechtung,* an extremely significant contribution of German federalism.

The Bundesrat's strong administrative role is a crucial component of the government. In different ways, this system avoids the shortcomings of both the fragmented legislative practices of the United States and the overly centralized policies of previous German regimes. Because the Bundesrat is concerned with shaping the framework of implementation, its role is more purposeful than that of the U.S. Congress, where laws that overlap or contradict previous legislation are frequently passed. For example, the Bundesrat coordinates the regional and national links between economic policies, vocational education systems, and the components of a major television network (ARD). The Bundesrat tends to be closer than the federal government to the concerns and needs of the entire country and provides a forum for understanding how national legislation will affect each *Land.* While the Bundesrat was originally envisioned to be more technocratic and less politically contentious than the popularly elected Bundestag, debates in the Bundesrat became strongly politicized in the 1970s and 1980s. The most common occurrence was increased conflict when regional elections caused a change in control of the Bundesrat, especially when this change gave more influence to the party, or group of parties, that was in opposition in the Bundestag.

With the increasing significance of the European Union (EU), the Bundesrat has a role to play here as well. It promotes representation for the *Länder* in EU institutions, most notably in the Council of Regions. It also successfully insisted on the German federal government's accepting that it could have a veto power over certain German positions on EU decisions.

The Party System and Elections

The following section details the functioning of the robust German political parties and identifies key patterns in FRG elections.

The Political Party System

Germany has a multiparty system that has proved remarkably stable for most of the post–World War II period.[3] Until the early 1980s, Germany had a "two-and-a-half" party system, made up of the moderate-Left Social Democratic Party, the moderate-Right Christian Democratic grouping (the CDU in most of the FRG and the Christian Social Union, CSU, in Bavaria), and the small, centrist Free Democratic Party. The ideological distance among these parties was not wide. Beginning in the late 1950s, the SPD broadened its base from its core working-class constituency to include more middle-class supporters. The CDU-CSU is a political grouping that includes both Catholics (mostly from the Bavarian-based CSU) and Protestants. The FDP is liberal in the European sense and favors both free-market solutions to economic problems and extensive personal freedoms for individuals. Yet with only 5 to 10 percent of the electorate, it is a pragmatic party and almost always chooses to ally itself with one of the two large parties to form a government. During their time as the only parties on the political landscape (1953–1983), the SPD, CDU-CSU, and FDP presided over a stable, growing economy with a widely mixed public- and private-sector agreement on economic and social policies.

During the 1980s and 1990s, three new parties arose to challenge the two and a half major parties: the Greens-Bündnis '90, generally leftist and favoring ecology, environment, and peace; the PDS, the former Communist Party of East Germany; and the Republikaner, a sharply right-wing party, much more conservative than the CDU-CSU, that has emphasized nationalism and aggression toward immigrants and ethnic minorities. These additions have begun to complicate the comparatively tidy political landscape and promise to continue to do so. (See Table 19.2.)

The Greens-Bündnis '90 originated in 1979 and has been winning seats at national and regional levels; clearly it has become a permanent fixture. Because of the 5 percent rule, the Republikaner are not represented in the Bundestag, although the party has won seats in some local and regional bodies. The PDS is regionally concentrated in the five *Länder* of the former GDR and has received as much as 25 percent of the vote in the Eastern German *Länder*, but it draws well under the 5 percent mark in the states of the former West Germany.

Because the parties are so important in shaping state policy, Germany has often been called a party democracy. However, criticism of the major parties surfaced in the late 1980s and throughout the 1990s owing to several financial and political scandals involving members of all

---

Table 19.2 Political Parties

Party of Democratic Socialism (PDS) (former Communist)

Greens/Bündnis '90 (environment)

Social Democratic Party (SDP) (Left)

Free Democratic Party (FDP) (Center)

Christian Democrats (Right)

    Christian Democratic Union (CDU)

    Christian Social Union (CSU)

Republikaner (far Right)

three. For example, one major CDU state official was found dead in a hotel bathroom under suspicious circumstances, former FDP officials have been subject to financial investigations, and Helmut Kohl's financial scandal has been the most recent. Such developments have provided increased opportunities for the new parties and could possibly disturb the relatively tame political party landscape.

Social Democratic Party. As the leading party of the Left in Germany, the SPD has had a long history. Founded in the 1860s in response to rapid German (and Prussian) industrialization, the SPD survived Bismarck's attempts in the 1880s to outlaw it and grew to be the largest party in the Reichstag by 1912. The party was badly split by World War I, however, with the more "evolutionary" wing supporting the war and the imperial German government. The "revolutionary" wing saw the war as an opportunity to defeat capitalism in all countries; they viewed support of bourgeois governments' war efforts as representing a fundamental betrayal of the international working class.[4] Following World War I, the evolutionary socialists who controlled the SPD helped it become the leading party of the Weimar Republic during its early years. The revolutionary socialists joined either the Kommunistische Partei Deutschlands (KPD, the original Communist Party) or the short-lived Independent Social Democratic Party (USPD), a party that lasted only until the early 1920s. Such splits among the left-wing parties proved fatal for the SPD in the Weimar period. The lack of a united Left prevented a clear response to the growing economic and social turmoil and thereby indirectly helped the Nazis find a path to power.

When the SPD reemerged after 1945, it was initially in a strong position to play a dominant role in rebuilding Germany. Industrialists and the conservative Weimar parties had been discredited by their relationship with the Nazis, and the SPD retained its evolutionary commitment to both democracy and socialism. In the immediate postwar years, the SPD, under the leadership of Kurt Schumacher, led the call for the nationalization of industry under democratic control, the provision for a vast array of welfare state measures to rebuild the country, and a return to the participatory workplace structures (the workers councils) that had been curtailed by the early Weimar governments.

Despite its strong influence from 1945 to 1948, the SPD was able to obtain only about 30 percent of the popular vote from 1949 until the early 1960s. Some of its critics observed that the party's inability to achieve wider influence resulted from its continued emphasis on its working-class origins and reliance on a Marxist-based ideology. More sympathetic observers believed that the cold war, the Communist GDR just to the east, and the economic miracle of the 1950s all played a major role in reducing the party's influence. In any event, the SPD was politically marginalized in the 1950s. The party formed municipal governments in a few of the major cities and regional governments in several traditionally strong northwestern *Länder*, but it exercised little national influence.

In an attempt to broaden its constituency, the SPD altered its party program at a 1959 party conference in Bad Godesberg. Abandoning its heavy reliance on Marxism, its new goal was to become what political scientist Otto Kirchheimer has called a "catchall party."[5] The SPD neither relinquished Marxism completely nor ceased to be a party representing the working class, but it began to seek and attract support from groups outside the traditional blue-collar working class. Among these were service-sector workers, elements of the middle class, professional employees, and defectors from the Free Democrats or Christian Democrats. The Bad Godesberg conference transformed the SPD into a party more like other Western European social democratic parties.

The SPD finally won a place as the leading member of a majority coalition in 1969. It increased its share of the vote to 42.7 percent and was thus able to propose a new coalition government with the FDP, which had received 5.8 percent of the vote. (Although the two parties had less than 50 percent of the popular vote, they attained a bare majority of the apportioned Bundestag seats after the smaller parties with fewer than 5 percent of the vote were discounted.)

The Center-Left SPD-FDP coalition appeared shaky at first (it had a slim majority until its reelection in 1972), but it was able to stay in power for thirteen years.[6] The SPD brought to the coalition concern for increased welfare and social spending, arising partly from pressure by the Extraparliamentary Opposition (APO), and the FDP brought its support for increased individual freedom of expression at a time when young people in all industrialized societies were raising this issue. However, the one factor that helped cement together the interests of these two dissimilar parties for such a long time was the strong performance of the Federal Republic's economy. In fact, the coalition came apart in the early 1980s only as an economic recession prevented the increased social spending demanded by the SPD Left. The recession also induced the FDP to define individualism less in terms of free expression and more in terms of an antistatist, free-market economic position.

Its years out of power (1982–1998) gave the SPD the opportunity to formulate alternative policies to challenge the Center-Right CDU/CSU-FDP coalition. Unfortunately for the SPD, it did not take advantage of this opportunity. Under the leadership of Hans Jochen Vogel in the mid-1980s, Oskar Lafontaine in the late 1980s, Bjorn Engholm in the early 1990s, and Rudolf Scharping in the mid-1990s, it was unable to formulate clear alternative policies to make itself attractive to its members, supporters, and voters. Nor could it forge a durable coalition with the Greens to challenge the Center-Right coalition, develop positions on European integration that would induce supporters to turn in the party's direction, or take advantage of the opportunity to capture support in the former GDR during and after the unification process. After the 1994 Bundestag elections, the SPD remained uncertain about what kind of party it was. It continued to agonize over whether it should reemphasize its working-class roots and perhaps take support from the PDS in the east, or find some new synthesis of positions that could blunt the rising support going to the Greens. Its electoral support remained stuck in the upper 30 percent range. Options for the SPD seemed limited.

However, in 1998 the Kohl regime had exhausted its mandate and the costs of overpromising the speed of transformation in Eastern Germany finally came due. An effective Gerhard Schröder campaign to search for a *neue Mitte* enabled the SPD to step into the void created by the CDU's demise and increase the share of its vote by 5 percent over 1994 and emerge as Germany's leading party. Schröder's consolidation of power has come at the cost of distancing himself from some of the left-leaning members of the party rank and file. The forcing out of Oskar Lafontaine, the party's Left tribune, may have made Schröder's move to the middle easier in the short run. But running the risk of losing the support of the party's hard core may prove costly in the long run, much as it did for Helmut Schmidt in the early 1980s.

Christian Democrats. The CDU is found in all *Länder* except Bavaria; the CSU is its affiliated Bavarian grouping.[7] Unlike the other older parties in the Federal Republic, the CDU-CSU did not originate until immediately following World War II, when most nonleftist parties wished to avoid the bickering and divisiveness of the Weimar period and establish a counterweight to the SPD.[8] The moderate leaders of the nonleftist parties feared that after the war, the SPD would represent a partially united Left, while the forces of the Right were both fragmented and discredited by the close ties some of their members had had to the Nazi Party. Consequently, several of the moderate conservatives proposed the creation of a Christian party grouping, which not only would finally unite

Catholics and Protestants in one confessional (Christian) party, but would also serve as a catchall party of the Center-Right, incorporating the various nonleftist elements (including "rehabilitated" ex-Nazis).

Programmatically, the CDU-CSU stressed the social market economy (*Sozialemarktwirtschaft*). The social market economy was neither a social democratic state (such as contemporary Sweden) nor a pure market economy (as expounded by the Reagan and George H. W. Bush administrations in the United States and the Thatcher and Major governments in Britain). Rather, it blended elements of both forms to create a society that not only was capitalist but also had a paternalistic sense of social responsibility. In fact, this synthesis joined the interests of a wide range of the party's supporters. The most active supporter of the market side of the equation was Adenauer's economics minister for most of the 1950s (and later the chancellor), Ludwig Erhard. Favoring the social side were the Christian trade unionists whose ideology derived from the Catholic tradition, which celebrated the value of human work, and from the Protestant work ethic.

After the SPD and the FDP established their Center-Left coalition in 1969, the CDU-CSU spent thirteen years as the opposition party. During this period, the popularity of SPD policies and the unpopularity of the CDU-CSU leadership prevented the Christian Democrats from mounting a strong challenge to the SPD-FDP coalition. It was not until that coalition collapsed in 1982 over economic policies that the CDU-CSU returned to power in a coalition with the FDP. Political pundits called this *Die Wende* (the turnaround), but the Christian Democrats' return had more to do with the SPD's failure to manage the economy and the coalition with the FDP than with any new ideological tendency.

Despite the electoral rhetoric about change and a turnaround, the first CDU-led Kohl government (1983–1987) made no dramatic new programmatic overtures. In fact, many observers were predicting that the stolid and colorless

Kohl would either lose the next election or be challenged within the party for the chancellorship. Kohl was not an ideologue in the mold of Britain's Margaret Thatcher and the United States' Ronald Reagan, and many criticized him for his plodding, pragmatic style. How, then, was he able to maintain his leadership of both the CDU-CSU and the Center-Right coalition? It is important to stress that the nature of the German party system—in fact, of *any* parliamentary system—places a premium on the leader's ability to manage the party as an institution. In this task, Helmut Kohl was the consummate party leader. He reputedly knew the name of every Christian Democratic mayor (*Bürgermeister*) in the entire Federal Republic. With his mastery of such allegedly pedestrian skills, he maintained and reinforced his leadership of the Christian Democrats. There is, of course, nothing pedestrian about winning four consecutive federal elections.

During the mid-1980s, two additional factors played into Kohl's, and the CDU's, hands. One was the lack of a clear alternative position by the SPD opposition that could challenge the Center-Right coalition. The other was the strong CDU-CSU position in support of strengthening European integration. Taken together, these factors enabled the Christian Democrats and Helmut Kohl to find their stride as the dominant political forces in the Federal Republic through the early years after unification.

In the wake of the problems of the 1990s, some of the earlier criticisms of Kohl began to surface again, focusing on his apparent overselling of unification and his lack of leadership in the face of the challenges of resurgent racism and Germany's geopolitical position after the cold war. With the end of the cold war and the tensions surrounding European integration and German unification, some party divisions surfaced. The first originated from the Bavarian CSU, led by Finance Minister Theo Waigel, and addressed a more conservative policy toward immigrants and minorities. The second was the more independent position, in favor of government intervention, of the regional CDU branches in Eastern Germany. Concern also rose within the CDU/CSU-FDP governing coalition after the 1994 elections, because the FDP narrowly achieved only the 5 percent of the vote necessary for representation. The Christian Democrats reached political exhaustion with the 1998 federal election in which they lost power for the first time since 1982. While the party can point to the truly significant accomplishments of German unification and European integration, it also faces the daunting task of replacing both Helmut Kohl and his deputy Wolfgang Schäuble, both of whom were implicated in the disastrous fundraising scandal of 1999 and 2000.

As it came to grips with its opposition role early in the new century, the Christian Democrats found themselves undercut by Gerhard Schröder's *neue Mitte* policies. Long accustomed to seeing themselves as the party that supported Germany's organized capitalist economy, they found that Schröder's government had taken their primary base of support. As it searched for a new focus in opposition, it has unfortunately seized on a mild form of nationalism, stressing patriotism and German *Leitkultur* (guiding culture) as its new themes early in the new century. For most countries, such policies would be understandable—if not admirable—but the rules are different for Germany. At a time when new citizenship laws have been passed and German industry encourages increased immigration, particularly for information industry jobs, such calls for a stronger German culture are tinged with ugly memories of the Nazi period. Gerhard Schröder and even German business have criticized the Christian Democrats on this point, with the chancellor strongly stating, "The last time German conservatism gave into the seductions of nationalism, Social Democrats suffered and died fighting the fascists."[9]

The Greens. The Greens Party is a heterodox party that first drew support from a number of different constituencies in the late 1970s and early 1980s: urban-based citizen action groups (*Bürgeriniativen*), ecological activists, farmers, anti-nuclear-power activists, the remnants of the peace movement, and small bands of Marxist-Leninists. After making it over the 5 percent hurdle for the first time in the 1983 Bundestag elections, the party went on to win seats in most *Länder* in subsequent regional elections by stressing noneconomic, quality-of-life issues. The electoral successes of this "antiparty party" caused a new and serious internal division between the *Realos* (realists) and the *Fundis* (fundamentalists). In the mid-1980s the realists, who thought it important to enter political institutions to gain access to power, won the upper hand over the fundamentalists, who unalterably opposed any collaboration with existing parties, even if some goals of the Greens could thereby be attained.

This choice was no guarantee of long-term success for the Greens, as all of the other parties began to include environmental and qualitative issues in their party programs. The position and direction of the Greens remained uncertain in the early and mid-1990s. To be sure, they were successful in continuing to win seats in regional and local elections. But like the SPD, they were caught off guard by both the process of European integration and, especially, the rapid move toward German unification during 1990. Many Green Party members were opposed to both developments, and the party lost strength as the twin processes of unification proceeded.

Until the merger with Bündnis '90, the Greens' position looked bleak. The party's squabbling about *fundi* or *realo* positions undercut its credibility among potential new supporters. Its inability to grasp the seriousness of unification and develop relevant positions made it appear unwilling to deal with reality. The ability of other parties to address what had formerly been Green issues, such as the environment, made the Greens' specific appeal less distinctive. Finally, the Green Party's failure to motivate its own core constituency ultimately proved the party's undoing. Electoral turnout for general elections in the Federal Republic averaged between 84 and 90 percent for every election between 1953 and 1987. However, electoral turnout for the 1990 federal election reached only 78 percent, and in 1994 it was up slightly to 79 percent. Several postelection analyses found that a disproportionate share of the nonvoters were previously Greens' supporters. Further embarrassing the party in 1990 was the success of Bündnis '90 in attaining seats by virtue of obtaining 6.0 percent of the vote in the former GDR territory. Before the general election, the Western Greens had spurned an offer from Bündnis '90 to run a joint ticket. Had the Greens done so, the resulting Green alliance would have won 5.1 percent of the vote, enough for representation in the Bundestag. It was this embarrassment for the Greens that eventually led to merger with Bündnis '90.

The persistent ecological problems of the five *Länder* of the former GDR have presented the Greens with a tremendous opportunity to gain strength. With the Greens-Bundnis '90 merger in 1993, a 5 percent electoral share and a position in parliament appeared certain for the foreseeable future. In the 1994 elections, however, the Greens attained a somewhat disappointing 6 percent of the vote after preelection polls had them closer to 10 percent. In 1998, however, the Greens raised their share of the vote to 6.7 percent and became the junior coalition partner of the SPD in the first democratic Left government since the beginning of the Weimar Republic. Party leader Joschka Fischer is the coalition's foreign minister, and the Greens have four of the fourteen cabinet ministries, the other three being the interior, health, and environment ministries. Six percent appeared to be a firm base for the party, and it is likely to remain a permanent fixture in the German Bundestag whether in coalition or on the opposition benches.

Party of Democratic Socialism. The PDS (known as the Sozialistische Einheits Partei, Socialist Unity Party—SED—in its GDR days) is concentrated in the five *Länder* of the former GDR. It has had a long and tortuous history. It sprang from the KPD's founding immediately after World War I, at the time of the Russian Revolution, when all socialist and labor parties split on the issue of evolutionary or revolutionary socialism. The KPD split from the SPD in 1919, following the success of the Russian Revolution, and continually attacked the SPD until both were outlawed and suppressed by the Nazis.

Following World War II, the KPD reappeared only briefly in West Germany and eventually disappeared in 1956, banned by the Constitutional Court. Several factors were responsible for its demise. Prior to Hitler's rise to power in 1933, a major area of the KPD's support was in the northeastern part of Germany. After World War II, this area became the GDR. Within the newly defined West Germany, there remained a much smaller constituency for the KPD. In addition, the onset of the cold war in the late 1940s seriously eroded the KPD's support in West Germany, although the party did receive 5.7 percent of the vote in the Federal Republic's first election in 1949. However, the intensity of the postwar anticommunist thrust was particularly damaging to the KPD in West Germany. West German leaders took advantage of these events to propagandize against communism, and the KPD's support diminished continually until the party was banned by the Constitutional Court.

Some members of the KPD organized themselves as the Deutsche Kommunistische Partei (DKP) following the ban, but the "new" communist party received even less support than the KPD. In 1968, the ban on the KPD was lifted, and its name was appropriated by Maoists and the New Left. It had a brief period of influence during the social turbulence of the late 1960s. The new KPD split in the early 1970s, and a Marxist-Leninist KPD also appeared. By the late 1970s, there were numerous tiny communist parties and sects, none of which came close to achieving 5 percent of the electoral vote (although most of these tiny parties regularly contested elections). By the early 1980s, many of the sects had officially disappeared, with many former members gravitating to the Greens and occupying a minority wing within that new party.

In the GDR, on the other hand, the KPD had a very different history. In the late 1940s, the KPD flourished in the Soviet zone and, with Soviet acquiescence, forced a merger of the KPD with the SPD, which had also sprung up after the war in this region of traditional SPD strength. The name of the merged Communist Party was the SED. This party dominated all aspects of life in the GDR under the successive leadership of Walter Ulbricht, Willi Stoph, and then Erich Honecker and was considered the most Stalinist and repressive of the Soviet client Communist parties. It was under this leadership that the dreaded Stasi secret police grew and ran roughshod on the GDR citizens. During the 1980s, elements in the SED favored establishing a dialogue with elements of the SPD in the Federal Republic.[10] Some of this built on the legacy of Willy Brandt's *Ostpolitik,* which was forged in the 1970s. Such attempts by the SED under Stoph to broaden its contacts and appear less repressive than under the Honecker regime ultimately proved unsuccessful. Thus, it is no wonder that the SED quickly changed its name to the PDS in 1990 as the process of unification gathered speed. Under the leadership of post-unification party leader Gregor Gysi, the PDS showed considerable immediate strength in the five *Länder* of the former GDR, winning between 9 percent and 15 percent of the vote during the October 14, 1990, *Ländtag* elections and 11.1 percent of the vote in these *Länder* in the first all-German elections on December 2, 1990. The new PDS was plagued, however, by the legacy of corruption and wasteful extravagance under the Honecker regime and the secret transfer of millions of deutsche marks to the Soviet Union after unification had taken place in October 1990.

By the mid-1990s, the difficulties of unification had created renewed strength for the PDS. In regional and local elections in Eastern Germany, it attained over 20 percent of the vote and

won four directly elected seats in the 1994 federal election. The winning of four individual seats on the direct portion of the ballot gave the party representation in the Bundestag even though its overall vote percentage on the party portion of the ballot in the entire country fell just under the 5 percent threshold. In the 1998 election, the PDS won not only the same four individual seats, but it also crossed the 5 percent threshold to 5.1. Thus, the PDS remained a strong force in German politics. It even formed a coalition government with the SPD in the *Land* of Saxony during 1994, a phenomenon that caused the Christian Democrats to return to some of their anticommunist rhetoric of the 1950s and 1960s.

While the idea of the PDS's participating in governing coalitions in other *Länder* or at the federal level seems beyond the pale to many observers, this "permanent" political pariah status once was believed to prevent the Greens from participating in governing coalitions. Both the Greens and the PDS quite likely have benefited from the democratizing influence of a multi-party parliamentary democracy that allows all significant parties to find their democratic voice. To some observers, the most interesting development regarding the PDS is that it is not really a communist party anymore. Rather, it has become a regionally based party beseeching the national government for greater resources. In this sense, it seems to be a left-wing, Eastern German mirror image of the right-wing, Bavarian-based CSU. In the new century, the PDS's primary challenge is not so much being seen as a legitimate party as much as its need to deal with its demographic problem. The average age of both PDS members and voters is between fifty and sixty. Until and unless the party is able to replenish itself with younger supporters, it might still have to worry about the 5 percent threshold.

Free Democratic Party. The FDP's philosophy is Germany's closest equivalent to the individualistic impulses of the British liberal movement.[11] Here we emphasize again that *liberal* is used in the European context to mean an emphasis on the individual, as opposed to an activist state tradition.

The FDP's major influence is its role as a swing party, since it has allied with each of the two major parties at different periods since 1949. In fact, it has been included in the governing coalition for almost the entire history of the FRG. Clearly, the influence of the FDP has been disproportionate to its electoral strength of 5 to 10 percent of the voters. The primary reasons for the party's key position are the discrediting of the central state after the Nazi abuses, the role of the U.S. occupation forces and their preference for free-market economic arrangements, and the effects of the cold war. These factors increased the importance of nonleftist parties in the eyes of both the Allied powers and the citizens of the Federal Republic, and the FDP was happy to play the nonleftist role.

The FDP's perspective is an expression of two ideologies, broadly characterized here as economic liberalism and social liberalism. During the postwar period, the FDP has relied on both philosophies to ally with the CDU-CSU and the SPD. Until 1998, the FDP was out of the cabinet only twice since 1949: during the CDU-CSU majority from 1957 to 1961 and during the Grand Coalition from 1966 to 1969. Moreover, the FDP has almost always had either the economics ministry or the foreign ministry, or both, in the various coalition governments. The leading politicians in the FDP have been Walther Scheel (former federal president), Otto Graf Lambsdorff (former economics minister), Hans-Dietrich Genscher (long-time foreign minister in both Center-Left and Center-Right governments), and Martin Bangemann (FDP party leader during the late 1980s and early 1990s).

The party has carefully nurtured its centrist position in the Federal Republic's politics by applying one or another of its political leanings to soften the ideological profile of the major party with which it is allied at the time. For example, in the early 1980s, during the latter years of the Center-Left Schmidt governments, the FDP acted as a strong counterweight to the leftist demands for more public spending made by many of the SPD rank and file. In fact, many of these SPD members described the FDP as the tail that wagged the SPD dog. On the other hand, after the Center-Right Kohl government took office in 1983, the FDP resisted the CDU-CSU's desire to increase the government's capacity for surveillance of individual citizens of the Federal Republic.

By adopting a strategy of allying with first one major party and then the other, the FDP has occasionally been accused of lacking strong political conviction. Critics view the FDP as a small collection of notables whose primary adherence to the party has been as a vehicle to gain important cabinet posts. Each time this accusation has been prominent, generally after a change of government, the FDP seems to have so disillusioned its voters as to fall below the 5 percent necessary for representation in the Bundestag. In fact, during the early and mid-1990s, the FDP failed to reach the 5 percent minimum in several *Land* elections. However, the Federal Republic's voters have generally been reluctant to give either of the two large parties an absolute majority. This occurred only from 1957 to 1961.

Throughout the history of the FRG, voters have always been induced to turn to the FDP as a buffer against the SPD and the CDU-CSU. But its flirting with the 5 percent electoral hurdle and falling below it in numerous *Länder* elections have been a constant worry for the party since unification. For years, many individuals have foretold the demise of the FDP, but the party has regularly frustrated these predictions. In fact, the party's stock rose considerably during the late 1980s and early 1990s, as it took leading and forceful positions, owing largely to the efforts of Hans-Dietrich Genscher, on European integration and German unification. Yet just before the 1994 election, the FDP was again dropping badly in preelection polls. Under the leadership of Klaus Kinkel, the FDP survived the election with 6.9 percent of the vote, thus retaining its representation in the Bundestag.

The FDP's electoral drop from 1990 (when it

received 11 percent) was very worrying for the party, especially when its electoral support dropped to 6.2 percent in the 1998 election (below the level of the Greens) and went into opposition for the first time since 1969. The party's fortunes looked especially bleak until the CDU financial scandal in 1999 when moderate German voters began searching for political alternatives. Under the leadership of Wolfgang Gerhardt, the party has rebounded in several *Land* elections since 1998 and once again seems to have avoided demise. Of course, what is different in the new century for the FDP is that it is no longer the balance wheel between the two large parties, serving as a constant coalition maker. Rather, the emergence of both the Greens and the PDS as contenders for non-SPD and non-CDU voters means that the political space for the FDP is threatened. Similarly, the emergence of other small party alternatives means that the FDP will no longer have the luxury of serving as the political kingmaker in the FRG.

Republikaner. The Republikaner were formed in the late 1980s when increasing numbers of non-Germans began arriving in Germany as European integration started.[12] There had been various splinter-group right-wing parties throughout the Federal Republic's history, but with the exception of the National Democratic Party of Germany (NPD), which received 4.3 percent of the vote in 1969, they had never seriously threatened to win seats in the Bundestag. The Republikaner's strength in local and regional elections in 1989 suggested that this right-wing party might finally break through the 5 percent threshold.

But the pace at which the Kohl government conducted the unification process in the early 1990s had a devastating impact on the far-Right Republikaner and its leader, former Nazi SS soldier Franz Shönhuber. In effect, Kohl's speedy and comparatively pragmatic process of unification had stolen the very essence of the Republikaner appeal. Just as the Greens complained that the other parties were stealing their issues—that is, embracing Green issues in the other party platforms—the Republikaner found their primary goals of curtailed asylum and restrictions on immigration already achieved without their input or influence.

As the difficulties of European integration and German unification mounted in the mid-1990s, the Republikaner became a "safe" political outlet for the neo-Nazi sentiments that people did not publicly admit. In fact, in *Land* elections during 1992 and 1993, the Republikaner continually surpassed preelection predictions, because some of the party's voters did not tell pollsters how they would actually vote. In the mid-1990s, this far-Right party apparently once again threatened to achieve the 5 percent threshold necessary for Bundestag representation. The continuing difficulties of unification should have been a major advantage for the Republikaner. One of the party's primary appeals had been to those in both the eastern and the western parts of the Federal Republic who wished to see the renewal of a resurgent German nationalism to counter the rising tide of internationalism that European integration represented. Prior to the 1994 elections, the party seemed to be taking advantage of Kohl's drift and indecisiveness on issues such as political asylum, immigration, racism, and taming the renewed nationalist impulses. Because of the Kohl government's apparent lack of direction in the 1990s, most observers felt the Republikaner remained a serious threat to Kohl and the Christian Democrats in the 1994 elections. However, the elections were a disaster for the Republikaner, who fell to less than 1.7 percent of the vote. And in 1998, the Republikaner failed to approach 5 percent again. Only in the *Land* election in Baden-Württemberg in 1996 did the party break through and achieve 9 percent of the vote in a regional election. The only other far-Right party to obtain seats in a *Land* election was the Deutsche Volksunion (DVU) in the East German state of Saxony-Anhalt, when it received 12.9 percent of the vote in April 1998. However, this was discounted as a protest vote since the DVU obtained only 3.2 percent of the vote in the 1998 federal election only five months later. For a country that has had such a heinous history of right-wing extremism, modern German voters have been remarkable in failing to allow such parties into elected office.

Electoral Procedure and Results

The German electoral system has produced two significant outcomes. The first is coherence among the parties, since the system—and the constitution itself for that matter—specifically supports the parties as essential organizations for political democracy. Second, the 5 percent hurdle ensures that only parties that command sufficient support attain seats in the Bundestag. This rule has helped Germany avoid the wild proliferation of parties in such democracies as Italy and Israel, which has made coalition formation difficult in those countries.

As Table 19.3 suggests, Germany has had no volatile electoral swings. There were four major periods of party dominance since 1949: the CDU/CSU-FDP coalition from 1949 to 1966; the Grand Coalition "interregnum" (1966–1969); the SPD-led coalition (1969–1982); and the CDU-CSU-led coalition from 1982 to 1998. And with the election of the Red-Green government in 1998, Germany could be poised for a fourth period of stable rule. The major uncertainty will be how well the two new parties in the Bundestag in the past fifteen years (Greens and PDS) find their niche.

Collective Identities

With respect to the politics of collective identity, organization of interests, and social movements, Germany remains a country of organized collectivities, never having developed as a country with a strong individualistic ethos. This is the case not only among major economic producer groups, but also among political parties (in which participatory membership is high) and a wide range of social groups. However, in its collective identities and their relationship to democracy, Germany is similar in many respects to other advanced capitalist countries. The political community is defined as all adults over age eighteen, and citizenship is based primarily on the ethnicity of one's parents. However, the granting of citizenship to non-German ethnics remained problematic until the Schröder government changed the law in 1999 to allow easier immigration. Prior to this significant change, Germany had taken a comparatively restrictive—some even say racist—position.

Social Class and Cleavage Structures

In analyzing Germany's social forces since industrialization in the late nineteenth century, class was and is a primary category. Germany's working class remains larger and more prosperous than those of Britain, France, or Italy, and it has thrived as postwar Germany's high-wage, high-skill, export-oriented industries have provided substantial material benefits to its mostly unionized workforce. While class remains a salient cleavage, other significant social divisions have been based on religion and region. The population in the southeast, portions of the southwest, and along the Rhine as far north as Düsseldorf is predominantly Catholic. In the northwest, northeast, and portions of the southwest, one finds predominantly Lutheran Protestants. Collective identities are also determined on regional bases, which sometimes are based on religious cleavages and sometimes not. Many of the pre-1871 German states have retained considerable autonomy, which is often manifested in different traditions and customs. In many respects, the creation of a *Federal* Republic of Germany was due to these regional divisions. Of course, during the late nineteenth century, and particularly during the first half of the twentieth, ethnicity and race were major lines of social demarcation, with monstrous consequences.

Interest groups behave differently in the Fed-

Table 19.3 FRG Election Results, 1949–1998

Year	Party	Percentage of Vote	Government	Year	Party	Percentage of Vote	Government
1949	Voter turnout	78.5	CDU/CSU-FDP	1980	Voter Turnout	88.6	SPD-FDP
	CDU/CSU	31.0			CDU/CSU	44.5	
	SPD	29.2			SPD	42.9	
	FDP	11.9			FDP	10.6	
	Others	27.8			Others	0.5	
1953	Voter turnout	86.0	CDU/CSU-FDP	1983	Voter turnout	89.1	CDU/CSU-FDP
	CDU/CSU	45.2			CDU/CSU	48.8	
	SPD	28.8			SPD	38.2	
	FDP	9.5			FDP	7.0	
	Others	16.7			Greens	5.6	
1957	Voter turnout	87.8	CDU/CSU		Others	0.5	
	CDU/CSU	50.2		1987	Voter turnout	84.3	CDU/CSU-FDP
	SPD	31.8			CDU/CSU	44.3	
	FDP	7.7			SPD	37.0	
	Others	10.3			FDP	9.1	
1961	Voter turnout	87.8	CDU/CSU-FDP		Greens	8.3	
	CDU/CSU	45.3			Others	1.3	
	SPD	36.2		1990	Voter turnout	78.0	CDU/CSU-FDP
	FDP	12.8			CDU/CSU	43.8	
	Others	5.7			SPD	33.5	
1965	Voter turnout	86.8	CDU/CSU-SPD		FDP	11.0	
	CDU/CSU	47.6	Grand		Greens	3.8	
	SPD	39.3	Coalition		PDS	2.4	
	FDP	9.5			Bündnis '90	1.2	
	Others	3.6			Others	3.5	
1969	Voter turnout	86.7	SPD-FDP	1994	Voter turnout	79.0	CDU/CSU-FDP
	CDU/CSU	46.1			CDU/CSU	41.5	
	SPD	42.7			SPD	36.4	
	FDP	5.8			FDP	6.9	
	Others	5.4			Greens	7.3	
1972	Voter turnout	86.0	SPD-FDP		PDS	4.4	
	CDU/CSU	44.9			Others	3.5	
	SPD	45.8		1998	Voter turnout	82.3	SPD-Greens
	FDP	9.5			CDU/CSU	35.1	
	Others	16.7			SPD	40.9	
1976	Voter turnout	90.7	SPD-FDP		FDP	6.2	
	CDU/CSU	48.2			Greens	6.7	
	SPD	42.6			PDS	5.1	
	FDP	7.9			Others	6.0	
	Others	0.9					

Source: German Information Center, 1998.

eral Republic than they do in the Anglo-Saxon countries. In the Federal Republic, interest groups are seen as having a societal role and responsibility that transcends the immediate interests of their members. Germany's public law traditions, deriving from Roman and Napoleonic legal foundations, specifically allow private interests to perform public functions, albeit within a clear and specific general framework. Thus, interest groups are seen as part of the fabric of society and are virtually permanent institutions. A social premium is placed on their adaptation and ability to respond to new issues. To speak of winners and losers in such an arrangement is to misunderstand the ability of existing interest groups to make incremental changes over time.

By being structurally integrated into the fabric of society, German interest groups have an institutional longevity surpassing that of interest groups in most other industrialized countries. But how does the German state mediate the relationship among interest groups? Peter Katzenstein observes that in the Federal Republic, "the state is not an actor but a series of relationships," and these relationships are solidified in what he has called "para-public institutions."[13] As noted in Chapter 18, the para-publics encompass a wide variety of organizations; among the most important are the Bundesbank, the institutions of codetermination, the labor courts, the social insurance funds, and the employment office. Under prevailing German public law, rooted in pre-1871 feudal traditions, they have been assigned the role of "independent governance by the representatives of social sectors at the behest of or under the general supervision of the state." In other words, organizations that are seen as mere interest groups in other countries are combined in Germany with certain quasi-government agencies so that together they have a much more para-public role in the Federal Republic.

Employer associations and trade unions are the key interest groups within German society, but they are not alone.[14] Other, less influential groups include the Protestant and Catholic churches, the Farmers Association (Deutscher Bauernverband), the Association of Artisans (Handwerk Verein), the Federal Chamber of Physicians (Bundesaerztekammer), and the now nearly defunct League of Expelled Germans (Bund der Vertriebenen Deutschen, BVD), which has represented the interests of emigrants from the GDR and Eastern Europe. Each of these groups has been tightly integrated into various para-public institutions to perform a range of important social functions that in other countries might be performed by state agencies. These organizations are forced to assume a degree of social responsibility in their roles in policy implementation that goes beyond what political scientist Arnold Heidenheimer has called the "freewheeling competition of 'selfish' interest groups."[15]

For example, the churches, through the state, assess a church tax on all citizens who have been born into the Protestant or Catholic Church. This tax provides the churches with a steady stream of income and ensures institutional permanence, but it also compels the churches to play a major role in the provision of social welfare and in aiding the families of *Gastarbeiter*. The Farmers Association has been a pillar of support for both the FDP and the CDU-CSU and for decades has strongly influenced the agricultural ministry. It has also resisted attempts by the EU to lower the agricultural support provided to European farmers in the form of direct subsidies as part of the EU's common agricultural policy. The Association of Artisans is a major component of the DIHT (the German chamber of commerce, to which all firms in Germany *must* belong), and the Chamber of Physicians has been intimately involved with both the legislation and implementation of social and medical insurance (social security and general welfare).

These interest groups and the para-public agencies within which they function attempt to contain social conflict through multiple, small-scale corporatist institutions. The Federal Republic's corporatist variant in the 1980s was much more regionalized and industry specific, and much less centralized, than earlier national-level conceptions of corporatism. Yet this system of interest groups and para-publics is subject to the same problems that have plagued macrolevel corporatism in more centralized industrial societies, such as Sweden and Austria: The system still must express the concerns of member organizations, channel conflict, and recommend (and sometimes implement) public policy.

Citizenship, Ethnicity, and Identity

The political parties represent a broad ideological spectrum and produce wide-ranging political debate in Germany. This diversity is also reflected in the media, as newspapers have similarly wide ideological reach appealing to a broad spectrum of political opinion. The major print media range from the mass-market tabloid *Bild Zeitung* (literally, "picture newspaper") on the Right, through more conservative and liberal broadsheet newspapers like *Die Welt* of Hamburg, the *Süddeutscher Zeitung* of Munich, and the *Frankfurter Allgemeine Zeitung*, to the *Frankfurter Rundschau*, which is close to the SPD in its editorial positions, and the *TAZ* of Berlin, which is closest to the Greens. There is now a wide variety of private cable television channels, but the three main networks are public channels, and they are careful to provide proportional balance on major party positions. In fact, only recently have some of the political parties chosen to advertise on the private channels. Until the past few years, the prevailing pattern on the public channels during the two-month electoral campaigns has been to prohibit paid TV campaign commercials. Instead, the networks present one- or two-hour-long roundtable discussions in which all parties participate in debates. This practice has prevented the larger and richer parties from "buying" a larger share of the popular vote.

The wide variety of public opinion has helped dispel the view that Germany's high voting turnout rate results from a sense of duty and not from a real commitment to democracy.[16] Perhaps during the Weimar years, and certainly during the period of the Second Reich (1871–1918), the commitment to democracy in Germany was suspect. However, the post–World War II period contains examples that sharply challenge the perception that Germans participate in politics only out of a sense of duty. German society holds evidence of a strong participatory ethic among the democratic Left. There are various opportunities for participation at the workplace, such as corporatism, codetermination, and the works councils, which exist in virtually all firms. Moreover, one of the primary appeals in the formation of the Greens has been its emphasis on increased rank-and-file democratic participation (*Basisdemokratie*), particularly in such technical issues as energy policy.[17] The strength of the Greens, and now of the PDS, has forced the traditional parties to make even greater attempts to mobilize their supporters and potential supporters through appeals to participatory democracy.

Germany's educational system has also changed in the years of the Federal Republic, particularly in terms of the socialization of German citizens. The catalyst was the student movement in the university system during the 1960s. The university system was elitist and restrictive at that time and undertook insufficient critical analysis of Germany's bloody twentieth-century history. Not only did the student mobilizations of the 1960s open up the educational system to a wider socioeconomic spectrum; they also caused many of the "'68 Generation" (called that since 1968 was the year of the most significant demonstrations) to challenge their parents about attitudes shaped by the Nazi period and before. Yet even at the turn of the century, many critics of the German educational system argue that some of the older attitudes toward non-Germans remain and that the educational system should increase its efforts to build an educated and tolerant citizenry.

Germany's social market economy enjoys broad acceptance among most Germans, with the possible exceptions of isolated minority positions of the extreme Left and Right. The social market economy provides universal benefits to almost all segments of the population, including public transit, subsidies for the arts, and virtually free higher and vocational education, among many others. Thus, a general tolerance for a wide variety of political and artistic opinion means there is very little of the squabbling and acrimony over public funding of the arts that is common in some other countries.

However, in the late 1980s and the 1990s, some of the optimistic views that Germany had become a "normal" parliamentary democracy were challenged by the nature of anti-ethnic and anti-immigrant violence. The attacks on foreign immigrants, and even on guest worker (*Gastarbeiter*) families who had lived in Germany for more than thirty years, raised questions among some observers regarding how tolerant the Germans really are. Owing to Germany's history of repression toward Jews and all non-Germans during the first half of the twentieth century, such concerns must be taken extremely seriously. More disturbing to many was the lack of leadership coming from the Kohl government at the time and the apathy—and in some cases enthusiasm—of some Germans toward the intolerant violence. To be sure, Germany was not alone among industrialized nations in racist violence, but Germany's history causes it to bear a special burden. The Schröder government has been more aggressive in using both the bully pulpit of the chancellor's office as well as the German legal system to pursue racist attacks aggressively. On the tenth anniversary of German unification, a group of neo-Nazis attacked a synagogue in Düsseldorf, and the Schröder government issued a statement calling on German citizens to rise up against the "brown scum" in a "revolt of the righteous."

The full development of citizenship, democracy, and participation in Germany is not blemish free, however. Germany has only recently altered an extremely restrictive position on immigration. Immigrant workers have generally fared better in German society than those non-

Germans outside the protection of organized worker representation and the democratic Left political parties. Without the granting of German citizenship, such workers remain marginalized residents of the FRG. Unlike many other European nations, Germany until 1999 had made it difficult for immigrants to be naturalized, no matter how long they were in the country, and generally denied citizenship to offspring of noncitizens born on German soil. This prejudice was exacerbated by the end of the cold war and the demise of the Soviet Union. For example, "ethnic" Germans whose ancestors had not been in Germany for centuries were allowed to enter Germany legally and assume citizenship rights immediately. Yet the *Gastarbeiter* who had lived in Germany for decades—and at the express invitation of the German governments of the 1960s—were not given the same opportunities for instant citizenship.[18] The new law, which took effect on January 1, 2000, provided for German citizenship for all children born in Germany provided their parents had resided lawfully in Germany for eight years or had an unlimited residence permit for three years. Naturalization now is possible after eight years of residence instead of the previous fifteen.

Perhaps the most contentious issue of citizenship and identity has surrounded the political asylum question. Following World War II, Germany passed one of the world's most liberal political asylum laws, in part to help atone for the Nazis' political repression of millions. The German government granted immediate asylum status to all those who claimed persecution or fear of persecution based on violated political freedoms and allowed those asylum seekers to remain in Germany, with considerable monetary support, until each individual's case was heard. Often this process took years. With the end of the cold war and the opening of East European borders, the trickle of asylum seekers turned into a flood in the minds of some Germans. This sentiment caused the Kohl government to curtail drastically the right of political asylum, a step that called into question whether Germany's democracy was as mature and well developed as it claimed during the stable postwar period. Germany's commitment to democratic rights appeared to contain some new conditions, and many of them involved a definition of identity that looked remarkably insular in a Europe otherwise becoming more international.[19]

Examples of this restrictive aspect of naturalization are evident in the wake of the breakdown of the Eastern bloc. The immigration of ethnic Germans, the presence of *Gastarbeiter* who have been in Germany for two generations and are only now slowly obtaining citizenship, and the volatile political asylum question have all placed strains on the concept of citizenship in the postunification years.

Gender

Gender did not appear to be a politically significant cleavage in Germany until the 1960s, as women remained politically marginalized for most of the first half of the Federal Republic's history. In other words, gender did not produce political divisions because many women appeared to accept their unequal position in postwar West German society. Taking to heart the Catholic admonition of *Kinder, Kirche, Küche* (children, church, and kitchen), many German women were socialized into believing that their status as second-class citizens was appropriate. To be sure, there were pre-FRG exceptions to this pattern—such as the socialist activist and theorist Rosa Luxemburg and the artist Käthe Kollwitz from the 1910s—but until the social explosions of the 1960s, very few women held positions in society outside the home.

Even with the spread of feminism since the 1970s, German women have generally lagged behind their American counterparts by some five to ten years in terms of advancement in business and politics, at least on an individual level. The differences between East and West

Germany on social policy affecting women provoked great controversy after unification. Women in the former East Germany had far more presence and influence in public life and in the workplace than did their counterparts in West Germany.

In areas outside the formal workplace, the differences between the laws in the GDR and the preunification FRG created a firestorm of controversy. In the former East Germany, women had made far greater social and economic progress (relatively speaking) and enjoyed greater government provision for such services as child care and family leave. In fact, one of the hottest items of contention in Germany during the early 1990s was whether to reduce East German–style benefits to women (including abortion) in favor of the more conservative and restrictive ones of the Federal Republic. The more restrictive Western German law prevailed after unification, to the consternation of many women.

Protest and Social Movements

To be sure, Germans engage in significant strikes and demonstrations on a wide range of economic and noneconomic issues. But rather than being seen as a sign of instability or a failure of public institutions, they should be seen as a success. Political institutions sometimes are mistakenly seen as fixed structures that are supposed to prevent or repress dissent or controversy. A more helpful way to analyze such conflicts is to take a "new institutionalist" approach. This theory argues that political organizations shape and adapt to social and political protest and channel such action in ways that are not detrimental to democratic participation, but in fact represent its essence.[20]

This distinction has important implications for the role of interest groups and social movements in the Federal Republic. Rather than encouraging fractious competition, this system creates a bounded framework within which these groups struggle tenaciously yet usually come to an agreement on policy. Moreover, because they are encouraged to aggregate the interests of all members of their association, their policy total—the general interest of the group as a whole—will be greater than the sum of its parts—the aggregated concerns of individual members. They are not omnipotent, however. If they fail and allow conflict to go unresolved, the failure challenges the effectiveness of the institutions and may allow elements of society to go unrepresented. A partial failure of certain interest groups and institutions led to the rise of a series of social movements during the 1960s and 1970s, particularly around university reform, wage negotiations, and foreign policy. The very existence of the Green Party is a prime example of a movement that arose out of the earlier inability of existing institutions to address, mediate, and solve contentious issues.

With respect to extrainstitutional participation and protest, a general system of inclusionary proportional representation has left few outside the political arena until recently. Those who are outside belong to political groups that fail to meet the 5 percent electoral threshold. The Republikaner, as well as other right-wing groups, might seem to fit into this category. Similarly, the substantial Turkish population, which accounts for over 5 percent of Germany's inhabitants, might be included here. First arriving as guest workers, many have now resided in Germany for decades. And compared to *Gastarbeiter* from EU countries such as Italy and Spain, Turkish residents have fewer rights in Germany. Finally, the once-active leftist community of revolutionary Marxists still retains a small presence, mostly in large cities and university towns. Some of these left-wing parties contest elections but never get more than 1 percent of the vote.

Still, during the years since the student mobilizations of the late 1960s, Germany has witnessed considerable protest and mobilization of social forces outside the established channels of political and social representation. Among the most significant forces in the postwar FRG have been the feminist, peace, and antinuclear movements. All three, in different ways, challenged fundamental assumptions about German politics and pointed to the inability of the institutional structure to respond to the needs and issues that these groups raised. From challenges to a restrictive abortion law in the 1970s, to demonstrations against stationing nuclear missiles on German soil in the 1980s, to regular protests against nuclear power plants since the 1970s, the spirit of direct action has animated German politics in ways that were not possible in the years before the late 1960s.

The 1990s, however, witnessed protest less from the Left than from the Right. Although the Republikaner are a legitimate party, illegal neo-Nazi groups have been responsible for numerous racist attacks, increasing since the summer of 2000, the most reprehensible one taking place at a Jewish synagogue on the tenth anniversary of German unification. Significantly, many of these attacks by the right-wing fringe have been met with spontaneous, peaceful marches, sometimes producing demonstrations of from 200,000 to 500,000 people in various cities. This reaction suggests that social protest, as part of an active democratic political discourse, has matured in the face of this new threat from the Right. The challenge for German politics is to maintain a system of democratic participation that encompasses both extrainstitutional groups and specific organized political institutions in a way that enhances democracy rather than destroying it.

Notes

1. Frank Louis Rusciano, "Rethinking the Gender Gap: The Case of West German Elections," *Comparative Politics* 24, no. 3 (April 1992): 335–358.

2. Ralf Dahrendorf, *Society and Democracy in Germany* (Garden City, N.Y.: Anchor, 1969).

3. Christopher S. Allen, ed., *Transformation of the German Political Party System: Institutional Crisis or Democratic Renewal?* (New York: Berghahn, 1999).

4. Carl E. Schorske, *German Social Democracy, 1905–1917: The Development of the Great Schism* (Cambridge, Mass.: Harvard University Press, 1983).

5. Otto Kirschheimer, "The Transformation of the Western European Party System," in Roy C. Macridis, ed., *Comparative Politics: Notes and Readings,* 6th ed. (Chicago: Dorsey, 1986).

6. Gerard Braunthal, *The German Social Democrats Since 1969: A Party in Power and Opposition,* 2d ed. (Boulder, Colo.: Westview Press, 1994).

7. Aline Kuntz, "The Bavarian CSU: A Case Study in Conservative Modernization" (Ph.D. diss., Cornell University, 1987).

8. Geoffrey Pridham, *Christian Democracy in Western Germany: The CDU/CSU in Government and Opposition, 1945–1976* (New York: St. Martin's Press, 1977).

9. Roger Cohen, "Is Germany on the Road to Diversity? The Parties Clash," *New York Times,* December 4, 2000, p. A13.

10. Ann Phillips, "Seeds of Change in the German Democratic Republic," in American Institute for Contemporary German Studies, Research Report 1 (December 1989).

11. David Broughton and Emil Kirchner, "Germany: The FDP in Transition—Again?" *Parliamentary Affairs* 37 (Spring 1984): 183–184.

12. Hans-Georg Betz, *Radical Right-wing Populism in Western Europe* (New York: St. Martin's Press, 1994).

13. Peter Katzenstein, *Policy and Politics in West Germany: The Growth of a Semi-Sovereign State* (Philadelphia: Temple University Press, 1987).

14. German industry is represented by the BDI (Federal Association of German Industry), and employers are represented by the BDA (Federal Association of German Employers). The former addresses issues pertaining to industry as a whole; the latter focuses specifically on issues of concern to employers. German workers are represented by sixteen different unions, organized by industry, which belong to the DGB (German Trade Union Confederation).

15. Arnold J. Heidenheimer, *Comparative Public Policy: The Politics of Social Choice in America, Europe, and Japan,* 3d ed. (New York: St. Martin's Press, 1990).

16. Dahrendorf, *Society and Democracy in Germany.*

17. Carol J. Hager, *Technological Democracy: Bureaucracy and Citizenry in the German Energy Debate* (Ann Arbor: University of Michigan Press, 1995).

18. Turkish *Gastarbeiter* are disadvantaged because if they accept German citizenship, they generally surrender property rights in Turkey.

19. Joyce Marie Mushaben, "A Search for Identity: The 'German Question' in Atlantic Alliance Relations," *World Politics* 40, no. 3 (April 1988): 395–418.

20. Sven Steinmo, Kathleen Thelen, and Frank Longstreth, eds., *Structuring Politics: Historical Institutionalism in Historical Perspective* (New York: Cambridge University Press, 1992).

C H A P T E R

20

German Politics in Transition

Is contemporary Germany best represented by a revitalization of democracy symbolized by the renovation and return of the capital to Berlin, with the city once again becoming a vibrant world capital to rival London, Paris, and Rome? Or is Germany again becoming a place hostile to foreigners and to all that does not seem "German," as suggested by the attack on a Jewish synagogue on the tenth anniversary of German unification?

As we try to understand which Germany we have today, we should keep in mind that an accurate picture of contemporary German politics lies between these two extremes. But the important point is that both images are recognizable parts of modern Germany, and it remains a political challenge for all German citizens to see if the spirit of the former image becomes more prevalent than that of the latter.

Which path German politics takes will be determined by the resolution of the four themes around which this book is organized. The more optimistic assumption would take the form of the continued integration of East Germany into the fabric of the Federal Republic as a whole. But as we have seen, mutual suspicions between Eastern and Western Germans remain high. The former resent the "elbow society" of the West, in which material goods seem to stand high in the hierarchy of societal goals, while the latter resent the huge costs—and increased taxation—required to rebuild the eastern *Länder*.[1]

If a successful economic, political, and social integration occurs, it will take patience, a sound institutional foundation, and the ability of both *Ossis* and *Wessis* (Easterners and Westerners) to understand much more fully the context of each other's values. Once these domestic transitions are accomplished, Germany can devote more attention to the larger issue of European integration.

The more pessimistic assumption could see a less than robust economy and resultant social tensions and conflict. Germany's political landscape now contains five political parties represented in the Bundestag, not just the three of the period from the late 1940s to the early 1980s. Can Germany's organized society (*Organisierte Gesellschaft*) and institutional political structure sustain the increased cooperation necessary to maintain a vibrant democracy? And what of Germany's "economic giant, political dwarf" syndrome? Can Germany take the political responsibility that its economic stature would suggest it should? Do its European neighbors really want it to do so? And what of Germany's high-wage, high-welfare structure in the face of increased economic competition from lower-wage countries in Eastern Europe, Asia, and elsewhere? Negative outcomes to one or more of these questions could produce a much less satisfactory outcome for both Germany and its neighbors.

Continuities, Transitions, and Changing Agendas

For many years Germany was touted as a model for other industrialized societies to emulate. Yet in the years since unification, we have seen increases in racial intolerance, as well as the partial erosion of the country's formerly vaunted economic strength. What is the state of German democracy in the face of racist attacks and rising intolerance, and what is the state of the German economy in the face of contemporary structural challenges?

The continuity of democratic institutions has clearly balanced participation and dissent effectively, as the country's turbulent and often racist past came to be offset by almost fifty years of stable multiparty democracy. For example, Germany has evolved a stable system of alternation between a coalition of moderate Left and moderate Right parties in the fifty years of the Federal Republic of Germany (FRG). And yet rather than the "stop-go" policies that characterized the alternation in power of British Labour and British Conservatives, Germany's alternation between a moderately conservative Christian Democratic Party and one of the most powerful and respected social democratic parties in the world has produced more continuity than sharp change. Despite the deregulatory and new information economy challenges, Germany has maintained its unique and successful industrialized democracy. The country is a bastion of advanced capitalism, yet it also possesses an extensive welfare state and government-mandated programs of worker, trade union, and works council participation in managerial decision making. Moreover, these economic and political successes have helped Germany participate more effectively in the wider world of other nation-states.

Let us briefly review the major contemporary transitional challenges that the Federal Republic faces. First, German unification has been both a tremendous accomplishment and a daunting challenge for all Germans. Few other countries could so quickly add 20 percent to their own population from an adjoining country with a completely different economic and social system. Such a challenge would likely have produced either a much less successful unification or far greater social chaos, or both, in most other countries. That official political unification took place within a year of the breaching of the Berlin Wall is an accomplishment of significant proportion. And the formal integration of the former GDR into the FRG as five new *Länder* is a tribute to organizational and political skills that combined both vision and pragmatism.

United Germany's democracy seems well established after almost fifty years of the Federal Republic and ten years of unification. It boasts high voter turnout, a stable and responsible multiparty political system, and a healthy civic culture.[2] Many observers now believe that Germany's broad-based political participation is part of the fabric of political life. However, several issues merit concern as Germany's political institutions are being extended to the five new *Länder*. How well have Eastern Germans understood and internalized democratic practice after so many years of authoritarian Communist rule? For many such individuals, dissent was not political participation; it was treason. Similarly, can Eastern Germans who have lost jobs and benefits in the transition to capitalism understand that ethnic minorities are not the cause of their plight? Can tolerance and understanding develop in all of Germany at a time when a right-wing fringe is preaching hatred and looking for scapegoats to blame for the costs of unification? Also, is the legacy of a bureaucratic state that as recently as the 1970s, under a social democratic–led government, purged individuals who appeared to have radical tendencies completely gone? In other words, if social tensions continue to rise in the new century, how will the German state respond?

Beyond the immediate institutional features of this unification lie the more difficult issues of integration of economic and social systems and of the quite different political cultures of Eastern and Western Germany, which will take years to blend together. Furthermore, after the initial wave of construction and the economic miniboom that followed in the first years after unification, a more sobering mood set in. As unemployment has remained much higher in the five new states than in the others into the new century, Germans have realized that unification was far from a quick fix. The process of fully unifying the disparate parts of Germany will continue well into this century.

Second, Germany's famed social market economy, with its characteristic organized-capitalist features and strong emphasis on manufacturing over services, its privileged position for trade unions, and its generous social welfare provisions, faced renewed pressures in the post-unification years. Not only did German public and private officials continue to face criticism from countries that had more fully embraced postindustrial (service-sector-driven) economic models; they also were criticized for maintaining the generous social welfare provisions that had eroded much further in countries such as the United Kingdom and the United States. Here too the pressures of unification added to the strains. Clearly these pressures were driving the push for the Schröder government in the summer of 2000 to pass the broad sweep of tax and pension reforms to help alleviate the so-called *Standort Deutschland* (Germany as an attractive location for investment) problem. The continuing heavy costs of rebuilding the East have taken the form of infrastructural investments (in transportation, communications, housing, and new plant), large transfer payments to those in the East who could not find work or did not possess skills needed for the twenty-first-century capitalist economy, and now the immigration of Indian computer programmers. Although Germans refused to give up the generous welfare state benefits they have enjoyed since the 1950s, they found that paying for these benefits in the new *Länder* did not come cheaply.

Germany's economy clearly faces transitional

challenges in the new century. For many years it has been characterized as "high everything," in that it has combined high-quality manufacturing with high wages, high fringe benefits, high worker participation, and high levels of vacation time (six weeks per year).[3] Since the first oil crisis in the 1970s, critical observers have kept insisting that such a system could not last in a competitive world economy.[4] Yet for most of the twenty-plus years since then, the German economy has remained among the world's leaders. More recently, however, the huge costs of unification have caused many of the old criticisms of an extended and overburdened economy to surface again.

Pessimistic observers have begun to suggest that the stresses of the 1990s have placed the German political economy in a precarious position. This "anti–German model" consists of several related arguments.[5] The first is that Germany's economic prowess has resided in certain manufacturing industries, such as automobiles and machine tools, whose goods are exportable but whose technologies are decidedly low. Yet wage costs in these sectors have continued to rise. Second, the costs of the social market economy, as witnessed in the costs of unification, have pressed on the upper limits of Germany's capacity to pay for them. In addition, economic tensions remain at the heart of the conflict between former East and former West Germans. While Eastern Germans have resented the slow pace of change and the high unemployment, West Germans are bitter about losing jobs to East Germans and paying increased taxes for the cleanup of the ecological and infrastructural disaster inherited from the former East German regime.

Third, racist movements and far-Right parties, however marginal they were in the 1990s, still retain a presence in modern unified Germany. The far-Right Republikaner Party threatened to break the 5 percent electoral threshold in the late 1980s and early 1990s, but by the 1998 federal elections it clearly had peaked as a political movement able to gain representation

A cynical western German view of money spent to rebuild Eastern Germany.

Source: Janusz Majewski/*Frankfurter Allgemeine Zeitung.*

in parliament (at least for the time being). And the attacks on foreigners, thought to have peaked in the early 1990s, returned again in the mid-1990s when a hostel for foreign refugees was firebombed and Jewish synagogues were attacked. While representing a tiny minority of the population, they nonetheless represent a significant concern for a democratic country with its catastrophic past. Further to the right is the National Democratic Party of Germany (NPD), which came close to gaining Bundestag representation in 1966 with 4.3 percent of the vote. Although it is gaining less electoral support now than even the Republikaner, the NPD has shown an increased extraparliamentary presence in demonstrations in large German cities, including several in East Germany.

In other words, in the area of collective identities, Germany faces numerous unresolved challenges. For example, the country's guest workers, a large number of whom are Turkish, remain essential to Germany's economy. But will the citizenship reforms of 2000 prove sufficient to integrate them into the fabric of German political and social life? The opening of East Germany produced an influx of refugees and asylum seekers beginning in the late 1980s. This influx placed great strains on a country that paradoxically has had generous political asylum laws but significant restrictions on non-Germans' attaining citizenship. Are some groups disadvantaged by being intentionally or unintentionally excluded from Germany's corporatist institutional structure? These factors have helped produce increased ethnic tensions as German nationalism, understandably suppressed since the end of World War II, has shown some signs of resurgence. In fact, the unification of Germany has partially contributed to this resurgence, as some younger Germans—two generations after the end of World War II—are asking what being *German* actually means. The dark side of such a development is manifested by the various extremist groups, which though still small in numbers, preach exaggerated nationalism and hatred of foreigners and minorities. Contributing to this climate is the reluctance of some German firms to settle reparation payments to aging workers who were slave laborers in World War II. Such tendencies are quite incompatible with a Germany that wishes to play a leading role in European integration.

The future of German politics depends greatly on how the country addresses these challenges, which relate clearly to the four primary themes that we have used to organize our analysis of the countries covered in this book, a world of states, governing the economy, the democratic idea, and the politics of collective identities. For much of the post–World War II period, Germany enjoyed a spiral of success, in that dealing well with one of these thematic issues enabled the country to confront others successfully. For example, problems of collective identities were handled in a much less exclusionary way as women, ethnic groups, and newer political parties and movements all began to contribute to a stable and healthy diversity in German politics that had been missing for most of the country's history.

However, in closely examining all four of these major themes, we find Germany at a crossroads. Can the country continue its successes in all four areas, or will tensions and difficulties undermine these successful patterns to produce a period of economic, political, and social instability?

There has been a significant change in the nature of German politics in the twenty-first century. Clearly the term *Modell Deutschland* used in the 1970s and 1980s is much less appropriate today. In the four preceding chapters, we reexamined the theme of democratic tolerance and respect for positions of other individuals and groups. The question remains, Can Germany evolve peacefully and democratically in a region where increased integration will become more likely? The expansion of the European Union (EU) in the 1990s enabled more European citizens to live and work outside their home countries. What happens to German collective identity? Can the elaborate and, for fifty years, effective institutional structure that balances private and public interests be maintained and supported? Will the EU augment or challenge Germany's position in Europe? Will these challenges threaten Germany's enviable economic position in the face of increased competition from newly industrializing countries?

The Challenges of European Integration

The challenge that the EU presents offers both opportunities and dangers to the Federal Republic. Although the creation of a single market clearly can benefit the strongest European economy, Germany faces unique problems as it attempts to integrate its economy with the Continent's. Clearly the weaker countries, such as

Portugal and Greece, will look to strong countries such as Germany for assistance. Moreover, Germany's brand of organized capitalism is clearly out of step with the more free-market sentiments of other European countries. Defenders of the German model might rightfully say, Why shouldn't the economy of all of Europe be modeled on Germany rather than on the much weaker, free-market-oriented United Kingdom? However, transferring the deeply embedded structures of German capitalism to countries that do not understand how they work is much easier said than done. Furthermore, the transition from the redoubtable deutsche mark to the uncertain euro adds further worries to the minds of German citizens. The precipitous fall in value of the euro (some 25 percent) after its introduction in 1999 until late 2000 threatened to raise inflation fears once again, because a weak euro means increased costs for imported goods from outside the euro zone.

The completion of the single market of the EU has also complicated Germany's relationship with other states. The EU was supposedly the grand culmination of a post–cold war spirit of German and European unity. But unity has proved more difficult to establish than first anticipated. The EU's first immediate outcome has only strengthened the trends toward decentralization and deregulation already under way in Western Europe, rather than initiating faster integration. More significant for the German economy, such deregulatory tendencies, if spread throughout Europe, could potentially disturb the organized capitalism of Germany's small and large businesses. In addition, the wholesale deregulation in European finance threatens Germany's distinctive finance-manufacturing links. In short, the trend toward Europeanization may be incompatible with the highly consensus-oriented and coordinated nature of Germany's adjustment patterns. Moreover, as Europe becomes more open to the rest of the world economy, how well will Germany's "high-everything" system be able to withstand increased economic competition from Asia and elsewhere? Politically, can Germany emerge from its political dwarf status and play a leadership role in integrating the East-Central European states into a wider EU?

For much of the post–World War II period, Germany's growing international economic prowess was not complemented by a similar level of international political responsibility. Yet in the 1990s and into the new century, Germany has confidently, and with the support of its neighbors and allies, taken a leading role in European integration. It is firmly anchored in Western Europe but uniquely positioned to assist in the transition of the formerly Communist East-Central European states toward economic and political modernization. Initial doubts concerning the capacity of Gerhard Schröder to continue Helmut Kohl's commitment to both a deeper and wider EU have been resolved as Schröder seems to be speaking with an even greater sense of the projection of German responsibility in the EU than did his predecessor.

Germany in Comparative Perspective

Germany offers important insights for comparative politics in several respects. First is the issue of the role of organized capitalism. Germany has a model of combining state and market in a way that is unique to many advanced industrialized nations. Many models of political analysis choose to emphasize the distinctions between state and market. Debates about whether nationalized industries should be privatized and whether welfare should be reduced in favor of private charity, for example, are symptomatic of the conflict between state and market that animates the politics of most developed countries. Germany's organized capitalism, together with the social market economy, has effectively blurred the distinction between the public and private sectors. The FRG has refused to see public policy as a stark choice between these two alternatives, preferring to emphasize policies in which the state and market work together. Within the general framework of the model of governing the economy (outlined in Part I), the German state effectively pursues development plans that benefit from its cooperative interaction with a dense network of key social and economic actors. Despite Germany's prominence as a powerful advanced industrialized economy, this model remains surprisingly understudied. And despite the current economic difficulties, largely brought about by unification and the strains of European integration and Anglo-U.S. deregulatory policy styles, it is a model worthy of comparative analysis.

A second area of comparative interest is Germany's evolution of the principle of democratization and participation in a collectivist democracy. In many developed states, one thinks of democracy in the sense of individual rights, often taking the form of a series of individual choices, much as a consumer would choose to buy one product or another in a supermarket. Germany, on the other hand, has seen the evolution of a different model that, although it sometimes underplays a more individualistic democracy, does offer insights for participation and representation in a complex society. German democracy has emphasized participation within different groups. In other words, it has stressed the role of the individual not as a consumer in isolation from the rest of society, but as a citizen in a wider set of communities, organizations, and parties that must find ways of cooperating if the nation-state is to maintain its democracy. It is clearly within this complex of political actors that Germany is wrestling with its treatment of different groups within the Federal Republic.

Third, Germany offers insights concerning the question of tolerance and respect for civil rights for ethnic minorities. Can Germany's group-oriented democratic practices open up to include the opportunity for former *Gastarbeiter*, apparently now to become German citizens, to participate and make a meaningful and significant contribution to German democracy? Can ethnic tensions be resolved in a way that enhances democracy rather than undermines it? Clearly, collective identities of Germans and non-Germans alike offer both powerful obstacles and large opportunities to address one of the most crucial noneconomic issues that Germany faces in the twenty-first century.

Fourth, can Germany really remake its political culture in the wake of the Nazi past? Many hoped so for the first fifty years of the FRG, but now some are less certain. To what extent have the educational system, the civil service, and the media addressed the Nazi past? To what extent do they bear some responsibility for the persistence of right-wing violence throughout Germany? Have the reforms in the educational system since the 1960s provided a spirit of critical discourse in the broad mainstream of society that can withstand the rise of right-wing intolerance? Can judges effectively sentence those who abuse the civil rights of ethnic minorities? Will the news media continue to express a wide range of opinion and contribute to a healthy civic discourse? Or will strident, tabloid-style journalism crowd out the more reasoned discourse that any democracy must have to survive and flourish?

Fifth, what is the role of a middle-rank power as a potential leader of a regional world bloc of some 400 million people? To some extent, Japan also faces this issue, as it too struggles to take on political responsibilities commensurate with its economic successes. Into the new century Germany not only faces intense pressures from within its borders, such as conflict among ethnic groups, but also from a complex mix of external influences. Germany's role as both a Western European and an Eastern European power pull at the country in different ways. Should the country emphasize the Western-oriented EU and build a solid foundation with its traditional postwar allies? Or should it turn eastward to step into the vacuum created by the demise and fragmentation of the former Soviet Union? Can it do both? Can Germany's twentieth-century history allow either its Western or Eastern neighbors to let it begin to play the geopolitical role that its low-profile postwar political status has only postponed?[6] To some extent the "political cover" of the EU will allow Germany to do more as the leading country in a powerful international organization than it ever could as a sovereign nation-state with its unique twentieth-century political baggage.

Finally, Germany's historical importance on the world political stage during the past 150 years means that understanding its transition is essential for comparative purposes. It was late to achieve political unity and late to industrialize. These two factors eventually helped produce a catastrophic first half of the twentieth century for both Germany and the rest of the world. Yet the country's transition to a successful developed economy with an apparently solid democratic political system would seem to suggest that other countries, as they attempt to achieve economic growth and develop a political democracy, particularly in the Third World, may be able to look at the successes and failures of countries such as Germany.

Notes

1. Robert Rohrschneider, *Learning Democracy: Democratic and Economic Values in Unified Germany* (New York: Oxford University Press, 1999).

2. Gabriel A. Almond and Sidney Verba, eds., *The Civic Culture Revisited* (Newbury Park, Calif.: Sage, 1989).

3. Lowell Turner, *Democracy at Work: Changing World Markets and the Future of Labor Unions* (Ithaca, N.Y.: Cornell University Press, 1991).

4. Bruce Nussbaum, *The World After Oil* (New York: Simon & Schuster, 1983); and Michael Moran, "A State of Inaction: The State and Stock Exchange

Reform in the Federal Republic of Germany," in Simon Bulmer, ed., *The Changing Agenda of West German Public Policy* (Brookfield, Vt.: Gower, 1989), pp. 110–127.

5. Peter Neckermann, "What Went Wrong in Germany After the Unification?" *East European Quarterly* 26, no. 4 (1992): 447–470.

6. Peter J. Katzenstein, ed., *Tamed Power: Germany in Europe* (Ithaca, N.Y.: Cornell University Press, 1997).

Bibliography

Allen, Christopher S., ed. *Transformation of the German Political Party System: Institutional Crisis or Democratic Renewal?* New York: Berghahn, 1999.

Berger, Stefan. *The British Labour Party and the German Social Democrats: 1900–1931.* Oxford: Oxford University Press, 1994.

Braunthal, Gerard. *The Federation of German Industry in Politics.* Ithaca, N.Y.: Cornell University Press, 1965.

———. *The German Social Democrats Since 1969: A Party in Power and Opposition.* 2d ed. Boulder, Colo.: Westview Press, 1994.

———. *Parties and Politics in Modern Germany.* Boulder, Colo.: Westview Press, 1996.

Craig, Gordon. *The Politics of the Prussian Army.* Oxford: Oxford University Press, 1955.

Dahrendorf, Ralf. *Society and Democracy in Germany.* Garden City, N.Y.: Anchor, 1969.

Eley, Geoff. *Reshaping the German Right: Radical Nationalism and Political Change After Bismarck.* New Haven, Conn.: Yale University Press, 1980.

Evans, Peter B.; Rueschemeyer, Dietrich; and Skocpol, Theda. *Bringing the State Back In.* Cambridge: Cambridge University Press, 1985.

Gerschenkron, Alexander. *Bread and Democracy in Germany.* 2d ed. Ithaca, N.Y.: Cornell University Press, 1989.

Hager, Carol. "Environmentalism and Democracy in the Two Germanies." *German Politics* 1, no. 1 (April 1992): 95–118.

Hesse, Joachim Jens. "The Federal Republic of Germany: From Cooperative Federalism to Joint Policy-Making." *West European Politics* 10, no. 4 (October 1987): 70–87.

Hirschman, Albert O. *Exit, Voice, and Loyalty.* New Haven, Conn.: Yale University Press, 1970.

Inglehart, Ronald. *Culture Shift in Advanced Industrial Society.* Princeton, N.J.: Princeton University Press, 1990.

Jacoby, Wade. *Imitation and Politics: Redesigning, Modern Germany.* Ithaca, N.Y.: Cornell University Press, 2000.

Katzenstein, Peter J. *Policy and Politics in West Germany: The Growth of a Semi-Sovereign State.* Philadelphia: Temple University Press, 1987.

———. *Tamed Power: Germany in Europe.* Ithaca, N.Y.: Cornell University Press, 1997.

Kemp, Tom. *Industrialization in Nineteenth Century Europe.* 2d ed. London: Longman, 1985.

Markovits, Andrei S. "Political Parties in Germany: Agents of Stability in a Sea of Change." *Social Education* 57, no. 5 (September 1993): 239–243.

Moore, Barrington. *Social Origins of Dictatorship and Democracy.* Boston: Beacon Press, 1965.

Piore, Michael, and Sabel, Charles. *The Second Industrial Divide.* New York: Basic Books, 1984.

Rein, Taagepera, and Shugart, Matthew Soberg. *Seats and Votes: The Effects and Determinants of Electoral Systems.* New Haven, Conn.: Yale University Press, 1989.

Rueschemeyer, Dietrich; Stephens, Evelyn Huber; and Stephens, John D. *Capitalist Development and Democracy.* Chicago: University of Chicago Press, 1992.

Rusciano, Frank Louis. "Rethinking the Gender Gap: The Case of West German Elections." *Comparative Politics* 243 (April 1992): 335–358.

Schmidt, Manfred G. "West Germany: The Politics of the Middle Way." *Journal of Public Policy* 7, no. 2 (1987): 135–177.

Schmitter, Philippe C., and Lembruch, Gerhard, eds. *Trends Toward Corporatist Intermediation.* Beverly Hills, Calif.: Sage, 1979.

Shirer, William. *The Rise and Fall of the Third Reich.* New York: Simon & Schuster, 1960.

Tilly, Charles, ed. *The Formation of National States in Western Europe.* Princeton, N.J.: Princeton University Press, 1975.

Thelen, Kathleen. *A Union of Parts.* Ithaca, N.Y.: Cornell University Press, 1992.

Wever, Kirsten S. *Negotiating Competitiveness: Employment Relations and Industrial Adjustment in the U.S. and Germany.* Boston: Harvard Business School Press, 1995.

Web Sites

American Institute for Contemporary German Studies, Johns Hopkins University, *www.aicgs.org.*

German Embassy, German Information Center, *www.germany-info.org/sf_index.html.*

German Studies Web, Western European Studies Section, w*ww.dartmouth.edu/~wess/.*

German News (in English), 1995–present, *www.mathematik.uni-ulm.de/de-news/.*

Max-Planck Institute for the Study of Societies, Cologne, *www.mpi-fg-koeln.mpg.de/inhalt/ index_ e.html.*

WZB, Social Science Research Center, Berlin, *www.wz-berlin.de/default.en.asp.*

PART

VI

Italy

Stephen Hellman

C H A P T E R

21

The Emergence of the
Modern Italian State

Italian Politics in Action

From the late 1940s until the 1990s, Italian politics appeared hopelessly blocked. The same parties, dominated by the Christian Democrats (DC), won every election between 1948 and 1992. From the 1980s on, their most important coalition partner, the Socialist Party (PSI), tried to crowd the DC off center stage, but at the end of the day, these warring allies, joined by two or three minor coalition partners, formed yet another government, under yet another DC prime minister, and effectively did as they pleased. Between 1947 and 1992, Italy had over fifty governments, but only a handful departed from the established pattern of constant turnover and, beginning in the 1980s, increasingly tawdry struggles for power.

And then with stunning speed, the entire party system, starting with those whose grip on power had seemed most permanent, disintegrated. A party that did not even exist a year earlier won elections in 1994 and became the largest party in the country. Its leader, Italy's richest man, a flashy entrepreneur named Silvio Berlusconi, owner of Italy's largest private TV networks as well as its largest advertising agency, became prime minister of a Center-Right coalition. The neofascist party, which had been a political outcast for nearly fifty years, not only became the third largest party in the country but held several ministries in Berlusconi's cabinet.

Berlusconi's government lasted barely seven months. Following an interim government, new elections were held in 1996, and a Center-Left coalition, called the Olive Tree (Ulivo), won a narrow victory, dramatically altering the political landscape for the second time in two years. This was the first time in the republic's history that the alternation of government and opposition had taken place. In yet another dramatic first, the largest party in the Ulivo—and Italy—was the Democratic Party of the Left (PDS), heir to the Italian Communist Party (PCI), systematically excluded from power since 1947. By 1998, its leader, Massimo D'Alema, was prime minister. He was the first former communist to lead the government of a Western power.

The collapse was astonishing. When Parliament was dissolved for the 1994 elections, a fifth of its members were under investigation or indictment. Corruption was so rampant that commentators referred to *Tangentopoli* ("Bribesville"), and the country's leaders were met everywhere by jeering crowds who pelted them with coins. The once-invincible DC, in a last-ditch effort to maintain credibility, renamed itself the Popular Party (PPI), its original title seventy years earlier. By the watershed 1994 elections, the PPI tried to run independent of the large Left and Right blocs and plunged to 11 percent of the vote. The PSI fared even worse; from around 15 percent in the early 1990s, it fell to 2 percent in 1994 and then dissolved into

Italy

mini-groups that dispersed across the political spectrum.

Italian politics is truly in transition. In less than a decade, Italy has gone from what many observers called a "blocked democracy" to a state of extraordinary political fluidity. In the past, increasingly referred to as the "First Republic," critics used to assume that if only the opposition were not dominated by a communist

party, the ruling Christian Democrats would be forced to change, since they would then face the very real threat of being thrown out of office. A clear bipolarity would be allowed to emerge and, with it, the possibility for parties to alternate with one another between government and opposition. These wishes have finally been granted, and although both bipolarity and alternation have in fact emerged, things have not gone quite as smoothly, or predictably, as many experts assumed. Profound changes are underway, but the transition to a Second Republic is proving far more complicated and arduous than expected.

Geographic Setting

Its distinctive boot shape may give Italy the most immediately recognizable outline of any country in the world. Jutting into the Mediterranean, with 4,750 miles (7,600 kilometers) of coastline, it has been a strategic crossroads almost since humans began traveling, and conquering each other, for it dominates the central Mediterranean as well as the southern approaches into western and south-central Europe.[1] Phoenicians, Greeks, Normans, North Africans, Spaniards, and, more recently, Austrians, French, and Germans have all conquered or occupied areas they considered essential.

Except for the flat, fertile Po Valley, Italy is extremely mountainous. Europe's largest mountain range, the Alps, runs across the entire north of the country, and half of all the Alps are found in Italy. The rugged Apennines run down the rest of the boot, and smaller ranges cover most of the rest of the land. The Po is the only navigable river of any significance. Italy has been poorly endowed with the natural resources most central to the age of heavy industry such as coal, iron, oil, and natural gas.

These physical characteristics have profoundly marked Italy's history and evolution. Italy is the most marginally located of the largest European countries. And this marginality was reinforced by the lack of resources that delayed the country's industrialization. Italy was both a late industrializer and, in West European terms, a latecomer to the family of nation-states. Because its weakness and strategic location had made it easy prey for more powerful neighbors, it remained carved up until 1870. Not surprisingly, the newly unified state was marked by extreme regional differences that

reflected centuries of different political, social, and cultural legacies. Italy's rugged terrain also helped reinforce regional and local differences until well into the twentieth century, when a modern rail and highway system, and, above all, radio and television, finally unified the country culturally and linguistically.

With nearly 58 million inhabitants, Italy has roughly the same population as the United Kingdom and France; its territory is a bit larger than that of the United Kingdom and about the same bit smaller than Germany (France is nearly twice the size of Italy). The populations of all these countries are rapidly aging, and deaths are now outstripping births; Italy and Spain have recently been neck-and-neck for the lowest birthrate in the world. These trends, evident in all advanced capitalist countries, lend a sense of urgency to the need to confront questions of pensions and welfare state restructuring, as well as immigration.

To be sure, Italy's location gives it continuing strategic importance. Even today, some major U.S. air bases are located in the northeast, and the U.S. Sixth Fleet has its home in Naples. Even with the end of the cold war, this has meant that Italy remains a vital staging area for the United States and the North Atlantic Treaty Organization (NATO), as military operations in the Balkans in the late 1990s demonstrated. During NATO's campaign against Yugoslavia in 1999, numerous air attacks were launched from bases in the northeast of Italy, to the consternation of many of the Center-Left government's allies of the time.

Critical Junctures

The discussion of Italy's strategic location should remind us how prominently this country has figured in the history of Western civilization. The Romans established an advanced urban society and conquered most of the known world two thousand years ago. Their direct and indirect impact on the rest of Europe was profound, most apparently in the Latin-based languages spoken where their presence was most significant, but also in the codified legal system, which the Romans invented. Christianity spread rapidly into the Continent after becoming the religion of the emperor and became the most powerful force shaping medieval Europe. Fiercely independent city-states in the north-center left important commercial and exploratory legacies, as well as establishing early democratic traditions.

But the rise of the nation-state found Italy lagging behind most of its neighbors. Precisely because of its historical importance and strategic location, the country had been fought over and carved up by successive waves of emerging powers. By the nationalist era of the nineteenth century, the glorious past served mainly as a unifying myth to patriots who chafed under rulers who were either foreign or, as in the case of the Papal States, considered backward and illegitimate by large segments of educated opinion. It is significant that the nationalists called their movement the *Risorgimento*, for this means "resurgence."

The Risorgimento and Liberal Italy (1848–1922)

In the mid-1800s, *Italy* expressed a nationalistic dream rather than a sovereign nation. The North was divided between the Kingdom of Sardinia under the Savoy monarchy (Piedmont and Liguria) and the Austrian-controlled northeast (Lombardy and Venetia). In the north-center, numerous small duchies and principalities led an uneasy existence. Across the entire middle of the boot, dominating most of central Italy, were the Papal States. Just south of Rome, embracing southern Italy and Sicily, was the Kingdom of the Two Sicilies, ruled by descendants of the Spanish Bourbons. This arch-conservative realm remained secure because, as a ruler once put it, it was surrounded "by salt water on three sides and holy water on the fourth."[2]

The Risorgimento finally triumphed in the second half of the 1800s. The king of Piedmont, Victor Emmanuel II, and his skilled prime minister, Camillo Cavour, attracted middle- and upper-class moderate nationalists with their enlightened liberalism. Italy was thus created by extending Piedmontese hegemony over the entire boot.

Outside intervention determined the unification of the peninsula. Austria's defeat by France forced the Habsburgs to cede part of the north to Victor Emmanuel II in 1859. In exchange, Piedmont gave Nice and Savoy to France. Eager to strike a deal with the fledgling Italian state, the French tolerated Piedmont's annexation of some of the territory of the Papal States, despite earlier promises to defend the pope.

The most colorful figure of the Risorgimento, Giuseppe Garibaldi landed in Sicily with 1,000 red-shirted volunteers and swept northward, inspiring the hopes of democrats and republicans—and the fears of the Piedmontese that he might actually carry out land reform. Cavour outmaneuvered Garibaldi militarily and politically. His army rushed south, annexing most of the Papal States (avoiding Rome with its French garrison). Plebiscites were quickly organized to join the newly liberated south to Victor Emmanuel's regime.

A parliament, elected by very limited suffrage, proclaimed the Kingdom of Italy in March 1861. Victor Emmanuel II of Savoy was its first monarch. No new constitution was drawn up: Piedmont's 1848 *Statuto albertino* (named for King Charles Albert of Piedmont, Victor Emmanuel II's father) was extended over the whole country. It was an enlightened document but a far cry from the more democratic republican constitutions of 1848, allowing extensive powers to remain in the king's hands.

The remainder of modern Italy's territory (save for Trento and Trieste, obtained at the end of World War I) was annexed thanks to Prussian military victories over Austria (1866) and France (1870), as the map of the unification of Italy shows. After the French withdrew from

The Unification of Italy, 1859–1870

Legend:
- Area unified in 1859
- Added in 1860
- Added in 1866
- Added in 1870

SWITZERLAND

AUSTRIA

SAVOY

Ceded to France in 1860

PIEDMONT

LOMBARDY

Milan

PARMA

MODENA

VENETIA

Venice

NICE

Nice

TUSCANY

PAPAL STATES

Rome

Adriatic Sea

OTTOMAN EMPIRE

Corsica (France)

SARDINIA

Naples

KINGDOM OF THE TWO SICILIES

Tyrrhenian Sea

MEDITERRANEAN SEA

Sicily

0   100 Miles

0   100 Kilometers

Rome, Italian troops seized Italy's historic capital. The defeat of the Church, and the seizure of almost all its territory, guaranteed problematic church-state relations, for the pope refused to recognize the new state.

Because of its narrow, and privileged, bases of support, the Risorgimento left basic social and political problems untouched. Italy's largest social group, the peasantry, was excluded from the independence movement and was then ignored by the new state. And the new country's leaders were in no hurry to extend democratic participation in a society with 60 to 80 percent illiteracy rates.

Economy and Social Relations. Italy's rulers consistently preserved existing property relations. Northern elites guaranteed the loyalty of southern landlords by repressing restive peasants and introducing tariffs to protect inefficiently grown southern crops. But they otherwise pursued laissez-faire industrial policies, serving their own interests while devastating struggling new firms in the less developed parts of the country.

By the mid-1870s, the drawbacks of limited state intervention in a country with so much economic ground to make up made Germany's impressive advances appear to be a more appropriate model for a new state to follow. In the course of the 1880s, a new economic policy evolved: taxes were lightened, tariff barriers were erected, and the state became more active in the economy.

Italy was an overwhelmingly agricultural country well into the twentieth century.[3] Only in 1930 did industrial output finally exceed that of agriculture, and not until the 1950s did industrial employees outnumber those in agriculture. This slow growth produced staggering emigration in the first half-century following unification. In peak years, over half a million people left Italy (800,000 emigrated in 1913), mostly for the United States and South America. Massive emigration affected the entire country, but it was greatest in the south. The outflow of so many young, able-bodied people distorted the population profile. But the drastic reduction of the workforce served as a social safety valve and was welcomed by both local and national leaders, who had good reason to fear the often brutal class warfare that periodically erupted in the countryside.

In 1906, trade unionists founded the CGL (General Labor Confederation). The CGL took a pro-worker stance but avoided direct affiliation with any one party. It only flourished after World War I, when its membership leaped to more than 1 million in 1919 and to 2.2 million in 1920. It then declined rapidly amid capitalist retrenchment and economic crisis.[4] A year later the Fascists came to power, and, with union-busting a top priority, the CGL was soon abolished.

Italy in the World of States Through World War I. Italy's location, late entry into the community of nations, and slow development made it a marginal European actor. When World War I broke out, Italy remained neutral, consistent with its policies over the previous fifteen years. Yet within a year, a secret agreement was signed with the Allies: in exchange for declaring war on Austria, Italian claims to Trento and Trieste would be secured at war's end. In May 1915, in a move that pleased only hard-core nationalists, Italy entered the war; a declaration against Germany came a year later. Although the Italian front was secondary by the standards of 1914–1918, it visited all the horrors of trench warfare on the millions (mostly peasants) who were conscripted and the approximately 600,000 who died.

The war extended Italy's border to the Brenner Pass in the north and to Trieste and Istria on the Adriatic. When more ambitious claims were not satisfied, the Italians abandoned the peace talks, which helped legitimize the extreme Right. Wars expose the weaknesses of the countries that wage them and are especially hard on losers. It is indicative of Liberal Italy's rickety underpinnings that although the regime emerged from the slaughter of World War I on the winning side, its days were numbered.

Liberal Italy's Political Contradictions. The Liberal regime collapsed because it lacked both the culture and the institutions that could attract mass support or regulate modern class conflict. Such mechanisms are never easy to develop, but the Liberal system barely recognized the demands of the emerging social classes as legitimate. The Statuto albertino made Roman Catholicism the official state religion, but the Vatican rejected all overtures and forbade believers to take part in politics. As an additional complication, Victor Emmanuel II's successors were, to put it bluntly, not very bright.

Trasformismo. *Trasformismo* refers to building a majority in Parliament by winning over enough deputies, irrespective of political affiliation, by whatever means prove most effective. What is ultimately "transformed" is the very meaning of the differences between parties, groups, and traditional ideologies. If the opposition is absorbed into the government itself, so much the better. This backward, corrupt system of representation explains why the ruling elite was in no hurry to extend the franchise. *Trasformismo* enabled the ruling Liberal Party (PLI) to rely on local power brokers rather than attempt to build modern parties or strengthen civil society.

"Liberal" Italy was unworthy of the name. The polarized mass politics that followed World War I put the finishing touches on the old system of local power and also demonstrated the flimsy commitment to democracy of vast segments of the PLI. War's end accelerated demands for change: in the 1919 general elections Italy's two mass parties, the PSI and the Catholic Popular Party (PPI), won more than half the votes cast. The PSI then swept to victory in more than 2,000 municipalities, depriving the ruling parties of their power bases.[5]

Then in 1920, widespread occupations of factories by workers struck profound fear in the hearts of the industrialists and the urban middle class. Frightened bourgeois looked to the extreme Right when they felt the state could no longer keep peasants and workers in line. In other words, the classes that supported the original post-Risorgimento coalition grew increasingly distant from what was supposed to be their own regime. Armed Fascist squads created reigns of terror in the countryside of Italy's central regions and then openly attacked the unions and the PSI in the cities of the North. This open violence was tolerated by the regime.

The Roman Question. The Church fiercely opposed liberalism for doctrinal reasons, but it also resented its loss of control over one-seventh of Italy's territory and population. In 1874, Pope Pius IX explicitly forbade Catholics from participating in the politics of the new state in his *non expedit* (noncooperation) decree. But practical considerations, and a less intransigent pope, saw the openly Catholic PPI able to win slightly more than 20 percent of the vote by 1919. The PPI—the name chosen again in the 1990s as the DC scrambled to salvage its credi-

bility—was socially and ideologically heterogeneous, and its left wing made the Vatican extremely uncomfortable. The Vatican's weak commitment to the Popular Party and democracy was revealed as soon as Mussolini, upon taking power, showed a willingness to compromise with the Church and extend it financial aid. Pope Pius XI eventually abandoned the PPI in 1924 when a pro-Fascist group seceded and formed its own Catholic party.[6]

Fascism (1922–1945)

Liberal indifference to democracy and postwar fears of social disruption or even revolution provided fertile terrain for the Fascist movement. The Socialists did not help matters by using inflammatory rhetoric while behaving rather moderately. Benito Mussolini, a charismatic ex-Socialist, built up a quasi-military party organization that both preached and practiced violence. Within a few years, his denunciations of Italy's "betrayal" after World War I, his open contempt for democracy, and his willingness to attack the Left head-on had won him widespread support on the Right and, more important, among masses of urban and rural property holders who had grown impatient with Liberal Italy's inability to adjust to the era of mass politics.

The Liberal system's fate was sealed when it handed power over to Mussolini following the March on Rome in October 1922. This march was a successful act of intimidation. Tens of thousands of armed Fascist "Blackshirts" (the militia's uniform) paraded through the capital, and King Victor Emmanuel III asked Mussolini to form the next government. With only 32 of 530 seats in Parliament, the Fascist Party (PNF) received support from the entire political spectrum (including the PPI), with the exception of the Left.[7] The Liberals and their allies thought they could restrain Mussolini, but they were wrong. Intimidation and widespread brutality made the elections of 1924 semi-free at best and gave the Fascists a huge majority. In 1926, following the murder of Socialist leader Giacomo Matteotti by Fascist thugs, a dictatorship was in place. Opposition parties were banned, the independent press was closed or brought to heel, and political opponents—mainly Socialists and Communists—were jailed or forced into exile.

As a movement, Italian fascism combined diverse and often contradictory elements, but complexity and inconsistency help explain its broad appeal. Mussolini was openly contemptuous of the old political system; more important, he convinced people he would act decisively—especially to make sure that the Left and the trade unions would be firmly put in their place. Denouncing the "decadence" of democracy, fascism claimed it would reclaim Italy's rightful place in the world as a great power and constantly invoked the glory of the Romans. (*Fasces*, a Roman symbol of power and authority, are a bound bundle or sheaf of rods symbolizing strength in unity.)

Italy's Fascist regime was the first of its kind, although similar movements quickly sprang up in Europe in the 1920s and 1930s. Italian fascism had a particularly aggressive foreign policy and ultimately was allied with Nazi Germany and Imperial Japan in World War II. But Italy's militaristic adventures began earlier. Italy's conquest of Ethiopia in 1936 led to its condemnation by the League of Nations—and embrace by Hitler. When the military and the Right attacked the elected Spanish Republican government in 1936, Mussolini and Hitler joined the rebels in the Spanish Civil War, which lasted three years and has been called the dress rehearsal for World War II. As Italy and Germany drew closer together, Mussolini passed anti-Semitic racial laws in 1938 stripping Jews of their rights and property. Finally, and most important, the wartime alliance with Hitler disgraced Italy and brought suffering and devastation to millions.

A generation of dictatorship that ends in disgrace and defeat does nothing to legitimize the state or nurture democratic traditions. Italy's legal and administrative apparatus, centralized

Coadiuvato

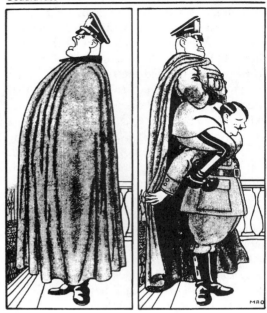

"Look at me, I'm a giant." Mussolini's reliance on Hitler is mocked in a 1939 cartoon.

Source: From Niciolo Zapponi, *Il fascismo nella caricatura* (Bari: Laterza, 1981).

and autocratic under the Statuto albertino, emerged from fascism with its oppressive aspects accentuated. To cite two key examples, the educational system was completely restructured under fascism, and the criminal code was rewritten. Both reforms were intended to remold Italy into a totalitarian society. When a democratic regime emerged following World War II, it inherited these structures—and the personnel who had administered the Fascist state for over twenty years.

Political Trade-Offs. We must always distinguish between a regime's claims and its accomplishments. Fascism's ambitions were openly totalitarian: Society was to be regimented from top to bottom. Mussolini, called *il Duce,* or

"Leader"—the living embodiment of all Fascist virtues—was at the very top of the pyramid. Citizens were to be made over in a new image: tough and uncorrupted by the materialistic softness represented by liberal democracy (or capitalism, for the really radical Fascists).

In practice, Mussolini was more maneuverer than dedicated ideologue. As a result, most of Italy's deep structural and institutional problems continued under the dictatorship; for example, the regular army personally swore allegiance to the king, who remained head of state. This was not an abstract consideration, for the monarch and his officers deposed Mussolini in 1943 after the Allies liberated Sicily and then invaded the peninsula. On another level, Mussolini inherited a top-heavy state structure and centralized it even further. At the same time, local party officials often ran personal fiefs, and il Duce tolerated this as long as these leaders did not grow overly ambitious or directly challenge his popularity.

Another trade-off was the Lateran Pacts, a series of three separate agreements between Church and state signed in 1929 that formalized the Church's privileged position in Italy. The first was a treaty recognizing the Vatican as a sovereign city-state headed by the pope. The second, and most important, was the Concordat, which made Roman Catholicism the official state religion of Italy, thus entitling the Church to special social and legal privileges, above all control over the compulsory weekly hour of religious teaching in Italy's public schools. The third part of the pacts was a large indemnity paid to the Vatican for property seized during the Risorgimento.

In return, the Fascist state obtained the recognition of the ecclesiastical authorities, which meant praise from thousands of pulpits every Sunday. The Vatican's approval of specific policies helped generate enthusiastic support for the regime and some of Mussolini's more questionable adventures. Pope Pius XI and most of the Church hierarchy applauded the conquest of Ethiopia when world opinion (save for the Na-zis) condemned Fascist aggression, which took on overtly racist tones and included such barbarities as the use of poison gas. The pope also supported Mussolini's intervention on the side of Franco in the Spanish Civil War, calling it a crusade against communism. And the Vatican was silent about the 1938 racial laws.

Governing the Economy Under Fascism. Fascism extolled the virtues of small producers in agriculture and industry but pursued policies that favored large firms. The Great Depression and League of Nations sanctions finally ended the fiction of a hands-off policy. By the late 1930s, Mussolini took protectionism to its logical conclusion: autarky, or complete economic self-sufficiency. He intended to carry on with his militaristic foreign policy, which required the arms that only a heavy industrial sector could provide. If other countries were going to try to dictate policy to him, he would show that Italy could go it alone.

Given Italy's shortages of key raw materials, these decisions forced more state involvement in economic affairs, especially as the Great Depression took hold. The Institute for Industrial Reconstruction (IRI) was created in 1933 as a holding company for bank stocks that the state had been forced to buy to avoid their bankruptcy. As more companies failed, the state continued to buy them up. Rome thus became increasingly involved in the ownership, and eventually the management and restructuring, of these firms. In 1937, IRI became a permanent holding company geared to furthering the policies of rearmament and autarky. By 1940, about one-fifth of all capital assets in all joint stock corporations in Italy were in IRI's hands, and important sectors of the economy, such as iron, steel, shipbuilding, and banking, were effectively monopolized by the state.

The Politics of Collective Identity Under Fascism. Italy lacked a strong sense of national identity before Mussolini came to power, and his efforts to create this help explain some of the broad support he received. Moreover, before Italian nationalism took such a belligerent turn, this really was the first time Italians from every region of the country genuinely felt they were part of the same nation. But Italy did become extremely belligerent. The Roman Catholic Church, while hardly responsible for these developments, reinforced the regime's aggressive nationalism with its overt shows of support, or with its silences. Thanks to this legacy, nationalism remained suspect throughout the postwar period.

Fascism's End and the Republic's Birth (1945–1948)

By deposing Mussolini and coming to terms with the Allies, Victor Emmanuel III hoped to spare Italy further suffering and salvage the monarchy in the bargain. But it took so long for the new monarchist government to declare war on Germany that neither goal was accomplished. Anticipating Italy's turnaround, the Nazis rushed in, set Mussolini up in a puppet regime in the north, and dug in along most of the length of the peninsula. The war ended only two weeks before Germany's final surrender.

The declaration of war did legitimize the Resistance against the Nazis and their Fascist allies. In areas under Nazi and Fascist control, the Resistance was a brutal conflict with overtones of civil war. Its symbolic importance for the country, especially for the Communists and the Left in general, cannot be stressed enough. Because of the prominent role of the Left, particularly the rapidly growing Communists, the Resistance helped salvage national pride and honor and legitimized the Left as democratic and patriotic.

The war reinforced historic north-south divisions. The south, also called the Mezzogiorno (noon, in an obvious reference to sunshine), was spared the worst of the conflict, as well as the brutal German occupation and the unifying liberation struggle. It was thus once more cut off

from any direct role in some of Italy's most significant moments. This estrangement was apparent in the 1946 referendum to abolish the monarchy. The rest of the country could not forgive the king's role in supporting fascism and voted solidly for a republic, while the Mezzogiorno opted for the monarchy, making the overall vote quite close (53 percent to 47 percent).

The parties of the Committee of National Liberation (CLN) agreed that Italy should be a republic but were deeply divided over almost everything else. Unity against a foreign invader and a thoroughly discredited fascism was one thing; unity in favor of new institutions and policies was quite another. In the brief period (1946–1947) before the full onset of the cold war, a fragile, tense unity produced a constitution that reflected the few points of agreement and the many divisions of its writers. Remarkably, the rules of the game that emerged from this compromise lasted into the 1990s.

At war's end, the Communists and Socialists were close allies. Together, they dominated the industrial north as well as the "red zones" of central Italy, where the Left has always been strongest. They also dominated the country's only trade union, the General Confederation of Italian Labor (CGIL). In the elections that accompanied the 1946 referendum, the Left won roughly 40 percent of the vote (see Table 21.1). The DC was the largest party but garnered only 35 percent of the vote. Its favored status in the eyes of both the Church and the United States, combined with a social base in the small-holding peasantry and urban middle classes, ensured that the DC would tolerate cooperation with the Communists and Socialists only as long as there was no alternative.

The 1946 vote, Italy's first exercise in truly universal suffrage, abolished the monarchy and elected, by proportional representation, a Constituent Assembly that was to serve as a temporary parliament and write a republican constitution within eighteen months. In 1947, as the constitutional exercise drew to a close, Christian

Table 21.1 Vote Obtained by Italian Parties in General Elections under Proportional Representation During the "First Republic," 1946–1992 (Percentage Obtained by Each Party List in the 1946 Constituent Assembly and in the Chamber of Deputies thereafter)

Party	1946	1948	1953	1958	1963	1968	1972	1976	1979	1983	1987	1992
Far Left[a]	—	—	—	—	—	4.5%	2.8%	1.5%	2.2%	1.5%	1.7%	5.6%
PCI/PDS	18.9%	31%[b]	22.6%	22.7%	25.3%	27.0%	27.2	34.4	30.4	29.9	26.6	16.1
PSI	20.7		12.7	14.3	13.9	14.5[c]	9.6	9.6	9.8	11.4	14.3	14.5
PR	—	—	—	—	—	—	—	1.1	3.5	2.2	2.6	1.2
Greens	—	—	—	—	—	—	—	—	—	—	2.5	3.0
PSDI	[d]	7.1	4.5	4.6	6.1	[d]	5.1	3.4	3.8	4.1	3.0	2.9
PRI	4.4	2.5	1.6	1.4	1.4	2.0	2.9	3.1	3.0	5.1	3.7	4.7
Leagues[e]	—	—	—	—	—	—	—	—	—	—	0.5	8.7
DC	35.2	48.5	40.1	42.4	38.3	39.1	38.7	38.7	38.3	32.9	34.3	29.7
PLI	6.8	3.8	3.0	3.6	7.0	5.8	3.9	1.3	1.9	2.9	2.1	3.0
Far Right[f]	8.1	4.8	12.8	9.6	6.9	5.8	8.7	6.1	5.9	6.8	5.9	5.4
Others	4.4	2.3	2.7	1.4	1.1	1.3	1.1	0.8	1.2	3.2	2.8	3.2
Total	**100.0**	**100.0**	**100.0**	**100.0**	**100.0**	**100.0**	**100.0**	**100.0**	**100.0**	**100.0**	**100.0**	**100.0**

[a] For 1964 and 1968, includes the PSIUP, which split from the PSI; from 1992, includes Rifondazione comunista, which split from the PCI-DS.
[b] Result of united PCI-PSI list (Democratic Popular Front).
[c] Result of united PSI-PSDI list (Unified Socialist Party).
[d] Social-Democrats were part of the PSI in 1946, split in 1947, then temporarily reunited with them 1966–1969.
[e] Lombard League until 1992; Northern League thereafter.
[f] Uomo Qualunque and monarchists in 1946; Neo-Fascists and monarchists until 1972; MSI (Neo-Fascists) until 1992; AN thereafter.

Key: DC = Christian Democracy; PCI = Italian Communist Party; PDS = Democratic Party of the Left; PSI = Italian Socialist Party; PSIUP = Socialist Party of Proletarian Unity; PR = Radical Party (until 1992; Pannella List thereafter); PSDI = Italian Social-Democratic Party; PRI = Italian Republican Party; PLI = Italian Liberal Party; MSI = Italian Social Movement; AN = National Alliance.

Source: For 1946 and 1948, Giuseppe Mammarella, *Italy After Fascism: A Political History 1943–1965* (Notre Dame, Ind.: University of Notre Dame Press, 1966), 116 and 194. Data since the 1953 elections compiled by author from newspapers.

Democrat prime minister Alcide De Gasperi ejected the Communists and the pro-PCI Socialists from the government. The Socialist Party had split over how close its relation to the PCI should be, and De Gasperi and the DC would eventually be able to count on the breakaway Social Democratic Party (PSDI) as a reliable, if small, coalition partner. With cold war tensions at their peak, the DC won a crushing victory in 1948; for the only time in the history of the republic, one party won an absolute majority of the seats and did nearly as well in the percentage of the vote (48.5 percent). In a climate of complete polarization, Italians flocked to the DC as the surest defense against communism, firmly setting the foundations of the postwar regime.

After a generation of il Duce, there was a strong consensus that the legislature, and not the executive, should be the supreme branch of government. The legacy of fascism, plus the multiplicity of parties—large and small—that collaborated at war's end ensured that Italy's electoral system would be a permissive form of proportional representation. (Until 1994, 1.5 percent of the vote usually guaranteed a party seats in Parliament.) From the beginning, a weak executive and fragmented party system produced unwieldy and unstable governing coalitions.

An especially sensitive constitutional issue was the place that the Catholic Church should formally occupy in postwar Italy. As the cold war increasingly divided East and West, the Communists made a conciliatory gesture to the DC, thus ensuring that Article 7 of the constitution included the Lateran Pacts. Notwithstanding this gesture, the PCI and PSI were soon in the opposition. Within a year, Pope Pius XII declared it a sin to uphold Marxist doctrine; by 1949 active Communists and Socialists were excommunicated. The country was ideologically polarized, with the Right and the Church on the offensive. In fact, the Church under Pius XII went well beyond the considerable powers granted by Article 7 in the spheres of education and marriage to involve itself directly in Italian politics for a generation. Only in the 1980s, under a Polish pope and a Socialist prime minister, was the Concordat finally revised.

The DC-Dominated Postwar Republic (1948–1994)

Most Western European democracies saw postwar settlements between capital and labor, but in Italy, as in France, Communist leadership of the workers' movement produced a policy of *labor exclusion*. This was less a settlement than a lopsided truce: The Left enjoyed political freedom and such influence as it could muster in the field of labor relations, with the tacit understanding that it was condemned to the role of permanent political opposition. This was better than its fate under fascism, but the Left had expected far more at war's end. It was clear by the late 1940s that the country would develop within the Western sphere of influence, within a more or less liberal-democratic institutional framework with little concern for the workers' principal representatives. In the 1970s, the workers' movement made great gains, and the PCI contributed decisively to the stabilization of Italian democracy, but even when the Communists rose to over a third of the vote in the mid-1970s and their support was needed in Parliament, they were still denied a full share of political power. By the 1980s, union and PCI influence was again reduced as the tide turned in favor of capital and the center of the political spectrum. Only the end of the cold war, massive scandals, and a total restructuring of the party system finally finished the DC-centered system of power in Italy and once more put the question of full governmental participation by a no-longer-communist Left on the agenda.

Variations on the Theme of Christian Democratic Dominance. From the expulsion of the

Left into the 1960s, the DC governed with the support of several small nonreligious parties of the Center-Left (Social Democrats and Republicans) or Right (Liberals). During this period, De Gasperi courageously resisted pressure from the Vatican and his own right wing to push Italy much further in the direction of a clerical, semi-authoritarian state. Despite the notable achievement of presiding over the beginnings of Italy's "Economic Miracle," these centrist coalitions barely commanded a majority (see Table 21.1). Parliamentary arithmetic and hopes of increasing working-class support pointed to bringing the PSI—which grew increasingly distant from the Communists in the 1950s—into the government. This finally occurred in the early 1960s, against considerable conservative resistance.

But the Socialists' alliance with the DC cost them votes and credibility, as a booming economy strengthened the unions' hand. Communist support grew steadily into the 1970s, and when the PCI reached its historic high of 34.4 percent in 1976, the DC was forced to make a number of concessions, including, for a time, accepting Communist votes in order to continue governing. The DC's sense of self-preservation, not to mention the unacceptability of formal Communist participation in a Western government, thwarted PCI secretary Enrico Berlinguer's more optimistic ambitions of a historic compromise between the PCI and DC. By the end of the 1970s, a frustrated PCI was back in the opposition, where it languished and steadily lost votes.

Socialist Party leader Bettino Craxi's aggressive strategy appeared to be paying off. When scandals weakened the DC, Craxi became prime minister in 1983, although his own party commanded barely 11 percent of the vote. His first government was the longest-lived of the entire postwar period, and he could boast important achievements, including the renegotiation of the Lateran Pacts in 1984. But his strategy was fatally flawed. His aggressive attacks on the PCI and the unions undermined Socialist credibility

as a party of the Left. At the same time, the DC-PSI partnership degenerated into a shameless, increasingly corrupt, struggle over political spoils.

Following its great victory in 1948, the DC leadership was eager to establish more independence from the party's major supporters: southern notables, the Church, private industry, and U.S. largesse. The leaders quickly found that they could use Italy's many public resources to build a patronage structure to solidify the party organization and serve as an independent source of funding and favors for the party faithful—beginning with members of one's own faction. These measures gave the DC the glue that held its heterogeneous constituencies together.

The groundwork was laid for what one writer aptly called the DC's "occupation of power."[8] This colonization of state and para-state apparatuses accelerated throughout the 1960s and 1970s. In periods of steady growth, the wasteful use of public resources could be overlooked. But these practices contributed immensely to Italy's huge public sector deficits and also set the stage for truly prodigious amounts of corruption.

Governing the Postwar Economy Through the 1970s. Chapter 22 addresses this topic in depth, but it is important here to understand the social and political foundations of Italy's postwar development. *Labor exclusion*, in cold war conditions, meant that the unions were not only weak but also politically divided. The CGIL's left-wing identity doomed its fragile unity once the Left was expelled from the government. Catholics eventually founded the Italian Confederation of Free Trade Unions (CISL), which remained closely tied to the DC. A year later, Social Democrats and Republicans exited the CGIL to form the Italian Labor Union (UIL), the smallest of the major confederations. By 1950, the partisan divisions that would keep the unions divided, and thus reinforce their weakness, were in place.

Although the 1960s began with much fanfare

and hopes that workers would finally obtain a more equitable share of the country's growing wealth under the new Center-Left coalition, its innovative period was brief. It was not the workers' representatives in Parliament who improved their lot but their militancy on the shop floor and in the streets.

The term *Hot Autumn* is commonly applied to the struggles that convulsed Italian society from 1968 through 1970. The period began with a mass-based students' movement and then spread to the factories. The workers knew better than anyone else that what was referred to as Italy's "Economic Miracle" had been built on low wages and scanty social services, and they rapidly set about redressing historic imbalances now that nearly full employment gave them a powerful bargaining position. Divided and demoralized employers were forced to make concessions that drove up production costs and quickly compromised Italy's competitiveness in export markets. Weak governments granted most of the workers' demands, and then made costly commitments to the self-employed and other middle-class categories to guarantee their continuing support. The Italian welfare state mushroomed. The price of this politically motivated generosity soon would be evident in Italy's distressed public finances, a legacy that lingered through the 1990s and threatened the country's membership in the emerging new Europe.

The Politics of Collective Identity. As social mobilization and gains for the Left continued, it appeared as if democracy itself might be compromised. Terrorists from both the extreme Right and Left tried to destabilize the political system and provoke either a coup (Right) or a revolution (Left). Although they failed miserably in their broader goals, these groups shook the country to its foundations throughout the 1970s and into the 1980s.

Terrorism was the most extreme, and distorted, symptom of the profound changes that Italian society was undergoing and that its deadlocked political system was demonstrably unable to resolve. Workers, students, and women were erupting onto the political stage, sweeping aside entrenched but increasingly out-of-date values and practices. Nowhere is this more evident than in the 1974 referendum to repeal Italy's new divorce law. The referendum failed by a 40-to-60 margin, a gap that shocked everyone. The Church, claiming to speak for the mass of Italians, was humiliated. The DC was stunned. (A 1981 referendum on abortion produced an even more lopsided defeat for the Church.)

1994–The Present: Toward a Second Republic?

There was no love lost between the DC and PSI, but their hold on the reins of power appeared secure through the 1980s. Yet within a few years, the collapse of communism set in motion a chain of events that found them fighting for their very survival—and losing. What accounts for this apparently sudden turnaround in the fortunes of the old system of power?

In one sense the turnaround really was not so sudden; the 1980s had contained important warning signs that the old system of power was in trouble. In the broadest sense, however, the answer can be found in the four themes that inform the organization of this book. *The world of states* impinged most directly on Italian events at the end of the 1980s. The first, and most obvious, factor was the collapse of communism. Within days of the fall of the Berlin Wall, the largest communist party in the Western world announced that it was dissolving itself to become an entirely new political formation. Despite a troubled start, the PCI's transformation into the PDS set powerful forces in motion. The removal of the anticommunist alibi undermined the DC's claim to be Italy's perennial governing party. And it certainly encouraged prosecutors to pursue corruption in governing circles with far more purpose, and courage, than they had in the past.

The other way in which Italy's international placement had a direct impact on the course of events overlapped with the theme of *governing the economy*. Precisely as the DC-PSI rivalry intensified, with an increase in Italy's already-profligate public spending habits, the global and European tide decisively shifted in the opposite direction. As the move toward more Europe integration gained momentum, Italy simply could not continue with business as usual. Changes in the *democratic idea* were most evident in the increasingly rapid erosion of support for the ruling parties, whose credibility plummeted under these combined pressures, particularly since they could not grasp the changes taking place around them. The rapid erosion of old *collective identities*, including the political loyalties that had shaped the country's postwar history, was accompanied by the rise of entirely new identities.

Important signals should have drawn the ruling elite's attention to growing unrest, and outright disgust, with the old style of politics.

Warning Signs (I): The Lega Nord. The major beneficiaries through the early 1990s were newcomers who stood outside the established party system. In fact, various Leagues sprang up in the north, and did best in historic DC strongholds in the Catholic northeast. Their origins were separatist, and in some instances ethnically based, but their major attraction was unquestionably an antiparty and anti-Rome rhetoric that appealed to the "little people" who saw greedy, corrupt politicians squandering their hard-earned money (especially on the south). Politically negligible through most of the 1980s, in the 1990s the Leagues literally exploded onto the political scene and quickly extended their influence throughout most of the north. By 1992 they had united into the Northern League (Lega Nord) and, with a quarter of the vote, were the largest party in Lombardy and the Veneto. Significantly, this wider appeal coincided with the emergence of a stronger sense of regional identity and demands for more autonomy for the north.

Warning Signs (II): Critical Referendum Campaigns. Italy's abrogative referendum (see Chapter 24) has mainly been used to put issues openly on the agenda when Parliament proves unable or unwilling to do so. It is a crude instrument, for it can only abolish a law. But in so doing, public opinion can send a powerful signal to lawmakers. And this occurred with increasing frequency starting in the late 1980s.

Tapping widespread public disaffection, reformers used referenda twice in the early 1990s to force changes on the electoral system. In 1991, the worst aspects of proportional representation (PR) were abolished. In 1993, another referendum effectively altered the system for choosing senators from PR into a first-past-the-post system. Most dramatic of all was the sheer size of the abolitionist vote: 96 percent in 1991 and 83 percent in 1993.[9]

The 1993 referendum resulted in a predominantly first-past-the-post system for 75 percent of the seats and a less permissive variant of PR for the remaining quarter. A new French-style electoral law for municipal elections was also instituted. Mayors are now directly elected, with a second, runoff, ballot guaranteeing a clear mandate, thus bypassing the parties in favor of individuals and their platforms. Local elections held under this system in 1993 and 1994 were devastating for the DC and PSI. The once-mighty DC failed to make it to the second ballot in every important city, and the PSI was all but wiped out.

Warning Signs (III): Bribesville and Clean Hands. The parties in power barely won the 1992 elections, but as that campaign unfolded, so did evidence of a degree of corruption that shocked even hardened observers. These revelations obliterated the prestige of the parties, especially the DC and PSI, and turned investigators and prosecutors into folk heroes. The task of forming a government was given to Giuliano

Amato, a Socialist with a clean reputation. Still, within barely six months, five ministers had resigned under a legal cloud. Within two years, roughly a fifth of the members of Parliament elected in 1992 were in some form of legal trouble, and it was clear that the old style of politics was in terminal crisis. "Operation Clean Hands," as the entire anti-corruption campaign was called, did not cause the ruling parties' downfall, but it certainly delivered the coup de grâce.

Groping Toward Bipolarity? Amato's first term as prime minister lasted only a year, but it marks the end of the so-called First Republic. During his tenure, the lira's weakness forced Italy's withdrawal from the European Monetary System (EMS), raising serious questions as to whether the country would ever get its currency stable enough and its budget deficits low enough to meet the restrictive Maastricht convergence criteria for membership in the Economic and Monetary Union (EMU). Amato responded with the most rigorous budget in living memory and is widely credited with setting Italy on the financial path to recovery.

It says everything about how seriously Italy took its economic plight to note that Amato was followed by Carlo Azeglio Ciampi, a former governor of the Bank of Italy. Ciampi's appointment clearly was a signal to foreign markets that the economy remained in capable hands. Ciampi's was an explicitly nonpartisan technical government of specialists whose mandate was to address pressing economic problems and prepare the country for new elections.

As the scandals ground on, the Left began to rejuvenate, sweeping local elections late in 1993. The most important of these took place in Rome and Naples, where the now-moribund DC failed to make either runoff. Dramatically, the neofascist Italian Social Movement (MSI) appeared to be the only party able to fill the vacuum on the Right. Running Mussolini's granddaughter in Naples and its own telegenic leader, Gianfranco Fini, in Rome, the MSI shattered its previous pariah status by making it into both

runoffs. Silvio Berlusconi, a swashbuckling entrepreneur and media magnate closely tied to the former ruling parties, announced that he would happily vote for Fini if he lived in Rome. In the runoffs, the MSI exceeded 40 percent, but the Left won handily and appeared poised to do the same in what many were thinking of as the first general elections of the Second Republic.

Berlusconi and Forza Italia. Frightened by the Left's successes, Berlusconi entered politics with his own new party, called Forza Italia (FI), "Go Italy," which is the cheer for the national soccer team. He might have owed his dominant media position to Italy's discredited former leaders (above all Craxi), but Berlusconi really did represent something new on the Italian political scene. In 1994, the two largest public networks remained in the hands of sycophantic DC and PSI appointees, and because Berlusconi owned the three largest private networks, he received constant, flattering coverage during the 1994 campaign.

But Silvio Berlusconi was more than a media phenomenon: he was the Center-Right's political lifeboat. Now a respectable alternative to the League and MSI existed, and veterans from the old ruling parties flocked to Forza Italia, ready to trade their much-needed experience for a continued place at the center of power.

Berlusconi and his staff set about finding attractive candidates to stand in Italy's new single-member districts. His major achievement was to consolidate the Center-Right. He quickly came to terms with Fini; in the south and part of the center, Forza Italia and the National Alliance (AN), as the MSI was rebaptized, presented a joint slate, known as the "Pole of Good Government." Hard bargaining then produced a "Freedom Pole" for the north-center of the country, which was primarily an FI–Lega agreement that gave the League 70 percent of the candidacies in the north.

Berlusconi Wins—and Loses. Berlusconi ran a slick ad-based campaign. He called the PDS "communists," sidestepped questions about his own neofascist allies, and made vague promises. The March 1994 elections really did seem to mark the definitive end of the First Republic. The Center-Right pole(s) won an absolute majority in the Chamber of Deputies and a near majority in the Senate (see Table 21.2).

As anticipated, the new electoral law produced a rough bipolarity: the Pole and the left-wing Progressive Alliance accounted for the vast majority of votes and seats alike. The PPI, which, as the DC, had dominated the republic's entire political history, tried to run as a centrist force. It managed 11 percent of the vote and was able to win precisely four of Italy's 475 single-member districts. Even allied with another ex-DC group, it obtained only 7 percent of the seats in the Chamber. The PSI fared even worse. The largest vote getter in the country, Forza Italia, had not even existed five months earlier.

Yet for all the apparent change, many classically Italian political dilemmas remained. There might now be two large political blocs, but each was deeply divided. The new Parliament was actually more fragmented than the old. More parties were present after the 1994 vote than there had been after 1992, and further splits soon increased their numbers. Forza Italia might have been the largest party, but it commanded the support of barely 20 percent of the electorate.

The Freedom Pole proved more adept at campaigning than governing. Even Berlusconi's allies, above all Lega leader Umberto Bossi, publicly wondered how a leading businessman could make policy decisions while owning some of Italy's most powerful conglomerates. The government's ineptitude and divisions soon produced a classic cabinet crisis. Bossi pulled the League out of the coalition, and Berlusconi resigned without a confidence vote after only seven months in office. In the face of the ensuing stalemate, worried that new elections might produce further destabilization, President Oscar Luigi Scalfaro actively stepped into the fray. He named Lamberto Dini, treasury minister under Berlusconi and former director general of the Bank of Italy, to head Italy's second technical government in three years—headed by yet another former bank official.

Dini's government lasted just over a year, supported by the Center-Left, Bossi, and the PPI. Berlusconi initially appeared to accept Dini as an interim leader but then led a fierce campaign from the opposition, arguing that the government was illegitimate (which it was not) and that it represented a reversal of the outcome of the elections (which it certainly did).

The Ulivo's Victory. Learning from its 1994 defeat, the PDS put together a coalition in 1996 with a clear and attractive leader. Romano Prodi was a prestigious economist, as well as a Catholic who could appeal to more middle-of-the-road voters. Berlusconi denounced him as a "useful idiot" under the control of the "communists," an epithet he later hurled at Amato in 2000. But with the support of middle-of-the-road politicians like Dini, Ciampi, and many former Christian Democrats, who could hardly be accused of radicalism, the Ulivo eked out a narrow electoral victory in 1996.

The largest party of the Left was finally in government after nearly half a century of exclusion, but the 1996 vote did not represent a dramatic shift to the Left by the electorate. On the contrary, the Right won more votes than it had in 1994. But with the League running separately, the split conservative vote in the north allowed the Center-Left to reap a harvest of single-member seats where the Left had come up empty two years earlier. For all its flaws, the new electoral system had produced another winning coalition, and the former opposition was now in power while the former government was in the opposition. For the first time, just as reformers had hoped, Italy had experienced a democratic alternation of power.

But institutional engineering could not alter the fact that the Ulivo was almost as heterogeneous as Berlusconi's Center-Right had been. It initially commanded a majority only with the support or abstention of Rifondazione comunista, with which it had been forced to strike a stand-down agreement in 1996 to avoid split-

Table 21.2 Election Results in the Chamber of Deputies, 1994–2001: Results since the Adoption of the New, Mixed, Electoral System

List or Bloc	1994			1996			2001		
	Single-Member Seats*	PR List Seats	Percentage of Vote**	Single-Member Seats*	PR List Seats	Percentage of Vote**	Single-Member Seats*	PR List Seats	Percentage of Vote**
Freedom Pole[a]	**301**			**169**			**282**		
Forza Italia	(69)	30	21.0	(85)	37	20.6	(127)	62	29.4
MSI/AN	**1**+(84)	23	13.4	(64)	28	15.7	(73)	24	12.0
Ex-DC	(29)	b		(18)	12	5.8	(41)	—	3.2
Minor Lay Parties	(8)	—	3.5	(2)	—	1.9	(11)	—	1.0
Lega Nord (part of Pole in 1994 and 2001)	(106)	11	8.4				(30)	—	3.9
Lega Nord (alone in 1996)				**39**	20	10.1			
Pact for Italy (1994)	**4**								
PPI (split in 1995)		29	11.1						
Segni Pact		13	4.6						
Progressives (1994)/ Olive Tree (1996, 2001)	**164**			**246**			**184**		
PDS/DS	(71)	38	20.4	(124)	26	21.1	(107)	31	16.5
Ex-PSI, Lay Parties	(14)	—	2.2	(24)	8	4.3	d	—	
Verdi	(11)	—	2.7	(14)	—	2.5	(18)	—	2.2
Other Leftist Groups	(30)	—	3.1	(19)	—	4.0	(9)	—	1.7
"For Prodi" (1996)	—	—	—	(63)	4	6.8			
Daisy List (2001)							(49)	27	14.5
Rifondazione Comunista	(28)	11	6.0	15[c]	20	8.6	—	11	5.0

Note: First used in 1994, the electoral system consists of 475 single-member constituencies (75% of all seats) and the remaining 155 seats distributed according to the proportion of votes obtained by party lists. Numbers may not add up to 100 percent or 630 seats because lists and blocs are selective.

* Boldfaced numbers indicate all single-member seats won outright by a bloc or list; numbers in parentheses refer to the distribution of single-member seats assigned to various parties within blocs.

** Percentage of vote is that obtained by individual lists on the separate proportional ballot.

a In 1994, ran as Freedom Pole (North) and Pole of Good Government (Center-South); in 2001 ran as Freedom's Home.

b Did not present a separate list in this election.

c In a stand-down agreement with the Olive Tree, but not officially part of the alliance.

d With Daisy List.

Source: Compiled by the author from various press and Web sources.

ting the left-wing vote. After 1998, Rifondazione withdrew its external support and forced Prodi from office. Only a fence-jumping maneuver (by former Christian Democrats) from the Center-Right to the Center-Left kept the coalition alive. And as they had been doing since 1994, the parties in Parliament continued to show a tendency to split, form, and recycle themselves.

Considering the underlying weakness of the coalition, its achievements under both Prodi and D'Alema appear all the more impressive. A highly ambitious effort to rewrite much of the constitution failed when Berlusconi abandoned the process. But the Ulivo carried out important educational reforms, revamping the requirements, structure, and curriculum of the public school system and the universities. The health system was also restructured. Administrative reforms began to streamline and simplify one of the Western world's most inefficient and unresponsive bureaucracies. It changed Italy's entrenched (and, many argued, tyrannical) criminal justice procedures, amending the constitution to ensure that the rights of the accused have equal status to those of the prosecution. Another constitutional amendment changed the way the governments of the regions are elected and then devolved considerable powers to them, as well as to other levels of local government. And a federal reform was set in motion in 2001 in the last days of the Center-Left.

Undoubtedly the Center-Left's most striking achievements were economic and financial. Against the confident predictions—and smug expectations—of many European leaders, Italy met the Maastricht convergence criteria in mid-1998 and was thus present among the (eleven) founders when the euro was officially adopted in 1999.

Italy in the Era of the Euro

When the Ulivo took power in 1996, Italy was still a long way from meeting the criteria for inclusion in the establishment of the EMU. With an accumulated public debt over 125 percent of gross domestic product, there was never any question of meeting—or even coming close to—the limit of 60 percent established at Maastricht. (Although the Italians were the worst offenders, they were hardly alone in this category.) The real sticking point was the annual budgetary deficit, which had been steadily reduced since Amato's restrictive measures for 1993, but it remained a long way from the target of 3 percent.

As the leader of a coalition that depended on the goodwill of the unions and the (external) support of a party that still called itself Communist, Romano Prodi faced a daunting challenge. Deficit reduction means cutting spending programs, and the unions and Rifondazione comunista were adamant about defending existing levels of social spending, particularly on Italy's expensive pension programs. Or else it means raising Italy's already-high taxes, which would threaten economic expansion and any hope of quickly creating jobs in an economy already suffering from high unemployment. During the campaign, Prodi had explicitly promised not to raise taxes. But after discovering that his European Union (EU) counterparts would not give Italy special concessions, Prodi's budget doubled previously announced tax increases and spending cuts.[10] When his budget was presented, not only did Rifondazione vote for it, but Forza Italia and the Lega abstained.

This outcome can be understood only in terms of Italy's obsession with qualifying for the EMU from its earliest stages and, more broadly, with being considered a serious country among its peers. Once this milestone was reached, Prodi and his successors would continue to impose far more restrictive budgets—in the name of maintaining Italy's commitments—than would have been imaginable a few years earlier. There is no doubt that Prodi's impressive achievements as prime minister paved the way for his election as president of the European Commission once he was pushed out of the prime minister's office in 1998. Rivals within his own coalition were of course delighted to kick him upstairs into such a prestigious post, but the rest of the EU would never have accepted him without his track record. As the domestic problems of both Prodi, and his successor, D'Alema, show, Italian parliamentary bickering and maneuvering remain quite capable of paralyzing legislative initiatives and bringing down governments, suggesting disturbing continuities with the so-called First Republic. Yet, the "European imperative" had obviously introduced a series of constraints on the entire political class inside Parliament, as well as on significant actors, like the unions, outside the legislature.

At the same time, Italy remains a long way from the free-market orthodoxy that reigns on both sides of the Atlantic. Pension expenditures remain extremely high, as do tax rates. The labor market is considered far too rigid; more flexible forms of work and working hours are slow to be implemented. Privatization remains hampered by an undeveloped capital market as well as deeply entrenched past habits that make it hard for the state to part with cherished holdings.

The fact that the 1996 election marked the first time in the history of the Italian Republic that opposed political blocs won successive elections, and that the Center-Right won again in 2001, suggests that Italy's long transition from First to Second Republic is practically complete. Even Prodi's resignation (the only time that an Italian government had ever resigned after losing a vote of confidence) had a sort of silver lining: he was succeeded by Massimo D'Alema, the leader of the largest party in the coalition that had been supporting the Ulivo. There was thus significant governmental continuity in this legislature—a marked improvement over Berlusconi's first government.

But D'Alema was able to command a majority thanks only to defections from the Center-Right. In short, representatives originally elected with the opposition had switched sides to keep the governing coalition in power. This was not quite as blatant as the League's 1994

flip-flop. But it was also not exactly a model of disciplined parliamentary behavior and hardly promised a rosy future. The fact that roughly one in seven members of Parliament had formally changed their party affiliation by the time D'Alema was brought down[11] also provides scant cause for optimism about the consolidation of a bipolar political system nearly a decade after the political earthquake that started in the early 1990s. Indeed, by Parliament's dissolution in 2001, Italy had more parliamentary groups than it had at any other time in its history. And all of the label shifting and fence jumping led observers to argue that there was more *trasformismo* apparent in Italian politics than at any time since the beginning of the twentieth century.

Themes and Implications

Historical Junctures and Political Themes

This chapter has concentrated on two of the four broad themes that inform this book: the challenges of democratization and the *democratic idea* and Italy's involvement in a *world of states*. At the same time, we have seen that any discussion of Italy's struggles to join the EMU necessarily raises questions that concern *governing the economy*, although that topic is addressed more fully in the next chapter. *Collective identities* are addressed more fully in Chapter 24. We can quickly review all four themes here.

The democratic idea is no abstraction in Italian political history. Each of Italy's critical junctures has been marked by deeply rooted differences over the very meaning of democracy and how much of it is desirable. The Risorgimento saw the victory of those with an extremely limited definition of democracy against their more radical collaborators, but also the overt hostility of the Church. The Church's opposition to democracy continued throughout the Liberal regime, which tolerated blatant corruption and backroom deals *(trasformismo)* to avoid enfranchising the masses—and then to avoid responding to their demands when men, at least, were given the vote. Fascism crushed the workers' movement, which had attempted to broaden the meaning of democracy to include social issues, and it also crushed conservative democrats. Because of the painful past, the mass parties that built the postwar republic in the wake of war and Resistance defined democracy as, above all, a proportional principle of representation with an assembly-style legislature that strictly limited executive powers. Although cumbersome and prone to paralysis, this system survived cold war polarization, when the DC was able to pose itself as democracy's most reliable defender against communism.

The end of the cold war, changing economic realities, and the corruption that grew out of the DC's uninterrupted domination of Italy's postwar governments finally led to a break with the past. This break was framed as permitting the country to become a mature democracy in which government and opposition could alternate in power and in which voters would be able to translate their choices into effective political action. A classical conflict between conflicting visions of democracy—a participatory but fractious (and often paralyzed) conception of democracy versus more efficient and stable governments (with strong executives)—has been part of the Italian political agenda since the 1980s.

The world of states is a theme that Italy, from unification onward, has been unable to avoid. Powerful neighbors dictated the timing of unification and the country's eventual borders. National leaders consciously imitated Prussia's interventionist behavior as a more suitable model for a latecomer, and leaders tried, with less success, to imitate their neighbors' colonial triumphs. Exaggerated international ambitions had the most profound effects on fascism's behavior, leading to international isolation, adventurism, and eventually complete disaster in World War II. In the postwar world, Italy played

a modest international role, often abjectly subservient to the United States. But by placing itself squarely in the Western camp, the country's political leadership ensured that the major opposition party—identified with the *other* major camp—would remain excluded from a governing role. Because its party system, based on this division, lasted so long in essentially unchanged form, the collapse of the state socialist systems of Eastern Europe had a profound effect on Italy's domestic politics—not as great as on Germany, to be sure, although the party system certainly has changed more than in any other country.

Governing the economy meant, from the 1870s until the triumph of free-market ideology in the 1980s and 1990s, extensive state involvement in economic affairs. It is worth recalling how uneven-handedly the state governed the economy, first against the peasants and then excluding the workers. Fascism may appear to be the strong state par excellence, but the dictatorship arose only because class conflict had become so intense that a radical antidemocratic alternative became acceptable not only to landlords and factory owners but to the middle class as well. The DC's domination in the postwar period was built largely on the marginalization of the working class, and it was the workers' and other social groups' militancy during the Hot Autumn that marked a turning point for the old system of power.

Italy came out of World War II with the largest public sector of the economy in the West. The "occupation" of this state by the DC (and its allies) profoundly shaped the evolution of the postwar political economy. The system that evolved eventually produced a level of budget deficits and accumulated debt unrivaled among the major economic powers of the West. The profligate practices of Italy's ruling parties made the country extremely vulnerable in the changed international economic situation of the 1980s and played an important role in creating the crisis of the political system in the 1990s.

The politics of collective identity has been an

elusive, problematic concept for Italy through most of its history. Italy at the time of unity was considered to be more a geographical expression than a true nation-state, and this generalization seemed to hold true well into the late twentieth century. In Almond and Verba's pioneering study of political culture, Italians stood out for their lack of any sense of pride in the state or its institutions and instead identified with Italy's artistic heritage and natural beauty.[12] The Italian term for localism—*campanilismo*—expresses the sense that the world that matters is within sound of the town bell tower *(campanile)*.

Stereotypes may reflect a partial reality, but they also glide over uncomfortable facts. Mussolini's excesses were enthusiastically supported by most Italians until Allied bombings and invasions brought the war's brutal costs home. Healthy second thoughts as well as outright embarrassment might account for some of the lack of nationalistic pride in the postwar period. It is also true, as many have observed, that Italy's political institutions and elites have not done much to win citizens' allegiance.

Postwar Italy was characterized by intensely held identities that underpinned cold war polarization for nearly two generations. These were explicitly *political* identities, built around mutually antagonistic subcultures (Catholic and "red," i.e., identified with the Socialist and Communist traditions). Deeply rooted class divisions fed these subcultures, but neither had a very pure class base. The DC, and even the PCI to a striking degree, were able to win support across social groups on the basis of political allegiance. This explains the longevity of their appeal: Each was rooted in and dominated specific areas of the country, guaranteeing a powerful political base and sources of bedrock strength. Only the dissolution of cold war polarization, compounded by a rapidly modernizing society that weakened traditional political organizations and practices, finally undermined these subcultures, though it has not eliminated them altogether.

What has replaced the old identities? At times nothing, or, more exactly, what Italians tellingly call a more laical sense of politics. This means a politics based not on identifying with tradition or ideological commitment, but with parties' platforms and, once elected, with their concrete policies. In other cases, as the success of the League indicates, new identities based on regionalism have filled the vacuum left by the collapse of DC hegemony. The League's appeal varies considerably, ranging from ethnic-based chauvinism in some areas to a more general regional self-righteousness and revulsion against central political authority.

The League initially targeted southern Italians, reproducing one of Italy's oldest cleavages. But as the movement unified and tried to expand, it increasingly focused on a new "other": dark-skinned immigrants. Parties like the Northern League and AN have been quick to fan the flames of economic, religious, and racial suspicion and intolerance, and this issue has come to rest near the top of the political agenda.

Implications for Comparative Politics

To study Italy is to take a continuing course in comparative politics. For many of its earlier historic junctures, interesting and fruitful comparisons could be drawn with Germany. Unified at about the same time, Italians consciously copied Prussia's interventionist model of development after laissez-faire policies (copied from Britain) failed to move the economy ahead at a satisfactory pace. Italy then was itself the pioneer; it invented fascism. Both countries had this grim legacy to overcome in their postwar democratic experiments, and both were dominated, though in different degrees, by Christian Democracy.

But despite these provocative parallels, comparisons with France in the postwar period are even more telling. Tripartite collaboration followed by the isolation of the Communists characterized both countries at war's end. But whereas the new rules of the game under

France's Fifth Republic laid the groundwork for reshaping the party system, Italy kept the same rules and resembled the Fourth Republic's assembly-style democracy through the 1990s. In France, the Socialists became the dominant party on the Left by joining the Communists, as the two-ballot electoral system required. In Italy, the Socialists tried to imitate Mitterrand's success by keeping the PCI at arm's length and were themselves crushed in the collapse of the old system.

In the area of policy, Italy, like all other advanced capitalist democracies, faces daunting challenges in adjusting to the new international economy. It does so with a pair of distinct (and linked) handicaps and one possible advantage. The first handicap is that in addition to considerable economic difficulties, Italy faces a full-fledged transitional crisis in the political sphere. The old party system has disintegrated, and a new one is struggling to be born. The process is fascinating, but it is chaotic and disruptive, with parties forming, dissolving, splitting, and showing little inclination to work together and coalesce into neat blocs according to the unrealistic projections of protagonists and observers alike. It is extraordinary that under these constraints, the Center-Left governments of Prodi and D'Alema were able to accomplish as much as they did.

The second handicap aggravates the first. Italy's economic challenges are greater than those of other European countries. Its accumulated debt is enormous. And although it has moved, under unrelenting pressure from EU watchdogs, to divest the state of its considerable ownership of the economy, the very speed of this privatization guarantees that the process will be rather slapdash and not provide the country with the maximum benefits. Many other members of the EU face similar problems, but none is in worse shape along either of these dimensions.

Finally, Italy may have an advantage that grows, ironically, out of its historic shortcomings. Because the state has always been so weak and coherent direction of the economy so problematic, vast sectors of the Italian economy have flourished by taking advantage of local and international conditions. This remarkable resiliency has been much commented on, sometimes in exaggerated fashion, but there is no question that the demands of the new global economy reward these qualities.[13] The state and political sphere may stumble and stagger, but the economy seems, mercifully, to flourish despite its alleged political masters.

Notes

1. Geographic details were obtained from the CIA's on-line factbook at www.odci.gov/cia/publications/factbook/it.html.

2. Luigi Barzini, *The Italians* (New York: Atheneum, 1964), p. 241, quoted in Sidney G. Tarrow, *Peasant Communism in Southern Italy* (New Haven, Conn.: Yale University Press, 1967), p. 21.

3. Giuliano Procacci, *History of the Italian People* (Harmondsworth, England: Penguin, 1968), p. 391.

4. Daniel L. Horowitz, *The Italian Labor Movement* (Cambridge, Mass.: Harvard University Press, 1963), p. 75.

5. Of just over 8,000 municipalities in all. For the 1914–1920 electoral figures, see Frank M. Snowden, "From Sharecropper to Proletarian: The Background to Fascism in Rural Tuscany, 1880–1920," in John A. Davis, ed., *Gramsci and Italy's Passive Revolution* (New York: Barnes and Noble, 1979), p. 165.

6. Charles S. Maier, *Recasting Bourgeois Europe* (Princeton, N.J.: Princeton University Press, 1975), p. 548.

7. Paolo Farneti, "Social Conflict, Parliamentary Fragmentation, Institutional Shift, and the Rise of Fascism: Italy," in Juan J. Linz and Alfred Stepan, eds., *The Breakdown of Democratic Regimes: Europe* (Baltimore: Johns Hopkins University Press, 1978), pp. 23–26.

8. Ruggero Orfei, *L'Occupazione del potere. I democristiani '45–'75* (Milan: Longanesi, 1976).

9. For 1991, see Patrick McCarthy, "The Referendum of 9 June," in Stephen Hellman and Gianfranco Pasquino, eds., *Italian Politics: A Review,* vol. 7 (London: Pinter, 1992), pp. 11–28. For 1993, see Piergiorgio Corbetta and Arturo M. L. Parisi, "The Referendum on the Electoral Law for the Senate: Another Momentous April," in Carol Mershon and Gianfranco Pasquino, eds., *Italian Politics: Ending the First Republic* (Boulder, Colo.: Westview Press, 1995), pp. 75–92.

10. James I. Walsh, "L'incerto cammino verso l'Unione monetaria," in Luciano Bardi and Martin Rhodes, eds., *Politica in Italia, Edizione 98* (Bologna: Il Mulino, 1998), pp. 117ff.

11. For details on the 145 members who had switched affiliation by the end of 1997, see Table C4 of David Hine and Salvatore Vassallo, eds., *Italian Politics: The Return of Politics* (Oxford: Berghahn Books, 2000), pp. 265–270. There were by no means over 100 members who moved from one end of the spectrum to the other: most of these changes reflect splits in existing parties or the creation of altogether new groupings (see Chapter 23).

12. Gabriel Almond and Sidney Verba, *The Civic Culture* (Boston: Little, Brown, 1959).

13. See Richard M. Locke, *Remaking the Italian Economy* (Ithaca, N.Y.: Cornell University Press, 1995), esp. chap. 6.

C H A P T E R

22

Political Economy and Development

It is important to remember that Italy did not really have a settlement between capital and labor in the same sense as most other Western countries following World War II. A policy of labor exclusion meant that postwar growth took place in a tense and polarized atmosphere.

The Postwar Settlement and Beyond

Italy finally implemented many of the policies and practices of other welfare states, but often only after considerable social conflict. The breakdown of Italy's postwar arrangements has to be viewed as occurring in two distinct stages. The first, in the 1960s and 1970s, saw the workers' movement achieve extensive benefits, wresting a stronger role for itself even though the Communist Party (PCI) remained politically isolated. The second stage, beginning in the late 1970s, followed a pattern found in all of the other Western European countries examined in this book: The exhaustion of the Keynesian model and the restructuring of capitalism witnessed significant inroads into—and occasional reversals of—the achievements of the previous period.

These problems, common to all advanced societies, were aggravated by the degeneration growing out of almost two generations of the ruling parties' uninterrupted occupation of power. The Christian Democrats (DC), joined by the Socialist Party (PSI) in the 1980s, had colonized great chunks of the state-owned parts of the economy, which these parties increasingly used for their own partisan, and at times personal, ends.

In difficult economic times, such mismanagement added to the country's growing financial woes, contributing to record deficits and debts. By the 1980s, even the ruling parties finally began to act, but as they did, they undermined some of their own bases of support. It was only in the 1990s that the situation was attacked in systematic fashion. A severe financial crisis in 1992, and the very real fear that Italy might be excluded from the foundation of the Economic and Monetary Union (EMU), finally produced sustained action. By the end of the twentieth century, Italy's economy remained distinctively Italian, but it had been set irreversibly on a new path.

With this overview in mind, we can turn in more detail to the trajectory of Italian political economy in the postwar period.

Economic Interventionism Within Postwar Polarization: From Reconstruction to Miracle

The postwar republic inherited from fascism very weak markets and a lopsided industrial structure that favored the heavy industries that had been essential parts of Mussolini's military ambitions. It also had the largest public sector among the Western economies. In some ways, this was an advantage: The challenge of postwar reconstruction could never have been met by reliance on free market forces alone. Moreover, because the major parties were either hostile to free market principles (Communists and Socialists), or at least not opposed to interventionism (Christian Democrats), laissez-faire ideas were in a distinct minority. Long after the Left's expulsion from government, the state continued to play an active role in Italy's economy. This interventionism helped set the stage for the impressive period known as Italy's Economic Miracle.

Yet for all its interventionism and high degree of public ownership of the economy, Italy never elaborated policies comparable to France's concerted *dirigisme*, or tradition of state-directed economic leadership. Even as the DC and its allies increasingly occupied the state and used public resources for partisan ends, important decision-making centers such as the Bank of Italy maintained their independence, often pursuing goals diametrically opposed to the politicians'. As a result, Italy's economic policies tended to be fragmented and uncoordinated, although they managed to produce impressive results starting in the 1950s.

Wartime devastation, the Resistance, and Italian capitalism's compromised position under fascism had initially favored the workers' movement. But cold war polarization and conservative economic policymakers quickly changed that situation. Once the Left was expelled from the government in 1947, Italy's recovery was built around low wages, a large surplus labor pool, and limited social spending. Administrators of the European Recovery (Marshall) Plan openly criticized the Italians for, among other things, diverting hundreds of millions of dollars in aid earmarked for investments in order to bolster foreign reserves.[1]

The State and Private Sectors. Despite the prevalence of conservative policies, traditional economists did not completely carry the day even with the Communists and Socialists in the op-position. Some leaders, including Prime Minister Alcide De Gasperi, favored at least limited long-range planning and state intervention. Furthermore, the Marshall Plan required that recipient nations tell how their massive infusions of aid were being spent, and this aid was intended to stimulate the economy. (Italy eventually received $1.3 billion.)[2] Most important of all were far-sighted initiatives set in motion by a selective direction of credit to more dynamic firms, using the huge state holdings and banking and financial levers inherited from fascism. Over the protests of both protected oligopolies and free marketers, huge sums were invested in key industries such as steel and chemicals. Successive governments gave free rein to public sector entrepreneurs, allowing them to reinvest dividends in state-held stocks. Before the DC seriously distorted the public sector of the economy for partisan (and private) ends, these policies paid handsome dividends. As Andrew Shonfield put it:

> It was another one of the characteristic Latin conspiracies in the public interest, of which France, in particular, has provided some outstanding examples. In Italy such things have to be done with greater stealth, because there is neither the instinctive French respect of the high public official, nor any of the confidence in his moral purpose.[3]

Public sector initiatives meshed well with the most dynamic parts of the private sector. Fiat became Europe's largest auto manufacturer by the late 1960s. Italian industry expanded enormously following Fiat's lead in mass-producing small cars, making the country a society of mass consumers. Aggressive export-oriented firms provided state-of-the-art products at low prices to increasingly affluent Europeans. By the mid-1950s, these companies were poised for maximum expansion. Thanks to earlier public sector intervention, abundant steel, fuel, chemicals, and other goods enabled rapid expansion without the hitches that inevitably would have occurred had free marketers won earlier debates about dismantling publicly owned firms. The groundwork for Italy's Economic Miracle was complete.

The Economic Miracle. In the 1950s and 1960s, only Germany enjoyed greater economic growth than Italy.[4] Gross national product doubled between 1950 and 1962, finally making real inroads into the country's chronically high unemployment rates. By the early 1960s, unemployment fell to 2.5 percent and stayed low through the decade.[5] Italy was forever altered in this period. In the early 1950s, a parliamentary committee of inquiry had described terrible living conditions. One family in eight lived in "utter destitution"; one house in ten had a bath; fewer than half of all Italians had an indoor toilet; and fewer still (38 percent) had indoor running water that was drinkable.[6] By the 1970s, illiteracy was halved. Industrial workers surpassed the entire agricultural population in the 1960s, and the latter finally fell to a fifth of the total workforce by the 1971 census (see Table 22.1). New car registrations more than quadrupled in the 1960s.[7] By other measures as well, such as televisions and telephones per capita, Italy was finally on a par with other large West European countries by 1971.[8]

But for all these achievements, the miracle left important problems unresolved. In the immediate postwar period, only a steady exodus of (mainly southern) workers had kept unemployment rates from depression-era levels. Between 1946 and 1955, net emigration totaled 1.6 million.[9] And even through the miracle's peak years, southern development was further distorted by northern-driven expansion and the DC's use of the state as a patronage agency. Uncontrolled growth in the 1950s and 1960s also created, or aggravated, many problems in the north as the mass migration of workers into the big cities put intolerable strains on housing and social services, particularly education, health, and transportation.

Moreover, much of the miracle was built on labor's weakness. Economically, labor market conditions hurt the workers' movement until near-full employment was achieved in the 1960s. But market conditions alone could never have marginalized the movement so thoroughly. As we have seen, the Left's isolation was a necessary precondition for the government to carry out its policies, and the political division of the unions left them badly weakened.

Because of dramatic losses in membership (see Table 22.2), the General Confederation of Italian Labor (CGIL) steadily lost ground to the CISL, the predominantly Catholic General Confederation of Italian Labor through most of the 1960s despite the CGIL's dominance among industrial workers.[10] The drop in the 1950s was hastened by the overt repression of union and left-wing militants, but the CGIL contributed to

---

Table 22.1 Occupation in Italy, by Sector of the Economy, 1951–1999

Economic Sector	1951 Employees	1961 Employees	1971 Employees	1981 Employees	1991 Employees	1999 Employees
Agriculture	43.9%	30.7%	20.1%	13.3%	8.4%	5.5%
All industries	29.5	34.9	39.5	37.2	32.0	32.6
All services, including government	26.6	34.4	40.4	49.5	59.6	61.9
Total	100.0	100.0	100.0	100.0	100.0	100.0
Number (000s)	(19,693)	(20,427)	(19,295)	(20,751)	(22,623)	(23,180)

Source: For 1951, Kevin Allen and Andrew Stevenson, *An Introduction to the Italian Economy* (London: Martin Robertson and Co., 1975), p. 104. For 1961, CISL, *CISL 1984* (Rome: Edizioni Lavoro, 1984), p. 56. For 1971–1999, ISTAT (Italian Statistical Institute), *Italia in cifre,* 2000: Lavoro, at www.istat.it, p. 2.

Table 22.2   Total Union Membership, Excluding
Pensioners, in the Major Confederations, Selected
Years, 1950–1999 (in 000s)

	CGIL	CISL	UIL
1950	4,314	1,094	
1955	3,741	1,166	
1960	2,212	1,158	
1965	2,158	1,318	
1970	2,513	1,674	
1976	3,551	2,537	1,016
1980	3,484	2,507	1,145
1983	3,134	2,224	1,121
1986	2,825	1,967	1,046
1991	2,706	2,071	1,136
1995	2,488	2,010	1,338
1999	2,328	1,935	1,336

Note: Reliable figures for the UIL are not available for
1950 through 1970.

Sources: For 1950–1970: Guido Romagnoli, ed., *La sindacalizzazione tra ideologia e pratica. Il caso italiano 1950–
1977* (Rome: Edizioni Lavoro, 1978), vol. 2, Table 1.2. For
1976: Guido Romagnoli, "Sindacalizzazione e rappresentanza," in Guido Baglioni et al., eds., *Le Relazioni sindacali
in Italia. Rapporto 1981* (Rome: Edizioni Lavoro, 1982),
Table 2. For 1980–1991: CESOS, *Le relazioni sindacali in
Italia. Repporto 1992–93* (Rome: Edizioni Lavoro, 1994),
Table 3, p. 76. For 1995, *Corriere della sera*, February 26,
1996, p. 15. For 1999, CGIL Web site (www.cgil.it/cgi-bin/
tesseramento/), CISL Web site (www.cisl.it/iscritti/
iscritti.htm),and Ufficio Organizzazione of the UIL.

its own decline by dogmatically insisting that
capitalism was on its last legs. During the most
intense period of the cold war, the Communists
kept the unions under tight control. Instead of
encouraging the CGIL to come to grips with
rapidly changing conditions, the PCI used it as a
megaphone for policies that often had very little
to do with the workplace.[11] When the CGIL began to lose elections in key factories, it finally
corrected its errors. It increased its independence from the PCI and began to pay more attention to local conditions.

The 1960s: The Tide Turns. The improved labor
market of the 1960s produced an increasingly
militant labor force, eager to assert itself after
more than a decade in isolation. Political divisions persisted, but the unions learned that
unity of action could produce impressive
benefits. The PSI's entry into the government in
1963, with the declared purpose of isolating the
PCI and undermining its working-class support,
initially created severe tensions within the
CGIL, in which Communists and Socialists were
supposed to work side by side. But by 1969, the
DC's sabotage of all but the Center-Left's weakest reforms had thoroughly disgusted Socialists,
who had hoped to build a more modern welfare
state and system of industrial relations.

During the Hot Autumn of 1968 through
1969, the unions used extremely disruptive tactics to make impressive gains. The politically divided three major union confederations were
not only cooperating but speaking of reunification. The Workers' Charter of 1970 guaranteed
civil rights on the shop floor and entrenched the
major confederations as bargaining agents. General strikes forced passage of a very generous
pension scheme. Through the 1970s, Italy led
the industrialized world in both the number and
the intensity of strikes and other labor disputes.
Contracts were so pro-labor that wages out-
stripped productivity (and inflation) through
the 1970s, and overtime, layoffs, and even plant
modernization became nearly impossible without negotiations with the unions. Wage differ-
entials were compressed, at the expense of more
skilled workers, with the introduction of a 100
percent cost-of-living escalator *(scala mobile)* in
1975. This mechanism calculated the cost of an
average basket of consumer items. Several times
a year, the absolute amount by which these
items' prices rose was added to workers' paychecks. The increase was equal for everyone and
was thus bottom weighted: It pulled the lowest
salaries up more than the highest. In an era of
very high inflation like the late 1970s and early
1980s, the impact of the *scala mobile* was
greatly magnified.

Table 22.3   Broad Performance of the Italian Economy, 1970–1999

Year	Percentage Change of Real GDP over Previous Year	Percentage Rise in Consumer Prices over Previous Year	Percentage of Total Labor Force Unemployed	Year	Percentage Change of Real GDP over Previous Year	Percentage Rise in Consumer Prices over Previous Year	Percentage of Total Labor Force Unemployed
1970	5.3	5.0	5.4	1985	2.3	9.2	10.3
1971	1.6	4.8	5.4	1986	2.5	5.9	11.1
1972	3.2	5.7	6.4	1987	3.0	4.7	12.0
1973	7.0	10.8	6.4	1988	4.2	5.1	12.0
1974	4.1	19.1	5.4	1989	3.2	6.3	12.0
1975	−3.6	17.0	5.9	1990	2.1	6.5	11.4
1976	5.9	16.8	6.7	1991	1.2	6.2	10.9
1977	1.9	17.0	7.2	1992	0.7	5.1	11.5
1978	2.7	12.1	7.2	1993	−0.7	4.5	10.4
1979	4.9	14.8	7.7	1994	2.1	4.0	11.1
1980	3.9	21.2	7.6	1995	3.0	5.2	11.6
1981	0.1	17.8	8.4	1996	1.1	4.0	11.6
1982	−0.3	16.5	9.1	1997	1.5	2.0	11.7
1983	−1.2	15.0	9.8	1998	2.1	1.9	11.8
1984	2.6	10.8	10.4	1999	2.1	1.7	11.4

Sources: Real GDP and consumer prices through 1984: OECD and ISTAT figures cited in CISL, *CISL 1984* (Rome: Edizioni Lavoro, 1984), pp. 28, 32. Unemployment figures: ISTAT, *Annuario Statistico, 1983* (Rome: ISTAT, 1984), Table 292 for 1970–1982. For 1985, Ferruccio Marzano, "General Report on the Economic Situation of the Country in 1989," *Journal of Regional Policy* 10 (April–June 1990: 267–268. For 1986–1993: OECD, *OECD Economic Surveys: Italy* (Paris: OECD, 1995), pp. 144, 150. For 1994–1999, ISTAT and OECD figures from various Web sites, but mainly the 1999 ISTAT Yearbook: www.istat.it/Anumital/cifre.pdf, pp. 10, 20.

Crisis: The Late 1970s and Afterward

Italy's reliance on imported fuel made the oil shocks of 1973 and 1979 especially severe, (see the inflation figures in Table 22.3). But by the mid-1970s, capitalist economies had a good deal more to worry about, and Italy was no exception. Growth slowed, unemployment rose, and militancy declined. It was under these circumstances that the unions and the Communists promised restraint should the PCI, the workers' strongest representative, enter the government.

But as we know, this was a concession the DC refused to grant in 1977–1978.

The worst aspect of the crisis was—and remains—the fiscal problems of the Italian state. As Italy began to approximate a modern welfare state, expensive benefits won by workers were quickly granted by the DC to its own constituencies. The costs for these benefits were slapped onto an inefficient and irrational bureaucratic and fiscal structure that could neither deliver services effectively nor pay its own way. The problem can be appreciated in comparative context. President Reagan's budget deficit caused justifiable alarm in the United States when it broke the $100 billion barrier in the early 1980s; at about the same time, Italy's deficit, without colossal defense outlays and in a far smaller economy than that of the United States, reached $53 billion. Italy's deficit hit $100 billion in 1988, and the accumulated national debt eventually soared to almost 125 percent of gross domestic product by the early 1990s.

The state managed to avoid alienating its major supporters by running up immense annual deficits, and hence the overall debt. By the 1980s, as successive governments had to face the consequences of their past actions, they began to raise taxes while making evasion much more difficult. These measures aggravated the government's supporters, further undermining the ruling parties' legitimacy on the very eve of the *Tangentopoli* scandals.

The Tide Turns Again: Labor and Management Since the 1980s. Union weakness and the disappearance of hundreds of thousands of industrial jobs by the mid-1980s undercut militancy and emboldened management, which set out to reverse its defeats since the Hot Autumn. Forced to make numerous concessions, by the early 1980s labor began to rely on government mediation in contract negotiations, hoping the government would make up part of what was conceded to management.[12] The PCI was cut out of these negotiations; its isolation in the opposition made the party step up its pressure on the unions, aggravating tensions between the major confederations. Union unity unraveled, and PCI–PSI relations reached a new low. By the time Socialist leader Bettino Craxi became prime minister, the stage was set for a showdown.

In 1984, Craxi forced a confrontation with the PCI and the Communist majority in the CGIL by imposing a ceiling for the *scala mobile*. The Socialist minority in the CGIL, along with the Italian Confederation of Free Trade Unions (CISL) and Italian Labor Union (UIL), supported the agreement, which was then rammed through Parliament over fierce PCI and far-Left opposition. In June 1985, the PCI and Communists in the CGIL tried to use a referendum to win back what Craxi had taken. The PCI's isolation made many Communists uncomfortable, while PCI unionists were also unhappy with the way the party had aggravated intra-union tensions. The referendum to abrogate Craxi's decree failed by the narrow margin of 47 to 53 percent. With their electoral strength at barely 30 percent of the vote, the Communists and the far Left claimed a moral victory. Yet this was a decisive political defeat and the beginning of the end of the *scala mobile*.

The Unions' Crisis. The major confederations began to decline in the late 1970s: Table 22.2 shows especially dramatic losses for the CGIL in the 1980s. This confederation's prominence has been due to its strength in the industrial workforce. Yet there is a reason that modern economies are called *post*industrial. In 1983, pensioners replaced industrial workers as the largest single group in the CGIL. By the end of the 1990s, of the 5.3 million members claimed by the confederation, well over half were retired. This trend is found in the CISL as well.[13] Table 22.1 shows that there were roughly equal numbers of service sector and industrial employees in the 1960s and into the 1970s, but by the 1990s, services outnumbered industry by two to one. And even where industrial expansion has taken place, it has done so in small firms and in geographical regions (e.g., the Catholic northeast) where unions have historically had less organizing success.

Since the mid-1980s, most labor conflicts have involved white-collar and service sector workers, who often do not even belong to a major confederation. "Autonomous" unions, so called because of their independence of the CGIL–CISL–UIL, have become common in the public sector. They criticize the confederations as too tame and undertake extensive job actions, often with considerable public disruption. Even more militant are the Committees of the Base (COBAS), which appeared in the mid-1980s in key state sectors such as railroads, air transportation, medicine, and education.[14] Finally, the PCI's increasing moderation and eventual transformation into the Democratic Party of the Left (PDS) led many hard-line Communists who refused to join the new party and created Rifondazione comunista to form a more militant faction within the CGIL that is consistently critical of the major confederations.

Organized labor was thus presenting an increasingly fragmented face at the same time that its real weight in society was diminishing. Disruptive tactics fed rising public impatience with, and resentment against, unions. This weakness helps explain why, in the early 1990s, the major confederations agreed to a reform of labor relations that institutionalized tripartite negotiations with management and the state. In terms of content, as we will see with regard to pension reforms, this framework of concertation guaranteed that the unions would be consulted and would be able to defend their interests in hard bargaining. In terms of formal structures, it gave them a solid representational base at a time when their fortunes had been on the wane.[15] And yet the unions, although weakened, remained relatively strong by international standards, still managing to organize roughly 40 percent of the labor force.

State and Economy

The very large state sector of the economy and the political uses to which it was put by the ruling parties ensured that Italy's embrace of laissez-faire, deregulation, and privatization would begin later (often against considerable resistance from within the ruling *Pentapartito* coalition) and be more limited than that of many other Western democracies in the 1980s.

Economic Management Since the 1980s

As we saw in the case of labor relations, truly significant departures from earlier policies only began in the 1980s.

The Public Sector. When Craxi brought the PSI back into the government, he demanded more leadership positions for Socialists in the public sector, which led to intense battles between the PSI and DC over political spoils. But economic reality increasingly intruded into the infighting. The most dramatic changes came at the helm of both IRI and ENI, the huge energy holding company, and produced dramatic turnarounds in the course of the 1980s before the privatizations of the 1990s.

Privatization, Italian Style. With its governing parties entwined in the reins of economic power, there was no rush to sell off Italy's public holdings in the 1980s. Privatization proceeded at barely a quarter of the rate in Britain or France.[16] In the 1980s, state-owned enterprises still accounted for 38 percent of the entire workforce in industry and services and an even larger proportion (45 percent) of sales in those sectors.[17] But changes did begin in the 1980s.

Italian privatization has had a distinctive character, due to the (related) facts of the enormity of the state sector, the weakness of Italian capital markets, and the domination of the private sector by a handful of large firms. The biggest companies worked closely with the country's largest private investment bank, Mediobanca, to dominate a stock market in which small investors—and, above all, powerful competitors from outside Italy—find it difficult to exert much influence. Acting in concert, these groups have been able to influence share prices or acquire controlling shares in state holdings and then stack directing boards with cronies who carry out policies that serve the large firms' interests.[18] Such collusion frustrated Romano Prodi when he headed IRI in the 1980s; his public outspokenness cost him his job. It is one of Italy's many ironies that a crusading privatizer became prime minister with the support of the Left, while Mediobanca and big business remain relatively hostile to privatization unless they can control it, to the detriment of a more open economy.

Until the 1980s, Italy had poured its own, and

European Community (EC), funds into salvage operations to save state-owned industries. But in that decade, the EC changed its policies, explicitly forbidding bailout operations and making continued aid contingent on restructuring troubled companies. Once privatization truly got underway in the 1990s, it was done rather indiscriminately. Even when Mediobanca's scheming could be avoided, the tendency simply was to obtain cash in the quickest way possible, for the overall concern, driven by the Maastricht convergence criteria, had become the reduction of the country's deficits and accumulated debt.[19]

When Italy began selling publicly owned companies in earnest, the state at first continued to keep a controlling share of these firms. Then, in an effort to circumvent European Union (EU) policies, it adopted a "Golden Share" policy (using the English phrase). This amounts to a treasury veto in key companies when their sale might compromise national security, as in defense-related industries, or where a private monopoly might result, as in utilities. These practices served domestic political functions, such as softening the rapid selloff of so many firms, and reassuring more left-leaning members of the governing coalition. Of course, such practices angered watchdogs in Brussels, who constantly threatened to take Italy to the European Court of Justice for violating EU rules.

Complaints will no doubt continue for a long time, but the trend is clear and irreversible. The die was cast by the first Amato government, which abolished the Ministry of State Holdings in 1993. The most extensive sales took place under Prodi's government. By the end of the 1990s, once-sacrosanct areas of state intervention such as electric energy (nationalized under the first Center-Left government of the 1960s), steel, fossil fuels, telecommunications, rail transport, autostradas, and innumerable industrial enterprises were sold off or were well on their way to being transferred out of state hands. When Italian Telecom was sold in 1997, it brought 26 trillion lire, or over $15 billion, into the Treasury and was the largest such sale

in West European history, dubbed "the mother of all privatizations." Telecom had been one of IRI's holdings, and its sale dropped IRI from the 35th-ranked corporation in the world to 157th.[20] Even more significant, by 1997, IRI's fate, along with the rest of Italy's public industries, had been sealed, and by 2000 this symbol of Italian public enterprise had been totally liquidated.

The financial system was progressively deregulated starting in the 1980s. Mediobanca managed to sabotage the privatization of two banks, but some of the most significant market-oriented changes occurred in this sector of the economy. The Bank of Italy obtained its independence from the Treasury early in the decade. Up to that point, the bank had been obliged to buy government bonds not sold in the open market. Following this "divorce," higher interest rates were required to make the bonds more attractive. The policy also resulted in a tighter money supply, something the bank had always wanted.[21] In the mid-1980s, rules governing investment and borrowing abroad were liberalized. Toward the end of the decade, exchange regulations were loosened and banks were deregulated, greatly easing the flow of capital into and out of the country. By the end of the decade, experts called the financial sector "Anglo-Saxonized."[22] By the end of the 1990s, all financial markets had been privatized, and the system of taxing investments had been dramatically simplified.[23]

The Private Sector and Changing Industrial Relation. Increasing international competition, not to mention a desire to roll back labor's achievements, nurtured militant and often hostile management attitudes. The most hostile, and vulnerable, firms were in the private sector, led by Confindustria (the Confederation of Italian Industries, the leading peak organization for private capital). They pressed, above all, for an end to the *scala mobile* and the introduction of much more flexibility into the labor market, which is another way of saying they wanted to see union power reduced dramatically. Although they won some political battles in this period, most notably on the *scala mobile*, their real advantage came from the fact that they had resurgent market forces on their side. Restructuring began later in Italy than elsewhere, but by the mid-1980s, industrial jobs were disappearing in such large numbers that not even the vigorous small firms of the north, or the huge submerged economy, could absorb all the displaced workers. The most devastating drop came in the early 1990s. In the first four years of the decade, half a million manufacturing jobs disappeared.[24] These trends created enormous difficulties for capital, and their consequences were even more problematic for organized labor.

Given labor's vulnerability and Italy's history of fierce class conflict, why did the Italian unions not face the sort of onslaught that Margaret Thatcher unleashed on British unions? As we have seen, in the early 1990s, the Italians adopted a policy of concertation, which involves cooperation among labor, management, and the state. Labor's weakness and fragmentation provided ample incentives for the unions to seek a more conciliatory stance, but what explains a similar orientation among the other major actors in this triad?

The answers to these questions can be found in Italy's political history, both throughout the postwar period and then in the unraveling of the party system starting at the end of the 1980s. But answers are also to be found in the dynamics of Italy's political economy from the 1980s onward.

There could be no all-out conservative onslaught on labor because Italy lacked a genuine conservative party into the 1990s. Recall that Italy's historically weak and divided bourgeoisie never produced a strong bourgeois party or political tradition. Compromised by its collusion with fascism, Italian capitalism delegated the defense of its interests to Christian Democracy at the end of World War II. The DC never won the bourgeoisie's deep allegiance and, with its strong peasant and middle-class base—not to mention a significant working-class component—it had numerous, and contradictory, in-

terests to reconcile. It was not ideologically committed to laissez-faire policies, and its habit of lavishing public funds on pork-barrel projects never pleased business. Still, the DC was the unchallenged bulwark of the system and therefore enjoyed the capitalists' unquestioned, if critical, support.

The rationales for this support dissolved in the late 1980s and early 1990s. The Communist threat simply disappeared when the PCI (and the Soviet Union) ceased to exist. During the same period, the margins for maneuver that had permitted the old wasteful and corrupt practices were dramatically reduced by global pressures and the move toward a more integrated EU. After the 1992 exchange rate crisis forced Italy's withdrawal from the European Monetary System (EMS), the entire political elite became more persuaded than ever before of the need for a stable framework of labor relations. The collapse of the party system then made such an arrangement even more essential in terms of Italy's international credibility.

In the course of the 1980s, Italian entrepreneurs had begun to feel their own growing strength at the same time that they saw a weakened, divided, and isolated labor movement. The paralysis and then the terminal political crisis of the ruling party led Confindustria to declare its effective political independence from the DC.[25] But a number of changes on the entrepreneurial front and in the international economic situation soon persuaded many capitalists that concertation might be, if not the best, then the most prudent, path to follow.

In the first place, Confindustria had grown much more diverse. Once dominated by large export-oriented firms, it had increasingly given voice to the small, extremely dynamic industries that have been the backbone of Italy's industrial dynamism in the past two decades. Although often not very hospitable to trade unions (except in the historic "red belt," the left's areas of greatest strength), these firms were far more interested in fighting for government deregulation and a lighter tax burden than they were in confronting the unions.

At the same time, galloping privatization was eliminating a historical division among the ranks of Italy's employers. Many of the largest, and most unionized, companies had been in public hands, and the management of these companies had evolved far more cooperative relations with unions, going so far as to organize their own managers' association. With Italy's formal commitment to the elimination of state-owned industry in 1992–1993, the rationale for separate management representatives disappeared, and in fact Confindustria basically absorbed these other organizations.[26] It could not, however, impose its own attitudes about unions on them, and although this expansion increased Confindustria's representativeness, it also made it far more heterogeneous. Concern over maintaining the unity of its newly expanded base made the employers' organization far more circumspect in its relations with the unions.

There were also more strictly political reasons for managerial caution in the early 1990s. *Tangentopoli* had injured the parties' credibility, but also that of entrepreneurs. With revelations of millions of dollars poured into party coffers by companies seeking to curry favor, Italian capitalism, not for the first time, found itself suffering from an image problem. Weakened by scandal, the employers found it necessary to present a more united front than ever before.

Finally, and significantly, employers and the government quickly learned, after the 1992 exchange rate crisis, that many old mechanisms no longer operated as they had in the past. For instance, under the pressures of increased competition and globalization, manufacturers found that they needed to worry about the quality of their products (and not just prices) or their skilled workers' job satisfaction, which are of course related. And these employers concluded that having a stable, predictable framework for negotiating with workers was preferable to confrontation.

Manufacturers also found that their ability to discipline their own workforce's wage demands did not necessarily produce lower overall wage levels. After the 1992 crisis, wages continued to rise, but not because of private sector demands. As workers in the private sector became more quiescent, the pattern setters for wage settlements became *public* service sector workers who were relatively insulated from international competition. This was a result not of the *scala mobile* but of different segments of the Italian labor force acting according to an unanticipated new pressure. So one had the rather ironic situation, following 1993, of Confindustria's demanding a stable negotiating framework for discussions between unions and management (and the state).[27]

These trends challenge the common wisdom that the move to a single market and increased competition means that unions will necessarily be severely weakened and that Britain (and the United States) represent organized labor's future. It is too early to tell whether Italian events are a reaction to the country's unique political crisis or an alternative path for labor relations, but they certainly do not conform to the Anglo-American pattern of unfettered neoliberalism.

Labor Relations Reforms of the 1990s. Reforms enacted in the 1990s represent the most dramatic departures in labor relations since the 1970s. Most were passed in 1993 when concertation was established.[28] The old *scala mobile* was abolished; wage increases now must be negotiated within projected inflation guidelines. National negotiations continue to cover issues that affect sectors or categories as a whole, with two annual meetings between representatives of labor, management, and the state formally required. But wages are now basically determined on a local level and are tied to rises in productivity rather than the cost of living, as was previously the case. The new agreement satisfied many of management's long-standing complaints and gave it more flexibility in hiring and layoffs. Furthermore, a larger share of benefit contributions will now come from workers' paychecks rather than management's pockets, bringing Italian practices in line with the rest of Europe.

The 1993 reforms also reshaped workers' workplace representation. More inclusive shop floor institutions have been constructed. Two-thirds of the members of the new bodies are elected (by all workers), and the remaining third are appointed by any union taking part in contract negotiations. These changes are intended to increase the representativeness of shop floor organizations (ensuring a place for autonomous unions and COBAS, for instance), in the hope of revitalizing and relegitimizing the unions. There were signs that some of these hopes were being realized; the first elections held under the new system saw high turnout rates and striking victories for the confederations.[29]

The new framework served the unions well in negotiations with the government over pensions, starting with Lamberto Dini in 1995. The unions have made concessions, but—particularly when negotiating with Center-Left governments that rely on their continued support —they have clearly bought considerable time for their members, ensuring that changes are weakened and introduced over extended periods. These may seem like minor victories, but they are the sort of achievement that helped the unions regain a measure of legitimacy and support in the shop floor elections of the mid-1990s.

As a final illustration of a changed climate of labor relations, legislation was passed in the spring of 2000 putting more teeth into a 1990 law regulating strikes in "essential" public services. These services are primarily in transportation, where wildcat strikes by the so-called autonomous unions have long bedeviled Italians, and tourists, since trains, ferries, and airports during peak travel periods are preferred targets. Several things stand out about the new rules. One is that public services are broadly defined, for instance, to include the self-employed in certain circumstances (truck drivers, for example). Another is that the major confederations agreed to these changes at the end of 1998, after Massimo D'Alema became prime minister. The

legislation is a compromise, but it represents a breakthrough for Italy. Strikes are not forbidden, but they are restricted, including the introduction of mandatory cooling-off periods before labor disruptions can be enacted. If a strike does occur in an essential service, 50 percent of services normally delivered must be guaranteed, as must the presence of 30 percent of regular personnel.[30]

These regulations were fiercely opposed by Rifondazione comunista, which presented 600 amendments in a vain effort to block the law's passage. But most people in the major confederations welcomed the changes. These unions have always been sensitive to public opinion and generally try to avoid strikes that disrupt the lives of citizens and, especially, fellow workers. Those most affected by the new rules are the autonomous unions and COBAS, whose militancy has won them much support within the workplace but antipathy among the public. Already weakened by general trends in the economy, the major confederations assume that a more predictable and peaceful climate of labor relations will better serve their long-run interests.

Welfare all'italiana

Maurizio Ferrera, perhaps the leading authority on the Italian welfare state, has shown that it conforms to the general pattern found along the Mediterranean rim of Europe.[31] These welfare states have fragmented social services and generally provide cash transfers rather than services in kind. Abundant direct cash payments render such systems particularly susceptible to clientelistic abuses and corruption. Most important, following the distinctions introduced by Richard Titmuss,[32] the underlying logic of these systems is particularistic; that is, benefits go to people as members of specified (and privileged) categories, in contrast to institutional welfare states, which provide (universal) benefits as a condition of citizenship. An example of a universal benefit would be so-called family checks (payments to all families with children), which originated under fascism and eventually gave way to means-based subsidies.

Historically, the state provided limited benefits, leaving most services in the hands of the workers' movement and the Catholic Church. Under fascism, as unions and democratic institutions were repressed, many benefits were initially rolled back. As the state got more engaged in the economy, it also assumed more responsibilities in the area of social security, reinforcing the fragmentation of an already haphazard structure. Given fascism's "corporate" ideology, benefits tended to be granted on an industry-wide basis, with the result that some clerks and workers enjoyed reasonable treatment, while others were totally bereft of coverage. When fascism fell, there was nothing like a national system of benefits; those who lived off the land (the majority of Italians in 1945) had no entitlements at all.

Earlier patterns were reinforced and then expanded as the DC sought to consolidate its bases of support, for example, among the peasantry. Small farmers, small businesspeople, and professionals gradually were added to the rolls, and their benefits were increased in the 1970s and 1980s. In contrast to, say, Scandinavia, the Italian workers' movement never pressed for universalistic benefits. Reflecting the Marxist orthodoxy of the period, they demanded that benefits be distributed to people as workers, not citizens, and thus did not challenge many of the Italian system's underlying assumptions. In the course of the postwar period, the DC's "occupation of the state" meant that many services became intimately interwoven with partisan political considerations and, finally, blatant corruption.

The expansion of the earlier fragmented system had long-lasting implications. First, because groups were included for partisan reasons, in piecemeal fashion, there was no sense that the system should be made to pay its own way. On the contrary: favored groups such as the self-employed could count on minimal contributions. During the Economic Miracle, when benefits were quite limited, this was not so important, but as the welfare state expanded, it became critical. Second, the emphasis on privileged, already employed groups and cash transfer payments meant that historically underdeveloped areas remained perpetually underserved. To cite one telling example, Italy traditionally provided a tiny "subsistence" check for the chronically unemployed, paid out of public assistance funds, compared to a guaranteed 80 to 90 percent of the preceding wage, paid out of the main pension fund, for unemployed workers. Southerners, people with large families, and young people (especially women) have been least well served by the system's built-in biases.

The Italian welfare state expanded from the late 1960s onward, pushed by the first Center-Left government's reformist impulses and pushed even more by the workers' struggles during the Hot Autumn. Every time the workers won concessions for themselves, the DC hastened to lavish similar benefits—with no concern as to how they would be funded—on its most important constituencies. By the 1980s, Italy resembled other Western countries in the proportion of gross domestic product (GDP) spent on social programs. But the Italian welfare state spends far more on pensions, and far less on all other benefits; Italy's nonpension welfare expenditures are less than half that of other members of the EU.[33]

Deficit Reduction and Welfare State Reform. High inflation and ballooning deficits in the 1980s forced some moderation on the pork-barreling DC and PSI. But fierce political competition between these parties ruled out changes that would hurt their key constituents. This is why Craxi focused on industrial workers and the *scala mobile* more than on rampant middle- and upper-class tax evasion or pension reform.

Indeed, he and his DC counterparts actually increased middle-class pension benefits while ostensibly fighting to bring down rising deficits. Moreover, by this point, well over a tenth of the entire population—as many as one in three adults in some parts of the South—was receiving disability pensions; 180,000 new ones were being awarded every year.[34] These and other minor pensions may be quite modest in what they provide individual pensioners and reflect the lack of benefits for the structurally unemployed. But nearly 10 million pensions of all types are distributed in Italy, and the cost of maintaining this level of support is crushing.

The greatest fiscal threat comes from old age and retirement pensions. Italy's pension schemes are exceptionally generous, particularly in the public administration. In the past, public servants, including school teachers, could retire after fewer than twenty years on the job; Italians, using English, called these "baby pensions." Retirement benefits have been funded out of general revenues, not contribution-based funds, and payments have also been protected from inflation by cost-of-living escalators.[35]

When Italian budget deficits climbed above 12 percent of GDP in the 1980s, they represented a record for Western Europe and a serious threat to continuing economic growth, let alone aspirations to adhere to EU standards. It took *Tangentopoli* and the collapse of the ruling parties, as well as the exchange rate crisis of 1992, for truly decisive action to be taken. The governments of Giuliano Amato and Carlo Ciampi, notable for the number of "technicians," or nonpolitical specialists, in their cabinets, pushed through extensive budgetary reforms and imposed numerous cuts and slowdowns in the growth of welfare programs.

These reforms were achieved after lengthy negotiations with the unions, leading many critics to complain that they did not go far enough. The critics have a point. For instance, those with eighteen years of contributions under the old seniority-based system were allowed to remain in the old system. The new contribution-based system will therefore not apply to everyone collecting a pension until 2036.[36] Every government and almost every annual budget has attempted to reopen pensions to further negotiations. The unions, and Rifondazione comunista, dig in their heels, and progress, if there is any at all, is very slow.

By the 1990s, advances were also being made in eliminating fraudulent pension and other welfare-related benefit claims. The figure for new disability pensions had fallen by over 100,000 per year by 1993,[37] and this obviously did not mean that Italians were suddenly healthier or more careful on the job.

Tax Evasion. The *Economist*, certainly no enemy of private enterprise, noted years ago that Italy is "a country where cheating on taxes by the self-employed is regarded as their entrepreneurial privilege."[38] The problem would be amusing were it not so serious. The total amount of income tax that goes unpaid each year has recently been estimated at a whopping 220 to 250 *trillion* lire, or $125 to $150 billion.[39] The inequities produced by rampant evasion are staggering; roughly half of national income is earned by dependent workers, and the other half goes to the self-employed, above all, shopkeepers and small businesspersons, professionals, and the like. But dependent workers, whose taxes are withheld at the source, pay 80 percent of all personal income tax.[40] Italy may have tax rates far above EU averages, but only some groups actually pay their taxes.

Tax evasion has received lip-service since the early 1980s. But only since the 1990s, with an intolerable debt burden and governments less beholden to offending groups, has significant progress been made. Finance Ministry figures for 1999 claimed the recovery of 36 trillion lire ($18 billion), an increase of almost 15 percent over 1998. If we recall that the record-setting Telecom privatization brought the Treasury

26 trillion lire in the same period, it is clear that these are truly substantial numbers.

Deficit Reduction. Sums like this help us understand how successive governments finally began to reduce annual budget deficits and, eventually, the national debt. Even without draconian measures, the deficit had been brought down to 7.5 percent of GDP by 1995. In 1996, Prodi had campaigned with the Left's support and reassured his allies that the welfare state would be spared any head-on assault. At the same time, he was utterly committed to Italy's meeting the Maastricht convergence criteria. He created an economic "superministry," subsuming the budget portfolio under the Treasury, entrusting it to Carlo Ciampi. Under Prodi and his successor, Massimo D'Alema, inflation fell to 2 percent by 1997. Similar successes were achieved in deficit and debt reduction, aided greatly by the money that poured into the Treasury thanks to extensive privatizations and improved tax collection. Further help was provided by an economic upturn, but there can be no doubt that the rigor of successive governments played an important part in these achievements. By the turn of the new century, the accumulated national debt had been brought down by over 10 percent, although it was still well above 100 percent of GDP.[41] Italy's economic problems were a long way from being solved, but these were impressive accomplishments, considering where the country had been just a decade earlier.

Society and Economy

Modern Italy has been marked by profound regional differences, none more serious than those between north and south, which were exacerbated under successive regimes. Late industrialization and the powerful presence of the Roman Catholic Church meant that it encountered modernity later and in different ways than other advanced countries. Italy also suffered from seriously polarized class relations—fascism arose as a response to militancy in the factories and fields—which were then perpetuated and entrenched by cold war divisions.

A Legacy of Polarized Class and Political Relations

For much of the postwar period, Italy was among the world's leaders in strikes. From the Left's expulsion from government in 1947 through the 1980s, Italian labor relations mainly revealed whether labor or capital had market conditions in its favor. When labor was weak, it was all but ignored; when it was strong, it played catch-up with a vengeance. When labor's fortunes flagged, capital would leap back onto the offensive and undo or ignore what had come before.

Successive governments, lacking strong ties to the labor movement and themselves internally divided, generally remained bystanders unable to produce a more institutionalized, less conflictual framework of labor relations. The welfare state, already fragmented and very uneven in the way it distributed resources, became even more so and was increasingly awash in a sea of red ink. Employed and organized workers, in the public and private sectors, did relatively well but carried a crushing tax burden. The self-employed did even better, particularly when authorities looked the other way at tax time. But historically unprotected groups remained so and often were able to achieve benefits only thanks to willful distortions of the system (e.g., disability pensions). It took the end of the cold war, the collapse of the postwar party system, and a disastrous economic inheritance further constrained by external (EU) guidelines before a sustained attack on this legacy could be mounted. Progress over the last decade of the twentieth century was significant, but it will be some time before it is clear whether the new regime of industrial relations was a short-term response to an unavoidable political and economic crisis or whether it is genuinely the start of something new.

A Legacy of Gender, Generational, and Regional Differences

Italy's social problems have deep and complex roots, but it is nevertheless clear that this legacy has had a clear impact in these three areas.

Gender Inequities. A discussion of society and economy can only briefly address the legally sanctioned discrimination against women that lasted well into the postwar period. It is important to underscore the ingrained prejudice of a society where adultery was a crime that only a woman could commit; women could not apply for passports without their husband's or father's permission; and rape was defined as a crime against public morality. That such a society would not pay much attention to women's educational or employment opportunities is hardly surprising, nor, for that matter, would one expect much concern about providing day care or other facilities for working parents. In many societies of this type—and they are especially common in southern Europe—women are often actively dissuaded from working at all. Traditionally, the state expected them to produce children, not goods or services.

Indeed, the state's slowness to offer many services can be understood only in terms of ingrained assumptions about the family's ability to provide these services. And, in this context, "family" is really a euphemism for "women." The result has been a welfare state skimpy in its provision of services in kind, and hence in its modern infrastructure. More specifically, the results of the entrenched biases of Italy's political economy can be seen in the extremely low participation rate (the proportion of employed or those seeking employment as a proportion of all adults) of women (35 percent) in the Italian economy, as opposed to 62 percent for men, which is also low. At 16 percent, women's unemployment rates are nearly double the rate for men (9 percent).[42] And this despite the fact that women have for some time outnumbered men

in university attendance and the completion of degrees.[43]

Numerous implications follow from this state of affairs. The most serious, in the medium to long run, is that Italy has one of the lowest active populations, and hence tax bases, of all advanced capitalist nations. Past practices have also left it particularly unsuited to the challenges of persistently high unemployment, above all in economically weak regions.

Generational Inequities. Italian women are disadvantaged when compared with men, but this is hardly the only inequality built into the Italian labor market and welfare state. Young people as a whole—both men and women—are badly disadvantaged when compared to their elders. The unemployment rate for youth is extremely high in Italy; in fact, in the EU, only Spain has a higher rate than Italy's official 33 percent (39 percent for women).

This does not mean that a third of all young men, or two-fifths of all young women, have no work at all, for they often find many part-time or "under-the-table" jobs. But it does mean that they are much less well paid and have few, if any, of the guarantees that those with steady full-time employment enjoy. It also means that young people feel little attachment to trade unions, which defend many of the rigidities in the labor market, or sympathy for immigrants, who are portrayed as stealing jobs from Italians by accepting low wages and poor working conditions.

Regional Inequities. A north-south gap existed when Italy was unified, and it has persisted through the postwar period despite the massive infusion of resources. Almost every important social and economic indicator not only shows the south lagging behind, but the data often suggest that entirely different economic and social logics are at play in these two broadly defined parts of the country. Sidney Tarrow argued more than thirty years ago that the south was not so much "backward" as systematically distorted by the way the DC had created a clientelistic network using the levers of a modern capitalist economy.[44] The effects of this distortion are very much present today.

In the course of the 1990s, for instance, the Italian economy grew at a modest but sustained rate, while managing not to make much of a dent in the unemployment figures (see Table 22.3). But in the northernmost parts of the country, unemployment was steadily dropping, while it actually increased in the south. Put another way, since the Economic Miracle, the north generally enjoyed an unemployment rate roughly half that of the nation as a whole, while the Mezzogiorno was roughly one and a half times the national average.[45] By the mid-1990s, regional differences had *increased*, with the south rising to 21 to 22 percent, or roughly twice the national average, while the north dropped to around 5 percent (central Italy was at 8 to 9 percent). In other words, the most advanced part of the country was approaching full employment, while the south fell further behind; if it had traditionally suffered three times the unemployment levels of the north, this was now better than four to one. And this regional difference compounds the gender and generational differences.

There are many other ways in which the south stands out from the rest of the country, ranging from birthrates and family size to migratory flows. In the south, births exceed deaths, and the population would in fact grow were it not for a net exodus of inhabitants. In the north, the dynamic is precisely the opposite: deaths exceed births, yet the population continues to increase because of the influx of migrants from the south and immigrants from outside Italy.[46] As with the employment data, the north and south are at the extremes, while the center tends to resemble the north more than the south.

The Politicization of Regional Identity. Regional differences have been central to many aspects of postwar politics; the red zones of the north-center and the Catholic white zones of the northeast served, respectively, as the PCI's and DC's subcultural anchors (see Chapter 24). But except for a short-lived separatist movement in Sicily at the end of World War II,[47] local identities never served as the foundation of political movements or parties—that is, until the rise of the Leagues. We will discuss this phenomenon at length in the next chapter, but introduce it here.

This phenomenon arose only in the 1980s and took off only at the end of that decade for the same reason that so many other changes matured at that time: the simultaneous end of the cold war and collapse of the DC. Anticommunism had displaced other potential sources of political identity. And despite the ruling party's shortcomings, its "Christian" message muted and moderated many of the nastiest antisouthern prejudices in the north. After all, millions of southerners migrated northward in the 1950s and 1960s, creating tremendous social tensions, including quasi-racist discrimination. But these tensions never found explicitly political outlets. As the DC lost political and moral credibility and as growing deficits and the national debt drew attention to the bankruptcy of its policies, the fortunes of the various Leagues rose.

Some earlier Leagues made an unabashed ethnic appeal, first against southerners and then against foreigners. Others expressed more of the middle-class, populistic tax revolt mentality that has recently appeared in many advanced capitalist nations. The truly disastrous state of Italy's finances, and northerners' sense that the country's prosperity was based on their hard work while its problems were based on spendthrift central governments that channeled their hard-earned money into an insatiable—and lazy—south helped give these disgruntled citizens a strong sense of regional identity. The northeast, where the League is strongest, finds the most polarized attitudes concerning demands for greater local autonomy and the most negative attitudes toward the welfare state and aid to the poorest regions of the country.[48]

Umberto Bossi created the Northern League out of various regional Leagues, and it has become the largest party in the northeast, and occasionally the north as a whole. Bossi has fluctuated between separatism and federalism, and between more or less xenophobic announcements, depending on political circumstances and, apparently, his own whims. Bossi may be an untrustworthy, unpredictable, and demagogic politician, but he is also the representative of a new political cleavage that shows no signs of fading from the scene, as the League's exceptional showing in the 1996 election, and its rejuvenated alliance with Berlusconi in 2000 emphatically demonstrated.

From a Country of Emigrants to One of Immigrants: Ethnic Tensions

Bossi has also helped keep immigration near the top of the political agenda in Italy, aided by other parties, including the ex-Fascist National Alliance and, increasingly, Forza Italia. Italians were used to thinking of themselves as a country of emigrants and therefore highly sensitive to the plight of strangers in a new land. But the rising tide of immigration, initially from Eastern Europe and then the Third World, forced them to confront their own intolerance and lack of preparedness for this issue.

The dimensions of immigration, both legal and illegal, are minuscule compared to France or Germany. In 1999, the legal number of foreign residents was 1.2 million; reliable estimates for undocumented immigrants put the figure at a few hundred thousand.[49] In all, this is less than 3 percent of the population, and many foreigners in Italy (e.g., art students from North America) are hardly the sort of people to get anti-immigration forces upset. But even such limited numbers have made some sectors of society react as if a flood of foreigners was invading the country, taking Italian jobs and boosting crime rates. At the same time, there have been undeniable connections between some immigrants and drug trafficking, forms of petty crime, and prostitution, and public opinion has shown growing sensitivity to immigration-related issues. Vio-

lent racist episodes have increased. Politicians, led by the League, have not hesitated to politicize the issue. After effectively avoiding systematic measures to regulate immigration, the Italian government passed three separate laws in the period between 1986 and 1998, tightening rules and increasing penalties on each occasion.

Italy at any rate would have had to address this issue because of its desire to be part of the EU's agreements on borders, which require standardized laws, controls, and restrictions on immigration among all participants. The most recent law was enacted under Prodi's government, which had to balance its humanitarian impulses against European imperatives.[50] Like laws of similar inspiration, many aspects of the current legislation are quite unrealistic, establishing arbitrary annual quotas and pretending that immigration can be made to conform neatly to the needs of the labor market. In fact, the demand for labor in the north was so great in 2000 that halfway through the year, the annual quota had already been achieved. It was promptly raised at the insistence of local employers, who are, ironically, among the League's staunchest supporters.

Public tolerance and bureaucratic incompetence will probably keep Italy from turning into a country that tracks down and expels dark-skinned foreigners, although the growing willingness of politicians to exploit popular fears is not encouraging. Recent developments show that decision makers are only beginning to grasp the implications of economic trends and migration patterns that have become integral parts of a radically transformed, increasingly interdependent global economy.

The Dilemmas of European Integration: Italy and the International Political Economy

The weight of international considerations in Italian economic policymaking is underscored by recalling that two of Italy's recent prime ministers were previously top officials of the Bank of Italy, one of whom, Ciampi, then went on to be elected president of the republic. Their selection told the international financial community that Italy took its obligations seriously. But any balanced assessment of economic trends would have to put these developments within the broader context of change. By the early 1990s, the same forces undermining the politics of the First Republic were also pushing economic policy in new directions; as the status quo collapsed, so did the attitude that had prevented numerous reforms from being realized. By the end of the decade, having made Italy's conformity to the Maastricht convergence parameters the central plank of their platform, successive Center-Left governments had enacted more dramatic changes in Italy's political economy than in any other period since the end of World War II.

In some areas, such as privatization, despite continuing pressure, progress remains slower than the EU's oversight authorities would like. And it can be argued than even where important changes can be documented, these have represented less a radical departure than the maturation of trends that began years earlier. Union strength had been declining for some time, and management had been moving toward more independence from the DC long before the ruling party imploded. Similarly, many policies that had long been paid lip-service were now carried forward, or at least addressed, more decisively.

Significant external factors were simultaneously hastening the demise of old political and economic arrangements. Changes adopted in the early 1980s, above all Italy's membership in the EMS, exposed the lira and monetary policy to greater international pressure. These pressures worked in a double sense. Most directly, from the mid-1980s on, Italy, like all other EU members, had to meet guidelines concerning the exchange rate, inflation, and budgetary deficits and accumulated debt (all of them related). When Italy had to withdraw from the EMS in 1992, getting the financial house in order became an even more explicit priority. This is precisely when Giuliano Amato's government became the first of several that finally attacked these long-standing problems in aggressive fashion.

But external factors have also worked indirectly. For example, Italian capitalists grew increasingly restive about very high, and therefore uncompetitive, payments for workers' benefits compared to their European counterparts. This was an old complaint, but with the approach of a single market, it could no longer be ignored. Similarly, Italy's grindingly slow bureaucracy and chronic governmental crises had always frustrated industrial and financial elites, but they now felt increasingly vulnerable without an efficient executive to defend their interests.[51] And observers of all stripes acknowledge that while Italian political institutions retain many of their more problematic characteristics, Prodi's adroit playing of the "European card" enabled him to achieve what few believed would be possible.

These illustrations show how hard it is to isolate domestic or international factors as the primary explanation for changes in policy. Even when we can say with certainty that one came first, it is the interaction between both that produces the final outcome. But given Italy's long history of political paralysis in the face of difficult decisions, and stalemated and polarized social relations, it is safe to say that the external pressure broke the deadlock, and internal political dynamics then determined just how far the reforms could go. It also appears safe to argue that—whether due to domestic or international pressures, or both—Italy's economic governance, and fortunes, were radically, and irreversibly, altered in the course of the 1990s.

Notes

1. Alan S. Milward, *The Reconstruction of Western Europe 1945–1951* (Berkeley: University of California Press), pp. 78–79, 98, 197–198.

2. Kevin Allen and Andrew Stevenson, *An Introduction to the Italian Economy* (New York: Harper & Row, 1975), p. 10.

3. Andrew Shonfield, *Modern Capitalism* (Oxford: Oxford University Press, 1969), pp. 186–187.

4. Gisele Podbielski, *Italy: Development and Crisis in the Postwar Economy* (Oxford: Clarendon Press, 1974), pp. 15, 100.

5. Allen and Stevenson, *Introduction to the Italian Economy*, p. 109.

6. Ibid., pp. 11–12.

7. Eugenio Scalfari, *L'Autunno della Repubblica* (Milan: Etas Kompass, 1969), p. 58.

8. For example, 180 televisions per 1,000 population (versus 293 in the United Kingdom and 272 in the Federal Republic), or 174 telephones (versus 269 and 226, respectively). Allen and Stevenson, *Introduction to the Italian Economy*, p. 28.

9. George H. Hildebrand, *Growth and Structure in the Economy of Modern Italy* (Cambridge, Mass.: Harvard University Press, 1965), p. 117.

10. Guido Romagnoli, ed., *La sindacalizzazione tra ideologia e pratica. Il caso italiano 1950–1977*, vol. 2 (Rome: Edizioni Lavoro, 1978), Table 2.2.

11. For a summary of the unions' programs and platforms in the first decade following the war, see Peter Lange, George Ross, and Maurizio Vannicelli, *Unions, Change and Crisis: French and Italian Union Strategy and the Political Economy, 1945–1980* (London: George Allen and Unwin, 1982), pp. 100–117.

12. For a good summary, see Gino Giugni, "Recent Trends in Collective Bargaining in Italy," *International Labour Review*, no. 123 (September–October 1984): 602. See also Miriam Golden, *Labor Divided* (Ithaca, N.Y.: Cornell University Press, 1988).

13. The CGIL's figures were: 5,260,412 total members, of whom 2,805,304 were pensioners. The CISL, with 4,000,524 members, reported 2,012,614 pensioners. The much smaller UIL reported a total of 1.8 million members, of whom 441,000 were retired. All data refer to 1999. Figures for the CGIL and CISL were found at those confederations' Web sites: www.cgil.it/cgil-bin/tesseramento/Results.asp and www.cisl.it/iscritti/iscritti.htm. UIL data were provided by the Ufficio Organizzazione of the UIL.

14. Lorenzo Bordogna, "'Arcipelago COBAS': frammentazione della rappresentanza e conflitti di lavoro," in Piergiorgio Corbetta and Robert Leonardi, eds., *Politica in Italia: Edizione 88* (Bologna: Il Mulino, 1988), pp. 260–262.

15. Marino Regini and Ida Regalia, "Employers, Unions and the State: The Resurgence of Concertation in Italy?" in Martin Bull and Martin Rhodes, eds., *Crisis and Transition in Italian Politics* (London: Frank Cass, 1997), p. 226.

16. Patrizio Bianchi, Sabino Cassese, and Vincent Della Sala, "Privatisation in Italy: Aims and Constraints," *West European Politics* 11 (October 1988): 88.

17. Anthony C. Masi, "Il complesso siderurgico di Bagnoli: la ristrutturazione e le relazioni industriali," in Raimondo Catanzaro and Raffaella Y. Nanetti, eds., *Politica in Italia: Edizione 89* (Bologna: Il Mulino, 1989), p. 213.

18. Alan Friedman, "The Economic Elites and the Political System," in Stephen Gundle and Simon Parker, eds., *The New Italian Republic: From the Fall of the Berlin Wall to Berlusconi* (London: Macmillan, 1996), p. 269.

19. When the Treasury is the seller, any funds obtained *must* immediately be applied to the national debt. Fiorella Padoa Schioppa Kostoris, "Excess and Limits of the Public Sector in the Italian Economy," in Gundle and Parker, eds., *The New Italian Republic*, pp. 284–285.

20. Guglielmo Raggozino, "Italia i miliardi delle privatizzazioni," *il manifesto*, July 21, 1998.

21. Jeffry Frieden, "Making Commitments: France and Italy in the European Monetary System, 1979–1985," Working Paper 1.14, Political Economy of European Integration Research Group, 1993, pp. 22–23.

22. Gerald Epstein and Juliet Schor, "The Divorce of the Banca d'Italia and the Italian Treasury: A Case Study of Central Bank Independence," in Peter Lange and Marino Regini, eds., *State, Market and Social*

Regulation: New Perspectives on Italy (New York: Cambridge University Press, 1989), p. 147.

23. Giacomo Vaciago, "Finance Between Markets and Politics," in David Hine and Salvatore Vassallo, eds., *Italian Politics: The Return of Politics* (Oxford: Berghahn Books, 2000), p. 198.

24. OECD Economic Surveys, "Italy" (Paris: OECD, 1995), Table H, p. 151.

25. Liborio Mattina, "Abete's Confindustria: From Alliance with the DC to Multiparty Appeal," in Stephen Hellman and Gianfranco Pasquino, eds., *Italian Politics: A Review*, Vol. 8, pp. 151–164.

26. Regini and Regalia, "Employers, Unions and the State," pp. 221–222.

27. Sofia A. Pérez, "From Decentralization to Reorganization: Explaining the Return to National Bargaining in Italy and Spain," *Comparative Politics* 32 (July 2000): 449–452.

28. Richard M. Locke, "The Abolition of the Scala Mobile," in Carol Mershon and Gianfranco Pasquino, eds., *Italian Politics: Ending the First Republic* (Boulder, Colo.: Westview Press, 1994), pp. 185–196.

29. Regini and Regalia, "Employers, Unions and the State," p. 219.

30. Riccardo De Gennaro, "Scioperi, da oggi si cambia," *La Repubblica*, April 19, 2000, p. 28.

31. "Il modello sud-europeo di welfare state," *Rivista italiana di scienza politica* 26 (April 1996): 67–101. For an overview in English, see Ferrera, "The Uncertain Future of the Italian Welfare State," in Bull and Rhodes, *Crisis and Transition in Italian Politics*, pp. 231–249.

32. Richard Titmuss, *Social Policy: An Introduction* (London: Allen and Unwin, 1974).

33. Ferrera, "The Uncertain Future of the Italian Welfare State," pp. 232–233.

34. *L'Unità*, December 3, 1994, p. 9.

35. Giuliano Cazzola, *Lo stato sociale tra crisi e riforme: il caso Italia* (Bologna: Il Mulino, 1994), 66.

36. Marco Mira D'Ercole and Flavia Terribile, "Spese pensionistiche: sviluppi nel 1996 e 1997," in Luciano Bardi and Martin Rhodes, eds., *Politica in Italia: Edizione 98* (Bologna: Il Mulino, 1998), p. 2260.

37. *L'Unità*, December 3, 1994.

38. "Will *la dolce vita* Turn Sour?" *Economist*, January 5, 1985, p. 58.

39. "L'evasione facile," *La Repubblica*, December 29, 1998, p. 12; "Evaso un terzo delle tasse," *La Repubblica*, January 25, 2000, p. 33.

40. Enzo Forcella, "Un paese senza ricchi," *La Repubblica*, January 4, 1990, p. 8.

41. OECD, *Rapporto economico sull'Italia*, Policy Brief (Paris: June 2000), p. 3, available at www.oecd.org/publications/Pol_brief/.

42. ISTAT, *L'Italia in cifre* (Rome: Istat, 1999), p. 12, available at www.istat.it/cifre.pdf.

43. Ibid., p. 19, for enrollment figures; for data on graduation rates, see Stella Conte, "Il marito costa due ore di lavoro in più," *La Repubblica*, February 9, 1999, p. 10.

44. Sidney G. Tarrow, *Peasant Communism in Southern Italy* (New Haven, Conn.: Yale University Press, 1967).

45. All figures obtained from ISTAT, *Serie storiche: TAVrev9_17.doc* (Rome: ISTAT, 2000), Table 17, available at www.istat.it.

46. ISTAT, *L'Italia in cifre 1999*, pp. 7–8.

47. There was also a separatist movement in the German-speaking Alto Adige in the 1960s, but this took the form of terrorist incidents rather than a mass movement.

48. Ferrera, "The Uncertain Future of the Italian Welfare State," pp. 245–247.

49. ISTAT figures for 1999 reported in *Il manifesto*, November 25, 2000.

50. David Hine, "Drafting the 1998 Legislation on Immigration: A Test of Government Cohesion," in *The Return of Politics*, Hine and Vassallo, pp. 175–193.

51. Vincent Della Sala, "Capital Blight? The Regulation of Financial Institutions in Canada and Italy," *Governance*, July 7, 1994, pp. 251–252.

CHAPTER

23

Governance
and Policymaking

On three occasions since the early 1980s, special committees of Parliament were created to overhaul Italy's institutions and, if necessary, rewrite the constitution. All three efforts ended either in failure or with only token changes. There actually have been important changes in Italy's institutional framework, as we will see in this and the following chapter. But these changes have been sporadic and piecemeal and have only begun to address long-standing obstacles to more efficient and democratic government.

Yet it is important to remember that many problems originated as understandable reactions to earlier abuses. Italy had been unified by force, and the Piedmontese *Statuto albertino* had been imposed on the entire country. The country's rulers did not enjoy great legitimacy among the lower classes, especially out in the periphery, and they acted accordingly, keeping tight control in the capital and often resorting to outright repression. The Liberal regime was succeeded by Fascist dictatorship. Although Liberal Italy was a constitutional monarchy, the king had much more discretion than did his counterparts in more democratic regimes. Victor Emmanuel III's naming Mussolini prime minister was remembered angrily when the monarchy was abolished in the 1946 referendum.

Mussolini governed for a generation without feeling any need to rewrite the Statuto albertino. The high degree of discretion it vested in the executive and its concentration of power in the hands of the national government and administration at the expense of the provinces served him well—and were not forgotten by his enemies when they drew up a new constitution in 1947. The postwar founders were driven by a dual desire: to put democracy on a firm footing and to avoid what they understood to be the worst mistakes of the past.

Constitutional Principles and the Organization of the State

The desire to break with the past is most evident in the role assigned to the parties and Parliament and in the limitations placed on the executive. The democratic idea took a distinctive form in republican Italy thanks to fascism's legacy. Politicians were so wary of executive abuses of power that anything challenging the primacy of Parliament and the parties was viewed with suspicion. (These were solidly organized mass parties, not the parties of notables of the Liberal epoch.)

Legislative (as opposed to executive) supremacy proved problematic from the start, since coalition governments were often rendered even more unstable because of the parties' considerable powers. Over time, the ruling parties' occupation of power and corruption produced widespread public revulsion, a rejection of the existing party system, and calls for stronger executive powers as well as other significant institutional changes. But the system's eventual degeneration should not blind us to its origins and the reasons Parliament and the parties were originally assigned such an important role.

The postwar period did not witness a desire to reject every aspect of the past. On the contrary: Left and Right alike were at first committed to a strong, centralized state. A belief in decentralization matured very slowly. Quite modest powers were finally devolved to the regions, and federalism has become a serious topic of conversation only since the rise of the Northern League in the late 1980s.

The Constitution of 1948

The republican constitution is the second basic law of the land since unification. Its drafting spanned the most tumultuous period in postwar history and therefore reflects the ideological tensions and the shifting balance of power within the country between mid-1946 and early 1948. It was drawn up by a Constituent Assembly elected by proportional representation at a time when the Communist Party (PCI) and Socialist Party (PSI) commanded 40 percent of the vote and the Christian Democrats (DC) had 35 percent.

One of Italy's foremost legal experts neatly summed up the situation by observing that the Right blocked the radical changes the Left wanted, but allowed the Left to include the promise of a revolution in the final draft.[1] Some articles (41 and 42) assert the right to private property but then add that this right may have to give way to broader social needs. Elsewhere, the qualifier comes from the opposite side of the spectrum: Article 40 guarantees the right to strike but notes that strikes may be regulated in the public interest. The constitution is also replete with broad principles but no means to ensure their enactment. For example, Article 34 asserts that eight years of education are compulsory and free, and Article 38 states that the disabled have a right to education and vocational training.

Collaboration among the PCI, PSI, and DC ended while the constitution was still being drafted. It is remarkable that the text nonetheless obtained an 81 percent majority when approved in December 1947. If it is tension ridden, contradictory, and incomplete, that is because Italy's republican constitution is the most that could have been produced under such difficult circumstances.

The document's key provisions reflect the painful Fascist experience and the desire to avoid a similar disaster. Mindful of Mussolini's usurpation and concentration of executive power, the framers tried to ensure that the legislative branch would at all times be the supreme level of government (see Chapter 24). Like the Fourth (and for that matter the Third) French Republic, the Italian Republic is a good example of an assembly-type parliamentary regime. To the framers' conscious design we must then add the actual evolution of the political system during the postwar period, in which political fragmentation and cold war imperatives produced highly unstable governing coalitions that further strengthened the parties at the expense of the prime minister.

Bureaucratic inertia and ideological inflexibility delayed, sometimes for decades, the implementation of some of the most innovative provisions. The Left initially suspected any limitations on Parliament's supremacy, whereas the Right was entrenched in the old system and resisted change. Similarly, Italy had always been a unitary state, modeled quite explicitly on France's centralized control—all the way down to prefects in each province who reported directly to the Ministry of the Interior in Rome. After World War II, regional agitation (and a short-lived separatist movement in Sicily) combined with a reaction to Fascist overcentralization to produce more sensitivity to the need to devolve power downward. The constitution thus explicitly establishes a regionalist structure, although it hardly is federalist. Still, naked partisan calculation stalled the implementation of even these limited concessions for a full generation following the war.

Chronic Problems of Governance:
Stable Parties, Unstable Cabinets

Since World War II, the Italian Parliament has seen ten or more parties regularly seated following elections. Governments have, on average, been extremely short-lived coalitions, lasting less than one year. (From the foundation of the republic in 1946 through 2000, Italy had fifty-nine governments and twenty-three different prime ministers.) Until the collapse of the old party system in the early 1990s, this apparent instability actually masked the remarkable stability of the Italian party system. The same parties, indeed the same people, ended up in the key ministries of every government for forty years. This reflected simple arithmetic: 35 to 40 percent of the seats in Parliament were regularly won by parties (Communists and neofascists) excluded from joining the government. Coalitions had to be built from among the remaining 60 percent, which was extremely heterogeneous though always dominated by the DC.

This paradox of stable instability, in which a parliamentary majority had to be found within a very limited pool of acceptable partners, profoundly shaped the contours of Italian politics and reinforced the major parties' already strong role in public life. The utter predictability of elections meant that the governing parties jockeyed constantly for marginal positional advantages in relation to their coalition partners and with respect to rivals within the same party. The mathematical certainty about who would hold power made it difficult for any government to enact serious reforms, for the resistance of just a few key figures could bring the government's support below 50 percent or precipitate crises and cabinet reshuffles that consumed weeks or even months.

Ironically, the end of the old party system, and the disappearance of the rationale for the stable instability of the First Republic (the pariah status of the Communists and neofascists), has produced a worse situation in some ways than the one that existed before. The party system is actually more fragmented and unstable than it used to be. At the same time, governing coalitions have proven to be as unstable as in the past.

The Principles of Italian Parliamentarism

Recent electoral reforms complicate the story of Italian parliamentarism somewhat, but there is nothing unusual about the way Italians create their governments. Parties must form a government that commands a majority in each of Parliament's two chambers. The president of the republic, after consulting party leaders, designates the most likely prime minister (whose official title is president of the council of ministers). The designee then constructs a cabinet by consulting the leaders and important figures of the various parties that will support the proposed government. The entire government, not just the prime minister, must then win the confidence of both the Chamber of Deputies and the Senate. Governments are sworn in and remain in office until they no longer command Parliament's confidence or, much more common, the support of the governing coalition. In fact, only once since 1946 (Romano Prodi in 1998) has a government been brought down on a no-confidence motion. All the other cabinet crises have been the result of internal divisions in the governing majority. When he no longer commands a majority, the prime minister notifies the president, who can choose the incumbent or someone else to form a new government. If no coalition then obtains a majority or if the normal term (five years) of Parliament draws to a close, the president, after further consultation, dissolves the legislature and calls general elections, which must be held within a maximum of ten weeks of dissolution (Article 61).

The Executive

Italy is a parliamentary republic, and thus has a dual executive: The head of state (the president), and the government (the prime minister and cabinet, formally known as the Council of Ministers). Although the presidency is supposed to be a largely ceremonial office, it has recently exerted considerable influence in the formation, and even the composition, of Italian governments.

President of the Republic: An Increasingly Controversial Role

The president is the head of state and representative of national unity. He (the presidency, as well as the prime ministership, has only been occupied by men) is elected by secret ballot of a joint session of both chambers of Parliament, with an additional sixty representatives from the regions. On the first three ballots, a two-thirds majority is required; from the fourth, a simple majority suffices. The term of office is seven years, and although the constitution does not forbid reelection, no one has served more than one term. The president's powers include designation of a prime minister and use of a suspensive veto, which sends a law back to Parliament unsigned with a note explaining the president's reservations, but this can be overridden by a simple majority vote. The president is also the chair of the Supreme Defense Council and the Supreme Council of the Judiciary. The most important presidential power is the ability to name a potential prime minister, for there have often been several plausible contenders for the role. As the party system went into crisis in the 1990s, prime ministers were chosen from outside the parties in an even clearer assertion of presidential prerogative.

Presidential discretion will probably be reduced if the Italian party system evolves into a truly bipolar system. The consultations that followed both Silvio Berlusconi's and Romano Prodi's electoral victories were very brief, since each was the unquestioned leader of the winning electoral bloc. For the same reason (preconstituted coalitions had contested each election), there was much less time-consuming negotiating with various coalition partners to produce a cabinet. Prodi was able to name all his ministers within a day of being designated prime minister, and even Massimo D'Alema and Giuliano Amato, his successors, named their cabinets within a matter of days, in contrast to the weeks that were often required in the past.

The office of the presidency became increasingly controversial from the 1970s onward. Some incumbents were clouded by scandal, and then the 1980s witnessed increasing outspokenness in an office that had previously not been noted for taking public stances. This outspokenness usually involved denunciation of the slow rate at which Parliament was producing reforms, and it became particularly pronounced in the course of *Tangentopoli* and the collapse of the governing parties' credibility. This is hardly surprising: because almost all significant power rests in Parliament, and hence the parties, so a crisis of authority inevitably resulted when their legitimacy crumbled. The resulting power vacuum created considerable freedom to maneuver in other branches of government. Into this vacuum stepped not only the president but the judiciary as well.[2]

By far the most significant developments involving the powers of the presidency occurred during the term of Oscar Luigi Scalfaro, a Christian Democrat who served from 1992 to 1999. While insisting that he was acting strictly within the constitution's limits, Scalfaro exercised unprecedented discretionary powers. In 1992, he informed Prime Minister Amato that politicians under a judicial cloud, no matter how strongly supported by their parties, would be unacceptable as members of cabinet. In 1993, he chose Italy's first nonpolitical prime minister (Carlo Azeglio Ciampi, former head of the Bank of Italy) to lead the country to general elections, and he then played an unprecedentedly active role in choosing members of Ciampi's cabinet of nonpolitical specialists.[3] Finally, and most important, he resisted a furious campaign by the Center-Right in 1994 to call new elections as soon as Berlusconi was forced to resign. A more cautious president might well have immediately dissolved Parliament. But Scalfaro believed that new elections would simply reproduce the paralysis that followed the 1994 vote.

When Scalfaro's term expired in 1999, he was succeeded by Ciampi. As a former governor of the Bank of Italy and a nonpartisan prime minister, Ciampi had earned considerable respect across the political spectrum. But because he had served as minister of the treasury under both Prodi and D'Alema, he was opposed by the Center-Right. Nor was he the original choice of many in the governing coalition, since he had no party affiliation, and several of the smaller parties were eager to enhance their own visibility. Ciampi's first two years in office were notable above all for his low profile and apparent desire to make his office less visible and controversial.

Scalfaro had been roundly denounced for exceeding his constitutional powers. Ironically, the Center-Right favors strengthening the powers of the presidency and would like to see Italy adopt something similar to that of the French Fifth Republic's semi-presidentialism. This, they argue, would provide stronger executive direction and enhance the government's legitimacy and ability to act decisively. As noted, the Left has historically been suspicious of anything that threatens Parliament's prerogatives. It also takes a dim view of a head of state who might use a popular mandate to appeal to the people over Parliament's head and would prefer that the prime minister's role, and not that of the president, be strengthened. But even the Left, although with considerable internal division, now accepts that the executive branch of government must have its powers reinforced. Indeed, the failed 1997 Bicameral Committee on constitutional reform proposed, with the support of all major parties, that the president be directly elected.

The Prime Minister and the Cabinet

The constitution's framers tried to ensure the collective responsibility of the government: The cabinet, not the prime minister, must obtain Parliament's confidence. In fact, with the consolidation of the Italian party system after World War II, key ministerial figures obtained more leverage than even most framers could have imagined. The permanent presence of the same parties in government meant that every cabinet would be dominated by the DC and its minor allies. This gave the governing parties, or the most powerful factions within them, complete control over the ministries. Governments often rose and fell because of struggles over the distribution of spoils within the majority. But because the opposition was never going to replace the government, the dust would settle to find precisely the same people in place. In the first thirty years of the republic, despite nearly forty changes in government, more than one-third of all top cabinet positions were held by only thirty-one people.[4] Some of those whose names still cropped up in the 1980s and 1990s (Fanfani and Andreotti, for instance) had been stalking the corridors of power back in the 1940s.

The situation also reflected some of the perversities of coalition governments, Italian style. One side effect of political longevity has been that politicians often develop proprietary attitudes toward their ministry. This created small groups with formidable ability and considerable expertise in several areas. (It also allowed opportunists and maneuverers of no special talent to rise and remain at great heights, but this is hardly a problem limited to Italy.) This situation makes the creation of coherent or coordinated policies nearly impossible, as powerful and ambitious ministers follow their own agenda with little concern for broader governmental objectives. Ministers constantly jockey for position with one another and with the prime minister, for they often have a vested personal, factional, or party interest in seeing a rival's plans fail. Secretaries of governing parties have been known to decline cabinet posts in order to maximize their freedom to criticize their ostensible allies and keep themselves in the spotlight. When powerful party leaders do accept ministerial posts, they may then veto, or badly undermine, the prime minister's policies.

Factiousness is built into the Italian cabinet system, for many of the leading politicians in the governing coalition are in constant rivalry with one another. Some of the system's worst aspects were eliminated in a 1988 reform that had languished in Parliament for over a decade before being passed.[5] The date of its passage is significant, for by 1988 four of the previous six governments had been headed by non-Christian Democrats. These leaders had often found it all but impossible to assert their authority amid the ferocious infighting and obstructionism within the cabinet, above all coming from the DC's ranks. (Christian Democrat prime ministers were presumably better able to mediate among factions of their own party, or they may simply have accepted the infighting with more equanimity.)

The 1988 reform addressed many issues, including the use and abuse of governmental decrees, which we examine in a later section. It also tackled the problem of how to make cabinets more collegial. It gave the prime minister for the first time ways to resolve disputes between ministers and to vet public declarations by ministers that involved broader governmental policies. It also established the Cabinet Council to coordinate interministerial activities and regulate collegial issues.

Following these reforms, experts noted that serious progress would require a streamlining of budgetary procedures and practices. At the end of the 1990s, some of the worst irrationalities were finally addressed in substantial administrative reforms implemented under Prodi and D'Alema. An economic "superministry" was created, combining the previously divided budget and treasury ministries (Ciampi was the first incumbent), and budgetary procedures were restructured and modernized.[6] Other ministries were combined, and more coordination was established among ministries with overlapping interests. Something roughly akin to an inner cabinet was established in 1999, with more regular coordination established between the ministries charged with economic and security-related affairs. In the course of the 1990s, the powers of the prime minister in relation to his cabinet colleagues were also extended, albeit very slowly.

Because of the overriding need to divide positions between parties and factions, Italian cabinets have frequently been politically fragmented and cumbersome. Every minister remains a member of the cabinet, and there were roughly thirty ministers through the early 1990s, when the number was reduced to about twenty. In addition, into the 1990s, two junior ministers (undersecretaries) existed for each portfolio, and they had to represent different parties or factions from the minister. This guarantees the representation of diverse interests and the distribution of patronage and influence, but it obviously undermines coherent policymaking.

Not surprisingly, as the solidity of the Center-Left coalition began to crumble, some of the old patterns appeared to resurface. D'Alema's cabinets and Amato's second government contained more ministries (twenty-four or twenty-five) and undersecretaries (more than fifty) than had their immediate predecessors, and there was no question that bloated cabinets were a price the leaders had to pay to keep fractious partners happy.[7] Despite unquestioned progress in the course of the 1990s, there were more than a few reminders that old practices, if given half a chance, would find ways to persist.

The Prime Minister. The Italian prime minister is one of the weaker heads of government in Western Europe, in part by design but especially by the nature of Italian coalition governments. On those occasions when the dominant party was united or even when it had an uncontested leader, the prime minister's power was enhanced. But as the DC and its system of power first fragmented into factions and later weakened, so did the prime minister's position, which was rarely associated with a strong sense of policy direction. The first half of the 1980s even saw a predominance of non-DC prime ministers, unthinkable until then. Craxi's leadership showed that force of personality and pressing an agenda can make a difference, and his two governments at least gave the impression of decisiveness and action. But no amount of prime ministerial dynamism can change the fact that under the existing rules, ministers owe their major debts to their own parties and factions, not to the head of government. When governmental crises occur, it is the party secretaries and faction leaders who work out a compromise or, failing that, agree to elections. Despite all the presumed changes since 1994, these basic rules have remained in place. They cost Berlusconi his job after only seven months in power, and although Prodi and D'Alema managed to remain in office a good deal longer by Italian standards, they were also brought down by intracoalition intrigues.

The 1988 reform and further adjustments in the 1990s addressed some of the weaknesses of the executive branch but left the basic balance of power unaltered. The idea of giving more power to the prime minister (and even to the president) is now accepted by all of the largest parties, whereas such suggestions used to be dismissed out of hand with reminders about Mussolini. The 1997 Bicameral Committee's final draft called for the direct election of the president as well as enhanced powers for the prime minister, but this agreement fell apart when Berlusconi argued that it did not go far enough in the direction of presidentialism. Although informed observers agreed that presidentialism was used as a pretext to scuttle the *Bicamerale*, it is revealing that this was the argument the Center-Right chose for a public justification.[8]

The underlying idea is both simple and time honored in democratic theory: If officials are chosen directly by the voters, they will be held more accountable for their actions—or, all too often in Italy, for their inaction. This idea informed the 1993 referendum that produced the mostly single-member system for parliamentary elections. It also contributed to the systems

adopted for mayoral elections in towns with a population greater than 15,000 and for the regions, where voters cast a ballot (with a premium) for a preferred designated executive.[9] The municipal and regional reforms have been successes, although they have hardly been the magic bullet that some reformers—irresponsibly—have promised since 1993. It is easy to smile at naiveté that suggests that the proper institutional tinkering will give Italy the efficiency of Britain or Germany. But that such serious changes are proposed without much thought about how they might work in the Italian context does reflect the frustration felt across most of the spectrum at the current state of prime minister–cabinet and executive–legislative relations.

Decree Laws. One area that received considerable attention in the 1988 reform was the use of executive decrees: The cabinet issues a pronouncement that has the force of law, although this is temporary and must be converted by a vote of Parliament within sixty days. This practice had been abused increasingly from the 1970s (see Chapter 24). Although decrees are constitutionally reserved for emergencies and times of extreme necessity (Article 77), by the 1980s nearly a fifth of all legislation originated in this fashion.[10] In a fragmented system where clear governmental programs and legislative time-tables were nonexistent, "emergency" measures had become a way to ensure that legislation dear to the prime minister and key cabinet members got Parliament's attention. There were, moreover, abuses that revealed the executive's impatience with Parliament's powers, most notably the practice of continually reissuing decrees when Parliament did not pass them within the prescribed sixty days.

The reform addressed the worst abuses by limiting the subject matter on which decrees can be issued: Electoral laws, budgets, legislative powers, and international treaties are totally excluded. The reform also forbids reissuing a decree that has not been passed in the required period if one chamber has voted it down. The old practice of tacking numerous unrelated riders onto decrees has been eliminated as well, putting an end to omnibus decrees. The content of decrees now must actually correspond to their title and be phrased in such a way as to be immediately applicable.[11] One gets some sense from these provisions of the extent of the abuses that used to take place, but many abuses continued despite the 1988 law. For example, only a 1996 decision of the Constitutional Court finally put an end to the continued reissuing of decrees, despite the earlier legislation. And because of this ruling, the conversion of decrees was often achieved only by making their approval a question of confidence in the government (thus forcing an end to debate—and interminable stalling), although this rather desperate practice was hardly unknown prior to 1996. A leading expert on the subject has concluded that in recent years, the executive has clearly augmented its power in relation to the legislature, but only by resorting to this and similar measures, such as pressuring its own majority in Parliament to delegate to the cabinet the enactment of specified legislation.[12] As is so often the case in Italy, the problem is not only the weakness of the executive but its problems in managing warring factions within the majority.

Public Administration and Para-State Agencies

Few institutions enjoy much public respect in Italy, but the bureaucracy is especially reviled, and with reason. Centralized and inflexible traditions, outmoded recruitment, grossly inadequate pay and working conditions (and a ridiculously short working day), ironclad job security, and practically every other shortcoming known to complex organizations are all combined in Italy's public administration. Its problems are so widely acknowledged that a Ministry for Bureaucratic Reform was long a fixture on the political scene—and the butt of sarcasm. The administrative system of the Italian state hardly

ends with the formal ministerial bureaucracies and the career civil servants who staff them, however. Its most unique aspects are found in the state-owned firms, holding companies, autonomous agencies and enterprises, and special institutions that still saturate the country, despite the accelerating pace of reforms since the 1990s.

This sprawling structure is highly politicized *and* extraordinarily fragmented; it is also the key to understanding the paralysis built into the entire political system. From the early 1950s, the DC consciously tried to create a political base autonomous from the Vatican, business interests, and the United States. While the DC overwhelmingly dominated its coalition partners, it doled out thin slivers of the pie. As its hegemony weakened, the DC was forced to provide its partners with larger shares. By the late 1970s, it even had to distribute limited shares to the organized labor movement and the PCI. But the system is the DC's creation, and that party retained the lion's share of the spoils as long as it existed. The system was fragmented from the very beginning, not so much because of limited power sharing among coalition partners but because the DC itself was divided internally, and this immense spoils system further stimulated the creation of independent power bases within the ruling party. Forty-five uninterrupted years at the center of the system, at least thirty-five of which were spent carving it up, created a dynamic that did not end with the collapse of the DC and PSI.

The Regular Public Administration

With slightly more than 2 million people employed by central ministries and another 2 million scattered throughout all other levels of the public administration, the number of state employees in Italy may seem high at just under 20 percent of the total workforce, but it is not out of line with the rest of Western Europe.[13] The main problem lies in the way ministries are organized; they seem designed to maximize inefficiency and demoralization through the ranks; they are overcentralized and rule bound; promotion disregards merit and rewards seniority and political connections; and the pay and working conditions are terrible. Especially at lower levels, absenteeism is widespread, second jobs are more the rule than the exception, and service is arrogantly delivered and appallingly slow. It is also widely believed that corruption is rampant.

Like the judiciary branch, the bureaucracy's upper reaches in the first generation of the republic were staffed with Fascist appointees, which helped entrench intolerance toward ordinary citizens. A reform got much of the old guard to take early retirement in 1972, but it also swept out the most professional civil servants in the highest ranks of the bureaucracy. The new top cadre, like the old, was highly sensitive to the political balance of power and the desires of the leaders of Italy's ruling parties. With politicians loath to delegate power and bureaucrats afraid of taking independent initiatives, the old system was perpetuated, though it became increasingly rule conscious as unionization spread through the lower administrative ranks and gave workers a new awareness of their rights. Another reform in 1980 attempted to break down the extremely rigid series of job classifications that have contributed to the bureaucracy's inflexibility. But this reform, like so many others, was met with stiff internal resistance. One sensitive observer says these reforms were "ingested" and integrated into the system's old structures and processes.[14] Thanks to political favoritism and its own self-serving behavior, there is one way in which the Italian bureaucracy does stand out: Its top grades are far more bloated than the upper levels of other Western democracies. Fully one of every eight Italian civil servants is found in the top ranks of the bureaucracy.[15]

The system is also perpetuated by its formalism: Entrance examinations stress abstract concepts and knowledge of legal minutiae rather than technical skills. This, along with the low pay, helps account for the high proportion of southerners at all levels of the civil service. Given tradition and the lack of other options in the Mezzogiorno and given as well the high enrollment of southerners in legal and philosophical faculties in the universities, the civil service has historically offered a chance to those who hope to earn a living without moving to the north or leaving the country.

Yet despite all the legal-rational trappings, the civil service, with a few exceptions, is highly fragmented and shot through with influence and patronage. Ministries set their own entry requirements and supervise their own examinations. A tradition of autonomous, centralized little empires was reinforced under the republic, as ministries were "colonized" by the ruling parties, often by one or two power groups within the DC. Especially for upper-level appointments, where long essays and oral exams are the allegedly objective basis on which candidates are judged, favored applicants easily get past the hurdles.

This colonization perpetuated fragmentation at the top of the system and penetrated down to the grass roots, making the bureaucracy an effective patronage machine but a much less satisfactory mechanism for the delivery of services. The results are disastrous all along the line: division, incoherence, and infighting at the center and indifferent service on the delivery end. A series of reforms at the end of the 1990s was meant to streamline and decentralize the bureaucracy, and it did produce important innovations in center-periphery relations. At the same time, the really important functions—control over personnel and the purse strings—remained firmly in the hands of the central government.

State Enterprises, Autonomous Agencies, and Special Institutions

Italy's public agencies have counterparts nearly everywhere in the advanced capitalist world, although Italian agencies are astonishingly prolific. Their number ranges anywhere from 40,000 to 54,000, depending on how one

counts.[16] State monopolies in Italy may historically have covered a few unusual sectors (salt
and bananas come to mind) and some public
corporations may have slightly different structures elsewhere, but the state-run, nonstock
corporation is a stranger to few modern capitalist societies. In Italy, the key industries of this
type, such as the railroads and telephone and
telegraph services, date back to the turn of the
century.

Health, pension, social security, and welfare
agencies and institutions are also commonly nationalized services, although in most advanced
societies many of these are under direct ministerial control. In Italy they evolved as autonomous agencies, parallel to Catholic and other
charitable institutions. They are organized under the umbrella of the Ministry of Labor and
Welfare, but the major institutions maintain autonomous control over the investment of their
own funds, which amount to billions of dollars.
They operate under strict controls, but their potential leverage over the economy is immense.
The largest agency is the Social Security Institute (INPS), and for at least twenty years there
have been discussion and halting steps toward
reorganizing and making the entire range of
welfare agencies under INPS more efficient.
This process has accelerated since the mid-
1970s, but it has been resisted fiercely by thousands of local mini-agencies representing a variety of special interests.

All Western societies contain abundant examples of the political use of state services, but
Italy is unique in the degree to which the control of state and para-state agencies, as well as
the allocation of payments, became flagrant instruments of political patronage. Italy is also
distinguished by the degree to which the political parties have been the direct agents (and
beneficiaries) of such practices.[17] A classic case is
the political use of the disability pension. By the
early 1980s, the total number of such pensions
reached 7.2 million, accounting for 4.5 percent
of GDP.

The extent and variety of public ownership of

industry has made Italy unique among West
European democracies. The Institute for Industrial Reconstruction (IRI) was not disbanded or
its holdings privatized at war's end; its role in
the economy steadily expanded, and other holding companies, most notably ENI, an energy
conglomerate, and EFIM, covering state-owned
industries in the south, were also created. The
degeneration of the holding companies, combined with unrelenting pressure from the European Union (EU), finally resulted in the formal
dissolution of IRI in 2000, although much of its
stock still remains in the Treasury rather than
in private hands.

These extensive resources played an active
role in Italy's reconstruction and in laying the
groundwork for the Economic Miracle. From
admirable beginnings, the picture increasingly
became one of narrow partisanship and the indiscriminate distribution of positions to key
power groups' numerous constituencies. Positions of immense influence were doled out in
proportion to parties' (or factions') political
leverage—a phenomenon the Italians call
lottizzazione. The result was a system where
purely political, or extremely shortsighted, criteria govern decisions. As the DC's hold on
power slipped, squabbling over the debt-ridden
system grew. By the 1980s, two of the DC's fiefs,
the Ministry of State Participation and the chair
of ENI, passed to the Socialists. Deregulation
and very limited privatization began in the
1980s, with both ENI and IRI moving away
from bailout operations and back toward more
market-oriented decisions. But while the PSI
portrayed itself as a champion of the free market, it used its positions of power to consolidate
and extend its own political networks. Only
with the collapse of the old party system and the
establishment of more rigorous technical governments under Amato, Ciampi, and Dini in the
1990s was privatization undertaken in a more
serious and sustained fashion. Even then, it was
often sabotaged or ferociously opposed by entrenched interests inside the public firms as well
as by powerful banking and industrial interests

in the private sector who were in no rush to see the economy become too competitive.

Other State Institutions

Few institutions have proven as controversial in the transition to Italy's so-called Second Republic as the judicial branch of government. And no institutions have been as central to debates about reforms than Italy's subnational levels of government.

The Judiciary

Like the rest of the political system, the judiciary was plagued by blatant and cynical political manipulation from the earliest days of the republic. For a full generation, its top echelons were filled with people who openly rejected most of the constitution's innovations. Even under conditions of normalcy, the fight against organized crime and political corruption was often hampered when investigations got too close to centers of political power. Since 1992, corruption scandals have shown how effective judicial investigators can be when they are not held back. The corruption scandals turned prosecutors into national heroes, but they also reinforced trends toward an increasingly politicized judiciary and raise troubling questions about the role of the courts in a modern democracy. Here, as elsewhere, Italy's institutional framework is by no means fully consolidated.

The Slow Implementation of the Constitution. Article 104 of the constitution affirms the judiciary's independence from other branches of government, but it took fifteen years for many of its provisions to be enacted. The DC simply stalled the creation of the Constitutional Court and the Superior Council of the Judiciary as long as it could. These departures from continental tradition were inspired by the ease with which fascism had trampled Liberal Italy's legal structures. The DC defended judicial au-

'A LIVELLA

In 1993, the leaders of the four major parties are all portrayed as involved in Tangentopoli. The executioner is the leading prosecutor of that period, Antonio Di Pietro.

Source: Reproduced by permission of Giorgio Forattini from Giorgio Forattini, *Mascalzonate: Il Meglio di Forattini a Colori.*

tonomy in the Constituent Assembly, but it promptly abandoned the principle once it was in power.

The Constitutional Court has fifteen members, appointed on a rotating basis to nine-year nonrenewable terms. A third of its members are named by Parliament, a third by the president of the republic, and the remaining third by the highest courts in the country. Much like the U.S. Supreme Court, it can only review cases on appeal. It cannot, in other words, rule on the constitutionality of a law after it has been passed but before it is promulgated, as in France, nor can it be directly petitioned, as in Germany.

In the early postwar period, the highest-ranking appeals judges, mostly Fascist appointees, interpreted the constitution on extremely narrow grounds. These legal conservatives never accepted the principle of judicial review and often flouted the rulings of the Constitutional Court once it was established. They greatly delayed the evolution of the legal and judicial system until, by the end of the 1970s, they had largely faded from the scene.

A major reason for leaving the previous system of justice intact through the late 1950s had nothing to do with legal principles. It was during this time that efforts were made to marginalize the Left and weaken it in every possible way, and a Fascist penal code simplified that task. Because the 1931 code was intended to outlaw all political activity, it does not take much imagination to realize how thoroughly the labor movement could be obstructed and harassed by the state's legal apparatus.

Pressures from above and below finally forced the system to change. The Constitutional Court eventually established itself as an autonomous body that would strike down national or regional laws that contravened the constitution, including large chunks of the penal code. Parliament's immobility enabled the court to take the initiative by eliminating old laws and codes to such an extent that legislators were forced to act, for example, in extending women's rights and in reforming family law. In general, the court's activism and relative independence (in spite of the fact that most of its members are political appointees) have made it one of the more respected political institutions in the country. This is much less true of the higher levels of the regular criminal courts: investigations take blatantly false and politically motivated paths for years, powerful judges shift the venues of investigations to sabotage them, decisions are rendered for extremely obscure motives, and so on.

Formally, the judicial branch is insulated from direct political interference by the Superior Council of the Judiciary, which was instituted in 1959. This is a thirty-member body, two-thirds of whose members are directly elected by members of the judiciary, thus further reinforcing its independence. The remaining third is chosen by Parliament from practicing lawyers and legal academics. It is presided over by the president of the republic, though its vice president, chosen from within the council's ranks, is the effective chief executive.

Changes in the judiciary were stimulated from below when increasing numbers of judges entered the system at the lower levels. By the 1960s, young recruits brought social ferment to the profession. The stranglehold of the conservative old guard was gradually broken, and the profession is now governed by civil service rules (e.g., tenure and de facto automatic promotion based on seniority) in a setting that can be highly politicized. The judiciary is divided into numerous organized factions, which break down into three broad political tendencies. In the late 1990s, conservatives represented about a fifth of the judges, the centrist faction had a commanding (60 percent) majority, and the left-wing faction accounted for roughly a fourth of the *magistratura*.[18] Since the 1970s, judges have engaged in strikes and job actions. The Superior Council has been the site of highly politicized disputes that break along classic left-right lines but also of more corporate struggles in which the judiciary as a body tries to assert its rights or prerogatives against outside interference.

The willingness of the judiciary to organize and promote itself aggressively, combined with numerous privileges granted it by law, has given this body immense power, raising serious questions about the judiciary's insulation from the political process.[19] The bureaucracy of the Ministry of Justice is, notoriously, the creature of the judges, who are legally entitled to its top positions. Judges are allowed to lobby external agencies with little concern for what would be considered a conflict of interest in other countries. Nor is there a ban on judges' standing for political office or participating in arbitration panels or other semipublic agencies. These privileges—or abuses—have produced numerous efforts over the years to cut down their power, further politicizing their role.

Delayed Reform. All advanced capitalist democracies face serious problems in their systems of justice, but the Italian situation truly seems to be more acute. Texts written a quarter-century ago wondered how the system had managed to survive into the 1970s, and matters have become much worse since.[20] Irrationality is at the very heart of things. Remnants of a Fascist legal code coexist with a progressive constitution, and structures that evolved under a highly centralized state must contend with judicial review, which assumes the separation of powers.

Judges themselves evoke contradictory public responses. There is immense sympathy for prosecuting magistrates, who literally risk their lives when they exercise the duties of office. In the late 1970s and early 1980s, they were the targets of left-wing terrorists; since then, threats and murders have been carried out by the mafia. At the same time, the arbitrary workings of the regular courts are legendary. Wrongful prosecutions, endless delays, and damaging leaks to the press without the possibility of response by the accused have ruined many reputations. Public resentment reached a head in 1987 when a referendum was held to abolish the laws that limited the civil responsibility of judges to a few highly circumscribed situations. More than 80 percent of the voters supported the referendum, to the dismay of the judges and the embarrassment of the major parties, all of which had originally opposed the vote and then vacillated shamefully when it became clear that public opinion favored making judges more accountable.

In 1989, after a decade of delays and an additional four years of parliamentary debate, a new code of penal procedure was finally enacted in the wake of the referendum. It has been modified considerably since then by rulings of the Constitutional Court, continued tinkering on the part of Parliament, and even constitutional amendment. Although some critics condemn it as an amalgam of two different legal systems, it still is an improvement over the old (Fascist) code, which permitted, among other things, situations in which the accused was not informed of the charges or evidence until a trial date was set. Pretrial investigations and trial deliberations are now far more open. The new code also entrenches the principle of the equality of the accused and the prosecution, as the constitution had insisted for forty years. Preventive detention, which in the past could be drawn out for as long as ten years, has been reduced. Its counterpart, conditional liberty—the release of suspects when it is determined they are unlikely to flee and represent no threat to society—has been expanded considerably. Another significant change was the elimination of the formerly all-powerful prosecuting magistrate.

But public prosecutors remain part of the judiciary in Italy and retain more police powers than similar figures in other Western constitutional democracies, where, moreover, they are under the control of the executive branch of government. During *Tangentopoli*, the liberal use of preventive detention enabled prosecutors to hold suspects for as long as ninety days, producing far speedier confessions than would have been the case had a more civil libertarian approach been followed. These techniques, combined with some prosecutors' penchant for self-promotion and well-timed leaks of privileged information to the press, turned many of these figures into instant heroes while convincing many politicians that the prosecutors had a clear political agenda. The worst abuses are sufficient to give pause to sober observers on all points of the political spectrum.

There are deep-seated problems that institutional reforms can hardly touch, but any improvement in the situation is long overdue. Cases are so backlogged, the machinery grinds so slowly, and the system is so inefficient that the intolerable becomes the norm. To cite but one example, when the new penal code was formally instituted in 1989, there was a backlog of

2.7 *million* criminal cases that would have to be tried using the old system in force when these arrests were made.[21] Those unfortunate enough to be jailed for minor offenses regularly serve the maximum sentence before coming to trial, and even those accused of more serious crimes may languish in pretrial detention for years. An incredible 60 percent of Italy's prison population is awaiting trial, a situation that is regularly denounced by the European Court of Human Rights and the Council of Ministers. Lawyers regularly stall their clients' cases, knowing that amnesties are issued every few years to clear the docket. When sentences finally are handed down, they are often so lengthy and obscure that even experts have trouble deciphering them. In a country that produces a sarcastic remark for almost every occasion, few are as telling as, "Italy is the cradle of the law and the grave of justice."

Local Government

There are three main levels of subnational government in Italy: *comuni* (the Italian term for all municipalities, towns, and cities), provinces, and regions. As political entities, the *comuni* were by far the most important through the 1970s, and they remain the liveliest site of local politics in the country, especially following important reforms in the 1990s. In terms of administrative importance, however, the province has historically been the major subdivision of the country, linked directly by the prefect, a member of the national bureaucracy, to the Ministry of the Interior in Rome and run at times like colonial offices. Because their boundaries are often arbitrary and the implementation of the regions seems to make them unnecessary, there is strong feeling that the provinces should be eliminated altogether. The regions, although steeped in history, had no formal status until the formation of the republic, and only the Special Regions had any significant powers until the 1970s. This situation has also changed, al-

though not as dramatically as many had hoped. As federalism has moved to the top of the political agenda, the regions occupy an increasingly important place in subnational politics.

The Comuni

There are roughly eight thousand *comuni* in Italy. The large size of the average *comune* means that towns are generally populous enough to reproduce most of the parties, and the partisan conflict, found at the national level. Until 1992, towns with more than 5,000 inhabitants voted according to proportional representation, with the size of the city council varying (from twenty to eighty) according to the size of the *comune*. In 1993, a new law for towns with populations greater than 15,000 maintained list voting but introduced a separate, more important ballot for individual mayoral candidates.[22] Mayors are now directly elected. If no candidate obtains an absolute majority on the first ballot, a runoff is held between the top two candidates. Significantly, the victorious candidate on the second ballot is guaranteed a working majority of the seats in city council. Parties must therefore support a candidate, and they are assigned seats proportionally from the winners' (60 percent) or the losers' (40 percent) column. The high voter turnout in general elections (80–85 percent) is nearly matched in local elections, which occur every five years on a schedule that must not conflict with general elections.

This new system, introduced during the collapse of the old ruling parties and the rise to prominence of the Leagues in the North and the ex-MSI National Alliance in the South, has greatly hastened a dramatic political turnover on the municipal level. Since the mid-1990s, the mayors of Italy's larger cities have enjoyed very high visibility and legitimacy because they were directly elected. Some of them have used this leverage to vault onto the national political stage.

Before the regional reforms, *comuni* were often heavily monitored by the prefects, who had immense power at their disposal. They could veto budgets, dissolve local governments, and install prefectorial commissions of nonpolitical specialists if local crises dragged on too long.

Municipal government has been important for the opposition in Italy. Its exclusion from national power led the PCI from the start to place great symbolic importance, and expend a great deal of energy, on local politics. At a minimum, the Communists tended to govern honestly and efficiently, and this alone attracted attention. Increasingly in the 1960s and 1970s, the Communists used their local administrations more aggressively as showpieces. They did not originate the idea of decentralizing services to neighborhoods, banning traffic in historic areas, and greatly multiplying cultural and recreational facilities, but they did put these experiments into effect and keep them operating. Ultimately their record helped earn a considerable measure of legitimacy for the PCI. In the 1990s, the PDS/DS cleverly used the new electoral rules to create broad Center-Left alliances, often built around attractive mayoral candidates without machine politics backgrounds. This enabled the Left to return to the government of most of Italy's largest cities and foreshadowed the coalition that won the 1996 general elections.

The Regions

The PCI's historic strength in the red zones, where it regularly obtained more than 40 percent of the vote, explains why the DC dragged its heels in devolving power to the regions, thus depriving the major opposition party of an important political lever. This was not the only instance of constitutional sabotage by the ruling party, but it was the most nakedly partisan in motivation. Although the regions were recognized in the constitution, enabling legislation allowing them to function was passed only in 1970.

Two types of regions were anticipated by the constitution. The five Special Regions, established in the 1940s, consist of the two major islands of Sardinia and Sicily and three areas on the northern border of the country with strong French, Germanic, and Slavic cultural characteristics. The fifteen ordinary regions were the source of all the foot dragging. Like the larger city governments, Regional Councils vary in size according to population. They are elected for five-year terms and, as has happened at every level of Italian political life in the 1990s, a new electoral system, different from all the others, is now in place. Through 1990, Regional Councils were chosen by proportional list systems. A complicated dual ballot was introduced for the 1995 regional elections, and in 2000 it was refined by recourse to a constitutional amendment that now allows for the direct election of regional presidents in a single ballot. (The direct election of mayors had a powerful influence on these changes.) Alliances are constructed by party lists around presidential candidates, with each list declaring its support of one or another candidate. These alliances are important, for only 80 percent of the seats are distributed proportionally to the lists. The remaining seats on the Regional Council serve as a premium to "top up" the winner's share, thus guaranteeing that the victors receive a working majority—generally a minimum of 55 to 60 percent—of all seats in the council. Moreover, the winning majority is "blocked" for two years; that is, those who declared their alliance must stick to it or call new elections. This precaution is intended to avoid coalitions of convenience that would divide the winner's premium and then immediately dissolve, with each party keeping the additional seats for itself.

Rome has historically kept the regions, like the *comuni*, on a tight leash, although there has been an unmistakable move away from centralization since the 1990s. Because Italy does not have a federal system, taxes go into the center and then come back to the regions—through an eye dropper, complain local politicians. There were high hopes that the 1997 Bicameral Committee would produce a truly federal constitution. For a while, there was even talk of converting the (totally redundant) Senate into a "Chamber of the Regions," much like the German Bundesrat. But the *Bicamerale*'s final draft fell far short of this goal. Indeed, its rather wishy-washy semi-federal proposals were themselves a response to the regions' anger at its even weaker original proposals.

In the absence of thoroughgoing constitutional reform, Italy nevertheless did pass a series of laws in 1997 and 1998 that extensively overhauled the central government's relations with local government, and especially the regions.[23] Article 117 of the constitution had reserved numerous policy areas for the regions, but as was so often the case, many of these provisions were left unrealized for decades. Until these reforms, regional legislation was straitjacketed by guidelines firmly established in Rome. Now, at least in some areas (public education, universities, transportation), there is more true autonomy at the local level. The reforms also establish, for the first time, a permanent structure, called a "United Conference," in which representatives of the various levels of government must coordinate relevant policies.

These are important innovations, and the momentum would appear irreversible, but this is still a long way from federalism. Rome continues to disburse about 90 percent of the funds the regions are permitted to spend and further specifies where the bulk of these funds must be spent. When the regions were made operational in the 1970s, certain areas of competence passed from Rome to the regions, and so did many bureaucrats. Even with the new legislation, the final decision in hiring or firing many public servants—teachers, for example—remains in Rome's hands, limiting local initiatives and flexibility. Above all, at a time when a strong sense of regional identity has been growing, particularly in the north, those in power at the center have shown themselves to be extremely timid in terms of innovative policies and new institutional arrangements.

Evidence that the regions have become rooted in Italy is that they tend to reproduce the country's historical cleavages in their own operations. In a famous, and controversial, study, political scientist Robert Putnam argues that by almost all relevant measures—from how efficiently they deliver services to whether they even manage to spend the funds earmarked for their use—the south lags behind the rest of the country, while the red regions and the northern industrialized areas show the most initiative. Innovative policies often give way to a rather crass division of spoils among the governing parties, but the regions have been far more than a pork barrel in the northern half of the country.[24] It is hard to argue with the evidence. Enactment of legislation to put the 1997–1998 reforms into practice has once again seen the north and center in the lead, with the south well in arrears. Yet recent developments suggest that the situation in the south might not be quite as irreversible as Putnam sometimes seems to suggest. For instance, the Campania region, and its capital city, Naples, have, by general agreement, made amazing progress since the mid-1990s.

Federalism has remained high on the political agenda ever since the Northern League's rapid rise put it there. The Center-Left's last act before Parliament was dissolved in 2001 was to begin to amend the constitution, introducing a more formal federal restructuring of the Italian state. The Center-Right pledged to defeat or, if necessary, to revoke this proposal and replace it with one of its own. The stage is thus set for a protracted conflict that is likely to last well into the first decade of the twenty-first century.

The European Dimension

Italy's efforts to enter the Economic and Monetary Union (EMU), and then to remain a member in good standing, required modifications not only of the country's policymaking processes, but many of its structures as well. To ensure compliance with EU directives, the Department for the Coordination of Community Policies was established and given ministerial status. The same pressures led to the deregulation of financial markets, the abolition of the Ministry of State Holdings early in the 1990s, and, perhaps more subtle, even the creation of the Treasury and Budget superministry later in the same decade. These long-overdue actions reflected the need to streamline and modernize economic decision making, but once EU standards had become imperative, such streamlining could not be avoided any longer.

This is most evident with regard to privatization, although Italy is still under pressure from European institutions to conform more fully to EU policies. Still, no serious observer of Italy's political economy could doubt for a moment that such a momentous step as the dissolution of IRI would ever have occurred without the persistent pressure that came from the EU. European pressures are even more unambiguously responsible for dramatic changes in Italian policymaking processes. Budgetary structures were not only changed, but budgetary decision making was profoundly altered, at the direct expense of the once all-powerful Parliament. With deficits and public spending under intense external scrutiny, governments had little, if any, maneuvering room of the kind that used to allow them to run up deficits, and spread largesse, with impunity.

Policy Processes: Continuity and Transition

On paper, the Italian Republic's strong unitary tradition and bureaucratic structures, its history of extensive involvement in the economy, and a single party that dominated the executive branch for nearly two generations would appear to guarantee it most of the components needed for a decisive and coherent system of government. But this was almost never the case. The consequences of a divided and sometimes paralyzed executive are often most visible in re-

forms that come very slowly indeed, or in economic and tax policies that seem more intent on not enraging constituents and clients than on achieving any clearly defined goals.

In strictly economic terms, Italy has in many ways been extremely well served by the lack of a strong commanding hand on the helm of the economy. The famous adaptability of the Italian private sector, particularly the numerous smaller firms of the north-center, has long been admired for enabling Italy to adjust so rapidly to changing market conditions. Even the state sector was left to pursue autonomous economic policies for much of the postwar period. It is only one of Italy's many ironies that fragmentation and lack of coordination at the top led to a policy that was far more laissez-faire than in many societies with much larger private sectors and a much less explicit commitment to economic planning. This hands-off policy may not have made the machinery of government function better or addressed major social injustices, but it did allow the country's entrepreneurial spirit to flourish.

Laissez-faire, however, is a notoriously risky political approach, especially when conditions change dramatically in a short time span. The policymaking process was fragmented and paralyzed even when the labor movement was on the defensive, the Left was isolated, and the economy was in its most robust phase of expansion. For the existing system, the crunch came following the late 1960s, when previously excluded groups (e.g., the workers' movement, women, young people, and pensioners) forced major breaches in the system that had earlier repelled their demands. Simultaneously, the expanding economy that had enabled the system to that point to pay at least most of its bills suffered a sharp downturn. State-owned enterprises in the vanguard of development just a decade earlier increasingly became drains on an already strapped budget by the 1970s.

As the 1970s proceeded, the DC found parliamentary arithmetic, the social climate, and its own slipping bases of power all working against it. At that point it fell back on the technique it had always employed: *lottizzazione* was extended to those (especially the PCI and the unions) whose social leverage was greatest and whose political demands could no longer be denied. Following the decline of the unions and the PCI at the end of the 1970s, a weakened DC surrendered increased leverage to the PSI. This response to political and social pressure was a shrewd survival tactic that enabled the DC to keep the proverbial half a loaf (and more) while surrendering the minimum necessary to maintain its own hegemony.

The seriousness of the problem is perhaps most evident in the attention that institutional reform has repeatedly gotten. Since the early 1980s, three ambitious efforts to rewrite parts of the constitution failed for the same reasons that reforms are necessary in the first place: the underlying structural problems of the Italian parliamentary system, including a fragmented multiparty system with entrenched interests in no rush to undercut their own power, and heterogeneous coalitions and a highly fragmented cabinet system. Some changes, such as the reform of the executive in 1988 and the reshaping of both ministries and center-regional relations in the 1990s, have been implemented. Others have at least partially addressed the functioning of Parliament and relations between the executive and legislative branches. But reforms to date have been unable to address the nagging underlying issues of reinforced executive authority, on the one hand, and federalism and increased local autonomy on the other.

Change in these two areas will require much more than institutional tinkering. Yet the Italian political system has been in flux since 1992, and the collapse of the *Bicamerale* in 1997 underscored the need for serious institutional transformation and the lack of the strong consensus required to guarantee the passage of truly extensive changes. Electoral reform in 1993 and the elections of 1994 initially appeared to set the country on a new path, but the bitter experience of Berlusconi was almost a caricature of the cabinet instability of the First Republic, and Prodi and D'Alema, with supposedly more solid majorities, fared only slightly better. Given the unlikelihood of any side's winning an overwhelming electoral victory under the existing rules, it is probable that basic disagreements about the proper role of Italy's major institutions—and these institutions' ability to generate policies that are more coherent, in more timely fashion—will remain unresolved for some time.

Notes

1. Piero Calamandrei, cited in P. Vercellone, "The Italian Constitution of 1947–1948," in S. J. Woolf, ed., *The Rebirth of Italy 1943–1950* (New York: Humanities Press, 1972), p. 124.

2. For details, see Enzo Balboni, "President of the Republic, Judges and the Superior Council of the Judiciary," in Stephen Hellman and Gianfranco Pasquino, eds., *Italian Politics: A Review*, vol. 7 (London: Pinter, 1992), pp. 49–67.

3. Gianfranco Pasquino and Salvatore Vassallo, "The Government of Carlo Azeglio Ciampi," in Carol Mershon and Gianfranco Pasquino, eds., *Italian Poli-*

tics: Ending the First Republic (Boulder, Colo.: Westview Press, 1995), pp. 55–73.

4. Mauro Calise and Renato Mannheimer, *Governanti in Italia: Un trentennio repubblicano, 1946–1976* (Bologna: Il Mulino, 1982).

5. The discussion that follows draws on Pietro Barrera, "La prima riforma istituzionale: la nuova disciplina dell'attività di governo," in Raimondo Catanzaro and Raffaella Nanetti, eds., *Politica in Italia: Edizione 1989* (Bologna: Il Mulino, 1989), pp. 51–70, and on Paul Furlong, *Modern Italy: Represen-*

tation and Reform (London: Routledge, 1994), pp. 125ff.

6. David Felsen, "Changes to the Italian Budgetary Regime: The Reforms of Law No. 94/1997," in David Hine and Salvatore Vassallo, eds., *Italian Politics: The Return of Politics* (Oxford: Berghahn Books, 2000), pp. 157–173.

7. D'Alema's short-lived second cabinet contained a record sixty-six undersecretaries by the time it was dissolved. These numbers all come from the Italian press. See especially Barbara Jerkov, "Il valzer dei 54 sottosegretari dentro Minniti, Intini e Chiti," *La Repubblica*, April 28, 2000, p. 9.

8. Gianfranco Pasquino, "A Postmortem of the Bicamerale," in Hine and Vassallo, *The Return of Politics*, p. 105.

9. See Chapter 24 for details on the national electoral system; details on the regional and municipal systems are examined later in this chapter.

10. Vincent della Sala, "Government by Decree: The Craxi Government and the Use of Decree Legislation in the Italian Parliament," in Raffaella Y. Nanetti, Robert Leonardi, and Piergiorgio Corbetta, eds., *Italian Politics: A Review*, vol. 2 (London: Pinter, 1988), p. 11.

11. Salvatore Vassallo, "Le leggi del governo. Come gli esecutivi della transizione hanno superato i veti incrociati," in G. Capano and M. Giuliani, eds., *Il processo legislativo in Italia: continuità e mutamento* (Bologna, Il Mulino, 2000).

12. Barrera, "La prima riforma istituzionale," pp. 63–64.

13. David Hine, *Governing Italy: The Politics of Bargained Pluralism* (Oxford: Clarendon Press, 1993), esp. pp. 232, 237.

14. Furlong, *Modern Italy*, pp. 87–88.

15. Filippo Cavazzuti, "Finanza pubblica e pubblica amministrazione: caratteristiche e limiti della nuova legge finanziaria," in Catanzaro and Nanetti, eds., *Politica in Italia: Edizione 89*, pp. 104–105.

16. For the higher figure, see Furlong, *Modern Italy*, p. 88; for the lower number, see Hine, *Governing Italy*, p. 229.

17. Maurizio Ferrara, "Il mercato politico-assistenziale," in Ugo Ascoli and Raimondo Catanzaro, eds., *La società italiana degli anni ottanta* (Bari: Laterza, 1988), pp. 327–328.

18. Carlo Guarnieri and Patrizia Pederzoli, *La democrazia giudiziaria* (Bologna: Il Mulino, 1997), p. 136.

19. Giuseppe Di Federico, "La crisi del sistema giudiziario e la questione della responsabilità civile dei magistrati," in Piergiorgio Corbetta and Robert Leonardi, eds., *Politica in Italia: Edizione 88* (Bologna: Il Mulino, 1988), esp. pp. 108–113.

20. P. A. Allum, *Italy: Republic Without Government?* (New York: Norton, 1973), p. 184; Raphael Zariski, *Italy: The Politics of Uneven Development* (Hinsdale, Ill.: Dryden Press, 1972), chap. 9, esp. p. 319.

21. Hine, *Governing Italy*, p. 255.

22. For towns with fewer than 15,000 inhabitants, voters choose among lists. The list receiving the most votes, even a relative majority, receives two-thirds of the seats. The remaining third is divided proportionally among all other lists.

23. The discussion draws on Mark Gilbert, "The Bassanini Laws: A Half-Way House in Local Government Reform," in Hine and Vassallo, *The Return of Politics*, pp. 139–155.

24. Robert Putnam, *Making Democracy Work* (Princeton, N.J.: Princeton University Press, 1993).

24

Representation
and Participation

When Italy's 1947 constitution was written, everyone except the extreme Right believed that a strong legislature was the best guarantee against antidemocratic tendencies. Parliamentary primacy, it was believed, would thwart the ambition of any future Mussolini. The Italian Parliament thus has an unusual amount of power and discretion in relation to the executive. Moreover, from the very beginning of the republic, party-dominated politics strengthened Parliament's centrality. It would be unfair to blame all of Parliament's problems on institutional design, however. Many of its problems are the product of a party system that was stalemated for two generations.

The Legislature

Parliament's Powers and Anomalies

As in other parliamentary systems, Italy's Parliament votes governments into and out of office and has wide latitude in passing laws. Additionally, in joint session, it elects (and may impeach) the president of the republic; it chooses a third of the members of the Constitutional Court and of the Superior Council of the Judiciary; and it may amend the constitution. There are two constitutional limits on parliamentary abuses of power. One is judicial review, discussed in the previous chapter. The other is the abrogative referendum, discussed in a later section, which permits the nullification of all or part of some laws by popular vote. Parliament did not pass the relevant enabling legislation for referenda until 1970.

Parliament has several characteristics that seem designed to drag out operations, diffuse authority, and maximize potential mischief. It represents a case of pure bicameralism: the two chambers, with a combined total of roughly 950 members, have *identical* powers. It also has committees that are able to pass laws directly without referral back to the floor of Parliament. Government-sponsored bills enjoy no special status, such as limits to the number of amendments that can be proposed. Since the 1970s, the parliamentary agenda and legislative timetables must be agreed to by all parties, including the opposition; the same holds for decisions to refer legislation to committee. Until recently a secret ballot was required on all final votes for bills in the Chamber of Deputies. Each of these anomalies is worth further attention.

Pure Bicameralism

This clumsy arrangement was produced by Christian Democrat (DC)–Left differences in the Constituent Assembly. Neither side got what it wanted and could only agree on something with no apparent virtues. Despite the two chambers' equality, no standing committee exists to reconcile different versions of similar legislation; each chamber must pass identical versions of a bill before it becomes law. The potential for stalling or sabotaging legislation is most evident when controversial legislation is at stake (e.g., the abortion law in the late 1970s). Yet when the political will exists, party leaders can easily hammer out a compromise. Most observers agree that pure bicameralism is an absurd impediment in a system that already has enough problems. Reform proposals range all the way from outright abolition of the 315-member Senate to making the upper body a "chamber of the regions."

Committees That Legislate

Standing committees' areas of competence parallel the major ministries. As in other legislatures, these bodies can take proposals and amend them beyond recognition or simply bury them by refusing to refer them to the floor of the Chamber or Senate. But committees can also pass a wide variety of proposals directly into law under conditions far less open to scrutiny than on the floor of Parliament. When a committee receives a bill under these conditions, it meets with deliberative powers *(in sede deliberante)*. Upon a request by the cabinet, a fifth of the relevant committee's members, or a tenth of the members of the chamber, the bill must be brought to the floor and voted up or down without debate, an option that is exercised only on highly controversial laws.

The numbers have dropped considerably since the mid-1970s, but the great majority of all legislation is still passed in committee. With so many sites of legislation, the Italian Parliament generated far more laws than any other European legislature in the postwar period: Over a thousand laws are passed in a five-year legislature, yet even this represents a huge drop compared to the past.[1] Despite its prodigious output, the legislature has historically avoided the truly important issues facing the country; the vast majority of laws passed in committee deal with minor matters.

The Parties' Powers

In the early 1970s, new rules gave Parliament and the committees more power while limiting private members' bills, which were previously unlimited. Committees were given the power to hold hearings, subpoena bureaucrats, and deliberate in public.[2] The most striking changes concerned setting agendas. For complex technical reasons as well as to ensure predictability and order in parliamentary operations, these procedures were changed to require agreement of the leaders of all groups in each chamber, including the opposition. If unanimity cannot be achieved, the president (speaker) of each chamber must impose a solution to guarantee the legislature's continued functioning.

The Secret Ballot

The Chamber of Deputies originally mandated a secret ballot on all final votes. Although not strictly required in the Senate, secret ballots are often used there as well, as a small number of legislators can demand it. This practice is a carryover from the 1848 *Statuto albertino*, designed to check tyrannical party leaders, but its effect is to keep citizens from knowing how their representatives vote. In practice, secret ballots have been a license to sabotage one's own party or coalition with impunity. Italians call this sniping, and it has seriously embarrassed and disrupted many governments.

The 1988 reforms discussed in Chapter 23 limited secret votes; spending and revenue bills now require an open vote, and only constitutional amendments, electoral regulations, and questions of personal morality and family law are subject to secret balloting. Nonetheless, the secret vote can still disrupt Parliament and shield legislators from the consequences of their actions. Amid mounting scandals in 1993, Bettino Craxi kept his parliamentary immunity thanks to a secret ballot, which led to the resignation of several ministers, weakening an already discredited legislature.

Blurred Boundaries Between Government and Opposition

Parliament's rules and practices give far more leverage to parties, including the opposition, than is usually the case in parliamentary systems. If we recall that the opposition was dominated by the largest communist party in the Western world, these levers appear even stranger. This apparent paradox is the result of the Communist Party's (PCI) playing the system with great skill, using both porous rules and governing coalitions' chronic difficulties to maximum advantage.

Viewed against this backdrop, the inclusion of the opposition in setting the parliamentary agenda in the early 1970s appears less strange. The PCI had shown itself to be anything but obstructionist, even in a period of intense popular mobilization and polarization. To involve the opposition in procedural matters was one way of ensuring predictability in Parliament's operations.

Despite reforms in the 1970s and 1980s, parliamentary instability actually increased from the 1970s on. Between 1972 and 2001, only two legislatures lasted for a full five-year term. All others were dissolved in order to hold early elections. In addition, the period required to form a cabinet during a governmental crisis doubled after the mid-1960s, and executive decrees became routine until the Constitutional Court put an end to their worst abuses in 1996. These disturbing trends were well in place when the party system, though eroding, was still relatively stable. Since the early 1990s, that system has disintegrated. On the positive side of the ledger, the new electoral system appears to have reduced significantly the time required both for the president to choose a prime minister designate and for the candidate to present his cabinet to Parliament.

Representative Principles and the Electoral System

Adults over the age of eighteen are automatically registered to vote for the Chamber of Deputies. Suffrage for the Senate is restricted to those age twenty-five or older. Senators must be at least forty years old, and deputies must be at least twenty-one. Through 1992, elections were held under a permissive form of proportional representation (PR), especially for the 630-seat Chamber, where roughly 1.5 percent of the vote usually guaranteed seats to a party. This system, in which voters select a party list and seats are then assigned in relation to the total votes that party obtains, was often blamed for the many small parties in Parliament. It also had aspects that magnified infighting and divisions within the same party. Voters could write in as many as four names from their chosen list; candidates within each list were elected according to how many of these preference votes they received, enabling those far down the list to jump to the top. Designed to limit the power of party bosses (who set the order on the lists), preference votes became an instrument used by members of factions of the same party against one another or by organized crime to deliver blocks of votes to accommodating politicians. Abuses led to the 1991 referendum that limited voters' choice to a single name.

A 1993 referendum then forced sweeping changes on the entire electoral system. The original goal was to eliminate PR altogether. It was felt that a single-member, first-past-the-post system would reduce the number of parties and force elected representatives to be more responsive to their constituents. Finally, it was hoped that fewer parties contending in a winner-take-all system would help produce a bipolar party system; two parties might be an unrealistic aspiration, but even two clear clusters or coalitions of parties would be a big improvement.

The reform that followed the 1993 referendum was a cumbersome compromise, produced by the very parties that were the targets of the referendum (and sixteen parties sat in the Parliament that passed this law), and by a DC committed to proportional principles.[3] The result is a mixed single-member and proportional system. Three-fourths of all seats are assigned on a first-past-the-post basis, and the remaining quarter are distributed according to PR lists. The new law is less permissive than the old; parties must now get at least 4 percent of the vote to obtain any seats from the PR lists. Otherwise their PR votes go into a pool that is distributed only to lists that exceed the 4 percent floor.

In some ways, the new system has been a success. It produced the Freedom Pole and Pole of Good Government, led by Silvio Berlusconi, and the leftist Progressive Alliance for the 1994 elections. In 1996 a more simplified array was present as well, as (minus the League) a single Freedom Pole represented the Center-Right throughout the entire country, and the Olive Tree coalition represented the Center-Left, and the same two blocs faced each other again in 2001. The new rules effectively compel rival blocs to unite behind a candidate for prime minister, giving a personal dimension to general elections. In the past, in contrast, backroom intrigues often determined who would lead the government only after the votes were counted.

But electoral systems are not magic bullets. The blocs that have been forced to form out of the existing parties are extremely heterogeneous since the party system remains in a phase of dramatic transition. One need only think of the quick collapse of Berlusconi's alliance with Umberto Bossi's Northern League, or Romano Prodi losing a confidence vote when the far Left abandoned him, or Massimo D'Alema replacing Prodi only when a small centrist group deserted

the Freedom Pole to support the Center-Left. Moreover, much petty maneuvering typical of the First Republic has returned. Battles regularly erupt within coalitions over the assignment of the safest single-member seats or the highest positions on combined lists. And cynical deals between very different forces are a constant temptation. Both major blocs openly courted the League in 1996, before it decided to stand alone. As Berlusconi feared, the League cost the Center-Right many seats in the north by splitting the vote. In 2001, political reality brought these allies-become-enemies back together, aiding the Center-Right's return to power.

Reformers have failed to eliminate the remnants of PR. Two separate referenda (in 1999 and 2000) were nullified when the required 50 percent of registered voters failed to turn out. Following these failures, the survival of the existing hybrid system or a new compromise making the system even more proportional seem the likely scenarios.

The Abrogative Referendum as an Instrument of Protest and Change

One of the most distinctive aspects of Italian political life since the enabling law of 1970 has been the frequency with which the abrogative referendum has been used to challenge Parliament. The first, on divorce in 1974, was an unsuccessful attempt to roll back progressive legislation. Since then, with a few notable exceptions, this instrument has been employed to raise issues that Parliament could or would not address. The disruptive headline-grabbing aspects of referenda are beyond doubt, particularly when they deal with contentious topics, as they often do, or when they are promoted by flamboyant figures.

Referenda in 1991 and 1993 hastened the demise of the old party system, producing massive majorities in favor of changes in the electoral system. Applauded by many as a grass-roots antidote to political paralysis and the parties' suffocation of civil society, referenda are seen by others as single-issue politics that degrade political participation by forcing a yes-no vote on complex and even obscure questions. They were used so often and indiscriminately in the wake of the successes of the early 1990s that their future is now problematic.

A referendum's sponsors must specify the law, or parts of a law, that they wish to eliminate. Then they must convince five regional councils to pass identical motions requesting a referendum. This method was never used until 1993, when growing impatience with the central government finally provoked a flurry of regional resolutions. The most common procedure has been to obtain half a million valid voters' signatures, usually a political campaign in itself. If the signatures are obtained (upwards of 700,000 are collected for insurance), the courts then rule on the validity of the challenge, for not all laws are subject to abrogation, and technicalities can void the effort. If the referendum is declared admissible, a vote must be held within a prescribed period, with all the costs and disruptions that this implies. Should Parliament amend the targeted legislation before the vote, the referendum is nullified. If Parliament does not act in time, the vote is held, and if at least half the electorate turns out, the law is abrogated (a majority votes yes) or it stands.

Between 1974 and 2000, referenda were held on twelve separate occasions, with fifty-three items subjected to abolition. On several dozen other occasions, sufficient signatures were gathered only to be rejected by the courts or derailed at the last minute by frantic parliamentary activity. Significant laws, such as the two-ballot system now used to elect mayors, are the product of such last-minute scrambling. In a few instances, Parliament was about to amend a targeted law but was paralyzed by obstructionism, for the parties supporting the referendum wanted the issue to come to a vote.

Despite the positive role that the electoral referenda played, it is easy to understand why many people want to limit the topics that can be subject to a referendum, increase the number of signatures required, or both. After being used in selective fashion on issues of great moment such as divorce, abortion, and the *scala mobile*, their abuse has produced understandable impatience. Between 1974 and 1985, voters were called out on just four occasions to vote on nine questions (two of which overlapped). Between 1987 and 2000, there were eight separate trips to the polls, with a total of forty-four questions put to the voters. On the last three such occasions, all fifteen questions were nullified by insufficient voter turnout.

The turnout for referenda steadily declined through the 1980s. But in 1991 and again in 1993, when the electoral system (which everyone understood to mean the party system) was on trial, the turnout rate climbed again, demonstrating that the referendum remains a potent instrument when it is used judiciously.[4]

Political Parties and the Evolution of the Party System

The Italian political system was dominated for two generations by a handful of parties and a distinctive party system. All of the important old parties either no longer exist or have undergone profound changes. In addition, important new parties—and many marginal ones—have arisen, while the party system has become more fluid, and is likely to remain so for some time. It is important to understand the current dynamic, its most important actors and most likely scenarios. Yet ignoring the past would render the present incomprehensible, especially since so much of the present reflects conscious efforts to avoid the problems of the past. At the same time, many politicians appear nostalgic for bygone days. We therefore begin with the past and recall its most important characteristics.

*The Party System Through the Late 1980s:
Christian Democratic Centrality*

The centrality of the DC (Christian Democrats) refers to two things: its occupation of the center of the political spectrum and the fact that its size made it the key player in every governing coalition. Its centrality reflected the unacceptability of the large left-wing and smaller right-wing opposition parties as participants in any government, neither of which was considered loyal to the democratic rules of the game. These divisions, faithfully mirrored by proportional representation, created one of the most immobile party systems in the democratic world. Even as cold war tensions faded, the underlying dynamic determined the formation of every Italian government between 1947 and 1994.

For forty-five years, centrist or Center-Left coalitions governed Italy; the only mystery was which minor parties would be the DC's partner and share the booty. The Center, totally dominated by the DC, held stable at around 40 percent through the 1970s. Three small lay (non-Catholic) parties were the DC's satellites. As the DC's share of the vote dropped well below 40 percent in the 1980s, its reliance on the Socialists became absolute, a dependency the PSI (Socialist Party) was quick to exploit.

The Left was divided between Communists and Socialists but was dominated by the PCI (Italian Communist Party) from 1948 on. Several smaller formations—far Left, ecological, and civil libertarian—came to occupy a limited but growing space on this part of the spectrum. Even counting the PSI as part of the Left (an increasingly difficult task by the 1980s), the Left rose steadily to a high of more than 45 percent in the 1970s but slipped to closer to 40 percent thereafter.

The small but persistent extreme Right was represented exclusively by the neofascists after 1972 (when the fading monarchists joined the MSI, or Italian Social Movement). The neofascists were the real pariahs of the party system, and not only because of their dubious history. Their commitment to democracy remained questionable into the 1980s, and in the 1960s and 1970s, some of their more militant members seemed uncomfortably close to antidemocratic and even terrorist groups.

The End of the Old Equilibrium (1989 and Beyond)

The party system had grown less stable by the 1980s. The number of parties in Parliament and the proportion of the vote going to new parties rose steadily, especially at the end of the decade. A dozen parties held seats in Parliament at the beginning of the 1980s, and their number reached sixteen ten years later. More dramatic, the share of the vote going to new lists went from a tenth in 1987, to a quarter in 1992, to nearly half in 1994. Before the tumultuous events between 1992 and 1994, the Northern League, which had barely a handful of seats even as late as 1987, appeared destined to reap the benefits of the DC's weakening grasp on its traditional constituencies.

The crumbling old system then received three decisive jolts. First, and most important, was the PCI's decision, within days of the fall of the Berlin Wall, to end its existence and form the Democratic Party of the Left (PDS). This transformation took far longer than planned. It initially weakened the Left, but it undercut the anticommunist logic that had underpinned all previous governing coalitions. Then came *Tangentopoli*, beginning in 1992, which weakened and then shattered the DC and PSI—but only because the Left was no longer occupied by a powerful, united communist party. Finally, a new electoral system, introduced in 1993, frustrated the DC's ability to occupy the middle of the spectrum.

At first it seemed as if things would hardly change. At most, the League seemed poised to replace the DC as the north's dominant party.

As in the Soviet Union, no one imagined that things could change—indeed disintegrate—with such rapidity. By the 1994 vote, the PSI was all but wiped out. The once mighty DC lost its left wing, renamed itself the Popular Party, and then lost its right wing. It tried to run as a centrist alternative to the Left and Right in 1994, and obtained a mere 11 percent of the vote. It split yet again in 1995, as the old centrist option appeared closed forever. The neofascist MSI broadened its own appeal for 1994 and then made the changes more permanent in 1995. Berlusconi leaped to prominence at the head of Forza Italia, which did not even exist five months earlier, and led a Center-Right bloc to victory.

Berlusconi's victory in 1994 appeared to confirm that a more bipolar logic was emerging. The Left's defeat in 1994 convinced the PDS that the only hope of victory lay in a broad Center-Left alliance, which was duly constructed for the 1996 elections under the Olive Tree label. Headed by Romano Prodi, a Catholic with impressive economic credentials, the Olive Tree defeated a badly divided Freedom Pole. The PDS then attempted to create a broader-based party of the entire Left that would reduce the Left's fragmentation. Aside from a minor name change—the PDS became the DS (*Democratici di sinistra*, or Left Democrats)—and the absorption of a few very small groups, this effort was not a success. Smaller parties were discovering that they enjoyed more leverage as outsiders than they would if they were part of a much larger whole. (This explains why most small groups cling to what remains of PR.)

Despite important changes, the new party system is more fragmented than the old. Even after the League abandoned him, deep differences in style and content separated Berlusconi from his post-Fascist partners. The addition of the League to this mix renders it even more heterogeneous. The Left comprises one large party and myriad smaller formations and has been marked by both serious differences with the far Left, which split several times, and constant bickering and maneuvering among its more moderate elements. Moreover, several old and new political groups, remnants of the former DC and some lay parties of the center, clearly are unhappy with a logic of bipolarity. They are uncomfortable in either bloc and unhappy as junior partners to anyone. They dream of controlling the balance of power from the center, which so recently seemed destined to irrelevancy.

We now turn to an examination of the specific political groups, or broad political families, as they have evolved and as they currently appear in Parliament.

Christian Democracy and Its Successors

Italy's postwar political experience demonstrates that there is no simple connection between social change and electoral behavior. For nearly thirty years, some of the most turbulent socioeconomic changes to occur anywhere in Western Europe barely rippled the surface of the Italian party system. The country as a whole showed stable electoral patterns, while the vote for the largest party, Christian Democracy, was amazingly consistent. Between 1953 and 1982, the DC's vote remained between 38 and 42 percent. In the tumultuous 1960s and 1970s, its total wavered less than a single percentage point in five consecutive elections (see Table 21.1).

The DC's "secret," ironically, was its lack of internal coherence: Its catch-all, multiclass, composite nature allowed it to be all things to all people. This may have denied Italy a true conservative party, not to mention consistency in economic or social policy, but it was an impressive recipe for raw political success. Its guaranteed governing role kept the DC united, despite often bitter internal divisions.

The DC's support period rested on four pillars: religion, anticommunism, patronage, and the halo effect from being in power when Italy became a prosperous, highly developed country. As time wore on, each of these was undermined, and anticommunism disappeared altogether.

The halo effect always counted most among voters who remembered the wretched immediate postwar period and less among children of the Economic Miracle or the easier times that followed. Similarly, mounting scandals, combined with tougher economic prospects since the late 1970s, worked against the DC as the party in power, especially among younger people. Religion continues to count heavily in Italian politics, but active Church involvement, and thus its ability to influence voters, has waned. More important, religiosity has fallen steadily; the number of those who attend mass regularly has dropped from more than 50 percent in the 1950s to below 25 percent in recent times.

Anticommunism was crucial to the DC's appeal and helped it attract more secular conservative and moderate voters who otherwise would never have accepted its close ties to the Vatican. But from the end of the worst period of the cold war, and particularly starting with the PCI's moderation and success in the 1970s, public opinion polls showed a steady drop in the strongest anticommunist attitudes. Then came the end of communism.

The decline of the other supporting pillars gave patronage increasing importance in holding together disparate constituencies. But because its strength had slipped, the DC had to distribute larger shares of the spoils to its coalition partners (above all, the PSI). The 1980s also marked an era in which limits were finally imposed on state spending because of a ballooning deficit and accumulated debt, policed by the European Community. When the corruption scandals of the 1990s broke, the ruling party was vulnerable enough to be attacked head-on; this was more a political than a judicial vulnerability, for the DC and its partners had weathered past scandals with impunity. With the alibi of anticommunism finally exhausted, it was open season on the former political class.

The DC fell below the 30 percent barrier in 1992—*before* the most damaging revelations of *Tangentopoli*. It then went into free fall. In the mayoral elections of 1993, its support fell to under 20 percent; by year's end, it was barely above 10 percent and no longer the largest party in Italy. It had not only ceded ground to the League in its northern strongholds, a trend evident for some time, but it was being displaced by the MSI in the south.

The 1994 name change to the Italian Popular Party (PPI) represented an effort to salvage some respectability for this once mighty machine (this was the party's original name when founded after World War I). But it was too late.[5]

Both left- and right-wing elements abandoned the party in 1994 in response to the emerging bipolar logic of the new electoral system. The PPI was crushed between the Progressives and Berlusconi's Pole. It obtained a mere 11 percent of the vote and was even more severely punished in single-member contests, winning only four contests. After this debacle, the PPI's disintegration accelerated. The more conservative faction renamed itself the United Christian Democrats (CDU), explicitly choosing initials identical to its large and eminently successful German counterpart. It joined Berlusconi. The PPI won the right to keep its name after a bitter and embarrassing court contest and joined the Ulivo. Within the Center-Right Freedom Pole, former Christian Democrats often have made common cause and frequently show their discomfort with the inclusion of the post-Fascists in the alliance. But the bulk of the CDU jumped ship in 1998 and supported D'Alema, who desperately needed their support after Rifondazione comunista abandoned the Ulivo.

Between Left and Right: Minor Centrist Parties and Formations

The plight of the minor lay parties became acute in the 1980s, when Craxi moved the Socialists toward the center, crowding their already limited political space. Electoral reform and increasing bipolarity from 1994 on effectively sealed these parties' fates. As occurred with the DC, people tended to go where their ideological inclinations or political calculations led them. Most of those who went with Berlusconi joined his party, Forza Italia. Others were among the founders of the Ulivo in 1995, or else they joined with other left-leaning centrists in 1996. Like most other centrists (including the remnants of the DC and PSI), however, they often appear more comfortable in a looser alliance where their own pivotal role is magnified.

In 1996, many left-leaning centrists felt vindicated. Under Prodi's leadership, the Center, rather than the far Left, would hold the decisive balance of power in the alliance. But the centrists' strategy was not a complete success. Rifondazione comunista's external support was essential for the survival of Prodi's coalition, at least in the Chamber of Deputies. When Rifondazione withdrew that support, Prodi fell. But the centrist parties did prove decisive in Prodi's electoral victory. Lamberto Dini had used his prestige as interim prime minister following Berlusconi to create a new party, named Italian Renewal, but called the Dini List by everyone. Joined by Socialists as well as nonparty specialists, Dini's group exceeded the 4 percent proportional representation floor, guaranteeing eight seats for itself in addition to nearly twenty that it won in single-member districts as part of the Ulivo. The vital contribution of his party earned Dini the prestigious Ministry of Foreign Affairs in Prodi's government.

Other non-Catholic centrists joined the PPI in forming a list called "For Prodi." The personal prestige of the Center-Left's flag bearer reaped handsome dividends. This group won nearly 7 percent of the vote in 1996. Thus, a clear strategy of joining with the Left in 1996, as opposed to running alone in 1994, combined with the presence of attractive and strong personal leaders and candidates, seemed to give many centrists a new lease on life in 1996.

At the same time, political grudges and maneuvering for position within the Ulivo soon recalled the First Republic. Prodi's followers, furious when he was pushed out of office, formed their own Democratic Party, hoping to strengthen what they called the "centrist leg" of the coalition. They were joined by the famous former prosecutor Antonio Di Pietro, who has a considerable personal following thanks to his role in *Tangentopoli*. This party then spent much of the next two years trying to undermine D'Alema at every turn, for they blamed him for ousting Prodi. And when D'Alema was replaced by Giuliano Amato, a former Socialist and collaborator of Bettino Craxi, Di Pietro threatened to break with the coalition altogether, for he considers Amato the embodiment of all that was wrong with the First Republic.

The Left

Italy is unique in the West in having the Left dominated throughout the postwar period by a communist party or its successor.

The Communist Party (PCI)/Democratic Party of the Left (PDS)/Left Democrats (DS). A key reason for the cluttered and fragmented Center is that the Left continues to be dominated by the heir to the PCI. Despite its evolution before the end of communism and its total transformation since then, the DS's "original sin" is something neither its opponents nor its allies lets it forget. Berlusconi misses no opportunity to drag up the past, while the DS's allies argue that prime ministerial candidates who are ex-communists have little appeal to moderate voters.

The PCI, increasingly liberal and independent of the Soviet Union from the late 1950s onward, almost became a governing party in the 1970s, when it reached 34 percent of the vote. But following its near entry into government, PCI votes and members fell steadily, and Craxi pushed the party back into the political wilderness in the 1980s.

Reacting rapidly to the impending collapse of communism, in 1989 the PCI embarked on a radical revision of its name, symbol, and structure in an effort to reverse its fortunes. After two years of lacerating divisions and a schism, it formally became the PDS in 1991 and adopted an oak tree as its new symbol, relegating the old hammer and sickle to the base of the tree. Completing its break with the past, the new party was accepted as a member of the Socialist International, the worldwide organization of socialist and social democratic parties that communists used to denounce as insufficiently militant and radical.

In 1996, the PDS nosed out Forza Italia as the largest party in the country, though with a mere 21 percent of the vote. In 1998, in an effort to expand its base and appeal, the PDS was renamed, but aside from eliminating the hammer and sickle from its logo, the DS only succeeded in absorbing a few very small leftist formations, leading observers to refer to the oak tree surrounded by little "bushes." Later in the same year, its secretary, Massimo D'Alema, became prime minister—the first former Communist to lead a Western democratic government. But he did not win this post by leading his coalition to victory in elections, and when he was replaced, it was by a former Socialist. When the Ulivo chose a prime ministerial candidate for the 2001 elections, the victor was the centrist mayor of Rome; his main rival was the ex-Socialist prime minister, Giuliano Amato. The DS did not put forward a candidate of its own.

An Electoral and Strategic Dilemma. The PCI was in crisis long before communism collapsed in the East, as shown by declining votes and members and above all by its political isolation in the 1980s. It spent a lot of political capital in the late 1970s when it let down those who believed the party would finally bring real change to Italian politics. This disappointment was especially great among younger voters. The PCI's share of the youth vote was quite high through the 1970s (e.g., at least 40 percent in 1976). But after 1979, newer parties, such as the Radicals, the Greens, and even the revitalized PSI, attracted significant support from young people. Thus, the PCI actually did disproportionately

poorly among the young. The radical changes begun by Secretary-General Achille Occhetto, such as making ecology and feminism central planks in the party's platform, were an effort to make itself relevant to younger Italians while defining a new identity.

Nor did the 1991 split, when hard-line elements left to join Rifondazione comunista, solve the identity crisis. Even those who fully supported the break with the past are divided. Some (a majority) want the DS to represent a social democratic anchor in a broad alliance, whereas others are convinced that all old left-wing ideologies and identities have been bypassed by history. This group would eventually like to see the DS and other groups of the Center-Left join in a single, even less ideological Democratic Party, like the one in the United States. For them, the Ulivo was not just a coalition but the precursor of a new political party.

The PDS's beginnings were not very promising. Its membership dropped precipitously, and it did very poorly in the 1992 general elections, gaining a mere 16 percent of the vote. It rose to just over 20 percent in 1994, but Berlusconi's victory drove home the point that if the Left ceded the center of the spectrum to others, it would remain on the losing end of every election. In the middle of 1994, following yet another defeat in the European elections, Achille Occhetto, who had led the PCI's transformation, was forced to resign. He was succeeded by the far more tactically able Massimo D'Alema, who swiftly moved the party even further toward the center.

The Birth—and Death—of the Ulivo. In 1994, the Progressives had lacked a clear leader, in contrast to the role played by Berlusconi. The emergence in 1995 of Romano Prodi as the Center-Left's standard bearer redressed the imbalance. Prodi reassured Italian capital, and particularly big business, that the Ulivo was committed to the sort of enlightened austerity programs that had marked the Ciampi government. And it was also intended as a bridge to Catholics and other centrists, who would feel more comfortable voting for a coalition headed by a figure like Prodi rather than a former communist.

This helped the Ulivo win the 1996 elections, but did not resolve the major dilemmas that the coalition or its largest partner faced. While D'Alema's government racked up impressive achievements, these were not reflected in the DS's fortunes. If anything, the shift of attention to the party's governing role disoriented its shrinking rank and file and further weakened an already atrophied organization. It remains solidly rooted in the red zones, but it had suffered highly publicized defeats even in these strongholds by the end of the 1990s (most notably, losing the mayoralty of Bologna). By the time D'Alema resigned, the Ulivo had effectively ceased to exist, and the DS appeared to be floundering in search of a clear identity.

Smaller Parties and Groups on the Left. The rest of the Left in Italy was always conditioned by the PCI's dominant role. The PCI's transformation into the PDS only changed the name of the major party; the dynamic remained the same.

The Socialists. No other party was more devastated by *Tangentopoli* than the PSI. The third largest party in the country through the 1980s, when many saw it as the wave of the future, it barely managed 2 percent of the vote by 1994, after which several different mini-groups arose to claim the "true" mantle of Italian socialism. They have been squabbling incessantly ever since. If we devote any attention to the Socialists here, it is to recall the role this party once played, as well as to mark how thoroughly the party system has changed.

For most of the postwar period, the Socialists failed to define a distinctive role for themselves. This was a result of their own shortcomings, to be sure, but it also reflected the fact that the PCI's flexibility and powerful organization left it little room to maneuver. After a disastrous experience as the DC's junior partner, Craxi appeared to be leading his party in a fresh new direction in the 1970s. But the reversal of the PSI's fortunes under Craxi proved to be not only ephemeral but fatal. In remarkably short order, the PSI dropped the little that remained of its traditional left-wing ideology and identity. More important, its power struggles with the DC cost it its hard-won credibility as the party most in tune with a changing society.

As scandals broke all around Craxi and his closest collaborators, decency finally required that they resign. But the commanding heights of the party, after more than fifteen years of personalized rule, remained firmly in the hands of *craxiani*, who thwarted every effort at reform by a succession of new leaders.[6] By mid-1993, despite millions of dollars obtained through kickbacks and payoffs, the party was bankrupt; it had to sell its historic headquarters in Rome to meet its debts. At the same time, the PSI was mercilessly punished at the polls, plunging below 3 percent of the vote in local elections and then remaining there in the general elections.

Socialist bankruptcy was even more moral than financial, and with continued resistance to change from the *craxiani*, the PSI entered its terminal phase. Many key leaders denounced the party as hopeless and resigned. Even reformers were divided as to the party's future path. By 1994, a large group left the party to join the Progressive Alliance. When the reformist leadership of the PSI realized it had no choice but to follow, the *craxiani* split from them and formed a separate group in Parliament. Many of these figures became Berlusconi's partners and were rewarded with key positions in his new movement; others stubbornly tried to keep the PSI alive as a minuscule organization.

The Far Left. From the 1960s on, the PCI's increasing moderation gave more militant leftists cause to believe that they could outflank the Communists on their left. But even after the Hot Autumn, this space remained quite limited. New Left groups in the 1970s tended to be divided primarily by their attitude toward the PCI, and those who did not see the Communists as hopelessly compromised drifted back toward collaboration or even fusion with them by the 1980s. The most militant parts of the movements of the late 1960s and 1970s gravitated toward Proletarian Democracy (DP), as did hard-line trade unionists. DP picked up 1.5 percent and seven seats in 1983 and improved slightly on that total in 1987. On the eve of the schism that created Rifondazione comunista, DP was a small but well-established group, drawing strong support from young people. It had also evolved into an increasingly vocal exponent of feminism, antinuclearism, and ecology as these themes gained support in Italy.

The creation of Rifondazione comunista, or the Party of Refounded Communism (PRC), altered the nature of the far Left. The new party originally had a solid base of 150,000 members, close ties to the most militant trade unionists, and considerable mass appeal. But in addition to hard-line militants and radicals from the old PCI, it included the most closed and Stalinist remnants as well. When DP dissolved itself and joined Rifondazione en masse at its founding in 1991, the PRC became a grab-bag of everyone on the Left who was unhappy with the PDS, dominated at the base by ex-Communists with a small but influential party machine.

Rifondazione has polled between 5 and 9 percent of the vote in general elections, with well over 10 percent in many areas of historic Communist strength, giving it considerable leverage in Italy's fragmented politics. This much support can easily make the difference between victory and defeat in single-member districts, as the rest of the Left—and even the Center-Left— is aware. In 1994, the PRC ran as an integral part of the Progressive alliance. In 1996, with the more moderate Ulivo contesting the elections, the PRC agreed not to play a spoiler role by entering a "stand-down" (*desistenza*) agreement with the Ulivo. In exchange for a number of guaranteed single-member seats, in which the Ulivo instructed its voters to support Rifondazione, the PRC abstained from all the other single-member contests, instructing its supporters to vote for the Ulivo. Following the

victory in 1996, when Rifondazione earned an impressive 8.6 percent of the vote, it did not formally enter the Ulivo government. But it did provide external support, which guaranteed Prodi his majority in the Chamber of Deputies, while magnifying its own bargaining power on important issues like pensions and the retrenchment of the welfare state. Eventually, however, the PRC decided that its identity outweighed its practical influence and joined the no-confidence vote that forced Prodi to resign.

Rifondazione faces a delicate balancing act: maintaining its militant credentials while simultaneously attempting to influence a "friendly" government. Every time it threatened the government, it confronted serious internal opposition and outright refusals of some members to follow party discipline in Parliament. After one close call when it avoided precipitating elections only by walking out of Parliament (and thus not voting at all), Rifondazione suffered splits in 1995 and again in 1998 as dissidents broke ranks to support the government in power. These splits, and its divisive behavior, exacted a measurable political cost. In both the 1999 elections to the European Parliament and the general elections of 2001, Rifondazione's support fell, often to about half of its historic highs. But even in this weakened state, its support (or abstention) remains essential to the Center-Left's electoral prospects.

The Greens. The Green phenomenon evolved slowly in Italy. Only in 1987 did a Green List obtain as much as 2.5 percent of the vote and thirteen seats, a showing that remained fairly constant in 1992 and 1994. More important, Greens strongly challenged the government's nuclear energy policy, forcing a 1987 referendum that divided the ruling coalition and produced an overwhelming vote that severely limited Italy's use of nuclear energy. Other referenda on pesticides, land use, and hunting have kept their message in the public eye.

The late formation of the Green Lists means that many activists had considerable earlier political experience. The two major organizations united in 1990 after years of mistrust. More moderate Greens are suspicious of those with experience in DP or the Radical Party; there are also typical disputes over whether members should enthusiastically participate in existing political institutions or use them as a propaganda platform. Some differences have been personality clashes, but underlying political divisions are real. Intensely committed to their own independence, the Greens initially refused to join the Ulivo, but eventually supported Prodi and his successors, winning the environmental portfolio for themselves in three of four governments.

The Radical Party (PR)/Pannella List/ Reformers/Bonino List. This is another formation whose impact has been greater than its small size. Its leader, Giacinto (Marco) Pannella, has probably been Italy's most flamboyant political figure; he is given to hyperbolic statements and actions such as hunger strikes and was immodest enough to name the group after himself when he liquidated the PR in the early 1990s for egotistical reasons.[7] The PR deserves brief mention because of its importance in referendum campaigns and its occasional ability to attract unexpected amounts of popular support.

The PR established its identity in the 1960s by embracing causes ignored by others: women's rights, civil rights (of a libertarian sort), conscientious objection, and ecology. It also emphasized the developed countries' responsibilities to the Third World. But the party's individualistic and libertarian stances increasingly created conflict with the Left in the 1980s. This group's appeal has been to many of the same social groups as the parties of the New Left: young people and professional and white-collar strata. But the Radicals are hard to categorize using standard Left-Right criteria. For instance, Pannella supported Berlusconi in 1994 before growing uncomfortable with a departure from his usual gadfly role.

Starting in the 1970s, the PR used the referendum far more often than anyone else to bypass and embarrass the major parties, forcing

them to confront contentious issues.[8] If a single theme runs through all Radical initiatives, it is extreme individualism. When the Church tried to abolish abortion in 1981 so Italy would revert to the old legislation outlawing this procedure, the Radicals put forward their own referendum question abolishing *all* rules pertaining to the regulation of abortion. This would have totally liberalized abortion—but it also would have removed it from national medical coverage. Their adamant civil libertarianism makes Radicals vocal critics of prosecutors and the heroes of corrupt politicians. Their resistance to any interference with personal freedom led them to promote a referendum in 1995 to prevent unions from having members' dues withheld from their paychecks.

The Radicals once represented a modern, innovative form of protest politics. But they also had a limited repertoire of actions, as their constant falling back on multiple referendum proposals, and Pannella's often clownish attention-grabbing actions, suggest. After appearing to fade from view in the early 1990s, a list led by former European commissioner Emma Bonino racked up a surprising 8.5 percent of the vote in the 1999 elections for the European Parliament, but quickly fell back to insignificance in regional elections less than a year later.

The (Center-)Right

Precisely because of their centrist ideology, some heirs of the DC and the lay parties straddle the Left-Right divide. Indeed, some have already been on both sides and make clear that they would be most comfortable in a centrist "third pole." Undoubtedly a key source of their discomfort is the presence in the Center-Right of the National Alliance (AN), born in 1995 out of the dissolution of the neo-fascist MSI. Despite AN's embrace of democratic institutions, centrists within and outside the Freedom Pole argue that should AN be dropped and should Berlusconi move more decisively into the center of the spectrum, he would leave both AN and the DS and its "bushes" permanently out in the cold. This scenario would undercut the emerging bipolarity of the party system and would reintroduce the centrality of the First Republic, with Forza Italia replacing the DC.

Whichever logic prevails, there can be no doubt that truly profound changes have taken place on this side of the political spectrum in Italy. Two of these parties were insignificant or nonexistent during the First Republic; the third had to undergo profound transformation to become a major player.

The Lega Nord. Several regional leagues, concentrated in the northeast, formed the Northern League in 1991 under the leadership of the strongest, the Lombard League, led by the mercurial Umberto Bossi. It began marked by strong regional identities, which included quasi-racist antisouthern and overtly racist antiforeign undertones. Its official platform now calls for the introduction of federalism and a devolution of powers to the north, which it calls "Padania" (after the Po River), but separatist sentiments are never far from the surface. Bossi has in fact flip-flopped several times between a separatist, and even a secessionist, stick and a federalist or devolutionist carrot, depending on his assessment of the demands of the moment.

The Lega rose amid the growing crisis of the established parties in the early 1990s. It moderated its cruder arguments as its support expanded, though Bossi has groped, often comically and sometimes menacingly, for myths and symbols that would provide a foundation for a new, alternative social and political identity. His more colorful inventions have included medieval symbolism recalling resistance to barbarian invasions, torchlight parades and rallies, green-shirted "militias," and claims of links to Celtic forebears; he was impressed by the film *Braveheart,* and Scotland inspired his emphasis on devolution.

The Leagues first appeared where the DC was most well rooted, in the increasingly urbanizing countryside of the "white" Veneto and eastern Lombardy, areas historically hostile to the state and outside intervention. This expansion was a sign of the breakdown of the DC's representational and mediating abilities.[9] As Ilvo Diamanti, an acute observer, notes, the various Leagues were able to break with more traditional bases of identity and representation, such as religion versus secularism, or class, taking other long-standing cleavages (e.g., north-south, center-periphery, "common folks" versus big government) and expressing them in a new way, thus dramatically altering the political landscape.[10] In the words of another keen student of the phenomenon, the League turned the southern question into the northern question.[11]

By the mid-1990s the League was a significant force in most of the north. Its support comes disproportionately from small businesspeople, shopkeepers, artisans, and other self-employed categories. Although it occasionally does well in big cities, its strongholds are in smaller towns and villages. There are clear parallels between the League and populist, anti-welfare "get the government off our back" phenomena elsewhere in the West, but there are also clear differences.

The League's populism distinguishes it from more individualistic, purely free-market ideologies. It tends to define its constituency collectively, which often makes it protectionist with regard to local interests. It has criticized the "Americanization" of traditional culture, and what it considers the EU's catering to large banking and industrial interests. This is not simply a crass defense of its constituents' material interests but the expression of an alternative vision of the world.[12] The small businesses and industries it represents have been the most dynamic elements in Italy's resurgent economy. But for the League, they are also the repositories of traditional virtues in a rapidly changing world; they are the expression of family (as opposed to impersonal corporate) values and of deep roots in small communities. These concerns also help understand the Lega's unusually strong emphasis on environmental and quality-of-life issues; in the 1996 elections, it paid more attention to these themes than did the Ulivo.[13]

The League has been able to build an organization and a strong sense of identity, making it far more than a mere party of protest. And although it originally appealed mainly to younger men with lower educational attainment, its supporters' profiles have increasingly come to resemble society as a whole, with notable success among workers in newly industrialized areas.[14] Remarkably successful by the early 1990s, the Lega still could not extend its influence very far beyond the north-east: it made some headway in other parts of the north, but was effectively nonexistent everywhere else.

This lack of nationwide appeal—and Bossi's idiosyncrasies—helped pave the way for Berlusconi's entry into politics. There is no question that Bossi resented latecomers who reaped the benefits of his own earlier actions. He also had serious reservations about his future allies. Berlusconi had close ties to some of the most corrupt officials of the old regime, starting with Craxi, and was plagued by blatant conflicts of interest. Nor did Bossi relish any connection to the MSI, with its reprehensible past *and* its primarily southern power base.

In 1994, the League obtained the lion's share of the Pole's single-member seats in the north. The victory gave it the largest contingent in the Chamber of Deputies, several ministries, and the prestigious office of speaker. Bossi insisted throughout the election campaign that he would never form a government with "fascists," but that is precisely what he did, though these differences—and his fear that a governing role was diluting the League's message and identity—precipitated a crisis that ended Berlusconi's government within seven months.

Bossi appeared to have committed political suicide by isolating his party and thus exposing it to the bipolar logic of the new electoral law. But thanks to its geographically concentrated strength, the Lega confounded the common wisdom in the 1996 elections. Considered nothing but a spoiler early in the campaign, the League managed to win outright thirty-nine single-member seats, an extraordinary showing, and obtained more votes in the North than anyone else. It did play a spoiler role, splitting the moderate vote and allowing the Olive Tree to win a large number of three-way races in the north. These proved decisive in the Center-Left's victory.

On the heels of this success, and without having to worry about coalition partners, the party was officially renamed in 1997. Its official title now had "Northern League" followed by "for the Independence of Padania," instead of "Northern League Federated Italy." But Bossi's "go it alone" stance created tension within his own movement (as well as within the Freedom Pole). Despite insistence that traditional Left-Right distinctions do not apply to the League, many followers and activists feel far more kinship with the Right and worry that isolation will simply guarantee the Center-Left perpetual victory. Many northern *leghista* leaders wanted to ally with Berlusconi in local elections and openly challenged Bossi's isolationism.

Finally, pragmatism prevailed, as is seen in Bossi's emphasis on devolution rather than separation. His criticism of the Vatican had become fierce by 1997; three years later, Bossi was praising the pope and stressing traditional values. Then came yet another name change: it is now Lega Nord Padania, with references to independence expunged. The alliance between the Freedom Pole and the League was renewed in 2000. But since Forza Italia and the League tend to compete for some of the same voters and since Bossi has certainly not established a reputation for steadfastness, it will be interesting to see how long the second edition of this alliance can last.

Forza Italia. Although Forza Italia circles sprang up all over Italy following the announcement of Berlusconi's entry into politics, this party is entirely his creature. It was immediately dubbed the *partito-azienda*, or "Company Party," since it was staffed by lawyers, managers, and publicists from Berlusconi's Fininvest business empire. Forza Italia was not a mere facade, however; some of Italy's most skilled advertising people used their media expertise to create a formidable electoral machine. Berlusconi conducted a smooth American-style campaign informed by focus group research and extensive public opinion polling.[15] He avoided face-to-face debates, fired off sound bites, and revealed himself to be a masterful communicator.

This is not entirely surprising, for Berlusconi is best known for his ownership of the Milan soccer team and his extensive media holdings. Thanks to farsightedness, ruthlessness, and a willingness to go into debt, he ended up owning three of Italy's four private television networks. Then, thanks to friends in high places (Craxi above all), Parliament wrote a law that sanctioned the multiple ownership of private networks, giving him a de facto governmental concession, which created a blatant conflict of interest when he entered politics. Berlusconi also owns the advertising conglomerate Publitalia, which has exclusive rights to sell commercials to his own networks. He bought up the Rizzoli publishing group in 1990 but had to divest himself of a newspaper and a weekly newsmagazine that came with the package. When Parliament passed a law limiting newspaper ownership, Berlusconi "sold" his controlling shares in the Milanese daily *il Giorno* to his brother.[16]

That someone with so many interests would want to protect them is evident. That he would vault into Palazzo Chigi (the prime minister's residence) as head of the largest party in the country six months after entering politics is extraordinary. And that in the course of this unprecedented personal triumph he would also help radically reshape Italian politics, not least by bringing the MSI into the democratic fold and hastening its evolution, was yet another triumph for the man known as "Il Cavaliere" (for his honorific title, *Cavaliere del Lavoro*, or Knight of Labor). Forza Italia did exceptionally well across the north and in Sicily, attracting former DC, PSI, and Lega voters. It obtained notable support across all age groups and did best among young people and worst among those

over age sixty-five.[17] It also provided an outlet for the considerable political experience, which it sorely needed, of former Christian Democrats as well as many ex-Socialists. Forza Italia appeared to have a solid mandate.

But Il Cavaliere proved a better campaigner than prime minister, a better empire builder than politician. His brilliant tactic of forming separate alliances with incompatible political forces—the MSI–AN in the south and the League in the north—turned out to be short-lived. He took power with no apparent program, having campaigned on generic, feel-good slogans, and seemed more concerned with providing the faithful with pieces of the political pie than with instituting policies of any identifiable type. He also claimed not to understand why people thought it problematic that he owned three of four private networks and directly or indirectly controlled all three public networks.

Berlusconi's obtuseness and insincerity over conflicts of interest undermined his credibility even among supporters. After resigning late in 1994 to avoid a confidence vote he was certain to lose, Berlusconi called Parliament "illegitimate" when elections were not immediately called. From the opposition, he spoke of "an effective coup" having been engineered by the president and of Italy's "suspended democracy." He also minimized his own judicial problems or attributed them to a conspiracy by malevolent prosecutors who used "police state" tactics.

His ejection from the prime ministership hardly reduced Berlusconi to powerlessness. His networks proved more than capable of defending themselves; a series of referenda in June 1995 that would have severely limited ownership and advertising on commercial television was defeated after a ferocious campaign by the private channels. He also lobbied incessantly for greater legitimacy and was rewarded in 1999 when Forza Italia was formally made part of the European Popular Party (Christian Democrats) in the European Parliament.

To call Berlusconi's behavior erratic and unstatesmanlike is a considerable understatement. Despite his rhetoric about violations of democracy, Il Cavaliere has been selective in his concern about the democratic rules of the game. Yet he remains the dominant figure on the Center-Right and the only one capable of uniting its disparate forces, as the renewed agreement with the League in 2000 demonstrated.

The Far Right. Italy's Fascist past meant that no one except extremists would admit to being on the Right until the mid-1990s. From 1972 onward, the extreme Right was monopolized by the neofascist MSI. "Social Movement" explicitly referred to Mussolini's "Social Republic," the puppet regime installed by the Nazis in the occupied north in 1943. Claiming to return to fascism's pure origins, this regime presided over and actively took part in the repression of the Resistance, the deportation of Jews, and total identification with Hitler's Germany. Since the postwar republic was explicitly antifascist and formally banned the reconstitution of the Fascist Party,[18] the MSI was truly a pariah. It flirted with antidemocratic elements and maintained an ambiguous attitude toward democracy well into the 1980s.

As nostalgic evocations of fascism faded with the aging of its leadership and original constituency, the MSI's appeal centered on anticommunism and a hard-line call for law and order, including the reintroduction of the death penalty. Evoking fascism's past, it also called for a strong role for the state in the economy; it rejected free-market capitalism as antisocial. The MSI always championed family values, and despite the strong anticlerical strains in the original Fascist movement, this party was pro-life and generally conservative on matters of Church doctrine. It was—and remains—anti–European Union and anti-American, although its leader has traveled to London and New York to reassure international opinion. After reaching nearly 9 percent of the vote in 1972, when it capitalized on middle-class fears after the Hot Autumn, the MSI stabilized at around 6 percent into the 1980s and then appeared to fade even further.

The MSI was not a complete throwback, however. Most important, because it had been systematically excluded from sharing power during the postwar period, it could attack the degeneration of the party system. Its strong law-and-order stance also made it easy to root for the prosecutors who were filling Italy's jails with corrupt politicians. During Francesco Cossiga's presidency, thanks to Cossiga's own attacks on the party system—and his inexplicable softness toward the MSI—the neofascists found a new hero, though they tended to ignore Cossiga's constant attacks on the judiciary.[19]

The MSI was shaken by the end of communism and underwent lacerating leadership turnover and serious losses in local elections at the beginning of the 1990s. It lost a mere 0.5 percent in the 1992 elections, but neofascism's future appeared bleak as it became clear that proportional representation was on its way out. All the new electoral systems required alliances, and who would make common cause with Mussolini's heirs?

At this point, the collapse of the DC came to the MSI's rescue. Stepping into the vacuum, the party made unprecedented gains and vaulted to national prominence in the municipal elections in Rome and Naples in December 1993. Silvio Berlusconi gave the neofascists a big boost when he announced that he would comfortably vote for them against the Left. Although it lost both runoffs, the MSI obtained more than 40 percent of the vote, which sent its telegenic young leader, Gianfranco Fini (who lost in the runoff in Rome), scrambling to reassure the public. He set up an electoral front, the National Alliance, to contest the upcoming general elections, and he hastily tacked free-market rhetoric onto his speeches and presentations. These maneuvers gained credibility thanks to some recent refugees from the DC and PLI, but everyone knew that AN was the creature of the MSI.

The post-Fascists became Italy's third largest party in 1994, more than doubling their vote (to over 13 percent) and tripling their representation in the Chamber of Deputies (to over 100).

The largest party in southern Italy, AN became Berlusconi's most faithful ally, and its loyalty was richly rewarded in terms of cabinet seats, undersecretaries, and appointments to myriad patronage positions. After the government's forced resignation, AN maintained a facade of unswerving loyalty to Berlusconi, to whom it owes a great deal.

The MSI's transition to full democratic respectability had remained incomplete while it was in government. In the opposition, Fini forced the issue. Shortly after Berlusconi's resignation, the MSI was dissolved. A small hardline faction refused to break with the past and created a party called the Tricolor Flame (after the torch in the old MSI's logo). The speed and relative painlessness of this transition give one pause; compare the wrenching experience of the PCI–PDS. And AN often competes with the Lega in voicing virulent anti-immigrant views. Still, AN broke significant new ground. It explicitly embraced liberal democracy and denounced the racism and anti-Semitism that marked the Fascist regime from 1938. Even more astonishing, it recognized the fundamental contribution of the Resistance to the foundation of democracy in Italy in the postwar period.

Experts continued to harbor serious doubt about the sincerity of this conversion,[20] but the extreme Right ceased to exist as a significant political force in Italy early in 1995, while in 1996, AN consolidated its position as Italy's third largest party, with 15 percent of the vote.

AN often appears more serious about institutional reform than Forza Italia. Fini is uncomfortable with Berlusconi's attacks on the judiciary, as well as his constant use of epithets like "communist" to characterize his enemies. AN has its own reasons to want to leave the past behind, of course. Yet no matter how statesmanlike he may appear, Fini and his party are condemned to bob along in Berlusconi's wake and to follow the agenda set by Il Cavaliere. AN's antipathy toward all the League stands for is reciprocated by the League, and yet these enemies became allies again in 2000. Above all, Fini worries that Berlusconi may succumb to the siren song of centrists, who would love to see the isolation of AN. In many ways, then, the most solidly rooted party in the Freedom Pole often disagrees with its primary ally on many substantive issues and has reason to suspect its long-term intentions. This of course reflects not just AN's problems, but the heterogeneity of the Center-Right. That heterogeneity became even more extreme when Berlusconi included the hard-line Tricolor Flame under the roof of his "House of Freedom," as he renamed the Pole in 1999.

Elections

Because of the changes that have swept Italy since 1992, both general electoral trends and the landmark 1994 and 1996 elections have already been analyzed in depth in this and preceding chapters. Let us simply recall that the so-called First Republic, with its system of proportional representation, provided almost monotonously predictable electoral results from the 1950s through the 1970s, and the results were still astonishingly stable even in the 1980s (see Table 21.1). The largest three parties were exactly the same (DC-PCI-PSI) from 1948 to 1992, in the same exact order. And then, aided mightily by a new electoral system, the major governing parties were shattered, while new (and renovated) parties gave rise to a new party system. After no real change of governing formulas for forty-five years and no alternation in power at all, the elections of 1994, 1996, and 2001 saw alternation between two rival blocs.

Decades, and in some cases generations, of rooted political traditions do not disappear overnight. The "red" (Marxist) and "white" (Catholic) subcultures, although diminished, continue to be relevant. The PCI disappeared a decade ago, but the red zones remain the areas where the Left gets the highest vote and where the Progressives (1994) and the Ulivo (1996) swept all but a handful of single-member seats. Similarly, the white zones of the northeast were both Catholic and conservative before and after the DC. Since its demise, these areas, along with other historically conservative parts of the north, still choose between contending conservative forces: the League and Forza Italia. The south, penetrated more by the DC's politics of patronage, is more variegated. AN or Forza Italia tends to dominate, but the Center-Left, particularly where the PPI is strong, is competitive in many areas.

A notable trend that began in the late 1970s and has continued through every election since is a decline in voter turnout. Italy used to have one of the highest turnout rates in the world, at 92 to 94 percent. It dropped below 90 percent in the 1983 elections and has declined steadily ever since; in 2001 it was 81 percent, which is still quite high by comparative standards. Some observers consider this a sign of Italy's growing political maturity. They argue that extremely high turnout rates in the past reflected a polarized country in which people felt that democracy itself was at stake in every election. Those who are less sanguine see the decline as evidence of growing disgust with politics. They point out that when blank and spoiled ballots are combined with those who do not bother to vote at all, the resulting quarter (roughly) of the electorate is larger than any single party's vote since 1994, save for Forza Italia in 2001.

It is also important to recall that the Ulivo's 1996 victory was not the product of massive shifts in public opinion due to the fluid and ever-evolving party system. The great swing to the Ulivo in 1996 was really the result of the League's running separately in that election. When it rejoined the Center-Right in 2001, it once again played an important role in Berlusconi's victory.

If electoral behavior is less volatile than the fall and rise of so many political parties would suggest, what factors other than the League's fickleness in choosing partners help us understand the swing from the Center-Right to the Center-Left? In 1994 the Left ran (as the Progressive Alliance) against the Center-Right and some unreconstructed centrists from the old DC. In 1996, the Left engineered a Center-Left alliance and was fortunate enough to find its opponents divided. Detailed analysis of the platforms of the different blocs shows that the Ulivo did not simply ally with forces toward the center of the spectrum; it also embraced centrist, and at times downright conservative, policies.[21] In the 1996 elections, and, one might add, in the years of the Prodi and D'Alema governments, the only party consistently espousing traditional Left positions was Rifondazione comunista.

Collective Identities

The red and white subcultural cleavage lingers on. Of course, these divisions were never equal in strength or geographical distribution. Catholicism has been a more powerful and diffused force in Italy than the various strands of Marxism, and the Church's entrenchment was formalized in the Lateran Pacts, under both fascism and the republic. Furthermore, the strong subcultures were limited geographically to areas that sometimes surprise people unfamiliar with Italian history and politics. The red areas are not in the industrial heartland of the northwest but in the central regions of Emilia-Romagna, Tuscany, and Umbria. The white areas, where church and religion are most deeply rooted, are found mainly in the Veneto and eastern Lombardy. Political subcultures in Italy cut across classes more than is appreciated. This is not so surprising for the white zones, for Catholic social thought rejects class conflict, but even the leftist subculture has a broad class base, due to its agrarian (and anticlerical) origins. Italian Socialists and Communists were always less obsessed with the factory proletariat than were their counterparts elsewhere, such as France.

There are other divisions in Italian society. Class divisions historically ran very deep in Italy, even though they were always mitigated, or cross-cut, by religious and regional factors. Ironically, with the rise of the League and Forza Italia, class—in this case one's status as an independent businessperson—has become a more solid predictor of political preference than ever before.[22]

The Fascist experience appears to have inoculated Italians against nationalism. At least in part because of this, perhaps the most important divisions since the war have been regional, above all, between north and south. It is an oversimplification to speak of a southern culture or political style, but the area's dependent development and the resulting distorted class and social structures have had an undeniable effect on its political institutions. These structural weaknesses have rendered southern politics especially vulnerable to patronage networks and clientelistic patterns of politics.

In related fashion, the League's emergence and consolidation show that in an era of rapid change and the undermining of old certainties, local identities can assume increasing importance, including taking explicitly political form. Such sentiments were far more diffuse, or obscured by other cleavages, in the past. It is especially interesting to note that the League commands the strongest support, and has the deepest roots, in areas where the DC was strongest—but not among practicing Catholics, who continue to support the DC's heirs. Rather, the League's support comes from those who used to support the DC, but not for religious reasons.

These new territorial identities have occasionally been expressed in ethnic or racial terms against southerners or foreigners. Such prejudice certainly exists in Italy, and it occasionally explodes into acts of intolerance against immigrants. The League's most successful appeals have been those couched in terms of a distinctive "northernness" based on hard work, honesty, traditional values, and distrust of the state, but it was again expressing overt anti-immigrant sentiments after its poor showing in the regional elections of 2000.

Far weaker, until very recently, have been the variants of modern bourgeois subcultures, such as secular liberalism and conservatism, which never managed to acquire mass bases as they did in most of the rest of Western Europe and North America. These secular forces were stunted by *trasformismo*, repressed by fascism, and then delegated much of their role to the DC after 1945. Their historic political expressions survived and evolved in the form of the minor, so-called lay parties of the center. Since the late 1970s, the advancing secularization of Italy and the accompanying erosion of the major subcultures have opened up more political space that new formations (e.g., the Radicals and the Greens) have partially filled, while older parties altered their ideology and style in an effort to appeal to more modern, secular strata.

Interests, Social Movements, and Protest

Italy's political history, from unification through the cold war, is reflected in a civil society that has been far more volatile, and far more fragmented, than in most Western democracies.

Business Organizations

Late and unbalanced industrialization, state intervention favoring some sectors at the expense of others, the late growth of a broad stratum of small and medium-size firms, and the existence of a very large public sector of the economy have often divided, and at times led to fierce antagonisms within, Italian capitalism. These divisions were aggravated in the postwar period by political factors. Because of the fragmentation of successive governing coalitions and the factional nature of the DC, interest groups have had multiple, contending targets to lobby. Most groups in Italian society divided along Left-Right lines, but even the group that should have been largely immune to such division nonetheless found ample grounds for disunity along other dimensions.

The Major Peak Organizations: A Brief Review. The Confederation of Italian Industry (Confindustria), created early in the twentieth century, represents companies in the private sector. After the war, it continued to favor Italy's top-heavy, protected industry, as it always had. Other industrialists and managers, especially in technologically advanced firms and the large state sector of the economy, had ideas more in tune with changing times, and these divisions undermined Confindustria's unity and effectiveness through most of the postwar period.

In 1957, Intersind, the peak association of the state sector industries, was created strictly for the purpose of negotiating labor contracts. In 1962, it signed a national contract with the unions on terms that Confindustria had previously rejected. The management front dissolved shortly after, exacerbated by the increasing militancy of the late 1960s. The old oligopolies and the very numerous smaller firms (those with fewer than one hundred employees) were usually antilabor. The dynamic large firms that produced consumer goods favored rapid agreements with the unions. They also supported broader social reforms—not only because they were more enlightened but also because theirs were more labor-intensive industries. They needed society to absorb the costs of improving the conditions under which working people lived; otherwise firms would have to foot the bill alone.

By the economic downturn that followed the Hot Autumn, many state sector firms were in crisis, frequently due to mismanagement by political appointees. At the same time, the contribution of Italy's resilient small firms was finally being recognized officially. As labor weakened in the 1980s, the worst rifts in the capitalist front began to heal. Confindustria gave a much greater voice to some of its historically silenced members; its presidents in the 1990s were chosen from the Association of Young Industrial-

ists and then from the small-firm sector. By the early 1990s, its ranks were expanded with the dissolution of state enterprises (and Intersind). In the course of the 1990s, Confindustria was instrumental in the labor relations reforms, but it also became more politically assertive, demanding budgetary rigor, tax reform, and an overhaul of an inefficient bureaucracy and institutions. These demands were couched in terms of making Italy more responsive to European and international competitive pressures.[23] Divisions persist, but with capitalism and market values seemingly triumphant, Italian capitalists are pursuing their interests more aggressively and in more sophisticated and united fashion.

Organized Labor

Organized labor has had an even more violent roller-coaster ride than has business. It suffered from two related weaknesses throughout the entire postwar period: It was politically divided and, as a result of the exclusion of the Communists, no government was ever constructed in which labor's major representatives were all present. These limitations had a profound effect on every aspect of labor relations and reform legislation in Italy, but they did not always result in crushing defeats for the unions and the working class. Particularly when the unions were united, they often achieved more (in job security, guaranteed wage increases, and pensions) than counterparts in other countries did—even those who had the relative luxury of socialist or social democratic governments to defend them. The flurry of legislation and contractual guarantees that followed the Hot Autumn of 1969–1970 are obvious examples.

The Hot Autumn brought the major confederations—General Confederation of Italian Labor (CGIL), Italian Confederation of Free Trade Unions (CISL), and Italian Labor Union (UIL)—close to reuniting. Such were the anomalies of the Italian situation that the unions actually became direct political protagonists, often negotiating directly with government. By the end of the 1970s, however, with the Communists' failure to enter the government and renewed tensions between the PCI and PSI, strains grew not only among the three confederations but also within the CGIL, where Communists and Socialists coexisted. By the 1980s and early 1990s, the major confederations were again divided and faced a shrinking class base, declining membership, and growing competition from autonomous unions and the Committees of the Base (COBAS). All these factors contributed to the rollback of the most generous benefits won in the 1960s and 1970s and a revamping of industrial relations.

Chapter 22 discussed the establishment of tripartite consultation among labor, management, and the government in the accords of 1993, which were instrumental in guaranteeing orderly negotiations on sensitive issues such as wage and pension reforms, welfare state cutbacks, and industrial restructuring. Under Prodi, the trend continued and was widely recognized as having made a vital contribution to Italy's success in meeting the Maastricht convergence criteria. Leftist critics complained that organized labor had been too ready to compromise, but the major confederations did manage to slow down numerous cutbacks, maintain respectable membership levels, and reinforce their own presence in the workplace under the 1993 rules.

The Church and the Catholic World

No discussion of Italian social and political forces since the war can ignore the immense role this unique institution has played. Provided with the opportunity to intervene decisively in postwar Italy, the Church under Pope Pius XII did not hesitate to exercise its influence, often harshly. The Church was supposed to stay out of politics, but it did not, and its own pronouncements and the activities of the clergy—including 25,000 parish priests—represented a formidable organizational network. It regularly acted

at all levels of politics to promote its own candidates and its own agenda. Fascist censorship of material offensive to the Church's reputation, its moral standards (nudity or suggestiveness in magazines, films, or theater), or its dogma (e.g., information on contraception as well as the availability of contraceptives) was retained or expanded by the DC through the 1960s.

Blatant interference faded with the death in 1958 of Pius XII, whose anticommunism was matched only by his authoritarian methods and his beliefs that Italy should be made to adhere to Church law. Under John Paul II, as one might expect of a non-Italian pope, direct involvement in Italy's internal affairs has lessened, although the pope's conservative sympathies are well known.

Of course, the Church always had to act under constraints. If it went too far, it could divide Catholic opinion, threatening its own privileged position. Since the DC's collapse, the political unity of Catholics has become a moot point, though the Church is hardly silent on social issues it considers important. It has, to date, emphasized a compassionate approach to immigration, and this advocacy has helped soften the tones of public debate as well as produce less harsh legislation on a potentially inflammatory topic. Relentless pressure on Catholics within the Ulivo (especially the PPI and the Democrats) produced legislation far more favorable to religious schools than many secular members of the coalition would have liked. The Vatican's views on conception have created similar contrasts within the Center-Left on issues such as in vitro fertilization and artificial insemination.

Protest and Social Movements

Italy has a long history of spontaneous social movements. Extensive land occupations in the 1940s and 1950s, bloody rioting that closed the door to the Right in 1960, and regional riots in Calabria in the 1970s have been the most dramatic episodes of the postwar period. What these phenomena have in common with the new social movements that have appeared since the late 1960s is that they arose outside, or quickly escaped the control of, established parties. Where they differ is that the new movements—and this justifies the adjective—have raised demands that do not easily fit the platforms and identities of the traditional parties.

New movements have often taken extreme forms in Italy because of the country's notoriously slow political machinery. Serious reforms are inevitably delayed or sabotaged, aggravating underlying problems. Furthermore, for most of the postwar period, the major parties blanketed the social sphere very effectively; their effort to absorb everything, capturing and channeling social activity in their own organizations, left limited room for the development of autonomous interest groups or citizens' movements. This controlling capacity began to break down in the late 1960s and had effectively vanished by the end of the 1980s.

Workers' and Urban Movements. In terms of size and impact on society, the most significant movement in recent times was the workers' activism that began in the 1960s and peaked during the Hot Autumn. Because of the explosive social and political context of the late 1960s, the boundaries between the labor movement and broader social movements were almost nonexistent. Spilling out of the factories, workers took up the banner of all sorts of social reforms, such as housing, transportation, and medical and other social services.

The major cities also witnessed the growth of extensive urban protest movements that lasted well into the mid-1970s. Among other things, these movements helped to discredit Christian Democratic rule in the big cities and produced important reforms. The urban movements initially agitated against the severe shortage of affordable housing, which led to spectacular, large-scale occupations of public housing projects. They also focused on other services, such as schools, health, parks, and day care centers.

Student and Youth Movements. Student and youth movements have taken several completely different forms in Italy. In the late 1980s, they were sporadic, uncoordinated protests against barely functioning high schools and universities. But in the 1960s, they had a highly ideological, leftist character. They often originated around protests against the Vietnam War, an event that was especially important in radicalizing young Catholics, putting them side by side politically for the first time with youths from different backgrounds. These movements peaked in 1967–1968, eventually furnishing activists for the far Left that was emerging (or in some cases, had been revitalized) by the end of the 1960s. They provided critical contributions to factory and urban struggles and trained militants and future leaders for the traditional Left. For example, nearly a quarter of all Communist militants, and over one-third of those who joined the party in the 1970s, had some experience in movements or groups (excluding the unions) prior to joining the PCI.[24]

Autonomous Movements and Terrorism. A totally different movement surged later in the 1970s. Although much smaller than the 1960s movement, it left a significant impression. It was, broadly speaking, antipolitical with an extremist, nihilistic fringe, inclined to violence. It attacked all parties, as well as the unions and the more privileged sectors of the working class. Such violence was especially newsworthy in the late 1970s, when left-wing terrorist groups such as the Red Brigades and Front Line reached their peak. These groups were never a mass movement, but they attracted diffuse sympathy among many disillusioned leftists, especially the young, at least until the terrorism escalated from symbolic acts to kneecappings and then dozens of murders. Former prime minister Aldo Moro was the best-known victim, but others included judges, police, journalists, politicians, and left-wing trade unionists.

Ultimately, the most interesting thing about Italian left-wing terrorism was how long it lasted. In part this reflects the clumsiness and brutality of the Italian forces of order. But as the breadth of support clearly indicates, it also reflects the deeper crisis of Italian institutions and society when compared to other Western countries. At the same time, it is notable that Italy did not panic and enact a range of measures as repressive as those introduced by the West Germans when they faced a much less serious threat.[25]

The Women's Movement. As occurred elsewhere, the feminist movement of the 1960s and 1970s in Italy originated in the extra-parliamentary Left, which preached egalitarianism but relegated women to subordinate roles. The traditional Left was also slow to appreciate the strength and depth of the feminist challenge. It initially dismissed feminists as a middle-class, privileged fringe. Feminists within the parties and unions kept up the pressure, however, and events, especially the momentous 1974 referendum on divorce, rapidly converted the unpersuaded. In fairness to the traditional Left, the great referendum victories on divorce and abortion would never have been so lopsided without the Left's full mobilization of its forces. Nor would the dramatic gains represented by the complete rewriting of family law have been possible without the Left's active support in Parliament.

The ideas of the women's movement penetrated Italian society with striking speed, at least in the cities. This is, after all, a country where as recently as the 1970s adultery was a crime only a woman could commit. Since the late 1970s, the women's movement in Italy, as elsewhere, has fragmented, although there remain umbrella organizations that can occasionally mobilize women around specific issues, and certain strands of feminism have become very influential in the universities.

Ecological Movements. Until the late 1980s, environmentalism had no autonomous political base in Parliament. Prior to the election of Green deputies, the Radical Party had acted as a sort of clearinghouse and publicizer of environmental initiatives. Parliamentary representation is a potent tool in Italy with more than propaganda value, as parties that sit in Parliament are generously funded by the state (in proportion to their size). These funds allow groups like the Greens to underwrite the referendum campaigns that they use so frequently.

As a broader social movement, environmentalism was slow to develop in Italy compared with many other European countries. At first glance, this appears anomalous, for Italy has probably suffered more ecological disasters than any other country in Western Europe. Moreover, Italy's abominable environmental record is well known to the European Union, where it is at the bottom of the list of countries that obey Community directives.[26] In 1988, the government finally addressed a package of European Community directives it had been ignoring for years—but only after world attention had focused on an Italian ship laden with toxic waste trying to unload its deadly cargo in Third World ports.

Slow to emerge and hampered by political infighting, the environmental movement proved especially effective in mobilizing protest against industrial pollution and the civilian use of nuclear energy. It has created sharp divisions within the unions and some parties over these issues, while the nuclear energy question threatened more than one national coalition. A 1987 referendum effectively overturned the government's policy on nuclear energy; in the process, it split the governing coalition as several parties, led by the DC, flip-flopped to fall in line with public opinion. The vote showed the strength of antinuclear sentiment in the post-Chernobyl era. And while the 1990 referenda failed to mobilize the required 50 percent of the eligible electorate, over 90 percent of those who did vote were in favor of abolishing hunting and the use of chemical pesticides in agriculture.

Notes

1. In the early 1970s, the average was closer to 2,000 laws per full legislature. Paul Furlong, *Modern Italy: Representation and Reform* (London: Routledge, 1994), p. 129.

2. Robert Leonardi et al., "Institutionalization of Parliament and Parliamentarization of Parties in Italy," *Legislative Studies Quarterly* 3 (February 1978): 161–169.

3. For details of the reform, see Richard S. Katz, "The New Electoral Law," in Carol Mershon and Gianfranco Pasquino, eds., *Italian Politics: Ending the First Republic* (Boulder, Colo.: Westview Press, 1995), pp. 93–112.

4. The turnout in 1991 was 62.4 percent; in 1993 it was 77.1 percent. Piergiorgio Corbetta and Arturo M. L. Parisi, "The Referendum on the Electoral Law for the Senate," in Mershon and Pasquino, *Italian Politics*, p. 81.

5. Douglas Wertman, "The Last Year of the Christian Democratic Party," in Mershon and Pasquino, *Italian Politics*, pp. 142–143.

6. For an excellent summary of this period, see Martin Rhodes, "Reinventing the Left: The Origins of Italy's Progressive Alliance," in Mershon and Pasquino, *Italian Politics*, pp. 114–121.

7. Mark Donovan, "I referendum del 1997: Il troppo stroppia?" in Luciano Bardi and Martin Rhodes, eds., *Politica in Italia: Edizione 98* (Bologna: Il Mulino, 1998), p. 201.

8. PierVincenzo Uleri, "I partiti e le consultazioni referendarie in tema di giustizia e nucleare," in Piergiorgio Corbetta and Robert Leonardi, eds., *Politica in Italia: Edizione 88* (Bologna: Il Mulino, 1988), pp. 203–204.

9. Patrizia Messina, "Opposition in Italy in the 1990s: Local Political Cultures and the Northern League," *Government and Opposition* 33 (1998): 473.

10. Ilvo Diamanti, "The Northern League: From Regional Party to Party of Government," in Stephen Gundle and Simon Parker, eds., *The New Italian Republic: From the Fall of the Berlin Wall to Berlusconi* (London: Routledge, 1996), p. 113.

11. Roberto Biorcio, "La Lega nord e la transizione italiana," *Rivista italiana di scienza politica* 29 (April 1999): 56.

12. Ibid., p. 69.

13. Donatella Campus, "Party System Change and Electoral Platforms: A Study of the 1996 Italian Election," *Modern Italy* 6, no. 1 (2001): Figure 6, p. 12.

14. Ilvo Diamanti, *La Lega* (Rome: Donzelli, 1993), pp. 98–100.

15. Renato Mannheimer, "Forza Italia," in Mannheimer, ed., *Milano a Roma: Guida all'Italia elettorale del 1994* (Rome: Donzelli, 1994), p. 40.

16. Mark Gilbert, *The Italian Revolution: The End of Politics, Italian-Style?* (Boulder, Colo.: Westview Press, 1995), p. 170.

17. Mannheimer, "Forza Italia," pp. 32–36.

18. Item XII of "Final and Transitional Arrangements." This was never enforced.

19. Piero Ignazi, *Postfascisti?* (Bologna: Il Mulino, 1994), esp. chap. 6.

20. Ibid.

21. This discussion draws on the research presented in Campus, "Party System Change and Electoral Platforms."

22. Ilvo Diamanti and Renato Mannheimer, "Introduzione," in Diamanti and Mannheimer, eds., *Milano a Roma*, pp. 15–16.

23. Liborio Mattina, "La Confindustria di Abete: dall'alleanza con la DC all'appello multipartitica," in Stephen Hellman and Gianfranco Pasquino, eds., *Politica in Italia, Edizione 93* (Bologna: Il Mulino, 1993), pp. 269–272.

24. Stephen Hellman, "Militanti e politica nel Triangolo industriale," in Aris Accornero et al., eds., *L'identità comunista. I militanti, le strutture, la cultura del Pci* (Rome: Ed. Riuniti, 1983), pp. 400–405, 429.

25. For an interesting comparison, see Donatella della Porta, *Social Movements, Political Violence, and the State* (New York: Cambridge University Press, 1995), esp. chaps. 2–3.

26. *Economist*, September 24, 1988, p. 68.

C H A P T E R

25

Italian Politics
in Transition

For all its shortcomings, postwar Italy became one of the world's richest societies, and its political system managed to evolve into an exceptionally vibrant and open democracy. To say that the country achieved all this against great odds is an understatement. Fascism's legacy, and then a postwar opposition dominated by the largest communist party in the West, paralyzed governments headed by the same, increasingly corrupt band of politicians. Combined with a state machinery of legendary inefficiency, these represent intimidating obstacles even when considered separately. Taken together, they would seem to present an insurmountable challenge. Moreover, and in large measure as a result of the foregoing circumstances, Italy's democratic institutions have had to weather serious trials: deeply rooted organized crime that openly challenges state authority; renegade security services that have plotted against democracy, often colluding with right-wing terrorists; the most violent and efficient manifestations of left-wing terrorism to have afflicted any advanced democracy; and the infiltration of political and judicial apparatuses by all manner of secret political and criminal organizations.

Many challenges have been met over past decades by a combination of institutional and extra-institutional responses. Despite the political system's perennial immobilism, starting in the 1960s it did manage to produce serious reforms, thanks to mass mobilization and societal pressure. Pressures coming from outside Parliament produced a pension reform so generous it had to

be modified within a generation. These pressures also forced passage of the Workers' Charter, advanced divorce and abortion laws, and a complete restructuring of family law. Abrogative referenda, although unable to propose coherent legislation, call attention to issues that Parliament would often prefer to ignore. In the past twenty years, referenda have been used more in Italy than anywhere else in the West save Switzerland.

The most egregious example of successful institutional functioning has been the role of the judiciary in *Tangentopoli*. Civil libertarians can justifiably find fault with the aggressive way public prosecutors went after corrupt officials, and especially with the excessive use of preventive detention and leaks to the media. At the same time, it can be argued that excessive investigative zeal might be expected—and even welcomed—in a system that until recently was notorious for sabotaging and derailing inquiries into malfeasance in high places, or simply intimidating investigators into silence. In any event, the role played by prosecutors in discrediting and, in effect, demolishing the old system of power is undeniable.

Continuities, Transitions, and Changing Agendas

After more than forty years of immobility, the Italian political system became fluid and unpredictable in the mid-1990s. Optimism that the

VOTATECI, E'QUI CHE DOVETE PASSARE IL RESTO DELLA VITA.

"Vote for us, you have to spend the rest of your life here." Italy's governing parties are represented waist-deep in garbage for the 1985 local elections.

Source: Reproduced by permission of Giorgio Forattini from Giorgio Forattini, *Forattini Classic, 1985–1990*

fall of the old political elite would be followed immediately by a simplified party system and an improved, efficient government turned out to be premature.

Transition—and Continuity

The collapse of Silvio Berlusconi's Center-Right government after only seven months in power underscored that new faces and new political parties could not guarantee a smooth transition to a new politics. The election of Romano Prodi and the Center-Left Olive Tree coalition represented an important breakthrough. In the first place, it produced true alternation between opposed blocs for the first time in postwar Italian history. Second, with more time in office, Prodi and his successor, Massimo D'Alema (the first former Communist to head a West European government), were able to implement numerous reforms, as well as bring Italy into the new Economic and Monetary Union (EMU). But despite these accomplishments, many of the worst aspects of the First Republic remained in place, as Prodi, and then D'Alema, were forced to resign by divisions within their own majority.

The old elite has largely been swept away, and the parties that dominated Italian politics for nearly half a century have undergone profound changes, have been reduced to bit players, or have disappeared altogether. New electoral systems at all levels have helped speed the changes. But nothing has been able to prevent the fragmentation of the party system. The First Republic was considered to have had too many parties, with somewhere between ten and twelve gaining parliamentary representation by the early 1990s. What, then, was one to make of the Ulivo coalition that alone counted nine different political parties? With so many political forces competing for breathing space, the construction of coherent coalitions, always a problem for Italy, has become even more arduous than in the past. Constant squabbling within the Center-Left helped undermine its credibility and guarantee victory for Berlusconi and his allies in the general elections of May 2001.

It may only be natural for an unsettled period to follow the collapse of a system that was entrenched for so many years, but there are troubling signs that the fragmentation could become self-perpetuating. Some small parties (Rifondazione comunista and the Italian Popular Party, PPI) are ideologically committed to proportional representation. But even those that are not have discovered that they have much to gain by stressing their independence and then bargaining to maximize their own advantage. None of these groups has any incentive to support a reform that might simplify the party system. And should the party system remain as fragmented as it has become, the smaller parties of the center of the spectrum will be tempted to jump from one side to the other as opportunities present themselves, hardly a guarantee of coherent coalitions or clear alternation.

Aside from the frustration of further electoral reform, there are mixed signs concerning the future of other much-needed reforms of the political system and welfare state, and thus whether the "Second Republic," awaited since 1994, would ever truly be realized. Pensions, the health system, education, and center-periphery relations have all witnessed some restructuring. But informed observers consider most of these reforms to be at best mere beginnings. The most sustained effort at comprehensive institutional reform—the Bicameral Commission of 1997—ended in failure and an apparent hardening of positions that does not bode well for a future re-writing of important parts of the constitution.

It may well be the case that the Center-Right victory in the elections of 2001 will provide at least some reforms with a second wind. It is cer-tain in any event that the question of federalism will be high on the agenda, for the last act of the Center-Left before the 2001 elections was to ini-tiate a constitutional reform that introduced a mild version of federalism. But in many other areas, despite agreement that the existing rules of the political game needed serious overhaul, the likelihood of sweeping reform may well have diminished for the foreseeable future.

Unresolved Political and Institutional Questions

A number of issues deserve further attention, as they are likely to shape Italian politics, or at least lurk in the background, for some time.

The Media and Politics. Berlusconi's self-inter-ested entry into politics underscored the unreg-ulated, unbalanced nature of Italy's broadcast media. It is bad enough that the three largest private television networks are in one person's hands. It is even worse that this situation is con-doned by a law written by Berlusconi's cronies in the 1980s, making him the beneficiary of a governmental concession that amounts to a near-monopoly. When that person is leader of the opposition or prime minister, one need not be a political philosopher to see the prob-lems created for the democratic rules of the game.

The question of political commercials is thorny enough. During campaigns, Berlusconi is paid by his opponents whenever they buy time on one of his networks. Beyond overt po-litical ads, the media can manipulate opinion in many ways and, since 1994, Berlusconi's chan-nels have provided ample evidence of such methods, from overt editorializing on news broadcasts and unbalanced guest lists on talk shows to blatant campaigning by the teenaged hostess of the country's most popular daytime variety show. A similar employment of the for-midable means at his disposal during the 1995 referenda that challenged Berlusconi's privi-leged media position, and a media blitz during the 1999 European elections, confirmed the be-lief that this situation should not be allowed to continue. Yet the most that has been achieved have been ad hoc laws, for Berlusconi and his al-lies not only ferociously resist more serious leg-islation, but frequently try to barter for silence on this issue in exchange for reforms in other areas.

Berlusconi has never shown much concern over his conflict of interest, even when the Con-stitutional Court opined in 1994 that three net-works were too many for any single proprietor. His victory in the 1995 referenda reinforced his resolve. His insensitivity to this problem can be breathtaking; he has said that he "gets a rash" every time an equal-time doctrine is mentioned, and he has also insisted that his vast wealth should be reassuring to the public, since it pro-vides the best guarantee that he will not try to enrich himself at public expense. His conflict of interest is unique in Western democratic soci-eties and will persist as long as Il Cavaliere owns three networks and remains in politics. Since he has once more become prime minister, it is likely to move to the top of the political agenda again.

Revise—or Rewrite—the Constitution? Al-though the Bicameral Commission's failure showed that no consensus existed about consti-tutional change in Italy, most observers agree that changes are necessary. As we saw in Chap-ter 21, the republican constitution is the product of a compromise. In 1947, the Italian political system appeared permanently fragmented; proportional representation guaranteed fair representation to all parties and also made it nearly impossible for one party to obtain an absolute majority of seats in both chambers of Parliament. Thus, the provision (Article 138) for constitutional revisions and amendments—an absolute majority of both chambers must pass identical versions of the proposed change on two occasions at least three months apart—appears rather permissive to someone from Canada or the United States but was quite restrictive when written.

With a majoritarian electoral system, however, parliamentary majorities usually do not faithfully mirror popular sentiment. When the goal is to put together a government solid enough to last more than ten months, the trade-off is acceptable. But it is another matter altogether if an artificial (or extremely narrow) majority can then be used to alter the constitution. The elaborate amending formulas of most countries with single-member electoral systems reflect concern that constitutions not be able to be rewritten too casually. Even countries with proportional representation have established more restrictive conditions than Italy for altering their constitutions.[1]

On the surface, Article 138 appears to make it quite difficult to push through controversial changes to the constitution. It stipulates that should less than two-thirds of each chamber support a proposed change, a popular referendum may be called within three months to ratify it.[2] But whereas this guarantee against hasty or demagogic action seemed ironclad when written, it looks less secure fifty years later, above all when the person likely to be proposing constitutional changes also happens to own Italy's private television networks, with a proven track record of swaying public opinion.

The Electoral System. Aside from the issue of the amending formula for the constitution, the institutional change most discussed has unquestionably been the debate over whether the elec-

toral system requires further modification. Under the impetus of simplifying the party system and strengthening its bipolar tendencies, post-*Tangentopoli* discussion originally focused on the French two-ballot system, with no residual proportional representation (PR) at all. But political realities (above all, the intransigence of the minor partners in both coalitions) soon put an end to this prospect, and the failure of successive referenda to abolish the PR seats has actually stimulated the hopes of those who would like to see the system made more proportional. Despite general agreement that the current mix of three-fourths single-member districts and one-fourth PR, represents an ungainly and not terribly effective compromise, it is unlikely that anything better will replace it.

The Executive. Since Bettino Craxi's governments in the 1980s, there has been discussion of the need for a stronger executive. But the weakness of Italian prime ministers has not only been due to constitutional design but also to the fact that all governments have been hostage to the many parties (or factions) that composed them. Notwithstanding this rather basic fact, half-thought-out schemes are regularly brought forward with the promise that they will solve the country's problems in one fell swoop. These schemes tend to be overly ambitious or absurdly unrealistic.

On the unrealistic side, some people actually believe Italy would be better off as a presidential republic, such as the United States (South American examples or Russia are studiously ignored by proponents of this option.) Despite manifest evidence of the built-in tensions between the U.S. president and Congress, particularly when different parties control each branch of government, people seriously argue that this is the only way to undercut the parties' power in Parliament. More plausibly, others argue that a semi-presidential regime, such as France's Fifth Republic, would be far less fraught with problems and more in keeping with the European continent's parliamentary traditions. This view has come to be accepted by most of those on the Center-Left, although their first preference remains that of a largely ceremonial president, whereas the prime minister's powers would be enhanced. The PPI, for instance, implacably opposes anything that smacks of presidentialism.

More allegedly moderate proposals can be highly unrealistic. Several reformers, for example, have suggested that the prime minister be directly elected, a practice that currently exists only in Israel. This would presumably give the head of government a popular mandate that would make it easier to keep fractious coalition partners in line. But such a procedure would be far harder to implement than its supporters imagine and could prove especially clumsy to apply at a national level. As both Berlusconi's and Prodi's experiences in 1994 and 1996–1998 poignantly demonstrated, even the unquestioned leaders of opposed electoral blocs ultimately serve at the sufferance of their coalition partners. The "remedies" that have been suggested to guarantee executive stability in this case—an electoral premium to the winning candidate—leave the smaller parties on both sides, and especially the Center-Left, highly suspicious.

Federalism and Bicameralism. The League has been federalism's strongest proponent and is most responsible for this question's remaining high on Italy's political agenda. There is a strong consensus that the regions, and all local levels of government, deserve more decision-making (and taxing) autonomy, though, as usual, there is nothing like unanimity about what forms this autonomy should take. We saw in Chapter 23 that although reforms were passed in the late 1990s, they barely qualify as first steps on the road to federalism. Here, as in the case of disputes over proportionalism and the role of the executive, we find that underlying the many differences among the parties are profoundly different political philosophies, as well as a good deal of opportunistic political calculation. There are true differences over whether Italy should be a federal state or a more unitary one with strongly decentralized components. This question will take on great importance now that the Center-Right (including the Northern League) has won the 2001 elections. Even before the election, Bossi and Berlusconi were preparing to undo the Center-Left's reform, which they denounced as inadequate. But many questions remain. Will the League's most recent demand, devolution, prove capable of being accommodated any more easily than outright federalism? Will the National Alliance, which retains a strong centralist orientation from its neofascist past, not to mention its strongest base in the south, balk at something it feels undermines national unity and permanently disadvantages the Mezzogiorno?

The debate over decentralization or federalism is likely to determine how bicameralism is addressed. Some would like to eliminate the redundant Senate altogether and reduce the Chamber to about 500 members from its current 630. Others, particularly federalists, would like to convert the Senate into a "chamber of the regions," similar to the German Bundesrat. Even many who are not convinced federalists agree that reshaping the Senate in this fashion would be desirable. Serious changes at this level would extensively transform Italy's political institutions and machinery of state, and there exists at present no clear consensus for any reform, which makes this a potentially divisive, and even explosive, political issue.

Italy's Changing Social Profile

Old stereotypes are slow to die, and many people undoubtedly continue to think of Italy in terms that have little connection with reality. The image of a deeply Catholic country, tradition bound, has been out of date for a generation. Ireland may have narrowly approved divorce in a referendum in 1995, but Italy did so massively in 1974, while almost 70 percent of

Italians voted to uphold the country's very liberal abortion law in 1981. Another statistic demonstrates how much this country's problems have become those of a mature capitalist society: By the end of the 1980s, Italy had the lowest fertility rate in the world; since 1993, deaths have outnumbered births.

This phenomenon is closely tied to another old stereotype: that Italy is a country of emigrants. This certainly was true for the first century of its existence, but since the 1970s, Italy has seen more immigration than emigration. Most immigrants have been Italians returning home, but since the 1980s, the country has had to face a phenomenon typical of many other advanced economies: the massive influx of dark-skinned foreigners from developing countries. Were it not for them, the decline in population and the disproportionately high aged population would be even more marked.

Relations with the Church (and Catholics)

The Olive Tree's victory might lead the casual observer to conclude that with a Center-Left government in power, Italy's evolution in a secular direction would continue apace. Such a conclusion would be hasty: Prodi is a practicing Catholic, and both his and successive coalitions depended on the support of the Catholic PPI, as well as Catholics in other parties. Moreover, Prodi named a militant Catholic (Rosy Bindi) as minister of health, an office directly involved with such sensitive topics as abortion, embryonic research, and sex education, and she continued in that role in both of Massimo D'Alema's cabinets. And while Polish-born Pope John Paul II has hardly been as directly involved in Italian politics as his Italian-born predecessors, he has not hesitated to issue pronouncements on these and many other issues he considers important, and he has done so much more often in the waning years of his papacy.

The Church's formal and informal roles in Italian society have at times been immense, although the formal boundaries were brought up to date in 1983 (under a Socialist prime minister) when the Concordat was revised. Interestingly, during the long period of Christian Democratic (DC) domination, the question of state aid to Catholic schools never arose, largely because the republican constitution expressly forbids this (Article 33). In addition, the ruling party desperately needed its lay partners' support and knew that even to raise the question might well be fatal to the always fragile coalitions of the First Republic. With the end of DC hegemony and with explicitly Catholic political formations reduced to minority status in both blocs, this constraint was no longer in force. Moreover, the very fact that Catholic political formations are now scattered and weak makes them, if anything, even more responsive to the Vatican's pronouncements and wishes. It was thus only to be expected that when the entire structure of public schooling was reformed, starting in 1997, this thorny question would come to the fore.[3]

A compromise was eventually reached, involving finding elaborate formulas that subsidize private schools while at the same time respecting the constitutional injunction against the state's assuming any direct financial burden in nonpublic education. Debates in both chambers of Parliament dragged on through the end of 1999 and into 2000, with the sharpest differences of opinion expressed within the Center-Left majority. Catholics would threaten to vote against the government's proposal unless more were done for the private schools; these moves would be countered by threats from the Left Democrats (DS), Socialists, Greens, and others to withhold *their* support unless the Catholics backed off. The Center-Right, after initially supporting the government's proposal, upped the ante and increased political confusion by insisting on a voucher system, which would clearly be unconstitutional as things currently stand. At the end of the day, de facto support for private schooling was passed into law, and everyone was reminded of the divisiveness of this issue.

Italy's New Immigrants

By the 1980s, the influx of people euphemistically referred to as *extracomunitari,* that is, from outside the European Community, began to take on notable proportions. In that decade, foreign immigration tripled. By the turn of the century, estimates put the total immigrant population, legal and illegal, at roughly 1.5 million, or just below 3 percent of the entire population.

By the standards of Europe's other large countries, these numbers appear low. But the fact remains that in just two decades, a country that had mainly experienced foreigners as middle-class tourists now encountered large numbers of black or brown street vendors or menial laborers in most of its largest cities. The most highly visible minorities are North Africans and sub-Saharan Africans, and their presence has generated many reactions tinged with intolerance and racism. With the growth of these immigrant communities has also come the involvement of their more marginal elements in drugs, prostitution, and other crimes. The underside of immigration inevitably gets extensive coverage in the more sensationalist press, which plays into a growing public sense of insecurity, which appears to be related more to crime than to the threat of job loss.[4]

Ugly episodes have taken place in the cities, with the National Alliance and the League occasionally distinguishing themselves for anti-foreign pronouncements that spill over into outright racism. Forza Italia has been more cautious, emphasizing the need to limit the inflow of immigrants, while taking a strong law-and-order stance. But there have been signs that this issue might become more politicized than in the past. It is notable that one constraint against such politicization has been the Roman Catholic Church. Whereas some on the right have expressed the usual fears and prejudices, including a defense of Christian values against groups identified as predominantly Muslim, the Church has remained a strong voice for moderation and tolerance until very recently, when a few cardinals (but not the pope) began speaking in decidedly intolerant tones.

There are numerous reasons for the surge of immigration. Italians increasingly refuse to accept such jobs as low-paying work in the cities and backbreaking seasonal work in the fields. Economic expansion in the north, and especially the northeast, has created labor shortages and pleas by employers to increase the quotas permitted under the legislation of the late 1990s. (Another category filled by immigrants is female domestic servants, but these workers are less visible and less threatening.) Then there are refugees fleeing poverty, political repression, and instability, or all three. For all these groups, Italy is easier to enter and has a more tolerant (or inefficient) bureaucratic environment than the other large, rich members of the European Union (EU).

This situation creates external and internal tensions. Fears among other EU members that immigrants would pour into Italy before 1992 led to pressures on the Italians to make their borders less porous before the Maastricht Treaty was signed; interim agreements in 1990 pointedly excluded the Italians to drive the point home.[5] The 1998 reform was a response to the inadequacies of earlier national legislation, but its contours were profoundly shaped by European imperatives, starting with the requirements for inclusion in the Schengen area, which governs immigration and migratory flows, and extending to other standards as well.

The Challenges of European Integration: Changes in the Economy and Industrial Relations

If Italy's record of institutional reform was at best mixed, its achievements in the broadly defined economic arena were far more impressive—and surprising. It is worth recalling that *Tangentopoli* was preceded by a serious exchange rate crisis that forced Italy's withdrawal from the European Monetary System and that no one really expected Italy to be able to adhere to the Maastricht convergence criteria by the 1997 deadline.[6] The First Republic's legacy appeared too daunting to overcome in less than five years. The "colonization" of the state by the DC and its partners, the rampant use of public resources for patronage purposes, a reticence to force key constituencies to pay their taxes, and some of the highest rates of industrial conflict in the capitalist world had saddled Italy with seemingly insurmountable problems.

And yet, by the middle of 1997, Romano Prodi could justifiably boast that Italy had qualified as a full-fledged member of the new Europe. Inflation and the deficit had been brought within Maastricht's restrictive parameters, and even a stratospherically high national debt had begun to decline, though it remains above 100 percent of gross domestic product. The contentious issue of privatization, although proceeding too slowly and incompletely for critics in the EU, was being implemented at a pace that would have been unthinkable five years earlier. The Institute for Industrial Reconstruction (IRI), the state-owned holding company that was one of the motors of the Economic Miracle and was still one of the largest corporations in the world at the beginning of the 1990s, had been sold off by 2000.

It is increasingly difficult to isolate the domestic from the external stimuli in a modern economy, particularly in Western Europe a few years into the new century. Italy's economy was in such bad shape by the end of the 1980s that even without the EU at the gates, serious corrective measures would have been required. But there can be no doubt that both the speed of Italy's recovery and the extent to which former sacred cows were sacrificed must be attributed to the willingness of successive governments, starting with Amato's first cabinet in 1992, to attack these problems head on. And there can equally be no doubt that the primary reason for this political decisiveness was the pressure all these governments felt not to suffer the humili-

ation of being excluded from full partnership in Europe.

The seriousness with which this challenge was considered is nowhere more evident than in the choice of leaders in this crucial period—and hence the signals Italy wished to send to foreign observers. Carlo Azeglio Ciampi was the former governor of the Bank of Italy before heading a government of experts in 1993 and serving as minister of an immensely more powerful Treasury under Prodi; Lamberto Dini was director general of the Bank of Italy and then Berlusconi's treasurer before heading yet another "technical" government, after which he served the Center-Left uninterruptedly as foreign minister. Prodi was chosen to lead the Ulivo for several reasons, but one of the most important was his reputation as a highly competent economist who had headed IRI in the 1980s and tried to reform it. Ciampi's election as president of Italy and Prodi's selection as president of the European Commission provide some indication of the credibility these leaders earned while in office.

The other striking achievement in Italy's political economy can also be traced back to the early 1990s, and precisely to the labor relations accords established under Amato's first government in 1993. These accords, which implemented formal tripartite consultation among labor, management, and the state, were offered to the unions as partial compensation for the abolition of the *scala mobile*, the cost-of-living escalator that had been the bane of employers and the source of some of the fiercest labor conflicts of previous decades. It is safe to say that if successive governments were committed to implementing policies that would bring Italy into Europe at any price, these accords—specifically, a formal, institutionalized voice for labor—were one of the most important of these prices. Management, above all in the largest, most vulnerable firms, was also glad to have a formal framework of consultation and negotiation in a world that had become increasingly competitive and unpredictable.

This list of achievements is impressive, but it

hardly means that Italy has left its chronic economic problems behind. To take the case of labor relations as just one example, one can only wonder how long the unions, even in their relatively weakened state, will continue with the sort of sacrifices they have been making since the early 1990s, keeping their wage demands well below inflation rates, losing purchasing power. Particularly should unemployment levels continue to drop and Italy's budgetary picture continue to be rosy, the unions might well want to play a bit of catch-up. With the Center-Right again in power, it will be interesting to see whether that government will be as committed as its predecessors to maintaining good labor relations or whether it will take a more aggressive stance toward the unions.

The Broader International Dimension

Throughout the entire postwar period, Italian governments tended to keep a low and generally noncontroversial profile in foreign affairs, presenting their country as a reliable partner in the North Atlantic Treaty Organization (NATO) and an ardent proponent of European integration. With regard to NATO, many critics and even some sympathizers have noted that the Italians have shown a willingness to follow the lead of the United States to a degree that is sometimes slavish. Whether it reflected a realistic assessment of their own irrelevancy in foreign affairs or a tacit trade-off for the unconditional support of the Americans against the PCI, Italian pliability regularly served U.S. interests. When others balked over President Ronald Reagan's plan to deploy cruise missiles in the early 1980s, Italy agreed to accept them on its soil. When the Spaniards insisted that the Americans remove their F-16 fighters later in the same decade, Italy promptly provided a base, which figured prominently in operations against the Bosnian Serbs in the mid-1990s. And when NATO controversially waged war against Yugoslavia over Kosovo, Italy again was in the forefront, not only making its strategically critical

territory available but actively supporting the effort. This support was all the more striking in that it came during the leadership of Massimo D'Alema, the former Communist.

There is truth in the Italians' claim to be good European citizens, especially compared to the British or French. But while Italy has not been as publicly disruptive as some of its neighbors, its actual behavior has been far from exemplary. Until recently, it was among Europe's most flagrant violators of practically every economic and financial guideline. And in a broader sense, Italy's behavior as a citizen of Europe has often been little short of atrocious. It regularly leads the EU in its failure to implement directives, in directives that are completely ignored, and in the number of violations proceedings that are instituted against member countries. The only other countries with such abysmal records are less wealthy newcomers like Greece and Portugal.

There are various reasons for such a terrible record. The Italian bureaucracy is excruciatingly slow to implement anything; it regularly fails to spend funds earmarked by the EU, so we can hardly expect it to spring to life to enact directives. Parliament's inability to pass important laws is also well known, and many Community directives require enabling legislation. Finally, since directives often involve one or another of the interests that are entrenched in the bureaucracy or find representation in Parliament, conscious obstructionism is often added to the more routine obstacles that plague the system. Frustration over machinery that continues to move at a snail's pace is the major reason the business community has become increasingly outspoken in its demands for bureaucratic reform and for a more efficient executive.

There were marked signs of improvement through the latter half of the 1990s, including some reforms of both bureaucratic structures and decision-making processes (discussed in Chapter 23). Are these reforms—and the EU's watchdogs—sufficient to produce long-lasting changes? Or will Italy revert to form now that the immediate challenge of being included in the monetary union has successfully been achieved?

Italy in Comparative Perspective

One way to conceptualize the Italian case comparatively is by undertaking specific country-by-country comparisons. No one would hold Italy up as a model to be emulated, but different aspects of Italian history and politics are by no means exceptional or unique. Indeed, extensive literature exists on many of these comparisons.

Many of the most interesting historical comparisons can be made with Germany, above all concerning late unification as nation-states and the subsequent reliance on a far more interventionist pattern of industrialization than Britain's laissez-faire model. Indeed, late in the nineteenth century, the Italians self-consciously shifted from a British to a Prussian pattern. Another quite stimulating, if unsettling, series of comparisons with Germany can be made surrounding the social and political alliances that dominated both countries through World War I, including their ultimate capitulation in the face of Fascist challenges to democracy. Christian Democracy was a widespread phenomenon in the immediate post–World War II period in Europe, but, interestingly, it triumphed politically only in these two countries, although the sister parties increasingly diverged as time wore on.

Japan provides the only comparison among advanced industrial democracies completely dominated by a freely elected single party for two generations.[7] For similar reasons, this comparison brings to the light extraordinary levels of corruption, including collusion with organized crime. Comparativists who prefer cultural explanations for many political phenomena, including corruption, might want to pay special attention to this comparison and perhaps look to more straightforward political explanations such as the length of time a single party spends in power with no real opposition in sight.

France is the obvious point of comparison for Italy's most distinctive political feature, the postwar domination of the opposition by a communist party. In the French case, this situation lasted until the end of the 1970s, when the French Socialist Party finally surpassed the French Communist Party. In Italy, because of a far more flexible and nondogmatic party, the Communist Party's (PCI's) domination of the opposition lasted until the end of communism itself. The PCI's distinctiveness in turn conditioned the evolution of the rest of the Left, above all, the Italian Socialist Party (PSI). Groping for its own space, Italian socialism (at the cost of its ultimate survival) decided that its fate lay in the center of the political spectrum. Its path was not so different from that taken by socialists and social democrats throughout southern Europe (e.g., Portugal, Spain, France, and Greece), and this phenomenon itself invites further analysis. But these other socialist parties did not chronically hover between 10 and 15 percent of the vote, nor were they obliterated by corruption scandals, even though most of them have in fact been implicated in serious misbehavior. (The susceptibility of socialist parties to corruption as they abandon their old ideological identification is yet another interesting theme.)

On a broader level of comparison, Italian politics has been dominated for years by some of the classic questions of democratic theory: Which institutional arrangements provide the best guarantee of effective democratic government? What is the trade-off between stable government and the faithful representation of ideological and programmatic differences? Between stability and grass-roots initiatives like the referendum? Can institutional engineering or manipulation produce desired results? Discussion of these issues has been the subject of national campaigns and is continuously aired in both the print and electronic media.

Italy has become something of a laboratory for some of the most basic issues of comparative politics. But its current situation may well be unique. This is not a transition from authoritarianism to democracy, which Italy underwent in 1945, and so much of the less-developed (including formerly communist) world has undergone more recently. If carried forward, it will be a transition from a party-dominated, assembly-style democratic regime (with severe problems of political immobility) to another, ideally more efficient type of democratic regime.

This may prove to be the rarest sort of transition of all, for despite the supposed flexibility of democratic institutions, democracies almost never undertake major institutional overhauls. And they simply *never* seem to do so unless massively disruptive and traumatic events such as war, revolution, or deep national division force their hand. It is worth recalling that the French transition from the Fourth to the Fifth Republic occurred as a response to the paralysis

and trauma of decolonization and the Algerian War; *society* threatened to tear itself apart in a crisis that was far more than merely political. The Italian transition, in contrast, is exclusively political.

Italy has always lacked the French flair for political drama, although in its own crafty way it often manages to achieve more than its neighbor—like pension reform in the 1990s, but, even more tellingly, a comparison of 1968 in France with Italy's Hot Autumn, reveals. Will it achieve the unprecedented—a transition to a Second Republic that is a radical new departure—without the trauma that such changes seem to require? Or will Italy continue to be the country of The Leopard,[8] where everything seems to change so nothing in fact really changes at all?

Notes

1. Sweden, for instance, has a provision similar to Italy's requiring two separate votes, but an election must intervene between these votes.

2. In addition to stipulating the same methods employed for holding an abrogative referendum (collecting 500,000 valid signatures or having a motion passed by five regional assemblies), Article 138 also permits a referendum ratifying constitutional change to be called if a fifth of the members of either chamber of Parliament request it.

3. For the government's proposal and the subtleties surrounding the whole issue, see Giancarlo Gasperoni, "L'incerto rinnovamento della scuola italiana," in Luciano Bardi and Martin Rhodes, eds., *Politica in Italia: Edizione 98* (Bologna: Il Mulino, 1998), pp. 265–288.

4. Carl Ipsen, "Immigration and Crime in Con-

temporary Italy," *Journal of Modern Italian Studies* 4 (Summer 1999): 275. This review essay surveys recent work on the subject.

5. "Italian Survey," *Economist*, May 26, 1990, p. 25.

6. For a typical assessment of the mid-1990s, see Lionel Barber and Andrew Fisher, "Eight European States 'on Course' for Single Currency," *Financial Times*, November 23, 1995. Italy was not one of the eight.

7. Sweden, governed by the Socialists from 1932 to 1976, comes close.

8. The reference is to Giuseppe Tomasi di Lampedusa's classic novel of the Risorgimento, *Il Gattopardo* (The Leopard) (Milan: Feltrinelli, 1966), first published in 1958.

Bibliography

Blackmer, Donald L. M., and Sidney Tarrow, eds. *Communism in Italy and in France.* Princeton, N.J.: Princeton University Press, 1975.

Bufacchi, Vittorio, and Simon Burgess. *Italy Since 1989: Events and Interpretations.* New York: St. Martin's Press 1998.

Bull, Martin, and Martin Rhodes, eds. *Crisis and Transition in Italian Politics*. London: Frank Cass, 1998.

Chubb, Judith. *Patronage, Power and Poverty in Southern Italy: A Tale of Two Cities*. Cambridge: Cambridge University Press, 1982.

Clark, Martin. *Modern Italy 1871–1995*, 2nd edition. London: Longman, 1996.

Ferraresi, Franco. *Threats to Democracy: The Radical Right in Italy After the War*. Princeton, N.J.: Princeton University Press, 1996.

Furlong, Paul. *Modern Italy: Representation and Reform*. London: Routledge, 1994.

Gilbert, Mark. *The Italian Revolution: The End of Democracy, Italian Style?* Boulder, Colo.: Westview Press, 1995.

Gilbert, Mark, and K. Robert Nilsson. *Historical Dictionary of Modern Italy*. Lanham, Md.: The Scarecrow Press, 1999.

Ginsborg, Paul. *A History of Contemporary Italy. Society and Politics 1943–1988*. London: Penguin, 1990.

Gundle, Stephen, and Simon Parker, eds. *The New Italian Republic; From the Fall of the Berlin Wall to Berlusconi*. London: Macmillan, 1996.

Hellman, Judith Adler. *Journeys Among Women: Feminism in Five Italian Cities*. New York: Oxford University Press, 1987.

Hellman, Stephen. *Italian Communism in Transition: The Rise and Fall of the Historic Compromise in Turin, 1975–1980*. New York: Oxford University Press, 1988.

Hine, David. *Governing Italy: The Politics of Bargained Pluralism*. Oxford: Clarendon Press, 1993.

Italian Politics: A Review. London: Frances Pinter from 1986–1993; Boulder, Colo.: Westview Press, 1993–1998. London: Berghahn Books, 1999–.

Jemolo, Arturo Carlo. *Church and State in Italy: 1850–1950*. Oxford: Basil Blackwell, 1960.

Lange, Peter, and Marino Regini, eds. *State, Market, and Social Regulation: New Perspectives on Italy*. Cambridge: Cambridge University Press, 1989.

Lange, Peter, and Sidney Tarrow, eds. *Italy in Transition: Conflict and Consensus*. London: Frank Cass, 1980.

LaPalombara, Joseph. *Democracy, Italian Style*. New Haven, Conn.: Yale University Press, 1987.

Locke, Richard. *Remaking the Italian Economy*. Ithaca, N.Y.: Cornell University Press, 1995.

Lumley, Robert. *States of Emergency: Cultures of Revolt in Italy from 1968 to 1978*. London: Verso, 1990.

Lyttleton, Adrian. *The Seizure of Power: Fascism in Italy, 1919–1929*. London: Weidenfeld and Nicolson, 1973.

McCarthy, Patrick. *The Crisis of the Italian State: From the Origins of the Cold War to the Fall of Berlusconi*. New York: St. Martin's Press, 1995.

Procacci, Giuliano. *History of the Italian People*. Hammondsworth, England: Penguin Books, 1973.

Putnam, Robert. *Making Democracy Work: Civic Traditions in Modern Italy*. Princeton, N.J.: Princeton University Press, 1993.

Tarrow, Sidney. *Democracy and Disorder: Protest and Politics in Italy, 1965–1975*. Oxford: Clarendon Press, 1989.

Urban, Joan Barth. *Moscow and the Italian Communist Party: From Togliatti to Berlinguer*. Ithaca, N.Y.: Cornell University Press, 1986.

Woolf, S. J., ed. *The Rebirth of Italy 1943–50*. New York: Humanities Press, 1972.

Web Sites (in English)

ISTAT, Italy's national Statistical Institute: *www.istat.it/homeing.html* Contains current, as well as historical series, of social and economic data.

The Istituto Carlo Catteneo: *www.cattaneo.org/english/1index.html* Excellent archives of social and political data, often in historical series.

The Italian Studies Web: *www.lib.byu.edu/~rdh/wess/ital/polygov.html* Basic information, and links to Web sites of interest to students of politics and society.

VII

East-Central Europe in Transition

David Ost

CHAPTER

26

The Making of
Modern East-Central Europe

East-Central European Politics in Action

A few snapshots from the land that used to be Czechoslovakia provide a wonderful picture of the complex and fascinating events that have been shaping East-Central Europe in recent years.

Late 1989. Commentators around the world speak of the dawning of a new age of freedom and democracy, symbolized first by the fall of the Berlin Wall on November 9 and then by the "Velvet Revolution" unfolding immediately afterward in Czechoslovakia. It is in Prague that the sense of promise and hope is most evident. Velvet is smooth, soft, and friendly, more an aesthetic concept than a political one. And that is what makes the term so appropriate. The strikes that brought down the government, in fact, were begun by actors who announced that they would use the stage to press for political freedom. Within days, first students and then the majority of workers had joined in. The protesters demanded civic rights: freedom of the press and association, an end to the Communist Party's monopoly on power, a truly representative political system. Workers and intellectuals, urbanites and farmers, Czechs and Slovaks, liberals and conservatives: all came together behind the program of the new opposition. With a huge general strike showing the

unity of the population and the Soviet Union no longer ready to intervene, the government was powerless to resist. By the end of December, veteran playwright and dissident Vaclav Havel, only recently released from jail, is named the new president of Czechoslovakia. The country entered the new year and decade filled with hope, united behind a new leader promising tolerance for all and a velvet-smooth transition to a just, democratic, and prosperous new system.

Mid-1992. The Velvet Revolution is coming apart. The Civic Forum has broken into pieces, and the new voices speak the language not of tolerance but of blame. Slovakia's leaders blame the Czechs for Slovak problems and say they want to secede. Leading Czech politicians say a divorce is fine with them. They in turn blame "Communists" for ongoing Czech problems even though the Communists are no longer in power. Those who remain loyal to the original goals of freedom and tolerance warn against this new politics of witch-hunt and resentment. But this group is decisively beaten in the 1992 elections. Vaclav Havel resigns from the presidency as the country prepares to split apart. The revolution seems to have taken off its velvet gloves.

Early 1994. For all the tensions of the past year, the breakup of the country goes smoothly. It is a "velvet divorce," with the two sides agreeing amicably on dividing territory and property.

Vaclav Havel is elected president of the new Czech Republic (and presided still when the new century began). Optimism reigns as the new country's first parliamentary elections are held.

October 1999. The Velvet Revolution seems to have survived, but the country faces new problems. Economic growth slows, corruption scandals explode, and unemployment begins to rise just when it is falling elsewhere in the region. The North Atlantic Treaty Organization (NATO) and the European Union (EU) beckon, but citizens are skeptical. The country had entered NATO in April 1999 without great public support, and was largely critical of NATO actions in Kosovo. Now, in October 1999, the EU issues a scathing report, its second in two years, criticizing the Czech Republic for not doing what needs to be done for joining the EU. The Velvet Revolution survived the breakup of Czechoslovakia, but whether social cohesion can survive European integration remains unclear.

These few snapshots show the hopes and fears of the new Eastern Europe: the hopes that nonviolent revolution is possible, that border questions can be resolved amicably, that economic growth can embrace all; and the fears that nationalism will win out against unification, that no post-Communist economy can escape economic crisis, and that European integration creates as many problems as it solves.

While hope seems to have triumphed in the former Czechoslovakia, the fears have been borne out by the experience of the former Yugoslavia. In that country, the democratic aspirations of citizens came to fruition in 1990 with free elections in each of the six constituent republics. In contrast to Czechoslovakia, however, the language of blame pervaded the new system from the start. Citizens in each republic elected political leaders who claimed that local problems were the result of outside interference—meaning not foreign entities but the other republics making up the country. Within a year, Yugoslavia had not only divided into separate states but had exploded in civil war, and the fighting lasted

until 1999. By the time the new century began, hundreds of thousands had lost their homes and many their lives, and many more questioned whether freedom was worth such a price.

The 1990s was a decade of enormous transformation in Eastern Europe, with each country having to create entirely new political and economic systems. Many commentators say this is just a matter of doing what the West did in the past. In fact, it is something the West never even tried. Capitalism in the West began to develop in the sixteenth century, but political democracy had to wait a full four hundred years. Eastern Europe had to build capitalism and democracy at the same time. Economically, this meant abandoning the informal consensus of communism, by which workers were guaranteed jobs and a low but steadily increasing standard of living in return for their acceptance of Communist Party rule. In its place came a capitalist market economy, where people lost their economic security and suffered a painful economic crisis, but gained political freedom. Western Europe has also moved away from guaranteeing economic security to citizens. But this substitution of the "new political economy" for the "old postwar consensus" has been much more painful in the East, where people began from a poorer position and where the underdeveloped economy left them with fewer possibilities.

By the beginning of the new millennium, the worst part of the post-Communist transformation appeared to be over. Where the first years after 1989 saw economic declines greater than during the Great Depression in the West, most countries in the region have been growing since 1996. Poland's gross domestic product exceeded 1989 levels in 1997, and Hungary followed soon after. All the countries have now had several multiparty elections, and most basic freedoms are accepted everywhere. There is greater inequality than before, but also real political democracy. But not all the questions are resolved, and this is what makes the region still so fascinating to study. Having freed itself from dependence on the Soviet Union, how will it react to its new dependence on the EU? Can the many

Eastern and Central Europe

young people who lost job opportunities because of the economic crisis find their way, or will many turn to the kind of right-wing extremism that has emerged in recent years? After decades of legal equality but de facto discrimination, can women become full citizens? Democracy may prevail, but what kind of democracy will it be? These are the questions we will be exploring in the following chapters.

Geographic Setting

The borders of the countries in East-Central Europe have changed a great deal over the past century. Most of the countries discussed here did not even exist as independent entities when the twentieth century began, and all of them have seen their independence come and go over the course of that century. Even today, the process of state formation is not yet complete. What is East-Central Europe? Until 1989, it referred to the countries between West Germany and the Soviet Union that were ruled by communist parties. (Thus the term had an ideological as well as a geographical referent. Vienna, for example, is located east of Prague but was considered part of "the West.") According to this definition, the region encompassed East Germany, Poland, Czechoslovakia, Hungary, Yugoslavia, Romania, Bulgaria, and Albania. Since 1989, however, East Germany has disappeared. Czechoslovakia has split in two. Yugoslavia has split five ways, into Bosnia, Croatia, Macedonia, Slovenia, and a country still called Yugoslavia (made up of dominant Serbia and the small mountainous republic of Montenegro). Six more countries then arose in the region west of Russia after the collapse of the Soviet Union: Estonia, Latvia, Lithuania, Belarus, Ukraine, and Moldova. Altogether, that adds up to eighteen, three more than the number of countries in the EU today.

The terrain in the region is quite diverse, getting steeper and more rugged the farther south you go. It ranges from the flat plains of Poland in the north to the rugged hills, valleys, and mountains in the former Yugoslavia. Geography, of course, has its consequences, particularly in an area that has been the object of so much foreign intervention. The flat plains of Poland (*pole* means fields) have enabled strong armies to occupy the country with ease, while the sprawling mountains of the former Yugoslavia help explain why no single army (or even the official Yugoslav state) has ever been able to conquer it fully, leaving many different ethnic groups to coexist in the area. As you see on the accompanying maps, all of these countries are rather small. Poland is the largest in terms of population and territory, with a population of nearly 40 million (plus several million Poles living in diaspora) and a territory of over 300 thousand square kilometers (about the size of New Mexico). Slovenia is the smallest, with just over 20,000 square kilometers (slightly smaller than New Jersey) and a population of just 2 million. In addition, there are Hungary (10.2 million people and just under 100,000 square kilometers, just smaller than Indiana), the Czech Republic (10.3 million people and 78,000 square kilometers), and Slovakia (5.4 million people and under 50,000 square kilometers). Farther south, the totals for Romania are 22.4 million population and 237,000 square kilometers, while Bulgaria has 8.2 million people and 110,000 square kilometers. In the former Yugoslavia, the "new" Yugoslavia (made up of Serbia, including Kosovo, and Montenegro) is the largest, with 102,000 square kilometers (about the size of Kentucky) and 11.2 million people (only 700,000 in Montenegro), followed by Croatia, with 56,000 square kilometers and just under 5 million people, and Bosnia, with 51,000 square kilometers and about 3.5 million people.

Although each country has its own unique history, the Communist and post-Communist experiences of all have had numerous features in common. In this book, we focus on three countries making up the political and geographical heart of this area: Poland, Hungary, and the Czech Republic. We also refer frequently to the Yugoslav experience. Until 1990, Yugoslavia was considered one of the most successful Eastern

European countries, with a unique blend of socialist and capitalist features. Since 1990, it has shown us the darker potential of Eastern Europe's future. We cannot cover the Yugoslav region as systematically as the other countries, since the new states there do not lend themselves to a discussion of stable political systems. But insofar as it reveals future possibilities, we ignore the Yugoslav experience only at our peril.

Critical Junctures

We can identify five critical periods in the shaping of modern East-Central Europe: the long era of subordination to neighboring powers, the attainment of independence after World War I, the introduction of communism after World War II, the collapse of communism in 1989, and the process of European integration in the late-1990s.

Why did communism come to Eastern Europe but not to Western Europe? The standard cold war answer is to blame the Soviets. And of course they did play a crucial role. But this answer ignores the fact that Eastern Europe had been quite different from Western Europe for a very long time. Communism came to Eastern Europe not just because the Red Army imposed it, but because in many ways Eastern Europe was ready for it. Communism seemed to many people to be an attractive solution to the two problems that had plagued Eastern Europe for generations: economic underdevelopment and a weak state. As long as these two overriding issues persisted, democracy seemed of secondary importance. When the Communists came to power after World War II, they were but the latest in a line of modernizers trying to do something about poverty and state deficiency.

Underdevelopment and Subordination: From the Fifteenth Century to World War I

During the martial law period in Poland in 1982, the title of a popular protest song was "Let Po-land Be Poland." Some Poles, however, thought such a notion was precisely the problem. "Let Poland be Sweden," they said, "Let Poland be England! Let us be anything but Poland!"

What the naysayers chiefly had in mind was Poland's location: between Russia and Germany, countries that have always dominated it. The theme of wanting to be some other country, however, is a recurring refrain in Eastern Europe. And it points to three central problems: domination by other states, a multiplicity of nationalities on the territory of one state, and a long history of economic backwardness.

The roots of Eastern European underdevelopment go back to the rise of capitalism in the West. Most of Eastern Europe began turning to the West for its manufactured goods as early as the fifteenth century, and this early dependency had serious consequences.[1] Up until the nineteenth century, no part of Eastern Europe except the Czech lands was able to make much progress in industrialization. Eastern Europe's economic woes soon led to political ones. Lacking the economic base on which to build viable states, the nations of Eastern Europe fell under the influence, and frequently the outright occupation, of stronger neighbors all around: Prussia in the west, Russia to the east, and the Hapsburg and Ottoman empires in the south. The period of state formation in Western Europe therefore was a period of state erosion in Eastern Europe.

Poland stands as a classic example of this trend.[2] The largest country in Europe in the fifteenth century, Poland quickly began to decline as a state when the powerful gentry joined together to clip the powers of the monarchy. By the seventeenth century, the king was denied the right to raise taxes, create an army, dismiss officials, or enact any law without the explicit consent of the landowners. Poland's neighbors were creating strong absolutist states at the same time. In the inevitable ensuing conflicts with these absolutist neighbors, Poland rapidly unraveled. A series of wars decimated the country in the seventeenth century, destroying a large part of Poland's population and economy. Economic backwardness, political domination

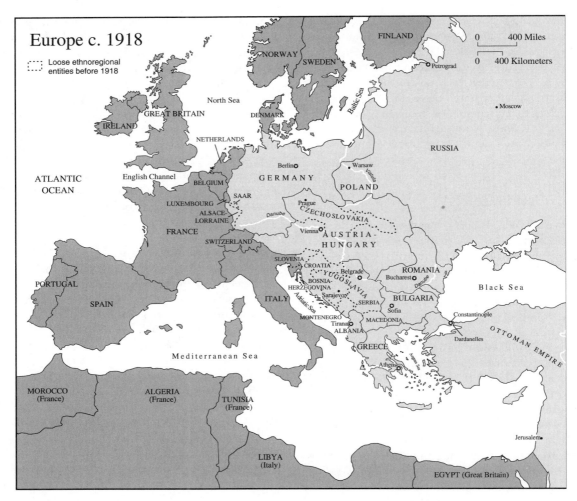

In 1918 the Czech Republic and Slovakia, former provinces of Austria-Hungary, united to form Czecho-slovakia; and Serbia, Croatia, Bosnia-Herzegovina, Slovenia, Montenegro, and Macedonia united to form Yugoslavia. The dotted lines on the map show the borders of each former entity. Poland's border with Russia was in dispute during this period.

by the large landowners, and the expansionary tendencies of other states led to a grim finale. Beginning in 1772, Russia, Prussia, and Austria divided the country among themselves. By 1795, Poland had ceased to exist as a state. It did not regain its independence until 1918.

Although Poland's encounter with the world of strong states was perhaps most dramatic, the other Eastern European countries also suffered from being small countries in a region of large states. Hungary, for example, was conquered by the Turkish Ottoman Empire in 1526, and by Austria 150 years later, before carving out semi-independence in 1867. The Czechs came under the control of the Austrian empire in 1620, al-though, alone among conquered nations, they were able to turn this to their economic advantage, becoming a nation of prosperous bourgeois producers. They sought independence only when the Austrian empire collapsed, and, together with the neighboring agrarian Slovaks, formed their own state in 1918.

Yugoslavia followed the most complex path to statehood. Long dominated by the Ottoman Empire, large parts of it were later conquered by the Austrians. Serbia finally fought its way to independence in 1878, and then, after the breakup of the occupying powers in World War I, took the neighboring republics under its wing to form an independent Yugoslavia in 1918. Although linguistically quite similar, the new country was extremely diverse in matters of faith, with Catholicism, Orthodox Christianity, and Islam (represented most significantly by Croatia, Serbia, and Bosnia, respectively) all figuring prominently. While the northern and western (and Catholic) republics of Slovenia and Croatia were the most highly developed economically, the country was dominated politically and militarily by the lesser-developed Serbia. These political, economic, and religious differences laid the groundwork for conflicts that would emerge first in the 1920s, then in the 1940s, and most recently in the wars of the 1990s.

When the region's four annexing empires of Austria, Germany, Russia, and Turkey all crumbled as a result of World War I, the small nations of Eastern Europe were finally able to gain their independence. Maintaining that independence proved to be almost as hard as achieving it.

Independence (1918–1939)

As this brief historical account makes clear, a key problem for Eastern Europe after World War I, as again in much of the region today, was not so much the world of states on the outside, but the dilemma of how to build stable states given the multiplicity of nations on the inside. Several million Hungarians, for example, lived outside Hungary's borders. Millions of Germans lived far from Germany's borders. Poland had a large Ukrainian minority, and it also had the largest Eastern European Jewish minority. All other East-Central European states also had large Jewish minorities, as well as large Roma, or Gypsy, populations.

The Western powers that directed the emergence of the new Eastern Europe after World War I wished to create states that were ethnically homogeneous. With so many nationalities living in such close proximity, however, this goal was impossible to achieve. The only way to accomplish it would have been to carry out a massive population transfer, with millions of people crisscrossing the region in a hundred directions, and most doing so against their will. Clearly no government or international organization was able or willing to carry out such a feat. Moreover, even then, East-Central Europe would have been left with a large Jewish minority lacking a state of its own, as well as an equally stateless Roma minority. It was the region's plethora of nations, not its plethora of states, that was the greatest obstacle to East-Central Europe's development.[3]

Historians have drawn a distinction between two types of nationalisms: *liberal*, which sees the independent state as a way to protect the needs of all citizens living in a given area, and *integralist*, which sees the state as championing the interests of all members of a given ethnic group regardless of where they live. Integralist nationalists claim their nation is better than all others and are ready to intervene in other countries to prove the point.

In interwar Eastern Europe, integralist nationalism got the upper hand, as it has more recently in the former Yugoslavia. In part, this attitude was inevitable in a region where so many new nations attained independence at the same time. Feeling understandably insecure in its new state status, each nation tried to guarantee long-term survival by bringing into government as many of its "own people" as possible and by keeping out all ethnic "others." With national loyalties as yet undeveloped, the members of a dominant ethnic group had reason to believe that the members of a minority group would use any power they might have on behalf of a foreign "mother" state to which they might hold greater allegiance. Indeed, ethnic Germans in Czechoslovakia in the 1930s did become avidly pro-Nazi, fueling Hitler's expansionary ambitions, which soon led to war. The pressures exerted by neighboring states, ostensibly concerned about their brethren abroad, as well as the internal pressures resulting from having so many minorities in such a small area, proved to be profoundly destabilizing for interwar Eastern Europe. The same conditions have come back to haunt contemporary Eastern Europe.

It was not only the harmful legacy of integralist nationalism that drove people to embrace the plans of the Left. The downward-spiraling economy also played a crucial role. Of course, East-Central Europe began its experience of independence with its economy in bad shape, suffering from the terrible and lasting effect of World War I. Then there was the problem of integrating these countries more fully into the world capitalist economy. This was no easy task. Small communities found themselves threatened by new economic pressures. The pursuit of profit by large landowners drove millions of peasants into poverty and landlessness and then into the cities. But the weakness of the industrial sector meant that it was hard to find work in the cities. The economies grew slowly, but unemployment grew even faster.

The state tried to promote industry but had little money with which to do so, because state building took most of the funds. Each new government had to come up with money for ministries, bureaucracies, embassies, border patrols, police, armies, and all the other trappings of statehood. A functioning economy might have been able to pay for these things, but independence came to Eastern Europe along with economic shambles. East-Central Europe's economy had been destroyed first by the war and then, paradoxically, by the peace, as the new national borders broke up old markets. For exam-

ple, Kraków and Prague both had been part of the Austrian Empire, and trade between them had been easy and plentiful. After the war, these two cities were located in two new countries, each promoting internal trade and busily imposing new rules to bring it about. The producer in Prague who relied heavily on purchases made by Kraków might now go bankrupt, while the consumer in Kraków now had nothing to buy. Independence therefore often made the local economy worse off than before, at least in the short term. But people live in the short term, and this economic disruption had important political consequences.

Continuing poverty, economic and social dislocation, and ethnic hatreds made it exceedingly difficult to consolidate democracy. The interwar years revealed the shakiness of liberal democratic institutions in Eastern Europe. For most of this period, Hungary and Poland were dominated by military leaders with only occasional respect for democratic government. In Yugoslavia, the king declared a dictatorship in 1926. When the Germans invaded Poland in 1939, setting off World War II, all of Eastern Europe except for Czechoslovakia had right-wing authoritarian governments.

There is no space here even to begin to tell the story of World War II's impact on the people, economy, society, and psychology of Eastern Europe.[4] Millions of people were killed and tens of millions were terrorized. Nazi occupation and then the Soviet-led liberation left the economic infrastructure almost totally destroyed. Apart from Yugoslavia, the "national problem" was partially "solved" in the most gruesome way imaginable: Nazi genocide against the Jews, a less organized but equally deadly roundup of Roma, and then the forced expulsion of Germans at war's end.

By 1945, East-Central Europeans could be forgiven for considering the interwar years of independence after 1918 as one vast failure. The Communists, who had rejected the status quo before the war and represented the victorious power afterward, reaped the benefits of the growing desire for a total break with the past.

Anti-Semitism and the New Global Economy

The first half of the twentieth century saw a sharp rise in anti-Semitism everywhere in Europe. The situation in interwar Eastern Europe was particularly bad, as anti-Semites demanded confiscation of Jewish property, expulsion of Jews from universities, and other restrictions on liberty. Racist and anti-Semitic newspapers and brochures, written by quack political theorists and disseminated by right-wing political parties, encouraged hatred against Jews. But this literature had the impact it did because of fertile economic ground. Jews had been living in Eastern Europe for hundreds of years (in part because they had been expelled from most of Western Europe). Since restrictive rules had largely kept them out of the countryside, they tended to congregate in towns and cities, making a living as shopkeepers, tavern owners, and moneylenders and in general catering to the needs of the native peasants in the surrounding villages. The arrangement worked reasonably well for both sides in the nineteenth century, when Eastern Europe was so rooted in the countryside. But when twentieth-century pressures of the global economy pushed the region toward capitalism and industrialism, Jews suddenly found themselves in the middle of the economic center, and often in a privileged position. Since they already lived in the cities, they easily found jobs as workers in the new factories. In addition, business activity had a bad reputation in much of the area (in the gentry states of Poland and Hungary, business was not considered a decent way for gentlemen to spend their time). As a result Jews, together with other minority groups such as Germans, were often among the leading capitalists. Local peasants, forced out of the countryside in search of economic well-being in the cities, suddenly found themselves confronting Jewish workers as competitors and Jewish industrialists as bosses. And so they became prone to the new racist propaganda of right-wing racist parties, who blamed the Jews for the problems of the capitalist economy. In reality, the dislocated peasants were angry at the changes caused by the new global economy, which favored urban industrial over rural agricultural areas. Fascist parties tried to take these economic angers and direct them at the Jews, and they proved to be quite successful at doing so.*

*On the connection between anti-Semitism and economic modernization, see Albert Lindemann, *The Jew Accused* (Cambridge: Cambridge University Press, 1991).

They promised an end to what they called the capitalist legacy of poverty and dictatorship. And so it was not just the Red Army that brought socialism to East-Central Europe. After too many years of poverty, dictatorship, national rivalries, and war, many East-Central Europeans were ready for it themselves.

The Beginnings of Communism (1945–1949)

Many Eastern Europeans thought and hoped that the Red Army's expulsion of the Nazis meant that the region had finally become free of foreign domination. Instead, the outside world bore down on them again, this time in the form of the Soviet Union. Stalin's Red Army occupied East-Central Europe as it expelled the Nazis during its march to Berlin in 1944–1945. Hoping to make sure the region would never again become hostile territory, Stalin sought to create a buffer zone between the Soviet Union and the West by imposing a Soviet-style socialism on all of East-Central Europe. Local socialists and Communists hoped the Soviets would aid them in building their own kind of socialism in accord with local traditions, and then leave. Stalin would not allow it. He imposed political systems that were essentially carbon copies of the one in the Soviet Union.

Europe, 1945–1990

The first years after the war saw some toleration of non-Communist parties and organizations. But by 1948, after the cold war had taken hold and the West had promoted the establishment of a new West German state, all pretense of tolerance disappeared. Stalin ordered the various Communist parties to eliminate all political rivals and to take power for themselves. From then on, East-Central Europe was governed just like the Soviet Union. Each country was ruled by the Politburo of the national Communist Party. Formally, each country had a single house of parliament, whose members were selected by Communist Party officials (though not all were Party members) and then "elected" by the people, who were all but required to show up on election day to vote for the sole candidate on the ballot. The judiciary was dominated by the Party, as was the civil service. The Party exercised control through the *nomenklatura* principle, meaning that it chose the people not only for nominally elected offices but also for key positions in the national bureaucracy, local government, industry, trade unions, educational institutions, and most other public organizations.

Millions of people supported the Communist program in the 1940s. Young people were particularly attracted to the new system, for communism offered them something grandiose to believe in: the struggle to industrialize the country and build a great new world.[5] The long legacy of weakness and underdevelopment was going to be conquered, and young people were to play the key part in the battle. At the same time, communism also offered plenty of good new jobs. Indeed, for young people from peasant and working-class backgrounds, the Stalinist years were a time of previously unimaginable social mobility. In contrast to the unemployment lines of the past, the Party had jobs to offer in industry, agriculture, the media, schools, the bureaucracy—anywhere one wanted. And the chief qualification for office was only that the applicant be committed to communism. Indeed, formal education often hindered chances for success, as it was considered a sign of a bourgeois background.

At the same time, the Stalinist years (approximately 1949–1955, though Stalin died in 1953) were an almost incomprehensibly brutal period. People were punished for their pasts, arrested for their private views, detained for telling jokes,[6] and even deported to Siberia without trial. Some defended these policies, saying that each country was engaged in a revolution and that enemies were lurking everywhere. But as the list of enemies kept getting longer and as police control embraced more and more of society, people turned increasingly against communism, seeing it as a betrayal of their hopes for a better world. Thus they entered on the long struggle for democracy.

The Rebirth of Democracy (1956–1989)

Prior to the mid-1950s, East Europeans seemed to treat independence and industrialization as more important than democracy. Yet by 1989, the very phrase "Eastern Europe" had become a synonym for democracy. Entire populations seemed to unite in the fight for democratic freedom, and the rest of the world looked on with awe and admiration.

In large part, it was the Communist experience itself that brought about the change. Communism had undeniably helped resolve the age-old problems of independence and economic backwardness. Despite Soviet influence, Eastern Europe was made up of independent entities with their own laws and armies. By the 1960s, no Eastern Europeans seriously expected their nations to disappear. Their economies may have been worse off than those in the West, but the debilitating poverty and monstrous inequalities of the past had been eliminated. Yet even after these accomplishments, communism continued to maintain a political repression that seemed increasingly inappropriate. People were ready to forgo democracy when the problems of independence and underdevelopment were central. As these old nineteenth-century problems dissipated, the struggle for democracy came to the fore.

Both concrete experience and conscious political activity contributed to this remarkable rebirth of democracy. Let us trace the evolution by looking at the events of 1956, 1968, 1970, and 1980.

Although no dissenting voices were tolerated during the peak Stalinist years beginning in 1949, that began to change soon after Stalin's death in March 1953. In June, pent-up anger broke out for the first time in East Berlin, sparking serious, if short-lived, working-class protests. Then, as new leaders in the Soviet Union began to abandon the policies of terror, a trickle of new voices began to be heard in Eastern Europe. These critics, known as revisionists, argued that socialism should be democratic and that Stalinism was an aberration of true socialism.

What began as a trickle turned into a torrent after the Twentieth Congress of the Soviet Communist Party in February 1956, when Soviet leader Nikita Khrushchev denounced Stalin as a tyrant and called for a return to "true Leninism." It is difficult to overestimate the impact of this congress on Eastern Europe. The region's rulers at the time all owed their positions directly to Stalin, who had picked them over rival Communist leaders during Soviet-sponsored purges of the late 1940s. The denunciation of Stalin constituted an endorsement of those who had been his victims and thus an invitation to Eastern Europe to make changes.

It did not take long for people to respond. Within months, protests inspired and led by the democratic socialist revisionists had gripped both Poland and Hungary. Soon the intellectual critique gave way to protests from below, as workers challenged the harsh rules, low pay, and poor working conditions endemic to Stalinist socialism as contrary to the principles of "real" socialism. By fall, both countries hovered on the brink of revolution. People first demanded the return to power of Stalin's victims: Imre Nagy in Hungary and Władysław Gomułka in Poland. When Nagy was restored to power in October, the old prewar parties immediately formed again, and Nagy became the leader of a genuine coalition that declared Hungary's intention to withdraw from the Warsaw Pact (the Communist states' military alliance) and separate completely from the Soviet Union. The Soviets responded by sending in the Red Army. After many days of fierce fighting and thousands of dead and wounded, the Soviets ousted Nagy and installed János Kádár as the new Hungarian leader. Even then, the Budapest Workers Council held out for a few months, acting as a kind of parallel authority in the capital.

Hungary acted as a cautionary tale for Poland. Gomułka was made head of the Party before the revolution in the streets got out of hand. He immediately used his authority, enhanced by tough words warning the Soviets against intervention, to consolidate the protests under his leadership. Then he defused them and reestablished Party control.[7]

Nevertheless, 1956 had changed Eastern Europe forever. Despite having repressed popular rebellions, neither Kádár nor Gomułka ever tried to reestablish the total control of the state over society that was the hallmark of Stalinist totalitarianism. Indeed, both countries soon experimented with economic reform and gradually allowed critics of the Party (including, in Poland, the Catholic Church) to take part in public life. Kádár's new motto—"Whoever is not against us is with us"—constituted a stunning reversal of Stalinist ideology and seemed to acknowledge that the new democratic longings of society could not forever be repressed.

In Yugoslavia, meanwhile, democratic socialist ideology made even further progress, thanks to Stalin's decision to expel Yugoslavia summarily from the list of Communist nations. The only "crime" of the Yugoslav Communist Party and its dynamic leader, Josip Broz Tito, was to have remained independent of the Soviet Union. Although Tito saw himself as a Stalinist and tried to reproduce the Soviet model, Stalin never reciprocated. He hated Tito's independence and in 1948 denounced him as a fascist counterrevolutionary. As a result, Tito was forced to find his own road to socialism, ultimately choosing a nonstatist socialism based on regional autonomy and worker self-management. Although the Party still retained control at the top and individual autonomy was allowed more in the workplace than in the political sphere at large, the Yugoslav reforms nevertheless constituted an important democratic innovation within socialism.

Then came 1968. The democratic fervor of 1989 cannot be understood apart from the legacy of 1968: the Prague Spring in Czechoslovakia and the student revolts in Poland and Yugoslavia. In the aftermath of both movements, a new generation rethought the whole strategy of revisionist opposition, developing an antistate orientation that would pave the way for the democratic revolutions of 1989.

The Prague Spring began as part of an effort for economic reform. The Stalinist economic program, developed as a crash industrialization strategy for a poor peasant country, had been particularly unsuitable for Czechoslovakia, with its strong industrial infrastructure and well-educated urban population. In 1962 Czechoslovakia became the first socialist country to record a decline in industrial output, sparking numerous calls for reform. Economists proposed a series of measures aimed at increasing managerial responsibility and promoting greater individual incentive. But inevitably in this country with strong democratic traditions, the call for greater economic freedom became a call for political freedom as well. Soon after Alexander Dubček became head of the Party in January 1968, Party reformers promulgated a program of thoroughgoing democratic reform, declaring freedom of speech indispensable to a modern economy and arguing that authority should derive from knowledge and expertise rather than Party affiliation.[8] By spring, Czechoslovakia had become a wide-open society, with censorship abolished and everyone speaking out on every possible issue.

The Soviets grew alarmed. Although set in motion by the Communist Party, the democratic changes seemed to make the Party irrelevant, something the Soviets viewed as a threat to their security. In August 1968, the Soviets sent Warsaw Pact troops into Czechoslovakia to crush this democratic socialist experiment, thrusting the country into a long, gloomy period of political repression that would end only in 1989.

Poland's 1968 began over cultural issues, after officials closed a theatrical production of a nineteenth-century Polish play because of its allegedly anti-Soviet character. Students reacted with a wave of protests, attacking government repression and demanding freedom of speech. The government responded by arresting student leaders, organizing goon squads of workers to beat up demonstrators, and launching a vast anti-intellectual and anti-Semitic campaign. Why anti-Semitism? Not because of any "Jewish problem" in Poland, but to root out the entire liberal intelligentsia, to whom anti-Semitism was anathema. By the end of the year, hundreds of students and professors were expelled, government administration was purged

of loyal civil servants, and the several thousand remaining Polish Jews were "invited" to leave the country for good.

The Party's ugly campaign had more in common with native fascist traditions than with anything coming out of the socialist camp. Yet the Party presented it as a "defense of socialism." Two years later, when shipyard workers in Gdańsk and Szczecin took to the streets to protest price increases and demand independent trade unions, Party authorities decided to "defend socialism" by shooting down dozens. For Eastern European oppositionists, the die had been cast. If official socialism could mean military invasion in Czechoslovakia and anti-Semitism and shooting down workers in Poland, perhaps it was time to stop looking to the Party to introduce "real socialism." Perhaps it was time to look inward for strength.

The new democratic oppositionists thus drew from 1968 the lesson that political change in Eastern Europe would not come from above. They now set out to force it from below through the promotion of a wide variety of independent social activity. The goal was to get people to do things—anything—just as long as they did it on their own, with no official mediation. Writing, printing, or reading an independent newsletter; organizing, publicizing, or attending an independent lecture series or discussion group: these were among the main forms of opposition activity. This was the time of the *samizdat* press (uncensored and self-published periodicals) and of "flying universities" (unofficial classes meeting in different homes each session). Such activity was considered the most important kind of political opposition possible. As conceptualized at this time, the aim of political opposition was not to take control of the state but to *democratize society*. If people felt and acted like free citizens, the opposition believed, then they would become free citizens. Eventually the state would have to follow along.

The Eastern European opposition thus rediscovered the concept of *civil society*: the idea that politics meant not just government but the whole sphere of daily social interactions. People began fighting not so much for free elections and parliamentary democracy, which seemed far removed and perhaps beside the point, but for the right to have some social space free from the state. Writers wanted space to write about what they were interested in; students wanted space to study what and how they wanted to study; workers wanted space to form their own trade unions.

A number of brilliant writers and theoreticians emerged in East-Central Europe in the 1970s to give voice to these new aspirations; among them were Vaclav Havel in Czechoslovakia, Adam Michnik in Poland, and George Konrad in Hungary.[9] Organizations soon emerged too, seeking to promote new civic activities and build an independent civil society. The most important and influential of these organizations was the Workers' Defense Committee, known by its Polish initials KOR. Formed by oppositionist intellectuals in Poland in 1977 to defend workers persecuted for going on strike the year before, KOR soon began sponsoring civic initiatives throughout the country, such as *samizdat* publications, lecture series, trade union organizing, and even some charitable work, often together with the Church. Combined with the independent workers' movement, KOR's activity helped bring about the remarkable Solidarity movement that spelled the beginning of the end of communism in East-Central Europe.

Polish workers had their own traditions too. In 1970, shipyard workers had struck for the right to form independent trade unions. Ten years later, they went on strike again. In the new environment of civic activism, intellectuals from all over the country flocked to their aid, helping them print pamphlets and negotiate with the government. The strike ended with the signing of the Gdańsk Accord on August 31, 1980, resulting in the formation of the "independent self-governing trade union Solidarity" headed by a thirty-seven-year-old electrician named Lech Wałęsa. It signified the beginning of the end of the state socialist system.[10]

Poland in the next sixteen months was the

site of a unique democratic revolution. Without making any attempt to seize state power, workers in Poland acted as if they were already citizens of a free and democratic state. Solidarity was perhaps the most democratic trade union that ever existed. The union leaders, all elected from below, were almost always in the public eye when discussing issues. All leadership meetings were attended by journalists, who published detailed accounts in the union press, carefully documenting who had said what. Although the union did push for wage increases, its main goal was simply to exist—to make sure the state respected the rights of social groups to organize on their own. Long years of political repression had convinced workers that political freedom was the most important goal of all.

Solidarity was threatening to the Communist system not because it demanded political power—in fact, it did not—but just because it existed. Communism was based on central planning. The Party made all public decisions and coordinated all public activities. Yet it could not do such things when millions of people gave their allegiance to an independent trade union that the Party could not control. And so on December 13, 1981, the Polish authorities declared martial law and banned Solidarity. For the next seven years, the Party tried to patch back together a system that had come apart at the seams. As it turned out, it could not be mended.

The Collapse of Communism (1989–1991)

In a breathtaking period of 1989, essentially from June 4 to December 20, Communist rule collapsed in one country after another in East-Central Europe. While everyone has heard of the fall of the Berlin Wall, which took place in November 1989, the real end to the Communist era happened not in Germany but in Poland, and it was a direct result of the decade-long struggle of Solidarity.

The denouement began in 1988. The government had been trying to introduce a painful economic reform and was having a hard time selling it to a skeptical public. This was because public support was still very much on the side of Solidarity, which, despite the imposition of martial law in late 1981, had survived as an underground organization. The turning point came when workers in several factories went on strike in the summer of 1988, against economic reforms and for the relegalization of Solidarity. The union's leaders actually supported the economic reforms, but they would use their influence to end the strikes only if the government would agree to reopen formal talks with the banned organization. Facing no other way to achieve economic reform, the Polish leadership, with the support of new Soviet leader Mikhail Gorbachev, agreed. The strikes ended at once, and, in February 1989, Solidarity and the Party entered into negotiations that ended two months later with Solidarity legal again and Poland preparing for its first real elections in the postwar period.

The Communists were guaranteed a majority in the lower house of parliament, but the newly created senate was up for grabs. In the elections of June 4, Solidarity proved so strong that its candidates won all but one of the seats it was allowed to contest: 35 percent of the lower house and ninety-nine of one hundred seats in the senate. Defeated so thoroughly, the Party could not even hang on to the formal state power it had been conceded. Although General Wojciech Jaruzelski, who had imposed martial law, became the new president, elected by parliament, Solidarity used its new power to force the selection of Tadeusz Mazowiecki, a veteran oppositionist and Solidarity adviser, as prime minister. Mazowiecki took office in September 1989, and Poland became the first Eastern European country after World War II to have a non-Communist government. After Poland, Communist power fell swiftly elsewhere in the region.[11]

Democratization in Hungary came peacefully but decisively. Actually, the reforms began there in 1968. Seeking to improve the economy, the government cut back the power of state bureaucrats, allowed non-Party intellectuals a greater role in public life, and improved the standard of living for ordinary workers. Everyone seemed to benefit. The intelligentsia reaped the benefits of power, workers earned tangible consumer rewards, and the government seemed to forestall the possibility of social protest. With the declining economy of the late 1980s, however, the deal was falling apart. In an effort to stave off a Polish-style crisis, the authorities initiated political reform. In 1984, Hungary became the first Communist country to experiment with multicandidate parliamentary elections. By 1987, opposition groups were forming political parties, and the government scarcely interfered. When the events of 1989 began, the government was ready to talk with those parties about managing a peaceful transition to democracy. These talks started in June 1989, just days after Solidarity's victory in the Polish elections. In September, both sides agreed to free parliamentary elections in the spring. Change came more peacefully in Hungary than anywhere else. With the elections of March 1990, a democratic political system was in place.

The changes in Hungary set off rebellion in East Germany (and then in Czechoslovakia, discussed at the beginning of the chapter). When Hungary opened up its borders on September 10, 1989, tens of thousands of East Germans, normally permitted to travel only within Eastern Europe, jammed the roads to Hungary, from there to cross over to the West. Ensuing mass demonstrations forced the ouster of Party chief Erich Honecker in October, the fall of the Berlin Wall in November, and the hasty collapse not just of the Party but of the entire state. In October 1990, East Germany merged into the Federal Republic of Germany to form a united Germany.

The day the Berlin Wall fell, so did Bulgarian Party leader Todor Zhivkov. A coalition of fledgling opposition groups, calling itself the Union of Democratic Forces (UDF), stepped in to fill the space. Although made up almost exclusively of urban intellectuals, the UDF was able to claim the anti-Communist mantle and won 38 percent of the vote in June 1990 parliamentary elections, a strong tally for an essen-

Frank Zappa, John Lennon, and the Velvet Revolution

Did music bring down communism in Czechoslovakia? Tough repression after 1968 ensured that no Solidarity-type organization could emerge in Czechoslovakia. In this land of Franz Kafka, political opposition tended to be expressed chiefly through culture, and above all, through music. In the 1970s, the Plastic People of the Universe, an avant-garde rock band named after a line from a Frank Zappa song, played its music and sang its politicized verses at enormous "private" jam sessions frequently raided by the police. John Lennon's music also served as a rallying point for antigovernment youth, especially each year on the anniversary of his death, which was observed more widely in Czechoslovakia, like an obligatory rite of urban youth, than anywhere else in the world. And the major political conflict of 1986 centered around the arrest of several jazz musi-

cians, charged with illegal commercial and publishing activity. So it is not surprising that the 1989 protests began with a strike by actors, who used the theaters to hold huge political rallies. When Civic Forum was created, it was led by the playwright Vaclav Havel, whose satiric accounts of duplicity and complicity among the elite and citizens alike cut straight to the heart of the existential damage caused by the long years of Party rule. After Havel became president, two of his first official acts were to invite the visiting Frank Zappa to his office for consultations and to ask the Rolling Stones to play a concert in Prague. And one of the first interviews he gave about the meaning of the Velvet Revolution was to Lou Reed—of the Velvet Underground. Rock 'n' roll retained its radical roots in Czechoslovakia long after going commercial in the West.

tially structureless organization. Two months later, Zhelyu Zhelev, a fifty-five-year-old historian and leader of the UDF, was elected president.

The most explosive transition of 1989 took place in Romania, a country that, next to Albania, most consistently embodied the totalitarian model that had been abandoned everywhere else. Since Party leader Nicolae Ceaușescu had suppressed all opposition activity, it was perhaps inevitable that bloodshed would accompany the final act, as there was no group with which Ceaușescu could negotiate even if he had wished to. Demonstrations in defense of a persecuted priest began in December 1989 in the western city of Timisoara and spread to Bucharest within days. As the army joined the rebellion, Ceaușescu and his wife fled the presidential palace in a helicopter, were arrested, and then executed on Christmas Day. The National Salvation Front, which took over from Ceaușescu, consisted mostly of ex-members of the Party—no surprise, since Party membership had been vir-

tually the only way for anyone to participate in public life. In parliamentary elections in May 1990, it won 65 percent of the vote.

Albania, the most economically backward and politically repressive of all Eastern European Communist countries, was the last one to fall. Angered by the absence of change, thousands of citizens jammed Western embassies in the summer of 1990 demanding the right to leave. After a long delay, the authorities granted permission and then set about introducing serious reforms. Opposition parties were allowed to form, and parliamentary elections were held in March 1991. The Communists won but, faced with massive strikes and protests, agreed in June 1991 to appoint a non-Communist cabinet. Considering the long years of stagnation, these changes were nothing short of extraordinary.

In the end, however, all these developments in Eastern Europe were quite extraordinary. And they were topped off, in the summer of 1991, with the fall of communism in Russia itself. How do we explain all this? Perhaps the best explanation is the one put forward by Moshe Lewin in relation to the Soviet Union.[12] According to this view, East European societies simply outgrew the political systems in which they were encumbered. Communism was done in by modernization. At the start of the Communist period, most of the region was economically and socially underdeveloped, and many citizens wanted a strong government to take control. As economic and educational levels improved, however, people sought more responsibility for their own lives and no longer believed they needed the state to set all the rules. Soon even the Party elite stopped believing that its rule was necessary for progress. Modernizing reformers started to chip away at Party rule and eventually found no one holding them back. In the end, the old Communist political system was no longer appropriate to the socioeconomic world the Communists had built.

The Road to European Integration: 1998–2001

Having shed its communist identity, Eastern Europe wanted nothing more than to "rejoin the West," in particular by entering the European Union. It took several years, however, before that could even be considered. First, the new governments had to begin reforming economic and political institutions, and to manage the clash between popular expectations and post-Communist realities. For most people in the region, democracy meant not only freedom of speech, association, travel, and free elections, it also meant a better economic life. For years the West had said that Eastern Europe could "be like us" if only they got rid of communism, and the "us" was advertised as a wealthy consumer society. After 1989, Eastern Europeans looked to capitalist democracy to provide the good life that communism was never able to deliver. Unfortunately, the region's severe economic crisis after 1989 meant that neither could the new capitalism.

The clash between expectations and reality laid the basis for a development that few expected to happen so soon: the revival of the Left.

Beginning in 1993, the parties that emerged out of the old ruling Communist parties came back to win a series of elections, and soon took control of parliament in both Poland and Hungary. Their most stunning symbolic moment of return came in the Polish presidential election of 1995, when a former Communist Party official defeated legendary Solidarity leader Lech Wałęsa.

In the end, what was significant about the return of the Left was not that domestic policies changed but precisely that they did not. These parties maintained pro-market policies and strict budgetary discipline, and they pursued privatization with the same energy as their predecessors had. In other words, they were not much of a classical Left at all, which had always opposed the market in the name of social equality. Or rather, they were very much like the contemporary social democratic Left in Western Europe, which has long since made its peace with capitalism and seeks only a slightly more socially concerned market economy. Despite their previous allegiances to Moscow, these former Communists also faithfully kept up the pro-Western orientations of the post-1989 governments, supporting entry into the EU and even NATO.

This political continuity led to the most recent critical juncture in East-Central Europe: the move toward integration with the West. When everyone could trust the old Communists to be as liberal, democratic, and pro-European as those who had toppled their rule half a decade earlier, it was clear there was no going back, and that integration could therefore go forward. The stage was now set for expansion of the EU. In the early twenty-first century, this is the most important issue in East-Central Europe.

The critical date here is March 1998, when the EU selected ten countries as possible new members. Not all countries are created equal, however. The EU divided the ten into two groups of five: those whose accession to the EU could be considered at once and those whose membership was conceivable but still a long way off. The top tier consists of Poland, Hungary, the Czech Republic, Slovenia, and Estonia. The second tier is made up of Romania, Bulgaria, Slovakia, Latvia, and Lithuania. Aside from Slovenia, the former Yugoslav republics were not even mentioned.

Even for the first group, however, accession is no easy thing. The EU has an 80,000-page collection of laws and regulations (the so-called *acquis communautaire*) that all countries must meet in order to become members, and when the new century began, even the top group was still scrambling to meet its conditions. By early 2001, the EU had still not set a date for admitting the first group, much less the second. Nevertheless, EU's formal commitment to expansion has dramatically changed East European politics. For example, all countries now make internal political decisions with a keen eye to how they will be perceived in the West. (The importance of this was brought home after the EU's ostracism of member state Austria in 1999 when a neofascist party became part of that country's ruling coalition.)

The recent EU commitment to integration has shaken the centuries-old divisions between East and West. Westerners are getting used to the idea that Warsaw, and possibly even Sofia, are proper European cities. Easterners, meanwhile, are on the verge of getting over their historical complex of being second-class European citizens. Although the process still has many tough times ahead, the historical magnitude of this process of European unification cannot be overestimated.

The EU is not the only sign of unification. At the time that the EU was making its offer to the select group of countries, NATO was inviting three of them to become full members of that military alliance. The East European countries had lobbied for inclusion ever since the demise of the Warsaw Pact in 1990, seeing inclusion as a bulwark against future Russian pressure and as a clear sign of membership in "the West." Russia, undergoing its own democratization, called for the dissolution of NATO now that the cold war had ended. But neither the United States nor Western Europe wanted the United States to lose its influence in Europe. So while trying to convince a skeptical Russia that the alliance was no longer directed against them, NATO decided not to disband but to expand. Poland, Hungary, and the Czech Republic—clearly East Europe's new elite—became full members of NATO in March 1999. Less than two weeks later, the new countries found themselves at war. This would be the first time NATO had fought a war, and it did so against another East European country, Yugoslavia, on behalf of autonomy for the province of Kosovo. This was not the kind of welcome the new inductees had hoped for. As it happened, though, the war opened opportunities for further NATO expansion. For when Romania and Bulgaria opened their airspace to NATO planes and saw their economies suffer as a result of joining the embargo against Yugoslavia, NATO rewarded them by promising to consider them for the next stage of expansion, along with the former Soviet republics of Latvia, Lithuania, and Estonia. The new century began with only three new NATO members, but the stage is set for future expansion. To be sure, there are potential dangers posed by expansion. When Russian president Vladimir Putin, elected in 2000, rescinded Russia's long-standing policy against no first use of nuclear weapons and made clear his intention of strengthening the military, some attributed this to a growing fear of isolation caused by NATO expansion.

What all this makes clear, in any case, is that East Europe's unification with Western Europe, symbolized by EU and NATO expansion, constitutes a critical juncture not just for Eastern Europe but for the West and for the rest of the world.

Themes and Implications

An old curse, attributed variously to Jews, Russians, or Chinese, goes like this: "May you live in interesting times!" Perhaps unfortunately for them, East Europeans have always lived in interesting times. The region has been in the center of all the great "isms" of the twentieth century: imperialism, nationalism, fascism, communism, democratization, and now global capitalism. Let us conclude this chapter by connecting this fascinating history with the main themes of this book.

Historical Junctures and Political Themes

Perhaps nowhere else in Europe is the link between this book's first two themes—world of states and governing the economy—clearer than it is in the countries of the East. While the international environment and global competition affects every state's ability to govern its economy, this has been starkly evident at every stage of East-Central Europe's recent past. Since the region entered the post-Communist era with a large foreign debt, it needed support from the West to get its economies going. The International Monetary Fund (IMF) offered help for the region's stabilization plans in return for commitments to open up their economies to foreign investment and products. Since these countries hoped to get into the "world of states" that make up the EU, they were particularly open to goods and investment from EU countries—even though the latter did not reciprocate. Ever since the process of entering the EU began accelerating in 1998, the supplicant countries have had to open up not only their markets but their legal codes. The EU's *acquis communautaire* must be adopted by desiring countries before entry. This meant that by 1999 and 2000, most of the laws passed by the parliaments of Poland, Hungary, and the Czech Republic were about changing the legal environment to conform to the EU. Critics saw the EU as hijacking the democratic process. The link between international influence and domestic economic governance has never been closer than in East-Central Europe's current historical juncture.

The connection is also quite close, though in a very different way, in the former Yugoslavia. It was an IMF restructuring plan that pressed the country to impose painful economic measures in the late 1980s, creating the social unrest that would explode in war. When the conflict in Bosnia ended in the 1995 U.S.-brokered peace play in Dayton, Serbia's economic options were limited by economic sanctions imposed by the United Nations. First Bosnia and then Kosovo came under direct U.N. (more accurately, U.S.) control. How this region governed its economy could be explained only by its role in a particular world of states.

Just as this book's first two key themes are so closely related in East-Central Europe, so are its last two themes: the democratic idea and the politics of collective identity. One thing the ruling Communist parties were never able to do was to instill among the people a strong pro-Communist identity. They succeeded in making people dependent on the state but not in getting them to feel grateful to the state. On the contrary, since state control was so all-embracing, it became common for people to think of the state as the enemy. People with a complaint about anything could plausibly place blame on the state rather than on some other social group or on themselves.

In 1989, this anti-Party collective identity came to the fore. People saw themselves now as "citizens" fighting for "democracy" against an oppressive state. To be a democratic citizen meant to have a voice in public life, in government. People did not organize in 1989 as workers or intellectuals, as urban or rural, as Czech or Slovak, as men or women, as gays or straights. They organized as citizens, united together and demanding democracy for all.

After 1989, this vision of democracy as entailing a grand sense of unity no longer made sense. Without a party and state to fight against, people had to develop new identities based on issues smaller (though not less important) than "us" versus "them." They still saw themselves as "democrats," but democracy for many people now meant the effort to build up the different social classes of a capitalist system. Democracy thus required that new collective identities come to the fore.

Class, paradoxically, is an identity that has not come easily. Communism discouraged class-based identities, since everyone was equal in relation to the state. The anti-Communist opposition also discouraged class identities, since everyone was supposed to be equal as citizens, fighting against the state. In the day-to-day workings of a democracy, however, class identities play a very important role. Workers organize as workers to win higher wages and better working conditions, and in the process they come to feel they have a stake in the entire economic and political system. Organizing along class lines thus helps the consolidation of a liberal democratic system, as it allows large groups of people to win concrete benefits. The absence of class identities up until 1989, however, has meant a weakness of class identities since 1989. Workers find themselves angry over their economic situation, but not well organized to defend themselves. Only new elites began to organize themselves as a class, fighting to make sure public policy serves its interests. In this way, however, many workers have been alienated by the post-Communist system, and a system without the support of working people cannot be very strong or very stable.

East-Central Europe has not seen a great deal of identification along gender lines either. Women certainly faced a great many problems under communism, owing to poorer educational opportunities and a strong macho culture. (Because of endemic shortages, shopping and cooking were even more of a burden than in the West.) Nevertheless women, like men, tended to see communism, and not gender relations, as the sole enemy. In fact, since communism claimed to have emancipated women, the struggle against communism was often seen to be a fight *against* the emancipation of women. Even women sometimes argued that communism was

a plot to take women out of the home in order to promote the indoctrination of children in the schools![13]

Just as class differences have become more potent in the post-Communist era, so have gender differences. As enterprises began to cut back on their workforces, women were the first to be fired. Where good new jobs were to be had, women were increasingly hired on the basis of their looks, not their qualifications. Such experiences are leading to the emergence of a women's movement and new gender identities, but the legacy of the past makes this a slow process.

Far more than along class or gender lines, people in Eastern Europe identify themselves along national lines. That is, we see a clash today between nationalism and internationalism—or, as it is frequently characterized, between nationalism and "Europeanism." The Europeanist is one who feels part of a new, upwardly mobile, economically productive community, moving collectively into the twenty-first century. The most obvious candidates for this identity are the budding capitalists, economic professionals, students studying business and foreign languages, and former dissident politicians who have moved into government. But even many people who have lost out economically subscribe to this identity. They believe their sacrifices are short term and feel pride in their country's path toward becoming "like the West."

The nationalist, on the other hand, is one who feels threatened by the new changes. To the nationalist, dependence on the East is being replaced by dependence on the West. Where communism once threatened traditional values, now liberalism, global capitalism, and secularism threaten those values. Those who embrace this new identity are usually those least able to prosper in the new environment, such as unskilled workers with few contemporary marketable skills or the elderly living in rural areas without much new investment. For these people, postcommunism is not very pleasant, and they have good reason for feeling threatened by "the West" and all it implies. Rejecting communism and capitalism alike, they find solace in and proclaim the merits of the nation instead. The "nation" is seen as a community of regular people—people just like them. Making policy in the interests of the nation means that state policy should benefit these "regular people," rather than the educated and the "cosmopolitans" who so like the West. We shall look more closely at the impact of these new identities in the chapters that follow.

Implications for Comparative Politics

Rarely can we see an entire region in such transition as in contemporary Eastern Europe, with so many exciting political, economic, and social experiments. Issues of democratization, globalization, privatization, and nationalism appear in this region in a way they appear nowhere else. While capitalism beckons, the old appeals of communism still tug. While the people are enticed by the opportunities to belong to a single global culture, their national pride and legacies of resistance keep them connected to small-scale values too. With the eruptions of ethnic nationalism existing side by side with the desire to join the EU, we see the tensions that political scientist Benjamin Barber has described as "jihad vs. McWorld" (the former referring to the desire to hold onto the local styles and traditions that "McWorld," or the push for global market uniformity, tends to sweep away).

The historic legacies of nationalism and communism have left East-Central Europeans feeling torn about their role in the world today. For the new elites, 1989 represented a chance to "join Europe," to become part of what they called the "normal world" of parliamentary democracies and a global economy dominated by large transnational corporations and international organizations. Many people in the area, however, still view the new global institutions skeptically. Echoing nationalist sentiments, they fear that in place of dependence on the Soviet Union will come dependence on the West. They feel that with their still weak economies, they can "join Europe" only as paupers, not as real players. They like the EU's record of peace and prosperity, but then they see Western European farmers organizing to keep out cheap Eastern European products. They like the promises of massive aid that they hear from organizations like the IMF and the World Bank, but then find these organizations demanding internal changes that could greatly upset political stability. They want to like the outside world, but they keep seeing evidence that the outside world may not like them or that it may treat them badly regardless of feelings, and then they wonder if joining Europe might not hurt national interests more than help them. East-Central Europeans still want to build their own strong states, and they fear that the international community is more interested in the region as a source of cheap labor than as a group of nations with interests of their own.

East-Central Europe faces an enormous number of pressing tasks in this post-Communist era. It must try to consolidate democratic political systems at the same time as it builds a market economy. It must build the complex institutions of a market society, such as regulatory agencies and a new social welfare network, to avoid the corruption scandals and poverty that can make people long for the past. It must try to avoid the dangers of fundamentalist nationalism by providing people with solid values to believe in now that the grand myths of communism no longer persuade. It must build a multiparty system so that differences of opinion can be expressed in a constructive way. Can East-Central Europe manage all these tasks? Can it privatize the economy in a way that serves the interests of both the employees and the economy as a whole? Can it integrate even economic "losers" into a new democratic society and thus keep people away from the lure of demagogues and potential dictators? Can it make good on the grand democratic ideals that inspired people as citizens in 1989?

In Eastern Europe, political scientists, sociologists, economists, and anthropologists have unprecedented opportunities for understanding the dynamics of social change. With all of the issues it faces and all of the transformations it is undergoing, East-Central Europe continues to be one of the most fascinating areas of the globe today.

Notes

1. See Jacques Rupnik, *The Other Europe: The Rise and Fall of Communism in East-Central Europe* (New York: Pantheon Books, 1989), esp. chap. 1.

2. For an account of Eastern European states and nations in the premodern era, see Perry Anderson, *Lineages of the Absolutist State* (London: Verso, 1974).

3. See Raymond Pearson, *National Minorities in Eastern Europe, 1849–1945* (London: Macmillan, 1983).

4. For a brief but excellent account, see Joseph Rothschild, *Return to Diversity: A Political History of East Central Europe Since World War II* (New York: Oxford University Press, 1989), chap. 2.

5. For a wonderful account of why Czech and Slovak intellectuals chose to join the Communist Party, see Antonin Liehm, *The Politics of Culture* (New York: Grove Press, 1968).

6. See Milan Kundera's novel, *The Joke* (New York: Harper and Row, 1982).

7. For an account of Eastern European protests up to 1980, see Chris Harman, *Class Struggles in Eastern Europe, 1945–1983* (London: Bookmarks, 1988).

8. For two inside accounts of the rise of reform communism, see Alexander Dubček, *Hope Dies Fast* (New York: Kodansha International, 1993), and Zdenek Mlynár, *Nightfrost in Prague* (New York: Karz, 1980).

9. Vaclav Havel, *The Power of the Powerless* (Armonk, N.Y.: M. E. Sharpe, 1985); Adam Michnik, *Letters from Prison* (Berkeley: University of California Press, 1986); George Konrad, *Antipolitics* (San Diego: Harcourt Brace Jovanovich, 1984).

10. On the Solidarity experience, from its early roots in the prewar period to the fall of the Communist government, see David Ost, *Solidarity and the Politics of Anti-Politics* (Philadelphia: Temple University Press, 1990).

11. See Timothy Garton Ash, *The Magic Lantern* (New York: Random House, 1990).

12. See Moshe Lewin, *The Gorbachev Phenomenon* (Berkeley: University of California Press, 1994).

13. On gender issues in postcommunism, see Nanette Funk and Magda Mueller, eds., *Gender Politics and Post-Communism* (New York: Routledge, 1993).

27

Political Economy and Development

We hear a great deal now about communism having been an economic failure. Yet as noted in Chapter 26, in 1945, for many Eastern Europeans, it was capitalism that was synonymous with failure. The term evoked memories of mass unemployment, economic depression, vast social inequalities, uncontrollable greed, and war. The reason that communism was able to win support, or at least grudging acceptance, from much of the population was that it promised something else: hope. Its proponents spoke of a planned economy with jobs for all, social mobility for society's poorest, stable prices, and general economic progress. To make good on this program, the new regimes would rely not on "outdated" market forces but on a massive use of state power.

The Peculiar Settlement and Beyond

In the postwar period, there was nothing so special about increasing the role of the state. Capitalist governments in Western Europe were doing the same thing; it was a key component of the postwar settlement beginning to emerge there. In the East, however, government sought not just to regulate the economy and promote cooperation between labor and capital, but to take over the economy completely so the state could plan everything in a "rational" way. The Communists had explicit totalistic aspirations: Only by planning the economy totally did they

feel they could eliminate the "anarchy" of capitalist production and build an economy that truly provided for people's needs. Total planning required complete ownership of factories, workshops, retail stores, and farms. It required ministries to determine how much of what products each firm should produce, as well as who should receive the finished products, and at what prices. Consumers were not compelled to buy the goods they found in the stores, but the absence of competition meant they had little choice but to do so. Constructing a planned economy—or, as it was often called, a *command economy*—therefore meant nationalizing all private property used for production and building a huge bureaucratic apparatus to administer all this property.

Clearly this approach was a very different kind of postwar settlement from the one that took hold in the western part of Europe. In Western Europe, the settlement was an attempt by the government to mediate the relationship between capital and labor. Both groups retained their autonomy (and capital retained its property), but they were persuaded to moderate their antagonisms by a state that showed itself able to advance the interests of the members of both groups. In East-Central Europe, the state abolished the relationship between capital and labor and essentially substituted itself for both groups. All property was taken over by the state, and trade unions were turned into arms of the state. This was not quite a settlement between capital and labor, since capital as such ceased to exist, but it ended up achieving the same basic goals as the settlement in the West: a growing economy and major social welfare benefits to workers. For a number of reasons, it never led to the levels of prosperity that it had in the West, but it did provide for social peace and regular growth.

The crucial difference, of course, was that the postwar settlement in the West was carried out on a democratic basis, whereas in Eastern Europe it entailed a suppression of democracy. In this way, it was a peculiar postwar settlement. No one was asked to accept it; instead, it was imposed by the ruling party. All political parties except for the Communists were banned. Newspapers, radio, and television had to follow the official line. There were elections, but only one candidate was on the ballot. The state tried to take workers' aspirations into account somehow, for it wanted to preserve social peace, but in the end it was answerable to no one. And with protests banned, strikes outlawed, and the media firmly under state control, there seemed to be no way for anyone to change the situation. Nevertheless, there is much evidence that people supported it. In Eastern Europe, as in the West, people saw the postwar era as a time for economic growth and political peace. Many were tired of politics and welcomed an interventionist state, provided it could get the job done. Most people surely wished such a process could occur while preserving political democracy, as in the West. But once it was clear that the Communists were not going to allow that, people were at least pleased that the social and economic arrangements of such a settlement would be put into place. (Indeed, the revival of the ex-Communists' popularity since 1993 shows that many people still want the social and economic commitments of a postwar settlement, although definitely not its political side.)

Some observers refer to the Communist system as being not so much a postwar settlement as a new social contract, by which the government agreed to guarantee workers a job and a slow but steady increase in the standard of living, and workers agreed to accept a nondemocratic political system. For the first two decades of Communist rule, the arrangement essentially worked. The protests that did arise concerned only the political aspects of the arrangement. Beginning around 1968, not only the political side but the entire settlement began to break down. The moves toward economic reform showed that signs of a new political economy were emerging in East-Central Europe as indelibly as they did in the West.

The Rise of the Peculiar Settlement

By 1949, the Stalinist transformation was largely accomplished: The state had effectively eliminated private property in the manufacturing and service sectors, with farming only slightly behind. From then on, the entire economy was to be managed by state-run institutions.

The state was able to accomplish several undeniably beneficial achievements. By concentrating resources, it was able to build up heavy industry very quickly. It eliminated unemployment by bringing millions into the workforce, including peasants from the countryside and women, who now entered the labor market at rates only slightly lower than men. Having obtained a job, moreover, a person had it for as long as he or she wished, as a job was considered a right, not a privilege. The state kept prices on most essential goods at a low and affordable level, one of the reasons people often had to stand in long lines. And it facilitated vast social mobility. By taking over the entire economy, Communist governments suddenly had hundreds of thousands of good jobs that had to be filled. They filled them not so much with the old specialists, most of whom the new governments did not trust, but with loyal political activists, regardless of their qualifications. In this way, hundreds of thousands of youths, unskilled workers, and illiterate peasants found that they suddenly had a future, if only they joined the Party (see Table 27.1). In Hungary, 60,000 workers were made enterprise managers during the 1949–1953 period alone.[1]

On Soviet insistence, Eastern Europe carried out its new policies without help from the rest of the world. For the first time in modern history, the region was largely cut off from the global economy. The West offered Marshall Plan aid, but the offer was rejected because it required recipients to open their economies to outside forces, and that would have prevented government planners from deciding just how the economy should be built. The West's response was to impose a boycott: no trade, no loans, and no exchange of technology. That symbolized relations between East and West until the détente of the late 1960s.

Forced to go it alone, the Eastern European states might have cooperated closely among themselves. However, for two key reasons that did not happen. First, each country wanted to build up its own heavy industry before working with anyone else; and second, Stalin opposed cooperation, seeing it as a potential threat to Soviet domination. Stalin wanted Eastern European economies to complement the *Soviet* economy, not each other's. Each country therefore worked to create a model Soviet economy at home, focusing on large-scale industry, with giant, sprawling factories taking up hundreds of acres of land, employing thousands of workers, and producing iron and steel goods used chiefly as intermediate products in the production of ever more industrial goods. Producing consumer goods was of only secondary concern. Just like the early Protestants and capitalists, Communists too said that hard work today brings gratification tomorrow.

The Stalinist economic strategy's main problem was that it did not take national particularities into account. Czechoslovakia, for example, already possessed a solid infrastructure. The Stalinist economic program of building everything anew meant duplicating what the economy had, and the political program of putting

Table 27.1 Communism Brings Mobility in Eastern Europe

	Agricultural Workforce (percentage)	
	1960	1980
Albania	71	62
Bulgaria	73	24
Czechoslovakia	38	13
East Germany	24	10
Hungary	49	24
Poland	56	26
Romania	74	30
Yugoslavia	70	33

Note: The way in which these data are collected suggests that the shift from agriculture is slightly underestimated by these statistics.

Source: Joni Lovenduski and Jean Woodall, *Politics and Society in Eastern Europe* (Bloomington: Indiana University Press, 1987), p. 130.

all decisions in the hands of the Party meant squandering the valuable experience of the experts and the enterprises. Hungary, however, with a small population and poor energy resources, had always relied heavily on foreign trade. The Communist program of striving for economic autarky or complete self-sufficiency was appealing to the national imagination, but it was never very viable as a strategy for development. Hungary had learned to prosper by international trade and would prosper again after the 1970s in the same way. The attempt at autarky thus obstructed the country's natural way forward. As for Poland, one of its chief problems, ironically, was that it did not follow the Communist economic program fully enough. Its inefficient agricultural sector stemmed in large part from the 1956 decision to allow private property in land, while doing everything possible to discourage private agriculture from becoming profitable. Investment went to the more inefficient state sector, and private farmers could not get the mechanical equipment needed to expand and develop. For unindustrialized areas like Romania, Bulgaria, and parts of Yugoslavia, the Stalinist economic strategy played a very constructive role by laying the basis of a modern industrial economy. Everywhere, however, the insensitivity to particular national characteristics led to severe problems that all countries would have to address in the future.

Failure and Demise

By the 1960s, the economies of East-Central Europe were in deep trouble, plagued by shortages, budget deficits, and lack of imagination. Employment guarantees remained, but workers often had little to do. Moreover, opportunities for social mobility had declined dramatically. Workers and peasants, whose predecessors had been able to move up rapidly in the initial postwar years, now found career advancement blocked by those who had advanced in the past and constituted a new elite that tried to pass on privileges to their children. These children, meanwhile, sought better and more creative jobs to match their levels of education, but the system, stuck in its old ways, could not generate such new opportunities.

The irony is that the economic problems of the system were a sign not of communism's failure but of its success. Communist leaders had wanted to build up big industrial economies. Having done so, they just did not know what to do next. Party authorities, in accord with the plan, had built up an economy that was very successful at producing large volumes of standardized goods, and very unsuccessful at producing specialized goods for particular markets. Quantity, not quality, was key. The entire economic system came to resemble one giant hierarchical enterprise, where decisions are made by a few at the top and executed by the majority at the bottom. The goods were produced, but initiative and imagination were smothered, fatal flaws in the high-tech global economy that was

just emerging. As Daniel Chirot has noted, by the 1970s this region had created

> the world's most advanced late nineteenth-century economy, the world's biggest and best, most inflexible rust belt. It is as if Andrew Carnegie had taken over the entire United States, forced it into becoming a giant copy of U.S. Steel, and the executives of the same U.S. Steel had continued to run the country into the 1970s and 1980s![2]

Eastern Europe needed reform, but how could government take away the things people expected from the system without jeopardizing the unwritten social contract on which it depended? Could the government cut down on guaranteed jobs, low prices on essentials, free education, and cheap housing without giving way on one-party rule as well? This would be the conundrum facing all of Eastern Europe in the last two decades of Communist power. Beginning in 1968, the various governments began their various experiments, the first tenuous shadows of an emerging new political economy.

Indeed, the Prague Spring itself should be understood as a first attempt to abandon the peculiar Communist postwar settlement. The main proponents of reform were self-proclaimed economic reformers who felt that the Party needed to let managers run businesses on a more market-oriented basis, without constant instructions from the bureaucratic center. But if the managers were going to try to make a profit, that would mean eliminating some of a firm's social welfare subsidies to its employees. Since that would break the regime's end of the social contract, how could the workers' end (political obedience) be maintained? The reformers proposed precisely that it not be maintained. Thus, the Prague Spring tolerated and even encouraged political freedom as a kind of quid pro quo, offered to society in return for giving up the social contract.

In the end, the whole matter was not very well thought through by the Czechoslovak leadership. Internal divisions were rife. Some reformers favored abandoning Party rule altogether; others did not. Some favored exchanging their peculiar settlement for the standard Western European one of a Keynesian welfare state; others aimed for a more radical evisceration of the welfare state. As it happened, the Soviets invaded the country before either side could prevail. But the word was out: The peculiar settlement would have to be revised.

Hungary was the next to try to do so. In 1968, it introduced the "new economic mechanism" that reduced the role of the ministries and made individual enterprises more responsible for their own affairs. Unlike in Czechoslovakia, however, political reforms were not part of the bargain. That is one of the reasons the reforms soon ran into trouble: different groups expressed their objections within the Party, and the leadership backed off its radical plans so as not to promote political discontent.

In 1970, Poland was the next country that felt it needed to moderate the peculiar settlement and reduce the extensive subsidies leading to chronic budget deficits. But instead of trying to reduce waste and make management more efficient, as the Czechs and Hungarians had tried to do, the Poles attempted to solve their problems by challenging the workers head on.[3] In May, the Party launched a propaganda campaign against alleged worker laziness and then began increasing work norms, cracking down on absenteeism, and cutting pay by reducing overtime. Key industries, such as shipbuilding and aircraft manufacturing, were slated for virtual elimination. And all this was carried out *without the approval* of the workers. The idiocy of such a policy was made clear in December. When Polish leader Władysław Gomułka suddenly announced a dramatic rise in food prices, shipyard workers in the port cities of Gdańsk and Szczecin responded with massive strikes. Gomułka suppressed the strikes immediately, leaving dozens dead. The price hikes were rescinded, but the economic problems remained, and workers remained mobilized. The experience demonstrated that the peculiar settlement could not be broken on one side only. Painful

economic reform might be tolerated only if political reform went along with it. Since neither East-Central Europe's governments nor the Soviet Union seemed ready for political reform, the crisis began to seem unresolvable.

Just as despair began to mount, a temporary solution was found. It was devised by Edward Gierek, who replaced Gomułka as Party leader in Poland soon after the 1970 massacres. We can sum up Gierek's strategy as "Let the West pay for it!" Eastern Europe would voluntarily reenter the global capitalist economy. The countries would turn to the West for the investment funds to help develop their stagnant economies and satisfy the appetites of their hungry consumers. Thus began a change throughout the region in the 1970s. (Only Czechoslovakia, looking inward after the suppression of the Prague Spring in 1968, maintained reservations about this new globalism.)

The West was willing to make loans to help finance its official enemy for three reasons. First, Eastern Europe was a good investment. Capitalist bankers paradoxically thought it safer to lend money to poor Communist countries than to poor capitalist countries, because in the former the political system was stable and labor was under firm control. Second, détente's temporary easing of the cold war, beginning in the late 1960s, made it politically possible to trade with Eastern Europe. Finally, the price hikes by the Organization of Petroleum Exporting Countries (OPEC) and the subsequent oil crisis made it economically possible to do so, as banks now held billions of so-called petrodollars (used to purchase oil at the new prices) that they needed to loan out. The West needed a market for capital just when the East needed a source.

So for a few years in the 1970s, Eastern Europeans lived rather well. Poland and Hungary, for example, imported not only machinery to make their industry more competitive, but also large volumes of Western consumer goods to placate the restive working class. But this "solution" in fact only sowed the seeds of a new crisis, for soon after all these goods were imported, the bills became due, and Eastern Europe had a hard time paying. Because the region was not part of the capitalist economy, it could not pay debts in its own currency. It needed hard currency, and for that it had to export goods to the West. Eastern Europe now learned that it was much easier to borrow from the West than to sell goods there. There was an internal reason for the export difficulties and an external one. The internal reason was that Eastern Europe was still producing inferior goods. Although it had imported much new technology, it had difficulty integrating the equipment into the production process. Because managers were paid according to output and because changes tend to make things worse in the short run, managers often let new machinery sit idle instead of trying to bring it on line. (In 1981, Polish TV showed whole parking lots filled with Western machine tools that had been rusting in the rain for years.) The external reason was that the West, reeling from the oil crisis, was going through a serious recession and was not anxious to buy even well-made products, such as metal goods from Poland, electronic goods from Czechoslovakia, or buses from Hungary.

By the end of the decade, Eastern Europe was deep in debt, with spiraling interest payments making the future look bleak. Poland's $20 billion debt led the way, though Hungary, with a much smaller population, had the highest per capita debt. East-Central Europe's entry into the global economy had failed. It had fallen into a "debt trap" similar to the kind that had been crippling the Third World.[4] And the debt precipitated a general economic crisis and a new round of shortages. These shortages came about for two reasons. First, Eastern Europe had integrated just enough Western technology to make its economy dependent on Western inputs, and the debt now prevented it from obtaining those inputs. (A 1981 toothpaste shortage in Poland occurred because Poland's toothpaste producers had signed an exclusive contract with a West German firm to supply essential ingredients, and when Poland failed to pay its debts, the firm

stopped shipping the ingredients.) Second, the debt burden forced Eastern Europe to export whatever would sell in the West, and the salable items tended to be items that the population needed itself, like ham from Poland or coal from Romania.

In other words, by 1980 it had become clear that Eastern Europe's attempt to borrow its way out of the crisis had failed. The crisis of the peculiar settlement now became even greater than before; not only was the economy in even more serious trouble, but popular anger had been stirred up, both by the continuing lack of political freedom and, perhaps even more, the sudden disappearance of the consumer goods that people were just getting used to.

In Poland, where the debt crisis had been worst, the attempt to raise prices sparked the general strike of 1980. Realizing that it could get the social support necessary for austerity measures only by easing the political monopoly of the past, the government legalized Solidarity in August 1980. Although it outlawed the union sixteen months later, it continued moving toward economic and political reform, culminating finally in the peaceful revolution of 1989.

While Poland was experimenting with political solutions to the crisis, Hungary experimented with economic solutions. Instead of giving workers political freedom, it gave workers the chance to make money. For example, workers were allowed to band together in the factories where they worked, forming their own quasi-enterprises using state machinery, after hours, to fill orders that they had contracted for independently. Enterprises were given more autonomy than ever before, and the small private sector (called the *second economy*) expanded considerably. By the end of the decade, Hungary had some of the highest consumption rates in Eastern Europe, as well as some of the most profitable large firms, such as the Tungsram plant, which sold light bulbs on the Western market, and the Ikarus bus company, which produced for hard-currency customers as far away as Latin America. Hungary also had some of the most overworked workers; according to some estimates, it had more "moonlighters" (workers holding two or more jobs) than any other country in the world.

Romania chose yet another way of dealing with its debt crisis: paying off the debt as quickly as possible. The costs were horrific. Party leader Nicolae Ceauşescu slashed domestic consumption to prewar levels, exporting to the West essential items that the population itself needed in order to survive. Electricity was shut off for several hours each day, with heating nonexistent even in winter, while the government exported coal and oil to earn the money to pay back the debt.

By 1989, the peculiar settlement had collapsed completely. One by one, Eastern European countries turned to a democratic market economy, and Eastern Europe's peculiar postwar settlement gave way to a rapidly emerging new political economy.

State and Economy

The fall of communism can thus be traced in part to the woes that befell East-Central Europe when it sought reintegration into the global economy. Once a society seeks to play on capitalist turf, it is difficult to play only halfway. In the years since communism has fallen, East-Central Europe has moved decisively toward the creation of a full market economy and has eagerly sought integration into the global economy.

Economic Management

Since 1989, managing the economy has first and foremost meant marketizing it. But each country has moved toward marketization in its own particular way. The differences have had to do with political parties, political culture, and the level of social support enjoyed by reform-oriented programs. In Poland, radical economic reform was made possible by the strong support

it received from the trade union Solidarity. In Hungary, the first post-Communist elections were won by a party that promised to undertake reforms slowly to minimize pain. In the Czech Republic, rapid marketization efforts were promoted by a political culture highly sympathetic to entrepreneurialism and Western willingness to invest large sums of money, whereas in Slovakia, market transition lagged behind because of a large rural population and an unusually large number of old, unprofitable factories. (In this respect, Slovakia is similar to Russia. In each country, numerous towns and cities are entirely dependent for their livelihood on the survival of a single, giant industrial plant that cannot easily be made profitable.)

In 1990, Poland embraced a series of marketization policies known collectively as *shock therapy,* or *neoliberalism.* Although not all of these measures have been adopted elsewhere in the region, they do represent a model of economic reform that other governments measure themselves against. Let us look at some of this model's main features.

The main aim of post-Communist economic transition is to get the state out of the business of managing the economy and to allow the market to make the most of the decisions that state planners used to make. This means disbanding the planning ministries and granting firms full autonomy. Companies are no longer told what to produce, whom to produce for, or what prices to charge for their products. They themselves decide all these issues. A firm that is not making a profit must make the necessary adjustments so it does make a profit or else go bankrupt. Firms are to do whatever it takes to survive—even fire their workers. The abolition of the old employment guarantee meant the end of the old social contract. (Of course, things do not always work quite this way in practice, even in Poland. See the "Shock Therapy in Practice" box.)

The aim of the state's withdrawal from the economy is to force enterprises to compete and become more efficient. But simple withdrawal is not enough. The old socialist economies fre-

Shock Therapy in Practice

Shock therapy is supposed to mean that uncompetitive firms simply go bankrupt. The market is supposed to determine who will survive. In practice, however, it has not worked out quite this way. The government has found it impossible simply to sit by and let a giant industrial enterprise go bankrupt, because all too often, an entire city would go bankrupt along with it. Take the example of the WSK-PZL plant in Mielec, Poland, which used to manufacture fighter planes, agricultural planes, and turbine engines for the old Soviet bloc. The factory employed 20,000 people in a city with only 60,000 total inhabitants. With the collapse of the Soviet bloc, it lost its old market. Even after cutting the workforce in half and switching some production lines to civilian products, the plant could not sell enough to make a profit. After much effort, it won a contract to build doors for new Boeing 747s, but this job supplied work only for a few dozen employees. According to market rules, the plant should fold. But if it did, so would the city's entire economy, and then the state would have to make large welfare expenditures just to keep the population alive. So contrary to shock therapy, the state continued to fund the plant, though on a vastly reduced level. In the Czech Republic, Prime Minister Vaclav Klaus also combined shock therapy rhetoric with quiet maintenance of unprofitable enterprises. Nowhere in East-Central Europe does market logic alone prevail.

quently relied on one giant firm to produce everything the country needed; that is, they created monopolies. Freeing prices alone would mean that these monopolies would charge higher prices without having to become more competitive. Competition therefore needs to be brought from the outside. Thus, an essential part of Eastern European market reform is to reduce drastically or even eliminate tariffs on imported goods, particularly from the West. Until new firms arise to create internal competition, existing firms have to compete against external competition.

Internal competition is to be created by taking the state out of the business of management and empowering a new wealthy class to do the job instead. In this sense, Eastern Europe's new economic policy is very much a "wager on the elite." Despite the fact that labor protest precipitated the overthrow of the Communist system, the new leaders seek to create a new monied, propertied elite to lead the way into the promised new world. Thus, we have Eastern Europe's current focus on privatization.[5] The aim is to create a new class of property owners who will have a personal interest in maintaining and developing the economy.

There are two kinds of privatization processes in Eastern Europe, usually referred to as small and large. *Small privatization* is concerned with the retail sector, particularly small shops like groceries, bakeries, and repair shops. This sector has been privatized relatively quickly, sometimes by selling the shops to the highest bidder, more often by leasing them to those who work there. This process has not been very contentious in Eastern Europe, largely because there is not a great deal of money (or power) at stake. The real conflicts have come in the area of *large privatization*, concerned with the ownership transfer of the large state enterprises, with their large labor forces, enormous capital stock, and huge markets.

In Hungary, large privatization began even during the Communist era. Those who took the lead in privatizing the economy were not the new capitalists but the old Communist managers. The process is often referred to as *spontaneous privatization*, or *nomenklatura buyouts*, because it was carried out by the old managers themselves (members of the former *nomen-klatura*, or bureaucracy), without coordination by the state. The state supplied only the legal framework: laws allowing managers of state firms to create spin-off private firms with no starting capital, followed by laws permitting the transfer of assets from state firms to these new firms. As a result of these laws, managers simply got together to set up a new firm, transferred assets of the state firm to this new firm, and suddenly became new capitalist entrepreneurs. After 1990, the post-Communist government cracked down on this practice. Nevertheless, large privatization in Hungary has remained very much an elite affair. Firms have been sold to Western companies and domestic investors, and the population has had little to do with it. In the end, foreigners appear to be the main beneficiary. Hungary has gone furthest of all the countries in East-Central Europe toward inviting foreign ownership. By 2000, even such a crucial sector for development as banking was about 80 percent foreign owned.

One of the reasons Hungary could afford to leave the population out of this process was that economic reform providing benefits to workers had already progressed far before 1989. In Poland and Czechoslovakia, where previous opportunities were more limited, governments made special efforts at least to appear to include more people in the privatization process.

In Czechoslovakia, aside from the sale of some major plants to Western buyers, the government decided to privatize industry through the use of a voucher system. In 1992, all citizens were allowed to purchase, at a nominal price, a booklet of stock shares, called points, that they could then invest in a company of their choice. By involving ordinary people in the privatization process, the government hoped to break the ethos of dependence on the state fostered by the old regime and to teach citizens the concepts of risk, profit, and ownership. By making people co-owners, the government hoped individuals would feel they had a stake in the entire process of marketization.

There were two problems with the Czech solution. First, voucher privatization proved not to be so inclusive after all. Within a short period of time, investment funds and banks still run largely by the state quickly bought out most of the citizens' vouchers. Formal citizen ownership, in other words, covered for continuing state control. Second, this lack of real private ownership reduced the pressure on firms to restructure. As a result, Czech firms avoided painful restructuring in the early 1990s, only to have to do so in the latter part of the decade, just when its neighboring economies were starting to benefit from changes they had made earlier.

Poland began privatization with a law in July 1990 that spelled out several possible paths and set up a ministry of property transformation to oversee the process. Over the next three years, Poland experimented with several kinds of privatization programs. First, it began selling firms on the open market. But there were not enough buyers, and the government usually ended up with majority ownership anyway. Then it began selling firms to single Western buyers, such as a food processing plant to Gerber or a chemical plant to Procter & Gamble. This practice, however, drew stiff opposition. Critics charged that the best firms were being sold at a fraction of their real value, in return for kickbacks or to ingratiate the authorities with the West. It is impossible to verify these charges. Part of the problem, of course, is that no one knew what these firms were really worth, since they were built on the basis of the artificial prices of the past and have been inadequately tested in the market competition of today. Government defenders reject the critics' charges, saying that firms are worth only what people are willing to pay for them. The fierce criticism, however, required the government to take more care before selling firms to foreigners. All East-Central European countries have had to deal with similar complaints.

Seeking to win popular support, Poland in 1995 introduced a plan known as *general privatization* in which ownership of several hundred state-owned companies was transferred to private investment firms in which individual citizens could buy shares. Whereas in the Czech plan a buyer purchases shares of the company itself, the Polish plan offers people shares of investment firms that are given ownership of various companies. The Poles chose this indirect method because they felt that what was important was not just privatization but good management. By the end of the 1990s, however, this plan too had run into serious problems, largely due to the poor quality of the firms selected for privatization and the limited capital at the disposal of the investment firms.

In the end, the most common method of privatization in Poland has been to sell or lease firms to their employees. This method was particularly popular with workers, who thereby became formal co-owners of the firm. However, since managers usually put up most of the money, and therefore got most of the shares, workers usually did not get more influence or more money.

This de facto exclusion of labor was a problem in all the privatization methods. In the initial privatization program, the elite sought to win labor support by reserving a small percentage of shares for the workforce at special prices. When the shares proved unaffordable to many workers even at discount prices, a 1996 law gave the workforce 15 percent of the shares of a privatized firm for free. Workers therefore got more money, but not necessarily more influence. Privatization in Poland has always been an elite-run affair, despite the powerful role played by Solidarity.

Finally, we have the many experiences of *bandit privatization*. Not a precise concept, the term refers to the illegal, semilegal, underhanded, nepotistic, coerced, and just plain criminal ways in which government elites have passed on property to themselves or their friends. All countries have had their share of these. Even Czech privatization, so admired by the West in the early 1990s, turned out by the late 1990s to have been bastions of corruption in

which allies of the ruling Civic Democratic Party gained fortunes from plundering state wealth. One of the worst epidemics of bandit privatization occurred in Croatia, whose president tried to put virtually the entire economy in the hands of a few dozen loyal families. One friend of the president was able to "buy" 157 companies with no money of his own.[6] Only after the president's death in 1999 and new elections in 2000 was the public able to learn all this. Dealing with the consequences will not be easy.

Welfare State

Over the past decade, Eastern European governments have radically changed their welfare state profiles. In place of the state socialist tradition of cradle-to-grave services for everyone, their new aim is to mesh with Western Europe's policy of providing assistance chiefly for those whom the market economy leaves behind.

In the communist era, the main social welfare benefit was provided for all: a guaranteed job. That is definitively over. Table 27.2 shows the rapid increase of unemployment throughout the region. The appearance of unemployment in East-Central Europe has meant the appearance of unemployment insurance. The general pattern is a percentage payment for a set period of time, followed by possible help from the general public assistance fund. In Poland, for example, laid-off workers receive 36 percent of the average national wage for twelve months. If after a year they are still unemployed, they then become eligible for public assistance for the indigent. Public assistance includes long-term welfare assistance for the very poorest (at 28 percent of the average wage, which still leaves the recipient impoverished), as well as one-time-only payments to help buy clothing or pay rent. Active labor market policies such as retraining and public works have also been common ways of fighting unemployment, particularly in the Czech Republic. (The comparatively low rates of unemployment in the Czech Re-

Table 27.2 Unemployment in the Post-Communist Era

	Registered Unemployment (percentage of labor force)						
	1990	1994	1995	1996	1997	1998	1999
Bulgaria	1.8	12.8	11.1	12.5	13.7	12.2	16.0
Croatia	—	17.3	17.6	15.9	17.6	18.6	20.8
Czech Republic	0.7	3.2	2.9	3.5	5.2	7.5	9.4
Hungary	1.7	10.9	10.4	10.5	10.4	9.1	9.6
Poland	6.5	16.0	14.9	13.2	10.3	10.4	13.0
Romania	1.3	10.9	9.5	6.6	8.8	10.3	11.5
Russia	—	7.5	8.9	10.0	11.2	13.3	12.2
Slovakia	1.6	14.8	13.1	12.8	12.5	15.6	19.2
Ukraine	—	0.3	0.6	1.5	2.8	4.3	4.3
Yugoslavia	—	23.9	24.7	26.1	25.6	27.2	27.4

Note: Yugoslavia includes Serbia and Montenegro.

Sources: *Economic Survey of Europe* (New York: United Nations, 2000), no. 2/3.

public can be explained not just by such policies but also by the location of the worst plants in Slovakia and the government's initial resistance to radical enterprise restructuring. When restructuring began in the late 1990s, unemployment began increasing there just when it was declining elsewhere.)

Free health care constituted another key benefit of the old system. Its scope and quality were deteriorating even before 1989, and they have only gotten worse since then. Governments tried to reform the health care sector by imposing hard budget constraints on hospitals and clinics and encouraging better-off individuals to purchase private health insurance. Private doctors now operate everywhere in the region, leading to a situation in which the wealthier people have access to care that the poor do not. Of course, the old system had inequalities too. Whereas political connections were the ticket to better health care in the past, now money makes

the difference. By the time the new century began, health care was still nominally free, but many procedures, operations, and medicines were in fact available only when citizens paid.

Higher education has been reformed in a similar way. Formally, it remains free for those who pass the tough entrance exams, but student aid has been substantially reduced, and the imposition of fees has become ubiquitous. For those who do not pass the exam, public universities now admit many of those students if they pay their own fees, and private universities also fill the gap. As a result, the number of students in universities has increased substantially in East-Central Europe, but the increase has been almost entirely in the paid sector.

Reforming old-age pensions was one of the key issues in the 1990s throughout Europe. In the West, this was due chiefly to demographic trends showing a growing number of retirees relative to wage earners. In East Europe, it was not demographics but the economic depression of the early 1990s that created a pension crisis. In Hungary, Poland, the Czech Republic, and Slovakia, that depression led to the loss of some 5 million jobs between 1989 and 1996. With millions of near-retirement-age workers allowed early retirement and young people not hired in the first place, the imbalance between wage earners and retirees grew considerably in the early 1990s. In 1997, Hungary and Poland followed an international trend and adopted a new pension system. Instead of paying guaranteed benefits on the sole basis of contributions from current workers, younger workers now pay part of their social security contributions into a private investment fund. Subsequent retirement benefits will be based largely on market performance. Given the booming international stock market of the 1990s, most people supported this reform. If, however, markets fail to maintain such spectacular growth rates in the future—and, indeed, 2000–2001 saw a considerable slowdown—the reforms might become much less popular and promote a new crisis in the future.[7]

In sum, East-Central Europe continues to maintain a broad social security network, rivaling that of Western Europe and surpassing that of the United States. In comparison with the Communist era, however, many social benefits have been reduced or even eliminated. In the old system, for example, the enterprise usually subsidized things like housing and vacations, but today citizens have to pay on their own. Even with the social security net, poverty remains high. In Hungary and Poland, two of the more prosperous countries, about 20 percent of the population live below the official poverty level (compared to about 14 percent in the United States). In Bulgaria and Romania, that number is about one-third.

Who is gaining and who is losing in the new Eastern Europe? Those with higher education and relative youth are doing best. Of course, not just any higher education will do. It helps to know foreign languages, particularly English, and also to know business or engineering rather than literature. It also helps to be a man, as a backlash against women in the workplace has resulted in a wave of discrimination. Those doing worst in the new Eastern Europe are the pensioners above all, followed by workers more than forty-five years old who are employed in old state enterprises and have little formal education. In 1993, to give one example, unemployment stood at about 17 percent in Poland. Among those with a university education, however, the figures were 3.4 percent for men and 4.4 percent for women. For those with only a basic high school education, the figures rose to 12.9 percent for men and a tragic 27.3 percent for women. Education, class, and gender are paying higher returns in the post-Communist era than they ever did in the past.

Society and Economy

Economic hardship always affects politics. It is commonly accepted, for example, that dissatisfaction with the economy led the American peo-ple to vote out both Jimmy Carter and George H. W. Bush after only one term in office for each. But it is also true that economics is far from the only influence on politics. Many political scientists explain the American population's turn away from the Democratic Party in the 1980s as resulting in large part from an increasing cultural gap between professional and college- educated Democrats and the voters of mainstream America. Where the former cherished the principles of diversity and questioning authority, the latter emphasized the values of order and discipline; where the former emphasized the rights of minorities, the latter defended the demands of majorities; where the former sought environmentally sound growth, the latter favored old-fashioned economic production above all else. Noneconomic factors are as important as economic ones for understanding a nation's politics.

Are the people of East-Central Europe attached to democracy as a value? Which do they consider more important: individual rights or the rights of the nation? What about the rights of minorities? Do Eastern Europeans believe in capitalism as a legitimate and desirable economic system? Do they believe in the separation of church and state? What do they think is the proper role of women in public life? Answers to these questions tell us a great deal about how social and political life in East-Central Europe will develop.

Inequality and Minorities

The people of East-Central Europe have had a curious relationship with the problems of minorities. On the one hand, since virtually all of the region was under foreign jurisdiction less than a century ago, people have a sense that they can *all* be considered minorities—that their national identity is inherently fragile. The Czech writer Milan Kundera has written that to be a Central European is to be aware that nationhood is not eternal; one's own nation can potentially disappear.[8] We might imagine that such a history makes people sensitive to the problem of national minorities. At the same time, however, it makes people more committed to solidifying their own national identity whenever they have the chance. And it is this that has continually created problems for minority rights in the region.

Most of East-Central Europe's nationalities first had the chance to consolidate their nationhood only after World War I. As the former occupying powers collapsed and the new world powers espoused national self-determination, former minorities now became titular majorities, committed to building a state (government, administration, and military) to serve the interests of their newly dominant national group. The problem, however, was the situation facing citizens of *other* nationalities. With the state now officially promoting the interests of a dominant nationality, members of other nationalities automatically became second-class citizens; the new state sought to defend the interests of a nation different from theirs. As the new states doled out new jobs and leadership positions, they tended to privilege citizens belonging to their "own" national group rather than citizens of "others." The national enmities this created—among both those whose national group had its "own" state nearby (such as Germans and Hungarians) as well as those that were stateless (such as Jews and Ukrainians)—contributed in large part to tearing the new states apart internally before the Nazis came along to finish the job.

As an ideologically internationalist party, committed to the famous line from *The Communist Manifesto* that "the working class has no nationality," the Communists were seen by many as the answer to the minority problems of the past. And indeed, in Yugoslavia, the Communists succeeded in stemming, though not eliminating, the fierce ethnic conflicts of the past. Elsewhere, however, it was the war itself, and not the Communist Party that transformed minority politics. By 1945, most of the region's

Jews had been killed, and Germans expelled. In Poland, new borders placed Ukrainians and Lithuanians in the Soviet Union instead. With few of the old minorities left, the new governments prevented the introduction of new minorities by maintaining a closed economy, thus sharply restricting immigration. As a result, East-Central Europe during the Communist era was more ethnically homogeneous than it had ever been in the past. Communist governments frequently spoke a patriotic-nationalist line in order to boost popularity, but there were few nationalities at hand to persecute. In officially multiethnic countries like Czechoslovakia and Yugoslavia, the government continually preached unity, although material inequalities among the nationalities certainly existed.

Minority problems reemerged only in the post-Communist era. They began when official minority elites in the official multiethnic states (Czechoslovakia, Yugoslavia, and the Soviet Union) took advantage of the new rules to break away into independent states. And when Slovaks, Croats, and Latvians (not to mention Slovenians, Lithuanians, and Estonians) declared their new states, they recreated in miniature the situation after 1918, when new states meant new minorities. In the global and multicultural age in which we live, individuals who kept silent about their national identity during the Communist years feel increasingly comfortable embracing it today. Although outside the Baltic republics and the former Yugoslavia, national minorities are still quite few—most prominent are the approximately 10 percent Hungarians in Romania and Slovakia, 9 percent Turks in Bulgaria, and a large Roma population in Hungary and Slovakia—those that are there are increasingly assertive of their identities. At the same time that this renaissance creates a cultural richness that many citizens of the dominant nationality appreciate, it always has the potential of creating tensions too, especially in the hands of ambitious politicians.

Finally, tensions begin to arise precisely as the region gets freer and richer. With "Eastern

Europe" increasingly perceived just as "Europe" and with limited European Union (EU) accession imminent, the region has begun to attract refugees from authoritarian countries and immigrant laborers from poor countries. Some local residents appreciate being able to provide political and economic refuge to others, remembering that they often sought this themselves during the Communist years. Such people see the resulting diversity as a positive good. But many others, particularly poorer citizens, are susceptible to the view spread by newly emerging right-wing parties that such immigrants are "taking our jobs." As it happens, the EU itself sees the new immigration as a problem, fearing it will lead to even greater influxes of people, and it is asking the region to tighten control of its borders as a condition for joining the EU. Thus, a host of factors contribute to create new minority problems and inequalities that had not existed before.

Inequality and Women

Another critical noneconomic factor shaping Eastern European politics today is the role of gender. In contrast to the feminism that has transformed Western politics, however, the phenomenon here can best be seen as what Peggy Watson calls *masculinism*—the policy of using power to boost men's chances in the world by cutting back the chances for women.[9] It is a peculiar kind of reaction against communism, for one of the first things communism did was to bring women en masse into the workforce. Since 1989, as the threat of unemployment has hovered over all of East-Central Europe, some men say it is necessary to "reverse the legacy of communism" and fire women first. And indeed, women were the first to be let go when enterprises started cutting back. In part this was because, owing to educational patterns, women were more likely than men to be unskilled workers. Yet even when such a criterion was ir-

relevant, women were more likely to be laid off. Men argue that jobs are more important for them than for women, since their role is to support a family (even though many women are also heads of households). Men also contend that they work harder on the job (despite the fact that productivity has traditionally been higher for women, who are less likely to drink on the job).

Besides this, women increasingly are being hired on the basis of their looks. Companies do not even hide this fact; job notices for white-collar jobs often specify a woman under thirty as the desired candidate and require photographs as part of the application. Working-class women often find that "beauty school," rather than trade school, is their ticket to a good job. What seem to be operating here are not rational economic criteria but old patriarchal stereotypes and old moral and religious norms. In other words, attitudes about gender represent one more way in which noneconomic factors are profoundly shaping post-Communist politics.

The loss of jobs for women has had more dire consequences as well, leading to a boom in prostitution throughout the region and beyond. Police in Western Europe report an alarming rise in the number of Eastern European women being exported to the West to work as prostitutes. Typically the cash-poor woman, with declining opportunities at home, is recruited by a dashing man who promises her a fancy "hostess" job in a chic Western European establishment. The woman flies to the West, hands her documents to her new "employer," and is promptly told that the hostess job is "unavailable" and that she is already in debt for the cost of the airfare and room and board. She is then offered "another way" to pay back the money. Without her documents, afraid of her "hosts" and the local police, and often unfamiliar with the language of the country she is in, the woman usually finds there is no choice. This international trafficking of women, sparked by the region's economic crisis as well as by a high external "demand" for white-skinned prostitutes (of which East Europe has, since 1989, become the world's largest supplier), now counts as one of the biggest and most nefarious of post-Communist "growth industries."[10]

The Generation Gap

Generational differences have been greatest in the region at the moment of grand systemic change. In the two great social experiments of the last half-century—the building of communism after World War II and the building of capitalism after 1989—young people strongly supported the changes while older citizens had many reservations. Young people tended to be early communism's main bastion of support because of the great social mobility that it promised. A new regime suspicious of those whose worldview had been shaped by tradition turned to fresh faces to help introduce a new style of rule. It had loads of good jobs for them, too—as managers, experts, policemen, and Party officials—jobs that were harder for middle-aged citizens to get, who first had to prove they could be trusted. This generation gap extended itself to the factory line too, where older workers resisted the speed-up and high work norms characteristic of Stalinism, which younger workers often embraced as sport. (Indeed, the state organized "socialist competitions" for young workers to see who could work the hardest, with big prizes for the victors.)

If young people gravitated disproportionately to communism in the late 1940s, they also gravitated heavily to capitalist democracy in 1989. Just as in earlier times, the new system offered them enormous new possibilities, for if Communists did not trust older workers after 1949, capitalists did not trust them after 1989. Many new companies wanted to hire only young people "untainted" by communism, filled with individual ambition rather than collectivist loyalties. This does not mean, however, that all young people have benefited. Education is more highly correlated with success than is age, with highly educated middle-aged people more likely to prosper than poorly educated youth. But young people *thought* they would do better, and had more opportunities to get the training necessary for the new economy. The new system also gave them the chance to travel abroad, an opportunity long denied them in the past. The early twenty-first century still finds many older citizens of the region nostalgic for the security of the past, but young people for the most part never look back.

Culturally the generation gap is not so great, since most of Eastern Europe had its own 1960s. The postwar generation, after all, came to embrace rock music and the sexual revolution as their own.[11] On issues like feminism and homosexuality, however, people in their twenties are far more open than others. Unlike in the West, where feminist organizations tend to be led by middle-aged women who came of age in the 1960s, those in the East are run mostly by women aged twenty to thirty-five, who became active only after 1989. And the fact that gay and lesbian issues can now be discussed openly is a direct result of the changed attitudes of young people.

Perhaps the major generational difference today is that young people are highly skeptical of politics. More than a decade after 1989, they are tired of hearing about the "heroes" who "overthrew" communism, and they believe that many of the new leaders are as corrupt as the old ones ever were. There are few young people in political parties and even fewer in trade unions. Where they do get involved, it tends to be in nongovernmental organizations and new social movements. When the World Bank held its first meeting in a former Communist country, in Prague in September 2000, the demonstrations against it were led by activists in their twenties. Nevertheless, political activism remains quite low among East European youth as a whole. They still want to enjoy the new freedoms they have rather than struggle for more.

The Dilemmas of European Integration

The Eastern European countries have tried to solidify their new Western orientation by joining the two key Western international institutions: the EU and the North Atlantic Treaty Organization (NATO). For the three "elite" countries of the region—Poland, Hungary, and the Czech Republic—the attempt has been largely successful. These countries entered NATO in 1999 and will almost certainly enter the EU by the middle of this decade.

While NATO integration was relatively cost free, that is not at all the case for the EU. Entry into the EU means opening up borders to free trade, and many East Europeans fear that even with all the preparations, their countries will still not be able to compete. Poland and the Czech Republic, for example, maintain a large machine tool industry, but nothing in comparison to powerful German engineering, which could use EU's open borders to take over Eastern industry. The East might have an advantage in food production, but this is one area in which EU policy has been highly protectionist. In 1993, the EU reduced tariffs on Eastern European manufacturing goods but not on agricultural products. French farmers regularly stage mass disruptive rallies against agricultural imports even from other EU countries and are not likely to allow uncontrolled Eastern European access without a big fight. It is no surprise that rural Eastern Europeans tend to be those most worried about EU integration. Besides concerns about their export market, they fear also for their ability to maintain ownership of the land, since all ownership restrictions disappear with EU entry. With Westerners worried about the influx of cheap East European laborers and products and Easterners worried about the power of Western capital, it is clear that full integration into the EU will not be an easy or unconflictual process.

One way the West has tried to advertise its good intentions has been through numerous aid programs. Unfortunately for its recipients, this has not taken the form of outright economic grants as it did with the postwar Marshall Plan. Instead, it has come in the form of technical assistance, advice on marketization, loans for infrastructural projects, and partial debt annulment.

Aid from the EU has been channeled through an agency specially set up for the purpose, known as PHARE. An acronym for "Poland, Hungary: Assistance for Restructuring Economies," the agency was created in 1990; by the next year, its scope extended to all former Communist countries in the region. Its main aim is to promote the evolution of West European–type institutions in East-Central Europe. Its funds have been used to produce reports on industrial restructuring, support the region's privatization agencies, publicize West European–type labor relations, increase environmental awareness, sponsor student exchanges, and offer consulting on numerous other issues. Similar assistance has been delivered by the U.S. Agency for International Development (AID).

Most of what PHARE and AID do comes under the rubric of technical assistance. Western countries send specialists in budget financing, tax policy, privatization, banking, labor relations, marketing, and a host of other areas to teach East Europeans how to transform their economies. As for results, the record is mixed. The main problem with the programs is conveyed by the word *teach*. Eastern Europeans appreciate the aid but not the condescension with which it is usually delivered. They complain that Western specialists are often too unaware of East European conditions to be of much help. They charge that Western agencies impose their own agendas on the East, taking little heed of what the recipients say they need. Indeed, some Westerners have been frank about their disrespect. One official defended the EU's practice of unilaterally deciding which projects to fund on the grounds that "it takes much longer for the recipients to specify their priorities than . . . for the donors to impose theirs."[12] East Europeans charge that the real beneficiaries of aid delivered like this are the Western specialists earning high consulting fees.[13] And indeed, the dollars expended in such aid programs often consist almost entirely of these consulting fees and do not go toward helping Eastern European economies directly.

Besides aid agencies, international financial institutions have played a crucial role in shaping Eastern Europe's relations with the West. The IMF has contributed to stabilization funds to maintain the value of local currencies against the inflationary trends of shock therapy caused by the elimination of subsidies and price controls. The World Bank and the new European Bank for Reconstruction and Development, specially created to aid in the economic rebuilding of Eastern Europe, offered loans for infrastructural projects like highways to Western Europe or installation of pollution controls. Yet another aid program has come in the form of debt reduction. With the exception of Romania, which imposed harsh costs on its people to pay back foreign debts, all East European countries entered the post-Communist era burdened with enormous foreign debts. By 1990, Poland owed nearly $50 billion, mostly to foreign governments. As a reward for its shock therapy program, Western governments reduced Poland's debt by half and persuaded private banks to do the same. Not all countries, however, got the same treatment. Hungary was not as successful in negotiating debt reduction, partly because it owed more of its money to private commercial banks, which cannot swallow losses as easily as big governments can, and partly because the IMF was not as happy about its record of market reform. (Hungary, moreover, cannot appeal simply to Western Europe; by the mid-1990s, about three-quarters of its foreign debt was held by Japanese banks.)

All in all, the benefits of the various aid programs have been far less than Eastern Europe expected. Economically, the East, not the EU, has made most of the concessions. It is clear that the East European countries are more eager to enter the EU than the EU is to have them.

East-Central Europe and the International Political Economy

Small states cannot shape their environment like large ones can. They must exist in a world where political and economic rule making are dominated by those large states. East-Central Europe has always been aware of its subordinate status. Whereas the Soviet Union and China each undertook grand autarkic development programs (such as the crash industrialization program of the 1930s in the Soviet Union and the Great Leap Forward in China), East-Central Europe has had to work together with great foreign powers.

From 1945 to 1989, it worked closely with the Soviet Union. In the early years, the Soviet Union exercised clear economic control over the region, confiscating raw materials and sometimes even dismantling entire factories for reinstallation in Soviet territory. By the 1970s, terms of trade became favorable for Eastern Europe, which received cheap oil from the Soviets in return for consumer goods of questionable quality. By not having to produce high-quality goods, however, the region suffered in the long run.

Since 1989, East-Central Europe has turned decisively to the West. It tries to sell its goods to the West and coordinates its economic development programs with the West. The change in orientation began after the upheaval of 1989, and intensified following the collapse of the Soviet Union. In 1988, Eastern Europe sent 27.2 percent of its exports to the former Soviet Union and 38.7 percent to all developed market economies. Ten years later, the respective figures were 7.5 percent and 71.6 percent.

The chief architect of Eastern Europe's integration into the global economy has been the IMF, whose main role is to be chief enforcer of "good" (i.e., pro-market) behavior. To get grants from Western governments or new loans from banks, East European countries must get the IMF seal of approval. The IMF seeks to make sure that the loan-seeking government will reduce its budget deficit by cutting subsidies to industries and consumers and pursuing a program of rapid privatization.[14] Aware of the possibility of severe social unrest when these cuts are made, the IMF recommends the establishment of new social welfare programs and unemployment insurance. Nevertheless, it gives its all-important seal of approval only when governments follow its advice on budget-reduction policies. Countries had to get this approval before either the EU or NATO would consider them for entry.

Western money has also entered East-Central Europe as a result of direct foreign investment. The specific patterns of investment are different in the different countries. Whereas Poland and Hungary have supported full Western ownership, the Czech and Slovak republics have preferred joint ventures. In the first five years after the fall of communism, Hungary received the most direct foreign investment, followed by the Czech Republic and Poland. This international investment has created new managerial jobs and has helped modernize existing factories. By the mid-1990s, however, direct foreign investment began to generate criticism among some Eastern Europeans as they learned that multinational corporations can change their plans and their investment strategies with remarkable speed. The Czech government in 1990 was delighted to accept Volkswagen's bid to help rebuild the Skoda autoworks, one of the strongest industries in the country. In 1994, however, the Czechs complained bitterly when Volkswagen decided to scale down the size of its investment considerably and move some production to plants in other countries. Hungary, meanwhile, began quarreling with General Electric, which took over Hungary's famous Tungsram light bulb company, and then gutted it. And Poland fell out with the Italian Lucchini concern after the company, having bought majority ownership in the Warsaw steel mill, drastically scaled down its commitment before it even began to invest. Of course, many foreign companies have invested more than originally planned, too. On the whole, East-Central Europe has benefited from foreign investment. But fears linger that the newly independent countries are selling off scarce resources and placing domestic policy under foreign control, including control by the IMF. Foreign investment is no longer seen as the unconditional good that it was viewed as in 1989.

Consequences of Globalization

Integration in the new global economy has brought new possibilities for growth and expansion to East-Central Europe. But it has also brought a set of new problems. First, it brought a major economic depression, the largest in peacetime since the Great Depression of the 1930s.

The recession began as soon as the state decided to free prices, end subsidies and tariffs, and allow goods from abroad to compete with those produced at home. Presented with Western goods and homemade goods at comparable prices and having heard for so long about the superiority of the former, consumers jumped at the chance to feel themselves part of the West by owning its products. Many economists called for stiff tariffs to protect weak domestic industry, but Eastern Europe instead chose greater openness than the West. As a result, domestic production plummeted. Industrial output fell about 30 percent throughout the region in the first year after the fall of communism. Rarely have modern economies seen such dramatic declines. Unemployment, meanwhile, went from zero to well over 10 percent in Poland and Hungary, often reaching 30 percent or more in the small industrial towns where the large factories of the Communist era were grinding to a halt. Only the introduction of unemployment benefits and the growth of small retail trade prevented a complete economic and human catastrophe.

Global integration has contributed to the recession in other ways too. Let us look briefly at three of them:

Table 27.3   Transformation by Numbers: Real GDP, 1989–1999 (1989 = 100)

	1990	1991	1992	1993	1994	1995	1996	1997	1998	1999
Bulgaria	90.9	83.3	77.2	76.1	77.5	79.7	71.6	66.0	68.9	70.6
Croatia	92.9	73.3	64.7	59.5	63.0	67.3	71.3	76.2	78.1	77.9
Czech Republic	98.8	87.3	86.9	86.8	88.8	94.1	97.7	98.0	95.5	95.3
Hungary	96.5	85.0	82.4	81.9	84.4	85.6	86.8	90.7	95.1	99.4
Poland	88.4	82.2	84.4	87.6	92.1	98.6	104.5	111.7	117.1	121.9
Romania	94.4	82.2	75.0	76.2	79.2	84.8	88.2	82.8	78.3	75.8
Russia	97.0	92.2	78.8	71.9	62.8	60.2	58.2	58.7	55.8	57.6
Slovakia	97.5	83.3	77.9	75.1	78.7	84.2	89.7	95.6	98.6	100.5
Ukraine	96.4	88.0	79.2	68.0	52.4	46.0	41.4	40.1	39.4	39.3
Yugoslavia	92.1	81.4	58.7	40.6	41.7	44.2	46.8	50.3	51.5	41.6

Note: Yugoslavia includes Serbia and Montenegro.

Source: *Economic Survey of Europe* (New York: United Nations, 2000), nos. 2/3.

Energy Costs. Except for Romania, East-Central Europe does not have much in the way of oil reserves. In the past, the Soviet Union took care of this problem, selling its allies plenty of oil at a fraction of its real market value. Freedom has its price, however, and as soon as Eastern Europe broke out of the Soviet bloc, the Soviet Union demanded full global prices, payable in hard currency, to meet the region's oil needs. Whereas the West experienced its own energy-based recession in the aftermath of OPEC price hikes in the 1970s, Eastern Europe began going through a similar experience only in the early 1990s.

Gulf War. For East-Central Europe, the West's 1991 war against Iraq, precipitated by Iraq's invasion of Kuwait, could not have come at a worse time. Iraq was an important trading partner for much of the region—far more so than for any Western member of the anti-Iraq alliance. Before the war intervened, East European teams worked there on numerous projects, installing modern machinery and receiving high salaries in return. Iraq was one of the few countries with which Eastern Europe ran trade surpluses, and it was willing to pay debts in oil, which Eastern Europe needed more than ever before. Overnight, that relationship ended. East-Central Europe's new location in the global economy made it imperative that it halt all ties with Iraq in 1990, in line with the international embargo that preceded and followed the Gulf War. Altogether, East-Central Europe lost tens of billions of dollars as a result of this war. Sanctions against Yugoslavia in the mid-1990s proved equally costly.

Arms Trade. Eastern Europe has had to agree to cut back drastically on its arms manufactures as a condition of receiving Western aid. But what is to replace this revenue producer? Weapons plants can be retooled to produce other goods, but the process takes a lot of time and money. In the meantime, disrupting production in this sector adds to the general economic collapse. It is especially painful because arms plants are frequently located in small cities far from the capital. When factories die in these areas, nothing takes their place. Perhaps not coincidentally, the

United States has used this opportunity to increase its own portion of the world arms trade. The U.S. share of arms sales to Third World countries, for example, increased from 56 percent in 1992 to 73 percent in 1993.[15]

Altogether, the first decade of transformation has been very difficult for East-Central Europe. As Table 27.3 shows, only Poland and Slovakia have managed to regain and even exceed their gross domestic product (GDP) level of 1989, although Hungary and the Czech Republic have come close. These countries have seen steady improvement since 1993 or 1994, and in this sense it can be said that by the beginning of the new century, life was beginning to get better. The same cannot be said for Bulgaria or Romania, or the former Yugoslavia (with the exception of Slovenia). Bulgaria suffered a devastating economic crisis in 1996, and Romania's attempts to grow were set back again in 1998. Serbia, reeling from sanctions and the effects of war, saw its GDP cut in half in the decade after 1989, while Croatia "recovered" to where, ten years later, its GDP hovered at about three-quarters its 1989 level. Ukraine, meanwhile, has suffered a depression of truly historic and painful proportions.

If we look at one classic indication of whether life has gotten better or worse, life expectancy, we see that the situation for the region is mixed (see Figure 27.1). By the late 1990s, people in the Czech Republic could expect to live about three and a half years more than they did in the Communist era, while those in Bulgaria now live about two years less. The more industrial-

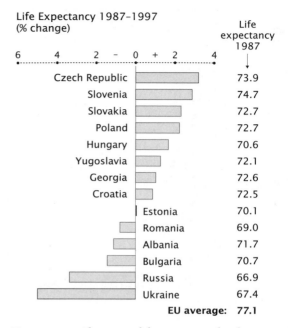

Figure 27.1   Changes in life expectancy for the region are mixed, roughly reflecting changes in basic economic conditions in the different countries.

ized northern countries of the region are clearly doing better than the lesser developed countries in the south, while even the latter are still doing better than Russia or Ukraine.

By the beginning of the twenty-first century, Eastern Europe had definitively reentered the global economy, although in a very divided way. With the elite countries of the north poised to become full, albeit weak, players in the EU, the southeastern countries are still, unfairly, treated more as paupers than as players.

Notes

1. Hans-Georg Heinrich, *Hungary: Politics, Economics, and Society* (Boulder, Colo.: Lynne Rienner, 1986), p. 44.

2. Daniel Chirot, "What Happened in Eastern Europe in 1989?" in Daniel Chirot, ed., *The Crisis of Leninism and the Decline of the Left* (Seattle: University of Washington Press, 1991), pp. 5–6.

3. See Roman Laba, *The Roots of Solidarity*

(Princeton, N.J.: Princeton University Press, 1991), pp. 15–18.

4. See Cheryl Payer, *The Debt Trap* (New York: Monthly Review Press, 1974).

5. For an overview of the initial process, see "Privatization: A Special Report," *RFE/RL Research Report*, April 24, 1992, pp. 1–90. For a detailed account, see Roman Frydman, Andrzej Rapaczynski, and John S. Earle, *The Privatization Process in Central Europe* (Budapest: Central European University Press, 1993). For a critical account, see Josef Poschl et al., *Privatization in Eastern Europe* (Vienna: Friedrich Ebert Stiftung, 1992). An interesting scholarly interpretation of the process is David Stark, "Path Dependence and Privatization Strategies in East Central Europe," *East European Politics and Societies* 6, no. 1 (Winter 1992): 17–54.

6. Tim Judah, "Croatia Reborn," *New York Review of Books*, August 10, 2000.

7. On pension reform, see the contributions by Maria Augusztinovics and Jerzy Hausner in *Economic Survey of Europe 1999*, no. 3 (New York: United Nations, 1999).

8. Milan Kundera, "What Is Central Europe?" abridged version available in Gale Stokes, ed., *From Stalinism to Pluralism* (New York: Oxford University Press, 1991).

9. See Peggy Watson, "The Rise of Masculinism in Eastern Europe," *New Left Review*, no. 198 (March–April 1993): 71–82.

10. To follow developments on international trafficking and Eastern Europe, see and subscribe to "Stop-Traffic" Web site at www.stop-traffic.org

11. On the lure of early rock-and-roll in Eastern Europe, see the wonderful Hungarian film *Time Stands Still* (directed by Peter Gothar, 1981). Interestingly, recreational drug use never caught on as in the West, both because of supply problems (tight border controls dissuaded potential smugglers, and low Eastern pay levels meant it was hardly worth the effort) and demand problems (alcohol has always been the drug of choice).

12. Cited by Peter Gowan, *The Global Gamble* (London: Verso, 1999), p. 218.

13. For a powerful critique of Western aid programs to Eastern Europe, see Janine Wedel, *Collision and Collusion: The Strange Case of Western Aid to Eastern Europe, 1989–1998* (New York: St. Martin's Press, 1998).

14. For two critical views on the role of financial institutions in the rebuilding of Eastern Europe, see John Feffer, *Shock Waves: Eastern Europe After the Revolutions* (Boston: South End Press, 1992), and Peter Gowan, "Old Medicine, New Bottles: Western Policy Toward East Central Europe," *World Policy Journal* 9, no. 1 (Winter 1991-1992): 1–33. For a more general critique of Western policy toward Eastern Europe and of the human costs of such policy, see Peter Gowan, *The Global Gamble* (London: Verso, 1999).

15. Eric Schmitt, "US Arms Merchants Fatten Share of Sales to Third World," *New York Times*, August 2, 1994.

C H A P T E R

28

Governance
and Policymaking

It is one thing to overthrow Communist Party rule. It is something very different, however, to construct a new system to take its place.

The paradox of the Eastern European revolutions of 1989 was that the next day, all the old state officials, save a few at the very top, went to work in the same way and in the same place as before. The police, the mayors, the journalists, the generals of the Warsaw Pact, and the functionaries in the ministries all stayed in place when the Communist Party lost power. There was no violent revolutionary upheaval anywhere in Eastern Europe; even in Romania, street fighting lasted only a few days and did not concern the old bureaucracy, which stayed at its posts. In this sense, every country, not just Czechoslovakia, had a Velvet Revolution.

This institutional continuity could not last indefinitely. One of the first tasks of the former dissidents who came to power in 1989 was to recreate government. It was not so much a matter of getting rid of old officials as of rethinking the very structure of the state, creating institutions appropriate to the kind of democracies the creators hoped to build. The new leaders had come to power in extraordinary, revolutionary ways, but they needed to devise ordinary methods for the transfer of power. They had to create new organs of power, devise rules for the relationships between the president and parliament, the executive and legislature, citizens and the state, parties and the state. Suddenly institutions were important. All the issues of state

building—issues that students in the West tend to see as matters settled long ago—had to be confronted as if for the very first time.

It might seem that politicians, in conditions like these, could calmly look around, take stock of the world's political institutions, and choose those that worked best. But although some lawyers and scholars did do just that, the new political arrangements that emerged had more to do with the domestic political battles of the day than with considerations of ideal democratic institutions. (For example, countries with strong single individuals leading the fight against communism, such as Poland and Russia, began to develop presidential systems; those where the struggle was more diffuse, such as Hungary and the former Czechoslovakia, produced parliamentary systems.) The rule seems to be applicable to the drafting of constitutions in all countries at all times: The pull of the present is at least as powerful as the lure of the future.

Organization of the State

Contrary to what many Americans believe, there are various types of democratic systems. The U.S. system, in fact, as a strong *presidential system*, is rather unusual, with its popularly elected president as the indisputable political leader who is responsible for forming a government, naming a cabinet, and shaping the legislative agenda. Most democratic systems are *par-*

liamentary systems, in which a single house of parliament is responsible for electing the country's political leader, who then rules in close cooperation with parliament and can be removed by parliament at any time. Some countries, like France, have a *semi-presidential system,* in which executive power is divided between a popularly elected president and a prime minister enjoying the support of the legislature.

In East-Central Europe, the clear preference so far has been for a parliamentary system, not a presidential one. Of the four central European countries, Hungary, the Czech Republic, and Slovakia all have strict parliamentary systems; the deputies, freely elected by the people, choose a prime minister to form a government. Even in Poland, Lech Wałęsa was able to push through only a semi-presidential system. The absence of a strong president, however, does not indicate a weak executive branch. On the contrary, *executive authority*—the power to carry out decisions—is strong throughout East-Central Europe, as befits a region undergoing rapid transformations where decisions need to be made fast and there is general agreement on the move to a market economy. There is not much check on the power of the executive either, as the judiciary tends to be weak in former Communist states.

One of the main criticisms heard from democratic activists was that the Communist system led to overcentralization of power. Such overcentralization occurred because Communist states, for the most part, were unitary as opposed to federalist. In a *unitary state,* the country is governed as if it were one giant unit, whereas in a *federal state,* only overarching affairs like defense and monetary policies are centralized; on other matters, local units have considerable autonomy. In the unitary states of Eastern Europe, power was extremely centralized. Authorities in the capital made all the important decisions. Local leaders were appointed from above and, deprived of their own tax base, had neither the funds nor the authority to take much action on their own. Whether they wanted to build a new school or increase support for local cultural activities, they needed approval from the center. Yugoslavia and Czechoslovakia, as well as the Soviet Union, were only formal exceptions to this rule. The diverse nationalities making up these countries formally had their own local governing bodies. Yet these were not true federalist arrangements; the central authorities still appointed local leaders, and the center alone exercised the power of the purse.[1]

One might assume, therefore, that postCommunist politics would entail new federalist structures, in which local regions and communities would take vast responsibility for their own affairs. In fact, that has not been the case. Three factors seem to be responsible for continued centralization. First, the new governments have been anxious to see their broad economic reform plans embrace the entire country, and so have been reluctant to cede power to local regions. Second, local regions themselves often fear the loss of state funds that might result from decentralization. Federalism is good for local political activists looking for a new institution to control, but regular people tend to fear new and costly experiments. The former Communists have successfully appealed to these fears. When the Democratic Left Alliance won power in Poland in 1993, for example, it cited local fears about the costs of taking over public schools as justification for its abandonment of regional decentralization schemes.

Finally, federalism has not taken hold for the simple reason that regional autonomy has traditionally been one of the area's greatest problems, as evidenced by the breakup of Czechoslovakia and the disintegration into chaos of the former Yugoslavia and Soviet Union. Countries that have already experienced regional division have been the most anxious to maintain strong central control. In the Czech Republic, for example, the Klaus government tried to block the creation of new regional self-governing bodies even after the constitution of December 1992 explicitly required that such bodies be formed.

Allowing real decentralization, the government felt, would re-create the kind of administrative dualism that precipitated the breakup of Czechoslovakia in the first place. This episode also serves to remind us that just because a constitution requires a particular arrangement does not mean that such an arrangement actually exists.

In general, relations between the legislature and the executive have not been highly contentious in post-Communist East-Central Europe. The legislatures have generally been supportive of a strong executive office, both because they agree that rapid decisions are necessary in the chaotic post-Communist environment, and because a strong executive is simply the usual European way.

The Executive

Poland was the first East European country to undergo major political transformation. It did so, however, before its politicians were sure just how far change would be allowed to go. The result was initial instability, as institutions were created for a political situation that almost immediately became obsolete. Poland's path to postcommunism began with the 1989 roundtable negotiations between the Communist party and the opposition solidarity union, still many months before the fall of the Berlin Wall. Opposition negotiators had a very delicate objective: to ease the Communists out of power and establish a foundation for full parliamentary democracy, while assuring party hardliners and the Soviet Union that their interests would still be taken into account. The goal was to engineer a stable transition, and that meant offering benefits to all sides.

The two sides worked out an arrangement for partially free elections, in which the Communists would be guaranteed a majority in the lower house, while a newly created upper house would be contested in full. In return for the government's final approval of the deal, Solidarity also agreed to the creation of a presidency. Because the president would be elected by parliament and the first parliament would be dominated by the Communists regardless of how people voted, the roundtable negotiators knew that General Wojciech Jaruzelski, who had imposed martial law banning Solidarity in 1981, would become Poland's president. They debated the powers of the presidency with this in mind. Solidarity wanted a weak president—someone to be little more than a reassuring symbol to the Soviet Union and domestic hard-liners. The Communists wanted a strong president who had the right to dissolve parliament and rule by decree. The rules that were finally drafted favored Solidarity's vision. As expected, General Jaruzelski was elected by parliament (though with only one vote to spare) and became essentially a figurehead president who helped keep the hard-liners at bay while allowing democratization to proceed on its own.

The situation was changing so suddenly, however, that even this arrangement soon became obsolete. A Solidarity official became prime minister in August. In November, the Berlin Wall came down, followed soon by the downfall of the governments of East Germany, Bulgaria, Czechoslovakia, and Romania. By the end of the year, it was clear that neither the Soviet Union nor local hard-liners would be needing the guarantees Poland's arrangement had left them. At the vanguard of political innovation ever since 1980, Poland now seemed to be lagging, so Lech Wałęsa decided that he would run for president—even though no elections were scheduled. He explained his decision as follows: "I don't want to, but I have to." Parliament duly changed the law, thus allowing for early presidential elections, and General Jaruzelski duly resigned. In December 1990, Wałęsa was elected president, this time in general elections open to all.

At this point the old arrangement proved intolerable, for Wałęsa had taken over a presidency with powers written for Jaruzelski. He wanted to be an activist president—a "president with an axe," he promised during the campaign—but the rules did not allow that. Wałęsa looked to the new parliament, elected in 1991, to ratify changes giving the presidency more power. But that was not so simple, for Wałęsa had alienated most of his political supporters by not attacking remnants of the old regime as vigorously as he had promised. The Center Alliance, for example, which had been created to promote Wałęsa's candidacy, became his fiercest opponent only months into his presidency. So although Solidarity supporters ostensibly won the 1991 parliamentary elections, the new parliament ended up in many ways more anti-presidential than before.

For the first six months of 1992, the president was in a virtually constant battle with the prime minister, and the existing constitution was useless in resolving the conflicts. On the contrary, it only made them worse. For example, the constitution implied, but did not explicitly state, that high-level military appointments should have the approval of the president. In fact, Wałęsa learned of them only from television news accounts. When he sought to maintain his own independent contacts with the military, the truculent defense minister accused Wałęsa of preparing a presidential coup d'état. Only when the prime minister and cabinet were forced to resign in June 1992 did parliament finally legislate a workable relationship between the president and parliament. The new arrangement, which the new constitution of 1997 formally enshrined, produced a semi-presidential system, in which power is distributed between the two authorities. This arrangement is a bit confusing (even for Poles), since it means there are basically two executive branches in Poland, the president and the prime minister, with the latter ultimately more important than the former. The president is weaker than in the United States or France but stronger than elsewhere in Eastern Europe except Russia.

In some ways, Poland's system seems to resemble that of the United States. The president is directly elected by the public to a five-year-term, has the right to propose legislation, and is in charge of foreign and defense policy. Parliament must pass all laws, but the president has the right to veto them. Parliament can override only by a two-thirds majority. The president can also demand that a constitutional tribunal rule on the constitutionality of legislation. The law is then suspended until the tribunal makes its decision.

Poland remains a parliamentary system, however, in that the chief executive is not the president but the prime minister, who is chosen by a parliamentary majority. The prime minister is responsible for the day-to-day workings of the government, such as drafting a budget or calling on the police to halt a demonstration. He or she can be ousted only if the government loses a parliamentary vote of confidence. Similar to Germany, Poland's system calls for a *constructive vote of no confidence*, meaning that the parliament must propose an alternative government at the same time it votes down the current one. In 2000, for example, the prime minister lost his parliamentary majority during midterm, but because parliament could not agree on a successor, he stayed on as head of a minority government.

Only in the former republics of Yugoslavia do presidents have greater power than in Poland, and that power has been due more to the war than to the constitution. The weakest presidency in Eastern Europe, however, can be found in the Czech Republic, owing both to the Czech Constitution and the behavior of its initial occupant, Vaclav Havel. According to the constitution, the president does not even have the power to propose legislation. Elected by parliament, not the public, the president can veto laws passed by the legislature, but the latter can override by a simple majority. Since this is the same number that was needed to pass the law in the first place, such a veto is not very effective. The president can dissolve parliament and call for new elections, but only if the lower house either votes out the prime minister or is incapable of passing legislation for more than three months. The president is not completely power-less. He or she appoints the prime minister, su-preme court, and constitutional court and is commander in chief of the armed forces. But for the first years of his presidency, Havel made lit-tle avail of the powers he had and did little to in-tervene in the workings of the government. In-stead, his was above all else a moral voice, attempting to guide the country's political as well as existential direction. So ingrained is the notion of a weak president, however, that when Havel intervened during a parliamentary crisis in 1998, this action led a sizable number of dep-uties to propose new legislation revoking the president's power of appointments.

Cabinet Government

In addition to the president or prime minister, the executive branch of government consists of the cabinet and the ongoing bureaucracy charged with implementing policy. Cabinet ministers in East European countries, as in other European democracies, are nominated by the prime minister and approved or rejected by par-liament. Once approved, they are largely free to pursue policy implementation vigorously in their areas of responsibility. Confrontations with parliament have been rare, as parliaments tend not to keep close tabs on the workings of the bureaucracy and the policies it implements.

This lack of attention is particularly evident in the crucial area of economic policy. The chief role of the legislature is to approve the annual budget proposed by the government. Legislative debates invariably change a few features, but by and large the budget is adopted in the form pre-sented by the government. Day-to-day eco-nomic management is also the prerogative of the executive office. Sometimes crucial decisions are made by one minister, without interference even from the prime minister. During the initial periods of post-Communist shock therapy, this practice of concentrating power—in this case, in the office of the Finance Ministry—reached

monumental proportions. In Poland, for exam-ple, Finance Minister Leszek Balcerowicz ran economic policy virtually as his own private fiefdom. Neither the prime minister nor presi-dent did anything to interfere.[2]

Since 1989, all East European governments have grappled with the question of how to pri-vatize the economy. This policy question has be-come almost the exclusive domain of the execu-tive branch. Government ministries were created to administer the extensive property transformation, and they have done so with only occasional intervention by the legislature. In Hungary, the State Property Agency decided which firms were to be privatized, to whom, and for how much. In Poland, firms in 1989 were le-gally governed by enterprise councils elected by the workforce, but once they conceded those rights to the Ministry of Property Transforma-tion, the latter decided on its own how to privat-ize those firms. In the former East Germany, a West German state agency, Treuhand, ran roughshod over all other interests in allocating state assets into private hands.

As noted in Chapter 27, the most difficult and controversial area of privatization concerns *re*privatization. Are people to be compensated for property taken over by the Communist par-ties? If so, how, and who decides the price? What form should compensation take, since the prop-erty itself, fifty years later, is not likely to exist in the form in which it was confiscated? These questions have aroused far more emotional dis-agreement than the issue of mere privatization. For that reason, governments decided that it was best for their own legitimacy to throw the issue into the legislatures' laps. Instead of proposing an unpopular policy that could bring down the government, why not make the elected repre-sentatives themselves suffer the consequences of such a controversial decision?

A major problem facing the executive bu-reaucracy as a whole is the absence of strict ethi-cal rules, which leads to recurring charges of conflict of interest. Ministers and their under-lings, for example, often sit on boards of directors of companies that they deal with in an official capacity. Publicly they explain this practice as a remedy for the shortage of sufficient experts in a given field. No doubt it also results from the comparatively low pay of government officials. They feel they are already sacrificing for the public good by agreeing to serve in government, and they see nothing wrong in earning a little extra on the side. For the public, however, what is going on is personal enrichment at public expense. Much of the time, of course, there may be nothing illegal going on. The practice does, however, lead to popular perceptions of wrongdoing and to much negative opinion about government. Close contacts between economic officials and Western banking elites have also led to charges that the bureaucrats are more interested in their own good than in what is good for the country, and the region has had its share of scandals that seem to substantiate such accusations. Suspicion is not likely to disappear until strict ethical rules are put in place.

Bureaucracy and Civil Service

Below the rank of cabinet minister and vice minister, we enter the ranks of the civil service bureaucracy. The term *bureaucracy* often carries with it a negative connotation, implying cronyism and routine decision making, but a well-functioning bureaucracy is a vital part of sound government. The classic definition was offered in the early twentieth century by the great German social scientist Max Weber (1864–1920), for whom the ideal type of bureaucracy is the group of neutral, well-trained civil servants who administer state policy continuously regardless of which party or government is in office. In the years since the fall of communism, one of East-Central Europe's main goals has been the construction of just such a bureaucracy. To try to achieve this goal, the new regimes have first had to attack the old system of state service known as *nomenklatura*. In that arrangement, the Party chose people for key po-

sitions in the state and economy on the basis of political criteria. The various levels of the Party kept lists of individuals suitable for appointment. When important jobs became available, such as the head of a local factory, manager of a housing cooperative, local police chief, mayor, or even deputy to the parliament, the candidates would come from these lists. Although the *nomenklatura* system abated over the years as increasing numbers of professionals were trained, it remained a continual source of friction between the state and society, a reminder that high qualifications and good work were not always enough for someone to get ahead.

The post-Communist system is supposed to be based on merit. People are supposed to obtain positions in the bureaucracies because of training or hard work or because they are elected to office. And for the most part it has worked this way. Many people who could not advance in the past, for political reasons, have been able to make careers in the post-Communist political, economic, and cultural spheres. The number of political appointments to state positions has been reduced by all governments in the region, and professional training for civil servants has been introduced as the rule. Countries seeking to enter the European Union (EU) must pass a civil service law as a precondition for consideration. Expertise, efficiency, and political neutrality are stressed as the ethos of the new public servant.

Transforming bureaucracies, however, is a slow process. In the first post-Communist years, attempts at change did not seem to be working out the way they should. On the contrary, bureaucrats from the past were holding onto their positions or even moving ahead. The old system was gone, but the same people who had made it in the old system were making it in the new one. For people at the top levels of the old bureaucracy, such as bankers and diplomats, perseverance was sometimes facilitated by complex personal ties, which created room for blackmail and corruption. For many civil servants, however, the reason was simply that the old officials had experience and better training. They may have gotten that experience and training for the wrong reasons, but if the new system was to be based on qualifications, these people had them.

Peggy Simpson, an American journalist living in Poland, told me a story that illustrates this scenario well. In one small town, a newly elected mayor, hoping to weed out purely political appointees and put together a staff of competent officials, ordered new civil service exams for the old staff and anyone else who wanted to take them. When the results came in, the old personnel had the best grades. The "democratic" bureaucracy thus came to look almost identical to the "Communist" bureaucracy, despite the abolition of *nomenklatura*. The old elite was managing to become the new elite.

This story reminds us that there was no violent revolution in Eastern Europe. It also reminds us of the problems a peaceful revolution can create. The old system was overthrown, yet those who had served it were not thrown in jail. This tolerance showed admirable restraint, rare among revolutionaries. But as economic conditions for the majority deteriorated, it also became a recurring source of anger. "We overthrew the system," people would say, "and the same old Communists reap the rewards." Politicians and parties soon tapped into these sentiments, and the result has been a call for "de-Communization" to get the old officials out of power. Notwithstanding the presence of former *nomenklatura* bureaucrats, however, East-Central Europe is well on its way to building a professional bureaucracy staffed with many new people trained in professional and nonpolitical ways.

Public and Semipublic Institutions

East-Central Europe emerged from the Communist system in 1989 with tens of thousands of state-owned enterprises (SOEs). Under the old system, and particularly in the early Communist years, the chief goal of SOEs was not to make a profit, and not even to make goods, but to help ensure social and political stability. State factories and enterprises "solved" the unemployment problem by providing jobs for all. They tackled housing problems by building apartment complexes for their employees. Trade unions at the work sites arranged vacations for employees and summer camps for their children, and often they distributed scarce food and appliances to their members. By acting much like social welfare agencies in the West, besides producing goods, SOEs were a crucial part of the entire political system.

Since 1989, the nature of Eastern Europe's state-owned enterprises has changed dramatically. In the first place, each country has embarked on a program of privatization. But even where an enterprise has retained its state-owned character, its role has been fundamentally transformed. State enterprises since 1989 are charged with making a profit and are threatened with closure if they cannot perform. Consequently, most of them are no longer the social providers they were in the past. They have sold their housing units, closed their vacation bureaus, and stopped procuring scarce consumer goods for their employees. Most important, they no longer guarantee citizens a job. Not all SOEs have cut all their services. In cities that are built around a single state enterprise and thus have an inflexible labor market, the enterprise typically maintains more services than in cities where the labor market is more open. Because of the difficulties in privatizing an entire economy, state enterprises have not completely disappeared. Indeed, the state has often needed the income they provide since, as noted in Chapter 27, private enterprises have been given extensive tax breaks.[3] Particularly for those countries entering the EU, however, the days of SOEs are numbered. Except in the health and education sector, the region will continue its radical privatization policies at least until a change in all of Europe's political culture back to a more statist fashion.

As enterprises become privately owned and

individually managed, the role of state regulation becomes increasingly important. This is particularly so in East-Central Europe, where an extreme reaction against state control has led to widespread neglect of working conditions and on-the-job safety. Governments have been so anxious to promote private business that they have offered not only tax breaks but also virtual immunity from regulations. Safety rules, overtime provisions, guaranteed vacations, and other benefits are violated with impunity, particularly in small, private firms. The situation is somewhat better in larger firms with a higher profile and in state firms where unions are still active. Even there, however, official accounts regularly report routine violations and lax regulation.

Willful neglect is not the only cause. Insufficient budgetary funds are also a key problem, and regulatory agencies tend to be at the bottom of the receiving line.[4] This neglect extends to pollution control agencies. While Eastern Europe has made some strides in fighting pollution, such as installing filters on smokestacks in the giant factories, agencies do not actively combat the dumping of toxic wastes or the lesser but steady polluting practices of small, private firms.

One reason there is little money in the coffers for regulatory agencies is that tax collection does not yet operate efficiently. Under the Communist system, governments got their funds simply by taking the revenues earned by the country's enterprises. The need for separate, elaborate taxation policies appeared only with the privatization of the post-Communist era. Within a few years, most countries in the region introduced a progressive personal income tax, levied through deductions and a year-end reckoning (as in the United States), as well as a host of disparate corporate taxes. The problem is collecting these taxes, particularly the corporate kind. While personal taxes are deducted from an individual's paycheck, business taxes are regularly avoided. In part, this is due to overly generous official tax breaks, an increasingly

common practice worldwide as governments scramble for new investment capital. A large part of the problem, however, stems from inadequate and underfunded state regulatory agencies, which are notoriously unable to collect taxes from small businesses, the fastest growing sector of the post-Communist economy. Economists estimate that millions of dollars in revenues are lost each year to unpaid taxes. More efficient collection depends on having more efficient bureaucracies, which in turn depends on more state revenues. Poor tax collection is likely to persist for some years to come, as long as governments continue to see the promotion of business activity as the number-one policy goal and turn a blind eye to the private sector's willful tax evasion.

Other State Institutions

In the communist era, East European citizens had frequent complaints about the police and the judicial system, and objected to the lack of true self-government. Since 1989, these institutions have all undergone thoroughgoing reform, although not always producing the most desirable results.

The Military and the Police

Most nondemocratic countries in the late twentieth century have had strong and independent militaries. This has been true for Latin America, which has seen a succession of military dictatorships, and even for China, where the military has frequently played a more important political role than the Communist Party. It has not been the case in Eastern Europe, however. From 1945 until 1989, the military played a secondary, subordinate role in the political system. In fact, it was doubly subordinate—first to the ruling Communist Party and then to the Soviet Red Army.

The Party established the principle of civilian

rule as soon as it came to power. But the subordination to the Soviet Union was especially painful. Each country's particular military history and doctrines were ignored as the Soviet Union became the model for everything. Generals were trained in Soviet schools and based their plans on Soviet interests. Overall strategy was determined by the Warsaw Pact, ostensibly a union for regional defense against NATO. In reality, the Warsaw Pact's chief goal was to uphold Soviet domination of the region. This reality was made dramatically clear in 1968, when the Soviets invaded Czechoslovakia and used East European troops to assist in the occupation. Only Romania refused to participate.

Perhaps because the military was not directly involved in government, it remained a popular institution in Eastern Europe. Even in Poland, when the military declared martial law in 1981, most people recognized that it was simply doing the bidding of the Party. This lingering support has helped the military redefine its role in the post-Communist era. The military is still subordinate to the civilian government (in this sense, the Communist past has been helpful for democracy). But it is being repackaged as a vital national institution. It is presented as a symbol of independence, an institution that has always served the nation loyally and will continue to do so in the future. The military is thus helping to legitimate the new political systems by linking them to the pre-Communist past.

The new prominence of the military might lead some to consider it a potential threat to the new democracies. If economic conditions deteriorate, might the military seize power, as it has done so often in other countries undergoing economic crisis? This possibility does not seem very likely, for three reasons. First, no discernible tendencies in East-Central Europe's military establishments are currently pushing in this direction. Second, civilians are still very much in control; the military's new public image is a result of government efforts to attract public support, not a campaign by the military itself. Third, as the military is breaking with its

Communist past, it is becoming increasingly integrated into the Western alliance. In 1999, Hungary, Poland, and the Czech Republic joined NATO, where civilian control of the military is an enshrined principle. During the Kosovo conflict and the NATO bombing of Yugoslavia, Bulgaria, Romania, and neighboring Albania, all opened their airspace to NATO planes, and NATO rewarded them by promising to consider them for membership in the future. All of the countries in the regions have gone along with Western sanctions against Iraq and Yugoslavia and have cut back military expenditures in line with Western requests. For all these reasons, the military is unlikely to pose a threat to civilian governments.

The exception to the story of a weak military is the former Yugoslavia. With the onset of civil war in 1991, the military emerged as a dominant political player in both Serbia and Croatia. That, however, has recently begun to change with the death of Croatia's President Franjo Tudjman in 1999 and the coming to power of liberals a year later, and the electoral defeat of Serbia's President Slobodan Milosevic in fall 2000. Until all the new borders of all the post-Yugoslav countries have withstood the test of time, however, and the causes of the war are finally eradicated, the military will likely remain more powerful than elsewhere in Eastern Europe.

Far more than the military, it was the police that was the feared institution of Communist society. Too often an unchecked power with vast secret networks and large numbers of citizen collaborators frequently blackmailed into service, the police penetrated every aspect of everyday life. This was particularly true in the Stalinist era, although even in the late stages of the Communist period, citizens needed police approval for all kinds of common requests, such as obtaining a passport to travel abroad.

In a very real sense, reforming the police was the first order of business of the post-Communist period. The first task was to impose restraint. New governments gave orders, effective immediately, instructing the police to desist from arresting political activists and to allow basic democratic civic expression. Comprehensive internal reform, however, has come more slowly. Although some police officials were fired for their previous activities, most, even those engaged in active persecution of the opposition, were judged to have merely been following orders. These have been given new training and allowed to stay on the force. Retention rates are even higher among the top espionage forces, whose services have largely been retained, with orders to redeploy those services against other enemies.

Today most citizens clearly have a very different view of the police than they did in the past and no longer see them as a feared enemy. On the other hand, not everything has changed. When protesters from around the world swarmed on Prague in September 2000 to rally against globalization and the International Monetary Fund, Czech police arrested and held incommunicado thousands of people, denying them food and the right to contact an attorney, and reportedly beating many detainees.[5] It is possible that such force was used at the request of the West (Seattle police were equally ruthless in their repression of similar demonstrations in late 1999), but clearly much of the old repressive apparatus still remains in place. Old traditions always die hard.

The Judiciary

Citizens often come into conflict with the state, and parliaments and executives often come into conflict with one another. And although constitutions may serve as the ultimate authority, people regularly disagree on just what the constitution actually means. Resolving these conflicts is the task of the third branch of government, to which we now turn.

Constitutionally, as well as in public opinion and popular expectations, the judiciary is the least powerful of the three branches of government—more likely to accept the decisions of the executive and legislature than to challenge them. This relative weakness is rooted in two factors: East-Central Europe's long affiliation with continental European traditions, by which the judiciary has always been weaker than in the Anglo-American model, and the experiences of the Communist era, when the courts too often acted as the arm of the Communist Party. The people in the region do not seem to want an activist judiciary.

In the United States, the judiciary's role is to make sure not only that the people abide by the laws but also that the government does so. As a check on government, the judiciary plays a much less substantial role in East-Central Europe—as it does, indeed, in all of Europe. Of course, it played an even more pliant role during the Communist era, particularly in the early years, when the Party regularly violated judicial independence and instructed judges how to decide particular cases. The courts have regained their full independence today. As appointed rather than elected officials, judges naturally tend to share the same broad policy orientations as the leading government officials. But they are fully free to decide cases in accord with their consciences and based solely on the rule of law.[6]

Even with this independence, however, the courts still play a less activist role than in the United States. The difference is rooted in the very nature of the legal systems. In most of Europe, law is strictly codified, and the judiciary's responsibility is to apply the law as it is written. In the United States, ever since the early nineteenth century, the judiciary has cast itself as a check on government, an authority charged with deciding whether the other two branches of government have a right to act as they do. The U.S. Supreme Court not only applies the law; its statements *become* the law. East European courts share the dominant continental view that lawmaking should be left to legislators rather than judges.

Nevertheless, the judiciary does provide some check on government. Constitutional courts, charged with assessing the constitutionality of laws, now exist in all East European countries. Typically the president appoints the constitutional court's members, who are confirmed by parliament and serve for a set number of years. This body, however, can only suggest changes in legislation, and its decisions can usually be overturned by a new parliamentary vote. The government is sensitive to the decisions of its constitutional court and usually makes some effort to abide by the court's rulings. But in the end, it is parliament, not the court, that has the ultimate decision on what is and is not the law of the land. It would be wrong, in other words, to equate East-Central Europe's constitutional courts with the U.S. Supreme Court.

Of course, the influence of each constitutional court depends on the specific country. So far, Hungary has had by far the most active judiciary, with the constitutional court pushing to get involved in political issues that elsewhere are the prerogative of parliament. Indeed, one of the reasons de-Communization, or "lustration" (see the box, "Jan Kavan and the Perils of Lustration"), has not gone far in Hungary is that the constitutional court took action to prevent it, invalidating a 1991 law that had lifted the statute of limitations so that former Communists could be brought to trial. The court has intervened heavily on issues of privatization as well. By the mid-1990s, some felt the Hungarian constitutional court had become too active— too much like the U.S. Supreme Court—and had tried to define its role more narrowly. Nevertheless, the court largely maintained its interventionist behavior into the new century.

One of the most glaring weaknesses of Eastern Europe's judicial system is that it has traditionally been difficult for ordinary citizens to use. In Communist as well as continental traditions, citizens do not have much chance to appeal to the courts against abuses of power by government or by other citizens.[7] In response to the mass popular protests of 1989, as well as in an effort to create governments more responsive to citizens, the difficulty of legal appeal has recently begun to change. One of the most im-

portant innovations has been the introduction of the post of ombudsperson, or civil rights officer. Borrowed from Sweden, this institution was first established in Poland under the Communist system, in 1987, as part of the government's reform program. The ombudsperson is appointed by the president, subject to parliamentary approval, and is a sort of free-floating civil rights troubleshooter. Citizens appeal directly to the ombudsperson when they feel their civil rights have been violated by the government, and the ombudsperson takes up the matter directly with the offending institution or refers it for a binding court decision. At the request of an individual citizen or a government body (or on his or her own), the ombudsperson can identify a law or policy as contrary to the civil rights of a certain group of people and refer it to the constitutional court for a ruling. In the Communist era, the Polish ombudsperson intervened in the defense of workers' right to strike; in more recent times, this official has intervened (unsuccessfully) against rules mandating religious instruction in the public schools.

This new institution has been quite successful in making the daunting world of legality more accessible and user friendly. Hungary adopted it in 1993. The Czech Republic stalled but finally passed an ombudsman law in late 1999. The ombudsperson plays an important role in legitimizing the new political systems in the eyes of the population by giving people a sense that their voices can be heard.

Finally, most of East-Central Europe has now adopted the European Convention on Human Rights and recognizes the jurisdiction of the European Court of Human Rights in Strasbourg. Citizens in countries that have passed association agreements with the EU can now appeal their national courts to a European-wide body, where the decision is final.

Subnational Government

East-Central Europe does not have a tradition of strong independent local self-government. This

Jan Kavan and the Perils of Lustration

In Czech writer Franz Kafka's harrowing novel *The Trial*, Joseph K. is arrested one day and thrown into jail, without ever knowing the charges against him. In March 1991, something similar happened to veteran political oppositionist Jan K. A commission charged with uncovering former collaborators of the Czechoslovak secret police made the astonishing announcement that Jan Kavan, a parliamentary deputy and one of Czechoslovakia's most prominent oppositionist politicians for over two decades, had been an informer for the secret police. Kavan vehemently denied the accusation but, as if in a scene from Kafka, he could not learn the exact charges against him for quite some time, leaving him unable to organize his defense.

With this unhappy episode began the era of de-Communization, or lustration—the attempt to force out of public life those who collaborated with the Communist police. To some, lustration was a way of making sure that those responsible for the evils of the past would not unfairly benefit in the present. Responsibility would be determined by a commission that would review the files of the former police apparatus. As critics pointed out, however, such methods do not necessarily lead to the desired results. First, they are based on the erroneous assumption that the old files make it easy to learn who was a collaborator and who was not. In fact, the files can be quite unreliable. Someone "invited" in for a chat with the police, for example, might be identified as a collaborator without ever even knowing it. (The police, after all, had a quota to fulfill.) Even an anti-Communist oppositionist might be listed as an informant if, during an interrogation, he or she provided false information to mislead the police, and the police did not know the information was false.

Another problem with lustration laws is that they leave many of the real beneficiaries of the old regime untouched. In particular, they do not affect those officials who quickly got out of government, using their connections to strike it rich in the new business world, which is immune from the law's sanctions.

Nothing was ever proved against Jan Kavan. Kavan himself said only that when he was working as a dissident student activist in exile in 1969, he met to discuss émigré student matters with a staffer from the Czech embassy who claimed, quite plausibly, to be a supporter of the Prague Spring. Nevertheless, soon after the accusation, Kavan was forced out of parliament and publicly disgraced without ever having had a proper trial. He was abandoned even by the majority of his own comrades, most of whom had contributed far less than Kavan had to the struggle for democracy.

In October 1991, the Czechoslovak parliament voted to formalize lustration, banning all former "collaborators" from working for the next five years in ministries or as senior administrators in universities or state enterprises. Germany has gone even further in trying to root out collaborators of the former East German security police—further than it ever went in rooting out former Nazis after World War II. Thousands of officials were fired or disgraced, including the first prime minister chosen *after* the fall of the Berlin Wall. In Hungary, the ruling Democratic Forum talked a great deal about "getting rid of the Communists," but took no legal steps to bring this about. Lech Wałęsa acted the same way in Poland, talking about the need to prosecute former Communists when he was running for president but dropping the issue after his election. Yet not everyone in Poland acted like Wałęsa. In June 1992, Interior Minister Antoni Macierewicz produced a list purportedly naming dozens of former agents who were now serving in the Polish parliament. The list included individuals with stellar oppositionist credentials, such as the leaders of militant anti-Communist parties and even Wałęsa himself. In January 1996, a prime minister was forced to resign on charges that he had spied for the Russians. In both cases, the charges were shown to be inaccurate, but they demonstrated that without a formal lustration process, a more dangerous informal one was inevitable. And so in 1999, Poland finally passed a lustration bill requiring judges and candidates for public office to declare whether they had ever collaborated with the Communist police. The penalty for those who lie (though not those who admit to having collaborated) is a ten-year ban on public service.

In Bulgaria, meanwhile, no lustration law was passed, although the government did prosecute selected officials of the old regime, including Party leader Todor Zhivkov. As for Romania, far from initiating any lustration, opposition leaders charged that the new government was actively using the services of people with "dirty hands."

Overall, what has been the result of lustration and de-Communization? Probably not much. The ostensible aim was not only to punish servants of the old regime, but also to cleanse the new government by removing sources of corruption and blackmail. There is no evidence that lustration has achieved such results. On the other hand, neither has it crippled the bureaucracy, as its critics feared. Although some individuals have been unfairly accused and forced out of their positions,

proponents of radical lustration have been kept in check by the critics. Most government employees survived in their posts, continuing to do the work they had done in the past. Lustration fever declined after the breakup of Czechoslovakia in 1993. Each republic had more pressing tasks at hand, and the controversy over the Kavan issue stifled some of the righteous indignation so evident at the beginning.

Perhaps the most dangerous consequence of lustration has been the way it legitimized the search for "enemies." If and when conditions decline in the future, demagogues may be able to win support for an antidemocratic program by promising to "root out" enemies, just as lustration offered to root out those responsible for communism. Witch-hunts are always an easy way to curry favor with a frustrated populace. At the same time, they are far more dangerous to democracies than the presence of a few former police agents. Politics based on the hunt for enemies always has unfortunate consequences for civil society and for a civilized sphere of public debate.

In January 1996, Jan Kavan was officially cleared of all charges. Two years later, he became the Czech Republic's foreign minister.

See the excellent report by Lawrence Weschler, "The Velvet Purge," *New Yorker*, October 19, 1992, pp. 66–96.

---

fact derives from both the region's long history of foreign occupation and the interwar years of independence, when each state dreamed up grand developmental schemes that could be implemented only by an interventionist central government.

One of the chief accusations against the Communist system was that too much power was concentrated in the center. As a result, post-Communist East-Central Europe has done some experimenting with decentralization. The process, however, is far from complete. For one thing, even the most committed decentralizers

in the national governments have not wanted to give up control all at once. They have preferred to institutionalize the new rules and procedures of a market economy and *then* hand over some power to local authorities. In addition, many leaders remain suspicious of local power, citing the Yugoslav, Czechoslovak, and Soviet examples in which regional governments turned into alternative power bases, leading to secession and, in two of the three cases, civil war.

There is an irony in the widespread desire to give local communities more control over their own affairs. Although they could not elect their own leaders in the old system, small communities actually did not do so badly. Communism was, in fact, rather congenial to local interests. Since investment decisions were made with political stability rather than profits in mind, the central government distributed resources widely. Small cities unlikely to receive investment funds in a private economy (and unable to find them today) had new factories literally thrust on them. Local authorities, rewarded based on how well they administered their areas, had a strong interest in forcefully representing local needs to higher authorities. And the higher authorities, wanting stability, kept doling out funds for wasteful factories and unnecessary cultural activities. Small towns therefore had clout for two reasons: because they were run by Party activists trying to make a career for themselves and because the government put money into projects just to keep people employed rather than to make a profit.

The transition to a market economy has changed this rather congenial arrangement. The new central governments needed to reduce expenditures and cut subsidies in their efforts to balance their budgets and please foreign lenders and potential investors. The first way they did so was by dramatically cutting aid to local communities. In Poland, for example, soon after the first free local elections in May 1990, the central government shifted to local governments the responsibility for funding day care centers, nurseries, cultural institutions, and local utilities. The problem was that the local communities were unable to support these services. Many towns do not even have regular revenues, both because the large enterprises in their areas are closing down and because tax collecting, where it exists at all, is so irregular. As former Solidarity officials took over local power, they had to make the kinds of tough budget decisions no politician wants to make. In two cities I visited in 1994, two former Solidarity activists who had become elected officials were fighting for their political lives because they had had to close a few sparsely used day care centers. "I didn't fight against communism in order to do this,"

they both told me. Inevitably, in the 1994 local elections, they were both branded as "anti-children" politicians and were defeated.

Local governments faced similar problems throughout Eastern Europe. Moreover, besides fighting with the central government, local officials also began to fight one another. The first free local elections in Hungary in 1990, for example, produced situations in which opposition parties won a majority in local councils while former Communists won election as mayors. Instead of trying to manage this outcome, quite common in democracies, the local councils in about one hundred small towns and villages made use of loopholes to prevent the mayors from taking office. Such activities would come back to haunt the non-Communist politicians in the form of accusations that they were obstructing stable government.

One of the reasons local affairs often became somewhat chaotic was the almost complete absence of political parties at the local level. The forty-five-year monopoly of power by the Communist Party, followed by a general dissatisfaction with parties afterward, meant that when Communist rule collapsed, no organized parties were ready to coordinate power anew. The new parties of the anti-Communist opposition were based in large urban centers. In small towns, the new elite consisted of isolated individuals with little experience in working together in complex organizations. The former Communists repeatedly harped on this theme of their opponents' political inexperience, in contrast to their own political seasoning. Opinion polls show that dissatisfaction with quarrelsome new politicians, and appreciation of the former Communists' more level-headed approach, were among the key reasons for the latter's electoral successes in the mid-1990s, and their likely renewed victories early in the new century.

It would be quite wrong, however, to concentrate on the negative features of post-Communist local politics. The other side of the coin is that local areas are now free to govern themselves. Where the central Party apparatus used to appoint mayors and the city council, now they are elected by the citizens. The new, democratically elected leaders can make decisions about the town that reflect their own interests rather than the interests of planners in Warsaw or Prague or Budapest. Small cities may no longer have friends in the capital always willing to throw money their way, but at least they are free to devise their own solutions to the problems they face. For a great many people, that is the most important feature of all.

The European Dimension

All of the other countries discussed in this book are members of the EU, and the tasks they face in the coming years are to deepen integration and make the transition to the euro without thoroughly diluting their national identities. For the countries discussed in this part, the great wish is to *become* EU members. They still see this as the culmination of a struggle for national identity—to be recognized as "Europeans" rather than, say, "Communists"—more than they see it as a challenge. Nevertheless, the process of actually entering the EU in the coming years will pose many tough challenges. Can the Eastern applicants persuade the EU to allow quick accession, or will they be forced to wait for many years? Can they convince their citizens that membership is desirable, even if it proves to be quite costly? Can they enter as fully equal members, or will they be condemned to second-class status?

The EU did not exactly welcome Eastern Europe's initial expressions of interest in joining after 1989. It had evolved in the era of a divided Europe and had become quite comfortable with the status quo. It had just gone through the process of admitting the poorer countries of Spain and Portugal and was not anxious to repeat the experience. Germany's annexation of the former East Germany was proving to be extraordinarily costly to the EU as a whole, and the price tag persuaded even sympathizers that the East

was not even remotely prepared for membership. Finally, the EU's initial concern after 1989 was maintaining good relations with the Soviet Union (which survived until 1991) and feared that EU enlargement would endanger those relations. For all these reasons, the EU was extremely hesitant about reaching out to new members after the fall of communism.

Yet the EU was in a dilemma. It had bandied about all-European unification as an ultimate goal ever since its foundation. Now that the East was ready to pursue it, the EU could not very well do nothing. Initially it tried to restrict itself to financial aid. In 1990 it created the aid agency PHARE and the European Bank for Reconstruction and Development, both aimed at providing assistance for market transformation. Events then pushed things along even further. In the summer of 1991, the Soviet Union imploded and soon disintegrated. Eastern Europe sought to use this moment to turn even more to the West, and the new Russian leaders made clear that they did not oppose this. Soon after, Yugoslavia broke apart in a violent war, and the EU realized it could not stay indifferent to what happens in the East.

Beginning in late 1991, the EU began offering "association" agreements with the Eastern European states, intended chiefly to placate the East while stalling on the key question of membership. Eastern Europe wanted to join the EU for its technology, prosperity, and democratic stability, but most of the benefits of these initial agreements went to the West. In return for these EU gestures, the East had to open up its markets and allow its firms to be privatized to Western buyers, but the EU maintained import restrictions in such key sectors for the East as textiles, coal, steel, and agriculture.

It was only in 1998, nearly a decade after the fall of the old system, that the EU finally announced it was ready to bring in new members. It could scarcely postpone matters any longer. The Eastern countries had maintained their new democratic systems, had accepted the new market rules, and had been vetted and accepted by the International Monetary Fund (IMF) (and some even by NATO). And so the EU now divided the region into "fast-track" and "slow-track" countries. The first group, consisting of Poland, Hungary, the Czech Republic, Slovenia, and Estonia, would be brought in first; the second—Bulgaria, Romania, Slovakia, Lithuania, and Latvia—would be considered only afterward. When all this will happen is still not clear. Fast-track countries wanted a precise date, but the West resisted. Sometimes it talks about 2003, but then backtracks and says that all depends on when the East is "fully" ready.

The stalling, in other words, continues, and the East can do nothing about it. As EU officials say, "The Eastern states are joining us; we are not joining them." Evidently the EU is still not fully convinced that joining is a good idea. It is not hard to understand why. If all ten applicants had been allowed to enter in 1997, the EU would have increased its population by one-third but its Gross Domestic Product (GDP) by only 5 percent.[8] The Western fear is that the poorer East will ultimately cost more in subsidies than they could contribute in GDP. The East counters that its large markets and access to Russia and Asia will be beneficial to the West too, but so far the latter remains unconvinced.

The second challenge facing the aspiring Eastern countries is to convince their citizens that the effort is worth the price. So far, the costs are both economic and political. The East has opened up its markets to Western goods and its parliaments to Western laws (most parliamentary activity in fast-track countries since 1998 has been about changing national law to conform to EU law) and has not yet seen much benefit. Domestic industry has lost customers to Western companies and ownership shares to Western capitalists, while the imposition of EU law, with virtually no discussion in parliament, means the export of the EU's notorious "democratic deficit" whereby rules are imposed from above rather than legislated from below. The economic costs of membership have many farmers and small businesspeople worried about

the future, and the "hijacking" of the legislature to EU law has led right-wing nationalists to mobilize against this "new dependency." Negotiating a way through this likely resistance will not be easy for Eastern European elites.

Finally, will membership really signify equal "European" status, or will the Eastern states be relegated to some kind of second-class citizenship? In the past, the EU has operated on the principle of formal equality, where every state is considered a fully equal member and important decisions must be made unanimously. Can it—and will it want to—maintain such rules with ten new and much poorer additions? Already the EU is talking about the new countries' entering with slightly different rules. The new applicants might not be able to join in as part of the new European Monetary Union, with the euro as their main currency. Or they might be excluded from the Schengen Accord, allowing unrestricted travel among EU countries (because of the latter's fear of a flood of refugees from the poorer East). Discussions such as these signify the continued resistance on the part of many Western elites and citizens to the incorporation of the new countries as full and equal partners. On the question of visa-free travel, some Eastern Europeans have reservations too—not because they do not want to travel freely in Europe but because they do not want to exclude their ethnic nationals farther east from doing the same. (The Schengen policy insists that member countries impose similar restrictions on entry from the rest of the world.) Since 1989, Hungary has had a very liberal entry policy for ethnic Hungarians living in Romania and Serbia, and Poland has maintained easy entry for people from neighboring Lithuania and Belarus. Both would have to be curtailed under the Schengen Accord.

Is the West willing to use its resources to improve the conditions of Eastern Europe in order to facilitate full equality? So far, it does not seem so. It did more to ease the entry of Spain and Portugal than it is currently doing for the Eastern applicants. For example, it allowed those countries to maintain import restrictions in order to help local industry but has insisted that the East open its markets fully. Scholars trying to characterize the nature of the relationship between the EU and the Eastern applicants have resorted to unflattering analogies: missionary-savage or priest-penitent.[9] Each dramatizes the profound economic and existential inequalities at the heart of this relationship. One way or another, the process so far entails the EU (and, of course, the United States, through the IMF and NATO in which the United States is the main party) whipping the East into shape. It may do so nastily (East as savage) or nicely (East as penitent), but either way, it is clear who is in charge. How each side deals with these inequalities will have a crucial effect on European politics in the next decades.

The Policymaking Process

For countries trying to enter the EU, which means virtually all of East-Central Europe, there are two dimensions of policymaking decisions: those related to EU accession and those focused on purely domestic policy. Policymaking for EU matters is something special. All applicant countries are required to make changes in their laws to conform to EU law if they wish to be considered for membership. This leads to a situation where special national commissions meet with special EU commissions to review national law and see where it needs adaptation. National parliaments then do the job in pretty much a pro forma fashion. This is what is meant by the export of democratic deficit. It also shows the power of the executive branch, rather than the legislature, to shape policy outcomes.

Aside from issues related to EU accession, most law is made by national parliaments or state agencies on behalf of national constituencies. Who has influence over these decisions? In the United States, the crucial informal policymaking role is performed by lobbies, which un-

dertake lavish campaigns promoting the interests of specific organizations or individuals and aimed exclusively at winning over a few legislators or regulators. Who tries to organize decision makers in East-Central Europe?

In the early post-Communist period, lobbying had a bad reputation in East-Central Europe, as it once did in the United States. No groups or organizations maintained separate, full-time lobbying organizations like those common in the West. Citizen groups and trade unions also refrained from lobbying because they believed that democratic parliaments would look out for their interests without organized pressure. Corporations or foundations, meanwhile, did not lobby for the simple reason that they were only beginning to function in this period.

The new politicians tended to offer a refreshing though naive vision of themselves as actors who vote solely according to conscience. The reality was quite different. Many legislators commonly maintained numerous ongoing connections with private businesses. Conflict-of-interest laws are still rare. Politicians and parliamentarians regularly sit on boards of directors of new private companies or have an economic interest in the success of a firm or branch that stands to profit from a specific piece of legislation. In such conditions, lobbies are quite superfluous.

Of course, groups influence policy without having formal lobbies. On concrete policy issues, such as health care or education, parliamentarians try to satisfy the wishes of the doctors' association or the teachers' union not because these groups have formal lobbies in Warsaw or Prague or Sofia, but because they have strong organizations that can potentially mobilize their supporters if they want to.

Certainly the most influential lobby in East-Central Europe has been the "lobby of the West," including the international business and financial community (IMF and World Bank), Western governments, and the EU. After 1989, each post-Communist country thought that its best chance for success was to be invited into the

West's institutions or to be chosen for investment by a multinational corporation. For this to happen, it had to win a seal of approval from Western banks and governments. Each country sought to convince the West that it, more than its neighbor, was the region's most stable and reform-minded country of all. Consequently, each tried to introduce whatever policies official Western advisory teams recommended.

This kind of influence extends not just to parliaments but to quasi-governmental organizations such as national tripartite councils, where representatives of business, labor, and the government meet to discuss issues of industrial relations. Despite the formal independence of these boards, they tend to limit themselves carefully to what international financial agencies deem acceptable. To cite one participant in the Bulgarian tripartite commission, the negotiations were "not tripartite but quadripartite, with the main partner [being] the IMF."[10]

Other strong pressures on parliaments come from nationalist groups in the multiethnic countries and from the church. These interest groups are able to influence policymaking far out of proportion to their actual numbers. Nationalists came to dominate policy discussion in Yugoslavia in the same way that militarists dominated policy debate in the cold war United States and Soviet Union: by exaggerating the threat from the other side and arguing that it is

better to be safe than sorry. As each side began mobilizing against "the other," the "other" mobilized back, thus "proving" to each that the other really was dangerous and setting in motion the vicious circle from which we still have not emerged. As for the Church, particularly in the strongly Catholic countries of Poland, Slovakia, and Croatia, where political parties are still weak, it exerts power through its direct access every Sunday to millions of citizens and through its control of several media channels. With organization such as this, no groups want to tackle the Church. Consequently, despite opinion polls showing strong public support for prochoice policies in all of these countries, it is the Church that has set the tone of the discussion on abortion.

When communism fell, these already organized interests had the most influence on domestic policy. That is now beginning to change, due to the emergence in the 1990s of many nongovernmental organizations. Working on behalf of civic, environmental, and gender issues, for example, such organizations were widely ignored during the first decade of transformation but are likely to become more influential. While politics in post-Communist Eastern Europe has so far been shaped largely by organized elites and foreign actors, social movements are likely to demand a more important role in the future.

Notes

1. On the nature of federalist institutions in former Communist Eastern Europe, see Rogers Brubaker, *Nationalism Reframed* (Cambridge: Cambridge University Press, 1996); and Valerie Bunce, *Subversive Institutions* (Cambridge: Cambridge University Press, 1999).

2. This style of authoritarian imposition has been characteristic of radical capitalist marketization policies not just in Eastern Europe but in Latin America too. See Bela Greskovits, "The Loneliness of the Economic Reformer," in his *The Political Economy of*

Protest and Patience (Budapest: Central European University Press, 1998).

3. See David Ost, "Shock Therapy and Its Discontents," *Telos*, no. 92 (Summer 1992): 107–112.

4. For a general discussion of East European budgetary problems, see John Campbell, "The Fiscal Crisis of Post-Communist States," *Telos*, no. 93 (Fall 1992): 89–110.

5. See accounts on www.praha.indymedia.org and www.undercurrents.org.

6. For a good account of the processes of building a new judicial system, see "Toward the Rule of Law," *RFE/RL Research Report*, July 3, 1992.

7. The United States is unique in both respects: in the number of lawsuits among citizens and in the ability of individuals to sue the government to force a change in the law, as in the landmark cases that abolished segregated schools (*Brown v. Board of Education*) and legalized abortion (*Roe v. Wade*).

8. Elena Iankova, "Converging with Europe? Central and Eastern Europe's Return to Capitalism," Institute for European Studies Working Paper 99.1, Cornell University, 1999, p. 2.

9. Andras Sajo, "Corruption, Clientelism, and the Future of the Constitutional State in Eastern Europe," *East European Constitutional Review* 6, no. 1 (Winter 1997); and Wade Jacoby, "Priest and Penitent: The European Union as a Force in the Domestic Politics of Eastern Europe," *East European Constitutional Review* 8, nos. 1/2 (Winter–Spring 1999).

10. Grigor Gradev, "Bulgarian Trade Unions in Transition," in Stephen Crowley and David Ost, eds., *Workers After Workers' States: Unions and Politics in Eastern Europe Since the Fall of Communism* (Boulder, Colo.: Rowman & Littlefield, 2001).

29

Representation
and Participation

In this chapter, we are concerned with how East-Central Europe's new systems of political representation actually work and how its citizens affect what happens in the political sphere. We go into considerable detail about the new parliamentary systems, focusing on Poland and Hungary in particular. We ask how parliaments make the new laws. What kind of people are members of parliament? What are the major parties? What do the parties actually do? Then we look at people's attitudes about politics, the role of the media, and the impact of trade unions, the Church, and other social organizations.

The Legislature

In the countries of East-Central Europe, as in most other parliamentary systems, the executive branch tends to shape public policy. Policies devised by cabinet ministries are presented for parliamentary approval. And since the cabinet already has parliamentary support (because such support was necessary for the government to be formed in the first place), the cabinet's proposals are usually approved by the legislature. In a parliamentary system, when one party has a majority, there can be no deadlock: The government passes those laws it wants to pass. When there is no majority party, however, and only a shaky coalition keeps the government in power, then the government either compromises or is removed.

How do Eastern Europeans choose their parliaments? How do the parliaments pass bills? Let us look at these processes in the context of parliament in Poland, since aside from Poland's relatively strong presidency, the process there is similar to what happens elsewhere in the region. The Polish parliament is made up of a lower house (Sejm) with 462 members and a 100-member senate. Elections for the lower house take place by a complex combination of proportional representation and individual selection. Unlike in the United States, districts are not represented by a single individual. Rather, the country is divided into several dozen electoral districts, each of which sends up to a dozen members to the Sejm. Citizens, however, vote for only one individual. The parties in each district run as many candidates as will enter the Sejm, and citizens put a mark by the name of their preferred candidate, listed under the candidate's party. In this way, the voter casts ballots simultaneously for an individual and a party. Seats are distributed first according to the number of votes received by each party. After that number is calculated, seats are distributed individually to those who received the greatest number of votes on the winning party lists. Elections to the senate are much simpler: Candidates in each district are listed on a ballot without their party affiliation, and the two candidates with the most votes in the district win.

The Procedures of Lawmaking

In Poland, as in most other parliamentary systems, parliament discusses chiefly bills submitted by the executive branch, rather than by individual legislators. Bills are first considered by the Sejm, the dominant body. If passed, the bill goes to the senate for possible revision. The revisions stand unless the Sejm overrides them by a vote of at least one more than 50 percent of its total members. As in the United States, the president can veto a law passed by parliament, which can then overturn the veto with a two-thirds majority. (In countries without a senate or a strong presidency, a majority vote by parliament is final.)

When the government has a strong majority in parliament, the outcome of debate is almost never in doubt. Indeed, parliamentary discussion plays a meaningful role, and opposition parties have real clout, only if the government lacks this majority. Hungary has had solid parliamentary majorities since 1990. The Czech Republic has also had strong parliamentary majorities, whereas Slovakia has had fragmented parliaments. Between 1989 and 1993, due to the large number of political parties, Poland regularly produced governments without a stable majority. As coalitions changed, so did the government; there were four of them during this four-year period. The country managed to produce a stable majority coalition only in 1993, after a new electoral law reduced the number of parties entering parliament. A different majority coalition came to power in 1997, but this broke down into a minority government in 2000.

The only way private citizens can directly influence the legislative process, apart from electing legislators and expressing opinions in the press and elsewhere, is through referenda.

For the most part, however, East European countries have discouraged the use of the referendum as a legislative tool. Except for binding plebiscitary votes, such as a yes or no to a new constitution (which is how Poland ratified its constitution in 1997), most referenda that are put on the ballot by civic groups gathering signatures are nonbinding on decision makers.

Parliamentarians

Parliaments can be either exciting arenas for passionate and policy-forming debate or boring chambers where deals worked out in the corridors are merely presented for ratification. We see some of each in East-Central Europe. Of the various post-Communist legislatures, the Polish parliament has had the most lively discussions, for several reasons: the large number of parties in parliament; the lack of a parliamentary majority from 1991 to 1993, which gave smaller parties a real chance to shape legislation; conflict with a president trying to expand his own powers; and a high degree of ideological antipathy between competing groups. (Some Poles add to this list a supposed "national inclination" for endless debate, citing the joke that whenever three Poles are talking there are at least four points of view.) Until 1998, the Hungarian legislature, on the other hand, was the most staid and predictable. This was particularly true in the initial post-Communist years, when a deal struck between the two largest parties (by which one held the prime minister's office and the other the presidency) meant that disagreements rarely came to the floor. (A 1997 deal between the two largest parties in the Czech Republic produced a similar lackluster Czech parliament in the late 1990s.) The presence of several dozen youthful deputies from the Alliance of Young Democrats (AYD) made Hungarian parliamentary sessions interesting to watch, but more for entertainment than for genuine insight into policymaking. This situation changed only after 1998, when the same AYD, now grown up, itself became the leading coalition partner and provoked a series of noisy fights with the other parties.

Parliaments have not been very well-liked in post-Communist countries. Within a few years after the fall of Communist rule, public opinion gave parliament some astonishingly low ratings—less than 10 percent public approval in Poland, Hungary, and the Czech and Slovak Republics. Such ratings reflected a general dissatisfaction with governments imposing painful economic changes. It also reflected the fact that many people who were elected to parliament after 1989 did not know how the institution was supposed to work. East European legislatures in the immediate post-Communist period were top heavy with writers and historians who could speak plenty about what was wrong with communism but did not know much about parliamentary procedure. For all the ridicule directed at Communist-era parliamentarians, who never had to stand for free elections, it turned out that they had a much better idea how parliamentary rules and procedures worked than did the dissidents who succeeded them. The former Communist deputies may never have voted a bill down, but they did negotiate with party circles on the inside, in corridors and in committees, to get specific clauses changed or have their local interests addressed. Indeed, this was one of the main reasons people began to vote the former Communist parties back into power: Voters appreciated the political professionalism that was lacking among the newcomers.

Parliament was also becoming much less attractive to potential newcomers. Highly skilled professionals are reluctant to run for office because of the low pay. Although higher than the average wage, the pay is substantially less than one can make, say, working in the new private sphere or for a multinational corporation. Polish parliamentary deputies in the mid-1990s earned about $500 per month plus a housing allowance, and more if the parliamentarian quit his or her other job (many do not). Low pay and the absence of conflict-of-interest laws have meant that parliamentarians try to supplement their income by being consultants and even members of the board of directors of private corporations. (Naturally, news about these connections leads to even lower popularity ratings for parliament.) By the mid-1990s, as a result of all this, many parties had to go searching for people willing to run on their tickets. (One candidate agreed to run on the Hungarian Socialist Party ticket in 1994 only because he was assured he would lose. Unfortunately, the party did so well that he won. He resigned the next day.) The parties often end up running people who are not even party members, but just upstanding citizens likely to have, or to be able to earn, popular support. This was standard practice in the Communist system too.

Parliamentary deputies do not get many benefits. Most do not even have their own offices or their own staffs. The parties they belong to have offices, but the individual representatives do not. Clearly such a situation does not make for strong, effective, self-confident parliamentarians. Parliament in the new Eastern Europe has been very much a male organization. Under the old system, women's share in parliament was about 25 to 40 percent. This relatively large number was due to the Communist system of "representation," in which the aim was to replicate in parliament the demographics of society. Workers, farmers, enterprise managers, cultural figures, and women all had their formal positions in parliament, even if real power was reserved for the top Party officials, almost all of whom were men. In the first free elections after 1989, the share of women parliamentarians dropped dramatically. Women won 7.3 percent of the seats in the first Hungarian parliamentary elections, 13.0 percent and 12.7 respectively in the 1990 Czech and Slovak elections, and 9.6 percent in the Polish elections of 1991. Women won 8.0 percent of the parliamentary seats in Bulgaria but only 3.0 percent in Romania. For the former Yugoslavia, figures ranged from a low of 4.8 percent in Croatia to a high of 10.0 percent in Slovenia.[1] At the same time, however, those women who are in parliament are no longer tokens. Some have attained real power, such as Hanna Suchocka, who served as Polish prime minister in 1992–1993. Nevertheless, politics clearly remains very much a men's affair in East-Central Europe.

Political Parties, the Party System, and Elections

Elsewhere in this book, there are separate sections on parties and elections. Here, we put them together. From the onset of Stalinism in 1949 to the fall of communism forty years later, the only party that existed was the official Communist Party; elections were merely ritualized forms of public participation, not meaningful choices among real alternatives. Since 1989, East-Central Europe has had both real elections and the emergence of real parties. Moreover, the two processes have been intrinsically connected, as parties have been shaped and reshaped continually in the past decade as a result of elections. For these reasons, we talk about these two phenomena together here.

Not long ago, all of Eastern Europe had the same kind of party system. The government was run by a Communist Party, and that is all there was to it. The party used different names in different countries (Socialist Workers Party in Hungary, United Workers Party in Poland, Communist Party in Czechoslovakia, League of Communists in Yugoslavia). In some countries, such as Poland and East Germany, other parties were permitted formally to exist, provided they did not oppose the government (that is, provided they did not act like real parties). But these minor differences did little to mask the essential similarity among countries of a single party governing the state and taking responsibility for all public policy.

If we look only at the Central European countries of Poland, Hungary, and the Czech Republic, we can divide post-Communist party development into two stages. In the first stage, lasting from 1990 to 1993, parties and politics were dominated by anticommunism. Liberal and conservative parties each claimed to be the most anti-Communist, and even the ex-Communist parties took great pains to prove their reformed status. In the second stage, since 1994, anticommunism is no longer sufficient to attract votes, as East Europeans began reacting to the realities of new capitalism rather than the memory of old communism. Social democratic parties won several elections in 1993 and 1994, leading some observers to talk about a "revival of the Left." But by the late 1990s, conservative and right-wing parties often recaptured power, as in Poland and Hungary. While ideological divides still remain strong, politics is becoming "normal" in the sense that parties now win or lose depending on their record (and their campaign strategies), and not just their stated beliefs.

Over the past decade, the party system in Eastern Europe has changed more completely and more thoroughly than in any other part of Europe. The plethora of parties today makes it difficult to recall that these were one-party systems until a short time ago. On the other hand, it is the very fact that new parties had to be created from scratch that accounts for their large number and for the fact that they are still not completely stable. For example, we know that in the next British election, the Labour Party will fight against the Tories, and in Germany the Social Democrats will be pitted against the Christian Democrats while the Greens try to maintain a presence. But in the summer of 2000, Poles were not even sure that the current governing party, Solidarity Electoral Action, would even run in the next election under the same name. Even in Hungary, with the most stable party system in Eastern Europe, the party that governed the country from 1990 to 1994, the Hungarian Democratic Forum, was reduced to a humiliating 3 percent of the vote in 1998 and was not at all a player in subsequent coalition talks. In the Czech Republic, meanwhile, the Social Democrats, who stood at the head of the country in 2000, could not even pass the 5 percent minimum threshold for entering parliament in the first post-Communist elections of 1990.

Yet while party shake-out is still likely in the coming decade, some parties have clearly established their record and their identity, and thus their staying power. In this section, we examine the main parties and recent election results in the three key Central European countries as of 2001 and the ideological tendencies in the elections so far. For shorthand reference, the election results in the three countries since 1990 look roughly as follows: in Hungary, the voting patterns have gone Right, Left, Right; in Poland, Center, Left, Right; and in the Czech Republic, Center, Right, Left.

Hungary is the best place to begin a discussion of parties because it entered 1989 with a party system apparently already intact. This was due to the prominence of two parties that seemed able to divide all the non-Communist vote between them: the Alliance of Free Democrats (AFD) and the Hungarian Democratic Forum (HDF). The AFD was formed and led largely by the liberal intellectuals who had led Hungary's democratic opposition movement since the 1970s. Maintaining their activities in the difficult years despite constant harassment by the police, AFD activists had accumulated the record, legitimacy, and intellectual firepower to make them the apparently natural successors once the Communist Party left the scene. Indeed, it was precisely this that led conservative intellectuals to form their own counterorganization, the HDF, in 1987. The HDF styled itself as a nationalist and populist movement, opposing communism less on grounds that it was hostile to democracy, as the ADF emphasized, than that it was contrary to the national and religious identities of Hungary. The liberal and conservative emphases of these two parties seemed to span the ideological divide with the non-Communist camp. The AFD entered the 1990 elections as a classic European liberal party, supporting rapid integration with the West and full individual rights for all citizens regardless of ethnicity or religion. The conservative HDF was more cautious about marketization, more focused on protecting ethnic Hungarians, and against substituting a dependence on the West for the old dependence on the East. With its 42 percent of the vote, the HDF came to power, while AFD's 24 percent made it the leading opposition. Together, with two-thirds of the total 1990 vote, the two parties thoroughly dominated the first post-Communist parliament.

Ten years later, however, both parties have become marginalized. The HDF compromised itself by its four years in power, characterized as a time of scandals, economic decline, and perceived governmental incompetence. By allowing widescale foreign takeover of industry, they lost much of their support on the right. By not severing ties with an extremist anti-Semitic faction in their midst, they lost support among many moderates. By 1994, their vote dropped to 9.5 percent and four years later to 3.1 percent. (See Table 29.1.)

The AFD, meanwhile, has been eclipsed by the former Communists. The Hungarian Socialist Party (HSP), as they were now called, received only 8.5 percent of the vote in 1990. Like most other such parties in the region, it paid a steep price for being identified with the old regime. As the new system developed a record of its own, however, and as the Socialists deftly distanced themselves from their past, their fortunes began to improve. While other parties spoke of the miracles of the market, the HSP noted also the high costs of market reform for the majority of the population. While other political leaders proved themselves incompetent politicians, prone to grandstanding for an audience, the Socialists earned respect for knowing the nuts and bolts of lawmaking and parliamentary procedure.

By 1993, the Socialists were already passing the liberals in the public opinion polls. Whereas both supported democratic rights and a market economy, the Socialists exhibited far more social

Table 29.1　Elections in Hungary, 1994 and 1998

Parliament: The National Assembly has 386 members, elected for a four-year term, 176 members in single-seat constituencies, 152 by proportional representation in multiseat constituencies, and 58 members elected to realize proportional representation.

Party	1998 Election (Voter Turnout, 57.0%)		1994 Election	
	Percentage of Vote	Seats	Percentage of Vote	Seats
Hungarian Socialist Party, socialist	32.3	134	54.1	209
Alliance of Young Democrats, conservative liberal	28.2	148	5.1	20
Independent Party of Smallholders, Agrarian Workers and Citizens, agrarian conservative	13.8	48	6.7	26
Alliance of Free Democrats, liberal	7.9	24	18.1	70
Hungarian Justice and Life Party, nationalist	5.5	14	—	—
Workers' Party, communist	4.1	—	—	—
Hungarian Democratic Forum, conservative/Christian-democratic	3.1	17	9.5	38
Christian-Democratic People's Party, Christian-democratic	2.6	—	5.7	22

Source: http://www.agora.stm.it/elections/election/hungary.htm.

concern than the liberals did. (It is important to keep in mind that in Europe, unlike the United States, *liberalism* implies individualism and promarket beliefs but not support for state intervention or strong welfare provisions.) And with class anger growing as a result of the new, inegalitarian capitalism, voters increasingly turned to the HSP as the best political alternative.

The only surprise in the 1994 elections was the extent of the HSP victory. From its miserable showing four years earlier, the party now received an astonishing 54.1 percent of the vote, winning an absolute majority of parliamentary seats all by itself. So thorough was the victory that prominent candidates of other parties found themselves defeated by political unknowns running on the Socialist ticket. Even the highly popular AFD chairman lost a head-to-head race with a little-known actress running as a Socialist. Although voters gave the HSP a convincing victory, opinion polls showed over-whelming support for a socialist-liberal coalition, and the liberals soon obliged. The AFD moved from being the most anti-Communist party in 1990 to being the governing coalition partner with the former Communists in 1994.

The emerging liberal-socialist alliance has been one of the most interesting developments in East-Central Europe of the past decade. Besides Hungary, it has occurred in the Czech Republic and Slovakia, in Slovenia and Croatia, and to a lesser degree in Poland. The reason has to do with the appearance of religious nationalism in the post-Communist era. As noted before, liberals opposed communism in the name of democracy, not in the name of church or nation. While cooperating with anti-Communist nationalists before 1989, they always had different views about the future. After 1989, everything changed. When reform Communists no longer opposed democracy, it turned out that liberals had more in common with them than they did with religious nationalists. Both favored a secular rather than religious system and opposed narrow ethnic nationalism. Both sought integration with the West and wanted an educational system teaching scientific know-how rather than moral purity. This liberal-socialist alliance began in Hungary and has become common throughout the region.

As it happened, the alliance hurt the AFD, which seemed to submerge its identity into the larger Socialist Party. So when the coalition government lost popularity due to tough austerity programs that contradicted its campaign promises, voters rejected the government, and particularly the bit-player liberals, who no longer represented any alternative. By 1998, the AFD sank to under 8 percent of the votes, and by the turn of the century its political influence was almost nil.

With the two prominent parties of 1990 marginalized ten years later, who has taken up the slack? The answer is the AYD. Having formed as sort of a youth group to the Free Democrats, the party emerged on its own in the early 1990s. While the other parties were compromising themselves with political infighting and responsibility for a chaotic economy, the AYD attracted support with shrewd political analysis, innovative policy proposals, and one of Hungary's best public speakers in party leader Viktor Orban. When the AFD entered a coalition government with the Socialists and the HDF saw its support evaporate, the right side of the political spectrum suddenly had a huge hole, and the AYD tried to fill it. Allying with the conservative agrarian Smallholders Party, the AYD rode dissatisfaction with the Socialist government into a stunning electoral victory in 1998. When the new century began, it was forty-year-old Prime Minister Orban who greeted it.

Despite the wide array of political parties populating the Hungarian scene since 1989, the result has been the genesis of a classic left-right split, as is common elsewhere in Europe. While the HSP seems assured of maintaining the man-tle of the Left, it is only the identity of the Right that remains unclear. In 2001, it is the Young Democrats that represent the Right, but its quick rise to power suggests that it is not yet a secure party. Just as the AYD replaced the HDF, another party might well supplant the AYD in the future. What seems clear, however, is that this Left-Right divide (with "Right" meaning pronationalist more than promarket) will stay as the dominant cleavage. In this sense, Hungarian politics has become "normal."

Parties had a harder time getting established in Poland than in Hungary, since until 1989 virtually all opposition politics was subordinated to Solidarity. When parties did begin to form after Solidarity started coming apart in 1990, they formed so fast that in the first free elections in 1991, sixty-seven different parties competed, and eighteen won at least one seat. With the subsequent introduction of a 5 percent requirement for representation, the number dropped to six parties entering parliament in 1993 and five in 1997. Since 1997, two parties have dominated Polish politics, the Alliance of the Democratic Left (ADL) and Solidarity Electoral Action (SEA), with the smaller Freedom Union (FU) playing an important role in the middle.

The ADL, like Hungary's Socialist Party, is the reformed version of the old ruling Communist Party. It was founded in 1990 (originally named the Social Democracy of Poland) after the demise of the old system. Despite the old ruling party's role in facilitating a smooth transition to democracy, its successor entered the new era without much popular support. Its presidential candidate won only 8 percent of the vote in 1990, and the party got only 12 percent in parliamentary elections a year later. Yet like the HSP, the ADL quickly increased its support thanks to their professionalism, the incessant quarreling of their opponents, their clearly demonstrated support for the new political and economic system, and their advocacy of better protection for the poor. By the 1993 parliamentary elections, the ADL had emerged as the leading party, with some 20 percent of the vote and 37 percent of the seats (because of electoral rules favoring large parties). It governed the country for the next four years in coalition with the smaller Polish Peasant Party, representing rural interests.

Solidarity Electoral Action did not exist in 1993. Yet it arose precisely because of what happened in 1993. The reason the ADL could become the dominant party with only 20 percent of the vote is that the vote of the old Solidarity supporters had been divided among several parties, only one of which got more than the 5 percent minimum necessary to enter parliament. Deprived of parliamentary representation, the conservative, Christian, and nationalist elements of the old opposition realized they had to unite their forces and that only the popular trade union Solidarity was in a position to lead that effort. Thus, Solidarity Electoral Action—a coalition of more than two dozen smaller right-wing political parties, mostly Christian democratic, conservative nationalist, and Catholic fundamentalist ones—led by leaders of the Solidarity trade union who have become more interested in politics than unionism. The coalition surged to nearly 34 percent of the electoral vote in the 1997 parliamentary elections (see Table 29.2) and took governmental power in a coalition with the Freedom Union.

The last of the important parties in Poland, the FU is the party of the old liberal intellectual dissidents, similar to the Free Democrats in Hungary. Although closely allied with Solidarity in the past—indeed, FU officials were the union's main negotiators at the 1989 round table talks that led to the fall of communism—the FU (from 1990 to 1994 known as the Democratic Union) broke with the Solidarity trade union in 1990, accusing the latter, and its leader, Lech Wałęsa, of pushing the country in a dangerous populist, authoritarian, and antimarket direction. FU support has regularly hovered between about 8 and 12 percent, with a social base consisting chiefly of professionals and intellectuals.

Although the liberals of the FU find much

common ground with the ADL and are critical of the religious nationalism of SEA, no liberal-socialist coalition has happened yet, due to the deep political conflicts of the past. Instead, when the SEA won the 1997 elections, the FU joined it in a coalition government, showing that the old glue of the old Solidarity still holds strong. Nevertheless, in 2000, FU broke with SEA, leaving the country with a minority government as it prepared for elections in 2001.

The beginning of the new millennium sees a shift back to the Left. President Aleksandr Kwaśniewski, who defeated Lech Wałęsa for the presidency in 1995, won easy reelection in 2000, and an ADL victory seems inevitable in the 2001 parliamentary elections. The easy alternation between the two parties, without any decisive change in policy, shows Poland's evolution to a two-party-plus system: two dominant catch-all parties on the Left and Right, with a couple of small interest group parties picking up the slack. As in Hungary, it is only the identity of the right-wing party that is unclear. Because it is formally a coalition, SEA may yet break down into rival groups again. Some party speaking in a religious nationalist tone, however, is likely to remain strong in Poland for the foreseeable future.

Politics in the Czech Republic is also dominated by right- and left-leaning parties, respectively known as the Civic Democratic Party (CDP) and the Social Democratic Party (SDP). The CDP traces its roots to the 1989 Velvet Revolution (though as in Poland, many liberal intellectuals broke away as the party turned increasingly conservative), while the SDP is a party revived from the pre–World War II era. (Unlike elsewhere, therefore, the main Left party is *not* the old Communist Party, chiefly because that party never fully converted itself into a democratic organization.) As Table 29.3 shows, CDP support has stayed fairly stable in the past decade while the SDP has grown dramatically, attracting support from all who oppose CDP dominance. The CDP stayed in power for a long time by combining tough-talking neoliberal rhetoric

Table 29.2   Elections in Poland, 1997

Parliament: Parliament has two chambers. The Sejm (Diet) has 460 members, elected for a four-year term—391 members elected by proportional representation in multiseat constituencies and 69 seats in a national constituency by proportional representation among parties obtaining more than 5 percent of the popular vote. The Senat (Senate) has 100 members selected for a four-year term in 47 two-seat constituencies and 2 three-seat constituencies.

| Party | *Results in the Polish Sejm Elections (Voter Turnout, 47.9%)* | |
	Percentage of Vote	*Seats*
Solidarity Electoral Action, conservative	33.8	201
Alliance of Democratic Left, socialist	27.1	164
Freedom Union, moderate liberal	13.4	60
Polish People's Party, agrarian	7.3	27
Movement for the Reconstruction of Poland, conservative	5.6	6
Union of Labour, social democratic	4.4	—
National Party of Old-Age and Disability Pensioners, pensioners' party	2.7	—
Union of Right of the Republic of Poland, conservative	2.3	—
National Agreement of Old Age and Disability Pensioners of the Republic of Poland, pensioners' party	1.5	—
German Social and Cultural Society, party of German minority	—	2

Source: NRC-Handelsbad/Reuter. The percentages of the parties under 5 percent are based on a prognose by Rzeczpospolita.

| Party | *Results in the Polish Senat Elections (Voter Turnout, 47.9%)* | |
	Percentage of Vote	*Seats*
Solidarity Electoral Action, conservative	—	51
Alliance of Democratic Left, socialist	—	28
Freedom Union, moderate liberal	—	8
Polish People's Party, agrarian	—	3
Movement for the Reconstruction of Poland, conservative	—	5
Nonpartisans	—	5

Source: http://www.agora.stm.it/elections/election/poland.htm.

Table 29.3   Elections in the Czech Republic, 1998

Parliament: The Parliament of the Czech Republic has two chambers. The Chamber of Representatives has 200 members, elected for a four-year term by proportional representation with a 5 percent barrier. The Senat has 81 members, elected for a six-year term in single-seat constituencies, in which one-third is renewed every two years.

| Party | *Results in Chamber of Representatives Election (Voter Turnout, 73.8%)* | |
	Percentage of Vote	*Seats*
Czech Social Democratic Party, social democratic	32.3	74
Civic Democratic Party, conservative	27.7	63
Communist Party of Bohemia and Moravia, communist	11.0	24
Christian and Democratic Union-Czechoslovak People's Party, Christian democratic	9.0	20
Freedom Union, conservative	8.6	19
Civic Democratic Alliance, conservative	—	
Rally for the Republic/Czechoslovak Republican Party, xenophobic	3.9	—
Pensioners for a Secure Life, pensioners' party	3.1	—
Democratic Union, conservative	1.4	—

Source: http://www.agora.stm.it/elections/election/czech.htm.

with a softer social democratic practice, but when the inegalitarian market elements began prevailing over the inclusive social democratic elements, the SPD grew as an alternative. Since 1998, the two parties have pretty much divided governmental power between themselves, much to the consternation of smaller parties, who feel increasingly shut out. Nevertheless, these two parties are likely to dominate in the 2002 elections as well.

Slovak politics has been a bit more complicated, due to the presence of the authoritarian nationalist, and ex-communist, Vladimir Meciar. His repressive internal policies made Slovakia a pariah in the region, delaying its entry into the North Atlantic Treaty Organization (NATO) and the European Union (EU) and earning the scorn of all committed democrats and socialists. In 1998, however, a coalition of liberals (Slovak Democratic Coalition) and reformed ex-Communists (Party of the Demo-

cratic Left) won enough seats to oust Meciar and put the country back on a democratic path. (See Table 29.4.) The new government has done much to restore public confidence and improve the economy, but the lingering presence of Meciar's populist party may yet present electoral surprises in the future.

The only country similar to Slovakia in this respect is Croatia. Dominated for ten years by the authoritarian nationalist and extreme militarist Franjo Tudjman and his Croatian Democratic Union, an electoral alliance of liberals and ex-Communists finally came to power in early 2000. As the new decade started, Croatia began moving toward the EU, though the authoritarian CDU may yet pose problems in the future.

Ten years after the collapse of the old regime, new party systems have emerged everywhere in all former Communist countries. Although the identities of particular parties may change, the basic framework appears to be set. We usually

Table 29.4   Elections in Slovakia, 1998

Parliament: The National Council of the Slovak Republic has 150 members, elected for a four-year term by proportional representation.

Party	*Results (Voter Turnout, 84.2%)*	
	Percentage of Vote	*Seats*
Movement for a Democratic Slovakia, authoritarian	27.0	43
Slovak Democratic Coalition, liberal	26.3	42
Slovak Democratic Coalition is supported by the following five parties:		
Democratic Party, conservative		
Democratic Union of Slovakia, liberal		
Christian Democratic Movement, Christian democratic		
Social Democratic Party of Slovakia, social democratic		
Slovak Green Party, ecological		
Party of Democratic Left, socialist	14.7	23
Party of the Hungarian Coalition, minority party	9.1	15
Slovak National Party, xenophobic	9.1	14
Party of Civic Understanding, social liberal	8.0	13
Slovak Communist Party, communist	2.8	—
Slovak Workers' Front, communist	1.3	—

Source: http://www.agora.stm.it/elections/election/slovakia.htm.

see the emergence of two dominant parties representing left- and right-wing tendencies, with "Right," as elsewhere in Europe, tending to mean pronationalist more than promarket. There is broad general agreement among most parties on the basic issues of the day, such as consolidating a market economy and entering both NATO and the EU. Rhetoric, of course, will continue to emphasize disagreements, with each party saying that its policies will best help accomplish the country's healthy integration into Europe. Once in government, however, each party is likely to continue to do largely what the EU and international business community tell it to do in order to take advantage of the historic opportunity before them. Thus, there was policy continuity when left-wing parties came to power in Poland and Hungary in the mid-1990s

and the same continuity when right-wing parties replaced them in the late 1990s. While such broad agreement can always help outsider parties come to power, the experience so far is that outsiders conform once in power themselves, largely due to international pressures and opportunities. Thus, the identities of the dominant parties may yet change but probably not the basic policy orientations. The bottom line is that no party wants to be responsible for squandering this historic opportunity to become part of the European mainstream and to end the centuries-old division of Europe into East and West. Such pressures, and opportunities, explain why extremist right-wing parties have largely been unable to succeed, as well as why, where they have come to power (Slovakia, Croatia), they have not been able to consolidate their rule. By the new millennium, basic European principles of liberal democracy and market economy were accepted as dogma in all the countries of the region.

The Importance of Parties

To say there is broad agreement on principles does not mean that the party system in the East is no different from that in the West. For one thing, party discipline is not yet very strong in East-Central Europe. Ironically, the reason is that it was too strong in the past. Communist Party discipline was so firm that not one bill proposed by the government was ever voted down in a Communist parliament. Even a few no votes were highly unusual. In Poland, parliamentary discussion became a bit more open after 1956, when several independent Catholic officials were allowed in as deputies (including Tadeusz Mazowiecki, who would become the first non-Communist prime minister in 1989). But the most these moderate critics could do was to ask a few questions publicly of Communist ministers. In Hungary, parliament began to have some critical discussion only in the 1980s. In Czechoslovakia parliament remained a unanimous body from 1968 to 1989. These experiences gave the notion of party discipline a bad reputation. Indeed, they gave the notion of "party" itself a bad reputation; many East-Central European parties do not even use the word *party* in their official name. After 1989, the widespread view among politicians as well as the general population was that representatives should vote their consciences. People viewed voting along party lines not as the way parliamentary systems worked, but as the way the Communist system had worked. This feeling was strongest in Poland, because the opposition was led by Solidarity, a highly diverse organization that could not have compelled unity even if it had wanted to. But elsewhere in the region, there was also a reluctance to impose party values on individual members. Such attitudes allow individual representatives to speak out more, but they also make parties weaker as organizations.

How crucial parties are for shaping state policy depends on which areas of policy one has in mind. Regarding economic policy, the answer seems to be not very crucial. Although the Democratic Forum, Socialist Party, and Young Democrats in Hungary were about as far apart as possible, at least in terms of their official programs, the transfers of power from the first to the second to the third party have been smooth and have not resulted in dramatic changes in economic policy. The same is true in Poland, where the ADL and the SEA took control of parliament without much change economically. Officially, left-wing parties tend to be more skeptical about the merits of privatization and more anxious to maintain social welfare payments, yet in power they have been perfectly willing to privatize companies and slash social benefits. Economic policy has largely been shaped not by the electoral programs of the competing parties, but by cabinet ministers facing the same domestic and international constraints as their predecessors and sharing the same desire to please the West.

Noneconomic policy, on the other hand, has been very much shaped by political parties. Each party brings its own style to government. Its spokespersons seek to focus public attention on different kinds of issues. Each party brings an ethos to public life that is unmistakably its own. Of course, politicians do not always live up to their words. The Democratic Forum in Hungary talked a great deal about retribution but never tried to turn its words into action. The FU in Poland talks of tolerance for all but often privileges the values and policy preferences of the Catholic Church. Nevertheless, words do count. Governing parties might not try to implement illiberal, intolerant laws, but by speaking kindly of such ideas, they encourage the actions of others who do not feel so constrained. Government statements set the agenda of public debate. Indeed, most people experience politics in their everyday lives through the kinds of issues that are discussed by the mass media. By shaping the environment in which policies are considered desirable or objectionable, parties ultimately play a crucial role in shaping the political realities.

Collective Identities

The ruling Communist parties tried to replace people's preexisting loyalties with loyalty to party principles but never came close to succeeding. They certainly influenced people greatly, but alternate identities—according to class, religion, nationality, or political ideology—have always remained prominent. Since 1989, old identities have combined with new ones to create fascinating and unusual concoctions with great implications for the political future.

Social Class

Because of the formally Marxist ideologies of the past, the countries of Eastern Europe have a peculiar relationship to class as an identity. In the early days of the system, class was an almost obligatory identity. Citizens got credits (or demerits) depending on their class background, and anyone who advanced up the social hierarchy had to swear loyalty to the working class, in whose interests the entire system was said to be run. Over time, the new elite managed to reproduce itself and get its children into good positions, but it was not allowed to develop a class consciousness of its own. Everything it did was still supposedly done for the working class. The impact was that most citizens were unable to think of themselves in terms of class. Since everyone was supposed to be a worker, no explicit class distinctions could arise, despite obvious social and economic inequalities.

This legacy has a strong impact on the post-Communist period. Although the new era is very much about the creation of a class soci-ety—building a capitalist system requires creating a capitalist class—class has remained an uncertain identity in the new era. Labor does not explicitly embrace a working-class identity (the very term *working class* is unpopular, conjuring up images of official old men in badly tailored suits) but sees itself as trying to become middle class. The emerging capitalist class meanwhile tries to underplay its wealth and power, conscious of the fact that its own right to privilege is not yet fully accepted by all. The limited scope of class identities is due also to the changing economy. The closing down of the old industrial factories in favor of small-scale service and white-collar jobs (everything from security guard to computer programmer) led to the erosion of class identities in the West and is now doing the same in the East. As we will see in the next section, this decline of class identity has led to minimal labor unrest despite the steep economic decline.

Citizenship and Nationality

Because of their long experience of foreign domination and the struggle against it, Eastern Europeans are extremely attached to their national identities. The Communist parties themselves recognized this and did their best to use national themes to their own advantage. The Ceauşescu government in Romania paid particular attention to playing up nationalist themes, as did the Polish government in the 1960s. Nevertheless, communism itself is treated in post-1989 Eastern Europe largely as a foreign imposition. Although all Eastern European countries, with the exception of the Baltic republics, were formally independent during the Communist years, they have treated the post-Communist period as a time in which to solidify their national communities. They do so through rituals, ceremonies, and new national holidays. Hungary, for example, has made October 23, the anniversary of the 1956 rebellion against the Soviets, a new national holiday, and Poland, having abolished commemoration of July 22, when the Soviet-supported government took power in 1944, now celebrates May 3 (for the 1791 constitution) and November 11 (for the 1918 declaration of independence) as its key national holidays. In a series of ways, countries have tried to emphasize their links with the pre-Communist past, sometimes acting as if the Communist period never existed. For his 1990 inauguration as president, for example, Lech Wałęsa received the official trappings of the presidency not from his legal predecessor, General Wojciech Jaruzelski, but from the so-called president-in-exile (recognized by no government in the world) in London. Jaruzelski was not even invited.

National and patriotic themes were quite evident in the struggle against communism. They played an especially crucial role in the Polish Solidarity movement in the 1980s.[2] Solidarity adopted the national anthem as its own union song, and the ever-present pictures of the Polish pope, John Paul II, also symbolized national aspirations. (Many decades of foreign rule made the Polish Church the only ongoing sign of national continuity, and so a powerful national as well as religious symbol.) And it was the nationalist revival in the Baltic states of Latvia, Lithuania, and Estonia that led to the final crisis of the Soviet Union.

A strong national identity can be conducive to political freedom, but it can also lead to the breakup of a country and to ruthless war, as we have seen in the former Yugoslavia. Eastern Europeans are quite aware of this dual nature of nationalism. For that reason, we see two competing tendencies coexisting in post-Communist East-Central Europe. The first is a tendency to instill among the population an impregnable sense of national identity. Eastern European countries want to do this because of their long history of foreign occupations. As the Czech writer Milan Kundera has noted, the people of East-Central Europe live with the ever-present awareness that statehood has been taken away before and can be taken away again. This awareness leads today's rulers, teachers, and writers to

emphasize nationalist themes and national triumphs, even at the cost of historical accuracy. This attitude can certainly lead to abuses, as in the way Serbian historians reinvented the past in the 1980s, turning Croatians into devils and Bosnians into Serbs. (The historians argued that Croatia had always taken advantage of Serbia and that Bosnians were really only Serbs who believed in Islam.) Yet the emphasis on nationalist history is also a necessary process of self-recovery after long years of subordination to the Soviet Union. And the globalization of culture that makes MTV or CNBC available in living rooms throughout Eastern Europe also makes national awareness seem necessary to guard against the "over-Westernization" of young people.

Along with this nationalistic tendency, however, the other strong tendency today is precisely toward globalism. All Eastern European countries talk endlessly about "joining Europe." They seek to join both NATO and the EU. They want their young people to travel to other countries, learn new languages, break free of local national biases, and become ever more cosmopolitan. In other words, they are trying to promote a new international identity at the same time they are promoting a new national identity. Sometimes the two tendencies are manifested at the very same time, such as when the schoolchild learns of the great contributions made to world history by some obscure (to the West) national hero and is asked to recite the tale of this valiant figure in English!

The nationalist tendency has been strongest where statehood is most tentative: in the Baltic Republics. Because these countries were part of the Soviet Union between 1940 and 1991, hundreds of thousands of Russians moved there. They came as Party officials and enterprise managers, as engineers or common workers, or simply as retirees. What they had in common was that they usually did not speak the native language, nor did they need to. As these countries have tried to establish statehood, however, they have often made knowledge of the language a condition of citizenship. In local elections in Latvia in the spring of 1994, 40 percent of the country's population and 60 percent of the capital city's (Riga) were not allowed to vote; as Russian speakers, they were not considered citizens of the country. Estonia, deciding that language was not enough, passed laws allowing citizenship only for people able to prove that their lineage in the country extended prior to 1940 (before annexation by the Soviet Union). These rules were attacked by Russian politicians as well as by international human rights organizations, and have since been modified.

Outside of the Baltic republics, no Eastern European country has passed such restrictive regulation of citizenship. Of course, none of them has the same problem of Russian residents either. Until recently, virtually the only people seeking citizenship in the Eastern European countries were ethnic nationals who had lived elsewhere, such as Poles from the Soviet Union or Hungarians from Romania, and these immigrants have been integrated without much difficulty. Same-nationality immigration can be a problem too. The former West Germany had difficulties incorporating former East Germans, and Hungary and Poland may yet face problems if there is mass immigration of ethnic nationals from Serbia and Kazakhstan, respectively. But these will be problems of logistics only. The immigrants will be accepted as citizens; the only problem will be how to accommodate them.

Increasing immigration from other parts of the world, however, means the region will soon have to confront the question of who exactly is a citizen. East-Central Europe's political freedom, relative prosperity, and proximity to Germany have made it an increasingly popular stop among emigrants from Asia, Africa, and the Middle East. In most cases, these people seek to use Eastern Europe only as a transit point. In the past, their main destination was Germany, whose liberal asylum law used to allow anyone who claimed to be politically persecuted to stay in the country until a court could review the case. In July 1993, however, Germany changed

its law. It now considers for asylum only alleged political refugees who enter Germany directly from the country in which they are being persecuted. Since all of Germany's neighbors are considered "safe," virtually all immigrants without proper visas are turned away at the border. As a result, of the tens of thousands of people who arrive in East-Central Europe hoping to enter Germany, thousands end up staying for months, if not years, in Eastern Europe.

In addition, tens of thousands of former Soviet citizens work illegally in the region, particularly in Poland. Many thousands of Roma, or Gypsies, have also left Romania and Bulgaria for Poland and the former Czechoslovakia, while thousands of refugees from Bosnia are living in neighboring countries.

Countries will define what it means to be a citizen in the light of these realities. For the time being, East-Central Europe, except for the Baltics, has accepted the civic rather than ethnic model of citizenship. The *civic model* accords citizenship to all people living permanently in the territory over which the state rules, whereas the *ethnic model*, as in the Baltic republics, allows only ethnic nationals—those deemed, by virtue of ancestry, as belonging to the dominant nationality—to become citizens. Whether the civic model remains dominant in the future will depend in large part on how immigration patterns develop, which itself depends on the future of the world economy.

Religion and Politics

During the Communist era, religious affiliation was discouraged but by no means forbidden. The first years of Communist rule saw the greatest pressure against organized religion, including the arrest of clergy and the closing down of houses of worship. By the 1960s, however, the authorities' chief concern was to keep religion out of public life. Schools taught that religion was an unnecessary and reactionary social construct—a myth by which people helped make sense of a prescientific world. People could and did have their own private religious values, transmitted chiefly by family tradition, but those who wanted to enter the political or economic elite had to keep such beliefs to themselves.

Of course, this general truth disguises various national particularities. Albania tried to suppress religion outright, closing down all churches and mosques. Poland, by the 1980s, had reached the other extreme, with the martial law government conciliating the Church at every opportunity in an effort to co-opt the Church as a substitute for Solidarity. Most of the region, however, stood somewhere in the middle, although more on the side of tolerance than proscription.

Religion became more important in the region in the 1980s. The inability to continue the growth rates of earlier times and the increasing self-organization of citizens committed to the expansion of democratic rights were signs of the economic and political crisis of communism, but they also sparked a crisis of identity. Religious feelings grew in this period as a way of holding onto something solid in a world of continuing change. (Only in the Czech Republic did religion fail to play an important role in recent political and social transformations.)

Because communism has always been officially antireligious, however, religious feelings in Communist Eastern Europe often reflected a political attitude more than a religious one. People liked what the Church stood for, as an institution opposed to communism, but had little intention of living their lives according to Church instructions. This attitude was most apparent in Poland. The overwhelming majority of Poles considered themselves believers in the 1980s. Yet few Poles lived by Church precepts regarding abortion, contraception, extramarital sex, and the like. (Contrary to the reputation of Catholics in each country, it is far more common to find Catholic families with eight or ten children in the United States than it is in Poland.) In public opinion polls, whereas Polish society gave better than 90 percent support to the

Catholic Church in the 1980s, that number had dropped by almost half by the mid-1990s. Findings like these suggest that religious identities are often more an expression of political values than of religious convictions.[3]

Religion has played the greatest political role in the historically Catholic countries of Poland, Slovakia, and Croatia. In each of these countries, Catholicism is intimately associated with national independence. In Poland, the Church kept Polish national traditions alive during the long years when Poland was under foreign rule (1795–1918). State and Church were also intimately connected in Croatia and Slovakia during the brief periods of World War II when each country attained formal independence under the tutelage of the Third Reich. When people were increasingly dissatisfied with communism, therefore, and identified communism as something alien, something Russian, their longing for a return to national traditions translated into a new attachment to Catholicism. Religious affiliation has expanded elsewhere in the region too—especially Orthodoxy in Serbia (and Russia) and Islam in Bosnia—as people seek new identities in the post-Communist era.

Many observers expected the collapse of communism to mean the rise of religious fundamentalism throughout the region. In fact, this reaction has not occurred.[4] It is true that people needed something else to believe in once communism was officially discredited. But religion and nationalism were not the only contenders for people's hearts and minds. The market was too. One of the most striking aspects of East-Central Europe in the immediate aftermath of the fall of communism was people's almost naive faith that the new capitalist system would solve all the problems of the past. People looked to capitalism to do the kinds of things that communism promised but could not achieve, such as making everyone equally wealthy. One of the reasons people did not join together politically on the basis of a religious identity is that they believed the market would solve their problems. Only in the mid-1990s did faith in the market begin to erode. Populations then began voting for left-wing parties. That people voted for the Left in Poland and Hungary, rather than for the religious parties already available, demonstrates that identity demands based on religion were not yet widespread. But they could still become so in the future. If existing parties prove unable to resolve economic problems and reduce inequalities, fundamentalist groups might succeed in mobilizing people on the basis of religious demands. And when that happens, political democracy is usually the loser. Since identity demands cannot usually be resolved by distributional means, they must be resolved by political means—for example, by establishing an official church and enforcing "religious values" in public life. By compromising on the protection of minority rights, however, such a solution compromises the principles of liberal democracy too.

Ethnicity

The famed ethnic heterogeneity of Eastern Europe has disappeared over the past sixty years in the most catastrophic of circumstances. After the Nazi genocide of the Jews, the forced migrations of Poles, Ukrainians, and Germans in 1945, and the "ethnic cleansing" in the former Yugoslavia in the 1990s, it is no surprise that the countries have been left with few ethnic minorities. Poland, the most ethnically diverse country before World War II, is the most homogeneous today, with some 98 percent of the population consisting of Poles. In the Czech Republic, 95 percent are Czechs; in Hungary, 90 percent are Hungarians; in Slovakia, 86 percent Slovaks. The only significant minorities left in the region are Hungarians in Romania and Serbia, Turks in Bulgaria, and Roma, or Gypsies, everywhere, particularly in Hungary, Slovakia, and Romania, where they make up from 5 to 10 percent of the population.

This high degree of homogeneity, combined with the ban on political protest, meant that there was little organizing on the basis of national identity during the Communist era. During that period, it was almost always the ruling

parties that played the nationalist card. Romania was the undisputed master here, using nationalism to buttress its own highly repressive rule. Through several highly publicized conflicts with the Soviet Union, the elite presented itself as the promoter of the Romanian nation, even as it fiercely repressed citizens. (This strategy worked abroad at least as well as it did at home. When Romania, alone among East European countries, refused to boycott the Los Angeles Olympics in 1984, it was hailed by the United States as a freedom-loving country.) Polish Communists also presented themselves as the guardian of Polish national identity. At various times of political crisis—1956, 1968, and 1981—it claimed that its own rule was essential to preserving Polish independence and that the political opposition was putting national sovereignty in question.

Nationalism has emerged strongly throughout the region since 1989, mostly in accordance with Mark Twain's old maxim about patriotism being the last refuge of scoundrels and fools. In this era, it has been deployed by elites as a way of protecting their own dominance by diverting the blame for political and economic crisis onto someone else. This was clearly the thinking of the nationalists in the former Yugoslavia, who promoted self-love (and "other-hatred") precisely at a time of great economic downturn. Slovak nationalists meanwhile rode economic dissatisfaction to an electoral victory in 1992 and then gave people an "independent Slovakia" (with the nationalists as its leaders) when all polls showed that people only wanted a better life.[5]

So while it can be a source of pride, national identity since 1989 has more often been a mode of humiliation and exclusion. One defines oneself by excluding others and gains an existential reward instead of a real, material one.

Gender

Gender identities, like class identities, have not come easily to East-Central Europe. It is not that former Communist systems were truly nondiscriminatory, as they claimed to be. On the contrary, women faced the same double burden of job and housework that they do in the West, made even more difficult by the need to stand in long lines to buy basic goods. Nevertheless, women did not feel subordinate to men. Rather, both men and women felt subordinate to the system. This was especially true in the last decades of Communist rule, when opposition movements were already growing. In the context of the struggle against the overarching system, even politicized women did not wish to undercut that unity by talking about gender issues.

But just as labor identities begin to grow in the postcommunist era, so do gender identities. Gender disparities are quite real in terms of educational possibilities, employment rates, and income—all important issues for would-be professional women trying to move up the hierarchy. By the mid-1990s, such conditions contributed to the emergence of a feminist movement in the region. In new journals and e-mail networks, women have begun to protest forcefully against these conditions. This has led to protests over abortion restrictions, fights for better birthing conditions in hospitals, demands for gender studies programs in universities, and efforts to stigmatize as well as criminalize domestic violence. One thing that has helped the emergence of gender consciousness is its relative prominence in the West. At a time when Western fashions in politics and economics have been picked up by all, feminism too has a "Western" aura that makes it increasingly acceptable in Eastern Europe. Not surprisingly, political parties, usually those on the Left, increasingly emphasize gender issues as a way of winning women's votes.

As in the West, gender identities have also been encouraged by business. Many daily newspapers have created special weekly women's sections, chiefly in order to sell advertising. But since these sections also frequently publish feminist pieces, they inevitably help generate a gender identity that can challenge the "masculinism" that has pervaded the region since 1989.

Protests and Social Movements

Given the way the populations of East-Central Europe united so spectacularly in 1989, it was only natural to expect that the new democracies would be marked by a high level of popular participation. We need only recall the images of 1989: the millions of Poles united behind Solidarity; the mass rallies in Leipzig and Berlin chanting "We are the people!"; the disciplined determination of the Czechoslovak people. The effort to recreate civil society seemed to have succeeded beyond all expectations as it helped topple a regime that had lost public support. Here was a new ethos of participation that it seemed nothing would be able to quell. Postcommunism would be an era of unprecedented popular involvement in politics, as citizens would militantly defend their interests through the same kinds of protests and movements that had worked so well in 1989.

Things have not worked out that way. Instead of being filled with well-organized social groups fighting for the interests of their members, post-Communist public life has been surprisingly quiescent. People went to the polls, elected those who initiated the democratic changes, and then largely retreated from public involvement, waiting for the benefits of democracy to pour in. Extrainstitutional protest played a minor role in the first years after 1989. Few rallies and demonstrations challenged government policies, and hardly any politically motivated strikes occurred. There was not even much lobbying activity by the kinds of nongovernmental organizations that help shape so much policy in the West, such as environmental groups, business associations, trade unions, and women's organizations.

Why has there been so little independent civic activity? One of the reasons has to do with the very success of such activity in the past. When the Communist governments were swept away, most former oppositionist activists and organizers themselves became part of the new governments. The outsiders became the insiders, and from their new inside vantage point, they urged citizens to trust the institutions that they used to distrust, to accept the bureaucratic ways they had formerly condemned. The paucity of extrainstitutional protest after 1989 was a result of the long honeymoon period that people were willing to give the new governments as they undertook the difficult work of transformation.

Labor, in particular, was for two reasons widely expected to be very active as an organized force in the post-Communist period. First, working people played a central role in toppling the old regime. This role was especially obvious in Poland, where the trade union Solidarity led the successful struggle against Communist rule. But in East Germany and Czechoslovakia, too, it was labor's participation in massive strikes in November 1989 that sealed the fate of the old regime. Second, postcommunism augured poorly for workers. Marketization meant severing the job guarantees and subsidized prices of the past. The labor movement presumably would organize early on to protect itself.

Yet labor was not very active in the first post-Communist years, despite falling living standards. The central reason has to do with ideology: Having rejected socialist ideology because of the experience of communism, workers embraced the ideology of their enemy's enemy and entered the new era as believers in free-market capitalism. Of course, workers did not have much experience with capitalism. They looked to Western Europe (rather than, say, Latin America) and saw workers living well. They did not know that they were seeing not so much the results of the market as the results of labor's having organized to defend itself against the market. West European labor succeeded in taming capitalism by organizing economically and politically. But East European workers saw only

the end result. If this is capitalism, they said, we'll take it. And since, as they were told, building capitalism required time, sacrifice, and a strong managerial class, workers accepted the decline in living standards as well as the declining power of unions at the workplace.

Another reason workers were not very active after 1989 was that they were not sure what the future would bring. To organize in defense of one's interests, one needs to know what one's interests really are, but such things are hard to know in the first years of a new system that promises so much. Workers knew they were losing out, with real wages declining and unemployment increasing. But if these were only short-term setbacks on the road to general prosperity, as the market reformers argued, then workers did not want to oppose them. Labor movements were quiescent because workers believed it was in their long-term interests to accept attacks on their short-term interests.

With trade unions disinclined to defend workers' interests, membership plummeted. In Poland in 1981, Solidarity alone had some 9.5 million members. By 1993, total union membership in the country was less that half that, with Solidarity numbering only 1.3 million. (Most of the rest were in the union federation created by the government in the 1980s to replace Solidarity.) Outside Poland, the old trade union federations also lost members, though they remained by far the largest union organizations in their countries. Throughout Eastern Europe, union membership became concentrated in the old state sector rather than in the new private sector. In part, this concentration developed because wages are often higher in the private sector (although so are violations of work rules and safety provisions). In part, it occurred because private companies regularly fire workers who begin to organize (even though doing so is against the law).

The labor situation began to change around 1993. Having experienced four years of a new market economy, labor learned the lesson Western labor movements had learned much earlier:

For wages and working conditions to get better, workers must organize to make them better. Sometimes the unions were simply responding to greater pressure from the rank and file. (Wildcat strikes in Poland, for example, forced unions to take a more militant line.) In Hungary and Poland, the ex-Communist trade unions played a key role in the electoral victories of the ex-Communist parties, and several dozen union officials entered parliament as a result.

New elites have tried to minimize labor input by granting symbolic instead of real representation. This has occurred chiefly through *tripartite councils*, or commissions bringing together labor, business, and government to discuss and decide economic policy. Such institutions have been common in Western Europe, where they have served as the linchpins of the neocorporatist arrangements that have stabilized labor relations and liberal democracy since the 1950s. According to such arrangements, the state guarantees that labor will have input in policymaking in return for labor's promise to limit strike action and exercise wage restraint. By mid-decade, tripartite councils were meeting in virtually every country in Eastern Europe. A big difference with the West European experience, however, is that tripartites in the East are for the most part mere discussion clubs, without the power to decide policy, whereas Western tripartites frequently come up with wage and income agreements binding on all. Because of this largely symbolic role, some have characterized the Eastern European experience as "illusory corporatism" only.[6]

Besides protests around economic issues, there has been some degree of political mobilization in East-Central Europe around gender, religious, and environmental issues. Particularly in the Catholic countries, women have staged rallies in defense of abortion rights and against domestic violence (also against the military violence perpetrated during the wars in the former Yugoslavia). They have begun publishing journals and establishing on-line networks in which to promote their ideas.[7] Partly as a response to

this, and in order to promote its own agenda, the Catholic Church has staged counterrallies calling for bans on abortion. Religious fundamentalist groups have also built their own organizations, such as the Hungarian Justice and Life Party in Hungary (led by Istvan Csurka), and a large extremist network in Poland grouped around the "Radio Maria" radio station.

As for environmental issues, Green parties have arisen everywhere in the region, though are not yet as well organized or widely supported as in the West. Contrary to the view that people experiencing hard times do not care about such matters, environmental debate has been particularly prominent in the economically depressed and heavily polluted industrial centers of the region, such as Silesia in Poland. In Bulgaria, meanwhile, with its old and weary nuclear plants, an ecological organization was one of the first to be active after 1989.

On the whole, the post-Communist world has seen far less protest than many had anticipated.[8] People have accepted the need for economic reform and have largely left politics to the politicians, hoping that the changes they introduce will make everyone better off. This is not to say that extrainstitutional protest has been absent.[9] Polish farmers have staged a number of actions and protests to publicize their plight, such as blockading roads and dumping potatoes in front of the presidential palace, and they are promising many more rallies to protest integration into the EU. A 1990 strike by taxi drivers in Hungary played an important role in reminding state leaders about the real social consequences of their economic program. And environmental organizations have scored a few local successes, such as closing down some noxious and inefficient polluters, and have used access to the airwaves at election time to at least keep ecological issues in the public consciousness.

Nevertheless, extrainstitutional protest plays much less of a role in East-Central Europe today than it does in the West. Protest, of course, is an important way in which people become integrated into the political system. Far from threatening democracy, protest is a way of strengthening it. The comparatively low level of protest suggests that many people in East-Central Europe do not yet feel themselves to be full citizens empowered with an array of democratic rights.

Notes

1. Figures taken from articles in Nanette Funk and Magda Mueller, eds., *Gender Politics and Post-Communism* (New York: Routledge, 1993).

2. Jan Kubik, *The Power of Symbols Against the Symbols of Power: The Rise of Solidarity and the Fall of State Socialism in Poland* (State College: Pennsylvania State University Press, 1994).

3. For an account of the Polish Catholic Church and its role in politics, see Adam Michnik, *The Church and the Left* (Chicago: University of Chicago Press, 1993); and Maryjane Osa, "Resistance, Persistence and Change: The Transformation of the Catholic Church in Poland," *East European Politics and Societies* 3, no. 2 (Spring 1989): 268–299.

4. Sabrina P. Ramet, "The New Church-State Configuration in Eastern Europe," *East European Politics and Societies* 5, no. 2 (Spring 1991): 247–267.

5. On nationalisms and other hatreds, see Paul Hockenos, *Free to Hate: The Rise of the Right in Post-Communist Eastern Europe* (New York: Routledge, 1993).

6. David Ost, "Illusory Corporatism in Eastern Europe," *Politics and Society* 28, no. 4 (December 2000).

7. See, for example, the Network of East-West Women, www.neww.org.

8. As to why this is so, see the discussion by Bela Greskovits, *The Political Economy of Protest and Patience* (Budapest: Central European University Press, 1998).

9. On protest in the first post-Communist years, see Grzegorz Ekiert and Jan Kubik, "Contentious Politics in New Democracies: East Germany, Hungary, Poland, and Slovakia, 1989–1993," *World Politics* 50, no. 4 (July 1998): 547–581.

C H A P T E R

30

East-Central Europe
in Transition

In the summer and fall of 1993, the embattled republic of Bosnia and its heroic resistance in the capital, Sarajevo, found itself confronted on all sides by forces calling on it to surrender. Serbia, Croatia, and the Western alliance all urged Bosnia to sign a treaty dividing the republic into three separate ethno-religious states—one for Orthodox Serbs, one for Catholic Croats, and one for Muslim Bosnians. The war had been raging since the Bosnian declaration of independence in 1991. Poorer Serbs living in the Bosnian countryside, frightened by Serbian nationalists into thinking they would be persecuted by Islamic fundamentalism, declared war against the government in Sarajevo, but their actual fighting was directed not against any Bosnian army but against individual Bosnian Muslims who had been their neighbors for years. The Serbs drove hundreds of thousands of Muslims from their homes, destroyed mosques and other signs of Muslim culture, and raped Muslim women as a way of terrorizing the community so it would vacate the land forever. Then they proclaimed the creation of an independent republic of Serbs in Bosnia. Using a similar ruse about the supposed rise of anti-Christian Muslim fanatics, Croatia joined in, urging ethnic Croats to carve out a Croatian Bosnia in the western part of the country. By 1993, archenemies Serbia and Croatia had begun to work together, for the first time since the breakup of Yugoslavia, to expel Muslims and divide Bosnia between the two of them.

There was, however, one problem: The Bosnian side was not simply the Muslim side. While Serbia and Croatia sought to root out all Muslim culture and people systematically from the areas they controlled, Bosnia did not respond in kind. The Bosnian president was a Muslim, but the head of the Bosnian parliament was a Serb. Many of the leading officers in the Bosnian army were Croats and Serbs. In Sarajevo, Serbs, Croats, and Muslims saw themselves first as citizens of Bosnia. Bosnia was keeping alive the hope of a multiethnic republic in which different nationalities could live together, just as they had been doing for hundreds of years.[1] By asking them to surrender, the world was asking them to betray the multiethnic principles that had been at the heart of Bosnia—the same multiethnic principles to which the world so often pays homage.

For as long as they could, the Bosnians held firm. Time and again, they rejected plans that would institutionalize the principle of separate countries for different ethnic groups. But in that fall of 1993, with their armies unable to hold out and the world demanding surrender, they finally accepted, grudgingly, the principle of division. Even then, many continued to hope the tide might turn—that the war would shift in Bosnia's favor, that the West would finally intervene on behalf of the multiethnic principles it regularly espouses. In the summer of 1995, the tide did turn. It did so, alas, in a way that only made things worse. First, the Serbs took over the eastern Bosnian cities of Srebrenica and Zepa, murdering and raping thousands en route to expelling all Muslims from the areas. Then the Croatian army expelled hundreds of thousands of Serbs from areas around western Bosnia, turning the region into a Croat stronghold. By late 1995, the war had changed population distribution so much that the once unthinkable ethnic partition now seemed all but inevitable. At this point, the West finally got militarily involved when the North Atlantic Treaty Organization (NATO) bombed Serbs as the latter began attacking Bosnian cities. The West did not push for a just settlement, however, but only for partition. In December 1995, a peace accord was signed in Dayton, Ohio, effectively dividing Bosnia-Herzegovina into three separate regions for the three different nationalities.[2] When U.S. troops entered Bosnia as "peacekeepers" in early 1996, they were enforcing the ethnic partition that Bosnian democrats had tried so hard to avoid. The nationalist fundamentalists had won.

Three years later, in 1999, the war spread to Kosovo. Or rather, it spread to NATO and became, by extension, an East European war. The southern province of Kosovo is the historic heartland of Serbia, but over the last half-century it has become almost completely Albanian. By the mid-1990s, fewer than 10 percent of the population was Serb, although the province formally belonged to Serbia. Unable to win sufficient autonomy, militant Albanian separatists began organizing an armed campaign, which intensified after a governmental breakdown in neighboring Albania made arms easily available. But the armed campaign led to even greater Serb repression, and by 1998 it looked to many that Kosovo would be the next Bosnia. In early 1999, the United States called the parties to a conference in Rambouillet, France, and demanded that Serbia allow NATO troops to monitor Kosovo. When Serbia, unsurprisingly, refused this violation of its sovereignty, NATO began bombing on March 24 and continued to do so for six weeks straight, until Serbia agreed

to a U.N. occupation. The bombing led to a mass exodus of ethnic Albanians. When the United Nations (though chiefly, as in Bosnia, the United States) occupied the country and Albanians began to return, ethnic Serbs began fleeing. By 2000, the province had been ethnically divided even more dramatically than Bosnia had.

There is, alas, no moral in the stories of Bosnia and Kosovo. The experience reminds us that brute force often still triumphs over the grandest dreams. By demonstrating the worst possible outcome of the breakup of communism, however, they serve as a model of what must be avoided. Even after partition, many citizens in Sarajevo are still trying to hold on to the city's multiethnic character, while a brave few in Kosovo try to do the same there. It will not be easy for them to succeed, but even war does not quench the desire for inclusive democracy. In the years to come, that truth may yet prove to be the real lesson of Bosnia. Indeed, the lesson seems to have been learned even in Serbia, where the Serbian people overcame great odds and in October 2000 pushed President Slobodon Milosević from office, first in a general election and then in a popular uprising when Milosević refused to recognize the outcome. As this book goes to press, the situation in Serbia looks more hopeful that at any other time since the early 1980s.

Continuities, Transitions, and Changing Agendas

In trying to understand the tragedy of Yugoslavia, we must go back to one of the fundamental issues we have been grappling with throughout the chapters on East-Central Europe: how to build a market economy and political democracy at the same time. This central challenge facing all of post-Communist Eastern Europe has been particularly difficult in the former Yugoslavia. Contrary to popular assumptions, the Yugoslav conflict has not revolved solely around nationalism. Rather, elites in Yugoslavia consciously appealed to nationalism in order to divert popular anger away from the economic problems caused by market reform. When democracy finally came to Yugoslavia, people were rebelling not just against communism but also against the market reforms that democratic reformers had already introduced to deal with the economic crisis. Local elites won people over with a promise that national independence would bring prosperity.

Yugoslavia began moving to a market economy and political democracy earlier than the other East-Central European states. Cut off from the Soviet bloc, it initiated programs of workplace democracy and began reorienting toward the global economy already in the 1960s. By the late 1980s, with its economic and political system in deep crisis, the country accelerated the pace of reforms.[3] Under the leadership of Prime Minister Anke Marković, Yugoslavia began experimenting with radical neoliberal market measures. And to secure the public support necessary for painful reforms, it began experimenting with political democracy too. People now had to determine for themselves a new political identity, and they had to do so at a time of severe economic crisis.

A few new political parties in post-Communist Yugoslavia tried to define themselves on the basis of a commitment to a market economy and universal rights. These parties were committed to building a liberal market democracy throughout the former Yugoslavia. Most of the new parties, however, made nationalism their central theme. These parties talked a great deal about how the economic policies of the Marković government were hurting the people. And the problem, they said, was that economic policy was being made in the interests of the wrong group of people—in particular, the wrong *nationality*. In the 1990 elections, people tended to vote for the party that promised to make things better for their own nationality. When the democratic elections were over, nationalist parties had won throughout the former

Yugoslavia. People had chosen a new post-Communist identity. But it was a nationalist one, not a liberal democratic one. They had used the ballot to vote for parties that blamed one nationality for the problems facing another. Instead of agreeing that all citizens should be free and endowed with inalienable individual rights, people voted to empower those of one nationality over those of another. In the former Yugoslavia, in other words, it has so far proved impossible to build a market economy and liberal democracy at the same time. Instead of liberal democracy, we have had ethnic hatred and civil war.

The challenge facing other countries in the region is to avoid the fate of Yugoslavia. Some have argued that structural problems are to blame for ethnic distinctions leading to war in Yugoslavia but peaceful secession in Czechoslovakia and the Soviet Union.[4] But if the region is to avoid a democratic breakdown in the future, it will have to do something about the dangerous ethnic tensions still prevalent. For example, there has been an alarming surge in skinhead gang violence against refugees and foreign workers alike, sometimes spilling over into attacks against homosexuals and even against centers for children with AIDS. The most significant and most chronic ethnic problem in the region, however, is the relationship of the dominant ethnic majority to the Roma, or Gypsies.[5]

In many ways, anti-Roma sentiment is a continuation of past patterns. But in some ways the situation has become worse after 1989. In the Communist era, governments outlawed Roma nomadic patterns, but created the many unskilled industrial jobs that allowed Roma to earn a living without constant migration. Since 1989, most of those jobs have disappeared. People are free to move, but many no longer know how to survive that way, as they had in the past. The result is that Roma now tend to stay in the communities in which they live, but are poorer and more discriminated against than ever before. Paradoxically, the situation is worse in the more developed countries such as Hungary and the Czech Republic, since these were more effective in creating the jobs that changed Roma ways in the past and more ruthless in cutting those jobs now.

One event in the Czech Republic in 1999 symbolized the problem dramatically. Local officials in the poor mining city of Usti nad Labem erected a wall in the city to separate Roma from the rest of the population. National politicians protested, but the local politicians were within their legal rights. Shattering the optimistic image of a New Europe in formation, the new millennium thus opened with a Roma ghetto in the heart of Europe. The fall of the Berlin Wall did not spell the end of divisions within Europe.

The protests of the national politicians were not only in vain but also somewhat hypocritical. Official Czech policy has been anti-Roma ever since the new state was founded in 1993. The government did its best to prevent Roma from becoming Czech citizens.[6] A 1969 law had defined all Roma as citizens of Slovakia regardless of where they lived. This did not mean much at the time, since the federation was effectively governed as a single country, but it had great significance after the breakup of the country in 1993. While citizens were legally entitled to request a new nationality at this time, most Roma residents did not know this. The result was that by 1994, hundreds of thousands of Roma became foreigners living in the Czech Republic without any legal basis. Policy such as this encouraged the racist practices of local officials that the government now abhors. With the Czech Republic and Hungary on the fast track to European Union (EU) entry, these countries' Roma problems will soon become the EU's.

The attacks on Roma are part of the way that "losers" in the post-Communist transition seek to negotiate their fate. The politics of blame is a powerful part of Eastern Europe's post-Communist reality. Of course, it is not only Roma who are targeted. Some people, and par-

ties, have sought to blame economic problems not on other nationalities but on former Communists and have proposed measures that would effectively ban former officials and Communist Party activists from participation in public life today. Others blame "corrupt" bankers and industrialists or the corrupting influence of "Western culture." Still others single out "secular humanism" as the problem and propose religious fundamentalism as the answer. In all its guises, this politics of blame is perhaps the chief threat to democratic consolidation in East-Central Europe today. When one group or way of life is held responsible for all the ills of the present, the danger is that that group or way of life may be banned in the future, or shut up in a ghetto like in Usti nad Labem.

The Challenges of European Integration

The EU's formal invitation to ten East European countries in March 1998 inviting them to stand for consideration for accession is a true historic juncture for East-Central Europe. The imminence of entry into what Eastern Europeans hope would be a veritable United States of Europe is, for most of them, the fulfillment of a dream that few would have believed possible just a short time ago. The challenges, however, are many. For example, can the applicant countries join the EU without giving away too much of the democracy they fought for in 1989? There have already been calls in the Czech Republic for the government to have "special powers" of decree to implement the laws of the EU. More generally, will it be possible to "enter Europe" as mainstream, fully dignified actors, without the second-class status in which many Westerners still view the newcomers?

This will not be easy. So far the accession process has been completely shaped by the West. For example, Eastern applicants were considered only after they followed International Monetary Fund (IMF) guidelines on structural adjust-

ment, entailing opening their markets to Western investors (and privatizers), refocusing
production toward exports to the West, and
moving quickly from state to private ownership.
Some countries have managed this prescription,
although with great difficulty; for others it has
been an economic disaster. Poverty levels in excess of one-third of the population, a huge con-
traction of gross domestic product, and massive
"bandit privatization" (corrupt sales to domestic
buyers) have hurt Romania and Bulgaria far
more than a more gradual transition would
have done. But since gradual transformation
was rejected by the West, they had no choice in
the matter. If the East's triumvirate elite of Poland, Hungary, and the Czech Republic are justifiably worried about entering the EU as second-class citizens, the next-tier entrants will do
so as third-class citizens—if they get in at all.
Despite the 1998 invitation, the EU still refuses
to give a precise date even for when the first
group might enter. (The earliest would be 2003.)
Whether the next group will enter the hallowed
body at all is still unclear.

There may yet come a time when people in
the region decide that they have been making
too many sacrifices for the cause of "entering
Europe" while reaping too few benefits. In
Chapter 28, we discussed how Western aid policy has reinforced this notion. Since the demise
of communism, numerous Western economic
experts, knowing little about the history or day-
to-day realities of Eastern Europe, have offered
textbook advice on how to introduce a market
economy—but without realizing that the actual
countries have national specificities that make
generic, one-size-fits-all measures completely
inappropriate.[7] Too often the aid has benefited
the donors, through consulting fees given to its
own advisers, far more than the countries it was
intended to help. As Janine Wedel has put it,
"Western 'help' meant mostly advice [that is]
not necessarily designed to benefit and serve the
needs of its recipients."[8]

A similar sense of neglect and condescension
fell on the region in the light of the NATO

bombing of Kosovo. With most EU countries
also in NATO, Eastern European countries felt
strongly pressured to give their full support despite public opinion. Even in the three Eastern
countries that had themselves become NATO
members barely two weeks before the bombing
began, public support was lukewarm, with Hungary particularly worried about NATO bombs
hitting ethnic Hungarians in northern Serbia
(some did). Reaction farther south was even
more negative, partly due to regional solidarity
and partly for economic reasons. (Some companies in neighboring Romania or Bulgaria had
exported virtually their entire output to Serbia,
meaning that the war brought further losses to
these already poor economies.) Nevertheless,
everyone understood that support for NATO
was an unstated condition of eventual EU accession, and so all countries ultimately gave their
support. The West promised that it would remember this support and help the region for
any economic losses incurred as a result. Yet
when the leading NATO countries convened a
high-profile meeting in Sarajevo in July 1999 to
come up with a Stability Pact for Eastern Europe, bringing together leading representatives
from some thirty different countries, little came
out of it. NATO promised money for rebuilding
Kosovo, not for the region.

If one of the challenges for East-Central Europe is to build a strong domestic economy
without becoming too dependent on other
states, this is a challenge for the international
community as well. It is not in the interests of
the West for East European governments to be
seen by their populations as serving Western
interests. In return for the numerous Eastern
concessions on economic and political issues
alike, the West must provide concrete rewards,
in the form of favorable tariff treatment for
Eastern European exports, aid funds administered by the receiving country alone, development funds for projects that benefit the poor,
and more precise promises on when they can
expect to join the EU.

Forced to compete in the global economy, the

East European states clearly do not have a great deal of flexibility. To sell their goods, they need to produce at a high technological level. To procure the new technology, they have to obtain loans. To be eligible for loans, they have to secure an IMF seal of approval and be completely willing to accept whatever terms for membership the EU puts forth. With no Soviet Union or any other source of funds for economic growth, governments do what they have to do to obtain that international approval.

All countries, of course, face similar constraints. The close EU integration of the euro era constrains the freedom of Western European countries too. Yet East-Central Europe is in a particularly difficult situation. As a collection of small states in a large world of states, East-Central Europe is extremely vulnerable to outside forces. With comparatively underdeveloped economies, insignificant military power, and a negligible resource base, it is unable to shape the outside world or cushion the impact of external forces on its domestic environment. We therefore see in East-Central Europe some of the consequences of the historical decline of the nation-state that social scientists have pointed to in recent years. Policy outcomes in East-Central Europe do not follow solely from the countries' own, autonomous decisions. They are in large part determined by demands from abroad.

All in all, East-Central Europe's governments must work to undertake the difficult task of adjusting their systems enough to enter the EU while maintaining the support of both regular citizens and foreign elites, of both working people and investors. This does not mean that all policies must be equally acceptable to all social groups. Such a consensus is impossible to achieve, and attempting to do so would be a recipe for stagnation. But governments must see themselves as the representatives of all and make sure that the interests of all groups are at least sometimes addressed in public policy.

To be successful, market reform and EU integration must serve the interests of the business community, whether domestic or foreign investors or international financial agencies. To these groups, East-Central Europe must show continuing commitment to establishing favorable investment climates, as well as an ability to maintain tight budgets. It must establish tax policies that promote investment while also guaranteeing the state sufficient resources to develop infrastructure and maintain social stability. At the same time, there will be no long-term stability without the support of labor. In the heavy industrial world that East-Central Europe remains, the working class still constitutes the largest potentially organized sector of the population. It is the group most affected by systemic transition and the one whose support is crucial if a democratic system is to survive.

Just as the political system must be transformed in a way that is compatible with economic reform, the economy must be transformed in a way that maintains support for political democracy. Economic reform, in other words, must be politically sensitive and socially aware. Citizens must come to feel that economic reforms are working for them and not just for the new or old elite. Creating this environment requires such things as a privatization program with shares for employees and citizens, anticorruption and antimonopoly measures, and strong regulatory agencies safeguarding safety, health, and environmental standards. Such policies are necessary not just to maintain a decent and growing standard of living for citizens, but for maintaining the stability of a democratic system. Eastern Europeans are well aware that change does not come without sacrifice. Indeed, what has been surprising in the years since the fall of communism is not how many strikes and protests there have been but how few. But if the post-Communist world comes to be perceived as being just as immoral and rotten as the old one, many people may lose all hope whatsoever. Society would then be overcome by a crushing sense of despair, giving rise to social pathologies like an increase in crime and violence and political pathologies like the emergence of fascist organizations.

So far, most countries in the region have avoided fundamentalist dangers by focusing on real economic issues. For the most part, the parties winning elections have been those that promise to make things better by proposing alternate economic policies, not by singling out one group of people for condemnation. There is, however, no guarantee that this democratic pattern of politics will continue. Party affiliation is still unstable in East-Central Europe. No party has succeeded in attracting majority support anywhere in the region. In particular, those who are suffering economically tend to feel left out. They are politically homeless—not yet loyal voters of any party. They are consequently accessible to any party that can win them over. Democracy has been a powerful lure in East-Central Europe. But the struggle for democracy does not end with the toppling of communism. People who lose out economically tend to feel that they still do not live in a "democracy," and they will eventually ally with whatever party seems best able to take their interests into account. If people become thoroughly alienated, governments lose their most precious asset: the goodwill of the citizens.

East-Central European Politics in Comparative Perspective

How can we best study East-Central Europe today? Until just a few years ago, students studied the region as little more than an afterthought to the study of the Soviet Union. Experts on contemporary Soviet society were treated as automatic experts on Eastern Europe as well. Introductory courses on European politics usually did not even mention the region, except as "the other" against which the "West" was pitted.

Today there is a danger of going too far in the opposite direction. With part of East-Central Europe already in NATO, against Russia's strong opposition, and much of it likely soon to be in the EU, scholars are beginning to treat the region as the kidnapped partner of the West finally returned home. European politics courses now regularly deal with democratic and market transition in Eastern Europe (though they speak not a word about events in Moscow). College students are discovering that a summer trip to Europe demands stops not just in Paris and Rome but in Prague, Budapest, and Kraków too (and maybe even Riga). In other words, little by little, Eastern Europe—particularly the three central European countries of Poland, Hungary, and the Czech Republic—is being readmitted to the fold, with Russia and Ukraine carved off as "the other." The East-Central Europe that was once viewed as "belonging" to Russia is increasingly seen as the rightful property of Western Europe instead.[9]

The reality is that East-Central Europe can be understood only in its connections to *both* Western Europe and Russia. It is trying to become more a part of the West today, but the very fact that it must try demonstrates that a chasm still remains. The main streets of downtown Budapest may seem like the main streets of downtown Brussels, but Hungary's dying industrial sector, just moving away from state ownership and Communist Party guidance, is experiencing problems more similar to those in Russia or China, which are also trying to build market economies, than to those facing a Belgium trying to find its place in a united Europe. We need to understand not only where Eastern Europe feels it is going, but also where it has been. As we saw in Chapter 26, Eastern Europe was not just "taken over" by communism; numerous internal factors pushed it in that direction. Today, numerous internal factors keep it from simply becoming another part of Western Europe. In some ways, it increasingly resembles not the West but the South, not Western Europe but South America and Southern Europe.[10] We need to be careful about how we "locate" countries or regions, so as not to fall into ideological wishful thinking. In this book, we have tried to highlight East-Central Europe's status as a set of countries in between, with inextricable links to both East and West, both liberalism and communism, both communism and capitalism.

One of the ways to look at these contradictory aspects of East-Central Europe is through the discussion of democratization. How can societies be democratized? How can a newly achieved democracy be consolidated? These questions have been at the center of research in comparative political science over the past two decades. Beginning in the mid-1970s in Latin America and southern Europe, a series of countries that had long been authoritarian or military dictatorships began the transition to democratic forms of government. By the mid-1980s, theorists had speculated on the causes of this transformation, argued about whether the new democratic systems could be consolidated, and suggested how democracy could best be strengthened. Mainstream political scientists, who had considered communism to be unreformable and totalitarian, thought it unimaginable that Eastern Europe would join this new wave of democratization anytime soon.[11] Within a few years, however, journals and conferences worldwide would be devoted to the new study of "comparative democratization," comparing democratic transformations in Latin America and East-Central Europe.

What can such comparisons teach us about how to initiate and consolidate democratic political transitions? What are some of the similarities and differences in transitions to democratic government from right-wing dictatorships and from Communist systems?

One common element is that democratic change is preceded by a revitalization of civil society. Indeed, the very term *civil society*, referring to the public sphere for civic and political interaction outside of government, has reentered the vocabulary of political science because of the experience of democratic transformations, particularly in East-Central Europe.[12] We can now see that one of the main weaknesses of mainstream political science was its focus on elites. Until recently, political scientists tended to have a very thin notion of citizenship. Citizens were considered insufficiently trained in public affairs and were advised to leave governing to the experts. "Acceptance of leadership," wrote Joseph Schumpeter, the influential economist and democratic theorist of the 1950s, "is the true function of the electorate."[13] In Latin America and particularly in East-Central Europe, however, it was precisely those citizens who refused to accept leadership who made democratization possible. Without Solidarity in Poland or the independent political activists in Hungary, the Communist governments would have had no reason to accept political democracy. Recent democratization movements have returned the study of citizens and civil society to the center of political analysis.

At the same time, comparative analysis also illustrates the importance of *conciliation* and *negotiation*. A mobilized and angry citizenry is not enough. The elites who control the guns must be persuaded that giving up power is in their interests too, or at least that it will not lead to their arrest and prosecution. The authorities need a reliable adversary to negotiate with. And that adversary, representing the citizens in their campaign for democracy, must be prepared to make concessions, even ones most citizens believe to be wrong, in order to persuade the authorities to go along.

What kinds of concessions must democratizers offer? First, they should agree to refrain from locking up the ousted dictator, at least right away. In Chile and in Poland, the respective military leaders Pinochet and Jaruzelski were even able to maintain their positions briefly as head of state after the first free elections. While some former leaders were eventually prosecuted—in Argentina, Bulgaria, and East Germany, for example—the charges and penalties were relatively minor, and all sides understood that the action was more a public relations campaign on the part of the new regime than an attempt to exact vengeance.

Supporters of the old system also remained

relatively free from persecution. Nowhere was democratization accompanied by an immediate purge of the bureaucracy, not even the military and police bureaucracies. The leading officials were retired, usually with generous pensions intact, but rank-and-file officials tended to retain their posts, at least for a while, until new recruits were brought in and the old guard could gracefully be retired.[14]

In Latin America, the need for conciliation of the old elite also meant a favorable attitude to capitalist big business, which had been the main social base of the dictatorships. Here, paths diverge.[15] For in East-Central Europe, there was no capitalist big business. If conciliation is necessary to calm the fears of potential opponents, then in a post-Communist context, conciliation means maintaining policies favorable to the working class. Few other groups are likely to be quite as dissatisfied by the post-Communist system—and certainly not former Party members and officials; most have been gracefully retired, quietly retained, or enabled to move on to lucrative careers in business and banking, fields they tended to know better than the old dissidents did. Far from suffering, this group has largely benefited from the building of a capitalist system. Most working people, however, have yet to benefit. That is why they represent a potential threat to democratic consolidation and why they must be conciliated.[16] If workers come to experience democracy as privation, they are likely to be susceptible to the appeals of demagogues and authoritarian nationalists. This was true in Latin America too, but the existence there of a powerful capitalist class, afraid to part with dictatorship because of its fear of labor militance, meant that business-friendly policies were more important in the short run than labor-friendly policies. In East-Central Europe, however, labor-friendly policies are more important as a way of consolidating the new system. Not all Eastern European democrats initially seemed to understand this. Growing support for populism and ethnic nationalism, however, and then the striking success of the ex-

Communists, eventually made the importance of winning labor support clearer. As East-Central Europe entered the new millennium, even ardent free-market supporters finally seemed to recognize the need to conciliate labor.

While working-class support for authoritarianism in Russia shows the importance of winning labor to democracy there too, we should note that the situations in Russia and China are actually quite different from that in East-Central Europe. Russian and Chinese authoritarianism has much stronger roots. Unlike in Eastern Europe, communism was experienced as part of the national tradition, not as something imposed from without. Under communism, both countries became superpowers. As a result, there is far more internal support for the old system than we see in Eastern Europe. Thus, in Russia and China, conciliating potential enemies of democracy requires efforts to change the underlying political culture, not just to reach out to those who may lose economically.

The international environment also plays a crucial role, or what this book refers to as the world of states. In Europe, whether Western, Southern, or Eastern, no country is fully accepted unless it is a democracy. Latin America could not gain Western acceptance unless it too adopted basic democratic forms of government. Western governments do not press all countries to democratize. If a country has a commodity the West wants to buy and a culture the West does not understand, the West does not care if it is a democracy or a dictatorship. (Kuwait, with an authoritarian government able to supply the West with oil, was not compelled to democratize even after the democratic world organized one of the century's greatest military campaigns in its defense.) East-Central Europe, however, with its cultural ties to the West and its attempts to join the European Union, will be accepted only on the condition that it is democratic. Political events of the past decade show that the people there understand and accept this fully.

In the end, whether a country can build a democratic system depends on a number of factors, such as its political culture, the nature and duration of its authoritarian experience, the degree of popular mobilization, the internal economic situation, international pressures, and the country's location in the global economy. In some countries, political mobilization from below plays the crucial role; elsewhere, a skilled negotiating strategy is key. In countries with a relatively homogeneous population, nationalism may help attract support for political democracy, whereas in multiethnic societies with a history of conflict, it may only damage chances for democracy. Where a capitalist class is strong, economic policy must be favorable to capital; where capital is weak and workers have historically been deemed the dominant class, economic policy must not be unduly harsh to working people.

But there is no one form of democracy either. Democratic countries can have a presidential or a parliamentary system, extensive or limited state intervention, strong or weak local govern-

ments, proportional or single-member-districts representation, broad or limited social welfare networks. They can allow unfettered capitalist development, or they can empower communities to restrict the privileges of private capital. What makes East-Central Europe so exciting today is that we see so many of these possible democratic forms in action. From the unprecedented civic involvement of the Solidarity movement in Poland to the creative ideas for involving citizens in economic reforms today, East-Central Europe has much to teach the West about democracy.

Whatever the form of democracy, however, critics can and will always demand greater democracy. People can always think of reasons and ways to be more involved in making decisions that affect them. Popular pressure for greater democratization is an inescapable feature of the world as a whole, and particularly of what used to be the Communist world. Democracy is, after all, an eternally unfinished project.

Notes

1. For a majestic history of Bosnia's multiethnic history over the ages, see the great 1945 novel by Bosnian Nobel Prize author Ivo Andrić, *The Bridge on the Drina* (Chicago: University of Chicago Press, 1984).

2. Formally, the accord speaks of a Bosnian-Croat federation governing both Muslims and Croats. In reality, the Bosnians and Croats have had their own distinct administrations from the very beginning. The formal breakup of the federation is probably only a matter of time.

3. For an excellent account of how economic developments led to the outbreak of war, see Susan Woodward, *The Balkan Tragedy* (Washington, D.C.: Brookings Institute, 1995).

4. Valerie Bunce, "Peaceful versus Violent State Dismemberment: A Comparison of the Soviet Union, Yugoslavia, and Czechoslovakia," *Politics and Society* 27, no. 2 (June 1999): 217–237. Some areas of the former Soviet Union, such as the Caucasus states of Ar-

menia, Azerbaijan, and Georgia, descended into civil war *after* the breakup of the country.

5. Anti-Gypsy hostility is widespread even far from Eastern Europe, of course. For example, millions of Americans use the word *gypped* without even being aware they are using an ethnic slur.

6. Jirina Siklova and Marta Miklusakova, "Denying Citizenship to the Czech Roma," *East European Constitutional Review* 7, no. 2 (Spring 1998): 58–64. More information on the East European situation is available on the Web site of the European Roma Rights Center, www.errc.org.

7. On the inadequacy of such generic measures, or what they derisively call "designer capitalism," see David Stark and Laszlo Bruszt, *Postsocialist Pathways: Transforming Politics and Property in East Central Europe* (Cambridge: Cambridge University Press, 1998).

8. Janine Wedel, *Collision and Collusion: The Strange Case of Western Aid to Eastern Europe,*

1989–1998 (New York: St. Martin's Press, 1998), p. 42.

9. For a critique of this view, see the last chapter of Valerie Bunce, *Subversive Institutions* (Cambridge: Cambridge University Press, 1999).

10. See Adam Przeworski, *Democracy and the Market: Political and Economic Reforms in Eastern Europe and Latin America* (New York: Cambridge University Press, 1991), esp. pp. 188–191.

11. One prominent scholar went so far as to virtually to rule out the possibility of democratic change in the Communist bloc. See Samuel P. Huntington, "Will More Countries Become Democratic?" *Political Science Quarterly* 99, no. 2 (1984): 193–218.

12. See John Keane, ed., *Civil Society and the State* (London: Verso, 1990).

13. Joseph Schumpeter, *Capitalism, Socialism and Democracy*, 3d ed. (New York: Harper & Row, 1950), p. 273.

14. The lustration process in Czechoslovakia was an exception, but even here many dismissed individuals were soon able to find good jobs again. More officials were sacked in East Germany, but this is a special case. East Germany was not an example of democratization from within but from without. Instead of confronting its former internal enemies, the East German elite had to confront an external enemy, a previous foreign power, which did not have to worry about unduly angering the old leaders, since the old leaders had simply become the vanquished side, and were thus unable to mobilize resistance to democratization. Significantly, in the year prior to reunification, there was no lustration in East Germany.

15. For more on these issues, see Melvin Croan, ed., "Is Latin America the Future of Eastern Europe?" *Problems of Communism* 41, no. 3 (May–June 1992): 44–57.

16. On the importance of conciliation, or "compensation," see Bela Greskovits, *The Political Economy of Protest and Patience: Eastern European and Latin American Transformations Compared* (Budapest: Central European University Press, 1998).

Bibliography

Ali, Rabia, and Lawrence Lifschultz. *Why Bosnia?* Stony Creek: Pamphleteer's Press, 1993.

Amsden, Alice, Jacek Kochanowicz, and Lance Taylor. *The Market Meets Its Match: Restructuring the Economies of Eastern Europe.* Cambridge: Cambridge University Press, 1994.

Bozoki, Andras, ed. *Intellectuals and Politics in Central Europe.* Budapest: Central European University Press, 1999.

Brubaker, Rogers. *Nationalism Reframed: Nationhood and the National Question in the New Europe.* Cambridge: Cambridge University Press, 1996.

Bunce, Valerie. *Subversive Institutions: The Design and the Destruction of Socialism and the State.* Cambridge: Cambridge University Press, 1999.

Callinicos, Alex. *The Revenge of History: Marxism and the East European Revolutions.* University Park: Pennsylvania State University Press, 1991.

Chirot, Daniel. *The Origins of Backwardness in Eastern Europe.* Berkeley: University of California Press, 1989.

Chirot, Daniel, ed. *The Crisis of Leninism and the Decline of the Left.* Seattle: University of Washington Press, 1991.

Crawford, Beverly, ed. *Markets, States, and Democracy: The Political Economy of Post-Communist Transformation.* Boulder, Colo.: Westview Press, 1995.

Crowley, Stephen, and David Ost, eds. *Workers After Workers' States: Labor and Politics in Eastern Europe After Communism.* Boulder, Colo.: Rowman & Littlefield Press, 2001.

Denitch, Bogdan. *Ethnic Nationalism: The Tragic Death of Yugoslavia.* Minneapolis: University of Minnesota Press, 1994.

Einhorn, Barbara. *Cinderella Goes to Market: Citizenship, Gender, and Women's Movements in Central Europe.* London: Verso, 1994.

Ekiert, Grzegorz, and Jan Kubik. *Rebellious Civil Society: Popular Protest and Democratic Consoli-*

dation in Poland. Ann Arbor: University of Michigan Press, 1999.

Elster, Jon, Claus Offe, and Ulrich K. Preuss. *Institutional Design in Post-Communist Societies: Rebuilding the Ship at Sea.* Cambridge: Cambridge University Press, 1998.

Eyal, Gil, Ivan Szelenyi, and Eleanor Townsley. *Making Capitalism Without Capitalists: Class Formation and Elite Struggles in Post-Communist Central Europe.* London: Verso, 1998.

Feffer, John. *Shock Waves; Eastern Europe After the Revolutions.* Boston: South End Press, 1992.

Frydman, Roman, Andrzej Rapaczynski, and John S. Earle. *The Privatization Process in Central Europe.* Budapest and London: Central European University Press, 1993.

Funk, Nanette, and Magda Mueller, eds. *Gender Politics and Post-Communism.* New York: Routledge, 1993.

Gardawski, Juliusz. *Poland's Industrial Workers on the Return to Democracy and Market Economy.* Warsaw: Friedrich Ebert Foundation, 1996.

Garton Ash, Timothy. *The Magic Lantern.* New York: Random House, 1990.

Gowan, Peter. *The Global Gamble: Washington's Faustian Bid for World Dominance.* London: Verso, 1999.

Greskovits, Bela. *The Political Economy of Protest and Patience: Eastern European and Latin American Transformations Compared.* Budapest: Central European University Press, 1998.

Hardy, Jane, and Al Rainnie. *Restructuring Krakow: Desperately Seeking Capitalism.* London: Mansell, 1996.

Hausner, Jerzy, Bob Jessop, and Klaus Nielsen. *Strategic Choice and Path-Dependency in Post-Socialism.* Hants, England: Edward Elgar, 1995.

Hockenos, Paul. *Free to Hate: The Rise of the Right in Post-Communist Eastern Europe.* New York: Routledge, 1993.

Jowitt, Ken. *New World Disorder: The Leninist Extinction.* Berkeley: University of California Press, 1992.

Kenney, Padraic. *Rebuilding Poland: Workers and Communists, 1945–1950.* Ithaca, N.Y.: Cornell University Press, 1997.

Kitschelt, Herbert, Zdenka Mansfeldova, Radoslaw Markowski, and Gabor Toka. *Post-Communist Party Systems: Competition, Representation, and Inter-Party Cooperation.* Cambridge: Cambridge University Press, 1999.

Kubik, Jan. *The Power of Symbols Against the Symbols of Power: The Rise of Solidarity and the Fall of State Socialism in Poland.* State College: Pennsylvania State University Press, 1994.

Legters, Lyman H., ed. *Eastern Europe: Transformation and Revolution, 1945–1991.* Lexington, Mass.: D.C. Heath, 1992.

Meardi, Guglielmo. *Trade Union Activists, East and West.* London: Ashgate, 2000.

Offe, Claus. *Varieties of Transition: The Eastern European and East German Experience.* Cambridge, Mass.: MIT Press, 1997.

Orenstein, Mitchell. *Out of the Red: Building Capitalism and Democracy in Post-Communist Europe.* Ann Arbor: University of Michigan Press, 2000.

Ost, David. *Solidarity and the Politics of Anti-Politics.* Philadelphia: Temple University Press, 1990.

Pearson, Raymond. *National Minorities in Eastern Europe, 1849–1945.* London: Macmillan, 1983.

Poznanski, Kazimierz. *Constructing Capitalism: The Reemergence of Civil Society and Liberal Economy in the Post-Communist World.* Boulder, Colo.: Westview Press, 1992.

Przeworski, Adam. *Democracy and the Market.* Cambridge: Cambridge University Press, 1991.

Ramet, Sabrina. *The Radical Right in Eastern Europe.* State College: Pennsylvania State University Press, 1999.

Ramet, Sabrina. *Balkan Babel: The Disintegration of Yugoslavia from the Death of Tito to the War for Kosovo.* Boulder, Colo.: Westview Press, 1999.

Rothschild, Joseph. *Return to Diversity: A Political History of East Central Europe Since World War II.* New York: Oxford University Press, 1989.

Schopflin, George. *Politics in Eastern Europe.* London: Blackwell, 1993.

Slay, Ben. *The Polish Economy: Crisis, Reform, and Transformation.* Princeton, N.J.: Princeton University Press, 1994.

Stark, David, and Laszlo Bruszt. *Postsocialist Pathways: Transforming Politics and Property in East Central Europe.* Cambridge: Cambridge University Press, 1998.

Stokes, Gale. *The Walls Came Tumbling Down: The Collapse of Communism in Eastern Europe.* New York: Oxford University Press, 1993.

Szacki, Jerzy. *Liberalism After Communism.* Budapest: Central European University Press, 1995.

Taras, Raymond. *Consolidating Democracy in Poland.* Boulder, Colo.: Westview Press, 1995.

Waller, Michael, and Martin Myant. *Parties, Trade Unions and Society in East-Central Europe.* Essex: Frank Cass, 1995.

Wedel, Janine. *Collision and Collusion: The Strange Case of Western Aid to Eastern Europe 1989–1998.* New York: St. Martin's Press, 1998.

Wheaton, Bernard, and Zdenek Kavan. *The Velvet Revolution: Czechoslovakia 1988–1991.* Boulder, Colo.: Westview Press, 1992.

Woodward, Susan. *The Balkan Tragedy.* Washington, D.C.: Brookings Institute, 1995.

Web Sites

For information on women's issues and organizations in Eastern Europe, see the Network of East-West Women, at *www.neww.org.*

For access and links to Eastern European newspapers and journals, in native languages and English, and to other relevant bibliographic material, see the University of Wisconsin, Madison's excellent Web site: *www.library.wisc.edu/guides/REECA/reeca.htm.*

"Transitions Online," an Internet journal covering Central and Eastern Europe, is available at *www.tol.cz.*

Information on Roma (Gypsy) issues can be found at *www.errc.org.*

For full-text editions of the excellent publication *Eastern European Constitutional Review,* go to *www.law.nyu.edu/eecr.*

Daily news from East-Central Europe and Russia is available also at Radio Free Europe's Web site: *www.rferl.org.*

Index